THE YEARS OF
MacArthur

Volume III
Triumph and Disaster
1945–1964

BY D. CLAYTON JAMES

Antebellum Natchez

South to Bataan, North to Mukden:
The Prison Diary of
Brigadier General W. E. Brougher
(ed.)

The Years of MacArthur
Volume I, 1880–1941

The Years of MacArthur
Volume II, 1941–1945

The Years of MacArthur
Volume III, Triumph and Disaster,
1945–1964

THE YEARS OF
MacArthur

Volume III
☆ Triumph and Disaster ☆
1945–1964

D. CLAYTON JAMES

*Illustrated with photographs
and with maps*

HOUGHTON MIFFLIN COMPANY

19 · *Boston* · 85

Library of Congress Cataloging in Publication Data
(Revised for vol. 3)

James, Dorris Clayton, date
The years of MacArthur.

Includes bibliographical references.
Contents: v. 1. 1880–1941. v. 2. 1941–1945. v. 3. 1945–
1964.
1. MacArthur, Douglas, 1880–1964. 2. Generals—
United States—Biography. 3. United States. Army—
Biography. 4. United States—History, Military—
20th century. I. Title.
E745.M3J3   355.3′31′0924 [B]   76-108685
ISBN 0-395-36004-8 (v. 3)

Printed in the United States of America

V 10 9 8 7 6 5 4 3 2 1

The author is grateful for permission to quote from the works listed below:

High Tension: The Recollections of Hugh Baillie. Copyright © 1959 by Hugh Baillie.
Reprinted by permission of Harper & Row Publishers, Inc.
A General's Life, by General of the Army Omar N. Bradley and Clay Blair. Copy-
right © 1983 by the Estate of General of the Army Omar N. Bradley and Clay
Blair. Reprinted by permission of Simon & Schuster, Inc.
War in Peacetime, by J. Lawton Collins. Copyright © 1969 by J. Lawton Collins.
Reprinted by permission of Houghton Mifflin Company.
Five Gentlemen of Japan: The Portrait of a Nation's Character, by Frank Gibney (New
York: Farrar, Straus and Young, 1953). Reprinted by permission of Farrar, Straus
& Giroux, Inc.
"Good Faith with Japan." Copyright © 1945 by the Christian Century Founda-
tion. Reprinted by permission from the October 3, 1945, issue of *The Christian Cen-
tury.*
The Riddle of MacArthur: Japan, Korea, and the Far East, by John Gunther. Copy-
right © 1950, 1951 by John Gunther. Reprinted by permission of Harper & Row
Publishers, Inc.

(Continued on page 818)

To J. Chester McKee, Jr.

Foreword

AFTER MORE THAN eighteen years of work on General Mac-Arthur, I still find him fascinating and can think of few other historical figures who would absorb my attention for so long a span. The main things I have learned during this interesting experience have been three: how little I know about MacArthur's inner self, how much material there is on his public life that no single researcher can cover, and how many people who never met him in life or research speak with great certainty about his traits as a commander and as a man. My nearly two decades of tracking him have led me only to a few fascinating shells along the edges of a long beach and a wide ocean, but the quest was worth it.

The reader will find no concluding chapter full of generalizations on the measure of MacArthur. Indeed, as my approach has been from the first volume onward, I have tried to use restraint in making judgments about his decisions and conduct, though I have not withheld bouquets or brickbats on some specific episodes and issues. I have tried to present his life as objectively and as comprehensively as possible, because, as a history professor first and a historian second, I should like college students to have access to a fair, full account of this man, who has been the subject of too much adulation and condemnation. I hope the serious reader will take the opportunity to form his or her judgments, using the many facts and the small guideposts I have provided.

A considerable number of military and civilian colleagues of

General MacArthur, along with other Americans and Japanese who had sundry connections with his commands of 1945–1951 and his later business ties, graciously gave of their time to talk to me, and some shared personal papers to assist my work. They are listed in the Bibliographical Note as well as in the chapter notes. Especially useful were various original and photocopied records given by Robert Sherrod, Samuel Milner, Frank Joseph Shulman, and George Dingledy, and some photographs supplied by Duane N. Diedrich. Excellent assistance was provided by the staffs of the MacArthur Memorial, the Diplomatic and Modern Military Records divisions of the National Archives, the Washington National Records Center, the Manuscript Division of the Library of Congress, the U.S. Army Military History Institute, the U.S. Army Center of Military History, the U.S. Army Command and General Staff College Library, the Naval Historical Center, the Marine Corps Historical Center, the Albert F. Simpson Historical Research Center of the Air University, the Harry S. Truman Library, the Dwight D. Eisenhower Library, the Oral History Research Office of Columbia University's Butler Library, the Hoover Institution on War, Revolution, and Peace at Stanford University, the Manuscript Department of Duke University's Perkins Library, the McKeldin Library's East Asia Collection at the University of Maryland, the Special Collections and Interlibrary Loan departments of Mississippi State University, the Japan Foreign Press Center and the United States Embassy in Tokyo, and the Japan Foundation and the Japan Embassy in Washington.

Until his departure from Mississippi State University in 1979, Vice President J. Chester McKee, Jr., to whom this book is dedicated, managed to find research funds to support this project strongly. Since then Professor William E. Parrish, head of the History Department, has given material assistance when possible. From 1973 to 1979, Mrs. Judy R. Hotard served as my right arm in performing a wide variety of secretarial and research chores. Miss Anne S. Wells worked as an able research assistant from 1974 to 1976 and during the past two years has emerged as a worthy successor to Mrs. Hotard as an indispensable helper on all phases of this project. Without these two ladies this book would still be years from completion. Others who have assisted me well on a part-time basis since 1975 are Miss Melinda L. Garner, Mrs. Susan E. Blackledge,

Miss Kelly P. Coggin, Mrs. Karen G. Capps, Miss Rebecca A. Spracklen, Ms. Wendy S. Hays, Miss Verna G. Woods, Miss Lona L. Lewellyn, and Mrs. Cornelia A. Lowe. Mrs. Ruth K. Hapgood of Houghton Mifflin Company has provided excellent editorial direction and well-timed encouragement. As on my previous four books, my wife, Erlene, has helped immeasurably in many ways, and my children, Sherrie, Ned, Judy, and Allie, have been understanding and supportive.

Mississippi State University   D. Clayton James
February 1984

Contents

Part IV. Fading Away

Illustrations

Arrival of the Joint Chiefs of Staff, January 1950. *U.S. Army*

Conferring with Ambassador Muccio and General Almond, June 1950. *U.S. Army*

With Generalissimo and Madame Chiang Kai-shek, July 1950. *MacArthur Memorial*

Talking to General Lowe, Tokyo, August 1950. *U.S. Army*

On board the U.S.S. *McKinley* during Inchon landings, September 1950. *MacArthur Memorial*

Going ashore at Inchon, September 1950. *U.S. Army*

At Kimpo Airfield, September 1950. *MacArthur Memorial*

Discussing operations with General Almond, September 1950. *MacArthur Memorial*

following page 592

With President Rhee, Seoul, September 1950. *U.S. Army*

Departing for Wake Island, October 1950. *U.S. Army*

President Truman awards MacArthur another Distinguished Service Medal, October 1950. *MacArthur Memorial*

Visiting Eighth Army's front, North Korea, November 1950. *U.S. Army*

With Dulles, chief U.S. negotiator on Japanese peace treaty, January 1951. *U.S. Army*

Leaving hq of 35th Infantry Regiment with General Ridgway, January 1951. *U.S. Army*

Greeting Mrs. MacArthur at Haneda Airport, Tokyo, January 1951. *U.S. Army*

Reading his controversial press statement in Korea, March 1951. *U.S. Army*

MacArthur confers with General Ridgway, April 1951. *U.S. Army*

The MacArthurs leaving San Francisco for Washington, April 1951. *U.S. Army*

Address to Congress, April 1951. *MacArthur Memorial*

Visiting with President Eisenhower at the White House, March 1954. *U.S. News & World Report and D. N. Diedrich*

Conferring with presidents of Remington Rand and General Electric, September 1954. *MacArthur Memorial*

With some Filipino veterans of World War II, July 1961. *MacArthur Memorial*

With President Kennedy, December 1961. *MacArthur Memorial*

Presentation to the general of the West Point yearbook, May 1962. *U.S. Army*

The MacArthurs at a Columbia College program, April 1963. *Wide World Photo*

His final birthday reunion dinner, January 1964. *MacArthur Memorial*

Rotunda of the MacArthur Memorial Museum, Norfolk, Virginia. *MacArthur Memorial*

Maps and Charts

PART I

The Occupation of Japan: Early Phase

CHAPTER I

Constraints on the New Shogun

1. The Conquered Nation

ON THE BRIGHT, CLEAR MORNING of September 8, 1945, General of the Army Douglas MacArthur journeyed by automobile from Yokohama to Tokyo. "The entire route is one of complete desolation," with "masses of rubble all along the road," observed Major General Clovis E. Byers, chief of staff of the American Eighth Army, who made the twenty-two-mile trip with MacArthur. Arriving at the United States embassy in the heart of Tokyo shortly after 11:00, MacArthur stepped from his car, walked up a slight incline to the edge of a picturesque lily pond on the terrace near the chancellery, and stood at attention facing the empty flagpole atop the bomb-scarred building. A colorful honor guard of the 1st Cavalry Division presented arms, and the cavalry band played the ruffles and a march. Lieutenant General Robert L. Eichelberger, commander of the Eighth Army, stepped to the front and faced MacArthur, who ordered, "General Eichelberger, have our country's flag unfurled, and in Tokyo's sun let it wave in its full glory as a symbol of hope for the oppressed and as a harbinger of victory for the right." The band played "The Star Spangled Banner" during the hoisting, and Eichelberger remarked of the occasion, "As the flag climbed slowly, gracefully, in Tokyo's sun, as the bell-like crescendos of the bugles rang out, there were many wet eyes in that martial assembly. It was a moment I am not likely to for-

get." The brief ceremony symbolized the movement of Mac-
Arthur, Supreme Commander for the Allied Powers (SCAP), and
his headquarters to the Japanese capital. The occupation of Japan, to last over six and a half years, was officially under way.[1]

The flag-raising ceremony, as well as MacArthur's lead role at
the surrender aboard the U.S.S. *Missouri* in Tokyo Bay six days
earlier, gave most Japanese the impression that he would possess
virtual autonomy and enormous powers in guiding postwar Japan. During the ensuing months, to MacArthur's delight and with
no small amount of cultivation by his public relations staff, the
majority of Japanese were overawed by SCAP and viewed him as
a sovereign with powers ranging from establishing occupation policy
to curing invalids. Kazuyoshi Yamazuki, a journalist, quickly wrote
a brief biography that projected an image of MacArthur as "a living god . . . a reincarnation of Emperor Jimmu [Japan's legendary first ruler]" and that sold 800,000 copies in Japan by March
1946. Letters from citizens of every walk of Japanese life poured
in to his office, beseeching him to work all sorts of wonders — to
bring back a soldier-husband from Soviet-occupied Manchuria, to
"put a stop to the black market," and to permit a hunter to keep
his rifle through the rabbit season. One farmer wrote, "My dear
Mack, Arthur, please lend us 2000 peaces of rolls which is to prepare us for cultivation," a request MacArthur might have granted
had he been able to figure out what the man wanted. Frequently
in such letters he was called "the new Shogun" or "the savior of
Japan." The superior of the Maryknoll mission at Kyoto reported
after a visit to the capital that "General MacArthur is such an idol
of the masses that hundreds gather in Tokyo every day just to see
him go to lunch."[2] Thus the occupation began with the dominant
image of MacArthur as the embodiment of hope and power.
Whether Japanese hopes would be realized depended, in part, on
whether his power was real or illusory, which will be considered
in the next sections of this chapter.

If at first MacArthur seemed omnipotent, Japan appeared to be
a shambles; in a physical sense, the latter was true. The view from
the chancellery roof, where the American flag flapped "in its full
glory," was, remarked a Tokyo resident, one of "desolate ex-
panses of gutted buildings as far as the eye could see." Tokyo's
time of terror had begun on the night of March 9–10, 1945, when

over 100,000 persons perished and sixteen square miles of the metropolis were burned to the ground in a fire-bombing raid by B-29s, called "the single most devastating fire the human race has ever known." By mid-August, after numerous air attacks, about 700,000 buildings had been destroyed in Tokyo, and the city's population shrank from nearly 7 million to fewer than 3 million as terrified, destitute civilians fled to the countryside. Among other raids on nearby Yokohama, a city of 900,000, one B-29 attack of less than an hour left 47 percent of its structures afire. All of Japan's urban centers were hit severely by B-29s or carrier-based aircraft, with the destruction of built-up areas averaging about 40 percent for the sixty-six largest cities. At Hiroshima and Nagasaki at least 110,000 persons were killed and over 85,000 structures destroyed by the atomic bombs, with hundreds of people there dying daily in September from radiation and blast-related wounds. World War II's toll in lives for Japan had been staggering: as many as 2 million Japanese, nearly a third of them civilians, had been killed. More than 15 million Japanese were homeless as the occupation began.[3]

As shocking as the human and physical devastation was, the long-range consequences were not as ominous as those of the collapse of the nation's economy. Industrial production by September 1945 was down to one third of the 1934–1936 level, crippled not only by the bombing of manufacturing facilities but also by the sinking of the merchant fleet, which ended the importation of raw materials and foodstuffs. With industry and commerce paralyzed in most areas, few jobs were available, large numbers of unemployed men roamed the streets and roads, and human misery was widespread. Raging inflation further diminished the already meager purchasing power of the masses: the yen dropped to less than a hundredth of its worth in late 1941, and Bank of Japan notes in circulation rose from ¥4.7 billion in December 1941 to ¥28.6 billion in August 1945 and ¥50 billion four months later. By the time of MacArthur's arrival, inflation and black markets were forcing city dwellers to travel to villages and farms to barter prized family belongings for rice and vegetables. Some Japanese wryly referred to the practice of peeling off layers of possessions to avert starvation as the "onion-skin economy." Agricultural production had declined sharply during the last year of the war, mainly because of the scarcity of farm workers, equipment, and fertilizers. The shortage of food, exacerbated by its high cost, reduced the average per capita intake to 1500 calories daily (compared with 3400 in the United States). Moreover, the Japanese diet was seriously deficient in fats, vitamins, and minerals. Not infrequently, a Japanese family had less to eat, in terms of both quantity and quality, in one day than a GI received at a single meal.[4]

Besides the heavy war casualties, physical ruination, and economic crisis, the plight of Japan was aggravated by a breakdown in social order and morale. Beginning months before the surrender, Japanese cities had been plagued by gangsterism and lawlessness on levels unknown before the war, as citizens defied the law and police in their struggle to survive. What could not be obtained . in black markets or through barter was gained by force or thievery by many Japanese who heretofore had never violated their country's rules of social behavior or its legal system. A sad commentary on the times was the emergence of black marketeers and operators in prostitution as the first significant groups of Japanese entrepreneurs in the postwar period.

When the Americans arrived in Japan, the people were still reeling from the news that their nation had lost in war for the first time in its history. In his surrender broadcast on August 15 the Emperor had told them that they must "bear the unbearable," and for two long weeks the Japanese people, exhausted and full of trepidation, had awaited the coming of the foreigners. But, to the pleasant surprise of both sides, Americans and Japanese quickly discovered that they did not fit the stereotypes of cruel conquerors or unyielding fanatics. Rather than castigating the Americans (or even the Emperor), most Japanese directed their bitterness against the militarists who had led the nation into aggression. Jiro Horikoshi, the engineer who designed the "Zero" fighter plane, probably expressed the sentiments of the majority of his countrymen when he wrote in his diary: "I cannot do other but to blame the military hierarchy and the blind politicians in power for dragging Japan into this hellish cauldron. . . . We must face our responsibilities of the future in a fashion entirely different from that adopted by the government which led us into the abyss of war and utter defeat." Disillusioned and desperate, the Japanese yearned for a leader in whom they could place faith and trust and from whom they could draw inspiration and hope. For various reasons, which will be discussed later, it is unlikely that any American officer of that time could have projected such an image of leadership as well as MacArthur.[5]

The vast majority of the Japanese were cooperative during the early phase of the occupation. Masayoshi Kakitsubo, a retired diplomat, suggests that it was part of a "bamboo strategy" of resiliency: "The bamboo bent with the breeze but did not break. With the passing of the breeze, the bamboo straightened again." This may account for the attitude of some individuals and groups, but it does not explain that of the masses. Undoubtedly important were the thoroughness and unexpectedness of their defeat in the war, which threw the Japanese off balance and made them more susceptible to new influences in a situation for which they were unprepared. So pliable did they seem that MacArthur was convinced that there was a "political, economic, and spiritual vacuum." The Japanese, he believed, "had suffered more than a military debacle, more than the destruction of their armed forces, more than the elimination of their industrial bases, more even than the occupation of their land by foreign bayonets. Their entire faith in the Japanese way of life, cherished as invincible for many centuries, perished in the agony of their total defeat." Occupied Japan, however, was not a tabula rasa on which American ideas were written, for later historical research has shown that virtually all the lasting reforms of the occupation were founded on prewar Japanese concepts and initiatives.

The cooperativeness of the Japanese was determined also by their initially favorable response to MacArthur and the American troops, as well as to the early occupation policies, which were generally seen as constructive, reasonable, and benevolent. Edwin O. Reischauer, an eminent historian and former ambassador to Japan, has suggested a number of other factors that affected the Japanese attitude: "their situational ethics, which permitted a sharp about-face; their respect for power and authority of any sort; the fact that they were fighting the war primarily out of a sense of duty and not because of personal hatred or fear; the underlying friendship and admiration in Japan for the United States, despite the prewar years of mounting friction; the realism of the Japanese, which made them recognize that cooperation was the only practical course; and their admirable willingness to accept new knowledge and admit past errors." Reischauer added, "But, whatever the causes for this cooperativeness, there can be no denying that it was the single most important factor in the history of the occupation, accounting in large part for the degree of success we had in Japan." Nevertheless, public compliance with the occupation was to be accompanied, as another scholar expressed it, by "determined and often successful underground efforts or delaying tactics employed to resist change and sabotage reform" by powerful interest groups.[6] Indeed, there were strong undercurrents, liberal as well as conservative, in Japanese society that would affect the course of the occupation as much as or more than anything the Americans did.

In his memoirs MacArthur stated, "I was thoroughly familiar with Japanese administration, its weakness and its strengths, and felt the reforms I contemplated were those which would bring Japan abreast of modern progressive thought and action." Actually neither he nor most Americans were aware that liberal, democratic movements had been alive, if sometimes dormant, in Japan since the late nineteenth century. The "freedom and people's rights movement" had resulted in the adoption of the Meiji Constitution in 1889, the establishment of the Diet (national parliament) the next year, and the development of political parties during the following decade. All three of these potentially democratic instruments, however, had been co-opted by the power elite of that era. A second major stirring of liberalism, "Taisho democracy," had begun during World War I, producing in 1918 the first Prime Minister from the ranks of bona fide party politicians, universal manhood suffrage in 1925, and Cabinets that until 1932 were controlled usually by political parties (not by the old cliques of aristocrats and military chiefs). Yet the conservatives had been successful otherwise in thwarting liberal endeavors in such areas as agrarian reform, revision of legal codes, and broader-based political participation. With the rise to power of the militarists in the 1930s, liberalism became moribund, but it was never dead in pre-1945 Japan. The SCAP seeds of political, economic, and social reform would fall on ground that had been at least partially prepared by decades of liberal efforts.

Although the wartime militaristic, supranationalistic leaders were already discredited and soon to be purged, the rest of the old-guard ruling class, which consisted mainly of big-business magnates, civil bureaucrats, landed gentry, and conservative politicians, emerged from the war with more unity and hidden power than most Westerners, including MacArthur, realized at first. An early warning came from George Atcheson, Jr., the State Department's astute political adviser in Japan, who wrote President Harry S. Truman in November 1945 that SCAP reformist attempts would encounter obstructionism from "the unregenerate and deeply entrenched bureaucrats" and the "big-business people," who were "fundamentally conservative and reactionary." According to Robert B. Textor, a SCAP civilian official, the old-guard leadership had already decided on one basic tactic, which was "to go through the motions of complying with G.H.Q.-sponsored changes in the legal structure, then capture the altered edifice, and proceed leisurely to sabotage the purpose for which G.H.Q. had demanded a restructuring." In a myriad of subtle ways the old guard was preparing to challenge threats to its interests while at the same time paying homage to the new shogun, General MacArthur.[7] The realities of power in occupied Japan were to evolve somewhat differently from what was expected by the Americans who had watched their nation's flag hoisted again over the embassy in Tokyo.

2. Emanations from Washington

Both during and after the occupation MacArthur, several of his top SCAP officers, and a number of journalists and biographers advanced the claim that MacArthur actually originated most of the significant occupation policies. For instance, Major General Courtney Whitney, who was to head the SCAP Government Section and who became the virtual alter ego of MacArthur, maintained that during their flight to Atsugi on August 30, 1945, MacArthur developed the basic objectives of the occupation: "I still recall vividly the sight of that striding figure as he puffed on his corncob pipe, stopping intermittently to dictate to me the random thoughts that crowded his mind and were destined to become the basis of the occupation. I can see now in retrospect that those terse

notes I took formed the policy under which we would work and
live for the next six years." MacArthur said in his *Reminiscences:*
"From the moment of my appointment as supreme commander,
I had formulated the policies I intended to follow, implementing
them through the Emperor and the machinery of the imperial
government." He listed fifteen objectives, which are nearly the same,
even in their wording, as those taken down by Whitney during the
trip from the Philippines to Japan: "First destroy the military power.
Punish war criminals. Build the structure of representative government. Modernize the constitution. Hold free elections. Enfran-
chise the women. Release the political prisoners. Liberate the
farmers. Establish a free labor movement. Encourage a free economy. Abolish police oppression. Develop a free and responsible
press. Liberalize education. Decentralize political power. Separate
church from state."[8]

Although most Japanese and perhaps a majority of the American public at the time thought that MacArthur initiated occupation policies, the truth is that for about two years before the end
of hostilities planners in Washington agencies, particularly the State-
War-Navy Coordinating Committee (SWNCC) and its Far East
Subcommittee, had been intensively debating and developing
principles and policies for the occupation. The Potsdam Declaration of July 26, 1945, by the United States, Great Britain, and China,
is best remembered for its ultimatum to the Japanese government
to surrender unconditionally or face "prompt and utter destruction," but most of the statement concerned the terms of surrender
and incorporated SWNCC concepts, including the two principal
objectives of demilitarization and democratization. Proclaiming that
"self-willed militaristic advisers" had seized control of Japan and
led the nation into aggression, the document stated that "there must
be eliminated for all time the authority and influence of those who
have deceived and misled the people of Japan into embarking on
world conquest," and "stern justice shall be meted out to all war
criminals." As for democratization, it said that "the Japanese government shall remove all obstacles to the revival and strengthening of democratic tendencies among the Japanese people. Freedom of speech, of religion, and of thought, as well as respect for
the fundamental human rights shall be established." In the economic realm, "just reparations in kind" would be exacted, "such

industries as will sustain her economy" in peaceful ways would be permitted, and "access to, as distinguished from control of, raw materials" would be allowed. The means of attaining the Allied objectives would include the limitation of Japan's sovereignty "to the islands of Honshu, Hokkaido, Kyushu, Shikoku, and such minor islands as we determine," and the occupation of "points in Japanese territory to be designated by the Allies," with the removal of the occupying forces "as soon as these objectives have been accomplished and there has been established in accordance with the freely expressed will of the Japanese people a peacefully inclined and responsible government." The fate of the Emperor and the imperial institution, of great moment to the Japanese, was not mentioned.[9]

Both the directive of August 15 designating MacArthur as SCAP and the Instrument of Surrender signed on September 2 contained similarly worded provisions for the authority of the Emperor and the Japanese government to be subject to MacArthur, who was empowered to issue whatever orders or directives he deemed proper and necessary to carry out the terms of surrender. Thus, although MacArthur would have supreme power in Japan, he was to administer the occupation through the instrument of the Japanese government, unless circumstances warranted direct intervention by SCAP.[10]

On August 29, while stopping at Okinawa en route to Japan, MacArthur received a radiogram containing the substance of a SWNCC-prepared document entitled "United States Initial Post-Surrender Policy for Japan," which, following Truman's approval on September 6, was sent in full to him as a directive from the Joint Chiefs of Staff. Although MacArthur was amenable to most of the ideas stated therein, he had not been consulted during its formulation and had no knowledge of it until the day before he landed in Japan. This statement set the tone for the early phase of the occupation and expressed in brief, general terms most of the policies that MacArthur was directed by the Joint Chiefs to execute, especially during the years 1945 to 1948. It was unilaterally interpreted and applied by the United States government until June 1947, when it was substantially reaffirmed by the Far Eastern Commission, representing eleven nations that had been at war with Japan.[11] Knowledge of the main points of "United States

Initial Post-Surrender Policy for Japan" is essential to an understanding of the occupation programs and an evaluation of
MacArthur's role as SCAP.

The first of the document's four parts consists largely of a re-
statement of the Potsdam terms, setting forth "the ultimate objectives of the United States in regard to Japan, to which policies in
the initial period must conform," and the "principal means" for
achieving them. In bringing about "the eventual establishment of
a peaceful and responsible government" in Japan, "the United States
desires that this government should conform as closely as may be
to principles of democratic self-government, but it is not the responsibility of the Allied Powers to impose upon Japan any form
of government not supported by the freely expressed will of the
people."

The dominant position of the United States is declared unmistakably in Part II, which, ironically, is entitled "Allied Authority."
Although "the occupation shall have the character of an operation
in behalf of the principal Allied powers" in the war against Japan
and participation by their forces "will be welcome and expected,"
all occupation units will be under "a Supreme Commander designated by the United States." The American government will attempt, "by consultation and by constitution of appropriate advisory bodies," to develop policies satisfactory to "the principal Allied
powers," but, "in the event of any differences of opinion among
them, the policies of the United States will govern."[12]

Most of Part II actually deals with SCAP's relations with the
Japanese government:

> The authority of the Emperor and the Japanese Government will be
> subject to the Supreme Commander, who will possess all powers nec-
> essary to effectuate the surrender terms and to carry out the policies
> established for the conduct of the occupation and the control of Ja-
> pan.
>
>   . . . The Supreme Commander will exercise his authority through
> Japanese governmental machinery and agencies, including the Em-
> peror. . . . This policy, however, will be subject to the right and duty
> of the Supreme Commander to require changes in governmental
> machinery or personnel or to act directly. . . . The policy is to use
> the existing form of government in Japan, not to support it. Changes
> in the form of government initiated by the Japanese people or gov-

ernment in the direction of modifying its feudal and authoritarian tendencies are to be permitted and favored. In the event that the effectuation of such changes involves the use of force . . . the Supreme Commander should intervene only where necessary to ensure the security of his forces and the attainment of all other objectives of the occupation.[13]

According to Part III, which covers "political" matters, "disarmament and demobilization are the primary tasks," to be executed "promptly and with determination." Japan's military establishment, including its military forces, Imperial General Headquarters, and General Staff, as well as its secret police, would be disbanded. Military matériel, aircraft, ships, and installations "shall be disposed of as required by the Supreme Commander." Persons who had been "active exponents" of militarism and supranationalism "will be removed and excluded from public office and from any other position of public or substantial private responsibility," including "supervisory and teaching positions." All societies and institutions, as well as educational doctrines and practices, of a militaristic or supranationalistic nature were to be banned. Individuals charged as war criminals "by the Supreme Commander or appropriate United Nations agencies" were to be "arrested, tried, and, if convicted, punished." Political democracy, obviously patterned along idealistic American lines, was to be encouraged:

> Freedom of worship shall be proclaimed promptly. . . .
>
> The Japanese people shall be afforded opportunity and encouraged to become familiar with the history, institutions, culture, and the accomplishments of the United States and the other democracies. . . .
>
> Democratic political parties, with rights of assembly and public discussion, shall be encouraged. . . .
>
> Laws, decrees, and regulations which establish discriminations on grounds of race, nationality, creed or political opinion shall be abrogated. . . . Persons unjustly confined by Japanese authority on political grounds shall be released. The judicial, legal and police systems shall be reformed . . . to protect individual liberties and civil rights.[14]

The final part of this important document deals with assorted economic matters, beginning with "economic demilitarization": "The existing economic basis of Japanese military strength must be destroyed and not be permitted to revive." To this end, there was to be an "immediate cessation and future prohibition of production of all goods designed for the equipment, maintenance, or use of any military force or establishment." MacArthur was directed to promote economic democracy: "Encouragement shall be given and favor shown to the development of organizations in labor, industry, and agriculture organized on a democratic basis. Policies shall be favored which permit a wide distribution of income and of the ownership of the means of production and trade." As one means of achieving redistribution of wealth, he was ordered to "favor a program for the dissolution of the large industrial and banking combinations." Economic rehabilitation, however, was not to be a SCAP responsibility: "The plight of Japan is the direct outcome of its own behavior, and the Allies will not undertake the burden of repairing the damage." Except where it might cause acute distress to the populace, "Japan will be expected to provide goods and services to meet the needs of the occupying forces." The Japanese authorities were to be allowed to administer "controls over economic policies" and direct "domestic fiscal, monetary, and credit policies," but these were "subject to the approval and review of the Supreme Commander." Reparations were to be exacted through the transfer of Japanese property in countries against whom Japan had committed aggression and of those "goods or existing capital equipment and facilities" in the Japanese home islands which were "not necessary for a peaceful Japanese economy or the supplying of the occupying forces." Restitution of "all identifiable looted property" was to be made promptly and in full. Although "eventually" Japan's foreign trade could be resumed on a "normal" basis, during the occupation Japan would be permitted only such exports as were necessary to pay for "approved imports" of raw materials and other goods "for peaceful purposes." However, "control is to be maintained over all imports and exports of goods, and foreign exchange and financial transactions," with the administration of controls "subject to the approval and supervision of the Supreme Commander."[15]

The fifteen reforms for which MacArthur claimed authorship, then, were incorporated, either directly or by implication, in the four key documents, all basically drafted by SWNCC, that pro-

ing a contribution to the advance of peace, I would gladly yield every honor which has been accorded by war."[17] But by posing before the Japanese and American publics as the architect of the occupation's objectives and policies, he would attract many rebukes by critics at the time and later for failures that were not wholly of his doing. Despite his carefully nourished image of power, the constraints on him were many.

3. A Minor But Revealing Confrontation

MacArthur's first postwar collision with authorities in Washington was not long in coming, but how much it had to do with the occupation is moot. Nine days after he entered Tokyo, he triggered a controversy that ultimately involved the State Department, the Pentagon, Congress, President Truman, several Allied governments, and most major editorialists — no mean feat. On September 4, Robert E. Wood, the Sears, Roebuck board chairman and an ultraconservative Republican leader who had backed the MacArthur-for-President movement in 1944, informed the general that "a very clever ruse on the part of the politicians in Washington" may be under way "to put the burden of blame on you if you should demand a very large army of occupation, which would have to be maintained through a draft." Wood suggested, "It would appear to me that once Japan is disarmed it would require a relatively small force, perhaps 200,000 to 300,000 men. . . . The commander who demands an exorbitant army will later be pilloried, in my opinion, in the eyes of the public."[18]

Wood was correct in assessing demobilization as an explosive issue, for its ramifications involved national security and a potential economic recession. At the end of May 1945 the United States Army's total strength had been nearly 8.3 million soldiers. The War Department's demobilization plan called for a gradual reduction to 6.8 million troops for the duration of the war in the Pacific. But the unexpectedly early capitulation of Japan produced popular outcries to "end the draft" and "bring our boys home." "The pressure here is terrific" to discharge the troops faster, Army Chief of Staff George C. Marshall wrote on August 14 to Eisenhower, commanding American forces in Europe. Pentagon authorities and the Truman administration favored a slower pace of demobilization than the public demanded, fearing that with sharp cuts the troop requirements for America's vastly enlarged global military commitments could not be met and that huge numbers of returning veterans could not be quickly absorbed into the civilian job market.[19]

An alarming acceleration of public pressure on Washington for speedier demobilization came in the wake of an announcement by MacArthur on September 17 that "the smooth progress of the occupation in Japan enabled a drastic cut in the number of troops originally estimated for that purpose," which had been 500,000. The cut would be made possible "by utilizing the Japanese Government structure to the extent necessary to prevent complete social disintegration, insure internal distribution, maintain labor, and prevent calamitous disease or wholesale starvation." He proclaimed, "Within six months the occupational force, unless unforeseen factors arise, will probably number not more than 200,000 men." Undoubtedly anticipating adverse reactions in Washington, he added that "the future of the Japanese politico-governmental structure on a national and international plane" is a matter that "necessarily awaits completion of the military phase of the surrender" and "unquestionably will be determined upon the highest diplomatic level of the United Nations."[20]

Dean G. Acheson, who was Acting Secretary of State while James F. Byrnes was attending the London Conference of Foreign Ministers, was outraged; he telephoned Truman, who was also upset and remarked that the general's pronouncement "would do a great deal of damage and was wholly uncalled for . . . and did not correctly reflect his policies." On September 18 Acheson issued a statement denying that "anybody can see at this time the number of forces that will be necessary in Japan" and declaring that "the occupation forces are the instruments of policy and not the determinants of policy." Harold Smith, the director of the budget, talked to the President that day and found that Truman viewed MacArthur's issuance as "a political statement." In his diary entry of the 18th, Eben A. Ayers, assistant press secretary at the White House, wrote, "The President . . . sounded off about MacArthur and said he 'was going to do something about that fellow,' who, he said, had been balling things up. He said he was tired of fooling around." Arthur Krock of the *New York Times* learned, however, that when someone proposed that MacArthur be relieved, Truman reportedly responded, "Wait a minute, w-a-i-t a minute." Indeed, his public response was temperate. At a press conference on the 18th he remarked, "I'm glad to see that the general won't need as many as he thought. He said first 500,000, later 400,000, and now 200,000. It helps to get as many more men out of the Army as possible." The next day he announced that over 2 million servicemen would be discharged by Christmas, and on the 23d he released to the press the text of "United States Initial Post-Surrender Policy for Japan," hoping to clarify public understanding of the administration's position.[21]

Meanwhile, the State Department received messages expressing consternation from the governments of the United Kingdom and New Zealand, insisting, respectively, that an Allied control commission be set up quickly in Tokyo and that troop reductions not lead to a "soft policy" toward Japan. With Truman's concurrence, Marshall sent MacArthur a telegram stating that the effect of his action was to "embarrass or prejudice War Department efforts" to preserve Selective Service, provide troop replacements overseas, and conduct an "orderly occupation." It also "jeopardized" the War Department's position "in the midst of a highly explosive Congressional situation" and produced "an adverse effect on our political position in the Far East." Henceforth MacArthur was to "coordinate" with the War Department, "prior to release, statements to press or visiting committees regarding strength of garrisons, rate of demobilization, and matters referring to replacement needs, etc." MacArthur replied, "There was not the faintest thought that my statement . . . would cause the slightest embarrassment. . . . I believed that I was acting in complete conformity with the War Department's announced policy of demobilizing just as rapidly as conditions permitted."[22]

A number of periodicals on current affairs and major newspapers in the United States felt compelled to enter the fray, but no pattern clearly indicative of public opinion emerged, because each editorialist addressed a different aspect of the multifaceted controversy. The Washington *Post* accused MacArthur of "mixing politics with statesmanship"; while the Chicago *Tribune* blamed the

furor on "the little jackasses in the State Department." Echoing
Soviet demands for a stern occupation, the New York *Daily Worker*
maintained that MacArthur's troop-reduction proposal was "bait"
to entice the American people to accept his "soft" handling of Japan. The San Francisco *Chronicle* found his "rosy plan to get
American boys home" to be "disquieting," for it "contains the threat
that many more American boys will be sent later to die in a welter
of unfinished business." The Philadelphia *Inquirer* criticized "the
general's unwise prediction," but concluded that "there is no reason to flay MacArthur alive." According to the Chicago *Daily News*,
the episode "indicates that, up to this point, the State Department
and the Army have not been working in close harmony" on occupation plans. The basic issue, commented *Forum*, is "the old
problem of civil vs. military control."[23] Trying to explain the excitement, *The Christian Century's* editorialist produced an interesting blend of perceptivity and naïveté:

> Millions of Americans must by now be asking, What caused such an
> uproar? Why did MacArthur's forecast of a small occupation army
> throw so many radio pundits, newspapers and Washington office-
> holders into such a frenzy? Of course there were many reasons, of
> which three may be mentioned.
>
> In the first place, the professional fighting forces were badly upset
> by this disclosure that a vast standing army would not be needed much
> longer. There are more than 1,600 generals who face reduction to
> their permanent ranks (most of them will be captains and majors) as
> soon as the present swollen army is demobilized. . . . In addition,
> however, the whole case of the army for a continued draft and for
> peacetime conscription has recently been made to rest on the alleged
> need for large forces to fulfill our occupation responsibilities.
> MacArthur's figure of only 200,000 for Japan pulverized that argu-
> ment. It also made the previous large figures for occupation forces
> in Germany — where Russia, Britain and France share the task — seem
> completely out of line, as was acknowledged when, within a week after
> MacArthur made his estimate, General Eisenhower revised his re-
> quirements downward to 400,000 men
>
> Again, there were those who suspected that in saying he could get
> along with 200,000 regulars MacArthur was making a bid for the Re-
> publican nomination in 1948. On its face that is scarcely credible;
> MacArthur will be 69 at the time of the next inauguration. There is
> every reason to believe that he was telling Hugh Baillie, president of

UP, the truth when he said in Tokyo last week: "I have stated before and reiterate now that I started as a soldier, and shall finish as one. I am on my last public assignment which, when concluded, will mark the definite end of my service." But those who are already preparing the groundwork for the Democratic campaign in 1948 feel that they dare overlook no opportunity, even this early, to make political medicine.

But of all the factors that entered into the outburst against MacArthur probably the most important, as it certainly was the most noisome, was the desire in some quarters thus revealed for a peace of revenge. There are some Americans who will be satisfied with nothing less than an occupation of Japan which never ceases for an instant to grind the faces of the Japanese people into the dust. It is the same spirit that once lofty-spirited *Nation* disclosed when, in commenting on Admiral [William F.] Halsey's desire "to kick each Jap delegate" that signed the surrender "in the face," it editorialized: "Not elegant. Not polite. But very exact and satisfying — and somehow reassuring."[24]

In retrospect, the effect of the incident on American demobilization seems to have been exaggerated. The rapid pace of troop reduction was probably unstoppable; by the end of 1945 the Army had 4.2 million troops, and a year later was down to 1.3 million. But the episode etched itself deeply in the memories of Acheson and Truman because of personal embarrassments associated with it. On September 19 the President sent Acheson's nomination as Under Secretary of State to the Senate, where confirmation was delayed mainly by Senators Kenneth S. Wherry of Nebraska and A. B. (Happy) Chandler of Kentucky, who charged that he had "blighted the name" of General MacArthur. Acheson recalled that the Senate debate was "supposedly on my confirmation but in reality on General MacArthur's position and authority in relation to the position and authority of the President of the United States. It was angry and bitter." Twelve senators voted in favor of Wherry's motion to recommit, but it was defeated handily. Acheson's appointment was finally approved on September 24, but it occasioned the only roll-call vote on a State Department nominee in the 79th Congress. Two days later the *New York Times* printed a comment by Tom Connally of Texas, chairman of the Senate Foreign Relations Committee, that the Senate would "never have voted for Mr. Acheson's confirmation unless it had been implicitly understood that he would not have a predominant voice in foreign policy." While the Senate was heatedly arguing over Acheson, a number of conservatives in the House delivered vituperative speeches against him, almost all referring to his alleged "insult" to MacArthur. Twenty-four years later Acheson wrote, "If we could have seen into the future, we might have recognized this skirmish as the beginning of a struggle leading to the relief of General MacArthur from his command on April 11, 1951."[25]

Truman was irked also because his invitation of September 17 to MacArthur "to return to the States to receive the plaudits of a grateful nation" was declined. The President later commented, "I felt that he was entitled to the same honors that had been given to General Eisenhower." MacArthur had replied that it would be "unwise" for him to leave Japan then because of "the delicate and difficult situation which prevails here." On October 19 Truman again invited MacArthur "to make a trip home at such time you feel you can safely leave your duties." He mentioned that plans were being made on the Hill to have the general address a joint session of Congress. Again MacArthur declined, citing "the extraordinarily dangerous and inherently inflammable situation which exists here." The general's effrontery so struck Truman that in his memoirs written in the mid-1950s he quoted in full the messages between him and MacArthur.[26]

An unusually revealing account of MacArthur's thinking in the early autumn of 1945 was recorded by Lieutenant General Robert Eichelberger, the Eighth Army commander in Japan, stationed in Yokohama. In his diary for October 20 he wrote:

> About a quarter of five last night I called on SCAP at his office in Tokyo. . . .
>
> When I told General MacA the ubiquitous Colonel [Julius] Klein was suggesting that he should quit now and had advised [Lieutenant General Robert C.] Richardson to write to SCAP . . . he said: "Don't think for a minute that I will quit now. At one time I might have done so but the President, the State Department, and Marshall (GCM) have all been attacking me. They might have won out but the Reds came out against me and the communists booed me and that raised me to a pinnacle without which they might have licked me. Thanks to the Soviets I am on top. I would like to pin a medal on their a——." . . .

SCAP said he did not intend to go home this fall or this winter but he added, "When I do go you are going with me." He said, "There has been a joint resolution in Congress [adopted on October 10] inviting me to appear before them and I intend to be the first man in our history to refuse to do so. I am going to tell them I have work to do and cannot spare the time." . . .

SCAP emphasized, "I do not intend to quit on this job. I can do it. I know I can succeed in it and I do not propose to be run out by anybody."

MacA said that Christmas would be a good time for me to go home although he wanted to warn me that if the Russians and other foreigners decided to come in about that time I might have to postpone it or go earlier. . . . He said, "I intend that these Russians, Chinese, and British will come under you as ground forces. Their air forces must come under FEAF [U.S. Far East Air Forces] and their Navy under [Admiral Raymond A.] Spruance. Any other condition would be chaotic." He said, "The Joint Chiefs of Staff have agreed with me that this must be done. I told the War Department I felt these foreign forces should be token forces but they say that they should be about 30,000 each." . . .

SCAP said, "Marshall wired in effect as follows: 'Going on the premise that the foreign troops will be the equivalent of your own troops, the President would like to know whether you can reduce below that minimum of 200,000 which you contemplate.' " SCAP added, "It seems funny that they should now be asking me to reduce below 200,000 when you think of all the fuss they made when I advanced the idea that 200,000 would be enough. I think that Truman promised England and perhaps Russia at Potsdam that he would keep a large army in Germany. When that didn't seem feasible he had to bawl me out because I stated that 200,000 would be enough. He had doubtless promised England and Russia that he would maintain a big army. At first they evidently hoped to keep a big army in Germany but because of the opposition they finally decided they would like to keep it in Japan. Not knowing these things at the time, I can see now why my remarks about the 200,000 startled Truman. Now he has to go before Congress in a day or so and plead for peacetime conscription and probably hates me because I didn't help him in this regard which I couldn't do because I didn't know what it was all about."

In speaking of Acheson, SCAP said, "As Acting Secretary of State he would never come out with that attack on me unless it had been directed by the President. His remarks were a trial balloon and the President later turned Acheson down. My remarks with reference to

an army of 200,000 wouldn't have been such as to have forced an
Acting Secretary of State to come out with an attack against a theater
commander. That is unprecedented and was evidently ordered by the
President."

SCAP said Truman is evidently starting out to fool the people just
like FDR did. In speaking of [Brigadier General Leif J. (Jack)] Sverdrup's visit [c. August 14] to the President, SCAP said that the President told Jack, "FDR was always afraid of MacA and seemed to think
he might have tremendous political power."[27]

The tone of MacArthur's remarks was hardly remorseful, but it
would be a long while before he again tested so brazenly the constraints imposed by Washington on his command authority.

4. Unwelcome Allies

"As I reflected on the situation during my trip home" in early August after the Potsdam Conference, Truman said, "I made up my
mind that General MacArthur would be given complete command
and control after victory in Japan." Convinced after this first
meeting with Premier Joseph Stalin that "force is the only thing
the Russians understand," the President concluded, "The experience at Potsdam now made me determined that I would not allow
the Russians any part in the control of Japan." The initial clash
with the Soviets over Japan came in September, during the London Conference of Foreign Ministers of the United States, the
USSR, Britain, France, and China. Although the meeting's purpose was to discuss European affairs, and Japan was not on the
agenda, Vyacheslav M. Molotov, Soviet Commissar for Foreign
Affairs, demanded suddenly on September 24 that Japan be added
to the agenda. He launched into a proposal for an Allied control
council of Soviet, American, British, and Chinese representatives
to be set up in Tokyo with functions similar to those of the control
council already established in Berlin. He angrily charged that
MacArthur was not executing the terms of surrender and was far
too lenient with the Japanese. He wanted all former Japanese soldiers used as slave labor, immediate destruction of all Japanese war
matériel, and punishment in short order of Japanese war crimi-

nals. Molotov also accused MacArthur of ignoring the Soviet mission in Tokyo, headed by Lieutenant General Kuzma N. Derevyanko, and he wondered aloud whether it would be "useful for the Soviet Government to continue having a representative in Tokyo." When Secretary of State Byrnes took a tough stance and blocked his effort to place Japan on the agenda, Molotov announced that the Soviet government was withdrawing its previous pledge to join the Far Eastern Advisory Commission that the United States had proposed in late August to make "recommendations" on policy for occupied Japan. The London Conference ended in a bitter deadlock on European matters as well, with the foreign ministers unable to concur even on a closing communiqué. Returning to Washington, Byrnes reported that Stalin and Molotov "were welching on all the agreements reached at Potsdam and at Yalta," and "it would not be wise for us to rely on their word today."[28]

There is no doubt that MacArthur and his staff were not treating the Soviet Union's chief representative in Japan with the respect that he felt he deserved. On several occasions Derevyanko appeared for scheduled appointments with MacArthur only to be told by a staff officer that he was mistaken about the date — a ploy that MacArthur may not have known about but would have enjoyed. Arrested by American military policemen for "reckless driving," the Soviet general, on his release after he had proved his identity, rushed to MacArthur and demanded an apology, but received instead a stern rebuke for violating the law. Derevyanko often complained that the American traffic controllers at Haneda Airport kept his plane circling unnecessarily long before granting landing clearance. According to MacArthur, when he refused Derevyanko's request to station Soviet troops on Hokkaido, "he went so far as to say Russian forces would move in whether I approved or not. I told him that if a single Soviet soldier entered Japan without my authority, I would at once throw the entire Russian Mission, including himself, into jail." Other than when encountering harrassments from GHQ, Derevyanko, "a bull-necked man who appeared to have been poured into his tight uniform," was known for "robust backslapping" and "became a friendly extrovert at frequent diplomatic parties" in Tokyo, observed William J. Sebald, later head of MacArthur's Diplomatic Section.

In October the Soviet government dropped its plan for a Soviet occupying force in Japan, rather than allow it to serve under MacArthur, and it recalled Derevyanko "to receive further instructions." When he returned to Tokyo, MacArthur reportedly "clapped him warmly on the back and exclaimed, 'Well, well, I never thought I'd see you again! I was sure that once Stalin got you back to Moscow he'd chop your head off.' " Contemporary observers differ on MacArthur's real opinion of Derevyanko; his quoted remarks about him ranged from "an officer of considerable ability" to "a peasant who made good as a general in the war." The correspondent John Gunther believed that the two had "a sneaking personal regard for each other." Whatever his views of Derevyanko as a man, however, MacArthur was not going to let him or the Soviet mission in Japan interfere with his programs. Stalin was right when he told Ambassador W. Averell Harriman in Moscow on October 25 that MacArthur treated Derevyanko like "a mere piece of furniture."[29]

On his return from the disappointing London Conference, Byrnes was successful in organizing the Far Eastern Advisory Commission in spite of the Soviet Union's refusal to participate and the deep discontent of Great Britain, Australia, and China with their merely advisory roles on policymaking for Japan. The body consisted of representatives of the United States, Britain, China, France, Australia, Canada, New Zealand, India, the Netherlands, and the Philippines. Major General Frank R. McCoy served as the commission chairman and American representative; Nelson T. Johnson, also of the United States, was secretary-general and ex officio member. Both McCoy, who had gained fame as a leader of the Lytton Commission on Manchuria in 1932, and Johnson, former ambassador to Australia and China, were old friends of MacArthur. Sir George Sansom and E. Herbert Norman, distinguished authorities on Japan, represented Britain and Canada respectively. The commission was to recommend to "the participating governments" — actually the United States — on the "formulation of policies, principles, and standards by which the fulfillment by Japan of its obligations under the instrument of surrender may be determined." Frank McCoy, one of the few persons to address MacArthur in letters as "Dear Douglas," wrote him on November 1, two days after the commission's first meeting in Washington, that he would be "kept informed of our formal doings here. . . . Nothing could be finer if I can help rather than hinder your splendid performance as Supreme Commander in Japan." MacArthur must have been relieved to know that his "devoted friend" was heading this potentially troublesome group.[30]

In late November, MacArthur invited McCoy's commission to visit Japan to "see at first hand actual current conditions" and to provide him the "greatest possible aid" through "consultation." Arriving the day after Christmas, the full commission spent three weeks in Japan, visiting Nikko, Sendai, Kyoto, Nara, Kure, Hiroshima, and Osaka on the weekends but spending most of the time "in daily conferences with General MacArthur's Special Staff Sections" in Tokyo. Three conferences with MacArthur were held at his office in the Dai Ichi Building, with a cordial atmosphere prevailing and a wide range of issues discussed. In the role of the charming host the Supreme Commander was unexcelled, and he won the commission members' plaudits for his hospitality and cooperation, as well as for his progress in the occupation.[31] In his memorandum to Byrnes accompanying the commission's official report on the trip, McCoy was glowing in his praise of MacArthur:

> The most satisfactory result of the Commission's visit, from the point of view of the United States, was the feeling of confidence in the Supreme Commander engendered in the minds of the foreign representatives. Regardless of their views concerning the policies established by the United States for the control of Japan, all delegates are convinced that those policies are being carried out effectively and with the utmost wisdom by the Supreme Commander and his staff. They were all impressed by General MacArthur's grasp of the problems which face him and by the statesmanship he has shown in performing his difficult task. They were particularly gratified by his consciousness of the international character of his position and the attendant responsibilities.
>
> Of equal importance was the ability of the Commission to erase from the minds of General MacArthur and his staff the natural suspicion which they harbored before they were able to establish personal contact with the representatives. There has now been established a mutual confidence and respect, a cognizance of each other's problems which will aid materially in furthering United States objectives not

only in the control of Japan but in the general field of international
cooperation.[32]

Seldom was McCoy's judgment so prematurely optimistic, for
MacArthur's attitude would change when the Allied role was altered to the making of policy.

For several weeks after the London Conference, Byrnes assumed that Molotov's attack on MacArthur's handling of the occupation was a maneuver to divert American claims for more influence in East Europe, where the Soviet Union continued to
act unilaterally and with impunity. In late October, however, Harriman talked at length with Stalin and reported to Byrnes that the
Soviet leader was greatly disturbed over the failure to create a four-
power Allied control commission for Japan. Moreover, Dr. Herbert V. Evatt, the Australian Minister for External Affairs, who
had been a leading spokesman for the small nations in the found-
ing of the United Nations Organization, launched a veritable crusade that autumn to get a greater voice for Australia in policy-
making for Japan. While discussing Evatt's demands for an
Australian occupying force in Japan at a meeting with Secretary
of War Robert P. Patterson and Secretary of the Navy James V.
Forrestal on October 30, Byrnes remarked, "Evatt wants to run
the world." As the strictly consultative nature of the Far Eastern
Advisory Commission became strikingly apparent during its early
meetings in November, several governments, with Australia in the
lead, became vociferous in wanting more than an advisory role in
dealing with MacArthur. Late in November, Byrnes called for another conference of the "Big Three" foreign ministers, and shortly
a meeting was scheduled for Moscow in mid-December. One of
Byrnes's main reasons for his proposal, states a foremost scholar,
was that he "had found it difficult to press for more authority for
American representatives in Rumania and Bulgaria while denying
Russian requests for a role in the occupation of Japan, and was
now prepared to arrange a compromise even over the objections
of General MacArthur."[33]

Through the autumn of 1945 there was growing suspicion on
the part of MacArthur and his inner circle of top GHQ officers in
Tokyo that SCAP authority might be sacrificed by the United States
government if it could obtain some concessions from Stalin in its

top-priority area, Europe. On October 10 the Tokyo bureau of Reuter's, the usually reliable British news agency, released a sensational bit of news that looks, in retrospect, like part of a SCAP counterstrategy: " 'General MacArthur will resign supreme command in Japan should a four-power commission be appointed to control Nippon,' a high officer stated here tonight, adding MacArthur would 'drop a few sticks of dynamite when he goes.' At the same time the officer asserted MacArthur's command had not received 'one iota of assistance or cooperation' from the Russian delegation here." Byrnes promptly called a news conference and stated that "there is no intention of changing General MacArthur's status. . . . The United States is opposed to the policy of a control council and will continue to pursue the present occupation policy at least for the time being." When queried later on the matter by the Senate Foreign Relations Committee, the Secretary of State gave similar assurances. Meanwhile the alleged threat of resignation produced sympathetic responses from some American newspapers, but not from an editorialist of the Baltimore *Sun*, who wrote: "Fortunately other American military leaders have refrained from statements in the press that they will resign if higher civil authorities of whom these leaders do not approve occupy posts with international affairs. The future of Japan is not an isolated question. It is clear that the United States is confronted by the large task of integrating its policy in Europe with its policy in Asia."[34]

The editorialist was not wrong about the Secretary of State's intentions, for at the Moscow Conference of December 16 to 26, Byrnes was concerned chiefly with projecting American influence into Soviet-dominated Eastern Europe, which had been his main interest at London also. With the backing of British Foreign Secretary Ernest Bevin, he hoped to secure Soviet agreement to concessions on democratic processes in Eastern Europe, especially in Rumania and Bulgaria, and to cooperate in starting multilateral negotiations on peace treaties for Italy, Hungary, Finland, Rumania, and Bulgaria. For a number of reasons, including Byrnes's increased willingness to compromise and to consider the treaties not in isolation but as part of "correlated negotiations" on other issues, Molotov finally agreed to a twenty-one-nation conference on drafting the peace treaties. Furthermore, in a private session with Stalin, Byrnes gained his reluctant and vaguely worded pledge to enlarge somewhat the political representation of the puppet regimes in Bulgaria and Rumania. In response to continuing Soviet insistence on a control council in Japan, Byrnes proposed the creation of two Allied bodies that would be involved with policy on the Japanese occupation: the Far Eastern Commission, to possess limited policymaking authority, and the Allied Council for Japan, to be merely advisory. Although they were aware that Byrnes's plan would not measurably loosen American control of the Japanese occupation, the Soviets gave approval, viewing it as a quid pro quo for their token concessions in the Balkans, which did not disturb Soviet influence there. China's concurrence for the creation of the two bodies was obtained quickly, and the agreement was announced on December 27. The writer Joseph Harsch commented that at least the Moscow settlement marked "the abandonment of a double moral standard by both America and Russia. Up to Moscow, America was trying to apply exclusive American control to Japan, but holding out for the principle of joint responsibility and authority in the Balkans. And Russia, equally, was urging joint responsibility and authority in Japan, but holding out for exclusive Russian control in the Balkans."[35]

The Far Eastern Commission (FEC), according to the Moscow Agreement, was to consist of representatives of the ten nations of the Far Eastern Advisory Commission with the significant addition of a Soviet member. Its two main functions would be "to formulate the policies, principles and standards" for Japan's fulfillment of the surrender terms and "to review, on the request of any member, any directive issued to the Supreme Commander for the Allied Powers or any action taken by the Supreme Commander involving policy decisions within the jurisdiction of the Commission." In its actions it was to "proceed from the fact that there has been formed an Allied Council for Japan and will respect the existing control machinery in Japan, including the chain of command from the United States Government to the Supreme Commander and the Supreme Commander's command of occupation forces." It could "take action by a majority vote, provided the representatives of the United States, United Kingdom, the Soviet Union, and China all concur in the action taken." The commission's headquarters would be in Washington, but it could "meet at other places as occasion requires, including Tokyo." That American dominance of policymaking was to continue virtually unimpaired was made obvious in a section entitled "Functions of the United States Government":

> The United States Government shall prepare directives in accordance with the policy decisions of the Commission and shall transmit them to the Supreme Commander through the appropriate United States Government agency. The Supreme Commander shall be charged with the implementation of the directives which express the policy decisions of the Commission. . . .
>
> *The United States may issue interim directives to the Supreme Commander pending action by the Commission whenever urgent matters arise not covered by policies already formulated by the Commission;* provided that any directives dealing with fundamental changes in the Japanese constitutional structure or in the regime of control, or dealing with a change in the Japanese Government as a whole will be issued only following consultation and following the attainment of agreement in the Far Eastern Commission. [Italics added.][36]

Under the provisions of the Moscow Agreement the Allied Council for Japan (ACJ) would be made up of "the Supreme Commander (or his Deputy) who shall be Chairman and United States member; a Union of Soviet Socialist Republics member; a Chinese member; and a member representing jointly the United Kingdom, Australia, New Zealand, and India." The council would have "the purpose of consulting with and advising the Supreme Commander in regard to the implementation of the Terms of Surrender, the occupation and control of Japan, and of directives supplementary thereto." The seat of the council was to be in Tokyo, and it was to "meet not less often than once every two weeks." The council's purely advisory relationship to MacArthur was not left open to question:

> The Supreme Commander shall issue all orders for the implementation of the Terms of Surrender, the occupation and control of Japan, and directives supplementary thereto. In all cases action will be carried out under and through the Supreme Commander, who is the sole executive authority for the Allied Powers in Japan. He will consult and advise with the Council in advance of the issuance of orders on matters of substance, *the exigencies of the situation permitting*. His decisions upon these matters shall be controlling. [Italics added.][37]

Carefully polished by Byrnes from an earlier SWNCC draft and not altered appreciably at Moscow, the FEC and ACJ terms of reference seemed to safeguard United States control, as well as MacArthur's authority, in the Japanese occupation. Or at least so Byrnes thought. After flying back to Washington in a jubilant mood, he delivered a radio broadcast on December 30 reviewing the work of the Moscow Conference, which actually covered many issues besides Japan and East Europe, and stating that the accord on Japan was designed "to assure that the outstanding and efficient administration set up and executed by General MacArthur should not be obstructed." But Truman was not pleased. Disturbed for two weeks because Byrnes had not kept him fully informed about the proceedings in Moscow, he was even more upset when the Secretary of State did not let him review in advance his radio address. According to Truman, he rebuked Byrnes for these derelictions and expressed strong disapproval of the results obtained at Moscow. Although Byrnes later disputed the President's account of their meeting, Truman said that he told the Secretary of State: "Unless Russia is faced with an iron fist and strong language another war is in the making. . . . I do not think we should play compromise any longer. We should refuse to recognize Rumania and Bulgaria until they comply with our requirements . . . and we should maintain complete control of Japan and the Pacific. . . . I'm tired of babying the Soviets."[38]

Truman had been agitated earlier by renewed rumors of MacArthur's threatened resignation. At a White House press conference on December 20 a correspondent asked, "Mr. President, a broadcaster out of Japan [Larry Tighe of the American Broadcasting Corporation's Tokyo bureau] today made the assertion that General MacArthur has threatened to resign — is upset about the possibility that Russia might have a part in the occupation of Japan. Could you say anything to bring that back into proper perspective?" Truman replied, "I know nothing about it. . . . I don't think General MacArthur has made any such statement." The next day MacArthur told reporters in Tokyo, "For the second time in recent weeks, it becomes necessary for me to deny any allegation that I have threatened to resign. I am here to serve, not to hinder or obstruct the American Government. It is my full purpose to see this thing through. The question of Russian participation in the occupation is a matter for other decision than my own." He added, "If Tighe made the statement he is alleged to have broadcast from Tokyo, someone must have been feeding him the funny type of 'hootch' being peddled around Tokyo on the black market."[39]

In his autobiography MacArthur maintained that "the action at Moscow was bitterly assailed throughout the United States. The outcry became so great that, in its alarm, the Administration sought to shift the responsibility to me." The incident that prompted this unjust criticism was a remark by a State Department public relations officer on December 30 that MacArthur "saw and did not object to the new Japan control plan before it was approved at Moscow" and "was kept informed throughout the conference on matters dealing with Japan and Far Eastern affairs." MacArthur immediately issued a rebuttal: "On 31 October my final disagreement was contained in my radio to the Chief of Staff for the Secretary of State, advising that the terms 'in my opinion are not acceptable.' Since that time, my views have not been sought. Any impression which the statement might imply that I was consulted during the Moscow conference is also incorrect." Although he had "no iota of responsibility for the decisions which were made there," he pledged that "whatever the merits or demerits of the plan, it is my firm intent, within the authority entrusted to me, to try to make it work." Byrnes, in turn, commented at a press conference on the 31st that MacArthur had "objected" to an early draft plan for the FEC and ACJ and that modifications had been made after conferences in Tokyo between the general and Assistant Secretary of War McCloy. Byrnes thought that the amended plan that he took to Moscow was workable from MacArthur's viewpoint. Byrnes continued, "The general has been doing a fine job, and I wanted to make certain that nothing adversely affected his administration. I was delighted to learn that he is determined to see that this plan works." But the Secretary of State replied with an emphatic "no" when a reporter inquired whether MacArthur "could properly concern himself on policy decisions to be taken by the Government."[40]

Having foreseen in early autumn that Allied voices would ultimately be heard in the formulation of occupation policy, MacArthur had been working himself and his staff feverishly on a counterstrategy of more substance than merely issuing objections through the press or messages to his superiors in Washington. He was determined to have his administration under complete control and in full operation and to implement as many reforms in Japan as possible before either of the new Allied bodies began functioning. He intended to present the "foreigners" with a fait accompli in Japan when the FEC held its first meeting in late February 1946 and the ACJ six weeks later. MacArthur might be bound by a multitude of constraints, but, after all, he had long been known as a master of strategic envelopment.

CHAPTER II

The World of GHQ

1. A False Start

WITH THE WAR in the Pacific fast approaching its end in the summer of 1945, MacArthur assumed that Japan, like Germany, would be under direct military rule at least during the early phase of occupation. Accordingly, on August 5 in Manila he established the Military Government Section of General Headquarters, United States Army Forces, Pacific (AFPAC). Brigadier General William E. Crist, who was appointed the section chief, hastily divided his new group into functional units, which began preparing initial proclamations, directives, and memoranda about the impending occupation. On August 28, as MacArthur prepared to fly to Japan and the day before he received the substance of the SWNCC-drafted "United States Initial Post-Surrender Policy for Japan," he indicated to Crist's section that he planned to use the Japanese government more than had been earlier anticipated: "Every opportunity will be given the Government and people of Japan to carry out such instructions without further compulsion. The Occupation Forces will act principally as an agency upon which SCAP can call, if necessary, to secure compliance with instructions issued to the Japanese Government and will observe and report on compliance."[1]

After signing the Instrument of Surrender aboard the *Missouri* in Tokyo Bay on the morning of September 2, Foreign Minister

Mamoru Shigemitsu went back to his office, but late that afternoon he was summoned to an advance-echelon office of Mac-
Arthur's GHQ at the Imperial Hotel. There he was told that at
10:00 the next morning MacArthur would issue three proclamations. The first would "establish military control over all of Japan," and "for all purposes during the military control," English
would be "the official language." The second proclamation stated
that any Japanese who violated the surrender terms or occupation
regulations, or "does any act calculated to disturb public peace or
order or prevent the administration of justice, or willfully does any
act hostile to the Allied Forces, shall, upon conviction by a Military
Occupation Court, suffer death or such other punishment as the
Court may determine." The third provided that "supplemental
military yen currency marked 'B' issued by the Military Occupation Forces is legal tender in Japan for the payment of all yen debts
public or private." Over ¥30 billion of the new currency had been
printed for issuance to the occupying troops on September 3.

Shigemitsu was "stunned," and the Cabinet, meeting in emergency session that evening, decided to try to persuade MacArthur
to suspend the three proclamations. Tadakatsu Suzuki, who was
serving in the Yokohama branch of the Central Liaison Office, set
up by the Japanese government to communicate with the occupation authorities, met early the next morning with Major General Richard J. Marshall, MacArthur's deputy chief of staff. An
appointment for Shigemitsu with MacArthur was arranged for
10:30 that morning. The proclamations would be held in abeyance pending the outcome of this first meeting between Mac-
Arthur and a Japanese official. The Foreign Minister arrived at
the New Grand Hotel in Yokohama, MacArthur's temporary
headquarters, and was "joyfully surprised" by "SCAP's graciousness" when he entered his office. Shigemitsu began by assuring
him that the Cabinet of Imperial Prince Naruhiko Higashikuni was
prepared to carry out the surrender terms completely and to cooperate fully with SCAP's administration of the occupation. But
the three proclamations, each of which was addressed "To the
People of Japan," would "totally destroy the people's confidence
in this Cabinet and lead to domestic disorder." He argued that
problems relating to violations and currency could be "solved by
mutual understanding" between SCAP and the Japanese govern-

ment. He continued, "Should the government fail to fulfill its duties, or should the occupation authorities feel the government's policies are unsatisfactory, then direct orders could be issued by the occupation officials." Shigemitsu concluded, "Issuing such proclamations immediately will not assist the Supreme Commander in achieving his purpose, however, or assist this Cabinet in putting his policies into practice."

Shigemitsu's record of the meeting states that MacArthur responded by reassuring the Foreign Minister that, "while the government must fulfill its duties," the Supreme Commander had "no intention of destroying the nation, or making slaves of the Japanese people." The purpose of the occupation, he said, was "to assist Japan in surmounting its difficulties, and if the government showed 'good faith,' problems would be solved easily." MacArthur then turned to Lieutenant General Richard K. Sutherland, his chief of staff and the only other person at the meeting, and told him that all three proclamations were to be "scrapped."[2]

Suzuki said that the Cabinet was pleased by the "very considerate" attitude of MacArthur, and he believed at the time that SCAP was motivated by the pacific behavior of the Japanese people: "Since the 28th of August, the beginning of the coming in of the troops, until the 2d of September, six days, there was no bloodshed, and it was quite peaceful. So it must have impressed him, and he must have changed his mind at that moment, agreeing not to issue the proclamations." In a recent work Justin Williams, Sr., then an officer in the AFPAC Military Government Section and later an able division head in the SCAP Government Section, contends that "MacArthur reversed himself then and there; until the Foreign Minister called, he had no way of knowing that the Japanese authorities were fully prepared and eager to do his bidding." But there was the precedent of MacArthur's instructions of August 28. Also, by the time of his conference with the Foreign Minister, nearly five days had elapsed since MacArthur had received the "Initial Post-Surrender Policy" statement from Washington, which clearly provided that the Japanese government, under MacArthur's authority, would be permitted "to exercise the normal powers of government in matters of domestic administration." It is difficult to believe that he intended to violate this policy, which would be incorporated shortly in a directive from the Joint Chiefs. A more likely explanation is that of Marshall, his deputy chief of staff, who recalled the incident only dimly many years later but suggested that probably during the first confusing days in Japan the prior plans for issuing the proclamations had not been reviewed. He also said it was unlikely that Crist and his staff had read the Washington document yet. Regardless, the incident served to benefit MacArthur; in the view of high-ranking Japanese officials, he appeared amenable to rational persuasion, sensitive to their need to preserve self-respect, and averse to unnecessary coercion.[3]

It seems more than coincidence that three days after his talk with Shigemitsu the following SWNCC-prepared directive was sent by the Joint Chiefs to MacArthur:

> 1. The authority of the Emperor and the Japanese Government to rule the State is subordinate to you as Supreme Commander for the Allied Powers. You will exercise your authority as you deem proper to carry out your mission. Our relations with Japan do not rest on a contractual basis, but on an unconditional surrender. Since your authority is supreme, you will not entertain any question on the part of the Japanese as to its scope.
>
> 2. Control of Japan shall be exercised through the Japanese Government to the extent that such an arrangement produces satisfactory results. This does not prejudice your right to act directly if required. You may enforce the orders issued by you by the employment of such measures as you deem necessary, including the use of force.
>
> 3. The statement of intentions contained in the Potsdam Declaration will be given full effect. It will not be given effect, however, because we consider ourselves bound in a contractual relationship with Japan as a result of that document. It will be respected and given effect because the Potsdam Declaration forms a part of our policy stated in good faith with relation to Japan and with relation to peace and security in the Far East.[4]

Apparently the favorable reaction in Japan to the MacArthur-Shigemitsu meeting caused concern among Washington authorities as to how far SCAP would go in accommodating Japanese interests.

In the meantime Shigemitsu, who was euphoric about his meeting with the Supreme Commander, indiscreetly disclosed some of the details at a press conference. According to a Japanese account, "MacArthur was reportedly upset at this disclosure, and there were indications that this was a major reason why Shigemitsu left the

Cabinet shortly thereafter." Responding to allegations in a number of American and Allied newspapers, MacArthur remarked in a press release on September 14, "I have noticed some impatience in the press based upon the assumption of a so-called soft policy in Japan. . . . The surrender terms are not soft and they will not be applied in kid-gloved fashion."[5] MacArthur was embarked on the rough waters between the rock of Scylla and the whirlpool of Charybdis.

2. Evolution of GHQ, SCAP

The Allied Council for Japan held its first meeting on April 5, 1946, in the paneled board room of the Meiji Insurance Building in downtown Tokyo, the structure then serving as headquarters of the Far East Air Forces. The second-floor room was crowded with newsmen, photographers, American and Allied military personnel, and a few Japanese. There was an atmosphere of excited anticipation, for many expected the new four-nation body to try to challenge MacArthur's autocratic handling of the occupation. At the polished mahogany table where the ACJ members sat, Lieutenant General Derevyanko, the Soviet representative, looked grim and ready for a confrontation. Chairman MacArthur opened the meeting with a sternly worded fifteen-minute speech. He quickly made it plain that "the functions of the Council will be advisory and consultative" only, and that, as Supreme Commander, he was "the sole executive authority for the Allied Powers in Japan." He emphatically set forth the objectives he had pursued since September, referring several times to "my administration." He looked directly at Derevyanko as he asserted that the ACJ was "charged to proceed in the full unity of purpose which characterized our common effort in the war just won." After making it clear that he would brook no interference by the council in GHQ, SCAP, administrative matters, MacArthur yielded the chairmanship to Major General William F. Marquat and quickly left the room. The Supreme Commander never attended another ACJ meeting.[6] Although physically near each other, the Dai Ichi and Meiji Insurance buildings would be light-years apart in the coming years as far as the ACJ's impact on SCAP was concerned.

Since the Dai Ichi headquarters was MacArthur's control center, a look at its organization and development is essential. Throughout September 1945 the AFPAC Military Government Section existed as an anomaly in MacArthur's headquarters while he worked on plans for a new administrative structure that would encompass the control of the occupation and the command of American Army forces across the Pacific. At the time of the American forces' entry into Japan, the section had nearly 300 officers who were graduates of the School of Military Government at the University of Virginia and of regional Civil Affairs Training schools elsewhere in the States, with occupation-related specialties in such fields as public administration, fiscal policy, and agricultural economics. About half of them were transferred to military government teams with the XXIV Corps in South Korea or with the Sixth or Eighth armies in Japan. Of the other half, some were retained in Crist's section, and the rest were assigned to the Economic and Scientific Section or the Civil Information and Education Section, both newly established in GHQ, AFPAC. On occupation matters during the first month in Japan, MacArthur relied heavily on the offices of his chief of staff and deputy chief, together with the four regular general staff sections of his headquarters. As was standard then in American military headquarters, the G-1 section developed policy and plans for personnel and administration; G-2, for intelligence; G-3, for operations and training; and G-4, for supply. Unlike Eisenhower's headquarters in Germany and Lieutenant General John R. Hodge's in Korea, MacArthur's general staff did not include a G-5 section, for military government. On any matter that claimed the interest of one of the general staff sections, Crist was required to obtain that section's approval on his group's reports or recommendations. "At no time during its two-month existence," states a former SCAP officer, "was the Military Government Section for Japan officially assigned specific duties and functions or given authority to act." MacArthur apparently felt that Crist's section was obsolete now that it was clear that the Japanese government would cooperate and the principal tasks of the occupation would be in non-military affairs.

On October 2 MacArthur dissolved the AFPAC Military Government Section and established General Headquarters, SCAP. The new organization comprised four general staff sections, several small functional offices, and nine special staff, or civil, sections, the last paralleling approximately the areas of responsibility of the main Japanese ministries and consisting initially of the specialists who had been retained in GHQ, AFPAC. General Richard Sutherland and General Richard Marshall, who had held their positions as MacArthur's chief of staff and deputy chief of staff throughout World War II, were to serve in those capacities for both GHQs. MacArthur decided to use the G-1, G-2, G-3, and G-4 sections, as well as the Public Relations Office and Adjutant General's Section, of GHQ, AFPAC, to perform similar functions in GHQ, SCAP, too. Also, he selected as chiefs of several SCAP civil sections officers who held roughly comparable positions simultaneously in GHQ, AFPAC, and all of the original SCAP division chiefs were AFPAC officers. Thus, some Army officers in MacArthur's favor gained dual or multiple roles of authority; one was Major General Charles A. Willoughby, a member of his "Bataan Gang" of key wartime staff leaders, who served as G-2, or intelligence chief, of GHQ, AFPAC, and GHQ, SCAP, besides later holding de facto control of the SCAP Civil Intelligence Section.[7] (The Bataan Gang was the group that had left embattled Corregidor in March 1942 and had gone with MacArthur to Australia to form the nucleus of his Southwest Pacific Area headquarters staff.) By placing in all the important SCAP positions trusted military officers, whose knowledge of the civil areas covered by their sections was a secondary consideration, MacArthur showed that he was obviously intent on keeping tight control of the administration of his new headquarters.

The nine special staff sections that MacArthur set up in October were Government, Public Health and Welfare, Economic and Scientific, Civil Information and Education, Civil Intelligence, Natural Resources, Civil Communications, Legal, and Statistics and Reports. Subsequently activated were the Diplomatic, International Prosecution, Reparations, Civil Transportation, and General Accounting sections. In addition, GHQ, SCAP, included the offices of Civilian Personnel, General Procurement Agent, and Civilian Property Custodian. Within a few months GHQ, SCAP,

GHQ, SCAP, 31 December 1947

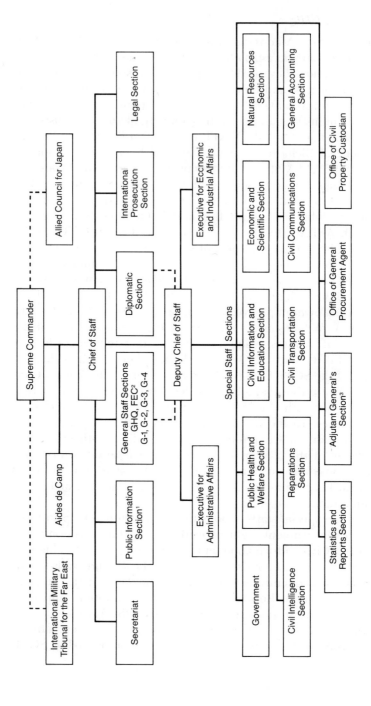

[1]SCAP section of PIO   [2]Limited functions for SCAP   [3]SCAP section of FEC AG

evolved into a considerable bureaucracy of over 2200 military and civilian staff members, nearly all of whom were Americans. During the first year or so a majority of the sections on civil affairs were staffed by reserve officers with military government training who had been recognized experts in their fields in civilian life. After one tour of duty in Japan, however, most of them returned to their civilian positions in the States, and their places were taken by civilians who, for the most part, had not been through the Army's training program in military government and civil affairs. One disappointed SCAP officer said of the latter breed, "Many were from defunct wartime agencies in Washington, few were qualified, and practically all lacked experience." By 1948 the GHQ, SCAP, staff numbered over 5000, but thereafter its personnel and operations were scaled down gradually as control was returned to Japanese authorities. Although there were some organizational changes between 1945 and 1951, the basic administrative structure remained about the same, and the chart of GHQ, SCAP, on the preceding page is fairly typical for the entire span.[8]

It would be impractical to delineate the functions of all the SCAP civil sections and their many internal units, but seven of the sections play such prominent roles in the following narrative that an introduction to them and their chiefs is important. At first the Government Section was led by Crist, but in December 1945 MacArthur replaced him with Brigadier General Courtney Whitney, by then his closest friend. Several of the section's officers later described Crist as simply "ineffective"; one remarked that he was "a lamb . . . too gentle a man to run this kind of operation." Whitney had known MacArthur in Manila's high society in the 1930s, when the former was a well-to-do lawyer, and he had served on his GHQ staff from 1943 to 1945, dealing with guerrillas and later civil affairs in the Philippines. He was admired strongly by his staff leaders in Tokyo as a sharp, highly capable section chief. But he could be aloof and abrasive, and he was intensely disliked by many GHQ officers. In large measure, the hostility stemmed from jealousy, for as one officer commented, "Whitney was very, very close to the Old Man." Short, stout, pink-faced, "with a pointed nose and small eyes," a detractor sneered, Whitney looked like "a stuffed pig with a mustache." He would continue as the section's chief and "strong man" until he returned to the States with

MacArthur in 1951. Under Whitney's leadership the section became the most powerful of the special staff organizations, possessing an extraordinarily competent senior staff and enjoying the strong support of MacArthur, who showed more interest in its work than in any other SCAP activity.

The Government Section was divided initially into the Korean Division and the Public Administration Division, but the former, primarily involving liaison with American military government programs in South Korea, was transferred to the deputy chief of staff's office in early 1947. The Public Administration Division, which was led by Colonel Charles L. Kades, a brilliant attorney, would be expanded later into five divisions because of the vast scope of its duties. As early as January 1946 its functions were, according to a GHQ chart, the providing of advice and recommendations to MacArthur on "planning and policy matters to include demilitarization and decentralization, elimination of feudal and totalitarian practices, elimination of relationships contributing to war potential, strengthening of democratic tendencies and processes, control of courts and procurators, limitation of sovereignty, expulsion of militant nationalists, dissolution of secret societies." It was also charged with preparing policy proposals on the "internal structure of civil government, reorganization and elimination of undesirable agencies, election campaigns, political parties, FEAC [Far Eastern Advisory Commission] liaison." In relation to Japan's foreign affairs, it advised MacArthur on the "transfer of external property and archives, recall of diplomats, Japanese expatriates, neutral nations' problems."[9]

MacArthur's first appointment as chief of the Civil Intelligence Section was Brigadier General Elliott R. Thorpe, who had headed counterintelligence ably in his wartime GHQ. Because of deep-seated personal differences and jurisdictional conflicts between Thorpe and himself, Willoughby persuaded MacArthur to discontinue the section in May 1946, and have its duties assumed by his G-2 section. When the Civil Intelligence Section was reactivated by MacArthur four months later, the new chief was Colonel H. I. T. Cresswell, who was followed, from 1947 to 1950, by Colonel Rufus S. Bratton. Both men were G-2 deputies; in reality, Willoughby maintained operational control of Civil Intelligence until 1951. Willoughby had been MacArthur's intelligence chief since

1941 and was one of the Supreme Commander's most trusted advisers, although he was never able to gain the relationship of informal camaraderie that Whitney enjoyed with MacArthur. Well over six feet tall, German-born, and "Old World in his manners," he was called "Baron Von Willoughby" by some colleagues in private. "He was so much the Prussian type," one remarked, "that all he needed was a spiked helmet." Generally he was regarded at GHQ as a brilliant but fiery individual who was opinionated and "prone to histrionics."

The Civil Intelligence Section's duties were in three areas: civil censorship, public safety, and counterintelligence. According to an official, if abbreviated, account of its activities, it "censors civilian communications and public information media; processes intelligence information derived from censorship controls; maintains security of Occupation forces; cooperates with Japanese law enforcement agencies in suppressing activities detrimental to the Occupation; collects information of intelligence value as required; controls, trains, and supervises Japanese public safety agencies on fire prevention, police protection, the maritime service, and the penal system." Its Civil Censorship Division, which became one of the most controversial SCAP units, was dissolved in late 1949 as controls began to be relaxed. Willoughby viewed the section as "primarily responsible for the dissolution and surveillance of ultra-nationalistic and militaristic organizations." But most of these groups were dissolved during the first few months, and much of the section's later intelligence and counterintelligence work was directed against Japanese radicals, especially Communists.[10]

Colonel Raymond C. Kramer, a former business executive in New York City who was known for his broad knowledge of economics, was chief of the Economic and Scientific Section until December 1945, when MacArthur, for unknown reasons, replaced him with another member of the Bataan Gang, Major General William F. Marquat. Having served in the coast artillery until the late 1930s, Marquat became the chief antiaircraft officer in MacArthur's Southwest Pacific headquarters. Actually he had had no training in any of the fields for which the Economic and Scientific Section was responsible, but MacArthur considered him "an excellent staff man," and he was widely respected and liked by the senior officers of GHQ. One colleague later recalled him as "extremely bright";

another thought him "not terribly intelligent." But most GHQ general officers agreed that he "had a tremendous capacity for work" and possessed "a great sense of humor." His paramount asset, as it would turn out, was his ability to select talented, qualified men for some of the key positions in his section. The responsibility of the section was to advise the Supreme Commander on "economic, industrial, financial, and scientific policies." The largest of the SCAP sections in personnel strength, it consisted of the Finance, Exports and Imports, Labor, Cartels and Antitrust, Industrial, Rationing and Price Control, Scientific, Statistics and Research, and Legal divisions.[11]

For the first nine months of the occupation Brigadier General Kenneth R. Dyke, a former radio and advertising executive, was the chief of the Civil Information and Education Section. When he went back to the United States in 1946 to become vice president of the National Broadcasting Company, an American correspondent in Tokyo learned that allegedly "the Bataan crowd was glad to see him go. Dyke's insistence that left-wing publications should have the same claims to news and newsprint sources as the more conservative press made him a radical in the eyes of MacArthur's men." His replacement was Marine Lieutenant Colonel Donald R. Nugent, who had taught once in a small-town school. According to one observer, he was "terrified" by MacArthur at first. Another noted that he "carries out orders brilliantly, rarely suggests or initiates." Still another of his GHQ colleagues commented, however, that "Nugent chose good people, and he gave them leeway . . . a chance to work."

Most of the efforts of the Civil Information and Education Section, states a SCAP report, were "concentrated on educational and sociological reforms, with particular reference to the democratization of the national school system. It made recommendations to insure the elimination of doctrines of militarism and ultranationalism, including juvenile military training, from all elements of the Japanese educational system." Among its other diverse functions, it advised the Supreme Commander on plans "to establish freedom of opinion, speech, press, and assembly by dissemination of democratic ideals and principles through all media of public information . . . to maintain freedom of religious worship and separation of Church from State," and to conduct "public opinion surveys and sociological research to provide factual information about public reactions to the Occupation."[12] Its experiments would include some that were among the most interesting but least effective of all those undertaken by GHQ, SCAP.

Throughout the occupation to 1951 the Public Health and Welfare Section was under the leadership of Colonel Crawford F. Sams, a distinguished Army neurosurgeon and researcher in preventive medicine who also proved to be a skilled administrator of the vast programs in health and welfare that were inaugurated by his section. Sams had served in the Middle Eastern and European theaters, so he did not meet MacArthur until he was assigned to the AFPAC Military Government Section at Manila in early August 1945. MacArthur developed a deep respect for his professional competence and gave him virtually free rein in administering his programs. Sams said simply, "I never had him turn me down" — a statement that few, if any, of MacArthur's other staff officers could make.

Because of critical shortages of well-trained personnel, modern equipment, and adequate supplies in Japanese health services, the many duties of Sams's section included establishment of training programs in preventive medicine, nursing, hospital administration, and veterinary medicine; control of narcotics production and distribution; administration of nationwide vaccination programs against epidemic diseases; formulation of new quarantine and sanitation regulations; organization of a modern system of recording health statistics; and production and distribution of dental, medical, sanitary, and veterinary equipment and supplies. In addition, the section was charged with "supervising and coordinating operations of the Japanese Government and private agencies dealing with social security," as well as establishing "essential activities necessary to maintain a minimum welfare standard and prevent disorder among the civilian population," including the setting-up of training programs in social work, child welfare, and rehabilitation of the physically handicapped. Although the fields of public health and welfare were "rather specialized and unrelated," according to an understatement by Sams, his section would become the one most appreciated by the Japanese people, yet inexplicably it is seldom mentioned by commentators on the occupation.[13]

Lieutenant Colonel Hubert G. Schenck of the Corps of Engineers headed the Natural Resources Section until late 1951. A Stanford geologist before the war, he was described by a GHQ officer as industrious and "capable but not outstanding." He did not develop close ties with MacArthur or his inner group, and, like Nugent, he remained a lieutenant colonel during six years in an administration where rank counted heavily. Yet interviews with a number of GHQ officers elicited no negative reactions to him, and General Matthew B. Ridgway, MacArthur's successor as SCAP, cited his "superb professional acuity and administrative competence" when awarding him the Distinguished Service Medal. Describing the functions of the Natural Resources Section, a SCAP report stated that it "investigates, recommends, and, as authorized, implements policies and programs" relating to "production, processing, distribution, and conservation" of agricultural, fishery, forestry, and mining products. The "primary concern" of his section, Schenck wrote, was "production from all the natural resources of Japan," and its missions were "(1) to maximize immediate production and promote efficient utilization of the materials produced in order to minimize import requirements, and (2) to maximize long-range production in order to reduce Japan's future dependence on foreign sources for its supplies." In 1948 the section was given the added responsibility of advising MacArthur on "policies and activities pertaining to agriculture, forestry, fishery, mining, and geology in the Ryukyus."[14]

Unlike the previously mentioned civil sections, the Diplomatic Section was not engaged directly in "reforming" Japan, but it is significant as the principal link between MacArthur and the Department of State. For the first nine months of the occupation the Office of the Political Adviser in Japan was administered by the State Department, though sometimes its message traffic was monitored by MacArthur's headquarters. This office, in essence, became the new Diplomatic Section in April 1946; thereby it came under MacArthur's authority, but it continued its political advisory function for the State Department while obtaining from GHQ, SCAP, the top-level access and logistical support that it had lacked often in previous months. Max W. Bishop, a member of the political adviser's staff, said that MacArthur, explaining the new arrangement, told him that "after the reorganization we would be a member of the team and he hoped that we would function as a member of the team" of GHQ, SCAP. The functions that Mac-Arthur assigned to the Diplomatic Section were "to make recommendations concerning the establishment of diplomatic missions and consular offices by foreign nations in Japan and Korea; to maintain liaison between [them] . . . and General Headquarters . . . and the Japanese Government; to maintain branches in Yokohama and in other cities to perform consular functions, and to supervise these branches and such other agencies of the State Department as might be established in Japan." The State Department's political adviser, who was also its senior representative in Japan, was to become the chief of the Diplomatic Section, and he would represent MacArthur as the chairman and American member of the Allied Council for Japan.

George Atcheson, Jr., who had been the political adviser since the occupation began, had been a Foreign Service officer in wartime China. He and two members of his staff, John S. Service and John K. Emmerson, were already under criticism in America for their alleged sympathy toward the Communist Chinese. To the astonishment of some of his general officers, MacArthur took a liking to Atcheson and often sought his advice as chief of the Diplomatic Section. In spite of some sharp differences of opinion between them, "Atcheson was very close to MacArthur, much closer than most people realize," said a State Department officer, but "he had to act with a great deal of discretion" at GHQ because "all the other top brass officials, of course, were very jealous of anybody who had close access to MacArthur." When Atcheson was killed in an airplane crash in August 1947, William Sebald, his successor as head of the section, visited MacArthur shortly and observed that "Atcheson's death was carved on his face. . . . The General was a deeply sentimental and sensitive man. . . . It was obvious that MacArthur had valued George A. as both a friend and one of his principal advisers." Sebald, who was a Naval Academy graduate and a naval intelligence officer in World War II, also had been an attorney in prewar Japan and spoke Japanese fluently. Reserved, intelligent, and tactful, he got along well with MacArthur, although, as in Atcheson's case, his job sometimes required him to differ frankly with the Supreme Commander, especially when representing the State Department's contrary position on a particular issue. Despite his usually harmonious relations with Atcheson and Sebald, however, MacArthur remained highly suspicious of their superiors in the State Department.[15]

In organizing GHQ, SCAP, the way he did, MacArthur devised an administrative framework that, at least on paper, covered the multitude of functions set forth in the "Initial Post-Surrender Policy." His structure demonstrates that he had studied that document carefully and intended to try to implement both its realistic and idealistic objectives. But it also indicates that, though formally acquiescing in the external imposition of high-level, or primary, policy, he realized that he had latitude at the internal, or secondary, policy level in interpreting Washington directives and determining their implementation. By entrusting his Tokyo administration to men whose loyalty to him was beyond question and by shrewdly, tightly controlling GHQ, SCAP, he would have the opportunity to make his distinctive imprint on the occupation. But the bureaucracy that he created would not become the "team" that he had hoped for, and many of its plans would be thwarted cleverly by the Japanese from the Diet down to prefectural and local levels. Moreover, although the demilitarization of Japan would be accomplished within reasonable expectations, its democratization was another matter. W. Macmahon Ball, an astute Australian who served on the Allied Council for Japan, believed that the concept of the occupation administration was based on a serious fallacy: "A military organization is perforce a hierarchy. In structure and in atmosphere, it does not seem to be well suited to foster democratic procedures. A military set-up, by its very nature, seeks to eliminate the individualism, the independence, the freedom of discussion and the atmosphere of equality which make the fabric of democracy." To MacArthur's credit, he too would realize this and in March 1947 would become an early advocate of terminating the occupation.[16]

3. GHQ in Action

MacArthur's organizational plan for GHQ, SCAP, looked rational and orderly on wiring diagrams, but it did not take long for the

new headquarters to manifest the typical ailments of a large bureaucracy. The special staff sections, complained a SCAP officer
in December 1945, "are stymied by red tape, taxed by duplication
of effort, and hampered by administrative growing pains."
MacArthur and his staff chiefs had no precedent to guide them
in administering this kind of organization; the experience of Eisenhower's occupation administration in Germany, begun five
months earlier, was of little help, because the structure and circumstances were far different. Especially during the first year, the
enormous turnover in SCAP personnel in the middle and lower
echelons at GHQ produced confusion at times, as did the large-
scale integration of military officers and civilians in the special staff
units. The situation was complicated further by personality clashes,
power struggles, and jurisdictional clashes between some senior
administrators, most of which were kept from MacArthur's
knowledge.[17]

One affair during the first half year, however, became so serious that MacArthur's intervention was necessary to resolve it. He
was eager to get as many SCAP programs activated as possible before Allied suggestions about policy became a reality, and some of
the civil sections were making the sort of progress he expected.
But at the same time, stated a former occupation officer, "there
was a quiet struggle by the traditional military general staff sections of MacArthur's headquarters to place the new functional
special staff sections under general staff control." According to
another account by a GHQ staff member, the general staff's "interposition in nonmilitary activities and purely civil affairs functions" reached the point of affecting GHQ's effectiveness: "The
unintelligent meddling by G-1 and G-2, along with the discouraging procrastinations of G-3 and G-4, critically delayed essential
action on many vital measures in the crucial first six months of the
occupation." The climax came when the G-3 section, headed by
Brigadier General William E. Chambers, proposed to MacArthur
that the whole headquarters structure be changed to place GHQ,
SCAP, which it viewed as "a civilian organization," under the "direct responsibility" of GHQ, AFPAC, the military headquarters.
Whitney and some of his irate Government Section leaders led the
way in convincing MacArthur that "his original command structure was sound," said Commander Alfred R. Hussey of Whitney's

section. "A 'palace revolution' nearly occurred in the Dai Ichi
Building during the first two months of 1946" before MacArthur
disapproved the G-3 plan, commented another GHQ officer. A
tenuous truce prevailed after MacArthur appointed a second deputy chief of staff, for SCAP affairs; he was Major General Lester
J. Whitlock, MacArthur's long-time G-4 chief. Thereafter special
staff business went to him for final action, bypassing the general
staff, whose authority over SCAP matters was limited to reviewing
"only those decisions of the SCAP special staff sections which were
of mutual concern." But a special staff officer, looking back three
years later, lamented that "if not directly, then indirectly, the general staff officers still exert by far the greatest influence in the Supreme Commander's headquarters."[18]

Although the threatened takeover of the special staff sections
was averted, the sections were plagued by intermittent friction between their military and civilian personnel throughout the entire
occupation period. A member of the Civil Information and Education Section remarked, "Civilian assistants were quickly recruited to bolster the military-headed sections, but, on the whole,
they were to have little authority and would not often be listened
to. MacArthur and his captains seemed to have a conditioned-re-
flex antagonism toward experts." Robert K. Hall, chief of the Education Division and a former professor, found that "civilians
without military backgrounds on occasion were resentful of the
military authority which was imposed on their work." An exception was the remarkable group of men at the top level of the Government Section; they had distinguished records in civilian pursuits and worked well with one another and with Whitney. Some
of them were civilians when they joined the section, but most held
temporary or reserve commissions, though they stayed on the job
long after reverting to civilian status. They included Kades, Williams, Frank Rizzo, Henry E. Robison, Alfred C. Oppler, Alfred
R. Hussey, Milo E. Rowell, Guy J. Swope, Blaine Hoover, and Cecil G. Tilton. Rizzo, out of uniform by 1951, eventually succeeded
Whitney as the section chief. But not all was harmonious even in
that section, as attested by a member who had been a sociology
professor: "We of the academic world were put into insignificant
places. . . . The occupation headquarters was marked by dissension. The Army was jealous of the civilians, as the civilians were

of the officers. The Army resented the presence of the civilians, whom they looked upon as spies."[19]

Offering a more balanced judgment, Harold S. Quigley and John E. Turner, University of Minnesota political science professors who worked in the Government Section, concluded, "Although there were many civilians in General Headquarters, and some sections in which their ideas were influential, in other sections their knowledge, ability, and enthusiastic interest often were well recompensed but poorly utilized." Most of the SCAP senior administrators were convinced that devotion to MacArthur was a vital unifying factor in GHQ, but in the middle and lower SCAP echelons, asserted Quigley and Turner, "There was no sense of being members of a community engaged in a great enterprise, though a man of MacArthur's magnetism and rhetorical powers might easily have stimulated a strong consciousness of individual importance and collective responsibility in so loyal and competent a body."[20] In truth, MacArthur probably could not have solved this problem, because most civilian specialists employed in large military bureaucracies, before and since that time, have had to combat the malaise of discouragement of their initiative and the lack of a sense of belonging.

Hans H. Baerwald, a junior officer in the Government Section and later a distinguished political scientist, maintained that "a doubtful and confusing albeit high-minded combination of premises and goals were included in the basic policies on which the vast superstructure of SCAP was built. That was probably its basic flaw." The strange mixture of liberal and conservative thinking that molded the external, Washington-originated policy for the occupation was reflected in different blends, to be sure, in MacArthur himself, who might reveal a conservative bent on one issue but would be liberally disposed on the next. Likewise, in the planning of internal, SCAP-drafted policy, the ideologies of his staff ran the spectrum. Virtually all his general staff men were ultraconservatives who became disturbed easily over many of the reformist directives from Washington and the special staff plans for implementing them. The spokesman of the most reactionary group of regular Army officers at GHQ was Willoughby, who had never hidden his admiration of Francisco Franco since the Spanish Civil War and after the occupation ended visited Spain, paying homage to Franco as "the second greatest general in the world." Willoughby even believed that Thorpe, in counterintelligence, and Whitney were too liberal. On the other hand, Roger Nash Baldwin, a renowned liberal who headed the American Civil Liberties Union, served on an advisory mission to occupied Japan and found that GHQ, SCAP, had too many liberals, at least of one breed: "General MacArthur remarked that when he asked Washington to send him all those civilian assistants, that they sent him a boatload of New Dealers. Well, my impression was that a large number of them *were* New Dealers. As a matter of fact, some of them were such extreme New Dealers that they had to be sent home." Sir George Sansom, British FEC member and a scholar of Japanese history, decried the large number of impractical liberals at GHQ, SCAP, where sometimes "idealism seems to have outrun practical wisdom." Shigeru Yoshida, a leader of Japanese conservatives who served as prime minister for all but one and a half years of the occupation period, declared that "not only in the Government Section, but in all sections outside the General Staff, there seems to have existed a good sprinkling of radical elements" that "made friends with Japan's own Left-wingers."[21]

Having been compelled to adapt to President Franklin D. Roosevelt's New Deal when he was Army chief of staff and to Prime Minister John Curtin's Labour programs when he was in Australia during World War II, MacArthur did not seem to be upset by the ideological potpourri in his headquarters in Tokyo. George F. Kennan, perhaps the most influential Cold War strategist in the State Department, conferred with MacArthur in early 1948 and found that he was "aware" of widespread suggestions that the "curious pattern of achievement on the part of SCAP was in part the result of Communist infiltration within the headquarters." Kennan said that MacArthur "did not, if I understood him correctly, think it impossible that there might be party members among the thousands of persons attached to SCAP — on the contrary, he rather assumed that there were. 'We have probably got some of them. The War Department has some. So does the State Department. It doesn't mean very much,' I seem to recall his saying. He did not think that such minor influences as they could exert was of any great importance." MacArthur may have been correct regarding Communist influence, but he never seemed to be fully aware of the extent of the exploitation of "the internecine wars among Occupation personnel" by some Japanese leaders in side-tracking certain reform measures. "The evasions were made easier," as one authority affirmed, "by a sharp division between liberals and conservatives in the ranks of SCAP policymakers of which the Japanese took full advantage."[22]

Since every section had a division or branch specifically charged with collecting data on current Japanese conditions in its field, it would appear — and so it did at the lofty level of the Supreme Commander — that GHQ, SCAP, was in receipt of adequate information on which to base its planning. But, observed an unusually frank staff member, MacArthur's "top brass knew little of the situation. . . . Only a handful enjoyed more than casual knowledge of Japanese civilian affairs, and fewer still were ardent students." Whereas accurate data often were available through the research of specialists at the lower SCAP levels, too many section and division chiefs did not heed such professional research, but fed information to MacArthur that came from such sources as English-language editions of Japanese newspapers and periodicals; daily digests of translations from the cautious, censored Japanese press; conferences with Japanese politicians, bureaucrats, and wealthy businessmen, whose views ranged from conservative to reactionary; and a select corps of Japanese informers who were usually concerned with self-advancement and had ingratiated themselves through social contacts with SCAP officials. "The Old Man rarely turned down a sound progressive idea," said a SCAP civil section employee, "but it was hard to get the idea before him." The bulk of SCAP reformist programs that proved durable and worthwhile came from the unpublicized work of staff members at the lower levels who somehow sold their proposals to section administrators or, in rare cases, bypassed them and reached MacArthur through a friend on the general staff.

Since they conferred with and rendered reports directly to the Supreme Commander, special advisory missions of civilian specialists from the United States were among MacArthur's most reliable sources of information on Japan. He used such a large number of these visiting teams of expert consultants in education, industry, labor, and other fields that it seemed that one or more such groups were arriving or departing from Haneda Airport every month. Their proposals were often incorporated in the policy planning of the special staff sections. "The recommendations of these commissions," an authority stated, "have resulted in a substantial proportion of changes initiated. Their work is one of the outstanding features of occupation administration."[23]

In dealing with the Japanese government, MacArthur used all three of the principal courses of action that were open to him: administrative orders for changes to be made; formal and informal contacts between SCAP and Japanese officials to obtain the latter's conformity through education and persuasion, including personal letters and talks between MacArthur and top-level government leaders; and, most frequently, a middle course that comprised both directives and working-level conferences. Because of his sense of urgency to get reformist programs moving, he resorted extensively at first to administrative directives, or SCAPINs, with over 1000 of them issued by early June 1946. Since at that stage he was concerned primarily with the removal of obstacles to positive changes toward political, economic, and social democratization, many of these early SCAPINs were negative in the sense that they abrogated restrictive legislation, organizations, and practices. After the first year MacArthur used directives less often and increasingly turned to meetings between his administrators and Japanese officials.

Each SCAPIN was planned and drafted by the staff section that MacArthur charged with the responsibility of giving advice and recommendations on the particular matter. It then passed through administrative channels, normally from the drafting committee through the branch and division administrators to the section chief, who made the presentation before the deputy chief of staff for SCAP affairs. At the various levels en route changes were often made in the draft, and consultations with pertinent Japanese agencies were usual, especially after the first year. The deputy chief and the chief of staff might call conferences with administrators of other SCAP units whose interests were involved in the particular SCAPIN draft. MacArthur delegated a large amount of authority in resolving differences to his chief of staff, and that officer functioned like a lightning rod in grounding bolts of dissent within GHQ. If concurrence could not be reached among the officers concerned, the chief of staff took the matter to MacArthur, who frequently ordered detailed briefings on the various positions held, then studied the draft directive carefully, and rendered the final decision. The approved SCAPIN was issued in the name of the Supreme Commander by the chief of staff.[24] The subsequent "medium of control," in SCAP jargon, is explained briefly in a GHQ document:

> The Supreme Commander transmits his instructions through directives and memoranda to the Japanese Government. Army and Corps Commanders conduct investigations and make reports, and in cases of non-compliance by the Japanese Government take appropriate action as directed by this Headquarters.
>
> Directives and memoranda are transmitted through the Liaison Officer, G-2, to the Central Liaison Office (CLO) of the Japanese Government. The latter directs the proper course of the instructions to the appropriate Ministries for compliance. Close liaison and expedition is provided for through frequent informal conferences between Special Staff Sections of this Headquarters and the appropriate bureaus within the Japanese Ministries.
>
> On the prefectural and local levels the SIXTH and EIGHTH Armies perform such military government activities as directed by SCAP. . . . Armies and Corps [have] the following responsibilities in addition to those of a strictly military character: (1) the procurement of labor, and (2) the procurement of supplies, equipment, and facilities.
>
> Military government officers and units are assigned to Armies, Corps, and Divisions. Liaison Officers of the SIXTH and EIGHTH Armies and XXIV Corps [in Korea] are stationed with GHQ SCAP.[25]

Although he simply saw no alternative in many instances, especially during the formative stage, MacArthur realized that "rule by directive" had its shortcomings: "Nothing that was good in the new Japanese government was going to be done because I imposed it, or because of fear of me and what I represented. . . . I knew that the whole occupation would fail if we did not proceed from this one basic assumption — the reform had to come from the Japanese."[26]

But he comprehended dimly that not only in compliance by the Japanese, but also in execution by his forces, a far distance separated his Tokyo GHQ from the cities and villages of Japan's forty-six prefectures. Military government teams of the Eighth Army, more accurately designated civil affairs teams in 1949, were assigned to each prefecture. They were engaged chiefly in surveillance and in advising prefectural and local officials on the meaning and implementation of sundry SCAP directives and programs. Always undermanned, a typical team in an intermediate-size prefecture of about 1.5 million Japanese had thirty-two enlisted men and eight officers. The teams were also handicapped by belated or sketchy information about the SCAP directives they were expected to explain and enforce. In its normal routing a SCAPIN went from GHQ to the Central Liaison Office and then to the appropriate Japanese ministry. At the same time GHQ sent copies to Eighth Army headquarters, whence they had to go through corps and division channels to regional and prefectural military government offices before reaching the teams in the field. In many instances local Japanese officials received copies of a SCAPIN before the team in the area knew of its existence. Moreover, the team's commanding officer ordinarily was not acquainted with the reasons for the directive, because his line of communication went strictly through military echelons. The GHQ, SCAP, special staff sections were never permitted to establish contact with the prefectural military government units. The absence of contact between the teams and GHQ, SCAP, made it difficult also for the latter to obtain accurate, up-to-date information from the field.[27] MacArthur, who never saw anything of Japan other than Tokyo, probably did not know about this serious defect in the system.

4. The MacArthur Way

MacArthur's office was on the top floor, the sixth, of the Dai Ichi Building, a large granite edifice across from the south end of the moat surrounding the Imperial Palace in the center of Tokyo. Built just before World War II to house the central offices of a large Japanese life insurance company, the structure was one of the few left in the Hibiya business district that was partly air-conditioned and undamaged by air raids. Most of his top general staff officers, together with the Government Section and some personnel of other

SCAP sections, were located in the Dai Ichi Building. Other SCAP offices were situated in nearby structures commandeered from the proprietors or the Japanese government, such as the Forestry, Radio Tokyo, and Mitsui Bank buildings. At first most GHQ senior officers resided at the Imperial Hotel, which retained its atmosphere of grandeur, but some of them later moved into requisitioned private houses. MacArthur and his family lived in the elegant ambassador's residence atop Renanzaka Hill in the United States embassy compound, about a five-minute drive from his headquarters.

Spacious but not ostentatious in size or décor, MacArthur's office was walnut-paneled and contained two comfortable but plain leather couches, several large upholstered chairs, a glass-door bookcase, a stand of American and Allied flags, a pipe table, and a large desk covered with green baize. On the desk there was an in-and-out basket, some pencils, a note pad, and perhaps a document or two, all neatly arranged, but no telephones or gadgets.[28] The office was slightly expanded in preparation for MacArthur's occupancy, according to Kimpei Shiba, former editor of the *Nippon Times:*

> The custodian of the edifice was Yosaku Matsumoto. Col. Eastwood [Brigadier General Harold E. Eastwood] gave him the title of Japanese building manager and told him to turn the granite structure over to SCAP six days later, Sept. 15.
>
> Mr. Matsumoto's first and, as it turned out, biggest shock came when an American military truck began unloading a huge carpet for Gen. MacArthur's office. He had it laid out on the floor and discovered that it was too large for the room.
>
> The custodian expected Col. Eastwood, who was ordering him to hubba-hubba, to instruct him to cut the carpet to fit the room. The latter was dumbfounded at the suggestion.
>
> "Move the wall back," Col. Eastwood commanded.
>
> It was Mr. Matsumoto, this time, who was flabbergasted. He had heard of carpets being fitted to a room but not vice versa.
>
> "The door is made of steel," he explained.
>
> Col. Eastwood took the Japanese aside and explained that the carpet belonged to Gen. MacArthur; it was his personal property.
>
> "So move the wall, get the job done by the end of the week, and let me hear no more about this," the colonel said.

This was done, and the experience gave the Japanese new insight into the magical power of the name MacArthur.[29]

On the wall behind his desk hung portraits of Abraham Lincoln and George Washington, whom MacArthur sometimes called "my major advisers." Beneath the picture of Lincoln was a printed card bearing one of that President's often-quoted statements: "If I were to try to read, much less answer, all the attacks made on me, this shop might as well be closed for any other business. I do the very best I know how, the very best I can, and I mean to keep doing so until the end. If the end brings me out all right, what is said against me won't amount to anything. If the end brings me out wrong, ten thousand angels swearing I was right would make no difference."[30] Also conspicuous on the wall was a framed quotation recorded by the historian Livy and attributed to Lucius Aemilius Paulus, a Roman general who led a campaign against Macedonia in the second century B.C. Another copy had hung in MacArthur's office in prewar Manila. The lengthy quotation reveals much about his own attitude toward critics of commanders in the field, particularly one portion:

> I am not one of those who think that commanders ought at no time to receive advice; on the contrary, I should deem that man more proud than wise, who regulated every proceeding by the standard of his own single judgment. What then is my opinion? That commanders should be counselled, chiefly by persons of known talent; by those who have made the art of war their particular study, and whose knowledge is derived from experience; from those who are present at the scene of action, who see the country, who see the enemy, who see the advantages that occasions offer, and who, like people embarked in the same ship, are sharers of the danger. If, therefore, any one thinks himself qualified to give advice respecting the war which I am to conduct, which may prove advantageous to the public, let him not refuse his assistance to the state, but let him come with me into Macedonia. He shall be furnished with a ship, a horse, a tent; even his travelling charges shall be defrayed. But if he thinks this too much trouble, and prefers the repose of a city life to the toils of war, let him not, on land, assume the office of a pilot. The city, in itself, furnishes abundance of topics for conversation; let it confine its passion for talking within its own precincts, and rest assured that we shall pay no attention to any councils but such as shall be framed within our camp.[31]

Except for flights to Manila in 1946 and Seoul in 1948, Mac-Arthur's daily itinerary remained remarkably the same until the Korean War, consisting of the short drives to and from the embassy and his headquarters. Four times a day, seven days a week, including American and Japanese holidays, Japanese policemen manually switched all traffic lights in his path to green as his black Cadillac sedan (later a Chrysler) approached. Having spent several hours in the early morning studying messages and documents brought to the embassy by GHQ couriers, he went to his Dai Ichi office about 10:30 or 11:00 A.M.; returned to the embassy at 1:30 or 2:00, often to host a luncheon for visiting dignitaries, followed by a long nap; and went back to his headquarters about 4:00 P.M., staying there until 8:00 or later in the evening. His routine made a long work day for his immediate staff, who reported to their offices at 8:00 A.M. and usually dared not leave until the Old Man's final exit that night. His arrivals and departures at the Dai Ichi Building, reported a Japanese newspaper in November 1945, attracted "large crowds" and "on Sundays particularly the crowd includes several hundred soldiers, sailors, and Japanese all anxious to see the General and to take pictures of him. The respectful attitude of these crowds is itself an inspiration." A less deferential *New Republic* correspondent quipped that it was "the best show in Tokyo" and offered another reason for some onlookers' presence: "400 Japanese suck in their breath and bow low as the General descends. American spectators, who have been smoking nervously, toss away their cigarettes and fumble with their cameras. The Japanese make their traditional obeisance and at the same time pick up the butts. . . . It is the reward of the humble."[32]

MacArthur scoffed at some of the office aids that executives usually find indispensable. He refused to have a telephone installed in his office, maintaining that its ringing would be an unwarranted intrusion on his private work or his conversation with a visitor. His intercom system consisted of one small buzzer; he summoned an aide or his chief of staff by a particular number of buzzes. Incoming telephone calls for him were taken by one of his senior aides, usually Colonel Laurence E. (Larry) Bunker or Colonel Herbert B. Wheeler, who relayed the message to him or made an appointment for the caller to see the Supreme Commander.

Nor did MacArthur have a personal secretary, and he insisted on opening all mail addressed to him. He wrote answers to many letters in longhand on legal-size pads, which he gave to aides for typing. Because of the heavy volume of mail he received, he sometimes let aides compose replies if only pro forma responses were called for, but frequently he edited even those before adding his signature. "The General," said an observer, "is from this point of view extremely accessible. All anybody needs do to gain his attention is to write a letter." In addition, during his stay in Tokyo he composed all his public statements and speeches, the latter being rare, and many communiqués issued by his press relations officer were revised by MacArthur before their release.[33]

He abhorred large staff meetings and seldom conferred at one time with more than three or four staff officers, much preferring to operate on an individual basis in discussing GHQ matters. Although he readily welcomed visiting military and civilian VIPs and was generous in the time he gave to them, he made himself virtually inaccessible to all but a select group of general staff officers and SCAP section leaders among his GHQ personnel. Lieutenant General Edward M. (Ned) Almond, who served as his G-1 chief, then deputy chief of staff, and from 1949 to 1951 as chief of staff, defended MacArthur's seeming aloofness toward most of his GHQ staff as a necessity to protect his time and privacy. He explained that MacArthur "required that every staff member discuss with the Chief of Staff any important decision that he was expected to make. He, therefore, saw his staff as a whole very rarely. Every staff officer understood that to get his particular idea adopted, he was first scheduled with the Chief of Staff to find out General MacArthur's views before presenting the matter to General MacArthur in person." In a bureaucracy employing thousands of personnel this approach seems sensible, but in practice MacArthur's succession of chiefs of staff and aides cordoned him off from almost all contacts with middle- and lower-echelon staff members. Indeed, some senior officers completed their tours of duty at GHQ without having any substantial talks with the Supreme Commander. For example, Colonel Richard M. Levy, his adjutant general for two and a half years, met MacArthur twice — when he first reported for duty and when he departed for the States.[34] The experience of General Barksdale Hamlett, who spent over two years as a colonel in his G-4 section, was typical of that of many officers who were not members of the Supreme Commander's inner group:

> Most of the people who served on his headquarters had the highest regard for him, though there was a great deal of criticism too about his methods of operation. MacArthur was a very unusual person. . . . What were some of his failures? Well, in the opinion of many of us on his staff he never had enough contact with people on the staff. He did all of his business through his Chief of Staff. None of us ever saw him. During my period in GHQ, I actually spoke with General MacArthur only three times, and yet I was only two echelons away from him on the staff and had been in his [outer] office many times, talking with the Chief of Staff. But you never saw General Mac-Arthur; we didn't, people on his staff, except going and coming from the Dai Ichi Building to his quarters.[35]

During the occupation years the group of GHQ officers who were close friends of MacArthur changed, of course, as some of his old comrades retired or were transferred, but there were few additions, the most notable being Almond. By the autumn of 1945 Whitney had replaced Sutherland at the top of the list of Mac-Arthur's confidants, and he was the only one who had the privilege of entering the Supreme Commander's office without an appointment, except for the chief of staff and the senior aides. Sutherland returned to the United States in December 1945 and was succeeded as chief of staff by Marshall, his quiet, reserved deputy. Besides Whitney, Sutherland, and Marshall, the list of members of the inner group at the start of the occupation included Willoughby, Marquat, Bunker, Eastwood, Whitlock, Wheeler (all previously mentioned); Major General Stephen J. Chamberlin, deputy chief of staff for operations and wartime G-3 chief; Major General Hugh J. Casey, chief engineer officer; Major General Spencer B. Akin, chief signal officer and head of the SCAP Civil Communications Section; Brigadier General Bonner F. Fellers, military secretary of GHQ; Brigadier General Le Grande A. Diller, public relations officer and later general staff secretary; and Colonel Sidney L. Huff, a long-time aide. Eight of these fifteen officers were from the Bataan Gang. The other seven had joined his staff later in 1942 or 1943. All of them were intensely loyal to MacArthur and brooked no criticism of him. In turn, MacArthur displayed "a fanatic loyalty" toward them, commented an observer, adding: "It was almost impossible to criticize one of these people. He would stand up for them, no matter how wrong."[36]

MacArthur's office diary reveals that a large amount of his time in Tokyo, from the first week onward, was spent in conferring with a bewildering assortment of visitors — American and Allied political and military leaders, correspondents and publishers from many nations, entertainment celebrities from the States, and a few Japanese, nearly all of whom were high-level government officials and big-business magnates. Regardless of nationality, vocation, or ideological persuasion, most visitors were impressed by MacArthur as a masterly conversationalist and left his office at least momentarily convinced that their particular interest would receive just, even sympathetic, consideration by SCAP. Carl Mydans of *Life* remarked: "In his private talks MacArthur was a spellbinder. He spoke, with slow deliberation, a steady flow of grammatical and lofty language, his tone sonorous, building his stories or his exposition of a thesis to a faultless climax. In my more than four years of covering him during the occupation of Japan, I found very few men who did not admit to falling under his spell after such sessions." Roger Baldwin of the American Civil Liberties Union looked on MacArthur as a ham actor before they met, but when he came away from their first meeting, he exclaimed, "Why, that man knows more about civil liberties than I do!" According to Baldwin, MacArthur was "fascinating" because he spoke "with great conviction" and was "extraordinarily frank." The correspondent Richard E. Lauterbach was awed: "Emphasizing a point he would spring out of his chair, reach his desk in two giant steps, pick up a box of matches, and rattle them over his head like a saber. . . . With head reared back and chin jutting out, he would begin answering and the words rolled forth as if they were heaven's final dictum on the subject. For emphasis MacArthur employed a sort of breathless eloquence, almost whispering a word here, drawing out a word there, then clipping one very short." An Australian visitor was impressed by his "prodigious memory" of their meeting in Brisbane five years earlier and also by MacArthur's relighting of his pipe fifty times during a conversation that lasted less than an hour.[37] There are many accounts recorded by visitors who witnessed MacArthur's spectacular performances in his Dai Ichi office. The majority describe scenes quite similar to the following one recounted by Hugh Baillie, the head of United Press who interviewed many colorful leaders during his forty years in journalism, but was distinctly impressed by a visit with MacArthur in the autumn of 1945:

> As he uttered these words, in sonorous cadence, the Supreme Commander needed only a toga to become the picture of a Roman Caesar proclaiming a stupendous victory. His aquiline visage was stern and unrelenting. He rose, and his mien and bearing were majestic. He turned and paced slowly to the window, where he gazed meditatively over the burned and blasted ruins. He stayed on his feet after returning his attention to my questions, striding up and down the room, with a loping or gliding motion, puffing slowly on his corncob pipe with its very long stem. He seemed preoccupied and far away — but in fact, he was completely alert to what I was saying, and his answers were carefully phrased.
>
> MacArthur's parade up and down the big office varied in speed; sometimes he walked fast, sometimes with slow portentousness. Occasionally he would throw his tall frame into a couch or a deeply upholstered chair, sink into the cushions, and stare out as if peering into another dimension. When he was not answering questions point-blank, he followed his own chosen line of discourse. If you interjected a remark that was not precisely in point with what he had been saying, he would listen courteously and then resume his monologue where he had left off, as though nothing had been said and there was nobody in the room but himself. He was never in a hurry to finish a sentence.
>
> I had been raised in an atmosphere where you talked loud and fast and got to the point — otherwise you would find that your audience had departed, and you were left talking to yourself. No such compulsion ever bothered MacArthur. He said what he had to say, and would not be hastened, interrupted or ignored. If you didn't care to listen, that was your hard luck. He even had his own pronunciations, which were not to be corrected by any person — or any dictionary. If the dictionary disagreed, it had better change and get down to date. For instance, the word hara-kiri, which was frequently heard in Tokyo in those days. To MacArthur it was ha-*rick*-iri. And that was that.[38]

Obviously, the world of GHQ was ordered by MacArthur so as to allow him to maintain as complete control as possible, whether

over the sections that his trusted chiefs headed or over the course
of conversations in his office. That he viewed himself as an enlightened proconsul leading 70 million Japanese to a nobler destiny is also apparent, but the translating of his orderly administrative charts and grandiloquent statements into creative leadership
in reforming Japan would depend ultimately on powerful forces
beyond his control.

CHAPTER III

Military Matters

1. Command Complications

MACARTHUR WAS A MASTER at staging grand performances for visiting dignitaries, whether at Dai Ichi meetings, embassy luncheons, or troop reviews. When he scheduled a review, unit commanders knew every detail had to be covered and all had to go off with split-second timing. On the occasion of former President Hoover's visit in May 1946, MacArthur ordered Major General William C. Chase to hold a review of his 1st Cavalry Division, one of the most distinguished outfits of the Southwest Pacific fighting. The review was to take place across the moat from the Dai Ichi Building on the wide-open space of the Imperial Palace grounds, south of the thick pine groves that hid the buildings of the palace complex. The cavalry troops were to wear yellow gloves and scarves (the traditional cavalry color), but their quartermaster could not locate nearly enough of the garments. Since there was a large supply of atabrine, the antimalaria medicine, left from the Pacific campaigns, Chase decided to have all the gloves and scarves dyed in an atabrine solution, which made them a bright yellow. The day of the review was an unusually hot one, and the cavalrymen were perspiring freely. The review went well from MacArthur's viewpoint, but for weeks afterward thousands of 1st Cavalry troops had their hands and necks stained yellow. Hoover left without knowing of the discomfort the cavalrymen suffered in order to stage a splendid show for him and the SCAP brass, nor did he know that the 1st Cavalry and all other American units in Japan were woefully understrength or that MacArthur's visible contact with the troops was through such reviews, for he never visited their bases.[1]

Previous writings on MacArthur's career between World War II and the Korean conflict have dwelled on his role as SCAP, usually ignoring his complex, far-ranging duties as a commander of military activities during that period. Yet a considerable amount of his time and energy was absorbed with military matters, sometimes compelling him to give less attention to SCAP business than he wanted to. Whereas most senior commanders of the Second World War either retired or undertook less onerous assignments in the post–1945 era, MacArthur's responsibilities expanded, and his problems were as challenging as those he encountered when he was a wartime theater chief. Indeed, rarely has a professional soldier been assigned as great an assortment of military and nonmilitary tasks as he faced simultaneously during his years in Tokyo.

The Joint Chiefs of Staff had reorganized the Pacific commands in April 1945, creating United States Army Forces, Pacific (AFPAC), with MacArthur as commander in chief, and designating Fleet Admiral Chester W. Nimitz as head of all American naval forces in the Pacific. Although large-scale fighting still lay ahead in the Philippines and Ryukyus, the directive's main purpose was to set up a more effective organization for the projected invasions of Kyushu and Honshu. After the capitulation of Japan, AFPAC's primary mission became "the conduct and support of the occupation of Japan and Korea," and its secondary missions were "the roll-up of wartime bases [mostly in the Southwest Pacific]; assistance in the organization, training and support of the Philippine Army; development of post-war bases in the Pacific; [and] post-hostilities mapping programs."

As the head of AFPAC in the autumn of 1945, MacArthur had six major commands under him: Eighth Army, led by Eichelberger (headquarters at Yokohama) and constituting the principal occupation force in Japan; Sixth Army, commanded by General Walter Krueger (headquarters at Kyoto) and stationed in Japan until its deactivation at the end of December 1945; United States

Army Forces in Korea (USAFIK), headed by Hodge (headquarters at Seoul); United States Army Forces in the West Pacific (AFWESPAC), under Lieutenant General Wilhelm D. Styer (headquarters at Manila) and including American ground units in the Philippines and Ryukyus, together with scattered detachments engaged in base roll-ups in the Southwest Pacific; United States Army Forces in the Middle Pacific (AFMIDPAC), led by Lieutenant General Robert C. Richardson (headquarters at Honolulu) and consisting of garrisons in the Hawaiian, Mariana, Bonin, and Volcano islands; and Pacific Air Command, United States Army (PACUSA), commanded by Lieutenant General Ennis P. Whitehead (headquarters at Manila and later Tokyo) and including the Fifth Air Force in Japan and Korea, the 1st Air Division in the Ryukyus, the Thirteenth Air Force in the Philippines, the Twentieth Air Force in the Marianas, and the Seventh Air Force in Hawaii. Altogether, MacArthur's AFPAC ground and air units had approximately 1.7 million officers and enlisted men in October 1945, but by the summer of 1946 massive demobilization reduced the total to about 400,000, of which half were in Japan and Korea. During 1946 about 36,000 Australian, New Zealand, British, and Indian soldiers and airmen of the British Commonwealth Occupation Force (BCOF), under Lieutenant General John Northcott (headquarters at Kure and later Eta Jima), arrived in Japan and added a token of international participation to the occupation, though they were under MacArthur's operational control and attached to Eichelberger's command.[2]

MacArthur's interest in Philippine affairs remained keen, but his military responsibility there was reduced sharply after the inauguration of the Republic of the Philippines in July 1946. AFWESPAC, however, continued to assist in training and equipping the Philippine Army, and a United States–Philippines agreement in March 1947 permitted the retention of sixteen American ground, naval, and air bases in the Philippines. USAFIK, which consisted mainly of Hodge's XXIV Corps in South Korea, reported directly to the Joint Chiefs of Staff from mid-1947 to its withdrawal in mid-1949. Nevertheless, MacArthur stayed in close communication with Hodge and Syngman Rhee, who became the President of the Republic of Korea when it was established in August 1948. Mac-

Arthur's relationship to the military activities of the Eighth Army and BCOF in Japan will be examined in the next section of this chapter.

Between 1942 and 1945 MacArthur had tried in vain to persuade the Joint Chiefs to adhere to the principle of unity of command in the war against Japan. "Of all the faulty decisions of the war," he wrote in his memoirs, "perhaps the most inexplicable one was the failure to unify the command in the Pacific. The principle involved is perhaps the most fundamental one in the doctrine and tradition of command." In Tokyo he continued to press Chief of Staff Marshall and his successor in December 1945, Eisenhower, to work toward the appointment of a supreme commander over all American ground, air, and naval forces in the Pacific. The interest of the Joint Chiefs, as well as the top officials and planners in the War and Navy departments, in the principle of unity of command was heightened in late 1945 and 1946 not so much because of MacArthur's arguments as because of several developments that all pointed toward a restudy of the issue: postwar studies by the armed forces of the waste and duplication resulting from the competition of MacArthur's and Nimitz's commands for scarce matériel and personnel during the war with Japan; the growing movement for unification of the armed services; the acute manpower shortages of the postwar Army and Navy, occasioned by pell-mell demobilization, disappointing results in recruitment, and the uncertain future of Selective Service at a time when America's global military commitments were greater than ever; mounting tensions with the Soviet Union over numerous trouble spots ranging from Berlin, Trieste, and Eastern Europe to Iran, Korea, and Manchuria; the Patch-Simpson Board's report calling for the reorganization of the War Department; and the strong recommendation of the Joint Congressional Committee on the Investigation of the Pearl Harbor Attack "that immediate action to taken to insure that unity of command is imposed at all military and naval outposts."[3]

Nimitz, who became chief of naval operations in November 1945 and, ipso facto, a member of the Joint Chiefs, proposed to his fellow chiefs in January 1946 that a unified command in the Pacific be accomplished by the abolishing of the current structure of control of Army and Navy forces along service lines in favor of West and Central Pacific theaters, with a supreme commander over each who would head all American ground, naval, and air units operating within the theater's territorial area. Eisenhower, who had grown to admire Nimitz as "a man of extraordinary qualifications" and "a friendly soul," supported the admiral's plan with some minor qualifications. But MacArthur, on being informed that the Joint Chiefs were seriously considering the proposal, angrily responded that it was "an attempt to secure permanent control by the Naval Command of the Ground and Air Forces within the Pacific Basin," which would "in effect destroy the basic reason for the existence of an Army and Air Force and render them merely adjuncts to and part of a unified defense system known as the Navy."

Stung by Eisenhower's failure to support his views fully on this issue and by continuing cuts that put his AFPAC personnel strength "far below" what he considered to be "minimum levels," MacArthur retaliated by remaining silent when the War Department repeatedly beseeched him to issue public statements in 1946 endorsing its position on Selective Service, universal military training, and unification of the armed services. Although Eisenhower wrote him after the Chief of Staff's visit to Japan, from May 10 to 15, that their reunion "was the real high-light of my entire Pacific tour," the AFPAC commander continued to insist that the entire Pacific be under a single commander's strategic direction and operational control.[4] On August 28 Eisenhower sent him a long, conciliatory message pointing out the assets of the two-theater plan:

> To summarize, this proposed plan:
> a. Achieves unified command in the Pacific.
> b. Gives you direct control of all United States forces involved in the accomplishment of your normal occupational mission.
> c. Vests in each commander the control of planning for all forces available and for such additional forces as the Joint Chiefs of Staff may indicate as prospectively available in case of emergency and assures unified command under him of all forces engaged in carrying out his mission in the event of an emergency.
> I believe that this solution is militarily sound, that it particularly strengthens your hand as United States commander, and enhances your position as SCAP.[5]

MacArthur was not convinced.

Nevertheless, the two-theater plan for the Pacific, considerably modified since Nimitz introduced it, was approved by the Joint

Chiefs on December 12, 1946, and by Truman two days later, in spite of MacArthur's adamant opposition. Effective January 1, 1947, Admiral John H. Towers and MacArthur were appointed commanders in chief of the Pacific (actually Central Pacific) and Far East (really West Pacific) commands respectively. The Far East Command (FECOM) included all American forces in Japan, South Korea, the Ryukyus, and the Philippines; China, in case of a general emergency; and with certain qualifications, the Marianas, Volcanoes, and Bonins. Although the Seventh Fleet now came under him as commander in chief of the Far East Command (CINCFE), the reorganization cost MacArthur control over the Seventh Air Force; the Army units in Hawaii, which had been the main ground forces of the former AFMIDPAC command; and responsibility for military and civil government, together with control of naval administration and naval logistics, in the Marianas, Volcanoes, and Bonins, which were assigned to the Pacific Command. The organizational change did not result, as MacArthur had warned, in a Navy "takeover" in the Pacific, but, on the other hand, it was not brimming with increased command advantages for him, as Eisenhower had promised. In a sense, it was a serious personal setback for MacArthur, because it ended his hope, nourished since 1942, of becoming the supreme commander of all American forces in the Pacific. Also, it reinforced his conviction that "Washington leaders" were conspiring to restrict his authority.[6]

The missions assigned by the Joint Chiefs to MacArthur as CINCFE were the military activities of the occupations of Japan and South Korea; "the military support of United States policies" in the Ryukyus, Philippines, Marianas, Volcanoes, and Bonins, as well as Japan and Korea; and plans and preparations, in case of a general emergency, to secure the above areas and to provide for the safety of American personnel in China. AFWESPAC was renamed Philippines-Ryukyus Command (PHILRYCOM), with Major General George F. Moore succeeding Styer; Moore had commanded Corregidor's defenses from 1941 to 1942, and then became a prisoner of war. The Marianas-Bonins Command (MARBO), which included the Volcanoes, was led by Major General Frank H. Griswold (headquarters on Guam); Vice Admiral Robert M. Griffin headed United States Naval Forces in the Far East (NAVFE),

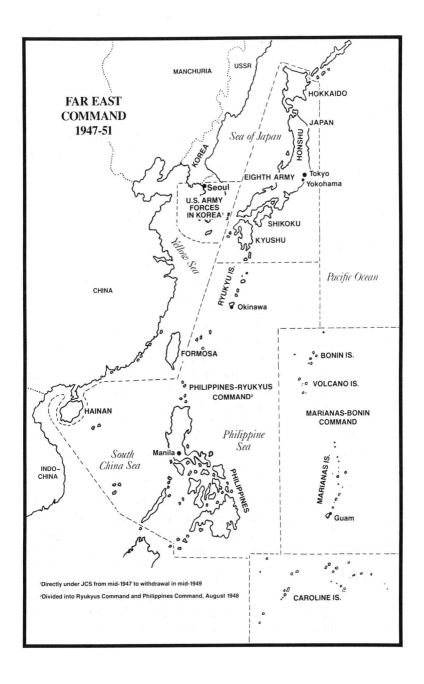

FAR EAST
COMMAND
1947-51

MANCHURIA

USSR

HOKKAIDO

JAPAN

Sea of Japan

KOREA

HONSHU

EIGHTH ARMY

Seoul

Tokyo
Yokohama

U.S. ARMY
FORCES
IN KOREA¹

SHIKOKU

KYUSHU

Yellow Sea

CHINA

RYUKYU IS.

Okinawa

Pacific Ocean

BONIN IS.

FORMOSA

VOLCANO IS.

PHILIPPINES-RYUKYUS
COMMAND²

MARIANAS-BONIN
COMMAND

HAINAN

*Philippine
Sea*

INDO-
CHINA

*South
China Sea*

Manila

PHILIPPINES

MARIANAS IS.

Guam

¹Directly under JCS from mid-1947 to withdrawal in mid-1949
²Divided into Ryukyus Command and Philippines Command, August 1948

CAROLINE IS.

with his headquarters at Tokyo. PACUSA, less the Seventh Air Force, became Far East Air Forces (FEAF); it was commanded still by Whitehead, who had led the Fifth Air Force during the latter part of the war in the Southwest Pacific. Other major commands under MacArthur remained the same in the change from AFPAC to FECOM.

The Joint Chiefs, together with leaders of the War and Navy departments, were particularly sensitive in early 1947 about communicating the spirit of unification and joint command as they established new theater commands around the world. Congress, the armed services, and the public were arguing heatedly the assets and liabilities of the national security bill, which became law that September and provided for a secretary of defense and an independent air force, among other things. Like those sent to its other theater commanders across the globe in December 1946, the Joint Chiefs' directive to MacArthur stated, "Each unified commander will have a joint staff with appropriate members from the various components of the services under his command in key positions of responsibility." But MacArthur remained distrustful of the Navy's leaders, and the GHQ organization that he set up for FECOM, as an official Army historian observed, "was essentially an Army headquarters, staffed almost entirely by Army personnel, and resembling the structure of General MacArthur's World War II headquarters" — and, he might have added, controlled by virtually the same set of senior officers. "The nature and duties of the [AFPAC] General and Special Sections," admitted Willoughby, "did not change with the order creating the Far East Command. The change was merely in nomenclature — for example, G-3, GHQ, AFPAC became G-3, GHQ, FEC."[7]

Some naval and air officers of FECOM were irritated by what appeared to be an administrative sleight-of-hand by MacArthur. FEAF and NAVFE headquarters were formally established in Tokyo, but MacArthur, claiming (though seldom using) the title of commanding general of United States Army Forces in the Far East (USAFFE), never activated USAFFE headquarters. Instead, he ordered the heads of each of the four FECOM ground commands — Eighth Army, USAFIK, PHILRYCOM, and MARBO — to report directly to him. Air and naval leaders felt that this system, in effect, put each of these Army headquarters on the same level as NAVFE and FEAF. MacArthur's explanation, which was not very convincing, was that the organization of a USAFFE headquarters "would duplicate the functions" of GHQ, FECOM, and "detract from the essential and cohesive relationships" between the positions of CINCFE and SCAP.

With criticism continuing about his alleged apathy toward joint command, MacArthur authorized Willoughby in January 1948 to expand his G-2 Section of GHQ, FECOM, on a "joint basis" by inviting FEAF and NAVFE to appoint one "suitably qualified" intelligence officer each "to act as the Air and Naval representatives and experts, for the various publications of Theater Intelligence." In August of that year he took another step toward the creation of a joint staff by establishing the Joint Strategic Plans and Operations Group (JSPOG) to "assist and advise" him on affairs relating "to the exercise of unified command over Army, Navy, and Air Forces allocated to the Far East Command." Headed by Major General Edwin K. (Pinky) Wright, MacArthur's G-3 chief, the group was made up originally of eight general officers — three Army, three Navy, and two Air Force. Wright said that MacArthur and Almond hit on the idea of JSPOG "while searching for a way to satisfy the Joint Chiefs and the other services, who were pushing for a joint staff in Tokyo. At the start they did not visualize that it would attain an important position, but it was definitely the top planning group all during the Korean War."[8] Nevertheless, many Navy and Air Force officers in FECOM remained less than content with MacArthur's Army-dominated headquarters and would have concurred probably with the following judgment in an official Air Force chronicle:

> The JSPOG was frequently cited as evidence that GHQ FEC was a joint staff, but it was apparent both from the statement of JSPOG's functions and from the small number of assigned personnel that the group could not serve in lieu of the joint staff contemplated by the JCS. . . . Unification, at the highest command headquarters level, had never reached the Far East; yet General MacArthur later testified [in May 1951]: "In the Far East the integration of the three fighting services has been as complete as I could possibly imagine."
> . . . Practically all of the inter-service difficulties during the Ko-

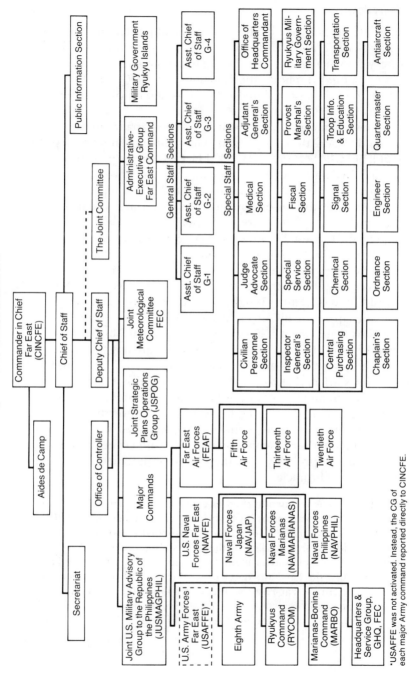

GHQ, Far East Command, December 1949

rean conflict could be traced to misunderstandings which probably would never have existed had . . . [MacArthur's GHQ] possessed a joint staff at the beginning of hostilities.[9]

Although not too pliable on matters of joint command, Mac-Arthur displayed commendable flexibility and innovation in attempting to alleviate some of his theater's vexing logistical difficulties. Until the outbreak of the Korean War, FECOM received no new military equipment, whether trucks, tanks, artillery, rifles, ammunition, field radios, or other matériel essential for combat readiness. This was owing not to negligence by the Pentagon but rather to niggardly defense appropriations by Congress. Army expenditures fell from $50.5 billion in 1945 to $27.9 billion in 1946 and averaged only $8.3 billion annually for the years 1947 to 1949. MacArthur inaugurated a program in 1947, nicknamed Operation Roll-up, to reclaim huge quantities of American Army equipment and supplies that had been left on various Southwest Pacific islands. After extensive surveys to classify usable items, he had the serviceable matériel moved to Okinawa and Japan. Relying heavily on Japanese labor, for want of American troops with appropriate specialties, and on rehabilitated Japanese facilities for repairing and rebuilding many types of equipment, MacArthur pushed the renovation program energetically. Although FECOM's supply status was far from adequate when hostilities erupted in Korea, MacArthur's far-sighted efforts and constant prodding of his field commanders made available much renovated matériel that was invaluable during the early phase of the war in 1950. "Almost 90 percent of the armament equipment and 75 percent of the automotive equipment in the hands of the four combat divisions" in Japan when the invasion of South Korea began "was derived from the rebuild program," according to the Army's official history of that war.

The drastic budget slashes suffered by the Army after World War II, of course, were reflected in serious declines in its total personnel strength — from 8.3 million in 1945 to less than 600,000 in the spring of 1950 — and in the personnel strength of FECOM, which shrank from about 300,000 in January 1947 to 142,000 the following year and only 108,500 by June 1950. MacArthur, as might be expected, often protested vigorously, but

the Pentagon could offer him little hope, so acute were the shortages in funds. Although he retained the Eighth Army's four divisions, each was woefully understrength, and, states an official
account, "over 150,000 Japanese personnel were being employed
in roles normally performed by service troops." Personnel problems were compounded by the excessive turnover rate, which averaged 43 percent a year in FECOM from 1947 to 1949, and by
the declining intelligence scores of the enlisted replacements, which
sometimes produced critical problems in training, discipline, morale, and relations with the Japanese populace. Training had to be
limited largely to battalion-level exercises because of the understrength and turnover situations and the lack of large training areas
in heavily populated, land-scarce Japan. With the relaxation of occupation controls that began in the spring of 1949, the Eighth Army
was able to return large numbers of officers and troops from duties in military government and civil affairs to their regular combat units. MacArthur ordered his forces in Japan that June to
launch an intensive training program, which was aimed at bringing about "the rapid integration of Army, Navy, and Air Force
components into an efficient team capable of performing its primary military mission" of ensuring the security of Japan.

But the American forces did not attain a satisfactory state of
combat readiness before the North Koreans struck across the 38th
Parallel the next June. The basic fault, MacArthur was convinced,
lay in the absence of strong leadership and sound strategic policies in Washington: "How, I asked myself, could the United States
have allowed such a deplorable situation to develop? I thought back
to those days, only a short time before, when our country had been
militarily more powerful than any nation on earth. . . . But in
the short space of five years this power had been frittered away in
a bankruptcy of positive and courageous leadership toward any
long-range objectives." [10] Not unlike the plight he had faced nine
years earlier when charged with the defense of the Philippines, he
was saddled in Japan, from 1947 to 1950, with the august title of
FECOM commander in chief, though he was agonizingly aware
that he lacked the resources to fulfill his assigned missions during
a general emergency.

2. *Military Activities*

Whatever animosity MacArthur felt toward Washington's naval brass, he cultivated amicable relations with the successive commanders of American naval forces in the Far East, who, from 1945 to 1950, were Vice Admirals Griffin, Russell S. Berkey, and C. Turner Joy. Their achievements evoked messages of high praise from him and deservedly so, for the Navy's functions were vital to the occupations of Japan and South Korea, as well as to the security of the West Pacific. Naval missions had to be executed often despite treacherous waters or severe weather, an extreme instance of the latter being Typhoon Louise in October 1945. Described by a naval historian as "the most furious and lethal storm ever encountered by the United States Navy," it struck American vessels anchored in Buckner Bay, Okinawa, sinking 12, seriously damaging 32, and grounding 222 ships, besides destroying about 80 percent of the island's buildings. Nevertheless that autumn and later, the Navy continued its various assignments, which included moving occupation troops to Japan and Korea; converting combat ships into temporary transports and using them to transport American servicemen from Pacific locales to the States (Operation Magic Carpet) — nearly 700,000 in December alone; moving Chinese Nationalist forces to Manchuria in an effort to prevent the seizure of that region by the Chinese Communists; and executing rapidly and with minimum losses the huge, difficult job of clearing mines from the waters off Japan, South Korea, the Ryukyus, and the Philippines. The worst tasks in minesweeping were in the seas around Japan, where there were an estimated 112,000 mines, laid by both the Japanese and the Allies. Using about 400 American and 100 Japanese minesweepers, Rear Admiral Arthur D. Struble's minecraft fleet had virtually all the ports and shipping channels cleared by March 1946. In addition, the Navy made a considerable contribution in the repatriation of millions of persons of various nationalities in East and Southeast Asia, mainly Japanese returning to their homeland, and in suppressing illicit sea traffic between Japan and Korea, which principally involved smuggling of drugs and of persons with more than the authorized allowance of personal goods. American patrolling was reduced later with the establishment of a small Japanese coast guard under NAVFE supervision. MacArthur maintained operational control, with NAVFE assistance, over the management and activities of the war-ridden Japanese commercial fleet through the United States Naval Shipping Control Authority for the Japanese Merchant Marine (SCAJAP). As will be seen later, he became a zealous advocate of reviving Japan's fishing and whaling fleets as key steps in that nation's economic rehabilitation.[11]

Ever since his staff had gained General George C. Kenney, who brought vigorous leadership to his Southwest Pacific air operations during the dark days of mid-1942, MacArthur had been an air-power enthusiast and enjoyed a strong rapport with his air commanders, who subsequently were Whitehead, from 1945 to 1949, and Lieutenant General George E. Stratemeyer, from 1949 to 1951. Like the ground and naval services, American air power in the Far East suffered from too-rapid demobilization and drastic cuts in funds after World War II, but Whitehead and Stratemeyer were unusually able air leaders who introduced innovative technical training programs, developed challenging unit exercises, and kept their air and ground crews in a relatively high state of readiness. The FEAF boasted thirty-nine major bases and the largest aggregation of American combat aircraft outside the United States. Its primary missions, as set forth in an FEAF report in 1948, were the "maintenance of a balanced Air Force in the occupied areas of the theater" and the "provision of air defense of military and naval installations throughout the Far East Command." Its secondary missions were "provision of search and rescue operations in coordination with the Navy; provision of aerial photography in support of the Army's post-hostilities mapping program in the Pacific; assistance in operations to alleviate human suffering and preserve order in the event of disaster, and to quell disorders, riots, or other disturbances requiring use of the US armed forces; establishment and control of military air routes, and operation of an internal air transport service in the Far East Command area." Its transport operations in support of the occupation of Japan were impressive; during a typical month its aircraft flew 4.5 million passenger miles and carried 250,000 ton miles of cargo involving SCAP personnel and programs. The conversion of its fighter squadrons to the new F-80 jet aircraft in 1949 pointed up the need for longer landing strips and of heavier load capacity, but Air Force funds were insufficient for the new construction. On one of the few occasions when he decided against his air staff, MacArthur disapproved an FEAF request for Japanese funds to build fields for the jets; he had ruled earlier that "no resources from the Japanese economy would be used for military construction not involving the occupation of Japan." FEAF leaders were still in quest of funds for the needed fields when war came in the summer of 1950.[12]

Under MacArthur in the Southwest Pacific war the Australian high command had complained often that he did not use their forces properly and refused to recognize their achievements. From the Australian viewpoint, the situation did not improve in postwar Japan, where the BCOF was made up largely of Australian troops, commanded first by Northcott and after May 1946 by Lieutenant General H. C. H. Robertson, both of the Australian Army. Despite MacArthur's statement in early 1946 extending "the heartiest possible welcome" and pledging that "the reception of the entire force will be of the warmest," BCOF personnel were not enthusiastic about their experiences in Japan. At first located in Hiroshima prefecture and later given eight other prefectures in south Honshu and all of Shikoku, the BCOF was charged by MacArthur with responsibility "for the demilitarization and disposal of Japanese installations and armaments and for exercising military control over the area, but not for its military government, which remains the responsibility of United States agencies." In June 1948 he told Eichelberger that the BCOF was "not to be included in planning or operations for the defense of Japan against external attack since their occupational function does not in any way include such activity, which is the exclusive, unilateral duty of US forces." An Aussie journalist in Japan remarked bitterly, "Humanly B.C.O.F. means bored young men in digger hats, in tommy and kiwi berets . . . living well at Japanese expense in an American-run Japan." Besides "parades, showing the flag, guard duties and the big job of disposal of enemy equipment," observed Brigadier Ronald Hopkins of the Australian 34th Infantry Brigade, "one of our interesting and very necessary jobs, more particularly during our first year, was to supervise the repatriation of demobilized Japanese soldiers, who were brought back to Japan from various

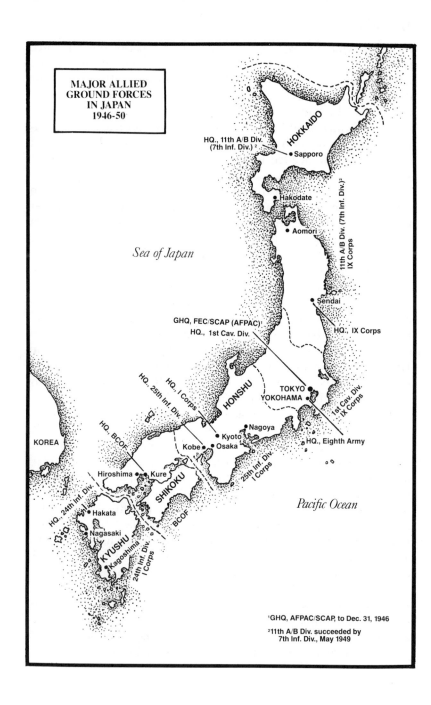

MAJOR ALLIED
GROUND FORCES
IN JAPAN
1946-50

HOKKAIDO

HQ., 11th A/B Div.
(7th Inf. Div.) ²   ● Sapporo

● Hakodate

● Aomori

Sea of Japan

11th A/B Div. (7th Inf. Div.)²
IX Corps

● Sendai

GHQ, FEC/SCAP (AFPAC)¹
HQ., 1st Cav. Div.

HQ., IX Corps

HQ., 25th Inf. Div.

HQ., I Corps

HONSHU

TOKYO ●
YOKOHAMA ●

1st Cav. Div.
IX Corps

HQ., BCOF

● Nagoya
● Kyoto
Kobe ● ● Osaka

HQ., Eighth Army

KOREA

25th Inf. Div.
I Corps

Hiroshima ● ● Kure

SHIKOKU

Pacific Ocean

HQ., 24th Inf. Div.

● Hakata

BCOF

● Nagasaki

KYUSHU

Kagoshima ●

24th Inf. Div.
I Corps

¹GHQ, AFPAC/SCAP, to Dec. 31, 1946

²11th A/B Div. succeeded by
7th Inf. Div., May 1949

overseas places. . . . Altogether, 700,000 were repatriated through the BCOF Area." In late 1947 the various Commonwealth governments began reducing or withdrawing their contingents in Japan, and by early 1949 only about 2000 Australian troops were left. When they departed in May 1950, MacArthur praised them for having "rendered model service worthy of the luster of the great nation that bred them," but it is unlikely that they or their BCOF predecessors had felt much of a sense of belonging in "MacArthur's Japan."[13]

While leading the I Corps and Eighth Army in the Southwest Pacific, Eichelberger had resented his seemingly unjust treatment by MacArthur, Krueger, and Sutherland on assignments and recognition, but he also admired MacArthur as a gifted leader. These ambivalent feelings were intensified during his stay in Japan, and his relations with MacArthur were alternately cordial and strained. Several times while he was Army chief of staff, Eisenhower appealed to MacArthur to release Eichelberger for other positions, including deputy chief of staff, but MacArthur always responded that his services were indispensable at the particular time. Eichelberger finally left Japan in August 1948, retiring from the Army with a now thoroughly embittered view of the "Big Chief," under whom he had served for six years.[14] On July 30 he journeyed from Yokohama to Tokyo for their last meeting alone. The end of their friendship is sadly evident in the words Eichelberger penned in his diary that evening:

> Arrived at Gen MacA's at 11:30 and had to wait about 10 minutes before I could get in. Our conversation was not in very high order. He did say that I was the last of the combat commanders in the Pacific to go home and that this was the end of an epoch. . . .
>
> I did not express any gratitude to him upon leaving him — nor regret. I did not thank him for anything. On the other hand, I must say that I don't recall any particular regret expressed by him. So [I] would say it was 50–50.
>
> He mentioned no award of any kind which only seems ridiculous. . . .
>
> This is a very interesting phase of his character that he would let an officer who has run his occupation for so many years and who has been in my opinion largely responsible for its success leave here without recognition of his services.

It has been unusual for him even after successful combat to praise one orally while at the same time claiming his own glory as a fighting field soldier, a thing which he certainly was not during World War II. . . .

In the words of Shakespeare, "He may have been a poor player but he has certainly been a player." This boy has certainly been a player on the stage of history. A strange character who probably wonders why he has so few friends and eternally blames the other fellow.[15]

Both Eichelberger and his successor, Lieutenant General Walton H. (Johnny) Walker, worried about the understrength condition of the Eighth Army, which was reduced from over 250,000 troops at the start of the occupation to fewer than 83,000 by June 1950. Eichelberger warned MacArthur in March 1948 that "it is already nothing but a supply organization with no combat soldiers, just a cadre," but there was little MacArthur could do except to inform him that he had "appealed directly to the President in this matter."[16] The responsibilities of the Eighth Army in Japan, however, continued to be enormous, as is evident from the FECOM inspector general's report for fiscal 1948:

The mission of the Eighth United States Army is complex. In addition to the mission of a tactical army, it has an occupation mission of great scope and responsibility. It executes all occupational responsibilities for Japan proper except small areas allotted to the Commander, Naval Activities in Japan.

Among its varied activities, it supervises the compliance of local Japanese government officials with orders received from SCAP; encourages the development of an economy which will meet peacetime requirements of the Japanese population for subsistence, clothing, and shelter; supervises production, procurement, and allocation of the construction materials from the Japanese government to occupation forces; supervises certain activities of the Japanese repatriation program; keeps forces prepared for action in the event of sabotage, disaster, disorders, riots, or other disturbances endangering personnel, property, or installations of the allied nations; requisitions, receives, stores, and distributes U.S. Army supplies throughout Japan; evacuates United States personnel from Japan to the United States; provides hospitalization and medical care for all United States personnel in Japan; and provides dependent housing facilities for all allied forces in Japan except those which are the responsibility of General Headquarters.[17]

The vast majority of Eighth Army soldiers had little or no official contact with the Japanese. They were assigned to training and guard duties related to the military missions of their tactical units, but, of course, informal relationships with Japanese citizens developed, especially in leisure activities. Although occupation critics have assailed the undue attention that the GIs devoted to Japanese prostitutes and black-market operators, the bulk of the evidence about their conduct generally supports MacArthur's boast that they "were truly ambassadors of good will."

The number of Eighth Army troops assigned to military government or civil affairs teams was never large, usually about 400 officers and 1500 enlisted men, to which were attached 600 civil service personnel. But, as a former military government officer observed in 1949, "it is this group of field service administrators who, living close to the citizenry, have daily contact with native government officials and are in an unparalleled position to impress the Japanese." He added that their performance "will be of no little importance in judging the final success of the occupation," but unfortunately little scholarly research has been done on this subject. The teams, though not empowered to undertake corrective action, were reasonably effective, for the most part, in the supervision and oversight of compliance with SCAP directives, the reporting of instances of noncompliance, and "the rendering of informal, nonmandatory advice and assistance to Japanese prefectural governments." The larger teams had separate staff officers assigned to the fields of natural resources, commerce and industry, education, money and banking, public health and welfare, and legal and governmental matters. In addition to the limitations mentioned in the previous chapter, however, the teams' officers were usually naïve in political affairs and too often were awed or outmaneuvered by prefectural officials. According to one authority, they "tend to become so allied with the government that in subtle and unintentional ways they lend support to the status quo against changes initiated by liberal elements or even by SCAP." In late 1949, as part of the plan to return SCAP controls and supervision gradually to the Japanese government, MacArthur abolished the prefectural teams and transferred their duties to eight regional civil affairs teams made up mainly of civilians.[18]

The "investigative arm" of the Eighth Army's military government system consisted of Counter Intelligence Corps (CIC) detachments, which operated in every prefecture in coordination with military police units. In December 1948 there were 117,600 FECOM personnel stationed in Japan, of whom 1200 were in the CIC and 3500 in the military police. Occupation critics in America and Japan thought the CIC and military police strength was excessive, but Willoughby maintained that with the population of Japan then at 78.6 million, the FECOM intelligence and security forces were "insufficient to counter a serious public disturbance or an aggressive fifth column," particularly since there was only one Japanese policeman for every 640 people. The Civil Intelligence Section, according to Willoughby, "played a dual role in the Occupation, as a SCAP Staff Section (CIS) and as an operating agency (Counter Intelligence Division); with its various components distributed throughout Japan, this agency became a sort of FBI for the Occupation in its special field of security surveillance." MacArthur allowed Willoughby and his lieutenants an almost free administrative hand, and their security and intelligence measures were not executed without injustice and bad feeling among the Japanese, as will be related in specific instances later. With the close links between Willoughby's G-2 staff, the SCAP Civil Intelligence Section, and the Eighth Army's CIC and military police units, "occupation intelligence" became the one exception to the poor communications between the SCAP field operators and GHQ. Civil intelligence personnel were active in such areas as low enforcement, security surveillance, modernization of Japan's police system, apprehension of war criminal suspects, and civilian censorship. CIC reports claimed that the most serious security threats stemmed from internal subversion, Communist infiltration of repatriates, and illegal, sometimes violent activities of the Japanese Communists and of the 600,000 Koreans in Japan. Though the need for aggressive efforts in civil intelligence were sharply disputed by critics, they were justified by Willoughby, with MacArthur's endorsement, on the grounds of "the deterioration in [the] national economy, the rising spiral of inflation, the increasing importance of the labor movement, the unrest in disaffected groups, and Communist penetration," especially in the ranks of the 6.4 million demobilized and often jobless Japanese servicemen. In mid-1947 eager CIC investigators charged that a number of SCAP civilian employees, notably in the Government Section, were allegedly "subversives" or "leftists," which led to some dismissals and to renewed enmity between Whitney and Willoughby. After this episode even MacArthur could not mediate between them, though both remained intensely loyal to him.[19]

During the early months of the occupation MacArthur pushed his ground, air, and naval commanders to carry out the disarmament of Japan's war machine "promptly and with determination." It took several years in some cases to locate caches of arms and ammunition hidden by die-hards near the end of the war, but Japanese military and naval units, all in process of demobilization, generally cooperated well in turning over their weapons, equipment, and supplies. The destruction of military matériel, carried out mainly by the Sixth and Eighth armies during the first autumn, included 1.3 million rifles and carbines, 1.2 million tons of ammunition of all types, 190,000 coastal and field artillery guns, 100,000 tons of chemical warfare supplies, 8000 combat aircraft, and 2500 tanks. Most of the remaining ships of the Japanese Navy were taken out to sea and sunk, but 420 vessels that were under repair or construction at the war's end were scrapped, with the salvaged metals turned over to the Japanese government for sale to peacetime industries; 408 ships were used for repatriation and minesweeping; 135 vessels of destroyer size or smaller were disposed of as reparations; and about 2000 craft of 100 tons or less were returned to the Japanese for fishing, cargo-carrying, ferrying, and other pacific pursuits. MacArthur ordered that all the large Japanese Army and Navy stores of clothing, food, construction materials, and medical supplies, together with much of the military's engineering and automotive equipment, be turned over to the Japanese for relief and rehabilitation. In the fall of 1945 many military and naval facilities, ordnance depots, arsenals, and factories formerly producing combat matériel were demolished or dismantled for scrap, although in January 1946 MacArthur announced that he was taking "nearly 400 Japanese aircraft plants, army and navy arsenals, and war material laboratories into SCAP custody to insure their availability, intact and in good operating condition, for reparations." In July 1947 he reported with considerable hyperbole that the disarmament program had been so thorough that "Japan could not rearm for modern war within a century."[20]

The disposal of Japanese war matériel was executed generally without press criticism of wanton ruin of equipment that could have peaceful uses, but a glaring exception was the destruction of Japan's five cyclotrons. In early November 1945, Major General Leslie R. Groves, who had commanded the Manhattan Project and now headed a military advisory board on atomic energy, concurred too hastily in a proposal by one of his staff officers to demolish the cyclotrons, located at Tokyo, Osaka, and Kyoto. MacArthur, who earlier had approved their operation for peaceful research in "the fields of biology, medicine, chemistry, and metallurgy," was astounded when he received a subsequent order from Secretary of War Patterson to destroy them. He protested to Eisenhower, but, says Groves, the new Army chief of staff "apparently. . . never saw this message" and "no action was taken" to countermand the order, which actually neither Groves nor Patterson had studied. The destruction was carried out in late November at MacArthur's reluctant command, precipitating widespread outcries in the American press and in scientific circles. Dr. Yoshio Nishina, the dean of Japanese nuclear physicists, who had spent many years constructing the largest of the cyclotrons, was "heartbroken" over the abrupt termination of his research, which he believed would have had valuable practical applications in biology and agriculture for postwar Japan. Dr. Karl T. Compton, president of the Massachusetts Institute of Technology, told Patterson that it was "an act of utter stupidity." In a public statement Patterson frankly admitted that "General MacArthur was directed to destroy the Japanese cyclotrons in a radio message sent to him in my name. That message was dispatched without my having seen it. . . . I regret this hasty action on the part of the War Department." In the meantime, however, some of the press had attacked MacArthur. Writing nearly two decades later, MacArthur was still bitter about the episode: "It was an unhappy affair, and the attempt of the War Department to falsely shift the blame left a bad taste in my mouth." But no evidence has been uncovered to support his allegation that the War Department intentionally made him the scapegoat.[21]

During his first year in Japan one of MacArthur's most time-consuming and least remembered missions was the administration of repatriation programs. Immediately after Japan's surrender, he set in motion plans to locate, supply, and return American and Allied prisoners of war and civilian internees in camps scattered through Japan, Formosa, Korea, Manchuria, and China. Thanks to prompt, well-organized action by special recovered-personnel units of the air and ground forces under his command, supported by American naval ships, all the known prison survivors were on their way home or were in American-run hospitals in Japan or the Philippines by the end of September 1945. The total number of POWs and internees recovered was nearly 104,000, of whom about 33,000 had been located in 93 camps in Japan.

Next came a far larger, more complex job of repatriation: about 6.6 million Japanese military and civilian personnel situated in the regions of East and Southeast Asia and the Pacific Islands that had been seized earlier by Japan, along with approximately 1.2 million non-Japanese nationals in Japan — mainly Chinese, Formosans, Ryukyuans, and Koreans (excluding the "permanent" Korean minority) — who had been brought there forcibly during the war and wanted to go home. The Potsdam Declaration called for the return of overseas Japanese servicemen only, but the program that MacArthur launched ultimately produced the repatriation of virtually all the above, the major exception being over a million Japanese held by the Soviet Union. Repatriation was welcomed by Japanese troops, but since it was compulsory for all Japanese in most of the formerly occupied countries, many civilians of long prewar residence were forced to abandon houses, lands, and businesses in the move to Japan. Political authorities in most of those nations feared that otherwise the Japanese civilians might "exert an adverse influence on the economic and political recovery of the countries concerned." During the peak period of Asian repatriation, September 1945 to June 1946, 188 Japanese ships, mostly old and battered, together with 191 American Liberty ships, LSTs, and transports carried 4.4 million Japanese back to their home islands and evacuated nearly a million non-Japanese from Japan in what has been called "a waterborne migration in scope without parallel in history." American and BCOF troops assisted Japanese officials in the reception centers at various Japanese ports where the incoming repatriates, by far the majority of persons in the move-

ment, were processed through customs and (if servicemen) demobilization and were given physical examinations, inoculations,
hospitalization (if needed), food, clothing, and railway passes to
their home areas. During a busy three-week period in the spring
of 1946 the centers arranged rail transportation in Japan for
550,000 repatriates from China alone. MacArthur masterminded
the vast repatriation program, which, though marred by some cases
of delay, confusion, mistreatment, lost belongings, undue over-
crowding, and outbreaks of disease, was, all in all, planned well
and carried out rapidly and efficiently. It was a logistical accomplishment of gigantic proportions, and as a humanitarian achievement it earned for MacArthur and his forces continuing grateful
remembrance in millions of Japanese and other Asian homes.[22]

Almost every week during his time in Tokyo MacArthur was
engaged in some aspect of the frustrating battle over the Soviet
Union's refusal to release Japanese. During and immediately after
its one-week participation in the war with Japan in August 1945,
the USSR had seized over 1.3 million Japanese military and civilian personnel in Korea and Manchuria. In spite of persistent efforts by MacArthur and the Japanese government, no Soviet-held
Japanese were returned during the first fourteen months after
World War II. Following long and difficult negotiations, Major
General Paul J. Mueller, MacArthur's chief of staff, and General
Kuzma Derevyanko, the Soviet representative on the Allied Council for Japan, signed an agreement on December 19, 1946, whereby
the repatriation of Japanese in Soviet territories would be carried
out at a minimum rate of 50,000 per month, with MacArthur providing the shipping and the Japanese government bearing all costs
incidental to the repatriates' delivery at designated Soviet Far
Eastern ports. MacArthur offered to transport 360,000 repatriates a month, but the Soviets consistently failed to meet even the
minimum monthly quota. The unsatisfactory progress of Soviet
repatriation became a hotly debated, perennial issue in the ACJ,
where George Atcheson and William Sebald, with strong backing
from MacArthur, repeatedly demanded an accounting of the fate
of the Japanese still imprisoned by the USSR. In the summer of
1949 the Soviets began delivering repatriate groups of considerable size, but most were found to have been thoroughly indoctri-
nated in Communism. After their arrival in Japanese ports, these

repatriates sang Communist songs loudly as they left the ships, displayed "crass disregard" of their waiting families, and became activists of the Japanese Communist Party.[23] On December 21, 1949, Derevyanko angrily walked out of an ACJ session at which the Soviet repatriation issue was being discussed. On the next day, MacArthur issued the following statement:

> I have accepted the wise recommendation of the British Commonwealth member, made at yesterday's meeting of the Allied Council, to seek the help of a neutral nation such as Switzerland, or of the International Red Cross, to gather the fullest possible details of the tragic fate of the 376,000 missing Japanese prisoners. To this end I am requesting the U.S. Government to attempt to negotiate the necessary arrangements. I can well understand the reluctance of the Soviet member yesterday to listen to so gruesome and savage a story in all its harrowing barbarity. It could well chill and sicken even a hardened soldier.
>
> The Soviet member has now given the press a letter containing charges of oppression by the Japanese Government. These moth-eaten charges have been so often made by the Soviets and so often irrefutably shown to be completely prejudiced, if not actually false, that their continued repetition could well be ignored under normal circumstances as merely blatant propaganda. But when, at this moment, they are again taken from the shelf and freshly dusted off to act as a smoke screen to distract attention from the investigation of the dreadful fate of hundreds of thousands of Japanese prisoners probably dead on Soviet soil, they represent a callousness of hypocrisy I cannot fail to denounce.[24]

Moscow usually ignored such tough-worded pronouncements by MacArthur, as well as other protests by the ACJ. The Soviet Union proclaimed in April 1950 that its repatriation of Japanese had been completed, but two decades later the Japanese government insisted that nearly 300,000 Japanese who had been imprisoned by the Russians in 1945 and presumably were still alive remained unaccounted for, and its many requests for information about them had brought only stony silence from Moscow.[25]

When Japan surrendered, its military and naval forces totaled almost 7 million officers and men, of whom about half were stationed in Japan proper. At first MacArthur vested responsibility for demobilization in the Japanese Imperial General Headquarters and Army and Navy ministries. On October 15, 1945, he proclaimed: "Today the Japanese Armed Forces throughout Japan completed their demobilization and ceased to exist as such. . . . I know of no demobilization in history, either in war or in peace, by our own or by any other country, that has been accomplished so rapidly or so frictionlessly." Actually, he did not abolish the Imperial General Headquarters until December, and at that time, while formally disbanding the Army and Navy ministries also, he retained nearly 200 former senior generals and admirals to serve as the First (Army) and Second (Navy) Demobilization ministries. With demobilization nearly finished by June 1946, these successors to the Army and Navy ministries were downgraded to bureaus and placed under the authority of the newly established Demobilization Board, whose members had not been career military and naval officers. In contrast to the unemployment turmoil that came next for Japanese veterans, the process of demobilization did progress with relative smoothness.[26] The following incident, which occurred in early September 1945, is typical of the amazingly cooperative attitude that most Japanese servicemen displayed during the demobilization program:

> A jeep bearing a 43rd Division lieutenant was spinning along the road from Kazo to Kumagaya when an approaching cloud of dust resolved itself into a Japanese tank company moving to a demobilization center. As the lead tank stopped to permit passing, the jeep driver cautiously skirted it to the left on the narrow road. The soft shoulder crumbled and the American found himself tilted at a perilous angle with his vehicle mired in the soft muck of a rice paddy. Climbing out, the officer scratched his head and pointed to a cable attached to the side of one tank. Meanwhile a Japanese officer had come running up and asked in passable English if the tank driver had been at fault. Assured to the contrary, he barked orders to his men and the tank driver jockeyed his tank into position, hooked the cable on the jeep, and pulled it back on the road. The Japanese captain bowed his apologies, accepted an American cigarette with thanks, ordered his tank column to continue, and, waving amiably to the American, disappeared in a cloud of dust.
>
> A month earlier these men would have shot one another on sight. Significantly, the Japanese armored unit was travelling without guard to be demobilized.[27]

This episode, and numerous similar ones on record, suggest that the success in the quick and uneventful demobilization was attributable more to fortunate Japanese responses than to initiatives by the occupation commander and his forces.

3. The Victors' Tribunals

In the growing literature on war crimes trials, MacArthur has been associated by many chroniclers with the inflicting of "victors' justice," really injustice, on a number of Japanese accused as war criminals. In truth, the vast majority of such trials, as well as those involving the worst miscarriages of justice, occurred in Far Eastern territories outside MacArthur's jurisdiction, particularly China, Malaya, Singapore, and the Netherlands East Indies. At the Potsdam Conference, the Combined Chiefs of Staff had decided to transfer the Southwest Pacific Area, except the Philippines, from MacArthur's authority. The change became effective on September 2, 1945, when Borneo, Java, Madura, and Celebes were attached to Vice Admiral Louis Mountbatten's Southeast Command and the remainder of the theater was placed under Australian command. In the ensuing months an estimated 5000 Japanese were tried as war criminals in China and Southeast Asia, of whom about half received life sentences and perhaps as many as 900 were executed. There has been little published research on these trials, but, as understated by one historian, "there were, inevitably, in view of the different nationalities of the local courts and the different procedures followed, some inconsistencies in the sentences." The available evidence indicates that when the full story is known, the proceedings and sentences at the Manila and Tokyo war crimes trials may seem less harsh in comparison. In fact, there were some postsurrender butcheries in China and Southeast Asia, where Japanese troops were not given even the pretext of "kangaroo trials." In British North Borneo, for example, 6000 Japanese soldiers who had surrendered and turned over their arms to an Australian infantry unit were marched into the jungle, supposedly en route to internment at Beaufort, only to be ambushed and massacred by vengeance-bent Borneo tribesmen while the Australians stood by and did nothing to protect the victims.[28]

During Japanese defensive operations in the Philippines in 1944–1945, commanded by General Tomoyuki Yamashita, troops committed widespread atrocities against hapless Filipino citizens and American prisoners of war, the number of victims variously estimated at 60,000 to over 100,000. About half of these people were murdered, wounded, or raped immediately before and during the battle of Manila in January and February 1945. In late September of that year MacArthur ordered Wilhelm Styer, his former G-1 chief and now AFWESPAC commander, to appoint a military commission to try Yamashita for "violation of the laws of war." The formal charge did not accuse him of committing or ordering atrocities; it stated that he had "unlawfully disregarded and failed to discharge his duty as commander to control the operations of the members of his command" and had "permitted them to commit brutal atrocities and other crimes" while he was in command of the Japanese Army in the Philippines. The twenty-two rules governing the conduct of the trial were dictated by MacArthur on the basis of recommendations by the GHQ, SCAP, Legal Section. Thereby the commission, which was made up of five American Army generals, none of whom was trained in law, was permitted to admit any evidence that it believed "would have probative value in the mind of a reasonable man." It could include hearsay testimony, affidavits, diaries, letters, and other documents of persons not present at the trial or not necessarily living, as long as such data "appeared" to relate to the charge against Yamashita.

The trial began on October 29 in the large reception hall of the high commissioner's residence near the Manila Bay front. Within sight to the east lay the heavily damaged Walled City (Intramuros) and a large expanse of ruined government buildings where many of the worst atrocities had taken place. Wrathful Filipino crowds taunted the heavily guarded Yamashita as he was transported to and from the makeshift courtroom, and most high-ranking officials of the Philippine Commonwealth regime, already alarmed by public discontent over dismal economic conditions and collaborationist allegations against prominent politicians, seemed quietly pleased to have a spectacle that would distract the populace. Although the five American Army legal officers who were appointed to defend Yamashita worked with skill and zeal in his behalf, the trial soon turned into an almost steady procession of prosecution witnesses and exhibits, with the outcome a foregone conclusion to most onlookers. MacArthur's unexplained but apparent desire for a speedy trial became obvious in early November, when the commission at first granted a request by the defense for a continuance to develop its case better but suddenly reversed its ruling after Styer received a radiogram from Tokyo GHQ saying that MacArthur was "disturbed" about "reports of a possible continuance" and "doubted" the "need of defense for more time." Not until an enormous amount of evidence on atrocities had been admitted did the commission permit Yamashita to testify that he had ordered his units out of the Manila vicinity in January 1945 because he felt the city was indefensible and that all the atrocities there had been committed subsequently by fanatic troops of a naval special landing force whose admiral defied Yamashita's orders and chose to defend the city. According to Yamashita and other defense evidence, he learned this after he and his forces had been pushed into distant mountain areas of Luzon and could not affect the situation in Manila. Rendering its decision on the probably more-than-coincidental date of December 7, the AFWESPAC military commission declared him guilty on the grounds that "where murder and vicious, revengeful actions are widespread offenses, and there is no effective attempt by a commander to discover and control criminal acts, such a commander may be held responsible, even criminally liable, for the lawlessness of his troops, depending upon the nature and circumstances surrounding them." Yamashita was sentenced to death by hanging — a humiliating method of capital punishment from the Japanese viewpoint.

In Tokyo a petition signed by 86,000 Japanese citizens was presented at GHQ; it asked that MacArthur either grant clemency to Yamashita, a popular hero in Japan since his conquest of Malaya and Singapore in 1942, or allow him to commit hara-kiri, considered by the Japanese to be an honorable way of dying for such a respected warrior. MacArthur made no comment on the petition. In Manila the trial record, findings, and sentence were reviewed and approved by Styer and the AFWESPAC judge advocate's staff on December 26. When the data were forwarded to MacArthur, he appointed a review board of five senior officers of his judge advocate general's office, which also recommended approval of the findings and sentence. Meanwhile the defense team for Yamashita filed petitions for writs of habeas corpus, prohibition, and certiorari with the American and Philippine supreme courts, the main contention being that the military commission was established by MacArthur and Styer "without jurisdiction," because there was "no martial law, no military government of occupied territory and no active hostilities in the Philippines at the time of the appointment of the Commission." Both courts rejected the petitions. The United States Supreme Court listened to the Yamashita defense team's argument on January 7–8, 1946, but its majority opinion, written by Chief Justice Harlan F. Stone and issued on February 4, sustained the commission's jurisdiction. The vote was six to two, with one absence. The concurring associate justices included three whose position surprised some observers, since they often championed liberal interpretations of civil rights and liberties — William O. Douglas, Felix Frankfurter, and Hugo L. Black. The dissenters, Frank Murphy and Wiley Rutledge, wrote minority opinions eloquently attacking the nature and proceedings of the trial.[29]

In Tokyo the next day MacArthur made his final decision on the Yamashita case, although he had received only a brief summary by a War Department official of the Supreme Court's action and knew that copies of the majority and minority opinions were being prepared for shipment to him. He issued the following statement to the press:

> It is not easy for me to pass penal judgment upon a defeated adversary in a military campaign. I have reviewed the proceedings in vain search for some mitigating circumstances on his behalf. I can find none. Rarely has so cruel and wanton a record been spread to public gaze. Revolting as this may be in itself, it pales before the sinister and far-reaching implication thereby attached to the profession of arms. The soldier, be he friend or foe, is charged with the protection of the weak and unarmed. It is the very essence and reason for his being. When he violates this sacred trust, he not only profanes his entire cult but threatens the very fabric of international society. The traditions of fighting men are long and honorable. They are based upon the noblest of human traits — sacrifice. This officer, of proven field merit, entrusted with high command involving authority adequate to

responsibility, has failed his duty to his troops, to his country, to his enemy, to mankind; has failed utterly his soldier faith. The transgressions resulting therefrom as revealed by the trial are a blot upon the military profession, a stain upon civilization and constitute a memory of shame and dishonor that can never be forgotten. Peculiarly callous and purposeless was the sack of the ancient city of Manila, with its Christian population and its countless historic shrines and monuments of culture and civilization, which with campaign conditions reversed had previously been spared. . . .

No new or retroactive principles of law, either national or international, are involved. The case is founded upon basic fundamentals and practices as immutable and as standardized as the most natural and irrefragable of social codes. The proceedings were guided by that primary rationale of all judicial purposes — to ascertain the full truth unshackled by any artificialities of narrow method or technical arbitrariness. The results are beyond challenge.

I approve the findings and sentence of the commission and direct the Commanding General, Army Forces in the Western Pacific, to execute the judgment upon the defendant, stripped of uniform, decorations and other appurtenances signifying membership in the military profession.[30]

Yamashita's defense asked President Truman to extend executive clemency, but he refused to do so. The "Tiger of Malaya" was hanged at Los Baños, a town near Manila, on February 23.

MacArthur was never more wrong than when he asserted that "the results are beyond challenge"; the trial's aftermath was marked by cries of unfairness that still echo. In 1949 the University of Chicago Press published a study of the Yamashita case written by A. Frank Reel, who had been a member of the defense in Manila; the book is a devastating indictment of both the military commission and MacArthur for obstructing justice in the case. MacArthur refused to allow its publication in Japanese and had Whitney prepare a treatise, printed and distributed by GHQ, that attempted to refute the "gross misrepresentations" by Reel. Over the years numerous articles have appeared in both legal and popular periodicals, criticizing the origins, procedures, findings, and sentence; a persisting theme has been that Yamashita was hanged for reasons other than that he was guilty of the charge against him. The most telling criticisms of MacArthur's role are still the dissenting justices' opinions. Justice Murphy concluded that the trial

was the manifestation of "an uncurbed spirit of revenge and re-
tribution, masked in formal legal procedure." The charge was
"speedily drawn," and "the trial proceeded with great dispatch
without allowing the defense time to prepare an adequate case,"
all of which resulted from MacArthur's pressure for a hasty trial.
One of Justice Rutledge's most effective attacks was on Mac-
Arthur's directive to the commission: "A more complete abrogation of customary safeguards relating to the proof, whether in the
usual rules of evidence or any reasonable substitute and whether
for use in the trial of crime in the civil courts or military tribunals,
hardly could have been made. So far as the admissibility and probative value of evidence was concerned, the directive made the
commission a law unto itself. It acted accordingly."

Unfortunately, in the research for this volume no evidence was
uncovered that reveals MacArthur's real motives or feelings about
the Yamashita case. Several officers close to him at the time later
offered guarded speculations: one suggested that he probably opposed the death sentence but yielded to the demands of Philippine political leaders who were old friends of his; another believed that MacArthur was so busy then with a myriad of other
problems in the occupation of Japan and West Pacific military activities that he may not have reviewed the findings as closely as he
should have. But his memoirs show that he never changed his mind
about the rightness of the trial and the sentence. Perhaps future
research may turn up manuscripts that will shed more light on his
motivation and complicity, but it is more likely that the controversy will never be settled. In the denial of justice to Yamashita,
however, the blame must be shared not only by MacArthur and
the AFWESPAC commission, but also by the American and Philippine supreme courts and President Truman.[31]

Manila residents did not have long to wait for the convening of
the next war crimes trial at the high commissioner's residence. On
January 3, 1946, began the trial of Lieutenant General Masaharu
Homma, who had led the Japanese Army's conquest of the Philippines in 1941–1942. Two formal charges were brought against
Homma: first, he had refused to grant quarter or to accept the
surrender of the Corregidor garrison in May 1942, allowing his
soldiers to kill unarmed Americans and Filipinos there; second,
he "did unlawfully disregard and fail to discharge his duties as . . .

commander to control the operations of members of his command, permitting them to commit brutal atrocities and other high crimes" during and immediately after the infamous Bataan Death March of April 1942. Over 8000 American and Filipino troops were killed by Japanese troops or died on the forced march from south Bataan, herded without food, water, rest, or medical attention for over a week; about 2000 American and 26,000 Filipino survivors of the march died in Luzon prison camps during the next seven weeks. MacArthur ordered Homma, who was in Japan at the end of the war, taken into custody in September 1945; he was held at Sugamo Prison in Tokyo until December, when he was moved to the Los Baños detention center, south of Manila, to await trial. As in the Yamashita case, MacArthur ordered Styer to appoint a commission of five United States Army generals, and, on the recommendation of the Legal Section of GHQ, SCAP, he approved and sent to Styer a directive containing virtually the same rules for trial procedure and evidence as those used in the Yamashita trial. Major General Leo Donovan, who had served on the commission that tried Yamashita, was appointed president of the Homma commission. The justification for the military commission was that Homma, like Yamashita, was being tried for "violation of the laws of war."

With Yamashita already found guilty of failing in his command responsibility for the conduct of his troops, Homma had little chance of escaping conviction and capital punishment. Major John H. Skeen, chief defense counsel, made an early move for dismissal on similar grounds to those of Yamashita's defense team — that the military commission was without legal jurisdiction under the circumstances — but the effort was futile. Because the case against Homma was considerably stronger than that against Yamashita, besides appearing anticlimactic in the wake of the previous trial, the Homma proceedings did not generate as much interest in Manila or abroad. When Skeen made his move for dismissal, however, a retired Army colonel in Arizona wrote him: "Your move for the dismissal of the charges against this Japanese fiend on the grounds that General MacArthur had no authority to appoint a trial commission looks like you were trying to make a cheap play to the galleries by tweaking the nose of the great MacArthur. It smacks of the spectacle of a small cur-dog, which from behind the shelter of his master's legs barks his defiance at a mastiff." During the five-week trial hearsay testimony and other questionable evidence were used freely by the prosecution. Homma frankly admitted that his troops committed the specified atrocities, but he denied knowing about them, much less ordering such action. He was found guilty on February 11 and sentenced to "be shot to death with musketry" — at least a more honorable form of death, in Japanese eyes, than that of Yamashita. His defense counsel appealed to the United States Supreme Court, but it refused to hear Homma's plea, since it had just ruled on similar arguments in the Yamashita case. Dissenting votes were cast again by Justices Murphy and Rutledge.[32] In his minority opinion, Frank Murphy wrote:

> It may well be that the evidence of his guilt under the law of war is more direct and clear than in the case of General Yamashita. . . . But neither clearer proof nor the acts of atrocity of the Japanese troops could excuse the undue haste with which the trial was conducted or the promulgation of a directive containing such obviously unconstitutional provisions. . . . To try the petitioner in a setting of reason and calm, to issue and use constitutional directives and to obey the dictates of a fair trial are not impossible tasks. Hasty, revengeful action is not the American way. . . . Those principles which were established after so many centuries of struggle can scarcely be dismissed as narrow artificialities or arbitrary technicalities. They are the very life blood of our civilization.[33]

Earlier, it will be recalled, MacArthur had praised the Yamashita commission's pursuit of "the full truth unshackled by any artificialities of narrow method or technical arbitrariness." To Justices Murphy and Rutledge, and to many others, MacArthur's shadow hung dark over both Manila trials. They were right when they attacked his unfair rules and his pressures for haste, but they were wrong in asserting or implying that the sentences of Yamashita and Homma were equally unjust or might have been more lenient had there been another AFPAC commander in Tokyo.

On March 11 Homma's wife met with MacArthur in his Dai Ichi office. She requested the meeting not to beg for General Homma's life but to thank MacArthur for letting her visit her husband in the Philippines and to urge the American commander "to consider carefully all the facts in the case." According to an American Army officer who was on the defense team and accompanied her,

MacArthur responded that "he would consider the record of the trial carefully" and "understood and sympathized with her position." Ten days later MacArthur announced his approval of the findings and sentence in the Homma case. In his press statement he noted the dissenting opinions of Justices Murphy and Rutledge, which he said he had "carefully studied." Then he boldly declared, "No trial could have been fairer than this one, no accused was ever given a more complete opportunity of defense, no judicial process was ever more free from prejudice." A subsequent defense appeal to Truman for clemency was refused, and on April 3, 1946, Homma was executed at Los Baños by a United States Army firing squad.[34]

By that summer apparently some members of the Supreme Court had second thoughts about the Yamashita and Homma cases, but too late to help the two generals. Colonel Frederick B. Wiener was then working in the Solicitor General's Office of the Department of Justice on the Uyeki and Cantos cases, "similar in all outward respects" to the cases of the two Japanese generals but involving two Japanese civilians found guilty by AFWESPAC military commissions of murdering Filipinos. That fall MacArthur, "much against his inclination," was ordered by Secretary of War Patterson to turn over Uyeki and Cantos to the government of the Republic of the Philippines, which had been established in July. Wiener said that in a discussion with Justice Black in June relating to the Uyeki and Cantos cases, he and Black had talked about the "doubtful legal underpinning" of the Yamashita and Homma cases, as well as of the Quirin case of 1942, involving the trial of German saboteurs, "in respect of the way that the Congressionally prescribed Articles of War expressly dealing with military commissions had been brushed off and indeed disregarded." Wiener recalled that "the conversation with Justice Black in his chambers had strongly indicated that at least four members of the Court would now be prepared to vote against the rationale of the earlier decisions — Justices Murphy and Rutledge, who had dissented in the Japanese cases; Justice Black, who now doubted their correctness; and Justice Douglas, who almost invariably concurred with Justice Black. And those four would probably have had but little difficulty in attracting a fifth Justice to form a majority." In Articles

85 and 102 of the Geneva Prisoner of War Convention of 1949 the "procedural rationale" of the Yamashita and Homma trials was "deliberately repudiated."[35]

In the autumn of 1945 MacArthur had recommended that former Prime Minister Hideki Tojo and his Cabinet members of 1941 be tried before an American court for "causing the murder of nationals of a country with which their nation was still at peace" in the attack on Pearl Harbor. The War Department's reply was that, "in accordance with the desire of the President," high-ranking Japanese charged with war crimes would be tried by an Allied court operating on "flexible procedures" patterned after those of the Nuremberg trial of German war criminals. Pursuant to the Potsdam Declaration, which said that "stern justice shall be meted out to all [Japanese] war criminals," and acting on SWNCC-originated directives issued by the Joint Chiefs, MacArthur announced on January 19, 1946, the establishment of the International Military Tribunal for the Far East (IMTFE). By its charter, which he proclaimed that day, he was empowered as SCAP to appoint its eleven judges from names submitted by the governments represented on the Far Eastern Commission. By charter authority also he appointed the tribunal's president, Sir William Webb of Australia, and the chief prosecutor, Joseph B. Keenan of the United States, both of whom were long-time friends of his. About 5100 lesser war crimes cases in Japan, categorized by SCAP as "Class B and C" trials, were judged by Eighth Army military commissions convened in Yokohama; the IMTFE met in Tokyo to try the "Class A" cases, or those involving "major war criminals." The IMTFE's jurisdiction covered "crimes against peace, conventional war crimes, and crimes against humanity." Twenty-eight high-ranking political and military leaders of Japan during the period of 1938 to 1945 were named in the fifty-five-count indictment on April 29.

From the start Sir William made it clear to MacArthur that he was not another Styer, however close their friendship. On March 5 he threatened to resign from the IMTFE if, as he wrote MacArthur, what Keenan had told him was true — "that you hold the view that, if any doubt arose as to the interpretation to be placed upon the Charter, it was your intention to direct the Tribunal what you intended the Charter to mean, and that the Tribunal would be bound to follow your direction." MacArthur quickly assured him that he would "respect the Tribunal's complete independence." The Tokyo trial began on May 3, 1946, and lasted two and a half years. Although it was an improvement over the Manila trials, the IMTFE was criticized at the time and since by journalists, historians, and legal scholars. The conclusion of the most thorough, scholarly study of the IMTFE is less than enthusiastic: "We have found its foundation in international law to be shaky. We have seen that its process was seriously flawed. We have examined the verdict's inadequacy as history." On November 4, 1948, Sir William read the judgment of the majority of the judges who found all the defendants guilty and sentenced seven to death by hanging, sixteen to life terms, one to twenty years in prison, and one to seven years' imprisonment. (Two of the defendants had died before the end of the trial, and one had been declared insane.) R. M. Pal, the IMTFE judge from India, wrote a stinging minority opinion, assailing particularly the practice of trying the leaders of a defeated nation for violation of ex post facto law proclaimed by the victors.[36]

Between November 9 and 21 MacArthur conferred separately with five of the IMTFE judges, including Pal, and consulted with the heads of the major Allied missions in Tokyo, excluding Derevyanko, about their governments' views on the trial. The IMTFE charter authorized him to review the court's verdict and, if he saw fit, "at any time reduce or otherwise alter the sentence except to increase its severity." A petition with 30,000 Japanese signatures asking leniency for former Prime Minister Koki Hirota was submitted to him, but he declined to comment on it.[37] He announced his review of the IMTFE's findings and sentences on November 24:

> No duty I have ever been called upon to perform in a long public service replete with many bitter, lonely and forlorn assignments and responsibilities is so utterly repugnant to me as that of reviewing the sentences of the Japanese War Criminal defendants adjudged by the International Military Tribunal for the Far East. It is not my purpose, nor indeed would I have that transcendent wisdom which would be necessary to assay the universal fundamentals involved in these epochal proceedings designed to formulate and codify standards of international morality by those charged with a nation's conduct. The problem indeed is basically one which man has struggled to solve since

the beginning of time and which may well wait complete solution till
the end of time. In so far as my own immediate obligation and limited authority extend in this case, suffice it that under the principles
and procedures prescribed in full detail by the Allied Powers concerned, I can find nothing of technical commission or omission in the
incidents of the trial itself of sufficient import to warrant my intervention in the judgments which have been rendered. No human decision is infallible but I can conceive of no judicial process where
greater safeguard was made to evolve justice. It is inevitable that many
will disagree with the verdict; even the learned justices who composed the Tribunal were not in complete unanimity, but no moral
agency in the present imperfect evolution of civilized society seems
more entitled to confidence in the integrity of its solemn pronouncements. If we cannot trust such processes and such men we can trust
nothing. I therefore direct the Commanding General of the Eighth
Army to execute the sentences as pronounced by the Tribunal. In
doing so I pray that an Omnipotent Providence may use this tragic
expiration as a symbol to summon all persons of good will to a realization of the utter futility of war — that most malignant scourge and
greatest sin of mankind — and eventually to its renunciation by all
nations. To this end on the day of execution I request the members
of all congregations throughout Japan of whatever creed or faith in
the privacy of their homes or at their altars of public worship to seek
Divine help and guidance that the world keep the peace lest the human race perish.[38]

Just after midnight on December 23 at Sugamo Prison, with only
the four members of the Allied Council and a select few American
Army doctors and soldiers allowed to attend, the traps were sprung
and the seven Japanese leaders, including Hirota, were hanged.
MacArthur ordered that their bodies were to be cremated and the
ashes scattered, lest fanatic ultranationalists try to turn their burial
places into shrines. "During the morning hours following the ex-
ecutions," wrote Sebald, "the bells of Buddhist temples and Shinto
shrines and Christian churches summoned their members to prayer.
What the faithful said, God alone knows."

A State Department intelligence officer in Tokyo reported to
Washington that MacArthur's "failure to reduce any of the penalties, particularly that of capital punishment for Hirota, deeply
disappointed those Japanese who had relied on his 'benevolence.'

Some Japanese reportedly had speculated that the sentences by the tribunal had deliberately been fixed with severity to permit commutations by SCAP. They had reasoned that such a gesture on MacArthur's part would augment his prestige." Ever the moralist, MacArthur seems to have hoped that the workings of the IMTFE would convince the Japanese people of the wrongness of the aggressions and atrocities that their past leaders had precipitated. But, stated one authority on modern Japan, "the International Tribunal for the Far East failed to accomplish its objective, in the sense that its activities and decisions failed to impress most Japanese." Another scholar observed, "By the time the judgments were finally handed down . . . the attitude of the Japanese public had turned from anger against these discredited old men to pity."[39]

Responding to what seemed to be a ground swell of anti-Japanese sentiment across the nation at the end of World War II, Congress passed a joint resolution in late September 1945, "declaring that it is the policy of the United States that Emperor Hirohito of Japan be tried as a war criminal." Numerous demands were voiced by official and unofficial groups in various Allied nations, especially the Soviet government and press, that Hirohito be branded a war criminal and that the Japanese imperial institution be abolished. Through the autumn of 1945 the Far East Subcommittee of SWNCC was split, with some members arguing to retain and exploit the Emperor in furthering occupation objectives and others urging that he be arrested and tried. After the Emperor's first call on MacArthur, on September 26, during which he assumed full responsibility for his nation's transgressions, MacArthur was convinced that Hirohito should be retained. "I was brought up in the democratic tradition," he remarked to an aide, "but to see someone who is so high reduced to such a position of humility is very painful." To a visitor in his Dai Ichi office he commented, "I came here with the idea of using the Emperor more sternly. But it hasn't been necessary. He is a sincere man and a genuine liberal." On November 30 Eisenhower sent him a Joint Chiefs' directive, born in SWNCC, stating that Hirohito was not immune from trial as a war criminal and that he was to collect the evidence necessary for Washington officials to make a decision for or against trying him. Later MacArthur received word that at the meeting of the United Nations War Crimes Commission, in session in London, the Australian delegate was planning to introduce a motion charging Hirohito as a war criminal.[40] Obviously aroused, MacArthur sent the following telegram to Eisenhower on January 25, 1946, setting forth unmistakably his views on the issue and the potential consequences of any actions that contravened the course he favored:

Since receipt of WX 85811 investigation has been conducted here under the limitations set forth with reference to possible criminal actions against the Emperor. No specific and tangible evidence has been uncovered with regard to his exact activities which might connect him in varying degree with the political decisions of the Japanese Empire during the last decade. I have gained the definite impression from as complete a research as was possible for me that his connection with affairs of state up to the time of the end of the war was largely ministerial and automatically responsive to the advice of his counsellors. There are those who believe that even had he positive ideas it would have been quite possible that any effort on his part to thwart the current of public opinion controlled and represented by the dominant military clique would have placed him in actual jeopardy.

If he is to be tried great changes must be made in occupational plans and due preparation therefore should be accomplished in preparedness before actual action is initiated. His indictment will unquestionably cause a tremendous convulsion among the Japanese people, the repercussions of which cannot be overestimated. He is a symbol which unites all Japanese. Destroy him and the nation will disintegrate. Practically all Japanese venerate him as the social head of the state and believe rightly or wrongly that the Potsdam Agreements were intended to maintain him as the Emperor of Japan. They will regard Allied action [to the contrary as the greatest] . . . betrayal in their history and the hatreds and resentments engendered by this thought will unquestionably last for all measurable time. A vendetta for revenge will thereby be initiated whose cycle may well not be complete for centuries, if ever.

The whole of Japan can be expected, in my opinion, to resist the action either by passive or semi-active means. They are disarmed and therefore represent no special menace to trained and equipped troops but [it] is not inconceivable that all government agencies will break down, the civilized practices will largely cease, and a condition of underground chaos and disorder amounting to guerrilla warfare in the mountainous and outlying regions result. I believe all hope of introducing modern democratic methods would disappear and that when military control finally ceased some form of intense regimentation probably along communistic line would arise for the mutilated masses. This would represent an entirely different problem of occupation from those now prevalent. It would be absolutely essential to greatly increase the occupational forces. It is quite possible that a minimum of a million troops would be required which would have to be maintained for an indefinite number of years. In addition a complete civil service might have to be recruited and imported, possibly running into a size of several hundred thousand. An overseas supply service under such conditions would have to be set up on practically a war basis embracing an indigent civil population of many millions. Many other most drastic results which I will not attempt to discuss should be anticipated and complete new plans should be carefully prepared by the Allied powers along all lines to meet the new eventualities. Most careful consideration as to the national forces composing the occupation force is essential. Certainly the US should not be called upon to bear unilaterally the terrific burden of manpower, economics, and other resultant responsibilities.

The decision as to whether the Emperor should be tried as a war criminal involves a policy determination upon such a high level that I would not feel it appropriate for me to make a recommendation; but if the decision by the heads of state is in the affirmative, I recommend the above measures as imperative.[41]

A copy of the strongly worded message was sent to the State Department from the War Department. MacArthur's exaggeration must have been obvious and his intimidation grating to officials of those two departments, SWNCC, and the Joint Chiefs, but who was to gainsay the commander in Japan? The suggestion of supporting "a million troops" and "several hundred thousand" civilian personnel in an occupation of Japan "for an indefinite number of years" must have had a quick, disconcerting effect. Five days later the State Department notified the United States embassy in London of MacArthur's "negative" response and, according to the State Department's record, "suggested any action 'appropriate in order to forestall such development,' namely, publicity on the Emperor as a war-criminal suspect." The issue quietly died in American and Allied official circles, except in Moscow, whose views on things Japanese were already held in disdain by MacArthur and most United States government leaders. In the American press and scholarly writings it continued to be debated sporadically but ineffectually. Whether it was through his rhetoric or his logic, MacArthur was instrumental in saving the Emperor from a humiliating trial for war crimes and in preserving one of the most effective instruments for securing Japanese cooperation during the occupation.[42]

CHAPTER IV

An Avalanche of Political Reforms

1. The First Four Months

AT THE END of the first week of September 1945, when Mac-
Arthur was preparing to move from Yokohama to Tokyo, he drove
to the capital and made a tour of the American embassy grounds,
apartment buildings, chancellery, and ambassadorial residence, the
last of which would be the MacArthurs' home for the next five
years and eight months. Colonel Sidney F. Mashbir, an intelligence officer then serving as one of his aides, accompanied the
Supreme Commander on his first visit to the embassy. The only
damaged structure was the chancellery, whose roof had been hit
during a B-29 fire-bombing of Tokyo in early February. Mashbir
was alone with MacArthur as they walked from room to room
through the chancellery. From the library they went down the
corridor to the ambassador's office, which had apparently not been
occupied since Joseph C. Grew was ambassador, from 1932 to 1941.
A portrait of George Washington still hung on the office wall. According to Mashbir, MacArthur "walked in and squarely up to the
picture of General Washington. He faced it, clicked his heels together, saluted, and said, 'Sir, they weren't wearing red coats, but
we whipped them just the same.' "[1] The Supreme Commander was
about to introduce Japan to large portions of the American heritage that he thought were transferable, especially political democracy as it had evolved in the United States.

From the beginning MacArthur maintained a studied aloofness toward most Japanese leaders of whatever walk of life, particularly those outside the conservative-dominated high echelons of officialdom. During the first four months he met with only nineteen Japanese — and with few of these more than once. They were Emperor Hirohito, Prime Ministers Naruhiko Higashikuni and Kijuro Shidehara, Foreign Ministers Mamoru Shigemitsu and Shigeru Yoshida, and Deputy Prime Minister Fumimaro Konoye (former three-time Prime Minister), as well as the Finance Minister, the speaker of the House of Representatives, the mayors of five large cities, the archbishop of the Roman Catholic Church in Japan, and the heads of the Central Liaison Office, the First and Second Demobilization bureaus, and the Japan Political Association (a brief-lived, restructured successor to the Imperial Rule Assistance Association, which had replaced the political-party system in wartime Japan). Yoshida met with MacArthur five times from September through December 1945; Higashikuni, Shidehara, Shigemitsu, and Konoye each conferred with him twice; the rest had one SCAP appointment each. It is unlikely that from this group MacArthur gleaned many insights into either liberal and radical currents of thought in the nation or the true sentiments of the conservatives. All the available information about these talks, which is meager and largely secondhand, indicates that they were polite and amicable but formal, with MacArthur doing most of the expounding and the Japanese revealing little of their underlying reluctance to participate in any drastic reordering of Japan's political, economic, and social ways.[2]

Prince Higashikuni, Hirohito's uncle, served as Prime Minister from August 17 until October 5, when he and his entire Cabinet suddenly resigned. According to MacArthur, the Emperor concluded that the Prime Minister should be replaced because Higashikuni's "relationship" to "the traditional ruling class" was "detrimental to the reforms being initiated by the occupation." Shigemitsu and Yoshida both stated later, however, that the en bloc resignation was provoked by MacArthur's so-called Civil Liberties Directive of October 4. SCAP peremptorily ordered the Japanese government to abrogate all laws and ordinances restricting freedom of thought, religion, speech, assembly, or press and all measures discriminating against persons on grounds of creed, race,

nationality, or political views; release everyone detained or imprisoned for his political or religious beliefs; dissolve the secret
police organs and the other departments involved in surveillance
or control of thought, religion, speech, or assembly; and remove
from office the Minister of Home Affairs, his police bureau chief,
and nearly 5000 police officials ranging from central government
to prefectural levels. "At that time our Government," as Yoshida
explained mildly, "had not yet become acclimatized to the stringent requirements of the Occupation authorities." Actually Higashikuni and his colleagues left in a state of shock.[3]

Three days after the Higashikuni Cabinet quit, Atcheson, the
SCAP political adviser and chief representative of the State Department in Japan, recommended to MacArthur that Higashikuni
be arrested as "a suspected war criminal." Atcheson argued that
"a strong advantage to be gained from the early arrest of *former
high officials* such as Higashi-Kuni is that the sooner such arrests
are completed, the more quickly will other high officials and personages who are worried about their own status in connection with
war crimes attain a peace of mind to enable them to devote their
abilities, such as they may be, to the task of reforming and reha-
bilitating the government in this country." Whether MacArthur
rejected this as convoluted reasoning or for some other reason,
Higashikuni was not arrested. In mid-December, however, Prince
Konoye was able to avoid imprisonment and trial as an alleged war
criminal only by committing suicide.[4] Shigemitsu, who had been
succeeded by Yoshida as Foreign Minister in late September, bitterly described the plight of leaders like himself who could not
adapt to the new circumstances of postwar Japan:

> Those who had fawned on the Army and Navy, and hastened to an-
> ticipate their wishes, now turned their coat. They loathed their Army
> and Navy and sang hymns of praise of the Army of Occupation. . . .
> Toadyism was rampant. However natural and inevitable this was in
> the hour of defeat, it sickened the heart of thinking people. Those
> who were content with the golden mean — behaving properly to all
> but fawning neither on military circles nor on the Army of Occupa-
> tion — gradually disappeared from public life.[5]

When Baron Shidehara was chosen as Prime Minister to succeed Higashikuni, Foreign Minister Yoshida had the task of in-

forming MacArthur and asking for his approval of the appointment. He was taken aback by the SCAP commander's queries: "General MacArthur asked me how old he was, and when I answered that he was a little over seventy, replied that this seemed terribly old. General MacArthur then inquired whether the Baron could understand English. . . . I answered that he spoke English well, and made a mental note to tell the Baron some day about the General's question." Obviously MacArthur knew little about Shidehara, although he had earned worldwide distinction and respect as an enlightened, conciliatory Foreign Minister and envoy in the 1920s and early 1930s, valiantly resisting the tides of Japanese militarism and expansionism. Widely known abroad for his polished English and probably the most admired of all Japanese leaders in the eyes of American and West European statesmen between the world wars, he reputedly "enjoyed an almost unrivaled position in the confidence of Western governments."[6] Contrary to the myth of MacArthur's mastery of things Oriental, at the time of this conversation with Yoshida there were still some gaps in his knowledge of Japan.

The SCAP commander demanded "immediate" action to implement his directive of October 4 and required the Japanese government to "submit a comprehensive report to this Headquarters not later than 15 October 1945 describing in detail all action taken to comply with all provisions of this directive." The sweeping changes thus ordered by SCAP became the first order of business for the new Shidehara ministry. Among other upheavals occasioned by the directive, as Atcheson estimated on October 10, "the removal of restrictions on political, civil, and religious liberties should cause the abolition of fifty percent of the positions in and under the Home Ministry," which had been occupied mostly by bureaucrats of "reactionary attitudes" who were bent on "passive resistance" to the occupation.[7] Although MacArthur seems to have been pleased with the overt signs of obedience to his Civil Liberties Directive, a State Department report of April 1, 1946, based on a study by Atcheson's office reviewing "the problem of civil liberties" in Japan during the previous half year, was less sanguine:

> Both the Higashi-Kuni and the Shidehara Cabinets have paid considerable lip service to the cause of civil liberties. Indeed, until it became

fully apparent to the Japanese Government that Allied policy called for a constitutional revision, the restoration of civil liberties alone tended to be emphasized as the method by which Japan might fully meet the political requirements of the Potsdam Declaration. Actual measures for insuring civil liberties have, however, been undertaken almost exclusively on the orders of the Supreme Commander, the Japanese authorities having taken little initiative in withdrawing restrictive laws and practices. Moreover, statements made and measures taken by some Japanese Government officials suggest that some individuals at least are making a conscious effort to prevent general exercise of civil rights, either through a desire to remain in power or through a misunderstanding of the conception of civil liberties which Allied Headquarters regards as essential.

Some attempts have been made to retain controls over individual liberty on the plea that they are necessary for peace and order. On October 19, the Shidehara government was reported to have announced that "freedom of speech and press, assembly and association, if detrimental to society" would be controlled, and plans for such controls were discussed in the Cabinet meeting. The suppression of newspapers carrying the story of the Emperor's visit to General MacArthur and the petition to SCAP for a greatly enlarged police force indicate the direction of Home Ministry policy in the early period of the Occupation.

Recent attempts to curtail civil liberties have been somewhat more subtle, but present a continuing threat. For example, athough the Japanese Government complied with the Allied order to release political prisoners, civil rights were not restored to all those released. At the time, Communist sources complained that releases were being delayed in order to prevent ex-prisoners from being registered in time for the coming elections, and it was not until December 29, 1945, in accordance with a SCAP directive of December 20, that an Imperial Ordinance was issued to restore the civil rights of many of those released in October.[8]

Actually Shidehara was burdened from the start of his ministry with the implementation of more changes than the government could cope with realistically in a short time. On October 11, two days after he took office, MacArthur summoned him to his Dai Ichi office and, states an official SCAP chronicle, "informed" the Prime Minister that "suppression of the people and repressive measures by the Government must cease and steps must be taken to liberalize the constitution."[9] MacArthur somberly read the following to Shidehara and gave him a copy of the document:

> I expect you to institute the following reforms in the social order of Japan as rapidly as they can be assimilated:
> 1. The emancipation of the women of Japan through their enfranchisement — that, being members of the body politic, they may bring to Japan a new concept of government directly subservient to the well-being of the home.
> 2. The encouragement of the unionization of labor — that it may have an influential voice in safeguarding the working man from exploitation and abuse, and raising his living standard to a higher level.
> 3. The institution of such measures as may be necessary to correct the evils which exist in the child labor practices.
> 4. The opening of the schools to more liberal education — that the people may shape their future progress from factual knowledge and benefit from an understanding of a system under which government becomes the servant rather than the master of the people.
> 5. The abolition of systems which through secret inquisition and abuse have held the people in constant fear — substituting therefor a system of justice designed to afford the people protection against despotic, arbitrary and unjust methods. Freedom of thought, freedom of speech, freedom of religion must be maintained. Regimentation of the masses under the guise or claim of efficiency, under whatever name of government it may be made, must cease.
> 6. The democratization of Japanese economic institutions to the end that monopolistic industrial controls be revised through the development of methods which tend to insure a wide distribution of income and ownership of the means of production and trade.
> 7. In the immediate administrative field take vigorous and prompt action by the government with reference to housing, feeding and clothing the population in order to prevent pestilence, disease, starvation or other major social catastrophe. The coming winter will be critical and the only way to meet its difficulties is by the full employment in useful work of everyone.[10]

Despite the quixotic nature of some of the above objectives, MacArthur claimed that "the Prime Minister was in full and enthusiastic agreement, and acted promptly and energetically." In truth, neither the will nor the capability of the Japanese to achieve these goals left much room for optimism in GHQ, SCAP, in the fall and winter of 1945, as can be seen in the less-than-eager Japanese participation in constitutional revision, to be discussed in the next section of this chapter.

Many of MacArthur's early directives were aimed at destroying the ideological props of Japanese ultranationalism, which he considered to be the most serious impediment to the development of political democracy. A series of SCAP directives facilitated the flow of news and information by divesting the government of its control of newspapers and news agencies and by eliminating wartime censorship regulations. Newspapers and periodicals, however, were forbidden to publish items deemed by SCAP to threaten public order or to disparage the occupation authorities. Ultranationalistic and militaristic organizations, together with secret and terroristic societies, were banned, and their properties were confiscated. In October the teaching of militaristic and ultranationalistic ideology in schools was prohibited, and all textbooks, as well as teachers, advocating such beliefs were removed from the schools in order, as MacArthur's directive stated, "to eliminate from the educational system of Japan those militaristic and ultranationalistic influences which in the past have contributed to the defeat, war guilt, suffering, privation, and present deplorable state of the Japanese people." A SCAPIN in December prohibited the teaching of all courses in Japanese morals, history, and geography, which SCAP's education experts decided were contaminated ideologically.[11]

A SCAP directive on December 15 disestablished state Shinto in order "to prevent a recurrence of the perversion of Shinto theory and beliefs into militaristic and ultranationalistic propaganda designed to delude the Japanese people and lead them into wars of aggression." No government funds or agencies were to be used to promulgate Shinto teachings or to support Shinto shrines and activities. The directive also included a sweeping denunciation of the doctrines supposedly central to Japan's unique national polity (*Kokutai*):

> (1) The doctrine that the Emperor of Japan is superior to the heads of other states, because of ancestry, descent or special origin. (2) The doctrine that the people of Japan are superior to the people of other lands because of ancestry, descent, or special origin. (3) The doctrine that the islands of Japan are superior to other lands because of divine or special origin. (4) Any other doctrine which tends to delude

the Japanese people into embarking upon wars of aggression or to glorify the use of force as an instrument for the settlement of disputes with other peoples.[12]

Two weeks afterward MacArthur capped his assault on the ideological underpinnings of ultranationalism by requiring the Emperor to issue a public statement denying that he was divine. In his rescript on January 1, 1946, Hirohito made the denial, if obliquely: "The ties between us and our people have always stood upon mutual trust and affection. They do not depend upon mere legends and myths. They are not predicated on the false conception that the Emperor is divine and that the Japanese people are superior to other races and fated to rule the world." Some Japanese subsequently tried to minimize the rescript's significance by pointing out that in Japanese polity the Emperor had never been regarded as divine in the Western sense of that term, which is true. But Hirohito's rescript did undermine the principal ideological pillar of the traditional national polity. A distinguished authority on modern Japan explained: "The state had claimed its authority to impose unquestionable obligation [on its citizens]. It could not do this without trying to establish the fiction that over it hovered a special source of final truth. For the Japanese system of things, this existed in the person of the emperor, in whom resided an inherited sacredness which made his will irresistible."[13] Perhaps more important at the time, Hirohito's self-effacing act unmistakably signified to his people that he, and therefore they, had an obligation for the sake of the nation's future to work with, not against, the will of MacArthur.

In his most direct assault against ultranationalism MacArthur launched the first phase of a purge program on January 4, 1946, ordering the "removal and exclusion of undesirable personnel from public office." He explained that the purpose of this directive and of the one abolishing ultranationalistic organizations was "to strike the shackles from the efforts of the Japanese people to rise toward freedom and democracy." He had hoped that "Japan itself would clean its own stable," but he had been compelled to act "in direct and forthright fashion" when "the inertia, if not the active opposition within the government itself, blocked all attempts. Centuries of feudal submission and the complete, untrammelled and irresponsible freedom of the executive proved obstacles too great to be overcome by the people themselves." The screening committees were ordered to make their decisions for purging on the basis of certain categories of "undesirable" positions held rather than on the evidence of individual responsibility and action. Directed primarily against ultranationalists and militarists in the Diet and the ministries of the central government, this initial phase of the purge produced the removal of nearly 400 persons in the Ministry of Home Affairs and over 170 members of the House of Peers. It disqualified about 90 percent of the Diet for re-election, together with 200 leaders of the Progressive Party, the strongest conservative political organization. Causing temporary disruptions in public administration, it barred virtually all public servants who had held office between July 1937 and September 1945.[14]

Even more sweeping were the second and third phases of the purge in 1946–1947, which removed or barred not only more politicians and bureaucrats but also many leaders of commerce, industry, and mass media. Ultimately 210,787 persons, or 0.3 percent of the Japanese population, were removed or excluded from office. In contrast, in the American zone of Germany 418,307 individuals (2.5 percent of the zone's population) were purged. A specialist on the two purges concludes that, despite SCAP's purge by categories, which brought injustice to many Japanese, "the volume of the effort in Germany was not only many times greater, it was also performed much less efficiently." MacArthur commented in his memoirs, "I very much doubted the wisdom of this measure, as it tended to lose the services of many able governmental individuals who would be difficult to replace in the organization of a new Japan. I put the purge into operation with as little harshness as possible." He did not add, however, that he successfully resisted a proposal of the National Security Council in late 1948 that called for relaxation of the purge.[15]

Although the purge in Japan was moderate compared with that in the United States zone in Germany, most scholarly writings on the SCAP program are not complimentary. One specialist on postwar Japan maintains that, though "all known ultranationalists were for a number of years barred from holding public office of any kind," in actual practice "their places were often taken by less well-known people holding much the same views, but careful not to express them in public." In the long run the purge, he finds, was not as successful in eradicating ultranationalism as were "the indirect Occupation measures — those that served to attack the ideological and material foundations on which extreme right-wing elements had been able to build their strength." Hans Baerwald, who served in the Public Service Qualifications (or "Purge") Division of the Government Section and later wrote the principal book on the purge, said that the temporary purge of the overwhelming majority of militarists and ultranationalists in high political offices was achieved, but the secondary effort to remove antidemocratic elements from the bureaucracy, political parties, business, and mass media was less effective. The trouble lay in the criteria for purging, for no sure and consistent way was devised to prove antidemocratic sentiments. Baerwald concluded, "In the field of leadership, the purge did effectuate some changes; its impact could have been greater. Its contribution to democratization was not impressive primarily because the purge as a concept proved antithetical to liberal democratic theory. For the achievement of democratization, greater success might have been possible if tutelage [reeducation] had played a large role." [16]

The early months of the occupation had been marked more by some hopeful signs of altering Japanese public attitudes than by actual progress in lasting political reforms. Analyses of Japanese press opinion in the Civil Information and Education Section suggested that most Japanese would be receptive to democratic changes, but it is not easy to gauge how accurately newspapers operating under occupation controls reflected public feelings. In December the Diet passed an election law providing for lowered ages for voting and office-holding, women's suffrage, and more proportional representation, but it is doubtful that the measure would have been enacted at the time without SCAP pressure. Nevertheless, MacArthur exuded confidence and optimism in his first New Year's message to the Japanese people: "A New Year has come. With it, a new day dawns for Japan. No longer is the future to be settled by a few. The shackles of militarism, of feudalism, of regimentation of body and soul, have been removed. . . . The masses of Japan now have the power to govern and what is done must be done by themselves." On the other hand, John K. Emmerson, a Foreign Service officer working under Atcheson, observed in a report to the State Department the following month "that the struggle for livelihood was uppermost in the mind of every subject of the Japanese nation, that political parties, elections, democracy, the emperor, were all of academic importance when the rice bowl is empty. Political factors could therefore be understood only against this economic background. . . . By February 1946 it was clear that the emphasis in the Occupation should shift from the *destructive* to the *constructive* phase."[17] Although amelioration of Japan's economic problems was not in the offing when Emmerson penned his report, MacArthur and his Government Section leaders could foresee positive and far-reaching political changes from the movement toward constitutional reform already under way.

2. An Abnormal Birth

A primary objective of the occupation, as set forth in the Potsdam Declaration, was "a peacefully inclined and responsible government" based on "the freely expressed will of the Japanese people." Not long after setting up his headquarters in Tokyo, MacArthur became convinced that "no political reform that did not encompass revision of the Meiji Constitution would be worth serious consideration." But in September 1945, he did not envision that he and his SCAP staff would become directly involved in the creation of a new Japanese constitution. On the other hand, Japan's leaders at the start of the occupation did not believe that it would be necessary to amend, much less replace, the revered Meiji Constitution, which had served the nation since 1868. "Its place in their political thinking," states an authoritative study, "was second only to that of the imperial dynasty, from which, in legal theory, it had been received." Although conservatives in Japan "preferred to have it interpreted in practice as the embodiment of enlightened and benevolent monarchy," Japanese liberals thought that "it would permit the development of democracy if interpreted by advocates rather than by antagonists of democracy. Above all other considerations in the minds of educated Japanese was the desire to avoid an imposed revision in the guise of one contrived by themselves."[18]

An inept interpreter inadvertently assisted in the start of constitutional reform when MacArthur and Prince Konoye of the Higashikuni Cabinet conferred on October 4, 1945. The SCAP commander did not inform the prince about the sweeping Civil Liberties Directive to be issued later that day, but listened quietly as Konoye delivered an "impassioned plea for gradualism in democratizing Japan." Toward the end of the meeting, according to one Japanese source, Konoye asked whether MacArthur had any instructions or proposals "about the make-up of the government. The interpreter translated the Japanese word for 'make-up' into English as 'constitution.' . . . The interpreter said, 'He's asking about the constitution of the government.' MacArthur, taken by surprise, replied in a grandiose manner that constitutional changes would, of course, be necessary." The interpreter translated this "in such a way that Konoye took it to mean that MacArthur had commissioned him to prepare the draft of a new constitution." Indeed, the Japanese text of Konoye's memorandum on the meeting interprets MacArthur as saying, in part, "We hope the necessary steps will be taken by the Japanese Government through reasonable procedures; however, they must be taken as promptly as possible, or else we will carry them out ourselves, even at the risk of friction. . . . If you were to rally the liberal elements around you and lay before the public a proposal for constitutional revision, I think the Diet would go along." A week later the Privy Council appointed Konoye to head a committee to determine whether the Meiji Constitution needed revision and, if so, what changes should be made. Konoye and his committee, including Professor Soichi Sasaki, an eminent constitutional specialist, went to work with zeal.[19]

During the next two weeks the prince conferred several times on the matter with George Atcheson and Bonner Fellers, the latter being both a member of MacArthur's inner group of advisers and a friend of Konoye's. MacArthur was kept informed of Konoye's work by Atcheson and Fellers and, claims one scholar, "tacitly endorsed the arrangement." Japanese and Western press coverage of the Konoye Committee's activities was full. As the direction of the project began to emerge, whether alleged or actual, the committee's efforts came under increasing attack from the Shidehara Cabinet and the Diet for supposedly proposing the Emperor's abdication, and from influential American newspapers that criticized Konoye's ties with militarists when he was Prime Minister. Konoye's tactless remarks in press interviews contributed to the mounting opposition in Japan and America. MacArthur was especially riled by the criticisms of Konoye that appeared in late October in the *Times* and *Herald Tribune* of New York. Nathaniel Peffer, an East Asian expert writing in the former paper, charged that "the worst blunder we have committed" in Japan was permitting Konoye to take the lead in constitutional revision. A *Herald Tribune* editorial described his selection as "the equivalent of choosing a gunman to devise rules for a reform school." On November 1 MacArthur issued a statement attributing Konoye's alleged mandate from SCAP as a "misunderstanding" and dissociating SCAP from the committee's work. The Konoye Committee continued, however, and Konoye and Sasaki each submitted a preliminary report to the Privy Council. It will be recalled that Konoye committed suicide in December, just before he was to be arrested as a war crimes suspect.[20]

MacArthur was eager to remove from the arena of constitutional revision not only Konoye but also Atcheson and the State Department. On October 17 the State Department sent to Atcheson detailed instructions on constitutional reform to guide him in his talks with Konoye. Since GHQ, SCAP, intercepted all messages between Atcheson's office and State, MacArthur knew of the guidelines and suspected that the department was preparing to encroach farther into what he considered to be his bailiwick. Shortly after his statement dissociating himself from Konoye's project, he "ordered" Atcheson to cease his discussions with Konoye and to confine his office's activities to Japan's "external affairs." Atcheson wrote Under Secretary of State Dean Acheson on November 7, "It is obvious to us now that General MacArthur, or his Chief of Staff and other members of the Bataan Club who act as his Privy Council or *genro* — wish if possible to keep the State Department out of this matter."[21] Atcheson had not misunderstood MacArthur's strategem.

When Shidehara became Prime Minister on October 9, MacArthur had "pointedly advised" him of the necessity for "liberalization of the Constitution." With the Konoye Committee beginning its work under the aegis of the Privy Council, Shidehara set up a Cabinet committee on constitutional revision on October 13 under the chairmanship of Minister of State Joji Matsumoto, a seventy-year-old former law professor at the University of Tokyo. Dr. Matsumoto's group was given the same charge by the Shidehara Cabinet as the Konoye Committee had received from the Privy Council: to determine "whether the Constitution needed to be revised and if so to what extent." The Matsumoto Committee worked independently and seems not to have taken into consideration the Konoye-Sasaki reports, which were completed in late November. Atcheson was forbidden by MacArthur to advise the Matsumoto Committee, too, though his counsel was not requested by the Japanese group. The SCAP Government Section, established in early October, had no contact with the Matsumoto Committee until the beginning of February. An official SCAP chronicle says that "as the winter progressed numerous bodies and individuals undertook to set down on paper their own ideas for such revision. The Matsumoto committee worked behind closed doors, but the political parties and other interested persons and groups of persons did not hesitate to make public their views." Some of these unofficial Japanese proposals included liberal and even radical concepts, and GHQ, SCAP, analyses of Japanese newspapers suggested that the people were amenable to major political changes as long as the Emperor was retained. MacArthur apparently assumed that Matsumoto's group would seriously consider ideas for democratization, incorporate some of them in its draft, and produce a revision reasonably acceptable to SCAP and the Allied governments. But the Matsumoto Committee was responsible to the Shidehara Cabinet, whose key members were not speaking out forcefully for major changes in the Meiji Constitution; for example, Shidehara told the House of Peers that "only those sections of the constitution which had been abused" would be revised, and Foreign Minister Yoshida declared that the Meiji Constitution already provided for democratic government and needed only such revision as "to prevent misuse of certain provisions by militarists and other recalcitrant elements."[22]

Despite MacArthur's efforts, the State Department refused to be denied a voice in the reshaping of the Japanese constitution. On December 13 Atcheson sent the following memorandum to the SCAP commander:

This Mission has just received from the Department of State copies of (1) a preliminary report "Reform of the Japanese Governmental System," October 22, 1945, prepared by the Department for the consideration of the State-War-Navy Coordinating Subcommittee for the Far East; and (2) a revision of the "Conclusions" of the above report prepared in the Department at the Subcommittee's request and submitted for its consideration on November 13, 1945. . . .

The recommendations in both documents, the latter being a revision in form rather than in substance, are generally the same as set forth in the Department's telegram of October 17. . . .

Since the discontinuation in early November of this Office's informal conversations with Konoye, there have been no further discussions to our knowledge of constitutional revision by American and Japanese officials at a working level. There would seem real danger if an effective liaison at this level is not reestablished, that the Japanese Government, working in ignorance of specific American desires and requirements, may arrive at an advanced stage in the preparation of a draft revision which fails signally to satisfy those desires and requirements. There would then arise the need which the preliminary State-War-Navy documents warn against, of formally ordering the necessary changes, reducing the possibility of their long-range acceptance and support by the Japanese people.[23]

The final form of the above report, "Reform of the Japanese Governmental System," was sent by the Joint Chiefs to MacArthur as SWNCC 228 on January 9. The document was forwarded to him ostensibly for his information and guidance, but, as a specialist on the subject notes, "the phraseology made it clear that the United States government expected the Supreme Commander to carry out the policies contained in the paper." Justin Williams, a political scientist and division chief in the Government Section, maintains that "SWNCC 228 is the master key to an understanding of what happened to the Meiji Constitution." The new Japanese constitution "was outlined in SWNCC 228," according to Williams, "and anybody who mistakes that cannot interpret properly what happened out there in 1946. It was a State Department document that MacArthur put into effect. He said at the time, 'It's in the record clearly, but everybody has missed it.'" In reference to SWNCC 228, MacArthur told the Joint Chiefs, in May 1946, "I have acted meticulously in accord with the instructions received from the United States Government, and been guided throughout by its policies in assisting the Japanese Government and people in the development of constitutional reform."[24] Because of the singular significance of SWNCC 228, the section on "Conclusions" in that document is provided here in full:

It is concluded that:

a. The Supreme Commander should indicate to the Japanese authorities that the Japanese governmental system should be reformed to accomplish the following general objectives:

(1) A government responsible to an electorate based upon wide representative suffrage;

(2) An executive branch of government deriving its authority from and responsible to the electorate or to a fully representative legislative body;

(3) A legislative body, fully representative of the electorate, with full power to reduce, increase, or reject any items in the budget or to suggest new items;

(4) No budget shall become effective without the express approval of the legislative body;

(5) Guarantee of fundamental civil rights to Japanese subjects and to all persons within Japanese jurisdiction;

(6) The popular election or local appointment of as many of the prefectural officials as practicable;

(7) The drafting and adoption of constitutional amendments or of a constitution in a manner which will express the free will of the Japanese people.

b. Though the ultimate form of government in Japan is to be established by the freely expressed will of the Japanese people, the retention of the Emperor Institution in its present form is not considered consistent with the foregoing general objectives.

c. If the Japanese people decide that the Emperor Institution is not to be retained, constitutional safeguards against the institution will obviously not be required but the Supreme Commander should indicate to the Japanese that the constitution should be amended to conform to the objectives listed in *a* above and to include specific provisions:

(1) That any other bodies shall possess only a temporary veto power over legislative measures, including constitutional amendments approved by the representative legislative body, and that such body shall have sole authority over financial measures;

(2) That the Ministers of State or the members of a Cabinet should in all cases be civilians;

(3) That the legislative body may meet at will.

d. The Japanese should be encouraged to abolish the Emperor Institution or to reform it along more democratic lines. If the Japanese decide to retain the Institution of the Emperor, however, the Supreme Commander should also indicate to the Japanese authorities that the following safeguards in addition to those enumerated in *a* and *c* above would be necessary:

(1) That the Ministers of State, chosen with the advice and consent of the representative legislative body, shall form a Cabinet collectively responsible to the legislative body;

(2) That when a Cabinet loses the confidence of the representative legislative body, it must either resign or appeal to the electorate;

(3) The Emperor shall act in all important matters only on the advice of the Cabinet;

(4) The Emperor shall be deprived of all military authority such as that provided in Articles XI, XII, XIII, and XIV of Chapter I of the Constitution;

(5) The Cabinet shall advise and assist the Emperor;

(6) The entire income of the Imperial Household shall be turned into the public treasury and the expenses of the Imperial Household shall be appropriated by the legislature in the annual budget.

A caveat to MacArthur appears in the sentence following the "Conclusions":

Only as a last resort should the Supreme Commander order the Japanese Government to effect the above listed reforms, as the knowledge that they had been imposed by the Allies would materially reduce the possibility of their acceptance and support by the Japanese people in the future.[25]

Unfortunately little is known of MacArthur's thoughts and feelings during the next three critical weeks of January. He ignored Atcheson's plea and continued his hands-off attitude toward the deliberations of the Matsumoto Committee. Three days after receiving SWNCC 228, he directed the Japanese government to hold the first postwar general elections "not earlier than March 15"; they were subsequently scheduled for April 10. "I had expected that the new constitution would be finished by then," MacArthur later

commented, "and that the voting would, in fact, be a plebiscite."
In a meeting on January 17 with Government Section leaders, the
visiting Far Eastern Advisory Commission found that group was
not engaged in or planning toward any direct involvement in the
revision process. At that time, as Williams attests, "there was no
thought of amending Japan's constitution. With General Whitney
furnishing close liaison between his staff and General MacArthur,
Government Section's views were, willy-nilly, those of SCAP." At
his final meeting with the Advisory Commission on January 30,
MacArthur told the delegates that he "had ceased to take any action in regard to the revision," for the matter "had been taken out
of his hands by the Moscow Agreement." The Moscow Conference, as mentioned previously, had provided for the establishment of the Far Eastern Commission, which, unlike the Advisory
Commission, would include the Soviet Union. Undoubtedly
MacArthur was anxious to have the progress of revision as advanced as possible before the new commission's first meeting, set
for February 26. He fully expected the Soviet member to push for
more severe measures against Japan, including abolition of the
imperial system, and to try to obstruct SCAP's reformist plans.[26]
All in all, however, MacArthur's actual conduct in January provided little inkling of his sudden change of course in early February.

The *Mainichi Shimbun,* one of Japan's largest newspapers, published on February 1 what was said to be the Matsumoto Committee's tentative revision draft. That same day the committee submitted to SCAP two documents entitled "Gist of the Revision of
the Constitution" and "General Explanation of the Constitutional
Revision Drafted by the Government," but offered no actual constitutional draft. Studying the two committee papers and the alleged draft published in the *Mainichi,* MacArthur concluded that
the Matsumoto Committee's version was "nothing more than a re-
wording of the old Meiji constitution." In the next few days most
Japanese newspapers were critical of the extremely conservative
nature of the draft. MacArthur told Whitney at first to "prepare
a detailed answer, rejecting the Matsumoto draft" (though that
document had not been submitted to SCAP). Also on February 1
Whitney quickly prepared for MacArthur a memorandum setting

forth the Government Section's opinion on the extent of his authority "to deal with fundamental changes in the Japanese constitutional structure, either by approving or disapproving proposals
made by the Japanese Government or by issuing orders or directives to that Government." The memorandum emphasized that
MacArthur had authority from both the Allied powers and the Joint
Chiefs to "proceed with constitutional reform." Whitney commented, "In my opinion, in the absence of any policy decision by
the Far Eastern Commission on the subject (which would, of course,
be controlling), you have the same authority with reference to
constitutional reform as you have with reference to any other matter
of substance in the occupation and control of Japan."[27]

MacArthur did not wait for the Matsumoto Committee to submit a formal draft of its revision plan. Instead, on February 3 he
reversed his decision on a statement of repudiation and instructed
Whitney to have his section immediately "prepare a draft constitution" as "the most effective method of instructing the Japanese
Government on the nature and application of these principles he
considered basic." He assured Whitney that he was extending "full
discretion" to his section in drafting the "guide," but "wished" that
certain points be included. While orally stating that he favored a
unicameral national legislature, he gave Whitney a handwritten list
of the other provisions he wanted:

I

The Emperor is at the head of the State.

His succession is dynastic.

His duties and powers will be exercised in accordance with the
Constitution and responsible to the basic will of the people as provided therein.

II

War as a sovereign right of the nation is abolished. Japan renounces it as an instrumentality for settling its disputes and even for
preserving its own security. It relies upon the higher ideals which are
now stirring the world for its defense and its protection.

No Japanese Army, Navy, or Air Force will ever be authorized and
no rights of belligerency will ever be conferred upon any Japanese
force.

III

The feudal system of Japan will cease.

No rights of peerage except those of the Imperial family will extend beyond the lives of those now existent.

No patent of nobility will from this time forth embody within itself any National or Civic power of Government.

At the bottom of the note MacArthur added: "Pattern budget after British system."[28]

Justin Williams maintains that "MacArthur's sudden decision to revise the Meiji Constitution resulted from Japanese procrastination, the imminent Diet election, and the prospect of filibustering in the FEC." Whitney believed that after the Moscow Conference, where the United States "surrendered the unilateral authority we were then exercising over Japan to an eleven-nation policy-making commission and gave the Soviet Union veto power over all policy incident to Japan, MacArthur realized the urgency of immediate action under the powers he then held." In December 1958, Dr. Kenzo Takayanagi, then chairman of the Japanese government's Commission on the Constitution, wrote MacArthur that his "impressions formed after due study of the materials" were that, "in view of the international situation then prevailing," the general's "very prompt action taken in February 1946 . . . greatly contributed to the welfare of the Japanese. . . . The condominium by eleven nations would have been disastrous to us."[29] In his reply MacArthur affirmed that his haste on revision was motivated significantly by his concern over potential Allied interference in Japan:

> The political situation in Japan was desperate. Its old Constitution, relatively liberal and wholesome in many respects, had been so warped in interpretation and so deprecated in public opinion by the results of the war, that a new charter was immediately imperative if the structure of Japanese self government was to be sustained. The choice was alien military government or autonomous civil government. The pressure for the former by many of the Allied nations was intense, accompanied by many drastic concepts designed to fracture the Japanese nation. My fixed determination and purpose was to avoid such violent discrimination and to reconstruct Japan's sovereignty along modern and liberal lines as soon as practicable. Had the Japanese people, the Japanese Emperor and the Japanese government not supported me as they did, the results would have been catastrophic.

Likewise, he was referring primarily to "the international situation" when he commented to Takayanagi: "The preservation of the Emperor system was my fixed purpose. It was inherent and integral to Japanese political and cultural survival. The vicious efforts to destroy the person of the Emperor and thereby abolish the system became one of the most dangerous menaces that threatened the successful rehabilitation of the nation."[30]

The first nine articles of the new constitution would provide for the maintenance of the emperorship as a state symbol but divested of sovereign power, which satisfied MacArthur. His desire to have the peerage terminated also would be realized in the new constitution. The elimination of some vestiges of feudalism, however, would require specific legislative measures and lengthy enforcement efforts, as in the case of land reform. Regarding his budget proposal, "no one in the Government Section understood what he meant by that," according to a constitutional scholar, "so that the instruction went largely ignored." The Government Section's draft would incorporate his suggestion of a unicameral legislature, but the Japanese Cabinet later won a concession to substitute its plan for a bicameral system with a weak upper chamber, to be called the House of Councillors. The Japanese provision met no objection from MacArthur, whose wish was fulfilled, namely, that "the House of Peers should be done away with, and nothing should be established that in any way resembled it."[31]

In the ensuing years MacArthur claimed repeatedly that the suggestion of a constitutional article renouncing war and armed forces came from Prime Minister Shidehara when they conferred on January 24, 1946. MacArthur, however, was surely responsible for its wording as conveyed in his note to Whitney on February 3. The clause would be revised by Whitney's section and the Diet, finally becoming Article IX of the new constitution. In spite of MacArthur's contention, questions about the proposal's origin have persisted, such as why Shidehara did not suggest it to the Matsumoto Committee also. Shidehara, Yoshida, and other contemporary Japanese political leaders later stated or implied that the concept originated with MacArthur. Such testimony, together with other bits of evidence that conflict with MacArthur's version, produced a large and still growing number of writings on the article's origin. It is impossible to summarize briefly the voluminous literature on the issue, and there is no definitive answer to the question of authorship. "Irrespective of the origin of the no-war clause," concludes one of the most respected American scholars on the subject, "there is no question that MacArthur's support for it was decisive in its adoption."[32]

MacArthur's original note to Whitney included the phrase "even for preserving its own security," which was deleted in the Government Section's draft and was not reinserted during the Japanese deliberations on the revision bill of 1946. Because of Article IX, considerable debate and litigation would develop over the constitutionality of the Self-Defense Forces established by the Japanese government in the 1950s. Writing to Kenzo Takayanagi near the end of that decade, MacArthur happily professed to see no problem: "Nothing in Article 9 prevents any and all necessary steps for the preservation of the safety of the nation. I stated this at the time of the adoption of the Constitution and later [1950] recommended a Defense Force be organized of ten divisions with corresponding elements of the sea and air forces. The article was aimed entirely at foreign aggression and was intended to give spiritual leadership to the world. It will stand everlastingly as a monument to the foresight, the statesmanship, and the wisdom of Prime Minister Shidehara."[33] Unfortunately Japanese courts have not found the issue to be as simple as MacArthur did.

From the time that the Government Section went to work on its draft, February 4, until the promulgation of the new constitution that autumn, MacArthur conceived his chief responsibility in the matter to be coping with external threats to the revision process, especially those posed by the new Far Eastern Commission. While eagerly following every step toward a new constitution, he displayed restraint in not interfering with the work of the Government Section or with the later deliberations of Japanese governmental bodies. Therefore the story of the drafting and passage of the constitutional revision bill, though fascinating and important, will be told briefly.

Upon receiving MacArthur's charge on February 3, Courtney Whitney set up a steering committee consisting of his three principal lieutenants: Charles Kades (chairman), Alfred Hussey, and Milo Rowell. Nine working committees, involving twenty-one members of the section, were organized to prepare drafts on the preamble, Emperor, legislature, executive, judiciary, civil rights, finance, local government, and treaties and enabling provisions. None of the participants seems to have been an expert on Japanese constitutional law. As a later researcher found, "for so fundamental and critical a task, their qualifications left a good deal to be desired." Nevertheless, working against time and with a paucity of source materials, Whitney's group demonstrated remarkable dedication, energy, and intelligence. Relying heavily on SWNCC 228, MacArthur's points, and an old volume of various nations' constitutions, borrowed from the University of Tokyo, the Government Section's "constituent assembly," as Whitney once called it, produced its draft constitution by February 10. MacArthur quickly approved it after making one minor change, which was the deletion of an article "prohibiting an amendment to the constitution impairing or altering the provisions of the bill of rights."[34]

Whitney and his steering committee presented copies of the draft to a group of Cabinet officials, including Yoshida and Matsumoto, on the 13th. In a ploy that MacArthur approved of but was informed about only after the meeting, Whitney told the Japanese that "if the cabinet were unable to prepare a suitable and acceptable draft before the elections, General MacArthur was prepared to lay this statement of principle directly before the people." The indignant Japanese took the SCAP draft to Prime Minister Shidehara, but it was another ten days before the Cabinet agreed in principle to prepare a revision based on the terms of the "MacArthur Draft," as some of them derisively referred to it. During the Cabinet discussions that followed the meeting on February 13, says Yoshida's recent biographer, "Yoshida sided with Matsumoto in opposing compromise; Shidehara advocated a more conciliatory position; and the issue appears to have been resolved only when the emperor personally endorsed the American draft." When the new Japanese version was submitted to GHQ on March 4, there followed a thirty-six-hour session between officials of the Government Section and the Cabinet to work out textual differences. Except for a concession to the Japanese on a bicameral legislature, the resulting document involved little compromise. As one authority asserts, it "conformed very closely to the original Government Section draft in both essentials and nonessentials."[35]

Late on March 5, after the marathon negotiations were done,

Hirohito issued an imperial rescript endorsing the new draft, though aware that it was a slightly modified version of the GHQ "guide." About an hour afterward, the Cabinet reluctantly agreed to support it. Shidehara told them, "I believe we are following the only possible course in view of the situation confronting us." That body, like the Privy Council and the Diet later, seemed to be convinced that support of the American-inspired draft was essential to bring an early withdrawal of the occupation forces, ensure MacArthur's continued backing of the imperial institution, and avert all sorts of potentially harsh FEC-imposed terms. The draft constitution was published the next day, along with a Cabinet statement supporting it and implying that it had been drafted by Cabinet officials on SCAP's orders.[36]

Also on March 6, MacArthur issued a statement that showed his elation but revealed little of GHQ's actual involvement:

> It is with a sense of deep satisfaction that I am today able to announce a decision of the Emperor and Government of Japan to submit to the Japanese people a new and enlightened constitution which has my full approval. This instrument has been drafted after painstaking investigation and frequent conference between members of the Japanese Government and this headquarters following my initial direction to the cabinet five months ago.

Extolling its main progressive features, he emphasized that it "places sovereignty squarely in the hands of the people," assures "fundamental human liberties which satisfy the most exacting standards of enlightened thought," and enables Japan through the "foremost of its provisions," the no-war clause, to "chart a new course oriented to faith in the justice, tolerance, and understanding of mankind."[37]

For the next month public attention in Japan was centered on the general elections that were held on April 10. A host of local and mundane issues surfaced to prevent the proposed constitution from being the all-consuming central issue, thereby frustrating MacArthur's hope of exploiting the first postwar elections as a popular referendum on the revision. But he obtained unexpectedly valuable assistance from the elections, for they ended the domination of the House of Representatives by members elected during the war and gave a majority of that chamber's seats to

Yoshida's Liberal party, with the other leading conservative party, Shidehara's Progressives, next in strength. On May 23 Yoshida succeeded Shidehara as Prime Minister; he and his new Cabinet proved surprisingly loyal in their commitment to the revision, ably defending it before the Diet.[38]

The constitutional revision bill was debated freely and extensively in both houses of the Diet. It was passed by overwhelming margins by the House of Representatives on August 4 (a vote of 421 to 8) and by the House of Peers on October 6 (298 to 2), and gained final approval from the Privy Council on October 29. The Japanese deliberations had produced some additions, deletions, and revisions of articles, but the essential features of the draft were not affected. In order to provide "legal continuity," the Japanese government's enactment of the revision bill was in the form of an amendment to the Meiji Constitution. The promulgation by the Emperor of the new constitution, which it actually was, took place on November 3, and it became effective on May 3, 1947. At the time of the promulgation MacArthur stated in a message to the Japanese nation: "The adoption of this liberal charter, together with other progressive measures enacted by the Diet, lays a very solid foundation for the new Japan. Like the product of all human endeavor, it has its frailties but by and large it shows how far we have come since hostilities ended. It represents a great stride forward toward world peace and good will and normalcy."[39]

The liberal, democratic constitution of 1946 is founded on the principles of popular sovereignty and of the individual's worth and dignity. Its preamble begins appropriately, "We, the Japanese people . . ." and its first article states, "The Emperor shall be the symbol of the State and of the unity of the people, deriving his position from the will of the people with whom resides sovereign power." Of the 103 articles, 39 deal with basic rights and freedoms of the citizens. Besides incorporating most of the American Bill of Rights, the Japanese constitution provides some remarkably progressive guarantees, such as universal adult suffrage; labor's right to organize and to bargain collectively; free and equal education; academic freedom; the right to "minimum standards of wholesome and cultured living"; no discrimination in "political, economic, or social relations because of race, creed, sex, social status or family origin"; equality for women in choice of spouse, property rights, inheritance, and divorce settlements; and the important guarantee that all the wide-ranging rights set forth in the constitution are "eternal and inviolate."

The governmental system more nearly resembles the British than the American. Executive power is vested in the Cabinet, headed by the Prime Minister, but the Cabinet is "collectively responsible to the Diet." According to Article XLI, "the highest organ of state power" and "the sole law-making organ of the State" is the Diet, which consists of two chambers, each elected by popular vote — the House of Representatives and the House of Councillors. The former is granted far more power than the latter; for example, it originates appropriations measures, has greater authority over the Cabinet, and possesses certain veto controls over the House of Councillors.

Among its other features, the constitution of 1946 includes a supreme court, modeled somewhat after the American body, and a system of inferior courts. The judicial branch is independent of the legislative and executive arms, and the Supreme Court possesses the power of judicial review of the constitutionality of "any law, order, regulation, or official act." The constitution also provides for a system of democratic government at the prefectural and local levels. Certainly the document's most unusual feature is Article IX, which renounces war and standing armed forces. An amendment requires a two-thirds majority in each house, whereupon it then must be approved by a simple majority in a popular referendum. To date, Japan has not amended its postwar constitution.[40]

MacArthur did not initiate or directly influence the drafting of any of the articles on civil and social rights, but he approved them as they came to him from the Government Section, and he appeared proud to support all sections of the constitution during its progression through Japanese channels to final promulgation. Seventeen years later he rated the constitution as "probably the single most important accomplishment of the occupation," and he singled out the provisions on women's rights and their subsequent legal implementation as the achievements most satisfying to him as SCAP: "Of all the reforms accomplished by the occupation in Japan, none was more heartwarming to me than this change in the status of women." Like some of the other important reforms, the impetus for women's rights within the GHQ bureaucracy actually came from some able middle-echelon civilians. Miss Beate Sirota, a brilliant twenty-two-year-old woman whose fluency in Japanese had won her a position working in the Government Section, was the principal author of the provisions on women's rights. Austrian by birth, she had lived in Japan for a decade before moving to America prior to World War II. She and the other two members of the section's Civil Rights Committee, Dr. Harry Emerson Wildes and Lieutenant Colonel Pieter K. Roest, effectively mobilized opinion in behalf of their sundry draft articles and, observes one historian, "took advantage of the fact that so much else was going on at the time." Another scholar suggests that the women's rights and other progressive articles were approved by the senior SCAP administrators because their decision-making was "supported by the full power of military law and isolated from Japanese groups and individuals with high stakes in the outcome. . . . They were able to carry out their radical experiment because they were in somebody else's laboratory." Moreover, the concept of democracy that most of the senior GHQ officers had was sufficiently diffused, generalized, and vague that it could encompass the ideas of Sirota and her committee colleagues. This was true for MacArthur, too, whose views even within the confines of Army reforms had ranged from radical when he was West Point superintendent in the early 1920s to reactionary during his tenure as the Army's Chief of Staff a decade later.[41]

In the birth stage of the constitution in 1946, MacArthur saw his main responsibility to be "protecting" the process from interference or obstruction by the Far Eastern Commission. He later remarked, "I am certain that it [adoption of the constitution] would never have been accomplished had the occupation been dependent on the deliberations of the Far Eastern Commission — with the Soviet power of veto!" He and other SCAP officials convinced many influential Japanese political leaders that the SCAP-sponsored draft was preferable to the alleged alternative of an FEC-dictated constitution, which would surely require the abandonment of the imperial institution. On the other hand, the FEC was determined to assert its authority, granted in the Moscow Agreement, to establish policy for the occupation, and declared its intention to review the draft constitution to ensure that it conformed with the Potsdam Declaration and the Instrument of Surrender.[42] Thus the initial collision course between MacArthur and the FEC was set in the spring of 1946.

The FEC, which had not become fully operative until after the Japanese Cabinet had approved the SCAP-originated draft, advised MacArthur in late March that the first postwar general elections, set for April 10, should be postponed. Holding the elections "at such an early date may well give a decisive advantage to the reactionary parties," the FEC maintained; besides, the constitution had become "at this late stage an election issue, upon which there can be little time for consideration by the Japanese people." MacArthur dismissed the FEC's apprehension as unwarranted and allowed the elections to be conducted as scheduled. On April 30 the FEC, which routed its messages to MacArthur through the Joint Chiefs, as required, requested him to send a staff representative to Washington to confer with the commission on "broad questions" of the constitutional issue.[43] Responding in turn through the JCS, MacArthur was indignant and arrogant: "In the first place, as Supreme Commander I have given my personal attention to the matter of constitutional reform, and there is no other officer in position to express in detail my views on that subject. In the second place, my key officer personnel situation has become so critical, due to the rapid demobilization of officer personnel, that the release of a key officer for such a purpose could not be effected without impairment to the command." In the same message of May 3, he boldly expressed his opinion on what he saw as the FEC's attempt to usurp his executive authority:

> The Far Eastern Commission, by its terms of reference, is a policy-making body with no executive powers, functions or responsibilities in the administration of Japan, which are reserved exclusively to the Supreme Commander. While it has the right of review of any action taken by the Supreme Commander which involves its own "policy decisions within its jurisdiction," it is not empowered, in my belief, to require prior approval of any action taken either by the Supreme Commander or the Japanese Government to implement, fulfill or enforce the terms of surrender. It thus far has formulated no action setting up "policies, principles and standards" to govern the revision of the Japanese constitution. It has not given the slightest indication of whether it concurs or non-concurs with the stated American pol-

icy, other than that contained in its apparent reversal of American policy [by requiring FEC approval before formal adoption of the constitution], designed to maintain the voluntary character of Japanese action on constitutional reform. Approval or disapproval of acts of the Japanese Government as a prerequisite to their validity is a function wholly executive in character. For the Far Eastern Commission to assert such power seems a clear violation of the terms of the Moscow Agreement and the interpretation of the American Government thereof, as publicly stated by the Secretary of State. To the contrary, it appears patently clear that the function of the Far Eastern Commission in the matter of constitution reform for Japan is limited to the formulation of guiding policy within the framework of the Potsdam Declaration and the surrender terms. In the absence of any such policy statement from the Far Eastern Commission, the Supreme Commander is clearly unrestricted in his authority to proceed in the implementation of the Potsdam Declaration and surrender terms as he interprets them or may be guided by developed American policy in point. In this matter speed is of the essence due to the fact, too readily lost sight of, that the Japanese people are now subject to their present wholly undemocratic constitution and will remain subject thereto so long as reform is delayed. Such delay, furthermore, but serves the interests of those who would much prefer that such reforms be not instituted at all.[44]

When the FEC decided that it should review the constitutional draft before its submission to the Diet, MacArthur ignored the international body and permitted the Diet to begin its deliberations on the document in June. In his charge to the Diet, however, he did emphasize the three principles set forth in a recent FEC directive: " a. Adequate time and opportunity should be allowed for the full discussion and consideration of the terms of the new Constitution. b. Complete legal continuity from the Constitution of 1889 to the new Constitution should be assured. c. The new Constitution should be adopted in such a manner as to demonstrate that it affirmatively expresses the free will of the Japanese people." All three were subsequently observed, at least to the satisfaction of MacArthur and the Japanese government.[45]

As first the House of Representatives and then the House of Councillors debated the various articles "in unrestrained fashion" that summer and early autumn, the FEC and MacArthur, communicating through the Joint Chiefs, engaged in a number of skirmishes over the commission's suggested revisions of certain words or phrases. MacArthur successfully opposed an FEC effort to force a plebiscite on the constitution immediately following its approval by the Diet and the Privy Council. But in late October the FEC directed that "not sooner than one year and not later than two years after it goes into effect, the situation with respect to the new constitution should be reviewed by the Diet," as well as by the FEC, with the possibility of "a referendum or some other appropriate procedure for ascertaining Japanese opinion with respect to the constitution." MacArthur won a temporary respite on the issue of publication of this directive in Japan, which the FEC had wanted to be done immediately. Drawing on his reservoir of mixed metaphors, he contended, "It would reduce the very essence of durability upon which the instrument has been built to a frail skeleton of temporary expedience overshadowed by the threat of forced abrogation or revision at the point of Allied bayonets."[46]

In retrospect, it is difficult to view the majority of the FEC members in the sinister light in which MacArthur cast them at the time. Both sides' best intentions were aimed at ensuring that whatever constitutional form was adopted would represent "the free expression of the Japanese people." The menace to that goal, according to MacArthur, was the FEC's intrusion; the FEC regarded SCAP as the threat. The end of the matter was rather anticlimactic, as described by a Japanese scholar writing in 1952:

> Our Constitution has functioned smoothly since its coming into force on May 3, 1947.
>
> In July and August, 1948, the general attention of the people was turned again to our Constitution, owing to reports that the Far Eastern Commission had taken a decision to permit the Diet to re-examine the Constitution after a lapse of a year or two after its coming into force. In the summer of 1948, the press carried reports concerning the Attorney General's views on an eventual revision and especially eventual abdication of the Emperor. The speaker of the House of Representatives began consultations with party leaders and the question of eventual revision of the Constitution came to be discussed among interested circles.
>
> The points of discussion chiefly concerned: 1) power of the Emperor in connection with Article 7; 2) fundamental human rights in connection with the limitative clause of public welfare contained in

Articles 12 and 13; and 3) advisability of war renunciation in view of the existing world situation.

However, the question did not go beyond the discussion stage, and no revision of the Constitution was demanded by the people.[47]

The "MacArthur Constitution" had taken firm root. In his self-appointed role as guardian of the constitutional process Mac-Arthur undoubtedly added to Cold War tension, but from his viewpoint and that of many Japanese his achievement had been worthwhile: neither the Far Eastern Commission nor the Soviet Union had had any impact of consequence on Japan's monumental constitutional revision.

3. Democracy à la Japan

During the seven months between the constitution's promulgation in November 1946 and its coming into effect in May 1947, legal draftsmen of the Japanese government, with advice and assistance from Whitney's Government Section, worked feverishly to prepare amendments or substitutions for much existing legislation in order to bring it into conformity with the new constitution. "Through sheer physical volume of work," says a SCAP report, "only the most urgent legislation could be enacted by May 3, 1947. . . . In later months the less urgent laws were enacted, and interim measures replaced with long-term legislation. A whole body of law which under normal conditions would have required ten years or more was enacted within less than two years."

MacArthur again assumed the role of guarding the process from what he predicted would be obstructionism if the FEC were allowed its wish to review the implementing measures before the Diet voted on them. According to Secretary of State James Byrnes, in September 1946 an FEC "drive for disapproval of [the] constitution was avoided" when Frank McCoy, the American representative on the FEC, informed his fellow commissioners of Mac-Arthur's assurance that copies of draft bills would be sent to the FEC for review prior to Diet action. After the first four implementing measures were introduced in the Diet on December 3, however, copies of them were not received by the FEC until the

27th of that month, by which time they had been passed by the Diet. The FEC's Australian representative was especially outraged and accused MacArthur of a "gross breach of faith." But the occupation commander continued his stratagem of forwarding draft legislation slowly to Washington, so that it was usually too late for the FEC to see a bill before its enactment into law. His high-handed manner was reprehensible, but it helped to make possible the rapid passage of many of the laws needed to implement the new constitution.[48]

The Diet that met from November 1946 through March 1947 was the last one under the old constitution. Politicians of the Liberal and Progressive parties, both conservative but now purged of many extreme rightists, held nearly half the seats. "Most of these men [and women]," observed a scholar of postwar Japanese politics, "were new to the Diet parties and marked a greater personal break with the prewar parties than the previous Diet because very few had ever been Diet members in the prewar parties." Eighty laws were passed as part of the package of enabling legislation. Among them were measures revamping the Diet's structure, election procedures, control of imperial properties, labor standards, government corporations, and the educational and judiciary systems. Despite its prodigious output, the Diet was under frequent criticism by Japanese leftists, who charged that it was "still reactionary and needs to be purged of a substantial portion of its make-up." MacArthur countered with encouragement of the Diet, which, he claimed, was demonstrating "much promise of becoming a genuine agency of popular government." Yet he himself interposed a significant undemocratic step. Usually the bills originated in the ministries, which sent rough drafts to the Cabinet's Bureau of Legislation, whence, often after revisions negotiated with the ministries involved, they were forwarded to the Diet. MacArthur refused, however, to permit the Diet to consider bills that had not gained previous approval by his GHQ or even to amend SCAP-approved measures without favorable SCAP reviews of the amendments.[49]

Although some Japanese liberals in the 1920s had pressed for decentralization of governmental authority, until 1946–1947 prefectural and local administrations had been largely extensions of the national government in Tokyo, with officials outside the capital functioning as appointed agents of the central government, mainly its Ministry of Home Affairs. MacArthur firmly believed that political decentralization and local autonomy were fundamental in developing democracy at the grass-roots level in Japan. With his prodding and the Government Section's advice and counsel, the Diet passed four local-government reform bills in the fall of 1946, enacted the Local Autonomy Law the next spring, and dissolved the Home Affairs Ministry near the end of 1947. Delighted, MacArthur saw these actions as vital steps toward Japan's reliance on "individual and community responsibility as the source of national political strength." Democracy, he averred, "must well up from the people's will to be free, from their desire and determination to govern their own local affairs without domination by individual strong men, by minority pressure groups or by entrenched bureaucracy."

The SCAP-inspired reforms at the prefectural and local governmental levels produced popularly elected officials and assemblies and led to broader-based political participation. But MacArthur never ventured into the countryside, and he accepted optimistic staff reports on the program at face value; he always thought it was one of the occupation's grandest achievements. In truth, the reforms were "less than a complete success," concluded Kurt Steiner, who worked in the Government Section and later became a noted political scientist. As he pointed out, "For one thing, the piecemeal opposition of conservative Japanese governments, closely allied with the prewar bureaucracy, sapped the effectiveness of the program from the start. For another, the reformers failed to tackle early enough and vigorously enough such vital problems as the reallocation of governmental functions and the establishment of an independent and viable local finance system." The governmental units at the prefectural, city, town, and village levels usually were restricted by inadequate tax bases and were excessively dependent on the central government for financial assistance. Although in 1949 a group of American tax experts helped to establish local fiscal policy on a sounder basis, the problems of government below the national level continued to be numerous and serious during the occupation, despite GHQ's sweeping claims to the contrary.[50]

In accord with his identification of democracy with decentralization, MacArthur pushed the Japanese government to break up its national police system. In the fall of 1945 the Kempeitai, the dreaded special police, had been disbanded, and subsequently thousands of regular police personnel had been purged. In early 1946 MacArthur obtained the temporary services of two respected American police commissioners to study the Japanese police system and make recommendations for its reorganization along more democratic and modernistic lines. The Diet and the Yoshida Cabinet were reluctant to implement the recommended reforms, particularly decentralization, for fear of weakening police effectiveness at a time when radical violence and unrest seemed to be growing. Within GHQ there were differences of opinion, with Whitney and his Government Section leaders generally favoring decentralization and Willoughy's G-2 staff and Civil Intelligence Section arguing for retention of the centrally controlled system but with limited reforms and augmented personnel. After the Socialist leader Tetsu Katayama succeeded Yoshida as Prime Minister in May 1947, MacArthur pressured him strongly for action on police reform. On September 16 he approved Katayama's plan to increase the police force to 125,000 men, but added: "I am not in accord, however, with the idea of, nor the necessity for, delaying the decentralization of the police power now existing, as I feel that the preservation of that power in its present centralized form is wholly incompatible with the spirit and intent of the new Constitution and inimical to democratic growth."[51]

MacArthur's proposals to Katayama, basically as enunciated in this letter, were incorporated in the Police Reorganization Law, passed by the Diet in December 1947. The new program called for local police forces in municipalities of 5000 or more people, with each unit under a local public safety commission comprising citizens. About a quarter of the total police personnel was assigned to the National Rural Police, which was under a national public safety commission and was independent of the local forces, except in emergencies. Police powers were reduced to apprehension of criminals and preservation of law and order. The new law was aimed at "deconcentrating the powers of police agencies, decentralizing such agencies, putting them under local control, and neutralizing them politically." As in the case of local government, however, funding for police units at the municipal level proved to be a serious obstacle, and local police were often ill trained and inadequately equipped to deal with such crises as Communist-incited riots. The SCAP reforms in the police field were a mixed blessing, and the system was overhauled and considerably centralized again two years after the occupation ended. MacArthur himself, as will be discussed later, precipitated the movement away from the 1947 reforms when he authorized the creation of the quasi-military National Police Reserve of 75,000 men at the beginning of the Korean War. In his memoirs he admitted that throughout the occupation the police system remained "a knotty problem." Nevertheless, after 1947 policemen functioned more responsibly as public servants, and as one scholar observed, "it was certainly apparent the police would play a diminished role in Japanese life."[52]

The Diet enacted a number of measures during 1946 to 1948 that drastically altered the legal and judicial system of Japan. The judiciary became an important guarantor of individual rights and freedoms, and the revamped civil and criminal codes became, in essence, instruments of social change. In practice as well as in principle, the judiciary was made independent of the legislative and executive branches; it had previously been under the administrative authority of the Ministry of Justice, but that agency was now abolished. Such Western principles as habeas corpus and the presumption of one's innocence until one is proven guilty were adopted, and such Japanese legal traditions as lèse majesté and the nobility's legal privileges were dropped. Radical changes in the family system followed the passage of the revised civil code implementing the equal-rights provisions of the new constitution. In legal contracts the responsible party now became the individual, not the family as in former times. Long accustomed to the Confucian principle of the rule of men, the Japanese began a slow but sure adjustment to and acceptance of the rule of law. Even the Supreme Court, though enjoying prestige and power, was cautious and restrained at first in exercising its authority, particularly in judicial review. It took a while for judges, procurators, and attorneys to adjust to the changes in jurisprudence, but jurists and citizens alike seemed to be supportive of the new system. One problem not anticipated by most SCAP officials was that the Japanese simply were not accustomed to resorting to adjudication. "There persists among most Japanese," remarked one observer, "a strong inclination toward compromise, conciliation, and mediation by informal methods rather than adversary litigation in courts."[53]

The most important SCAP official in advising and assisting Japanese jurists on legal and judicial reforms was Alfred C. Oppler, a division chief in the Government Section who had been a judge in Germany but fled to America before World War II. His approach in dealing with the Japanese was to propose and persuade, not to impose and direct. Under his wise and tactful guidance the Japanese developed a new structure of courts and legal procedures that conformed to the new constitution, was relatively well suited to changing Japanese values, and represented an eclectic blending of democratic legal concepts from Continental, as well as Anglo-Saxon and American, legal systems. Whereas the SCAP attempts to Americanize local government and police were not impressively effective, the SCAP influence on revising the administration of justice was more significant, thanks in part to Oppler's tactics and his adamant refusal to try to convince the Japanese that the American way was the best for Japan. Oppler gave much of the credit to the Japanese for the reforms in his field and others that were lasting: "The relative success of the Occupation efforts . . . has various reasons, the principal of which was the maturity of the Japanese civilization and the fact that we merely pushed forward existing reforming and liberalizing trends that would have effectuated similar results, though at a slower tempo." As for his contact with MacArthur, Oppler simply said that he had "little opportunity to deal with him personally." It is regrettable for MacArthur's sake, because Oppler would have counseled him more realistically than some in the GHQ inner circle who thought Japan should be compelled to adopt American values and methods. Despite their valuable contributions to the occupation, Oppler and Sirota and others like them in the SCAP civil sections receive no mention in the memoirs by MacArthur or Whitney.[54]

MacArthur played only a limited direct role in judicial and legal changes, the following instances being perhaps the most conspicuous. In late 1946 he denounced lèse majesté as contrary to the principle that "all men are equal before the law, that no individual in Japan — not even the Emperor — shall be clothed in legal protection denied the common man." During the revision of the penal code in early 1947 he rejected Yoshida's proposal that the punish-

Organization of the Government of Japan, July 1948
(From: GHQ, SCAP, Government Section, *Political Reorientation of Japan*, I, viii)

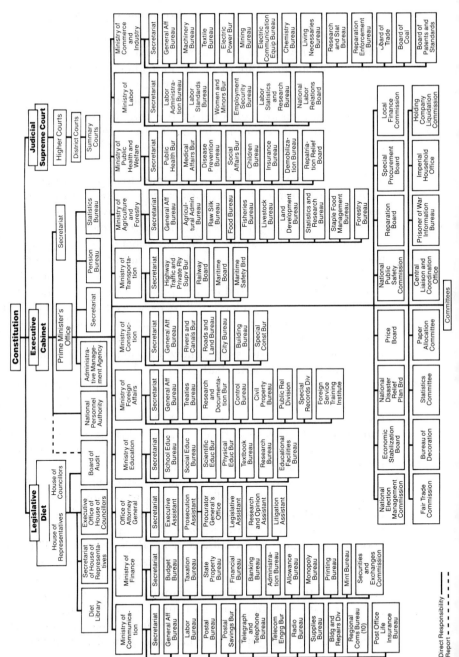

ment for an act of violence against the Emperor or certain members of the imperial family should be more severe than for the same crime against "an ordinary individual." MacArthur concluded that such a provision "would violate the fundamental concept, clearly and unequivocably expressed in the new Constitution, that all men are equal before the law." Moreover, since the new code provided the death penalty for murder and "severe penalties for acts of violence against persons," he felt that articles on crimes against the imperial house were "surplusage." That April he blocked a move by the Yoshida Cabinet to appoint the new Supreme Court. In the Diet elections earlier that month Katayama's Socialists had won a narrow plurality of seats over Yoshida's Liberals and the newly formed Democratic party, which was a merger of the old Progressives and a defecting Liberal faction led by Hitoshi Ashida. MacArthur decreed that "midnight appointments" to the Supreme Court by the Yoshida Cabinet "could not fail to arouse public suspicion and disturb public confidence in the court at a time when full confidence will be most needed. . . . The first panel of the supreme bench should be named by the first cabinet selected under the new constitution." As it turned out, the Katayama Cabinet's selections were more judicious than Yoshida and his conservative colleagues had expected.[55]

Reform of the bureaucracy, the "fourth branch" of the government, was not seriously addressed by MacArthur and his Government Section during the first year of the occupation. Other problems seemed more pressing; besides, the SCAP staff at first lacked experts on civil service. GHQ was forced to rely heavily on the bureaucracy, moreover, because of the weakened state of the Japanese legislative and executive machinery, which had been riddled by purges of prominent politicians and dissolution of some formerly powerful agencies. Although politicians and businessmen bore the brunt of the purges, only about 145 of the more than 3000 bureaucrats were removed from their positions. The bureaucracy that manned the sundry ministries, divisions, bureaus, boards, and commissions of the central government was strongly entrenched through a self-perpetuating system, efficient and opportunistic in exploiting power vacuums in the legislative and executive realms, and extremely valuable in the role of middleman between GHQ and Japanese politicians, as well as between the

politicians and the business leaders of Japan. "Absolutist bureau-
cratism," claimed a Japanese scholar of that time, was stronger in
Japan than in any other major nation. Another said, "The truth
of the matter is that the politicians and Diet members are completely at the mercy of the bureaucracy, since without the help and
support of the career officials and ex-bureaucrats they are unable
to operate at all." The main political parties, which were still weak
in organizational and operational skills, depended on the bureaucrats in formulating policies and platforms. Frequently former
bureaucrats worked their way into top party positions and into Diet
and Cabinet seats. In fact, Prime Ministers Shidehara and Yoshida,
as well as Hitoshi Ashida, who succeeded Katayama in March 1948,
were former bureaucrats, as would be most of Japan's future pre-
miers.[56]

Despite SCAP's practical need for their services, the bureaucrats
posed a challenge to MacArthur's goals of democratization. As a
group, they were notoriously arrogant and reactionary; their personnel system was elitist and, by American civil service standards,
"feudalistic"; and they seemed oblivious of the new constitution's
stipulation that they were expected to be "servants of the whole
community." A SCAP public administration official reported in early
1946: "Of all the major bulwarks of feudal and totalitarian Japan
only the bureaucracy remains unimpaired. . . . All our evidence
indicates that without constant pressure and guidance from this
Headquarters the present bureaucracy is neither willing nor competent to reform the system . . . [or] to manage a modern democratic society." In November of that year MacArthur obtained
through the War Department the services of a team of American
specialists in personnel management; it was headed by Blaine
Hoover, president of the Civil Service Assembly of the United States
and Canada. After thoroughly studying the system in Japan, the
Hoover Mission rendered its report to MacArthur in June 1947.
It concluded that the Japanese civil service was in desperate need
of modernizing and democratizing, and it made extensive proposals for remodeling it, largely along the lines of the United States
system. Hoover later commented that "the vast majority of old-
line Japanese bureaucrats" constituted a "danger to the successful
democratization of Japan's institutions of public administration."
He feared that unless the system was drastically overhauled, "ide-

ologically hostile bureaucrats would by administrative sabotage nullify Occupation policies or the programs of Japanese political leaders evolved pursuant thereto."

Based in large measure on the Hoover Mission's recommendations, which MacArthur fully endorsed, the National Public Service Law was passed by the Diet in October. Although not as sweeping in its changes as SCAP wanted, it provided the legal foundation for establishing "a democratically oriented merit service" that would, if properly administered, promote fairness and efficiency. The law also established the National Personnel Authority to enforce the standards and policies of the new civil service program. MacArthur persuaded Hoover to remain in Japan to head a new "watchdog" agency, the Civil Service Division of the Government Section. But by mid-1948 the rising militancy of government employees' unions would prompt MacArthur to call for revision of the 1947 law. Attention was diverted from the Tokyo bureaucrats to unionized workers in government-owned enterprises in transportation and industry. Since the issue of civil service became entangled with labor controversies in 1948, this account will be resumed in connection with the next phase of the occupation, when the SCAP focus on political reform dimmed. Through both the early and later phases, however, the bureaucracy managed to escape major surgery.[57]

Studying his staff's reports on political parties and elections from 1945 to 1947, MacArthur was pleased with the manifestations of widespread zeal for political activities, though perturbed by the sometimes rowdy behavior of the new, inexperienced party politicians of the Diet. In the half-year from his issuance of the Civil Liberties Directive in the autumn of 1945 to the first postwar national elections the following April, the number of political parties had grown to 368, though most were small, and even the larger parties were characterized by confusing flux, often merging and splintering. Over 70 percent of the eligible voters, including large numbers of women, turned out for the general elections in April 1946 and again in April 1947. Candidates were numerous and contests keen for most of the local and national elections; for example, nearly 2700 candidates competed for the 466 seats in the House of Representatives in 1946, including 38 women who won.[58]

Whether MacArthur was merely trying to encourage the Japanese as they took their first steps along the road toward SCAP's version of political democracy or whether he actually believed that their progress was remarkable, his public statements about the election results in 1946 and 1947 were filled with unbounding optimism. He was particularly impressed by the voters' seeming preference for "moderate" or "middle-of-the-road" candidates and parties. After the elections of 1946, he said of the Japanese electorate: "Given the opportunity for free expression of their popular will, they responded wholeheartedly; and, rejecting leadership dedicated to the political philosophies of the two extremes, both of the right and of the left . . . they took a wide central course which will permit the evolvement of a balanced program of government designed best to serve their interests as a people. Democracy has thus demonstrated a healthy forward advance." Following the elections of 1947, he again interpreted the outcome optimistically: "This is democracy! . . . [The Communist party] had its full chance and on the merits has failed. The Japanese people have firmly and decisively rejected its leadership and overwhelmingly have chosen a moderate course, sufficiently centered from either extreme to insure the preservation of freedom and the enhancement of individual dignity."[59]

The elections of 1946, it will be recalled, gave the Liberals and Progressives a predominance of seats in the Diet and resulted in Yoshida's premiership with a Liberal-Progressive coalition Cabinet. The 1947 elections brought a slight increase in the proportion of Diet seats held by the Liberals and Democrats (formerly Progressives), but permitted Katayama to form a weak, short-lived coalition Cabinet of Social Democrats (Socialists), Democrats, and Cooperatives. The following table of percentages of seats held by various groups in the House of Representatives after the elections of 1946 and 1947 substantiates MacArthur's assertion about the Communists' small successes, but does not clearly demonstrate a "moderate course" in national politics:[60]

Party	*1946*	*1947*
Liberal	30.4	28.1
Progressive (1946); Democratic (1947)	20.0	26.6
Social Democratic (Socialist)	20.0	30.7
Communist	1.1	0.9

Party	*1946*	*1947*
Cooperative (1946); People's Cooperative (1947)	3.0	6.7
Independents	17.3	2.8
Minor parties	8.2	4.3

If ideological labels like "moderate" and "conservative" are often misused in defining American politics, Westerners observing the political scene in occupied Japan tended to use such terms even more loosely and erroneously. Political parties in Japan evolved out of the distinctive, complex national character, and analogies to the American organizations were misleading. Even the major Japanese parties changed names and slogans with perplexing frequency and with no apparent correlation to policy. A foremost Japanese political scientist explains that in Japan "parties remain 'personality centered' and 'leader centered' organizations in which loyalty is primarily to persons rather than to principles or policies . . . . Personal loyalty provides the indispensable basis for bossism which pervades practically every level of politics from the lowest level of the village assembly to the highest level of the national Diet."

On the level of national politics in postwar Japan the bureaucracy and big-business elite provided the principal authority figures (aside from the Emperor and MacArthur), the organizational skills, the fund-raising capabilities, and the commitment to resisting change in the fundamental distribution of power and wealth. Most scholarly studies of politics in occupied Japan unmistakably link the bureaucrats and businessmen with the leadership of the Liberals and Progressives (or Democrats). Also, the Cooperatives and perhaps a majority of the independents in the Diet, according to many scholars, were conservative in the sense of opposing Socialism or Communism. Thus it appears from the percentages of the preceding table that in both the 1946 and 1947 elections the trend was definitely conservative if the figures for the Liberals, Progressives (Democrats), Cooperatives, and at least half of the independents are added together. Since there was no longer an ultranationalistic alternative, having been blocked by occupation directive and repudiated by the Japanese majority, the extremes of the political spectrum were now occupied by the Liberals on the right and the Communists on the left. Through shrewd coalition maneuvering Yoshida's Liberal party would play the paramount

role in national politics throughout the occupation era, except for
the short span of Katayama's premiership, May 1947 to March
1948. Unless the contrivance of a nonexisting ultranationalist extreme is introduced, it is difficult to interpret this as a middle-of-
the-road pattern.[61]

Apparently MacArthur based his conclusion on the assumed accuracy of such Government Section data as the following abbreviated analysis of the main parties' positions in 1947 on the state's
relationship to business and industry:

Conservative
  Liberal Party: Laissez faire.
Middle-of-the-road
  Democratic Party: Modified capitalism (meaning stringent government con-
        trols).
Opposition
  Social Democratic Party: State control as a preliminary to government owner-
        ship (e.g., key industries, coal, iron, steel, fertilizer).
  People's Cooperative Party: Cooperative unionism.
Extreme left
  Communist Party: People's control of Zaibatsu-owned enterprises and the key
        industries.[62]

At the least, the above classification is an oversimplification that
does not suggest the deep-seated reluctance of many politicians
allied with bureaucrats and corporate leaders to cooperate on SCAP
reforms any more than was necessary to ensure their interests and
an early end to the occupation.

Unless attracted away from his basically ethnocentric (though not
racist) outlook by some appealing, workable proposal in another
direction, MacArthur was prone to consider Japanese situations in
terms of analogies from American experience: if it worked in the
United States, it will work in Japan; if these are the needs or interests of the American people, then those of the Japanese people
are the same or similar. Thus, when a Brooklyn citizen wrote him
requesting a brief statement on his "pattern" for the occupation,
the Supreme Commander replied in early 1948:

> The pattern of my course in the occupation of Japan lies deeply rooted
> in the lessons and experiences of American history. For here I have
> merely sought to draw therefrom the political, economic and social
> concepts which throughout our own past have worked and provided

the American people with a spiritual and material strength never before equalled in human history.

There is no need to experiment with new and yet untried, or already tried and discredited concepts, when success itself stands as the eloquent and convincing advocate of our own — nor is there factual basis for the fallacious argument occasionally heard that those high principles upon which rest our own strength and progress are ill-fitted to serve the well-being of others, as history will clearly show that the entire human race, irrespective of geographical delimitations or cultural tradition, is capable of absorbing, cherishing and defending liberty, tolerance and justice, and will find maximum strength and progress when so blessed.[63]

By then the main rush of inaugurating political reforms was done, and MacArthur was well satisfied with Japan's progress. Now the Japanese were freely tossing about words like "democracy," "liberty," and "rights," and some SCAP officials assumed that both they and the Japanese had the same definitions in mind and nourished the same expectations for the future of the nation. The early phase had been characterized politically by stirring idealism and promising beginnings, but erroneous assumptions and false hopes would contribute to disillusionment for many Japanese during the later phase of the occupation. The constitution, however alien its origin, would stand as the most durable monument to the early bright hopes for Japanese democracy. Fortunately, some of the other political reforms would also take root, in spite of American ethnocentrism, because MacArthur had another side, which yielded to the wise proposals of men like Oppler when their voices could be heard, and because the Japanese had another side, which, in the words of an authority on the period, "eagerly subscribed to the noble aims of the Occupation, contributing mightily to all its accomplishments."[64]

CHAPTER V

Efforts Toward Economic Relief, Recovery, and Reform

1. The Economic Aftermath of Defeat

WHEN THE CHRYSANTHEMUMS began blooming in the early autumn of 1945, Yosaku Matsumoto, the custodian of the Dai Ichi Building, put some of the flowers in a vase on MacArthur's desk, which greatly pleased the Supreme Commander. The following day General Sutherland, the chief of staff, requested that Matsumoto place chrysanthemums on his desk also. Soon other officers at GHQ were asking for them, and Matsumoto found himself making daily deliveries to virtually all the many offices in the building. When MacArthur asked who was paying for the chrysanthemums, Matsumoto replied that the bills for them were being taken care of by the Japanese government through occupation procurement orders. MacArthur decreed that henceforth any officers at GHQ who wanted floral arrangements were to pay for them personally. GHQ quickly lost its flower-shop appearance. Knowing that the Japanese government was being required to devote a sizable portion of its budget to paying for many of the essential expenses of the occupation forces, MacArthur was not about to invite press criticism over flowers for his and other GHQ offices. Undoubtedly the Japanese government wished he had assumed a similar watchdog role over more expensive tabs for nonessentials that his occupationnaires continued to bill as procurement orders. War-ravaged Japan was hardly in a position to provide the material luxuries that some high-living SCAP personnel expected.[1]

The early postwar directives that General MacArthur received from Washington did not address the issues of relief and economic rehabilitation. In accordance with the occupation objective of demilitarization, SCAP's initial intervention in the Japanese economy was negative, consisting of restrictions to ensure that Japan would not possess the economic potential to wage war again. Plants that had been producing war matériel were closed or dismantled, with much heavy equipment impounded for possible use as reparations later to Allied countries. In fact, the physical devastation caused by air raids and naval shellings during the final months of the war had left Japan so prostrate economically that, as one SCAP officer observed, "there was damned little industry left to restrict." In the autumn of 1945, and in some areas of Japan for many months thereafter, a state of paralysis gripped much of the nation's industry, commerce, banking, transportation, and agriculture, and foreign trade, so vital to the prewar economy, was nil.[2]

The most immediate and critical problem from the Japanese view was unemployment. The destruction of many factories and shops, together with SCAP's shut-down of the remaining war-related businesses, left more than 4 million workers without jobs. Demobilization in the home islands threw over 2 million former servicemen on the job market, and by late 1946 the SCAP repatriation program had returned another 6 million overseas Japanese, all desperately in need of livelihoods. About 3 million repatriates and jobless urbanites went back to family farms to try to eke out an existence, but there still remained over 10 million unemployed Japanese in a nation whose shattered economy showed no early signs of revival nor afforded hope of new job opportunities.[3]

Another menace was wildly rising inflation. Advised and prodded by SCAP, the Japanese government established the Economic Stabilization Board and inaugurated a number of measures to combat inflation, including wage controls, rigid price ceilings, rationing of certain commodities, heavy levies on capital assets, and impoundment in frozen savings accounts of incomes above a modest living scale. But SCAP and Japanese efforts in the war against in-

flation were largely ineffective before 1949. A survey by the Tokyo Chamber of Commerce and Industry found, for example, that
the average level of legal retail prices in that city, with the level
for 1930 as 100 on its index, had risen to 304 by mid-1945 but
had soared to 13,009 by July 1948.[4]

For the Japanese, the winter of 1945–1946 was one of the cold-
est in recent times, its severity made worse by serious shortages of
nearly all essential commodities. Common sights were shop shelves
barren of manufactured goods and markets with no or pitifully
few items of meat, fish, vegetables, or fruit to sell. Black markets
spread like plagues in the metropolitan areas. Desperate city residents were forced to barter away family jewels, art objects, and
other prized possessions to obtain the bare necessities for survival — food, clothing, and coal for heating. The first postwar rice
crops and fish hauls were disappointingly poor, and coal production fell off sharply after the surrender. Many of the miners had
been forced-labor Koreans and Chinese, most of whom now refused to work and wanted their repatriation. Besides making the
winter miserable for house dwellers, the critical coal shortage
crippled the operations of businesses and the railway system.[5]

MacArthur had been told by SWNCC through the Joint Chiefs,
"The only responsibility on our part for the Japanese standard of
living is the purely negative one prohibiting us from requiring for
the Occupation Forces goods or services to an extent which would
cause starvation, widespread disease, and acute physical distress."
From his first days in burned-out Yokohama, when he was ap-
palled by the extent of the ruin and suffering, MacArthur, acting
without Washington's advice, ordered his units to utilize their field
kitchens and food services to feed starving local residents as long
as such activities did not hinder the proper feeding of the occupation troops. When SCAP studies showed that winter that the daily
food intake of the average Japanese was hovering between 1000
and 1500 calories, he called for a massive roll-up of food supplies,
totaling 3.5 million tons, that were stored in American Army ware-
houses and lockers in his theater, principally in the Philippines
and Ryukyus, where they had been stocked to support Operation
Olympic (the invasion of Kyushu that had been set for November
1945 and cancelled by the sudden Japanese capitulation). Invasion stocks helped many hungry Japanese.[6]

In subsequent years MacArthur crusaded persistently for the inclusion of relief funds in the Army's annual appropriations. When the Appropriations Committee of the United States House of Representatives requested his justification for funds to feed the former foe, he replied strongly:

> The great lesson and warning of experience is that victorious leaders of the past have too often contented themselves with the infliction of military defeat upon the enemy power without extending that victory by dealing with the root causes which led to war as an inevitable consequence.
>
> Under the responsibilities of victory the Japanese people are now our prisoners, no less than did the starving men on Bataan become their prisoners when the peninsula fell. As a consequence of the ill treatment, including starvation of Allied prisoners in Japanese hands, we have tried and executed the Japanese officers upon proof of responsibility. Can we justify such punitive action if we ourselves, in reversed circumstances but with hostilities at an end, fail to provide the food to sustain life among the Japanese people over whom we now stand guard within the narrow confines of their home islands? To cut off Japan's relief supplies in this situation would cause starvation to countless Japanese — and starvation breeds mass unrest, disorder, and violence. Give me bread or give me bullets.[7]

Herbert Hoover, MacArthur's long-time friend and now chairman of the Emergency Famine Relief Committee, visited Japan in May 1946. He added his voice to MacArthur's in stressing the need for increased American food shipments to that nation in order to avert "starvation and unrest throughout the country," which would "hamper and endanger the occupation." In spite of the continuing complaints of some congressmen, the efforts of MacArthur and Hoover helped bring about a more humanitarian policy on Japanese relief, and by the time MacArthur left Japan the United States had provided over $2 billion in relief and welfare goods and services to Japan. One Japanese, then in his teens, remembered MacArthur's persistence and success in getting American food for the Japanese people as "the general's most noble and perhaps his most important achievement during the occupation."[8]

The foodstuffs, fertilizers, raw cotton, and other essential imports from America, financed largely through GARIOA (Government and Relief in Occupied Areas) grants, were appreciated by the Japanese, but even more the stricken nation needed progress toward economic recovery. No less so than the British, the Japanese economy had always been inextricably linked to the sea. As a Japanese official in the Ministry of Commerce and Industry expressed it, "Many of our business and government leaders were resigned to the fact that substantial, long-term recovery would have to await the revitalization of the merchant fleet, foreign trade, and fishing industry." The once large merchant marine had been virtually wiped out by Allied submarines and air attacks, and the flow of oil, rubber, tin, bauxite, and other raw materials from Southeast and East Asian territories had been effectively cut off well before Japan's surrender. It would be many years before Japanese shipyards would be bustling again; in the meantime, vessels of foreign registry would carry the bulk of Japan's export-import trade.

From the fall of 1945 through 1947, over 90 percent of Japan's imports came from the United States. Exports were minuscule compared with the prewar era, amounting in 1947 to less than 10 percent of the annual export trade in the early 1930s. About 60 percent of Japanese postwar exports, mostly textiles, went to Asian markets. For the foreseeable future, Japan had lost her traditional sources of raw materials and of markets for her manufactures, because of the crippling effects of World War II on the European and Asian nations with whom she had traded, the chaotic conditions in Asian countries beset by nationalist revolutions, and the outright war-bred hostility of some nations, especially Australia and the Philippines.

Under the terms of the Potsdam Declaration, Japan was to be allowed "access to, as distinguished from control of, raw materials." The American-drafted "Initial Post-Surrender Policy" statement stipulated that Japan would "be permitted eventually to resume normal trade relations with the rest of the world," but that while the country was occupied, raw materials or other goods purchased from abroad and exports would be controlled. The matter of control was vested in MacArthur, who was to see that "all proceeds of exports" were "made available in the first place for approved imports." With SCAP controls strict and with a continuing unfavorable trade balance, Japan's foreign trade prospects were not promising. For the first two years of the occupation all of Japan's international trade was on a government-to-government basis, with MacArthur, through his Economic and Scientific Section's trade officials, acting for Japan in selling goods abroad. The Japanese Board of Trade was established in December 1945 to oversee purchases of exportable goods produced in Japan and sales of imports in Japan. Revival of foreign trade was hindered, both because Japanese exports were insufficient to pay for imports and because the foreign exchange system set up by SCAP was, according to Japanese trade officials, too complex, not uniform or consistent, and unfair in the yen-dollar valuation.[9]

The Inter-Allied Trade Board for Japan, created by the Far Eastern Commission in October 1946, advised SCAP and the Japanese Board of Trade in facilitating export-import matters. MacArthur permitted the entry of two official representatives from each nation desiring trade ties with Japan; they were to stay only as long as it took them to negotiate trade agreements on behalf of their governments, with all such transactions subject to SCAP approval. MacArthur encountered some difficulties with the British government's trade agents, who, according to Colonel Laurence Bunker, a trusted aide to MacArthur, were at times overeager: "The British were very anxious to get back into Japan at the earliest possible date, well ahead of other countries, if possible, in order to re-establish the British domination of much of the Oriental markets. MacArthur was completely opposed to that . . . and was not willing to allow the British to come in before the other countries."[10]

MacArthur announced in June 1947 that limited private trade with Japan would be resumed shortly. On August 15 he permitted the entry of 102 foreign businessmen, mostly American, British, French, Dutch, and Australian, though none from the Soviet Union. They were under strict SCAP regulations and could stay only six months. During the next two years, coinciding with the acceleration of the Cold War and Washington's realization that Japan, rather than war-ridden China, was the best bet as a bulwark against Communist expansion in East Asia, restrictions on Japan's foreign trade were steadily relaxed.[11] MacArthur was pleased as opportunities increased for Japan's international commercial relations. At the time of his inauguration of limited trade in 1947 he had made clear his sympathy for Japan's economic plight and envisioned the ultimate solution as linked to an early peace treaty and end to the occupation:

> This is a step which partially lifts the economic blockade of Japan, a sound step but only a partial one. Japan is a country so lacking in indigenous materials that it must trade or starve. Despite this action its economy will remain precarious until trade is completely restored to normal channels which means private trade channels. While the present measure is merely palliative, it is probably the best that can be done until we have peace. It will give some measure of relief to all concerned but falls far short of a full economic solution. This can only be attained through the medium of a peace treaty and the sooner this is accomplished the better, not only for Japan but for the world.[12]

MacArthur's advocacy of Japanese interests in matters such as relief, foreign trade, and termination of the occupation brought charges of "softness" from a considerable number of editorialists and writers of letters to editors in American and Allied newspapers and periodicals who wanted Japan to undergo a long, harsh occupation. At governmental levels, however, his championing of Japanese fishing rights provoked the most controversy. George H. Blakeslee, an American delegate on the FEC, commented, "The right of the Japanese during the occupation to fish and to whale in the high seas presented an issue between the Far Eastern Commission and the U.S. Government which continued throughout nearly the entire history of the Commission." He added, "It aroused acerbic discussion within the Commission and led probably to more hard feelings on the part of some of the FEC countries than any other issue."[13]

A JCS directive of November 1945, issued prior to the FEC's creation, authorized MacArthur to control Japanese fishing but stated that it "should not be permitted near areas under Allied jurisdiction without prior permission from the country concerned." About 85 percent of Japan's prewar fish hauls came from the coastal waters around the four main islands. But Japanese officials convinced Colonel Donald Nugent, head of the SCAP Natural Resources Section, and through him MacArthur that the postwar food crisis could be alleviated in part by letting the pelagic, or deep ocean, fishing boats go to sea again. Thereupon MacArthur opened a large expanse south and east of Japan to the pelagic fishermen, but warned them to stay out of waters to the west and north near Soviet territories, where some individual Japanese boats had already ventured and been confiscated. In the next three years MacArthur approved gradual extensions of the fishing areas, ultimately allowing them to reach southward to the waters off Formosa and eastward to the 168th Meridian. Various nations represented on the FEC that had fishing fleets operating in the Western Pacific objected heatedly to each of his extensions, especially since he did not consult them in advance.[14]

When MacArthur approved the sending of a Japanese whaling expedition to Antarctic waters in the summer of 1946, FEC protests were loud; the Australians proclaimed it a threat to their security, and other delegates recalled prewar Japanese violations of international whaling agreements. Although eventually opposed by most of the other nations represented on the FEC, the United States government — the Joint Chiefs, the State Department, and the American FEC delegation, as well as General McCoy, MacArthur's old friend who was the FEC chairman — steadfastly supported MacArthur's position in authorizing the pelagic whaling. After catching repeated protests on the issue, State Department leaders put the question to their legal office: "Has SCAP the authority, vis-à-vis the Far Eastern Commission, to conduct a 'SCAP-administered, Japanese-manned' whaling expedition to the Antarctic?" An affirmative answer came back: his authority "is inherent in his position as Supreme Commander." Besides, the FEC, confronted by stiff United States opposition, had not formulated a policy on the matter. MacArthur's own position was that Japanese whaling was justified by "the continuing acute shortage of necessary food products in Japan and the importance of maximizing foreign exhange resources for the procurement of essential imports for Japan." He reported that the whale meat provided the Japanese people with up to a third of their protein intake, and the sale of whale oil to other countries was brisk and helped to relieve the trade imbalance.

Continuing to ignore objections, particularly from Australia, MacArthur authorized annual whaling expeditions to Antarctic waters. When he proposed in 1948 to enlarge the expedition's number of factory ships, Sir John Balfour, the British chargé d'affaires in Washington, protested to the State Department that this "would not only place Japan in an equal position relative to the U.K. and Norwegian whaling fleets but in proportionately a better position than she had been prior to the war and that on any moral grounds this seemed to the British iniquitous." MacArthur yielded on this point, but he continued to support strongly the resurgence of Japanese pelagic fishing and whaling, winning the gratitude of many Japanese for himself and for the United States.[15]

2. The Reparations Threat

Casting a shadow over the attempts of SCAP and the Japanese to get the economy moving was the threat of reparations. The Japanese fully expected to be assessed in some form for war damages, and the early occupation guidelines clearly anticipated reparations. The Potsdam Declaration said that "the exaction of just reparations in kind" would be required. The "Initial Post-Surrender Policy" stated that "reparations for Japanese aggression" would be made not only through the transfer of Japanese property in her former colonies and occupied territories but also in the home islands "through the transfer of such goods or existing capital equipment and facilities as are not necessary for a peaceful Japanese economy or the supplying of the occupying forces."

The claims against Japan by some of the Allied nations were enormous. The Philippines, for instance, at first demanded $8 billion in reparations. Nationalist China wanted at least 40 percent of whatever total reparations were decided on by the FEC. Following its whirlwind conquest of Manchuria in the last week of the war, the Soviet Union had removed from that area huge amounts of Japanese military and industrial equipment; estimates of the total value ranged as high as $2 billion. Nevertheless, Moscow still insisted on a considerable share of reparations from Japan's internal industrial resources. Britain, France, and the Netherlands expected to utilize Japanese industrial equipment, shipped from the home islands as reparations, in the reconstruction of the war-wrecked economies of their colonies in the Far East. At first, even the United States government insisted on up to 29 percent of the ultimate reparations pool of "surplus" Japanese industrial assets.

Were all the claims of the nations formerly at war with Japan to be satisfied, the Japanese economy, already in a state of stagnation and near ruin, would have faced utter collapse. Some SCAP officials, as well as MacArthur, feared that Japan, like Germany after World War I, might be saddled with a staggering reparations burden that could help those who wanted to sow the seeds of militarism in the future.[16]

In November 1945 President Truman sent Edwin A. Pauley to the Far East to investigate and recommend a reparations program for Japan, as he had done for Germany. Pauley and his technical staff spent several weeks of November and December (returning to Japan briefly the next May) surveying Japan's industrial situation and visiting with Philippine and Nationalist Chinese officials, who pictured their devastated nations as greatly needing reparations from Japan's machine-tool, steel, chemical, electric-power, and shipbuilding industries. Pauley took a tough stance in his subsequent report to Truman, recommending that, in effect, Japan's heavy industry should be kept at about 10 percent of its level in the mid-1930s, with large amounts of the remaining industrial equipment to be removed as reparations. All of her war-related industrial facilities should be declared surplus, and Japan's industrial capacity should be limited to a level necessary only to maintain a standard of living on par with those of the countries she had conquered. Pauley envisioned using reparations as an instrument to help in eliminating Japan's economic potential for waging aggressive war and in assisting in the economic recovery of the nations damaged by the war. MacArthur and Japanese officials protested that Pauley's recommendations were unrealistic and harsh, but Truman gave his approval to the Pauley Report.[17]

Orders from the Joint Chiefs of Staff went to MacArthur in January 1946 for him to "take into custody" an initial group of 394 industrial plants whose equipment was earmarked as reparations, although no one yet knew to which Allied nations it would go. In March the FEC began its deliberations on Japanese reparations, with most of the delegates favoring exactions as severe as Pauley had proposed. Early in its debates, the FEC declared that reparations should be exacted especially from the assets of the Zaibatsu in order to cripple the large combines that had allegedly been vital to the promotion of Japanese aggression from 1931 to

1945. "More time was given," remarked Blakeslee, "by the Far Eastern Commission and its committees to Japanese reparations and related topics than to any other subjects which came before the Commission." From the spring of 1946 onward FEC members often fell into bitter wrangling over such questions as what production levels were essential to Japan's subsistence and how to determine the percentage of reparations to be allocated to each country. Soviet intransigence in regarding as "war booty" the Manchurian equipment it had confiscated slowed the FEC's development of a reparations policy; the other members argued that this equipment should be counted as part of the USSR's share of whatever reparations pool was finally determined. The failure to settle the reparations issue retarded economic recovery in Japan, for her industrialists were reluctant to invest in capital expansion as long as they were uncertain about what plant facilities might be seized for reparations. In turn, Washington officials began to realize that the United States would be stuck with the ultimate reparations bill of all the FEC member-nations. As Japan shipped out reparations, handicapping her own recovery, American relief assistance to the Japanese would have to be continued and even augmented.[18]

MacArthur informed the War Department in late 1946 that Pauley's earlier estimates of Japan's industrial capacity were "exaggerated" and that actually there was little excess capacity, or surplus, in most industrial fields for possible reparations. He urged that the United States position on reparations be realistically adjusted "to permit and assist Japan to raise its lagging productivity to something approximating its minimum needs." He recommended that "the industrial levels prescribed in the interim removals program should be accepted with minor modifications as the final levels and that Japan's economic recovery should be permitted to develop up to the industrial levels in the interim levels program." These interim removal levels were viewed by the FEC as tentative and intended only to govern early emergency shipments to FEC nations whose economies were in dire straits. Most FEC members envisioned that these levels would be considerably raised later, meaning larger exactions from Japan.

In January and February of 1947 Clifford S. Strike, president of a large American engineering firm, together with four other

American engineering experts, visited Japan as a special reparations committee appointed by the War Department. The department had ignored the FEC in deciding the Strike Committee's composition and functions. In its report to the War Department on February 24 the Strike Committee virtually contradicted the severe, punitive principles on which the Pauley Report and the thinking of the FEC's majority were based. Strike and his colleagues recommended that "the present reparations program in respect to plant removals be abandoned" and that "a new program should be formulated" that would drastically scale down the demands on the Japanese economy.[19] The Strike Report concluded:

> The Committee does not believe the program recommended herein constitutes any softening of attitude but does give recognition to conditions and problems as they exist at present. This program provides both an adequate control over the level of Japanese industry and an opportunity for that level to be developed to a point of self-sufficiency. . . .
>
> In summarizing the findings of the foregoing report, the Committee believes that the program recommended provides the following improvements over the present situation: (1) a simplification of the work to be done by SCAP, (2) a removal of large segments of Japanese industry from the present doubtful status which is now delaying recovery, (3) an acceleration in the process of making some reparations available, (4) reduced expense to the United States Government, and (5) elimination of the threat of disaster to the Japanese economy by too drastic reparations removals.

In longhand at the bottom of the report to the War Department, MacArthur, obviously jubilant, wrote: "To the Secretary of War: This report represents an outstanding contribution to the complex problems involved. It is presented in a comprehensive and authoritative manner and should receive due consideration in the solution of a situation which brooks no further delay."[20]

That April, with no FEC policy on advance, or interim, transfers yet formulated, the United States government instructed MacArthur to make available to certain especially needy nations 30 percent of the industrial equipment that had been declared surplus to Japan's economic needs according to the FEC's interim criteria. Under the Advance Transfer Program, administered by

MacArthur's Reparations Section, about $43 million worth of machine tools and other industrial equipment went out as interim reparations to China ($20 million); the Philippines ($11 million); the United Kingdom, for Malaya and Burma ($7 million); and the Netherlands, for its East Indies ($5 million). The total represented about one fifteenth of the total reparations bill then under discussion in the FEC.

Also in April 1947, a SWNCC-drafted document on reparations was presented to the FEC as an American policy paper. Though not consonant with all MacArthur's points on reparations, it supported his position, in essence, on holding at the interim levels. Thus, according to Blakeslee, "the United States abandoned the idea which it had previously held that the final schedules of reparations from Japan should be much more severe than those in the program of interim reparations removals." The FEC members, however, could reach no consensus on whether to follow the American line. In June the FEC finally adopted its fundamental statement on the occupation, entitled "Basic Post-Surrender Policy for Japan," but the document's section on reparations was couched in general terms that gave no indication as to how severe the final exaction would be. That July the War Department commissioned Overseas Consultants, Inc., to undertake a half-year detailed investigation in Japan of that nation's industrial capacities and make recommendations on future reparations policy. The group consisted of experts from eleven distinguished engineering firms and research organizations in the United States. Most promising to MacArthur and Japanese leaders, it was to be headed by Clifford Strike.[21] The return of Strike brought hope, but as of the autumn of 1947 the unsettled reparations issue left Japan still braced for harsh treatment.

3. Target: Zaibatsu

The Zaibatsu had been crucial in Japan's rise from a quasi-feudal state in the 1850s to a modern military-industrial power in the twentieth century. The fifteen or so families that constituted the Zaibatsu (literally "financial clique or combines") had formed a complex but mutually beneficial relationship with the central government over the years, providing, among other things, huge governmental subsidies for the combines and, in turn, forceful, efficient, and rational organization by the Zaibatsu of the bulk of Japan's industry, finance, commerce, transportation, and foreign trade. Through holding companies, interlocking directorates, and a host of other corporate stratagems that limited free competition, the Zaibatsu, especially the four largest combines — Mitsui, Mitsubishi, Yasuda, and Sumitomo — accumulated vast holdings that included factories, banks, mines, railroads, steamship lines, and shipyards. Although not as agreeable to the militarists' aggressive policies of 1931–1945 as most Westerners imagined, the Zaibatsu were indispensable in producing the matériel for the Japanese war machine of that era. An authority on postwar Japan estimates that "through 67 holding companies and over 4,000 operating subsidiaries and affiliates, the Zaibatsu families at the end of the war asserted effective control of 75 percent of Japan's financial, industrial, and commercial activities."[22]

For at least the first year and a half of the occupation, most top leaders of the FEC's member-nations, including the United States, viewed the Zaibatsu as past and potentially future warmongers and agreed with Pauley's assessment: "Not only were the Zaibatsu as responsible for Japan's militarism as the militarists themselves, but they profited immensely by it. Even now, in defeat, they have actually strengthened their monopoly position. . . . The 'little men' are not only ruined, but heavily indebted to the Zaibatsu. . . . As long as the Zaibatsu survive, Japan will be their Japan." The American "Initial Post-Surrender Policy" provisions concerning the Zaibatsu, later endorsed in slightly modified form by the FEC, stipulated that MacArthur was to give "encouragement" to reorganizing industry "on a democratic basis." He was to promote policies permitting "a wide distribution of income and of the ownership of the means of production and trade." The policy directive, approved by Truman on September 6, 1945, stated further that MacArthur was "(a) to prohibit the retention in or selection for places of importance in the economic field of individuals who do not direct future Japanese economic effort solely toward peaceful ends; and (b) to favor a program for the dissolution of the large industrial and banking combinations which have exercised control of a great part of Japan's trade and industry."[23]

With Colonel Raymond Kramer's Economic and Scientific Section still in its formative stage and lacking SCAP personnel knowledgeable about the intricacies of the Zaibatsu system, MacArthur hastily approved "in general" a plan submitted by the Yasuda combine in late October 1945 for voluntary but limited dissolution. A scheme to avert more drastic action by SCAP, the Yasuda Plan provided for withdrawal of the Yasuda family from its positions in industry and banking; dissolution of the principal Yasuda holding company; cessation of the Yasuda Bank's control over subsidiary banks; resignation of officials in controlled companies who had been appointed by the Yasuda family or its chief holding company; and sale of all shares in controlled companies held by the Yasuda family and its main bank and holding company to a control commission made up of Japanese appointed and supervised by MacArthur. The commission would supervise the public marketing of the securities. Because of the interfamily ties, the ingenious methods of direct control, and the questionable ability of the public to purchase the securities, the Yasuda Plan was fraught with loopholes that would allow the combine to escape full deconcentration. Mitsui, Mitsubishi, and Sumitomo quickly agreed to dissolution on the terms of the Yasuda Plan. In a directive on November 1, the Joint Chiefs of Staff approved the initial steps toward the Zaibatsu dissolution, but told MacArthur to "require the Japanese to establish a public agency responsible for reorganizing Japanese business" and to "require this agency to submit, for approval by you, plans for dissolving large Japanese industrial and banking combines or other large concentrations of private business control."[24]

Several SCAPINs, or "instructions" from MacArthur to the Japanese government, were forthcoming later that fall on the impending breakup of the Zaibatsu. Until the Holding Company Liquidation Commission (HCLC) was organized, which would be the next summer, MacArthur told the government initially to enforce a freeze on the sale or transfer of securities of fifteen Zaibatsu holding companies and their subsidiaries. By the time the HCLC began its work, SCAP's list of such "restricted companies" numbered several hundred, all Zaibatsu-controlled. MacArthur also put pressure on the government to draft legislation for a graduated capital levy that would especially hit the top 5 percent of property-holders and for a statute proscribing government payment of claims to individuals and corporations (mainly Zaibatsu) for unpaid war contracts and government-ordered war-plant expansions. These measures were enacted in 1946, and, as intended, their impact was sorely felt by the Zaibatsu.[25]

Realizing that he needed more expert advice on the Zaibatsu problem, MacArthur requested Washington to send a group of antitrust specialists to study the Japanese situation and recommend further courses of action. In January 1946 the resulting State-War Mission on Japanese Combines arrived in Tokyo to begin a ten-week investigation. The eight-man mission was headed by Corwin D. Edwards, an economics professor at Northwestern University and consultant on cartels to the State Department. The Edwards Report of March 1946 criticized the Yasuda Plan as "obviously insufficient to destroy the power of the great Japanese combines," because, among other defects, it did not affect corporate ties below the holding-company level nor did it ensure against Zaibatsu members controlling company policies and stocks through loyal corporate officials. The report, as one commentator concluded, "recognized that MacArthur had not really prepared anything but a superficial juggling of the Japanese economic set-up, preferring to leave any basic changes to a Japanese Government which itself was not basically altered." The mission's recommendations were sweeping, clearly intended to break the dominance of the Zaibatsu, prevent their revival, and ensure the growth of free, fair, and competitive trade practices.[26]

In submitting the Edwards Report to Washington, MacArthur sent along a critique prepared by him and General William Marquat, now chief of the Economic and Scientific Section. It included a number of concurrences on specific proposals but also numerous comments like "too liberal," "unwise," "unworkable," and "too sweeping" on other particulars. Some of the main negative points were: (1) In order to implement all the mission's proposals, "not only would the [Japanese] Government have to be increased to several times fold, but Occupation personnel also would have to be increased to several times the number then employed."

(2) MacArthur feared that "some of the reforms proposed by the Mission might create chaotic conditions in the Japanese economy." (3) He expressed concern, too, that "instead of creating free enterprise, the reforms would place business in a strait-jacket of governmental controls. Such a situation would be entirely foreign to American democratic concepts."[27] Although MacArthur was agreeable to using the Edwards Report as "a general guideline," Mark Gayn, a liberal American correspondent in Tokyo and a savage critic of MacArthur, recorded in his diary on June 24, 1946:

> Told today by two distressed Headquarters men that MacArthur has in effect rejected Professor Edwards' master-blueprint for the destruction of the zaibatsu. The rejection, sent to Washington early this month, expressed agreement with most of the Edwards report "in principle," but insisted that a way less painful to Japan's economy could be found.
>
> MacArthur's critique, my informants said, reflects the feeling in top Headquarters that:
>
> Any drastic steps taken now against the zaibatsu would seriously hamper the revival of Japan's economy, thus prolonging the period of social stress;
>
> Any directives aimed at the zaibatsu would embarrass the Yoshida cabinet; and
>
> These directives must give the zaibatsu a fair deal, and provide for the continuity of the Japanese business tradition.[28]

In spite of MacArthur's less-than-enthusiastic support of the Edwards Report, it became the basis for a SWNCC policy paper (SWNCC 130/2), called "Excessive Concentrations of Economic Power in Japan," which was sent to MacArthur and in May 1947 transmitted to the FEC as the American position on the Zaibatsu dissolution. The confidential document was designated FEC-230 and placed under consideration by the FEC as that body's policy statement. Closely following the wording of the Edwards Report, FEC-230 stated that "the over-all objective of occupation policy in dealing with excessive concentrations of economic power in Japan should be to destroy such concentrations as may now exist, and to prevent the future creation of new concentrations." FEC-230 stipulated, in addition to the dissolution of monopolistic business, that "all individuals who have exercised controlling power in or over any excessive concentration of economic power" should be purged from business or government posts and "divested of all corporate security holdings, liquid assets, and business properties." Such holdings should be disposed of "as rapidly as possible to desirable purchasers . . . even if it requires that holdings be disposed of at a fraction of their real value."[29]

In August 1946 MacArthur gave the Japanese government ninety days to dissolve all trade control associations, which had been dominated by the Zaibatsu and had seriously retarded free enterprise. That same month the MacArthur appointed, Japanese-manned Holding Company Liquidation Commission began work. With no great pressure from MacArthur, the HCLC had not made much progress by September 1947: "Of 67 designated holding companies," according to Eleanor M. Hadley, a SCAP economist, "3 were in process of dissolution, 2 had been ordered dissolved, and 62 were working on plans. Of some 1,100 subsidiary companies, not a single stock reorganization plan had as yet been set in motion."[30]

Following Whitney's advice and rejecting the counsel of Yoshida, Marquat, and Willoughby, MacArthur launched an economic purge in early January 1947. He decreed that "key officials," ranging from board chairmen and presidents to managing directors, of 250 designated companies were barred from those jobs or "any position in the public service." Moreover, the purge was to be applied to all relatives of such persons "to the third degree." About 2200 business leaders were purged by mid-1947, the bulk of all those who were ultimately ousted. Actually the economic purge did not mightily affect the Zaibatsu nor cost Japan most of its managerial talent. Since the purge affected only high-level officials in a select group of firms, many able and loyal ones remained in subsidiaries or moved up to the vacated positions. Moreover, many of the purged Zaibatsu members continued to exert considerable, if now indirect, influence in business and government. As for the impact of the purge on the economy, Sherwood M. Fine, of the SCAP Economic and Scientific Section, believed that "far more substantive barriers to reconstruction lay in deficiencies of raw materials and the inflationary backdrop."[31]

In the first significant American attack on the SCAP administration, *Newsweek* published in late January a scathing article on the economic purge, written by Compton Pakenham, its Tokyo bureau chief. About "25,000 to 30,000" of Japan's "businessmen, financiers, and industrialists," charged Pakenham, "faced removal from their jobs. Furthermore, all their relatives to the third degree were also forbidden to hold such posts, thus making a total of 250,000 victims." He asserted that Willoughby and Marquat had opposed the purge but had lost to Whitney, who was portrayed as "a red-faced man . . . inclined to be portly and short-tempered" and who enjoyed "direct access to the throne" of MacArthur. Pakenham probably echoed the dismay of many of the American corporate elite, so heavily represented on *Newsweek*'s board, when he called for a congressional investigation "to discover why American capitalist principles are being undermined by American occupation authorities."[32]

Stung by the criticism, which in private he called "a smear," MacArthur issued an immediate rebuttal. As in the past when his hypersensitivity to criticism was aroused, he may have overstated his defense, for his previous behavior had not suggested a fervent commitment to an offensive against the Zaibatsu. The article, he claimed, "reflects a complete lack of knowledge and understanding of the basic facts and issues involved." He quoted extensively from the Joint Chiefs' directive that authorized the economic purge. He went on to defend strongly the purge and to accept full responsibility for it:

> In the implementation of the above directive, I used the normal discretion of a field commander in the matter of both details and timing, having due regard to the exigencies of the local situation both in its economic and political aspects. . . .
>
> While there have been natural differences of views on detail, throughout there has been complete unity of purpose by the staff sections concerned, and every decision has been personally made by me. I have aggressively furthered this objective, not alone because to do so is in compliance with the basic directive by which my course of action as Supreme Commander is bound, but because any other course would be to ignore those very causes which led the world into war, and by so doing to invite the recurrence of future war.
>
> It was these very persons, born and bred as feudalistic overlords, who held the lives and destiny of the majority of Japan's people in virtual slavery, and who, working in closest affiliation with its military, geared the country with both the tools and the will to wage aggressive war. . . . Those are the persons who, under the purge, are

to be removed from influencing the course of Japan's future economy. . . .

Petitions and letters have been received by the thousands from the people of Japan calling for the extension of the purge to which "Newsweek" objects, and since its announcement the press of Japan has been practically unanimous in applauding its purpose. . . .

The details of the purge program have been carefully evolved so as not to disturb the ordinary businessman. . . . It is fantastic that this action should be interpreted or opposed as antagonistic to the American ideal of capitalist economy. In my opinion, and I believe in the opinion of truly responsible Japanese as well, the action will not unduly disturb the development of a future peaceful industrial economy. But even if this should prove not the case — even if, as "Newsweek" avers, this cleansing of the economy of Japan of undesirable influence is destined seriously to handicap industrial revival for lack of essential leadership — or even if such revival is wholly impossible without the guidance of those several thousand persons involved who directly contributed to leading the world into a war taking a toll of millions of human lives and effecting destruction of hundreds of billions in natural resources — then, in that event the interest of those other hundreds of millions of people who want and seek peace leave no alternative than that Japan must bear and sustain the consequences, even at the expense of a new economy geared down to the capabilities remaining.[33]

The SCAP offensive against the Zaibatsu reached its zenith in 1947. Besides the continuing purge and HCLC proceedings, the deconcentration drive included the enactment of the Anti-Monopoly Law in April. This measure defined and prohibited "unreasonable restraints of trade," "unfair methods of competition," and "excessive concentration of power," while also outlawing interlocking directorates and mergers and creating the Fair Trade Commission to enforce the provisions. With the support of Katayama, the nation's first Socialist Prime Minister, a bill providing for limited coal nationalization was enacted, despite brazen attempts by the "coal barons" to bribe key members of the Diet. In July, MacArthur took perhaps the most drastic anti-Zaibatsu action yet, ordering the immediate dissolution of the huge Mitsui and Mitsubishi trading companies, which had been the linchpins of those Zaibatsu empires. So gigantic had been these two firms that subsequently about 200 successor companies were formed from each one.

In December 1947 two significant deconcentration steps were taken by the Diet, under heavy pressure from SCAP, with the passage of the Zaibatsu Family Control Law and the Deconcentration Law. By the terms of the former, for the first time statutory authority was provided for the removal of Zaibatsu officials from all companies within their own combines. The Deconcentration Law (actually entitled the Elimination of Excessive Concentration of Economic Power Law) "placed on the statute books the strongest law in the complex pattern of postwar legislation relating to business," commented Thomas A. Bisson of SCAP's Antitrust Division. Before then "MacArthur obtained inadequate authority for dealing with restrictive contractual arrangements among combine subsidiaries," Hadley remarked, but with the Deconcentration Law he now had "the authority to deal with this problem." The law gave the HCLC the authority to define, designate, and dissolve "excessive concentrations of economic power." The HCLC was to cite the designated enterprises before October 1948, requiring them to submit reorganization plans; if such plans were unsatisfactory, the HCLC was to supervise their reorganization under a plan of its own devising. Shortly, the HCLC had prepared its initial list of 325 companies that were designated "excessive concentrations." Commented one SCAP staff member, "The list reads like a *Who's Who* of Japanese business." After the *Newsweek* incident MacArthur seemed to be more zealous in the attack against the Zaibatsu. Whereas he had not wholeheartedly endorsed the Edwards Report in the spring of 1946, the Deconcentration Law twenty months later had his strong backing, though it was an implementation of proposals in the Edwards and FEC-230 reform plans. When questioned about this apparent change in MacArthur's attitude, Charles Willoughby responded, "The General was never really sold on going after Japanese big businessmen. As for the stepped-up attack in 1947, he may have been too busy with other things and gave his antitrust people too much leeway."[34]

There was a portent of future policy change when, shortly following the Japanese House of Representatives' passage of the Deconcentration Bill, William H. Draper, Under Secretary of the Army, cabled MacArthur to "delay implementation until the questions we have concerning this legislation and the United States position taken in SWNCC 130/2 (FEC-230) are settled here at cabinet level."[35] By then, a considerable number of leading businessmen and conservative politicians in America were expressing uneasiness about the anti-Zaibatsu program, and State and Pentagon officials were seriously questioning the wisdom of pursuing it further. As will be seen later, American policy toward Japan was about to undergo a "reverse course" that would emphasize recovery, not reform.

4. The Pandora's Box of Unionism

Although MacArthur's early directives from Washington opposed the continuance of the industrial and financial combines, they favored the growth of trade unionism, which had been weak in prewar Japan. The "Initial Post-Surrender Policy" did not directly address labor policy, but it did say that MacArthur was to promote civil liberties, democratic organizations in labor, and redistribution of income and ownership. A Joint Chiefs' directive in early November 1945 instructed MacArthur to "require the removal of all legal hindrances to the formation of organizations of employees along democratic lines" and "prevent or prohibit strikes or other work stoppages only when you consider that these would interfere with military operations or directly endanger the security of the occupying forces." MacArthur told Prime Minister Shidehara that his government was to stress "the encouragement of the unionization of labor — that it may be clothed with such dignity as will permit it an influential voice in safeguarding the working man from exploitation and abuse and raising his living standard to a higher level."[36]

A number of early political reforms, previously discussed, proved beneficial to labor: the Civil Liberties Directive; the purge of police officials, as well as the termination of police control over labor administration; and the freeing of political prisoners, some of whom were veteran leaders of the prewar labor movement. MacArthur instructed the government to abolish several wartime government-controlled labor associations, which had been notorious in exploiting workers, and to ban their officials from future labor administrative posts. Besides protecting citizens' fundamental rights, the new constitution, as mentioned before, guaranteed the rights to work, organize unions, and engage in collective bargaining.[37]

During the first two years of the occupation the Diet passed fourteen labor bills, though often only after much behind-the-scenes effort by the SCAP Labor Division and pressure by MacArthur himself. Altogether, these measures gave Japan a sound statutory foundation for a free, democratic labor movement that was even more progressive than American labor had been able to get into legislation. Five of the acts of 1945 to 1947 were particularly significant: (1) The Trade Union Law of December 1945 guaranteed the rights of workers to organize trade unions, to bargain collectively, and to strike; protected workers from unfair management practices; and established labor relations committees at the national and prefectural levels to handle labor-management disputes. (2) The Labor Relations Adjustment Act of September 1946 provided procedural machinery for conciliation, mediation, and arbitration under the auspices of the labor relations committees. Some union leaders unsuccessfully opposed the inclusion of a section that placed restrictions on strikes by public utility employees and prohibited strikes by certain classes of government workers. (3) The Labor Standards Law of April 1947 prohibited forced labor, which had been widely used formerly; and it set up comprehensive standards relating to wage scales, overtime pay, vacations, rest periods, employment of women and minors, and safe and sanitary working conditions, with stiff penalties for violators of the standards. (4) The Labor Ministry Law provided for the creation of the Labor Ministry, which was established in September 1947, with five bureaus covering labor policy, labor standards, women's and minors' employment, employment security, and labor administration. (Labor had been under the Welfare Ministry since the abolition of the Home Ministry.) (5) The Employment Security Law of November 1947 established a system of free public employment exchanges, vocational training, and job assistance for handicapped persons. The Employment Security Bureau would administer these programs and regulate hiring practices. The feudalistic boss-henchman *(oyabun-kobun)* relationship of reciprocal obligations was outlawed, but the hierarchical arrangement actually was continued in labor arrangements, as in other facets of Japanese personal relations.[38]

"The effects of these laws, bureaus, and the atmosphere of democracy," a Japanese scholar states, "were instantaneous. The union movement mushroomed."[39] From the struggling prewar unions, whose membership totaled about 100,000, the growth of Japanese trade unions between 1945 and 1948 was phenomenal, as the following table demonstrates:[40]

	Number of local unions	Number of union members
Oct. 1945	5	707
Dec. 1945	707	378,481
June 1946	11,579	3,748,952
Dec. 1946	17,265	4,849,939
Dec. 1947	28,013	6,268,432
June 1948	33,940	6,636,710
June 1949	34,688	6,655,483

By the end of 1947 an estimated 48 percent of Japan's nonagricultural work force was unionized. At first, unions were seldom organized above the local level; varied greatly in structure and program; and, in view of their inadequate funds, planning, and leadership, were not very effective in local confrontations with management. In August 1946, however, two large national labor federations were founded: the Socialist-dominated General Federation of Trade Unions (JFL, or Sodomei) and the often pro-Communist National Congress of Industrial Unions (CIU, or Sanbetsu), each boasting over a million members by the end•of 1947. About a third of the unionized workers were government employees, their largest unions by then being the Government Railway Workers' Union (600,000 members), Japan Teachers' Union (500,000), and Communications Workers' Union (350,000).

The Japanese government employed 175,000 of its citizens performing services for the occupation at the various Allied installations — army, air, and naval bases and, of course, the sprawling GHQ complex in Tokyo. Nearly half these employees belonged to locals of the JFL or CIU, each of which had a federation of occupation forces' workers' unions. At the large United States Navy station at Yokosuka especially, but also at other Allied military facilities, the base commander sometimes was hostile to such unions. But they were tolerated, because MacArthur endorsed the idea of the unions at the bases as long as their activities did not interfere with military security and operations. For a while the Japanese government discriminated against the occupation workers, keeping their pay at about half of what similar union members were getting in nonoccupation work. In May 1947, however, the occupation forces' unions finally negotiated a new wage scale with the government that brought their pay on par with other workers.[41]

The explosive growth of trade unionism, the ignorance of most members about the functions of unions, the increasing absorption of many labor leaders in political goals and militant tactics rather than in economic objectives and peaceful bargaining, and the takeover of some of the main unions by Communists or extreme-left Socialists — all these trends made some of the GHQ generals fearful that the occupation's liberality on unionism had opened a Pandora's box of troubles. In early April 1946 several policemen were injured when they clashed with a group of union demonstrators who had gathered outside the Prime Minister's residence to protest late food rations and to demand Shidehara's resignation. MacArthur himself became uneasy when at least a million people participated in May Day demonstrations three weeks later in several cities, including a huge march in downtown Tokyo. Leaders of the Tokyo demonstration later circulated to members of the Allied Council for Japan a manifesto of grievances, mainly against alleged police violations of workers' rights. General Derevyanko, the Soviet delegate on the ACJ, defended the manifesto's charges at a meeting of the council, but Atcheson vehemently rebutted the allegations. On May 14 an angry mob was stopped by guards when it tried to enter the Imperial Palace grounds to protest the government's delay in issuing rice rations. A large turnout of Japanese, though guilty of few disorders, staged a food protest in Tokyo on the 19th. Some GHQ officers saw the mounting unrest as a Communist scheme. Willoughby, MacArthur's intelligence chief, was sure that "the crowds were led by Reds and made up mostly of their loyal followers in the unions." Kyuichi Tokuda, a leader of the Communist party, headed a group of thirty who forced their way into the Prime Minister's residence on May 20 and staged a sit-down protest.[42] Enough was enough for MacArthur, who that day issued to the Japanese people his first major warning against disorder:

I find it necessary to caution the Japanese people that the growing tendency towards mass violence and physical processes of intimidation, under organized leadership, present a grave menace to the future development of Japan. . . . The physical violence which undisciplined elements are now beginning to practice will not be permitted to continue. They constitute a menace not only to orderly government but to the basic purposes and security of the occupation itself. If minor elements of Japanese society are unable to exercise such self-restraint and self-respect as the situation and conditions require, I shall be forced to take the necessary steps to control and remedy such a deplorable situation.[43]

When they heard MacArthur's somber message by radio, Tokuda and his group quickly left the Prime Minister's residence. Other demonstrations planned for the rest of the week were promptly cancelled. Some leftist leaders ruefully concluded that "the fight was lost." Meanwhile Yoshida, just appointed to succeed Shidehara as premier, confidently announced his conservative selections for the new Cabinet. Correspondent Mark Gayn wrote in his diary on May 20: MacArthur's "statement had a startling effect. I could actually recall no American move that matched this pronouncement in its repercussions. There was consternation in union headquarters and in the offices of the left-wing parties. In conservative quarters, there was undisguised jubilation."[44]

Economic conditions were so bad in 1946 that, though MacArthur had won a respite from demonstrations with his tough warning, he and Yoshida realized that the fast-growing radical wing of the labor movement would get widespread support when it challenged the establishment again. While labor organized nationally that summer, unemployment and inflation continued to increase, food shortages prevailed, and industrial production sagged at one-third its level in the early 1930s. A rise in strikes in August brought another public warning from MacArthur: "Strikes, walkouts, or other work stoppages which are inimical to the objectives of the occupation are prohibited."

But that autumn incidents of labor disputes, demonstrations, strikes, and sporadic violence rose alarmingly. By October unionized miners, seamen, railwaymen, electricians, newspaper and radio workers, teachers, and postal employees were either striking or threatening to do so. Many were fighting for higher wages and better workers' benefits; others, especially the radicals, were demanding the ouster of the Yoshida ministry. During the "October Offensive" of militant labor activities, Yoshida publicly branded it "a movement by small minorities aiming at the establishment of dictatorial government." The two main conservative parties, Liberal and Democratic, issued a joint statement backing Yoshida against the labor "faction" that was disrupting the economy and public order. In New Year's Day messages to the Japanese people, Yoshida denounced strike leaders as "recalcitrant" and "lawless elements"; in his statement MacArthur complimented the "exemplary approach" of "the great majority of Japan's leaders" in implementing SCAP programs. One observer said of MacArthur's plaudit, "To the public this meant a benediction for Yoshida."[45]

The Joint Struggle Committee, which represented a number of JFL and CIU unions of public workers, especially of the national railway, postal, and communications systems, began earnest planning in January 1947 for a general strike. Heading the committee was Yashiro Ii, a Communist who had been a leader in organizing the railway workers. After weeks of bitter, futile negotiations with Yoshida's labor officials, Ii and his committee demanded on January 11 that Yoshida apologize publicly for his recent insulting remarks about labor leaders. When the Prime Minister refused, the Joint Struggle Committee broke off the negotiations, branding Yoshida as insincere toward labor and a lackey of the big industrialists. On the 18th, Ii announced that a general strike would begin on February 1. Supporting the call were thirteen unions and federations representing 2.6 million members. Other unions were recruited in the following days as the demands for Yoshida's resignation and for improved wages and benefits attracted a broadening spectrum of organized labor, not just its radical groups. Theodore Cohen, who headed the SCAP Labor Division, urged MacArthur to "issue a statement" opposing the general strike, but the general told him that he "chose to wait." Tensions heightened on January 21, when the prostrike president of the CIU was seriously wounded in a knife attack by members of a reactionary society that threatened to attack other labor leaders unless the strike was cancelled.

Desperately endeavoring to avert the nationwide strike, both the government's Central Labor Relations Committee and SCAP officials, particularly Marquat and Cohen, spent long hours talking to the Joint Struggle Committee. A brief sign of hope came when the JFL, feuding with the CIU and Ii's committee over strike plans, withdrew from the projected action. But on January 28 the chances for a negotiated settlement worsened when 400,000 workers in Tokyo staged a demonstration calling for the "immediate overthrow" of the Yoshida ministry. On the 30th, Marquat summoned Ii and his committee to his GHQ office, where he told them firmly to call off the strike before midnight of the 31st. The labor leaders gave no indication that they would comply.[46] At 2:30 P.M. on January 31, nine and a half hours before the deadline, MacArthur issued a "bombshell" order, flatly forbidding the general strike, set to begin the next day:

> Under the authority vested in me as Supreme Commander for the Allied Powers, I have informed the labor leaders, whose unions have federated for the purpose of conducting a general strike, that I will not permit the use of so deadly a social weapon in the present impoverished and emaciated condition of Japan, and have accordingly directed them to desist from the furtherance of such action.
>
> It is with the greatest reluctance that I have deemed it necessary to intervene to this extent. . . . I have done so only to forestall the fatal impact upon an already gravely threatened public welfare. . . . [Japan's] cities are laid waste, its industries are almost at a standstill, and the great masses of its people are on little more than a starvation diet.
>
> A general strike, crippling transportation and communications, would prevent the movement of food to feed the people and of coal to sustain essential utilities, and would stop such industry as is still functioning. The paralysis . . . would produce dreadful consequences upon every Japanese home. . . .
>
> The persons involved in the threatened general strike are but a small minority of the Japanese people. Yet this minority might well plunge the great masses into a disaster not unlike that produced in the immediate past by the minority which led Japan into the destruction of war. . . .
>
> While I have taken this measure as one of dire emergency, I do not intend otherwise to restrict the freedom of action heretofore given labor in the achievement of legitimate objectives. Nor do I intend in any way to compromise or influence the basic social issues involved. These are matters of evolution which time and circumstances may well orient without disaster as Japan gradually emerges from its present distress.[47]

With the pressure of deciding which course to take in this crisis, it is perhaps more understandable why MacArthur had reacted so much when the *Newsweek* attack was published on the 27th. The maintenance of order, whether it meant curbing excesses by reactionaries or radicals, stood high on his list of occupation priorities. In private, MacArthur remarked to his chief of staff on the 30th, "If they start anything, I am going to have Eichelberger [Eighth Army commander] arrest them and that includes those lower down" in organized labor's leadership. But the Joint Struggle Committee, in an atmosphere of "bitter disappointment," quickly met and decided to call off the general strike. Cohen later observed: "Ii misunderstood Occupation policy. We could never have let the railway and communications industries go out on strike because that would have interfered with the functioning of the Occupation. Our problem was not whether or not to permit the general strike but how to avoid it."

The FEC, which had adopted a liberal statement on labor policy in December, was critical of MacArthur's strike ban but even more of his action without consulting that body. In official Washington and across the United States his strong stand was generally admired. Although greatly oversimplifying American views, Atcheson, who was then in the States, reported to the new Secretary of State, General of the Army George C. Marshall, that the opinions he had been hearing were "unanimous in supporting General MacArthur's intervention and stoppage of the strike." William Green, president of the American Federation of Labor, publicly defended MacArthur's labor policy as "above reproach" in allowing "maximum freedom of action to Japanese trade unions." American liberal periodicals, on the other hand, generally were critical — "shockingly reactionary," one of them judged his order.[48]

As for Japanese conservatives' reactions, a respected biographer of Yoshida says: "In Yoshida's appraisal, SCAP did not begin to come to its senses until the threatened general strike of early 1947. Business leaders and other opponents of the early reform agenda also commonly cite SCAP's prohibition of the strike as the first unequivocal step in the abandonment of reformism." Kichisaburo Nomura, the former admiral who had been the ambassador to the United States during the peace negotiations in 1941, wrote

MacArthur on February 1 that "his wise statesmanship at the last stage of the crisis" had "saved" Japan from "national calamities" and "imminent anarchy." In the aftermath of the incident, most Japanese apparently were critical of the participating unions. Barred by SCAP regulations from soliciting opinions of MacArthur, a Japanese newspaper polled nearly 4000 Tokyo citizens in mid-February as to whether the unions or the government had been more "unreasonable" in the crisis. The unions were blamed by 44 percent of the respondents; 26.4 percent chose the government. (The rest checked "no interest," 8.6 percent, or "don't know," 21 percent.)

Ii, the chairman of the Joint Struggle Committee and later a member of the Central Committee of the Japanese Communist party, delivered a moving radio address the day after Mac-Arthur's order. He declared his determination to continue the struggle and said that he viewed the strike cancellation as "one step backward in preparation for moving two steps forward." He also interpreted MacArthur's action as a shift in direction, for "until then, SCAP had been sympathetic to labor."[49]

Ii proved correct on both counts, in part. In the first place, union militancy, dormant for a while, erupted again with serious labor disturbances in the spring of 1948. In the second place, though supportive of the important measures in behalf of labor that the Diet enacted later in 1947, MacArthur became increasingly intolerant of labor radicalism and disorder. To try to avoid strike bans in the future, he authorized the SCAP Labor Division to take a more active role in labor-management disputes before a strike stage was reached. The principal immediate consequences of the general strike affair were MacArthur's instructions to Yoshida the next week to conduct general elections, which led to Socialist Kataya-ma's ascendancy to the premiership that spring; and the formation of the Council of Labor Unions in March, an effort by the federations to present a united front on as many crucial issues as possible in future confrontations with the government. The council was to serve as a liaison political action body representing 5.8 million workers then belonging to unions affiliated with the CIU, JFL, and Japanese Congress of Labor, a new middle-of-the-road federation. Both MacArthur and the Japanese government were aware that more threats to public order and economic recovery lay ahead, once the large radical portion of organized labor had regrouped and devised new strategies. As Russell Brines, a veteran American reporter in Tokyo, observed, "Both sides of the controversy recognized the general strike as unfinished business."[50]

5. *New Hope for the Peasants*

One day in October 1946, Colonel Charles Kades, deputy chief of the Government Section, rushed into MacArthur's outer office and asked Colonel Herbert Wheeler, aide to the Supreme Commander, whether he knew the whereabouts of General Whitney. When told that he was in conference with MacArthur, Kades asked Wheeler to tell Whitney that he had "some important information." Wheeler went in to inform Whitney, who came to the door and invited Kades to join him and MacArthur. Entering, Kades announced, "You'll be glad to know, sirs, that the Diet has passed the Land Reform Bill." According to Kades, MacArthur, who was seated at his desk, "leaned back in his chair and said, 'How am I doing, Dad?' I didn't see what he was looking at, but he was looking up. I said to Whitney later, 'What was he looking at? Was he talking to his Father in heaven?' He said, 'No. He was looking at a picture of his father.' It was probably on the wall or on a bookcase." Afterward Whitney explained to Kades that when Major General Arthur MacArthur was military governor of the Philippines in 1900–1901 he had instituted several reforms that benefited the Filipino peasants. The sweeping land reform that MacArthur the son was instrumental in obtaining for Japan's agrarian populace, however, would overshadow all the reform endeavors of MacArthur the father in the Philippines.[51]

When MacArthur arrived in Japan, seven out of ten Japanese farmers were tenants, renting all or part of the land they worked. Only 54 percent of the nation's farmland was cultivated by its owners. As agricultural depressions produced growing debts for peasants during the earlier part of the century, many had sold their farms to landlords but remained as tenants, living under a feudal system in which the landlord demanded two fifths to one half of the value of the tenant's produce as rent. Even with a bountiful rice harvest, the tenant had little hope of ever buying back his land, not only because of the exorbitant rent in kind but also because of the low prices he received for his produce, the ever-rising land values, and his continuous state of indebtedness. Though often guilty of using hyperbole, MacArthur was accurate in describing the peasants' plight: "Japan's feudalistic regime was most evident in the matter of landholding. As late as the end of the war, a system of virtual slavery that went back to ancient times was still in existence. Most farmers in Japan were either out-and-out serfs, or they worked under an arrangement through which the landowners exorbited a high percentage of each year's crops."

The need for revamping the farm tenure system was recognized by the government from the early 1920s onward, as periodic peasant revolts and widespread tenant unrest made the ruling groups uneasy. Peasants had long constituted the backbone of conservatism in Japan, and with the rise of the militarists in the 1930s the government became even more concerned about alleviating rural discontent, especially since the bulk of the Army's enlisted men came from the peasant class. Several measures were enacted to help tenant farmers, including provisions for small loans, some protection against eviction, and conciliation procedures for tenant-landlord disputes. A limited plan for land reform was under consideration when the war with China interrupted in the late 1930s. But the prewar measures had not provided the peasant with much hope of gaining a farm of his own, for landlords were not required to sell land, and the government did not attempt to place ceilings on rent or land prices.[52]

The democratization of Japan had to include progress toward economic democracy for the peasants, as both Washington and SCAP leaders early realized. W. Macmahon Ball, an Australian political scientist and a zealous exponent of land reform when he was the British Commonwealth representative on the Allied Council for Japan, explained: "The emancipation of the peasant must be the first and most important step in any programme for the economic and spiritual emancipation of the Japanese people. . . . Their importance lies not only in their numbers [nearly half the population in 1945], but in the fact that they represent what is most backward in Japanese society. . . . No democracy can be built on a foundation of agricultural serfdom." MacArthur's early directives clearly established his responsibility to promote economic democracy in agriculture, as well as in industry and labor: he was to favor policies permitting "a wide distribution of income and of ownership of the means of production and trade," it will be recalled, and "the development of organizations in . . . agriculture on a democratic basis." MacArthur did not have mixed feelings on this matter, as he had on Zaibatsu dissolution: "I felt that any man who farmed the land should, by law, be entitled to his crops, that there should be an end to sharecropping, and that even more fundamental, perhaps, was the need to make land itself available to the people."[53]

On its own initiative in November 1945, the Japanese government launched a study, headed by Hiroo Wada of the Ministry of Agriculture and Forestry, to investigate the agricultural land situation and to recommend a plan for land reform. The Shidehara Cabinet's subsequent bill was under deliberation in the Diet, though meeting fierce opposition from large landholding interests, when MacArthur issued a SCAPIN on December 9 instructing the government to undertake land reform. He called for an end to "the economic bondage which has enslaved the Japanese farmer for centuries of feudal oppression" and gave Shidehara the deadline of March 15, 1946, for submitting a plan. The specifics of MacArthur's directive were derived from a comprehensive study of the land situation that had been prepared by Robert A. Fearey and Wolf I. Ladejinsky, who came to GHQ on loan from the State and Agriculture departments, respectively. His SCAPIN, says a Japanese historian, "undercut the opposition that had been building in the Diet" to the land reform bill, and on December 29 it was passed. Among other provisions, the measure reduced the amount of land that a single owner could hold to a maximum of 12.3 acres (or five *cho*, one cho equaling 2.451 acres), and it required farm rent to be paid in money instead of in kind (rice), as formerly. On the advice of Colonel Hubert Schenck, chief of the SCAP Natural Resources Section, MacArthur refused to accept the measure, because, among other flaws, it would affect only a third of the tenants, it allowed up to five years for the land transfers, and it did not require the government to act as agent in landlord-tenant negotiations on transfers.

The question of land reform remained stalemated for the next half-year as SCAP and Japanese agricultural officials tried in vain to reach a consensus on a new plan. On one of the rare occasions when he made use of the Allied Council for Japan, MacArthur referred the issue to that body and in mid-June largely concurred in its proposed plan. The ACJ recommendation was the work of Ball, and it helped to break the logjam, with many of its ideas incorporated in the second bill on land reform. During the ACJ's deliberations, Derevyanko had offered a counter plan that would have required the confiscation of all tenant-worked farmland without compensation to the owners. "The knowledge that such a proposal had been advanced," said Yoshida, "probably helped in reconciling the landowners to the actual terms of the second land reform."[54]

The bill that finally emerged as reasonably satisfactory to both sides was formulated through the efforts of a talented group of American and Japanese agricultural experts, who worked well together and came to respect each other's professionalism. On the SCAP side, they included Wolf Ladejinsky, Laurence I. Hewes, Robert S. Hardie, and William Gilmartin of the Agriculture Division of Schenck's Natural Resources Section. Wada, now Minister of Agriculture and Forestry, took an active, constructive role, and his specialists on land reform, particularly Iwozumi, Tokoro, and Owada, were able and cooperative. "To both groups this period served to prove as nothing else can prove," Hewes attested, "that men who work hard together, even though in disagreement, cannot remain hostile indefinitely." As for MacArthur's role, he said: "Without the continued firm backing of the Supreme Commander, the task of the [civilian] specialists would have been almost impossible, if for nothing else than the lack of mutual understanding with the [SCAP] military. The offsetting factor therefore was the weight of the personal responsibility of MacArthur." Hewes added that "the personal factor" contributed by MacArthur "had to serve as the main carrier channel through which decision and action were implemented. The prompt, forthright nature of these decisions and the continued firm confidence in the work of the agricultural technicians was a source of encouragement to them and this alone was indispensable to the success of the project."[55]

After numerous revisions by SCAP and the Ministry of Agriculture and Forestry, followed by lengthy debates in the Diet, the complex program was finally enacted in October 1946 in the form of two complementary statutes, the Owner-Farmer Establishment and Special Measures Law and the Agricultural Land Adjustment Law. They became identified collectively as the Second Land Reform Law, or the Land Reform Law of 1946. As summarized by SCAP, the legislation was designed "to eliminate the feudal system of land tenure and remove obstacles to the redistribution of the land on an equitable and democratic basis." Absentee landlordism was abolished, with lands of noncultivators bought by the government and sold to tenants at lower prewar prices, payable in thirty-year installments at 3.2 percent interest. Rent payment in kind was prohibited; rent maximums were set at 25 percent of the crop value on paddy fields and 15 percent on upland fields. A landlord could retain up to about 2.5 acres (one *cho*) that he actually cultivated (a concession to the hundreds of thousands of "little landlords"). With slight variations to allow for terrain and climatic differences, farmers who cultivated their own land were allowed a maximum of 7.5 acres for their own use, along with 2.5 acres that could be rented out. Agricultural land commissions were to be elected at the local and prefectural levels, including representation by tenants, owner-cultivators, and landlords. The commissions were crucial to the program's success, since they were responsible for such functions as selecting lands and purchasers and supervising the land transfers. At the national level the Central Agricultural Land Commission was established to coordinate and oversee the work of the 11,000 local and 46 prefectural commissions. "The Diet's passage of the Land Reform Bill," MacArthur remarked in a public statement on October 12, "is one of the most important milestones yet reached by Japan in the creation of an economically stable and politically democratic society. . . . It penetrates far deeper to root out existing evils than has yet been attempted in most lands."

More than 400,000 Japanese participated at some administrative level in the organizational structure devised to execute the land reform. The redistribution of land was an exercise in economic democracy, and the administration of it, especially at the town and village levels, produced a bonus in providing rural folk with practical experience in grass-roots political democracy through the election of and participation on the land commissions and various ad hoc committees that were found to be necessary. In early 1947 the commissions were elected, and the government began buying farmland. By the end of 1948, 4.5 million acres of farmland had been purchased by the government and 4.3 million acres of it sold to tenants. Through an amendment to the Land Reform Law in 1947, the government also acquired 540,000 acres of pasture land and began reselling it to tenants. New and fairer leasing procedures were inaugurated for the 1.7 million acres of agricultural land still in tenancy. By December 1949, when most of the land transfers had been completed, the total figures stood at 4.7 million acres bought by the government, of which 4.6 million had been resold. Most impressive, 89 percent of all agricultural land was then owner-operated and only 11 percent tenant-operated. Thus, all but a small number of Japan's 3.8 million farm-tenant families had become farm owners in the short span of two years. The achievement was remarkable, particularly in view of the chaotic workings of some of the local commissions and the opposition of many landlords as manifested in taking their grievances to the Diet and the courts.[56]

In October 1949, as the major portion of the land reform was nearing completion, MacArthur wrote to Yoshida, who had become Prime Minister again in October 1948, praising "the people of rural Japan for the magnificent accomplishment which their devotion to this task has made possible." Although most of the program had been executed during the premierships of Katayama and Ashida, MacArthur lauded Yoshida's role as the supportive Prime Minister at the beginning and the end of the land reform: "The world watched your work skeptically, in belief that the job was too big, that you would not approach it with sincerity, that feudalistic interests would render it only a token reform. Your progress shows no deviation from the high objective enumerated." He added, "As Japan works toward re-entry into the family of nations, this achievement stands as one of the most important single demonstrations of her approaching maturity as a democratic nation." Emphasizing that "it was the Japanese Government that took the initiative" in land reform, Yoshida nevertheless later admitted, somewhat grudgingly, that "it is quite possible that without occupation backing, agricultural land reform might not have been realized." Even Whitney, not known for his humility, said that land reform, rather than constitutional revision, would be "the one MacArthur accomplishment in Japan that will probably be ranked higher by the future historian than any other." And, indeed, the historians, whether Japanese or American, liberal or conservative, generally have given the land reform high marks.[57]

There is no question that the land reform was a giant step forward for rural economic democracy in Japan, but contemporary and later evaluations have found flaws in this perhaps "best-laid plan" of the occupation. To mention only several of the recurring criticisms: in the first place, the rampant postwar inflation and consequent high land prices meant that the landlords lost heavily in being forced by the government to sell their lands at ridiculously low 1939 prices. Kazuo Kawai, editor of the *Nippon Times,* whose opinions were usually moderate, maintained that for the "hard hit" landlords "the actual effect was hardly distinguishable from the outright confiscation advocated by the Russians and vigorously denounced as immoral by SCAP." The *Asahi Shimbun* staff uncovered an undoubtedly rare case wherein "a former tenant farmer who made a fortune from selling the land he had acquired through the reform offered part of his new wealth to his impoverished former landlord as a gift." In the second place, the land reform led to "a high degree of fractionalization of farmlands into small patches, separately owned and farmed." Although landownership greatly increased, the average size of farms decreased, with over 1 million farmers cultivating fewer than 1.5 acres. The average farm was tiny, only 2.4 acres, in contrast to an average of 47 acres in the United States. Japanese productivity even then was among the highest in the world in rice yield per acre, but Andrew J. Grad, who served in the SCAP Natural Resources Section, found in 1952 that "the majority of peasants are extremely poor and live very close to the starvation point . . . and possibilities of improving one's status [are] practically absent." Third, Laurence Hewes, a key SCAP figure in formulating the land reform plan, warned that it "must be reinforced by adjustments in related phases of the farm economy." The government, he felt, needed to realize that only part of the agrarian problem was solved by land reform and that a comprehensive agricultural policy was required to promote farmer cooperatives, a farm credit system, sound and fairer agrarian taxation, improved rural education, and greater participation by farmers in politics.[58]

The reputation of the land reform as one of the most worthwhile reforms of the occupation period rests not only on the changes wrought at the time but also on its permanence, in contrast to many other SCAP reforms. An American economist, viewing it in retrospect over three decades, sees the long-range success of the land reform as linked to postoccupation urban migration and general economic prosperity:

> There are . . . some nagging questions in my mind about the permanence of the land reform. . . . 1) What if there had not been the population shift to the cities from the rural areas? Would the presence of a large agricultural population over time [have] not resulted in a reversion to feudal-like conditions as the members of this large agricultural population competed with each other for increasingly scarcer and more valuable land to till? . . . 2) What if, in the period 1951 to the present [1980], the economy of Japan had not been as dynamic, innovative, economical, and efficient as in fact it was? Suppose that instead it had been depressed, stagnant, unproductive, and/or Malthusian-like in character, so that peasants shared with the rest of the nation not national prosperity over nearly three decades but rather tight money, depressed incomes, and a propensity for insurmountable indebtedness? Would not that have caused a reversion to great dependence on landlords by former owners now reduced to tenant status? Would not that kind of environment have been a rerun of the 1930's in Japan and the quality of life endured by so many agriculturalists in that period?[59]

Such what-if questions did not bother MacArthur then or later, for land reform was a success in limiting the spread of Communism in occupied Japan, an increasingly important priority to him and to Washington policymakers: "The redistribution formed," he later commented, "a strong barrier against any introductions of Communism in rural Japan. Every farmer in the country was now a capitalist in his own right." An American scholar concludes that, in fact, the land reform's main success was not in contributing toward economic recovery but rather in creating in rural Japan "a mass political base for anti-Socialist parties and against any proposal for agricultural collectivism. In retrospect, this political effect seems to have been the principal purpose of the reform all along" for both the Japanese and American governments.[60]

Besides the land reform and the American relief assistance, which included large amounts of fertilizer, MacArthur and his GHQ agricultural staff assisted the Japanese farmers in other ways less well known. In the spring of 1946 MacArthur, in his capacity as head of the Far East Command, obtained the Joint Chiefs' authorization to take over the mining of phosphate rock on Angaur from a departing American mining firm, at the same time also acquiring the company's remaining stockpiles of phosphate rock. MacArthur stated that his purpose was "to supply Japan with required fertilizer to increase indigenous food production and reduce the amount of United States appropriated funds required to meet the food deficit in Japan." The island of Angaur is located in the Carolines in the Western Pacific, which had been formerly mandated to Japan but seized by American forces during World War II and later placed under American trusteeship. The Angaur phosphate industry employed Japanese technicians and laborers "under the strict supervision and control of the Supreme Commander," MacArthur reported. When the Australian government raised questions about the security aspects of the operation in mid-1947, the State Department backed MacArthur, maintaining that the activity "does not threaten the security of or otherwise injure any nation, while permitting a significant saving in occupation costs."[61]

From the early months of the occupation MacArthur promoted the development of farmer cooperatives, which the agrarian populace welcomed but which, except for enabling legislation, the Japanese government supported in only niggardly fashion. In early December 1945 MacArthur instructed Shidehara "to foster and encourage an agricultural co-operative movement free of domination by non-agricultural interests and dedicated to the economic and cultural advancement of the Japanese farmers." A law was enacted later that month establishing a system of cooperatives along the lines of those developed by American farmers. The measure eliminated the former government-controlled agricultural associations, which had seldom considered peasant needs and interests. The properties of the 10,400 prohibited agricultural associations were transferred to the new farmer cooperatives, which were free of landlord domination. In the period 1946–1949 the farmers voluntarily organized over 33,000 "democratically constituted" cooperatives, with a total membership of 8.2 million. About 1000 federations of cooperatives were also formed. At the local level the cooperatives, which sprang up in nearly every village and town, became the principal credit, purchasing, marketing, and service instruments for the millions of new farm operators under the land reform program. In December 1949 MacArthur issued a statement praising the cooperatives' contribution to ending "the monopolistic and repressive practices of the past" that had beset rural Japan. "The farmers of Japan," he said, "have carried through an organizational task perhaps unsurpassed in the history of the world cooperative movement. In so doing they have demonstrated their growing capacity to handle the tools of democracy."[62]

The troubled status of Japan's economy after two years of occupation could not have left MacArthur feeling as confident and proud as many of his public pronouncements suggested. After a hard fight he was beginning to convince Washington authorities that Japan was in desperate shape, still unable to stand on her own economically, and in great need of American relief aid. So far efforts to curb inflation had failed badly. The question of reparations stood unsettled in 1947, and he knew that severe exactions could cause the stagnant economy to collapse. From the start he had been of two minds about the economic purge and the Zaibatsu dissolution programs; his orders were to implement them, yet he was aware that such actions would undoubtedly retard economic recovery. As directed, he had encouraged trade unionism, had been delighted by its astounding growth, and then had been compelled to act against its excesses, fully realizing that the battle with the radical elements of labor was far from done. It is little wonder that he singled out the land reform, though it was hardly flawless, as "one of the most far-reaching accomplishments of the occupation."[63] Thanks to the fortuitous trends of Japan's demography and economy after the occupation, the land reform still stands today as the most enduring SCAP reform in the economic field.

CHAPTER VI

His Second Political Misadventure

1. The Lure of the White House

NO QUESTION ABOUT IT; MacArthur was a political animal. Yet he and Whitney, often called his alter ego, felt compelled to deny in later years that MacArthur had political ambitions or had endorsed futile campaigns in 1944, 1948, and 1952 to get the Republican presidential nomination for him. "The insistence by MacArthur and his aides," suggests one historian, "that the General had only a superficial interest in presidential politics is partly explained as an attempt to answer the equally insistent counterclaims of partisans of the Truman Administration." Indeed, Truman himself compared him with General George B. McClellan, who ran against Abraham Lincoln in the 1864 presidential election.[1]

It is true that the evidence implicating MacArthur directly in the presidential campaign in his behalf in 1944 is slim. He remained well in the background, never publicly revealing an interest in the Republican nomination and allowing trusted staff officers, such as Whitney, Willoughby, Lloyd A. (Larry) Lehrbas, and Philip F. La Follette, to act as liaisons with dedicated activists in the United States. While the McCormick, Hearst, Patterson, and Scripps-Howard publications promoted his command feats in the war against Japan and his attributes as presidential timber, Robert E. Wood, the Sears, Roebuck board chairman and former head of the isolationist America First Committee, and Senator Arthur H. Vandenberg, the influential Republican leader from Michigan,

plotted a low-key strategy that would have the convention delegates primed to choose MacArthur as a dark horse when the expected stalemate occurred between Thomas E. Dewey and Wen-
dell L. Willkie. But the pro-MacArthur excitement spread beyond
their control, with MacArthur-for-president organizations spring-
ing up in several states and a number of notorious reactionaries,
like Gerald L. K. Smith, joining the cause. Contrary to the wishes
of MacArthur's key political advisers, in April 1944 a delegate slate
in his name was entered in the Republican primary in Wisconsin,
where it finished behind Dewey's and Harold E. Stassen's tickets
and virtually killed the MacArthurites' chances at the convention.
As a coup de grâce, Representative Albert L. Miller of Nebraska,
a MacArthur enthusiast, released an exchange of letters between
him and the general in which MacArthur appeared to endorse
Miller's extreme right-wing criticisms of the Roosevelt administration. MacArthur shortly issued statements saying he was not a
candidate and would not accept the presidential nomination if offered. His monumental ego had been badly burned by this political misadventure, but, amazingly, he continued to keep a close
watch on the American political scene and always enjoyed discussing national politics with the numerous congressmen, editors,
publishers, and business leaders who visited him at his Dai Ichi
office or embassy residence in Tokyo.[2]

After a chat with MacArthur in early February 1946, Eichelberger recorded in his diary:

> . . . MacA said he does not intend to leave until the job is over but
> did not state when he thought that would be. He did say he does not
> intend to go home for a visit, although urged to do so by Secretary
> of War [Robert P.] Patterson, who apparently was acting for the
> President in asking him. . . . MacA also told me he had received a
> message stating that Postmaster General [Robert E.] Hannegan would
> like to visit Japan but would not come without MacA's consent. SCAP
> sent word by some visitor that Hannegan would always be welcome
> and said, "Tell Hannegan that I said if the Republicans nominate any
> army officer for the next election it will not be MacArthur but will
> be Eisenhower." [3]

When Chief of Staff Dwight D. Eisenhower visited MacArthur
in May 1946, their afterdinner conversation quickly turned to the
next presidential race. Many years later Eisenhower recounted to

the author MacArthur's surprising proposal: "He kept me in his study from dinner until 1:00 A.M., trying to persuade me to run for President in 1948. When I suggested that he was the one to be a candidate, he merely dismissed the notion with the remark that he was too old for the job." Later Truman told James V. Forrestal, then Secretary of Defense, that he "had been amused to have Ike tell him upon his return from Japan that he thought the President would have to face the prospect of MacArthur's returning here in the spring [of 1948] to launch a campaign for himself." Truman continued, "Another visitor to MacArthur had returned the message from MacArthur warning the President that Eisenhower would be the candidate for the presidency!" He felt that both generals were suffering from "either 'Potomac fever' or 'brass infection.' "[4]

Apparently MacArthur was still feeling the sting of the 1944 political fiasco when he journeyed to Manila in July 1946 for the inauguration of Manuel Roxas as the first President of the Republic of the Philippines. There he met General George C. Kenney, head of the Strategic Air Command and his Army Air Forces chief in the Southwest Pacific war. When Kenney asked when he planned to return to America, MacArthur replied, "When I have finished here, or they fire me. This is my last job for my country." Kenney then inquired what he intended to do when he did return. MacArthur said, "I expect to settle down in Milwaukee, and on the way to the house I'm going to stop in a furniture store and buy the biggest red rocker in the shop. I'll set it up on the porch and alongside it put a good-sized pile of stones. Then I'll rock." Curious, Kenney asked, "What are the stones for?" MacArthur's eyes "twinkled" as he responded, "They are to throw at anyone who comes around talking politics."[5]

Nevertheless, at some point in the ensuing months MacArthur began to reconsider and within a year and a half gave, in essence, the go-ahead to Stateside leaders who wanted to make him the next Republican presidential candidate. Besides his own supreme self-confidence in his understanding of presidential politics, MacArthur seems to have been influenced by four principal factors in his thinking about making a bid for the presidency in 1948: (1) political trends in America in 1945–1947, (2) the status of the occupation and the political convertibility of his SCAP role, (3) results of selected American polls, and (4) incessant pressures and optimistic analyses by his GHQ and Stateside advisers on political affairs.

For the first time since 1928, the Republicans gained control of both houses of Congress in the 1946 elections. Capitalizing on inflation, labor disputes, Cold War anxieties, and Truman's alleged bungling, the Republicans had been effective that fall with their slogan "Had enough?" In the aftermath of the elections Democratic Senator J. William Fulbright of Arkansas even proposed publicly that Truman should resign in favor of a Republican so that the country might be spared the futile battling between a Democratic President and a Republican Congress. Republican party leaders were looking forward eagerly to ousting Truman or any other Democratic presidential candidate in 1948. But from the perspective of MacArthur and his "political advisers," the main Republican hopefuls — Dewey, Willkie, Stassen, and Senator Robert A. Taft of Ohio — each had serious weaknesses in presidential vote-getting. If ever MacArthur had a chance to gain the Republican nomination and win the presidency, it seemed to be in 1948. That election appeared to be his last opportunity, because by 1952 he would be seventy-two and probably too old to receive serious consideration.[6]

A keen student of history, MacArthur knew that virtually all military occupations had been dark periods to be endured by the occupied peoples and portrayed negatively in their national chronicles. He was determined that the occupation of Japan would be remembered by the conquered and the conquerors as a relatively progressive, cooperative experience from which came a lasting bond of amity between Japan and America. But that depended, he was convinced, on the occupation's being of short duration; once the basic occupation objectives had been achieved, prolongation of the SCAP authority over Japan's government, economy, and society would bring diminishing returns. This sincerely held belief motivated his call in early 1947 for a peace treaty as soon as possible. Some scholars and contemporary critics have alleged that this move to try to hasten the treaty negotiations was politically motivated, but the evidence does not indicate that he was convinced by that time that he should try for the 1948 nomination.

MacArthur's SCAP record could be a more important political asset in 1948 than his wartime theater command had been in 1944. After all, what other contender besides Truman possessed experience as a virtual head of state? And, as the Supreme Commander in Japan, he had demonstrated leadership in nonmilitary activities that was enlightened and humanitarian, yet decisive and, for the most part, effective. Liberals in America might be attracted by the land reform, the expansion of women's rights and the broadening female participation in politics, the new constitution, the promotion of trade unionism, the offensive against the business elite, and the demilitarization program. Conservatives might find appealing his support of Yoshida and the conservative government, his efforts in behalf of economic recovery, and his stalwart opposition to the Soviet Union's attempts to have more voice in occupation policymaking and to the disorders of mobs led by Japanese leftists. Realistically, his main support would have to come from the conservative Republicans, to many of whom his principal asset was his strong anti-Communist stance. In the new era of the Cold War he appeared to them to be the kind of leader who would stand tough in dealing with Stalin. Already Truman was catching flak for not doing more to thwart the spread of Communism at home and abroad, and none of the other potential candidates for 1948 seemed likely to be any more effective in confronting Moscow. Such were some of the considerations fed to MacArthur by his advisers as he deliberated. Among other erroneous estimates, they did not understand how tough Truman could be, nor did they fathom how deeply anxious about some SCAP reforms, especially the anti-Zaibatsu program, were many influential conservatives in American politics and big business, some of whom feared MacArthur was "out-dealing the New Deal" in Japan.[7]

Apparently MacArthur and his inner circle in GHQ, as well as his confidants in the States, read the Gallup, Roper, *Fortune,* and other American polls with rose-tinted bifocals. They focused on those demonstrating that MacArthur was much admired, and such poll results were impressive in 1945–1946. A Gallup survey in late 1945, for example, found that the choices of the people polled as "the greatest person, living or dead, in world history" were (1) Franklin Roosevelt, (2) Lincoln, (3) Jesus, (4) Washington, and (5)

MacArthur. A poll by the American Institute of Public Opinion in June 1946 placed MacArthur first, followed by Eisenhower and Truman, as "the most admired living person in the world."

But the polls offered a mixed reading on the people's feelings about MacArthur as a potential presidential candidate. A mid-1945 survey showed that MacArthur was first and Eisenhower second in the responses to the question "What persons not in politics might make a good President?" Probably of special notice at GHQ was the 1946 Gallup poll series that inquired, "What [Republican] man would you like to see elected President in 1948?" They showed that MacArthur's stock was on the rise: he was picked by 3 percent in April, 6 percent in May, and 12 percent in July. But by the last date Dewey was the choice of 42 percent and Stassen of 25 percent, leaving the general a distant third. A survey in December 1946 found that, in selecting only between Eisenhower and MacArthur as to which would "make the better President," 43 percent chose Ike and only 24 percent MacArthur, the rest having "no opinion." That same month a *Fortune* poll among World War II veterans uncovered some data that should have disturbed the MacArthurites. The same question was asked separately to each participant about Eisenhower and MacArthur: "Would you like to see him become a candidate for President in 1948?" Of those who responded "yes" to either question, the distribution was as follows:

	Total	*Pacific theater veterans*	*European theater veterans*
MacArthur	16.1%	13.7%	17.3%
Eisenhower	30.6%	28.3%	33.2%

The veterans' data were destined to be an omen of trouble later, when they would embarrass MacArthur and plague the efforts of his campaign leaders. In the meantime, however, the pro-MacArthur prognosticators concluded from the polls that there were possibilities of transforming the people's widespread admiration for the general into votes and of overcoming the early popular lead of Dewey. As long as Ike did not enter the race, the main problems appeared to be beating Dewey for the Republican nomination, for "Haberdasher Harry" Truman certainly could be beaten in the November election. As it turned out, the MacArthurites would not be the only Republicans overly optimistic about defeating Truman.[8]

In 1946–1947 several GHQ officers made trips to the United States and provided MacArthur with reports, by letter or later in person, on the "political climate," usually described in highly favorable terms. Brigadier General Bonner F. Fellers, his military secretary, reported in January 1946 that he had meetings with seventeen influential political, business, labor, and newspaper leaders. The main ones who would figure in the 1948 MacArthur campaign were Wood, who had been a key financier of the 1944 movement; La Follette, the Wisconsin Progressive leader; Robert R. McCormick, the Chicago *Tribune* publisher; and Herbert Hoover, who as President in 1930 had chosen MacArthur as Chief of Staff. From these talks Fellers drew some general conclusions: "MacArthur sentiment is strong; especially is the Middlewest pro-MacArthur. . . . MacArthur opposition is gradually being identified as coming largely from the ranks of Communists, Jews, Administration, and in some instances British. . . . There are no leaders of stature actively seeking the 1948 presidential nomination." From Hawaii, en route back from a trip to the States in February and March of 1946, Willoughby wrote that he had met with House Speaker Joseph E. Martin; Clare Boothe Luce, wife of Henry R. Luce, the *Time-Life-Fortune* publisher; and Thomas W. Lamont of J. P. Morgan and Company, among other persons. This "very rich and influential group," as Willoughby characterized them, "feel that the General ought not to continue his stay in Japan too long. . . . Frightened as they are by the Russians, they feel that no one can handle this situation with the same dignity and force as the General." Colonel Laurence E. Bunker, a trusted aide, wrote MacArthur from Washington, D.C., in November: "Everywhere I go, people tell me what a grand job they think you are doing. . . . Often they refer to incidents or situations elsewhere and say: 'I wish we had MacArthur in command of that situation, too.'" Eichelberger of the Eighth Army informed MacArthur late in 1946 that his brother, an attorney in New York City, found the consensus of his friends to be that "MacArthur could, if he [properly] timed his return and announcement, have the [Republican] nom-

ination and election handed him on a platter."[9] Such reports would
be heady stuff for anyone, much less for an ambitious general with
an already large ego.

A number of former Southwest Pacific staff officers who had
supported the MacArthur-for-President activity in 1944 continued a lively effort to secure his candidacy. For example, in October 1945 La Follette, now back in Wisconsin, wrote that Mac-
Arthur's critics in America were mainly "the extreme Nationalists,
those sometimes classified before Pearl Harbor as 'Intervention-
ists' " and "Communists and their fellow travelers." He assured his
former chief, however, that "both in the Country and the Congress you have a solid and certain backing. . . . Let nothing deter
you from the high course you have set for yourself." Also that
month Major General George Van Horn Moseley, now retired but
a key officer under MacArthur when he was Chief of Staff, expressed his hope that MacArthur would run but warned: "There
are a great many enemies within our gates who . . . are afraid of
you. . . . Among this number are the members of the C.I.O., the
Communists and Jews, and such skunks as Walter Winchell and
Drew Pearson." As for 1948, he commented, "To date the Republicans have no one who seems to have the ability or the chance of
election." Julius Klein, now a public relations executive in Chicago, reminded him that December: "Colonel McCormick is your
devoted friend," and "Senator [R. Owen] Brewster of Maine has
been your ambassador of good will," and Herbert Hoover, "like
all of us, hopes and prays that when the time comes you again will
answer the country's call." MacArthur must have been moved by
the encouragement from Hoover, such as his message in late 1945:
"You might do a service to this country comparable to that of John
the Baptist when he came out of the wilderness. . . . The whole
nation will listen to you as to no other man." Hoover envisioned
MacArthur as the leader of a crusade against the nation's "greatly
degenerated" morals, "left-wing regimentation," and "frustration
in international relations." Without much subtlety, Hoover, like
others who knew MacArthur well, pitched his appeal to the general's strong sense of duty, honor, and country.[10]

Lansing Hoyt, a dissident Republican in Wisconsin who opposed Thomas Coleman's Republican "political machine" in that
state, informed Wood in March 1947 that he planned to organize

a MacArthur-for-President drive, as he had done in 1944, and file a full slate of MacArthur delegates for the state primary in April 1948. Speculation about MacArthur's political plans rose markedly in newspapers and periodicals in the spring of 1947. For instance, *Newsweek* devoted an article to the general's potential candidacy, apparently stemming solely from a reporter's question to MacArthur about what his favorite song was, to which the general had answered, "Home, Sweet Home." Wood reported to MacArthur in June that, though Dewey was leading in the polls, he "is bitterly opposed by the western Republicans." He dismissed Taft and Governor John W. Bricker as lacking "sufficient appeal to the masses." Several prominent senators had told Wood, he recounted, "that in their opinion the time is ripe for a compromise candidate and you [MacArthur] would be the ideal compromise candidate." He suggested that MacArthur should "return to this country sometime in the late fall of '47 or early spring of '48 so the people could see you." Wood's key message was "I would like to see you become a candidate and I would be prepared to go all out in your behalf and you, on your side without committing yourself in any way, shape or manner, could decide whether you were willing to sacrifice yourself for your country by serving."[11]

About the same time McCormick also wrote the Supreme Commander, praising him as "one of the few men who will remain famous throughout history, not only as a great general but as a great organizer and humanitarian." He added, "Your career has not paralleled Washington's or Lincoln's, but in its own particular sphere is as great as either of theirs." In August *United States News* reported, "The MacArthur sentiment is rising in Wisconsin and Illinois," citing promotion in McCormick's Chicago *Tribune* and Hoyt's activities in Wisconsin. Late that month McCormick notified MacArthur that he planned to make a week's visit to Japan in November, to which MacArthur responded that he was "delighted." Eichelberger, visiting in the States, informed MacArthur in September that in a conversation he had had with McCormick, the *Tribune* publisher had remarked, "There is only one functioning statesman in America today and that is your Chief. There may be others but they have not proved themselves."[12]

The possibility of securing Taft's support at least at the convention probably weighed heavily in MacArthur's thinking. He and the senator, leader of the main body of conservative Republicans, were not friends on a personal basis but by correspondence had expressed mutual admiration and shared many common views of current national trends and foreign affairs. In May 1946, for example, Taft had written him: "Your course in Japan meets with the approval of all those I talk with. . . . There is general disapproval of the State Department's policies but they are operated in such darkness that very few understand them." He assured MacArthur, "We are doing the best we can to keep the left wing from taking over the government." In the fall of 1947 General Albert C. Wedemeyer, a Taft adviser who had formerly headed the American forces in the China theater, wrote MacArthur: "I predict, that should you return early next spring, you will be acclaimed by a vast majority as the logical man to be President in this critical period of our history. . . . I know Bob and Martha Taft quite well and I am quite certain that he would throw his support in your direction."[13]

Hanford MacNider, a retired general who had served under MacArthur in both world wars and now was a well-to-do cement manufacturer in Iowa, told MacArthur in September 1947 that his leadership was needed "if we are to save this republic." Not having received an answer to his June letter, Wood wrote the general again in October. He observed that "whatever city I go to, I am visited by many prominent businessmen or professional men . . . who are tremendously anxious to see you nominated." He pleaded for some indication of MacArthur's position, because to the many inquirers "I can only state that I know nothing whatever of your plans, that I do not know what your ideas are on the subject, I do not know when you will come back and I do not know at the present time how to start a boom though I would be prepared to support such a movement with all my influence and with plenty of money if it is needed."[14]

Their letters crossed in the mails, for MacArthur had written Wood on October 15, finally committing himself to accept a presidential nomination. The previous day he had sent a similarly worded notification to MacNider, confidentially channeled through Brigadier General Harold E. Eastwood, a mutual friend and MacArthur's G-4, or assistant chief of staff for supply. The general made three main points. First, he did not "covet or actively seek" the presidency "or any other office." Second, if the Mac-Arthur-for-President movement should demonstrate strong popular backing, "there would be no other course open to me but to accept it as a mandate and risk the hazards and responsibilities involved." Just as he wanted the letters held "in the highest confidence," he also felt that "it is yet premature to make any decision or to commit myself" publicly to seeking the Republican nomination.[15]

In his reply to MacArthur, Wood, who had been in close touch with MacNider and La Follette, provided the general with "an estimate of the situation" that is an enlightening synopsis of their thinking on the strategy of the projected MacArthur campaign and its evolution to that stage in the fall of 1947:

> There is an increasing number of men, some of them very important men both in business and politics, who are swinging over to the belief that you are the one man best qualified to lead this country in the four years of great decisions that lie ahead of us. This movement, as yet, is unorganized and I, personally, do not believe the time is right to organize. I think your greatest danger lies in the misplaced enthusiasm and loyalty of your friends, not alone in this country, but among your staff in Tokyo.
>
> If a national movement for you is launched too soon, all it means is that the smearing, sniping, and belittling campaign will be started by your opponents, and you have no organization to reply to such a campaign. . . . I do not think any movement should be started until one, two or, at most, three months before the convention. However, I do think that the movement in Wisconsin is all right, because it is essential that we have at least one delegation from one state that will present your name, and I think that is well taken care of. From all I hear, you will get 20 to 27 of the 29 Wisconsin delegates. In Wisconsin you have Lansing Hoyt with one set of followers, you have Phil La Follette who commands most of the old Progressive Party, and you have Fred Zimmerman, one of the shrewdest Republican politicians in the state. He led the Dewey forces in 1944, but he is today very strongly in favor of supporting you and will work in the state of Wisconsin.
>
> Another reason why I believe it is inadvisable to organize nationally at the present time is the effect on the other candidates. Coalitions would be formed and the general attitude would be unfriendly. On the other hand, if you were to appear only as a compromise candidate, certainly the Taft forces, in the event of a deadlock, would be

willing to throw their strength to you. This might not be possible if a national political movement in your behalf were started at the present time.

Outside of Wisconsin, I do not think the time to strike has yet come. I talked with Lansing Hoyt in Milwaukee yesterday and told him that, in my opinion, it would be a very great mistake to launch a national organization at the present time, at least one with any publicity. I believe a little later we can call a secret meeting and get one man of substance, ability and political skill in each state who is devoted to your interest, and who would be ready to set up an organization when the proper moment arrives. I do not believe the time has yet come for it to be stated publicly that you would accept the nomination. . . .

The one great question is whether you should return and the time of your return. . . . It is the one point on which I disagree with Phil La Follette. I do believe it is essential for you to make a visit to the United States and at least show yourself to the people of the United States, but that visit should be timed sometime in March, April, or May.[16]

MacArthur's response to Wood indicated that he went along with the proposed strategy generally, but he recoiled at the notion of returning before the Republican convention in June. It seemed to him "unwise" and "politically unsound" to make such a trip, for "it would instantly project me actively into the political arena, regardless of how scrupulously I sought to avoid political implications." Undoubtedly thinking of the need to be in good stead with Taft at convention time, he stressed that his premature return "would crystallize the bitterness in other Republican camps." He declared, "Should I be selected as the standard bearer of the Republican Party by the National Convention, I should, of course, look upon it as a mandate" and would "actively enter the ensuing campaign to win the election."[17] In other words, he wanted to be President, but he was not willing to make that desire public until he was chosen by the convention. Of course, this stand, if held inflexibly in the coming months, would enormously handicap the efforts of those working in his behalf.

As the lengthy selection from Wood's letter sets forth by implication, four of the key questions that would determine whether the MacArthur-for-President campaign had any hope were already in the minds of Wood, MacNider, and La Follette: (1) Could an effective organization be established in time at the ward, county, and state levels? (2) Was the Wisconsin situation, where the crucial primary test would take place, as secure as reported? (3) In case of a convention deadlock in June, would Taft and his followers support MacArthur? (4) Could MacArthur be persuaded to return and campaign for the nomination? At least they had obtained more from the general than his 1944 campaign leaders had gotten: they had his written pledge, though yet confidential, that he would be agreeable to serving as the Republican candidate if, in effect, he were drafted. Confronted by severe limitations and uncertain possibilities, MacArthur's national "political advisory committee" of Wood, MacNider, and La Follette decided to move ahead, but cautiously.

On November 15, 1947, however, just nine days after Wood's letter, Hoyt defied the counsel of Wood and convened a well-publicized meeting in Milwaukee of thirty-nine delegates from MacArthur clubs in ten states. In his opening speech, which even the *Nippon Times* quoted, Hoyt proclaimed, "We have reason to believe General MacArthur will accept the presidential nomination when it is offered to him. Otherwise, we would not engage in this great cause." Joseph Choate, a Los Angeles attorney and 1944 supporter, read a letter that MacArthur had sent him, though it was of unknown vintage and did not mention presidential politics. Some policy resolutions were enacted, and a loose national organization was set up. It was announced that a MacArthur delegate slate would be entered in the Wisconsin and Nebraska primaries. Elsewhere the MacArthur clubs, for the most part, were to work on persuading their state delegations to the Republican convention to accept MacArthur as their second preference.[18] Hoyt and his group were off in one direction; Wood and his colleagues preferred another route. It was not the best of beginnings for the MacArthur campaign.

2. *Thwarted Again*

When "Colonel" McCormick visited Japan in November 1947, he met with MacArthur three times: at lunch on the 2d, dinner on the 9th, and a late afternoon session on the 12th. In a press inter-

view shortly after his arrival in Tokyo, he avowed that he "would
certainly support General MacArthur for President if the Chief
would be a candidate." At some point during their talks, however,
he told the general that Taft was his first preference and Mac-
Arthur second, but he would support the latter if a convention
stalemate developed. Wood later wrote MacArthur that Mc-
Cormick had said this to him, too. After returning to Chicago,
McCormick publicly announced that Taft was his first preference.
He and his Chicago *Tribune* continued to support MacArthur over
Dewey, Stassen, and other contenders, but not as avidly as before
the publisher's trip to Japan. McCormick's visit had coincided with
SCAP's push to secure enactment of the deconcentration bill, the
main anti-Zaibatsu measure. An early study of MacArthur suggests this was an important factor: "McCormick expressed to
MacArthur his concern over the 'socialistic economic policies' he
was implementing in Japan. MacArthur replied to this effect: 'This
is not socialism. But it would be better for Japan to have real socialism, than the socialism of the monopolies.' " Perhaps having
McCormick in mind, Eichelberger confided to Roy W. Howard, of
the Scripps-Howard newspaper chain, that in MacArthur's
"squabble" with *Newsweek* over his anti-Zaibatsu program "a great
mistake has been made, which may be far reaching."[19]

Other unexpected turns lay ahead for the MacArthurites on the
long road to the convention. In a sudden move on January 22,
1948, Eisenhower sent a public letter to the editor of the Manchester, New Hampshire, *Union Leader,* who had recently endorsed Ike for the presidency, announcing, "I am not available for
and could not accept nomination for high political office." This
was good news to the MacArthur camp, but Ike's further exposition in the letter seemed to reflect against MacArthur: "It is my
conviction that the necessary and wise subordination of the military to civic power will be best sustained, and our people will have
greater confidence that it is so sustained, when lifelong professional soldiers, in the absence of some obvious and overriding reasons, abstain from seeking high political office." He continued: "In
the American scene, I see no dearth of men fitted by training, talent, and integrity for national leadership. On the other hand,
nothing in the international or domestic situation especially qual-
ifies for the most important office in the world a man whose adult

years have been spent in the country's military forces." After a flurry of public protests from MacArthur supporters, Eisenhower explained in a National Press Club speech in early February that his earlier statement had not been "intended as a slap at General MacArthur's possible candidacy. . . . I resent any implication that any army officer is ready to crucify another officer. . . . I hope he [MacArthur] feels the same friendship for me that I do for him. I would never knowingly do anything to damage him." Nevertheless, Roy E. Larsen, a *Time-Life* executive, predicted accurately in a letter to Eichelberger that Ike's remarks had hurt the Mac-Arthur cause: "I think it makes it very tough for MacArthur to encourage any talk of himself for the job, and it seems to me that, if there should be any 'draft,' Eisenhower has clinched his hold on the American people with his pronouncement."[20]

In the New York *Journal-American,* the San Francisco *Examiner,* and other Hearst papers across the country on March 1, a bold-type front-page editorial was published under the large headline THE MAN OF THE HOUR. Marking the all-out entry of the Hearst press in the campaign, it proclaimed: "None of the avowed candidates for the Presidency meets the public need. . . . If we are to save ourselves from our own follies, we must DRAFT General MacArthur for the Presidency." *Time* dismissed it as "one last try" by "gaunt old William Randolph Hearst, who always hankered to be or make a U.S. president." The Pittsburgh *Press* editor felt pity for "the Man of the Hour": "It looks as if MacArthur has been booby-trapped. . . . He's too smart to ask for a political kiss of death. . . . Some weird things have happened already in the campaign . . . but nobody else has suffered so extreme an embarrassment as that of becoming 'the Hearst candidate.' " On the same day as the Hearst endorsement, the Republican National Committee made public a letter from MacArthur commending the drive to establish Young Republican clubs on college campuses. But most of his message was filled with plaudits for the Republican party, which "has never deviated from the proposition that all political power resides in the people." Representative Albert Miller, who was busy setting up a MacArthur slate of delegates for the Nebraska primary in mid-April, said the message would "dispel any doubts" that the general was a Republican and insisted "I know" he would accept the party nomination if it was tendered. At the time far more attention was paid to the sensational Hearst kick-off.[21]

As it turned out, his message to the Republican brass was a harbinger, for MacArthur suddenly announced on March 9, 1948:

> I have been informed that petitions have been filed in Madison, signed by many of my fellow citizens of Wisconsin, presenting my name to the electorate for consideration at the primary on April 6th. I am deeply grateful for this spontaneous display of friendly confidence. No man could fail to be profoundly stirred by such a public movement in this hour of momentous import, national and international, temporal and spiritual. While it seems unnecessary for me to repeat that I do not actively seek or covet any office and have no plans for leaving my post in Japan, I can say, and with due humility, that I would be recreant to all my concepts of good citizenship were I to shrink because of the hazards and responsibilities involved from accepting any public duty to which I might be called by the American people.[22]

What motivated him to "go public" at this particular time? Whitney maintained that MacArthur was angered by mounting attacks on him as "the man on horseback" by William Z. Foster, head of the American Communist party, and by its organ, the *Daily Worker;* he said MacArthur gave him the draft statement and remarked, "That will be my answer to Mr. Foster." Another view is that "the assertion in mid-February by David Lawrence [editor of *U.S. News & World Report*] that MacArthur was preparing formally to withdraw himself from contention for the GOP nomination brought the question of an availability announcement to a head." The day after the announcement Hoyt, who was "jubilant at the news," told reporters "the General had been informed that petitions bearing more than 100,000 signatures had been entered for MacArthur delegate-candidates in next month's Wisconsin primary," and he believed "that factor had influenced the General's decision." Probably most crucial to MacArthur's timing, Wood had recently informed him that the Wisconsin situation was deteriorating and a primary defeat was likely unless he made a public statement that he would accept the nomination if it was offered.[23]

Of course, the announcement was enthusiastically received by MacArthur campaigners and extolled by the Hearst and McCormick papers. Some reactions, however, were more sober. In Tokyo the Pacific edition of *Stars and Stripes* had given the announcement a front-page spread that began, "General Douglas MacArthur will run for the Presidency of the United States!" A sarcastic *New Yorker* writer wondered how *Stars and Stripes* "had managed to boost the General over the troublesome hurdle of the nominating convention with such dispatch." *The Nation* reported that MacArthur's announcement "has been received with no more enthusiasm by professional Republican politicians than they accorded the unofficial boom for General Eisenhower. MacArthur's supporters, like Eisenhower's, will have to depend on a ground swell in the country and a miracle at the convention."[24]

An American correspondent in Japan observed that in that country the reaction to MacArthur's announcement was me. "with a mixture of approval and regret." The general's "pronouncement was issued on the day that Japan's new Prime Minister, Hitoshi Ashida, revealed the line-up of his Cabinet. . . . Almost without exception, Japanese newspapers played the MacArthur statement in the lead spot on Page One and shoved the Cabinet story into a secondary position." Actually public reactions are difficult to evaluate, because Japanese publications were forbidden by SCAP regulations from printing anything derogatory about MacArthur.[25] Many years later the *Mainichi Daily News* provided a glimpse of some of the favorable and amusing public manifestations:

> Journalistic tones were barely sufficient to reflect the enthusiastic sentiments of the Japanese people, however. Local MacArthur supporters joined the bandwagon in droves, and hand-painted signs began appearing all over Tokyo. One read "Pray for Gen. MacArthur's Success in the Presidential Election," while another ambitiously declared, "We, the Japanese people, hope to see Gen. MacArthur as the President of the United States in order to prevent the annihalation (sic) of humauity (sic) and for overcoming the world crisis." One sign was apparently authored by someone afflicted with the "r-l" bugaboo; it simply read, "We want Gen. MacArthur erected."[26]

Skeptics may wonder whether the people behind such efforts may not really have been placating their military overlord or even assisting in his more rapid departure. At least one GHQ officer thought MacArthur's politics harmed his image in Japan. Major General William A. Beiderlinden, the crusty assistant chief of staff for personnel and administration (G-1) of the Far East Command,

maintained that in Japanese public respect "MacArthur was second to the Emperor up until he tried to get nominated for President. . . . He lost a lot in Japanese opinion." His stock would have
been higher among some of his officers, too, asserted Beiderlinden, if he had not been so absorbed in politics: "That MacArthur
was, in fact, politically motivated in everything that he did, and
was avid to become President, was well recognized in FECOM
headquarters. This was one aspect of things that one had always
to reckon with in dealing with him."[27] For want of available evidence thus far, the intriguing questions of how much the presidential factor influenced MacArthur's decision-making or affected
the tactics of Japanese leaders in dealing with him must remain
moot.

Besides those who have been previously mentioned as active in
the MacArthur-for-President movement in the States, influential
people who supported the cause, at least through the Wisconsin
primary, included Representative James Van Zandt of Pennsylvania; Juan Trippe, president of Pan American Airways; news-
paper-chain publisher Frank Gannett; John C. O'Laughlin, editor
of the *Army and Navy Journal;* Robert M. Harriss, New York bro-
ker; and Louis B. Mayer, Hollywood producer, to name a few.
Chicago activists included Alfred O'Gara, business executive; Edward A. Hayes, attorney and past national commander of the
American Legion; Henry A. Regnery, book publisher; and Thomas
S. Hammond, industrialist. Hayes and O'Gara formed a Chicago
organization to inaugurate a vigorous nationwide campaign and
file MacArthur slates in numerous primaries. The Wood group,
however, was able to convince them in November 1947 to move
with less haste and to concentrate initially on the Wisconsin primary. In California, Choate, Allen Worcester, Gaetano Faillace
(MacArthur's former staff photographer), and other MacArthur
enthusiasts were dissuaded from plans to enter the general's name
in the California primary, where the heavy favorite already was
Governor Earl Warren. In Arkansas and Illinois plans to file in
primaries were considered by MacArthur activists but shelved for
various reasons. In Nebraska Mrs. Mary Kenney, backed by Representative Miller, succeeded in getting a MacArthur slate of delegates qualified for the April primary there. A full slate in
MacArthur's name was filed for the Republican primary in Wis-

consin. There La Follette and Hoyt had attracted a few able Republican politicians, notably William J. Campbell, Fred R. Zimmerman, and Ralph J. Immell, but most prominent Republicans remained loyal to Coleman's organization, which was backing Stassen. According to the findings of one historian, the typical local or state leader in the MacArthur movement was wealthy, conservative, and, up to 1941, isolationist; he was a businessman, resided in the Midwest, had served in the Army, and was sympathetic to the views of the Taft wing of the Republican party.[28]

"The nuttiest state in the Union" was the way McCormick once characterized Wisconsin politically. Defeat in the Wisconsin primary had been instrumental in dooming the MacArthur-for-President drive in 1944, and now, four years later, the Wisconsin primary was again crucial for the MacArthur camp. The general's campaign leaders thought that he could be portrayed there as a "native son," giving him an advantage over Dewey and Stassen, the other two contenders in the primary. MacArthur's grandfather had served as judge, lieutenant governor, and (very briefly) governor of Wisconsin; his father was reared in Milwaukee, led the 24th Wisconsin Volunteer Regiment in the Civil War, and moved back to Milwaukee in retirement. But Douglas had lived in Wisconsin only for the nineteen months preceding his entry into West Point in 1899. It is doubtful that many Wisconsin voters were swayed by the native-son pitch.

On the surface, the union of Philip La Follette's Progressives and Lansing Hoyt's anti-Coleman Republicans looked promising, but the coalition did not prove effective in coordinating tactics, raising funds, or persuading voters. The MacArthur forces in Wisconsin were unable to win the backing of any of the state's pro-Republican newspapers except the Milwaukee *Sentinel,* a Hearst publication. "Boss" Coleman and his regular Republicans scored heavily from the start in portraying La Follette as an exploiter of the MacArthur cause to resurrect his declining political career. In the 1930s Philip La Follette had been elected governor three times, first as a Republican and then twice as a Progressive. After he was defeated for re-election in 1938, he became an ardent isolationist spokesman for the America First Committee and later joined MacArthur's staff during the war. His Progressive organization was in disarray when he returned from the Southwest Pacific. In 1946

Senator Robert M. La Follette, Jr., his brother, lost in the primary
to Coleman's candidate, Joseph R. McCarthy. After MacArthur's
statement of March 9, the Coleman machine, states an authority,
"raised an issue which ultimately overshadowed all others — that
[Philip] La Follette, the Progressives, and the dissident Republicans were using MacArthur as a popular vehicle to take over the
Republican Party" in the state.[29]

Not only the absence of MacArthur himself but also the lack of
any statements by him on the issues raised in the Wisconsin campaign seriously handicapped the La Follette–Hoyt forces. The
Progressives stressed the general's liberal accomplishments in Japan; Hoyt's group, mostly conservatives, followed the line of the
Milwaukee *Sentinel* in emphasizing his qualities as an anti-Communist leader. Not convinced that MacArthur would really run for
the presidency, some Wisconsin critics, prior to his announcement
of March 9, charged that his backers were merely providing a
"stalking horse" for Taft. Returning to campaign for Stassen,
Senator McCarthy took some pot shots at MacArthur, referring to
his divorce (in 1929) and maintaining that at his advanced age he
was "ready for retirement." The most scathing attacks by Coleman's politicians and papers, however, were levied against the slate
of MacArthur primary delegates, who were pictured as extreme
rightists or persons of no standing in their communities. Most of
the delegates, in fact, represented a fair cross-section of classes and
beliefs in Wisconsin, but nearly all the state papers except the Hearst
journal denounced them as unfit.[30] A fundamental weakness of
the MacArthur drive in Wisconsin was inadequate funding, as explained by the principal authority on the campaign:

> Surprisingly, although the MacArthur movement had a reputation
> for being supported by the wealthy, the MacArthur campaign in
> Wisconsin did not do as well financially as the two opposing cam-
> paigns. . . . Several explanations exist for this phenomenon. Basic is
> the fact that MacArthur's opponents each possessed comprehensive
> national organizations on which they could rely to channel funds to
> Wisconsin. Only with great difficulty could potential MacArthur con-
> tributors be turned from concentration upon the national picture. Most
> simply failed to understand the crucial importance of the Wisconsin
> race to the overall strategy. Another likely explanation is that con-

servative Republican contributors simply preferred the more traditional Taft candidacy.

Wood, La Follette, and Immell raised the majority of the funds for the Wisconsin campaign from groups outside Wisconsin, primarily Wood's associates in Chicago and a group of New York businessmen. In view of the wealth of these men, their contributions are surprisingly modest. . . .

All of this meant that the campaign suffered continually from a lack of field people, campaign literature, and newspaper and radio publicity. . . . An even more unfortunate aspect of the lack of funding was that as a result the Hearst and McCormick press, over which the MacArthur organizations had no control, directed the majority of the publicity.[31]

Harold Stassen, former governor of neighboring Minnesota, crisscrossed Wisconsin repeatedly in robust rounds of stump speaking. Coleman's organization and its supporting newspapers, especially the Madison *Wisconsin State Journal,* gave the Stassen campaign powerful backing while viciously assailing the MacArthur delegates and Philip La Follette's attempt to return to power. The Madison *Capital Times,* a Democratic paper, joined in the criticism of La Follette; it also pointed out that Robert La Follette was "keeping a significant silence" about the MacArthur drive. The Veterans Against MacArthur organization, which was active at the University of Wisconsin, was a further embarrassment to the MacArthurites, especially since chapters were spreading in at least six other states, mostly on college campuses. In early April, Dewey, anxious about the challenge by Stassen, arrived in Wisconsin for several days of campaigning. Despite a host of negative signs, the MacArthur camp thought its candidate's chances had improved since his statement of March 9 and was extremely optimistic on the eve of the primary voting. Even the *New York Times* predicted a MacArthur triumph, possibly because out-of-state reporters concentrated on Milwaukee, where MacArthur's support was the strongest.[32]

To say the least, the MacArthur forces were shocked by the primary results in Wisconsin on April 6: Stassen won easily, getting nineteen delegates to eight for MacArthur and none for Dewey. None of the MacArthur delegates-at-large was elected, including

Philip La Follette, who received fewer votes than any of Stassen's delegates-at-large. The popular vote looked better, but could not have been of much consolation to the general's followers: Stassen, 40 percent; MacArthur, 36 percent; Dewey, 24 percent. In Tokyo the following day William Sebald, the State Department's top man in Japan, came to the Dai Ichi Building for a conference with MacArthur. "But the Chief of Staff, Major General Paul J. Mueller, who had kept himself strictly aloof from politics," remarked Sebald, "held up a warning hand. 'The General is as low as a rug and very disappointed,' Mueller said. I decided to delay my visit until a more propitious time." With Representative Miller and various editorialists speculating publicly that the general might withdraw his name from further consideration, Wood, MacNider, and other friends wrote to MacArthur that the cause was not lost and urged him to stay in the running.[33]

But a week later, on April 13, Stassen was triumphant in the Nebraska primary; Dewey finished second, Taft third, Vandenberg fourth, and MacArthur fifth. As in Wisconsin, the MacArthur organization left much to be desired. But far more so than in Wisconsin, says one source, "most of the people who came forward were political novices, incompetents, or primarily associated with anti-Communist, extremist organizations." Mrs. Kenney, a virulent anti-Communist, and Representative Miller, neither of whom commanded much respect in the state's regular Republican hierarchy, spearheaded the disastrous campaign in Nebraska.

Wood now renewed his plea to MacArthur to return, but the Supreme Commander again adamantly refused. He said it would place him "in a most untenable position" and subject him to criticism for "projecting myself actively into the campaign." He obviously was stung by the Wisconsin and Nebraska setbacks but also seemed to be acutely conscious of the public's sensitivity to the military-civilian relationship that Eisenhower had stressed in his January statement of noncandidacy.[34] When the Senate Appropriations Committee asked him to testify personally in Washington on funding needs "affecting the Far East," he replied to Chairman Styles Bridges on May 28:

> In normal circumstances, I should respond at once to your present invitation as a citizen and servant of the Republic and sit in with you

frankly to state my views. . . . But the existing circumstances are not normal and my return at this time, however sincere its purpose, would be misunderstood and condemned by many as politically inspired and much that I might be obligated in good conscience to say would lose its effect under the impeaching process of doubt thereby aroused in the public mind. . . .

. . . It would be peculiarly repugnant to me to have it felt that I sought to capitalize to political advantage, as many have frankly urged, the public goodwill which might manifest itself upon my first return to American soil following the Pacific war. For such goodwill would find its inspiration in the victory which crowned our Pacific war effort to which countless gallant Americans, living and dead, contributed by unfailing and invincible devotion. Usurpation of such goodwill by me to serve a political end would be a shameful breach of their faith and a betrayal of the mutual trust on which was erected the cornerstone to the Pacific victory. . . .

. . . Were I permitted to give but one word of advice toward the safeguard of the national interest, I should elect to urge that we reaffirm the basic concepts which safely guided our past, and above all else regain some of Lincoln's faith in the wisdom of the people.[35]

At the Republican National Convention in Philadelphia in late June, the eight-man MacArthur delegation from Wisconsin was headed by Harlan Kelley, who was a blind Milwaukee attorney with a reputation as an eloquent speaker. Earlier, he had received MacArthur's approval to deliver the nominating speech. General Jonathan M. Wainwright volunteered to give the seconding address. Now an insurance-company president but in declining health, Wainwright, it will be recalled, had succeeded MacArthur in command of the unsuccessful defense of the Philippines in 1942 and, following the archipelago's surrender, had spent the rest of the war in Japanese prison camps. MacArthur had vented his wrath on Wainwright during the last days before Bataan's fall and had temporarily succeeded in denying him a Medal of Honor. But the two had become fast friends after their reunion on the occasion of the Japanese surrender ceremony in Tokyo Bay in September 1945. Wainwright concluded that MacArthur "will forever stand as one of the great captains of history" and, beginning in May 1948, had spoken out in support of him for the Republican nomination. At Philadelphia the nominating process began on the evening of June 25, but it moved slowly as the speeches and demonstrations followed the nominations of Dewey, Stassen, Taft, Vandenberg, and a number of favorite-son candidates. MacArthur's nomination had to await the roll-call progression finally to Wisconsin. By then it was shortly after 4:00 A.M., the convention hall was largely empty, and the two MacArthur speakers, Kelley and Wainwright, stood before "row upon row of empty chairs." When the voting began later that day, Dewey took a strong lead on the first ballot with 434 votes; Taft received 224 votes; Stassen, 157; Vandenberg, 62; and MacArthur, 8. On the third ballot Dewey got the nomination, and Earl Warren was subsequently selected as his vice presidential running mate.[36]

In Tokyo, Eastwood found MacArthur "keyed up" before the convention vote but "not so sharp" after the news of Dewey's victory arrived. Whitney observed that, on getting the results, the general "hung his head in deep emotional stress." MacArthur later wrote MacNider that "from the start I had no illusions concerning the prospects of my nomination, as I understood fully the strength of the forces opposed."[37] On June 26, the day the convention picked Dewey, MacArthur sent the following cable to Hearst:

> Now that the Republican convention has passed into history, I wish to convey my deep sense of gratitude to you for the public confidence and faith you so steadfastly and eloquently have voiced in the potentiality of my leadership. In so doing I am fully mindful of the fact that your stand, so firmly taken and magnificently supported, was dictated without the slightest consideration of personality, either yours or mine, but with sole need to the national interest as you viewed it. This is in keeping with your full life of selfless devotion to the American cause, and permits me to thank you not only as a beneficiary of your faith but as a citizen of the republic to which you have contributed so much in spiritual strength. May God bless and preserve you. MacArthur.[38]

On receipt of a prompt letter of gratitude from MacArthur for his seconding speech, Wainwright in his reply commented, "When I went to the Republican Convention in your behalf, I felt that it would be a forlorn hope, but you and I, side by side, have fought a forlorn hope before now." Later that summer MacArthur sent a wire seconding Wainwright's nomination as national commander of the Disabled American Veterans. After winning the election, Wainwright expressed his thanks to MacArthur and closed his letter by summing up his sentiments on the effort to make his former chief the Republican presidential candidate: "I felt that we did all that was humanly possible. . . . . The professional politicians had us beaten from the start with the big machine they had set up and the vast amount of money they spent in seeking their own nominations."[39] Though never professing to be politically astute, Wainwright had touched on the three cardinal failings of the MacArthur-for-President movement: the inability to attract the movers and shakers among the Republican leadership, the absence of an effective organization, and the lack of adequate funding, all of which proved to be interrelated.

Despite the convention defeat, MacArthur was not yet free of the political whirl. In early September La Follette notified Mrs. MacArthur, "There is a move on looking toward the General's being tendered the task of being Dewey's right hand in the whole field of National Defense if the latter is elected — and it is, I think, the consensus of opinion he will be elected." From another direction Wood reported that he had received communications from anti-Truman Democrats who wanted to nominate MacArthur on the Democratic ticket, but the general was not interested by then. Actually a Democrats-for-MacArthur organization had been formed in March 1948. The conservative Southern Democratic vote, some of which might have gone to MacArthur in November had he been the Republican candidate, was largely channeled to the States Rights (Dixiecrat) ticket headed by Governor J. Strom Thurmond of South Carolina. MacArthur had not encouraged a Democratic movement for himself, though some evidence suggests that he briefly considered the idea. "During the Spring of 1948," comments one scholar, "with Republicans and Democrats both supporting him for the presidency, MacArthur foresaw his nomination as a non-partisan president, beloved by all as the man to unite the nation and set it back on the right course. . . . One can hardly blame him for falling victim to the illusion."[40]

After a lackluster campaign characterized by Republican complacency, which was nourished by numerous polls predicting an easy victory, Dewey went down to ignominious defeat in November. At least MacArthur could say that, long before, he had labeled Dewey another Bryan. By the way, the fellow who won the presidential election that autumn was named Truman.

PART II

The Occupation of Japan:
Later Phase

CHAPTER VII

Entrenchment of Conservatism

1. "Reverse Course" in American Policy

WITH THE FULL ONSET of the Cold War in 1947, MacArthur's bailiwick again, as in World War II, was overshadowed by crises elsewhere that commanded higher priority in Washington. During the first half of 1947 alone the fast-breaking developments included Marshall's return from China, where civil war was raging anew; aid, under the new Truman Doctrine, to prevent Communist takeovers in Greece and Turkey; failure of the Moscow Foreign Ministers' Conference; rapidly growing Communist political strength in France and Italy; heightened East-West tensions over Berlin; proclamation of the Marshall Plan to assist European recovery; and spreading nationalist-Communist revolutions in Malaya, Indochina, and the Dutch East Indies. On the State Department's new Policy Planning Staff (PPS), which was headed by George F. Kennan, veteran diplomat and Soviet specialist, work was under way on developing an effective approach to what seemed to be an increasingly aggressive attitude of the Soviet Union. Kennan summarized the policy as one of "long-term, patient but firm and vigilant containment of Russian expansive tendencies" through the "application of counterforce" at "a series of constantly shifting geographical and political points, corresponding to the shifts and maneuvers of Soviet policy." It did not take long for the containment strategists to become alerted to Japan's vulnerability to internal and external Communist incursions and to her potentiality in furthering American political, economic, and military interests in the growing Cold War.

After receiving Marshall's somber assessment of the situation in China and other pessimistic reports from that beleaguered country, State Department leaders, according to Kennan, began to view Japan as "more important than China as a potential factor in world political developments." In an address at Cleveland, Mississippi, on May 8, 1947, Under Secretary of State Dean Acheson, foreshadowing both the European and Japanese recovery programs, called for "the reconstruction of those two great workshops of Europe and Asia — Germany and Japan — upon which the ultimate recovery of the two continents so largely depends." He asserted that the United States was prepared to undertake these missions unilaterally without awaiting support from the other major Allied powers. That summer and fall State and Pentagon officials weighed several SWNCC proposals for restoring Japan, including a $500 million American aid program to boost Japan's economy, partly through removing restraints on her industry and reviving her foreign trade, particularly with Southeast Asia. Under Secretary of the Army William Draper and Secretary of Defense James Forrestal, along with Kennan, strongly favored shifting the emphasis in Japan to recovery and away from reform, especially from the anti-Zaibatsu program enunciated in FEC-230 and now being implemented with vigor by MacArthur.

There was also agreement among these officials, as well as the PPS and SWNCC staffs for the most part, that an early peace treaty for Japan, as MacArthur had called for in March 1947, could launch Japan on her own before political stability and economic revival had been attained, making that nation an attractive target for Communist subversion or even an overt move by the Soviet Union. A preliminary draft treaty, mostly prepared by Hugh Borton of SWNCC, was rejected by Kennan's PPS, in part because of its alleged neglect of America's future need of Japan as a strong, stable, and dependable ally. Nevertheless, that summer the State Department invited the other FEC nations to participate in a preliminary treaty conference, but the meeting was aborted because of procedural objections largely raised by the Soviet Union and Nationalist China. In truth, the more American officials learned of Japan's economic plight, the more relieved they were to post-pone treaty negotiations.[1]

James L. Kauffman, a New York attorney representing a group of large American firms that had prewar investments in Japan, went there in August 1947 on their behalf to study the business situation. The Kauffman Report, dated September 6, went not only to his corporate clients but also, through unofficial channels, to high officials of the Pentagon and State Department. Kauffman, who had obtained a copy of the confidential FEC-230 document while in Tokyo, excoriated its anti-Zaibatsu provisions, along with MacArthur's current deconcentration and purge programs, and expressed dismay over the chaotic conditions in Japanese business and labor. He did not recommend that American investors return to Japan until the American government was willing to "put an end to the economic experiment being conducted in Japan" and "replace the theorists now there with men of ability and experience who can restore Japan's economy." Draper and Forrestal, both formerly with the prestigious Wall Street firm of Dillon, Read, were particularly impressed by the Kauffman Report. One historian describes the impact of the report on Washington as "staggering" and rates it as "one of the most decisive documents in Japan's 're-verse course.'" Kauffman's findings were confirmed by Draper, who flew to Japan later in September, meeting with MacArthur on the 19th and 26th and otherwise conducting his own check of the economic situation. Draper seems to have tried to dissuade the general from pushing the deconcentration bill, the crowning piece of anti-Zaibatsu legislation, but MacArthur allowed the measure to be introduced into the Diet on the 28th and continued to support it through its passage in December.[2]

As in the case of *Newsweek*'s criticism of the economic purge in January, MacArthur overreacted again, assuming a defensive stance regarding his implementation of the offensive against the Zaibatsu that does not appear characteristic of his true feelings, which were mixed but basically concerned for recovery. Colonel Charles Kades, Whitney's deputy chief in the Government Section, was instructed to prepare for MacArthur a detailed refutation of the Kauffman Report. Kades concluded that Kauffman was motivated by "a desire to defend vested interests of his Japanese and American clientele" and that his report presented "a wholly distorted and false view of the occupation." On October 24 Mac-Arthur sent a lengthy radiogram to Secretary of the Army Kenneth C. Royall, defending the Zaibatsu measures as essential to implementing the previous JCS, SWNCC, and FEC directives he had received. "Involved in the failure or success of this program," he argued, "is the choice between a system of free private competitive enterprise . . . [and] a system of private socialism largely owned and operated by and for the benefit of only 10 family clans." If he were compelled to change direction now, he claimed, it "would not only be extraordinarily embarrassing, but what is infinitely more important, it would introduce doubt and confusion in the program, delay and perhaps defeat its accomplishments, and play into the hands of those who have been bitterly opposed to it." When Kauffman later requested permission to return to Japan, Mac-Arthur refused to allow him to come back. His grounds for the exclusion, as he reported to the Pentagon, which backed him, were Kauffman's "security betrayal of a classified document [FEC-230]" and evidence that he was "closely allied in Japan with Zaibatsu and other recalcitrant elements."[3]

Forrestal, Royall, and several other ranking State and Pentagon officials met on October 31 to reconsider FEC-230. Like Draper and Kennan, who already felt it must be shelved, they reached a tentative consensus that the deconcentration drive would have to be halted if Japan was to progress economically. When the Deconcentration Law was enacted in December, it will be remembered, Draper told MacArthur that its implementation was to be held in abeyance pending a final decision on FEC-230. In the meantime, on December 1, *Newsweek* had outraged MacArthur again by publishing an article highly critical of the occupation's policy on big business; the piece included quotations from FEC-230, which was still classified, and from the Kauffman Report. Inflamed by the *Newsweek* account of the "socialist" attacks by the occupation authorities against the Japanese corporate structure, Republican Senator William F. Knowland of California delivered fiery speeches in the Senate in December and January castigating FEC-230 and demanding "a full-scale investigation of American policy in Japan." Knowland, a conservative who generally admired Mac-Arthur, saw the fault for FEC-230 "either originating among doctrinaire New Dealers who found their activities limited in Washington and signed up for overseas occupation service, or finding its fountainhead in the Far Eastern Commission." Nevertheless, the *Newsweek* article and the Senate debate precipitated by Knowland proved extremely humiliating to MacArthur, especially since they came during the critical phase in the passage of the Deconcentration Law.[4]

On February 17, 1948, as the Senate excitement over the issue continued, Senator Brien McMahon of Connecticut read on the floor a letter of February 1 from MacArthur to him. In it the Supreme Commander denied any responsibility for FEC-230's formulation but defended his duty to implement it until a contrary directive was issued. Dramatically predicting a revolution in Japan unless the Zaibatsu dissolution was carried to completion, he appeared to be determined on his course:

> In any evaluation of the economic potential here in Japan it must be understood that the tearing down of the traditional pyramid of economic power which has given only a few Japanese families direct or indirect control over all commerce and industry, all raw materials, all transportation, internal and external, and all coal and other power resources, is the first essential step to the establishment here of an economic system based upon free private competitive enterprise which Japan has never known before. Even more it is indispensable to the growth of democratic government and life, as the abnormal economic system heretofore in existence can only thrive if the people are held in poverty and slavery.
>
> The Japanese people, you may be sure, fully understand the nature of the forces which have so ruthlessly exploited them in the past. . . . These things are so well understood by the Japanese people that apart from our desire to reshape Japanese life toward a capitalistic economy, if this concentration of economic power is not torn down and redistributed peacefully and in due order under the occupation, there is no slightest doubt that its cleansing will eventually occur through a blood bath of revolutionary violence.[5]

It is true that MacArthur had not received explicit orders yet on the "reverse course," as the Japanese would later call the American policy shift away from liberalism. He also did not know that Kennan and Draper had collaborated with Harry F. Kern,

Newsweek's international affairs senior editor, on the controversial December article. But more than three weeks before he had written Senator McMahon, he had received a clear signal on the new policy in the making when Secretary Royall delivered a well-publicized address in San Francisco on January 6. He stated that since the early occupation directives had been issued, "new conditions have arisen — in world politics and economics, in problems of national defense, and in humanitarian considerations. These changes must now be fully taken into account in determining our future course" in Japan. He emphasized that "deconcentration must stop short of the point where it unduly interferes with the efficiency of Japanese industry. Earlier programs are being reexamined — as for example . . . FEC-230. We are not averse to modifying programs in the interests of our broad objectives." Subsequently, on March 12, the United States informed the FEC that it was withdrawing its support of FEC-230.[6]

Since MacArthur was apparently still opposed to or confused about the evolution of Washington thinking on the Zaibatsu dissolution, Kennan flew to Tokyo to confer with him, arriving on March 1. He later observed that relations between SCAP and the State Department "had been so distant and so full of distrust that my mission was like nothing more than that of an envoy charged with opening up communications and arranging the establishment of diplomatic relations with a hostile and suspicious foreign government." After forty-eight hours of travel and no sleep, Kennan met with the general on the day he landed. Kennan recalled that MacArthur subjected him to a two-hour monologue in which he proclaimed, among other things, that "the Japanese were thirsty for guidance and inspiration; it was his aim to bring them both democracy and Christianity. . . . The Communists were no menace in Japan." Kennan and General Cortlandt V. R. Schuyler, who accompanied him on the journey, were then given several days of briefings by SCAP officers on sundry activities of the occupation. Finally on March 5 Kennan obtained a private evening interview with the Supreme Commander and was able to get in more than a few words about Washington's changing outlook on occupation objectives.[7] The two got along amiably, and MacArthur seemed far less inflexible than his public statements suggested, as Kennan's version of the long session indicates:

We discussed — without exception, I think — all the leading problems of occupational policy as well as the problems of relations with our former allies in matters affecting the occupation and the peace treaty. He gave his views freely and encouraged me to do likewise. I could see that he was himself not unaware of some of the dangers that had suggested themselves to us, and that he felt, no less than we did, the need for changing and modifying a number of the occupational policies. What worried him particularly was the opposition that any such changes might be expected to encounter on the part of the Allies, as represented in the Far Eastern Commission. . . . I pointed out that the advisory capacity of the Far Eastern Commission related solely to the responsibility he bore for executing and enforcing the terms of the Japanese surrender. . . . These terms have now been carried out. He could thereby be said to have carried to completion that portion of his responsibility, flowing from the terms of surrender, with relation to which the Far Eastern Commission was qualified to advise him. The changes in occupation policy that were now required were ones relating to an objective — namely, the economic rehabilitation of Japan and the restoration of her ability to contribute constructively to the stability and prosperity of the Far Eastern region — the necessity of which did not flow from the terms of surrender but rather from the delay in negotiation of a peace treaty. There had been no international agreement on the policies and methods to be applied in this unforeseen situation. This being the case, the United States government and he as its commander in Japan had to exercise an independent judgment. I saw no need for him, in these circumstances, to consult the Far Eastern Commission or to feel himself bound by views it had expressed at earlier dates with a view to implementing the terms of surrender. . . .

This thesis appeared to please the general mightily; he even slapped his thigh in approval; and we parted with a common feeling, I believe, of having reached a general meeting of the minds.

From that moment things went very well.[8]

In his memoirs, however, Kennan says that, up to then, "the policies of SCAP had brought Japanese life to a point of great turmoil and confusion, and had produced, momentarily at least, a serious degree of instability." More harshly, he contends that "the nature of the occupational policies pursued up to that time by General MacArthur's headquarters seemed on cursory examination to be such that if they had been devised for the specific purpose of rendering Japanese society vulnerable to Communist political pressures and paving the way for a Communist takeover, they could scarcely have been other than what they were."[9] Undoubtedly he did not express these opinions to the general personally, or things would not have gone "very well."

On the day of Kennan's third and final visit with MacArthur, March 21, the Supreme Commander hosted a luncheon for Draper and an economic mission of corporate executives headed by Percy H. Johnston, board chairman of the New York Chemical Bank. The distinguished group also included Paul G. Hoffman, president of Studebaker Corporation and former Marshall Plan administrator. They had received the rather rare honor of being welcomed by MacArthur at Haneda Airport when they landed the previous day. Draper, Johnston, and some or all of the other mission members met with the general on five occasions between March 20 and April 2. According to one source, Draper "made it known to SCAP that the reform phase of the occupation had ended and that further dissolution of the Zaibatsu would hamper the realization of a self-supporting Japan as the foundation upon which the United States sought to build its policies in the Pacific." Like Clifford Strike's second report, in February 1948, which had favored higher production levels for Japanese industry and opposed severe reparations, the Draper-Johnston Report, released in late April, emphasized industrial revival and curtailment of reparations, along with considerable American aid to rebuild Japan's shipping and foreign trade.[10]

The "economic crank-up," as it was sometimes called by Washington planners, was manifested tangibly in June when Congress appropriated $530 million in assistance for Japan, much of it in the new Economic Rehabilitation of Occupied Areas (EROA) legislation. The EROA program, states one scholar, was "the capstone in the initial United States commitment to Japanese economic recovery," and Draper hailed it as a Far Eastern equivalent of the Marshall Plan, with Japan as the "focal point" of the entire region. Essentially, the program would provide funds for promoting Southeast Asian exports of raw materials to Japan which, in turn, would stimulate Japanese production of manufactured goods for export to Southeast Asia particularly, but also to other areas.[11]

After Kennan returned from Japan, he submitted his report to

Marshall on March 25 regarding changes in American policy in Japan. The document, designated PPS 28, gradually made its way through the State Department, Pentagon, and National Security Council channels and eventually became the basis (indeed, much of Kennan's wording was retained) for the formal policy statement issued that autumn on the change in emphasis from reform to restoration. Kennan later remarked, "I consider my part in bringing about this change to have been, after the Marshall Plan, the most significant constructive contribution I was ever able to make in government."[12] Some parts of the reverse course had started being implemented in March, but the explicit directive MacArthur had needed came with the National Security Council's adoption of the Kennan-originated document, NSC 13/2, on October 7, 1948, and its approval by Truman two days later. NSC 13/2, which bears the title "Report by the National Security Council on Recommendations with Respect to United States Policy Toward Japan," is ranked with the "United States Initial Post-Surrender Policy" of September 1945 as the two most significant directives on the occupation.

The opening sentence clearly reveals the Cold War's impact on the altered United States viewpoint toward Japan: "In view of the differences which have developed among the interested countries regarding the procedure and substance of a Japanese peace treaty and in view of the serious international situation created by the Soviet Union's policy of aggressive Communist expansion this Government should not press for a treaty of peace at this time." On a future settlement, it adds, "it should be our aim to have the treaty, when finally negotiated, as brief, as general, and as nonpunitive as possible."

American tactical units and bases should be retained in Japan at least until the peace treaty becomes effective, but "every effort . . . should be made to reduce to a minimum the psychological impact of occupational forces on the Japanese population." The post-treaty retention of American troops and stations in Japan should await the peace negotiations and should be decided "in the light of the prevailing international situation and of the degree of internal stability achieved in Japan." In the meantime, however, "the Japanese Police establishment, including the coastal patrol, should be strengthened by the re-enforcing and re-equipping of the present forces, and by expanding the present centrally directed police organization."

By the terms of NSC 13/2, MacArthur was "to inform the Japanese Government informally that no further extension of the purge is contemplated and that the purge should be modified" to permit several large categories of purged persons to apply for reexamination of eligibility for public positions. As for war crimes trials, since all the "Class A" (major) cases had been tried, "we should continue and push to an early conclusion" the remaining "Class B" and "C" (lesser) suspects' cases. The occupation costs paid by the Japanese government "should continue to be reduced to the maximum extent consonant with the policy objectives." (Such costs took a third of Japan's budget in 1948.) Protection against a revived "economic war potential" should now involve only restrictions on "stockpiling of designated strategic raw materials" and "prohibition of the manufacture of weapons of war and civil aircraft." Among sundry other matters covered in NSC 13/2, "precensorship of the Japanese press should cease"; American government radio broadcasts to Japan should be undertaken, possibly from Okinawa, "with a view to developing an understanding and appreciation of American ideas"; and "the interchange between Japan and the United States of scholars, teachers, lecturers, scientists, and technicians should be strongly encouraged."

Although there should not be "any major change in the regime of control," and MacArthur's "existing rights and powers" should be maintained, NSC 13/2 stipulates that "responsibility should be placed to a steadily increasing degree in the hands of the Japanese Government." Moreover, "the view of the United States Government should be communicated to SCAP that the scope of its operations should be reduced as rapidly as possible, with a corresponding reduction in personnel, to a point where its mission will consist largely of general supervisory observation of the activities of the Japanese Government and of contact with the latter at high levels on questions of broad governmental policy."

The retreat from reform is clearly evident in NSC 13/2: "Henceforth emphasis should be given to Japanese assimilation of the reform programs." But MacArthur "should be advised not to press upon the Japanese Government any further reform legislation." He "should be advised to relax pressure steadily but unobtrusively on the Japanese Government in connection with" reform measures already enacted. MacArthur "should intervene only if the Japanese authorities revoke or compromise the fundamentals of the reforms as they proceed in their own way with the process of implementation and adjustment."

On the key matter of economic restoration, NSC 13/2 is explicit on the high priority it now commanded in official Washington: "Second only to U.S. security interests, economic recovery should be made the primary objective of United States policy in Japan for the coming period." Such recovery

> should be sought through a combination of United States aid program[s] envisaging shipments and/or credits on a declining scale over a number of years, and by a vigorous and concerted effort by all interested agencies and departments of the United States Government to cut away existing obstacles to the revival of Japanese foreign trade, with provision for Japanese merchant shipping, and to facilitate restoration and development of Japan's exports. In developing Japan's internal and external trade and industry, private enterprise should be encouraged. Recommendations concerning the implementation of the above points, formulated in the light of Japan's economic relationship with other Far Eastern countries, should be worked out between the State and Army Departments after consultation with the other interested departments and agencies of the Government. We should make it clear to the Japanese Government that the success of the recovery program will in large part depend on Japanese efforts to raise production and to maintain high export levels through hard work, a minimum of work-stoppages, internal austerity measures and the stern combatting of inflationary trends including efforts to achieve a balanced internal budget as rapidly as possible.[13]

The same month that NSC 13/2 was adopted, Yoshida returned to the premiership, succeeding Ashida, and three months later his Liberal party, for the first time, won an absolute majority of seats in the Diet. Once the conservatives were firmly entrenched in power, both the Japanese government and SCAP would become decreasingly tolerant of left-wing objections to the movement away from the occupation's earlier idealistic endeavors. A former Japanese bureaucrat recalled, "After 1948 the leftists would still be noisy nuisances, but never again would they think they had the blessing of the American authorities and never again would they seriously threaten conservative rule in Japan."

The shift in American policy also affected GHQ. In the years 1948 to 1950 the number of SCAP, GHQ, personnel was reduced from 3500 to 2000 (excluding Japanese employees); only a small percentage were Army officers, but they still held most of the top positions. During this period Whitney's Government Section was cut more than two-thirds in personnel. The Government Section was no longer pulsating with reform proposals, but, instead, quietly trying to protect the advances made in democracy and civil rights. It seems more than coincidental that the Government Section's two-volume history, *Political Reorientation of Japan,* ends in September 1948, a month before the promulgation of NSC 13/2. With the stress henceforth on economic restoration and political stability, Marquat's Economic and Scientific Section and Willoughby's Civil Intelligence Section became the most active SCAP civil agencies.[14]

Although officially charged with implementing rather than creating policy, MacArthur previously had enjoyed a larger degree of freedom in interpreting his orders than Washington intended, because, except for SWNCC, integrated planning was inadequate at the top levels of the armed services and between the Pentagon and the State Department. But the reorganization of the military establishment under the National Security Act of July 1947 had improved cooperation between the services and between the military and diplomatic agencies in policy coordination. SWNCC was reconstituted after the July act as the State-Army-Navy-Air Force Coordinating Committee (SANACC), and in August 1948 it was divested of its occupation responsibilities. Yet by late 1948 MacArthur had to look for guidance not only to the JCS but also to a fairly unified State-Army team on Japanese affairs, which was led by Kennan and Draper, the principal architects of the reverse course. Working closely together were the Army's Office of the Under Secretary and Civil Affairs Division and the State Department's Policy Planning Staff and Office of Far Eastern Affairs. Top-level planning now was to be integrated by the National Security Council.

Most crucial to MacArthur's exercise of power, he had lost the maneuverability he had formerly had as the wearer of "two hats" — an American general and an international commander. Alluding to MacArthur and to American officers with international commands in Europe, but especially the former, Kennan observed: "Pressed in the field of competence associated with one of these hats, they promptly took refuge under the other. This flealike agility and flexibility gave them extraordinary powers of resistance to any Washington-generated pressures which went contrary to their own views and inclinations." Of course, MacArthur had just employed this flea-hopping tactic in his disclaimer to Senator McMahon for FEC-230's formulation. As it dawned on MacArthur later, Kennan had proven to be the cleverer of the two at their March session in Tokyo, when MacArthur expressed delight to learn that, according to the new strategy plotted primarily by Kennan and Draper, he would no longer be held accountable to the FEC. Actually the subsequent increase in Washington's disdain for the FEC and the fading of that body from the arena of occupation policy-making cost MacArthur his main alternative refuge when he was not happy with a particular directive from his American superiors. From now on, the Supreme Commander for the Allied Powers would be, in reality, just the American commander in Japan and would be kept on a much shorter leash by his military superiors, who, on occupation matters, were now acting in close accord with the State Department, thanks to Kennan and Draper.[15]

Of course, the United States' dropping of FEC-230, its unilateral action to restore Japan as a Far Eastern power, its apparent indifference to further FEC deliberations on liberal changes in Japan, and its renunciation of American claims to reparations in May 1949 all created rumblings among the other FEC nations. Whereas before MacArthur had borne much of the FEC members' criticisms for ignoring or defying that body, now the majority of the delegations in the FEC directed their attacks on the United States government. Complex national interests were involved, too. The British were uneasy about future Japanese trade competition, especially in the world textile market, and about American intentions regarding some of their former trading areas in the Far East; and they resented their unequal partnership with America in formulating containment strategy. The Australians, New Zealanders, Filipinos, and Nationalist Chinese feared that Japanese industrial growth and trade expansion might produce the economic foundations for a Japanese military resurgence. The Soviets, as expected, interpreted the American move to restore Japan as an escalation of the Cold War and a blatant attempt to link Japan with the Western capitalist powers. Kennan, among others, later believed that the prospect of a strong Japan, particularly if a benevolent peace settlement and a security pact with the United States were in the offing, was a primary reason for "the Soviet decision to unleash a civil war in Korea" in June 1950.[16]

Apparently unknown to MacArthur in 1947–1948, an extensive and influential lobbying effort against FEC-230 and for a revived Japan with close American ties had been under way for some time. The American Council on Japan (not to be confused with the Allied Council for Japan) was "the most important pressure group," a respected researcher has found, and was "the organizational umbrella for what may properly be termed the Japan Lobby" during that period. Its leaders included Harry Kern and Compton Pakenham of *Newsweek;* several former State Department officials, such as Joseph C. Grew and William R. Castle, who had been ambassadors and under secretaries, as well as "old Japan hands" like Eugene Dooman and Joseph W. Ballantine; and attorney Kauffman, together with a number of corporate executives of firms interested in resuming or establishing business ties in Japan. When Eichelberger retired after leaving his Eighth Army command in August 1948, nursing some bitter personal grievances against MacArthur, he became close to Kern and spoke at programs of the American Council on Japan. Draper and Kennan frequently listened to the counsel of Kern's group and were sympathetic with most of their views. The council became inactive in 1953 after having achieved its basic goals, which, as summarized by the main scholar on the group's brief but important history, were "to reverse the reformist orientation of the early occupation, to make Japan a bulwark against communism in Asia, and to rivet Japan onto an American-dominated world capitalist system."[17]

Revisionist historians have made much of the United States' alleged postwar efforts to create a global capitalistic trading system that would not be dependent on American aid yet would amount to a vast sphere of influence whose trade benefits would accrue principally to American firms. "While a strategic component will

always, at some time and in varying degrees, enter the policy deliberations on nearly every critical question," states one of the most
noted revisionist works, "Washington's considerations in Japan were
first and foremost economic. . . . Politically the conservative ruling class was [to be] firmly entrenched in power . . . [but] above
all, the Japanese economy had . . . [to be] reintegrated into the
American economic orbit." Surely the economic factor was significant not only to the American Council lobbyists but also to the
key Washington decision-makers on occupation policy, many of
whom, like Draper, came from the business elite. But the strategic
factor underlying the containment policy seems to have been just
as important to the official and unofficial leaders who played crucial roles in the reverse course. Recent scholarship has shown that
the State and Pentagon planners were seriously developing a "great
crescent" strategy, wherein Japan would be the vital segment in a
great arc of containment stretching from Japan through Southeast Asia to India. In the nations along that arc American assistance would be used to develop integrated regional trade and security systems.[18] It seems unlikely that any researcher will ever be
able to delineate fully and rank assuredly the various theories —
ideological, strategic, political, and economic — that made up the
idea of the reverse course or the great crescent. As for Mac-
Arthur, though he resisted the change in policy direction for a short
while, he must have been pleased eventually with the new possibilities, because the advancement of Japan's position in the Asian
picture might somehow enhance his own leadership role, which
seemed to be reduced by NSC 13/2 to a caretaker's job. As it turned
out, he would return to center stage, but he would do so as a result of developments in Korea, not in Japan.

2. Unhappy Times for Japanese Leftists

Willoughby, never comfortable with the earlier latitude allowed to
leftists and radicals, interpreted the rightward policy shift after 1947
as a mandate for him to track all sorts of allegedly disloyal or suspicious persons. With increasing Japanese Communist agitation in
1948, as well as several leaks of GHQ documents to the press, he

became extremely security-conscious. On his orders one night a security check was made of every nook and cranny in the Dai Ichi Building. An overeager young lieutenant decided to examine MacArthur's office and found one of his desk drawers partly open, with a file marked "Confidential" showing. A note was left reminding the Supreme Commander of the need for tight security. On MacArthur's arrival at the office the next morning, Willoughby received a call from Bunker to report to the Supreme Commander at once. When he walked in, MacArthur exploded in rage, "Charlie, what's the matter with you? Are you out of your mind?" After thoroughly excoriating his intelligence chief, MacArthur explained that the particular file held correspondence regarding the MacArthur-for-President movement, and that it would be "deadly if that should fall into the hands of the press." Willoughby confessed that he "didn't blame him for being mad" and that the young security officer "was a nut." Later Willoughby commented, "That's the only time I saw him enraged." MacArthur agreed with most of his intelligence chief's measures to guard against "the enemy," but he laid down an iron-clad rule for security personnel. As Willoughby put it, "You don't make security checks on the Supreme Commander."[19]

The shift in emphasis of American policy, whatever Willoughby's narrow interpretation, did not mean that all matters related to the original objectives of demilitarization and democratization were now regarded as achieved or voided. Three major areas of activity in "liquidating the war" remained: war crimes trials, property restitution, and Soviet repatriation.

The IMTFE's trial of "Class A" war crimes suspects, like former Prime Minister Hideki Tojo, ended in late 1948. MacArthur announced the completion of the trials of "B" and "C" suspects in Japan in October 1949, by which time the British, Australian, Dutch, French, and Chinese trials of Japanese war crimes suspects in their territories were also largely finished. The trials succeeded in bringing a number of war criminals to justice, but the lack of fairness in some of the proceedings precipitated controversies that have not yet ceased. To MacArthur's disappointment, the trials in Japan were of questionable value in producing a sense of contrition in the Japanese people. Whereas there was nationwide shame over the atrocities that were revealed in the proceedings, most Japanese citizens did not seem to experience guilt over the initiation of the war or the perpetration of war crimes, blaming instead the individuals on trial or the discredited militarists in general. "Considering the nature of the prewar social and governmental structure," commented Robert Fearey of the State Department's Office of Far Eastern Affairs, "under which the people's relation to the government was one of duty and obedience with virtually no control over governmental policy, the man in the street saw no reason to blame himself." One Japanese recalled, "General Tojo and his group had brought Japan down to defeat and infamy, and now they were being held accountable for their mistakes. But the people believed our sons and brothers had fought an honorable war."

The restitution of properties looted by the Japanese during their occupation of Allied territories had been debated in the FEC almost from that body's beginning. By late 1949 the SCAP Civil Property Custodian's Office had processed about $50 million worth of claims for looted property, such as precious metals and cultural objects, leaving only 10 percent of the claims unsettled. A related problem was the restitution of business properties of Westerners that had been confiscated in Japan during the war. Much of the adjudication of these claims for return of properties or compensation for losses had to await the peace treaty and the postoccupation era. Meanwhile SCAP was charged with making sure that the Japanese government preserved such properties in their current condition.[20]

Except for land reform, MacArthur had referred few substantive issues to the Allied Council for Japan during the occupation's early years. Ball of Australia (the British Commonwealth representative), Derevyanko of the USSR, and Lieutenant General Chu Shih-ming of Nationalist China had often been so critical of SCAP policies that Atcheson and Sebald, the successive American representatives, usually had little constructive to report to MacArthur about the ACJ meetings. After its first few sessions the Supreme Commander, according to Sebald, decided to ignore the body and let it "wither into uselessness." As time went on, however, MacArthur came to see some value in the ACJ as a sounding board to expose the Soviet Union's retention of 380,000 Japanese troops and civilians whom it had seized at the end of World War II. By late 1949 Sebald's fervent crusading on the issue in the ACJ and

MacArthur's public blasts against the callous Soviet attitude toward the repatriates were receiving generous attention in the press in Japan and around the free world. Returning Japanese who had not been brainwashed by the Soviets provided accounts of hideous treatment in Siberian prison camps, which Sebald recounted in detail in ACJ meetings and the Japanese press avidly reported to the nation, pointing out that the huge number still imprisoned faced the same horrors.

The repatriation issue became so heated in the ACJ in the spring of 1950 that Derevyanko walked out of the session on May 10; the Soviet boycott lasted until November. A United Nations resolution in December calling on the Soviet Union to repatriate the rest of the Japanese was ignored by Moscow. A few more prisoners eventually were sent back to Japan, but the fate of the remaining ones in Soviet captivity was never revealed. MacArthur's image of the ACJ improved especially during 1949–1950, because on the dominant issue before the body in that period, Soviet repatriation, the ACJ could be exploited for propaganda purposes, and Sebald at last had a majority, the Soviet delegate standing alone. Sebald was convinced that those Japanese whom the Soviets released probably would not have been freed "without the pressures generated by the Allied Council." As for the Soviet intransigence and inhumanity toward the repatriates, he believed that "within Japan it was at this period one of the strongest influences restricting the growth of the Japanese Communist party and other leftist groups."[21]

Targeted for change under NSC 13/2 was another demilitarization program, the purge. By the autumn of 1948, about 220,000 Japanese had been barred or removed from public, corporate, or media positions because of alleged militarist or ultranationalist ties in the past. Over 80 percent of these people were former officers of the armed services. Whereas under the Potsdam Declaration and early directives, they were to retain their outcast status permanently, the reverse course in American policy helped many of them to appeal their cases successfully and to win reinstatement before the occupation ended. In February 1949 the Yoshida Cabinet established the Purge Review Commission; within less than ten months it had received over 30,000 review applications, and the number soared much higher in 1950. With MacArthur's approval, the first large group of those who had been purged — more than 10,100 — were released in October 1950, and two weeks later 3250 former military and naval officers who had not received their training prior to December 8, 1941, were freed. When Lieutenant General Matthew B. Ridgway succeeded MacArthur as SCAP in April 1951, one of his early actions was to approve the release of most of the 200,000 or so remaining purged personnel.

Besides being "probably the major factor undermining the success of the purge," maintains the leading authority on the purge, "the shift in Occupation policy also had the ultimate effect of switching the objective of the purge from removing militarists and ultra-nationalists to removing Communists and their sympathizers." In a public statement on July 4, 1949, at a time when Communist-led railway workers were resorting to violence against a new layoff policy, MacArthur said that Japan may have to face the question as to whether the Communists "should longer be accorded the validity, sanction, and protection of the law." Two months later, however, he commented publicly that the Communists' aggressive tactics against the railway dismissal plan that summer "were effectively repulsed — not by the repressive force of police power — but by the weight of an increasingly informed and active Japanese public opinion aroused to meet the threat to their free institutions." Apparently he had shelved the idea of outlawing the Communist party. But a new round of Communist criticisms of SCAP and Japanese governmental policies and another wave of Communist-incited demonstrations and acts of violence, including unprecedented attacks on American servicemen, occurred during the period from May Day to the early June elections of 1950.[22] In marked contrast to his nonchalant discounting of an internal Red menace when he conferred with Kennan in March 1948, now the Supreme Commander ordered the purge of all twenty-four members of the Central Committee of the Japanese Communist party and, in his letter to Yoshida on June 6, painted an ominous picture:

> [The Communists] have hurled defiance at constituted authority, shown contempt for the processes of law and order, and contrived by false and inflammatory statements and other subversive means to arouse through resulting public confusion that degree of social unrest which would set the stage for the eventual overthrow of consti-

tutional government in Japan by force. Their coercive methods bear striking parallel to those by which the militaristic leaders of the past deceived and misled the Japanese people, and their aims, if achieved, would surely lead Japan to an even worse disaster. To permit this incitation to lawlessness to continue unchecked, however embryonic it may at present appear, would be to risk ultimate suppression of Japan's democratic institutions in direct negation of the purpose and intent of Allied policy pronouncements, forfeiture of her chance for political independence, and destruction of the Japanese race.[23]

MacArthur followed up the next day by directing Yoshida to purge seventeen staff members of the Communist newspaper, *Akahata* ("Red Flag"), for printing "licentious, false, inflammatory and seditious appeals to irresponsible sentiment in an effort to provoke defiance of constituted authority." On June 26 the general ordered a thirty-day suspension of *Akahata* as an "instrument of foreign subversion," and he had a Communist member of the Diet branded as a purgee for his criticisms of MacArthur's recent actions against the Communists. One of MacArthur's long-time staff officers later remarked, "Purging the Reds was more the Old Man's style, really, than purging the Zaibatsu."[24]

In the area of democratization efforts initiated earlier, the implementation of the new constitution was progressing smoothly, except from a leftist viewpoint; the Diet, prefectural and local governments, and the court system, though not functioning as Americans might wish, were proving reasonably effective and were generally protective of the many new freedoms and rights bestowed on the citizenry; the Emperor's less exalted status had won wide acceptance, and he had become somewhat of a popular figure, seen far more in public than previously. In the matters of government employees' rights and the revamped police system, however, the reverse course's implementation left some Japanese cynical about the occupiers' intentions in democratization.

The bureaucracy, as mentioned earlier, had suffered few purges and generally had been successful in resisting SCAP changes. The National Personnel Authority had been established under the National Public Service Law of 1947 to administer an American-style civil service system. Written examinations were required, beginning in early 1950, of applicants for civil service positions in the central government from assistant section chiefs up to vice ministers. But most of the entrenched bureaucrats were still secure in their positions, partly because of the many loopholes in the law, and many of the senior bureaucrats had shifted into politics. With the onset of the reverse course, no serious SCAP pressures were brought to bear on the bureaucrats staffing the principal ministries, particularly the Ministry of International Trade and Industry (Ministry of Commerce and Industry until May 1949), which would be vital to economic restoration.

But another portion of the National Public Service Law was revised drastically, namely, that covering the large number of transportation, communications, and other service workers in government employment. Unions of such government employees, it will be recalled, had been in the forefront of the agitation for the general strike in early 1947. Again, in the spring and summer of 1948 there were strikes and labor violence by some of the big government-worker unions, especially of the railroad, telephone, and telegraph employees. In the midst of a spreading strike of public service workers, MacArthur sent a letter to Prime Minister Ashida on July 22, 1948, ordering the government to amend the 1947 National Public Service Law so as to prohibit strikes by government employees that threatened the public welfare. The railway and communications unions, led by radicals, were particularly vociferous and even violent in their protests. Within GHQ there was sharp disagreement over MacArthur's new policy, leading to the resignation of James S. Killen, who had followed Cohen as chief of SCAP's troubled Labor Division. Nevertheless, MacArthur persisted in pushing the Japanese government on the matter, and in November the Diet passed amendments to the 1947 law that denied the rights of collective bargaining and of striking to certain categories of government workers. Baron E. J. Lewe van Aduard, deputy chief of the Netherlands mission in Japan, asserted, "SCAP's persistence in enforcing restrictions in the Public Service Law was an unmistakable indication of the stiffening attitude of the Occupation."[25]

In accord with the early SCAP view that decentralization and local autonomy were part and parcel of the democratizing process in Japan, the police system, as discussed earlier, had been thoroughly decentralized. But NSC 13/2 called for strengthening the police, in part by expanding again the central police structure. At first MacArthur was reluctant to inaugurate changes that would reinstate the old centralized system, maintaining that they "could be expected to have very explosive international reactions," according to Justin Williams of the Government Section. In December 1948 and again the following June, in response to queries by the Department of the Army, he reported in optimistic terms on the training, resupplying, and general effectiveness of the Japanese police, asserting that they were able to cope with any internal disorders.

But increasing Communist-led violence in 1949, as well as inadequate local financing of police and instances of municipal police corruption, led to growing public criticism of the ineffectiveness of the police system as decentralized in 1947. Some of the notable incidents in 1949 that reflected the need for changes included the seizure of the Taira municipal police headquarters by a Communist-led mob of 700; the murder of Sananori Shimoyama, president of the Japanese National Railways, during the tense period of austerity layoffs of workers; and several sensational cases of train sabotage that resulted in heavy fatalities. Two weeks after the outbreak of the Korean War, as he prepared to send his four American divisions in Japan into combat, MacArthur was compelled to enlarge and centralize the police establishment. On July 8, 1950, he directed Yoshida "to establish a national police reserve of 75,000 men and expand the existing authorized strength of the personnel serving under the Maritime Safety Board by an additional 8000." The National Police Reserve was to be supplied with American Army weapons and supplies and, beginning that December, with a limited amount of heavy military equipment. Most historians have interpreted the creation of the National Police Reserve and the expansion of the coast guard service as the beginning of the Self-Defense Forces of postoccupation times. While acknowledging that the new Japanese units in 1950 constituted a "special Far East Command reserve," MacArthur saw no conflict with Article IX of the new constitution because the move was not a step toward Japanese rearmament. Instead, he insisted, it was a plan to provide constabulary forces during the Korean War emergency, when his American troops would not be able to provide backup support for the regular police in crises menacing internal order in Japan. In 1954 the Diet enacted a measure that completely revised the Police Law of 1947 and, in effect, returned the police to a strongly centralized system.[26]

A cardinal feature of NSC 13/2 for MacArthur's role was its demand for increasing transference of SCAP controls and functions to the Japanese. His first public pronouncement on the new stage of relaxed controls came in his message to the Japanese nation on May 2, 1949, the second anniversary of the constitution:

> The Allied purposes enunciated at Potsdam in many essential respects have been fulfilled, and you have worked diligently and faithfully to discharge your surrender commitments. That Allied forces still occupy your native soil is thus by no means due to fault of yours since the inception of the Occupation, but rather to events and circumstances elsewhere beyond your capacity to influence or control.
>
> In these two years the character of the Occupation has gradually changed from the stern rigidity of a military operation to the friendly guidance of a protective force. While insisting upon the firm adherence to the course delineated by existing Allied policy and directive, it is my purpose to continue to advance this transition just as rapidly as you are able to assume the attending autonomous responsibility. Thus progressive latitude will come to you in the stewardship of your own affairs.
>
> To such an end and to insure the continuity of a calm and well-ordered progress, I call upon every Japanese citizen on this anniversary of Japan's rebirth, to safeguard the commonweal by unrelaxed vigilance against the destructive inroads of concepts incredulous of human wisdom, prejudicial to personal dignity, and suppressive of individual liberty. There can be no higher purpose.[27]

There were probably few Japanese who did not interpret his final sentences as a warning that disorder and radicalism would bring an end to the relaxation.

A week later Major General Edward M. Almond, MacArthur's chief of staff, summoned all the SCAP section chiefs and ordered them to "inaugurate an intensive review of all Scapins (SCAP instructions), verbal orders, and other directives to the Japanese Government with a view to determining those which might be eliminated or modified" by the end of May. At the "express direction" of MacArthur, he said, "the general program of relaxing controls to which Headquarters had been devoted for some time might now be considered as having passed from an 'implied' to an 'expressed' stage." Cloyce K. Huston, who represented Sebald's Diplomatic Section, observed, "A general air of willing cooperation prevailed among the section chiefs." Marquat, however, opined that this would be a "tremendous task," in view of "the multitudinous directives calling upon him to implement the present intensive program of economic rehabilitation." In contrast, Whitney remarked that his section had "issued no directives during the past two years." Huston concluded that the SCAP staff's determination to screen the 17,000 SCAPINs and other directives issued to the Japanese government since September 1945 "seems to reflect an honest recognition in General Headquarters of the need for a genuine relaxation of controls and the progressive transfer of responsibilities to the Japanese Government." Indeed, nothing more clearly symbolized the drastic change that MacArthur was enforcing now than the requirement that the still large SCAP bureaucracy perform an unmentionable task for any bureaucrats — clearing the files of obsolete documents. Such housecleaning was needed, for few of the old SCAPINs seemed relevant after the birth of NSC 13/2.[28]

Most of the affected controls, as Marquat had noted, related to the economic sphere, but international relations was a realm in which all the Japanese could soon detect changes. Until 1949 only a handful of Japanese had been permitted to leave the home islands. That May the State Department recommended to the FEC that, "under SCAP's supervision, Japan be permitted to attend international meetings and conventions and to adhere to and participate in such international arrangements and agreements as other countries may be willing to conclude with Japan." MacArthur immediately began approving trips for Japanese political and trade leaders, and in August the State Department backed him for "correctly allowing Japanese international relationships of a limited character," since the FEC was still wrangling over the matter and had not acted. During the twelve months beginning in May 1949 increasing numbers of Japanese people and missions were permitted to visit other countries; most went to the United States on diplomatic, trade, or cultural matters. The United States government, for want of FEC action, provided MacArthur with interim directives to cover the occasions, with all such journeys "subject to his discretion and continued control." One such group in early 1950 consisted of fourteen members of the Diet and of various ministries, who spent three months in America visiting federal agencies and corporate headquarters. By May 1950, under SCAP supervision, Japanese governmental offices with diplomatic and commercial functions similar to consulates had been opened in New York, Seattle, San Francisco, Los Angeles, and Honolulu.[29]

Both external and internal factors contributed to the swing of the pendulum of Japanese national politics in a conservative direction from 1948 to 1951. Externally, the conservative politicians benefited from the American authorities' retreat from reformism and the SCAP offensive against those who would obstruct stability and recovery. Besides holding grievances over Soviet imperialist interests in Korea, Manchuria, and China, the majority of the Japanese people were alienated toward the Soviet Union because of the latter's seizure of southern Sakhalin and the Kuriles, fishing disputes in the Sea of Japan and Sea of Okhotsk, and the repatriation issue, all of which handicapped the recruiting efforts of the Japanese Communists. Most Japanese, like Americans, blamed Moscow for triggering the Korean War, and during that conflict they felt their nation benefited economically and in strategic security by its linkage with the United States. Many feared that if the South Korean republic was overrun, Moscow would direct its North Korean and Chinese puppets to attack Japan next.

Internally, the conservatives, especially Yoshida's Liberal party, which was reconstituted as the Democratic Liberal party in March 1948, profited in the aftermath from the unimpressive records of the Katayama (May 1947 to February 1948) and Ashida (March to October 1948) ministries. Socialist Katayama's regime was ineffectual, plagued as it was by labor difficulties and continually forced to compromise Socialist interests in order to retain the support of its coalition partners, the conservative Democratic and People's Cooperative parties. Hitoshi Ashida, the leader of the Democratic party, formed the succeeding ministry, but it comprised the same divisive coalition elements and faced even more serious economic and labor troubles, in addition to a series of shocking scandals involving members of the Cabinet and implicating Ashida. On returning to the premiership in October 1948, Yoshida brought several Democrats into his Cabinet, which helped to produce a split in the Democratic ranks between factions for and against a coalition with his party.[30]

The elections in January 1949 to the lower but more powerful Diet chamber, the House of Representatives, which would be the last until after the occupation was formally terminated in 1952, serve as a fairly accurate barometer of the course of Japanese national politics during MacArthur's stay in Japan. The Democratic Liberals not only became the first postwar party to gain an absolute majority but also had such an overwhelming lead over the combined total of seats obtained by the Democrats, Socialists, and Communists — 264 seats to 155 — that Yoshida and his party faced no possible parliamentary threat. The Democratic Liberal party's success was striking, too, when compared to its showing in the 1947 elections. In 1949 it more than doubled its number of seats and got 44 percent of the vote, compared with 27 percent in 1947. When the seats held by the three main conservative parties — the Democratic Liberal, Democratic, and People's Cooperative — were combined, the conservatives' strength in the Diet amounted to nearly 75 percent of all the seats. The three parties that had participated in the Katayama and Ashida coalition Cabinets suffered setbacks — the Democrats, People's Cooperatives, and especially Socialists. From 143 seats in 1947, the Socialists dropped to only 49 in 1949. This has been generally attributed to disunity among the right, left, and centrist factions of the Socialist party; the ineffectiveness of the Katayama government; and the scandals of the Ashida ministry, in which Socialists allegedly were involved. The Communists got 35 seats and 10 percent of the vote in 1949, in part because of their strong campaigning and also because of support from voters who had backed the Socialist party in 1947 and had subsequently become disillusioned after the Katayama ministry. Shortly after the 1949 election, *New York Times* correspondent Lindesay Parrott commented on the obvious, "What the election means is that power in Japan — insofar as power exists apart from General MacArthur — now has passed to the group that represents business, the conservative countryside, and that section of the prewar Japanese civil service that has not been eliminated from militarist leanings."[31]

Back in 1947 when the Socialists gained a plurality, MacArthur observed after the elections that the Japanese voters had "firmly and decisively rejected" the extreme left especially and had "over-whelmingly" chosen, instead, "a moderate course sufficiently centered from either extreme." Following the decisive conservative triumph in 1949, the Supreme Commander took an entirely different slant on the returns: "The people of the free world everywhere can take satisfaction in this enthusiastic and orderly Japanese election which at a critical moment in Asiatic history has given so clear and decisive a mandate for the conservative philosophy of government."[32] Both the GHQ administrators in Tokyo and the strategists of the reverse course and the Cold War in Washington must have breathed easier after the 1949 elections, assuming that a Japan ruled by Yoshida-type conservatives would be more likely in the post-treaty era to remain linked with the United States in its global causes of advancing capitalism and democracy. In the decades ahead Japan would advance from apt student to master teacher on the subject of capitalism. Unhappily, though, many Japanese never did quite figure out what the "occupationeers" meant by "democracy" — especially after the reverse course.

CHAPTER VIII

Stabilizing Japan's Economy

1. Easing Some Anxieties of the Corporate Elite

THE REVERSE COURSE was reflected in Washington's changing view on reparations. In early 1947, it will be recalled, Clifford Strike had headed a mission to Japan to investigate Japan's capacity to pay reparations. Subsequently the mission had recommended to the War Department that reparations should be scaled down sharply from the levels that the other FEC nations were considering in order to prevent "disaster to the Japanese economy." From July through December 1947, Strike led another investigative group to Japan, Overseas Consultants, Inc., which rendered an even more negative report on Japanese levels of industry and possibilities for reparations. The report of the Overseas Consultants to the Department of the Army in late February 1948 (publicly released in early March) concluded: "Removal of productive facilities (except primary war facilities) which can be effectively used in Japan would hurt world production; would reduce the likelihood of her becoming self-supporting, and in any case increase the time required for accomplishing this objective; would be expensive to the American taxpayer; and, in our opinion, would not be in the best interests of the claimant nations." MacArthur had been pleased by the findings of both of the Strike missions.

In his conversation with MacArthur on March 5, Kennan reported that the general spoke "at length, and with some vehe-

mence, about the impracticability of the reparations program."
MacArthur believed that the United States government should
"make it clear that there would be no reparations from Japan in
excess of the 30 percent program" of advance transfers then in
process of delivery to China, the Philippines, Burma, Malaya, and
the Netherlands East Indies. On the 21st he told Draper and Kennan in his Dai Ichi office that "the whole approach to the reparations problem, and particularly the discussion upon this matter
with the Far Eastern Commission," had been "totally unrealistic"
and it would be "utterly fantastic to reduce further Japanese economic potential by additional removal of industrial equipment for
reparations purposes." Again he emphasized that once "the present 30 percent program in which SCAP is now engaged" is completed, the United States should "abandon entirely the thought of
further reparations." In fact, MacArthur recommended that "in
affording other assistance to Foreign Nations, we require written
agreement from such nations to the renunciation of all claims for
future Japanese reparations." The report of the Draper-Johnston
Mission in late April 1948 maintained that the threat of severe
reparations was stifling the Japanese "incentive to restore and re-
construct." It added, "It is most important that the present uncertainty be removed and the reparations issue be finally settled."[1]

On receipt of a directive in December 1948 detailing a new economic stabilization program for Japan, to be discussed later,
MacArthur reminded his Washington superiors that the reparations issue must be resolved soon. Since economic stabilization

> has formally become a basic and primary allied objective in the oc-
> cupation of Japan, it would be entirely inconsistent for the United
> States as sponsoring government to support the removal of any fur-
> ther materials from Japan for the reparations account. For every
> pound of material so removed is a reduction in the resources avail-
> able to support the stabilization program and an added burden upon
> the economy by way of costs incident to preparation and transpor-
> tation, as well as a strong psychological brake upon the mustering of
> the Japanese will to support, however onerous it may appear, the
> American formula for stabilization.[2]

A number of State and Army planners who had been involved
in the evolution of the new policy emphasis on "economic crank-
up" in Japan, of course, were already having difficulty in recon-

ciling reparations and recovery. Max W. Bishop, chief of the State Department's Office of Northeast Asian Affairs, probably reflected their general sentiment when he commented on MacArthur's above statement: "Acceptance of his no-further-reparations position would be an earnest to him [MacArthur] and to the whole Japanese nation of how seriously we regard the stabilization goal and of how far we are willing to go in supporting his and the Japanese people's efforts to attain it." In early February Bishop flew to Tokyo to confer with the general, whom he found, in personal conversation, to be even more firmly convinced that "it was inequitable and contrary to our best interests to attempt to remove further resources from Japan."[3]

After lengthy arguments over what levels of industry should be the basis for reparations, the State and Army planners finally decided that no excess was available for reparations and that any further drain would seriously deter Japan's ability to recuperate economically. Draper and Kennan worked jointly in drafting the final United States position on reparations. On May 12, 1949, General McCoy, American member and chairman of the FEC, announced to that body the decision that MacArthur had long wanted:

> The United States is forced to the following conclusions:
>
> (a) The deficit Japanese economy shows little prospect of being balanced in the near future and, to achieve balance, will require all resources at its disposal.
>
> (b) The burden of removing further reparations from Japan could detract seriously from the occupation objective of stabilizing the Japanese economy and permitting it to move towards self-support.
>
> (c) There is little or no prospect of Far Eastern Commission agreement on a reparations shares schedule despite the repeated initiatives by the United States over the past three years to assist the Commission in reaching such an agreement. . . .
>
> (d) Japan has already paid substantial reparations through expropriations of its former overseas assets and in small degree, under the Advance Transfer Program.
>
> In light of these conclusions, the United States Government is impelled to rescind its interim directive of April 4, 1947, bringing to an end the Advance Transfer Program called for by that directive. It is impelled also to withdraw its proposal of November 6, 1947, on Japanese reparations shares [for the United States]. . . . Finally, the U.S. Government takes this occasion to announce that it has no intention

of taking further unilateral action under its interim directive powers to make possible additional reparations removals from Japan.[4]

The advance transfers, mostly machine tools, were completed in May 1950, and thereafter the United States withdrew from the picture, leaving the other FEC nations to negotiate postoccupation bilateral agreements with Japan on reparations. At last Mac-Arthur's long, hard-fought struggle on this issue was over, and for a change he and the Washington planners were in accord. On this matter at least, he had been arguing for Japan to be given a chance for economic recovery long before the shift in occupation objectives became official.

Japanese big business gained another windfall with the arrival in Tokyo of the Draper-appointed Deconcentration Review Board in May 1948. This group of American business executives and federal officials, headed by Joseph V. Robinson, president of a New York connector company, had as its primary functions "to review each reorganization order for a company prepared by the Holding Company Liquidation Commission and appraise its effect on the operating efficiency of the enterprise and on the Japanese economy." In September, however, the board revised the principles for designating a company as an "excess concentration," leading to a considerable relaxation in interpreting the Deconcentration Law of late 1947. "It has become clear," said the *New York Times*, "the occupation has jettisoned its policy of breaking up undue concentrations of economic power." The board's new principles, it noted, "make any deconcentration exceedingly difficult, although the board emphasized — apparently for Japanese consumption — that 'there is no change in basic policy.' " In quick order the board reduced the number of companies the HCLC had designated for dissolution from 325 to 30, then to 19, and finally to only 9 by December 1948. A SCAP official, according to the *Nippon Times* editor, "gave the Japanese press the tortured explanation that . . . there was no disagreement between SCAP and Washington, that there was no inconsistency between the actions" of the board and the HCLC. Rather, the GHQ spokesman explained, "The Japanese had been enforcing their fair trade laws so vigorously and so effectively that the aim of economic democratization had now already been achieved without need for further recourse to the Deconcentration Law." In early August 1949, MacArthur announced the end of the board's work and his implementation of all its recommendations, which marked "the completion of another major phase of the Occupation mission."[5]

Meanwhile, also in the summer of 1949, some of the more restrictive provisions of the Anti-Monopoly Law were revised, permitting a number of corporate devices and techniques that could lead to new restraints of trade competition (though holding companies were still prohibited). The most important change was the redefinition of "unfair methods of competition." As explained by an authority, "the circumstances in which two companies are to be considered in competition were more narrowly defined, with a resulting liberalization of the provisions in the law forbidding or setting restrictions on international contracts, intercorporate stockholdings, holdings of stock by company executives, mergers, and the like between competing concerns or officers of competing concerns." In other words, Japanese combines were allowed to resume some of their old monopolistic tactics. Hadley frankly concludes that the changes resulted in "largely emasculating" the Anti-Monopoly Law.[6]

Yoshida had already set up machinery for screening applicants for release from the purge. Many business leaders were among those released in the fall of 1950. By June 1951 nearly all the purged business group had been freed. When the "depurging" process had gotten under way earlier, Yoshida asked MacArthur in early 1949 to allow two men on the purge list to join his new Cabinet as Minister of Finance and president of the Economic Stabilization Board. Yoshida maintained that he was "encountering great difficulties in finding suitable persons for the economic posts in the new cabinet. . . . The field of choice is extremely limited owing to the purge of so many men of ability and experience." One of the men had been a Zaibatsu trading company executive and editor of a Zaibatsu trade journal; the other was a former director of the Bank of Japan and head of its overseas department during the war. MacArthur replied in a one-sentence letter to the Prime Minister: "It would not be within the proper scope of my authority to sanction purgees for Cabinet office without concurrence of the Far Eastern Commission which it would be quite impossible to secure." The general tolerated the depurging,

but the leap from "purgee" to Cabinet member was too quick for
him. (After the occupation many formerly purged people would
ascend to top governmental positions.)[7]

Although the anti-Zaibatsu program became a casualty of the
reverse course, it had already taken a toll of the monopolistic powers
of the main Zaibatsu families. Their holding companies had been
dissolved and extensive redistribution of their stocks had taken
place, making for broader-based ownership in the corporate sector. The wealth of the ten or so leading Zaibatsu families, besides
being reduced by capital taxes, was nearly immobilized for years.
But, as one authority points out, by the end of the occupation "a
massive process of recombination was in full swing, and a number
of the old networks had emerged in recognizable form. A few dikes,
holding back the flood at key points, still marked the strongest operations of the dissolution program, but these too were being
threatened. . . . And, meanwhile, new concentrations of economic power have taken the place of the old."[8]

On the fourth anniversary of the Japanese surrender ceremony
in Tokyo Bay, September 2, 1949, MacArthur issued a statement
to the Japanese nation citing the political, economic, and social accomplishments of the past four years. Despite the recent emascu-
lation of much of the anti-Zaibatsu program, he nevertheless ranked
them alongside the land reform as the outstanding achievements
in economic democracy:

> Both leaders and people are coming to understand that representa-
> tive democracy draws its strength from the support of a broad ma-
> jority of the people imbued with the belief that under it they may
> attain a standard of living commensurate with the capabilities of
> modern civilization — that a prerequisite of that condition is individ-
> ual freedom of activity in the field of economic enterprise, for no in-
> dividual bound in economic thralldom can be politically free. Thus,
> for the vast majority of those who earn their living in industrial and
> commercial pursuits there could be no political freedom so long as
> their economic destiny was determined by decisions made in the closed
> councils of the few families which formerly controlled the vast bulk
> of the productive and financial resources of Japan. Nor could there
> be any political freedom for those who work the soil so long as they
> were economic serfs under a feudalistic system of land tenure. The
> fruition during the past year of the plans laid down by the Occupa-
> tion and carried out by the Japanese Government to remove, through

the Economic Deconcentration Program on the one hand and the Land Reform Program on the other, these barriers to the existence of a free society, has established in Japan the economic basis for the existence of a broad middle class which, having a stake in the economic well-being of the country, will support the ideal of democracy as their way of life and will reject with scorn any will-of-the-wisp economic utopias which require the surrender of the individual's freedom to the State.[9]

To pronounce the assault on the agrarian landlords as a success at this stage was warranted, but to attribute similar success to the program against the corporate elite, especially when he knew the latter effort was being largely dismantled, seems impossible to justify. Perhaps he reasoned that the Japanese people, who put great store in saving face, would be sympathetic with his own face-saving gesture. After all, in this anniversary statement, which covered almost every activity of the occupation, he had to say something about the anti-Zaibatsu offensive. So why not just tell them that he had achieved his objective of deconcentration?

2. SCAP Gets a Stabilization Czar

A fallacious assumption of the SWNCC planners had been that while SCAP concentrated on demilitarization and democratization programs during the early phase of the occupation, the Japanese economy would gradually recover without external intervention. But by early 1948 industrial production was not quite half of the 1930–1934 average, inflation was still rampant, black-marketeering was widespread, price controls were ineffective, and foreign trade was badly unbalanced. The Katayama and Ashida ministries did not attempt any firm countermeasures to halt the economic deterioration, and the large-scale corruption and fiscal irresponsibility of government leaders during that period further undermined business and public confidence. Baron van Aduard, the perceptive Dutch diplomat in occupied Japan, believed that "a large group of Japanese, led by reactionary politicians and influential profiteers," opportunistically anticipated American aid for rehabilitation and realized that, with Cold War tensions rising, it was in America's self-interest to promote Japan's economic revival. But "they considered it wise to proceed slowly with the implementation of the American plans" and, meanwhile, "profit from the situation." As Aduard interpreted this Japanese strategy, the Americans would pour money into Japan in bidding for her as a future anti-Communist ally, and the Japanese themselves would have to do little toward recovery. "Sooner than they expected, however, the Japanese were to discover," remarked Aduard, "that America's patience was not so unlimited as they had thought." Aduard's theory may not be susceptible of proof, but one factor in the complex economic situation was the feeling of many Japanese that the United States would sustain the major burden of planning, funding, and leading in economic rehabilitation, which may have dulled the motivation of some in working toward their nation's economic recovery.[10]

Ralph A. Young of the Federal Reserve Board headed an American mission of businessmen and economists that the United States government sent to Japan in May 1948 to investigate and recommend on economic stabilization. The Young Report called for the Japanese government to operate on a balanced budget; develop effective, strict controls over prices, credit, and raw material allocations; stabilize wages; reform tax collections; and adopt a single general foreign exchange rate. In July, MacArthur urged the Ashida ministry to inaugurate a stabilization program based on the Young proposals. But no action had been taken by October when Ashida was forced to resign after several of his Cabinet members were accused of accepting bribes for obtaining excessively generous loans for the Showa Electric Company. Yoshida, who now became Prime Minister, had done little toward stabilization during his 1946–1947 ministry and was known to prefer less rather than more governmental controls over the economy.[11]

On December 10, MacArthur received a directive from Royall: "You will direct the Japanese Government immediately to carry out a program of economic stabilization by adopting whatever measures may be required rapidly to achieve fiscal, monetary, price and wage stability in Japan to maximize production for export." The following "special objectives" were set forth:

1. To achieve a true balance in the consolidated budget at the earliest possible date by stringent curtailing of expenditures and maximum expansion in total governmental revenues, including such new revenue as may be necessary and appropriate.

2. To accelerate and strengthen the program of tax collection and insure prompt, widespread and vigorous criminal prosecution of tax evaders.

3. To assure that credit extension is rigorously limited to those projects contributing to economic recovery of Japan.

4. To establish an effective program to achieve wage stability.

5. To strengthen and, if necessary, expand the coverage of existing price control programs.

6. To improve the operation of foreign trade controls and tighten existing foreign exchange controls, to the extent that such measures can appropriately be delegated to Japanese agencies.

7. To improve the effectiveness of the present allocation and rationing system, particularly to the end of maximizing exports.

8. To increase production of all essential indigenous raw material and manufactured products.

9. To improve efficiency of the food collection program.

10. To develop the above plans to pave the way for the early establishment of a single general exchange rate.[12]

The above goals were substantially those enunciated in the Young Report, the difference being that now MacArthur was to order, instead of urge and persuade, the Japanese government into action on stabilization; and he was directed to maintain close surveillance and demand prompt implementation. After several exchanges with Washington over clarification of the goals, MacArthur wrote to Yoshida on December 19, transmitting the gist of the directive and the objectives. He warned the Prime Minister that there would be no toleration of "political conflict over the objectives" or of "any attempt to delay or frustrate . . . accomplishment" of the stabilization program. Although he agreed only reluctantly with some of the objectives, Yoshida promptly pledged his commitment to the new drive to achieve stabilization. It was fortunate for the program that his party gained overwhelming dominance of the House of Representatives in the next month's elections, so the Yoshida ministry's bills implementing the directive were generally assured of passage without delay or serious modification.[13]

Secretary of the Army Royall notified MacArthur on December

11, the day after the stabilization directive was dispatched, that "the President is taking a strong personal interest in supporting you in the difficult stabilization of the Japanese economy that lies ahead. . . . Today the President personally asked Mr. [Joseph M.] Dodge to undertake [the] important responsibility [of] assisting you with the whole economic and financial program in Japan." Dodge was president of the Detroit Bank, president of the American Bankers Association, and formulator of the successful currency reform instituted in West Germany in June. MacArthur responded to Royall: "Delighted at [the] prospect of securing [the] assistance of Mr. Joseph Dodge. Please express to the President my appreciation of his interest." Nevertheless, MacArthur undoubtedly realized that he was being forced to accept as his financial adviser a man who would be, in effect, the President's special representative in Japan and who would be in charge of the economic recovery program, now the occupation's highest priority.[14]

Dodge was moving to Tokyo for an indefinite stay, and Royall decided to accompany him for a brief visit, probably mainly to see that Dodge and MacArthur got off to a harmonious start. Secretary Royall had learned "informally" in late January from the State Department that MacArthur was setting up a GHQ "economic council," consisting of Whitney as chairman, Marquat of the Economic and Scientific Section, and Major General Alonzo P. (Pat) Fox, the deputy chief of staff. This information had come to W. Walton Butterworth, head of the Office of Far Eastern Affairs in the State Department. On January 25 he told Dean Acheson, who that week had succeeded Marshall as Secretary of State, that this GHQ group allegedly was to function "as a buffer between Mr. Dodge and SCAP with a view to watering down any recommendations which Mr. Dodge may make before they reach General MacArthur." Acheson advised Truman of the supposed stratagem and urged that Dodge should enjoy "a direct relationship" with the Supreme Commander, not one "strained through the staff." Thereupon the President bestowed on Dodge the rank of ambassador extraordinary to ensure that as SCAP financial adviser he had "direct access to General MacArthur in order to achieve the best results." Apparently the GHQ economic council never functioned as such. Besides, shortly after Dodge arrived on February 1, he and MacArthur developed a mutual respect and liking that grew over the ensuing months, according to each man's later recollections. Oddly, however, they met only four times in the three months Dodge was there during his first trip to Japan.[15]

At his first session with Yoshida and his ministers, Dodge, who had been assured by both the American and Japanese governments that he would have almost dictatorial powers in launching the stabilization program, let it be known that he meant business: "Before anything else, the Japanese budget must be balanced," he told the ministers. "Forget your dreams and start with the most realistic, as well as the most merciless, measures." The "Dodge Line," as his overall plan was sometimes called, soon emerged in the spring of 1949 as a tough, anti-inflationary, austerity program, which he enforced unflinchingly — and successfully — with full backing from SCAP and Washington. The Japanese government's budget for fiscal 1950 (beginning in April 1949) was balanced — the first time the feat had been achieved in eighteen years. It was accomplished not by raising taxes, but by eliminating waste, utilizing sound fiscal methods, cancelling a number of needless subsidy programs, instituting more effective tax collections, and discharging about 300,000 surplus government employees. The old multiple exchange rate was dropped in favor of a single general rate of 360 yen to the dollar, which helped to curb inflation and in the long run assisted Japan's foreign trade. A counterpart fund, generated by the yen value of American aid to Japan, was set up under SCAP control for economic reconstruction and reduction of government debts. The machinery for raw materials' allocations was made more efficient, and credit controls were tightened, especially by stopping the loose loan practices of the Reconstruction Finance Bank. Fearey claimed that the Dodge program produced "one of the sharpest reversals of an economic situation in history, in the absence of a currency conversion."[16]

Of course, Dodge did not accomplish all this singlehandedly nor was it done without provoking opposition and creating other problems. Finance Minister Hayato Ikeda and his lieutenants, as well as the officials of the increasingly important Ministry of International Trade and Industry, headed by Kiichi Miyazawa, were cooperative, as were Marquat and his SCAP economic staff. On the negative side, according to some Japanese economists, the credit stringency and severe deflationary pressures hurt many small businesses and bankrupted some. The huge number of government personnel layoffs in the summer of 1949 was a major cause of the labor violence that season, particularly among the railway and communications workers, who were hardest hit by the reductions. Communists among them charged, with some truth, that this was actually a "Red purge," because they were the first to be dismissed and the locals they controlled were most severely affected.[17]

As he began his vigorous program, Dodge said in a public statement on March 7, 1949: "To live as a self-supporting and not a dependent nation Japan must produce more at less cost, it must accumulate capital by savings and economy, it must supplement its limited internal resources with materials and products only available from other sources, and it must be able to pay for them from expanding exports." Though economic indices within a year of his arrival generally showed progress toward stabilization, Japan's foreign trade, the key to long-range economic success, was reviving with disappointing slowness. And its immediate future remained uncertain because of a host of persisting problems that included the chaotic political and economic conditions in most of the rest of the Far East, where Japan's natural trade routes lay; continuing foreign resistance to Japanese trade overtures, partly born of wartime hatred and partly of fear of competition; the slow revival of Japan's shipping industry, which had been the world's third largest before World War II; and Japan's inability to attract foreign investments because of the nation's shaky economy since 1945, discriminatory taxes, and restrictive government and SCAP regulations. Most serious, according to a recent scholarly study, were the SCAP-imposed controls, which resulted in "the institutionalization of the most restrictive foreign trade and foreign exchange control system ever devised by a major free nation."[18]

When Dodge left Japan on May 2, 1949, MacArthur wrote to Royall that his departure was "a distinct loss to the occupation," and he hoped that the President would "convince him that he should return to Japan just as soon as practicable to see the work he has so ably started through to its successful conclusion." Dodge returned for five weeks in late 1949 and for two months in late 1950. On each visit, according to *Asahi Shimbun*, Dodge continued "urging on hesitant government leaders the necessity of a balanced budget and sound planning." The Japanese paper also commented, "It is clear that the Dodge program proved successful only because it carried MacArthur's authority behind it."[19]

About the only area listed in the stabilization directive that Dodge did not enter was tax reform. That was left to a mission of seven American tax experts, headed by Dr. Carl S. Shoup of Columbia University, who came to Japan in June 1949 at MacArthur's invitation to study and make recommendations on Japan's tax structures at the national, prefectural, and local levels. The Shoup Report, based on four months of intensive work in Japan, took up four large volumes. The mission's recommendations, says one scholar, "resulted in a revolution in the tax system in Japan, transforming it from a basically Continental European type to an Anglo-American system in which national and local taxes are separated." A Japanese tax authority called the Shoup plan "the most advanced system in the world," but was not altogether sure about how "to foster the [Shoup] ideal . . . in this country where a number of [tax] abnormalities still exist." Among its other recommendations, the Shoup Mission emphasized that tax rates could be lowered if taxes were collected more efficiently. In the past there had been widespread evasion, with the actual tax often determined by negotiations between the collector and the taxpayer. Getting the Japanese to abandon this inequitable, if traditional, practice was merely one of the complexities involved in rationalizing taxation from the village to the central governmental levels.

In September, MacArthur strongly recommended the Shoup plan to Yoshida, praising it as "a vehicle for placing the finances of the national and local governments of Japan on a sound foundation" and calling for the "earliest possible action" on it. The Japanese government subsequently adopted some of the Shoup recommendations and found, through reforms in tax collection, that it could reduce or abolish a number of taxes and still maintain adequate revenues. But the Diet rejected a Shoup-based local tax measure in 1950 that SCAP officials considered fundamental to the reform program in taxation. MacArthur was "so angry," according to Justin Williams, that "he called to account the chiefs of SCAP's two most important staff sections and flayed the presiding officers of the two Diet chambers." After cooling off, however, he issued a press statement on the bill, concluding that "in a democracy it sometimes takes a little longer to get things done."[20] Ideally, the Shoup plan, like Dodge's program, was a good one, but in the end it was up to the Japanese, not the occupiers, to fit it to their needs and make it work.

3. Firing from the Rampart

From April to December 1949, MacArthur encountered more than the usual number of attacks that he considered serious enough to demand responses. The assaults came from three different quarters of "the rear," as he sometimes referred to the United States: popular periodicals that concentrated on the occupation's economic efforts; the House Appropriations Committee and the Bureau of the Budget, which threatened to decrease funding for Japan; and leaders of the State and Army departments, who were considering revision of the regime of control in Japan. MacArthur, who was not hard to convince that there were conspiracies against him, probably saw links among all three maneuvers. Indeed, there may have been more than coincidence in the attacks by the periodicals, with the American Council on Japan involved again, but there is not enough available evidence to justify a claim that there was a connection between them and the moves afoot in Congress and the federal agencies.

In the early part of 1949 Harry Kern of *Newsweek* and other leaders of the American Council on Japan had been actively speaking in private and public to business and government groups and individuals on the urgent need to restore Japan. On April 18 *Newsweek* published an article by Kern entitled "What's Wrong with Japan? Plenty, Blasts Survey Expert." Most of the piece consisted of criticisms of SCAP economic policies by Frederick Pope, a former New York chemical company president who had just returned from Japan, where he had headed a group studying Japan's chemical industry. He had submitted his report to MacArthur on April 2. In the article Pope is quoted extensively on the flaws in the economic purge, the deconcentration program, reparations, and inaccuracies in SCAP economic figures. Both Kern and Pope, by the way, made sure that Dodge was fully informed of their views. Apparently his previous confrontations with *Newsweek* were enough for MacArthur; he chose to ignore this latest barb.[21]

The general expressed surprise when *Fortune* published a ten-page article in its issue of April 1949 under the title "Two Billion Dollar Failure in Japan." MacArthur considered *Fortune's* essay of March 1947 "a comprehensive, informed, and balanced exposition of conditions in Japan." Herrymon Maurer, the author of the 1947 piece, had concluded that Japan's was an "economy of survival." MacArthur contended two years later that "it is still by all standards an 'economy of survival.' " The anonymous writer of the 1949 article said most of his data came from American businessmen "who have tried to do business in Japan since the war." The main scholar of the American Council on Japan says the group was "probably behind the publication" of the 1949 essay. In it the author contends that after three and a half years of the occupation 80 million Japanese were living on 53 percent of the production levels that the nation had "barely existed on" during the Depression years of 1930 to 1934, when the population was 60 million. He admits there had been improvement since 1946, when the production index figure was 32.5 percent of the 1930–1934 level, but argues that "even this shallow gain has come about almost entirely by Japanese efforts. . . . In fact, a great many SCAP actions can be shown to have harassed and frustrated even this feeble revival." He then expounds on eight points to demonstrate his thesis that the Japanese economy was stagnant or worse and the SCAP bureaucracy was largely responsible for the chaotic situation.[22]

In its June issue *Fortune* published MacArthur's response, which was about the same length as the original article. He claimed that if the occupation had been ended after two years he could report "mission accomplished" on the original objectives of demilitarization and democratization and that not until late 1948 was SCAP assigned the additional objective of economic restoration. Moreover, whatever economic progress that had taken place up to the end of 1948 had been achieved without direct American aid for economic rehabilitation, in contrast with the generous assistance of the United States to German industrial recovery. "On a per capita basis the total financial aid received by Japan from the U.S. since the Occupation began," MacArthur pointed out, "has been but one-fourth of that extended to Germany, not counting the cost of airlift operations [during the Berlin blockade of 1948–49]."[23]

The criticisms by *Fortune*'s essayist, as well as the rebuttals by MacArthur, covered eight areas of Japan's postwar economic situation: inflation, industrial production, taxation, export markets, business climate, occupation costs, controls over raw-material allocations, and dependence on American imports.[24] Each side was highly selective in its use of statistics, and much more data would have to be considered to determine which one, if either, got the edge in this debate. It must have been nettling to MacArthur, who considered himself a Hoover conservative and a champion of capitalism, to be assailed particularly by *Fortune* because not only was its stature prestigious among top American businessmen but also it was part of the empire of the husband of one of his fondest admirers, Clare Boothe Luce.

In its October issue *Fortune* resumed the attack in an article entitled "SCAPitalism Marches On: Japan's Economy Will Be Better Off When It Comes Marching Home." The target this time was mainly Marquat's Economic and Scientific Section: "SCAP's team of economists, admittedly second-rate . . . is torn by disagreement and dissension." They "appear unable or unwilling to implement the whole Dodge plan." The anonymous writer also pictures the Japanese economy as beset by increasing Communist-led labor troubles, unemployment, and trade deficits, as well as lagging industrial productivity. This time MacArthur did not reply to the editor but issued a lengthy press statement, addressing the criticisms point by point. He also sent a letter to Under Secretary of the Army Tracy S. Voorhees, expressing his perturbation over *Fortune*'s latest insults and closing with the question "What can be the motive behind the continuance of such irresponsible and venomous attacks?"[25]

Another piece that elicited a strong response from MacArthur was written by Helen Mears, who had visited Japan in 1946 with a labor advisory group. It appeared in the *Saturday Evening Post*'s issue of June 18, 1949, under the catchy title "We're Giving Japan Democracy, But She Can't Earn Her Living." MacArthur replied with an essay of similar length in the *Post*'s issue of July 30, following which the editor added some telling comments in defense of his writer. Mears' article, like the previously discussed ones in

Newsweek and *Fortune,* followed closely the line of the Japan Lobby. The suspicion among Kern's group and some State Department officials that SCAP might not fully support Dodge may be the explanation for their timing, which coincided with the critical phase of inaugurating the Dodge Line.

Mears made three principal points, and MacArthur offered a rebuttal to each. First, she maintained that the Japanese government since 1945 had "huge" budgets, "largely due to the very high cost of the occupation and our reform program." MacArthur retorted that this charge was "unrealistic and misleading in that it ignores the fact that through food and other relief supplies alone the United States is contributing to the Japanese economy far more than enough to balance the cost of the Occupation." (He might have added that Japanese costs for occupation support dropped from 33 percent of the national budget in fiscal 1946 to 18 percent in fiscal 1950.) Second, Mears argued that, though SCAP thrust a host of new freedoms and democratic changes on the Japanese, "these liberated peoples can no longer earn even a prewar standard of living." MacArthur responded, "The conclusion finds its complete refutation in progress thus far made toward economic stability under which . . . Japanese industrial production has recovered decisively toward its average prewar level." Third, Mears said that MacArthur, in effect, "told the Japanese that when we say 'democracy' we don't mean a decent standard of living. Democracy, the general said, is a 'spiritual commodity' that 'springs from hardship, struggle and toil.' Maybe the general is right, but we can't expect the communists not to laugh their heads off." MacArthur replied heatedly, "No such laughter has been detected here, but rather the despair of complete frustration due to the firm and enthusiastic absorption of these very liberties which are so cynically 'derided' by the Communists." Overall, MacArthur dismissed Mears's attack as based on "almost fantastic" ignorance, for "practically everything discussed occurred after her departure [in July 1946]."[26] For the general, this must have seemed like a skirmish compared to the *Fortune* assaults, but even they were not as menacing as the other threats from the rear he had to counter in 1949.

Congressional appropriations for relief and nonmilitary occupation expenses in Japan had been steadily rising: 1946, $108 million; 1947, $294 million; 1948, $357 million; 1949, $503 million. The amount for fiscal 1949 included $107 million for economic rehabilitation, the first such funding for that purpose, though, according to MacArthur, "up to the end of [calendar] 1948 none of the supplies purchasable with these funds had yet arrived in Japan." As has been noted, pressures from Congress, the Japan Lobby, and various interest groups for decreasing the burden of Japanese aid on American taxpayers had been growing. The persistent efforts of MacArthur and, said Voorhees, the "potent support" of former President Hoover had been of great value in the annual budgetary battles over assistance for Japan. With the inauguration of the reverse course and particularly after Dodge's early successes in 1949 in producing Japanese governmental retrenchment, American congressmen began to think that the time had arrived when United States aid could be cut drastically.[27]

Voorhees, who agreed with MacArthur that the aid program could not yet be reduced without harming the Japanese situation, notified the general in late May 1949 that the House Appropriations Committee was contemplating "drastic slashes . . . below the levels recommended by the Department of the Army" for Japan that, if enacted, would have a "devastating effect upon U.S. objectives" in that country. MacArthur sent word to the House committee that such cuts as its members were considering would result in Japan's economic recovery being "materially undermined if not actually completely vitiated." He reminded them that "the severe domestic financial stabilization program outlined by the Dodge mission was imposed as a prerequisite of United States economic recovery fund contributions." The congressmen were convinced; the fiscal 1950 appropriation for aid to Japan was set at $438 million, which was less than for the previous year but not nearly as great a reduction as originally contemplated.[28]

A new threat to funding for Japan loomed in late 1949, when Frank Pace, Jr., director of the Bureau of the Budget, proposed severe cuts in monies for Japan, with the GARIOA funds to be reduced from the Army's proposed $320 million to $140 million and economic aid from $300 million to only $97 million. MacArthur told Voorhees on December 16 that such action would constitute "a most devastating attack against the objectives of this Occupation and the United States program of world political, social and economic readjustment. . . . The realistic basis for slashing 70 percent from carefully prepared budget estimates for Japan defies comprehension and can only be construed by the Oriental mind as an abandonment of [American] policy." Later Voorhees happily notified him that the desired GARIOA budget had been saved, thanks to the efforts of Gordon Gray, the Secretary of the Army since June 1949, "the value of which I cannot overestimate." Dodge, who was to make his third trip to Japan in 1950, also came in for praise from Voorhees: "Joe Dodge was of immeasurable value to us in getting the budget restored to the full $320,000,000. I am sure that we could not have done this without him." Among other assistance, Dodge "saw [Secretary of the Treasury John W.] Snyder personally, appeared before the Staff Committee of the National Advisory Council, appeared at the hearing before the Bureau of the Budget, and also had a long personal talk with Frank Pace himself."[29] Voorhees was undoubtedly aware that such information would benefit Dodge in his next rounds with SCAP.

For fiscal 1951, however, the best endeavors of MacArthur, Voorhees, and others concerned about aid to Japan were to no avail, and the appropriation was reduced to $288 million. After testifying before the House Appropriations Committee in a futile defense of the Army's proposed larger amount, Voorhees wrote to MacArthur, trying to point out the brighter side: "The reductions in GARIOA costs and in personnel — military and civilian — backed as they were with dramatic figures of economic recovery and by cultural progress and reorientation toward peace and democracy, constituted convincing evidence of a real triumph of American policy." As for the "attitude" of the committee, he reported "there was not a word of expressed or implied criticism of any kind" of the occupation. Voorhees' support of MacArthur on the funding issue was one of several differences between him and his Pentagon superiors that led to his resignation as Under Secretary of the Army in April 1950. Later he confided to MacArthur: "I regret that you have not been receiving the support from Washington that you feel you need for the occupation. . . . I write this . . . so that you would know that I had not intentionally let you down."[30] Actually, with the Korean War in full sway, the surge of procurement orders placed by the United Nations Command with Japanese suppliers was boosting the economy of Japan more by the end of fiscal 1951 than all previous attempts to promote recovery had done.

Besides defending his occupation administration against hostile journalists and economy-minded Washington officials, MacArthur was also firing from the rampart in 1949 at those who seemed desirous of removing him from his position — and had the power to do so. With the creation of the Federal Republic of Germany in May 1949, the regime of control in the American zone of occupation shifted from the jurisdiction of the Department of the Army to the State Department. General Lucius D. Clay, who had served as military governor, was succeeded by High Commissioner John J. McCloy, who had been Assistant Secretary of War from 1941 to 1945 and then president of the International Bank for Reconstruction and Development. The change had been percolating at the State and Army planning levels for over a year, and officials of both departments involved in occupation affairs had been giving serious thought to a shift to civilian control in Japan, too. MacArthur's first inkling came in June 1948, when Draper asked for his comments on NSC 13/1, the first revision of NSC 13, which stemmed from Kennan's recommendations on policy toward Japan. The final section of the document called for an American ambassador in Japan acting directly under the State Department and only in a secondary capacity under MacArthur. "An independent State Department representative reporting directly to Washington," MacArthur responded, "would introduce into Japan a divided command responsibility." He contended that it "could only result in friction and unsettlement of the coordinated balance heretofore existing between the several executive departments in the orientation of American policy," and it would "do much to undermine that efficiency in operation which heretofore has resulted from application of the principle of unity of command." Besides, he pointed out, "the Japanese would play the ambassador against the Supreme Commander, and vice versa, until the present orderly administration yielded to disorder and intrigue." During the continuing revision of NSC 13 that summer and fall, the proposal of an ambassador in Tokyo was dropped; and Mac-

Arthur was satisfied with the statement on control and responsibility as it was worded in NSC 13/2, which was adopted in October.[31]

Because of disagreements among the planners, however, NSC 13/2 had three unfinished sections — on West Pacific island bases, on the FEC, and on reparations. The wording was the same for each of these sections: "Recommendations on this subject are to be submitted separately." NSC 13/3, or the third revision of the "Report by the National Security Council on Recommendations With Respect to United States Policy Toward Japan," was adopted on May 6, 1949. The only changes from NSC 13/2 were the additions of the three incomplete sections. NSC 13/3 stated that the United States should retain "on a long-term scale" strategic control of the Ryukyus (mainly Okinawa), as well as Nanpo and Marcus islands to the east. In the section on the FEC it declared, in essence, that more American independence of that body was in order: "We should not hesitate to use the interim directive. SCAP should also be encouraged to make greater use of his authority as sole executive for the Allied Powers." It also stated that "the reparations question should be reduced to the status of a dead letter" and worded the position on United States withdrawal almost exactly as General Frank McCoy presented it to the FEC that month, which was quoted earlier.[32]

In the process of completing the official position on these three matters for NSC 13/3, however, the State Department's Office of Far Eastern Affairs reopened in early March the discussion about an ambassador and even talked of completely "civilianizing" the occupation administration in Japan. The new round apparently began when, on the 2d of that month, Maxwell M. Hamilton of the Far Eastern Office, with Max Bishop's collaboration, presented the office chief, W. Walton Butterworth, with a draft plan entitled "State Department Assumption of Control of Non-Garrison Aspects of Military of Japan: Full Implementation of NSC 13/2." The American ambassador, according to the document, would report "directly to the Secretary of State on all political and economic matters in Japan and on all matters affecting American interests in general." Beginning on July 1, 1949, "control of all non-garrison aspects" of the occupation "would be transferred to the State Department," and "instructions to SCAP on all non-garrison aspects . . . would be issued by the State Department." The SCAP civil sections "would be discontinued," and their staffs would be replaced by State appointees, who would report to the ambassador. The positions of SCAP and CINCFE, both then held by MacArthur, would be separated, with the headquarters of the Far East Command relocated outside Tokyo and preferably outside Japan. The proposal concluded:

> If the foregoing program should be adopted, it is recommended that the President order General MacArthur to Washington for consultation, at which time the President would inform General MacArthur of the new program. If General MacArthur were agreeable, he could continue as SCAP. He could remain in residence at Tokyo, or he might take up residence at some point such as Honolulu, paying periodic visits to Japan and turning over immediate charge there to his deputy, a high-ranking military officer. Should General MacArthur prefer to resign, it is suggested that consideration be given to appointment as his successor Major General Maxwell Taylor, a graduate Japanese-language officer with an outstanding combat record.[33]

Somewhere in the maze of State-Pentagon planning channels, possibly before it left "Foggy Bottom," this bold scheme was killed. As in NSC 13/2, the next edition of NSC 13 made no mention of an ambassador or of control changes. If they had a chance to comment on this plan, of course, the Army planners involved in NSC 13 revision did not have to be pro-MacArthur to object; the audacity of State officials proposing which officer should succeed MacArthur would have cost the plan most Army support. As seems to be a tradition in relations between officials and journalists in Washington, however, there were leaks to the press. It was said that MacArthur's regime might be replaced by a civilian one, and in short order the word reached GHQ in Tokyo. According to one of MacArthur's staff generals, the initial surface reaction of the Supreme Commander and his top officers was to dismiss it as "the most outlandish of many crackpot ideas from those State Department loons."[34] But given his long-standing distrust of those "loons" and his feud with Dean Acheson dating from the fall of 1945, MacArthur probably doubted that the idea was dead even after the adoption of NSC 13/3 in early May.

If he harbored such a doubt, it was confirmed on June 3, when General Omar N. Bradley, the Army Chief of Staff and a favorite of Marshall and Eisenhower, notified him rather matter-of-factly: "For some time, our trend of thought here has been that we should try to get the State Department to take over the Military Government in Japan in a similar manner [to that in Germany] as soon as the State Department is organized to handle it. We hope to take up this matter again with the President and the Secretary of State as soon as the German Government is established and functioning." Later Bradley remarked, "Inasmuch as MacArthur was still urging a Japanese peace treaty, thus allying himself with State against Defense, I thought this was a fairly reasonable proposal to which he would probably have no objections. How wrong I was! Back came a scathing diatribe the like of which I have seldom read." Bradley claimed that at that time he was not aware of "the deep distrust with which MacArthur viewed our State Department in general and Dean Acheson in particular. He must have viewed me as a traitor too, 'selling out' to State."[35] For the military head of the Army, Bradley displays here surprising naïveté (or ignorance) about both MacArthur and the State Department.

On June 16, the day he wrote to Bradley, MacArthur sent almost the same 1500-word letter (except for different opening and closing paragraphs) to Acheson, Voorhees, and Deputy Secretary of Defense Stephen T. Early, who had been his fast friend since World War I and had served as President Roosevelt's press secretary. The selections from his letter to Bradley represent the substance of his message to all four men:

> Here there is no military government. . . . I have permitted the Japanese government in all of its branches and sub-divisions to function, subject only to the close observation and inherent authority of the Supreme Commander. . . . Such United States personnel as are required to carry on the civil phase of the Occupation consist for the most part in specially qualified civilians recruited in Washington. Thus, in the SCAP Headquarters organization, out of 2796 persons on duty, 2443 are civilian.
>
> The situation here is thus entirely different than that prevailing in the United States zone of Germany where Mr. McCloy is about to enter upon his duties as High Commissioner. There the American forces have actually governed through an established and functioning military government, with a civil German government only just about to be inaugurated. In addition, the United States has maintained unilateral control over policy and administration from the start in its zone

of Germany. Here in Japan, to the contrary, such unilateral control was yielded at the Moscow Conference in late 1945 when an Allied set-up was agreed upon. . . . This set-up embodied . . . the Far Eastern Commission . . . the Allied Council for Japan . . . and the Supreme Commander for the Allied Powers. . . .

The United States could, with respect to the American zone of Germany, alter the regime of control at will, but, by the express terms of the Moscow Agreement, any change in the regime of Occupation control in Japan . . . to permit the State Department to assume a position in Japan analogous to that it is about to assume in Germany, would require the consent of a majority of the Far Eastern Commission. . . . It is most unlikely that such an agreement would be forthcoming. . . .

But apart from this, and of infinitely greater importance, no move could be more calculated to destroy the remaining prestige of the United States in the Far East than a serious effort toward such a change. Nothing would give greater impetus to the Communist drive to bring all of Asia under control. . . . It could not fail to be regarded as a decisive step toward yielding in the face of Communist successes in China and as a tacit acknowledgment of our inability to maintain our position, support our responsibilities, and defend our rights and interests in the Far East. . . .

The United States has emerged through three and a half years of a predominantly American Occupation to occupy a unique position in the hearts of the Japanese people. It is a position of respect bordering on reverence and veneration [that would be lost by such a change in the regime of control]. . . .

The estimate I have made is so conclusive in evidentiary support that I earnestly request that if the suggested change is seriously considered, I be advised in time to permit me to place my views in full detail before Secretary Acheson, who, you may recall, as Undersecretary was one of the principal architects of the present international set-up, and the President, both of whom have previously indicated opposition to any fundamental change in the existing structure.[36]

MacArthur had heard nothing official about further developments on this matter when Sebald, who had just returned from a visit to the State Department, conferred with him on July 23. In a message to Butterworth marked "Personal and Top Secret," Sebald reported: "The General asked me whether consideration is being given to a change in the regime of control of Japan. I replied that I was unable to discover any definitive thought on this matter . . . and that, barring a treaty of peace, I very much doubted that the regime of control would be changed." Later in their conversation Sebald shared with the general a Washington rumor that Truman had accepted Clay's resignation as military governor in Germany in early May, "presumably because of his failure to carry out United States policy. This interested the general greatly." He also tried to assure MacArthur of "the earnestness with which all levels in the [State] Department strive to meet and reconcile SCAP's views with realities of the situation in Washington." But Sebald admitted that "one thought in the Department is along the line of establishing a civilian deputy under the Supreme Commander, with broad powers separate and distinct from the military." The general asked, "Who would this gem of a person be?" Sebald said Dodge had been mentioned, but MacArthur did not believe Dodge would take such a job. The general added, according to Sebald, that he, MacArthur, "would not be party to an arrangement" in which he was forced to "sit idly by and let someone else run the Occupation for him." In summing up for Butterworth, Sebald said of the Supreme Commander's current disposition, "I sensed a new willingness to 'play ball,' an attitude which contrasts favorably with his former criticisms of the Department."[37]

In an interview on August 5 with William R. Mathews, editor and publisher of the *Daily Star* of Tucson, MacArthur ranged over a variety of topics. He was "in fine humor," Mathews later informed John Foster Dulles, and "physically he looked better than he did in 1945," when Mathews had first met MacArthur, in Manila. "He loves to talk," said Mathews, and "the general is just about as artful a dodger as any politico I have met." When Mathews asked whether he thought America should continue to help Chiang Kaishek, MacArthur replied, "Why, certainly. . . . He may be on his way out, but as long as he will fight, I believe in helping him, as I would help anyone else who will fight the Communists." Then the general suddenly inserted, with no follow-up or amplification, a surprising suggestion: "What we need out here is someone to unify and direct all of our policy in the Orient. He should have the rank of a High Commissioner." Farther on in his letter to Dulles, Mathews altered the sequence of the remarks. After they had discussed how American officials "had messed things up pretty badly" in trying to mediate in the Indonesian revolution, "it was at that

Headed for the flag-raising ceremony at the U.S. embassy, Tokyo, September 8, 1945. *Left to right:* Generals Sutherland and Giles, Admiral Halsey, and Generals Eichelberger, MacArthur, and Chase.

Entering the U.S. embassy, Tokyo, September 8, 1945. *Left to right:* Generals Eichelberger and MacArthur, Admiral Halsey, and General Fellers.

The first meeting of General MacArthur and Emperor Hirohito, U.S. embassy, Tokyo, September 27, 1945. Both men autographed the picture.

Ah Cheu, Mrs. MacArthur, and Arthur outside the embassy residence, Tokyo, c. 1947.

OPPOSITE PAGE
Top: A commander with contrasting traits, Tokyo, winter of 1945–1946.
Bottom: At his desk in the Dai Ichi Insurance Building, then SCAP/AFPAC General Headquarters, Tokyo, February 26, 1946.

Manuel Roxas, first President of the Republic of the Philippines, greets
MacArthur at Nichols Field, Manila, July 2, 1946.

OPPOSITE PAGE
Addressing the first meeting of the Allied Council for Japan, Tokyo,
April 5, 1946.

MacArthur and an aide leaving the Dai Ichi Building on the day of the
declaration of the new constitution of Japan, Tokyo, November 3, 1946.

Accompanied by Colonel Bunker, MacArthur leaves the Dai Ichi Building, Tokyo, April 2, 1948.

Conferring with Ambassador Muccio and General Almond at Suwon, Korea, June 29, 1950.

Top: Inspecting the honor guard at the U.S. embassy, Tokyo, with Captain Kenneth G. Groom, the honor guard's commander, and Colonel Huff, on MacArthur's seventieth birthday, January 26, 1950.
Bottom: Arrival of the Joint Chiefs of Staff at Haneda Airport, Tokyo, January 31, 1950. *Left to right:* Generals Bradley, MacArthur, Vandenberg and Stratemeyer, Admiral Sherman, and General Collins.

With Generalissimo and Madame Chiang Kai-shek at Taipei, Formosa
(Taiwan), July 31, 1950.

Talking to General Lowe, President Truman's special representative, at Haneda Airport, Tokyo, August 8, 1950.

At Kimpo Airfield, near Seoul, Korea, September 20, 1950. *Left to right:* Generals Almond, MacArthur, Fox, and Wright.

OPPOSITE PAGE
Top: On board the U.S.S. *McKinley* during the Inchon landings, September 15, 1950. *Left to right:* Generals Wright, Whitney, MacArthur, and Almond.
Bottom: Going ashore at Inchon, Korea, September 16, 1950. *Left to right*: General Whitney, Admiral Struble, and Generals MacArthur and Smith.

Discussing operations with General Almond at Kimpo Airfield, Korea, September 21, 1950.

point when he made the recommendation about a High Commissioner to be in authority over all of our political and military effort in the Orient."[38] Since he knew Mathews had some ties among journalists and officials in the national capital, perhaps MacArthur, who was being kept in suspense about his very job, wished to create a bit of puzzlement himself in Washington circles.

No response by Bradley to MacArthur's strongly worded letter of June 16 has been located in any records, but on August 16 Bradley, who had just been elevated to chairman of the Joint Chiefs, wrote him expressing his "gratitude for the assistance and loyal support you have given me during my tour as Chief of Staff of the Army." MacArthur waited nearly three weeks before answering, and when he wrote he used the salutation "Dear Bradley" in contrast to Bradley's "Dear General MacArthur." He wished Bradley "a most successful tenure" in his new position, but also commented on the fact that, as Chief of Staff, Bradley had not visited Japan, and that he hoped the new JCS chief would "find the opportunity for an on-the-ground view of this sector of the world" soon.[39] It was a mere exchange of innocuous pleasantries, since Bradley had nothing to report about the status of the proposal to change the occupation's system of control.

MacArthur's long wait ended when he received a lengthy, conciliatory letter from Acheson, dated September 9, 1949, and bearing the notation that it was "sent with the concurrence of Secretary of Defense [Louis] Johnson and the approval of President Truman." The Secretary of State did not delve into the processes of decision-making on the proposal for a State Department takeover in Japan, but, instead, treated the matter as one that MacArthur had taken more seriously than Washington planners had:

> First, may I allay the concern expressed in the opening sentence of your letter. You say, "I have been rather disturbed recently over recurrent Washington datelined dispatches reflecting a trend of thought in official circles . . . [regarding] a change in the regime of control in Japan. . . ."
> I remember seeing some newspaper stories along these lines. But so far as I know they do not reflect any trend of thought in official circles — certainly not in the Department of State.
> As you correctly state, the situation in Germany was and is very different from that in Japan. . . .

In a situation so different from that in Germany and so much more favorable from the point of view of accomplishment of United States policy, no one in a position of responsibility would, I think, find developments in Germany a pattern. These newspaper stories to the contrary were what newspapermen call "think pieces" — with little or no stress on the "think."[40]

Acheson devoted the latter half or more of his letter to the topic that had become a high priority for the Secretary of State, the negotiation of a Japanese peace treaty. "We now have this treaty question under active consideration," he told MacArthur. "It seems not at all improbable that it will prove impossible to draft a treaty acceptable to us and to all of the other interested powers," particularly the Soviet Union. Undoubtedly catching MacArthur by surprise, Acheson asked for his advice in writing the treaty and added, "Before long I should like to send one of our most trusted officers to discuss some of these questions with you." He also complimented the general for his role in NSC 13/3, "to the formulation of which you contributed so helpfully." As for its implementation, "here, again, we in the Department of State would be greatly helped by a thorough talk with you." Acheson confessed, "In this connection I am conscious of a defect, without being able to suggest a remedy, in the liaison with you." The Secretary closed disarmingly: "I am sorry to inflict upon you so long a letter. . . . Your own kindness in giving me your own reflections, as well as your thoughtful invitation to come and see for myself, I most deeply appreciate."[41] Since MacArthur was a master at blowing smoke, too, he undoubtedly viewed Acheson's unusual friendliness as the cover for a strategic withdrawal by the State Department from its takeover scheme, which had been rejected finally, perhaps by the National Security Council or by Truman himself. Secretary of Defense Johnson, who admired MacArthur and despised the State Department with about equal intensity, probably had had a hand in defeating the plan. The general must have enjoyed a chuckle when he contemplated how drastically the State Department leaders' intentions had apparently changed over the summer season — from shipping MacArthur to Honolulu or the States to seeking his counsel in the formulation of a Japanese peace treaty.

CHAPTER IX

Social and Cultural Encounters

1. Society in Transition

JAPANESE AND AMERICAN PERCEPTIONS of each other's civilizations undoubtedly were molded more by the relationships between local Japanese and off-duty GIs than by all the decrees emanating from GHQ. Next in importance probably were the contacts between the citizens and the Eighth Army's prefectural civil affairs teams (discontinued in 1949). Again, the most meaningful communications may have occurred during the civil affairs troops' off-duty time rather than when they were explaining SCAP regulations at village meetings. There are countless anecdotes about the soldiers' leisure activities, ranging from romances and sightseeing trips to brothel patronage and drunken brawls, but, other than what venereal disease records indicate, there is little way to measure the myriad ways in which the GI (and a few BCOF) conquerors and the Japanese people communicated and interacted with each other. It is no wonder that, though scholars acknowledge the era as important and unique in modern Japanese social history, there is a paucity of serious studies about the impact of the occupation on Japanese society and culture, or vice versa. A major reason is the difficulty of reconciling that which is essentially administrative and manifested in directives and legislation with what is basically nonadministrative and traceable in elusive ways through mores and values. This chapter is not a pioneering effort to tackle this problem, which may be insoluble; instead, it is a modest attempt to look at a few areas of Japanese life where SCAP, as the occupation administration and, less often than wished, as MacArthur, was influential, for better and for worse.

The SCAP program that touched the most people, literally and figuratively, was Colonel (later Brigadier General) Crawford F. Sams's war against major communicable diseases. The intensive American air raids had ruined medical facilities and water and sewage systems, besides forcing people into unsanitary underground shelters, where they were exposed to growing hordes of pestilential insects and vermin. Widespread malnutrition made the Japanese vulnerable to disease, and the collapse of medical services during the last months of the war made it almost inevitable that massive epidemics would strike the nation. Moreover, the return of millions of Japanese repatriates from the Asian mainland and the Pacific islands, many of whom were disease bearers, to an already overcrowded, devastated homeland increased the possibility of unprecedented plagues unless quick, effective preventive actions were taken. Sams, who had strong support from MacArthur and enjoyed excellent rapport with him, organized and directed enormous antiepidemic campaigns that may have been unequaled in size in history.[1]

A typhus epidemic was already under way among the large Korean population of Japan when the occupation forces arrived, and it spread rapidly as hundreds of thousands of Koreans began moving to the port cities for repatriation. Sams therefore set typhus control as his immediate priority. He quickly organized 80,000 Japanese and American medical and public health personnel in 800 newly established district health centers, from which teams fanned out across the country to disinfect people by DDT dusting, to vaccinate, to decontaminate water supplies, and to teach preventive measures. Sams, recalled a Japanese doctor who served in the program, "worked like the devil himself" and "was a pragmatic idealist devoted to getting things done." In Osaka, which was hard hit by typhus, Sams oversaw the dusting of a half million people in four days. About 50 million Japanese were dusted with DDT, and nearly 13 million were vaccinated during the antityphus drive. From 31,141 cases of typhus in 1946, the number of cases dropped to only 121 by 1949. Dr. Lauren V. Ackerman, a member of an American medical mission that visited Japan, remembered Sams as "an extremely efficient individual" who used "authoritarian methods" and was not always tactful. But perhaps such a dynamic, hard-driving leader was needed during those critical days. The Japanese who worked with Sams in the war against typhus nicknamed him "Dr. Lice."[2]

During the first months of the occupation there were no problems with cholera, but, despite quarantines of ships carrying repatriates, somehow cholera entered Japan in 1946 with some of the Japanese returning from China. By August of that year there were over 1200 cases, mainly in port cities. Sams and his immunization teams were in full action against the dread disease by then, however, and vaccinated nearly 35 million people. The battle against cholera was won quickly; no cases were reported after December 1946. MacArthur called it "our greatest triumph" in the struggle against communicable diseases in Japan. Remarkable progress was achieved against other highly contagious diseases, too. Over 17,000 smallpox cases were reported in 1946, but after enactment of a preventive vaccination measure and massive immunization of infants and schoolchildren, smallpox ceased to be a major problem by 1949; there were only 124 cases that year. The combined efforts of American and Japanese public health personnel between 1946 and 1949 reduced typhoid and paratyphoid by 90 percent, diphtheria by 86 percent, and dysentery by 79 percent. Tuberculosis had long been "extremely prevalent" in Japan, where the death rate from it was one of the highest of any nation. Sams mounted a strong campaign against tuberculosis, vaccinating over 35 million people; the result was a reduction of the death rate by 40 percent between 1946 and 1949. In all, an estimated 96 percent of Japan's people underwent immunization or DDT dusting during the occupation. At the time, of course, no one knew that DDT, used against several diseases, was carcinogenic. A Japanese writer charitably, though without proof, states that "certainly" the DDT dusting "prevented many more deaths from epidemic diseases than it may have caused . . . through cancer."[3]

The influx of millions of repatriated Japanese, besides several hundred thousand American and Allied troops, magnified the problem of venereal diseases in occupied Japan. The returning Japanese troops especially "were riddled with VD," says one ac-

count, and the whores who had traveled overseas with the imperial forces and now went back to work in Japan were found to be
90 percent infected. The American military set up multitudes of
prophylaxis stations near its bases, and Sams directed the establishment of over 1700 Japanese clinics to treat venereal diseases,
the production of effective anti-VD drugs, and the distribution of
education programs on preventive measures. In January 1946
MacArthur ordered the Japanese government to abolish licensed
prostitution and to void all contracts whereby girls were sold into
bondage. But the house and "open-air" girls managed to continue
their lucrative trade, despite all official efforts to the contrary. The
brothel prostitutes in Tokyo even organized a union and sent a
letter to MacArthur asking him to "take steps against the street-
walkers," who were cutting into their profits. The Supreme Commander chose not to intervene. Unit orders declared red-light areas
off limits, but GIs bent on whoring were not greatly impeded. "The
Japanese government and Occupation authorities cooperated,"
according to a reliable source, "in creating official brothels ('rec-
reation and amusement' areas) for the American victors." It is
doubtful, however, that MacArthur was apprised of this activity.
In the winter of 1945–1946 the VD rate among American troops
in Japan reached 27 percent, but, thanks mainly to the efforts of
Sams and his public health forces, it was cut to about 13 percent
by the next July and remained at approximately that level. The
incidence rate was commendable in comparison with the rate of
nearly 31 percent among American troops in Germany in August
1946 and even higher rates among some Stateside military units.[4]

Besides its work in preventive medicine, the SCAP Public Health
and Welfare Section oversaw a host of programs that included improvement of water and sewage systems; reorganization of the
Japanese Medical Association, Red Cross, and Institute of Public
Health; establishment of district public health centers and of district training schools in nutrition, public health, and sanitation;
nationwide educational programs in public health through films,
lectures, and pamphlets; modernization of Japan's medical, dental, nursing, and veterinary schools, as well as its hospital facilities
and management; regulation of pharmaceutical manufactures;
supervision of the distribution of relief supplies through the Licensed Agencies for Relief in Asia (LARA); administration of dis-

aster relief; free school lunch programs for needy children, which were providing daily meals for over 7 million school children by 1949; compilation of health and various social statistics; narcotics control; and assistance in drafting legislation on a number of public health and welfare matters, ranging from child welfare to health insurance.

The school lunch programs, the SCAP promotional campaign for better nutrition, and the gradually improving standard of living in Japan contributed to a population of taller, heavier, and healthier children by 1950. In addition, nearly all the fearsome epidemic diseases of old were under control, and the death rate dropped from an average of 18.7 per 1000 persons in 1933–1940 to 8.1 in 1950–1951. One of the best measures of the SCAP success in public health was that the Japanese in the postoccupation era expanded and improved, but did not abolish or radically alter, the major programs Sams had inaugurated. In his memoirs Sams commented, "The benefits . . . in the lowered death rates and lowered disease incidence and improved standards of living will go on for many, many years as these programs are continued. They have been continued. Had we attempted to impose on the Japanese our way of doing things just because we do it a special way in our own country I am quite sure we would have failed."[5]

Unfortunately, these humanitarian and successful programs in public health aggravated what had been Japan's chief problem for a long time, namely, too many people. One of the main reasons for Japanese expansionism in the 1930s had been the pressures of overpopulation. And the problem greatly worsened during the occupation years. Between 1945 and 1950 the Japanese population rose from 71 million to 83 million, some of the rise due to repatriation but more than half the result of natural increase at a rate of over 1 million per year. The differences between relatively high birthrates and sharply reduced death rates in occupied Japan "produced the highest rates of natural increase in Japan's history," states a noted demographer. Overpopulation added pressures to the already volatile labor situation, accelerated the consumption of the nation's scarce natural resources, and gave rise to serious ramifications for the political, economic, and social future of Japan. "It was hardly practical," observed an American journalist in Japan, "to take measures that would drastically reduce the death rate in an already overpopulated country without at the same time paying attention to the need of reducing the birth rate."[6]

Several American experts who came to Japan as consultants to the SCAP Natural Resources Section pointed out that the population and natural resources problems were closely related. Most notable were Dr. Edward Ackerman of the University of Chicago and his team of specialists, who spent nearly two years in Japan and prepared a well-researched two-volume report on the nation's natural resources. In several passages the report stressed the need for limiting population growth to keep Japan from facing starvation conditions, social unrest, and continued dependence on American assistance. When the report was printed, in the late spring of 1949, copies were obtained by several American religious groups in Japan who were opposed to birth control. They protested to MacArthur, and he replied with a public release saying that "the problem of Japanese population control . . . does not fall within the prescribed scope of the Occupation, and decisions thereon rest entirely with the Japanese themselves. . . . Birth control, with its social, economic, and theological sides, is, in final analysis, for individual judgment and decision." The issue continued to provoke public controversy that summer, and after a strong complaint from the Catholic Women's Club of Tokyo and Yokohama, an American women's organization that was upset about the Ackerman study, MacArthur was stirred into action. He recalled the copies of the report that had been distributed and had all copies put in a vault; a new edition was commissioned, with the offending passages deleted. He allegedly reprimanded Lieutenant Colonel Hubert Schenck, chief of the Natural Resources Section, whose foreword to the work, referring to the problem of "too many people on too little land," was one of the expurgated passages. The Supreme Commander cancelled an impending survey by the SCAP Civil Information and Education Section on Japanese public opinion about the population issue, and he refused an entry permit to Dr. Margaret H. Sanger, the famed American birth-control advocate, who had been invited to Japan to give a series of lectures.

When asked about MacArthur's actions, one SCAP official explained simply, "Mac didn't want to be caught in the middle." A distinguished authority on Japanese demography concludes that MacArthur may have been wise not to take a position favoring family limitation, for such advocacy "might well have furthered the already strong identification of population policy with militarism and war rather than with peace and welfare," and it would have "permitted the accusation of genocide." Later in 1949 the Diet enacted the Eugenics Protection Law, which legalized abortion for both health and economic reasons; made lawful the manufacture, sale, and use of contraceptive devices; and established government-controlled marital counseling offices, where information on birth control, among other services, was to be made available.[7]

If the size of the family had become a lively issue by 1949, the structure of the traditional family system had been shattered by the reforms under the new constitution and civil code of 1946–1947. The postwar Japanese constitution may be unique among such documents in its stipulation that "marriage shall be based only on the mutual consent of both sexes, and it shall be maintained through mutual cooperation with equal rights of husband and wife as a basis." The new civil code abolished the legal disability of married women (formerly designated "incompetents"), and it established the legal equality of the sexes in marital choice, divorce, property settlements, and parental rights. "The new civil code was one of the postwar legal revisions least influenced by SCAP," said one of its Japanese drafters, adding: "Both the Americans and the Japanese were of the same mind on this issue [of abolishing the old family system]. . . . All of us on the commission considered it the logical step to bring the civil code into conformity with the new constitution's emphasis on the dignity of the individual and the equality of the sexes."

Under the traditional system of the extended family, or house, the head, who was normally a patriarch, had exercised virtually absolute authority over the other members not only of his immediate family but also of his children's families. The family head arranged marriages, governed where members might reside, and decided matters of property and estate succession. But under the new democratized family system, the nuclear family, which consisted of a couple and their unmarried children, became more significant than the extended family, and in many cases the influence of the house patriarch collapsed. With the stress now on individualism and sexual equality, the divorce rate rose markedly — from 48,832 divorces in 1943 to 83,689 in 1950 — as did the incidence of "love marriages" and "unarranged" changes of residence. Generally young people consulted family elders less often about their decisions, and some felt the new system liberated them from the traditional responsibility of caring for aged, infirm members of the house. The legal reforms affecting marriage, women, and the family surely furthered the principles of the worth of the individual and the equality of women, but some critics believed that such democratization also was a prime factor in exacerbating problems of housing shortages, inadequate care of the aged, domestic instability, social rootlessness, and juvenile delinquency. For many young adults in occupied Japan, the de jure shift from the extended to the nuclear family became a de facto change from the family altogether to the individual as the fundamental unit of society. According to one Japanese who was in his young adulthood in the late 1940s, "The breakdown of the family, the scorning of old values, the sense of not belonging, the foolish imitation of GI tastes and behavior — these things all made it a time of social chaos for us. We were living in between — the old ways were fading, but we had not yet embraced anything new of substance that was ours, that was made in Japan."[8]

MacArthur, who repeatedly endorsed greater participation by Japanese women in public affairs, apparently thought the democratic reforms that had led to progress in women's rights had also resulted in strengthening, not weakening, the family as the basis of Japanese society. In October 1946, Dr. Mary R. Beard, the wife of the historian Charles A. Beard and an eminent scholar herself, drew the following conclusions from some beliefs of the general that she had obtained on request in connection with her research on modern woman's role in society:

> I've got something in this document indicative of General MacArthur's conception of the family as the core or heart of society and of woman as its prime guardian, which I would otherwise almost have to go back to Confucius to get. . . . That General MacArthur should associate the care and nurture of the family with political democracy . . . gives him a standing in my mind which is at the top of . . . statecraft. I need this very kind of statement to help me . . . to so-

cialize our ultra-feminists who so tragically overlook the role of the family even in a democracy. I say "tragically" because the American family is suffering almost disastrous injuries.[9]

Many of Japan's older generation would have said that the family in their country, too, was tragically declining in influence.

In the history of Japanese women the occupation period is a watershed, and, as in the case of land reform, the progress achieved during that era undoubtedly would not have been as rapid or substantial without the intervention of SCAP. But, also like land reform, female emancipation was not altogether a SCAP innovation but had roots in earlier Japanese efforts. In 1931, for instance, the House of Representatives passed a bill granting civil rights to women, but it was defeated in the House of Peers. Voting and running for office for the first time in the elections of April 1946, women demonstrated surprising strength at the polls in gaining seats in the House of Representatives. Soon female candidates were winning representation in prefectural and local assemblies. In 1948 Chiyo Sakakibara, a Diet member, was appointed the nation's first woman vice minister (of Justice). Despite difficulties posed by males on the job and discrimination in pay, women steadily moved into the work force, constituting 39 percent by 1951; they also had gained a bureau in the Ministry of Labor charged with serving their needs. Socially, their push for equality was not overly successful in those early years, for male feelings about the subordination of women were deeply instilled and could not be eradicated simply by legislation. But, as an American observer commented in 1949, "it seems improbable that they will be forced back into their traditional position of complete subservience to men."[10]

The principal leadership in the women's sundry causes in occupied Japan, of course, was borne by Japanese, such as Mrs. Fusae Ichikawa in the suffrage movement, Mrs. Shizue Kato in birth control advocacy, and Mrs. Yukika Soma in various crusades. Two American women who worked in GHQ distinguished themselves in the struggle for Japanese women's rights. One was Miss Beate Sirota, the young woman in the SCAP Government Section who wrote the provisions on women's rights that eventually were incorporated in the new constitution. She also contributed significantly to the overall drafting of the bill of rights that was included in that document. The other American woman of distinction was

First Lieutenant Ethel B. Weed of the Women's Army Corps, who served ably as chief of the Women's Subsection of the SCAP Civil Information and Education Section. Among many achievements, she was responsible for the creation of the Women's and Minors' Bureau of the Labor Ministry, and she traveled extensively from Hokkaido to Kyushu, lecturing on women's rights, counseling women who were moving into public affairs or the labor market, and assisting Japanese women in organizing their own political, civic, cultural, labor, and social organizations. An *Asahi Shimbun* publication in 1972 described her as "an extremely energetic advocate of increased rights and privileges for Japanese women. . . . Although she mothered and nursed the postwar Japanese women's movement during her seven busy years in Japan, Miss Weed is all but unknown in her own country."[11]

On numerous occasions MacArthur issued public statements praising the progress of Japanese women, particularly on each anniversary of their startling success in the 1946 Diet elections. When those pioneer female politicians took their seats in the House of Representatives that summer, many of their male colleagues treated them coolly. Their prestige was suddenly boosted, however, when MacArthur took action after learning of their unhappy reception in the Diet. He invited all the newly elected women to his Dai Ichi office, shook hands with each one, chatted amiably, and delivered a short inspiring address, which he then released to the press to make obvious his enthusiastic endorsement of their presence in the Diet. In his speech he praised them and all the women of Japan for "responding magnificently to the challenge of democracy" and "discarding the age-old bonds of convention which have so long denied them the fundamental democratic right to participate in communal affairs beyond the home." As the leader of the group of women, Mrs. Kato then spoke, expressing to the general their "gratitude for your noble effort to bring democracy to this country" and "for granting us suffrage and educating us as to the use of it." She said they were pledged to support peace, the new constitution (then under debate), legislation protecting women and children, the furtherance of civil liberties, and the elimination of "feudalistic family systems."[12]

Prince Higashikuni, the former Prime Minister, maintained that "MacArthur was deeply concerned with women's suffrage." A scholar of the movement recently contended, however, that "there is little evidence that MacArthur himself played a key role in initiating reforms concerning women's rights," although he did perform "an important role in supporting the proposed changes when they reached the highest levels of SCAP," where his approval "was crucial in moving these measures through." His pressures on the Japanese government were important, too, in behalf of various measures benefiting women. But perhaps his principal contribution was hortative and symbolic, one that inspired and encouraged women's leaders to continue their crusades and communicated to potential obstructionists that the women had his blessing. An instance of his symbolic gesturing was recalled by an American in Tokyo at the time: as usually happened when he entered or left the Dai Ichi Building, "a crowd of Japanese" had assembled "to witness the pageant of the MPs with polished helmets and the great man himself, in battered hat and open shirt, returning their salutes; and this day a woman in a kimono broke from the crowd and suddenly prostrated herself before MacArthur. Gently he picked her up, smiled, and said, 'Now, now — we don't do that sort of thing any more,' patted her on the shoulder, and sent her on her way."[13] No one who witnessed that simple incident was likely to forget it — or the Supreme Commander's message.

Although MacArthur found it necessary to send a letter to all American army chaplains in Japan in 1946 to ask their help in curbing the "widespread promiscuous relationships between members of the occupying forces and Japanese women of immoral character," he was strongly supportive of fraternization in the more congenial, wholesome sense of GIs mixing with the Japanese people. Colonel Roger O. Egeberg, his physician during the Southwest Pacific war and the early part of the occupation, described MacArthur's reaction to a directive from the War Department in early September 1945 that said fraternization should be discouraged:

> This distressed General MacArthur deeply. As we were driving along in the jeep, where so many of our conversations occurred, he said: "Doc, what is fraternization? Fraternization by our soldiers means they they will be going into Japanese homes or maybe hovels because we bombed their homes, bringing some gum, some candy, some K-ration or food they saved from their own mess for the kids; of being nice

to the people in that home, of coming back, of gradually becoming a part of this household or that. Oh, some of our men just want a woman for the night, but most of our boys don't. Here they have fought their way through the jungle of New Guinea, the Admiralties and down the Central Luzon Plain, and now they are through with fighting. They are our ambassadors, they are our true ambassadors, and they want even more to bring to the people of this recent enemy country that we are occupying the real feeling of the people of the United States. And they will do a better job of it than an ambassador or minister sitting in a fine residence talking with the upper hierarchy. No, Doc, I cannot stop fraternization. They can recall me, but I won't do that" — and he didn't.[14]

The crime statistics that MacArthur saw, like some of the other data fed to him by SCAP underlings, did not jibe with those compiled by the Japanese police, and the American combat veterans who entered Japan in the fall of 1945 were not all looking for nice Japanese families, as the general rather idealistically pictured them. But with the rotation home to the States in 1945–1946 of most of the wartime forces, the American troop replacements in Japan dropped markedly in age, maturity, and self-discipline. It was these "high school commandos" who, far more than their predecessors, overindulged in whoring, drunkenness, and fighting, and when scholars eventually determine the accurate figures on GI crimes in Japan, it is likely that they will conclude that most were committed by the younger replacements. Eighth Army commanders had to tighten regulations on their off-duty activities until the opportunities for almost any form of fraternizing became severely limited. When Roger Baldwin visited Japan in 1947, he found that "no American could stay in a Japanese home overnight, not even a Nisei [second-generation Japanese-American] with his grandmother; and giving presents to Japanese was strictly taboo — to control black marketing." Baldwin told MacArthur he "thought the regulations too tough" and should be relaxed, including the prohibition against marriages between the soldiers and Japanese women. MacArthur expressed surprise and said he had not known how strict the rules had become. In July of that year the Supreme Commander lifted the ban against marriages of occupation personnel and Japanese, and he had the regulations revised to permit "moral" forms of fraternization. The consequence in the next several years, as one scholar expressed it, was "probably the largest number of legally sanctioned interracial marriages in such a brief space of time in American history."[15] As suggested earlier, it was at the level of such relationships and the many informal liaisons between the soldiers and the Japanese people, especially the young women, that the most significant and least measurable social and cultural interactions occurred. MacArthur may have been idealistic in his view of fraternization, but at least he was wise enough to understand that the GIs, not he and his GHQ officers, were "our true ambassadors" in occupied Japan.

2. MacArthur's Spiritual Mission

American ethnocentrism was evident in the attempts to democratize Japan's political, legal, economic, and social systems, but it was blatant in the interventions in Japanese culture. Most SCAP culturally related incursions stemmed from Washington directives, but in the field of religion MacArthur exploited his latitude as Supreme Commander to venture far beyond what his superiors intended. Amazingly, Pentagon and State officials do not seem to have called him to task on his religious stewardship.

The Potsdam Declaration and the "United States Initial Post-Surrender Policy," as well as subsequent directives in the fall of 1945, called for the establishment of religious freedom and the elimination of ultranationalistic, militaristic organizations. To SWNCC planners and to MacArthur the logical corollary to religious liberty was the separation of church and state, which led to the directive of mid-December 1945 disestablishing Shinto and the Emperor's statement two weeks later repudiating the doctrine of his divinity. The new constitution stipulated that "freedom of religion is guaranteed to all. No religious organization shall receive any privileges from the State."

But MacArthur, who became obsessed with the idea of Christianizing Japan, believed that so long as "no religion or belief was oppressed, the Occupation had every right to propagate Christianity." He proceeded to make a "unique contribution to religious policy," commented William P. Woodard, an official in the

Religions Division of the SCAP Civil Information and Education Section, who at times was astounded by MacArthur's "outspoken support of Christianity and the Christian movement in Japan and his negative approach to the indigenous faiths of the country." Although the Religions Division was supposed to advise the Supreme Commander on religious matters, Woodard said "there was practically no prior consultation" with the unit by the general in his Christian offensive.[16]

MacArthur never attended church and counted few chaplains among his friends during his long career, yet he was deeply religious in his own way, possessed a good layman's knowledge of the Bible, made frequent references to Christian principles in private talks and public statements, and welcomed visits by high-ranking Protestant and Roman Catholic clergymen from the United States. In expressing his theological beliefs, he rarely went beyond the ethical precepts in Christ's teachings, particularly those in the Sermon on the Mount. MacArthur's zeal to convert the Japanese appears to have been rooted in five convictions that he held firmly by the time he lived in Tokyo: (1) He believed that history should emphasize his efforts as a peacemaker rather than as a warrior. At the surrender ceremony in Tokyo Bay on September 2, 1945, he had asserted in a moving address aboard the battleship *Missouri* that the problem of peace henceforth "basically is theological," and he envisioned himself as the inspiring leader in Japan of the "spiritual recrudescence and improvement of human character" that he mentioned in the speech. (2) He believed that Christianity and democracy together formed the foundation upon which America's greatness lay and upon which postwar Japan's future should be built. "I am absolutely convinced," he told the editor of a religious periodical in 1948, "that true democracy can exist only on a spiritual foundation. It will endure when it rests firmly on the Christian conception of the individual and society." Father Edward Flanagan, the Boys' Town founder, said after a talk with him in Tokyo, "General MacArthur feels democracy can never succeed in Japan until the country is Christianized." (3) MacArthur saw Christianity also as an effective Cold War weapon against Communism. "Japan is a spiritual vacuum," he remarked to a group of Protestant leaders. "If you do not fill it with Christianity, it will be filled with Communism." When Katayama became Prime Minister in 1947, MacArthur praised him, along with Generalissimo Chiang Kai-shek and Philippine President Manuel Roxas, as Christian heads of state who afforded "hope for the ultimate erection of an invincible spiritual barrier against the infiltration of ideologies which seek by suppression the way to power and advancement." (4) He thought that the Japanese people, who now seemed to have no regard for the militarists who had led them to defeat, had repudiated their old religions along with militarism and ultranationalism. On various occasions he derided Shinto and Buddhism for their "complete failure" to satisfy spiritual needs and for their allegedly inferior moral standards in comparison with those of Christianity. (5) He was convinced that the time was ripe for Christianity in Japan, where, he predicted to a minister, it could win "one of its outstanding victories of all times." In 1946 he wrote the president of the Southern Baptist Convention in the United States that the Japanese were primed for conversion and "Christianity now has an opportunity without counterpart in the Far East." The situation seemed uniquely opportune, too, because for the first time Japan was subject to control by outsiders; the United States, long the main source of personnel and funds for Christian missions, had the dominant position in the occupation control system; and the occupation commander was ready to use his considerable influence to Christianize the Japanese.[17]

And mightily exert his influence he did. MacArthur promoted Christian missions in Japan through numerous press releases, messages to American church organizations and publications, personal letters to and interviews with prominent church leaders, and even in communications to Pentagon officials and congressmen. An Episcopalian by christening, if not in church attendance, the Supreme Commander was utterly nonsectarian in his pitch to Christian groups about the opportunity in Japan and avidly supported the activities of such diverse organizations as the National Conference of Christians and Jews, American Bible Society, Gideons, Pocket Testament League, Foreign Missions Conference of North America, and several Roman Catholic societies. In May 1949 he issued a communiqué promoting the 400th anniversary of the arrival in Japan of Jesuit missionary Francis Xavier and welcomed pilgrimages by Westerners for the occasion.

"It is the policy of this theater to increase greatly the Christian influence," he informed the Joint Chiefs in November 1946, "and every effort will be made to absorb missionaries as rapidly as the church can send them into the area." He made direct appeals to various missionary boards asking first for 1000 missionaries and later pleading for a "hundredfold" increase over the number sent. "I asked for missionaries, and more missionaries," he recalled. By 1950 there were 2500 serving in Japan. Announcing that the "demand for Bibles, testaments, and gospels is insatiable" in Japan, MacArthur launched a drive to have 10 million Bibles given to the Japanese people. Through gigantic fund-raising efforts by church groups and assistance by Bible societies in America, together with the use of military transport ships to carry the Bibles, he reached his goal, calling the drive a "demonstration of practical Christianity." Probably he never knew that many Japanese, as one historian discovered, "accepted the Bibles because the paper served as a cheap substitute for the high-priced cigarette paper on the black market." MacArthur also made vigorous appeals for contributions for the International Christian University, and, beginning in late 1948, he served as the honorary chairman of the foundation planning the school, which opened in 1953 at Mitaka, near Tokyo.

Not only were Christian missionaries admitted to Japan sooner and under easier permit procedures than other Westerners desiring entry, they also received preferential treatment from both SCAP and Japanese officials who were eager not to appear to be obstructing the Supreme Commander's "pet project." When Dr. Toyohiko Kagawa, Japan's outstanding Christian evangelist, was appointed to the House of Peers in early 1946, some SCAP staff members questioned whether he should be seated, since they allegedly had evidence that he had backed Tojo's regime and had made some critical remarks about the occupation. The final GHQ decision was to permit his seating, because SCAP's disapproval of Kagawa might "undermine the Protestant evangelistic movement in Japan." Later Kagawa became an ardent admirer of MacArthur's, lauding him as "an honest Christian" who would have "a high place in Japanese history." In the SCAP censorship of Japanese school textbooks, statements derogatory about Christianity were deleted and favorable ones added. MacArthur set up a board of chaplains to review religious references in textbooks. Colonel Hubert Schenck later reported proudly to MacArthur, "There is more Christian content in the Japanese course-of-study and text-books than there is content relating to any other religion." Army chaplains, spurred by the Supreme Commander's crusade to convert Japan, often undertook evangelistic work among the Japanese in addition to their task of providing spiritual nourishment to interested GIs. In assisting missionaries to meet needs in transportation, housing, supplies, and other matters, SCAP officials, eager to please their commander, frequently went well past the second mile in helping the Christian movement in Japan. Dr. William K. Bunce, chief of the SCAP Religions Division, said in 1947, "The privileges extended missionaries by SCAP have . . . not been enjoyed by any other persons not attached to the Occupation."[18]

When the correspondent John Gunther visited occupied Japan, he quipped that MacArthur "goes so far as to think of himself and the pope as the two leading representatives of Christianity in the world today." Indeed, if all the plaudits and honors that were bestowed on him by grateful Protestant and Catholic groups in America were the criteria, MacArthur seems to have accomplished the "spiritual revolution" in Japan that he frequently claimed was under way, particularly in 1946–1947. *Ave Maria,* a Catholic periodical in the United States, suggested MacArthur and Pope Pius XII for the Nobel Peace Prize in 1947. Bishop Fulton J. Sheen called him "America's greatest citizen," and numerous Protestant and Catholic organizations requested inspirational messages from him to be read at their national gatherings. An official of the Evangelical Missions Association of Japan told the general, "We believe that God has sent you in 'His place' . . . for the redemption of the Far East." A cynic, of course, might point out that it was perhaps more than coincidental that his Christian crusading and especially the publicity about it reached a zenith about the time that the MacArthur-for-President campaign began anew.

MacArthur's optimism about Christianity in Japan apparently did peak in 1947, with Katayama the Christian as Prime Minister and four other Christians in his Cabinet and with the evangelist Kagawa completing a 427-day campaign for Christ across Japan, during which he spoke to over a million people. MacArthur boasted to a mission board official, "I could make the Emperor and seventy million people Christians overnight, if I wanted to use the power I have." He later told the evangelist Billy Graham that the Emperor had personally "declared his willingness to make Christianity the national religion," but the general "had rejected the offer because he felt it was wrong to impose any religion on a people." Some time that year the story began circulating that the Emperor himself was about to become a Christian. Woodard stated, however, "To one with whom he was somewhat closely associated, he [MacArthur] said that His Majesty would be accused of outrageous cynicism if he became a Christian." In February 1947, MacArthur reported to Chief of Staff Eisenhower that "a spontaneous development which offers both encouragement and inspiration" was "the increasing number of the Japanese people — already estimated at over two million — who, under the stimulus of religious tolerance and freedom, have moved to embrace the Christian faith as a means to fill the spiritual vacuum left in Japanese life by the collapse of their past faith." The gist of this message also went into a SCAP press release. When a woman missionary questioned his figure for the total of Japanese Christians, MacArthur responded, "Two million was no exaggeration, in fact four million might be a more accurate number to give."[19]

Although most Protestant and Catholic opinions were highly favorable toward the Supreme Commander's eager pushing of the Christian cause, some missionaries in Japan felt their special treatment and identification with GHQ handicapped their evangelistic efforts among the Japanese. "Most of his written statements endorsing the Christian movement," Woodard said, "appeared to the Japanese to be a violation of the official policy. Any government official making similar statements, particularly in respect to Shinto, would have been disciplined." Non-Christian missionaries were not welcome in MacArthur's realm; when one Indian Hindu group complained to GHQ about the discrimination, the Supreme Commander dismissed its grievance as based on "sadly misinformed" sources. Of course, Buddhists and Shintoists were upset not only by his seeming lack of sincerity about religious liberty and church-state dissociation, but also by his disparaging remarks about their faiths.

As the occupation shifted direction in 1947–1948 toward more dependence on the Japanese, MacArthur apparently realized he needed the support of the large numbers of Buddhists and Shintoists. They had been antagonized especially by his frequent references to Christianity in his public statements. In his New Year's Day message of 1948 to the Japanese nation, he mentioned religion but dropped "Christianity" and never used the term again in such pronouncements, though he continued to refer to moral and religious values. In his draft of a statement in 1949 promoting the projected International Christian University, he first wrote, "Japan must move strongly toward Christianity and Christian leadership in order to achieve democracy." In the final copy, however, he changed the words "Christianity" and "Christian" respectively to "spirituality" and "moral."[20] The general's more realistic attitude toward the religious situation in Japan was evident to Dr. Bunce of the Religions Division when they conferred in November 1949, as Bunce's memorandum to Colonel Donald Nugent about the conversation shows:

> Near the end of the conference General MacArthur turned abruptly from world affairs to religions in Japan. He made the observation that Japan would not be Christianized in any conceivable period of time — that pride of race, if nothing else, would prevent most Japanese from becoming Christian — and inquired whether the Buddhists and Shintoists are accepting those fundamental principles of moral conduct and right living which he has so often attributed to Christianity. . . . He stated further that perhaps the greatest contribution Christians could make would be to awaken leaders of other religions to a more positive and progressive role. . . .
>
> I gained the definite impression that while the General is still a strong proponent of Christianity . . . he might have good words for Buddhists and Shintoists too if he felt that they were promoting the same broad moral principles he finds in the Christian ethic. He is definitely anxious for evidence of this broader support of his program.[21]

The results of the Christian crusade in occupied Japan in terms of increase in church membership must have been discouraging to the missionaries and MacArthur, though it is not certain that the latter learned how poor the figures actually were. In 1941 there had been about 233,000 Protestants and 120,000 Roman Catholics in Japan. By 1951 the number of Protestant Japanese was about the same as ten years earlier, and the number of Roman Catholic

Japanese was 157,000. Thus Christians made up only about a half of 1 percent of Japan's population of 83 million by the time of MacArthur's departure. In defense of the evangelists' effort, it should be added that their achievements in educational and medical work, if not evangelism, were impressive and their contribution of leaders to national and local government was far out of proportion to their numbers. But in comparison with the two main religions of Japan, the figures on adherents of Christianity looked minuscule: by 1951, the Shinto sects had 17 million members, and there were 45 million Buddhists. Moreover, during the occupation era there had been an astounding proliferation of new non-Christian religious sects, whose total membership may have reached over 4 million by 1951. Of all the religious bodies in occupied Japan, however, the fastest growing was Soka Gakkai, a Buddhist sect based on the humanistic tenets of Nichiren Daishonin, a thirteenth-century priest. (In the ensuing two decades it would grow to 20 million and develop a potent political arm, Komeito, or the Clean Government Party.)

Why, despite all the support MacArthur mounted and the various advantages it was given, did the Christian movement not make any appreciable headway? A respected student of the subject suggests three basic reasons: (1) Buddhism and Shinto were "hardier and more deeply ingrained" than Westerners realized. (2) The missionaries "deluded themselves by accepting superficial evidence" of Japanese interest, not delving, for example, into the motives of those who attended their meetings or accepted their literature. (3) "Outraged Japanese citizens" often judged Christianity by the "social and sexual behavior" of miscreant GIs.[22] Two other reasons warrant consideration: (1) The Japanese have never been attracted to religions that could not be adapted to their cultural heritage. Islam and Hinduism were even less successful than Christianity in Japan. Buddhism had arrived in the fifth century, when the Japanese were absorbing portions of Chinese culture and language (by way of Korea). In post-1945 Japan, Buddhism was accepted as a "native" religion and, like sectarian Shinto, was enmeshed with some of the finest aspects of Japan's long cultural tradition. (2) Some missionaries perceived, in the close identification of their cause with MacArthur and his GHQ regime, a liability to the success of their evangelism. The general's overzealous

crusading, his denigrating of Buddhism and Shinto, and his ignoring of religious freedom and church-state separation were not
the wisest tactics to use among a people who could be as ethnocentric as their American overlords and over half of whom were
Buddhists.

3. The Right Ways and Words

MacArthur's imprint on educational policies is less discernible than
on religious affairs. He felt "deep concern," he said, about the
"thought control" underlying the old Japanese educational system, and he strongly endorsed nearly all the reforms, no matter
how costly and unrealistic, that were advocated by his educational
staff and the American experts brought in for consultation. He
would have agreed with the following assessment by the editor
Kawai: "The Occupation might impose sweeping changes in the
political, economic, or social organization of Japan, but the permanent acceptance of these changes depended ultimately on how
successfully the Japanese were educated to appreciate them. The
role of education was in this respect fundamental to the whole
Occupation program."[23]

MacArthur's primary instructions regarding education were
spelled out in several SWNCC and JCS directives from September
to November 1945. Dr. Robert K. Hall, a former professor of
comparative education at Columbia University who served as chief
of the Education Subsection of Nugent's Civil Information and
Education Section, summarized these instructions as a four-part
SCAP "Basic Education Plan":

> First: To eliminate militaristic and ultra-nationalistic propaganda, of-
> ficial sanction of and support of Shinto, and unacceptable teachers.
> Second: To introduce democratic ideas and principles, democratic
> tendencies in social organizations, information on the Japanese de-
> feat and its implications and knowledge of the responsibility of the
> Japanese to maintain their own standard of living without assistance.
> Third: To safeguard religious freedom and, within the limits of se-
> curity, freedom of opinion, speech, press, and assembly.
> Fourth: To control the curricula of educational institutions, the eli-

gibility of persons to hold public office or important positions in private organizations, and the opening of schools.[24]

Hall believed "the first two years were overwhelmingly the most important" in SCAP educational reforms, and "after that, the influence of the Occupation, so far as education was concerned, followed an asymptotic cycle as American influence waned." The highlights in policy evolution during that early period were the recommendations of the Stoddard Mission in March 1946 and the subsequent implementing legislation of March 1947, the Fundamental Law of Education and the School Education Law. Dr. George D. Stoddard, commissioner of education in New York State, headed the United States Education Mission of twenty-seven educators, who, on MacArthur's invitation, spent several weeks investigating the Japanese system and made recommendations to SCAP in the areas of educational aim and content, administration, teaching and teacher training, primary and secondary schools, universities and colleges, adult education, and language reform. Yoshida observed that press releases on the plans for overhauling education "aroused public enthusiasm," but he and other top Japanese officials thought they were "highly unrealistic," in light of "the stringent financial situation" and the wartime destruction of "so many school buildings." But under heavy pressure from SCAP the Japanese government began to try to implement all but language reform among the major proposals of the Stoddard Mission. Besides the two key measures of March 1947, the Diet enacted thirty-seven other educational laws between 1947 and 1951. The Ministry of Education often acted slowly and reluctantly in implementation, and it sometimes successfully obstructed reform efforts. The principal impediment, however, was the dire shortage of funds at the national and local governmental levels.[25]

The Stoddard Report heavily emphasized the need to simplify Japan's written language, one of the most complicated ever devised. But its recommendation to phase out the old ideograph-based language in favor of *romaji,* a much simpler syllabic-based Romanized form, was not adopted. According to Hall, the change was opposed by "a powerful minority in SCAP's headquarters and the Department of State, as well as by traditional and conservative Japanese." If "powerful," the SCAP opponents must have been close to MacArthur; the Supreme Commander's view is believed to have been less than enthusiastic. Stoddard and his colleagues later were highly complimentary of MacArthur's interest and support, but he actually conferred with them only once, on March 20. In a press release later he praised the Stoddard Report as "a document of ideals high in the democratic tradition," but added, "Some of the recommendations regarding educational principles and language reform are so far-reaching that they can only serve as a guide for long range and future planning."[26]

Only a few of the many changes that SCAP forced on the Japanese educational system can be mentioned here. Compulsory attendance was extended from six to nine years, and an American-style plan of six years of elementary school, three years of junior high school, three years of senior high school, and four years of college was introduced. Progressive teaching methods were inaugurated, involving less rote work and more problem-solving and independent thinking by students. Curricula and textbooks were extensively revised to exclude militaristic, ultranationalistic views, and instruction in "morals" and military science was dropped. Courses in social studies, physical education, nutrition, and vocational subjects were added, and more emphasis was placed on extracurricular activities, all in the name of preparing precollege students better for "life in a democratic society." Much of the power of the Education Ministry was stripped away; decentralized administration based on elected local school boards, as in America, was inaugurated. Parent-teacher associations were eagerly promoted as democratizing agencies. Though most were only at beginning or formative stages during the occupation years, efforts were undertaken to broaden educational opportunities by promoting women's education; setting up programs in adult education; improving learning skills for the blind, deaf, and other handicapped persons; expanding public and school library holdings and services; and, beginning in 1949, developing a student exchange program with American schools and colleges.[27]

Teacher education was stressed, too, but there was a serious shortage of qualified teachers at all levels. About 116,000 teachers and school administrators had resigned or been removed by Japanese authorities in anticipation of the purge directive of January 1946; an estimated 80,000 or more left teaching in the ensuing three years. Nearly 6000 educators were purged or lost their jobs during the screening process in the year following the start of the purge, and thousands of others were fired during the anti-Communist campaigns of 1949–1950 that hit hard the ranks of the militant Japan Teachers' Union. Dr. Hall, SCAP's education chief during the early years, did not like the punitive changes: "The censorship of the textbooks suffered from the same shortcomings as did the purge of the teachers. What the Occupation took out, the Japanese could later put back. The act of removal actually called attention to and made attractive the very things the Occupation wanted unnoticed. Worst of all, the purge and censorship had a bad smell so soon after the defeat of Nazi Germany."[28]

Japan's system of state-sponsored higher education also was drastically changed. Before 1945, elitism characterized admissions and standards of the small number of prestigious imperial and private universities, and competition to gain entry into their student bodies was severe. But SCAP, acting on a Stoddard Mission recommendation, compelled the Japanese government to reorganize as four-year colleges nearly all of the former technical and other institutions of learning above the secondary level, with each prefecture to have its own "national" university and several so designated in each large metropolitan area. During the years 1945–1950, the number of "national" and "public" universities grew from 21 to 104, but there was no appreciable elevation in the quality of the faculties or programs of the newly designated universities, primarily because of lack of funds, though American-style graduate schools were added to many of these schools. Moreover, an ambitious system of over 200 junior colleges was begun.[29]

In December 1949, MacArthur reported to the Commission on Occupied Areas, an advisory body on culture and education, that in the past four years "Japanese and American educators cooperated in building from the ruins a new educational structure, soundly conceived and based on concepts as democratic as those which prevail in any country in the world." At his instigation, another American education mission came to Japan in August 1950 to evaluate "the progress and results of the recommendations made in 1946." The mission was headed by Dr. Willard E. Givens, the executive secretary of the National Education Association, who, along with all four of the other members, had participated in the Stoddard Mission. The 1950 report hailed "the remarkable accomplishments of General MacArthur and his staff" and concluded that "the educational program outlined by the 1946 Educational Mission is working successfully," except for language reform, which they again recommended be undertaken.[30]

Contemporary and later critics of the educational reforms, however, found many flaws. Four main points have been stressed over the years by Japanese and American scholarly critics: (1) the impossibility of financing so many changes during such economically troubled times, with just the three-year expansion of compulsory education proving shockingly costly; (2) the often irrelevant or unnecessary implantation of American pedagogy and methods when much of the old Japanese system, with modifications, would have worked more smoothly and efficiently; (3) the resort to decentralization when financial and administrative considerations at the time indicated the impracticality of local educational boards and the need for a strong, if liberalized, Ministry of Education; and (4) the abolition of moral education, under the rubric of discarding the old emphases on filial piety and loyalty to the Emperor, when instruction in ethics, basic human rights, and traditional nonmilitaristic Japanese values could be valuable in training youth in a time of social stress and flux. Though much of the criticism came from the Japanese and later from American scholars, not all contemporary American educators were blind to the faults of the SCAP reforms. Hall, for instance, concluded that "the greatest mistake was that of confusing punitive action with implementation of the democratic philosophy." Dr. Verna A. Carley, a Stanford professor who served as a SCAP adviser on teacher education, was especially critical of the dabbling in university education without adequate funding: "By edict to raise schools to four-year universities without providing libraries, professors, or qualified students was just shocking, especially when the Japanese had high standards in higher education."[31]

Within a decade after the end of the occupation the Japanese discarded the local boards, revitalized the Education Ministry, restored moral education, and put more emphasis on fundamental subjects like mathematics and the sciences. Superior Japanese youth continued to try to earn their degrees from the same prewar elite group of universities in order to obtain the best openings in government and business. A Japanese scholar pointed out, however, that "all that [SCAP's] New Education brought Japan has not necessarily been lost." He cited the improved communications between teachers and pupils, the continuing popularity of extracurricular activities, the effective merging of problem-solving with "systematic learning," the growth of coeducation, the widened access to education for adults and handicapped persons, and the absence of a "return to super-nationalism in education." Looking back on the changes in American education over the three decades since World War II, not many of which he saw as advances in teaching and learning, Hall grimly asked, "What would SCAP have directed the Japanese to do [in education] if the Occupation had taken place in 1975?"[32]

Censorship of school textbooks was merely one of the many SCAP attempts to control or mold Japanese thought and expression. Of course, ever since the rise of the militarists to power in the 1930s and especially during the war, the Japanese people had been subjected to much thought control and curtailment of freedom of speech. As the occupation evolved, it seemed to many of them that at times the SCAP restrictions were nearly as severe as those of the militarist regime and surely more ludicrous, since one of the occupation's aims was to teach democracy to the Japanese. SCAP efforts to maintain such controls originated mainly with the Civil Censorship Detachment of the Civil Intelligence Section, the Press and Publications Division of the Civil Information and Education Section, and MacArthur's Public Relations Office, which handled, respectively, actual censoring functions, relations with the Japanese press and publishers, and dealings with foreign correspondents. Controls on freedom of expression were aimed first at eliminating militarism and ultranationalism, then at curbing irresponsible journalism, and finally at combating Communism.[33]

In accordance with guidelines from Washington, MacArthur set forth his basic policy on Japanese media expression on September 10, 1945:

  1. The Japanese Imperial Government will issue the necessary orders to prevent the dissemination of news, through newspapers, ra-

dio broadcasting or other means of publication, which fails to adhere to the truth or which disturbs the public tranquillity.

2. The Supreme Commander for the Allied Powers has decreed that there shall be an absolute minimum of restrictions upon freedom of speech. The freedom of discussion of matters affecting the future of Japan is encouraged by the Allied Powers, unless such discussion is harmful to the efforts of Japan to emerge from defeat as a new nation entitled to a place among the peace-loving nations of the world.

3. Subjects which cannot be discussed include Allied troop movements which have not been officially released, false or destructive criticism of the Allied Powers, and rumors.

4. For the time being, radio broadcasts will be primarily of a news, musical and entertainment nature. News, commentation, and informational broadcasts will be limited to those originating at Radio Tokyo studios.

5. The Supreme Commander will suspend any publication or radio station which publishes information that fails to adhere to the truth or disturbs public tranquillity.[34]

Within a month MacArthur ordered Domei, the government's news agency, to be closed for violating the above directive; compelled Japanese journalists and publishers to subscribe to a code of professional ethics; terminated Japanese governmental control over and censorship of news, now SCAP prerogatives; and incorporated freedom of the press in the Civil Liberties Directive of October 4. In the new constitution, safeguards for the future were provided in Article XXI: "Freedom of assembly and association as well as speech, press, and all other forms of expression are guaranteed. No censorship shall be maintained, nor shall the secrecy of any means of communication be violated." The catch was that so long as Japan was under occupation SCAP could invoke the principles of military security and public order to permit its censors wide latitude in interpreting the media's treatment of many topics. "Criticism of the Allied Powers" quickly came to mean primarily negative comments about the Supreme Commander and GHQ policies.[35]

"SCAP officers first had to fight to take the press away from the reactionaries," comments an authority, "and then battle to protect it from the Communists." In between those struggles they were confronted by an outburst of "yellow journalism," reminiscent of the Hearst-Pulitzer rivalry at the turn of the century, as Japanese newspapers, after years of repression under the militarists, engaged in wild circulation battles. Even the "big three" of Japanese newspapers, each with a circulation several times larger than the *New York Times* — *Asahi, Mainichi,* and *Yomiuri* — were guilty of reckless journalism, despite the new code of ethics. One editor later admitted, "Many of the newspapers indulged in an outburst of undisciplined sensationalism, carelessly and irresponsibly mixing rumor with fact." Stories about GI crimes against Japanese, especially rapes, particularly boosted sales, but at the same time provoked GHQ leaders, who saw the potential for "disturbing the public tranquillity." Thus, MacArthur felt justified in ordering prepublication censorship in October 1945; it was not lifted until mid-1948. Another threat came from the newly organized unions of newspaper employees, some of which were led by Communists. *Yomiuri,* the third largest newspaper, was briefly taken over by radical employees in a mutiny in 1946, and for a while its editorial slant was clearly Marxist. MacArthur intervened on the side of the *Yomiuri*'s former management; in short order the radicals were ousted and the paper's policy returned to a middle-of-the-road position. After the union's defeat in the *Yomiuri* crisis, the press, especially the major newspapers, "settled down to a condition of sensible normality," generally reflecting the nonextremist attitude of the majority of Japanese, according to a contemporary journalist. But the editors found that the number of their items held up by SCAP censors increased in the next two years. Kawai blamed the trend on GHQ replacements "who knew virtually nothing about newspapers" and made the censorship "capricious and onerous" at a time when "the success of the Occupation had long been assured, and the friendliness of the Japanese had long been proved."[36]

Probably the most infamous and ridiculous case involving an alleged affront to MacArthur that was censored occurred in October 1946, after the newspaper *Jiji Shimpo* carried an editorial admonishing the Japanese for viewing MacArthur with an "adoration that verges on idolatry" and urging them to stand on their own feet. The editorial was prompted by a recent Japanese-language biography of MacArthur by a journalist, Kazuyoshi Yamazuki, that had sold over 800,000 copies and portrayed him as almost "a living god." The SCAP Public Relations Office had given the editorial its prepublication approval, and the *Nippon Times* decided to print an English translation. But Willoughby learned of the editorial for the first time when the *Nippon Times* was starting its press run, and he quickly decided it "was not in good taste." He dashed to the *Nippon Times* offices and ordered the presses stopped. Learning that a train was about to leave with some early copies aboard for distribution outside Tokyo, he had American military policemen halt the train and remove the papers. The *Nippon Times* staff was then required to substitute another editorial and make a new press run. MacArthur "did not know of Willoughby's action until later," asserts one of the principals in the episode. But Japanese and American journalists of that era have left so many accounts of SCAP censors' prohibitions of items even slightly critical of the Supreme Commander that surely he was not altogether ignorant of such antics.[37]

A surprising number of Japanese journalists agreed with Kawai's view that, though insulting and irritating, SCAP censorship "left few serious ill effects" on the Japanese press, and in light of the huge number of press items screened, "the ratio of foolish decisions was low" in the Civil Censorship Detachment. Of more long-range significance was the generally good working relationship that evolved between the Japanese press and Major Daniel C. Imboden's Press and Publications Division. Although his journalistic experience was limited to a small-town newspaper in California, Imboden made up for his lack of technical expertise by his sincerity in trying to get Japanese journalists to aspire to higher standards of editorializing and reporting. Partly through his encouragement and his staff's assistance, by the end of the occupation period the main newspapers were approaching the level of excellence of some of the better large newspapers of America and Europe. In a public statement in September 1949, MacArthur paid tribute to the Japanese press for the "impressive strides" it had taken in the past four years. "The progressive marshalling of its full power and influence behind the forces of law and order and good government has been one of the most encouraging developments of postwar Japan," he emphasized. The principal historian of the press in occupied Japan maintains, "Nowhere was his Occupation more successful than in its work with the press of Japan," which in the early postwar days had been "the most sensational press in the world." SCAP policy for the Japanese press "was sometimes brilliant, sometimes plodding, but always aimed toward the democratic ideal."[38]

But the same scholar, together with many other students of the subject, has scathingly denounced SCAP's attitude toward critical foreign correspondents, the epithets ranging from "arrogant" and "obnoxious" to "uncooperative" and "inconsiderate." Whereas the Japanese reporters often had access to news about GHQ happenings but could not print it, the foreign correspondents in Japan complained that usually they were not able to obtain access to such news, or if they wrote about the news unfavorably they were barred from learning anything beyond the bland GHQ press releases and had to rely on the Japanese press. Especially damned were MacArthur's public relations officers, who were, successively, Brigadier Generals Le Grande A. Diller and Frayne Baker, and Colonel Marion P. Echols. Although MacArthur himself bore the ultimate responsibility for his headquarters' strained relations with the foreign press, "the unfriendly attitude toward the foreign correspondents," claims one authority, "developed almost entirely on a level below General MacArthur. The loyal ring of staff officers about him shielded the Supreme Commander from the truth about abuses of press freedom." Unhappily for his record, however, the correspondents who felt maligned by SCAP usually became bitter toward him, too, and later were not shy in recounting their experiences in Japan. But the Supreme Commander cannot escape culpability in the abusive treatment of some correspondents, as was clearly demonstrated in the case of his vindictiveness toward Compton Pakenham of *Newsweek*. By October 1950, seventeen foreign correspondents had been expelled from his theater; all such actions required his final decision.[39] His attitude toward the press that was critical of his policies was revealed when he replied to Chief of Staff Eisenhower in late 1946 about a possible visit to Japan by a large group of American journalists:

> While continuing my doubts as to the advisability of the contemplated trip, in view of the insistence of the War Department, I will withdraw my objection. I would like to have an opportunity to pass

upon those contemplated for selection before their invitation is accomplished. I believe the list should not include actual writers but should be limited to publishers and editors and should not include those of known hostility to the occupation. Such papers are the Christian Science Monitor, [New York] Herald Tribune, Chicago Sun, San Francisco Chronicle, PM, Daily Worker, and others of this stamp whose articles and editorials have not only been slanted but have approached downright quackery and dishonesty.[40]

On the other hand, MacArthur cultivated good relations with some of the foreign correspondents in Japan, for example, Russell Brines, the head of the Associated Press bureau, who found the Supreme Commander usually amiable and cooperative.

But the cases are numerous of foreign, especially American, reporters who were harassed in various ways by GHQ, perhaps sometimes at MacArthur's instigation but more often through the machinations of his loyal lieutenants, particularly in the Public Relations Office. As much as possible, these officers tried to restrict the correspondents' sources about GHQ to official press releases and unclassified section reports; digging behind the scenes for additional information was discouraged. Critical or uncooperative correspondents sometimes found themselves losing their offices or quarters in Tokyo, commissary privileges, permits to travel outside certain areas, or access to top GHQ officials for interviews. Diller even set up a quota system to limit the number of representatives admitted from news services, newspapers, and periodicals, but the War Department, reacting to outraged journalists in America, "suggested" to MacArthur that the quota scheme be dropped, which it was. Subsequently he replaced Diller with Baker, whom some correspondents found even more abusive. Baker, in turn, was succeeded by Echols shortly after the public release in February 1948 of a scathing letter from the Tokyo Foreign Correspondents Club to the Committee on Freedom of Press of the American Society of Newspaper Editors. It charged SCAP on eight counts for actions against reporters who had shown "marked antipathy" toward occupation policies or procedures; the reprisals included threats of various sorts, raids on residences, derogatory letters to employers, and branding as "security risks." Echols proved less hostile than his predecessors, but the foreign correspondents' difficulties with MacArthur and his headquarters continued and would increase during the Korean War. Besides the Pakenham incident, the most celebrated cases of SCAP vengeance against critical reporters involved Malcolm Muggeridge of Reuter's, Frank Hawley of the *Times* of London, David Condé of Reuter's and the International News Service, Mark Gayn of the Chicago *Sun,* Andrew Roth of *The Nation,* Keyes Beech of the Chicago *Daily News,* and William Costello of the Columbia Broadcasting System, some of whom attained the distinction of being expelled from Japan. Often expulsion came on short notice: Condé said Willoughby gave him the word that "he had ten days to get out of the country."[41]

SCAP censorship and control were extended also to magazines, radio programs, motion pictures, books, dramas (including the famed *kabuki* plays, which were banned for a time), and the importation of American and other Western publications and films. SCAP censorship of mail was selectively applied, though MacArthur denied any knowledge of it when Roger Baldwin brought up the subject in a conversation in May 1947; later that year the Supreme Commander ordered the practice halted. Japanese radio broadcasting was a favorite target of the SCAP censors both because it was regarded as an important "tool for democratization" and because Japan had more radios than any other country except the United States, the Japanese being avid radio listeners as well as newspaper readers. At times the censors' criteria went beyond security matters; they included also moral judgments, for instance, in banning "erotic" dramas and films. For various reasons, some American classics were banned, including the movie *Citizen Kane* and John Steinbeck's novel *The Grapes of Wrath.* As mentioned previously, the purge was applied also to people in the information media; the first ousted were those with militaristic or ultranationalistic ties, and later radicals and Communists were removed. After MacArthur's suspension of the Communist newspaper *Akahata* in the summer of 1950, over 500 Communists and "fellow travelers" among the various newspapers' employees were dismissed, along with some radio station workers.[42]

Ironically, though subjected to military occupation and a host of restrictions on freedom of expression, the Japanese had "an almost compulsive fascination" for public opinion polls. Among the earliest were those conducted by the major newspapers; later in the occupation the Japanese government established the National Public Opinion Institute. (SCAP had a public opinion staff busily collecting data, too.) Kawai believed that "such great concern with what the public thinks is another manifestation of the democratic trend of postwar Japan." It might also reflect the fact that SCAP censorship and other controls on freedom of speech left the Japanese in frustrating silence, which SCAP could and often did accept as acquiescence, and the polls offered a means of at least expressing one's opinion honestly through anonymity.[43]

Interestingly, however, the Japanese polls did not reveal widespread animosity toward the occupation. A *Yomiuri* survey in April 1951, just after MacArthur's relief from command, inquired, "Do you think the occupation has been beneficial to Japan?" Of 783 respondents, an overwhelming 92.8 percent replied "yes," only 1.0 percent said "no," and the rest marked "don't know." When asked by *Yomiuri*, "Do you think the resignation *[sic]* of General MacArthur is good for Japan?" 7.2 percent of the same respondents said "yes," 46.7 percent answered "no," and 18.1 percent "no effect," with 28 percent indicating "don't know." An *Asahi* poll of May 1952, shortly after the end of the occupation, asked, "Do you think the UN Occupation has had good effects on the people?" Of 2523 answers, 47 percent responded "yes," 14 percent "no," and 39 percent "don't know."[44]

If these polls are indicative of honest opinions rendered under the protection of anonymity, the majority of the Japanese people at the time did not believe, contrary to what some Japanese and American scholars have since maintained, that the occupation had been a "tragic encounter" in which the Japanese had suffered greatly in lost cultural values, national pride, talent, and opportunity because of the ethnocentric SCAP reforms and interventions. Perhaps the poll results suggest, too, that most of the Japanese believed that the American authorities meant well, even when they presented "democracy by fiat" and used military officers to administer democratization. Many of the Japanese people of the occupation era may well have concurred with the following conclusion of a recent American study of the period: "The greatest paradox of all was that despite intense American ethnocentrism, despite profound American ignorance of Japanese culture and society, despite every reason for failure in terms of the goals

Americans defined, the Occupation of Japan was extraordinarily successful, a landmark in human history."[45] If contemporary Japanese could forgive SCAP's blunders and admire the idealistic goals, maybe historians and biographers henceforth will grant MacArthur's wish, after all, and record that his career reached its zenith in Japan.

CHAPTER X

Affairs of State

1. Relations with the Prime Ministers

IF MACARTHUR ENJOYED better rapport with publishers than
with correspondents generally, he found his most satisfying
professional dealings at the very highest levels, with heads of state.
Except for Truman, whom he personally met only once, for a few
hours on Wake Island in 1950, the general's connections with
American, Philippine, Australian, and Japanese heads of state, from
1930 to 1951, rank as his most harmonious working relationships
beyond the inner circle of his own staff. When he served under
Hoover as Chief of Staff of the Army, from 1930 to 1933, he and
the President developed a deep friendship that lasted until
MacArthur's death. As Chief of Staff under Roosevelt, from 1933
to 1935, and as a theater commander under him in World War
II, MacArthur, though he disliked the New Deal and some of the
President's subordinates, got along surprisingly well with FDR and
secured from him some of the principal appointments of his career. As Philippine military adviser, from 1935 to 1941, he was
extremely close to President Manuel Quezon and his wife, who were
the godparents of his son. MacArthur's chief admirer and warmest friend in the Labour government of Australia from 1942 to
1944 was Prime Minister John Curtin. Likewise, in occupied Japan his relations with Emperor Hirohito and his Prime Ministers,
particularly Shigeru Yoshida, were assiduously cultivated by both

sides as models of smooth and cordial, if often formal, ties. For MacArthur, in view of his many other tempestuous relations, dealing with heads of state must have been like sailing a ship in the eye of a hurricane.

Although all of the Emperor's meetings with MacArthur, usually two or three a year, took place at the general's embassy residence, MacArthur's conferences with the five men who served as Prime Minister from 1945 to 1951 occurred at his Dai Ichi office. The following data on the number of sessions with the Prime Ministers are based on the general's office diary:[1]

Prime Minister	Time in office	Meetings with MacArthur	Total
Higashikuni	Aug.–Oct. 1945	1945(2)	2
Shidehara	Oct. 1945–May 1946	1945(2); 1946(2); 1949(2); 1950(3)	9
Katayama	May 1947–Mar. 1948	1947(4); 1948(2); 1949(2)	8
Ashida	Mar.–Oct. 1948	1947(1); 1948(7)	8
Yoshida	May 1946–May 1947, Oct. 1948–Dec. 1954	1945(5); 1946(9); 1947(11); 1948(11); 1949(19); 1950(16); 1951(4)	75

It will be noticed that some of the above meetings occurred before or after the individual was Prime Minister, including six with Yoshida, when he was Foreign Minister under Shidehara; five with Shidehara, when he was speaker of the House of Representatives; two with Katayama; and one with Ashida. The Supreme Commander and the Prime Ministers met on average only every two or three weeks. Most of their communications were through intermediaries or by correspondence. The frequency of their meetings rose in correlation with the implementation of the reverse course and the relaxation of SCAP controls, declining, as expected, with the onset of the Korean War and MacArthur's priority on military matters. By far, most of MacArthur's meetings were with Yoshida, which is not surprising, since he served as Prime Minister during forty-four of the General's sixty-eight months in Japan and for fifty-six of the eighty months of the entire occupation, which formally ended in April 1952. Not unexpectedly, too, much more information is available about MacArthur's relations with Yoshida than with the other men who held the premiership during the occupation.

Prince Naruhiko Higashikuni served as Prime Minister only seven weeks, from mid-August to early October 1945. "The primary purpose of the 'Imperial Family Cabinet,'" said Shigemitsu, his Foreign Minister, "had been to bring the war safely to an end." As uncle of the Emperor and an army general, the suave little premier suppressed the army elements in Japan that had initially rebelled against the decision to surrender; arranged the main surrender details, culminating in the Tokyo Bay ceremony; persuaded the far-flung units of the imperial forces to cease fighting; and cooperated with the occupation forces in ensuring law and order during the first critical weeks after MacArthur arrived. He proved "surprisingly adept at the rough and tumble game" of handling "sharp and sometimes hostile questions" at press conferences with foreign correspondents, according to an American reporter. Nothing specific is known about his two meetings with MacArthur, on September 15 and 29, but several Japanese who knew him said later that the Prince believed he and MacArthur quickly established "mutual respect." MacArthur left no comments in writing about the Prince, but he was convinced that the Emperor could be a valuable instrument in assuring a successful occupation, and, one of his GHQ officers attested, he "treated Higashikuni as his first contact with the Imperial family — politely and wisely." After the Prince left the premiership, some Washington officials favored his arrest as "a suspected war criminal," allegedly for ordering the execution of American airmen, but the idea was dropped when MacArthur opposed it.[2]

Baron Kijuro Shidehara was Prime Minister for the next seven months, during which many of the basic SCAP reform programs were inaugurated, including constitutional revision. Seventy-two years old when he became premier in October 1945, Shidehara was the son-in-law of the founder of the Mitsubishi combine, an internationally respected diplomat and pacifist who had been one of the founders and early leaders of the League of Nations, and remarkably vigorous and sharp for a man of his age. MacArthur recalled him as being in "full and enthusiastic agreement" with the general's early reform ideas, on which he "acted promptly and energetically." A Japanese friend remembered Shidehara's outstanding trait as "cleverness in bending and outlasting the American winds." Grateful to MacArthur for quickly supplying penicillin during his serious illness in December 1945, he was also indebted to the general for supporting his continuation as Prime Minister during a Cabinet crisis in early 1946, when several members resigned. Later Shidehara became a leader of the conservative Democratic party, helped in forming the Democratic Liberal party in March 1948, and was House speaker when he died of a heart attack in March 1951. MacArthur, who had come to respect greatly his counsel and his influence among leading conservatives, issued a statement within an hour of his passing: "I deeply regret the death of Speaker Shidehara. His wisdom and wide experience have been a great asset to this country in its readjustment and his loss cannot fail to be keenly felt at this critical moment of world tension."[3]

After the first premiership (May 1946 to May 1947) of Shigeru Yoshida, who will be discussed last among the five occupation Prime Ministers, Tetsu Katayama was premier for almost a year, from May 1947 to March 1948. At the time he was elevated to the position, he was sixty years old and serving as secretary-general of the Social Democratic (Socialist) party. A lifelong Christian, he had served in the Diet for five years, but much of his career had been spent as a legal consultant on labor cases. He was unaggressive and mild in temperament, and ideologically he represented the Socialist right wing. On Katayama's selection as premier following his party's success in the Diet elections in April 1947, MacArthur publicly hailed the turn of events as reflecting the triumph of "middle of the road" politics and declared that "of possibly even greater significance . . . are its spiritual implications." Ignoring the fact that Katayama was the nation's first Socialist Prime Minister, he pointed out that "for the first time in history, Japan is led by a Christian leader — one who throughout his life has been a member of the Presbyterian church." In his early addresses the new Prime Minister also referred to the religious aspect, telling the Diet, for instance, that "democratic government must be permeated by a spirit of Christian love and humanism . . . [and] guided by a Christian spirit of morality." With Katayama's elevation to the premiership coming at the height of the general's optimism about Christianity's chances of converting the Japanese, MacArthur "expected great things somehow from Prime Minister Katayama," observed a SCAP official. Ball, the Australian member of the ACJ, noted that the Katayama government unmistakably "had the sympathy and moral support of SCAP."

But Katayama faced serious economic crises, aggravated by inflation, labor militancy, and food shortages, that proved unsurmountable, as related earlier. With its initial widespread popular support disappearing by early 1948, the Katayama ministry was in dire straits after the left-wing Socialists split from the premier's fragile three-party coalition. When Katayama informed MacArthur of his intention to resign after losing a confidence vote in the Diet, the Supreme Commander issued a sympathetic statement, recognizing his "conscientious and patriotic leadership" and his struggles to solve the problems of "serious political, economic, and social dislocations," which "are not novel but are inherent in the Japanese situation" in the wake of war and defeat. Actually, commented Dr. Harry Wildes of SCAP, "the general liked the fact that Katayama had a Bible in his right hand but was uncomfortable about the Socialist baggage he carried in his left hand."[4]

Hitoshi Ashida, who served as Prime Minister from March to October 1948, had a versatile background, having been a diplomat abroad for many years, publisher of the *Nippon Times*, and member of the Diet as a Democratic leader. After their merger in early 1948 as the Democratic Liberal party, the forces of Yoshida and Shidehara controlled the Diet and obstructed most attempts by Ashida to get measures he wanted. Wildes, who got to know Ashida, characterized him as "intensely ambitious," which, if accurate, must have meant that he was a very frustrated gentleman by the time of his resignation amid whirls of rumors of corruption that autumn. Ashida appeared especially deferential toward MacArthur; in his letters to the general, for example, he always referred to MacArthur as "Your Excellency," using the honorific several times in the body of a normal letter. But except for a comment by one of Ashida's friends that the Prime Minister thought he and MacArthur "supported each other as best as possible under the conditions," little is known about their relationship, neither the general nor Ashida having left any known written impressions of the other.[5]

Shigeru Yoshida first became Prime Minister in May 1946 at the age of sixty-eight (two years older than MacArthur), following his

Liberal party's dominance in the Diet after the April elections and
SCAP's purging of the main Liberal leader, Ichiro Hatoyama (Prime
Minister from 1954 to 1956). Yoshida's background and views made
liberals in GHQ and among the Japanese think, as one source
phrased it, that "he was hardly the ideal candidate to carry out the
projected reform program" of the occupation. Like Shidehara, he
came from a wealthy, aristocratic background, was respected internationally as an able veteran diplomat, and was accused by Japanese leftists of being "in league" with the bureaucrats, conservative politicians, and big-business elite. But he had opposed the
militarists since the Manchurian aggression and had been jailed in
early 1945 for favoring a negotiated peace. Between the world wars
and afterward he believed Japan needed to nourish close ties with
the West, especially with America and Britain. He viewed the age
of the militarists, from around 1930 to 1945, as an aberration from
Japan's normal evolution; the curtailment of militarism and ultranationalism was the essential change needed to set the nation
on the right course again. Reforms that would restore Japan's institutions to what they were before about 1930 were opposed by
him as threatening, in the words of his biographer, "the very heart
of all that had been positive in Japan's successful emergence as a
modern nation." Thus, with the advent of the Cold War and the
reverse course, he welcomed America's recognition of Japan's
unique business structure and its desire for close bilateral relations after the occupation. A solid patriot and a firm believer in
tradition and order, he intensely hated Communism, the Soviet
Union, and all forms of radicalism. It is little wonder that, after
the flurry of early occupation reforms, he thought MacArthur was
finally acting with common sense when he thwarted the radical-
planned general strike of 1947.[6]

Interviews with Japanese who knew Yoshida produced the following brief descriptions of what they considered to be his main
traits of personality and leadership: "A very good leader . . . [but]
misread by some of the people at the time." "He liked some people and disliked others. He knew only two kinds of people." "Un-
compromising with his political opponents." "A gambler, where
Shidehara was not, in dealing with General MacArthur." "Very
blunt — he said what he thought." "An affable gentleman." "Very
witty . . . and considerate if he liked you." Because of his high-

handed manner of operating as Prime Minister, he was often called "the one-man Cabinet" or "one-man Yoshida" by Japanese of the opposition parties. He once advised Nobusuke Kishi, who later was premier from 1957 to 1960, "A good Prime Minister must permit democratic elections. But when the elections are over, he must assert his full authority." A noted Japanese historian characterized Yoshida as a leader of "aristocratic disposition" who possessed "strong conviction and patriotism" and who "stuck to a stubbornly conservative stand in the midst of the postwar social turmoil, where wild street demonstrations demanding food were the order of the day." Wildes remarked, "Like MacArthur, Yoshida kept aloof from the people, talking to few and listening to fewer."[7] One of the best brief portrayals of Yoshida by a Westerner was penned in 1952 by Frank Gibney, a *Time-Life* correspondent:

> Locked into his pince-nez and his old-fashioned wing collars, Yoshida looks like the perfect trustee. . . . He is one of the few prominent Japanese statesmen who forthrightly opposed the military and lived to tell about it. He is better equipped than most to deal with Westerners, with a long residence in European countries behind him. . . .
>
> Yoshida's qualities, however, transcend those of the respectable trustee. He is a stubborn and cantankerous man, scrupulously honest, who expresses himself without fear. . . . Yoshida is a patriotic man; his admiration of long cigars, polite English conversation and Churchillian phrases has not taken away his Japanese tastes and the Japanese code by which he lives. Although he had known the West, he never depreciated Japan. During the occupation period, he set his goal: independence and sovereignty as soon as possible and did not deviate from it.
>
> He alternately resisted the American occupation and gave it his support. . . . When his own party attacked him, he replied with a simple set of alternatives: "Do what I say or I'll get out." The party, until the peace treaty was signed and for a good time thereafter, did exactly as Yoshida said. There was no other man to replace him, no one willing on the one hand to defend what he felt to be Japanese rights against an occupying authority — and to risk the stigma of being called a "foreign puppet" on the other. . . .
>
> In action he looks more like a Gladstonian Liberal suddenly parked into a world of violent and un-British social change. "Mr. Yoshida understands what liberalism is," one of his young supporters once

admitted, "I do not think he understands what democracy is." Almost all Japanese, when they criticize, feel that another man could have done a better job than Yoshida; but they begin to stammer, when pressed for names.[8]

Yoshida reputedly began his first meeting with MacArthur with great self-assurance, offering the Supreme Commander one of the expensive Havana cigars that he had preserved from prewar days. But during his first premiership, from May 1946 to May 1947, though reluctantly implementing a host of SCAP reforms, he was not impressive in tackling the nation's foremost problem, the troubled economy. In fact, he was opposed in principle to most governmental intervention in economic affairs except to assist big business. The Liberal party's setback in the Diet elections of April 1947 reflected public dissatisfaction with the Yoshida government's meager efforts to cope with inflation, food rationing, and labor grievances. MacArthur was not at all satisfied by his first performance as Prime Minister, and in early 1948 told E. H. Norman, a Canadian diplomat, that Yoshida was "monumentally lazy and politically inept." According to Norman, the general "feared that the Japanese would have to endure mediocre and uninspiring leaders" until the postoccupation era, when Japan would have "greater access to the world" and "leaders might appear with greater imagination and energy." Sharp disagreements between Yoshida and MacArthur were frequent in 1946–1947, and the former, "when overruled, yielded ungracefully," said a SCAP official. "At one point, Yoshida reportedly asked MacArthur directly if his intention was to turn Japan Red," maintains an authority on the period.

When Ashida and his Cabinet resigned in October 1948, some officials in the SCAP Government Section who viewed Yoshida as reactionary were opposed to his return to power, and a move was started to get the leaders of the Liberal party to nominate someone else for the premiership. But Yoshida quickly rallied the party brass behind him and brought "a decisive end to the movement" to nominate another Liberal politician. "I then visited General MacArthur," he related in a matter-of-fact manner, "informed him of my resolve to head the next Government and obtained his approval."[9]

Yoshida served as Prime Minister during the last two and a half years of MacArthur's time in Japan, and his style of leadership and political philosophy proved well suited to the conservative, anti-Communist priorities of the later stage of the occupation. He and the general gradually learned to work well together and weathered many storms in combating labor radicalism, implementing the new economic recovery measures, curbing liberal initiatives without yielding altogether the basic advances in democratization, and steadily transferring more responsibilities from SCAP to the Yoshida government, particularly when MacArthur's attention turned to the new war in Korea. Yoshida became a master in applying the advice given to him by the last wartime premier, Admiral Kantaro Suzuki: "It is important to be a good winner in a war, but it is equally important to be a good loser." Yoshida later said of his dealings with MacArthur and GHQ:

> Where policies drafted by the occupation authorities appeared to me to be mistaken through ignorance of the facts, or where they were not compatible with the actual situation in Japan at the time, I would clearly state my views. But if, in spite of my suggestions, the decision remained unaltered, I would abide by their wish and wait for the time when, having realized their mistake, they might reverse the policy. In short, General Douglas MacArthur never issued orders to me. We discussed matters fully, after which the supreme commander reached a decision, which I carried out.[10]

With NSC 13/2 and the advent of the reverse course, undoubtedly there were fewer occasions when Yoshida left GHQ feeling that the Americans had made another "mistake."

After late 1948, Yoshida and MacArthur seemed to enjoy and respect each other's challenges and maneuvers. The Prime Minister "played a carefully contrived cat-and-mouse game with MacArthur," as one correspondent observed. "The two men had a mutual respect and dealt bluntly and openly with each other." When Robert D. Murphy, perhaps best known for his negotiations with the French in North Africa preceding the Allied invasion in late 1942, arrived as the first postoccupation American ambassador to Japan in the spring of 1952, he, too, came to appreciate Yoshida — his maturation as Japan's pre-eminent statesman, his fight to preserve what was worthwhile in his nation's traditional ways, and his ability to work with MacArthur in securing what seemed best for both Japanese and American national interests. Yoshida "played his cards right," said Murphy, "and his efficient administration delighted MacArthur. . . . He was by no means a yes-man. He was friendly to the United States and he knew when to yield."

Yoshida's favorite saying, according to a Japanese historian, was "Many a nation lost the war and won in diplomacy" — his modification of Suzuki's maxim. Recent scholarship indicates that Yoshida "played on American fears of Soviet expansion to win for Japan an elevated role in international affairs and rebuild Japan's fortunes." He and MacArthur concurred in their eager anticipation of a peace settlement that would be benevolent. The San Francisco Conference of September 1951, where such a liberal peace treaty was signed, as well as a security pact between America and Japan, and the revitalization of the Japanese economy with the coming of the Korean conflict all marked the beginning of the realization of Yoshida's dreams for a future Japan that would be affluent, peaceful, and oriented to the West.[11]

In 1960, when President Eisenhower was planning a trip to Japan (later cancelled) and sought MacArthur's advice about that nation's leaders, the former Supreme Commander there remarked about Yoshida that "there would have been no war if he had been Prime Minister just before Pearl Harbor." MacArthur added that Yoshida "is probably the only man that fills the criteria of what we used to call the elder statesman" and urged Eisenhower to seek his counsel. In his memoirs MacArthur singled out Yoshida as the only Prime Minister of the occupation period that he judged to be truly "able." Thus far had his opinion of Yoshida changed since their troubled encounters of 1946–1947.[12]

Yoshida, in turn, came to appreciate MacArthur's role in occupied Japan, particularly his efforts to protect the Emperor and the imperial institution. In January 1952, H. Alexander Smith, a New Jersey Republican on the Senate Foreign Relations Committee, who had just returned from Japan, wrote the general to convey

> a very special message from Prime Minister Yoshida of whom I saw a great deal and who told me a number of times of the high regard he had for you. He said he felt that he could confide in you and get the best advice on the problems that faced him and that he missed you no end. . . . He also said that you were the one who had saved the Emperor's household from destruction and the whole Emperor

tradition which meant so much to the Japanese people. He spoke especially of your wisdom and vision in realizing the important place the Emperor held in the hearts of the people.[13]

According to Yoshida's biographer, the Prime Minister believed MacArthur deserved credit as one of the "great benefactors" of Japan also because of his opposition to Soviet occupation of Hokkaido, his restraints on SCAP liberals, his assistance in food relief, his repatriation program, and his support "in opposing pressure from Washington for more rapid Japanese rearmament."[14]

The most recent evaluation of the MacArthur-Yoshida relationship, interestingly, is offered by former President Richard M. Nixon. In his 1982 study of the seven "leaders who changed the world" in the twentieth century, he includes both Yoshida and MacArthur (the only American on his list); he had first met each of them in 1953. A believer in the great-leader theory of history, Nixon oversimplifies the causal factors underlying Japan's spectacular rise over the past three decades, but his analysis is perceptive and provocative. Of their "unique partnership," which "produced modern Japan," he writes:

> The impressions I received from these encounters [in 1953] were borne out by later ones. MacArthur was a hero, a presence, an event. Those who were invited to meet with him, as I was during his retirement years in New York, listened in deferential silence as he paced around the room, declaiming upon whatever subject happened to be on his mind at the moment. Yoshida was as human and accessible as MacArthur was remote. Sitting low in a chair, his roguish grin sometimes hidden in a cloud of cigar smoke, he reveled in the good-humored give-and-take of a well-informed conversation.
>
> They had their similarities. Both were well-read intellectuals. Both were in their seventies when they exercised their greatest powers. Victorians by birth, each carried himself in public with a certain old-world dignity and austerity. But MacArthur never softened his bearing. A one-time assistant said, "Even in reproof and rebuff, he kept the lofty manners of a gentleman." Yoshida, in contrast, could be refreshingly coarse when the moment demanded it, as when he called a Socialist in the Diet a "damned fool" or when he poured a pitcher of water over the head of an annoying photographer.
>
> If I had had to guess from my first encounters with MacArthur and Yoshida which man was the lofty idealist and which was the stubborn pragmatist, I think I would have guessed right. As it turned

out, postwar Japan needed both. Without MacArthur's vision, the necessary reforms might not have taken place. Without Yoshida's meticulous attention to detail, those reforms might have jarred Japan from confusion into chaos.

In essence MacArthur was an Occidental whose life unfolded East, while Yoshida was an Oriental whose life unfolded West. They shared a vision of the way their culture could meet on the crowded archipelago of Japan and produce a new and powerful free nation.[15]

2. The General and the Emperor

From the outset MacArthur realized that, though he would have to work through the Prime Ministers to use the Japanese government effectively, it was crucial to establish good communications with the Emperor in order to get the people's support. The Emperor whom he helped to protect from war crimes trial was the same Hirohito who had ruled Japan since 1926, but the imperial institution after the early SCAP reforms differed greatly from the prewar one. As discussed earlier, the Emperor voluntarily repudiated the divine origins of the imperial institution and began making public appearances that were unprecedented in number and informality; criminal punishment for lèse majesté was dropped; titles of nobility were abolished for all but Hirohito and his immediate family, so a large number of princes of royal blood became commoners overnight; the imperial household's staff and budget were sharply cut, and the Diet set up controls over imperial property holdings and levied a stiff capital tax on imperial wealth; and the new constitution reduced the Emperor's position to that of a state symbol, stripping away the broad, if rarely used, imperial powers under the Meiji Constitution and reducing his functions to formal, ceremonial ones. No SCAP actions, however, could (or tried to) lessen the enormous prestige the Emperor still possessed with the people, which, though not consisting of actual power, as now bestowed on the Cabinet and Diet, was a continuing and vital force socially and psychologically in the Japanese spirit and national pride. Hirohito and his family lived simply and adhered scrupulously to the new constitutional role for the imperial house. But, as was clear to MacArthur, the Emperor had lost no respect among the vast majority of his people, to whom he was symbolic of what was good and precious in the Japanese heritage.[16]

The first meeting between the Emperor and MacArthur was a historic occasion, for it set the tone of their relationship for the next five and a half years. MacArthur said that some of his GHQ officers urged him, shortly after the occupation began, to "summon the Emperor to my headquarters as a show of power." He refused, believing that "in time the Emperor will voluntarily come to see me," whereas a summons would "outrage the feelings of the Japanese people and make a martyr of the Emperor." Several weeks after MacArthur's arrival, Hirohito requested a meeting; arrangements were made through Foreign Minister Yoshida. At 10:00 A.M. on September 27, 1945, Hirohito arrived in his 1930 Rolls-Royce; Marquis Matsudaira, the court chamberlain, rode with him, and in several following automobiles were other members of the Emperor's staff. Entering the American embassy, which was guarded by 1st Cavalry Division troops, the Emperor was accompanied by Matsudaira, his physician, and an interpreter. General Bonner Fellers, MacArthur's military secretary, escorted them to the seventy-foot-long room, where the Supreme Commander waited at the opposite end beside a massive table. MacArthur dismissed everyone after inviting the Emperor and his interpreter to be seated beside the marble fireplace, where a crackling fire was going. When he offered Hirohito a cigarette, the general recalled, "I noticed how his hands shook as I lighted it for him. I tried to make it as easy for him as I could, but I knew how deep and dreadful must be his agony of humiliation."

According to MacArthur's version of the conversation, the Emperor said, "I come to you, General MacArthur, to offer myself to the judgment of the powers you represent as the one to bear sole responsibility for every political and military decision made and action taken by my people in the conduct of war." The general remembered being moved "to the very marrow of my bones" by "this courageous assumption of a responsibility implicit with death. . . . He was an Emperor by inherent birth, but in that instant I knew I faced the First Gentleman of Japan in his own right." The general said that he had "stoutly resisted" moves to place Hirohito on trial and had advised Washington that the Japanese people's response would be so violent that "I would need at least one million reinforcements should such an action be taken." MacArthur offered in his memoirs nothing else about the forty-minute session, except for noting that he learned afterward that his wife and son had been peeking from behind a curtain.[17]

Almost all Western accounts of this meeting have relied on MacArthur's version, ignoring the one offered at a press conference by a spokesman of the Ministry of Home Affairs four days later. The official said MacArthur had made a "tremendous impression" on the Emperor, who, in turn, stated that he was "well satisfied" with the occupation's progress. The general responded that "the smooth occupation was really due to the Emperor's leadership" and that "he was most thankful it had not resulted in any bloodshed." According to the government spokesman, "The Emperor was particularly impressed that General MacArthur did not make any reference as to who was responsible for the war. . . . The Emperor expressed, as his personal opinion, that final judgment would have to be left to future historians, but General MacArthur did not comment." They "then discussed various occupational measures to be taken," and MacArthur "told the Emperor he would welcome any suggestions the Emperor might make concerning the reconstruction of Japan." The Home Ministry official closed by saying that the Japanese "were all confidently looking forward to the Supreme Commander's returning the courtesy of the Japanese Emperor by calling on him at the Imperial palace." So much for what might have been said at a meeting where no minutes were taken. A biographer of Hirohito later added a bit, finding in his research that the general had presented his guest with a box of chocolate candy, "one of the Emperor's favorite foods," and, in return, Hirohito "sent Mrs. MacArthur a Japanese confectionary in the shape of a huge chrysanthemum, the imperial symbol."[18]

Actually the meeting's principal immediate impact on the populace resulted from the photograph taken by MacArthur's staff photographer, Lieutenant Gaetano Faillace, during a break in the session. Appearing in many Western newspapers in the next few days, it showed the two principals standing beside each other in front of the large table in the reception room. The general, looking relaxed and confident, was dressed in a casual khaki uniform with no tie or ribbons; he appeared to tower over the tiny Emperor, who was in formal attire and looked nervous and worn. The obvious contrasts in their expressions, heights, and outfits so horrified Home Ministry officials that they suppressed the next day's editions of *Asahi, Mainichi,* and *Yomiuri,* which contained the allegedly disrespectful picture. MacArthur, however, countermanded the ban and permitted the newspapers to include the photograph in their next press runs. No amount of printed or spoken words impressed most of the Japanese people as much as did that one photograph with what a startling change had occurred in their history in September 1945. Reactions varied; some Japanese bitterly, if quietly, resented the publication of the photograph. To the shocked majority, said one source, "it seemed that the Son of Heaven had stepped down to a very earthy earth," and "as nothing else could, the imperial homage to MacArthur told the people that Japan was truly beaten." [19]

The general and the Emperor met at least twice a year thereafter, but always at the American embassy. At their second session they discussed the need for emergency food shipments, but nothing is known about their later conversations. MacArthur apparently accepted the counsel of George Atcheson, the State Department–appointed SCAP political adviser, who suggested two weeks after the first meeting and following an indirect inquiry from the Emperor as to when the general might return his visit: "It would be inadvisable for you to return Hirohito's call. Not only would such a gesture be likely to cause widespread adverse comment in the American press, but it would, I believe, offend the sensibilities of the American people in general." As for "the question of the Emperor's loss of face and a possible consequent feeling of humiliation on the part of the Japanese Government," Atcheson concluded that such reactions were anticipated as "merely axiomatic" in the aftermath of Japan's defeat, and, besides, "some loss of face by the Emperor is not necessarily undesirable from our point of view but . . . to a reasonable extent, the contrary is true." When Atcheson sent a copy of his memorandum to MacArthur to the State Department, Under Secretary Dean Acheson noted in the margin: "Good for George. He is 100% right." Atcheson and Acheson reflected a lack of sympathy for the Emperor and misunderstanding of his prior role in governmental decision-making that was prevalent among American and Allied leaders immediately after the war.[20]

Mrs. Elizabeth Gray Vining, who, on the Emperor's initiative, came to Japan in 1946 to tutor Crown Prince Akihito and eventually other members of the imperial family, was impressed by the remarkably sincere relationship that developed between MacArthur and Hirohito. "They really, genuinely were friends," she remarked. It was "a measure of the magnanimity of both men," she felt, "but more remarkable in the case of the Emperor." She saw in Hirohito a "largeness of spirit that can enable a man to accept impoverishment and humiliation . . . without bitterness, to meet the invading enemy without fear, to enter upon friendship with the triumphant General: this seems to me to partake of nobility." Each Christmas the Emperor sent a handsome gift to MacArthur, and the Empress gave presents to Mrs. MacArthur and young Arthur; on the General's dismissal in 1951, the Emperor sent him two silver vases. When Roger Baldwin of the ACLU interviewed Hirohito in 1947, he was struck by the Emperor's supportive attitude toward MacArthur and the occupation. Hirohito commented to him, "On the whole, I think the American Occupation is doing the country good. . . . I hope General MacArthur will not make the mistake of leaving us too soon, because many of the things that the Americans have started should be completed before you go."[21]

Mrs. Vining, an unusually gifted American teacher and writer, visited MacArthur seven times at his Dai Ichi office, including one occasion when she accompanied her prize student, the teen-age Crown Prince, in June 1949. She commented regarding MacArthur's view of the Emperor, "Always the General spoke of His Majesty with liking and admiration, praising his scholarly interest in biology, his simplicity and sincerity, his innate fineness and 'high character.'" MacArthur once remarked to a visitor, "I came here with the idea of using the Emperor more sternly. But it hasn't been necessary. He is a sincere man and a genuine liberal." To Major Faubion Bowers, his aide, he said of Hirohito, "I was brought up in the democratic tradition, but to see someone who is so high reduced to such a position of humility is very painful." To Eisenhower in 1960, he commented, "The Emperor's actions in support of the American occupation were probably the greatest factor in the successful foundation we laid there. . . . He has a unique fund of common sense and is far and above most of the politicians." When MacArthur was relieved of his commands, the Emperor paid him a final visit. According to a member of the Emperor's staff, the news of the dismissal "shocked and grieved . . . His Majesty, who had had such a personal respect and attachment to him." Although he omitted the crucial factor of Hirohito's positive role in the relationship, Yoshida may well have pinpointed the general's chief contribution in occupied Japan when he observed, "I have no hesitation in saying that it was the attitude adopted by General MacArthur towards the Throne, more than any other single factor, that made the Occupation an historic success."[22]

CHAPTER XI

War, Diplomacy, and New Hope for Japan

1. Impact of the Korean War on Japan

WHEN THE KOREAN CONFLICT BEGAN in late June 1950, Japan ostensibly was still under Allied occupation, with policy determined by the thirteen-nation Far Eastern Commission, which included the Soviet Union. In truth, the administration of control in occupied Japan from the beginning had been firmly under American direction, and after the reverse course began in 1948 United States authorities, whether in Washington or Tokyo, barely paid lip service to the FEC and more boldly than ever repudiated Soviet protests over occupation policies. In the months following the outbreak of hostilities along the 38th Parallel in Korea, Japan was transformed into the forward staging base for the United Nations Command's operations on the mainland of East Asia.

This transformation occurred with the full support, not merely the acquiescence, of the Yoshida government, which was vehemently anti-Communist and anti-Soviet. The secretary of the Yoshida Cabinet hinted to the press a week after the war started that the Japanese government, "in compliance with Occupation orders," would find it "natural" to undertake certain activities to back the "United Nations police action" in Korea. "Formal cabinet approval," states an authority, "to cooperate with the United States in Korea followed on July 4." The Cabinet secretary told reporters on the 21st of that month, "If we can make no direct contribution, we, at least, can maintain order here, act as General MacArthur will want us to act, and free American soldiers from occupation duty so they can take to the field of battle where they are needed." Of the Japanese, MacArthur remarked in late August, "I can think of no finer tribute to their full acceptance of the rights and responsibilities of liberty than their conduct during this difficult war in Korea. . . . My faith in them is such that I am now cannibalizing the last division of occupation forces and sending the majority of its men and equipment to Korea." William Sebald, Atcheson's successor, observed, "Japan was in full accord and sympathy with the United Nations action in Korea, and both the government and the people responded as fully as the situation required."

Like the nonbelligerent status of the United States in 1940–1941, when the Roosevelt government was aiding Great Britain with almost everything short of troops, Japan became America's "arsenal of democracy" in the Far East from 1950 to 1953 and provided invaluable assistance in many ways during the war against the North Korean and Chinese Communists. While thereby committing herself to the West, Japan profited enormously from the conflict, at last achieving economic recovery and an end to the occupation. One scholar contends that "a regional military and economic integration of the basic U.S.–Japan dependency relationship . . . was, ultimately, the most enduring legacy of the Korean War." If so, it would surely have pleased both Yoshida and MacArthur.[1]

The war brought a huge increase in the number of foreign troops and bases in Japan. MacArthur's Far East Command personnel stationed on the main four Japanese islands in the spring of 1950 numbered fewer than 60,000, most of whom were in four understrength army divisions. The wartime buildup of American troops in Japan and Korea was rapid; by the end of September 1950 the total was 250,000. The ground, sea, and air forces of the United Nations Command numbered 768,000 by January 1953, including 350,000 Americans, 44,000 Allied personnel, and the rest South Koreans. Japan became the advance training area for all the Western forces bound for the war zone; many South Korean soldiers also were sent to Japan for training. By 1952, besides Allied facilities, there were 2500 American "military installations" in Japan, consisting of training camps for ground forces, naval stations, air bases, special military schools, practice ranges, hospitals, recreational centers, embarkation port areas, and large depots of ordnance, engineering, signal, chemical, transportation, medical, and quartermaster supplies and equipment. Massive construction programs were undertaken all across Japan, primarily with American funding and engineering and with Japanese labor, to meet the many building needs of the rising military population. American engineers and Japanese workers also teamed up in vast projects to improve and expand Japan's highways, railroads, and ports so that they could meet the demands of the military traffic.[2]

MacArthur "was confident that the Japanese Government would furnish a secure and orderly base," said Ambassador Robert Murphy, "and the Japanese with amazing speed did transform their islands into one huge supply depot, without which the Korean war could not have been fought." In 1947 MacArthur had been far-sighted in launching Operation Roll-up, a program to reclaim large quantities of American military equipment left throughout the Central and Southwest Pacific islands at the end of World War II. After much of this matériel was collected at depots in the Philippines, Marianas, and Ryukyus, it was shipped to Japan, where Far East Command personnel repaired, rebuilt, or overhauled the vehicles, artillery pieces, and ammunition and stored them under controlled conditions for a future emergency. When war came in Korea, most of the service troops involved in Roll-up were needed for more immediate tasks, so the reconditioning of such equipment, as well as the repair of reusable vehicles and ordnance from the Korean fighting, was contracted to Japanese firms. During the first four months of the war the rebuilding and overhaul program, now largely handled by Japanese industry and labor, "turned out 489,000 small arms, 1418 artillery pieces, 34,316 pieces of fire control equipment, 743 combat vehicles, and 15,000 general purpose vehicles," states an official American Army history. "The program . . . saved the tactical situation in all probability [and] dollars as well — and the resources and time which those dollars represented."

MacArthur faced a dire shortage of service troops in the Korean War, but the situation was relieved to a large extent by the recruiting of Japanese workers for noncombatant chores, such as maintenance of base facilities, transportation, and storage and handling of supplies. MacArthur's logistical headquarters in Japan, according to an official chronicle, "estimated that if all the supply and service functions of the command had been carried out without the use of Japanese workers, an additional 200,000 to 250,000 service troops would have been required." Japanese personnel also assisted in the combat zone, even when the United Nations forces advanced into North Korean territory, some participating in dangerous minesweeping operations on vessels of the Maritime Safety Agency (Japanese coast guard) and others in engineering, technical, and stevedore jobs behind the lines in Korea. Murphy observed, "The Japanese were not asked or permitted to recruit soldiers to help us, but Japanese shipping and railroad experts worked in Korea with their own well-trained crews under American and United Nations commands. This was top-secret, but the Allied forces would have had difficulty remaining in Korea without this assistance from thousands of Japanese specialists who were familiar with that country." Shortly before his dismissal, MacArthur even used Japanese intelligence agents, transported on American submarines, to "infiltrate" Sakhalin and the Kuriles, both under Soviet control. According to one historian, "While retired Japanese admirals and generals served in SCAP's Tokyo headquarters as 'consultants,' lesser ranking Japanese military experts served in Korea with the Eighth Army." Moreover, in Japan's home islands and coastal waters the new National Police Reserve and the enlarged fleet of the Maritime Safety Agency proved to be a not inconsiderable home defense force. The National Police Reserve, commented Sebald, "looked as though it had been made in the United States. On a visit to one of the training camps, I thought at first I had stumbled into an American base, for everything from guns to fatigues was GI."[3]

During the Korean conflict, Yoshida and his conservative leaders pushed the depurging program, secured revisions of tax and antitrust legislation to unshackle big business from the earlier reformist restrictions, and tried to undo as many of the liberal SCAP advances as MacArthur would tolerate, but the Japanese government's main target seemed to be the nation's Communists. As mentioned before, some 22,000 Communists and other radicals in public and private employment were summarily dismissed in the summer of 1950. The General Council of Japanese Trade Unions (Sohyo), a middle-of-the-road federation, was formed in July 1950 and soon became the foremost national labor organization, particularly after the government ordered the dissolution of the Communist-led Japan Congress of Trade Unions (Zenro) later that summer. Subsequently several measures were enacted by the Diet aimed at combating subversive activities, especially in labor and political action groups. The war emergency provided Yoshida with a rationale for offensives on several fronts against the menace of radicalism.[4]

Although the Dodge Line had helped in controlling inflation and balancing the budget, the American banker's deflationary program had brought Japan near the edge of depression by May 1950. "The war enabled us to deflate the deflation," said a Finance Ministry official. The sudden and huge inflow of American special procurement orders for military matériel and services contracted with Japanese firms provided the stimulus the economy needed. The anxieties of labor over unemployment and of management over accumulating inventories of products vanished during the first summer of fighting in Korea. At the start, special procurements were processed through the Eighth Army headquarters in Yokohama, but with that headquarters' move to South Korea and the growing volume of requisitions, in late August MacArthur established the Japan Logistical Command, with Major General Walter L. Weible as its head. The new command's main functions were procuring and transporting all supplies and equipment requisitioned by the Eighth Army, now fully committed in combat. Soon American expenditures for special procurements, mainly contracted with the big industries of Japan that had once been favorite targets of SCAP "trust busters," greatly exceeded in dollar value the American aid under the GARIOA and EROA programs for Japan, which were terminated in mid-1951. Military procurements contracts with Japanese firms totaled $184 million for the last half of 1950, $592 million in 1951, $824 million in 1952, and $806 million in 1953. (The Korean truce was signed in July 1953.) With large numbers of American forces remaining in Korea and Japan after the armistice, the five-year total of special procurements in Japan was $1.7 billion by mid-1955.[5]

The American special procurements negotiated with Japanese suppliers were not only for United States forces but also for Allied and South Korean troops and for civilian relief in the war-ravaged areas south of the 38th Parallel. The principal funding sources were the Department of Defense, the Mutual Defense Assistance Program, and the Economic Cooperation Administration. The scale and variety of the procurement orders placed with Japanese businesses are bewildering, as evidenced by the following random selections from Japan Logistical Command records of September to December 1950:

Floating cranes and harbor boats (Sept. 3).

1,320 Red Cross flags; 3,784 canvas tarpaulins; 103,000 wool blankets (Sept. 11).

Teletype test boards from Oki Electric Co. (Sept. 20).

9.6 million fuel-heating tablets (Sept. 26).

15 semi-trailer vans with telephone and telegraph carrier equipment from Nippon Electric Co. (Oct. 16).

Communications circuits from Nagamura Takkosho Co. and Nippon Electric Co. (Oct. 20).

19 locomotives from Central Japan Heavy Industries, Kisha Seizo KK, Kawasaki Sharys KK, Nippon Sharys Seizo KK, and Hitachi, Ltd. (Oct. 21).

75,000 40-yd. bolts of khaki twill cotton cloth; 680 metric tons of cotton clothing padding; 135 metric tons of wool-rayon worsted spun yarn (Oct. 25).

9,280,000 200-yd. spools of white thread; 300,000 prs. of cotton socks; 7,830 DDT hand dusters; 773,000 lbs. of DDT powder (Oct. 28).

Coaxial patch cords and jacks for transmitting stations from Nippon Electric Co. and Nihon Dengo Kosaku Co. (Oct. 29).

150,000 prs. of cotton underwear; 90,000 lbs. of wool-rayon knitting yarn; 25,000 sq. yds. of flannelette; 7 million lbs. of cotton waste; 260 metric tons of soap; 750,000 sewing needles; 7 million sq. yds. of cotton sheeting (Oct. 29).

Inflatable sleeping pads (Nov. 27).

100,000 prs. of Arctic felt boots from Nakashima Co. (Nov. 28).

75,000 prs. of cold-weather rubber shoepacs (Dec. 11).[6]

Other items procured from Japanese suppliers included trucks, automotive parts, building supplies, bridging sections, machinery and tools, chemicals, coal, medical equipment, and pharmaceutical supplies. The impact of the big American orders on some Japanese businesses was dramatic. For example, Toyota, which made 304 trucks in June 1950, received its first special procurement order, for 1000 trucks, the next month; by March 1951, the automotive company was producing over 1500 trucks a month, mostly under military contract. Shotaro Kamiya, the Toyota president at the time, said the special procurement orders "were Toyota's salvation. I felt a mingling of joy for my company and a sense of guilt that I was rejoicing over another country's war." An estimated 10 percent of the value of the procurement orders up to early 1951 were for Japanese-made light weapons, ammunition, and ordnance equipment, which, says one source, "reestablished the Japanese arms industry." According to a Japanese history, "More than 1000 plants and factories of the war industry, which had been closed down by SCAP at the time of Japan's defeat . . . were ordered by the same SCAP to resume business." Apparently Article IX of the new Japanese constitution was not on the minds of anyone except liberals and leftists. As early as August 1950, the American Joint Chiefs of Staff concluded that "if global war should eventuate, the war potential of Japan should be available to the United States." After MacArthur's departure Japanese manufacturers produced increasing amounts of the ordnance used in the war, which, contends a not-too-sympathetic scholar, was "one of the concrete ways in which the United States spurred Japan's illegal rearmament and eventually locked Japanese industry into the role of arsenal for anti-communist Asia" in the following years.[7]

When the Department of the Army's Occupied Areas Office questioned the high prices being paid to Japanese contractors, MacArthur's deputy chief of staff responded in February 1951 by setting forth the Supreme Commander's position on pricing and on the broader implications of the procurement program:

> Surely it was to be expected that $200 million in emergency procurement over a period of only seven months would have a serious effect on price structure in Japan. This effect has been aggravated by urgency with which orders have been placed, by small short-term orders rather than a sustained demand and by the many cancellations that have been effected when conditions in Korea changed.
>
> I have never pressed for procurement in Japan where prices were not competitive with U.S. prices after including freight to destination, usually Korea, although I consider that it will be unquestionably

to U.S. advantage to pay as much as 10% additional for procurement in Japan.

Industrial mobilization plan for Japan now in preparation by ESS [SCAP Economic and Scientific Section] can be expected to secure strong Japanese support since their government representatives voluntarily opened this subject in our treaty discussions and themselves proposed industrial mobilization. ESS plan will insure adequate Japanese capacity will be reserved for normal trade with Southeast Asia which it is essential that Japan maintain.

I believe you should orient your efforts toward:

a. Orienting military orders to be placed in Japan toward items that will be of use in MDAP [Mutual Defense Assistance Program] in Far East so as to develop a long-term demand.

b. Securing placement in Japan of orders large enough to permit cost of industrial conversion to be amortized.

c. Arranging assignment of staff here of appropriate procurement agencies when and if requested. Consideration is being given here to requesting ZI [Zone of Interior]–type procurement districts.

d. Arranging for allocation of raw materials.[8]

Obviously MacArthur viewed special procurements as part of the big picture of Japan's long-range economic development and its future trade relations in the Far East, which Washington planners also were contemplating.

The surge in Japanese prosperity during the Korean War stemmed not only from the procurement orders but also from the personal spending by the thousands of American and Allied servicemen who were in the country for training, logistical functions, combat-related duty at air and naval bases, convalescence, or rest-and-recreation periods. Japanese commerce suddenly emerged from its prewar sluggishness and was barely able to supply the demands of the soldiers, sailors, and airmen for souvenirs, liquor, food, clothes, cameras and other gadgets, and entertainment of all sorts. Prostitution flourished as never before; Yokosuka alone had 1500 brothels, mainly to serve the sailors of the big American naval station there. "At the height of things GHQ financial officers estimated that individual spending by troops alone (spending exclusive of procurement, that is) amounted to about a million dollars a day. That was a lot of pump-priming," commented a SCAP official.[9]

When the Korean War started, the index of Japanese manufacturing production was about one-third that of the 1934–1936 average. By the end of 1950 it was up to 94 percent of that prewar standard, rising to 128 percent in 1951 and 171 percent by the end of hostilities, in mid-1953. The production of ingot steel in 1951 was 6.5 million tons, which was more than triple the 1949 output of 2.1 million tons and considerably larger than the 1937 level of 5.8 million tons. Japan was again the world's leading exporter of textiles by 1951, SCAP having abolished its ceiling on cotton spindles when the Korean fighting began. The real wage index for manufacturing industries (using the 1960 average as 100) rose steadily: 45.6 in 1949, 59.5 in 1950, 65.6 in 1951, 73.5 in 1952, and 77.4 in 1953. Although an unfavorable trade balance continued and export inflation became a wartime problem, Japan's export trade grew from $510 million in 1949 to $820 million in 1950 and $1.4 billion in 1951. Through the income generated from both exports and special procurements, Japan was able to raise its imports from $905 million in 1949 to $2 billion by 1952. This meant, as a Japanese economic historian explained, "The key industries which depended on imports of raw materials could virtually double their scale of production" by 1952. When the war began, in June 1950, the Tokyo Stock Exchange's prices generally reflected a "very uncertain" outlook, but by late summer the average of select stocks was gradually climbing, and subsequently a boom developed. Whereas in June 1950 daily trading on the exchange averaged 1.2 million shares valued at 94.7 million yen, by the time the boom hit its peak in February 1953, 10.8 million shares valued at 2.4 billion yen were traded daily. Most other economic indicators likewise demonstrated that the Japanese economy had definitely broken out of its 1945–1949 coma.[10]

In order to spur rapid and continuing economic growth, Japanese economic and financial officials, particularly in the Ministry of International Trade and Industry, inaugurated a number of measures to promote rationalization and capital expansion in industry and to stimulate foreign trade. The Japan Development Bank was established by the government to provide low-interest loans for plant and equipment expansion and technological innovations, especially in key industries that, because of inadequate capacity, had been "bottlenecks" in the late 1940s, such as steel, shipping, coal, and electric power. The Japan Export-Import Bank was set up to provide low-interest funds to assist exporting firms. Capital accumulation by business was assisted also by a variety of favorable tax revisions. The foreign exchange allocation system, begun in 1949 after the Young Mission's study and recommendations, was a complex plan for restricting imports, protecting and fostering domestic industries, and helping to solve the trade deficit problem. With the end of the occupation in 1952, many of the remaining antitrust regulations were evaded, sometimes with the concurrence of the government, as new cartels were formed.

In an understatement Yoshida remarked during an address before the Diet in early 1951, "It is gratifying to us all that of late Japan has made notable progress on the road to recovery and reconstruction." If World War II did more to pull the American economy out of the Great Depression than had the host of New Deal measures, the Korean War provided more stimulus for Japan's economic resurgence than did all the occupation efforts. But just as the unprecedented New Deal interventions in the economy prepared the way and helped to make possible the 1941–1945 boom in America, so the strivings of MacArthur, Dodge, Washington planners, and Japanese authorities during the occupation cannot be discounted altogether in explaining the economic upswing of the Korean War period.[11] The Japanese economic authority on that era who is quoted below is right in looking backward and forward to understand the significance of what happened to his nation's economy during the Korean conflict:

> The externally imposed Occupation reforms greatly changed the fixed system of the prewar Japanese economy and ended by preparing a rich soil not only for "democratization" but also for economic growth. For example, the rise in both farmers' and workers' incomes and the expansion of consumption capacity, as well as the zaibatsu dissolution and the elimination of excessive concentration, combined to produce the competitive market conditions that were indispensable for this growth. Over and above this . . . policies favoring capital accumulation and the introduction of foreign technology were adopted along with the decision to hold down military expenses and take the "rich country" path, dispensing with the "strong army." In this sense the course of subsequent economic growth had been virtually charted by the early 1950s. Hence I believe it is appropriate to lump together the years from 1951–1952 to about 1970 as the period of rapid economic growth.[12]

It should be remembered, too, that a factor of incalculable but great proportion in the return of business confidence in Japan was the negotiation of the benevolent peace settlement in 1951, which will be examined next.

2. *"A Happy Ending to a Great Task"*

One of the most effective, attractive American emissaries of good will in occupied Japan was Mrs. Elizabeth Gray Vining. The tutor of the Crown Prince and sometimes of other members of the imperial family was one of the few persons who had the confidence and friendship of both MacArthur and Hirohito, and she may well have been a primary factor in the amiable relationship that developed between the Supreme Commander and the Emperor. When Mrs. Vining visited MacArthur, they would discuss frankly their personal views on many topics, most of them dealing with problems of the Japanese nation. From her accounts of their meetings, MacArthur apparently was unusually sincere and open with her, staging none of the histrionics that many distinguished male visitors remembered. During her visit at his Dai Ichi office in mid-May 1950, the conversation turned to the negotiations on the Japanese peace treaty. The general said he hoped she would stay in Tokyo until its signing and added, "I am going to." She asked, "When will it be?" He responded, "If it were only between Japan and the United States, it could be settled in a very short time. Unfortunately, Japan's interests have gotten sidetracked, and the struggle is between the Allies. But, even so, if we could get some honesty in this, the peace treaty could be made in a rather short time. We owe it to Japan. We made an agreement with her, and she has lived up to her part of it. Now we are in honor bound to do ours." By the time of the signing of the treaty, however, neither MacArthur nor Mrs. Vining was still in Japan.[13]

MacArthur's involvement in the Japanese peace planning began with a bang in 1947 and ended with a whimper in 1951. In between, the State Department kept him well informed on developments and often sought his opinion, despite the differences on other matters that had marred relations between the two sides and the mutual suspicion between the general and Acheson, who became Secretary of State in January 1949. MacArthur's role was augmented when the State Department decided to bring the Japanese government into the treaty-making at its formative stage and when John Foster Dulles became the chief American negotiator. Ironically, more often than not, MacArthur found himself siding with the State Department or Yoshida against the Defense Department and the Joint Chiefs.

As related earlier, a State committee headed by Hugh Borton prepared a draft peace treaty in early 1947, which Borton showed to MacArthur. The general criticized it as "imperialistic in concept, in purpose, and in form." Shortly afterward, on March 17, he showed up at the Tokyo Foreign Correspondents Club ("Shimbun Alley"), surprised everyone by agreeing to his first and only general press conference of the occupation period, and while fielding questions, issued a call for a Japanese peace treaty "as soon as possible." An American-sponsored preliminary treaty conference was cancelled that summer because of Soviet and Nationalist Chinese objections to the proposed voting procedure. For the next two years the United States government essentially let the matter ride, because State and Defense planners were at odds over post-treaty Japanese security and because both departments believed Japan needed to be strengthened economically and politically before being launched on her own again. Meanwhile MacArthur continued to drop suggestions to Washington that treaty negotiations should be started soon. He and William Sebald often talked about the future peace settlement; according to Sebald, the general believed the treaty "should be simple and should be written in general terms." In September 1949 he told Sebald that the matter of Japan's post-treaty security "should be arranged by bilateral agreement with the United States."[14]

During the last half of 1949, State and Defense leaders found themselves stalemated over the security issue, with the military wanting to postpone the drafting of the peace treaty until agreement could be reached regarding the retention of American bases in post-treaty Japan and the promotion of Japanese rearmament. MacArthur sided with the State Department in favoring the earliest possible return of full sovereignty to Japan and in thinking that American bases in the Philippines and on Okinawa would be adequate to defend Japan. In December 1949, Under Secretary of the Army Tracy Voorhees and Lieutenant General Alfred M. Gruenther, assistant chief of staff for operations, went to Tokyo to persuade the Supreme Commander to shift sides in the security controversy, but, remarked Sebald, "there was no sign the Washington emissaries made any progress whatsoever in altering his views." Nevertheless, neither MacArthur nor Sebald liked the latest draft treaty, prepared by the State Department that November. Probably voicing the general's sentiments in addition to his own, Sebald criticized "its patronizing tone," besides noting that it was "too long and too complex."[15]

From mid-December 1949 through mid-March 1950 Ambassador-at-Large Philip C. Jessup, Sr., made a fourteen-nation "fact-finding" tour of the Far East for the President and the State Department, in part to ascertain the views of leaders in that region regarding a Japanese peace settlement. For six days in early January he was in Tokyo, conferring with MacArthur, Sebald, and Japanese officials. After three lengthy sessions with the general, he notified Acheson on January 10 that

> General MacArthur is quite outraged by the views of the Joint Chiefs of Staff in regard to the postponement of arrangements for negotiating the Japanese Peace Treaty. He spoke very strongly on this subject and feels that the view does not really reflect a military judgment but that General Bradley is merely speaking for Secretary Johnson. . . . He said he hoped that you would take the matter up with the President and have the Joint Chiefs overruled. As you know, he feels very strongly that we should go ahead with the negotiation of the Treaty. I fully agree with him. In this connection, he stressed a point . . . namely, that the negotiation of the Peace Treaty would be one of the dramatic steps by which we could recapture from the Russians the initiative in terms of general Asiatic thinking. . . .
>
> On several different occasions he stressed the excellent cooperation which he had received from the State Department and indicated that his difficulties had been due almost entirely to the Department of Defense. . . . I wonder whether on a matter so important as the negotiation of the Japanese Peace Treaty it would not be possible for the President to take the matter into his own hands and request General MacArthur to report directly to him his views on this question. In terms of American thinking, SCAP's support on this would be of great importance and it would seem too bad if it were necessary to

have his views remain secret. . . . I would stress again that I would venture to suggest such a procedure only in a matter of very great importance. I think the negotiation of the Peace Treaty is such a matter.[16]

Nothing came of Jessup's novel proposal, and the treaty preparations continued to move with agonizing slowness because of the deadlock between the State and Defense departments over security aspects.

A turning point came in April 1950, when Acheson appointed dour but sharp John Foster Dulles, a respected Republican authority on international affairs, as his special adviser; the next month Dulles was charged with handling the preliminary planning for the Japanese peace treaty. A kinsman of two past Secretaries of State, a distinguished international attorney, and a veteran of the diplomatic and intelligence services, as well as of the Senate, Dulles had participated in the Versailles Conference of 1919 and the United Nations Conference at San Francisco in 1945, and served as United States delegate to the United Nations General Assembly from 1946 to 1950. Scholars differ on the reason for Dulles' appointment as treaty negotiator in 1950. One contends that it was the Democratic administration's "effort to shore up an almost disintegrating structure of bipartisanship" in the aftermath of the Communist triumph in China in late 1949 and the emergence of Senator McCarthy's raucous anti-Communist crusade in early 1950. Another scholar suggests, "In part, Dulles' selection represented an effort to exclude Japan from the furor enveloping the administration's East Asian policy; in part, it reflected Acheson's desire to reserve his own energies for Europe, the area of first priority," where NATO was in its critical beginning stage. Although "well-polished and well-skilled in international affairs," Sebald observed, "Dulles was little known at that time in Japan," but both the Japanese and MacArthur would come to respect him as "a hard-working, knowledgeable, and busy emissary who negotiated the peace treaty with the skill of a master craftsman."[17]

On June 17, only eight days before the Korean War erupted, Dulles arrived in Tokyo, accompanied by John M. Allison, head of the State Department's Office of Northeast Asian Affairs and soon to become Dulles' deputy in the treaty negotiations. Dulles and Allison stopped briefly at Haneda Airport for a talk with Sebald, then flew on to Seoul. Arriving also on June 17, shortly after Dulles had left for Korea, was a Defense Department group led by Secretary Louis Johnson and General Omar Bradley, the JCS chairman. Since the State-Defense impasse had not been resolved, Sebald wondered "whether the two delegations had purposely planned to avoid meeting."

Johnson, Bradley, and the officers in their party met with MacArthur and some of his GHQ leaders on Sunday, June 18. Sebald, who was present as chief of the SCAP Diplomatic Section, said that Johnson delivered a "shocking" denunciation of "the State Department crowd" and of Dulles for pushing for an early treaty, which the Defense Secretary assumed would force the withdrawal of American forces from defenseless Japan. He "sharply criticized" the notion that Japan had fulfilled the Potsdam terms. MacArthur apparently remained quiet through Johnson's tirade, but, Sebald commented, the Defense Secretary "must have been upset when later he was given a memorandum by General MacArthur on the peace treaty issue" that contained quite different views than Johnson's.[18]

Actually Johnson, who left Tokyo for the States on the 23d, received two "top secret" memoranda written by MacArthur, and Dulles also was given copies when he came back to Tokyo from Korea on the 21st. The first document, dated June 14 and over 4200 words in length, was called "The Peace Treaty Problem"; the second, entitled "Concept Governing Security in Post-war Japan," was about 600 words and bore the date June 23, so Johnson may have received the latter after his return to Washington. The two memoranda contain the essence of MacArthur's general thinking about the peace treaty and security arrangements. Dulles later claimed that they were of "invaluable assistance" to him. Indeed, in his response to the general after studying them, Dulles commented, "I follow very closely your own line of thinking on these matters." In early 1951, Dulles stated that "the security proposals which the Mission would be presenting to the Japanese are directly based on a memorandum submitted by General MacArthur last June." In view of the significance that the chief American negotiator attached to them, it is in order for us to examine some of MacArthur's main points therein.[19]

The general began his peace-treaty commentary with a reminder: "Three years ago I publicly expressed the view . . . that the Allied Powers should proceed at once in the formulation of a peace treaty for Japan. . . . I added that a post-treaty unarmed Japan should be able to look to the machinery of the United Nations for the safeguard of her political and territorial integrity." He pointed out that recently the Soviet Union and Communist China had found propaganda "ammunition of destructive value" in press allegations that the treaty's delay was due to "conflicts in viewpoints between the Defense and State Departments." The press emphasized "the idea that the conflict lies in the insistence by the Defense Department that Japan be held as a vital security adjunct of the United States."

MacArthur disagreed with the Joint Chiefs' position, "which requires that the Soviet [Union] and Communist China be among the signatories of the final treaty." This would "foreclose any possibility of treaty action" if the United States wanted "adequate security reservations" in the document and maintained its "present political policy vis-à-vis Communist China." Moreover, he argued, "it does not necessarily follow that all action leading to a treaty must be suspended pending assurance of their agreement."

Appearing to take dead aim at Johnson's assertion about the Potsdam terms, the general asserted, "The Japanese people have faithfully fulfilled the obligations they assumed under the instrument of surrender and have every moral and legal right to the restoration of peace." He added, "For this reason and irrespective of the issues joined and ultimate policy objectives, we should not allow ourselves to be deterred from moving invincibly forward along a course which we ourselves and the entire world recognize to be morally and legally right. We should proceed to call a peace conference at once." He avowed that America's "most impelling need" in the Far East was "the regaining of our lost initiative over the events which are stirring all of the Asian peoples" who "respect and follow aggressive, resolute, and dynamic leadership but quickly turn from a leadership characterized by timidity or vacillation." He maintained that "the resolute move toward the holding of a peace conference because it is morally right . . . would go a long way toward reasserting that leadership and regaining that initiative."

On the other hand, "our continued delay in calling a peace conference . . . cannot fail to result in a progressive deterioration of our position here and abroad."

As he understood the Washington stalemate, "State's position is based primarily upon political considerations, while that of Defense finds its direction in overall security requirements. The solution sought is that which will serve the one without doing violence to the other." Having taken his stand boldly against the Defense Department's efforts to halt treaty preparations for the present, MacArthur next attacked the two main security proposals put forward by Defense officials. The first provided for a collective security pact among the Allies, to be signed at the time of the peace treaty's consummation, allowing American bases in Japan by Allied edict, not by Japanese agreement. He said the Japanese would be filled with "bitterness and resentments" over such "a move toward the 'colonization' of Japan," as intense nationalists and Communists both would regard it there. The second Defense proposal provided for restoration of only partial sovereignty to Japan in the peace treaty, with the United States retaining tight control over security and defense affairs. He contended that the Japanese would view such as "a betrayal by the United States" after the recent trend of relaxing occupation controls. The failure "to restore full autonomous authority" to Japan would provide the Communists "with a propaganda weapon against which there would be no defense."

Writing only days before the sudden outbreak of war along the 38th Parallel, MacArthur was opposed to the idea, often expressed by Pentagon officials since NSC 13/2, that Japanese rearmament would be essential in the post-treaty era to deter external Communist threats. "Any effort to reverse Allied policies toward the rearmament of Japan at this time would be accompanied by convulsions in Australia, New Zealand, Indonesia, the Philippines and throughout Asia," he claimed. It would produce "no less convulsive reactions in Japan itself where the people with irrefutable sincerity have turned scornfully from the militarists and militarism." Besides, Japan would have to depend on "billions in American aid to build military strength" to an adequate level.

MacArthur reasoned that, "from every standpoint, it is more essential that Japan be denied to the Soviet than that she be an active military ally of the United States. Such denial can best be assured through a firm political alignment resting upon the good will and faith of the Japanese people, with our access to military and naval bases and other available facilities adequate to meet the needs of our security operations." The peace treaty should reserve to the Allies — and here MacArthur uses phrases from the Potsdam Declaration — the right to continue occupying "points in Japanese territory" until "irresponsible militarism is driven from the world" and threats to "peace, security, and justice" are gone. But he wanted the retention of American forces and bases in Japan provided for in a separate security pact, entered into voluntarily by Japan after the signing of the peace treaty. He felt it should be ratified "not only by the Government of Japan . . . but through a plebiscite by the Japanese people as well."[20]

Sebald later remarked, "MacArthur had thus offered an ingenious compromise to what appeared to be an insoluble problem. . . . This was, in fact, the genesis of the final disposition of the security question which Dulles later worked out." The Defense-State impasse over the security arrangements was resolved in September 1950, when agreement was reached on a bilateral formula that Dulles developed from MacArthur's basic ideas. George Marshall, who succeeded Johnson as Secretary of Defense that month, was undoubtedly a major factor in easing tensions between the two agencies.[21]

In his supplementary memorandum on Japanese security, written only two days before the surprise North Korean invasion began and two weeks before he directed Yoshida to form the National Police Reserve, MacArthur was already qualifying his interpretation of Article IX: "In any study of the Japanese problem it must be understood that despite Japan's constitutional renunciation of war its right to self-defense in case of predatory attack is implicit and inalienable. In such a situation Japan would muster all of its available human and material resources in support of the security forces committed to its defense." The self-defense provision would be incorporated in the peace treaty.[22]

Although the State Department frequently consulted MacArthur through correspondence and personal representatives, the Defense Department, on the contrary, seemed less solicitous of his views on the peace and security issues, in part undoubtedly because it already knew through State of his opposition to some of its views. The fullest request by the Defense Department for MacArthur's opinions arrived at the Tokyo GHQ during the height of the Chinese offensive in December 1950. MacArthur's responses to the nine questions set forth by the JCS, on behalf of Marshall, were understandably brief, since he was then wrestling with the worst crisis of the Korean fighting. Below is an interpolation of the questions from the Joint Chiefs' message of December 18 and MacArthur's answers in his reply of the 28th:

(1) JCS: From the military point of view, are there any objections to seeking an early conclusion of a peace settlement with Japan without awaiting a favorable outcome of the situation in Korea?

MacArthur: To the contrary, there is every reason why we should proceed at once to call a peace conference for Japan. We are fully committed to such action, the Japanese have earned the right to a treaty of peace, and our failure to proceed cannot but cause loss of faith in our moral integrity and leadership, not only in Japan but throughout Asia.

(2) JCS: From the military point of view, are there any objections to discussing this peace settlement with the assumption that the United States intends to commit substantial armed force to the defense of the island chain of which Japan forms part?

MacArthur: No objection.

(3) JCS: From the military point of view, are there any objections to leaving the Ryukyu and Bonin Islands under Japanese sovereignty, subject to the provisions of the contemplated military security agreement which would presumably take special account of the position in Okinawa?

MacArthur: Leaving the Ryukyu and Bonin Islands under Japan's sovereignty is highly objectionable from a military point of view. The Japanese are fully resigned to the loss of these areas as a penalty for waging war. They form a vital segment of our littoral defense line and our control thereof is formally established and universally recognized. It would be unthinkable to surrender control and render our use of these areas, fortified at the United States expense, subject to treaty arrangement under Japanese administration. It would but be to transform strength to weakness without the slightest moral or legal reason for so doing.

(4) JCS: From the military point of view, are there any objections to exploration at this time of a possible Pacific Pact along the lines

outlined in paragraph 4 of the attached memo? [This proposes "a mutual assistance arrangement among the Pacific Island Nations (Australia, New Zealand, the Philippines, Japan and the United States, and perhaps Indonesia) which would have the dual purpose of assuring combined action as between the members to resist aggression from without and also to resist attack by one of the members, e.g., Japan, if Japan should again become aggressive."]

MacArthur: No objection. The foregoing views [on the first four questions] apply with equal force whether or not it is contemplated that the armed forces assigned to this theater will be materially increased.

(5) JCS: Should the United States unilaterally seek an early conclusion of a peace settlement with Japan without assurances of participation by friendly FEC nations and in spite of lack of their support?

MacArthur: The United States should fulfill her moral and legal obligations vis-à-vis the restoration of Japanese peace whether acting alone or in consonance with other Pacific powers.

(6) JCS: Would Japan accept rearmament without your leadership?

MacArthur: It is impossible to predict what, if any, influence personalities might have upon Japan's future course with respect to rearmament. It is patently clear, however, that the degree of such influence on such matters by the United States or any of its representatives is dependent in large measure on the future course of American policy in Asia, and specifically the manner in which we meet the present crisis in Korea.

(7) JCS: If USSR is not a party to the treaty, in view of terms of armistice relative to Allied military controls over Japan through SCAP, could or should CINCFE retain functions of SCAP in order to counter possible USSR action seeking to assume those functions?

MacArthur: I regard it as utterly impossible to formulate an acceptable peace treaty for Japan without restoring in full the sovereign power. The post-treaty retention of powers now vested in SCAP would render such a treaty wholly unacceptable and invalid in the eyes of the Japanese.

(8) JCS: If peace treaty eventuates quickly, what long-term and short-term military measures would, in your opinion, be necessary in order to insure security of Japan against USSR?

MacArthur: Under normal conditions, in the absence of a threat of imminent hostilities, an army of four divisions with other T/O [table of organization] components, all at full strength plus marine and air detachments and comparable Navy and Air Force complements, would suffice for the security of Japan. This should be a basic security force subject, however, to immediate reinforcement upon any increase in international tensions to the point that hostilities aimed at Japan become imminently threatened. In such eventuality, the extent of reinforcement should be guided by global studies of points of enemy concentration indicating the nature of the threat and the potentiality of possible enemy action. When any such threat of imminent hostilities has subsided, the security force should be reduced to its basic strength. Long-term military security of Japan should obviously be based on placing all possible reliance upon the United Nations acting in collaboration with the Government and people of Japan in which Japan will be expected to develop and maintain such indigenous forces as will assure her internal security and assist in her defense.

(9) JCS: Have you other comments, from the military point of view, on the general subject of a Japanese peace treaty now?

MacArthur: My views with respect to a Japanese peace treaty are fully on record and I know of nothing further that I could helpfully add at this time.[23]

Except for his views on retention of the Ryukyus and Bonins and on a Pacific collective security pact, MacArthur's position had not changed appreciably from where he stood prior to the start of the Korean conflict. His main message was surely the same: quickly negotiate a peace treaty restoring full sovereignty to Japan.

During the latter half of 1950 Dulles worked with State Department officials on revising a draft treaty and busily conferred on a one-on-one basis with numerous representatives of the FEC nations in Washington and at the United Nations headquarters in New York. In January 1951, Truman appointed him a special presidential representative with the rank of ambassador and authorized him to visit all the FEC nations, as needed, to complete his treaty task. After discouraging her government's initial desire for post-treaty economic penalties on Japan, Dulles got good cooperation from Britain; in fact, the British Foreign Office went to work on a draft treaty with the understanding that it would later be merged with the American text. As expected, the Soviet Union refused altogether to work with Dulles. So great was some allies' uneasiness about a future security menace from a resurgent, sovereign Japan that Dulles had to promise American security treaties with the Philippines, Australia, and New Zealand as the price of their support on the Japanese peace settlement.[24]

Dulles, who worked diligently with congressmen for bipartisan support of his treaty efforts, early realized, states an authority, that "General MacArthur was important not only because of his wide experience in the Far East and Japan, but also because of his heroic stature in the eyes of Congressional Republicans." He was careful to keep the general fully informed, to solicit his advice at almost every turn (even on speech drafts), and to treat him with the utmost cordiality. The two men "shared a lofty yet practical idealism" that "made their cooperation easy," says one scholar. Also, both men were born in the 1880s, espoused conservative political philosophies, saw issues starkly in either-or, good-evil dichotomies, closely identified Americanism with Christianity, and envisioned a future world community rid of Communism and led by the United States. Always pleased when his counsel was sought, MacArthur responded enthusiastically to Dulles' overtures. They developed a solid friendship and, except on Japanese rearmament, shared similar views about the treaty issues.

Their correspondence of 1950–1952 is full of very cordial, courteous, and complimentary expressions, each man seeming to try to outdo the other, yet a tone of genuine liking and respect for the other comes through clearly. After his visit to Tokyo in June 1950, Dulles expressed gratitude to the general for "the long intimate talks which we had," and later that summer MacArthur thanked Dulles "for keeping me abreast" and declared he would "support your position completely" on the treaty negotiations. In mid-November, after the first battles with Chinese forces in Korea, Dulles wrote that he was seeking MacArthur's "judgment *first* as to whether in the light of the new Korean and Chinese Communist developments we should push on steadily for the Japanese Peace Treaty." Following his visit to Tokyo in early 1951, Dulles wrote the general several letters brimming with gratitude for his "indispensable cooperation," "wise counsel," and "invaluable" work in laying the "foundation" for the treaty. In March he told MacArthur, "Your own position is central, dominating, and indispensable. For that I am grateful." The Supreme Commander responded, "Your untiring energy and determination to advance the treaty against odds of which I am quite aware have been magnificent, and I am confident that the enthusiasm which you have brought to the task cannot fail to see it through to early consummation." After a visit with the general at his Waldorf-Astoria Hotel apartment in New York in January 1952, Dulles wrote him, "As always, I find your thoughts and their expression stimulating and elevating." Dulles had won a strong ally, but so had the general.[25]

When Dulles returned to Tokyo in late January 1951, he spent two busy weeks meeting with MacArthur, Yoshida, the Emperor, government officials, leaders of all major political parties, business executives, editors, university presidents, labor spokesmen, and Japanese of other vocations, acquiring responses on treaty issues from persons of all conceivable shades of opinion and ideology. In a meeting with Yoshida and MacArthur, Dulles suggested to the Prime Minister that the United States might expect post-treaty Japan to support an army of 350,000 troops and to assume some of the responsibility for strategically containing Communism in the Far East. Yoshida balked, however, on the grounds that his nation's economy could not afford a large military establishment; besides, he contended, the new constitution's Article IX forbade rearmament, and the majority of the people would not tolerate it. MacArthur, with whom Yoshida later said he had a "secret understanding" if this topic was raised, spoke out in support of the Prime Minister's position, stating that "rearmament is impossible for the moment." According to one source, "When MacArthur sided with Yoshida on the impossibility of such large-scale armament, Dulles gave way." The later security pact, however, did contain a statement that Japan would be expected to "increasingly assume responsibility for its own defense against direct and indirect aggression." Allison, Dulles' deputy, observed, "While Mr. Yoshida was a firm anti-Communist and was much more realistic than the Socialists, he nevertheless had a genuine fear of re-establishing a Japanese military machine." Yoshida had earlier concluded that a security pact with the United States was the better of the alternatives Japan faced, which were, as stated by his biographer, "sovereignty with continued U.S. military presence in Japan or no sovereignty at all." He had also reconciled himself to the establishment of the National Police Reserve but, like MacArthur, wanted to keep its growth gradual and limited. Neither he nor the Supreme Commander regarded that force as the start of "Japanese rearmament."[26]

When Dulles was informed by Acheson of MacArthur's abrupt dismissal in April, he told the Secretary of State that, in his opinion, "the responsibility for bringing this situation to pass lay very largely with the Administration and particularly with the Joint Chiefs as they had not found a way to give General MacArthur or the public the impression that General MacArthur's thinking was a factor in decisions." He added, "Where General MacArthur had been fully consulted, as in relation to the Japanese Peace Treaty, there was complete harmony and not the slightest evidence of disposition on General MacArthur's part to make private utterances through correspondence or through newspaper correspondents." The general's relief from his commands unleashed such public outcries in America that Dulles feared the bipartisan treaty support that he had assiduously cultivated might be destroyed. He quickly conferred with Republican leaders in Congress and got their promises to keep the peace treaty considerations free from the controversy that was already mounting over the general's removal. He also anticipated "a very serious effect upon Japanese public opinion," as did also Truman and Acheson, who decided it was "imperative" that he return to Japan and reassure the Yoshida government that the treaty process would not be affected by the sudden turn of events. Dulles arrived in Tokyo on April 16, the day of MacArthur's departure. Much to his relief, he found that General Matthew Ridgway had quickly established good rapport with Japanese leaders, and the public, though uneasy about the portent of the command change, seemed to be in a stable mood. Having convinced the Japanese government leaders that MacArthur's exit meant no change in American occupation policy or planning for the treaty, Dulles returned to Washington with a deeper respect for the amazing resilience of the Japanese.

During the remainder of the spring and through the summer Dulles continued his travels and talks with leaders of the FEC nations, negotiating with each government separately. He was also busy with the revision of the draft treaty; in May the sensitive job of blending the Anglo-American texts got under way in earnest, and by July a final treaty text was ready after a host of minor changes proposed by various FEC nations. The United States and the United Kingdom then issued a joint invitation to fifty-five nations to send delegates to a peace conference at San Francisco in early September for the purpose of signing the treaty, a copy of which was included with each formal invitation. The delegates would be allowed to make statements, but substantive changes in the treaty were not expected. When Yoshida received the final text in July, he wrote MacArthur, "It is gratifying that your efforts and exhortations have borne fruit. A fair and magnanimous treaty has been written embodying the principles as laid down first by you." MacArthur responded, "I rejoice with you and the Japanese people."[27]

When the delegates assembled in San Francisco to approve, in effect, the document that the major Western powers had already agreed on, only three of the invited nations did not send representatives — India, Burma, and Yugoslavia. President Truman made the opening address on September 4, emphasizing that the peace treaty was one "of reconciliation, which looks to the future, not the past." MacArthur would have been satisfied with the President's highly favorable remarks about the occupation and the conduct of the Japanese in cooperating and carrying out its objectives. Acheson presided over the ensuing session, fending off with shrewd reasoning and parliamentary deftness the obstructionist tactics of the Soviet, Polish, and Czechoslovakian delegates. As speech after speech was offered by the various delegates, it became clear that the vast majority was satisfied with the treaty. Yoshida's address was sincere and moving; he praised the treaty as "unparalleled in history" in its "fair and generous" terms. He declared, "We are determined to take our place among the nations who are dedicated to peace, to justice, to progress and freedom, and we pledge ourselves that Japan shall play its full part in striving toward these ends." The Japanese Treaty of Peace was signed on September 8 at the San Francisco Opera House by all the nations' representatives attending the conference, except the delegates from the USSR, Poland, and Czechoslovakia.[28]

In hailing the treaty's magnanimity as unprecedented, Yoshida may have been historically correct, for it would be difficult to name another peace treaty over the centuries that was more conciliatory. Among its main provisions, it required Japan to pledge to apply for United Nations membership and to conform to the principles of the UN Charter in the meantime. Japan assented to the judgments of the International Military Tribunal for the Far

East on its war criminals, and, though not required to pay a consolidated reparations bill, it agreed to negotiate bilateral agreements with FEC countries desiring reparations. The treaty recognized Japan's "inherent right of individual or collective self-defense" and stated that she "may voluntarily enter into collective security arrangements." As for the main home islands and adjacent territorial waters, Japan's full sovereignty was restored. But she had to renounce all claims to her former empire. These territories included Sakhalin and the Kuriles, which the Soviet Union held; Korea, which was recognized as independent; Formosa and the Pescadores, now under Nationalist Chinese control; the Marshalls, Carolines, and Marianas in the Central Pacific, held by the United States under United Nations trusteeship; and, at least for the time being, the Ryukyus and Bonins, where the United States retained administrative authority, though not residual sovereignty. The occupation was to end ninety days after the treaty went into effect, but Japan could enter into agreements with "one or more of the Allied Powers" for "the stationing or retention of foreign armed forces in Japanese territory" even before the peace treaty became effective.

With the signing of the peace treaty at the Opera House on the morning of September 8, that afternoon the Japanese and American representatives journeyed to the San Francisco Presidio, a historic Army post. There they signed the security treaty between the United States and Japan, providing for the stationing of American forces in Japan for an indefinite period. On February 28, the two nations concluded an administrative agreement permitting American military bases in independent Japan for defensive purposes and an exchange of notes regarding interim security arrangements. The United States Senate, by large majorities on each vote, approved the peace and security treaties on March 20. Truman issued a presidential proclamation formally terminating the state of war with Japan on April 28, 1952, and that day the occupation officially came to an end.[29]

More than any other single person, MacArthur had been responsible for guiding the Japanese nation to the point where forty-eight nations were prepared at San Francisco to restore sovereignty and independence to Japan and to welcome her as an equal member of the family of nations again. The general's contribu-

tions to the peace and security settlements were significant, if indirect, consisting chiefly of his unceasing pressures on Washington for moving ahead more rapidly on the matter, his advocacy of
a nonpunitive treaty guaranteeing complete restoration of Japan's
sovereignty, and his counsel to Dulles that led to breaking the Defense-State deadlock on the security problem. Nevertheless,
MacArthur was not present at the peace conference nor at the
signing of the security pact. His presence at the latter event would
have seemed particularly appropriate both because of his role in
the security negotiations and because the commanding officer at
the Presidio was Lieutenant General Joseph M. Swing, Mac-
Arthur's old friend, who had been a division and corps commander in the Southwest Pacific war and in occupied Japan. After
the signing of the Treaty of Peace, Yoshida sent MacArthur a
message: "My heart and the hearts of all Japanese turn to you in
boundless gratitude, for it is your firm and kindly hand that led us,
a prostrate nation, on the road to recovery and reconstruction. It
was you who first propounded the principles for a fair and generous peace which we now have at long last." An hour before the
historic signing ceremony at the Opera House, Dulles sent the
general a telegram: "You will be present in spirit for the signing,"
for without "your great leadership" in World War II and the occupation, "the results achieved here would not have been attain-
able."[30]

On August 21, two weeks before the San Francisco assembly
convened, Colonel Bunker, MacArthur's aide, issued a press release from the general's small New York office: "General Mac-
Arthur has received no invitation to attend or address the San
Francisco Conference. . . . The General was not included in the
Delegation selected by President Truman . . . and this would seem
to foreclose upon any appropriate appearance short of a direct invitation by the Peace Conference itself." In his memoirs all that
MacArthur said about the matter was that "perhaps someone just
forgot to remember" to invite him. It had been a short span from
April, when Truman summarily relieved him, to September, when
the San Francisco Conference met, and many of the general's
faithful followers concluded from the press statement that the
President and Acheson were still trying to humiliate the old hero.
MacArthur's statement in his memoirs seemed to confirm the no-

tion of a conspiracy to deprive him of his rightful place at San Francisco. So the legend was born and perpetuated; it continues to enjoy a long life in popular works that depend too heavily on the writings of MacArthur and his lieutenants.[31]

In truth, MacArthur was invited to address the San Francisco Conference. On August 11, Dulles called the general's New York office and informed Bunker that "there was now agreement from the White House and State Department to the idea of the General's coming out and making a speech at San Francisco." After the President's opening-day address, MacArthur "would be the first speaker at the first business session," with Dulles speaking after him. "The thought was that he and I between us would cover the background of the Treaty," said Dulles, "he dealing with the occupation and I picking up with the Treaty negotiations." Dulles read to Bunker over the telephone a draft statement suggested by the State Department as a basis for the general's address, which the aide copied down. Dulles told him to "submit this text to the General, and let me know whether it was acceptable, or what modifications seemed to him desirable." Two hours later Whitney called Dulles to report "that the suggested statement was totally unacceptable, that it seemed to put General MacArthur in a position of an attendant to the U.S. Delegation, a role which was unacceptable and incompatible to that which he had played in Japan, where he had been the Supreme Commander for the Allied Powers and not a United States official." Dulles said he was "disappointed" and suggested that he could come to New York and "talk the matter over further personally with General MacArthur." Later Bunker called back to say that the general "would be glad to see" Dulles but "thought it was hardly worthwhile discussing the matter" unless Dulles "felt it possible to find an international basis for the invitation." Bunker and Whitney duly reported their talks with Dulles to the general, who made no direct contact with Dulles about the matter. Dulles had no recourse except to drop the subject.[32]

When reporters asked Truman on August 16 about a rumor that MacArthur might speak at the San Francisco meeting, the President replied, "I don't know. It will be all right if he wants to address the Conference. I would have no objection to it whatever. And if the State Department invites him, he undoubtedly will." It was five days later that Bunker issued the statement that Mac-

Arthur had not been asked to attend or to speak. Dulles then responded with a press statement pointing out that "obviously, the U.S. is not in a position to issue an invitation on behalf of the Conference. . . . I would not want to speculate on what, if anything, the Conference will do in this respect." Acheson, who presided over the San Francisco Conference, said that Bernard M. Baruch suggested to him that MacArthur be invited, but since the general "would appear only on invitation by the whole conference," the Secretary of State responded, "I had not provided for this in the rules and was not inclined to do so." Acheson's concern was over possible Soviet machinations, and he intended to be the absolute parliamentary master over the proceedings. Thus MacArthur was invited by his own government but not by the conference. Sebald's reasoning probably reflected that of most of the conference delegates: "General MacArthur was without official status, and he could have been invited only by creating a special precedent. In fact there would have been no proper role for him . . . even if he had continued to be the Supreme Commander, an international military position. The peace delegates, on the other hand, were national representatives." Sebald observed that Ridgway, who had been SCAP since April, was not invited either, and "this was probably the reason" in his case, too.[33]

Actually the happenings at San Francisco in September 1951 were deeply satisfying to MacArthur despite the hurt he felt over his dismissal and over the conference's failure to make a place for him. Before the Senate voted on the peace and security treaties in March 1952, Knowland wrote the general, asking for his views. MacArthur replied that "f he were in the Senate he would vote for the ratification of the Treaty." He was likewise warmly supportive when other senators and public leaders solicited his opinion on whether the treaties should be approved. After the overwhelming Senate votes in favor of the Japanese treaties, Dulles wrote to MacArthur, thanking him once more for "his inspiration and support" in the long and tangled treaty negotiations. By then MacArthur had recuperated emotionally from his setbacks, and he responded to Dulles with obvious joy and sincerity that the ratification of the Japanese peace and security treaties marked "a happy ending to a great task."[34]

CHAPTER XII

Personal Life in Tokyo

1. Controls and Conflicts

DURING THE NEARLY FIVE YEARS that he presided over the occupation of Japan before the Korean War erupted, MacArthur was able to manage his personal environment more firmly than perhaps ever before in his life. "He worked harder than ever at his job," observed Colonel Sidney Huff, his faithful assistant and aide from 1936 to 1951, but the general's personal life was "probably more pleasant than any since the prewar days in Manila." Unlike the period of the Southwest Pacific war, now he could be with his family every day, and he was able, to a large extent, to control whom he saw, what he did, where he went, and how the public viewed him. There are striking parallels between the orderliness and happiness of his private world in the idyllic settings atop the Manila Hotel from 1935 to 1941 and at the Tokyo embassy from 1945 to 1950. Both of these peaceful, pleasant eras ended the same way, too, with the shattering intrusion of sudden war. The principal differences between the two periods were the more accentuated aloofness of his Tokyo years and his less flexible adjustment to the demands of war in 1950. During his Tokyo residency, age must be reckoned as a factor — he was seventy on January 26, 1950 — and the unique nature of the Korean conflict, a limited war fought under United Nations auspices, made his command decisions more complex than those of World War II. The fact that at an advanced age for a commander he was compelled to move quickly from his best controlled situation to the least controlled of his life in 1950 has not been fully appreciated by most historians of the Korean War.

The beautiful United States embassy in the middle of Tokyo, which became the MacArthurs' home after the arrival of his wife and son on September 19, 1945, was conducive to the tranquil, well-ordered life the general desired. The embassy compound was situated on a wooded, hilly tract in the downtown area, about a mile and a quarter southwest of the Dai Ichi Building. Though much of the city had been devastated by air raids, the embassy structures had suffered comparatively little damage and were soon repaired. The grounds were enclosed by a handsome but formidable combination of masonry wall topped by fancy iron grill; the large main gate, flanked by twin guard buildings, led into the courtyard facing the chancellery. Near its rear were two buildings that housed nine or ten apartments for guests and members of MacArthur's personal staff, such as aides like Huff and the general's physician, Colonel Douglas B. Kendrick (succeeded in 1949 by Lieutenant Colonel Charles C. Canada). Atop a small hill behind the apartment buildings lay the ambassador's residence, or the "Big House," which contained seven bedrooms, four bathrooms, three salons, a banquet hall, a private dining room, a smoking room, a loggia, and a generous number of utility rooms for ironing, sewing, cloaks, and storage, besides a large kitchen. From the house MacArthur had a superb view of the heart of the city with the Diet Building looming to the north. Near his residence were a swimming pool, a large reflection pool, and formal gardens. All the embassy buildings had attractive exteriors of white trimmed in black ironwork at the windows and balconies. "The buildings are all impressive," Huff remarked, "and the grounds and gardens beautiful." Even in 1932, when Ambassador Joseph C. Grew had arrived, he had been impressed by the embassy's magnificence and isolation; he called it "a real oasis in the more or less ugly surroundings of the new-grown city" — an analogy even more apt in the bomb-wrecked Tokyo of the fall of 1945.[1]

MacArthur's daily routine, described in Chapter II, hardly varied from Sunday through Saturday every week, with no days off whatsoever during the entire time he was in Japan, except for two days he spent in bed with a throat infection in 1946. His daily arrival at the office in late morning, long midafternoon break at the embassy, and return to the Dai Ichi until well into the evening were extremely trying on the staff officers, who had to report at 8:00 A.M. and stay until he left that night, which might be 9:00 or 10:00. When a visitor once observed to MacArthur that he was "killing" his immediate office staff with such long hours, the general merely replied, "What better fate for a man than to die in performance of his duty?"

His travel was severely restricted before the Korean War; he made only two brief trips outside Japan, one to attend the inauguration of Manuel Roxas as President of the new Republic of the Philippines in July 1946 and the other to be at the swearing-in of Syngman Rhee as the President of the new Republic of (South) Korea in August 1948. MacArthur did not visit the bases of the occupation forces, though some were nearby, such as the large American naval station at Yokosuka, only thirty-eight miles south of Tokyo. Huff, an ardent admirer, even admitted that "Jean [MacArthur] accompanied Lt. Gen. Robert Eichelberger and later Lt. Gen. Walton H. Walker [successive Eighth Army commanders] on a number of inspection trips around Japan, acting as unofficial representative of the General because he wouldn't spare the time from his office." It is hard to believe, but nevertheless true, that in sixty-eight months in one of the most fascinating countries on earth the only sights of Japan he saw were from his automobile as he was driven between the Dai Ichi Building and the embassy and on the Haneda Airport route.[2]

The MacArthur quality that his detractors have had the most difficulty accepting as genuine was his courage, perhaps because his physical acts of valor in both the world wars were so often flamboyant. Since he was primarily in an administrative role in Japan, physical courage would seem to be one of his least demonstrable traits. But his arrival in Japan in August 1945, when only a small American force had preceded him, brought accolades, even from Churchill, as a supreme act of boldness and bravery. Three weeks later he refused an escort when he drove to Atsugi Airfield to pick up his wife and son. He detested the idea of being escorted to and from his office by a jeep with armed guards, which the military police first assigned to him. After running arguments with his security-wary senior officers, he got the guards removed and even refused to allow Japanese motorcycle policemen to precede his car to and from Haneda Airport. After he thought he had won his battle against escorts, however, Willoughby made sure that a jeep with two guards in fatigues always trailed him a block or so, though the Supreme Commander never learned of it. From MacArthur's viewpoint, what he was doing was not courageous; he was demonstrating to the Japanese people his faith in their good will and peace-loving intentions. He refused to alter his regular route on May Day, 1946, even though demonstrators waving red flags had to move aside to let his car pass and American counter-intelligence reported a foiled assassination plot by a former kamikaze pilot against him only a few days earlier. Had he known more about the frequency of political assassinations in Japanese history, it is still unlikely that he would have been deterred.[3]

Although before 1941 he had built a reputation as a dandy, now in Japan he eschewed dress uniforms, no matter how distinguished the visitor. His attire in Tokyo was the same as that for which he had become well known as a World War II commander: the open-necked khaki shirt, battered braid hat, sunglasses, and pipe, with no decorations or insignia except his five-star circles on each collar tab and jacket shoulder strap. Faubion Bowers, an aide who often rode with him, noticed that "the famous hallmark, the hat vizored with scrambled eggs, was tarnished, sweat-stained, almost tattered." His next most familiar appurtenance was the long-stemmed corncob pipe, which he still used in public; however, in private he usually turned to a fine-quality briar or meerschaum pipe. According to Bunker, he used "a tremendous variety of pipes," but often "as something to keep his hands busy"; he did not actually smoke them as much as people thought. He "smoked cigarettes very rarely" and sometimes after dinner enjoyed "very mild Filipino cigars." Much idle speculation was spent on whether the Old Man used black hair dye; his hair was obviously thinning, but on his passport as late as 1961 it was described as "black hair streaked with gray." The passport also reveals, by the way, that he had gray eyes, not brown, as commonly thought, and he was five feet, eleven inches tall, which was shorter than most people imagined.[4]

Visitors to MacArthur's headquarters during the Second World

War often commented on the youthful appearance of the South-west Pacific theater commander, who reached the statutory retirement age of sixty-four in January 1944. Such observations became more frequent among those visiting him in Tokyo, since they were prepared to accept the reality that as he approached his seventies, even he could not defy the relentless process of aging. But when Assistant Secretary of War John McCloy visited MacArthur in late 1945, he exclaimed afterward to an officer in the outer office, "My God! How does he do it? He's in better health than when I saw him before the war . . . more fascinating than when he was Chief of Staff. . . . What a man!" Mrs. Vining said he had "a look of almost youthful freshness" in 1947; she described him as "handsome, tall, vigorous, magnetic, commanding with a high forehead, deep-set, keen, seeking eyes, a clear, fresh, smooth skin, a firm, fine sensitive mouth." Bowers commented, "He was really very beautiful, like fine ore, a splendid rock, a boulder." In 1949 the newspaper editor William Mathews said he was "vigorous" and "looked better than he did in 1945." John Gunther, who had lunch with him in early June 1950 and had not seen him for a long while, was astonished by MacArthur's seeming control over the signs of aging: "He is extraordinarily handsome . . . not merely from the point of view of conventional good looks, but with a magnetism, a vitality, that come from within. Also he looks amazingly young." Although noticing that his "sensitive, slim hands . . . tremble slightly," Gunther maintained that the general's "appearance as a whole (I am not exaggerating) is that of a man of fifty, not seventy, moreover, a man of fifty in the very best physical condition and at the top of his form." In October 1950, when MacArthur was still elated over his Inchon triumph and advance into North Korea, William Courtenay, a reporter, remarked after a visit with him at his office: "I never saw him look so fit and well, so alert and youthful and full of color and mental vigor. . . . Last year . . . his face was looking more worn and tired as if his age was catching up with him. But this week he appeared back to the form of 1941."[5]

MacArthur told Gunther and probably many other visitors that his good physical condition was due to his regular afternoon naps, his moderation in eating, drinking, and smoking, and his ability to fall asleep quickly. Although the general was fighting a com-

mendable delaying action against the onset of the physical manifestations of aging and was projecting to visitors a convincing image of permanent youthfulness, those who worked with him were
beginning to see some effects of the years on him physically, if not
mentally. To Sams, a neurosurgeon by profession, the general
"showed . . . definite signs or symptoms of Parkinson's disease.
He was somewhat embarrassed by the muscular tremors which
developed in his hands, causing them to shake. The tremors seemed
to be more evident toward the end of his stay in Japan." Since the
tremors usually came when his hands were not in use, some friends
felt that was why he kept his hands in almost constant motion in
the presence of others, either gesticulating as he talked and paced
or handling his matches, pipes, or tobacco in the oft-repeated
process of lighting up.[6]

The general counted his successive physicians among his better
friends and often employed them really as senior aides, but he
found little use for them as doctors except to treat his family and
staff members. Sams recalled that "neither I nor any physician, to
my knowledge, was able to get General MacArthur to undergo a
physical examination." Colonel Egeberg, his physician in the
Southwest Pacific and during the early phase of the occupation,
was able to put a stethoscope on his chest once briefly while ex-
amining an officer seated beside the general on a wartime B-17
flight. On the one occasion when MacArthur was forced to miss
work, in 1946, because of a streptococcus throat infection, Colonel
Kendrick could not treat him until the general had stubbornly tried
his favorite patent medicine first and found it did not cure him,
his temperature having reached 101 degrees by the time he let the
doctor examine his throat. In early 1951 Colonel Canada, his last
physician in Japan, stated that MacArthur "has the physiological
and mental age of a man forty-five years old." Sams, however,
qualified his assessment: "He seemed to be generally in good health,
although he was beginning to have some problems often associated with advancing age. His waistline was expanding. He did not
stand quite as erect or walk as crisply as in the old days. He could
not read fine print without glasses." Whitney often gave him memos
in extralarge type or handwriting, because MacArthur was reluctant to use his glasses. Bowers believed that "his hearing was im-
paired"; he often had to repeat statements loudly to him.

Also by late November 1950, when the massive Communist Chinese offensive hurled his forces back in Korea, MacArthur's legendary ability to go to sleep easily had left him. From then until the next April, he often did not go to bed until he had paced for hours, thinking out his latest command problems, and then, going to bed in the early morning hours, slept from sheer exhaustion. Huff noted that the Supreme Commander's usual pacing route at his residence in the late evenings was from the curving staircase near the front door through the long hall and large drawing room: "He had about a hundred and twenty-five feet of wide-open pacing space and, night after night, he made the most of it." Somehow he retained his good health in spite of, not in the absence of, midnight worrying during the tense period when he commanded both the occupation in Japan and the United Nations forces trying to stop the Chinese armies in Korea.[7]

MacArthur had been a fairly good athlete in several sports, particularly baseball, and had continued to play tennis in prewar Manila, but he had reduced considerably the amount of exercise he got by the time he was in Tokyo — not surprising for a man in his late sixties and early seventies. In his bedroom each morning he went through a simple program of calisthenics; the regular spectators at this ritual were Arthur's three dogs and Huff's cocker spaniel. Sometimes at the Dai Ichi, according to Bunker, MacArthur would climb the six flights of stairs to his office at a pace that left anyone with him "out of breath." His principal daily exercise came in his pacing, which his subordinates variously estimated came to as much as four miles per day. At his office he often paced while delivering a monologue to whoever was present, but he also did a lot of walking alone; Whitney, who had access to the general's office by a side door without having to clear through the chief of staff or aides, said that he frequently entered to find MacArthur by himself rapidly walking back and forth across the room. And, as mentioned above, he indulged in hours-long pacing sessions at night in his residence. With the Korean War and numerous flights to the peninsula, MacArthur got in more pacing time. According to Colonel Anthony F. Story, his long-time pilot, MacArthur "paces up and down in the plane nearly all the way from take-off to destination, to an extent where he is the only man I know who covers twice the distance when he flies between two points. . . . I had to operate on instruments to compensate for the constant shifting in weight, back and forth, back and forth." Such a mannerism may have helped his thinking, but it also was a good health habit for the Old Man.[8]

It will be recalled that even before MacArthur was chosen to head the United Nations Command in the Korean conflict, he already held another important position, in addition to his SCAP role in the occupation, namely, commander in chief of the Far East Command of American ground, air, and sea forces. Because of his multitude of high-level responsibilities, he found it necessary to forego many of the social affairs, held by the various Allied diplomatic missions, that the highest-ranking American official in a foreign land would normally attend. During his first year in Tokyo he went to a party, dinner, or reception at the FEC missions on each one's national day, but thereafter, according to Huff, "he never again made a social appearance outside of his own home." Although some viewed his withdrawal from social activities as an indication of his haughtiness, it was mainly the result of his official duties, which were overwhelming. He wisely chose to conserve his energy for higher-priority calls on his time. One GHQ officer suggested another motive: "General MacArthur got used to his open-collar casual attire during World War II and never wanted to wear a dress uniform and decorations again." But Huff may have been closer to the truth in saying that "there weren't enough hours in the day or enough days in the week to suit him." Put simply, he was busier than ever before, was not getting younger, and was aware of both facts.

MacArthur tried to compensate somewhat for his absences from social functions by having his wife, usually escorted by Huff, attend as his representative, which proved a good idea, because Mrs. MacArthur's vivacious, amiable personality was well received. The MacArthurs also gave luncheons (but seldom dinners) at the embassy, sometimes almost every day and for groups up to thirty individuals; the guests were usually Allied and American military, diplomatic, and political dignitaries residing in or visiting Japan. He also was generous with his office time in receiving all the Allied representatives in Japan except the Soviet. It will be noticed in the appendix listing the people who had the most contact with

MacArthur by appointment were the heads of the United Kingdom, New Zealand, Australian, Canadian, French, and Netherlands missions in Japan. In fact, next to William Sebald, the senior State Department representative, the person who had the most office appointments with MacArthur in Tokyo between 1945 and 1951 was Sir Alvary D. Gascoigne, who was the chief of the United Kingdom liaison mission.[9]

"The official dining room of the Embassy," said Whitney, "looked out on the lawn, pool, and gardens. It contained a long table capable of seating up to thirty guests. On the wall behind MacArthur at the head of the table was a Japanese painting of two white cranes; over Mrs. MacArthur at the foot of the table was another painting, this one of a shimmering green waterfall." According to another source, "The table is laden with flowers and lit with candles. Luncheon is served by eight Japanese manservants, clad in dark brown kimonos with the United States seal on them."[10] Numerous people invited to lunch with the MacArthurs at the embassy have left accounts, most varying little from the description provided by Huff, who often served as much as aide to Jean MacArthur as to her husband:

> If there were guests for luncheon, Jean and I would have them assembled in the big drawing room before two o'clock and she would quietly count noses and worry about whether there were enough places set at the table. . . .
>
> At approximately two o'clock the General would come in the big front door. Jean would have had a telephone call that he was en route, but she would look up in surprise and usually say, "Oh, here's the General!" He would walk over to kiss her. "Hello, Sir Boss," was her routine greeting. "I didn't hear your car arrive."
>
> The General would walk around the room, greeting his guests, and then return to Jean and ask, "Got anything for us to eat?"
>
> Jean always led them into the dining room without much delay. Most of the guests — usually distinguished visitors — were persons who wanted to get MacArthur's views of important problems or vice versa, and the luncheons often lasted until close to four o'clock. Sometimes the General would talk very informally, but almost without interruption for an hour or so. . . .
>
> [On the guests' departure] MacArthur always went to his bedroom, took off his clothes and slept after luncheon. Normally, he would

awaken after an hour, but if not, Jean would awaken him, he would look at the evening paper, and return to the office around five o'clock.[11]

Gunther and other guests found that Mrs. MacArthur was helpful in getting some speaking time for the visitors, "in the event that the General's eloquence is in full majestic flow, by interrupting gently and saying, 'But, General, Mr. X wants to ask you about This-or-That.' Previously, before he entered, she had found out tactfully what subjects the guest is most eager to discuss." It is to be hoped that in most cases the general already knew the topic the guest had in mind, though it was said by many such visitors that at times only Mrs. MacArthur was successful in interrupting one of his monologues to give others a voice.[12]

In view of his lifelong interest in sports, it is surprising that MacArthur did not attend any athletic events, especially the Japanese national tennis and table tennis championships, whose winners, beginning in mid-1947, received MacArthur Cups, bearing his signature. The general, however, did enjoy following West Point football in the newspapers, by radio broadcasts of the big games, and through correspondence with the U.S. Military Academy's renowned coach, Earl (Red) Blaik, who had been a cadet at the academy when MacArthur was the superintendent from 1919 to 1920 and had made the school's football teams into consistent winners. MacArthur often offered advice to Blaik on football strategy, kept up with the statistics on all of his players, and sent inspiring messages to the team before crucial games, such as those with Notre Dame and Navy. Blaik took the general's counsel in the right spirit and encouraged the correspondence. In April 1948 MacArthur wrote the coach that his letters gave him "one of the few bright moments of relaxation that fall to my lot." MacArthur's continuing devotion to West Point was further demonstrated daily by his wearing of "a regular cadet robe," which, according to Mrs. MacArthur, "we ordered . . . all these years from the Cadet Store at the Academy, even during the war years. His 'A' was always put on at the Academy (this . . . he won in baseball as a cadet)."[13]

Although his eyesight was poorer and his rapid-reading ability was on the wane, MacArthur still tried to keep up his old hobby of reading military history and biography. Most such reading, as well as his poring over the early day's messages from his office, was done at the embassy before his daily departure for the Dai Ichi Building about 10:00 or 11:00 A.M. Another form of relaxation was playing with Arthur, usually early in the morning, which almost invariably involved the boy's three dogs: Blackie, a cocker spaniel, Uki, a white Akita dog, and Brownie, a Shiba terrier. Blackie, the general's favorite, was permitted to sleep in his bedroom chair and to stay with him during his morning shave. In terms of hours per week, MacArthur's principal leisure activity was the same as in prewar Manila, namely, watching movies, usually six evenings per week. All the personnel in the compound were invited, including the servants and honor guards; the usual nightly audience in the banquet hall was about fifty. MacArthur always sat in his old red wicker rocker, with Jean on his left and Huff on his right. According to Mrs. MacArthur, he wore "the monogrammed smoking jacket [that] was a birthday gift to the General in Tokyo by the Honor Guard. They gave it to him to wear during the movies at the Embassy, which he always did." He preferred light films, which for his relaxation meant comedies, musicals, and Westerns. On Sunday evenings he and Jean listened to records in the small library room. General George Kenney, his air chief in the Pacific war and later head of SAC, visited his old boss five times in Tokyo and concluded that MacArthur would be active for quite a long while to come, because "the way he lives agrees with him so well."[14]

MacArthur's efforts during his Tokyo years to master his immediate environment through a routine based on simplicity, orderliness, and aloofness were his way of adjusting to and succeeding under the enormous pressures of his manifold responsibilities, though he was acutely aware that aging would eventually take its toll of his energy, health, and sharpness. But just as the captain who has his crew and ship in top condition must still reckon with the vagaries of the sea and the elements, MacArthur could not control, but only react to, such external factors that impinged on his success or failure as trends in Japanese political and economic affairs, Washington strategy shifts, and Cold War developments in East Asia and the rest of the world. He could only trust that his vessel was prepared to meet any unexpected storms. Unhappily, though he succeeded fairly well in attaining control over much of the physical context of the world in which he daily moved, he was never able to master the complex, contradictory traits that made up his own personality and character.

The nearly 180 colleagues and contemporaries of his who were interviewed over the years of research on this project provided altogether an interesting collection of impressions and interpretations of MacArthur the commander and the man. Of these people, the largest group comprised senior officers who served with him, but many others, nonmilitary as well as military, who knew or dealt with him or his GHQ inner circle were included, too, and their opinions of MacArthur ranged from adulatory to condemnatory. Most agreed on three basic points: (1) MacArthur was the most complicated person they had ever met, and they knew of no one who fully understood him and of only a few who were genuinely close to him. (2) Regardless of whether their general views of him were favorable, they believed there were sharp discrepancies between the public image of the general and the man himself. (3) For the most part, the closer and longer the interviewed person had worked with MacArthur, the more affirmative were his or her impressions of him; the most negative opinions were expressed by those having the least personal contact with him. The only major defector whom the interviewees could recall among those who served under him for a considerable time was Eichelberger, who retired in 1948 with bitter feelings toward MacArthur that dated back to the Papuan campaign of 1942–1943. Eichelberger, however, was even more sour toward several of MacArthur's generals.[15]

The picture of MacArthur that emerges from these interviews is a montage of contradictory attributes. Some described him as courageous, bold, strong-willed, decisive, and self-confident; others found him vacillating, indecisive, and insecure. He was intensely conscious of himself as a "man of destiny," but he refused to fire incompetent staff members, shifted the blame for blunders to others, and fretted over his tenure and his image. Depending on the viewer, he appeared humble, shy, and self-sacrificial, or, on the other hand, arrogant, egotistical, and narcissistic. He would invite a startled young lieutenant to ride in the Dai Ichi elevator with him, yet boldly reject invitations to confer in Washington with the President or with congressional committees. He impressed some colleagues as charming, amiable, tactful, and considerate; others saw him as obnoxious, haughty, and calloused. He would be the friendly, courteous host to newspaper publishers at a luncheon and shortly afterward order one of their correspondents out of Japan on a few days' notice. He was capable of appearing both movingly sincere and gratingly theatrical, both austere and flamboyant. It was the same man who dressed casually and refused to wear ties, yet rode in a long black Cadillac bedecked with his five-star flag and five-star license plate. Some praised him as honest, high-principled, noble, and judicious; others believed him to be deceitful, mendacious, petty, and scheming. He was strict in refusing special privileges for his officers in general, but looked the other way when some of his favorites obtained undue advantages. Loyalty to and from his staff was a high priority for MacArthur, but his own dealings with superiors sometimes bordered on insubordination. He enjoyed others' jokes and could be witty, yet he did not possess the ability to laugh at himself. His role-playing, discussed in Volume II of this series, was developed to a high art in Tokyo, though the part in which he seemed most natural, according to most interviewees, was still that of the chivalrous officer-aristocrat. Some suggested that the enigmas posed by his many conflicting traits and role assumptions contributed to his charismatic appeal. Of the sundry attributes that others saw him as possessing, courage was the virtue most esteemed by MacArthur. Thus he counseled an officer-student at the U.S. Army Command and General Staff College in 1956:

> Moral courage — true leadership — is based upon a fundamental but simple philosophy — to do what you think is right as opposed to what you think is wrong irrespective of the popularity or unpopularity which may result, and always with the realization that being human you may be wrong in your decision. Do this and you will always be a little lonesome although it will render you immune to two of the greatest frauds in the world, triumph and disaster — the roar of the crowd either in the acclaim of victory or in the disapproval of defeat.[16]

If students of psychohistory face a morass of contradictory data on his personal characteristics, researchers studying his beliefs will be hard put to find consistency or a systematic philosophy. In Japan he appeared at times to be liberal, reformist, or idealistic, but on other occasions and issues seemed conservative and even reactionary. A staunch capitalist, he encountered his fiercest opposition in America from big-business leaders, who feared he was "socializing" Japan. An outspoken anti-Communist, he was amazingly tolerant of Communist activities in Japan during the early phase of the occupation, and before the reverse course he expressed the hope that Japan might become a neutral in the Cold War — "the Switzerland of Asia." Extremely patriotic and proud of America, he refused to go back to the States for fourteen years and was darkly alarmist in his estimates of postwar national leadership and trends. As political-minded as any American general since Leonard Wood or perhaps even George McClellan, he had a deep distaste for politicians and campaigning, and, as attested to by a number of interviewees, he was less than wholehearted in his acceptance of the principle of civilian supremacy over the military. He often spoke of God and even sparked a zealous crusade to Christianize Japan, but he never attended church himself. His decisions were often based on intuition, yet he frequently lashed out at Washington leaders for their lack of policies and plans arrived at rationally or empirically. In such accusations he could be brutally frank, but he was hypersensitive about any criticism of himself, his staff, or the administration of the occupation.[17]

In the versatility of his skills, knowledge, and experience, MacArthur came as close as any American military leader to approximating the Renaissance ideal of excelling in a number of areas. In bygone days his mother had envisioned him as an executive with E. H. Harriman's railroad empire, and his first wife, Louise, had tried to interest him in a position with J. Pierpont Morgan's investment banking firm. Neither job was appealing to him, but most of his peers believed that he was one of the few officers who could have made it to the top in those fields or several others. Most interviewees, whether they liked him or not, expounded at length on MacArthur's superior mind. His forte was an uncanny ability to analyze a problem quickly and focus on essential points or options, relating them to broader, more long-range considerations than did others who had worked on the problem. Several of his colleagues used the same analogy about his intellectual grasp: MacArthur could see both the trees and the forest. His communicative skills were exceptional, too, particularly as a persuasive conversationalist and a moving speaker, though neither his printed speeches nor his other writings usually could stand the tests of good style, especially on clarity, coherence, and conciseness. Yet his "purple prose" at its best possessed an old-fashioned eloquence and vividness that surely distinguished it from the pedestrian writing of most generals.[18] As related previously, he was a superb administrator, demonstrating unusual ability in organizing and planning, as well as in selecting and motivating his staff leaders. His GHQ certainly suffered from some of the usual snarls and legalisms of bureaucracy, but for its considerable size and unprecedented mission it was well administered.

MacArthur was at the zenith of his career between 1945 and 1950, and the respect he commanded as an authority figure, together with his versatile talents and varied command experiences, made him the best-suited officer the United States had for the task of overseeing the occupation of Japan. Although some other senior officers may have been better liked in the role of SCAP, none would have had the influence he had with key people and groups in America and Japan. Pentagon and State leaders may have disagreed with him on occasion, but time after time they deferred to his judgment because it made good sense, because his record of achievement since becoming a general in 1918 was long and solid, or because the majority of his half-century of service to the nation had been spent in East Asia. The reform measures that were undertaken in occupied Japan and the American relief and economic assistance provided that country might have been impossible were it not for the support MacArthur had from the coalition of conservative Republicans and Southern Democrats that controlled Congress during the Truman administration. If, as has often been alleged, Eisenhower succeeded where Truman failed in terminating the war in Korea because the latter was considered too liberal, in post-1945 America the success of the occupation of Japan was in no small measure due to the respect its commander had in conservative circles. The majority of the Japanese admired those traits of MacArthur which alienated many Americans, and never in his lengthy career was he more effective at image projection than he was in Japan. At a time when the Japanese had become disillusioned with their leaders of 1931 to 1945 and needed someone to look to for inspiration and hope, MacArthur provided them with the image of the dramatic, dynamic, and dedicated leader. Generally the Japanese had deep respect for his strong will, his firmness, his austerity, his sense of destiny, and — in a society where personal loyalty meant much — his demand for strict loyalty from his subordinates and even from the press.[19]

Although MacArthur's assets were many in his multiple role as head of the occupation and of the Far East Command, increasingly since 1948 questions had been raised about his liabilities. In retrospect, that year seems to have been a pivotal one in his career because of three crucial developments: the MacArthur-for-President campaign, the departure of Eichelberger, and the adoption of NSC 13/2. Both in America and Japan, at the time and ever since, disturbing questions arose regarding how much MacArthur's political ambition affected his positions on, for example, the anti-Zaibatsu offensive, the Christian crusade in Japan, the early termination of the occupation, the need for further toughening of America's stance against the Soviet Union, and the allegedly deteriorating state of the American nation under Truman's leadership. When Eichelberger left Japan, MacArthur lost his principal remaining confidant from World War II who had dared to disagree with him and to dissent from the concurrence-seeking, "groupthink" behavior of the inner circle of senior officers around the Supreme Commander. Although that group contained men who could be strongly individualistic on other matters and in confronting one another, the strong bond that they had in common was a deep devotion to MacArthur. It had been true earlier to some extent, but more and more after Eichelberger's exit MacArthur's channels of information narrowed and his sources of fresh, objective thinking declined. The shift in policy emphasis that came with NSC 13/2 made MacArthur appear in the eyes of some key leaders in Washington to be anachronistic and inflexible as he responded with slowness in implementing some of the changes. The often poor communications between him and the post-1945 leaders in the Pentagon, State Department, and White House; the absence of any personal relations with many of the "new breed of Europe-firsters and Eastern establishment types," as one of his GHQ officers described the men now in the high echelons of Washington decision-making; and the lack of strong MacArthur supporters in key positions in the executive branch any longer — all these conditions had led to tensions over occupation matters but could spell serious trouble for MacArthur if a dire emergency arose, such as the coming of war or, worse, the prospect of defeat.

Had Napoleon Bonaparte examined MacArthur's career up to the eve of the Korean War, he undoubtedly would have concluded that he passed the first and foremost test of a commander: he was lucky. Indeed, MacArthur's fortune had been incredibly good at timely moments in his past. But the main difference between the MacArthur of old and the general during his final half-year in Tokyo was that his luck finally ran out. In the terrible process he lost control of some of the environmental conditions he had so carefully ordered in his life, and the contradictory traits that had once seemed so charismatically appealing now pulled and twisted him toward a tragic end.[20]

2. *Home in the Embassy*

General MacArthur achieved the quiet, simple private life he wanted in Tokyo mainly because of the unending, selfless efforts of a slight, pretty lady named Jean MacArthur. Deeply devoted to her husband, she did everything possible to make his time at home in the embassy as happy and peaceful as possible. Under her watchful eye the Japanese and Filipinos who largely made up the household staff kept every detail of living as smooth and methodical as possible. "No details escape her attention," one observer remarked, "and concurrently no small details ever have to concern the General." His unusual schedule left her day virtually consumed once she had cared for all of his and Arthur's needs. Besides running a tranquil, efficient household, Mrs. MacArthur helped her husband in numerous other ways, representing him at official social functions, charitable events, Japanese ceremonies, and inspection tours; giving countless luncheons with unfailing graciousness; reporting her detailed impressions of Japan from her travels in the city and countryside; taking early morning dictation from him, to be typed later at the office; making unofficial telephone calls in his behalf, since he abhorred phones; clipping newspapers and magazines for him; always being ready for his evening meal but seldom knowing when he would arrive; sitting

through movies of his choice evening after evening, though not
without dozing, especially during reruns; and, perhaps hardest of
all, listening to him talk out his problems as he paced into the early
morning hours when the Korean situation worsened. The general
could not have had a more ideal mate.[21]

One of the rare occasions when Jean MacArthur's attempts to
have all the details in order did not work out took place shortly
after the family moved into the embassy. The garden pool had
not been cleaned for years and was full of mud and slime. She
scooped out all the rare goldfish and put them carefully into con-
tainers of pool water until a crew finished scrubbing the basin.
"When the pool was clean again," according to one source, "she
called out the embassy staff and made a little party of returning
the fish to their home. Every fish promptly turned belly-side up
and died. U.S. Army engineers, it developed, had chlorinated the
water supply."[22]

While the general's strong personality stirred highly favorable
or unfavorable reactions in others, Mrs. MacArthur seemed to have
been universally liked. Mrs. Vining found her to be "a genuinely
sweet person" who "absolutely adored" and "lived for" her husband and son. Le Grande Diller described her as "a perfectly
charming individual. She is gracious to an extreme and just good
company to be with at any time — a good talker and smart as a
whip. But her mouth was closed like a clam; she never discussed
what she knew." William Mathews wrote to Dulles that she possessed "distinguished grace and cordial feminine dignity. She is a
delightful hostess and a charming table companion." Larry Bunker
commented, "She played her role to perfection, as far as I was
concerned. I know that she was a tremendous help to the General
because he always, all through his career apparently, needed to
have someone close to him with whom he could talk. . . . It was
just one of those marvelous situations where the right person was
in the right spot at the right time."[23]

On shopping trips, which she made unescorted or with one of
the general's aides, Mrs. MacArthur stood in lines at sales like all
the other shoppers and refused offers of special privileges at the
post exchange, such as inspecting goods before they went on public sale — a practice of some of the generals' wives. Only once in
Tokyo did she deliberately identify herself, and that was to keep

some Japanese from being disappointed. As she left a store one day, she noticed a crowd gathered outside. Curious, she joined them to await the exit of the unknown celebrity inside. After a while one of the general's aides found her and informed her that the people were expecting Mrs. MacArthur to come out. She slipped back into the building, telephoned to have her car driven to the entrance, and then emerged with the aide, to the crowd's delight. Walking down the aisle that the people had left between the door and the street, she was, said one account, "a superb and charming actress playing the part of the supreme commander's wife. Some recognized her from the place where she had stood with them. They bowed and she returned their bows, a twinkle in her eyes."[24]

Mrs. Phyllis Gibbons, the Englishwoman who was Arthur's tutor from 1945 to 1951, claimed that Jean MacArthur, who was only two years older than she, was a dear friend to her and "one of the most considerate persons you could ever meet." Mrs. MacArthur was particularly adept at appearing happy to be doing what others wished to do, though it might not be her preference. Ah Cheu, the elderly Chinese lady who had served as Arthur's nurse since shortly after his birth, in 1938, and had become a permanent member of the household, enjoyed table games, especially checkers and mahjong, which Jean MacArthur played with her every day, even though she was not an enthusiast of table games. Mrs. MacArthur, who turned fifty in 1949, was concerned about keeping her trim figure, yet she had to sit down to six meals a day, three each with her husband and son, who ate at separate times. Apparently she ate very little at each meal, for she managed to remain strikingly slim.[25]

Arthur MacArthur lived at the Tokyo embassy from the time he was seven until he was thirteen, or through his transition into adolescence. The boy, unusually handsome and bright-eyed, possessed some of the best facial features of each parent. Interviews with the general's colleagues who knew Arthur during this period produced the following descriptions: "delicate," "sweet," "lively," "frail," "gentle," "sensitive," and "nice." His parents, Ah Cheu, and Mrs. Gibbons tried to ensure that he grew up as normally as possible, despite the fact that his childhood had been different ever since he celebrated his fourth birthday between the bombardments on besieged Corregidor Island. Huff, whose book provides the most intimate glimpse of the MacArthurs' family life, maintained that "he did all of the things that interest the average American boy," and Mrs. Gibbons, or "Gibby," likewise asserted, "He is just an ordinary American boy." Arthur enjoyed romping with his dogs, swimming, rowing, tennis, croquet, horseback riding, ice skating, and Cub Scout activities. Finding playmates was a problem until the officers' families began to arrive; one of his chums was Charles Canada, Jr., the son of the general's physician, who lived in the embassy compound. Arthur's best friends, aside from his parents, however, continued to be Ah Cheu and Gibby.

Unlike a typical American youth, however, Arthur had a slight British accent, probably picked up from Gibby or during his years in Australia. He had never seen the United States and had never been enrolled in a public or private school. Later qualifying her assertion about his ordinariness, Mrs. Gibbons said that he was "very intelligent, reserved, and shy." She noted that his "outstanding talent" was his "gift for music," which he had demonstrated at an early age. He excelled at the piano, and sometimes he presented programs of classical concerts for the embassy staff and their families, usually including a composition or two he had written. His interest in music also extended to learning to play the squeeze box, ukulele, drums, recorder, and zither. An American Army officer who was Arthur's equitation instructor in the spring of 1947 believed that "General MacArthur preferred riding lessons for Arthur rather than piano lessons, but music was the preference of the boy and of his mother."[26]

Describing his feeling toward Arthur to some reporters in 1949, MacArthur exclaimed, "He is the apple of my eye." Those who observed the general with his son testified to the mutual affection, but some thought he was overindulgent toward the boy. Despite their love for each other, MacArthur and his son were confronted by far more obstacles than the usual generation gap between parent and child. For one thing, when the general was seventy, Arthur was but twelve, which made them not the best pair for pitching ball. For another, MacArthur was burdened with more awesome responsibilities than almost any American other than a President had shouldered. He tried to spend some time with Arthur each morning, but their time together was brief — far short of the needs of a boy during that critical span of years. Also, as Arthur reached the age of discretion, between eleven and thirteen, the realization must have begun to dawn on him, a delicate lad with a love of music, that he was named for a grandfather who had won the Medal of Honor and had risen to become the senior-ranking officer in the United States Army and that his own father was almost a living legend in the world of warriors. It is somehow difficult to imagine Arthur sharing with his father his latest piano composition. The mutual love was there, but the time and the common interests, alas, were not.

Just as FDR seemed to feel that somehow his public statements of support for China made up for the inadequate American aid to that nation in World War II, so MacArthur became excessive at times in his public displays of concern and affection for Arthur, as if he were trying to compensate for their lack of time together. While ice skating with Colonel Story in 1947, Arthur fell and broke his left arm. He was taken to St. Luke's Hospital, where the general visited him two to five times every day. (The number depends on which source is followed.) One version claims that MacArthur demanded dozens more x-rays than necessary, left the hospital staff "turned upside down," and forbade Arthur to go ice skating again. The general could be too proud, as well as too protective, of his son. On MacArthur's birthday each January, Arthur made him something special that had obviously taken considerable time and effort: a pair of wooden bookends for his sixty-ninth birthday, a pastel painting of flowers and a pair of hand-carved ashtrays for his seventieth birthday, and an ivory letter opener "shaped like an Egyptian dagger with a fitted hand rest and a series of carvings that give it a jeweled effect" for his seventy-first birthday. The general treasured these handmade gifts and kept them on his desk. All well and good so far. But each year the general's birthday doings, highlighted by detailed descriptions of his son's gifts and the father's proud comments thereon, were prominently featured in the next day's issue of *Nippon Times* and other papers, including the *New York Times*.[27] Whether this was the work of MacArthur or of his overzealous public relations staff, it is doubtful that it favorably impressed the shy, sensitive boy who had given the presents in sincere love. The fundamental problem between this father and son was surely not a lack of love; rather, it had to do with reconciling the priorities of such things as little rowboats and huge aircraft carriers, pianos and howitzers, dreams and duties, privacy and fame, adolescence and old age.

The seemingly idyllic life of the MacArthur family was suddenly disrupted in late November 1950 by the massive intervention of Communist Chinese armies in the Korean War and the forced withdrawal southward of the United Nations forces to avoid envelopment and destruction. Criticism of MacArthur's leadership became widespread in the American and Allied press, and there were demands for his removal from command. The general worked harder and harder as the criticisms mounted. His hours at the office became longer, starting earlier in the morning and ending later at night; his pacing at the embassy went on night after night; his flights to Korea, despite worsening weather and battle conditions, became more frequent; his moods in the office and as expressed in messages to Washington veered sharply from buoyant to depressed. If the general was worried or gloomy, then Jean mirrored his mood. The period around Christmas 1950 was especially distressing for the family. The intense pressures on the general will be dealt with later in the account of the Korean War. No one recorded the agonies that young Arthur must have undergone, but at least Huff provided a glimpse of the distress that Mrs. MacArthur suffered:

> For a couple of weeks it seemed to me that she was likely to collapse. She lost weight. She couldn't sleep. She picked at her food. She hardly left the embassy. . . .
>
> She would be awake in the morning long before MacArthur arose and she would stay as close to him as possible until he left for the office. Before lunch she would come down the hill to our apartment to talk to Keira [Mrs. Huff] and me, to ask our opinion about the General's health, to discuss the day's developments in Korea, to vent her anger at the critics. . . .
>
> Often she called me at the office and asked if I was going to be home soon, because she wanted to talk. "I feel as if the walls are closing in on me," she said. "I feel I must talk to someone." I went home and Keira and I would talk to her for an hour or so until word came that the General was on the way home.
>
> "You're not getting enough sleep, Jean," Keira insisted. "Why don't you take a sedative at night or go see the doctor?"
>
> She shook her head. "If I took a sedative I wouldn't be awake if the General wanted me," she replied. "I'm not going to see a doctor.

He'd probably want me to go to bed." Sometimes we could get her to sip at a glass of sherry, but most of the time she wanted nothing. . . .

At night, after the General had paced himself into readiness for bed, Jean would . . . be at his door every ten minutes until she was sure he was sleeping.

On days when MacArthur flew to the Korean front, Jean always waited tensely for word that his plane had started back to Tokyo, and then I would take her out to the airfield to greet him.[28]

Mrs. MacArthur "again became more like her old self" and the embassy atmosphere began to appear normal once more in early 1951, when the United Nations forces went on the counteroffensive. The worst crisis for the MacArthur family, however, was yet to come.

3. Changing of the Guard

The most dependable way of judging which men were closest to General MacArthur during a given period is to look at his immediate staff. He had long been a compulsive worker, and his friends had usually been chosen from those colleagues with whom he worked daily, because virtually the only worlds in which he moved were his job and his home. Since he had become a general officer in World War I, the officers who had served on his various command staffs stretched over several generations. When he was the Army Chief of Staff in the early 1930s, his subordinates in the War Department who had been good friends of his, such as Generals George Moseley, Hugh Drum, and George Simonds, had been in his age range. But by World War II the age gap had widened between him and his staff leaders; it was then that his Southwest Pacific GHQ began referring to him in private as the Old Man. The difference in years became more pronounced in Japan; most of the key officers at his Tokyo GHQ were much younger than he. Because of his seniority and distinguished record in two world wars, it is little wonder that most showed such deference to him that informal relations were difficult, especially in view of his remote and aristocratic demeanor. By early 1950 Willoughby, Marquat, and

Huff were the only members of the Bataan Gang who remained on his staff. Among the other officers who had become part of his inner group during the war against Japan, all except Whitney had left his command by 1950. In fact, so many of his former staff comrades were back in the United States that they began in 1949 to hold reunion dinners on the general's birthday, January 26 (and continued the practice for many years, with MacArthur joining the annual gathering after his move to New York).

By the eve of the Korean conflict, MacArthur's inner circle consisted of twelve officers of his GHQ staff. Six of them were especially good friends of his. They will be discussed briefly in the approximate order of their closeness to him, as judged from available oral and documentary evidence. No attempt will be made to rank the second echelon of six. Of course, information about many of these men has appeared already in this book or in the two previous volumes of this work, to which the reader may wish to turn and refresh his or her memory.

Brigadier General Courtney Whitney had succeeded Lieutenant General Richard K. Sutherland in the winter of 1944–1945 as the Supreme Commander's principal confidant and would retain that position until MacArthur's death, in 1964. Every fifth year exactly to the day that he joined the Southwest Pacific GHQ staff on May 24, 1943, MacArthur presented Whitney with a photograph of himself, usually in his five-star uniform and always bearing an affectionate inscription. On the commemorative photograph for 1963, less than a year before MacArthur died, he wrote, "Twenty years have passed, dear Court, since you joined me, and each has but increased my esteem for your loyal and devoted service." On another photograph that final year MacArthur paid tribute to Whitney, "who, as so many times in the past, has been my 'right arm' in this venture." The Supreme Commander once explained that he and Whitney got along so well because "their minds just meet." Whitney's writing style became so similar to his boss's that few colleagues could distinguish between them. He also seemed to be able to anticipate many of MacArthur's needs. John Gunther claimed, "MacArthur never has to ask or explain anything twice" to Whitney. A considerable number of interviewees believed that Whitney became, indeed, "MacArthur's alter ego."

Many officers at GHQ saw more differences than similarities in the temperaments of MacArthur and Whitney, particularly in view of the latter's tendency to be impatient and blunt. Contemporaries and later writers have speculated on Whitney's attraction for MacArthur, but amid such conjecture they have often overlooked two important factors: (1) MacArthur's friendship with Whitney long predated his ties with any other person on his staff; the two first met in the early 1920s. (2) MacArthur appreciated first-rate intellect and achievement; Whitney was mentally very sharp, and he had been outstanding in his leadership of the SCAP Government Section. Though Whitney was admired by MacArthur and by most of his own section members, his obvious closeness to the Supreme Commander created an undercurrent of ill will among some GHQ officials. Envy by others who also were devoted to MacArthur explains much of this negative sentiment, but some claimed that Whitney could be arrogant and rude. Later, partly by default, Whitney was often cast in the role of MacArthur's spokesman, and unfortunately, in trying to protect his boss, he did not communicate well with some reporters. His most valuable role was as the person who, next to Jean, MacArthur valued most as a trusted friend who would listen, advise, and keep utterly confidential whatever was discussed with him. Whitney may have alienated some of the GHQ staff, but to MacArthur he was always "dear Court."[29]

By the later phase of the occupation, and afterward in New York, the next highest position in the MacArthur hierarchy of officer-friends was held by his aide-de-camp, Colonel Laurence E. Bunker. In 1950 he was forty-eight, four years younger than Whitney. Before the Second World War, Bunker had practiced law with a distinguished New York firm; Whitney was a successful attorney in Manila. Bunker was a bachelor from a socially prominent family of Wellesley, Massachusetts. He had been awarded a Phi Beta Kappa key while earning his bachelor's degree at Harvard, and he had degrees from Cambridge University and New York University Law School. During the war in the Pacific he was a staff officer under Major General Richard J. Marshall, who was MacArthur's deputy chief of staff and successor to Sutherland as chief of staff in Tokyo. He became MacArthur's aide in the late spring of 1946, when Marshall returned to the States. On the job Bunker was industrious and efficient; his intense loyalty to MacArthur was matched only by Whitney's. Ideologically, he was much farther to the right than Whitney. Like Willoughby, he was passionately anti-Communist; in later years he became a national official of the John Birch Society. Dexterous, urbane, and well read, he possessed all the social graces. An excellent pianist, he sometimes helped Arthur with his lessons. Willoughby remarked, "Larry Bunker was naturally clever. . . . He would have done wonderfully well as a courtier at Versailles under Louis XIV." Brigadier General Charles J. West, who was on MacArthur's headquarters staff in 1945–1946, commented, "Bunker was an aristocrat; it showed. . . . He was bright, polished, smooth . . . with a very dry sense of humor. . . . He was always very much himself. . . . he was very close to Mrs. MacArthur and the boy." Bunker and Whitney, who by 1950 were in a category somewhat above the rest as intimates of MacArthur, differed greatly in personality and viewpoint and often did not get along with each other, but they had in common three traits that appealed to the Supreme Commander: both were bright, loyal, and hard-working.[30]

Whereas neither of the top two friends was a career soldier, Major General Edward M. Almond already had nearly thirty years of service as an infantry officer when he joined MacArthur's GHQ as assistant chief of staff for personnel and administration (G-1) in June 1946. Ned Almond had been a major in the Aisne-Marne and Meuse-Argonne campaigns in France in 1918, and he had been wounded in combat. During World War II he was a division commander in Italy. He was a graduate of the Army Command and General Staff College, Army War College, and Naval War College. Ambitious and highly competent, he rose fast in the GHQ hierarchy in Tokyo, becoming deputy chief of staff of the Far East Command in January 1947 and chief of staff of both SCAP and the Far East Command in January 1949; in the latter position he succeeded Major General Paul J. Mueller. Almond was the strongest chief of staff since Sutherland and was greatly respected by MacArthur. Major General William Beiderlinden, who served as his G-1, said Almond was extremely self-confident and often overrode his subordinates' decisions: "Staff actions meant nothing to him; he delighted in doing things on his own and deciding things for himself." Major General Edwin K. Wright, his assistant chief of staff for operations (G-3), said, "General Almond was one of the most aggressive officers I have ever known. . . . He was very positive in his opinions." Terms used by other colleagues to describe Almond included "peremptory," "tough," "energetic," "short-tempered," "professionally well qualified," and "completely devoted to General MacArthur." Almond frequently crossed swords over policy and personal differences with Whitney and with Lieutenant General Walton H. Walker, who had succeeded Eichelberger as Eighth Army commander in 1948. Long before the Korean hostilities began, it was said at GHQ that Almond was restless at his desk job and was eager for a field command and his third star; he was soon to get both.[31]

Certainly the most interesting, colorful character of the group was Major General Charles A. Willoughby, assistant chief of staff for intelligence (G-2) of the Far East Command and, in effect, in control of the SCAP Civil Intelligence Section, too, since its successive chiefs were G-2 officers subordinate to him. He had performed creditably, sometimes brilliantly, as MacArthur's intelligence chief in the war with Japan. Clever, cocksure, and temperamental, Willoughby was easily upset and could stage a dramatic show of emotional fireworks. His most fiery displays were reserved for his confrontations with Chiefs of Staff Sutherland and Mueller. One of his fellow officers observed that he could be "impressive, elegant, and dignified when calm, but fearsome when angered." Very tall and broad-shouldered, he was fifty-eight in 1950 and still spoke with a German accent, though he had left Germany four decades before. To many at GHQ he was the personification of "the old-school Prussian army officer," but those whom he counted as friends found him quite warmhearted behind his autocratic, formal front. Bunker, along with a number of interviewees, was impressed by the "tremendous intellectual capacity" of Willoughby, and Fellers thought he was "just a terrific professional soldier from the ground up." Among the favorite nicknames for him in private among less respectful officers were "Sir Charles" and "the Count." Willoughby's showmanship alienated some of his colleagues, one of whom summed up the negative opinion of him concisely and brutally: "an arrogant, opinionated sycophant." John Gunther accurately captured the essence of the MacArthur-Willoughby relationship: "MacArthur is the only man in the world about whose opinion he cares anything. The Supreme Commander thinks that some of his eccentricities may be annoying, but he has complete confidence in him as an officer."[32]

From the viewpoint of probably the majority of the GHQ staff, the most popular member of MacArthur's inner circle was Major General William F. Marquat, chief of the SCAP Economic and Scientific Section. The following impressions of him were typical of the interviewed GHQ officers: "always joking," "easy to talk to," "a good sport," "one of the most good-hearted men I have ever known," "a cheerful and hard worker," "never looked down on anyone who wasn't one of the old Bataan Gang." One of his fellow officers observed, "Bill Marquat obviously had General Mac-Arthur's personal affection as well as his confidence." Actually his most remarkable attribute was not his amiability; it was his adaptability. On the eve of World War II, MacArthur picked Marquat to be his chief antiaircraft officer, though his career had been in coast artillery. He so impressed MacArthur that he took him to Australia in 1942 and put him in charge of antiaircraft defenses in the Southwest Pacific theater; he did a commendable job for the next three years or so. In late 1945, dissatisfied with his first chief of the SCAP Economic and Scientific Section, MacArthur suddenly gave the job to Marquat, who had no experience or training for such an assignment. Astonishingly, for the most part he administered the section reasonably well. One SCAP official maintained that Marquat's secret was that "he played his cards superbly." Whitney credited him with being "able and resourceful," and Lieutenant General Alonzo P. Fox, then SCAP deputy chief of staff, emphasized that Marquat had "an enormous capacity for work." As related earlier, by the later phase of the occupation his section was the most important and active in SCAP, yet he managed to get the job done satisfactorily, if not superbly. At least he was still not only liked but admired by MacArthur even through the confusion of the changes that came with the reverse course. Whatever his secret, Marquat knew how to adapt; he may not have possessed traits of distinction, but he was a survivor.[33]

In terms of length of service under MacArthur, Colonel Sidney L. Huff, another of the Bataan Gang, ranked second with nineteen years (1935–1951, 1952–1955), compared with Whitney with twenty-two years (1943–1964). Huff was the only officer still with MacArthur in 1950 who had belonged to his staff in late 1935, when he was beginning as military adviser to the Philippine Commonwealth. (Willoughby joined the staff in mid-1941.) Huff had retired as a United States Navy officer after a heart attack and then joined MacArthur's staff in Manila as naval adviser from 1935 to 1941. He served him as aide-de-camp in World War II with an Army commission. He had known Mrs. MacArthur since her first dates with MacArthur in Manila in 1935–1936; during much of his post-1941 service he really was an aide to Jean, especially in escorting her, at the general's request, to social and public events in Brisbane, Manila, and Tokyo. Huff was generally viewed by other GHQ personnel as a pleasant, poised individual "with a stronger sense of etiquette than most military men." At MacArthur's GHQ in Tokyo his principal duties were as a sort of chief of protocol, whereas Bunker was really the Supreme Commander's senior aide for regular office activities. In 1946, Huff, who was then fifty-two, married a lady whom he had met in Australia; as previously indicated, they lived in the embassy compound and provided valuable companionship to all three of the MacArthurs, particularly Jean. Huff's friendship with the general was based on a deep loyalty that ran both ways. Huff retired in the summer of 1951, but rejoined MacArthur's staff in New York in late 1952 and served him for another three years. The MacArthurs guarded their privacy so carefully that Huff's memoir is invaluable in providing the only accurate picture in any detail of what their family life was like; it is also a moving testimony to the depth of Huff's love for all three of the MacArthurs.[34]

Another group of six individuals who might be regarded as forming a second echelon of the MacArthur inner group by 1950 were (1) Lieutenant General George E. Stratemeyer, a distinguished leader of the China-Burma air war of 1943–1945 who now commanded the Far East Air Forces; (2) Major General Doyle O. Hickey, the able deputy chief of staff of the Far East Command who would later succeed Almond as chief of staff; (3) Major General Alonzo P. Fox, a veteran of both world wars who had served well as SCAP deputy chief of staff (and whose daughter married a lieutenant on duty in Japan named Alexander M. Haig, Jr.); (4) Major General Edwin K. Wright, MacArthur's G-3, or operations officer, who had been an armor leader in the war against Germany from 1944 to 1945 and later deputy director of the Central

Intelligence Group, which preceded the CIA; (5) William J. Sebald, the astute chief of the SCAP Diplomatic Section who somehow managed to hold MacArthur's friendship and trust while also serving as the State Department's main representative in Japan; and (6) Lieutenant Colonel Anthony F. Story, a colorful individualist who had been MacArthur's personal pilot through World War II and the years in Japan and was warmly regarded by all the MacArthur family. Of this group, only Stratemeyer and Story rivaled the first echelon in their extreme devotion to MacArthur. In view of MacArthur's strong attachment to the United States Military Academy, it is interesting that Stratemeyer was the only West Pointer among the twelve men who were closest to the Supreme Commander by the eve of the Korean conflict (though Sebald was a Naval Academy graduate).[35] Notably absent from the inner circle was General Walker, commander of the Eighth Army. His sometimes hostile relations with several GHQ officers, especially Almond and Willoughby, may have affected MacArthur's attitude toward him, which was professionally correct but personally rather distant. As events turned out in the latter half of 1950, the lack of good communications and personal understanding between MacArthur and Walker had a profound impact not only on the course of the Korean War but also on the future of the Supreme Commander.

PART III

Korean War:
Command and Controversy

CHAPTER XIII

The Road to War in Korea

1. Internal and External Stresses

THE MONSOON SEASON was beginning in Korea, and rains drenched the rice paddies and mountains along the 38th Parallel in the predawn darkness of Sunday, June 25, 1950. About 4:00 A.M., North Korean artillery and mortar barrages began hitting South Korean positions along the 150-mile width of the peninsula, shortly followed by invasion forces totaling over 90,000 troops and 150 Soviet-built tanks that struck in smoothly coordinated assaults into South Korea. The main North Korean thrust, including most of the tanks, was aimed at the South Korean capital, Seoul. Amphibious landings were made meanwhile at points along the east coast up to forty miles below the 38th Parallel. Caught by surprise, in lightly held defenses, the South Korean soldiers fell back, some after valiant resistance but others in total disarray. With the daylight hours the North Korean Air Force went into action, bombing and strafing chiefly in and around Seoul. At 11:00 A.M., Radio Pyongyang in the North Korean capital announced that its nation had declared war because "the bandit traitor Syngman Rhee" had launched his forces across the parallel first that morning, allegedly invading near Haeju on the west side of the peninsula. By 3:00 P.M., Radio Pyongyang was claiming that Rhee's troops had been hurled back and that the North Korean Army had advanced ten to fifteen miles into South Korea all along the 38th Parallel.

The first news of the invasion to reach the American mission in Seoul came at 6:00 A.M. from five American soldiers on the Ongjin Peninsula at the west end of the front, next to the Yellow Sea. They reported the South Korean regiment to which they were assigned as advisers was under heavy attack; they were flown out before the unit was overrun. At 9:25 that morning GHQ in Tokyo got the news by way of an information copy of an emergency message from the military attaché at the embassy in Seoul to the Department of the Army headquarters in the Pentagon. John Gunther, who was then in Tokyo, observed that the "South Koreans and Americans in Korea, to say nothing of SCAP in Tokyo, were taken utterly by surprise. They were as blankly astonished as if the sun had suddenly gone out." MacArthur received the word by telephone in his bedroom from a GHQ duty officer. After he put the phone down, he recalled the shocking news nearly nine years earlier of the Pearl Harbor attack and thought to himself, "Not again! . . . How . . . could the United States have allowed such a deplorable situation to develop?"[1]

Perhaps it began with the stirrings again of nascent Korean nationalism during the Second World War, when the major Allied powers pledged Korea's future freedom. In the Cairo Declaration of December 1943, Roosevelt, Churchill, and Chiang Kai-shek stated that "in due course Korea shall become free and independent." This was reaffirmed in the Potsdam Declaration of July 1945, and the Soviet Union committed itself to support Korean independence in its declaration of war against Japan that August 8. With the Japanese offer of surrender two days later, SWNCC, with help from other Pentagon and State officials, drafted General Order No. 1; it was to be Supreme Commander MacArthur's directive governing the surrender arrangements for all Japanese forces across the Pacific and Asia. As for Korea, it stipulated that Japanese troops above the 38th Parallel would surrender to the Soviet Army, and the American Army would receive the surrender of Japanese units south of that parallel. The Red Army conquered Manchuria with lightning speed and entered Korea on August 12, pushing south to Seoul. The 38th Parallel may not have been a wise division of the peninsula, but with the nearest American ground forces in Okinawa and the Philippines, the Soviet troops could have seized all of Korea before the Americans arrived, had not a demarcation line been drawn quickly. The British, Soviet, and Chinese governments agreed to the division of Korea as set forth in General Order No. 1 for surrender and temporary occupation purposes, and the order was issued by MacArthur on September 2, the day the Instrument of Surrender was signed aboard the battleship *Missouri* in Tokyo Bay. The officially expressed goal set forth by the United States government was that both American and Soviet forces were to withdraw from Korea after the disarmament and repatriation of the Japanese personnel there and the formation of a united, independent government freely chosen by the Korean people.[2]

MacArthur, who had been appointed Supreme Commander for the Allied Powers in mid-August, was designated by the Joint Chiefs of Staff to oversee the surrender of Japanese forces in regions for which the United States was responsible, which included South Korea. But whereas Washington planners, especially SWNCC, had spent much time on plans for the occupation of Japan and Germany, Korea had been scarcely considered in postwar planning. It could hardly be viewed as an enemy country, but no one seemed quite sure how Korea should be treated. The result was that MacArthur received almost no guidance at first, and no formal directive from Washington regarding the occupation of South Korea was forthcoming until October. If the Washington planners had not given Korea much forethought, MacArthur's attention by late August was on the multitude of problems associated with the Japanese surrender negotiations and with the logistics of moving his ground, air, and sea forces to Japan. At the time Korea was a low priority, indeed, an afterthought, to him and his Washington superiors.

Happenstance seemed to determine two of the early crucial developments in the occupation of South Korea. First, MacArthur appointed Lieutenant General John R. Hodge to head the United States Army Forces in Korea (USAFIK). A tough, hard-working division and corps commander in the Pacific war, Hodge was already known for his tactlessness, impatience, and aggressiveness. Moreover, he had no experience in civil affairs, received virtually no instructions from MacArthur or Washington at the outset, and, when he requested a political adviser, was given a low-level Foreign Service official with little knowledge of Korea. The stocky, pugnacious Hodge was chosen primarily because he commanded the XXIV Corps, which was on Okinawa and was the nearest ground force that could be dispatched to South Korea. One authority quipped, "General Hodge was very possibly the first man in history selected to wield executive powers over a nation of nearly twenty million on the basis of shipping time." Second, the priority on shipping went to the movement of American units to Japan, and MacArthur did not make vessels available to transport the XXIV Corps until the first week of September. Hodge's corps, which consisted of the 6th, 7th, and 40th Infantry divisions, was not able to get to Inchon until September 8, nearly a month after the Soviet entry into Korea. As the Americans began to disembark, the Soviet troops in the Inchon-Seoul area quietly withdrew and moved north of the 38th Parallel. Despite their seeming cooperation, the Soviets had had ample time to sow some seeds of mischief in South Korea.

Besides the outright promotion of Communism, the Soviets had encouraged the formation of "people's committees" to help maintain order, to confiscate and redistribute Japanese properties and the holdings of some well-to-do Korean collaborators with the Japanese, and to establish a leftist-controlled government before the Americans arrived. A few days before Hodge's corps disembarked, the Korean People's Republic was proclaimed by what appeared to be a coalition of South Korean Communists and liberal nationalists who wanted immediate independence and reforms in the distribution of wealth, among other aims. In late August General Nobuyuki Abe, the wartime Japanese governor-general of Korea, notified MacArthur that he was alarmed by the potentially revolutionary situation developing in South Korea. MacArthur authorized him "to preserve order and safeguard property" until the American forces arrived.[3]

By early September, the Korean People's Republic, though commanding probably the largest popular following, was only one of many political factions, ranging from radical to reactionary, that were vying for power. All that most of them had in common was a desire for the prompt ouster of the Japanese and for the freedom and independence of Korea. MacArthur contributed to the political turmoil when on September 7 he issued Proclamation No.

1, an unwisely worded decree announcing the establishment of American military government in South Korea:

To the People of Korea:

As Commander-in-Chief, United States Army Forces, Pacific, I do hereby proclaim as follows:

By the terms of the Instrument of Surrender [signed Sept. 2 in the Tokyo Bay ceremony] . . . the victorious military forces of my command will today occupy the territory of Korea south of 38 degrees north latitude.

Having in mind the long enslavement of the people of Korea and the determination that in due course Korea shall become free and independent, the Korean people are assured that the purpose of the occupation is to enforce the Instrument of Surrender and to protect them in their personal and religious rights. In giving effect to these purposes, your active aid and compliance are required.

By virtue of the authority vested in me as Commander-in-Chief, United States Army Forces, Pacific, I hereby establish military control over Korea south of 38 degrees north latitude and the inhabitants thereof, and announce the following conditions of the occupation:

ARTICLE I

All powers of Government over the territory of Korea south of 38 degrees north latitude and the people thereof will be for the present exercised under my authority.

ARTICLE II

Until further orders, all governmental, public, and honorary functionaries and employees, as well as all officials and employees, paid or voluntary, of all public utilities and services, including public welfare and public health, and all other persons engaged in essential services, shall continue to perform their usual functions and duties, and shall preserve and safeguard all records and property.

ARTICLE III

All persons will obey promptly all my orders and orders issued under my authority. Acts of resistance to the occupying forces or any acts which may disturb public peace and safety will be punished severely.

ARTICLE IV

Your property rights will be respected. You will pursue your normal occupations, except as I shall otherwise order.

ARTICLE V

For all purposes during the military control, English will be the official language. . . .

ARTICLE VI

Further proclamations, ordinances, regulations, notices, directives, and enactments will be issued by me or under my authority, and will specify what is required of you.[4]

The harsh tone of the decree, more suitably addressed to a defeated enemy nation, must have come as a shock to the Koreans, who had felt enslaved and exploited since Japan had annexed their country in 1910 and who had eagerly awaited the arrival of the Americans as liberators and friends. Surely one of the most ill-advised documents of MacArthur's career, the proclamation proved to be a distinct liability to Hodge from the start.

In stumbling into trouble with the South Korean populace, Hodge proved during his first few days in Seoul that he could match MacArthur. After presiding over the Japanese surrender ceremony in Seoul on September 9, Hodge reluctantly agreed to talk with the President of the Korean People's Republic. It was a brief session: angered by his demands, the American general told him that neither he nor any other Korean possessed governmental authority and then ordered him to leave his office. Later in a statement that, unhappily, was much quoted, Hodge remarked that "these Koreans are the same breed of cat as the Japanese." In accord with Article II of MacArthur's proclamation, Hodge announced that temporarily he would retain General Abe as governor general, along with most of the other Japanese who were in governmental or administrative posts, about 75,000 in number. Outraged Koreans began to protest in street demonstrations, several of which resulted in clashes with American soldiers. On September 12, Hodge relieved Abe, and by December virtually all the Japanese officials had been replaced by Koreans. Since the Japanese had dominated all governmental activities in Korea since 1910, Hodge had thought a transition period would be needed to identify or train Koreans for public positions. He had badly misjudged the nationalist sentiments of the people, however, who preferred their own inexperienced countrymen to even a brief retention of the Japanese. Next, Hodge blundered by moving into the residence that Abe had occupied; the Koreans resented the continuing reminder that Hodge had early supported the hated Japanese general. On the day he relieved Abe, Hodge appointed Major General Archibald V. Arnold, commander of the 7th Division, as head of the United States Army Military Government in Korea (USAMGIK). Arnold's qualifications were no better in civil affairs than Hodge's, though, like his superior, he had been a well-regarded troop commander in the Pacific campaigns. Battle leadership counted for little, however, in the complicated political, economic, and social conditions Hodge and Arnold faced in South Korea.[5]

Frequently Hodge reported conditions of unrest and disorder in South Korea to MacArthur, requesting his counsel on what courses to pursue. His communications often were lengthy and detailed, but usually MacArthur's responses were brief and vague. For example, when Hodge asked his advice in November 1945 on how to counter the latest disruptive tactics of South Korean "pinkos" and the continuing agitation for recognition by the Korean People's Republic leaders, MacArthur replied: "Use your own best judgment as to what action to be taken. I am not sufficiently familiar with the local situation to advise you intelligently, but I will support whatever decision you may take in this matter." Over the course of his nearly three years in South Korea, Hodge, who worked hard and worried much over what he called "the worst job I ever had," journeyed to Tokyo only four times for conferences with MacArthur, one of which was his farewell call in late August 1948. MacArthur, in turn, came to South Korea only once during that period, and it was primarily to participate in the South Korean presidential inauguration, not to confer with Hodge or to visit the USAFIK units. According to Faubion Bowers, Hodge sent "plea after plea" to MacArthur to come, but the latter always replied that he was "too busy, too preoccupied in Japan," though in private the Supreme Commander admitted he "didn't want any part" of the "messy" Korean situation. In July 1946, Hodge, who was both discouraged and ill from ear and sinus troubles, asked MacArthur to have him transferred elsewhere, but the Supreme Commander refused his request, told him to "go home" for forty-five days and "forget Korea," and expressed "every possible confidence" in his leadership.[6]

The continuing political confusion, together with wild inflation and massive economic dislocation, prompted Washington authorities to believe that order might be established in South Korea if some of the prewar leaders of the independence movement, long living in exile in China and America, were returned to the country. Accordingly, in mid-October 1945, Kim Koo and Dr. Syngman Rhee, thought to be strong conservative nationalists with wide public support among South Koreans, were flown to Seoul on American planes. Rhee stopped en route for two days in Tokyo, where he conferred with MacArthur, who endorsed the idea of his return and let him travel on his plane to Seoul. About the same time SWNCC sent the first detailed directive to MacArthur regarding South Korea; it anticipated a three-phase development from the current dual occupation to a period of four-power trusteeship (United States, USSR, United Kingdom, and China) and finally to Korean independence. At the Moscow Foreign Ministers' Conference in December a Soviet-American commission was set up to work toward a provisional unified, democratic government in Korea and to formulate a plan for a five-year four-power trusteeship. But the commission's efforts on both scores were fruitless, and South Koreans intensified their protests against the proposed trusteeship while the Soviets, working through Korean Communists trained in Moscow and Peking, tightened their control over North Korea. The continuing division of Korea was proving disastrous economically; most of the industry was in the north and the principal agricultural production was in the south. MacArthur commented to the press in March 1946 that the trusteeship decision at Moscow had produced "a boiling cauldron of political activity" among "all Korean factions," who were "resentful" of the postponement of independence. There was so much disorder in South Korea in the ensuing months that he ordered some troop units in Japan on alert for a possible move to assist Hodge's forces in restoring public tranquillity. Meanwhile Tass, the Soviet news agency, charged that MacArthur's "irresponsible" criticisms of the Moscow plan had further agitated the Koreans.[7]

In November 1947 the United Nations General Assembly adopted an American-sponsored resolution establishing a temporary UN commission to supervise elections and form a national government in Korea, to be followed by the withdrawal of all foreign troops. The commission was denied entry into the Soviet zone, but elections under its auspices were held in South Korea in May 1948 for a 200-seat national assembly, with rightist parties gaining a majority. Seats were reserved for North Korean delegates, but none was sent. The assembly then proceeded to draft a constitution and to elect government officials, choosing seventy-three-year-old Dr. Rhee as President. Subsequently Rhee issued an invitation to MacArthur to speak at the inauguration of the Republic of Korea (ROK) on August 15, which the general promptly accepted, calling it "a signal honor."[8]

On the morning of the 15th, a Sunday, MacArthur and his party, consisting of his wife, Whitney, Bunker, and Huff, flew into Kimpo Airfield, between Inchon and Seoul, where he was greeted by Hodge, Rhee, and a host of South Korean dignitaries. The Supreme Commander greeted Rhee warmly, saying, "I'm glad to see you. Indeed, I wouldn't have missed this for the world." After reviewing an honor guard of Korean and American troops, the group left in an automobile caravan for the palace at Seoul. Before the inauguration ceremony began, MacArthur put his arm around Rhee's shoulder and remarked loudly enough for nearby correspondents to hear, "If Korea should ever be attacked by the Communists, I will defend it as I would California." In his inaugural address Rhee spoke ominously about the possibility of a war to overthrow the Communist regime of North Korea: "Our joy is clouded with sorrow as we look to the north. . . . No nation however powerful should be allowed to occupy the territory of its weak neighbors." MacArthur said in his speech: "I am profoundly moved to stand on the soil of Korea in this historic hour, to see liberty reborn, the cause of right and justice prevail. . . . Yet in this hour, as the forces of righteousness advance, the triumph is dulled by one of the greatest tragedies of contemporary history — an artificial barrier has divided your land." He continued rather bellicosely, "This barrier must and shall be torn down. Nothing shall prevent the ultimate unity of your people as freemen of a free nation. Koreans come from too proud a stock to sacrifice their sacred cause by yielding to any alien philosophies of disruption." Four days later Rhee flew to Tokyo for two days of talks with MacArthur; he told newsmen afterward that the general again had said that he would protect South Korea "as I would protect the United States." This caused no small degree of consternation in Washington, where Pentagon and State leaders were sharply divided over contingency plans for American military support of South Korea in case it became involved in hostilities, particularly since many felt the belligerent Rhee might instigate a war against North Korea.[9]

Since "acute personal animosity" had characterized his relations with Rhee from the autumn of 1945 onward, Hodge requested and obtained his own relief as USAFIK commander after the presidential inauguration; he was succeeded by his deputy, Major General John B. Coulter. The American military government structure (USAMGIK) ended on August 15, and within a month the gradual withdrawal of all American forces began. That December the UN General Assembly recognized the ROK government as the only lawful one in Korea, called for the withdrawal of foreign troops, and created a permanent UN commission to oversee the evacuations and to work toward a unified government based on the people's freely expressed wishes. Formal United States recognition of the Republic of Korea came in January 1949, with John J. Muccio, Truman's special representative in Seoul since August, becoming the first American ambassador in March. At the end of June, USAFIK's last troops left and its headquarters was deactivated. By agreement with Rhee's government, Brigadier General William L. Roberts headed an American Army force of nearly 500 enlisted men and officers that remained to assist the ROK military establishment; it was called the United States Military Advisory Group to the Republic of Korea (KMAG).[10]

In the meantime the People's Democratic Republic of Korea had been inaugurated to the north of the 38th Parallel in September 1948, its capital at Pyongyang and its Prime Minister a Moscow-trained Communist named Kim Il Sung. Like Rhee's regime, Kim's government claimed sovereignty over all of the Korean peninsula. The Soviet Union and its satellites quickly granted diplomatic recognition to the new North Korean government, and the Soviet Army began withdrawing from the country. On December 25, 1948, the Soviet Union announced that all its troops had left North Korea. It did not admit, however, that the remaining Soviet military advisory force in the north was much larger than the American one in the south, nor that the Soviet regulars had left behind large quantities of heavy weapons and armor, though the ROK Army inherited from the departing USAFIK only light weapons suitable for constabulary functions.

With the deactivation of USAFIK on June 30, 1949, the overall responsibility for administrative and operational control of the remaining American agencies in South Korea shifted from Mac-Arthur to the State Department. The American Mission in Korea (AMIK) was headed by Ambassador Muccio; under him were the United States embassy, Roberts' advisory force (KMAG), the Economic Cooperation Administration (ECA) office, and the Joint Administrative Services (JAS), a logistical support agency for the AMIK. MacArthur's only direct connection now with the Korean situation was through JAS, which requisitioned its supplies from Far East Command depots in Japan.

The Pentagon's original plan had called for MacArthur to have operational control over KMAG, but he did not want it. As explained in the official KMAG history, "MacArthur's experience with the Joint U.S. Military Advisory Group to the Republic of the Philippines (JUSMAGPHIL) made him reluctant to accept a similar arrangement for KMAG. In the case of JUSMAGPHIL, the JCS had laid out the group's missions and MacArthur's role had been limited to minor matters having little to do with the major task of advising the Philippine forces." He recommended that KMAG be under Muccio "unless he [MacArthur] were granted authority to assign the objectives" for Roberts' force, though he felt all KMAG communications should be forwarded through him. Thus operational control over KMAG went to John Muccio, and William Roberts was to report directly to the Pentagon on strictly military command and administrative matters. According to the official history, MacArthur's "responsibility was limited to the logistic support of KMAG to the water line of Korea and to the emergency evacuation of U.S. personnel from the country if the need arose." KMAG, however, "did maintain close liaison with MacArthur's headquarters" through periodic visits by Roberts and his representatives and through message traffic, including information copies of communications to the Department of the Army headquarters in Washington.[11]

For over two years before he became President, Rhee had served with other rightist leaders on an advisory council to the American military government. United States troops and the 25,000-man Korean police force had been used to repress dissident groups on numerous occasions; the protestors had ranged from labor unionists calling for action against inflation and tenant farmers demanding land reform to students outraged by the lack of progress toward democracy, unification, or independence. As President, Rhee ruled from the beginning with an iron fist; police brutality against his political opponents increased markedly, and popular discontent in South Korea steadily mounted. The economic situation continued to deteriorate, aggravated after May 1948 by North Korea's refusal to transmit hydroelectric power, which it monopolized, causing many light industries in the south to close. Revisionist historians have charged that Hodge and USAFIK had implemented a deliberate policy of the United States government to suppress "popular revolution" and establish a "rightist police state" under Rhee. In truth, however, the chaos of South Korea's politics, economy, and society was almost equaled by the disordered state of American policymaking on Korea. Rhee appeared to have gained political power in spite of the muddled Americans, not because of a well-planned scheme of Washington. Indeed, Rhee repeatedly accused Hodge of trying to put the South Korean Communists in power.

Whereas Hodge and Rhee had strong personality differences, Muccio managed to work out a modus vivendi with the strong-willed ROK President. "Rhee had a very genuine awe of MacArthur," according to Muccio, "and we had little difficulty with him so long as MacArthur remained in command." Muccio found Rhee to be "very intelligent," with "an excellent historical perspective." However, "when he got emotional, then he reverted to his long-standing instincts of self-survival. . . . And with the experience he had had he was very distrustful, inordinately so." Muccio added, "The similarities and the relationships between MacArthur, Chiang Kai-shek, and Syngman Rhee intrigued and baffled me. I think they were all of the same school — egomaniacs." Neither Muccio nor the Pentagon and State leaders trusted Rhee not to unleash his army, when he felt it was strong enough, against North Korea. Truman was "deeply concerned," too, over Rhee's lack of progress toward democracy and economic stability.[12]

The worse conditions became in the south, the more Rhee seemed to try to divert his people's attention to the goal of reuniting Korea by force, which he mentioned in numerous public statements. Radio Pyongyang, on behalf of Kim's regime, responded in kind with bitter denunciations of Rhee's "reactionary" rule and with threats to bring all Korea under Communist rule.

The American and Soviet forces, which had tensely faced each other across the 38th Parallel for three years, seemed, in retrospect, to have deterred hostilities. "The most remarkable aspect of the entire political process leading up to the outbreak of the Korean War," declares an authority on post-1945 Korea, "is that domestic Korean forces were always more inclined toward armed unification than were external forces." No sooner had the American and Soviet units departed than both the North and South Korean armies began to conduct raids across the parallel, some resulting in pitched battles of considerable magnitude. Both sides carried on extensive propaganda and subversive activities, but the North Koreans were especially adept at infiltration tactics. By late 1949, Radio Pyongyang claimed that over 77,000 Communist partisans were operating in South Korea, mostly organized and led by North Korean infiltrators.[13]

Although civil war seemed inevitable after the pull-out of the foreign forces, with the fiery Rhee as likely to precipitate it as Kim Il Sung, the United States government appeared to be committed to assisting Rhee's regime economically and militarily. Between 1945 and 1947 $99 million in GARIOA funds for relief and rehabilitation had been spent on South Korea; in 1948–1949 another $257 million was invested. Moreover, $110 million in ECA grants was earmarked for South Korea during fiscal 1950. On leaving, in mid-1949, USAFIK turned over to the South Korean Army $110 million in military equipment. In October 1949, Congress appropriated $10.2 million in military aid for Rhee's ground forces under the new Mutual Defense Assistance Program, though only a few pieces of signal equipment arrived before the war began.[14]

During the autumn of 1949 MacArthur revealed little concern over the mounting tensions and border clashes between North and South Korea. His attitude was influenced undoubtedly by the monolithic concept of global Communism, which he, along with most Washington leaders, then accepted. If war came to Korea, he assumed it would necessarily be by North Korean aggression on orders from Moscow or by South Korea acting unilaterally. His focus was on the former possibility; he gave little consideration to the possibility of a civil war started without external stimulation. In September he confidently told a visiting five-man congressional committee: "South Korea is in no danger of being overrun by North

Korea. The Kremlin has South Korea outflanked and knows that eventually it must go the way the continent of Asia goes. As long as South Korea is not a threat to North Korea, no action will be taken by the Kremlin to absorb it as there would be nothing to gain by taking it over. However, if South Korea tries to take over North Korea, retaliatory measures could certainly be expected. If the United States by default fails to support South Korea, the consequences will be most devastating to the United States interests." In late 1949 Rhee tried to enlist MacArthur's help in getting MDAP grants for the establishment of ROK air and naval forces, but the general was reluctant to argue for American aid beyond the strengthening of the ROK Army with defensive weapons. His reasoning against a ROK Air Force was that "such a force was not essential to the maintenance of internal order in Korea, would increase the possibility of war between North and South Korea, and would lend credence to Communist charges that the United States was fostering an armaments race in Korea."[15]

As early as May 1947, with demobilization having weakened America's armed services alarmingly and with the Soviet-American commission on Korea at an impasse, Secretary of War Robert Patterson had urged withdrawal of the United States Army divisions from South Korea not only because of the tight military budget and their need elsewhere but also because of the relatively unimportant strategic value of the peninsula. SWNCC and the State Department objected, however, on the grounds that an American evacuation would lead to a quick Communist seizure of South Korea. That September Lieutenant General Albert C. Wedemeyer, former China theater commander who had recently returned from an investigative trip to China and Korea, recommended that American troops should remain in South Korea for the time being, especially since Russian forces were still in North Korea. Nevertheless, that same month the Joint Chiefs of Staff went on record favoring withdrawal because "the United States had little strategic interest" in Korea and in case of a general war in the Far East "our present forces in Korea would be a military liability." In March 1948 the JCS stated that the United States government should provide no guarantee of military security to South Korea. Soon afterward Truman approved a policy statement, originating in SANACC (formerly SWNCC), that "the United States should not become so irrevocably involved in the Korean situation that an action taken by any faction in Korea or by any other power in Korea could be considered a 'casus belli' for the United States." That June the Joint Chiefs, after still another review of Korean policies, concluded again "that Korea is of little strategic value to the United States and that any commitment to United States use of military force in Korea would be ill-advised and impracticable."[16]

Soon after American troops had begun the phased withdrawal from South Korea in September 1948, widespread disorders led Rhee to ask that the evacuation be halted. The State Department favored the retention of at least a reinforced regimental combat team in South Korea. When the Pentagon requested his opinion in January 1949, MacArthur reported that the ROK Army and the South Korean constabulary forces were sufficiently strong for assuring internal security in the country, so he recommended the withdrawal of the remaining American troops by May. He warned, however, that it was "not within the capabilities of the United States to establish Korean security forces capable of meeting successfully a full-scale invasion from North Korea supported by Communist-inspired internal disorder." In a press interview in early March he omitted both Korea and Formosa, the latter soon to be the refuge of the retreating Nationalist Chinese forces, from what he thought should be the American defense line: "Now the Pacific has become an Anglo-Saxon lake and our line of defense runs through the chain of islands fringing the coast of Asia. It starts from the Philippines and continues through the Ryukyu archipelago which includes its broad main bastion, Okinawa. Then it bends back through Japan and the Aleutian Island chain to Alaska." He repeated this in another interview later that month.

MacArthur had long been known for voicing views on strategic matters that did not always jibe with official positions, but in January 1950 the Truman administration went public on the extent of America's defense commitments in the West Pacific, or so many commentators interpreted the remarks by the President and the Secretary of State. In a speech on the 5th, Truman stated that he was opposed to sending military assistance to Formosa, where the forces of Chiang Kai-shek had fled after being driven from the Chinese mainland the previous autumn. That both Korea and Formosa were viewed as of little worth strategically to Washington

leaders was proclaimed by Acheson in an address on the 12th to
the National Press Club in Washington. Although excluding them
from the westernmost area considered vital to American strategic
interests, the Secretary did seem to affirm that if either was attacked American forces might be committed under the aegis of
the United Nations. But to many Americans and probably to leaders in Pyongyang, Moscow, and Peking, Acheson appeared to say
that the United States would not act unilaterally in the defense of
Korea or Formosa. It is debatable whether the Communists interpreted his remarks as an "invitation to aggression against South
Korea," as one editorialist maintained, but the public delineation
of the American line of strategic commitment in the Pacific was
not necessary or wise. In his memoirs, wherein he indulged in frequent exercises in rewriting history, MacArthur said of Acheson's
speech, "I felt that the Secretary of State was badly advised about
the Far East." In later years both Acheson and MacArthur would
try to explain what they meant, with the general sometimes con-
veniently forgetting his own remarks of March 1949. But neither
man was ever wholly convincing about why he had felt compelled
to specify publicly that critical line in the West Pacific.[17]

2. *Too Many Noises from Other Directions*

Despite the unprecedented global obligations of the American
military after the Second World War, Congress had provided such
niggardly appropriations that by 1948–1949 the United States could
not have deployed forces to respond effectively to overt aggression, whether in West Europe or East Asia. The actual strength of
the American armed forces was down to 1.4 million men by 1948,
including only 631,000 ground troops in both the Army and the
Marine Corps. The fiscal 1950 budget, determined, of course, long
before the Korean War began, totaled $13.5 billion for the mili-
tary, a slight rise over the previous year. But owing to inflation,
the budget still required the Pentagon to cut nearly 200,000 personnel, and it provided for only 238 capital ships for the Navy, 48
groups for the Air Force, and 10 Army divisions, including 4 divisions in Japan and 2 in Germany. The strength of MacArthur's

Far East Command, despite his persistent objections, had been pared from over 300,000 in 1947 (including 42,000 in the FEAF) to 120,000 for fiscal 1950, which began in July 1949. His Eighth Army, which had an authorized strength of 87,000 troops, possessed an actual combat strength of under 27,000. In October 1949, Chief of Staff J. Lawton Collins informed MacArthur that, because of the acute shortage of funds, the number of Army divisions would probably be reduced from ten to nine, with the loss to be absorbed by his command. After stormy protests from MacArthur, the Pentagon decided to retain all ten divisions but to cut their strength further.

Despite the United States' nuclear monopoly for four years following World War II, the Strategic Air Command was a "hollow threat," as one authority phrased it, because its delivery capability was inadequate. The American military's conventional weapon stocks by 1949 consisted largely of leftovers from the war of 1941–1945. Also dismaying, the National Security acts of 1947 and 1949 had not yet produced significantly improved coordination between the armed services. Indeed, their leaders had clashed frequently over contingency war planning, with no consensus on military strategy for the new era of containment and atomic weapons. In the summer and fall of 1949 the senior Air Force and Navy officers were locked in an ugly wrangle over the question of spending on supercarriers or on B-36 long-range bombers. To make matters worse, Louis Johnson, who had become Secretary of Defense in March 1949, was an imprudent man, ill-suited to mediate between the services or to coordinate planning with the State Department. Also, he seemed to be as parsimonious about defense budgets as some of the worst Pentagon critics in Congress or the Truman administration.

During the latter half of 1949, when the American military establishment had sunk to its postwar ebb in morale, it was rocked by two portentous shocks: the explosion of the first Soviet atomic bomb and the triumph of the Communists in the Chinese civil war. The Soviets successfully detonated their first nuclear explosion in August, about four years sooner than most American authorities had predicted. Pentagon leaders were unsettled by the event's revelations of the inadequacy of intelligence on Soviet research, the gross underestimation of the scientific capability of the Russians, and the need for a crash program to develop an American hydrogen, or thermonuclear, bomb. From the onset of the massive Communist offensive in the spring of 1949, the fast-crumbling Nationalist defenses and the rapid advances of Mao Tse-tung's forces made it clear that the Chinese civil war was nearing its end. Chiang Kai-shek's government began preparations for the withdrawal of its forces to Formosa in July, and by early December the movement to the offshore island was completed. In the meantime the State Department issued its "White Paper" on China in August, defending American policy since 1944 and criticizing the Nationalist leaders for mismanaging military operations, relations with the Chinese masses, and earlier aid from the United States. In October the People's Republic of China was proclaimed; it was quickly recognized by the Soviet Union and its satellites, as well as by a number of other nations, including the United Kingdom. In February 1950, Communist China and the USSR negotiated a thirty-year treaty of amity, alliance, and mutual assistance.[18]

The ominous Soviet and Chinese developments prompted some important responses in Washington. Congress established the Mutual Defense Assistance Program in October 1949 and appropriated over $13 million the first year for military aid to America's allies in Latin America, East Asia, and particularly West Europe. Plans were speeded up for organizing the military arm of the newly created North Atlantic Treaty Organization. In December, the JCS approved the Joint Outline Emergency War Plan, which gave top priority to West Europe as the most likely theater of initial operations in a war between the West and the Soviet Union, but also stipulated that the United States would defend Japan, Okinawa, and the Philippines and "would attempt to deny the enemy the use of Taiwan [Formosa]," though it did not mention Korea. The Joint Chiefs recommended that a survey by a MacArthur-appointed mission be made of the Nationalists' defensive needs on Formosa, but Truman, on Acheson's advice, rejected the idea. Also in December, the President approved NSC 48/2, a general policy statement on containment strategy in East Asia that stressed regional economic and political stabilization of friendly Asian nations with American aid, together with a strengthening of security arrangements in that area, especially Japan, Okinawa, and the Philippines. On January 30, 1950, Truman gave his approval to a program to develop the hydrogen bomb and also ordered the State and Defense departments "to make an over-all review and re-assessment of American foreign and defense policy in the light of the loss of China, the Soviet mastery of atomic energy, and the prospect of the fusion bomb."

Partly because Secretary of Defense Johnson was not supportive of any reappraisal that might call for more military spending and because the military departments were still hassling over the supercarrier-bomber issue, leadership in the ensuing strategic review was assumed by the State Department. In fact, the chairman of the project's State-Defense team was Paul Nitze, director of State's Policy Planning Staff. The draft document that emerged in April 1950 and, with revisions, eventually became NSC 68, says a scholar, was "the first effort to define an overall strategy and supporting military programs for the Cold War." In brief, it stressed the increased danger of war with the Soviet Union, now nuclear-armed, and predicted that the Soviet military could be ready for hostilities against the West by 1954. NSC 68 recommended an immediate, large-scale expansion by both the United States and its allies in conventional and special weapons and forces. Although Nitze's group did not spell out the expected costs, the American buildup was estimated by the State Department at $35 billion annually, or nearly three times the military budget for fiscal 1950. The document's recommendations did not seem to have much chance of implementation in view of the economy-mindedness of both the Truman administration and the Republican-dominated Eightieth Congress. Also, the Joint Chiefs now joined Secretary Johnson in criticizing the proposed program's costliness, with Bradley asserting that "the appropriations request which we would have to recommend would be out of all proportion to that which we believe this country could afford at this time." The report of Nitze's group was awaiting action (and probable rejection) by the National Security Council when the North Korean invasion began in late June. Among the many consequences of the ensuing war was a sudden about-face by the White House and Congress on military spending that would make possible much of the buildup called for in NSC 68, as well as substantial funding for the arming of NATO.[19]

Contributing to the low level of attention on Korea and to renewed public and official concern over Formosa was the virulent anti-Communist crusade that Senator Joseph McCarthy launched in February 1950. Speaking at Wheeling, West Virginia, on the 9th, McCarthy waved his now infamous sheet of paper before an audience of Republican women and proclaimed that thereon were the names of over 200 Communists who worked in the State Department. He became an overnight sensation with the press, gaining headlines almost daily for the next four years in the wildest orgy of witch-hunting in the nation's history. On February 20 the senator took his attack against Acheson's department before the Senate in a long harangue, this time, though, cutting his list to eighty-one suspects. The Senate thereupon set up a committee headed by the venerable Millard F. Tydings of Maryland to investigate McCarthy's charges. The Tydings Committee began its hearings in early March, and McCarthy and his accusations got front-page attention until the North Koreans upstaged him in June. The hearings ended in July somewhat anticlimactically, the Tydings Committee reporting no evidence of Communists in the State Department.

But during the critical six months before the Korean War, McCarthyism spread like wildfire, forcing the Truman administration, particularly Acheson and his department, to defend its foreign and security policies repeatedly. The government's position on Nationalist China, which had been under attack by pro-Chiang groups in America for several years, was a favorite target of McCarthy and his supporters from the start. The repeated charges of the administration's softness on Communism and its inadequate support of the Nationalist Chinese cause focused attention on Formosa more intensely than before, and public pressure became so strong that Truman and Acheson would have had to review their hands-off policy for reasons of political survival, even if the thinking of their strategic planners about Formosa had not been changing. The President and his Secretary of State, so it seemed by the late spring of 1950, were being challenged to demonstrate to the nation and America's allies that they, not McCarthy, conducted American foreign policy and that they would not tolerate a Communist attack against Formosa. Walter Lippmann may not have exaggerated when he remarked of the McCarthyism onslaught against Acheson in 1950, "No American official who has represented this government abroad in great affairs, not even Wilson in 1918, has ever been so gravely injured at home."[20]

In January, after both Truman and Acheson publicly had appeared to dismiss the possibility of military aid to Formosa, much less unilateral intervention on Chiang's side in case of attack, Secretary Johnson and the JCS recommended that the $75 million in MDAP funds recently authorized for use in "the general area of China" be used to aid the French against the rebels in Indochina. By early May, however, the Joint Chiefs had changed their minds and decided that American military assistance to Chiang should be granted. According to the official JCS history, the situation had been altered by Communist China's growing expansionist activities. The Joint Chiefs were concerned over evidence that Red China was assisting the Vietnamese insurgents in Indochina, it had seized Hainan Island, off the southern coast of China, and it was receiving aircraft and amphibious vessels from the Soviet Union. The JCS repeated their December proposal that MacArthur be authorized to send a mission to Formosa to survey Chiang's military needs. No decision had been made on the JCS recommendations prior to the outbreak of the Korean War. Meanwhile, in April, Acheson had received an ominous report from Sebald in Tokyo that intelligence data at GHQ indicated a Communist Chinese "amphibious operation to bring about [the] final destruction of [the] Nationalist force on Formosa" was "highly possible" in "coming months."[21]

During the half-year before the Korean conflict started, MacArthur also changed his view about supporting Formosa. When Canadian Minister of External Affairs Lester B. Pearson visited him in January 1950, he said that MacArthur "was not alarmist about the spread of communism on the mainland and surprised me by stating that with a chain of island bases in the Pacific from which American air power could be brought to bear on the continent, the United States had little to fear. In this strategical chain he did not seem to include Formosa, which also surprised me." When Cyrus L. Sulzberger of the *New York Times* talked to the general on May 18, MacArthur predicted that "there will not be a war soon," but did not mention Formosa. Two days later, however, when Sulzberger conferred with Willoughby, the Far East

Command's intelligence chief asserted that Formosa was strategically important and that he was disturbed that "the United States had virtually extended an invitation to the Communists to capture that island when we delineated the Japan-Okinawa-Philippines line." Willoughby rarely differed from MacArthur on strategic views, so it is not surprising that on May 29 the latter urged the Joint Chiefs to reconsider the strategic position of Formosa, which "is the equivalent of an unsinkable aircraft carrier and submarine tender" for whichever side holds it. He did not offer specific recommendations about assisting Chiang, but stressed that steps needed to be taken by the United States to avert a Communist Chinese conquest of Formosa. Admiral Arthur W. Radford, commander in chief of the Pacific Fleet (CINCPACFLT), conferred with MacArthur on June 2–3 and found him "quite unhappy with . . . the failure of the United States to support General Chiang Kai-shek."[22] When Johnson and Bradley arrived in Tokyo for conferences with him on June 18–23, MacArthur presented them with copies of his "Memorandum on Formosa," dated June 14. The main points of that document, the stubborn adherence to which would have no small bearing on his later controversy with Truman, are given below:

1. . . . The strategic interests of the United States will be in serious jeopardy if Formosa is allowed to be dominated by a power hostile to the United States. . . .

2. The front line of the Far East Command as well as the western strategic frontier of the United States rests today on the littoral islands stretching from the Aleutians through the Philippine Archipelago. Geographically and strategically Formosa is an integral part of this offshore position. . . .

3. The geographical location of Formosa is such that in the hands of a power unfriendly to the United States it constitutes an enemy salient in the very center of that portion of our position now keyed to Japan, Okinawa, and the Philippines. At the present time there is on Formosa a concentration of operational air and naval bases which is greater than any similar concentration on the Asiatic mainland between the Yellow Sea and the Strait of Malacca. Additional bases can be developed in a relatively short time by an aggressive exploitation of World War II Japanese facilities. . . . Formosa bases are 100 miles closer to Okinawa than any point on the Chinese mainland and are

150 miles closer to Clark Field and Manila than any other area which could be acquired by Communist military forces. . . .

4. . . . Formosa in the hands of the Communists can be compared to an unsinkable aircraft carrier and submarine tender located to accomplish Soviet offensive strategy and at the same time checkmate counteroffensive operations by United States Forces based on Okinawa and the Philippines. This unsinkable carrier-tender has the capacity to operate from ten to twenty air groups . . . as well as to provide forward operating facilities for the short-range coastal submarines which are predominant in the Russian Asiatic Navy. . . .

5. Current estimates of Soviet air and submarine resources in the Far East . . . satisfy me that the Russians have the capability to extend their forces southward from their present positions. . . . Pending the actual outbreak of hostilities United States military forces will be unable to prevent the stockpiling of essential military supplies on Formosa if that area is acquired by the Communists.

6. Historically Formosa has been used as a springboard for military aggression directed against areas to the south. . . .

7. In addition to its military value . . . in normal times Formosa held the position of a food surplus area in a generally food-scarce locality. . . . Such a factor . . . may be of considerable importance in reestablishing the economies of those Oriental nations now largely dependent upon United States assistance.

8. . . . There is every basis from a moral standpoint to offer the Taiwanese an opportunity to develop their own political future in an atmosphere unfettered by the dictates of a Communist police state. . . . The future status of Formosa can well be an important factor in determining the political alignment of those national groups who have or must soon make a choice between Communism and the West.

9. There can be no doubt that the eventual fate of Formosa largely rests with the United States. Unless the United States political-military strategic position in the Far East is to be abandoned, it is obvious that the time must come in the foreseeable future when a line must be drawn beyond which Communist expansion will be stopped. . . . It is apparent to me that the United States should initiate measures to prevent the domination of Formosa by a Communist power. . . .

10. At this time I am unable to recommend the exact political, economic, and military measures which should be taken to prevent the fall of Formosa. . . . I concur wholeheartedly with the recommendation of the Joint Chiefs of Staff on 23 December 1949 [reaffirmed on 4 May 1950] to the effect that the Commander-in-Chief Far East should make an immediate survey of the need and extent

of the military assistance required in Formosa in order to hold Formosa against attack. . . .

    11. . . . There are conflicting reports as to the capability and will of the Chinese Nationalist Forces as now constituted and equipped to prevent either the military or political conquest of the island of Formosa. I cannot predict what the cost may be of preventing Communist domination of that island, although I have advised the Joint Chiefs of Staff what the cost may be if such an event transpires. I am satisfied, however, that the domination of Formosa by an unfriendly power would be a disaster of utmost importance to the United States, and I am convinced that time is of the essence. I strongly believe that the Commander-in-Chief Far East should be authorized and directed to initiate without delay a survey of the military, economic and political requirements to prevent the domination of Formosa by a Communist power and that the results of such a survey be analyzed and acted upon as a basis for United States policy with respect to Formosa.[23]

Returning to Washington only hours before the Korean War erupted, according to the JCS history, "General Bradley drafted a memorandum for Secretary Johnson to send to the President, urging the sending of an aid mission to Taiwan, but it was overtaken by events and never used."[24] It will be noticed that in his Formosa memo of June 14, MacArthur again did not include South Korea within the West Pacific defense line of the United States. In fact, he never sent any message to Washington from 1945 to the beginning of the Korean conflict suggesting that the loss of South Korea would be "a disaster of utmost importance to the United States."

In the public furor over the alleged "loss" of China from the fall of 1949 through the spring of 1950, which McCarthy ruthlessly exploited to promote his "Red Scare," little attention was paid by the American press or by Congress to the escalating border raids and bombastic pronouncements by North and South Korea against each other. Indeed, American economic assistance to South Korea was nearly cut off because of the excitement over Formosa and McCarthyism. The House of Representatives defeated a bill in January 1950 appropriating $60 million in economic aid to South Korea. According to an official source, "The opposition was ascribed partly to a conviction that the money would be wasted, but also to irritation at the Administration's refusal to provide military aid to the Chinese Nationalists." After pressure from the White House and the State Department and after it had been incorporated in a combined China-Korea aid bill, the appropriation for economic assistance to South Korea was approved finally by Congress. Truman noted in his memoirs that Republicans had constituted a majority of those who had voted against the first bill and that "Congress was in no hurry to provide the aid which had been requested for Korea by the President."

In early 1950, MacArthur continued to be reluctant about helping Rhee to establish ROK naval and air forces. When Rhee learned that the FEAF's propeller-driven fighters were being replaced by jet aircraft, he asked MacArthur for some of the obsolete planes being phased out at bases in Japan. But MacArthur would not plead his case with the JCS and Air Force authorities in Washington, perhaps fearing that Rhee might use them for offensive, not defensive, purposes. Desperately trying to find ships for a Korean coast guard, Rhee again did not find MacArthur helpful when he requested him in January to secure the return of 600,000 tons of South Korean ships that the Japanese allegedly had taken between mid-August 1945 and the arrival of Hodge's corps in South Korea. MacArthur did not return the vessels, then in Japanese ports, but referred Rhee to Washington, saying, "I am without authority to effect a change in the existing policy."[25] The South Korean government was finding it difficult to get much attention from Washington or Tokyo leaders, who seemed preoccupied with more important matters.

In the spring of 1950 Soviet shipments of military matériel to North Korea increased markedly, though even earlier Kim's forces possessed arms and equipment superior to those of the ROK Army in quantity and quality. The North Korean Army was supplied by the Russians with 122-mm. howitzers and guns, 76-mm. howitzers and self-propelled guns, as well as 45-mm. antitank guns and 120-mm. mortars; the ROK forces' main ordnance types were 105-mm. howitzers, 37-mm. antitank guns, and 81-mm. and 60-mm. mortars. The North Koreans had 150 Soviet T-34 32-ton medium tanks; the South Koreans had no tanks. North Korea had about 180 military aircraft, including 120 combat planes (fighters and attack bombers), all of Soviet make; South Korea had no combat aircraft and only 22 liaison and training planes. Neither of the Koreas had a real navy, each possessing 20 to 30 patrol boats and other small craft. The North Korean Army was about 135,000 men strong, including 89,000 combat troops, the bulk of which were in 7 infantry divisions of 11,000 men each and a 6000-man tank brigade. The ROK Army had approximately 98,000 men, including 65,000 combat soldiers, which were in 8 infantry divisions of 7000 to 10,000 men each. An important if not measurable difference between the two sides was the vastly superior training of the North Korean combat forces. Although they had assumed responsibility for intelligence in Korea after June 1949, General Roberts and his KMAG staff were not well informed about the North Korean military advantages. Several times in the late spring of 1950 Roberts confidently predicted that the ROK Army could repel a North Korean invasion. His often-quoted and undoubtedly most-regretted remark on the eve of war was that the South Koreans had "the best doggoned shooting army outside the United States."[26]

Offsetting the North Korean military edge over South Korea was MacArthur's Far East Command, most of it stationed a short distance away at bases in Japan. His ground forces numbered about 108,000 by June 1950, up slightly from the previous two years. Of these, 83,000 were in the Eighth Army, stationed in Japan; the rest were scattered in garrisons in the Ryukyus, Philippines, Marianas, and Bonins. Walker's Eighth Army was made up primarily of four divisions: the 1st Cavalry, 7th, 24th, and 25th Infantry, whose average strength was about 12,800 men, far below their authorized combat strength of 18,900. The nearest other sizable Army unit was the 29th Infantry Regiment on Okinawa. Stratemeyer's Far East Air Forces had 34,000 personnel and 1172 aircraft, including 639 fighters and bombers. They were spread between the Fifth Air Force in Japan, the Thirteenth Air Force in the Philippines, and the Twentieth Air Force in the Ryukyus. Vice Admiral C. Turner Joy's U.S. Naval Forces, Far East (NAVFE), had only 1 light cruiser, 4 destroyers, and an assortment of auxiliary ships. But stationed at bases in the Philippines and Ryukyus was Vice Admiral Arthur D. Struble's Seventh Fleet, consisting of 1 carrier, 1 heavy cruiser, 8 destroyers, 3 submarines, and various auxiliary craft. Equipment for MacArthur's ground forces was made up almost entirely of World War II vehicles, guns, and other items that had been overhauled in Operation Roll-up. The FEAF, however, had been able recently to replace many of its obsolete fighters with 542 F-80s and F-82s.[27]

The Joint Chiefs were impressed by what they judged to be "the present high standard" of the Far East Command forces when they visited the area in late January and early February 1950. Besides inspecting various units, they conferred with MacArthur on February 1–3. The JCS then consisted of the same four officers who would make up that body through the time of MacArthur's relief fourteen months later: General Omar N. Bradley, chairman; General J. Lawton Collins, Army Chief of Staff; General Hoyt S. Vandenberg, Air Force Chief of Staff; and Admiral Forrest P. Sherman, Chief of Naval Operations. A significant command alteration resulted from their sessions with MacArthur: when in an emergency (war) situation Pacific Fleet units operated in Far East Command waters, they were to come under MacArthur's control; this applied specifically to the Seventh Fleet, then under Admiral Arthur Radford, the CINCPAC at Pearl Harbor. Bradley later commented, "The JCS and MacArthur were in nearly full agreement on most specific Far East matters. We shared the view that Korea was still of little strategic interest and that in the event of 'trouble,' the ROK Army could handle North Korea." About the Far East trip, Bradley said "the JCS benefited greatly" from the journey, and added: "What stands out above all in my mind was the general amity established between MacArthur and the JCS. We had spent enough time together to get to know one another on a personal basis. All of us left the Far East considerably less awestruck by the man and his theatrical style."[28]

Shortly after his return to Washington, Bradley wrote MacArthur on February 13:

We [the JCS] were exceptionally well pleased with what we observed in your command. It was good to see soldiers with such a high state of morale; their every action showed the fine training they are receiving, which in turn reflected great confidence in themselves and in the duties they are performing. An excellent spirit of cooperation was in evidence every place we went.[29]

The Joint Chiefs must have been taken on a carefully guided tour, because Bradley's statements are contradicted by a number of studies of the combat readiness of the ground forces, especially on the eve of war and during their baptism under fire that summer. For example, the official U.S. Army history of the war states that generally the Far East Command units were "under-strength, inadequately armed, and sketchily trained," and the attitude of many of the men was one of "inertia imposed by the years of occupation." The chronicle concludes that the personnel of the Far East Command were, in general, "flabby and soft, still hampered by an infectious lassitude, unready to respond swiftly and decisively to a full-scale emergency" on the eve of the North Korean invasion.[30]

To repeat for emphasis, KMAG, not MacArthur's command, was chiefly responsible for intelligence about North Korea after mid-1949. State Department intelligence personnel and CIA agents also sent reports from Korea to Washington during the ensuing twelve months. The reports told of a significant buildup of North Korean forces and equipment just north of the 38th Parallel in the late spring of 1950, as well as continuing raids, infiltrations, and inflammatory pronouncements by both North and South Korea. Acheson later stated, however, that the various American intelligence sources indicated that "the possibility for an attack on the Korean Republic existed at that time, but they were all in agreement that its launching in the summer of 1950 did not appear imminent." The Joint Intelligence Committee reported to the JCS on June 27 that it had had some "prior indications" of potential hostilities, including evacuation of civilians in North Korea near the 38th Parallel, but the information was not judged "sufficiently significant, in view of the fluid military situation in the general area, to justify prediction of military action." Major General Lyman L. Lemnitzer, director of the Office of Foreign Military Assistance in the Department of Defense, later testified that the data he had seen prior to the start of the war, including CIA reports, warned that Korea was a likely trouble spot but not in the immediate future. An Air Force colonel who was on the Joint Intelligence Committee later reviewed the prewar CIA reports and concluded, despite the JIC's knowledge of border evacuations, that specific warning of an invasion in June had not been provided. Major General Alexander R. Bolling, G-2 of the Department of the Army headquarters, reviewed the prewar intelligence reports from all sources and likewise found no definite signals of an imminent attack.

Rather, he said, the data suggested that North Korea would continue its "guerrilla and psychological warfare, political pressure, and other means" to subvert Rhee's regime. Truman later commented that the intelligence reports he read that spring indicated that North Korea "might at any time" attack, but there were no clues as to when. He added, "These same [CIA] reports also told me repeatedly that there were any number of other spots in the world where the Russians 'possessed the capability' to attack." Johnson later testified that Iran was regarded by Pentagon leaders in the spring of 1950 as the most likely target of Communist aggression in the near future.[31]

Harold J. Noble, first secretary of the American embassy in Seoul at the time, recalled in his memoirs that much of the AMIK staff's attention in June was diverted by several clever ruses of the North Korean government to center attention on its alleged interest in a cooperative effort by both Koreas to achieve unification. Border observers of the UN Commission on Korea reported nothing to indicate that war was near. South Korean officials, particularly Defense Minister Sihn Sung Mo, were warning in May and June of a North Korean assault, but they had been issuing alarmist reports for so long that Americans in Seoul had come to discount their value. Dulles addressed the ROK National Assembly on June 19, assuring the South Koreans that they were "not alone" and implying that America would come to their support in case of war, which, of course, was only his opinion and quite contrary to prevailing official United States policy. Dulles also visited the ROK positions along the 38th Parallel and later reported no indications of an imminent outbreak of full-scale hostilities. Meanwhile, in Tokyo the Defense Secretary and JCS chairman were meeting with MacArthur, Willoughby, and senior Far East Command officers. Roberts, the KMAG head, joined the meeting on the 20th. Bradley later said that from what he and Johnson learned from Roberts and MacArthur's staff, they felt "greatly relieved that we had no cause for concern in Korea."[32]

Nevertheless, Rear Admiral Roscoe H. Hillenkoetter, the CIA director, told the Senate Appropriations Committee on June 26 that his agency's reports had shown that an attack was imminent but other federal officials had not paid proper attention to them, though he admitted that the CIA had not forecast an invasion timetable. MacArthur later claimed, "My intelligence section was increasingly aware of the distinct menace of an attack by the North Korean Communists in the summer of 1950. . . . Constant intelligence reports of increasing urgency were submitted to Washington, advising of a possible North Korean thrust. But little impression was made against the general apathy." Willoughby, who had set up a small intelligence unit on the peninsula called the Korean Liaison Office, vehemently asserted that he had provided adequate warnings to the Army G-2 in Washington. He maintained that on June 25 his Korean Liaison Office had sixteen operatives in North Korea compared to only four CIA agents above the 38th Parallel and that his agents "consistently turned in more intelligence reports than the CIA agents." In his memoirs of 1954, he quotes a number of his G-2 reports to Washington predicting a North Korean attack in June. But his reports were discounted in Washington, probably for three reasons: (1) Willoughby had been arrogant and irascible in his prior dealings with the Office of Strategic Services, CIA, and State Department intelligence efforts in his theater. (2) Korea had been declared outside the jurisdiction of the Far East Command since June 1949, so his Korean Liaison Office was regarded by some in Washington as a brazen, extralegal creation. (3) Most important, Willoughby's warnings were interspersed with assurances by him that no invasion was near. For instance, on March 10 he reported that "the North Korean P.A. [People's Army] will invade South Korea in June," but only two weeks later he notified Army intelligence in Washington, "It is believed there will be no civil war in Korea this spring or summer." Bolling, the Army G-2, told Collins that fall after reading some press comments by Willoughby critical of the Washington G-2 office, "The statements made by Willoughby [about a June attack] are correct in part, but he failed to indicate [in his press statements] his conclusions that definitely discount the report referred to." At the Senate hearings in May–June 1951 on MacArthur's dismissal, Acheson also pointed out the qualifications and contradictions in Willoughby's predictions.[33] Perhaps the most objective judgment on the intelligence breakdown appears in the Army's official study of its high-level policy and command during the first year of the Korean conflict:

American intelligence failed to predict the time, strength, and actual launching of the attack because of reluctance to accept all the reports rendered by Koreans, a distrust of Oriental agents and sources, and a belief that the South Koreans were prone to cry wolf. . . . Signs which marked the prelude of the North Korean attack had become accepted as routine communist activity. . . .

In the final analysis, the controversy over the intelligence failure in Korea is academic. The United States had no plans to counter an invasion, even had it been forecast to the very day.[34]

If North Korean records on the beginning of the war are ever opened to researchers, they may well show that Kim's government was heavily influenced in its decision to launch the invasion in late June by the outcome of the national elections in South Korea. On May 30, Rhee was dealt a serious political blow when, in the UN-supervised election of a new ROK National Assembly, Rhee's supporters won only 49 of the 210 seats, with 130 going to independents. "The regime was left tottering by lack of confidence, both in Korea and abroad," commented *U.S. News & World Report.* On June 8, the North Korean "Democratic Front for the Attainment of Unification of the Fatherland," a mysterious organization probably sponsored by the Kim regime, issued a manifesto in the main North Korean newspapers calling for a general all-Korea election on August 5 to choose a "Supreme Korean Assembly," representing both North and South Korea, to convene on August 15, the fifth anniversary of Korea's liberation from Japanese control. The Democratic Front also invited certain South Korean leaders (but not Rhee) to a meeting at the 38th Parallel to discuss unification plans; no South Korean officials went. On the 20th, the North Korean government called for the setting up of a united Korean assembly, branded Rhee and other ROK leaders as traitors, and demanded that the UN Commission leave the peninsula. In the meantime, starting about June 15, North Korean Army units began moving secretly into positions just above the 38th Parallel; by June 23–24 all the assault forces were poised at their lines of departure for the offensive. Attack orders were issued by the North Korean high command between June 18 and 22, as revealed in documents later captured by MacArthur's forces.[35]

Some revisionist scholars have argued that North Korea's military operations on June 25 were merely a counterattack to repulse a ROK invasion. This view was proclaimed by Pyongyang, Moscow, and Peking that summer, and it was repeatedly argued by delegates of the Soviet Union and its satellites in subsequent sessions of the UN General Assembly. Rhee, it is granted, may have been so desperate after his May disaster at the polls that he was considering an attack against North Korea to try to recoup his political fortunes. But the revisionists have never convincingly accounted for two factors that strongly implicate North Korea as the aggressor on June 25: (1) the attack orders issued up to a week before the start of hostilities, which have never been shown to be faked documents; and (2) the days, even weeks, of preparation required to launch a well-coordinated 90,000-man operation such as that which the North Korean Army undertook on the 25th and the following days. No one acquainted with logistics could accept the notion that the North Korean forces were merely responding that day to a ROK assault. Some revisionists, beginning with the pioneer work of the journalist I. F. Stone in 1952, have also asserted that the events of June 25 were the culmination of a Rhee-MacArthur conspiracy (Stone included Chiang, too) to salvage the rightist ROK regime. Indeed, MacArthur, whose last talks with Rhee had been on February 16–17 (and he had not yet met Chiang), may have wished later that he had "conspired" with the ROK president during that fateful spring when, in truth, he continued to be far more concerned about Formosa than South Korea. On this point, the revisionists, ironically, credit MacArthur with more foresight than he had.[36]

CHAPTER XIV

Holding the Naktong Line

1. "Time Is of the Essence"

SHORTLY BEFORE 9:30 P.M., Saturday, June 24, 1950, the official news of the beginning of the Korean War reached Washington when the State Department received a telegram from Ambassador Muccio, declaring that North Korea had launched an "all-out offensive." The first unofficial word had come earlier that evening from a United Press correspondent in Seoul. Muccio's message seems belated, since it was dispatched nearly six and a half hours after the invasion began, about 4:00 A.M., Sunday, Korean time. But he was known for careful reporting, and because of the many prior clashes along the 38th Parallel and because of the "fog of war," or confusion endemic to battle, he waited until he felt sure the action was more than another border raid.

(Time differences in the Korean War are important but confusing. In June 1950, when Tokyo and Washington were on daylight saving time, Seoul was thirteen hours ahead of Washington, and Tokyo was one hour ahead of Seoul and fourteen hours ahead of Washington.)

President Truman and some of his top diplomatic and defense advisers were out of the capital that weekend. When notified at his Maryland farm, Acheson telephoned Truman, who was at his home in Independence, Missouri. The President said that he would return to Washington on Sunday afternoon, and he agreed to

Acheson's proposal to request an emergency Sunday session of the United Nations Security Council to consider the crisis. Although only Bradley of the Joint Chiefs learned of the war's outbreak that Saturday night, State Department officials were busy throughout the night preparing a resolution for the Security Council meeting and receiving more reports, many still fragmentary, from the American mission in Seoul.

MacArthur's first message about the new war arrived at the Department of the Army headquarters about 5:00 A.M., Sunday, Washington time, or fourteen hours after the invasion started. He reported that much of the area from the Ongjin Peninsula to the Imjin River had been lost, including the city of Kaesong, but the ROK forces were preparing to make a stand on the south bank of the Imjin. Only minutes later, however, a more up-to-date report came to the Pentagon from KMAG, saying that the North Koreans had crossed the Imjin and were twenty-five miles north of Seoul. Receiving an urgent request from KMAG for munitions for the ROK Army, which had only a ten-day supply, MacArthur went into action on the first day of war, the 25th, without waiting for JCS authorization: he told Walker to have a cargo ship at Yokohama loaded with howitzer, mortar, and carbine ammunition for South Korea and instructed Stratemeyer and Joy to have their planes and ships provide protection for the vessel during its journey and unloading. In a message later that day to the Pentagon, MacArthur stated that he was shipping the munitions, called the invasion an "undisguised act of war," estimated the North Korean assault strength at three divisions (it was in fact seven infantry divisions and an armored brigade), and proposed that the Seventh Fleet be sent into Korean waters in case it was needed soon.

At Lake Success on the afternoon of June 25 the United Nations Security Council adopted an American-drafted resolution labeling North Korea's "armed attack" as "a breach of the peace," calling for a cease-fire and a withdrawal of North Korean troops to the 38th Parallel, and urging all UN members "to render every assistance to the United Nations in the execution of this resolution." American officials did not know in advance whether the Soviet delegate, absent since January, would appear at the session, but the Soviet Union continued its boycott of the Security Council in protest against the seating of Nationalist China instead of Communist China. In its UN tactics at least, Moscow did not appear to know much more than Washington about the specific timing of the North Korean assault.[1]

While Truman was flying back to Washington that Sunday afternoon, State and Pentagon leaders met and drew up a tentative set of proposals to present to the President regarding limited military support for South Korea. In a teletype conference, or "telecon," they discussed their conclusions with MacArthur, but they made it clear these had not been approved yet by Truman, and they did not imply that American intervention with ground forces was in the offing. That week and, indeed, often in the months ahead the telecon was an effective device for Washington and Tokyo leaders to communicate "instantaneously." The telecon involved the projection on large screens in the Pentagon and Tokyo GHQ of teletype statements and questions that could be seen by the assembled officials, who could discuss and respond by teletype. At Blair House that evening Truman conferred with thirteen key State and Defense officials about the Far Eastern situation. Johnson and Bradley opened the meeting by trying to focus the discussion on Formosa as strategically more significant than Korea; they even introduced MacArthur's memo of June 14 on the subject. But Acheson, who took the lead among the President's advisers, insisted on redirecting attention to the Korean crisis. He and Truman were strongly resolved that positive American action was needed, though short of the use of ground troops. The question of command came up briefly, but the President dismissed it as premature, remarking that he "was not yet ready to put MacArthur in as Commander-in-Chief in Korea." The three-hour meeting ended at 11:00 P.M., after Truman approved a four-point plan of limited action, largely suggested by Acheson with the others concurring.[2]

A half-hour later Secretary of the Army Frank Pace, Jr., and the Joint Chiefs conferred by telecon with MacArthur, conveying the following instructions, which had just been approved by the President:

> a. A survey party from Japan would be dispatched to Korea to consult with Advisory Mission in Korea [KMAG] and a report would be made as soon as possible as to the military aid which CINCFE [MacArthur] could furnish. This report was to include the possible

use of military forces available to CINCFE in order to hold the Seoul-
Kimpo-Inchon area;

   b. Such ammunition and equipment would be sent to Korea as
CINCFE considered necessary in order to prevent loss of the Seoul-
Kimpo-Inchon area. This authorization included appropriate use of
air and naval cover in order to assure arrival of this matériel;

   c. Such air and naval action as necessary to prevent the overrunning of Seoul-Kimpo-Inchon area was authorized in order to insure
safe evacuation of United States dependents and non-combatants; and

   d. The Seventh Fleet was ordered to proceed to Sasebo [Kyushu]
at once, at which point it would pass under operational control of
CINCFE.[3]

During this telecon, which began at 1:30 P.M., June 26, Tokyo time,
MacArthur was cautiously reassuring about the ROK defensive
situation after a day and a half of fighting. Although it would be
another five days full of high-level discussions in Washington before Truman made the fateful decision to commit ground forces,
the official Army chronicle maintains that "the authority to employ the Air Force and the Navy on June 25 rendered the later
decision one of degree rather than one of principle."[4] And the
decision on the 25th gave retroactive approval to actions Mac-
Arthur had already set in motion in sending a munitions ship with
air and naval escort.

   MacArthur's somewhat optimistic view during the telecon was
probably based on news that the ROK Army had begun a two-
division counterattack on the morning of June 26 to protect
Uijongbu and the corridor to Seoul. But one of the ROK divisions
was routed, forcing the other to fall back to avoid being outflanked; by nightfall the North Koreans had captured Uijongbu,
and no major South Korean forces stood between them and the
South Korean capital. On the 26th Muccio ordered the evacuation
of American civilians and dependents from Seoul. During the next
two days 2000 people, mostly American dependents, AMIK personnel, ECA employees, and Western missionaries, were evacuated to Japan. A commercial freighter at the port of Inchon carried some, and others were flown out by both commercial and FEAF
aircraft, operating out of Kimpo Airfield, which lay between Seoul
and Inchon. The first aerial battle between American and North
Korean fighters occurred on June 27 over Kimpo and Seoul, with

three Soviet-built YAKs shot down and no losses among the FEAF F-82s that were covering evacuation activities. Meanwhile Rhee and his officials fled southward, shortly followed by Muccio and his staff. The battle for Seoul began at dawn on June 28 with a North Korean artillery barrage; by that night the city had fallen. North Korean troops moved on quickly to seize Kimpo and Inchon.

In the meantime MacArthur's reports to Washington had become more and more pessimistic. John Allison, Dulles' deputy in Tokyo, observed, "I have never seen such a dejected, completely despondent man as General MacArthur was that Tuesday morning, June 27, 1950." By then MacArthur had most of the details of the disaster at Uijongbu. He reported to the Pentagon on the 27th that the ROK soldiers "have not shown adequate resistance capabilities or the will to fight and . . . complete collapse is imminent."[5] After another Blair House conference between Truman and the top State and Pentagon leaders on Tuesday evening, the 26th, a telecon was held between the JCS, Pace, and Air Force Secretary Thomas K. Finletter on the Washington end and MacArthur and several of his senior officers in Tokyo. MacArthur was informed of his latest directive, which was based on the decisions made at that evening's Blair House session:

> a. In order to clear South Korea of North Korean military forces, all military targets south of the 38th parallel were cleared for attack by the air forces. Similarly naval forces were authorized to operate against forces engaged in aggression against South Korea without restriction in coastal waters and sea approaches south of the 38th parallel;
>
> b. The Chinese Nationalist Government was called upon to cease offensives against the mainland. CINCFE, utilizing the Seventh Fleet which was assigned to his operational control, was directed to prevent, by naval and air action, any attack on Formosa or any sea or air offensive from Formosa against the mainland of China.[6]

He was also told that Admiral Radford, CINCPAC, was being directed to reinforce the NAVFE forces with "a carrier task group, together with submarines and necessary train" and that CINCPAC was "to support and reinforce CINCFE" further as directed by the JCS through the Chief of Naval Operations.

Apparently as soon as this telecon ended, which was in the early afternoon of June 27 in Tokyo, MacArthur gave George Stratemeyer orders to send his bombers and fighters into action against North Korean troop positions, convoys, supply depots, and other military targets south of the 38th Parallel. Within eight hours Stratemeyer's planes had flown 183 missions, and during the next two days they shot down 26 North Korean aircraft. Admiral Joy's NAVFE units also were sent out into the Yellow Sea and Sea of Japan and in South Korean coastal waters, but they found no targets the first few days.

In Washington on Wednesday, the 27th, Truman issued a statement announcing that he had ordered the interposition of the Seventh Fleet between Formosa and the Chinese mainland and the acceleration of military assistance to the Philippines and to the French in Indochina. He also said, "I have ordered United States air and sea forces to give the Korean Government troops cover and support." He asserted that the introduction of American air and naval units into combat south of the 38th Parallel was justified because North Korea "has defied the orders of the Security Council." That same day, in New York, the Security Council passed another American-sponsored resolution, this one recommending that United Nations members "furnish such assistance to the Republic of Korea as may be necessary to repel the armed attack and to restore the international peace and security in the area." Inexplicably continuing its boycott, the Soviet Union missed a cardinal opportunity to veto this resolution, whose adoption would provide the main basis for the forthcoming establishment of the United Nations Command. A veto would have presented Truman and Acheson with a quandary, but they would have undoubtedly continued to favor unilateral United States support of South Korea, though perhaps more gradually and with greater reliance on congressional approval. The following day the United Kingdom informed the Security Council that it was placing its naval forces in the Far East under MacArthur's control for use in the defense of South Korea. In Moscow, meanwhile, the Soviet government peremptorily rejected a United States note requesting that it use its "good offices" to try to get North Korea to halt its invasion and withdraw above the 38th Parallel.[7]

MacArthur's resumption of command over American military activities in Korea after a year's hiatus became a reality when his fifteen-man survey team, led by Brigadier General John H. Church, arrived in South Korea on June 27. By then authorized to use his air and naval forces in South Korea, MacArthur designated Church's mission as GHQ Advance Command and Liaison Group in Korea (ADCOM). Church and the ROK Army Chief of Staff set up a joint temporary headquarters at Suwon, a town with a primitive but usable airstrip located about thirty miles south of Seoul. Although his initial task was to ascertain the logistical needs of the ROK forces, Church soon found himself helping to plan a defensive line along the south bank of the Han River. He also sent situation estimates to MacArthur, including one on the night of the 28th bluntly advising that the North Koreans could not be driven back to the 38th Parallel without the intervention of the American Army. Moreover, Church had to report that on the 28th the bad news included not only the fall of Seoul but also the collapse of the South Korean central front, where the city of Chunchon was overrun that day. The next two days, however, marked a lull in the fighting as the North Korean units halted to regroup and bring up supplies and reinforcements.[8]

Apparently spurred by Church's report on the need for American ground forces, MacArthur decided to observe the frontline situation for himself. Shortly after 6:00 A.M., June 29, MacArthur's plane, a C-54 renamed *Bataan* (earlier called *SCAP*), lifted off the runway at Tokyo's Haneda Airport in a rainstorm and headed westward. Aboard with MacArthur were Generals Almond, Whitney, Willoughby, Wright, and Stratemeyer, Admiral Joy, and four correspondents; as always, the pilot was Colonel Story. They landed at the Suwon airstrip four hours later, just after North Korean aircraft had bombed and strafed some transport planes at one end of the runway. At a little schoolhouse at Suwon MacArthur and his party met with Rhee, Church, Muccio, and some ROK, ADCOM, and KMAG officers. Church opened the session with a briefing on the current military situation, which was dismal: between casualties, desertions, and stragglers, only 24,000 ROK troops could be located from an army that had numbered 98,000 four days earlier. Rhee's evaluation of conditions, said Almond, "amounted to about the statement that 'We are in a hell of a fix.'" The ROK Chief of Staff, soon to be replaced, suggested mobilizing 2 million ROK young men — a quixotic plan at a time when the ROK government was in flight and only a fourth of the current army could be found. After some brief but perceptive and realistic comments by Muccio, MacArthur said, "Well, I have heard a good deal theoretically, and now I want to go and see these troops that are straggling down the road."

Almond described their visit to the Han River front at Yong-dungpo, just southwest of Seoul:

> We got three old, broken-down cars and . . . drove to the south bank of the Han River, where we could see the enemy firing from Seoul to targets on the south bank. We were within probably a hundred yards of where some of these mortar shells were falling. . . . Going up that road from Suwon for a distance of 30 miles, we passed many trucks, many stragglers, many men in groups, all smiling, all with rifles, all with bandoliers of ammunition around them, all saluting, showing that they were disciplined — they recognized that some dignitary was coming along. We had . . . some Korean MP's . . . clearing the road. . . . General MacArthur made the remark . . . "It is a strange thing to me that all these men have their rifles and ammunition, they all know how to salute, they all seem to be more or less happy, but I haven't seen a wounded man yet." That indicated that nobody was fighting, that they had lost their leadership and that is what happened.[9]

MacArthur said that he stood for an hour on a hill only a mile across the Han from Seoul, observing the burning buildings in the capital and the lines of South Korean troops and refugees moving southward. "The scene along the Han was enough to convince me," he recalled, "that the defensive potential of South Korea had already been exhausted." While watching "the pitiful evidence of the disaster I had inherited," he said, he recognized two facts: (1) his troops in Japan would have to be thrown "into this breach," and (2) an amphibious envelopment, as later executed at Inchon, would be necessary to offset the North Koreans' superiority in manpower and to "wrest victory from defeat."

Returning to Suwon, MacArthur and his group departed on the *Bataan* about 6:15 P.M., immediately before another North Korean bombing of the airstrip. Rhee, Muccio, and their staffs then prepared to move south to Taejon, about 100 miles below Seoul. En route to Tokyo, MacArthur told the correspondent Marguerite Higgins, "The moment I reach Tokyo, I shall send President

Truman my recommendation for the immediate dispatch of American divisions to Korea." Since it was after 11:00 that night, however, when his C-54 touched down at Haneda, the seventy-year-old MacArthur, whose exhausting day had begun before 4:00 A.M., did not complete the drafting of his message to Washington until the next day.[10]

About 9:00 A.M., June 30, MacArthur received from the Joint Chiefs a new directive that summarized his previous instructions and also included some significant new ones that the President had approved after a session with the National Security Council, the JCS, and the service secretaries late on the previous afternoon:

1. This directive consolidates, broadens, and supplements existing instructions governing your actions with regard to situation in South Korea and Formosa.

2. In support of resolutions of United Nations, approved on 25 June . . . and 27 June . . .

a. You will employ naval and air forces available to the Far East Command to provide fullest possible support to South Korean forces by attack on military targets so as to permit these forces to clear South Korea of North Korean forces.

b. Employment of army forces will be limited to essential communications and other essential service units, except that you are authorized to employ such army combat and service forces as to insure the retention of a port and air base in the general area Pusan-Chinhae.

c. By naval and air action you will defend Formosa against invasion or attack by Chinese Communists and will insure that Formosa will not be used as a base of operations against the Chinese mainland by Chinese Nationalists.

3. Seventh Fleet is assigned to your operational control. CINCPAC and CINCPACFLT will support and reinforce you as necessary and practicable.

4. You are authorized to extend your operations into Northern Korea against air bases, depots, tank farms, troop columns, and other such purely military targets, if and when, in your judgment, this becomes essential for the performance of your missions as given in paragraph 2a and b, or to avoid unnecessary casualties to our forces. Special care will be taken to insure that operations in North Korea stay well clear of the frontiers of Manchuria or the Soviet Union.

5. You are authorized to send to Korea any munitions and sup-

plies from resources at your disposal which you deem necessary. You will submit your estimates of amounts and types of aid required from sources outside your control.

6. The decision to commit United States air and naval forces and limited army forces to provide cover and support for South Korean troops does not constitute a decision to engage in war with the Soviet Union if Soviet forces intervene in Korea. The decision regarding Korea, however, was taken in full realization of the risks involved. If Soviet forces actively oppose our operations in Korea, your forces should defend themselves, should take no action to aggravate the situation, and you should report the situation to Washington.[11]

Although much of this directive repeated earlier authorizations to MacArthur, the new decisions that brought the United States closer to full-scale intervention in the Korean War were, first, to commit ground forces to protect the Pusan area, and, second, to permit air and naval operations north of the 38th Parallel. Actually about twenty-four hours earlier MacArthur had ordered Stratemeyer to send his planes over North Korea. The two had discussed the decision en route to Suwon, and while in flight Stratemeyer had sent the following radio order to FEAF headquarters in Tokyo: "Take out North Korean Airfield immediately. No publicity. MacArthur approves."[12] This marked the second order by MacArthur in four days that preceded JCS authorization, the other being his premature dispatch of the munitions ship to South Korea with air and naval cover. Of course, in both cases he correctly anticipated his superiors' decisions. But, as the several references to the Soviet Union in the above directive suggest, Washington leaders were extremely concerned about potential Soviet responses to American actions in the Korean conflict. Were he to anticipate wrongly, MacArthur's issuance of orders in advance of JCS directives could greatly increase the risk of a hostile confrontation with the USSR or Communist China.

In the early afternoon of Friday, June 30, MacArthur sent to the Pentagon a recommendation that American ground forces be committed to combat on the Korean front; the message reached Washington shortly after midnight of June 29–30. As the "today" in the first sentence indicates, he had begun drafting it on the 29th; Whitney claimed he started working on it during the flight back from Suwon. For unknown reasons, he did not revise the time reference in the final copy nor did he allude to the JCS directive he received on the morning of the 30th. He probably finished the draft before the JCS message arrived, became involved in pressing matters at the office, and had his message to Washington sent out as he departed for lunch after a conference with Admiral Arthur Struble, the Seventh Fleet commander. Because it weighed so heavily in the considerations of his superiors regarding the decision to commit ground forces, MacArthur's message of the 30th is given here in full:

I have today inspected the South Korean battle area from Suwon north to the Han River. My purpose was to reconnoiter at first hand the conditions as they exist and to determine the most effective way to further support our mission.

The Korean army and coastal forces are in confusion, have not seriously fought, and lack leadership through their own means. Organized and equipped as a light force for maintenance of interior order, they were unprepared for attack by armor and air. Conversely, they are incapable of gaining the initiative over such a force as that embodied in the North Korean army.

The Korean army had made no preparations for a defense in depth, for echelons of supply or for a supply system. No plans had been made, or if made, not executed, for the destruction of supplies or matériel in event of a retrograde movement. As a result, they have either lost, or abandoned, their supplies and heavier equipment and have absolutely no system of inter-communication. In most cases the individual soldier, in his flight to the south, has retained his rifle or carbine. They are gradually being gathered up in rear areas and given some semblance of organization by an advance group of my officers I have sent over for this purpose. Without artillery, mortars, and anti-tank guns, they can only hope to retard the enemy through the fullest utilization of natural obstacles and under the guidance and example of leadership of high quality.

The civilian populace is tranquil, orderly, and prosperous according to their scale of living. They have retained a high national spirit and firm belief in the Americans. The roads leading south from Seoul are crowded with refugees refusing to accept the Communist rule.

South Korean military strength is estimated at not more than 25,000 effectives. North Korean military forces are as previously reported, backed by considerable strength in armor and a well trained, well directed and aggressive air force equipped with Russian planes. It is now obvious that this force has been built as an element of Communist military aggression.

I am doing everything possible to establish and maintain a flow of supplies through the air-head at Suwon and the southern port of Pusan. The air-head is most vital but is subject to constant air attack. Since air cover must be maintained over all aircraft transporting supplies, equipment, and personnel, this requirement operates to contain a large portion of my fighter strength. North Korean air, operating from nearby bases, has been savage in its attacks in the Suwon area.

It is essential that the enemy advance be held or its impetus will threaten the overrunning of all Korea. Every effort is being made to establish a Han River line but the result is highly problematical. The defense of this line and the Suwon-Seoul corridor is essential to the retention of the only air-head in Central Korea.

The Korean army is entirely incapable of counter action and there is grave danger of a further breakthrough. If the enemy advance continues much further it will seriously threaten the fall of the Republic.

The only assurance for the holding of the present line, and the ability to regain later the lost ground, is through the introduction of US ground combat forces into the Korean battle area. To continue to utilize the forces of our Air and Navy without an effective ground element cannot be decisive.

If authorized, it is my intention to immediately move a US regimental combat team to the reinforcement of the vital area discussed and to provide for a possible build-up to a two division strength from the troops in Japan for an early counter-offensive.

Unless provision is made for the full utilization of the Army-Navy-Air team in this shattered area our mission will at best be needlessly costly in life, money and prestige. At worst, it might even be doomed to failure.[13]

At 4:00 A.M., June 30, Washington time, Chief of Staff J. Lawton Collins, together with several Pentagon and State leaders, communicated by telecon with MacArthur and some of his senior officers. Collins said the regimental combat team (RCT) could be moved to the Pusan area under the terms of the JCS directive of the 29th, but the President would have to decide about its deployment in the combat area to the north and about the two-division buildup. MacArthur responded that the current authorization "does not give sufficient latitude for efficient operation" and "does not satisfy the basic requirement" to stem the North Korean offensive. "Time is of the essence," MacArthur asserted, "and a clear-cut decision without delay is imperative." Collins replied that he should be able to get a White House decision regarding the two divisions before the RCT's movement to Korea was completed. He asked, "Does this meet your requirement for the present?" According to an authority, "At this point MacArthur employed a technique no other officer in the United States military service would dare to use. He simply did not respond to the last statement of the Chief of Staff. The screen remained blank." Collins later said, "We took this to mean that General MacArthur stood by his emphatic plea for a decision 'without delay.'" The Chief of Staff then informed him by teletype that he would try to get an immediate decision; the telecon screen stayed blank, as again MacArthur did not answer. While the telecon continued with a general discussion of the military situation in South Korea, Collins left to telephone Pace, who, in turn, called Truman about MacArthur's requests. By then it was about 5:00 A.M., but Truman was already up when the Secretary of the Army phoned him. "I told Pace," said Truman, "to inform General MacArthur immediately that the use of one regimental combat team was approved." Collins hurried back to the telecon, informed MacArthur of the President's decision, and told him he would be advised later about the two divisions. The Chief of Staff closed the telecon by praising MacArthur's "prompt action" in going to Korea himself, and expressing "full confidence" in his leadership.[14]

On the morning of the 30th in Washington, there was a flurry of top-level meetings: Johnson, the JCS, and the service secretaries at 8:30; an hour later a White House conference involving the same men plus Truman, Acheson, and some other key presidential advisers; a JCS meeting about 10:15; and another White House session at 11:00 that included Truman, Acheson, Johnson, the Joint Chiefs, and seventeen Democratic and Republican leaders of Congress. At the 9:30 meeting Truman approved Admiral Forrest Sherman's proposal of a naval blockade of North Korea; later MacArthur was sent a directive about implementing it, which included a warning to keep his NAVFE units "well clear of the coastal waters of Manchuria and USSR." The President determined, too, that an offer by Chiang Kai-shek of 33,000 Nationalist

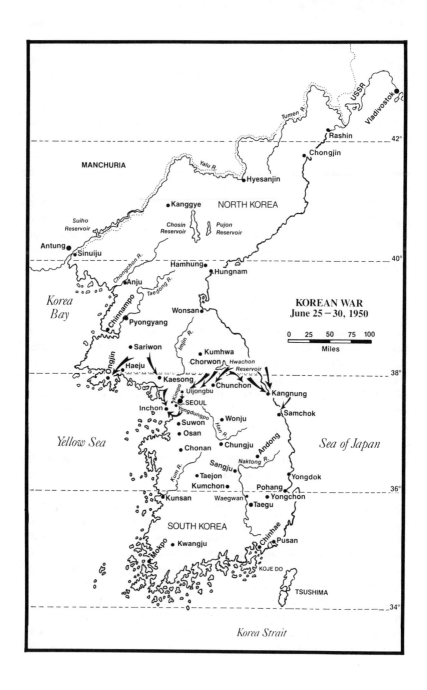

Chinese troops for use in defending South Korea should be "politely declined" because of potential diplomatic difficulties and logistical liabilities. Most important, Truman decided to give MacArthur "full authority to use the ground forces under his command" in combat. At the 11:00 gathering the President explained to the senators and representatives the decisions of that morning and the previous day. When one congressman inquired whether the American intervention was "within the framework of the United Nations," according to one source Truman "emphasized that it was, and said that MacArthur would be not just the United States commander but the United Nations commander, as well." Despite some legislators' grumbling that he had bypassed Congress in committing American soldiers to the war, Truman, says an authority, "concluded that, while he needed congressional support for the moves he made, he did not need congressional approval."

Early that Friday afternoon the JCS, with Truman's sanction, notified MacArthur, "Restrictions on use of Army Forces . . . are hereby removed and authority granted to utilize Army Forces available to you . . . subject only to requirements for safety of Japan in the present situation which is a matter for your judgment." The Army's official history states, "General MacArthur quite clearly had tipped the balance in favor of troop commitment." In a press statement that day, Truman announced that he "had authorized the United States Air Force to conduct missions on specific military targets in northern Korea wherever militarily necessary, and had ordered a naval blockade of the entire Korean coast." Almost parenthetically at the end, he added the news of his most crucial decision of the day: "General MacArthur has been authorized to use certain supporting ground units." Acheson's later observation was more realistic and frank: "Friday's decisions were the culminating ones of a momentous week. We were then fully committed in Korea."[15]

2. Halting the North Korean Offensive

By the time MacArthur received approval on July 1 to send his ground forces into combat, the North Korean offensive had resumed. Kim Il Sung's main force, spearheaded by tanks, seized Suwon on July 4 and continued down the Seoul-Taejon-Taegu-Pusan axis. MacArthur's three-phase strategy to counter the invasion consisted of (1) delaying actions necessitating rapid, if piecemeal, commitment of the first of his divisions from Japan; (2) establishment of a holding line above Pusan after the introduction of other Far East Command forces and the revitalization of the remaining ROK units; and (3) a dual counteroffensive, by amphibious landing far behind the enemy lines and by overland assault from the perimeter north of Pusan, after a sufficient buildup of men and matériel from the States.

While the regiments of Major General William F. Dean's 24th Division were preparing to move to Korea, a 540-man task force from that division, consisting of two rifle companies and a 105-mm. howitzer battery, was sent in advance to slow the enemy drive below Suwon. Led by Lieutenant Colonel Charles B. Smith, the tiny force, which had no effective antitank weapons, was overrun by enemy armor and infantry north of Osan on July 5 in the first battle between American and North Korean troops. For the next two weeks the 24th Division's regiments fought desperate, costly delaying operations, which bought time with lives as more American units began to arrive in South Korea. Dean was captured after the battle for Taejon, which fell on July 20; Church, the former ADCOM head, succeeded him as commander of the casualty-ridden 24th Division. Meanwhile, enemy advances to the east of the Americans were slow owing to mountainous terrain and to the ROK troops' resistance, now fiercer than it had been before.

With more American units and, he hoped, allied reinforcements preparing to enter South Korea, MacArthur ordered his Eighth Army commander to direct the operations of such forces. So leaving a rear headquarters echelon at Yokohama on July 13, Walker moved the main Eighth Army headquarters to Taegu, a city about seventy miles north of Pusan that had become the location also of the seat of the ROK government and of ROK Army headquarters. The next day Rhee notified MacArthur that he was placing all South Korean forces under his authority; henceforth the ROK Army would be under Walker's operational control. Between July 18 and 26, the 25th Infantry and 1st Cavalry divisions arrived in Korea from Japan and the 29th RCT from Okinawa.

By then, Stratemeyer's FEAF, reinforced by American carrier planes and an Australian fighter squadron, had won supremacy of the skies, almost annihilating the North Korean Air Force and thereafter concentrating on close ground support and interdiction of enemy supply lines, with some strategic bombing of targets in North Korea. American cruisers and destroyers helped to slow the North Korean push down the east coast with heavy shore bombardments.

Despite the preponderance of American air and naval firepower, however, the North Korean Army's superiority in troops, artillery, and tanks forced a continuing retreat of the defenders. By the end of July, North Korean forces had seized all the lightly held southwest portion of Korea, and the ROK and American troops withdrew into the Naktong, or Pusan, perimeter, a rectangular area in the southeast corner of the peninsula. On its west side the defensive line ran about eighty miles from the vicinity of Sangju down the Naktong River to its confluence with the Nam River and then to the Korea Strait coastline west of Masan; on its north side the line extended approximately fifty miles eastward from the Sangju area to the coast of the Sea of Japan above Yongdok. Walker positioned his three American divisions on the west and the five remaining ROK divisions on the north. From MacArthur's viewpoint, the holding-line phase was now beginning; to Kim and his commanders the battle for the Naktong perimeter was to be the final stage of their conquest of South Korea.[16]

As the North Korean Army advanced south of the Han River during the first days of July, separate but similar proposals were drafted by UN Secretary-General Trygve Lie and by State Department officials for a military organization to incorporate the forces to be contributed by UN members to assist in the defense of South Korea. Both plans called for a Security Council resolution to authorize the United States government to direct the unified command and select its head, and both provided for a special committee of the council to handle offers of military assistance and receive reports from the international force's commander. The State Department's version was studied by the Joint Chiefs, who objected to the special committee and to any direct link between the Security Council and the UN commander. Pentagon-State discussions led to a revised draft that satisfied the JCS and got Truman's approval. It was jointly introduced in the Security Council by the United Kingdom and France on July 7 and was passed that day with no negative votes, the USSR still boycotting the sessions. The resolution recommended that all UN members who decided to help South Korea provide "military forces and other assistance" to "a unified command under the United States," which also would "designate the commander of such forces." The United States government would render to the council "reports as appropriate on the course of action taken under the unified command." At his discretion the commander was authorized to use the UN flag concurrently with the national flags of the participating forces.[17]

Once the Security Council empowered the American government to control the international command and choose its leader, the chain of authority below Truman, who became the executive agent for the UN body, ran downward according to the American military structure, namely, through the JCS and the Army Chief of Staff to the UN commander. When Truman asked the Joint Chiefs to select a commander, they did so promptly, recommending MacArthur on July 8. The President gave his approval and announced the appointment publicly the same day. Apparently neither the President nor the JCS seriously considered any other officer for the position. In fact, the official JCS history says simply, "There was only one conceivable choice." The Joint Chiefs officially notified MacArthur on the 10th of his appointment as UN commander in the Korean conflict.[18] The following day he sent a radiogram to the President:

> I have just received the announcement of your appointment of me as the United Nations commander of the international forces to be employed in Korea and cannot fail to express to you personally my deepest thanks and appreciation for this new expression of your confidence. I recall so vividly and with such gratitude that this is the second time you have so signally honored me. Your personal choice five years ago as Supreme Commander for the Allied Powers in Japan placed me under an intimate obligation which would be difficult for me ever to repay and you have now added to my debt. I can only repeat the pledge of my complete personal loyalty to you as well as an absolute devotion to your monumental struggle for peace and good will throughout the world. I hope I will not fail you.[19]

Truman replied cordially on the 12th: "I deeply appreciate the letter and the spirit of your message relating to your appointment as the United Nations commander of the international forces in Korea. Your words confirm me, if any confirmation were needed, in my full belief in the wisdom of your selection."[20] It would be interesting to know whether either man reread this exchange of plaudits as their relationship deteriorated in the months ahead.

According to the diary of Eben Ayers, Truman's assistant press secretary, Dulles, who had been in Tokyo until June 27, told Truman on his return to Washington that MacArthur should be "hauled back to the United States immediately." Dulles, who had implied in a Seoul speech on June 19 that South Korea could count on American support if attacked, allegedly was upset by MacArthur's seeming lack of concern during the first three days of the North Korean invasion. As recorded by Ayers, Truman's response to Dulles was "that the General is involved politically in this country — where he has from time to time been mentioned as a possible Republican Presidential candidate — and that he could not recall MacArthur without causing a tremendous reaction in this country where he has been built up, to heroic stature." But Ayers' account does not jibe with the previous and later friendly relations between Dulles and the general when they worked on the Japanese peace treaty. And Ayers' story is contradicted by the following message Dulles sent MacArthur on July 10: "I hail your designation as the first commander of United Nations armed forces. The existence of such force is itself symbolic of the growing resolution, unity, and strength of the free world, and that world is fortunate in finding for its first commander one of your moral stature who will honorably and meritoriously lead in the way of righteousness."[21] It is hard to believe that Dulles changed his mind so quickly, or, on the other hand, was so grossly hypocritical.

On July 9, the day after Truman announced MacArthur's appointment, the correspondent James Reston warned in the *New York Times*, "Diplomacy and a vast concern for the opinions and sensitivities of others are the political qualities essential to his new assignment, and these are precisely the qualities General MacArthur has been accused of lacking in the past." Recalling the general's "old habit of doing things in his own way, without too much concern about waiting for orders from Washington" during World War II and in Japan, Reston noted that he had already shown the same tendency during the first days of the Korean conflict, when, on his orders, "his planes attacked the North Korean capital before President Truman authorized any such action." He characterized MacArthur as "a sovereign power in his own right, with stubborn confidence in his own judgment."[22] Reston might have pointed out, too, that, except for the political angle, the President and his military chiefs need not have felt compelled to add another enormous command burden to a general who was already overloaded with high-level responsibilities and who was only a half-year away from his seventy-first birthday. There was an ample reservoir of younger, highly capable generals — J. Lawton Collins, Matthew B. Ridgway, and Maxwell D. Taylor, to name a few — who had been distinguished commanders in the Second World War, who could have approached this unprecedented coalition assignment in limited warfare with a clearer understanding of recent Washington thinking on global and allied strategies, and who enjoyed more harmonious personal relations with most or all of the current Joint Chiefs and key Pentagon officials. MacArthur, it should be remembered, had not been on duty in the United States since 1935. The first step leading to the Truman-MacArthur confrontation of 1950–1951 may well have been the selection of the difficult, aging, and overburdened MacArthur, who should not have been ordered to prove his leadership ability in another military crisis.

The dual nature of MacArthur's position was evident in the early instructions the JCS sent him. In keeping with Truman's insistence that the military support of South Korea be "truly" an effort of the United Nations, the Joint Chiefs instructed him on July 12 to identify himself in communiqués as commander in chief of the United Nations Command and, whenever possible, to cite the participating international forces. They told him, "For world-wide political reasons, it is important to emphasize repeatedly the fact that our operations are in support of the United Nations Security Council." On the other hand, on July 28 the Joint Chiefs directed him to prepare reports covering about two-week intervals of operations and to submit them to the JCS, never directly to the Security Council. They cautioned that "certain political factors which must be determined in Washington" might necessitate revisions of his reports by them or by the State Department before they were sent to the Security Council. They assured him, however, that he would be notified in advance of any changes. As in their earlier opposition to the creation of a special Security Council committee, the Joint Chiefs were determined to have no direct communications between MacArthur and the Security Council. As the JCS history admits, "It was to prevent the United Nations from involvement in strategy or tactics."[23]

The Joint Chiefs' uneasiness had been precipitated by a report the general had sent to Truman on July 19, which was dramatically written and boldly predicted that the North Korean plan to conquer the peninsula had already failed. The President, however, liked it so much that he quoted it in full in a radio and television address to the nation that evening. The general's report ended: "He [the enemy] has had his great chance but failed to exploit it. We are now in Korea in force, and with God's help we are there to stay until the constitutional authority of the Republic is fully restored." After the JCS directive of the 28th, MacArthur's language became more circumspect; he made his first official report to the Joint Chiefs on August 16, covering operations of July 20–31, and duly submitted two-week reports thereafter. In his testimony at the Senate hearings in May 1951, he said a number of alterations were made in Washington before his reports were sent to Lake Success. He commented, "Many of those changes I accepted. There were at least in one case changes which I would not accept, changes which seemed to me to place a political slant upon a military officer's report, which were not warrantable." He could not recall the case, however, when Senator Richard B. Russell tried to pursue the subject further.[24] Earlier MacArthur had told the senators:

> My connection with the United Nations was largely nominal. There were provisions made that the entire control of my command and everything I did came from our own Chiefs of Staff and my channel of communication was defined as the Army Chief of Staff.
>
> Even the reports which were normally [in fact, never] made by me to the United Nations were subject to censorship by our State and Defense Departments. I had no direct connection with the United Nations whatsoever.

The controls over me were exactly the same as though the forces under me were all American. All of my communications were to the American high command here.[25]

During his first wartime visit to the Far Eastern theater, Collins presented MacArthur with a UN flag in a ceremony atop the Dai Ichi Building, where it was flown, along with the United States flag, from that day, July 14, on, throughout the war. Sebald, who was present, observed that MacArthur "looked tired and ashen-gray" but "alert to the importance of the occasion." MacArthur responded to Collins' presentation: "I accept this flag with the deepest emotion. It symbolizes one of the greatest efforts a man has ever made to free himself." The brief rooftop ceremony was, indeed, symbolic of a historic occasion, for, as Sebald expressed it, "this was the first time the United Nations had at its disposal actual and potential forces sufficient to withstand naked aggression."[26]

MacArthur issued a general order on July 25 formally establishing the United Nations Command (UNC), of which he was commander in chief (CINCUNC). Simultaneously he also held the positions of SCAP over the occupation of Japan; commander in chief of the Far East Command of American ground, sea, and air forces in that theater; and commanding general, U.S. Army Forces, Far East (USAFFE), a largely administrative division. The general headquarters of UNC was located in the Dai Ichi Building and nearby structures in downtown Tokyo that already housed his Far East Command staff, because, as the official Army history states, "with few exceptions, staff members of the Far East Command were assigned comparable duties on the UNC staff. In effect, the GHQ, United Nations Command, was the GHQ, Far East Command, with an expanded mission." Willoughby and Wright, for instance, who were the assistant chiefs of staff for intelligence (G-2) and for operations (G-3) of the Far East Command, served in the same posts for the new UNC. Some such officers, like Willoughby, retained key roles in the SCAP administrative structure also. In other words, MacArthur was continuing another old habit, stocking his principal GHQ positions with trusted American Army officers, usually of long service under him. To no avail had the Australian high command protested this tactic during the days of his Southwest Pacific GHQ, as had the Allied powers during the past years of his

SCAP, GHQ, in occupied Japan and as America's allies in the Korean conflict would do. But MacArthur managed to fend off all attempts to make his American Army–dominated GHQ staffs from 1942 to 1951 truly representative of the coalition commands they ran. Perhaps his feeling was that in all three periods — the Southwest Pacific war, the occupation of Japan, and the Korean War — the United States Army bore the main responsibilities in operations and logistics, so it was realistic to have its officers in the key GHQ posts. Of course, too, there was the vital consideration to him that such assignments go only to officers whom he trusted implicitly, which, as always, narrowed the number to those whom he found not only competent but also personally loyal. Shortly MacArthur would carry this to the extreme, when he appointed Almond as commander of the X Corps in Korea while allowing him to retain his positions as chief of staff of SCAP, Far East Command, and USAFFE — a total of four positions held at the same time by one member of his inner circle.[27]

While ROK and American forces were endeavoring to stop the North Korean drive toward Pusan that summer, MacArthur was demanding more and more troops and Pentagon leaders were frantically trying to provide them from the already weak American defense establishment. On June 30 he indicated that two divisions from his occupation forces would be sufficient in Korea, but two days later he asked the JCS for a Marine RCT with supporting Marine air units, as well as reinforcements for the FEAF. The Joint Chiefs responded swiftly, informing him the next day that the Marine troops and aircraft would be sent, besides over 200 more bombers and fighters for the FEAF. On July 5, MacArthur said he needed the 2d Infantry Division, an airborne regiment, and an engineer special brigade. The Joint Chiefs were worried about draining the General Reserve (forces in the United States and Hawaii reserved for a national emergency mainly), so they asked him for an estimate of the total force requirements to drive the North Koreans back to the 38th Parallel, in the meantime holding in abeyance the approval of his specific requests. Two days later he replied that because the enemy army was much greater in size and firepower than earlier thought, the "minimum without which success will be extremely doubtful" would be "4 to 4½ full-strength infantry divisions, an airborne RCT complete with lift and an armored group composed of three medium tank battalions, together with reinforcing artillery and service elements." He added, "Forward planning must anticipate a probable additional requirement for fighters and light bombers, as well as for another fast carrier task force." Pentagon officials planned ways to raise American military strength overall as soon as possible, but the JCS, Johnson, and Truman immediately approved MacArthur's latest and largest request yet, and the units were alerted for shipment to Korea in some cases while in others the units were designated for mobilization from the National Guard, their readiness for actual movement overseas not projected for months. Assuring MacArthur that his theater's needs had their "active sympathetic consideration," the Joint Chiefs nonetheless reminded him of three of the main "difficulties" they faced in meeting his requests: "A. To date there has been no authorization for an increase in personnel in any of the services. B. We must maintain a suitable United States military posture in other parts of the world. C. There is a shortage of shipping which makes it impossible for the units you have requested to meet the schedule indicated by you."[28]

Meanwhile, MacArthur had received on July 8 an alarming report about the North Korean Army's effectiveness from General Dean, the 24th Division commander, which seemed to show that even what had been requested in additional forces would not be adequate to repel the enemy. On July 9, MacArthur made his boldest demand yet of the JCS:

The situation in Korea is critical. . . .

This force more and more assumes the aspect of a combination of Soviet leadership and technical guidance with Chinese Communist ground elements. . . .

Our own troops . . . are fighting with valor against overwhelming odds of more than ten to one. To build up, under these circumstances, sufficiently to hold the southern tip of Korea is becoming increasingly problematical.

I strongly urge that in addition to those forces already requisitioned, an army of at least four divisions, with all its component services, be dispatched to this area without delay and by every means of transportation available.[29]

The same day Admiral Radford sent a message to the Joint Chiefs urging them to act immediately to raise MacArthur's Marine RCT to division strength and to send him large numbers of additional aircraft and combat ships, as well as amphibious craft.

With MacArthur raising his demand from four to eight divisions in two days and with only four divisions left in the General Reserve after committing the 2d Division to Korea, the JCS faced the problem not only of how much further to go in supporting the defense of South Korea but also of how to maintain a capacity to respond to potential aggression against the United States, West Europe, and other areas of strategic importance. When Johnson and the Joint Chiefs reviewed with Truman the risks involved in weakening further the General Reserve and American forces in other overseas regions, the President directed the JCS to send two of its members to the Far East to get a better estimate of the situation and the needs. Generals Collins and Hoyt Vandenberg, the Army and Air Force Chiefs of Staff, were designated to make the trip, accompanied by four Pentagon staff officers.

Arriving in Tokyo on the morning of July 13, Collins and Vandenberg were taken forthwith to MacArthur's office, where they had a long, earnest conference with him, Almond, Walker, Stratemeyer, and Radford. The main topic, of course, was the total reinforcement in men and matériel needed to stop the North Korean offensive and to drive the enemy out of South Korea. Not surprisingly, MacArthur tended to dominate the talking. Collins described him as "cool and poised as always. He spoke with confidence and élan as he paced back and forth in his customary fashion. He always gave me the impression of addressing not just his immediate listeners but a larger audience unseen." MacArthur praised the toughness, firepower, and professionalism of the North Korean Army, urged that the JCS give top priority to Korea and "grab every ship in the Pacific and pour the support into the Far East," and reiterated his need for eight additional divisions and another army headquarters. Collins made a brief trip with Walker to Taegu late on the 13th, and the conference at the Dai Ichi Building resumed the next day. Among other topics, the men considered MacArthur's plans for an amphibious assault in the Inchon area, with Collins venturing the opinion that the 1st Marine Division could probably be used but arguing against Inchon as the landing site because of its unusually high tides. MacArthur was advised by the two JCS members that he should shape his strategy realistically according to the forces he currently had and those reinforcements already approved, because little more could be expected, in view of the dangerous depletion of the General Reserve.

Collins and Vandenberg left Tokyo on the afternoon of the 14th and, on returning to Washington, briefed the other JCS members, Secretary Johnson, and President Truman on their visit. Collins said he expressed to them his "agreement with Generals MacArthur and Walker that the Eighth Army and the ROK Army would be able to hold a bridgehead covering Pusan, but I urged prompt reinforcements." Although MacArthur did not get all the forces he called for, the Joint Chiefs provided everything they could by way of reinforcements. For example, of major American ground combat units from outside the Far East Command, he received the 2d Infantry Division in July, the 5th RCT and the 1st Provisional Marine Brigade in August, the 1st Marine Division and the 187th Airborne RCT in September, and the 3d Infantry Division in November.[30]

MacArthur's many requests that summer for troop replacements, fillers, and reinforcements and for weapons and equipment in huge quantities forced Pentagon leaders to push for a rapid expansion of the armed services. Mobilization of reserve and National Guard outfits began on July 20, and a supplementary military appropriations request of $10.5 billion was sent to Congress four days later. In early August, Congress abolished the ceilings on military manpower. The personnel strength of American ground, sea, and air forces in Korea grew from 45,000 on July 31 to 148,000 on August 31 and 233,000 by September 30, and reached nearly 360,000 by the time of MacArthur's departure the next April. Matériel shipments to MacArthur's command mounted proportionately, and the additions in armored and ordnance items increased even more rapidly.

During the two weeks after the Security Council's resolution of June 27 calling on UN members to assist South Korea, there had been much talk but disappointingly few international contributions to the war effort. In early July the JCS accepted offers from Britain, Australia, New Zealand, Canada, and the Netherlands of naval or air contingents, mostly small units. On July 14, Secretary-

General Lie issued an urgent appeal to the UN members for military assistance, "particularly ground forces." That same day the Joint Chiefs requested MacArthur's advice on the type, size, and logistical support of the international forces most needed. He replied the next day, setting forth in detail his recommended criteria; for example, he suggested infantry units of reinforced battalion size (about 1000 troops) with their own artillery and with supplies for sixty days, to be supported thereafter by the United States with reimbursements by the respective governments. The JCS, according to that body's official history, "immediately applied General MacArthur's criteria in judging the offers of aid that began to flow in following the Secretary-General's message." Ultimately nineteen nations, besides the United States and South Korea, contributed ground, air, naval, or medical units to the United Nations Command, but up to mid-September 1950 the only non-American UN ground force was the British 27th Infantry Brigade from Hong Kong, which went into action northwest of Taegu on September 5.[31]

MacArthur's establishment of the United Nations Command coincided with worsening conditions at the front, where Major General Hobart R. Gay's 1st Cavalry Division and Major General William B. Kean's 25th Infantry Division had joined the 24th Division in trying to stop the North Korean drive toward Taegu. Sometimes, states the Army's history, these two fresh divisions retreated "in circumstances that seemed not to justify [such action], and with troops in panic and out of control." On July 26, when North Korean forces were within forty miles of Taegu at several points west and northwest of the city, General "Johnny" Walker issued a warning order for all units to prepare to withdraw southeastward to new defensive positions, their location and the time to be announced shortly. That day Walker telephoned GHQ in Tokyo and talked to Almond about the precarious situation. He asked Almond to get MacArthur's authorization to move Eighth Army headquarters from Taegu to Pusan. When Almond and MacArthur later discussed Walker's call, they concluded that he intended to withdraw not just his headquarters but all his combat forces to the vicinity of Pusan. Actually the defensive line Walker had in mind was along the Naktong River, with Taegu inside his perimeter. Nevertheless, MacArthur decided it was time for a talk with his Eighth Army commander; Almond notified Walker that he and MacArthur would fly to Taegu the next morning.

When the *Bataan* landed at the Taegu airstrip at 9:45 A.M. on July 27, according to one observer MacArthur emerged from the plane "grim-faced and business-like," though when he departed that afternoon "he was smiling and exuding confidence." Mac-Arthur and Almond went directly into conference with Walker. Almond, who was the only one of the three present to describe the session later, recalled that MacArthur said to Walker: "You can make all the reconnaissances you want. You can put your engineers to work if you desire in preparing intermediate trenches, but I will give you the order to retire from this position and there will be no Dunkirk in this command. To retire to Pusan will be unacceptable." After the conference of the three generals, they met with Walker's staff, at which time, as reported by Almond, "Walker said with a very commanding attitude, 'This army fights where it stands. There will be no retirement.' Most of his staff looked surprised because, evidently prior to that time, they had been hoping and recommending that a withdrawal be made." While at Taegu, MacArthur also conferred with Rhee and Muccio, attended Eighth Army and Fifth Air Force briefings, and visited the wounded soldiers at a nearby hospital. As he prepared to board the *Bataan* for the flight back to Tokyo, he told a group of correspondents: "The enemy has lost his great chance for victory in the last three weeks. . . . This does not mean that victory passes to us instantly or without a long hard row and the most difficult struggle. That we will have new heartaches and new setbacks is inherent in the situation, but I have never been more confident in victory — in ultimate victory — in my life than I am now." Two days later Walker visited his division command posts and told the officers to warn their troops that the Eighth Army had reached a "stand or die" point: "There will be no more retreating, withdrawal, or readjustment of the lines. . . . There is no line behind us to which we can retreat. . . . We are going to hold this line. We are going to win."[32]

In the following six weeks the desperate struggle to hold the Naktong perimeter was fought, and the American and ROK defenders found that "stand or die" orders from generals often meant for the combat soldiers lots of dying even in successful stands. The

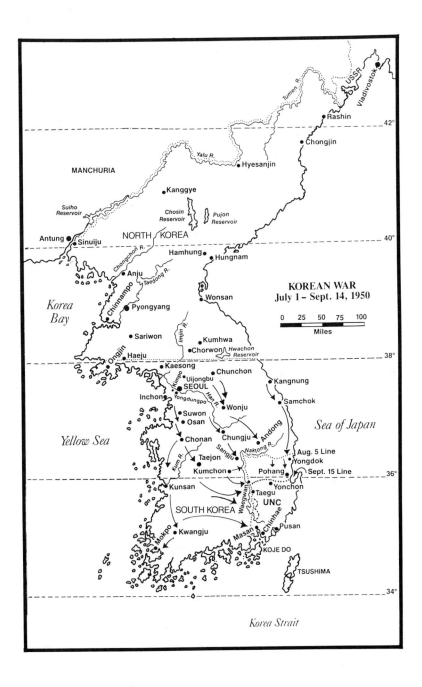

KOREAN WAR
July 1 – Sept. 14, 1950

first major enemy threat came in early August at the south end of the line, where the 25th Infantry Division and two recently arrived units, the 1st Marine Provisional Brigade from California and the 5th RCT from Hawaii, thwarted a North Korean drive toward Masan, which was only thirty miles west of Pusan. During the month of August, the enemy made several other major attempts to break through the perimeter elsewhere, but Walker was brilliant in exploiting his interior lines of defense to move reserves rapidly from one threatened area of the front to another. On the west side, enemy bridgeheads across the Naktong River were established northwest and southwest of Taegu, but they were contained, and most were reduced by the end of the month. On the north side, the ROK divisions were slowly pushed southward an average of fifteen miles in depth during the period August 6–26, but no serious enemy penetration was made. Along the east coast the North Koreans drove as far south as Pohang, cutting off a ROK division that had to be evacuated by the U.S. Navy, but by late August Pohang had been retaken and the line stabilized twelve miles up the coast.

During August Walker's reinforcements had included the Marine brigade and the 5th RCT and also Major General Laurence B. Keiser's 2d Infantry Division from the States, which relieved the exhausted 24th Division in the western defenses. Walker had also received over 500 Pershing and Sherman tanks, which meant, as one historian phrased it, "the single most valuable weapon the Communists possessed [the T-34 tank] had been checkmated." Walker got another kind of help, too: to free him of responsibilities not related to the battlefield, MacArthur created the Japan Logistical Command on August 24, headed by General Weible, as related earlier. Weible's headquarters was set up in the Yokohama buildings formerly occupied by Walker's staff. Undoubtedly, to the hard-pressed Walker this release from supply and service functions for his headquarters was welcome, if long overdue.[33]

Coordination of Air Force and Navy air operations, which involved over 28,000 sorties that summer, was direly lacking during the first month or so of the Korean conflict. In August 1949, MacArthur had created the Joint Strategic Plans and Operations Group (JSPOG), an eight-man body of Army, Navy, and Air Force officers headed by General Wright (G-3). Its job was "to assist and advise the Commander-in-Chief, Far East, on matters pertaining to his exercise of unified command over Army, Navy, and Air Force forces, allocated to the Far East Command." Under the stresses of war and with the rapid buildup of ground, sea, and air forces in the theater, Wright's little group tried valiantly but not always successfully to cope with the multiplying problems of joint staff planning and operations. Conflicts developed early between Air Force and Navy leaders over operational control of carrier strikes on inland targets and over the nature and procedures of the several committees that evolved to handle target selection. Lack of cooperation between the services produced in July a number of missions that were wasteful of time and equipment and, unhappily, lives, as a result of several air attacks on friendly forces. MacArthur delegated to Almond the task of working out with Joy and Stratemeyer and their staffs better arrangements for coordination of land-based and carrier air operations, which led to fairly satisfactory compromises on operational control and target selection. At first, MacArthur assured Stratemeyer that he could "run his show as he saw fit," but with the continuing inability of the ground forces to halt the enemy advance, he stepped into the picture in mid-July and told his air chief that strategic raids would have to become secondary for the FEAF Bomber Command, with priority going to air strikes in frontline areas.[34]

Some of the heaviest fighting in August took place in the mountainous region around Waegwan, a town on the east bank of the Naktong River only eleven miles northwest of Taegu. The defending forces in the area were the 1st Cavalry Division and the ROK 1st Division. Concerned about the growing threat to Taegu, MacArthur told Stratemeyer on August 14 that he wanted FEAF B-29 Superfortresses to deliver a carpet, or saturation, bombing raid on the North Korean positions near Waegwan. For weeks B-29s had been used against targets at or near the North Korean front-line positions, despite FEAF leaders' private objections to that misuse of the bombers that had been the backbone of the strategic air war against Japan in 1944–1945. MacArthur had told Stratemeyer to use B-29s "to strafe, if necessary," in order to stop the enemy advance. Stratemeyer relayed the latest MacArthur mission for the B-29s to Major General Emmett (Rosie) O'Donnell, Jr., head of the FEAF Bomber Command, who then plotted a 27-square-mile rectangle north of Waegwan for the saturation attack. Intelligence reports indicated that as many as 40,000 enemy troops were assembling in that area for a major assault toward Taegu. On August 16, 98 B-29s dropped nearly 1000 tons of bombs from 10,000 feet up on the supposed assembly area. An Air Force official historian said, "It was the biggest employment of airpower in direct support of ground forces since the Normandy invasion." But another official source found that "the UN Command could not show by specific, concrete evidence that this massive bombing attack had killed a single North Korean soldier." North Korean prisoners later avowed that none of their units had been in the target zone when the B-29s attacked. When MacArthur ordered a carpet bombing on another alleged enemy assembly area three days later, Stratemeyer persuaded him to cancel it for want of adequate intelligence data.[35]

The Joint Chiefs informed MacArthur on July 31 that strategic bombing of North Korean industrial targets was "highly desirable." He was not precluded from using B-29s on tactical support missions, but the JCS sent him a list of targets to be destroyed at North Korean cities from Pyongyang and Chinnampo on the west to Rashin, seventeen miles from the Soviet border, on the east. The Joint Chiefs told him two more B-29 groups were being sent, primarily to augment the strategic bombing campaign. The targets at Rashin included the rail yards, port facilities, and oil-storage tank farm. O'Donnell sent his B-29s to Rashin on August 12, but the bombing was ineffective because of poor weather. Ten days later another B-29 raid on Rashin was scheduled, but it had to be diverted to Chongjin because of heavy clouds. After State Department objections to bombing so near Soviet territory, Rashin was removed from the FEAF target list on September 1. Two weeks later Stratemeyer reported, "Practically all of the major military and industrial targets strategically important to the enemy forces and to their war potential have now been neutralized." By then the USSR and Red China were hotly protesting an accidental FEAF strafing of an air base near Antung, Manchuria; a possible Soviet aircraft, moreover, had been shot down by U.S. Navy carrier planes over the Yellow Sea. In his memoirs Kennan, like a number of contemporary American officials and reporters, indicated that he thought MacArthur had conceived the idea for the Rashin raids:

"This had caused me to doubt that General MacArthur was under any very effective control by anybody in Washington, or that anyone really knew what he was doing." In truth, the JCS had pushed for the Rashin attacks, though MacArthur, during those critical days of fighting along the Naktong, probably wanted to use all the B-29s, however unsuitable, in close support of ground operations.[36]

Near the end of August, when it seemed the North Korean Army had been so crippled by air and artillery bombardments and by its many costly piecemeal attacks that it could not mount another large-scale assault, the battle for the Naktong perimeter suddenly erupted as the enemy launched the heaviest attacks yet. The ferocious assaults hit the UNC defenses all along the perimeter. On the west, the North Koreans gained new bridgeheads across the Naktong River, but most were gradually eliminated within ten days after heavy fighting by the 1st Cavalry and 2d and 25th Infantry divisions, now joined by the British 27th Infantry Brigade. On the north side of the perimeter, the enemy forces almost achieved a major breakthrough on the ROK right flank. The North Korean drive was finally stopped after it reached Pohang and Yongchon, when the battered 24th Division was ordered from its reserve area to assist in the crisis. By September 10, the most savage of the North Korean attacks had subsided, and Kim's army had suffered over 10,000 casualties in ten days. Along the perimeter by then the North Korean Army numbered about 88,000 troops, while Walker's ground forces (including service troops) had grown to 180,000. The Eighth Army's strength in tanks now was five times greater than that of the North Korean Army, and Walker's artillery was vastly superior. Since it entered combat, the Eighth Army had received over 2 million tons of supplies and equipment; on the other hand, the North Korean troops at the front were short of all kinds of items, their supply lines being under constant attack by FEAF and carrier planes. Kim's air force had been all but wiped out and his few naval craft destroyed, but the FEAF and the Seventh Fleet held firm mastery of the skies and seas and were still adding more planes and ships. The North Korean gamble to reach Pusan before the Naktong perimeter could be sufficiently strengthened had failed.[37]

CHAPTER XV

From Formosa to Inchon

1. Beginning of Troubles

FOR SOME TIME before the Korean hostilities commenced, it will be recalled, not only MacArthur but also Secretary of Defense Johnson and the Joint Chiefs of Staff had favored a Far East Command survey of Chiang Kai-shek's defense capabilities and needs on Formosa, prefatory to the United States' sending military assistance to the Nationalist Chinese regime. During the high-level decision-making of the first week of war, the President had not offered much encouragement to those who wanted stronger American support of Chiang. He had decided on June 27 to use the Seventh Fleet to neutralize Formosa and, three days later, to decline Chiang's offer of troops for the defense of South Korea. When the State Department notified the Nationalist government on July 1 of the rejection of its troop offer, however, the message also said that MacArthur would be in communication with Chiang soon about the dispatch of a Far East Command mission to discuss Formosa's defense needs. In early July, Admiral Struble visited Taipei, the Formosan capital, to confer about the role of his Seventh Fleet in the Formosa Strait. When Collins was in Tokyo, on July 13–14, MacArthur remarked that he intended to visit Chiang when the Korean military situation became less critical, but he told the Chief of Staff that he did not want a Nationalist Chinese force in Korea both because its transfer would weaken Formosa's defenses and because, since the Eighth Army would have to support it with artillery and supplies, it would be "an albatross around our neck for months."

In view of increasing reports after mid-July indicating an imminent Communist Chinese invasion of Formosa, Johnson and the JCS recommended to the National Security Council that MacArthur be authorized to send reconnaissance flights over the mainland coast opposite Formosa and to dispatch a survey team to determine Formosa's needs in military matériel and that subsequently the United States supply arms and equipment to the Nationalist Chinese forces. On July 27 the NSC adopted the recommendations, and Truman gave his approval. With new alarming reports coming in about the Communist buildup along the Formosa Strait coast, the Joint Chiefs recommended the next day that Chiang's forces be allowed to launch pre-emptive air strikes and to mine mainland coastal waters to repel the alleged invasion armada. Acheson objected strongly, however, and the new JCS proposals were dropped. In the meantime, the JCS sent what Bradley said "amounted to a 'war warning' " to MacArthur on the 28th regarding the imminent Red Chinese assault and also informed him of their recommendations. The Joint Chiefs thought a Communist force of 200,000 troops and 4000 ships and amphibious craft was assembling along the shores opposite Formosa. MacArthur responded on the 29th: "I concur completely with the recommendation of the Joint Chiefs of Staff. I am proceeding to Formosa with a selected group of staff officers on July 31st to make a brief reconnaissance of the situation there." In reply, the JCS suggested that, pending the outcome of further discussions on Formosa policy between Pentagon and State officials, MacArthur might "desire" to postpone his own trip for a while and send one of his senior officers instead. But the Joint Chiefs added, "If you feel it necessary to proceed personally on the 31st, please feel free to go since the responsibility is yours." As they probably expected, MacArthur said he would go.[1]

On July 31, MacArthur, Stratemeyer, Struble, and thirteen other senior officers of the Far East Command flew on two C-54s to Taipei. After two days of conferences with Chiang and his top officers, they returned to Tokyo. Controversies began to swirl almost immediately about the nature of the journey. In a press statement the day after he came back from Taipei, MacArthur stated that the trip was "primarily for the purpose of making a short reconnaissance of the potentiality of its [Formosa's] defenses against possible attack." He praised Chiang Kai-shek's "indomitable determination to resist Communist domination," and he announced that "arrangements have been completed for effective coordination between the American forces under my command and those of the Chinese Government, the better to meet any attack which a hostile force might be foolish enough to attempt." On August 3 Sebald, who had not been invited on the Taipei trip, told MacArthur that Acheson wanted information about what had been discussed on Formosa. The general "made it clear," according to Sebald, "that he had no intention of providing details" to the Secretary of State, because "the talks were purely military in nature . . . and hence what was said and done was his sole responsibility, and not that of the State Department."[2]

But the Joint Chiefs were uneasy, too; he had not immediately sent them a report, and during his flight to Taipei he had radioed the Pentagon that he planned to dispatch three F-80 jet fighter squadrons to Formosa if the Communist Chinese invaded. The State Department's representative at Taipei learned of this plan, but erroneously relayed to Acheson word that MacArthur had already issued orders for the planes to go to Formosa. This news quickly found its way to the Joint Chiefs, Johnson, and even Truman. MacArthur received a strong message from the JCS on August 3 that such action involved "political" issues and required approval at the "highest levels" of the United States government. The general replied that he had not intended to send the fighters to Formosa unless it was attacked. The following day he got another sternly worded message, this time from Johnson on orders from Truman. After reminding him that the President's decision of June 27 on the neutralization of Formosa was still in effect, the Secretary of Defense said, "No one other than the President as Commander-in-Chief has the authority to order or authorize preventive action against concentrations on the 'Chinese' mainland. . . . The most vital national interest requires that no action of ours precipitate general war or give excuse to others to do so." MacArthur responded that he understood the President's policy on neutralizing Formosa and had been "operating meticulously in accordance therewith." He reassured Johnson: "I understand thoroughly the limitations on my authority as Theater Commander and you need have no anxiety that I will in any way exceed them. I hope neither the President nor you has been misled by false or speculative reports from whatever source, official or non-official."

On August 5, the Far East Command Liaison Group, headed by General Fox, MacArthur's deputy chief of staff, arrived on Formosa to begin a three-week survey of the defensive matériel needs of Chiang's forces. The Fox mission found, in effect, that in the National Chinese Army "enough arms and equipment could be collected to furnish completely around 40,000 men." From the Liaison Group's report in late August, MDAP officials figured the Nationalists on Formosa needed $271 million in arms, equipment, and supplies, particularly munitions. Nearly $10 million worth of ammunition was shipped to Formosa from United States stocks by November.[3]

Although Almond prepared a full report immediately after their return to Japan, MacArthur inexplicably waited until August 7 to send the Joint Chiefs his official report on the Formosan trip of July 31 to August 1 (and it was an abbreviated version of Almond's paper). As for the needs of Chiang's forces, the report to the JCS stated: "There is a real potential in the Armed Forces on Formosa, but a definite and substantial improvement in equipment, organization, communications, training and in developing sound methods of direct command responsibility is required." Chiang's defense plans "appear to be inadequate, incomplete, and undeveloped in certain respects. There are indications of a weak concept of joint operations." Decisions and actions by MacArthur, concurred in by Chiang, consisted of dispatch of the Far East Command Liaison Group to survey Formosa's military requirements, establishment of a Far East Command communications center at Taipei, continued patrolling of the Formosa Strait by elements of the Seventh Fleet, reconnaissance flights by American planes over coastal areas of mainland China "to determine the imminence of any attack" against Formosa, "familiarization flights for small groups" of FEAF fighters to Formosa with landings there for refueling only, and "immediate coordination in the defense of Formosa" of the planning of MacArthur's and Chiang's senior air and naval commanders.

Except for the FEAF fighters' flights to Formosa and the coordinated planning by Chinese and American air and naval officers, the JCS could have hardly taken exception to MacArthur's report. His decisions were in line with what had been previously authorized — and surely in accord with the Joint Chiefs' deep interest in the defense of Formosa. Had MacArthur simply sent his report to Washington promptly, his superiors would have been spared much anxiety during the needless six-day wait while Acheson and the press became unduly excited over a trip that really was not very controversial. Acheson, writing in 1969, remained convinced that MacArthur had actually "ordered" the three FEAF squadrons to Formosa without telling the JCS, cancelling the order after the tough JCS message of August 3 and before the aircraft departed. A number of contemporary and later accounts of his journey to Formosa have included the allegation that he went there in defiance of the Joint Chiefs or without their authorization, that he struck some kind of secret deal with Chiang for American combat personnel to be committed if Formosa were invaded, and that the episode was the first serious confrontation in the Truman-MacArthur controversy of 1950–1951.[4] Seldom has so minor an incident given rise to so many myths. (Oddly, no one has shown much interest in what happened to the 4000-ship Communist Chinese invasion fleet.)

At the time Truman did not appear especially disturbed over MacArthur's trip to Formosa, but he was concerned about the general's possible misunderstanding of the administration's policy on Formosa. So he designated Ambassador W. Averell Harriman, one of his most distinguished and trusted advisers, to "discuss the Far Eastern political situation" with the general. Harriman was in Tokyo on August 6 and 8 for sessions with MacArthur, and traveled to Korea on the 7th; he was accompanied by Generals Matthew B. Ridgway, Lauris Norstad, and Frank E. Lowe, and by several aides. Harriman pointed out to MacArthur that Chiang Kai-shek's overriding ambition was to reconquer the Chinese mainland, which the Generalissimo knew was impossible unless the United States could be drawn into a war with Communist China. MacArthur offered the facetious remark "It might be a good idea to let him land and get rid of him that way." Harriman later reported to Truman that his talks with the general had been "cordial," that MacArthur reaffirmed that he had discussed "only military matters" with Chiang, that he still thought we should quit "kicking Chiang around," and yet that he would, "as a good soldier, obey any orders that he received from the President." But Harriman cautioned the President, "For reasons which are rather difficult to explain, I did not feel that we came to a full agreement on the way we believed things should be handled on Formosa and with the Generalissimo. He accepted the President's position and will act accordingly, but without full conviction. He has a strange idea that we should back anyone who will fight communism." Harriman, Ridgway, and Norstad also discussed the Inchon assault plan with MacArthur, and Harriman said, "The three of us came back determined to recommend it, and did so in a memorandum to the President." Ridgway said he was "particularly impressed" during the Tokyo discussions on Korean military matters by MacArthur's presentations and attitude, which "did not reveal the slightest lack of loyalty to authority. . . . He was confident, optimistic, eloquent, and utterly without fear — yet he was completely a soldier, seemingly ready to implement, without cavil or complaint, whatever decisions his superiors communicated to him." MacArthur later remarked that Harriman "left me with a feeling of concern and uneasiness that the situation in the Far East was little understood and mistakenly downgraded in high circles in Washington."[5]

Both Truman and MacArthur made public comments on August 10 about the general's trip to Formosa, though they were quite different in tone and implication. Truman remarked at a news conference that day, "General MacArthur and I are in perfect agreement. . . . I am satisfied with what he is doing." In a press release MacArthur re-emphasized that only military topics had been discussed with Chiang during their Taipei talks; he had not gotten into political or diplomatic issues, such as the future of the Chinese government or "anything else outside the scope of my military responsibility."[6] He concluded bitterly that his trip to Formosa had been

maliciously misrepresented to the public by those who invariably in the past have propagandized a policy of defeatism and appeasement in the Pacific. I hope the American people will not be misled by sly insinuations, brash speculations, and bold misstatements invariably attributed to anonymous sources, so insidiously fed them both nationally and internationally by persons 10,000 miles away from the actual events, if they are not indeed designed, to promote disunity and destroy faith and confidence in American purposes and institutions and American representatives at this time of great world peril.[7]

Although it was undoubtedly not intended as retaliation for MacArthur's acerbic statement, the Joint Chiefs, at Truman's direction, sent him an order four days later that "no squadrons or other US forces be based on Formosa unless specific approval has been given."

About three hours after Harriman's plane took off on August 8 for the return flight to Washington, MacArthur had a private conference with General Lowe, an old friend and admirer of both MacArthur and Truman. Arriving on August 6 with Harriman's group, Lowe, in the unique position of presidential assistant for liaison with the United Nations Command, had come to serve as Truman's "eyes and ears." A reserve officer and veteran of both world wars, he was sixty-six when Truman called him at his Maine farm and said, "I want you to go to Japan and Korea and keep me informed." They had become fast friends during the Second World War, when Lowe served as the War Department's liaison officer with the Senate Committee to Investigate the National Defense Program, which Truman ably headed. When he became President, Truman sent Lowe on several secret missions, including ones to the Philippines and to Japan; while on the latter assignment, he conferred with MacArthur in Tokyo in January 1946.

Since Truman and MacArthur had never met in person, the unusual Lowe mission was a commendable effort by the President to avert breakdowns in communication with his Far East commander, and it began with good intentions on the part of all three men. Truman asked Lowe to tell the general "I have never had anything but the utmost confidence in his ability to do the Far Eastern job, and I think I've shown that by action, as well as by words."[8] On August 12, MacArthur, obviously well disposed toward the arrangement, wrote the President:

At my suggestion, General Lowe is returning to Washington for a few days in order to give you a firsthand and comprehensive picture of the situation out here which he has gathered from talks with me and members of my staff, formal briefings, a ground survey of the battlefront, and an aerial reconnaissance over vital sectors of Korea. It was my thought that he could give you his impressions much better orally than by written report.

I hold General Lowe in high esteem, and the direct liaison which he can effect will be of real value.[9]

Truman replied that he "had a very interesting conversation with him [Lowe] about his interviews with you and the Field Commanders in Korea. I am very happy that the General made the trip. He will be going back to Japan very shortly. . . . I am hopeful that the Korean matter will work out as successfully as your south[west] Pacific campaign did and I am sure it will."[10]

Lowe, who left Japan on orders from Truman in April 1951 about an hour after MacArthur's flight left Haneda, first talked publicly about his UNC mission in an interview in January 1952, at which time he told the reporter that he

> had nothing to do with policy and he took pains to have nothing to do with the strategy. To keep from appearing to be a spy on the latter, he meticulously stayed away from all briefing conferences and to avoid appearing to be a spy on MacArthur, he carefully sent duplicates of his constant reports to the President, to MacArthur. MacArthur saw every one of his reports but the last one, and MacArthur was already out when that one was made.[11]

Lowe said MacArthur permitted him "the greatest leeway. He could go where he chose." He was given an office only a few doors from MacArthur's on the sixth floor of the Dai Ichi Building, and in the GHQ organizational scheme he was listed as attached to the Office of the Military Secretary (Whitney). On Truman's instructions, he spent much of his time in Korea, reporting on the performances of commanders and units. During the UNC drive toward the Yalu River that autumn, Major General Oliver P. Smith, commander of the 1st Marine Division, found Lowe invaluable as "the only means of physical liaison between the X Corps and the Eighth Army," since each of those commands reported separately to MacArthur. The "gentleman farmer" from Maine, as Lowe referred to himself, left his mission with a deep, abiding admiration for both Truman and MacArthur, who "actually saw things alike" on many issues, but "the two were deliberately pulled apart and pitted against each other by third parties." Lowe believed that he "failed" in his mission of keeping the lines of communication open between the two leaders because some of his key messages to Truman were "sidetracked" and never reached him. He said that he simply "couldn't cope with that damned Pentagon crowd," who resented his assignment and "misled" the President about MacArthur.[12] Further research on Lowe's role in the Korean War should provide a fascinating story about his hitherto little-known mission.

On his first trip to Tokyo in August, Lowe was instructed by the President to report on "General MacArthur's physical condition and ability to withstand stresses incident to his duty." Lowe wrote that the general was "hale and hearty," and apparently Truman pursued the matter no further. The President's concern may have been prompted by a bizarre episode, revealed only recently. Brigadier General Thomas J. Davis, who had been MacArthur's aide in the 1930s and had served on Eisenhower's headquarters staff during and after World War II, prepared a memorandum for the JCS on his observations of MacArthur's alleged mental and emotional instability during off-duty hours while he was the Army Chief of Staff. The Joint Chiefs "did not act" on Davis' accusations, according to the writer who uncovered the document.[13] Indeed, the incident revealed more about the ugly side of Davis than of MacArthur.

Truman's troubles with MacArthur may have been exacerbated by the invitation to the latter from the Veterans of Foreign Wars, dated August 17, asking that he send a message to be read at their annual "encampment" in Chicago on the 28th. The topic was left up to the general, who could easily have picked the Japanese peace treaty or the heroism of the American boys on the Korean front lines but, instead, unwisely chose the sensitive issue of Formosa. On the 20th he sent his message to the VFW, explaining that it was intended to correct the "misconceptions currently being voiced concerning the relationship of Formosa to our strategic potential in the Pacific." Most of the statement was drawn almost verbatim from his memo of June 14, copies of which he had given to Johnson, Bradley, and Dulles and which had been read at the Blair House session on June 25. Again he used the analogy of Formosa as "an unsinkable aircraft carrier and submarine tender," which had appeared in his messages to the JCS as early as May. After fervently arguing the case for Formosa's strategic value to America's western defense line, he shifted to the attack against those who opposed aggressive American support of Chiang: "Nothing could be more fallacious than the threadbare argument by those who advocate appeasement and defeatism in the Pacific that if we defend Formosa we alienate continental Asia." He continued, resorting to another oft-used theme of his: "Those who speak thus do not understand the Orient. . . . It is in the pattern of the Oriental psychology to respect and follow aggressive, resolute, and dynamic leadership — to quickly turn on a leadership characterized by timidity or vacillation." In closing he cited as a notable case of decisive leadership the President's dispatch of the Seventh Fleet to the Formosa Strait, but he apparently viewed it only in terms of deterring a Communist invasion of Formosa: "The decision of President Truman on June 27th lighted into flame a lamp of hope throughout Asia that was burning dimly towards extinction. . . . It swept aside in one great monumental stroke all of the hypocrisy and the sophistry which has confused and deluded so many people distant from the actual scene."[14]

MacArthur's GHQ public relations office released his VFW message to the press in advance. It was published in full in the *New York Times* on August 29 and in *U.S. News & World Report* on September 1, as well as in excerpted form in many other papers and periodicals. The *U.S. News* issue, which went to press late on August 25, was brought to the attention that evening of Acheson, who became outraged. The next morning Truman, also upset by the message, read its contents aloud at a meeting with Acheson, Johnson, and the Joint Chiefs. He asked whether any of them had known about it in advance; none had. "The whole tenor of the message," Truman said later, "was critical of the very policy which he had so recently told Harriman he would support. . . . It was my opinion that this statement could only serve to confuse the world as to just what our Formosa policy was." For a while after the meeting Johnson hesitated to order MacArthur to withdraw it, as Truman had instructed during the session. Stephen Early, Johnson's deputy and an old friend of the general, was also reluctant to see such "drastic" action taken. After numerous talks between Johnson, Early, Acheson, and Harriman, Johnson's hesitation came to the President's attention. Thereupon, already short of patience with Johnson, whom he would dismiss in less than two weeks, Truman dictated to the Secretary of Defense the order to be sent promptly to MacArthur: "The President of the United States directs that you withdraw your message for [the] National Encampment of Veterans of Foreign Wars, because various features with respect to Formosa are in conflict with the policy of the United States and its position in the United Nations." Later in the day Johnson learned that MacArthur had sent his message to Chicago by Army communications. He went to the White House and informed Truman. According to Johnson, "The President was quite indignant. There was discussion at that time between the President and myself about relieving MacArthur as Korean commander, [but] not in any other field. . . . The conclusion [was] that we would do nothing about it at that time." Truman said he gave "serious thought" to "replacing him with General Bradley" as CINCUNC, keeping MacArthur as SCAP. He decided against such a change, because "it would have been difficult to avoid the appearance of a demotion, and I had no desire to hurt General MacArthur personally. My only concern was to let the world know that his statement was not official policy."[15]

When MacArthur received the Truman-dictated order from Johnson, he astoundingly sent back a protest, arguing that his VFW statement was in accord with Truman's policy, that the views were strictly his "personal" ones as a private citizen, and that a withdrawal statement after the message was already in process of publication would be a futile gesture. In case he lost his appeal, MacArthur enclosed a brief withdrawal statement for Johnson to forward to the VFW. In reply, Johnson simply notified the general that his withdrawal message had been sent to the VFW. Lowe, who considered himself "utterly loyal" to Truman, had read and approved MacArthur's message of August 20 for the veterans' convention. He said that both he and MacArthur were "shocked and surprised" by the withdrawal order, since "they believed the message expressed support of Mr. Truman's Far Eastern Policy." The episode marked the beginning of the alienation of Lowe from certain State and Defense officials, though it did not harm his relationship with Truman.

The President sent MacArthur a message on August 29 that was conciliatory. Hoping that it would help the general to understand the larger context, he enclosed a copy of a letter of August 25 from Warren R. Austin, U.S. ambassador to the United Nations, to Secretary-General Lie, setting forth the administration's position on Formosa. It stated that the United States had no territorial ambitions regarding the island, wanted Formosa neutralized for the present, and welcomed UN efforts to settle peacefully the permanent status of Formosa. Much of Austin's letter was based on a statement by Truman to Congress on Formosa policy on July 19. Both the President's and Austin's moves had been made to counter recent Moscow and Peking charges that the United States planned to occupy Formosa and promote an invasion of the mainland by Chiang's forces. Truman had also been agitated by a fiery speech by Secretary of the Navy Francis P. Matthews on August 25, in which he bluntly advocated a "preventive war" with the Soviet Union before that nation's nuclear and conventional weapons systems grew stronger. Truman noted that, unlike MacArthur, the Secretary of the Navy was "very contrite and full of regrets" about his irresponsible remarks. Nevertheless, Matthews soon was sent to Ireland as ambassador.[16]

Truman had become outraged not about the Formosa trip but about the VFW message. What upset him was not some new position the general had taken, for nearly all the phrases had appeared in previous MacArthur messages to Washington. The President was angered because MacArthur had switched channels in expressing his differences over strategy and policy — from classified messages to his superiors to a statement to the public. And the general had done so at a most inopportune time for the United States government in its strategy to counter Communist charges about America's interest in Formosa. At the Senate hearings on MacArthur's relief in the late spring of 1951, Bradley, Collins, and Acheson each pointed to different consequences of MacArthur's VFW message. Bradley told the senators that, though not an act of "military insubordination," MacArthur's statement was the first act in "an accumulation" that led to his recall. MacArthur's "various statements, without being cleared by the Government, were contrary to custom in the services, and, in my opinion," Bradley said, "if allowed to continue on indefinitely would jeopardize the civilian control of the military." Collins admitted that "there was . . . no clear-cut difference between the views of the

Joint Chiefs of Staff and those expressed by General MacArthur" in his VFW message regarding Formosa's strategic value, but "the thing that did disturb us . . . was the sort of imputation contained in the letter that we wanted Formosa as a military base." According to Acheson in his testimony, MacArthur's statement was "dangerous" because it resulted in "great damage" to America's world image and was exploited propagandistically by the Communists. Acheson quoted from a General Assembly speech by Andrei Vishinsky, Soviet ambassador to the UN, in which he distorted MacArthur's words to place the United States, said the Secretary of State, "in the eyes of the world into the role of an aggressor nation which was trying to take advantage of the situation in China and seize portions of that territory." Acheson maintained that MacArthur's action made it appear that on foreign policy there were "two voices speaking on behalf of the United States," the President and the general.[17] (Of course, MacArthur's defenders pointed out that the Communists had exploited more than just the propaganda angle of Acheson's own defense-perimeter address of January 1950.)

Truman, in trying to demonstrate to the American public that he, not Joe McCarthy, was the nation's chief executive, had found since January that it was no simple matter to control the Wisconsin senator. But as the commander in chief of the nation's armed services, he surely could act decisively to counter one of his generals. The forced withdrawal of the VFW message should have been a loud and clear signal to MacArthur that he was out of line. Unhappily, because of the general's personality and because of potential political reverberations that could cost him and his party dearly, Truman would discover that command and control of his Far Eastern commander were not the same thing.

2. *MacArthur's Plains of Abraham*

In the Southwest Pacific from 1943 to 1945, MacArthur had used surprise amphibious assaults behind strong Japanese defensive positions with impressive results. On the other hand, the most notable such operation in the war against Germany was the landing at Anzio, Italy, in early 1944, which was a costly near-fiasco that did not outflank the German main line to the south. Although neither was directly involved in the disappointing Anzio undertaking, Bradley and Collins, as commanders in the European theater, were in on many formal and informal analyses of that amphibious attack and were acutely aware of the high risks involved in such ventures. At the hearings of the House Armed Services Committee in October 1949, Bradley, who had recently become the JCS chairman, offered the unwise prediction "Large-scale amphibious operations . . . will never occur again." MacArthur, as early as his Suwon trip of June 29, 1950, quickly conceived of an amphibious thrust deep in the rear of the North Korean Army as the best way to win, but Bradley, Collins, and a number of other top Army officers in the Pentagon, who were predominantly veterans of the war in Europe, were wary and reluctant when the Far Eastern commander first began talking about a major amphibious operation in Korea.

MacArthur, Almond, and Wright's JSPOG began planning about July 2 for Operation Bluehearts, an amphibious assault on July 22 at Inchon, the port for Seoul, employing the 1st Cavalry Division and the Marine RCT that had just been requested. But Bluehearts was cancelled on the 10th, because the 1st Cavalry had to be committed against the North Korean drive; besides, it was learned the Marines could not reach Korea before early August. Meanwhile, MacArthur told Wright to keep his JSPOG staff working on other plans for a later amphibious operation, still preferably at Inchon but this time using the 2d Infantry Division and the 5th Marine RCT, both en route to the theater; the operation was codenamed Chromite. Revealing few details of his plan, MacArthur informed the Pentagon on July 23 that he intended to launch Chromite on September 15. But when the Marines and the 2d Division arrived a week or so later, he was forced to send them into action immediately, thus upsetting his Inchon plan again. After getting an early indication from the JCS that the 5th Marine RCT (to be redesignated the 1st Provisional Marine Brigade when it joined the Eighth Army in Korea) would be reinforced shortly by the rest of the 1st Marine Division, MacArthur received word in late July that only the 1st Marine Regiment would be added. Finally, on August 10, the JCS said he could also have the 7th Marine Regiment, thereby making possible for use in Chromite the full division, three regiments strong, counting the Marine outfit withdrawn from the Naktong perimeter.

Two days later MacArthur approved a new edition of the Chromite plan, calling for an amphibious attack at Inchon on September 15 by the 1st Marine Division and an unnamed Army division, which would move on to take Seoul while the Eighth Army was breaking out of the Naktong perimeter to link up with the Chromite force south of the capital. The Army division that was subsequently designated for Chromite was Major General David G. Barr's 7th Infantry; it was the fourth of the occupation divisions in Japan and had been cannibalized in July to strengthen the other three divisions already sent to Korea. On August 13, MacArthur instructed Walker to send him South Korean civilian youth to be trained quickly in Japan and incorporated into the 7th Division on a "buddy" system with the American soldiers. Within a month nearly 9000 South Korean recruits were added to the division, though their level of combat readiness was still low by the time of the Inchon invasion. Barr and his officers did an amazing job of training and integrating the South Koreans into the division, and the practice of using Koreans Attached to the U.S. Army (KATUSA) was applied later to other American ground units.[18]

Throughout July and into late August, the JCS had cautiously considered MacArthur's general concept of an amphibious landing in the enemy's rear area. Collins had returned from Tokyo in mid-July less than eager about it, but Harriman and Ridgway came back from their talks with MacArthur in early August rather enthusiastic about the Inchon scheme. The Joint Chiefs had tried to provide him the men and matériel for some sort of future amphibious operation, but they and other senior officers in the Pentagon expressed grave doubts about the wisdom of landing at Inchon, primarily because of the extremely high tides there, the narrow channel to the port, the drain on Eighth Army's reserves, and the distance from Walker's lines, which might result in a late link-up and another Anzio.

By the time General O. P. Smith, commander of the 1st Marine Division, reached Tokyo on August 22, Rear Admiral James H. Doyle had already been selected to head the Chromite attack force (Task Force 90). Doyle would be in charge of the amphibious phase of the assault, with Struble, the Seventh Fleet commander, in overall charge of the invasion armada. The Marine general found planning to be under way on all phases of the operation, though MacArthur had not yet obtained authorization to launch Chromite. After Smith conferred at length with Doyle, both men concluded that, because of nightmarish logistical problems and the many difficulties associated with the Inchon site, the target date for the landing should be postponed at least a week and the landing should be made at Posung-myon, about twenty miles south of Inchon. In a comment that summed up many Navy and Marine officers' sentiments, one of Doyle's staff members remarked, "We drew up a list of every conceivable and natural handicap and Inchon had 'em all." Late on the afternoon of his first day in Tokyo, Smith, his own assessment now supported by Doyle and his colleagues, went into his first conference with MacArthur ready to present a strong case against the UNC chief's pet scheme. According to an official source, Smith was ushered into MacArthur's office, where he "received not only a warm greeting, but assurance that the Inch'on landing would be decisive and that the war would be over in one month after the assault." Smith's argument fell on deaf ears. He later said of MacArthur's attitude, "It was more than confidence which upheld him; it was supreme and almost mystical faith that he could not fail."[19]

Besides Smith and Doyle, the Joint Chiefs had become increasingly anxious about what MacArthur was planning, particularly since he was telling them very little about the details. Smith's arrival in Tokyo coincided with a gathering of brass from Washington and Pearl Harbor for a detailed briefing on Chromite. From Washington came J. Lawton Collins and Forrest Sherman, accompanied by Lieutenant General Idwal H. Edwards (representing Hoyt Vandenberg) and a small party of Pentagon staff officers. From Pearl Harbor came Arthur Radford, the CINCPAC, who was a strong admirer of MacArthur's, and Lieutenant General Lemuel C. Shepherd, Jr., head of Fleet Marine Force, Pacific, who was predisposed in favor of an amphibious operation. Since his visit with MacArthur on July 10, Shepherd had been a prime mover in getting the 1st Marine Division sent to the Far East theater. In advance of the conference, set for the 23d, MacArthur thought that Admiral Sherman, Chief of Naval Operations, would be the key person he would have to convince. Arriving with Collins on August 21, Sherman traveled to Sasebo Naval Base to meet with Struble aboard his Seventh Fleet flagship, the heavy cruiser *Rochester*. There Sherman informed Struble confidentially, "I'm going to back the Inchon operation completely. I think it's sound."

The high-level meeting at the Dai Ichi Building on August 23 was a briefing session, but it was crucial regarding the fate of Chromite, because the final decision in Washington later would depend heavily on the impressions brought back by Collins, Sherman, and Edwards, as well as the responses solicited from Radford and Shepherd. Those present at the late afternoon conference were MacArthur, Almond, Wright, Hickey, Joy, Struble, Doyle, Stratemeyer, Major General Clark A. Ruffner (soon to be named X Corps chief of staff), three members of Wright's JSPOG staff, and nine briefing officers from Doyle's staff representing the Far East Command; Radford representing the Pacific Command and Pacific Fleet; and Sherman, Collins, and Edwards, together with some of their staff officers, representing the Pentagon. Oddly, Shepherd and Smith were not included. General "Pinky" Wright, the head of JSPOG and MacArthur's G-3, opened the session by outlining the basic Chromite plan, especially regarding the ground operations and objectives. Next, Doyle's officers presented a series of concise briefings on the naval, air, and amphibious aspects of the operation, covering intelligence, navigation, communications, naval and air bombardment, landing formations, and a host of technical matters. "Their remarks were decidedly pessimistic," states an official chronicle. Then Doyle got up and remarked, looking at MacArthur: "General, I have not been asked nor have I volunteered my opinion about this landing. If I were asked, however, the best I can say is that Inchon is not impossible." When Doyle later expounded on the difficulties of navigating Flying Fish Channel leading into Inchon, which might be heavily mined and well covered by enemy shore batteries, Sherman interrupted with the comment "I wouldn't hesitate to take a ship up there." MacArthur exclaimed, "Spoken like a Farragut!" Collins, who spoke later, said that he preferred Kunsan, about 100 miles south of Inchon, as the landing site because it was closer to the Eighth Army's Naktong line. The Army Chief of Staff pointed out that unless "a quick junction" could be made between the Chromite force and Walker's units, it might mean "disaster" for the Inchon operation. One historian suggested that Collins "probably had Anzio in mind."

More than an hour passed during the presentations by Wright, the nine briefers, Doyle, Collins, and some short comments by others, including Sherman. Except for making several one-sentence remarks, MacArthur had sat quietly puffing on his pipe. When everyone was finished, the group looked at the general for his reaction, but he continued to sit and smoke in silence for an estimated minute or longer. Then he slowly rose and began walking back and forth, gesturing with his pipe and speaking at first in a low voice but, said Collins, "gradually building up emphasis with consummate skill." He spoke for forty-five minutes, without notes.[20] Unfortunately the session was not tape-recorded nor were minutes taken, and the participants have left slightly varying accounts of what was said. Although his dramatic presentation and eloquence, perhaps the best of his career, cannot be recaptured, MacArthur's own account of the gist of his remarks vividly presents his main points:

> The bulk of the Reds are committed around Walker's defense perimeter. The enemy, I am convinced, has failed to prepare Inchon properly for defense. The very arguments you have made as to the impracticabilities involved will tend to ensure for me the element of surprise. For the enemy commander will reason that no one would be so brash as to make such an attempt. Surprise is the most vital element for success in war. As an example, the Marquis de Montcalm believed in 1759 that it was impossible for an armed force to scale the precipitous river banks south of the then walled city of Quebec, and therefore concentrated his formidable defense along the more vulnerable banks north of the city. But General James Wolfe and a small force did indeed come up the St. Lawrence River and scale those heights. On the Plains of Abraham, Wolfe won a stunning victory that was made possible almost entirely by surprise. . . . Like Montcalm, the North Koreans would regard an Inchon landing as impossible. Like Wolfe, I could take them by surprise.
>
> The Navy's objections as to tides, hydrography, terrain, and physical handicaps are indeed substantial and pertinent. But they are not insuperable. My confidence in the Navy is complete, and in fact I seem to have more confidence in the Navy than the Navy has in itself. . . .

As to the proposal for a landing at Kunsan, it would indeed eliminate many of the hazards of Inchon, but it would be largely ineffective and indecisive. It would be an attempted envelopment, which would not envelop. It would not sever or destroy the enemy's supply lines or distribution center, and would therefore serve little purpose. . . .

But seizure of Inchon and Seoul will cut the enemy's supply line and seal off the entire southern peninsula. The vulnerability of the enemy is his supply position. . . . The several major lines of enemy supply from the north converge on Seoul. . . . By seizing Seoul I would completely paralyze the enemy's supply system — coming and going. This in turn will paralyze the fighting power of the troops that now face Walker. . . .

The only alternative to a stroke such as I propose will be the continuation of the savage sacrifice we are making at Pusan, with no hope of relief in sight. Are you content to let our troops stay in that bloody perimeter like beef cattle in the slaughterhouse? Who will take the responsibility for such a tragedy? Certainly, I will not.

The prestige of the Western world hangs in the balance. Oriental millions are watching the outcome. It is plainly apparent that here in Asia is where the Communist conspirators have elected to make their play for global conquest. . . . Actually, we here fight Europe's war with arms, while there it is still confined to words. If we lose the war to Communism in Asia, the fate of Europe will be gravely jeopardized. . . .

If my estimate is inaccurate and should I run into a defense with which I cannot cope, I will be there personally and will immediately withdraw our forces before they are committed to a bloody setback. The only loss then will be my professional reputation. But Inchon will not fail. Inchon will succeed. And it will save 100,000 lives.[21]

According to several listeners, he concluded, "I realize that Inchon is a 5000 to 1 gamble, but I am used to taking such odds. . . . We shall land at Inchon and I shall crush them!" The group was so spellbound that a long pause elapsed after MacArthur sat down before anyone spoke. Sherman then rose and said, "Thank you. A great voice in a great cause."[22]

The next day, before departing, Sherman had a private session with MacArthur. The Navy Chief did not reveal the substance of their talk, but as he left the general's office, he commented to a staff officer, "I wish I could share that man's optimism." Collins later stated that he had been "favorably impressed" by Mac-

Arthur's "brilliant exposition" on the 23d, "but still had some reservations," fearing that the enemy might be able to reinforce the Inchon-Seoul area quickly. On the morning of August 24, Sherman, Radford, Joy, Doyle, Shepherd, and Smith met in Joy's office. They concurred that MacArthur had been articulate and persuasive, but most of them still preferred to stage the landing at Posung-myon, below Inchon. Shepherd went to MacArthur and pleaded their case for the alternative landing site, but the UNC commander would not yield. The Navy and Marine leaders gave up the fight and thereafter worked zealously to make the Inchon plan succeed. Returning to Washington, Collins and Sherman conferred with their JCS colleagues, Johnson, and Truman about Chromite. On August 28 the Joint Chiefs notified MacArthur of their conditional approval of the Inchon plan, suggesting, however, that he have "alternative plans" ready for an amphibious assault at Kunsan or "a favorable beach south of Inchon if one can be located." He was also told to keep them better informed in the future, "with timely information as to your intentions and plans for offensive operations."[23] The Joint Chiefs thus had given their tentative approval of Chromite, but only in lukewarm fashion.

Two days before this limp endorsement by the JCS, MacArthur established the X Corps as the Chromite ground force and named Almond its commander, letting him retain his positions as chief of staff of UNC, Far East Command, SCAP, and USAFFE. Hickey, Almond's deputy, became the acting chief of staff. MacArthur thought the war with North Korea would be over within a month after the Inchon assault and Almond could then resume his GHQ duties. But Almond was still head of the X Corps when MacArthur left Japan the next April, and Ridgway appointed Hickey his chief of staff.

On August 30, MacArthur issued his operations orders for Chromite, setting forth the forces to be employed and their various missions and objectives. Almond's X Corps of 71,300 troops, consisting of the 1st Marine and 7th Infantry divisions and supporting artillery and other ground units, would seize Inchon and Seoul; the assault was to begin on September 15. Until directed otherwise, the X Corps would be directly under MacArthur, not part of Walker's Eighth Army. Struble's armada was to be made up of 260 ships, divided into task forces and groups and assembled for loading at Yokohama, Kobe, Sasebo, and Pusan; as a whole, it was designated Joint Task Force 7. Of the forty-seven LSTs (landing ship, tanks), thirty-seven were manned by Japanese crews, a fact that was probably not passed along to Washington until well after the operation. Air cover would be provided over the Inchon-Seoul area by the planes of four American carriers and a British carrier, and FEAF missions would continue to be flown primarily in support of Walker's operations along the defense perimeter to the southeast. The battleship *Missouri* and other elements of the Seventh Fleet would stage diversionary bombardments along the east coast while landing feints were made at Kunsan and other points on both coasts to draw the enemy's attention away from Inchon as the landing target. The day following the Inchon assault, Walker's units were to launch an all-out offensive along the Naktong perimeter, concentrating on linking up with the Chromite force as rapidly as possible by way of the Taejon-Suwon axis.

Besides dealing with countless logistical problems that had to be solved somehow during the first two weeks of September in order for the massive operation to be launched successfully and on time, MacArthur faced controversy among some of his key commanders and continuing uncertainty in Washington. On August 30, Smith asked Almond to get the 5th Marines, now at the Naktong front, released from Walker at once. The Eighth Army commander informed Almond, however, that the Marines were the mainstay of his perimeter defense, and the North Koreans were now hurling their severest attacks ever against his lines. Almond tried to persuade Smith to accept a regiment of the 7th Division to fill out his 1st Marine Division, but the Marine general adamantly refused. Struble hit on a compromise that was accepted by the principals in the heated dispute: while the Marines shipped out of Pusan to join the Chromite armada at sea, a regiment of the 7th Division would be kept in floating reserve in Pusan harbor for a time in case the enemy broke through the Naktong perimeter.[24]

Meanwhile, in Washington the Joint Chiefs, having heard nothing further from MacArthur about Chromite, despite their explicit instructions of the 28th, sent a message to him on September 5 asking for any plan modifications he may have made. He replied briefly that "the general outline of the plan remains as described to you" and that a courier would deliver a copy of his detailed operational plans by the 11th. Worried about the drain on Walker's reserves just when the Eighth Army was confronted by the fiercest enemy attacks along the Naktong line, the JCS requested him on September 7 to reconsider the whole Chromite operation: "We desire your estimate as to feasibility and chance of success of projected operation if initiated on planned schedule." MacArthur said the Joint Chiefs' message "chilled me to the marrow of my bones," for it "expressed doubt of success and implied the whole movement should be abandoned."[25] He immediately and forcefully replied:

> There is no question in my mind as to the feasibility of the operation and I regard its chance of success as excellent. . . . It represents the only hope of wresting the initiative from the enemy. . . . To do otherwise is to commit us to a war of indefinite duration, of gradual attrition, and of doubtful results. . . . There is not the slightest possibility, however, of our forces being ejected from the Pusan beachhead.
>
> The envelopment from the north will instantly relieve the pressure upon the south perimeter and, indeed, is the only way that this can be accomplished. The success of the enveloping movement from the north does not depend upon the rapid juncture of the X Corps with the Eighth Army. . . .
>
> The embarkation of the troops and the preliminary air and naval preparations are proceeding according to schedule. I repeat that I and all of my commanders and staff officers, without exception, are enthusiastic for and confident of the success of the enveloping movement.[26]

Collins stated they were "impressed by this firm reiteration of confidence from the responsible field commander," so on September 8, exactly one week before the landing date, the JCS finally yielded altogether and gave the full authorization for Chromite that MacArthur, "with growing concern," had been awaiting: "We approve your plan and [the] President has been so informed." MacArthur, having wondered who was behind this "last-minute hesitancy," drew a conclusion, probably wrong, from the phrasing of the terse JCS message: "I interpreted this to mean that it had been the President who had threatened to interfere and overrule" the Inchon assault. On another occasion MacArthur said he thought

Sherman "must have been largely instrumental in influencing the ultimate decision" for Chromite.[27]

Actually the slowest ships of the Inchon invasion force had left Yokohama on September 5, three days before the operation's final approval in Washington. The 1st Marine Division sailed from Kobe on the 11th, and the 7th Infantry Division from Yokohama the same day; the 5th Marines departed from Pusan the following day. MacArthur, accompanied by Shepherd, Almond, Wright, Fox, and Whitney, left Haneda Airport on the UNC chief's new Lockheed Constellation, named *SCAP*, on the afternoon of the 12th. They flew to Itazuke Air Force Base on Kyushu and then traveled by car to Sasebo Naval Base. While on the road to Sasebo, they saw that the heavily overcast sky broke shortly before sunset and a rainbow appeared. Shepherd recalled, "General MacArthur turned to me and said, 'Lem, there is my lucky rainbow. This operation is going to be a success.'" At Sasebo they joined Doyle and Smith aboard the Task Force 90 flagship, *Mount McKinley*, which put out to sea just after midnight. During the first portion of the voyage to Inchon the seas were extremely rough, because they encountered the edge of Typhoon Kezia, which Doyle described as "one of the worst storms" he had met. Fortunately for the armada, Kezia, which packed winds of 125 miles per hour, shifted away from the path of the main body of ships. Only ten days earlier Typhoon Jane had struck the Kobe area with winds of 110 miles per hour, with forty-foot waves crashing across the city's waterfront. Jane totally disrupted the loading of the 1st Marine Division's supplies for thirty-six hours and did considerable damage to the dock facilities and to some of the fifty or so ships anchored in the harbor. Kezia, an even larger storm, could have created a major sea disaster and caused cancellation of the invasion if its full force had hit the Chromite armada. MacArthur's luck had not left him yet.

In the meantime, Lieutenant Colonel Lynn D. Smith, MacArthur's courier, who carried a copy of the detailed Chromite operational plan that was previously promised to the JCS, left Tokyo on September 10; MacArthur cautioned him not to arrive in Washington "too soon." Smith reached the American capital on the 13th, and the Joint Chiefs agreed to meet with him the following day. He presented the plan to the JCS on the 14th, but by the time he had finished his presentation and answered the many questions, it was too late for the invasion to be stopped, had that been the chiefs' decision. The first wave of Marines went ashore about 6:30 A.M., September 15, Korean time, which was approximately 5:30 P.M. on the 14th in Washington. It is not known whether Smith relayed MacArthur's oral message: "If they say it is too big a gamble, tell them I said this is throwing a nickel in the pot after it has been opened for a dollar. The big gamble was Washington's decision to put American troops on the Asiatic mainland."[28]

Air attacks on the Inchon area had begun on a daily basis on September 4. On the 13th, Struble's gunfire support group of ten American and British cruisers and destroyers entered Flying Fish Channel and about noon began bombarding Inchon and Wolmi-do, the latter a small island with a 335-foot hill that lay at the entrance to the harbor of Inchon. Enemy batteries on Wolmi-do returned fire at first, but when the ships came back on the 14th to shell the area again, the Wolmi-do guns were knocked out entirely by the time the ships ceased firing. During those two days the North Korean defenders had been subjected to intensive air strikes by carrier planes, which saturated Wolmi-do with napalm bombs. A few mines had been sighted in Flying Fish Channel and had been destroyed, but, as was learned later, the North Koreans had not had time to place the new shipment of Soviet mines they had stored nearby. In view of the impossibility of keeping the massive assault preparations secret in Japan, where the loading activities at the ports of Yokohama and Kobe were in public view, it is astonishing that Soviet intelligence agents or Japanese Communists did not alert the North Korean high command. Whatever the reason, Willoughby's preinvasion estimate of about 2000 enemy troops in the Inchon area proved accurate. Strategically and tactically, the North Koreans were caught by surprise.[29]

While MacArthur and the other senior officers observed with binoculars from the *Mount McKinley*'s bridge, the first wave of landing craft, carrying troops of a battalion of the 5th Marines, touched down on the north end of Wolmi-do about 6:30 A.M., September 15. Preceded by an hour and a half of furious air and naval bombardments of the little island, the landing met only light resistance. Within a half-hour the Marines had seized the main hill, where they ran up an American flag. By 8:00 mopping-up was under way on Wolmi-do, and Marines moved on to attack the small but stubborn enemy garrison on Sowolmi-do, an islet to the south connected to Wolmi-do by a causeway. By noon the fighting was over on both harbor islands. The Marines had suffered no fatalities and only 17 wounded, and had killed about 200 enemy soldiers and captured nearly 140. That morning after the flag was raised and the first reports from Wolmi-do left no doubt about its quick capture, MacArthur told Doyle to send a message to Struble, who was aboard the cruiser *Rochester:* "The Navy and the Marines have never shone more brightly than this morning. MacArthur." Then he turned to Doyle, Shepherd, Smith, and Almond, who were with him on the *Mount McKinley's* bridge: "That's it. Let's get a cup of coffee." While drinking coffee below deck, he drafted a message to be sent to the Joint Chiefs: "First phase landing successful with losses slight. Surprise apparently complete. All goes well and on schedule."[30]

By early afternoon the 31-foot tide off Inchon, one of the world's highest, rolled back, leaving the Marine battalion on Wolmi-do stranded by an exposed bottom of Yellow Sea mud that extended up to three miles out from the shoreline around Inchon. While waiting for the tide to start in again, the Marines aboard ship watched as Inchon was heavily pounded by naval shelling and aerial bombing. When the main assault started at 5:30 P.M. to establish two beachheads at Inchon itself, the Marines would be confronted by a high sea wall along the waterfront that required scaling ladders. Then they would have to secure footholds quickly in the city of 250,000, despite possibly heavy enemy fire from countless buildings and several excellent hill positions near the harbor. They were aware, too, that the huge tide would roll out to sea again about two hours after they landed, marooning them overnight until reinforcements and supplies could be brought on the next morning's high tide.

On Red Beach, which was on the northwest edge of the downtown district, the 5th Marines (less their Wolmi-do battalion) went ashore against strong opposition at first, secured positions along the waterfront, and shortly seized the two key hills overlooking their beachhead. In a daring move, eight heavily loaded LSTs, whose equipment and supplies were vital to the regiment, were grounded at Red Beach and stranded overnight on the mud flats. At Blue

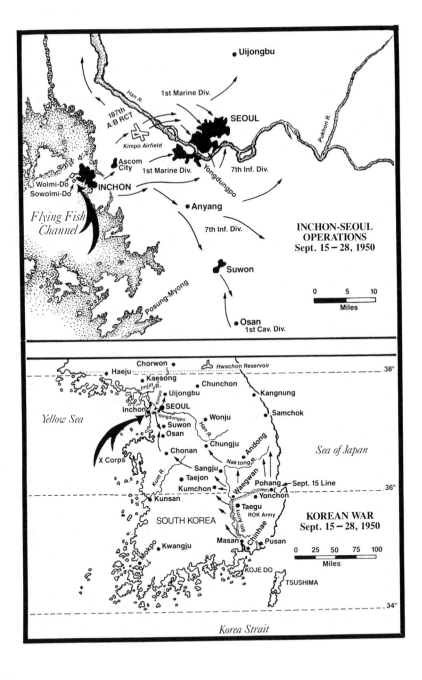

INCHON-SEOUL OPERATIONS
Sept. 15 – 28, 1950

Uijongbu

Han R.

1st Marine Div.

187th A/B RCT

Kimpo Airfield

SEOUL

Pukhon R.

Ascom City

1st Marine Div.

Yongdungpo

7th Inf. Div.

Wolmi-Do
Sowolmi-Do

INCHON

Flying Fish Channel

Anyang

7th Inf. Div.

Posung-Myong

Suwon

0   5   10
Miles

Osan
1st Cav. Div.

Chorwon

Haeju

Hwachon Reservoir

38°

Kaesong

Chunchon

Imjin R.

Uijongbu

Kangnung

Inchon

Kumpo R.

SEOUL

Yellow Sea

Yongdungpo

Suwon

Wonju

Samchok

Osan

Han R.

X Corps

Chonan

Chungju

Andong

Sea of Japan

Naktong R.

Sangju

Taejon

Waegwan

Pohang

Sept. 15 Line

36°

Kumchon

Yonchon

Kunsan

Kum R.

Taegu
ROK Army

SOUTH KOREA

8th Army

Masan

Chinhae

Pusan

KOREAN WAR
Sept. 15 – 28, 1950

Mokpo

Kwangju

0   25   50   75   100
Miles

KOJE DO

TSUSHIMA

34°

Korea Strait

Beach, which was south of the main part of the city, the 1st Marines meanwhile had also established a beachhead, though some landing craft had gone to the wrong places and the sea wall had to be dynamited to let later troop waves move inland. Shortly after midnight the Marine regiments had taken their first-day objectives, holding over a third of the city and losing 20 killed and 174 wounded. On the evening of the 15th MacArthur happily informed the JCS: "Our losses are light. . . . The command distinguished itself. The whole operation is proceeding on schedule."

The next morning the two Marine regiments made contact with each other and prepared to move eastward toward Ascom City and Kimpo Airfield, leaving the mopping-up in Inchon to a ROK Marine regiment. The following day the 7th Division disembarked at Inchon and began advancing eastward on the right, or south, flank of the Marines. On September 18 the Marines seized Kimpo, but enemy resistance was stiffening markedly. The 7th Marines, the third regiment of Smith's division, landed at Inchon on the 21st and joined the push toward Seoul. The next day, after the heaviest fighting yet, the 1st Marines captured Yongdungpo, situated just across the Han River to the southwest of Seoul, and the 5th and 7th Marines, having crossed the river farther west, closed in on Seoul from the north side of the Han.[31]

As had been true of the Southwest Pacific amphibious assaults that he observed, MacArthur was eager to go ashore not long after the first waves of Marines secured a foothold. On the afternoon of September 15, he, together with Struble, Shepherd, and others, took a barge from the *Mount McKinley* and traveled in for a closer view of Wolmi-do and the Red Beach landing site, moving as near as the exposed mud flats and the enemy gunners along the Inchon shoreline allowed. A nearby destroyer captain observed MacArthur standing at the front of the barge "in a Napoleonic pose." On the morning of the 17th, MacArthur, Struble, Shepherd, Almond, Whitney, Wright, and Fox went ashore at Inchon. After climbing into several jeeps, they and some other X Corps officers and some correspondents visited Smith's command post and then headed east along the Seoul highway toward Ascom City. MacArthur particularly wanted to tour the scene of an ambush during the previous night in which the 5th Marines had wiped out 6 tanks and 200 enemy troops near Ascom City. Several of the tanks were still burning as MacArthur and his party walked among the corpses. After they headed back toward Inchon, 7 enemy soldiers were discovered hiding in a culvert over which MacArthur's jeep had been parked. On September 20, MacArthur, together with most of the same officers who had been on the tour of the 17th, drove up to the Han River to watch the 5th Marines cross; then they headed south for visits to the command posts of Colonel Lewis B. (Chesty) Puller of the 1st Marines and General David Barr of the 7th Division. The battle for Yongdungpo was under way, and they could easily observe large fires in the city. Almond, who was driving MacArthur's jeep, went at such high speed during the daylong journey — at one point he nearly hit a large X Corps truck — that when they reached the Inchon waterfront, Wright, said one source, "with perfectly straight face asked Almond if he had a driver's license."[32]

The next morning MacArthur and Struble visited the battleship *Missouri,* which had joined the fire support ships off Inchon on the 19th after earlier participating in the diversion along the east coast. When MacArthur saw the plaque on the quarterdeck commemorating the Japanese surrender ceremony five years earlier, tears "rolled down his cheeks," and he stood silently for a long while, then turned to the ship's captain, shook his hand, and remarked, "You have given me the happiest moment of my life." That day Almond finally established his X Corps headquarters ashore; he was criticized then and later by the Marines for not having done so earlier. Meanwhile MacArthur and his GHQ party drove to Kimpo, where the *SCAP* was ready for the return flight to Tokyo. Before boarding, MacArthur staged a brief ceremony to award the Silver Star to O. P. Smith, praising him as "the gallant commander of a gallant division." During the flight that day, the 21st, he surprised Lem Shepherd by awarding him a Silver Star, too, commenting, "You have served your country with great distinction."

By the time MacArthur left Kimpo, the X Corps had ashore most of its troops, as well as over 25,000 tons of equipment and 6000 vehicles, including nearly 250 tanks. The 187th Airborne RCT would arrive on the 24th at Kimpo to guard that vital airfield and to undertake operations to the northwest of it. MacArthur was elated by the relatively easy conquests from Wolmi-do to Yongdungpo; the latter was secured the day after his departure. He was optimistic about a quick capture of Seoul as he chatted during the flight back to Japan. But Shepherd recorded in his diary aboard the *SCAP* that day, "I personally believe it will take a week of fighting before Seoul is secured." It must have dismayed him the next day when the Associated Press bureau in Tokyo sent out an erroneous dispatch that Seoul had just fallen.[33]

Unhappily, Shepherd's prediction about the Seoul operation was accurate. Though preinvasion intelligence estimated 4000 enemy troops in the South Korean capital, a North Korean division en route to the Naktong happened to be passing nearby to the east when news of the Inchon attack came; it, together with several smaller units in the area, was ordered to reinforce the Seoul garrison. The battle for Seoul developed into a costly fight from house to house and street to street against elements of three North Korean divisions totaling about 20,000 troops. The fiercest actions took place on the western edge of the city, where the 5th Marines progressed slowly and with heavy casualties. The 32d Regiment of the 7th Division had to be committed on the 25th; it attacked from the south into the city. The rest of Barr's division held a blocking position below Seoul to prevent enemy reinforcements coming from the south. Almond and Smith had several heated confrontations over the former's interference in tactics and his criticism of the Marine regiments' inability to take Seoul quickly. Clark Ruffner, the X Corps chief of staff, tried to mediate but was not successful; some deep resentments developed between the Marines and Almond, and they would worsen before Christmas. By the evening of September 28, Seoul was secured, though small pockets of enemy resistance continued. The remnants of the North Korean defenders retreated northward toward Uijongbu; a Marine attempt to block the enemy escape on the road to Uijongbu was unsuccessful. Actually, however, the bulk of the North Korean defenders had already died in the fighting in the city. During the period of September 15–28, the X Corps suffered 3500 casualties, of which 2400 were in the 1st Marine Division. About 14,000 North Korean troops were killed and 7000 were taken prisoner. During those two weeks most of the casualties suffered by both sides occurred during the battle for Seoul. No casualty figures were given for the 1.1 million civilians in Seoul, but, as in the battle of Manila in early

1945, the civilian toll probably far exceeded that of the military killed, wounded, and missing.[34]

Although the heaviest fighting during the Chromite operations took place at Seoul, the 7th Division, about a third of whom were recently recruited South Koreans, had its hands full not only assisting at Seoul but also holding the line to the south against an estimated 10,000 North Koreans between the Han River and the city of Osan. Barr's troops took Suwon on the 22d. When Walker, in the meantime, tried to launch his breakout from the Naktong perimeter on September 16, the North Korean resistance was so strong that the Eighth Army was not able to get across the Naktong River in force for three days. Apparently the enemy units along the perimeter had not yet received word of the disaster 180 miles to their rear at Inchon. Aboard the *Mount McKinley* on the evening of September 19, MacArthur had held a conference with Struble, Shepherd, Doyle, Almond, and other senior officers. The UNC commander expressed doubt that Walker would be able to achieve his breakout from the perimeter soon and told Wright to start preparing plans for another amphibious assault, this time at Kunsan, to relieve the pressure on the Eighth Army. About that same time, however, news of the Inchon landing reached the North Koreans along the Naktong; they started a general withdrawal northward that quickly deteriorated into a rout. Walker's forces began reporting sizable daily advances and large hauls of enemy prisoners. A spearhead of the 1st Cavalry Division linked up with the 7th Division north of Osan on September 27. The plan for a landing at Kunsan was shelved.

Later UNC figures showed that over 130,000 North Korean prisoners were taken and 200,000 enemy casualties suffered during the operations of Almond's and Walker's commands in September. The totals seem high, but the North Korean Army had added a number of units since June by draining virtually all available youth in North Korea and by forcing large numbers of South Koreans into its military ranks. With the meeting of Walker's and Almond's forces, some North Korean troops caught in the southwest corner of the peninsula fled into the mountains there and later undertook guerrilla operations; others managed to flee northward across the 38th Parallel. But, in truth, the North Korean Army had ceased to exist as an effective army-size fighting force, and, though it would be reorganized later to fight alongside the Chinese Communist armies, its combat strength during the war never again would be more than of corps size.[35] Thanks to his overwhelming ground, sea, and air firepower and his dogged determination to execute Chromite, MacArthur had succeeded, in spectacular fashion, in fulfilling his pledge to "crush" the North Korean invaders.

For some time Rhee and MacArthur had had an understanding that the ROK government would be re-established at Seoul as soon as the city was recaptured and the general would participate in the ceremony marking the return of the seat of government to the capital city of South Korea. When MacArthur mentioned to the JCS his intention to go to Seoul for the occasion, the word soon reached the State Department, where objections were raised, states an official account, to "any participation by the military commander in ROK government matters." On September 22, the Joint Chiefs told MacArthur to "submit without delay" his plans for restoring Rhee's government at Seoul, because "such plans must have the approval of higher authority." The general responded indignantly: "Your message is not understood. I have no plans whatsoever except scrupulously to implement the directives which I have received." He cited the Security Council resolutions of June 25 and 27 as intended, in part, to bring about a restoration of the ROK political establishment following the North Korean invasion. He went on to explain that he planned to "return" Rhee and his government "to domicile in Seoul as soon as conditions there are sufficiently stable to permit reasonable security." He argued that the ROK government had never ceased to function, so no actual governmental change was involved. On the 27th, the JCS authorized him to "facilitate the restoration" of Rhee's government, but they also warned him, as Acheson wished, not to get entangled in political issues regarding North Korea's future.[36]

Almond had pushed Smith to have Seoul secured by the 25th, which would be exactly three months since the war's start. Although three hard days of fighting remained, Almond brazenly notified MacArthur on September 25 that the city had been captured, and a Tokyo GHQ communiqué was issued the next day announcing the liberation of Seoul. On the 28th, when the capital was actually secured, Almond sent MacArthur a suggested program involving elaborate ceremonies for the next day, marking the restoration of the ROK government. Almond envisioned an honor guard for Rhee and MacArthur when they arrived at Kimpo, a parade, and a lengthy ceremony at the ROK Capitol building. MacArthur replied that he would handle the proceedings, which would be kept much simpler and briefer than Almond intended. About 10:00 A.M., September 29, the *SCAP* landed at Kimpo, with MacArthur, his wife, Whitney, Stratemeyer, and several other GHQ officers aboard. MacArthur immediately plunged into a conference with Almond and Walker, who were at the airfield. An hour later the *Bataan*, the C-54 that had been MacArthur's personal plane until recently, arrived from Pusan, bearing Rhee, his wife, Muccio, and a host of ROK officials.

The ceremony marking the return of the South Korean government to Seoul began promptly at noon in the National Assembly Hall of the Capitol, which was packed with ROK officials and civilians, as well as ranking officers of the ground, sea, and air forces — American, ROK, and British — that had participated in the campaign. Many in the audience carried side arms and steel helmets, and in the distance occasional small-arms and artillery fire could be heard, for the mopping-up was still under way after the week-long battle for the city. As MacArthur commenced the ceremony, concussions from nearby artillery blasts caused several large panes of heavy glass to fall from the overhead panels; people in the audience dodged barely in time, and those who had helmets quickly donned them. MacArthur later remarked that the scene reminded him of the program that he participated in restoring the Philippine government at battle-ravaged Manila in March 1945. In his five-minute address he emphasized that the restoration was made possible by "the grace of a merciful Providence" and by "our forces fighting under the standard of that greatest hope and inspiration of mankind, the United Nations." He expressed his confidence "that from the travail of the past there may emerge a new and hopeful dawn for the people of Korea." Then he led the audience in reciting the Lord's Prayer and closed by addressing Rhee: "Mr. President, my officers and I will now resume our military duties and leave you and your government to the discharge of civil responsibilities." Before delivering his prepared speech, Rhee responded extemporaneously to MacArthur: "We admire you. We love you as the savior of our race. How can I ever explain to you my own undying gratitude and that of the Korean people?" In a separate short ceremony in Seoul, MacArthur awarded the Distinguished Service Cross to Johnny Walker and Ned Almond, citing "their marked skill and courage in exploiting the decisive pincer movement." MacArthur and his party took off from Kimpo for Tokyo shortly after 1:30 P.M.[37]

Back at his Dai Ichi office, MacArthur soon received messages from both the Defense and State departments, admonishing him because the United States flag had been flown alongside the ROK flag over the Capitol in Seoul during the ceremony. The Washington officials felt the place of prominence should have gone to the UN flag in order to emphasize that the defense of South Korea was an undertaking of the United Nations. But there were also many congratulatory messages to MacArthur about Chromite. Truman said, "No operations in military history can match either the delaying action where you traded space for time in which to build up your forces, or the brilliant maneuver which has now resulted in the liberation of Seoul." The Joint Chiefs told him, "Your transition from defensive to offensive operations was magnificently planned, timed, and executed. . . . We remain completely confident that the great task entrusted to you by the United Nations will be carried to a successful conclusion."[38]

In his memoirs, written over a decade later, MacArthur obviously still relished the memory of what turned out to be his last great triumph: he included not only the praises from the President and the JCS but also congratulatory messages and laudatory comments about the Inchon operation from the British chiefs of staff, George C. Marshall, Louis Johnson, Frank Pace, Jr., Shigeru Yoshida, James Byrnes, Winston Churchill, Dwight D. Eisenhower, William Halsey, Carl Spaatz, John Foster Dulles, and Douglas Southall Freeman. The last may well have meant the most to MacArthur, for Freeman, the noted biographer of Robert E. Lee, was then considering a biography of the UNC commander. But MacArthur's grand victory at Inchon and his long, illustrious career would not be chronicled by Freeman, who later abandoned the idea. Perhaps he realized that his newest idol would have to be judged not only by the glory of Inchon, but also by later developments. Inchon may have doomed the North Korean Army, but it also was the beginning of the end of MacArthur's military career. The full measure of Inchon would not be revealed in the Chromite operations but in its consequences on MacArthur's self-confidence and on his superiors' sense of his unassailability in the following critical weeks. "The success of Inchon was so great," Collins commented, "and the subsequent prestige of General MacArthur was so overpowering, that the Chiefs hesitated thereafter to question later plans and decisions of the general, which should have been challenged." After the Inchon-Seoul operations, said Collins, MacArthur "seemed to march like a Greek hero of old to an unkind and inexorable fate."[39]

CHAPTER XVI

The Optimism of October

1. Advance into North Korea

BY THE END OF SEPTEMBER 1950, the initial objective of the United States and the United Nations, according to the Security Council resolution of June 25, had been attained: the aggressors had been repelled from South Korea. The second and more vague objective, incorporated in the council's resolution of June 27, was "to restore international peace and security to the area." Although the North Korean Army had been reduced to ineffectiveness as an army-level organization, scattered regiments and smaller units were still functional, the enemy high command had escaped MacArthur's pincers, and North Korea was capable of revitalizing its armed forces for a later try at conquering the south. When J. Lawton Collins and Hoyt Vandenberg visited him in mid-July, MacArthur stressed the need to oust the enemy from all territory below the 38th Parallel and to annihilate the North Korean military units entirely, which would probably entail pursuit of them across the parallel and occupation of North Korea. At the time of the visit of Collins and Forrest Sherman to Tokyo in late August, the two JCS members discussed future operations with Mac-Arthur; the three agreed that his forces should not be hindered by any restrictions on crossing the 38th Parallel. They apparently concurred, too, on the desirability of a limited occupation of North Korea after its military units were destroyed.

The idea of invading and occupying the Marxist state bordering both of the principal Communist powers, which would be a high-risk shift from containment to liberation, did not originate with MacArthur; it had been widely discussed and generally supported by State and Pentagon leaders well before the Inchon success. On August 17, and on other occasions that month, Warren Austin, American ambassador to the UN, spoke out in the Security Council in favor of UN endorsement of a new objective in the war: "establishing democratic government in the reunited Korea." In a nationwide radio broadcast on September 1, Truman also asserted that he was for a "free, independent, and united" Korea. Acheson seemed eager to exploit the opportunity that might come with military triumph to rid North Korea of Kim's regime and to reunite the two Koreas. In speeches in the British Parliament late that summer, a number of influential members affirmed anew their hope for Korean unification after North Korea was "liberated" from Communist domination.[1]

On September 11, the President approved NSC 81/1, a crucial policy formulation by the National Security Council based on earlier recommendations by the Joint Chiefs. Among its main provisions, NSC 81/1 stated that (1) UNC forces would be authorized to advance above the 38th Parallel in order to force the withdrawal of the North Korean Army from the south or to defeat it; (2) ground operations in North Korea would be prohibited if the USSR or Communist China intervened prior to the UNC forces' movement across the 38th Parallel; (3) UNC air and naval, as well as ground, operations "across" the Manchurian or Soviet borders would be forbidden; (4) "it should not be the policy" to use non-ROK forces in advancing into the northern border provinces of North Korea; and (5) MacArthur was to be authorized to develop contingency plans for the occupation of North Korea, with execution dependent on the President's approval. Oddly, the document said that in case of Soviet intervention north or south of the 38th Parallel, MacArthur was to order his forces to go on the defensive and was to consult Washington immediately, whereas if Red Chinese forces intervened south of the 38th Parallel (mention of movement into North Korea was omitted), he was to continue operations "as long as he believes his forces capable of successful resistance." In its conclusions, NSC 81/1 stated that "final decisions cannot be made at this time concerning the future course of action in Korea," because they would depend on "the action of the Soviet Union and the Chinese Communists, consultation and agreement with friendly members of the United Nations, and appraisal of the risk of general war." On September 15, the date of the Inchon assault, the JCS sent MacArthur the basic provisions of NSC 81/1, intimating that a directive would be forthcoming soon based on the new policy.[2]

On September 27 MacArthur received the crucial JCS directive authorizing the advance into North Korea. It was based on NSC 81/1 — indeed, it incorporated many of its phrases — and had the strong backing not only of the NSC but especially of Truman, Acheson, and Marshall; the last had become the Secretary of Defense on the 21st. According to a White House assistant, there had also been "some amount of inter-allied consultation" regarding the directive, probably with the United Kingdom, France, and some of the British Commonwealth nations, who favored the move across the parallel. The directive stated: "Your military objective is the destruction of the North Korean Armed Forces. . . . You are authorized to conduct military operations north of the 38th Parallel in Korea, provided that at the time of such operations there has been no entry into North Korea by major Soviet or Chinese Communist Forces, no announcement of intended entry, nor a threat to counter our operations militarily in North Korea." It went on to repeat from NSC 81/1 what his responses were to be in case of such intervention, and it included the prohibition, "as a matter of policy," of non-ROK troops in the North Korean provinces bordering Manchuria and the Soviet Union. He was told that armistice terms would be sent soon for him to broadcast to North Korea. His authorization to restore Rhee's government in Seoul was also in this directive. Additionally, MacArthur was instructed to submit promptly to the JCS his plans for military operations above the 38th Parallel and for the occupation of North Korea.[3]

The following day MacArthur sent the Joint Chiefs his plan for operations in North Korea, which JSPOG had been working on for some time. The Eighth Army would advance northwest from Seoul to Pyongyang, and the X Corps, with Almond's headquarters still reporting directly to MacArthur, would conduct an amphibious assault at Wonsan, a port on the east coast about 100 miles above the 38th Parallel, and then drive westward to link up with Walker's forces. Subsequently the UNC units would push north to a line running roughly across North Korea from Chongju to Hungnam, the narrowest part of the Korean peninsula. Only South Korean forces would be employed in the offensive beyond this line. The next day the Joint Chiefs gave their approval of his plan. Also on September 29, Marshall sent MacArthur a message advising against Walker's reported plan to announce that his forces would halt at the 38th Parallel until ordered forward; the Defense Secretary wanted no public pronouncements that might produce a UN vote on the issue of the parallel. Marshall included one sentence that he should have known from his World War II dealings with MacArthur was open to misinterpretation if taken out of context: "We want you to feel unhampered strategically and tactically to proceed north of the 38th Parallel." MacArthur, in replying, was supremely confident: "The logistical supply of our units is the main problem which limits our advance. . . . I regard all of Korea open for our military operations unless and until the enemy capitulates."[4]

The ROK 3d Division began moving in force across the 38th Parallel on October 1, heading up the east coast toward Kosong. MacArthur told his superiors that he wanted to make an after-the-fact public announcement about the ROK crossing, but the JCS immediately forbade it: "We desire that you proceed with your operations without any further explanation or announcement and let action determine the matter. Our government desires to avoid having to make an issue of the 38th parallel until we have accomplished our mission." On the other hand, the Joint Chiefs did authorize him to broadcast an unconditional surrender ultimatum to North Korea on October 1. Although there was no reply from Kim Il Sung's government, there was a response from Peking: on October 3 Premier Chou En-lai informed K. M. Panikkar, the Indian ambassador to Communist China, that in crossing the 38th Parallel, "the South Koreans did not matter, but American intrusion into North Korea would encounter Chinese resistance." When the warning was passed on by the Indian government to Washington, American officials dismissed it, some not trusting Panikkar's reports and others figuring Peking was either bluffing or trying to influence opinion in the UN about the war. Panikkar's message was duly forwarded to MacArthur, as had been sundry previous reports from other sources regarding possible actions by Red China. Meanwhile, the ROK Capital Division crossed the 38th Parallel on the east coast, and three other ROK divisions advanced into North Korea in the central sector of the front. By October 3, some ROK patrols had pushed over fifty miles into North Korea; the American and British forces, however, had not yet moved across the 38th Parallel.

Through its own and Nationalist Chinese intelligence channels, the United States government was aware that since April there had been large-scale movements of troops from South China to the north. By mid-July it was believed that a minimum of 180,000 Chinese regulars were in Manchuria. The estimates rose steadily thereafter, and three months later intelligence reports indicated that between 300,000 and 450,000 Chinese soldiers were there, including General Lin Piao's Fourth Field Army and elements of General Chen Yi's Third Field Army. (A Chinese field army was the equivalent of an American army group in organization, though smaller in size.) Other armies were moved to the region between the Shantung Peninsula and Peking, from which they could be deployed readily to Manchuria. Apparently Peking postponed its plans to seize Formosa after the North Korean offensive was halted at the Naktong line.

Besides the northward shift of its ground forces, which Washington considered precautionary on Red China's part rather than ominous for Korea, Peking also began a graduated mobilization of public opinion against the United States. From early July to late August the "hate America" campaign assailed America for supporting Rhee's and Chiang's regimes. During that period the Peking propagandists urged opposition to the American "imperialists," often using the verb *fan tuei,* which means "to resist," but in a nonviolent manner. From late August onward, however, Peking's intensifying anti-American campaign in publications, broadcasts, and speeches was marked by a small but significant change in verbs meaning "to resist": now *k'ang yi* was frequently used; it connoted resistance by violent action. In a Peking address on September 30, Chou issued his strongest public warning yet of Red China's possible belligerency, asserting that his people "will not tolerate foreign aggression, nor will they supinely tolerate seeing their neighbors being savagely invaded by the imperialists." In retrospect, this warning, together with his remarks to Panikkar three days later and the growing assembly of Chinese armies in and near Manchuria, should have signaled Washington clearly of the probability of a clash if American troops entered North Korea. Nevertheless, a CIA report of October 12, which was in line with its previous estimates, as well as with those of the American diplomatic and military intelligence groups, maintained that Red Chinese intervention in the war, though "a continuing possibility," was "not probable in 1950," and that Communist China's support of North Korea "will probably be confined to continued covert assistance."[5] In picking out the signals from the noises in intelligence data, the CIA was not any more helpful in the autumn of 1950 than it had been during the months preceding the North Korean invasion in June.

The secret movement of Chinese forces across the Yalu River from Manchuria into North Korea began about October 8–14, or shortly after the UN General Assembly's resolution calling for, in essence, unification of Korea by force and after the Eighth Army began its offensive into North Korea. With the return of the Soviet Union to the Security Council in August and the certainty of its veto of the unification resolution if it were introduced in that body, State Department leaders persuaded the UN General Assembly delegations of Great Britain and seven other nations to sponsor the resolution drastically altering the UN's political objective in the war. It was passed on October 7 by a large margin of 47 to 5, with 7 abstentions. Its principal recommendations were that:

> (a) All appropriate steps be taken to ensure conditions of stability throughout Korea;
> (b) All constituent acts be taken, including the holding of elections, under the auspices of the United Nations, for the establishment of a unified, independent and democratic government in the sovereign state of Korea. . . .
> (d) United Nations forces should not remain in any part of Korea otherwise than so far as necessary for achieving the objective specified in sub-paragraphs (a) and (b) above. . . .[6]

The political objective had been set forth in three UN resolutions since 1947, "but heretofore the UN had not as a body committed itself to the attaining of Korean unification by force," observes an authority. "The Rubicon of the Korean War," comments another, "had been passed with the enthusiastic support of the Western Allies." Available evidence indicates that Communist China's subsequent entry into the conflict was triggered, however, by the American troops' move into North Korea, not by the UN resolution. In the meantime, the JCS instructed MacArthur to issue a second ultimatum to North Korea to surrender; he did so on the 9th, but it went unanswered.[7]

According to MacArthur's operations orders of October 2, the X Corps was to begin its east-coast conquest with an amphibious assault at Wonsan about October 20. The 1st Marine Division embarked on October 9 at Inchon for the long sea trip around the tip of the peninsula, and the 7th Division traveled overland to Pusan and boarded transports there on the 17th for the voyage along the western edge of the Sea of Japan. In the meantime, however, the ROK 3d Division, moving rapidly against light resistance, took Wonsan on October 11; it and the ROK Capital Division then raced northward and captured Hungnam and Hamhung six days later. Before the X Corps had left the Inchon-Seoul vicinity, Walker had tried futilely to persuade MacArthur to incorporate it under his Eighth Army command for the drive toward Pyongyang. Failing in this effort, he and members of his staff tried unsuccessfully to get GHQ to deploy the X Corps in an overland advance to Wonsan, since the sea route was over six times longer. Walker flew to Wonsan after its seizure by the ROK troops; on his return to Seoul he attempted again to dissuade the UNC chief from shipping the X Corps to the east coast and splitting the forces in the advance northward. But MacArthur stubbornly stuck to his plan, partly because he favored Almond, who wished to retain his command separate from Walker's, and partly because he was convinced that the rugged Taebaek Mountains of central North Korea made the separate commands and axes of advance of the Eighth Army and the X Corps practical. In fact, not only Walker, his headquarters staff, and his unit commanders but also Turner Joy and Arthur Struble of the Navy and Doyle Hickey, Pinky Wright, and George Eberle of MacArthur's GHQ staff were opposed to the Wonsan operation, Almond's continued command independence, and the divided advance through North Korea. MacArthur later claimed that his plan "followed standard military practice in the handling and control of widely separated forces where lateral communications were difficult or impossible." But a senior UNC officer commented, "Almond got what he wanted, though it didn't make good military sense to some of the rest of us." As Walker's forces started moving forward on the Seoul-Pyongyang axis, they encountered the logistical consequences of the Wonsan move — temporary shortages of ammunition, supply, and equipment because of the congestion at the port of Inchon and on the Seoul-Pusan road and rail arteries, occasioned by the transfers of the X Corps divisions.

Sweeping operations began on October 10 to clear the more than 3000 mines discovered in the Wonsan harbor. Of the nineteen minesweepers used, eight were Japanese; several of the vessels were hit by mines during the dangerous work, including a Japanese minesweeper that sank with a loss of seven crewmen. The slow process of minesweeping was still under way when Struble's task force, bearing the 1st Marine Division, arrived off Wonsan on the 19th. For a week the troop transports sailed back and forth off the harbor entrance in "Operation Yo-yo," as the exasperated Marines nicknamed it. The division was finally able to go ashore at Wonsan on the 26th. Three days later the 7th Division made an unopposed amphibious landing at Iwon, about 120 miles up the coast.[8]

MacArthur, without consulting the JCS, announced on October 17 a new restraining line above which only South Korean troops would be employed. It ran from Sonchon, forty-five miles below the Yalu River on the west coast, to Songjin, fifty miles northeast of Iwon on the east coast. The new line was, on the average, thirty to forty miles north of and about twice as long as the more defensible Chongju-Hungnam line across the "waist" of the peninsula. The Joint Chiefs did not question MacArthur's judgment at the time, though Collins later viewed it as "the first, but not the last, stretching of MacArthur's orders beyond JCS instructions." In truth, however, though he should have sought his superiors' counsel in advance on the sensitive matter, MacArthur had set the earlier Chongju-Hungnam line; the JCS had directed him on September 27 to use only ROK units in the provinces bordering Manchuria and Siberia, with no specific line delineated.

In the October drive, Almond's X Corps, which consisted of the

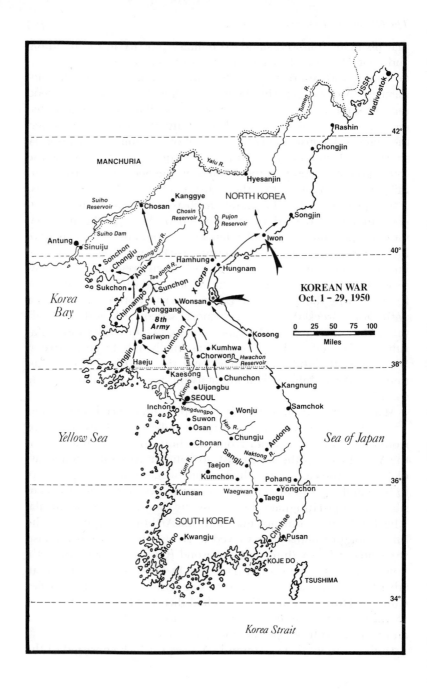

KOREAN WAR
Oct. 1 – 29, 1950

0 25 50 75 100
Miles

1st Marine and 7th Infantry divisions of the United States forces and the 3d and Capital divisions of the ROK Army, operated largely along the eastern coast, the main inland advances being about seventy miles above Hungnam and Iwon by South Korean units. No concerted effort was made to establish contact with the Eighth Army across the Taebaek Range, though MacArthur's plan had initially called for the X Corps to advance westward from Wonsan. By this time Walker had three corps, two of which he deployed in the advance up the west side of the peninsula, leaving the third in South Korea. Major General Frank W. Milburn's I Corps, made up of the American 1st Cavalry and 24th Infantry divisions, the 27th Commonwealth Brigade (the British force now joined by an Australian battalion), and the ROK 1st Division, moved along the Seoul-Sariwon-Pyongyang axis. On its right, or east, flank in the offensive was the ROK II Corps, consisting of the ROK 6th and 8th divisions. Major General John B. Coulter's IX Corps, which included the American 2d Infantry and 25th Infantry divisions and the ROK 7th Division, stayed below the 38th Parallel, in part because of logistical shortages but also for operations against guerrillas.

The Eighth Army's offensive began on October 9, but the spearheading 1st Cavalry ran into strong resistance not far above the 38th Parallel and took five days to overcome the North Korean garrison at Kumchon. After that battle the enemy opposition was more scattered and ineffective, and the Eighth Army units moved northward rapidly. On October 19, Pyongyang fell to the 1st Cavalry and ROK 1st divisions, and the now disorganized North Korean Army remnants, along with Kim and his top government leaders, fled toward Anju. The next day the 187th Airborne RCT staged the first parachute drops of the war near Sukchon and Sunchon, thirty miles above Pyongyang, but they failed to trap the retreating enemy troops and officials. Kim established the temporary seat of his government at Sinuiju, on the Yalu River opposite Antung, Manchuria; later he and his leaders moved to Kanggye, deep in the mountains to the northeast. Meanwhile, the ROK 6th Division, meeting negligible opposition, raced far ahead of the units on its flanks. One of its platoons arrived at the banks of the Yalu River near Chosan, less than fifty miles southwest of Kanggye, on October 26 (the same day the Marines landed at

Wonsan). In the general euphoria that gripped the UNC and ROK commanders during the first three weeks or so of October, it was thought the ROK 6th would be only the first of their divisions to reach the Yalu. As it turned out, they would be the only troops under Walker's command to see the river.[9]

On the morning of October 20, the sixth anniversary of his celebrated return to the Philippines, MacArthur, accompanied by Stratemeyer, Wright, and Whitney, flew to the Sukchon and Sunchon drop zones to witness from the air the parachute landings of the 187th Airborne RCT from 113 C-119 and C-47 transports. Most of the fleeing North Koreans had already moved north, as related earlier, so the drops did not entrap any sizable numbers. From the *SCAP,* this was not obvious, and MacArthur later told reporters joyfully, "I didn't see any opposition. It looks like it was a complete surprise. It looks like we closed the trap. Closing that trap should be the end of all organized resistance. The war is very definitely coming to an end." Landing later on the 20th at Pyongyang, which had fallen the previous day, MacArthur conferred with Rhee, Walker, Milburn, and some Eighth Army staff officers; took a drive through Pyongyang, where portraits of Stalin and Kim Il Sung were still displayed on streetside posters; and received from Stratemeyer the Distinguished Flying Cross for his "outstanding heroism and extraordinary achievement while participating in aerial flights" to Korea under "precarious" conditions on four occasions since the hostilities started. Though that ceremony may have made some veteran FEAF airmen wince, everyone present was genuinely moved when MacArthur reviewed F Company of the 5th Cavalry Regiment, the first American outfit to enter the North Korean capital. MacArthur asked all those who had been in the company from the time it entered combat ninety-six days ago to step forward. Of the nearly 200 soldiers with the unit when it went into action the first time, only 5 were left to come forward, and 3 of them had suffered wounds. After more discussions about impending operations and future occupation plans, MacArthur and his party left on the *SCAP* shortly after 3:00 P.M. for the flight to Tokyo. Back in the North Korean capital of 800,000 residents, I Corps troops tore down Communist propaganda displays, and Walker settled into the office formerly occupied by Premier and Commander in Chief Kim Il Sung.[10] The first Communist capital to be "liberated" would shed its Red trappings quickly — or so Walker and his men optimistically thought.

Off Wonsan, where Smith and his seasick, bored Marines were engaged in Operation Yo-yo, the Marine general learned from Admiral Joy on the 20th that with the imminent end of hostilities two of the 1st Marine Division's regiments would return to the States and the third would go to Japan. Three days later Smith was informed of MacArthur's intention to keep only a single American Army division in North Korea for the postwar occupation, the rest of the Eighth Army to be stationed in Japan. On October 21, MacArthur informed the JCS that he "envisioned" that the Eighth Army's movement to Japan "would start before Thanksgiving and be completed before Christmas." The next day he told Stratemeyer to release two of his B-29 groups for return to the United States. From about October 10 onward, messages went back and forth between MacArthur and the JCS relating to future problems of occupation administration and rehabilitation and to the degree of participation by Rhee's officials in North Korean affairs, pending all-Korea elections and unification. There was talk, too, about war crimes trials in the fighting's aftermath, because since the Naktong breakout the advancing UNC forces had come on grisly scenes of atrocities committed by North Korean troops against ROK soldiers and civilians and also against American troops. Most recently, they had found over seventy American prisoners bound and murdered near Sukchon after the airdrop. In Washington a principal concern as the war neared its end was the strengthening of the General Reserve and of NATO's military establishment. The JCS notified MacArthur on October 21 that he would lose before Christmas both the 2d and 3d Infantry divisions (the latter would reach Korea on November 10). His vociferous protests helped to postpone the 3d Division's projected departure from the theater until May 1951, by which time it was thought the Korean national elections would have been held.

Serving alongside the American and ROK troops in North Korea by late October were 9000 soldiers in British, Australian, Turkish, Philippine, and Thai units, the largest outfits being the 27th Commonwealth Brigade and the Turkish Brigade (both under Walker). Another 27,000 troops from various UN countries were preparing to depart or were en route to Korea. But Pentagon officials decided on October 24 that only 15,000 non-ROK, non-American troops were needed in the United Nations Command, so the contributing nations were notified that just 6000 of their impending reinforcements would be required. Some UN members that had intended to assist militarily had already reduced or cancelled their commitments of future forces, so encouraging was the prospect of a quick end to the war. As will be discussed in the next section, MacArthur's meeting with Truman and some of his top advisers at Wake Island on October 15 had, if anything, nourished the sense of elation over the nearness of victory.[11]

Despite the contagion of optimism in Seoul, Tokyo, and Washington, there were portents of trouble ahead with Communist China — and with the UNC commander in chief. On October 18, American planes spotted nearly 100 Soviet-built fighters at an air base near Antung, Manchuria, just across the Yalu from North Korea. This foreboding sign, together with a CIA report that Red Chinese forces might be thrown in to defend the Suiho Reservoir hydroelectric facilities near Sinuiju, North Korea, prompted the JCS to send an urgent, if unusual, message to MacArthur on the 21st. Partly acting on Acheson's suggestion, the Joint Chiefs "authorized" him, but at his own discretion, to make a public announcement stating that (1) his forces would not attack the Suiho power center and (2) the UN Commission for the Unification and Rehabilitation of Korea (UNCURK), set up after the resolution of October 7, would consult with "all interested parties," including Communist China, about Korea's political future. The general answered promptly that at present he had no plans to attack the Suiho hydroelectric plant but would not disavow the possibility of its future destruction if it was used to provide power for "hostile military purposes," such as munitions production. He also declined to make the UNCURK pronouncement on the grounds that he could not speak for that body and its future actions. He concluded that it was "inadvisable to issue any statement" on these matters "at this time." The Joint Chiefs did not press the issue further.

The JCS entered no objection either when on October 19 MacArthur ordered Walker, Almond, and their commanders to push forward to the new Sonchon-Songjin line with "maximum effort" and to be "prepared for continued rapid advance to the border of North Korea." It sounded, at least by implication, as if he was unleashing all his forces in the drive to the Yalu. On October 24 he issued another order to his commanders that no longer left any doubt: he abolished the restraining line for non-ROK units and exhorted the field commanders "to drive forward with all speed and full utilization of their forces." They were authorized by him to "use any and all ground forces" under their command "to secure all of North Korea," though non-ROK forces were to be "withdrawn from border areas as quickly as feasible and replaced by ROK units." This drew an immediate response from the Joint Chiefs, who told him that his order violated their directive of September 27 banning non-ROK forces from the border provinces. The message also said, "While the Joint Chiefs of Staff realize that you undoubtedly had sound reasons for issuing these instructions they would like to be informed of them, as your action is a matter of some concern here."[12] MacArthur responded to his superiors with an argument that, for its twisted logic and arrogance, was amazing:

The instructions contained in my [message to UNC commanders] were a matter of military necessity. Not only are the ROK forces not of sufficient strength to initially accomplish the security of North Korea, but the reactions of their commanders are at times so emotional that it was deemed essential that initial use be made of more seasoned and stabilized commanders. There is no conflict that I can see with the directive . . . dated 27 September, which merely enunciated the provision as a matter of policy and clearly stated: "These instructions, however, cannot be considered to be final since they may require modification in accordance with developments." The necessary latitude for modification was contained also in . . . [the message] dated 30 September from the Secretary of Defense which stated: "We want you to feel unhampered tactically and strategically to proceed north of the 38th Parallel."

I am fully cognizant of the basic purpose and intent of your directive and every possible precaution is being taken in the premises. The very reverse, however, would be fostered and tactical hazards might even result from other action than that which I have directed.[13]

As brazen as was his reply, the Joint Chiefs again decided, astonishingly, to let his judgment stand. The principle of trusting the field or theater commander was deeply ingrained in all four of them. According to the official JCS history, "The Joint Chiefs of Staff apparently accepted his defense of his latest action; at any rate, they did not countermand his order." At the Senate hearings the following spring, however, Collins maintained that this was MacArthur's first clear violation of a JCS directive during the war. The incident "was one indication among many others [later] . . . that General MacArthur was not in consonance with the basic policies" of his superiors, he said, and it "led us [the JCS] to fear that just as he violated a policy in this case without consulting us, perhaps the thing might be done in some other instance of a more serious nature." In his book on the Korean War, Collins stated lamely, "In any event, it was too late for the JCS to stop the movement of American forces north of the restraining line."[14] For not holding a firmer leash on their aggressive Far Eastern commander, the Joint Chiefs must share with him the blame for some of the disasters that followed.

2. Wake: Policies or Politics?

By the time he returned to the White House on October 7 after several days aboard the presidential yacht *Williamsburg* on Chesapeake Bay, Truman had decided to confer with MacArthur somewhere in the Pacific during the next week or so. The idea had been advanced by several staff members with him on the *Williamsburg*, particularly George M. Elsey, his administrative assistant. Truman told Marshall on the 9th to arrange the date and the place with MacArthur and to suggest in his message that the President preferred to meet on the 14th or 16th at Pearl Harbor. MacArthur promptly replied to Marshall that he "would be delighted to meet the President on the morning of the 15th at Wake Island." Truman was agreeable, and on the 10th Charles G. Ross, the White House press secretary, issued to reporters a statement from the President: "General MacArthur and I are making a quick trip over the coming weekend to meet in the Pacific. . . . I shall discuss with him the final phase of United Nations action in Korea

. . . [and] other matters within his responsibility." Although the President deferred to the general on the date and the location of the session, MacArthur said he was told "nothing of the purpose of the meeting" or of who would be present. On the 12th, however, he received word from Harriman that he was "looking forward keenly" to seeing him at Wake. When MacArthur learned through press reports that a chartered Pan Am airliner carrying thirty-five newspaper, radio, and television reporters and photographers would accompany the presidential entourage, he sent a request to the Pentagon to be allowed to bring some reporters from Tokyo with him on his *SCAP*. MacArthur said he "was surprised when the request was promptly and curtly disapproved."[15]

The President offered two reasons publicly for calling the Wake conference: to discuss crucial matters of Korean and other Far Eastern policies and to improve communication with MacArthur personally. In his communiqué at the end of the Wake meeting, the President stated, "I have met with General of the Army Douglas MacArthur for the purpose of getting first-hand information and ideas from him."[16] In what was billed as a major foreign policy address at the War Memorial Opera House in San Francisco on October 17, Truman made the following remarks about his motive for the Wake assembly:

> I understand that there has been speculation about why I made this trip. There is really no mystery about it. I went because I wanted to see and talk to General MacArthur. The best way to see him and talk to him is to meet him somewhere and talk to him.
>
> There is no substitute for personal conversation with the commander in the field who knows the problems there from first-hand experience. He has information at his fingertips which can be of help to all of us in deciding upon the right policies in these critical times.[17]

The course of events in the Korean War during the first nine days of October surely lent credence to the need for a detailed discussion between MacArthur and top Washington leaders about the situation and its explosive implications. On October 1, ROK troops had started moving across the 38th Parallel. Two days later had come Chou En-lai's saber-rattling against an American incursion into North Korea. On the day of the President's return from his Chesapeake Bay cruise, the UN General Assembly had adopted its momentous resolution on Korean unification, radically altering its objective in the war. The next day two FEAF fighters had strafed a Soviet air base sixty miles beyond the North Korean border and not far from Vladivostok. (The American government subsequently apologized and offered to pay damages.) On the 9th, the day Marshall had first approached MacArthur about a meeting with the President, the UNC chief had broadcast his second surrender ultimatum to North Korea in vain, and the Eighth Army had begun its drive above the 38th Parallel. Uneasy about Peking's possible reaction, Truman had instructed the JCS that same day to amplify MacArthur's instructions of September 27, to wit: "Hereinafter in the event of the open or covert employment anywhere in Korea of major Chinese Communist units without prior announcement, you should continue the action as long as, in your judgment, action by forces now under your control offers a reasonable chance of success." MacArthur was also directed to "obtain authorization from Washington prior to taking any military action against objectives in Chinese territory."[18]

Flying many thousands of miles from east and west to rendezvous at tiny Wake Island in the mid-Pacific, the Truman and MacArthur parties were quite different in their size and make-up. Those from the United States went to Wake in four groups: an advance party of White House staff members arrived on the 13th to make security and logistical arrangements; the press plane and the two aircraft carrying the Washington officials and their assistants reached the island early on the 15th. The major participants in the Wake conference from the twenty-four-person presidential group would be Truman; Harriman, special presidential assistant on foreign affairs; Bradley, JCS chairman; Pace, Secretary of the Army; Dean Rusk, Assistant Secretary of State for Far Eastern affairs; and Philip C. Jessup, ambassador-at-large. Radford, who was CINCPAC and Pacific Fleet commander, also participated, joining Truman for the flight from Oahu to Wake. With MacArthur on the flight from Tokyo were Muccio, Whitney, Bunker, and Canada; Story piloted the *SCAP*, as usual. The only ones from the Tokyo group who would be active participants in the Wake talks were MacArthur and Ambassador John Muccio.[19]

On October 11 Truman flew from Washington to St. Louis, where he attended the installation of his sister as head of the Order of the Eastern Star in Missouri. The next day he went on to Fairfield-Suisun (later Travis) Air Force Base, near Sacramento, to be joined there by his advisers from Washington. On the morning of the 13th the three aircraft of the presidential entourage arrived at Hickam Air Force Base, Oahu: the President's plane, a Douglas DC-6 called *Independence,* which bore him and his senior officials; an Air Force C-121 (Lockheed Constellation), carrying the rest of the staff from Washington; and a Boeing Stratocruiser, which transported the press representatives. Most of Truman's day on Oahu was consumed in touring defense installations and conferring with his advisers. Shortly after midnight the *Independence* departed from Hickam for Wake; the other two planes had taken off earlier. The three planes crossed the International Date Line about five hours out and made their arrival at Wake on Sunday morning, October 15.

Meanwhile, MacArthur and his small group had left Tokyo about 7:00 A.M. on the 14th aboard the general's Constellation. During the flight MacArthur "paced restlessly up and down the aisle of the plane," according to Whitney. Muccio observed that "he appeared irked, disgusted, and at the same time somewhat uneasy. In the course of his exposition, he used such terms as 'summoned for political reasons' and 'not aware that I am still fighting a war.'" MacArthur had voiced the same complaints when summoned suddenly from Brisbane to Pearl Harbor to confer with Roosevelt in July 1944. The *SCAP* touched down on Wake just after 6:00 P.M. that day; MacArthur and his officers were billeted overnight in a Quonset hut that was the residence of the local maintenance manager of the Civil Aeronautics Administration.[20]

It will probably be impossible for scholars ever to bury the myths about the Truman-MacArthur meeting that were propagated from 1973 to 1976 in a best-selling book, a popular stage play, and a television dramatization. Allegedly, the planes carrying Truman and MacArthur arrived over Wake at the same time on the 15th. When the *SCAP* continued to circle, Truman became angry and radioed MacArthur to land first. Then, claim the myth-makers, MacArthur did not appear to meet the President until forty-five minutes after the *Independence* had landed. When they finally met, the chief executive heatedly reprimanded the general for his disrespect.[21]

Actually, the *Independence* touched down at 6:30 A.M. on the 15th, the press aircraft and the Air Force C-121 had landed earlier that morning, and MacArthur had arrived the previous day. As Truman descended from his plane, MacArthur and his officers, together with the Washington personnel who had come on the C-121, were waiting to greet him. Later Truman did remark in a disapproving tone that MacArthur was attired in an open khaki shirt and "a greasy ham and eggs cap that evidently had been in use for twenty years." But on October 15 neither man, by word or deed, reacted negatively toward the other. When they met, for the first time ever, both leaders smiled broadly and shook hands vigorously. Truman said, "I'm glad you are here. I have been a long time in meeting you, General." MacArthur responded, "I hope it won't be so long next time, Mr. President." After posing cheerfully together for the photographers, they strode arm in arm to an old two-door Chevrolet sedan (the only car on the island) and chatted amiably as they were driven to the small building where MacArthur had stayed the previous night. The other visitors from Washington and Tokyo were transported by bus to a pink-colored one-story structure that was the newly constructed communications center of the Civil Aeronautics Administration. When the two leaders completed their private talk of forty or more minutes, they were driven to the building where the other officials were assembled. They appeared relaxed and cordial toward each other as they entered for the general conference. In their memoirs each expressed a favorable first impression of the other: Truman found MacArthur to be "a most stimulating and interesting person" and their private conversation "very friendly"; the general was impressed by the President's "engaging personality" and "quick and witty tongue." He added, "I liked him from the start."[22]

Not much is known about what Truman and MacArthur discussed before the general session. While they were talking on the back seat of the small Chevrolet en route to the Quonset, the Secret Service agent who was on the front seat beside the driver remembered that Truman asked about the probability of Peking's intervention in the Korean conflict. MacArthur replied that his intelligence did not indicate the Red Chinese would enter the war, but if they did his UNC forces could handle them. Truman said that at the Quonset the general "assured" him that "the victory was won in Korea" and reasserted that "there was little possibility of the Chinese Communists coming in." MacArthur also affirmed that "Japan was ready for a peace treaty." He remarked, too, that "he was sorry if he had caused any embarrassment" by his VFW message, to which Truman replied that he "considered the incident closed." According to the President's account, MacArthur maintained "he was not in politics in any way — that he had allowed the politicians to make a 'chump' (his word) of him in 1948 and that it would not happen again." Truman brought up plans for "the strengthening of Europe," and MacArthur responded that "he was sure it would be possible to send one division from Korea to Europe in January 1951." In his memoirs MacArthur did not mention his meeting alone with the President; when asked about it at the Senate hearings in 1951, he said he did "not feel at liberty to reveal what was discussed." In his book published in 1956, Whitney quoted MacArthur as calling it a "relatively unimportant conversation." Whitney, whose version undoubtedly came directly from his boss, generally affirmed Truman's version of each man's remarks about the VFW message, but claimed that "most of the rest of the conversation was devoted to, of all things at this time, the fiscal and economic problems of the Philippines."[23]

The general meeting began in the new communications building at 7:35 or 7:45 A.M., depending on which source one follows. Five small folding tables were pushed together to form an oblong table at which sat Truman, MacArthur, Radford, Muccio, Bradley, Harriman, Pace, Jessup, Rusk, and Whitney. Also at the table were Colonels Archelous L. Hamblen and Willis S. Matthews, Pace's special assistant on occupied areas and Bradley's executive officer, respectively. Others of the Truman and MacArthur groups were seated behind those at the table, including even MacArthur's pilot, Story. According to Whitney, when Bunker began making notes as the conference started, Ross, Truman's press secretary, told MacArthur that "no record was to be made of the talks," so Bunker ceased writing. There must have been a misunderstanding on this score, because throughout the session of about an hour and a half Bradley, Harriman, Jessup, Rusk, Hamblen, and Matthews all took

notes openly. In addition, Miss Vernice Anderson, Jessup's secretary, sat in a small room nearby with the slatted door partly open
and, on her own, made shorthand notes of the session.

The atmosphere of the general meeting was informal and congenial: Truman soon shed his coat, MacArthur puffed on a briar
pipe, and several quips by them and others during the ensuing
discussion produced general laughter. The session began with a
lighthearted touch when MacArthur asked whether Truman
minded his smoking and the President responded, "No. I suppose
I've had more smoke blown in my face than any other man alive."
Throughout the meeting the pattern of the conversation remained about the same, with Truman or one of his advisers asking for MacArthur's views, which sometimes produced supplementary comments by Muccio on topics relating to political and
economic affairs in Korea. About half the time was devoted to
problems involved in the political and economic reconstruction of
Korea after the cessation of hostilities that all assumed was imminent. With MacArthur fielding nearly all the questions and the
others contributing relatively short queries and remarks, the total
number of words spoken by the Far Eastern commander during
the session was larger than that of all the other participants combined, though he confined himself to responses that were comparatively short for him and did not launch into his usual extended monologues. Based on the Truman group's record, the
general session comprised 485 typescript lines of conversation by
9 people, distributed thus: MacArthur, 243 lines; Truman, 54;
Muccio, 52; Bradley, 34; Rusk, 30; Pace, 26; Radford, 24; Harriman, 15; and Jessup, 7. In that span of approximately 90 minutes,
over 30 questions were directed to MacArthur. At no point did
the discussion become argumentative, and no remarks were made
at which any participant could take offense. But also at no time
did the conferees probe in depth any issue raised; instead, they
skipped hastily and often disconnectedly from one topic to another. There was no agenda and no official minutes were kept;
the principal source on the session is a memorandum of the statements made as reflected in the notes taken by Truman's advisers
and Miss Anderson, which were later compiled by Bradley. Copies
of the compilation were sent to MacArthur on October 19, but it

should be remembered that he was not asked to contribute to, revise, or approve Bradley's memorandum.[24]

Truman led off the general session by asking for MacArthur's views on the problems of Korean rehabilitation after the fighting was over. The general began by presenting a résumé of the military situation, which he reminded them had to be resolved first. He confidently asserted that North Korea was "pursuing a forlorn hope" and that "formal resistance will end throughout North and South Korea by Thanksgiving." After the capture of Pyongyang, which would actually take place on the 19th, he thought any substantial enemy resistance would end. "It is my hope to be able to withdraw the Eighth Army to Japan by Christmas," he commented, though he planned to leave the American 2d and 3d divisions and some smaller UN units as an occupation force until all-Korean elections could be held, preferably early in 1951. He wanted to withdraw the non-ROK forces as soon as possible after the fighting stopped, for "all occupations are failures." He believed a 500-man KMAG should be left to assist the ROK military establishment, and he thought the United States should help to equip a ten-division ROK Army, as well as a "small but competent" ROK Navy and Air Force to "secure Korea" and to deter a future attack by Communist China, the latter being a possibility that "cannot be laughed off." As for economic assistance in rebuilding Korea, he and Muccio both felt that American aid amounting to about $150 million annually for several years would be needed. When the question of the future of Rhee's regime came up, MacArthur and Muccio each expressed concern lest Rhee's position be undermined. When Rusk pointed out that considerable anti-Rhee propaganda was circulating in the UN, Truman retorted, "We must make it plain that we are supporting the Rhee Government and propaganda can 'go to hell.' "[25]

Truman then turned the discussion back to the war, asking MacArthur, as he had done in private, "What are the chances for Chinese or Soviet interference?" According to Bradley's compilation, MacArthur answered:

Very little. Had they interfered in the first or second months it would have been decisive. We are no longer fearful of their intervention.

We no longer stand hat in hand. The Chinese have 300,000 men in
Manchuria. Of these probably not more than 100/125,000 are distributed along the Yalu River. Only 50/60,000 could be gotten across
the Yalu River. They have no Air Force. Now that we have bases for
our Air Force in Korea, if the Chinese tried to get down to Pyongyang there would be the greatest slaughter.

  With the Russians it is a little different. They have an Air Force in
Siberia and a fairly good one. . . . They can put 1000 planes in the
air with some 2/300 more from the Fifth and Seventh Soviet Fleets.
They are probably no match for our Air Force. The Russians have
no ground troops available for North Korea. . . . It would take six
weeks to get a division across and six weeks brings the winter. The
only other combination would be Russian air support of Chinese
ground troops. . . . I believe Russian air would bomb the Chinese as
often as they would bomb us. Ground support is a very difficult thing
to do. . . . Between untrained Air and Ground Forces an air umbrella is impossible without a lot of joint training. I believe it just
wouldn't work with Chinese Communist ground and Russian air.[26]

Both MacArthur's views and his figures were substantially the same
as those recently reported by the CIA and other Washington intelligence sources; Truman and his advisers knew of them and
concurred. A significant omission from Bradley's compilation, as
charged later by MacArthur, Whitney, and Willoughby, relying on
notes made by Whitney and Bunker during the return flight from
Wake, was MacArthur's important qualification that his opinion was
only speculative, because the question of whether other nations
would enter the war was a matter of political intelligence that was
properly in the realm of CIA and State intelligence groups, not
his military intelligence staff. The most astonishing fact about this
most-quoted portion of the Wake talks is that this was the whole
extent of the conferees' probe into the enormous implications that
the current UNC offensive might have for decision-makers in Peking and Moscow: one question by Truman, a single response by
MacArthur, and absolutely no follow-up questions, challenges, or
further mention!

  Indeed, as soon as MacArthur completed the above statement,
Harriman led the discussion into another direction by asking him,
"What about [North Korean] war criminals?" MacArthur responded briefly that those who committed atrocities would be tried
quickly by military tribunals, but war crimes trials like those at

Nuremberg and Tokyo, involving "crimes against peace," lengthy proceedings, and international tribunals, "were no deterrent." Truman next asked the general for his view on producing a Japanese peace treaty without Soviet or Communist Chinese cooperation. MacArthur answered, "I would call a conference at once and invite them. If they don't come, go ahead. . . . The Japanese deserve a treaty." Quickly the discussion moved on to MacArthur's views about arrangements for Japan's post-treaty security and the stationing of American forces there. Bradley interjected a statement about the need for American divisions in Europe, and MacArthur said he would make one of his available by January. He recommended the 2d Division, rather than the 3d, because it was "better trained." At a dizzy pace, the discussion whirled on to some brief remarks and questions about the future need for the SCAP administration and for GARIOA funds in Japan.

Pace seemed sincerely interested in trying to determine whether MacArthur had any grievances that his department could alleviate. When he inquired whether the general's directive on North Korean operations was "sufficiently comprehensive," MacArthur answered simply "yes" and the conversation moved on to another topic. Later Pace asked him, in the context of the discussion on Korean rehabilitation, "Is there anything in terms of ECA [Economic Cooperation Administration] and Army cooperation that we might do to help you?" MacArthur replied, "No commander in the history of war has ever had more complete and adequate support from all agencies in Washington than I have." Since MacArthur had apologized in private for his VFW message, Truman, in the spirit of the group's agreeableness, averted any review of the Formosa issue by stating, "General MacArthur and I have talked fully about Formosa. There is no need to cover that subject again. The General and I are in complete agreement." Later Truman repeated this to reporters, but, in truth, he and MacArthur had neither discussed fully nor concurred on any Formosa-related issue except the VFW message.

In the course of the general session Truman raised the idea of "a possible Pacific pact or some other arrangements similar to that in the Atlantic." MacArthur, backed by Radford, remarked that the United States needed a Pacific-Asian policy like the Truman Doctrine and "assurance of security from the United States" to the

Southeast Asian countries. But he contended that a collective security pact "would be very difficult to put into effect" because of "the lack of homogeneity" among those nations and because "they have no military forces" of their own. This led to a short discussion of the situation in French Indochina, which MacArthur found to be "puzzling. The French have 150,000 of their best troops there with an officer of the highest reputation in command. Their forces are twice what we had in the perimeter and they are opposed by half of what the North Koreans had. I cannot understand why they do not clean it up." Truman added, "I cannot understand it either. . . . We have been working on the French in connection with Indo-China for years without success. . . . This is the most discouraging thing we face."

Just as it seemed that the conferees might delve in some depth into the Indochina situation, even though it was far afield from Korea, they suddenly moved on to the economic problems of the Philippines. After raising one related issue, they left the matter hanging and hurried on to query MacArthur about whether additional forces from UN members were needed in Korea. The general said they would be "useless from a military point of view," but since "they give a United Nations flavor," he thought "the balance between these two considerations should be struck in Washington."

About 9:10 A.M., or after some ninety minutes of this disorganized bewildering talk, Truman announced, "No one who was not here would believe we have covered so much ground as we have been actually able to cover." He proposed to terminate the general session forthwith, continue informal talks with MacArthur and Muccio while he rested and some of his staff prepared a communiqué, reunite the group for lunch, and have everyone depart from Wake early that afternoon. Whether he was tired, desirous to get back to Tokyo before dark, or disgusted by the superficiality of the session, MacArthur remarked, "If it's all right, I am anxious to get back as soon as possible and would like to leave before luncheon if that is convenient." Truman consented after noting that Bradley and Pace particularly wanted to talk with MacArthur following the general session. Truman concluded the meeting with the comment "This has been a most satisfactory conference." [27]

While Truman relaxed at the Quonset residence of the Wake manager for Pan American World Airways, MacArthur and Muccio chatted with various officials for the next hour and a half. Rusk and Harriman discussed with MacArthur some further points about Indochina, North Korean war criminals, performance of ROK forces in combat, and possible Chinese Communist entry into the Korean War. Rusk asked the general his opinion of Peking's threat to intervene if the UNC forces invaded North Korea. According to Rusk, MacArthur "said he did not fully understand why they had gone out on such a limb and that they must be greatly embarrassed by the predicament in which they now find themselves." Bradley and Pace later talked with MacArthur at length, mainly about the logistical needs of his forces and the future redeployment of some of the Eighth Army. Bradley recalled, "He could not have been friendlier. He thanked me privately for the tremendous support the JCS had given him during the almost four months of the Korean War." Although the Far Eastern commander thought his theater should get top priority in "the fight against communism," Bradley believed MacArthur's profession that "he would cooperate to the utmost" in making troops available for transfer to West Europe. During the informal conversations after the general session, Harriman said MacArthur was "much impressed by the President" and was pleased that Truman had solicited his views.[28]

About 10:45, MacArthur and his officers went to the Quonset, where the President was resting. There Truman and MacArthur quickly approved without changes the conference communiqué, drafted by Truman's staff. Ross then distributed copies to the horde of waiting newsmen. The communiqué, which MacArthur initialed, was phrased as a first-person statement by the President; it mentioned several of the many topics touched on during the general session, misleadingly implying that a serious exchange of views had occurred but accurately conveying the spirit of optimism and congeniality of the conferees. Truman said that the conference had been "highly satisfactory" and "most helpful." He explained that "the very complete unanimity of view which prevailed enabled us to finish our discussions rapidly." The talks were "greatly facilitated" by "the excellent coordination which has existed between Washington and the field." The President asserted that, in reviewing the major Far Eastern problems, the participants were "fully aware of the dangers which lie ahead." He added, "I am very glad to have had this chance to talk them over with one of America's great soldier-statesmen." Truman and MacArthur returned to the airfield together in the Chevrolet. Their main topic was the presidential race of 1952. MacArthur denied interest in being a candidate but thought Eisenhower would run. Truman said Ike "doesn't know the first thing about politics" and would be worse than Grant as President.

At the air terminal Truman gave MacArthur a box of candy for his wife and son, and he awarded the general a fourth Oak Leaf Cluster for his Distinguished Service Medal, praising his "conspicuously brilliant and courageous leadership and discerning judgment of the highest order." He also presented the Medal of Merit to Muccio. In an aside to Whitney and MacArthur, the President promised to see that Whitney was promoted to major general (his second star came later that fall). MacArthur, though appearing in a pleasant mood, was unusually reticent when correspondents tried to question him outside the terminal: he remarked that he had "greatly enjoyed meeting the President," but said that "all the discussions of this meeting are in the hands of Mr. Ross." As Truman boarded his plane, MacArthur's final words to him were "Goodby, sir, and happy landings. It's been a real honor to talk to you." At 11:35 A.M., only five hours after his arrival, the President and his chief advisers took off aboard the *Independence* for Hawaii. Shortly afterward the *SCAP* left for Tokyo, and the C-121 and the Stratocruiser also departed, headed for Oahu. During the flight back to Oahu, according to Vernice Anderson, Bradley proposed that the participants in the general session work on their notes, which he would collect later and compile as "a composite record of this event for the official record," because it had been "an extremely important and historic meeting."

In his San Francisco speech two days later Truman again lauded MacArthur and spoke of the Wake conference as a significant discussion of Far Eastern policies. He assured the audience that "there is complete unity in the aims and conduct of our foreign policy," and he told them that "it is fortunate for the world" that MacArthur, "a very great soldier," was heading the United Nations Command. On the flight back to Tokyo, MacArthur also was in good spirits; Muccio thought he was at "his sparkling best." The *Nippon Times* reported that the general was "smiling and looking fresh" and "appeared in excellent humor" when he arrived at Haneda Airport at 4:00 P.M. on the 15th. After reading a press report later about Truman's San Francisco address, he sent the President a highly complimentary message about its inspiring impact on Asian peoples who opposed aggression and Communism. He thought the speech revealed Truman's dedication to "dynamic leadership based upon positive policy."[29]

Bradley summed up the favorable impressions of Truman's advisers on the trip when he wrote MacArthur on the 19th:

> It was positively refreshing to see and to talk to you again. I am only too sorry that I could not spend more time with you. The conference, I feel, was most satisfactory and profitable — all of us from here got a great deal out of it. I am inclosing five copies of the substance of statements compiled from the notes made by those of us who made the trip from Washington.
>
> We all think that you are doing a grand job — as exemplified in this morning's reports on the good news from Pyongyang [captured that day].[30]

For a fleeting period longer, Truman and MacArthur continued to exchange pleasantries about the Wake get-together. The President wrote MacArthur on October 23 that he was "pleased" and "happy" about their talks at Wake and added, "Our meeting has had a splendid reaction here in the United States, and I think it was well worthwhile, if for no other reason than that we became personally acquainted." MacArthur replied on the 30th: "I left the Wake Island conference with a distinct sense of satisfaction that the country's interests had been well served through the better mutual understanding and exchange of views which it afforded." But he closed on a somber note: "I hope that it will result in building a strong defense against future efforts of those who seek for one reason or another (none of them worthy) to breach the understanding between us."[31]

It will be recalled that Truman's avowed reasons for the Wake meeting were to discuss policy and to improve relations with MacArthur. Since the discussions ranged over a host of topics in an unorganized, superficial manner, it is farcical to claim that the conferees seriously reviewed policies on Korea and the Far East. On all the questions posed to MacArthur, the Washington authorities already had his positions well documented in his message traffic with the Pentagon. MacArthur was correct when he later maintained that the discussions involved "nothing on which my views were not known. No new policies, no new strategy of war or international politics, were proposed or discussed." Acheson, Marshall, Collins, Sherman, and Vandenberg, though key figures in policymaking related to the Korean situation, were invited to the meeting by Truman very late in the game, after he had consulted the others. Each of them declined. Acheson later said of the Wake conference: "The whole idea was distasteful to me. I wanted no part of it, and saw no good coming from it." In view of the "mile wide, inch deep" approach used in the meeting at Wake, chiefly determined by Truman as moderator, the added presence of the Secretaries of State and Defense and the other Joint Chiefs probably would hardly have transformed it into a penetrating and thorough reconsideration of American policies in Korea and elsewhere in the Far East.

When General Frank Lowe, the President's liaison with UNC, learned of the impending conference at Wake, he tried to persuade Truman to cancel or postpone it. Failing in this, Lowe suggested that he meet with Truman in Hawaii en route to brief him on MacArthur and the Korean situation. Lowe, who liked and respected both Truman and MacArthur, feared that a brief get-together, particularly with over sixty advisers and newsmen around them, would not be conducive to a sincere exchange of views between the two principals. Although the general and the President were favorably impressed with each other, their time together was far too brief for them to build a foundation for good personal communication in the trying times that lay ahead. In family letters of October 13 and November 17, Truman referred to MacArthur as the "Right Hand Man of God," indicating that Wake did not greatly alter his private opinion. Truman's public façade of unity with the general began deteriorating in a few short weeks, first over the Formosa issue. He continued to tell reporters that they were in agreement, but MacArthur, when asked by correspondents in Tokyo whether his position on Formosa had changed, emphatically stated that it had not. At the Senate hearings on MacArthur's relief and afterward, acrimonious comments would be exchanged between the Truman and MacArthur camps about a number of issues born at Wake, such as Bradley's composite record of the general session, Miss Anderson's role, and MacArthur's prediction about Red China. Some of these differences will be referred to in a later section on the hearings. In the long run, the Wake meeting contributed more to alienating Truman and MacArthur than to improving their relationship.[32]

If the conference did not seriously address policy nor build rapport between the two leaders, why was it called? Robert Sherrod, a *Time* correspondent on the Wake trip, reported at the time that, as the conference ended, "many a correspondent felt he had witnessed nothing but a political grandstand play." Whitney wrote six years afterward, "It was only later, when Mr. Truman made his amazing charge that MacArthur had misled him on the possibility of Red Chinese intervention and when the scandalous method of preparing the 'record' of the proceedings was exposed, that MacArthur realized that Wake Island was no longer an enigma — it was a sly political ambush." Dismissing the views of journalists like Sherrod as current opinion and Whitney as sycophantic and paranoiac, many respected scholars since then have written of Wake as a serious policy parley. Recently, however, two of the best-researched studies of the Wake conference, each written by a noted historian, have concluded, in part, that Truman's primary motive in convening the meeting was political. And in a recent interview Charles S. Murphy, Truman's special counsel at the time, stated that White House staff members proposed the idea of the meeting to the President because "it was good election-year stuff" and the Democratic candidates in the congressional elections of November 1950 generally were in need of a boost. It was thought that Truman's identification with MacArthur three weeks before election day might draw some conservative, anti-Communist voters away from Republican contenders. Also, it was felt that the President, who, unlike MacArthur and McCarthy, had been off the front pages for some time, could use the headlines, which the trip surely provided. A distinguished historian recently suggested that the Wake conference was really "an exercise in public relations" or "a piece of presidential theater," and not at all "a serious attempt to deal with serious questions of policy." Because most previous accounts have dealt with it as an important episode in the reappraisal of East Asian policies, he continued, historians "should be careful not to assume that historical personages generally exalted by history — in this instance, President Truman — always acted on the basis of exalted motives." Unhappily, he seems to be right about the President's dominant motive.[33]

But as a political tactic to assist the Democrats in the midterm elections, the Wake ploy was apparently of no benefit: though the Democrats came out of the elections still in control of both houses of Congress, the Republicans gained twenty-eight seats in the House and five in the Senate, with several powerful Democratic senators going down to defeat, including the majority leader and the majority whip. McCarthy was influential in helping to produce the defeat of two veteran Democratic senators, and in California's Senate race another Republican conservative exploiting the anti-Communist theme was victorious. His name was Richard M. Nixon.

Perhaps the principal consequence of the Wake episode was one that did not seriously enter Truman's considerations in advance. Afterward, however, Truman and a number of his officials used it to advantage, namely, MacArthur's erroneous prediction about Communist Chinese intervention in Korea. The general's well-known proclivity for expounding on subjects beyond his expertise had hurt him previously, for instance, his needless pontificating in the wake of the Bonus Army's ouster from Washington in 1932 about the ragtag group's Communist leadership and aims. The great majority of writings since 1950 that have mentioned the Wake affair have focused on MacArthur's poor judgment about Peking's intentions. The implication in many such works is that had MacArthur predicted the opposite, the direction of the war might have been different and its expansion might have been averted. Such interpretations are distorted and unfair, because Washington was already committed to the drive to the Yalu and the President and his advisers at Wake agreed with MacArthur's views.

Had Truman's motivation been other than political in calling the Wake meeting, the conference could have been of crucial importance. It afforded an excellent opportunity for sober reconsideration of what the United States and the UN were trying to achieve in the Korean War. And it was a chance for Truman and Mac-Arthur to begin to establish a personal rapport that might have prevented later misunderstandings. Instead, the Wake conference was added to a long list of heralded summit meetings at which opportunities to change a tragic course in history were missed.

CHAPTER XVII

"An Entirely New War"

1. Venturing into the Unknown

THE EUPHORIC FEELING that the Korean War was almost over, shared by all those who had met at Wake, was jolted on October 25 by sudden attacks on both the Eighth Army and X Corps fronts by Chinese Communist forces (CCF). On the west side of the peninsula that day, a regiment of the ROK 6th Division was engaged by Chinese soldiers near Onjong, about forty miles north of Anju; it was virtually annihilated in the next two days. The rest of the 6th Division, including the troops that had reached the Yalu, were wiped out or routed by Chinese forces lying in ambush farther north. The other two ROK divisions in the western advance, the 1st and 8th, were hit hard, too, producing, in Walker's words, a "complete collapse and disintegration of ROK II Corps" and dangerously exposing the right flank of the Eighth Army. By the end of their first week of combat the Chinese were threatening Unsan, southwest of Onjong, and were also pushing south of the Chongchon River toward Kunuri. In the farthest northward advance during the war of any American forces of the Eighth Army, a regiment of the 24th Division had reached Chonggo-dong, eighteen miles south of Sinuiju, by November 1. But with the menacing Chinese envelopment in the Kunuri area, the 24th Division and the British brigade, also well north of Anju, were ordered to withdraw southward, and the 1st Cavalry and 2d Infantry divisions were rushed north to help stop the CCF thrust. In three days of vicious fighting at Unsan the 8th Cavalry Regiment was decimated, but by November 5 the UNC troops had stabilized the front at Kunuri and north of Anju. The next day, as quickly as they had appeared, the CCF withdrew northward.

Across the Taebaek Range to the east on October 25, the ROK 3d Division encountered an armor-supported Chinese force at Sudong, south of the Chosin (Changjin) Reservoir. Smith sent his 7th Marine Regiment to relieve the hard-pressed South Koreans on November 2, and in the next five days they mauled the Chinese. Suddenly the enemy troops broke off the action and disappeared into the mountains to the north. On both the western and eastern fronts nearly forty Chinese soldiers were captured during the two weeks of combat. Under interrogation, many of them spoke truthfully, as was proven later, about the Chinese units to which they belonged and about the large number of CCF troops, allegedly "volunteers," that had crossed the Yalu, mostly in the past two weeks.

Despite the evidence, Walker, Almond, MacArthur, and their G-2 officers were not yet ready to accept the fact that Chinese forces of division and army size were already south of the Yalu. The battles, as well as the information gained from prisoner interrogations, were duly reported by MacArthur and Willoughby to Washington. On November 2, however, Willoughby estimated that only 16,500 CCF soldiers were in North Korea, and he figured about 316,000 Chinese regulars and 274,000 irregulars (security troops) were in Manchuria. In fact, at least 180,000 regulars in six CCF armies were then hiding in the mountains of North Korea. CIA reports in late October on POW interrogations were made available to the JCS, but the CIA expressed no great alarm, assigning the reports to the F-6 category, which was the lowest level of priority for content and source. In Washington, as in Tokyo, according to the JCS chronicle, "the belief prevailed that Communist China would have little to gain by intervening in Korea at that time" with major forces.[1]

When the Joint Chiefs asked MacArthur on November 3 for his "interim appreciation of the situation in Korea and its implications," he replied the next day expressing a blend of caution, reassurance, and puzzlement about the meaning of the Chinese presence in Korea. He speculated on four possible courses that Peking might be pursuing: (1) full-scale intervention, (2) covert military assistance to North Korea, (3) use of Chinese volunteers to strengthen the North Korean forces, or (4) provisional intervention predicated on encountering only ROK units in the border provinces. MacArthur thought the first contingency was not as probable as one of the others or a combination of the last three. "I recommend against hasty conclusions," he advised, "and believe that a final appraisement should await a more complete accumulation of military facts." On the following day, the 5th, he himself set the pace by submitting a special report for the Security Council on the CCF intervention that was remarkably restrained in its wording. He duly cited the instances of air and ground hostilities between UNC and CCF units as "matters which it is incumbent upon me to bring at once to the attention of the United Nations."[2]

But in a sudden, inexplicable change of mood that same day he ordered Stratemeyer to launch an intensive two-week bombing campaign to "destroy every means of communication and every installation, factory, city, and village" in North Korea between the front lines and the border. The only exceptions were to be hydroelectric plants, Suiho Dam, and the city of Rashin, and targets near the border were to be attacked only when visual bombing was possible to avoid erroneous strikes in Manchuria or Siberia. All bridges across the Yalu were to be destroyed at their Korean ends, which would require uncommon flying and bombing skills even if there were no enemy resistance. The main targets on the morning of November 7, the first day of the two-week aerial assault, were to be the twin bridges over the Yalu linking Antung and Sinuiju, which were thought to carry much of the military traffic from Manchuria into North Korea.

MacArthur did not believe he needed special permission for the attack on the Antung-Sinuiju bridges. The projected raid was mentioned in a routine teleconference between the G-2 staffs in Tokyo and the Pentagon on the 6th. The news also reached Washington that day via a message from George Stratemeyer to Hoyt Vandenberg. In a short while Deputy Secretary of Defense Robert A. Lovett was in touch with Acheson and Rusk; the three agreed that the mission should be cancelled for a host of reasons, such as the risk of bombing Antung, which might trigger all-out war with Red China and perhaps even the USSR (bound by a mutual-assistance pact); the chance of jeopardizing a resolution about to be brought to the Security Council, calling on Communist China to cease its military action in Korea; and the United States' "commitment not to take action affecting Manchuria without consulting the British." Acheson telephoned Truman, who was at his home in Independence. According to the President, "I told Acheson that I would approve this bombing mission only if there was an immediate and serious threat to the security of our troops." At a hastily summoned meeting the Joint Chiefs decided to countermand MacArthur's order for the strike; the message was radioed to him only eighty minutes before the bombers were scheduled to take off. The JCS told him, "Until further orders postpone all bombing of targets within five miles of the Manchurian border. Urgently need your estimate of the situation and the reason for ordering bombing of Yalu River bridges as indicated."

MacArthur was so upset by the JCS prohibition that he wrote out a request "for immediate relief from assignment to duty in the Far East," but he said that Hickey, his acting chief of staff, persuaded him not to send it because "the army would not understand my leaving at such a critical moment, and might become demoralized and destroyed." (At least Hickey was able to take advantage of his boss's egotism.) Instead, MacArthur vented his frustration by issuing a special communiqué and dispatching a return message to the Joint Chiefs, both of which were alarmist and strikingly at odds with his counsel against hasty decisions only two days before. In the communiqué he branded the Chinese intervention as "one of the most offensive acts of international lawlessness of historic record" and darkly pictured the front-line situation, where "a new and fresh army now faces us."[3] His wrath came through clearly in his response to the Joint Chiefs:

> Men and material in large force are pouring across all bridges over the Yalu from Manchuria. This movement not only jeopardizes but threatens the ultimate destruction of the forces under my command. The actual movement across the river can be accomplished under cover of darkness and the distance between the river and our lines is so short that the forces can be deployed against our troops without being seriously subjected to air interdiction. The only way to stop this reinforcement of the enemy is the destruction of these bridges and the

subjection of all installations in the north area supporting the enemy advance to the maximum of our air destruction. Every hour that this is postponed will be paid for dearly in American and other United Nations blood. The main crossing at Sinuiju was to be hit within the next few hours and the mission is actually already being mounted. Under the gravest protest that I can make, I am suspending this strike and carrying out your instructions. What I have ordered is entirely within the scope of the rules of war and the resolutions and directions which I have received from the United Nations and constitute[s] no slightest act of belligerency against Chinese territory, in spite of the outrageous international lawlessness emanating therefrom. I cannot overemphasize the disastrous effect, both physical and psychological, that will result from the restrictions which you are imposing. I trust that the matter [will] be immediately brought to the attention of the President as I believe your instructions may well result in a calamity of major proportion for which I cannot accept the responsibility without his personal and direct understanding of the situation. Time is so essential that I request immediate reconsideration of your decision pending which complete compliance will of course be given to your order.[4]

Responding with astounding deference to the irate theater chief, the Joint Chiefs decided to consult the President. Bradley read MacArthur's message to Truman over the telephone, whereupon the President, though aware of the "grave dangers" involved in such a raid, went against the advice of his Pentagon and State Department advisers: "Since General MacArthur was on the scene and felt so strongly that this was of unusual urgency, I told Bradley to give him the 'go-ahead' " to reschedule the mission. In their next message to MacArthur, the Joint Chiefs authorized him to bomb the Korean ends of the Yalu bridges, including the Antung-Sinuiju spans, but warned against attacks on dams or power plants along that river. They also noted that the situation as depicted in his message of the 6th was quite different from what he had described on the 4th, and they reminded him that "it is essential that we be kept informed of important changes in [the] situation as they occur." This time MacArthur, now somewhat calmer, responded with the more comprehensive report on the military situation that the JCS had requested on the 3d. Alluding to Willoughby's latest estimate of 40,000 Chinese troops in Korea and another 350,000 that could be deployed from Manchuria, he soberly admitted that the commitment of such forces could compel his command to make "a movement in retrograde." But he vowed to resume the advance toward the Yalu anyway, for "only through such an offensive effort can any accurate measure be taken of enemy strength." He also justified again the need to bomb the Yalu bridges "to prevent a potential build-up of enemy strength to a point threatening the safety of the command."

Bradley later observed, regarding MacArthur's brazen challenge to the JCS order, "Right then — that night — the JCS should have taken firmest control of the Korean War and dealt with MacArthur bluntly." The Joint Chiefs did not do so for two major reasons, he said: "The first was the traditional and customary reluctance of the JCS to meddle in the tactical operations of the theater commander. The second was the lack of clear-cut information on the extent of the Chinese communist threat; the actual threat was still unknown." He might have added that they were still somewhat in awe of the commander who had pulled off the Inchon operation so brilliantly. Moreover, MacArthur, not for the first time, was employing an effective tactic in human relations: to paraphrase an old adage, the world steps aside for a man who knows — or acts as if he knows — where he is going.[5]

In a gesture to lessen the tension between MacArthur and his superiors over the bombing issue, George Marshall sent him "a very personal and informal" dispatch on November 7. "We all realize your difficulty" in commanding a multinational army locked in battle in wintry, mountainous conditions and bound by "necessarily limiting" factors, Marshall said sympathetically, explaining: "Everyone here, Defense, State, and the President, is intensely desirous of supporting you," but adding, "We are faced with an extremely grave international problem which could so easily lead to a world disaster." The UNC commander in chief replied in a kindly spirit, thanking Marshall for his understanding and assuring him of his "complete agreement with the basic concept of localizing, if possible, the Korean struggle." MacArthur went on to say that he did not believe Peking's deployment of forces in Korea was motivated by concern over the Yalu hydroelectric facilities but, instead, by the Red Chinese regime's "lust for the expansion of power." He thought Communist China's recent seizure of Tibet and its aid to the rebels in Indochina were part of the same pattern now being manifested in Korea.[6]

On November 8, only one day off schedule, because of the Washington leaders' excitement, Stratemeyer's planes, including 79 B-29s and 300 F-80s and F-51s, struck the Antung-Sinuiju bridges and at the same time laid waste much of the city of Sinuiju. That day FEAF fighters engaged in history's first all-jet dogfight, when F-80s encountered Soviet-built MIG-15 fighters over Sinuiju and destroyed one of the latter. (MIG-15s of the Communist Chinese Air Force had been spotted over North Korea first on November 1.) Carrier aircraft also participated in the massive bombing campaign, which was directed mainly against twelve Yalu bridges, but by December 5, when the operation was suspended, only four of the bridges had been severed. The UNC planes were handicapped by flying in fixed attack patterns to avoid border violations along the winding river, by concentrated and heavy enemy antiaircraft fire, and by Chinese fighters that attacked and then fled back across the border. The bridge-bombing campaign was frustrating, too, because the Chinese proved adept at quick construction of pontoon bridges; besides, not long after the air assault began, the Yalu froze, enabling CCF units to cross the river on the ice. Unknown to MacArthur and Stratemeyer at the time, moreover, probably the bulk of the 300,000 CCF troops hiding in North Korea by the third week of November had arrived there before the bridge raids were under way in earnest.

As early as November 7, MacArthur began complaining to Washington about the prohibitions against FEAF planes pursuing enemy aircraft across the border. "The present restrictions imposed on my area of operations," he asserted, "provide a complete sanctuary for hostile air immediately upon their crossing the Manchurian–North Korean border." He maintained that "the effect of this abnormal condition upon the morale and combat efficiency of both air and ground troops is major." The Joint Chiefs were sympathetic with his grievance, which undoubtedly was backed by every FEAF airman flying missions along the Yalu, and they assured him that "corrective measures" were "being presented for highest United States level consideration." The "hot pursuit" issue, as it became known, was discussed often among Pentagon and State leaders in the ensuing days, and the opinions of the British and other allied governments were sought. Although the JCS favored allowing FEAF pursuit of enemy attackers up to eight miles across the Manchurian border, the State Department's canvass of other UN members involved in the Korean conflict determined that their reactions were overwhelmingly negative and that it might cost the United States support in several ways if hot pursuit were unilaterally approved. A factor for a while in November was the American-led move in the Security Council to obtain that body's call for Peking to remove its forces from Korea, but the resolution was vetoed by the Soviet Union. More important, the endorsement of hot pursuit would be at variance with several efforts by the United States government, in presidential statements and UN overtures, to signal Peking that the UNC operations in North Korea were not a threat to Communist China. Authorization for short-distance pursuit across the border was still discussed by Washington leaders long after November, but it was not granted, much to the disappointment of MacArthur, Stratemeyer, and especially the FEAF airmen, who did not fully appreciate the international implications of hot pursuit.[7]

During the first week of November, Pentagon and State officials began reviewing American policy in Korea, MacArthur's operational plans, and intelligence data on Communist Chinese moves and intentions. On the 8th, the JCS informed MacArthur that the CCF intervention, even if limited and seemingly suspended, might mean a revision of his directive by the National Security Council, which was to meet the next day. MacArthur heatedly responded, "It would be fatal to weaken the fundamental and basic policy of the United Nations to destroy all resisting armed forces in Korea and bring that country into a united and free nation." He declared that he was planning to start the final drive to the Yalu shortly and that the abandonment of the offensive "would completely destroy the morale of my forces" and would produce such strong resentment among the South Koreans that the ROK Army "would collapse or might even turn against us." Reacting to a mention in the JCS message of the need to consult Britain on policy changes relating to China, he depreciated the "Munich attitude" in London and roundly denounced "the widely reported British desire to appease the Chinese Communists by giving them a strip of Northern Korea."[8]

At the NSC meeting on November 9, the significance of the CCF actions of the previous two weeks and the implications for the future were discussed at length, as were the global ramifications of continuing or changing MacArthur's mission. As summarized in the official JCS history, "It was finally agreed that no change would be made in General MacArthur's directive; he would be free to act at his discretion (but not to attack Manchuria). At the same time, the Department of State would investigate the possibility of negotiating with the Chinese Communists." Dean Acheson remarked later, with the wisdom of hindsight, "Here, I believe, the Government missed its last chance to halt the march to disaster in Korea. All the President's advisers in this matter, civilian and military, knew that something was badly wrong, though what it was, how to find out, and what to do about it they muffed."[9]

As the CCF attacks mysteriously ceased, MacArthur anxiously pointed out to his superiors that the shipment of replacements and reinforcements should be augmented at once. "The alternatives are either a stalemate or the prospect of losing all that has thus far been gained," he warned the JCS on November 7. Fortunately for his case, Major General Charles L. Bolté, the G-3, or operations chief, of the Department of the Army headquarters, had been visiting the Far East Command in late October when the Chinese struck. After conferring with MacArthur, Wright, and the JSPOG staff in Tokyo and with Walker and some of his commanders in Korea, Bolté strongly recommended to Washington that MacArthur's command be supported as fully and quickly as possible.

By mid-November, MacArthur had assurances from Collins that the flow of troop replacements would be increased, with 40,000 to be sent in November and December, and that he would also get many of the service units he had requested earlier. Plans for redeployment of one or more of his divisions to Europe were postponed, and the UN members contributing forces in Korea were asked to suspend recent plans to reduce or terminate their military commitments there. In addition, Truman approved the Pentagon's recommendation to provide training assistance and logistical support for the buildup of the ROK Army to ten divisions (from five in July). An additional 20,000 South Koreans would be used in American units under the KATUSA program. The last division-size reinforcement to go to Korea while MacArthur headed the UNC was the U.S. 3d Infantry Division, which was at sea when the CCF assaults began and arrived at Wonsan on November 5. He was informed that no more large ground forces would be forthcoming until four federalized National Guard divisions were ready some time during the next year. MacArthur would not get all he wanted, but the CCF crisis had forced Washington leaders to shelve plans to reduce or redeploy his forces.[10]

Even while the Eighth Army was being hit by savage Chinese attacks, MacArthur, until better apprised of the situation, was pressing Walker to continue his advance above Pyongyang. As soon as the Chinese broke off contact, MacArthur again began to push his field commanders for a resumption of the drive to the Yalu. Almond's X Corps faced some supply shortages, but Walker's forces were encountering serious logistical difficulties. Milburn reported that his I Corps was operating with less than two days' reserves of ammunition and POL (petroleum, oil, and lubricants). After setting November 15 for the renewal of his offensive, Walker had to tell an impatient MacArthur that it would have to be postponed because of inadequate supplies. On the 22d he reported that the Eighth Army's logistical difficulties were solved. This was fortunate for Walker's position, because four days earlier MacArthur had told the JCS the offensive would be launched on November 24.[11]

While Walker was worrying about his supply lines, MacArthur was exhibiting an aura of confidence in Tokyo. On November 14 he expounded his views on the impending operations in a talk with William Sebald. He seemed sure that Stratemeyer's air campaign would succeed not only in knocking out the Yalu bridges but also, as Sebald reported the general's words to Acheson, in destroying "as much as possible of the built-up areas between the present UN front lines and the Yalu River, thus obviating any possibility of the Communist Forces living off the country." MacArthur said, according to Sebald, that once adequate supplies were brought forward, his ground units would launch an all-out offensive designed to drive the Communist Forces across the Yalu River. The UN Forces would, of course, stop at the boundary. If this can be accomplished during the next several weeks and before the river freezes, General MacArthur feels that the Korean campaign would be at an end. Should the planned operation fail and the Communist Forces continue to stream into North Korea from Manchuria, however, he saw no alternative, from a military point of view, to bombing key points in Manchuria. He said that if this should become necessary "the fat would be in the fire," because such operations would, in his opinion, bring about a counter-move by Soviet Russia. Such counter-move, he felt, could only lead to a spreading of the war and he therefore hoped that it would not be necessary to resort to such drastic action. . . .

General MacArthur felt that if his military operations, as envisaged above, are successful, the Korean campaign will be at an end. He expressed the opinion that the Chinese Communists would then feel that they had demonstrated their desire to be of assistance to the North Koreans, and had also proven to the world their ability to engage in a first-class war. He explained the late date of the Chinese assistance by saying that the Chinese Communists had not thought it necessary previously to enter into the war, as they had believed that the North Koreans would drive the UN Forces into the sea. It was only after the Inchon landings that it became apparent that something must be done. In consequence, considerable time was lost in the complete reorientation of the center of gravity of Chinese military force, requiring the shifting of Chinese armies and supplies from Central and South China to the northeast.[12]

In a conversation with Muccio three days later MacArthur again exuded confidence about the coming offensive. According to Muccio's record of the talk, the general's optimism was based on two principal assumptions: (1) "He was sure the Chinese Communists had sent 25,000, and certainly no more than 30,000, soldiers across the border. They could not possibly have gotten more over with the surreptitiously covert means used. If they had moved in the open, they would have been detected by our Air Forces and our Intelligence." (2) He believed that Stratemeyer's air power would destroy the Yalu spans and would wreak such destruction "between our present positions and the border" that "this area will be left a desert." Muccio continued in his report to the State Department: "The General stated that he is mounting an all-out offensive and is certain that the whole area still in the hands of North Koreans and Chinese Communists would be cleared within ten days."[13]

In contrast to MacArthur's sureness, Major General James H. Burns, who was assistant on foreign military affairs and aid in the office of the Secretary of Defense, prepared a memorandum for Marshall on November 14 in which he argued that the JCS and other top Defense and State leaders should go at once to Tokyo and seriously restudy the mission objectives with MacArthur before the UNC offensive started rolling. Burns was worried, he told Marshall, because "if we continue to pursue our present military objectives in Korea we are running a serious risk of becoming involved in the world war we are trying to avoid." Marshall was not eager about the Washington leaders' traveling to Tokyo then nor about interfering with MacArthur's operation, but he suggested that Burns get the reactions of State officials. Dean Rusk and Philip Jessup, with whom he met, admitted the need to review MacArthur's mission but were against the sort of meeting Burns proposed. They assured him that his idea would receive more consideration, but, states the JCS chronicle, "there was apparently no further discussion of it."[14]

While those like Burns in the Defense and State departments were unable to dissuade their superiors from their commitment to MacArthur's mission after the CCF attacks, an almost complete turnaround on Korean policy, bordering on panic in some cases, occurred in early November among a considerable number of top officials in London and other Western capitals who earlier had warmly endorsed united action to hurl back the North Korean invasion. Among other direct and indirect suggestions to Washington was that of the British military chiefs, who proposed pulling the UNC forces back to a defensible line across the waist of the peninsula; government leaders in Britain, Canada, and France supported the creation of a buffer zone along the Yalu border. Much of the concern in NATO nations stemmed from the fear that a major confrontation with Red Chinese forces would divert American assistance from the building of a defense system to deter Soviet aggression in Western Europe. (In December, Eisenhower would be appointed as head of the new NATO military establishment.) Whatever their motivation, however, British and other allied leaders felt helpless to stop MacArthur's drive at this late stage, particularly since his chain of command actually ran through Washington, not Lake Success.[15]

The last-chance gathering of Defense and State officials at which MacArthur's directive might have been altered took place at the Pentagon on November 21. The Defense Department participants included Marshall, Lovett, Pace, Bradley, Collins, Sherman, Vandenberg, and Bolté; the State representatives were Acheson, Rusk, Jessup, and H. Freeman Matthews; Harriman represented the President. They discussed the rising anxiety among UN members about Communist China's possible massive intervention in Korea, and they noted growing international support for the British version of a plan for a demilitarized zone along the border of Manchuria and North Korea. Acheson believed diplomacy could still avert a full-scale war with China, but he did not propose halting MacArthur's offensive. As on previous occasions, the military spokesmen were reluctant to interfere with the theater commander until his judgment had proven faulty; all of them seemed to be afflicted by the "Inchon syndrome." As Bradley summed it up, "Once more we adhered to the custom of yielding to the recommendation of the man on the scene." Out of the session came no revision of MacArthur's mission nor even a strong suggestion to change it. Later the JCS sent him an almost obsequious message summarizing the main topics discussed at the meeting and requesting his views on the postoffensive positioning of his forces and on preparations for reuniting Korea. "On the assumption that your coming attack will be successful," the Joint Chiefs briefly listed seven points related to the dilemma of how to bring about "the establishment of a unified Korea and at the same time reduce the risk of more general involvement." They meekly told MacArthur, "The above is suggested as a course of action upon which we would appreciate your comments." Neither the meeting nor the message marked high moments in the annals of Defense and State Department leadership.

This message was read by MacArthur late on November 24, after his return from a flight to North Korea as the UNC offensive got under way. In his reply the following day he assured the JCS that "the concern underlying the search for the means to confine the spread of the Korean conflict is fully understood and shared here."

He flatly rejected one of the JCS recommendations for reducing the risk of escalation, namely, withdrawal of his forces during the postoffensive period from the banks of the Yalu to hill positions south of the river valley. He dismissed such a move as "fraught with most disastrous consequences" both militarily and politically. He also repeated his opinion that large-scale intervention by Communist China or the USSR was unlikely if his command advanced in force to the Yalu. He concluded, "By resolutely . . . accomplishing our military mission . . . lies [the] best — indeed only — hope that Soviet and Chinese aggressive designs may be checked before these countries are committed to a course from which for political reasons they cannot withdraw." When his message reached the Pentagon, Bolté recommended on the 27th that the JCS endorse MacArthur's position and reiterate that body's approval of the drive to the Yalu. But before the Joint Chiefs' next meeting the situation in North Korea would change so drastically that MacArthur's and Bolté's thoughts on the matter were no longer relevant.[16]

If the midterm congressional elections of November 1950 were a key factor underlying Truman's convening of the Wake conference, some scholars have suggested that the Democratic reverses in those contests may have influenced the administration's reluctance to countermand MacArthur's drive to the Yalu. The impact of the exponents of McCarthyism, the pro-Chiang lobby, and other strident critics of Truman's foreign and military policies since 1945 was believed by some Democratic party leaders to have been limited to a minority of the American voting populace. As one commentator observed, however, "After November 7 there could no longer be any doubt that large numbers of Americans were out of sympathy with the Administration's methods and dubious about its objectives." Tightening the leash on MacArthur after the initial CCF attacks would surely have brought much more right-wing criticism of Truman and Acheson. Until future researchers find solid evidence to the contrary, however, the political factor does not appear paramount in the deliberations of Truman and his military and diplomatic advisers on the eve of the UNC offensive. The most obvious consequence of the Republican election gains that month was the emboldening of the Senators Robert A. Taft and Kenneth S. Wherry to begin the bitter hassle on Capitol Hill over

American policy toward Europe in general and military assistance to NATO in particular. The Great Debate, as it was soon called, would keep Congress in a state of agitation over foreign and military policies for several months. MacArthur would be privately pleased with the stirring of the controversy, particularly its Asia-first connotations by Taft and his supporters, but actually the Great Debate brought him no more divisions, though four were deployed to Europe, along with five-star Ike. If Truman was brave enough to stir his critics' rage by strengthening NATO when MacArthur was calling for more forces, it is doubtful that his refusal to restrict the UNC commander in chief in November was based on fear of political repercussions.[17]

Meanwhile, along the cold, bleak terrain of the Chongchon Valley and the barren mountains to the east, Walker's offensive began on the morning of November 24. The American I and IX corps, comprising four divisions and the British brigade, advanced in the western and central sectors of the Eighth Army's front, with the ROK II Corps on their right, or eastern, flank. During the first day and a half Walker's troops gained up to twelve miles, meeting only light resistance. Although the Eighth Army had been in holding positions for nearly three weeks prior to the offensive, Almond's X Corps, which was separated from Walker's units by over fifty miles of rugged, desolate terrain, had been probing in several directions, resulting in a wide dispersion of its divisions. The American 3d Infantry Division was northwest of Wonsan, and the 1st Marine Division, advancing with caution and sound preparations on Smith's orders and against Almond's wishes for greater speed, had made its way to the south end of the Chosin Reservoir and turned northwestward. From Iwon the American 7th Infantry Division had moved rapidly toward the Yalu, its 17th Regiment reaching the river at Hyesanjin on November 21. The two ROK divisions attached to Almond's corps, the 3d and Capital, had pushed northeastward almost to the port of Chongjin, sixty miles from the Soviet border. The X Corps had not faced serious opposition since the first week of November, but its soldiers were now suffering severely from the first winter storms, which dropped temperatures to 20 degrees below zero (about 30 degrees colder than on the west side of the Taebaek Range). The principal X Corps thrust set for the 24th was the renewed advance of the Marines

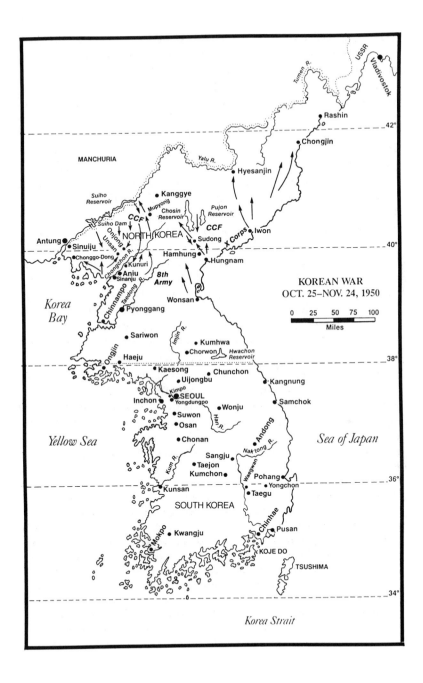

KOREAN WAR
OCT. 25–NOV. 24, 1950

0 25 50 75 100
Miles

northwest of the Chosin Reservoir. They were supposed to push on to Mupyong and eventually link up with Walker's right flank en route to the Yalu. As earlier, Smith's Marines moved out but with much greater carefulness than Almond desired, precipitating another in a long series of tense exchanges between the two generals.[18]

MacArthur, accompanied by Whitney, Willoughby, and Huff, flew to Walker's headquarters at Sinanju, in the Chongchon Valley, on the morning of the 24th. MacArthur and his party stayed about five hours, conferring with Walker and journeying by jeep to visit several American command posts near the Chongchon front. The UNC chief was in a buoyant mood, and to several officers, including Coulter, the IX Corps commander, he expressed the hope of being able to "get the boys home by Christmas." Several nearby correspondents pounced on his choice of phrases and soon nicknamed the operation the "Home by Christmas Drive." Although cheerful in appearance during the tour, MacArthur later maintained, "What I had seen at the front worried me greatly. The ROK troops were not yet in good shape, and the entire line was deplorably weak in numbers." That afternoon Story flew MacArthur and his group along the Yalu River for a considerable distance northeastward from Sinuiju. After looking from an altitude of 5000 feet for signs of the CCF, which were not detected, MacArthur told Story to head the unarmed *SCAP* back to Tokyo. The escorting fighter pilots were undoubtedly relieved to see the theater commander's plane turn away from the Yalu.[19] At GHQ in Tokyo that day the following communiqué, prepared by MacArthur before his flight, was released:

> The United Nations massive compression envelopment in North Korea against the new Red armies operating there is now approaching its decisive effort. The isolating components of the pincer, our air forces of all types, have for the past three weeks, in a sustained attack of model co-ordination and effectiveness, successfully interdicted enemy lines of support from the North so that further reinforcement therefrom has been sharply curtailed and essential supplies markedly limited. The eastern sector of the pincer, with noteworthy and effective naval support, has steadily advanced in a brilliant tactical movement and has now reached a commanding envelopment position cutting in two the northern reaches of the enemy's geographical potential.

This morning the western sector of the pincer moves forward in a general assault in an effort to complete the compression and close the vice. If successful this should for all practical purposes end the war, restore peace and unity to Korea, enable the prompt withdrawal of United Nations military forces, and permit the complete assumption by the Korean people and nation of full sovereignty and international equality. It is that for which we fight.[20]

It was destined to be the last of the long line of victory communiqués he had issued since the recapture of Papua, New Guinea, in early 1943.

2. A Real Crisis and a False Dilemma

MacArthur's "all-out offensive" to the Yalu and "massive compression envelopment" of the enemy died suddenly on the night of November 25, when strong Chinese forces unleashed a surprise assault against Walker's right flank. Within twenty-four hours the CCF had again smashed through the reconstituted ROK II Corps that it had struck severely a month before; the American IX Corps found itself facing large numbers of Chinese on its exposed right flank and soon in its rear. As was learned later, about 180,000 Chinese troops were committed against the Eighth Army. Many of them were used in the CCF's turning movement through Walker's shattered eastern flank in order to cut off the retreat route for the rest of the Eighth Army. Laurence Keiser's 2d Division and the Turkish brigade suffered heavy losses in trying to slow the CCF advance; their heroic resistance and the superior mobility of the American and British forces enabled the IX and I corps to escape envelopment north of the Chongchon River. Meanwhile, on November 27 the 1st Marine Division, slowly moving west of the Chosin Reservoir, and the U.S. 7th Division, to the east of the reservoir, were both hit by ferocious CCF attacks not only at their points of advance but also along their supply lines to the south. As determined later, approximately 120,000 CCF troops were involved in the operations against the X Corps. Both of the American divisions began rearward moves under intense enemy fire. To the northeast the two ROK divisions, having reached Chongjin, were ordered to start withdrawing down the coast before they were cut off from their main ports of supply, Songjin and Iwon.[21]

At first Walker and Almond were hesitant to report the Chinese operations as part of a massive offensive, but by the 28th the power of the 300,000-man CCF commitment was alarmingly apparent on both the Eighth Army and X Corps fronts. That day an agitated MacArthur informed the JCS: "The Chinese military forces are committed in North Korea in great and ever increasing strength. No pretext of minor support under the guise of volunteerism or other subterfuge now has the slightest validity. We face an entirely new war." He asserted that Red China was bent upon "the complete destruction of all United Nations forces in Korea" and that "our present strength of force is not sufficient to meet this undeclared war." He was ordering his forces to "pass from the offensive to the defensive with such local adjustments as may be required by a constantly fluid situation." He said new policy guidance was needed from Washington, because "the resulting situation presents an entire new picture which broadens the potentialities to world-embracing considerations beyond the sphere of decisions by the Theater Commander." Summoning Walker and Almond to Tokyo, MacArthur held a long conference with them, Hickey, Wright, Willoughby, and Whitney on the evening of November 28. They did not adjourn until 1:30 the next morning, having recognized the urgent need to preserve the Eighth Army and X Corps by retreating southward to avert envelopments. The former was to move toward Pyongyang and the latter toward Hamhung.[22]

The Joint Chiefs responded to MacArthur's alarming news by quickly approving his decision to go on the defensive and withdraw farther south. But they recommended that Walker's and Almond's forces develop a continuous line of defense across the peninsula when they reached its waist. MacArthur strongly disagreed; he foresaw a thinly manned cordon that could easily be penetrated. He preferred to pull the two forces back toward separate beachheads for possible defensive stabilization or evacuation, depending on the course of events, with the Eighth Army heading toward Pusan and the X Corps to Hungnam. With Truman's concurrence, the JCS authorized him on December 3 to go ahead with "consolidation of forces into beachheads," since "the preservation of your forces is now the primary consideration." MacArthur also renewed his suggestion to accept Chiang's offer of Nationalist troops for service in Korea. He pointed out that no other source of rapid reinforcement was available, and, besides, the previous arguments against using Chiang's forces were outmoded, because Formosa was not in imminent danger of invasion now and Communist China had entered the Korean War in enormous strength. Truman, Marshall, and Acheson all had a say in the reply sent by the Joint Chiefs, which told him that his proposal would be "considered" but "involves world-wide consequences," including possible "disruption of the essential Allied lineup" since the United Kingdom and the Commonwealth nations may find the idea "wholly unacceptable." Lieutenant General Matthew B. Ridgway, the Army's deputy chief of staff, asked Vandenberg after a high-level Pentagon meeting about this time why the JCS did not simply "send orders to MacArthur and *tell* him what to do." Ridgway was astounded by the Air Force chief's response: "What good would that do? He wouldn't obey the orders. What *can* we do?"[23]

Because the gravity of the battlefront situation could not be truly gauged from Washington, the JCS, with Truman's endorsement, delegated Collins to visit MacArthur and the commanders in Korea. The Army Chief of Staff reached Tokyo on December 4 and, after a brief conference with MacArthur, flew on to North Korea, where he visited Walker, Almond, and some of their commanders. While Collins was in North Korea, the Eighth Army evacuated Pyongyang in its continuing move southward, having largely broken contact with the slower moving CCF divisions. To the northeast, Smith's embattled Marines and the hard-hit 7th Division made their way toward the south end of the Chosin Reservoir and the road to Hamhung, facing heavy enemy pressure and constant threats of envelopment. Although both UNC forces were in retreat, Collins concluded that so far the retrograde movement of the Eighth Army was in good order, and Almond and his staff appeared confident that the Hamhung-Hungnam area could be held for a considerable period if the 1st Marine and 7th Infantry divisions escaped from the Chosin region without severe losses. The Marines were reported to be inflicting enormous casualties on the enemy.

Collins returned to Tokyo on December 6 for a lengthy meeting at the embassy with MacArthur, Stratemeyer, Joy, Hickey, Wright, Willoughby, and Whitney. The Chief of Staff sounded out MacArthur especially on three contingencies that might develop in the coming days. If the existing restrictions on his forces were continued and no reinforcements were forthcoming, MacArthur believed the UNC forces should be evacuated to avoid their destruction. If Red China were subjected to naval blockade and bombing and if Nationalist reinforcements were approved, MacArthur said his forces could hold in Korea. If Communist China agreed not to let its armies cross the 38th Parallel, MacArthur thought a UN-supervised armistice should be arranged. According to Collins, MacArthur "concluded by saying that unless substantial reinforcements were sent quickly, the United Nations Command should pull out of Korea." Judging from his observations while in North Korea, however, Collins thought differently: "While I did not presume to argue the point with General MacArthur, I did not feel that, even with the limitations likely to be placed upon the United Nations Command, the Chinese could force its withdrawal from Korea." During the session MacArthur provided Collins with a map delineating nine successive withdrawal lines down the Korean peninsula where the Eighth Army units would be expected to try to hold before reaching Pusan, with evacuation probably required if they were attacked by vastly larger forces at the Kum or the Naktong river line.

After returning to Washington on December 8, Collins confidently told inquiring reporters at the airport that "the United Nations forces would be able to take care of themselves without further serious losses." To his JCS colleagues, however, he recommended that if "an all-out effort in Korea" was not to be made, MacArthur should be authorized "to take the necessary steps to prevent the destruction of his forces pending final evacuation from Korea." With Truman's endorsement, the Joint Chiefs notified MacArthur on the 8th that they approved his plans for the phased withdrawal of Walker's forces toward Pusan, and they advised him to carry out the evacuation of X Corps from Hungnam as soon as possible.[24]

On November 28, only hours after Truman had learned that the UNC offensive to the Yalu had been stopped by powerful

Chinese forces, he convened the National Security Council to consider the sharp change in the war. No new directive for MacArthur was devised, but the President and his top advisers concurred at the session, according to Bradley, that "we had moved much closer to danger of general war with the Soviets," that "we should not commit more troops to Korea" because of their probable need elsewhere against a major Soviet thrust, and that "the long-pending recommendations of the April NSC-68 paper must be implemented" to strengthen America's defense system greatly. The discussion ranged over the possibilities of an armistice, an evacuation of UNC forces, and a successful defensive posture in Korea, but, alas for MacArthur's concerns, there was no enthusiasm over sending him substantial reinforcements or broadening the war against Communist China.[25]

Much of the American and West European press reacted with sensational, alarmist reports on the aborted Home by Christmas Drive, portraying MacArthur as blundering and warmongering and his forces as fleeing, panic-stricken, in the face of the Chinese attackers. American popular opinion, as measured in Gallup polls, dropped precipitously from 66 percent in July to 39 percent in December "in support of the war." Britain and other NATO nations retreated quickly from the United States' side when American officials talked of strong sanctions against Red China or a UN censure of the Communist Chinese intervention. At a press conference on November 30, Truman added to the anxieties of allied leaders when, in responding to reporters' queries, he remarked that use of the atomic bomb in Korea was under "active consideration." Some excited newsmen erroneously reported that the President had implied that MacArthur would be allowed to decide whether atomic weapons were used in the Korean conflict. A heated debate on foreign policy was under way in the British Parliament when distorted versions of Truman's comments reached that body, setting off a furor that Prime Minister Clement R. Attlee partially quieted by announcing that he was going to Washington to talk to the President.[26]

The Attlee-Truman talks of December 4–8 covered a range of Anglo-American and global problems, but the escalating Korean War was the chief topic. The leaders agreed on the need to uphold Korean freedom and unity, the United Nations' prestige, and

NATO's new military arm, and they agreed also on the necessity of avoiding a general war. Although both men favored a UN-supervised cease-fire in Korea, Attlee was willing to grant political concessions to Communist China, particularly UN membership, but Truman refused to dangle "rewards for aggression" before Peking in order to obtain an armistice. The most significant achievement of the talks was the recognition that the UN General Assembly resolution of October 7, calling, in essence, for the forceful establishment of a united and independent Korea, was unrealistic and that it was time to return to the original June objective of preserving South Korea. "In short, after a brief flirtation with the terrifying potentialities of a policy of liberation," observes a scholar, "a chastened, uncertain, but still stubborn Democratic Administration was returning to its true love — containment." Following the Attlee visit, little more was heard in official Washington about the grandiose goal of October 7, which had lasted only two months. Somehow, though, this drastic alteration of objectives was not communicated effectively to the United Nations commander in chief.[27]

During the first week or so after Red China's plunge into the war, MacArthur cast discretion to the wind and expressed his frustration and resentment publicly. In a number of interviews with journalists and messages to media executives he defended his thwarted drive to the Yalu as a wise move that located the Chinese armies and forced them into combat before they were fully prepared logistically; denied that his operations in North Korea had provoked the Chinese intervention or had exceeded his orders; argued that his forces were engaged in a skillful, orderly withdrawal, not a rout; and charged that Washington's restrictions prevented a short, successful end to the war. He also authorized Willoughby to issue several press statements that were critical of some correspondents' reports of the alleged rout of the UNC forces and that blamed Washington for the inadequate political intelligence on Peking's intentions. Particularly resented by Truman and Acheson were MacArthur's statements on December 1 in an interview with several editors of *U.S. News & World Report* and in a cablegram he sent to Hugh Baillie of the United Press. Excerpts from the interview and the Baillie message in full appeared in many American and European newspapers, beginning on the 2d, and

U.S. News & World Report carried the full interview in its issue of the 8th. The public excitement over MacArthur's criticisms was buzzing throughout Attlee's visit in Washington.[28]

MacArthur remarked to the magazine editors about his Yalu offensive, "Had we failed to assault and uncover enemy strength and intentions the opportunity secretly to build up from available resources of all China would inevitably encompass our destruction." Henceforth he took his cue from Walker's comment on November 29 that the UNC advance "probably saved our forces from a trap," and shortly MacArthur would substitute "reconnaissance in force" for "all-out offensive" in referring to the aborted drive. When queried about the impact of "the limitations which prevent unlimited pursuit of Chinese large forces and unlimited attack on their bases," he told the editors that the restrictions imposed by his superiors were "an enormous handicap, without precedent in military history." He wrote Baillie similarly, claiming that the failure of the UNC offensive "results largely from the acceptance of military odds without precedent in history — the odds of permitting offensive action without defensive retaliation." He castigated the "somewhat selfish though most short-sighted viewpoint" of many newsmen and political leaders in Western Europe, who opposed an aggressive retaliation against Communist China. As for guidance from Washington, he asserted, "I have received no suggestion from any authoritative source that in the execution of its mission the command should stop at the Thirty-eighth Parallel or Pyongyang, or at any other line short of the international boundary."[29]

As might be expected, Truman responded more angrily than he had even to the VFW message. In private he was greatly irritated by the latest incidents of MacArthur's "shooting off his mouth," but Truman penned a note to himself on his desk calendar: "I must defend him and save his face even if he has tried on various and numerous occasions to cut mine off. But I must stand by my subordinates." In his autobiography he said that he saw "no excuse" for the general's public criticism of Washington for "his troubles" or for his "quite plain" implication "that no blame whatsoever attached to him or his staff." Truman wrote, "I should have relieved General MacArthur then and there. The reason I did not was that I did not wish to have it appear as if he were

relieved because the offensive failed. . . . Nor did I want to reprimand the general, but he had to be told that the kinds of public statements which he had been making were out of order." On
December 5, during a break in his conference with Attlee, the
President issued two directives that, though generally applicable
to "officials of the departments and agencies of the executive
branch" in the United States and overseas, were in direct response
to MacArthur's outbursts. The first said that all public statements
by United States government personnel, civilian and military, regarding foreign policy must be cleared in advance by the State
Department and those on military policy by the Defense Department. His second directive ordered officials and commanders
abroad "to exercise extreme caution in public statements, to clear
all but routine statements with their departments, and to refrain
from direct communication on military or foreign policy with
newspapers, magazines, or other publicity media in the United
States." MacArthur quickly probed with a test case, asking the
Pentagon's permission on the 9th to release a communiqué that
included an indictment of American officials responsible for political intelligence because they had not provided sufficient warning of Peking's imminent belligerency. The JCS told him with unusual curtness that his proposed communiqué did not conform with
the President's directive and therefore could not be released. The
general was muzzled — at least for a while. In the meantime Rusk,
at a session of high-level State Department officials, suggested "the
possibility of using General Collins as a Field Commander with
General MacArthur spending full time on the Japanese Peace
Treaty." Acheson's response was not enthusiastic, and the idea apparently was not taken up with Pentagon leaders.[30]

Britain's eagerness for a cease-fire in Korea to the point of offering political concessions to Peking, as expressed by Attlee in
Washington and supported by many nations that America counted
on as allies, made it imperative for the United States to cooperate
as far as possible in UN efforts to obtain a peace settlement. Accordingly, the American government went along with an invitation from the Security Council to Communist China to send a
representative to address that body about Peking's grievances over
the Formosa issue. The result, on November 28, was a savage attack by General Wu Hsiu-chuan, the Red Chinese emissary, against

the United States' role in Formosa and Korea, which was followed by anti-American speeches by delegates from the Soviet Union and its satellite nations. The United States also supported a cease-fire resolution proposed by a bloc of thirteen Arab and Asian countries, though its wording was not what Washington wished. With American support, the resolution was passed in the UN General Assembly by a large margin on December 14. But Chou En-lai subsequently rejected any cease-fire negotiations that did not include as prerequisites withdrawal of American military assistance from Korea and Formosa, no United States or UN involvement in the Koreans' resolution of their political future, and replacement of Nationalist China by Communist China in the UN. Chou also proclaimed that the UNC invasion of North Korea had "obliterated forever" the 38th Parallel as a "demarcation line of political geography" and that now Communist China would produce the unification of Korea by force. The United States supported another UN cease-fire resolution that was approved by the General Assembly on January 13, but it, too, was rebuffed by Peking.[31]

By the time of Chou's harsh response on December 22 to the first UN cease-fire overture, the Eighth Army had fallen back to positions along the Imjin River, just north of Seoul. Far to the northeast, the 1st Marine Division had completed its harrowing, heroic withdrawal from the Chosin Reservoir to the Hamhung-Hungnam area by December 11. It had taken such an immense toll in enemy casualties that the CCF was unable to mount heavy pressure against the evacuation perimeter. At the port of Hungnam the withdrawal by sea of elements of the X Corps was already under way when the troops of the 1st Marine and 7th Infantry divisions arrived. On the 11th MacArthur flew to an airstrip at Yonpo, southwest of Hungnam, for a briefing by Almond's staff on the plans for the huge embarkation. On a short tour he also visited with some officers and enlisted men, and later told reporters that the morale of the X Corps was high and the soldiers had displayed "conspicuous self-confidence." Some X Corps elements were taken aboard ships at Songjin and Wonsan, and the 100 or more ships of Admiral Doyle's Task Force 90 evacuated from Hungnam about 105,000 American and ROK troops, together with over 90,000 Korean refugees and 350,000 tons of X Corps equipment and supplies in a well-executed operation that was completed on

KOREAN WAR
Nov. 25, 1950–Jan. 24, 1951

0 25 50 75 100
Miles

Christmas Eve. The X Corps units were transported by sea to Pohang and Pusan and immediately prepared to move overland to help Walker's units form a defensive line across the peninsula just below the 38th Parallel. MacArthur had earlier agreed, after prodding from the JCS, to place the X Corps under Walker's overall command when the continuous front was formed. But by the time the X Corps joined the Eighth Army, Walker was dead; he had been killed on December 23 when his jeep collided with a truck on the road between Seoul and Uijongbu.[32]

Because of Walker's frequent visits to front-line sectors, Collins feared he might be killed and had discussed with MacArthur, during their talks in Tokyo early that month, a possible successor to Walker if his fears were realized. They agreed that an excellent choice would be Ridgway, Collins' deputy chief of staff for administration and a highly respected division and corps commander in airborne operations during the war against Germany. On learning of Walker's death, MacArthur promptly called Collins and requested Ridgway as commander of the Eighth Army; approval of the appointment was quickly obtained from Marshall and Truman. MacArthur sent a message to his new army commander before he left Washington: "I look forward with keenest anticipation to your joining this command. Your welcome by all ranks will be the heartiest." Ridgway, who had accompanied Harriman on his visit to Tokyo in August, landed at Haneda Airport late on Christmas night. The next morning he conferred with MacArthur and his acting chief of staff, Doyle Hickey, at the former's Dai Ichi office.[33] Ridgway's account of the session follows:

> My meeting with MacArthur [and Hickey] began at nine-thirty. . . .
> I had known MacArthur since my days as a West Point instructor but, like everyone who had ever dealt with him, I was again deeply impressed by the force of his personality. . . . He was a great actor too, with an actor's instinct for the dramatic — in tone and gesture. Yet so lucid and so penetrating were his explanations and his analyses that it was his mind rather than his manner or his bodily presence that dominated his listeners.
> . . . His immediate instructions were to hold as far as possible "in the most advanced positions in which you can maintain yourself." I was to hold on to Seoul, largely for psychological and political reasons, as long as possible but not if it became a citadel position. . . .

Supply discipline in the U.S. forces, he told me, was not good
— a fact I was soon to confirm by firsthand observation. . . . Mac-
Arthur decried the value of tactical air support. It could not, he flatly
stated, isolate the battlefield or stop the flow of hostile troops and
supply. . . .

His chief concern at this conference seemed to be the fact that we
were then operating in a "mission vacuum," as he termed it, while
diplomacy attempted to feel its way. "A military success," he said, "will
strengthen our diplomacy." . . .

He urged me especially not to underestimate the Chinese. "They
constitute a dangerous foe," he warned me. . . . "The entire Chinese
military establishment is in this fight."

As for his own goal, the maximum he had in mind, he said, was
"inflicting a broadening defeat making possible the retention and security of South Korea."

"Form your own opinions," he told me in closing. "Use your own
judgment. I will support you. You have my complete confidence." . . .

My final question was simply this: "If I find the situation to my liking, would you have any objections to my attacking?" And his answer
encouraged and gratified me deeply:

"The Eighth Army is yours, Matt. Do what you think is best."[34]

MacArthur was generous in the latitude he gave Ridgway; he
had not extended it to Walker. But on December 26, 1950, there
was not much else he could give the new Eighth Army commander except the doleful news that a renewed CCF offensive was
anticipated within a week and that no substantial UNC reinforcements could be expected soon. Recent headlines, however, made
it seem that the United States was gearing up vigorously for the
"new war" in Korea. The President urgently requested, and Congress quickly granted, huge supplementary military appropriations that quadrupled the defense funding for fiscal 1951 to $52
billion. On December 14 the NSC approved the American Army's
expansion to eighteen divisions by June 1952. The following day
Truman issued a proclamation of national emergency, thereby
enabling him to exercise wartime executive powers and facilitating
the government's mobilization of manpower and industry. He also
issued directives freezing Communist Chinese assets in the United
States and banning the American merchant marine from the ports
of Red China. On the other hand, Truman added fuel to the

fire of the Great Debate in Congress over American policy toward Western Europe by announcing on the 19th that Eisenhower would be supreme commander of NATO forces and that additional American units would be sent to bolster Western Europe's defenses.

While the attention to NATO's military needs at the time of the worst crisis in the Korean War must have upset him, MacArthur favored any actions by the United States government that appeared to acknowledge the conflict in Korea as warranting higher priority than Truman's unfortunately worded phrase "police action" had earlier suggested. As he told General Wade H. Haislip, Army vice chief of staff, on December 18, he thought the Far Eastern crisis of such proportion as to "impel the immediate and complete mobilization of our full military potential." But his prospects for reinforcements were slim. He appealed to the JCS for the four National Guard divisions that had been called to federal duty, arguing that their training could be completed in Japan, but he was informed again that they would not be prepared for shipment to the Far East until the summer of 1951. The 33,000 troop replacements the Army Department had promised to send him in December, moreover, had to be scaled down to 23,000, despite his plea that the month's allotment be raised to 74,000 to offset recent losses against the CCF. His recommendation to reconsider Chiang's offer of 33,000 Nationalist soldiers for action in Korea was not approved. At least some of the ground units — though they were mostly of battalion size — that UN members had promised earlier began arriving in late November and early December, including forces from Canada, New Zealand, France, the Netherlands, Greece, and Thailand. But the total troop commitment by the UN members was far short of the 75,000 allied soldiers that he said were now needed. The State Department and the Pentagon concluded that not much more could be expected in combat units from America's allies in the war. Many of these nations had quite obviously lost much of their zeal for assisting in the Korean conflict after the entry of Communist China.[35]

Dr. John M. Chang, the ROK ambassador in Washington, and Dean Acheson separately suggested in December to the Pentagon that a possible means of reinforcing the UNC forces would be to supply American small arms to the 500,000-member Korean Youth

Corps, which already had some military training. But MacArthur, when asked by the JCS for his opinion, opposed arming part or all of the ROK youth organization. Instead, he maintained that any surplus light weapons could be put to more effective use by the new National Police Reserve in Japan and that the Youth Corps members could be employed as fillers in already existing ROK units. After the collapse of ROK divisions against the CCF, MacArthur was no longer enthusiastic about expanding the ROK Army. Using the occasion to push again for policy review in Washington, he wrote the Joint Chiefs in early January 1951 that the arming of more ROK forces was "dependent upon determination of the future United States military position with respect to both the Korean campaign and the general critical situation in the Far East." Expansion of the ROK Army would be of dubious value, because unless American policy was changed and the theater got a higher priority, he believed, evacuation of the UNC forces from the peninsula would become necessary soon.[36]

Ridgway, after reaching the Eighth Army's main headquarters at Taegu on December 26, quickly impressed his staff and field officers with his determination to avert destruction or evacuation of his forces. In fact, he talked of counterattacking instead of retreating farther south. But when touring the front-line positions, he noticed "a complete lack of that alertness, that aggressiveness that you find in troops whose spirit is high." By example and exhortation, and by transferring some officers, he quietly but quickly began instilling a new spirit of confidence in his army. A complete transformation, however, could not be wrought in time to meet what the CCF called its "third-phase offensive," which began on New Year's Eve. The heaviest assaults were aimed initially at the American I and IX corps positions along the Imjin River, north of Seoul, but the CCF was not able to achieve a breakthrough. On the other hand, the ROK forces on the central front virtually collapsed under ferocious attacks, leading to an enemy penetration through Chunchon that briefly threatened to outflank the Eighth Army. In view of the critical situation in the Chunchon area and the awesome strength of the CCF offensive, estimated to involve nearly 500,000 troops (including some reconstituted North Korean units), Ridgway was compelled to order his troops to retreat to a new defensive line, which was about seventy miles below the

38th Parallel, extending from Pyongtaek on the west coast to Samchok on the east. CCF troops occupied Seoul on January 5, marking the third time the South Korean capital had changed hands since late June. The first week of 1951 was the low point of the war for the UNC forces, but even as they pulled back to the Pyongtaek-Samchok line, Ridgway was expressing confidence that soon his soldiers would be moving out to counterattack.[37]

Whereas the new Eighth Army commander was not thinking in terms of withdrawing his forces to Japan, that contingency was much on the minds of MacArthur and the Joint Chiefs during the latter half of December. In the message traffic between Tokyo GHQ and the Pentagon, the questions of reinforcements, restrictions, defensive positions, evacuation plans, and cease-fire terms all pointed to the need to replace MacArthur's outmoded mission directive, drawn up in the immediate post-Inchon period, when times were happier. After getting advice and approval from Marshall, Acheson, and ultimately the President, the Joint Chiefs dispatched a new directive to him on December 29. The document began with the three principal conditions that had necessitated a revision of his mission: (1) Apparently "the Chinese Communists possess the capability of forcing UN forces out of Korea if they choose to exercise it," based on MacArthur's (but not Ridgway's) estimates of the situation. (2) Neither from the United States nor from other UN members would "significant additional forces for Korea" be obtainable in the near future. (3) The President and his State and Defense leaders, including the JCS, "believe that Korea is not the place to fight a major war." But if they could do so "without incurring serious losses," MacArthur's forces could make a contribution of "great importance to our national interests" by resisting and damaging the CCF as much as possible, thus producing "a deflation of the military and political prestige of the Chinese Communists." The JCS instructed him to go ahead with his plan, earlier presented to Collins in Tokyo, "to defend in successive positions," but if at the Kum River line the CCF amassed superior strength that could overrun the UNC positions, then he would be directed "to commence a withdrawal to Japan." The Joint Chiefs concluded by asking for his views on the "conditions which should determine a decision to initiate evacuation, particularly in light of your continuing primary mission of [the] defense of Japan."[38]

MacArthur later said, "This message seemed to indicate a loss of the 'will to win' in Korea. President Truman's resolute determination to free and unite that threatened land had now deteriorated almost in defeatism. . . . The thought of defeat in Korea had never been entertained by me."[39] This is a distortion of the record, for since late November his own messages to the JCS about the combat situation had ranged the spectrum from cautiously confident to highly alarmist. He had not been averse to using the false dilemma, and again in his reply to the Joint Chiefs on December 30, quoted below, his basic argument presented only the alternatives of adopting his proposed course of action or committing his forces to annihilation or evacuation, as if no other options existed:

> Any estimate of relative capabilities in the Korean campaign appears to be dependent upon political-military policies yet to be formulated regarding Chinese military operations being conducted against our forces. It is quite clear now that the entire military resources of the Chinese nation, with logistic support from the Soviet, is committed to a maximum effort against the United Nations Command. In implementation of this commitment, a major concentration of Chinese force in the Korean-Manchurian area will increasingly leave China vulnerable to areas from which troops to support Korean operations have been drawn. Meanwhile, under existing restrictions, our naval and air potential are [sic] being only partially utilized and the great potential of Chinese Nationalist force on Formosa and guerrilla action on the mainland are [sic] being ignored. Indeed, as to the former, we are preventing its employment against the common enemy by our own naval force.
>
> Should a policy determination be reached by our government or through it by the United Nations to recognize the state of war which has been forced upon us by the Chinese authorities and to take retaliatory measures within our capabilities, we could: (1) blockade the coast of China; (2) destroy through naval gunfire and air bombardment China's industrial capacity to wage war; (3) secure reinforcements from the Nationalist garrison on Formosa to strengthen our position in Korea if we decided to continue the fight for that peninsula; and (4) release existing restrictions upon the Formosan garrison for diversionary action, possibly leading to counter-invasion against vulnerable areas of the Chinese mainland.
>
> I believe that by the foregoing measures we could severely cripple

and largely neutralize China's capability to wage aggressive war and thus save Asia from the engulfment otherwise facing it. . . . I am fully conscious of the fact that this course of action has been rejected in the past for fear of provoking China into a major effort, but we must now realistically recognize that China's commitment thereto has already been fully and unequivocally made and nothing we can do would further aggravate the situation as far as China is concerned.

Whether defending ourselves by way of military retaliation would bring in Soviet military intervention or not is a matter of speculation. I have always felt that a Soviet decision to precipitate a general war would depend solely upon its own estimate of relative strengths and capabilities with little regard to other factors. If we are forced to evacuate Korea without taking military measures against China proper, as suggested in your message, it would have the most adverse effect upon the people of Asia, not excepting the Japanese, and a material reinforcement of the forces now in this theater would be mandatory if we are to hold the littoral defense chain [Japan, Ryukyus, and Philippines] against determined assault. Moreover, it must be borne in mind that evacuation of our forces from Korea under any circumstances would at once release the bulk of the Chinese forces now absorbed by that campaign for action elsewhere — quite probably in areas of far greater importance than Korea itself.

I understand thoroughly the demand for European security and fully concur in doing everything possible in that sector, but not to the point of accepting defeat anywhere else — an acceptance which I am sure could not fail to insure later defeat in Europe itself. . . .

So far as your tactical estimate of the situation in Korea is concerned, under the conditions presently implied, namely — no reinforcements, continued restrictions upon Chinese Nationalist action, no military measures against China's military potential, and the concentration of Chinese military force solely upon the Korean sector — [it] would seem to be sound.[40]

MacArthur added that a decision about evacuation could be postponed until the "beachhead line" was manned, which in a later message he explained as meaning the old Naktong perimeter. The JCS countered by informing him that the final decision on withdrawal would be made when the Davidson line was reached, an arc about thirty miles above Pusan proposed by the Eighth Army's chief engineer officer back in the dark days of August. Collins observed, "This was the first time that the Chiefs stepped in and gave the Commander in Chief of the U.N. Command a specific order on a matter of seeming detail . . . [but that actually] had not only military, but tremendous political significance."[41]

The response by the JCS on January 9 was negative regarding MacArthur's proposals, though he was assured they were still under "careful consideration." The Joint Chiefs' opening sentence conveyed the key message: "There is little possibility of policy change or other external eventuality justifying strengthening our effort in Korea." They went on to counter his proposals one by one. A naval blockade would take considerable time, because UN concurrence would be required and especially "negotiations with the British," in view of the effect on Hong Kong, their Crown colony. Air and naval bombardments of Chinese mainland targets would be authorized only if the Communist Chinese attacked American or UN forces outside Korea. Nationalist troops would not be employed, "in view of the improbability of their decisive effort on the Korean outcome and their probable greater usefulness elsewhere." Again the JCS directed MacArthur to "defend in successive positions . . . inflicting maximum damage to hostile forces in Korea, subject to [the] primary consideration of the safety of your troops and your basic mission of protecting Japan." As for withdrawal, they told him, "Should it become evident in your judgment that evacuation is essential to avoid severe losses of men and material you will at that time withdraw from Korea to Japan."[42]

Meanwhile, on January 8, Ridgway reported a "sense of apprehension in the ROK Army" and requested MacArthur to issue "some public statement designed to reassure these loyal comrades in arms." MacArthur told both Ridgway and the Joint Chiefs, however, that such reassurance "is impossible unless and until the basis for such a statement is established by policy determination at [the U.S.] Government level." On his own, Ridgway issued an unusual message to his troops on the 21st, setting forth his personal answers to two questions he found "uppermost" in the men's minds: "Why are we here? What are we fighting for?" It was a simply worded expression of his own convictions as one soldier to another, and his troops appreciated his effort as frank, noble, and inspiring.

MacArthur was in another kind of mood; he told the JCS on

the 10th that his new directive needed "clarification," because his command had "insufficient strength to hold a position in Korea and simultaneously protect Japan against external assault." He pointed out that "severe" was a relative term and could be widely interpreted in determining what losses would necessitate evacuation. He also wanted Washington to spell out "the political basis" on which his soldiers were being "asked to trade life for time" and to do so in a manner "clearly delineated, fully understood, and so impelling that the hazards of battle are cheerfully accepted." MacArthur passed to his Washington superiors the responsibility of deciding whether his forces were to stay in Korea or get out, for it was a matter "of highest national and international importance, far above the competence of a Theater Commander" to determine.[43] He concluded by again picturing the situation in terms of only two possibilities:

> My query therefore amounts to this: Is it the present objective of United States political policy to maintain a military position in Korea — indefinitely, for a limited time, or to minimize losses by evacuation as soon as it can be accomplished?
>
> As I have pointed out before, under the extraordinary limitations and conditions imposed upon the command in Korea its military position is untenable, but it can hold for any length of time up to its complete destruction if overriding political considerations so dictate.[44]

Needless to say, MacArthur's message upset Washington leaders. Marshall later remarked that "we were at our lowest point" when the Tokyo chief warned that, in essence, annihilation or evacuation were the only options if his recommended actions were not approved. According to Forrest Sherman, MacArthur's challenge produced a "very difficult" time for the Joint Chiefs, and they were nonplussed at being asked to clarify instructions that seemed lucid to them. Acheson concluded that MacArthur was "incurably recalcitrant and basically disloyal to the purposes of his Commander in Chief." Lovett saw his message as a "posterity paper." Truman said MacArthur's message "deeply disturbed" him. "The Far East Commander was, in effect, reporting," commented the President, "that the course of action decided upon by the National Security Council and the Joint Chiefs of Staff and approved by me was not feasible. He was saying that we would be driven off the peninsula, or at the very least suffer terrible losses."[45]

MacArthur's directive of December 29 was not changed by his superiors in spite of his tactics of intimidation, which had often worked in the past. On January 12–13 they did initiate four actions in response to his disturbing words of the 10th: (1) a JCS exposition of certain aspects of his directive, (2) approval by the JCS and forwarding to the NSC of a contingency plan of possible actions against Communist China, (3) a letter from Truman to MacArthur setting forth American objectives in Korea, and (4) the JCS decision to send two of its members to Tokyo and Korea.

The Joint Chiefs told MacArthur on January 12 that, "based on all the factors known to us," they had concluded the UNC forces could not "hold for a protracted period" in Korea against a "sustained major effort" by the CCF. But before MacArthur initiated a withdrawal to Japan they hoped that his forces could resist long enough "to gain some further time for essential diplomatic and military consultations with UN countries participating in [the] Korean effort" and that they could inflict "maximum practicable punishment" on the Chinese armies. While reminding him that their instructions of December 29 and supplementary ones of January 9 remained effective, they asked for his estimate "as to timing and conditions under which you will have to issue instructions to evacuate Korea."[46]

The JCS had studied the reports of their strategic survey and plans committees, as well as a special memorandum by Sherman, on contingency planning for actions against Communist China under certain worsened conditions: if the UNC forces were expelled by force from the peninsula; if the Eighth Army were cornered in a beachhead perimeter with no hope of breaking out; if the Red Chinese attacked American or UN forces beyond the bounds of Korea. On January 12 the Joint Chiefs approved a memorandum recommending to the NSC sixteen possible military and nonmilitary courses of action against Red China if one of these contingencies arose. The list included three of the four measures proposed by MacArthur on December 30: naval blockade, air and naval bombardment of mainland targets, and logistical support of and removal of restrictions on Nationalist forces for "effective operations against the Communists." The last referred to operations on the Chinese mainland of an unspecified nature, for the JCS rejected the employment of Chiang's troops in Korea. As the official Army history emphasizes, the cardinal difference between Mac-Arthur's and the Joint Chiefs' recommendations on the three actions was a matter of timing: "MacArthur wanted . . . [them] at once in order to halt the Chinese drive in Korea. The Joint Chiefs of Staff, taking a longer view, attached to some of their recommendations conditions which would not have stopped the Chinese in Korea but would have held them in Korea." Likewise, Vandenberg observed that the JCS viewed their memorandum only as "a study of possible contingencies," whereas MacArthur saw part or all of it as a plan of action to be "implemented without delay." Although the NSC was not due to deliberate this memorandum until its session on January 17, the JCS decided to send a copy along with Collins and Vandenberg, who were delegated to make an immediate trip to Tokyo and Korea to confer more fully with MacArthur about his new mission and to learn from Ridgway and his commanders the situation on the battlefield.[47]

The President wrote MacArthur on January 13 what Acheson called "an imaginatively kind and thoughtful letter," expounding at length on "our basic national and international purposes" in the Korean conflict. The epistle was one of Truman's noblest gestures in trying to improve relations with his theater commander. The President's letter and Ridgway's message to his troops on the 21st have remained the most eloquent expressions of the reasons for American participation in the Korean War. Truman set forth ten purposes to which the resistance to Communist aggression in Korea contributed, stressing the need to keep the war limited and to avoid alienating the allies on whom the United States would depend in a larger struggle against the Soviet Union. In perhaps his main point to the general, the President explained, "Steps which might in themselves be fully justified and which might lend some assistance to the campaign in Korea would not be beneficial if they thereby involved Japan or Western Europe in large-scale hostilities." He closed on a positive personal note: "The entire nation is grateful for your splendid leadership in the difficult struggle in Korea, and for the superb performance of your forces under the most difficult circumstances." MacArthur responded tersely, "We shall do our best." In private he told his GHQ confidants that the President's message means "there will be no evacuation."[48]

While communications laden with speculation about evacuating the troops to Japan continued between Tokyo and Washington, Ridgway suddenly launched Operation Wolfhound on January 15, a limited-objective advance by Lieutenant Colonel John H. (Mike) Michaelis' 27th Infantry Regiment of the 25th Division. The unit, built up to RCT strength and supported by tanks and tactical air strikes, moved against moderate resistance through Osan to Suwon, uncovering no major CCF concentrations, stationing a small covering force in the area, and withdrawing the bulk of the Wolfhound force southward into the I Corps lines again. The mission, though only a reconnaissance in force, tremendously boosted morale throughout the Eighth Army, demonstrated that at least in that region the Chinese were not assembling in great strength, and started Ridgway planning a two-division assault for January 25 code-named Thunderbolt. According to the Army's official chronicle, Wolfhound proved to be "a harbinger of the offensive spirit that General Ridgway was bent on developing in his new command."[49]

Wolfhound coincided with the visit to Korea by Collins and Vandenberg; the former spent two days touring the Eighth Army front, while the latter visited FEAF bases in Korea. In contrast to MacArthur's reports about the dismal morale of the soldiers, Collins discovered the men to be in "very good" spirits, revitalized, of course, by the success of Wolfhound. Though he was not pleased with the attitude of the ROK troops, who feared the Chinese greatly, Collins reported back to Washington that the Eighth Army was "improving daily under the vigorous leadership of General Ridgway." He told a group of correspondents at Taegu on January 16, "As of now, we are going to stay and fight." Of course, Ridgway had been convinced all along that he could get his army not only to stop the CCF advance but to push the Chinese back across the 38th Parallel. While at the front Vandenberg apparently got an overdose of the new confidence: he flew in a helicopter twelve miles behind the enemy lines, where he briefly joined an American infantry patrol before returning to safety.

Collins and Vandenberg had conferred with MacArthur on January 15, the day they arrived in Tokyo, before spending the two days in Korea. They returned to Tokyo for another conference with MacArthur and his senior GHQ officers on the 18th and departed for Washington on the following day. (General Walter Bedell Smith, the CIA director, came to Tokyo by another flight on the 15th and met separately with MacArthur and Willoughby on intelligence matters.) At the first session between the JCS members and MacArthur in the latter's Dai Ichi office, the UNC commander read aloud Truman's letter of the 13th and said, according to Collins, that "he interpreted the letter as a directive to remain in Korea indefinitely, which the UN forces could do, though in this case he could not assume responsibility for the risk of leaving Japan defenseless." The JCS representatives pointed out that Truman clearly said his message was not a directive and that the President had concurred with the Joint Chiefs that "the decision to evacuate Korea should be delayed as long as possible, without endangering the Eighth Army or the security of Japan." Collins later reported: "General MacArthur stated that a withdrawal from Korea would have repercussions throughout Asia. . . . He declared, with some emotion, that his command should not be held responsible for the defense of Japan while required to hold in Korea." He again appealed for the four National Guard divisions, but Collins told him that the JCS position on their shipment was not likely to change. At the second session MacArthur contended that at least two of those divisions should be sent to Japan, but Collins made no commitment. Also at the second meeting, after Collins shared with him his message to Bradley on the 17th expressing confidence that the UNC forces could hold in Korea, MacArthur spoke more optimistically, asserting that the Eighth Army could maintain "a beachhead in Korea indefinitely." But, according to Collins, MacArthur "reiterated his belief that a decision to evacuate Korea was a political matter and should not be decided on military grounds."[50]

Ridgway, who had set up his advance headquarters near the IX Corps's front line, had to go down to his main headquarters at Taegu on January 20 to confer with MacArthur and some of his GHQ generals, who came for briefings on the battlefield situation and to discuss Ridgway's impending offensive, Thunderbolt. The contingency of tactical success that MacArthur had told Washington was not possible without the adoption of his proposals on more reinforcements and fewer restrictions was obviously coming to pass: Ridgway had revitalized the Eighth Army and was preparing to advance northward soon. Collins and Vandenberg, on their return to Tokyo, were enthusiastic about the aggressive spirit Ridgway had infused in his army, and now MacArthur, who had not exercised close supervision over Ridgway's activities, saw for himself that the UNC forces were on the verge of a significant turnaround. With Ridgway sitting on the front row and probably bemused by his superior's words, MacArthur proclaimed to a room full of correspondents and staff officers at Taegu headquarters: "There has been a lot of loose talk about the Chinese driving us into the sea, just as in the early days there was a lot of nonsense about the North Koreans driving us into the sea. No one is going to drive us into the sea. This command intends to maintain a military position in Korea just as long as Washington decides we should do so." In his memoirs MacArthur added, "I ordered Ridgway to start north again." Years later when Ridgway was reading MacArthur's *Reminiscences,* he stopped at this sentence and wrote in the margin of his copy, "No such order was ever issued."[51]

Collins' message to Bradley on the 17th about the new spirit among Ridgway's forces was promptly shared with Truman and his top advisers. Largely on the basis of the news from the Army Chief of Staff that, in effect, the evacuation crisis was overblown, the NSC met on January 17 and decided to return the JCS memorandum on possible courses of action against Red China, directing the Joint Chiefs to revise it in light of the changed battlefront conditions in morale, if not yet in tactical positions. On the 24th the President and the NSC considered the revised JCS recommendations but made no decision then or later to implement them. Marshall remarked that it became "unnecessary" to continue deliberations on the JCS contingency plans: "Action with respect to most of them was considered inadvisable in view of the radical change in the situation which originally had given rise to them." In their personal reports on the 19th and their later written reports, Collins and Vandenberg told their JCS colleagues, Marshall, and Truman that there was no cause for great alarm about the Eighth Army. Collins remarked about the subsequently transformed outlook of Washington leaders: "For the first time since the previous November responsible authorities in Washington were no longer pessimistic about our being driven out of Korea and, though it was realized that rough times were still ahead of us, no longer was there much talk of evacuation. General Ridgway alone was responsible for this dramatic change."[52]

The prospects for combat success made possible by Ridgway and the findings of Collins and Vandenberg revealed as fallacious the threats of annihilation or evacuation MacArthur had posed if his strategy were not accepted. Thereafter, says an authority on the war, he "was increasingly bypassed by Truman and the JCS in dealing with Ridgway."[53] The official JCS history states:

> The imposing figure in Tokyo no longer towered quite so impressively. . . . His prestige, which had gained an extraordinary luster after Inchon, was badly tarnished. His credibility suffered in the unforeseen outcome of his late November offensive, and declined further when General Collins contradicted his assertions about the sinking morale of Eighth Army. . . .
>
> . . . General MacArthur's counsels no longer commanded the respect they had once enjoyed. Washington now exerted a closer and more direct control over the course of operations in Korea. Moreover, the misunderstanding between the General and his superiors was widening and his dismissal had moved a step closer.[54]

Indeed, the mid-January exposure of MacArthur's false dilemma marked the beginning of the end of his military career.

CHAPTER XVIII

The Furies of Self-Destruction

1. Clouds on the Horizon

AS PUBLIC CRITICISM OF MACARTHUR mounted in the wake of Red China's entry into the war, one of his secret adversaries was the Central Intelligence Agency, according to Lieutenant General Pedro A. del Valle. A distinguished officer with the 1st Marine Division in the war against Japan, del Valle claimed that CIA Director Walter Bedell Smith tried to recruit him to "establish a CIA intelligence office in Tokyo to pull the rug out from MacArthur." Then based in Buenos Aires as president of International Telephone and Telegraph in South America, the retired Marine leader journeyed to Washington in the late autumn of 1950 at the request of the JCS, to whom he had sent his own "plan for combatting communism on a world-wide basis." But the plan was forwarded by the Joint Chiefs to the CIA director, and on his arrival del Valle was directed to confer with General Smith, who, instead of discussing his anti-Communist plan, proposed the anti-MacArthur mission. According to del Valle, Smith said "he knew I had 'crossed swords' with General MacArthur out in the Pacific," but actually the Marine officer had served in MacArthur's theater only briefly, had had no personal dealings with the Southwest Pacific chief, and was a strong, if distant, admirer of his. Del Valle described his reaction:

I told him [Smith] that, far from being an enemy of General Mac-Arthur, I considered him the greatest soldier-statesman this country had. . . . I got up and said I regretted this interview had turned out badly. But I could not accept his offer to send me to Tokyo . . . because I certainly would do nothing to upset MacArthur's position in Japan.

On my way out I met Allen Dulles, second in command of the CIA. He was all smiles and greeted me cordially, saying he was glad I was joining them. I disabused him of this erroneous conclusion and departed.[1]

After returning to Argentina, del Valle wrote to MacArthur on December 14, 1950, and, without mentioning his "strange experience" with the CIA leaders, assured him of his "staunch support, admiration, and approval." He went on to denounce "the internationalist-socialist-communist mob which has seized our government from within." On February 10, 1951, he wrote MacArthur again, mysteriously thanking him for "accepting" him "to do a job of work out in the East," but adding that "it was decided that I should not go." Del Valle remarked, "It would have been a great thing for me to be associated in any way with our greatest soldier-statesman." He went on to tell MacArthur, "I had expected to have my plan studied instead of being sent out on an assignment which possibly did not even agree with my basic ideas," as he "explained quite frankly to Smith." Obviously MacArthur knew by then about del Valle's "plan," but probably not about Smith's idea of using the retired Marine general against him. Del Valle mentioned the CIA incident in a press interview in 1953, but it largely went unnoticed. Later he served as president of the ultraconservative Defenders of the American Constitution.[2]

Smith, who had established close friendships with Marshall, Eisenhower, and Bradley as a valuable staff officer in the Pentagon and European theater in the Second World War, subsequently had served as ambassador to Moscow and had become head of the CIA on October 1, 1950, shortly after Marshall had been appointed Secretary of Defense. In view of their reluctance about dismissing MacArthur the next April, to be discussed in the following section, it is doubtful that Marshall or Bradley endorsed Smith's alleged scheme to obtain MacArthur's removal. Smith himself possibly had a change of mind, assuming the validity of the del Valle allegation, because, it will be recalled, he traveled to Tokyo at the same time as Collins and Vandenberg in early 1951. He met with MacArthur alone on January 15 and two days later with him and his intelligence chief, Willoughby.[3]

Rumors of friction between MacArthur's intelligence staff and the CIA had surfaced periodically since the war began, but they intensified after the Red Chinese intervention and the failure of American intelligence services to predict it. Smith's trip to Tokyo, of course, prompted more press speculation. One journalist reported that MacArthur had excluded the CIA from his theater and that, as a consequence of Smith's visit, "General MacArthur's intelligence activities have been integrated with the various intelligence agencies in Washington." This interpretation of Smith's mission to Tokyo was reinforced by Truman at a news conference in May, when he charged that MacArthur "wouldn't let the Central Intelligence Agency work in Japan until just recently" and that on his January trip Smith "persuaded General MacArthur to let CIA intelligence get into his office." On the other hand, MacArthur wrote Roy Howard two weeks after Smith's visit that "Beedle Smith came to Japan in response to a personal invitation I issued him several months ago." During the Senate hearings in May, he asserted that "the purpose of [Smith's] visit was to perfect and expand the Central Intelligence Agency; it was not to iron out any friction, it was not because of any difficulties." MacArthur told the senators he had given the CIA "every possible assistance," which was echoed by Willoughby in his writings.[4]

Nevertheless, MacArthur's past record demonstrated a wariness of anyone operating in his theater and reporting directly to a Washington agency rather than to him. In World War II he had kept the Office of Strategic Services out of his Southwest Pacific Area, and in the occupation of Japan he had relied exclusively on Willoughby's intelligence and counterintelligence staff. Of course, from mid-1949 to the start of the Korean War, when limited CIA operations were begun in Korea, that peninsula was not then included within MacArthur's command. During the Korean War, as he testified at the May hearings, the one condition he imposed on the CIA was that when its agents "came into the theater, [they] would not act surreptitiously so they would coordinate with my own

Intelligence." During the period between the initial CCF attacks of late October and the massive intervention a month later, when intelligence on the CCF was particularly critical, MacArthur continued to discourage any interference with Willoughby's sphere. On November 15, the Joint Chiefs, evidently concerned over the conflicting reports by Willoughby about the Red Chinese, informed MacArthur that they planned to send to his command "a small Joint Survey Group . . . for the purpose of studying intelligence practices and procedures employed and developed at the several staff levels during the Korean situation, with particular reference to the higher staffs which are concerned with Joint Intelligence problems." In response to their request that he "suggest an appropriate time for dispatch of the Survey Group," MacArthur tartly told the JCS that, in effect, they should wait until the war was over.[5]

In early 1951 public and private charges continued to fly over the question of who was to blame for the failure of United States intelligence to predict the CCF intervention. MacArthur claimed that the Chinese entry into the war resulted from a political decision by the government of a nation not then a belligerent in the Korean conflict and that information about it was therefore the responsibility of "the Defense Department, the State Department or the Central Intelligence Agency, [the Far East Command's] only sources of political intelligence." As he emphasized at the May hearings, "The intelligence that a nation is going to launch a war is not an intelligence that is available to a commander limited to a small area of combat." The official Army history agreed with him that "normally, the intelligence evaluation of whether a foreign power has decided to intervene in a war in national force involves political intelligence at the highest level. Field and intelligence commanders could expect such an evaluation to be made by the government in Washington with the advice of its Central Intelligence Agency." But in reality, according to the Army chronicle, "of all the intelligence levels of the UN command and the American government, perhaps the most decisive in evaluating the intention and capability of Chinese intervention in the Korean War was that of the Far East Command in Tokyo" because of the default of the CIA and the Defense and State intelligence groups, which were either "undecided" or whose views apparently "coincided" with MacArthur's, as evidenced in his unchanged directives for so long.[6]

MacArthur was so disturbed by press accusations of his and Willoughby's misjudgment of Red China's plans in the fall of 1950 that he authorized his intelligence chief to prepare an extensive study of intelligence reports from Washington to Tokyo for the period August 10 to December 7, 1950. Willoughby's resulting report, "Trends of High Level Washington Estimates on Chinese Communist Intervention in Korea," dated February 23, 1951, concluded that "Washington failed to define or forecast Communist China['s] intentions for a major effort." Willoughby went on to frame what was to be the basic Tokyo GHQ position on the issue:

> Washington, with very considerable diplomatic resources and outposts throughout East Asia, was unable to define Chinese intentions as demonstrated, i.e., failure of political intelligence. On the other hand, military intelligence (i.e., in Korea) was limited from the outset by the prohibition of flights beyond the Yalu.[7]

Willoughby later stated that "the entry of Communist China into the war was a piece of political intelligence; it became military only at the point of collision."[8] The full story of the role of the Washington intelligence agencies in the forecast failures of both June and November 1950 must await the complete opening of their records on the questions.

On the basis of the limited documentation now available, it can be concluded that Washington did fail to predict the Chinese intention to enter the Korean War — both at the time of the initial attacks and a month later, when the main intervention occurred. During the crucial period in November between the two CCF attacks, however, MacArthur and Willoughby must share some responsibility for the intelligence failure, because at this time the CCF was already in North Korea in great strength and within the realm of UNC field intelligence. Had the Tokyo GHQ leaders been provided with more accurate estimates of the size of the Chinese commitment below the Yalu at that time, they should have realized that the magnitude of the CCF deployment meant imminent military operations.

In addition to blaming the Washington intelligence system for the failure to predict Peking's intentions, MacArthur later charged that the "perfidy" of British spies contributed to the UNC reversals in the late fall of 1950. In a 1954 interview with MacArthur, Jim G. Lucas, a Pulitzer Prize–winning journalist, recorded that the general believed "the Chinese knew in advance every step he proposed to take. The Chinese Communists decided to come into the Korean War, he said, 'after being assured by the British [spies] that MacArthur would be hamstrung and could not effectively oppose them.' " MacArthur later elaborated on this charge: "My campaign plans, including those of the Eighth Army, were transmitted daily to Washington. General Walker complained constantly to me that the enemy was receiving prior information of his movements. We could find no leaks in Korea or Japan." MacArthur maintained, "It was not until the recent exposure of the British spies, [Guy] Burgess and [Donald] Maclean, that the true facts began to unfold. These men with access to secret files were undoubtedly links in the chain to our enemy in Korea through Peking by way of Moscow." In 1956 he charged that "what may well have triggered my removal was my recommendation, made in January [1951] shortly before my relief, that a treason trial be initiated to break up a spy ring responsible for the purloining of my top secret reports to Washington. . . . One of my dispatches concerning the order of battle was published in a Washington paper within a few hours of its receipt." He was convinced that his "demand that this situation be exposed, coming after the Alger Hiss and Harry Dexter White scandals, caused the deepest resentment and that it probably was branded a political move to embarrass the administration."[9]

Burgess and Maclean were members of the British Foreign Office who acted as double agents for many years before their defection to the Soviet Union in May 1951. Along with H. A. R. (Kim) Philby, a third member of the ring, whose role did not become known until his defection in 1963, these agents all held positions that gave them access to classified information during the Korean War that the United States government shared with the United Kingdom: Maclean headed the American section of the Foreign Office in London; Burgess served as second secretary in the British embassy in Washington; and Philby, also in the Washington embassy, acted as a liaison between American and British intelligence.[10] It is not known how much war-related sensitive information was passed by the trio to Moscow and presumably then to Peking, and it is even less clear what effect, if any, such information had on Communist Chinese actions during the war. But the circumstantial evidence does allow for the possibility that MacArthur's claims about the "purloining" of some of his classified messages were true; however, the linking of his charges and his subsequent dismissal seems far-fetched.

Although MacArthur later focused on the damage done by British spies during the war, by late 1950 he was as concerned with the publication of sensitive data by Western journalists as he was with leaks overseas. At the beginning of the war he had refrained from imposing censorship on the correspondents, relying instead on "voluntary self-censorship." Although Communist publications were outlawed in Japan, Western reporters covering the war were, in effect, on their honor not to hinder military operations by disclosures of troop numbers, losses, dispositions, and plans.[11] By late September, MacArthur was still satisfied with the voluntary system, as he informed the Department of the Army:

> The policy and system governing reporting of military operations by war correspondents in the Korean theater have resulted in the most complete coverage for public information of any military campaign in history, without, as far as I know, a single security breach of a nature to provide effective assistance to the enemy.
>
> Correspondents assigned to war reporting are essentially responsible individuals as are their editors and publishers, and their ability to assume the responsibility of self-censorship has been amply and conclusively demonstrated.[12]

By the time of the disastrous UNC setback against the CCF, however, MacArthur became sufficiently alarmed over the publication of information endangering the Hungnam evacuation to take action. Following a meeting between Hickey and the Tokyo news bureau chiefs, at which the latter said their home offices were putting extreme pressure on them to report stories from the front more fully, MacArthur asked Collins on December 15 to get the Pentagon to call a "high-level conference" of publishers and managing editors to discuss "the gravity of security breaches." Three days later Marshall held such a meeting in his office, at which time the consensus of the group was that "security of information from [the] combat area is the responsibility of the military." MacArthur claimed to be shocked by the response, but he promptly used it as the grounds for imposing military censorship on correspondents in Korea, which he said "the Pentagon had long advocated." The responsibility for enforcing censorship in the field was assigned to Eighth Army headquarters, which was to use the rules on the matter as set forth in the Army field manual of 1942.[13] In response to a protest by Robert U. Brown of *Editor and Publisher*, MacArthur told him on January 18 that he preferred self-censorship but was compelled to act otherwise:

> The demand for censorship became so heavy, however, that I put the matter before a conference of leading publishers and editors held in Washington on December 18th last who made it unequivocally clear that military censorship should be imposed.
>
> It is indeed a screwy world, as you term it, when a soldier fighting to preserve freedom of the press finds himself opposed by the press itself.[14]

More frankly, he wrote the Army's chief of military history in 1957 that "the general unreliability of the press coverage of the incidents of war in the absence of censorship" had produced "grave concern at the front" in Korea where it had a "demoralizing effect on troop morale."[15]

In 1951, however, MacArthur usually let Willoughby run interference for him in criticizing irresponsible or inaccurate reporting of the war. In April, the Far East intelligence chief produced an attractive-looking, if poison-filled, booklet entitled *Aid and Comfort to the Enemy: Trends in Korean Press Reports*. In it he quoted extensively from sensationalist, erroneous dispatches by war correspondents, especially those written during the withdrawal of the UNC forces in December, setting in contrast "the facts" in each case. In the December issue of *Cosmopolitan*, Willoughby wrote a slashing attack against the journalists who "smeared" MacArthur and the Eighth Army, naming as the worst culprits the syndicated columnist Drew Pearson, Hal Boyle of the Associated Press, Hanson W. Baldwin of the *New York Times*, and Joseph Alsop and Homer Bigart of the New York *Herald Tribune*. In their later books Willoughby and Whitney stressed the negative impact of the press on Eighth Army morale and on Truman's impression of Mac-Arthur.[16]

In early 1951, besides controversies over intelligence and censorship, MacArthur was compelled to face the issue of racism in his command. With MacArthur's authorization and cooperation, Thurgood Marshall, special counsel for the National Association for the Advancement of Colored People and future Supreme Court justice, began on January 14 a five-week investigation in Japan and Korea of the courts-martial of black soldiers of the Eighth Army. He concluded that racial discrimination was prevalent and had influenced the court-martial process against blacks' cases. Marshall later commented that, although "MacArthur did not have official responsibility for the disposition of the individual courts-martial cases," in his final report he found it "necessary to place the ultimate responsibility for these courts-martial squarely upon General Douglas MacArthur. He had both the authority and the responsibility for maintaining or ending racial segregation in the Army's Far East Command."[17]

Integration of the American armed services had begun gradually before the Korean War, but it was accelerated after June 1950, partly because of immediate necessity in combat and because of an Army study which found that black troops performed better in integrated outfits. In the first year of the war blacks in the Eighth Army served in both integrated and all-black units, the most conspicuous of the latter being the 24th Infantry Regiment, which received poor reviews for some of its performances under fire. In part due to the smaller number of blacks involved, the Air Force's record at curbing segregation was better. While in Tokyo, Thurgood Marshall observed blacks on duty in FEAF headquarters but not in MacArthur's GHQ, three blocks away.[18]

In an interview with a reporter of the black Pittsburgh *Courier* on May 22, 1951, MacArthur said of Marshall's findings: "I was unaware of the prevalence of these courts-martial as far as race is concerned until they were called to my attention. . . . I am willing to concede that these courts-martial may have been excessive." On receiving Marshall's report, he "immediately ordered a complete investigation. The report I asked for had not reached me when I left Tokyo." MacArthur went on during the interview to praise the black soldiers who had served under him and declared that he had only "one criticism of Negro troops. They didn't send me enough of them." As on other matters, he shifted the blame for segregation to his superiors: "Negro units in the U.S. armed forces . . . were created in Washington and sent to me as already organized Jim Crow units. . . . I did not ask for men by race. . . . I asked Washington for *men*. . . . I don't believe that any theater commander in American war history accepted and integrated the number of Negro troops that I did." He concluded on an astonishingly idealistic note: "In my commands, if segregation exists [*sic*] . . . it exists [*sic*] as it may have been dictated from Washington; and certainly discrimination never existed." [19]

Though criticism of his command's problems in the areas of intelligence, censorship, and race relations got considerable press coverage, the development in early 1951 that produced the most public excitement and had a potentially crucial bearing on MacArthur's theater was the Great Debate. Truman's pre-Christmas news that Ike would head NATO forces and that more American troops would go to Europe produced a torrent of criticism from Taft and his supporters in Congress, as well as from such influential citizens as former President Hoover. Already evolving in the fall of 1950, the Great Debate had its formal beginning on Capitol Hill when Senator Wherry of Nebraska, the Republican floor leader, introduced a resolution on January 8 stating that "it is the sense of the Senate that no ground forces of the United States should be assigned to duty in the European area for the purposes of the North Atlantic Treaty pending the formulation of a policy with respect thereto by the Congress." Two weeks later the Senate Foreign Relations and Armed Services committees began hearings on the matter. Challenged by the Taft-Wherry faction were the administration's foreign and military policies and the President's right to commit troops to NATO without congressional approval.

During the Great Debate many who sided with Taft and Wherry were isolationist regarding European relations but aggressively interventionist on East Asian affairs. They included some fiscal conservatives who feared America was headed toward disastrous overspending in its NATO commitment and some self-styled realists who wanted to limit American military support to areas where the Communists had already plunged into armed action, namely, Korea and China. Some of MacArthur's public utterances of that period seem to have been intended to influence the outcome of the Great Debate and thereby gain a higher priority for his theater. But neither the efforts of the general nor those of the Taft Republicans seriously altered the administration's plans to strengthen NATO militarily: Secretary of Defense Marshall announced on February 16 that four American Army divisions would be sent to West Europe that year, and in April Eisenhower moved to NATO's supreme headquarters near Paris to assume his new command. The Wherry resolution was eventually tabled by the Senate in favor of the Connally-Russell resolution, which in its final amended form endorsed Ike's NATO appointment and the shipment of troops to Europe but also advised Truman to consult Congress before sending more troops to Europe, to render semi-annual reports to Congress on NATO's military establishment, and to endeavor to get larger contributions for NATO's forces from the other member nations. The Great Debate formally ended with the Senate's passage of the Connally-Russell resolution on April 4.

Although White House press statements and pro-Truman journalists made much ado about presidential leadership in foreign policy when French Premier René Pleven came to Washington to confer with Truman on January 29–30, some West European newspapers maintained that many officials in NATO countries believed the Great Debate revealed the President's weakness in controlling American foreign affairs and made him more reluctant to tighten the leash on MacArthur. Meanwhile, in the UN General Assembly on February 1, the Truman administration gained a triumph of sorts when that body adopted a resolution condemning Communist China for aggression in Korea. But it was widely reported in the foreign press that, in order to get its allies' support for the resolution, the United States government had conceded that it would not initiate any new aggressive measures against Peking that could obstruct a peaceful settlement in Korea. The tightrope that Truman seemed to be walking was described by a British journalist-historian: "The necessity of keeping NATO and the Allied front in the UN intact only emphasized that, while any Administration concession to the Taft-MacArthur alliance could destroy America's international coalition, too complete an alignment with the British attitude towards Peking could mean the disintegration of the Administration's precarious support in Congress."[20]

If the Great Debate had not resulted in the greater focus on his theater that MacArthur hoped for, his army's success in early 1951 did not buttress his continuing argument for reinforcements, fewer restrictions, and retaliatory measures directly against Red China. On January 25, Ridgway began Operation Thunderbolt, at first using a division each from the I and IX corps, located on the west side of the front. As CCF resistance increased, he threw in two more American divisions, along with the Turkish brigade and two ROK regiments. The severest fighting took place on and near Hill 440, north of Suwon, which elements of the 25th Division secured on February 9 after a four-day battle in which over 4000 Chinese soldiers were killed (compared to 70 American troops). The I Corps had reached the Han River west of Seoul by February 10, overrunning Inchon and Kimpo.

In the meantime, Almond's X Corps, with the ROK III Corps on its right flank, began Operation Roundup in the central area of the front on February 5, attacking toward Chipyongni and Hongchon respectively. But there was a strong enemy counteroffensive on February 11–14, involving both mass-wave assaults and infiltration behind the UNC lines. On the ROK front to the east the enemy penetrated to Chechon before Ridgway could commit enough reserves to stop the thrust. Falling back in good order to the west, the X Corps withdrew southward but left some forces to defend Chipyongni and Wonju. For several days a regiment of the 2d Division and a French battalion fought off five CCF divisions around Chipyongni before being relieved. Wonju also was held, despite repeated attacks by much larger enemy forces. Concentrated UNC artillery, armor, and infantry firepower, supported by the close strikes of Major General Earl E. Partridge's Fifth Air Force and of carrier aircraft, took such a high toll of the massive enemy assault formations that by the 18th the CCF and North Koreans broke contact and moved northward. In the battle for Chipyongni alone the enemy had suffered 5000 fatalities. Ridgway considered the stopping of the enemy counteroffensive to be a "turning point"; not until April 22 would the CCF be able to mount another offensive effort, so serious had been its losses.[21]

Ridgway's Operation Killer, an apt name in view of its "meat-grinder" tactics, aimed more at destroying enemy forces than seizing territory, was launched on February 21. The UNC-ROK order of battle now was Milburn's I Corps, occupying the west sector of the front and comprising the U.S. 3d and 25th divisions, the Turkish and 29th British brigades, and the ROK 1st Division; the IX Corps, now headed by Major General Bryant E. Moore (who succeeded Coulter on January 31), holding the west central sector and consisting of the American 1st Cavalry and 24th divisions, the 27th Commonwealth Brigade, a Greek and a Philippine battalion, the ROK 6th Division, and, just added, the 1st Marine Division; Almond's X Corps, located in the central mountain area and including the U.S. Army's 2d and 7th divisions, along with three ROK divisions; the ROK III Corps in the east central sector; and the ROK I Corps, manning the eastern, or coastal, sector next to the Sea of Japan. (The 1st Marine Division had been engaged earlier in destroying elements of the North Korean II Corps that had infiltrated as far south as Andong.) Within eight days after the beginning of Killer, the UNC and ROK units had recaptured Kangnung on the east coast and Hoengsong in the central region, moving in force to the Han River west, south, and east of Seoul. Bad weather and spring thaws slowed their advance more than did enemy resistance. Moore, the new IX Corps commander, was killed on February 24 when his helicopter crashed into the Han River; Smith, the Marine leader, served as acting corps commander until March 5, when Major General William M. Hoge took over the corps.

On March 7, Ridgway launched Operation Ripper; its secondary objective was to drive a salient into the enemy's central front while also achieving the primary aim of tearing enemy forces apart. The outer reaches of the salient, with Chunchon at the northern apex, were occupied by the 21st. Although not a stated objective, Seoul was occupied on March 15 without a battle — the city's fourth change of hands since June — when divisions of the I Corps, pushing north of the Han on each side of the capital, forced the CCF defenders to evacuate in order to avert encirclement. A parachute drop by the 187th Airborne RCT at Munsan, about thirty miles north of Seoul, failed to entrap the fleeing CCF troops. On March 22, the day after the fall of Chunchon, Ridgway kept up the relentless pressure on the enemy by ordering Operation Courageous to get under way. In the ensuing eight days nearly all of South Korea except the small area west of the Imjin River was cleared of Communist regulars, though thousands of guerrillas still caused havoc in several mountainous areas south of the 38th Parallel. Having no new directive regarding movement across the 38th Parallel but securing his superiors' guarded approval of its crossing by UNC and ROK forces to improve their tactical positions, if not to reconquer North Korea, MacArthur authorized Ridgway on March 23 to go ahead with his requested advance to a new phase line just above the parallel; he cautioned him, however, not to publicize the move. Four days later elements of the ROK I Corps crossed the parallel along the east coast and proceeded to capture the small port of Yangyang on the 31st. Advancing north of Uijongbu along the road to Chorwon, American patrols of the IX Corps pushed above the 38th Parallel on March 31.

The Seventh Fleet and allied naval contingents, meanwhile, kept the ports of Wonsan, Hungnam, and Songjin under almost daily bombardment. UNC naval units were also busy transporting and supporting commando raids on both coasts of North Korea, and small garrisons were placed on islands off the harbors of Wonsan, Songjin, Chinnampo, and Ongjin to assist in air-sea rescue operations and to man radar and radio stations. Considerable enemy manpower was tied down in all these coastal areas because of the threat of larger amphibious operations. Stratemeyer took great pride in reporting to MacArthur new records for total daily sorties by his air units; for example, he proclaimed an all-time high of 1025 sorties on February 15 and 1477 on March 16. FEAF, naval, and allied planes continued to control the skies over Korea, but Chinese MIGs were rising to challenge them in growing numbers by that spring. The largest air battle of the war so far came on April 12, when 80 MIGs attacked 48 B-29s and 75 FEAF fighters over Sinuiju (3 B-29s and 9 MIGs were shot down).[22]

By the end of March, the intelligence staffs at Ridgway's and MacArthur's headquarters were accumulating evidence that CCF reinforcements were moving into North Korea, presumably for a large counteroffensive. The main assembly area for the CCF was a rugged region about twenty miles above the 38th Parallel; bounded by Chorwon, Kumhwa, and Pyonggang (not to be confused with Pyongyang, the capital), it was soon nicknamed the Iron Triangle and would be the scene of many savage engagements during the next two years. In order to keep the massing enemy units off balance as long as possible and to secure a more advantageous defensive position to meet the anticipated enemy attack, Ridgway launched Operation Rugged on April 5 to advance to Line Kansas. By the 9th his forces had reached the new phase line, which gave them control of the high ground immediately south of the Iron Triangle. Ridgway was preparing to assault Chorwon, the southwest point of the CCF's assembly area, when he suddenly learned on April 11 that he was to move to Tokyo.[23]

True to his pledge to Ridgway the day after Christmas, MacArthur left the running of the Eighth Army and the planning of UNC-ROK operations to him and his headquarters. Nevertheless, MacArthur made eight trips to Korea in less than three months to confer with Ridgway and his commanders. His usual pattern was to leave Haneda in the early morning aboard the *SCAP*, spend six to ten hours on the ground conferring at army headquarters and touring the front, and return to Tokyo by nightfall. His first visit to Ridgway, it will be recalled, was at Taegu on January 20 to review plans for Thunderbolt. His later flights to the front were to Suwon on January 29, February 13, and March 7; to Wonju on February 20 and March 17; to Yongdungpo on March 24; and to Kangnung on April 3. Whitney always went with him, Hickey and Canada made most of the trips, and Wright and Stratemeyer went on some of the flights. Although he had passed his seventy-first birthday on January 25, 1951, MacArthur set an exhausting pace on such journeys. When he was not questioning commanders about upcoming operations or logistical problems, he was moving about by jeep, chatting with officers and enlisted men and usually getting near enough to the front lines at least to observe artillery barrages on enemy positions. On his expeditions to Korea he wore out his traveling companions and sometimes exposed himself and them to considerable risks. For example, during Operation Ripper, as the 1st Marine Division, operating in the central mountains, encountered "stiffening enemy opposition" above Hongchon, the UNC Commander in chief landed at the Wonju air strip on March 17 and went by jeep to the Hongchon area to visit the Marines and observe the action. Marines were still clearing enemy mines along the rough, narrow mountain road between Wonju and Hongchon, and the CCF was offering sharp resistance on the ridges near the town of Hongchon, which had fallen to the Marines only two days earlier.[24] Ridgway and Smith, both in top physical shape, accompanied MacArthur to the combat area and were impressed, as on other such occasions, by the Old Man's energy and endurance. As Smith described it:

> We got the word from Gen. MacArthur that . . . he was coming over by plane . . . to Wonju and wanted to be met there by a jeep, and he wanted to make a tour of the [1st Marine] Division without getting out of the jeep. So . . . I took my driver and we met the plane. Gen. Ridgway rode in the jeep with Gen. MacArthur and myself. We started out on the road and I said, "Now, General, we are scattered — I don't know how many miles we were scattered, 60 miles or so up the road — and you said you had 3 hours that you could spend here; and we can't make the rounds in 3 hours." He said, "I've got the time." I said, "All right, if you've got the time."
>
> So we went and picked up the reserve regiment [5th Marines] of the Division, which was the first unit we ran into — [Col. Richard W.] Hayward was in command of it at the time — and Gen. MacArthur didn't get out of the jeep; he talked to Hayward. We went on up by my CP [command post], and he didn't get out of the jeep; he shook hands with some of the staff officers. Then I said to him, "The 7th Marines are up the road, up by the Hongchon River; that's quite a distance." He said, "I've got the time." So we took off for the Hongchon River, and I was hoping that [Col. Homer L.] Litzenberg hadn't crossed the darn thing yet, because it was a deep and fast flowing river that we would have to ford in a jeep. But we got to the south bank of the Hongchon and Litzenberg had gone on, so we forded the Hongchon River. We actually floated at times, and we had to stop for a while and dry out the engine on the other side. We never got out of the car. We got it going again, and then we found Litzenberg and talked to him. Then Gen. MacArthur said, "I want to see an assault battalion." My gosh! We kept going up the road and found [Major] Webb Sawyer and his battalion, and all the Marines crowded around. . . . Nobody told these Marines it was Gen. MacArthur who was coming up the road, but all of them had cameras. My God, there were more cameras!
>
> After we talked to Webb Sawyer, we went back . . . to Wonju. I don't know how many miles that was, but if you've ever ridden for 4 or 5 hours in a rough-riding jeep you've got to go to the head. Well,

nobody ever suggested stopping . . . [before] we got to Wonju. The General marched majestically off to his plane, and all the rest of us just disappeared! General Ridgway came to me and he said, "Smith, why in hell didn't you suggest that we stop to take a leak?" I said, "Well, you were the senior, and I think it was up to you to suggest that!" Maybe the Old Man had a rubber bag, or something.[25]

Ridgway found that on each of his Korean visits MacArthur was generous in his praise and expressed "complete satisfaction with our performance and our tactical plans." Although he continued to get along well with his boss, Ridgway was annoyed by two of his habits. As he had done at Taegu on the eve of Operation Thunderbolt, MacArthur told a group of correspondents at Wonju on February 20, the day before Killer began, "I have just ordered a resumption of the offensive." The Eighth Army commander, who was standing nearby, said nothing to the contrary at the time, but in his book on the war he noted with lingering agitation that "no order at all concerning any part of the operation" had come "from CINCFE or from the GHQ staff in Tokyo. . . . Neither he nor any of his staff had had any part in the conception or in the planning of Operation Killer." It was, observed Ridgway, "a rather unwelcome reminder" of MacArthur's urge "to keep his public image always glowing." This, Ridgway was convinced, also motivated the Far East chief when he habitually visited Korea just before an offensive was about to begin. After MacArthur sent word that he planned to arrive on the eve of Operation Ripper "to fire the starting gun," as Ridgway put it, the Eighth Army commander finally felt compelled, for the security of his forces, to ask his superior to postpone his visit until the offensive was under way. Ridgway was relieved when MacArthur took it in the right spirit and good-naturedly agreed to arrive at Suwon about noon on March 7; Ripper had been launched early that morning. On the occasion of Operation Courageous, MacArthur cooperated and put off his visit until the offensive was two days old. On his last visit to Korea, however, he reverted to habit and arrived two days before Operation Rugged.[26] At least Ridgway had gotten him to make a temporary change, which was more than most accomplished in trying to get MacArthur to alter his ways.

Ridgway's battlefield successes, particularly the smashing of the

Chinese counteroffensive in mid-February, prompted MacArthur to appeal again to the JCS to remove some of the restrictions on his forces. After a strong pitch to him by Stratemeyer on its necessity, MacArthur asked the Joint Chiefs on February 15 to permit the FEAF's bombing of Rashin, which, he argued, was "imperative" to disrupt the supply line from the USSR to North Korea. The JCS, as well as State officials, still viewed such a raid as risking violations of the nearby Soviet border or sinking Russian vessels, which often were anchored in Rashin harbor. They also disagreed with his high evaluation of Rashin as a supply center. After discussing the matter for a week with Pentagon and State leaders, the Joint Chiefs notified him that the prohibition against bombing Rashin was to remain in effect. When he received another "urgent request" from Stratemeyer, MacArthur tried again, on February 26, to obtain authorization for the FEAF to attack hydroelectric power facilities in North Korea, but the JCS rejected the idea on March 1 for "political" reasons. The next day MacArthur submitted to the Joint Chiefs his report for the UN Security Council covering UNC operations during the last half of February. He closed by saying that "if and when" the issue of crossing the 38th Parallel arose anew, he did not plan to send his forces into North Korea again "if cogent political reasons against crossing are then advanced and there is any reasonable possibility that a limitation is to be placed thereon." Both Pentagon and State officials agreed that his concluding statement should be deleted, and he was so informed. According to the Army's official account, they "saw no profit in unnecessarily calling the attention of the United Nations to the 38th Parallel."[27]

A JCS report on discussions between that body and State Department representatives in February about "possible lines of action" in Korea said, "The Department of State would prefer not to express political objectives with respect to Korea until military capabilities there were established. On the other hand, the consensus of the opinions of the Joint Chiefs of Staff was that a political decision was required before there could be suitable determination of military courses of action." Similarly, the official Army history says, "Through March 1951, the United States . . . continued to fight without having elected any new political or military courses of action. . . . Frequent meetings took place between State and Defense representatives, but each Department deferred to the other for a clear statement of what should be done in Korea."[28]

While the State-Defense quest for a harmony of political and military objectives in Korea continued, MacArthur developed in the privacy — and unreality — of his office a new, grandiose strategy for winning the war "in a maximum of ten days." According to his memoirs, he planned, if the restrictions on his operations were removed, to subject the northern provinces of North Korea to "massive air attacks" and then to "sever Korea from Manchuria by laying a field of radioactive waste — the byproducts of atomic manufacture — across all the major lines of enemy supply." In 1954 he remarked of his plan, "A belt of radioactive cobalt . . . could have been spread from wagons, carts, trucks, and planes. . . . For at least sixty years there could have been no land invasion of Korea from the north." Subsequent to the spreading of the radioactive waste, MacArthur's fantastic plan called for the UNC to be joined by 500,000 Nationalist Chinese troops and two U.S. Marine divisions in "simultaneous amphibious and airborne landings at the upper end of both coasts of North Korea," which would "close a gigantic trap. The Chinese would starve or surrender." In light of prior JCS responses to his pleas for Chiang's troops and for approval to attack border targets, as well as his neglect of such crucial factors as allied and Soviet reactions, his superiors undoubtedly would not have wasted much time considering his plan and probably would have judged him as having succumbed to senility. But MacArthur never submitted his plan to the JCS, though he apparently conceived it in late February or early March of 1951.

The concept of using radioactive waste for military purposes did not originate with MacArthur and, in fact, appeared in contemporary publications. In early June 1950, Secretary of Defense Louis Johnson released a study of potential methods of radiological warfare, which pointed out that from the waste of atomic piles "militarily significant quantities of RW [radiological warfare] agents" could be obtained. Commenting on the study, Hanson Baldwin observed in the *New York Times*, "Theoretically, these dusts and gases, fluids and particles, radioactive and with differing chemical half-lives, could be packed in cylinders, lead-lined or otherwise shielded, and later could be released to contaminate any desired area." He believed they "might be used in ground warfare, much like gas or mine fields or fortifications, to deny any enemy the use of an area." Baldwin, a respected writer on military affairs and history, noted that military use of such waste posed technical difficulties and that similar effects of contamination could be produced by exploding an atomic bomb at or near ground level. MacArthur was probably aware of the study released by Johnson, but the idea was also suggested to him by a Seattle citizen in a cable of December 1, 1950: "Why not lay down radioactive mist along Yalu. Warn Chinese this has been done. Will prove we do not intend to cross border. Will trap Reds in Korea." The notion was also brought to Truman's attention. As MacArthur was en route to the States after his dismissal, Representative Albert Gore, a Democrat from Tennessee, proposed to the President that "radioactive by-products" be used to contaminate a belt across "the entire peninsula of Korea."[29]

MacArthur's enthusiasm for the radioactive-waste scheme was made public during his postdismissal years, but his views on the introduction of atomic bombs in Korea were less clear and consistent. The issue of using such weapons raised intense domestic and international anxieties, as demonstrated by Attlee's sudden trip to Washington in December. The JCS considered several contingencies involving possible use of atomic bombs in Korea, particularly in December 1950, but concluded that the mountainous terrain would nullify much of their effectiveness, and besides, America's allies would not countenance their employment, even if the President could be convinced, which was unlikely. Collins discussed the use of atomic weapons in Korea hypothetically when he visited MacArthur in early December, and later that month the JCS asked MacArthur to recommend potential Soviet targets for atomic attacks in case the USSR entered the Korean conflict. While he headed the United Nations Command, however, MacArthur ventured no clear-cut judgment on whether atomic weapons should be employed. After his dismissal his statements on the subject were ambiguous and sometimes conflicting. During the Senate hearings he said he had asked the JCS "what might be the potentialities and possibilities of the use of the atomic bomb in my own theater," but he denied having recommended its use, adding that "the use of the atomic bomb has, by fiat and order, been limited to the deci-

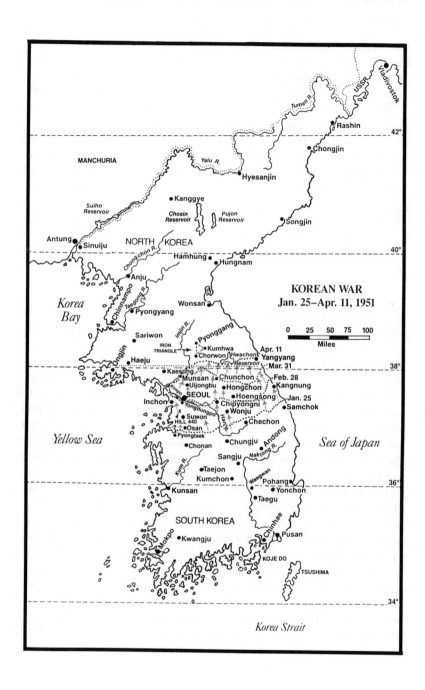

KOREAN WAR
Jan. 25–Apr. 11, 1951

MANCHURIA

USSR

Vladivostok

Tumen R.

Rashin

Chongjin

Yalu R.

Hyesanjin

Suiho
Reservoir

Kanggye

Chosin
Reservoir

Pujon
Reservoir

Songjin

Antung

Sinuiju

NORTH KOREA

Chongchon R.

Hamhung

Hungnam

Anju

Korea
Bay

Chinnampo

Wonsan

Taedong R.

Pyongyang

Sariwon

Imjin R.

Pyonggang

IRON
TRIANGLE

Kumhwa

Apr. 11

Chorwon

Hwachon
Reservoir

Yangyang

Ongjin

Haeju

Mar. 31

Kaesong

Chunchon

Feb. 28

Munsan

Uijongbu

Hongchon

Kangnung

Kimpo

SEOUL

Hoengsong

Jan. 25

Inchon

Chipyongni

Samchok

Yongdungpo

Wonju

Suwon

Han R.

Chechon

0   25   50   75   100
Miles

HILL 440

Osan

Pyongtaek

Chungju

Andong R.

Sea of Japan

Chonan

Sangju

Naktong R.

Yellow Sea

Taejon

Kumchon

Waegwan

Pohang

Yonchon

Kum R.

Kunsan

Taegu

SOUTH KOREA

Chinhae

Mokpo

Kwangju

Pusan

KOJE DO

TSUSHIMA

Korea Strait

42°

40°

38°

36°

34°

sion of the President." Under further questioning by the senators, he conceded that "the use of the atomic weapon would certainly represent a great reserve potential which we could exercise at the discretion of the Commander in Chief." To President-elect Eisenhower in late 1952, he proposed the atomic bombing of military targets in North Korea, and also the laying of radioactive wastes along her northern border. In an interview conducted in 1954 but not published until after his death, MacArthur stated that he had wanted to drop "between thirty and fifty atomic bombs" on enemy bases before laying radioactive waste material across the northern edge of North Korea. In a letter in 1960, he implied that America's atomic dominance should have been used to win the Korean War, but a few months later, in response to a charge by Truman that MacArthur had wanted to use atomic bombs during the conflict, the general stated that "atomic bombing in the Korean War was never discussed either by my headquarters or in any communication to or from Washington." Truman later said his own comment was merely an opinion and that he had no documentation of MacArthur's "advocating use of the A-bomb." The idea of using atomic weapons in Korea was not mentioned by MacArthur, Willoughby, and Whitney in their memoirs.[30]

That MacArthur would invent such a "victory" strategy in the late winter of 1951 indicated his increasing frustration over Washington's failure to develop new policies to prevent a war of stalemate and attrition. Though he was not so foolish as to send his grandiose plan to the JCS, he did provide glimpses of his growing dissatisfaction through public remarks that were critical of current policies and guidelines and that violated the President's "muzzling" directive of early December. With fierce battles under way at Chipyongni and Wonju during the enemy counteroffensive in February, MacArthur issued a press statement on the 13th after his return that day from Korea. "The concept advanced by some that we should establish a line across Korea and enter into positional warfare," he declared, "is wholly unrealistic and illusory." Because of the rough terrain and the numerical inferiority of the UNC forces, he maintained that such tactics "would insure the destruction of our forces piecemeal." As for crossing the 38th Parallel again, he asserted, "We must materially reduce the existing superiority of our Chinese Communist enemy engaging with impunity in undeclared war against us, with the unprecedented military advantage of sanctuary protection . . . before we can seriously consider major operations north of that geographic line." Although an obvious public criticism of the administration's prohibition on air operations beyond the Yalu, his statement, which was widely printed in American and allied papers, produced no reprimand from the Joint Chiefs.

After conferring with Ridgway and Almond at Wonju and visiting some front-line units to the north on February 20, he told reporters that, though the President "has indicated that crossing of the [38th] Parallel is to be resolved in accordance with my best judgment as theater commander," he would not "arbitrarily execute that authority" if his forces were to be restricted further or if there were "cogent political reasons" against entering North Korea again. Some of his phrases were exactly the same as those used in his subsequent report for the UN Security Council that, it will be recalled, were excised by his superiors, but, strangely, at this time his statements brought no remonstrance from Washington.[31] When he was at Suwon on March 7, MacArthur issued a statement to an assembly of correspondents at the air strip, predicting that the "savage slaughter" would continue and the war would evolve into one of attrition and indecisiveness unless Washington policies were changed:

> As our battle lines shift north the supply position of the enemy will progressively improve, just as inversely the effectiveness of our air potential will progressively diminish thus in turn causing his numerical ground superiority to become of increasing battlefield significance.
>
> Assuming no diminution of the enemy's flow of ground forces and materiel to the Korean battle area, a continuation of the existing limitations upon our freedom of counter-offensive action, and no major additions to our organizational strength, the battle lines cannot fail in time to reach a point of theoretical military stalemate. Thereafter our further advance would militarily benefit the enemy more than it would ourselves. . . .
>
> Vital decisions have yet to be made — decisions far beyond the scope of the authority vested in me as the military commander, decisions which are neither solely political nor solely military, but which must

provide on the highest international levels an answer to the obscurities which now becloud the unsolved problems raised by Red China's undeclared war in Korea.[32]

Reporters dubbed it his "Die for Tie" statement. The Joint Chiefs said nothing to him about it, but Ridgway, in essence, contradicted his gloomy assessment when he told the press on the 12th that if his forces were able to liberate South Korea, "a tremendous victory for the United Nations" and "a defeat of incalculable importance" for Communist China would have been achieved.

In answer to a cable query from Baillie, the United Press head, regarding how large a force would be needed "to hold the 38th Parallel inviolate," MacArthur responded on March 15, "The conditions under which we are conducting military operations in Korea do not favor engaging in positional warfare on any line across the peninsula. Specifically with reference to the 38th Parallel, there are no natural defense features anywhere near its immediate proximity." He concluded that "fundamental decisions" needed to be made at levels above him and that the decision-makers "must not ignore the heavy cost in Allied blood" that would result from a protracted stalemate in Korea. His statement to Baillie received prominent attention in the *New York Times* and other leading newspapers on the 16th, but, though he had not cleared it in advance, as required by Truman's December directive, the JCS did not confront him about the violation.

On his final visit to Korea — his fifteenth wartime trip to the peninsula — MacArthur flew to Kangnung on April 3 and then traveled by jeep along the coastal road beyond Yangyang, about fifteen miles north of the 38th Parallel, to observe the ROK Capital Division in action. After returning to Tokyo that evening, he told the press about his journey to North Korea but emphasized, in line with Washington thinking, that the significance of the 38th Parallel now was political, not military. He commented, "Our strategy remains unchanged and is based on maneuver and not positional warfare."[33] By then his units from the Imjin River westward to the Sea of Japan were crossing the controversial parallel in force and were preparing to attack the CCF concentration in the Iron Triangle. As he had repeatedly stated, MacArthur did not envision another attempt to conquer North Korea unless the

existing restrictions on his forces were removed and unless there
were significant changes in Washington policy. His forecast of
March 7 regarding a line beyond which it was not militarily advantageous to advance would prove accurate. When the armistice
would be negotiated finally in July 1953, the UNC and ROK forces
would be holding nearly the same positions across the peninsula
that they had occupied in early April 1951.

The *Times* of London printed a short article on March 10 based
on a dispatch from a Reuter's correspondent in Tehran, where the
Iranian Prime Minister had been assassinated the previous week;
many Iranians believed the United States was guilty of "interference" in their nation's affairs. The dispatch included a statement,
without elaboration, that "a crowd of 5000 demonstrated outside
the American Embassy for two hours and a half to-day, shouting
'Death to MacArthur.' "[34] If perchance Truman or Acheson saw
the brief article, he may well have pondered the state of the United
States government's global image when such people thought the
general decided even American foreign policy in the Middle East.
The time was fast approaching when the President would make
clear to the American public and to the world where the outspoken Far East commander stood in the making of Washington policy and in the constitutional system of the United States.

2. *The Storm Breaks*

As Ridgway's Operation Ripper pushed northward, exacting
enormous enemy casualties and regaining Seoul in mid-March, the
question of crossing the 38th Parallel again was discussed by State
and Defense officials; both they and allied leaders hoped to reach
a consensus on future policy in the Korean conflict. Acheson found
that nearly all the nations allied with the United States in the war
were reluctant to have the UNC forces invade North Korea again.
Washington planners concluded that, in view of the wavering support of the UN members and of the heavy losses the Chinese and
North Korean units were suffering, the time was opportune to attempt to get negotiations started toward an armistice. Since the
previous UN efforts to obtain a cease-fire had brought only neg-

ative reactions from Peking, State and Defense leaders and the NSC decided that a more effective approach might be through a direct appeal by President Truman to the Communist Chinese government to open talks about a military and political settlement of the Korean situation. On March 19 the draft presidential declaration was presented by the State Department to George Marshall and the JCS, who concurred, and State officials began consulting the other UN members with forces in Korea.[35] On the 20th the Joint Chiefs, though they did not send him a copy of the draft declaration, told MacArthur that the peace move was about to be initiated by Truman:

> State [is] planning a Presidential announcement shortly that with [the] clearing of [the] bulk of South Korea of aggressors, [the] United Nations [members with forces in Korea are] now prepared to discuss conditions of [the] settlement in Korea. United Nations feeling exists that further diplomatic efforts toward [a] settlement should be made before any advance with major forces north of the thirty-eighth parallel. Time will be required to determine diplomatic reactions and permit new negotiations that may develop.
>
> Recognizing that the parallel has no military significance, State has asked [the] Joint Chiefs of Staff what authority you should have to permit sufficient freedom of action for [the] next few weeks to provide security for United Nations forces and maintain contact with the enemy. Your recommendation [is] desired.[36]

Strangely refraining from any comment on the impending step toward peace negotiations, MacArthur replied the following day almost as if in response to another sort of message:

> [I] recommend that no further military restrictions be imposed upon the United Nations Command in Korea. The inhibitions which already exist should not be increased. The military disadvantages arising from restrictions upon the scope of our Air and Naval operations coupled with the disparity between the size of our command and the enemy ground potential renders it completely impracticable to attempt to clear North Korea or to make any appreciable effort to that end. My present directives, establishing the security of the command as the paramount consideration, are adequate to cover the two points raised by the State Department.[37]

Three days later, March 24, the JCS and, indeed, the world suddenly learned what MacArthur thought of the new peace initiative. He issued a public statement that, in effect, was an arrogant challenge to the pride of Communist China and also to the authority of his Washington superiors:

> Operations continue according to schedule and plan. We have now substantially cleared South Korea of organized Communist forces. . . .
>
> Of even greater significance than our tactical successes has been the clear revelation that this new enemy, Red China, of such exaggerated and vaunted military power, lacks the industrial capacity to provide adequately many critical items necessary to the conduct of modern war. He lacks the manufacturing base and those raw materials needed to produce, maintain and operate even moderate air and naval power, and he cannot provide the essentials for successful ground operations, such as tanks, heavy artillery and other refinements science has introduced into the conduct of military campaigns. Formerly his great numerical potential might well have filled this gap, but with the development of existing methods of mass destruction, numbers alone do not offset the vulnerability inherent in such deficiencies. Control of the seas and the air, which in turn means control over supplies, communications and transportation, are no less essential and decisive now than in the past. When this control exists as in our case, and is coupled with an inferiority of ground fire power as in the enemy's case, the resulting disparity is such that it cannot be overcome by bravery, however fanatical, or the most gross indifference to human loss.
>
> These military weaknesses have been clearly and definitely revealed since Red China entered upon its undeclared war in Korea. Even under the inhibitions which now restrict the activity of the United Nations forces and the corresponding military advantages which accrue to Red China, it has been shown its complete inability to accomplish by force of arms the conquest of Korea. The enemy, therefore, must by now be painfully aware that a decision of the United Nations to depart from its tolerant effort to contain the war to the area of Korea, through an expansion of our military operations to its coastal areas and interior bases, would doom Red China to the risk of imminent military collapse. These basic facts being established, there should be no insuperable difficulty in arriving at decisions on the Korean problem if the issues are resolved on their own merits, without being burdened by extraneous matters not directly related to Korea, such as Formosa or China's seat in the United Nations.
>
> The Korean nation and people, which have been so cruelly ravaged, must not be sacrificed. This is a paramount concern. Apart from

the military area of the problem where issues are resolved in the course of combat, the fundamental questions continue to be political in nature and must find their answer in the diplomatic sphere. Within the area of my authority as the military commander, however, it would be needless to say that I stand ready at any time to confer in the field with the commander-in-chief of the enemy forces in the earnest effort to find any military means whereby realization of the political objectives of the United Nations in Korea, to which no nation may justly take exception, might be accomplished without further bloodshed.[38]

MacArthur afterward tried to play down his statement as merely a "military appraisal" and a "routine communiqué," and he pointed out that he had issued two previous surrender ultimatums to North Korea without the "slightest whisper of remonstrance" from his superiors, though he failed to say that both had been on orders from the JCS. Whitney probably was close to the truth about MacArthur's principal motivation when he maintained that the UNC commander in chief's action thwarted "one of the most disgraceful plots in American history," whereby "in some parts of the UN and the U.S. State Department, and in some very high places in Washington, men were scheming to change the status of Formosa and the Nationalists' seat in the United Nations." A respected historian suggests, "With the perfectionist belief in total solutions he had shown throughout his life he was willing to risk ending his career if he could bring home to the American public the necessity for a showdown with Red China." By insulting Communist China and calling on it to admit that it had been defeated, he assuredly killed any hope that Peking might have considered the overture by the President. In that sense he succeeded, but in the process he brought his own military career to an end.[39]

The State Department and the White House were immediately bombarded by allied leaders wanting to know whether MacArthur's position represented a new policy direction of the United States government. Although he did not reveal his verdict to anyone at the time, Truman firmly decided on the 24th that MacArthur would have to be relieved, but he was not yet clear about the timing and the manner: "It was an act totally disregarding all directives," he wrote in his memoirs, "to abstain from any declaration on foreign policy. It was in open defiance of my orders as

President and Commander in Chief. . . . By this act MacArthur left me no choice — I could no longer tolerate his insubordination." Truman wrote to George Elsey on April 16, "MacA's Mar. 24 statement, after the Mar. 20 message to him, was not just a public disagreement over policy, but deliberate, premeditated sabotage of US and UN policy." When he learned of the general's proclamation, Lovett was in favor of removing him at once. Acheson was convinced that MacArthur's action constituted "defiance of the Chiefs of Staff, sabotage of an operation of which he had been informed, and insubordination of the grossest sort to his Commander in Chief." According to the Secretary of State, Truman was calm but "in a state of mind that combined disbelief with controlled fury" when he met with him, Lovett, and Rusk on the 24th to decide what step to take first.[40] They agreed, amazingly, on only a mild reprimand, which was sent by the JCS to the general that day:

> The President has directed that your attention be called to his order as transmitted 6 December 1950. In view of the information given you 20 March 1951 any further statements by you must be coordinated as prescribed in the order of 6 December.
> The President has also directed that in the event Communist military leaders request an armistice in the field, you immediately report that fact to the JCS for instructions.[41]

It seems that MacArthur had won by intimidation again, but seldom has a message so belied the strong feelings of a President.

One authority on the Truman-MacArthur controversy maintains, "It is possible that, in spite of MacArthur's open defiance of March 24 and the hardening determination of President Truman to dismiss him which resulted, this new crisis in American civil-military relations might in time have blown over." Hardly, for this view does not credit fully the seriousness with which MacArthur's offense was interpreted by the President and some of his key civilian advisers, especially Acheson. The Secretary of State undoubtedly expressed the feeling of Truman, too, when he charged that the general had "perpetrated a major act of sabotage of a Government operation." Nor does the above-quoted view do justice to the intense mood of self-destruction in which MacArthur apparently had enveloped himself. The general may have be-

lieved that he would achieve through his martyrdom a rallying of
support to his cause by the public and members of Congress, many
of whom had already expressed alienation from the Truman-
Acheson policies by supporting McCarthyism and backing Taft's
faction in the Great Debate. His objective was nothing less than a
major redirection of American foreign and military policies, particularly toward placing a much higher priority on what he believed to be national self-interests at stake in East Asia.[42]

If MacArthur's March 24 pronouncement convinced Truman
that the general must go, the decisions on how and when he would
be dismissed were inadvertently triggered by House Minority
Leader Joseph Martin, a long-time MacArthur admirer and an Asia-
first advocate. On March 8, Martin sent the general a copy of his
speech in Brooklyn on February 12, in which he criticized American policy on Formosa and urged that United States support be
given Chiang's forces "in the opening of a second Asiatic front" on
the mainland of Red China. Martin had been opposed to the Truman administration's plans to strengthen NATO, which, he averred,
would not necessarily make West Europe secure against Soviet incursions but would "weaken our position in Asia" by further
draining our support of anti-Communist nations·in that area. The
representative asked MacArthur to read his address and added, in
regard to American backing of a Nationalist assault across the
Formosa Strait, "I would deem it a great help if I could have your
views on this point, either on a confidential basis or otherwise."
MacArthur waited until March 20 to answer the Massachusetts
Republican representative, by which time he had probably received the JCS message about the proposed peace move. On
April 5, Martin, who was not told by the general to keep his words
in confidence, released copies of MacArthur's letter to the press
and also read it aloud on the floor of the House. The latter action
precipitated talk among some members of the House and the Senate
of sending a congressional mission to Tokyo to confer with him
about his views on solving the Far Eastern problems.[43] In Mac-
Arthur's letter, which follows in part, he actually said nothing his
superiors had not heard from him previously, but now, thanks to
Martin, his criticisms of the Truman administration's growing
support of NATO and limited-war strategy in Korea got bold
headlines:

My views and recommendations with respect to the situation created by Red China's entry into the war against us in Korea have been submitted to Washington in most complete detail. Generally these views are well known and clearly understood, as they follow the conventional pattern of meeting force with maximum counter-force, as we have never failed to do in the past. Your view with respect to the utilization of the Chinese forces on Formosa is in conflict with neither logic nor this tradition.

It seems strangely difficult for some to realize that here in Asia is where the Communist conspirators have elected to make their play for global conquest, and that we have joined the issue thus raised on the battlefield; that here we fight Europe's war with arms while the diplomats there still fight it with words; that if we lose this war to Communism in Asia the fall of Europe is inevitable; win it and Europe most probably would avoid war and yet preserve freedom. As you pointed out, we must win. There is no substitute for victory.[44]

At the Senate hearings in May, MacArthur would testify, "My letter to Congressman Martin was merely a routine communication such as I turn out by the hundreds. It made so little impression upon me . . . that when I heard one of my staff officers saying there had been some criticism of what I had said to him, I had to go into the files. I didn't even recall what the circumstance was." In his *Reminiscences* he professed that the letter "was intended to be merely a polite response couched in such general terms as to convey only a normal patriotic desire for victory." It was viewed altogether differently in Washington. Acheson asserted that it was "an open declaration of war on the Administration's policy." In his diary Truman wrote: "MacArthur shoots another political bomb. . . . This looks like the last straw. Rank insubordination." The President said in his autobiography: "The time had come to draw the line. MacArthur's letter to Congressman Martin showed that the general was not only in disagreement with the policy of the government but was challenging this policy in open insubordination to his Commander in Chief."[45]

The 5th of April was crucial for MacArthur's future not only because Martin made public his letter. The *Daily Telegraph* of London published that day an interview its military correspondent had with MacArthur, in which the latter allegedly said, "United Nations forces were circumscribed by a web of artificial conditions." The correspondent went on, "He found himself in a war without a definite objective. . . . The situation would be ludicrous if men's lives were not involved." *The Freeman,* a conservative Republican periodical, published in its issue of April 5 a statement by MacArthur that the ROK Army had not been expanded — despite a reservoir of South Koreans eager to serve, as a recent news dispatch had claimed — because of "basic political decisions beyond my authority." Truman was incensed by the general's remark, which he saw as another barb at his administration. He also saw it as another attempt by MacArthur to shift blame to Washington, for, as Truman pointed out, "the principal reason, of course, that the Republic of Korea's request for additional arms had been denied was that General MacArthur had recommended against it in his message of January 6."[46]

Also on April 5, the JCS, according to Bradley, drafted an order to CINCFE, later approved by the Defense and State departments and the President, authorizing him, in case "the Communists made a large air attack against our forces," to "immediately attack such air bases in Manchuria and the point of the Shantung Peninsula, if any of the planes came from that area." But for fear that MacArthur might "make a premature decision in carrying it out," stated the JCS chairman, "this order was kept in the JCS file for use in case of an emergency." The Joint Chiefs' trust in their Far East commander's judgment obviously was eroding fast. Later on the 5th, Bradley met with Sherman, Vandenberg, and General Wade H. Haislip, Army vice chief of staff (representing Collins, who was on a brief trip to several posts in the South). The JCS chairman alerted them that the President was "quite disturbed" about MacArthur and suggested that they start thinking about "possible lines of action." They reached no conclusions but discussed three courses, according to Bradley: (1) Truman should relieve MacArthur of his commands; (2) "a senior officer," preferably Marshall, should go to Tokyo and "talk to General MacArthur"; and (3) Marshall should write the Far East chief, "telling him how much his actions were embarrassing the government."[47]

The President summoned Acheson, Marshall, Bradley, and Harriman — "the Big Four," as Truman called them in his diary — to his office on Friday morning, April 6, to get their ideas on what to do about MacArthur. Secretary of Defense Marshall, as Truman recalled the discussion, pointed out that MacArthur's dismissal could make it "difficult to get the military appropriations through Congress." The sources differ over Harriman's and Bradley's views that morning. According to the President, Harriman said that the general should have been relieved in 1949 for refusing a request to return to Washington to discuss occupation policy and for supposedly being reluctant to disapprove a Diet measure that was contrary to the reverse-course program in Japan. But Harriman later asserted that Truman had misquoted him and that he had been more noncommittal on the 6th. Bradley said he expressed the need for more time to think about the matter and to discuss it with the Joint Chiefs, though in Truman's memoirs the JCS chairman was portrayed as firmly convinced that MacArthur "deserved to be relieved of command" for insubordination. In a memorandum for the record on April 24, summarizing the sundry high-level meetings on the MacArthur issue that took place on April 5–10, Bradley wrote about the April 6 session: "Secretary Acheson and Mr. Harriman thought he should be relieved at once. General Marshall and I recommended against such action." Acheson, the closest of the four to the President, came out most strongly for the general's dismissal, but he warned Truman that such action would "produce the biggest fight of your administration." He emphasized the need to have the unanimous backing of the JCS because of "the utmost seriousness" of the decision and its likely explosive public impact. "There was no doubt," remarked the Secretary of State, "what General MacArthur deserved; the issue was the wisest way to administer it." Truman directed the four advisers to meet together later that day and to confer with him again on the matter the following morning.[48]

The Big Four discussed the MacArthur issue again in Marshall's office on the afternoon of the 6th, but, said Bradley, "each of us was still of the same opinion as he had given the President that morning." Marshall suggested summoning MacArthur to Washington for consultations before making a decision as to his relief, but the other three opposed the idea. Acheson probably expressed their common feeling of uneasiness when he later commented, "This seemed a road to disaster. . . . To get him back in Washington in the full panoply of his commands and with his future the issue of the day would not only gravely impair the Pres-

With President Rhee at the ceremony marking the restoration of the
government of South Korea at Seoul, September 29, 1950.

Preparing to depart from Haneda Airport, Tokyo, October 14, 1950, for the following day's conference with President Truman on Wake Island. *Left to right:* Sebald, Colonel Huff, General MacArthur, Brines, Admiral Joy, and Generals Willoughby and Wright.

President Truman awards MacArthur another Distinguished Service Medal after their conference on Wake Island, October 15, 1950. *Left to right:* General Whitney, Colonel Bunker, General MacArthur, Ambassador Muccio (partly hidden), and President Truman.

With Dulles, chief U.S. negotiator on the Japanese peace treaty, Tokyo, January 25, 1951.

OPPOSITE PAGE
Visiting the Eighth Army's front in North Korea on November 24, 1950, the eve of the "Home by Christmas" offensive. *Left to right:* Generals Walker, MacArthur, and Mildren.

Leaving the headquarters of the 35th Infantry Regiment with General Ridgway near the Korean front lines, January 28, 1951.

Greeting Mrs. MacArthur at Haneda Airport, Tokyo, on the general's
return from Korea, January 28, 1951.

Reading his controversial press statement at Suwon, Korea, March 7, 1951. *Left to right:* General MacArthur, Lieutenant Colonel James T. Quirk, and General Hickey.

During his last visit to Korea, MacArthur confers with General Ridgway
at Kangnung, April 3, 1951.

Visiting with President Eisenhower at the White House, March 1954.

OPPOSITE PAGE
Top: The MacArthurs leaving San Francisco for Washington, April 18, 1951.
Bottom: Acknowledging applause on the occasion of his address to Congress, April 19, 1951.

With President Kennedy at the Football Hall of Fame banquet, New York, December 1961.

OPPOSITE PAGE
Top: Conferring with James Rand and Ralph Cordiner, presidents of Remington Rand and General Electric respectively, at the MacArthur suite in the Waldorf-Astoria Hotel, New York, September 1954.
Bottom: With some Filipino veterans of World War II during Mac-Arthur's visit to the Philippines, July 1961.

Presentation to the general of a copy of the 1962 *Howitzer*, the West Point yearbook, on the occasion of MacArthur's visit to the U.S. Military Academy to receive the Thayer Award, May 12, 1962.

Top: The MacArthurs at a Columbia College program honoring the general, New York, April 19, 1963.
Bottom: His final birthday reunion dinner, Waldorf-Astoria Hotel, New York, January 26, 1964. *Left to right:* a Waldorf-Astoria official, Colonel Bunker, General MacArthur, Colonel Egeberg, General Sverdrup, and the sergeant-at-arms.

Rotunda of the MacArthur Memorial Museum, Norfolk, Virginia. MacArthur's grave is on the left; the other is reserved for his wife.

ident's freedom of decision but might well imperil his own future." Having borne the brunt of the vicious assaults and media manipulations of McCarthy for the past year, the Secretary of State surely knew from personal tribulations how wildly the currents of public opinion ran. Moreover, "the effect of MacArthur's histrionic abilities," as Acheson phrased it, might well produce a revival of the Taft-Wherry crusade against the administration's foreign policy, just when the Great Debate had subsided in Congress. Marshall quickly dropped the notion, and after the others left, without reaching a consensus, he began studying the file of past correspondence between the JCS and MacArthur, as Truman that morning had suggested he do.

When the four top advisers went back to the President's office on Saturday morning, the 7th, they found Truman irritated now over MacArthur's assertion in *The Freeman* that his superiors bore the responsibility for failing to enlarge the ROK Army. In his diary entry of April 7, Truman recorded: "It is the unanimous opinion of all that MacArthur be relieved. All four so advise." He stated in his memoirs that at the session Marshall reported that after reading the back file of JCS-MacArthur messages he, like Harriman earlier, thought MacArthur "should have been fired two years ago." On the other hand, Bradley states that at the Saturday morning meeting Acheson and Harriman were still for relieving MacArthur, but he and Marshall were against it, though "our position was somewhat weakened by the statement reportedly made by General MacArthur to FREEMAN Magazine." The group, according to the JCS chairman, recommended that Truman "take no action until after the weekend, during which time he could confer with other governmental leaders." Besides, Bradley wanted to confer with the JCS on Sunday, since Collins would not return until Saturday evening. Bradley's account of each man's position at the meeting seems more reliable than others, because if the Big Four had been in unanimous agreement that day about dismissing the general, Truman probably would have revealed his own decision then. As it was, he did so on Monday, when he learned that the four key advisers and the JCS were all agreed on relieving MacArthur. Later on Saturday, Marshall and Bradley worked together on "a personal and confidential letter to General Mac-

Arthur, pointing out the difficult position in which he was placing the government." It was to be sent in Marshall's name, but events nullified its need and the letter was never dispatched.[49]

On Sunday afternoon, April 8, Bradley met with the Joint Chiefs in his Pentagon office on the "MacArthur problem." Among other courses of action, they considered the idea of relieving MacArthur of all his commands except the occupation of Japan, but, as Collins explained, "we all thought that the problems of occupation and defense of Japan were so intimately tied with Korea that it would be infeasible to have two commanders in Japan." All four officers participated actively in the discussion, finally reaching the unanimous conclusion that MacArthur should be dismissed from all four of his commands. Bradley said the group reached its decision on the basis of "a military point of view only," realizing that "the military considerations were only a small part of the question involved." Although Truman and Acheson at the time and later did not hesitate to accuse the general of insubordination, the JCS as a body and as individuals refrained from using that term. According to Bradley, "In point of fact, MacArthur had stretched but had not legally violated any JCS directives. He had violated the President's December 6 [5] directive, relayed to him by the JCS [on the 6th], but this did not constitute violation of a direct JCS order." After two hours of deliberation, the Joint Chiefs went to Marshall's office about 4:00 P. M., where Bradley reported the group's decision to the Secretary of Defense: "If it should be the President's decision to relieve MacArthur, the JCS concurred." According to the JCS history, the Joint Chiefs "agreed that if the President did not relieve General MacArthur, General Marshall should send General MacArthur a letter" like the one Marshall and Bradley had drafted jointly the previous day, telling the Far East commander, as Bradley put it, "to shut up."[50] In his memo of April 24, later endorsed by the other Joint Chiefs as accurate, Bradley said they informed Marshall on the 8th that "they would refrain from making a specific recommendation to the President for the relief of General MacArthur, and merely expressed their views." Bradley set forth "the principal reasons why they thought from a military point of view he should be relieved":

    a. That General MacArthur had shown plainly that he was not in sympathy with the decision to limit the conflict to Korea and might not be sufficiently responsive to the directives given him for this purpose.

   b. He had failed to comply with the instructions of the President to clear statements of policy with the Government before making public such statements and had taken independent action in proposing to negotiate directly with field commanders for an armistice and had made a public statement to that effect, knowing that the President still had such a proposal under consideration.

   c. That it was difficult to have General MacArthur do certain planning for eventualities. . . . [The reluctance of the JCS to inform MacArthur of the order authorizing across-the-border air strikes is cited as an example.]

   d. All members of the Joint Chiefs of Staff have expressed from time to time their firm belief that the military must always be controlled by civil authorities. They were all concerned in this case that if General MacArthur were not relieved, this civil control would be jeopardized.[51]

Marshall offered no opinions of his own, but thanked the JCS and asked Bradley to report the Joint Chiefs' position at the meeting of the Big Four and the President that was scheduled for Monday morning.

   Meanwhile, that Sunday, Truman met with several officials, including Acheson, Secretary of the Treasury John W. Snyder, House Speaker Sam Rayburn, and Chief Justice Fred M. Vinson. He also talked by telephone with Vice President Alben W. Barkley, who was hospitalized. Although he apparently discussed the MacArthur issue with each of them, he gave no indication that his mind was made up on the matter.[52]

   There had not been enough time since Martin's revelation of the MacArthur letter on Thursday for widespread reactions by allied governments, but an indication of the British government's attitude was evident by that weekend. On April 7 a Labour member of the House of Commons submitted a motion, not voted on that day, stating that "this House regrets that it no longer has confidence in General MacArthur as Supreme Commander of the UN forces engaged in Korean operations." Also that day Kenneth Younger, of the British government, lashed out in a public address against "such irresponsible statements as seem to come out at frequent intervals from highly placed quarters, without the authority of the United States or indeed of any member Government"; his target obviously was MacArthur. The following day *The Observer* of London stated that Younger's speech was "a mild version of what the Cabinet really thinks about General MacArthur's statements," that "the British Government has taken the strongest possible exception to General MacArthur's letter to Mr. Joseph Martin," and that the British embassy in Washington allegedly had asked the United States government for "a full explanation of how it is possible for such a statement, in complete variance with agreed policy, to be made by a serving officer." British officials, declared *The Observer*, viewed the general's comments "as foreshadowing an extension of the war to the mainland of Asia." The British response, both in itself and as a harbinger of likely reactions of other allies, was no doubt of great concern to Truman and Acheson.[53]

Acheson, Marshall, Bradley, and Harriman met again with Truman on Monday morning, April 9. After hearing that dismissal of MacArthur was the unanimous verdict of the four key advisers and of the Joint Chiefs, though their reasons and degrees of decisiveness differed, the President finally said, "I had already made up my mind that General MacArthur had to go when he made his statement of March 24." Truman gave his approval to the appointment of Ridgway as the successor to MacArthur's commands and of Lieutenant General James A. Van Fleet to replace Ridgway as head of the Eighth Army. Both men were recommended strongly by Marshall and Bradley, who had obtained prior agreement from the JCS and Secretary of the Army Pace. Truman instructed Marshall and Bradley to have the necessary orders drafted for the three officers; the task was delegated to Collins as the Army's military head.

When Acheson went to Capitol Hill on Tuesday, the 10th, on a matter related to the Senate Appropriations Committee's hearings, two members of that committee, Senators Patrick A. McCarran (Democrat, Nevada) and Styles Bridges (Republican, New Hampshire) asked the Secretary of State "to urge the President not to make any change in so far as General MacArthur's status was concerned." They maintained that, judging by what they learned in their correspondence and trips across the country, the general was held in "great regard" by much of the public. Acheson replied merely that he would convey the message to Truman. On Tuesday afternoon Marshall brought the draft orders to another session with Truman, Harriman, Bradley, and Acheson, where some minor revisions were made, and the President signed them. Truman told Joseph H. Short, his press secretary (since Ross's death in December), who was present at the meeting, to prepare a press release on MacArthur's dismissal. Bradley later assisted Short in its drafting. Since Secretary Pace was then touring the front in Korea, Truman decided to have him deliver the order of relief to MacArthur personally at the Tokyo embassy at 10:00 A.M. on the 12th (8:00 P.M., April 11, Washington time); the press statement from the White House was to be released soon afterward. Acheson was to send MacArthur's and Ridgway's orders to Ambassador Muccio for delivery to Pace, who was with the Eighth Army commander somewhere near the front lines. But the commercial cable line used by the State Department was not functioning properly through Pusan, so unknown for a while to the Washington leaders, Muccio did not get the message.

On Tuesday evening the Chicago *Tribune* correspondents at the White House and the Pentagon began asking officials whether a report their managing editor had received from one of the paper's Far East reporters was true — that MacArthur was about to be fired. The *Tribune* allegedly planned to publish the story in its first edition the next morning. (Actually it appeared in the paper's final edition on the 11th.) Truman "decided that we could not afford the courtesy of Secretary Pace's personal delivery of the order but that the message would have to go to General MacArthur in the same manner that relieving orders were sent to other officers in the service." The President had Short call a news conference at 1:00 A.M., April 11; the reporters were given copies of the President's announcement regarding the general's relief, the order of dismissal, and seven "background documents," as Truman called them. The relief order had been sent out by Army communications before the press conference, but commercial radio broadcasts about the command upheaval reached Tokyo first.[54]

The order of relief, dated April 10 and signed by Bradley, stated:

I have been directed to relay the following message to you from President Truman: I deeply regret that it becomes my duty as President and Commander in Chief of the United States military forces to replace you as Supreme Commander, Allied Powers; Commander in Chief, United Nations Command; Commander in Chief, Far East; and Commanding General, US Army, Far East.

You will turn over your commands effective at once to Lieutenant General Matthew B. Ridgway. You are authorized to have issued such orders as are necessary to complete desired travel to such place as you may select. My reasons for your replacement will be made public concurrently with the delivery to you of the foregoing order, and are contained in the next following message. Harry S. Truman.[55]

The accompanying message, Truman's public announcement, said:

With deep regret I have concluded that General of the Army Douglas MacArthur is unable to give his wholehearted support to the policies of the United States Government and of the United Nations in matters pertaining to his official duties. In view of the specific responsibilities imposed upon me by the Constitution of the United States and the added responsibility which has been entrusted to me by the United Nations, I have decided that I must make a change of command in the Far East. I have, therefore, relieved General MacArthur of his command and have designated Lieutenant General Matthew B. Ridgway as his successor.

Full and vigorous debate on matters of national policy is a vital element in the constitutional system of our free democracy. It is fundamental, however, that military commanders must be governed by the policies and directives issued to them in the manner provided by our laws and Constitution. In time of crisis, this consideration is particularly compelling.

General MacArthur's place in history as one of our greatest commanders is fully established. The nation owes him a debt of gratitude for the distinguished and exceptional service which he has rendered his country in posts of great responsibility. For that reason I repeat my regret at the necessity for the action I feel compelled to take in his case. Harry S. Truman.[56]

The "background documents" Short gave the reporters were (1) Truman's directive of December 5, sent to MacArthur in a JCS message on the 6th, regarding prior clearance of public statements; (2) the JCS message of March 20 to MacArthur about the impending peace move; (3) MacArthur's surrender ultimatum to the CCF on March 24; (4) the JCS message, at Truman's direction, to MacArthur on March 24, reminding him of the December directive on clearing statements beforehand; (5) MacArthur's letter to Martin of March 20; (6) the JCS message to MacArthur on January 5, requesting his advice about arming more ROK forces; and (7) MacArthur's reply to the JCS of January 6, counseling against such action. Inclusion of the exchange on ROK Army expansion seems petty and irrelevant in retrospect, but when he selected these documents on late Tuesday evening the President probably was not feeling especially generous.

In the meantime, rumors of MacArthur's imminent relief had been growing at Tokyo GHQ since late March. The rumor mill became most active on April 9 when Secretary Pace, Lieutenant Generals John E. Hull and Edward H. Brooks, deputy chief of staff and assistant chief of staff for administration and personnel of the U.S. Army respectively, together with four other Pentagon officers, arrived in Tokyo on April 9. MacArthur was host to Pace and his party at a luncheon that day at the embassy; it also included Lowe, Truman's special emissary, and fifteen senior officers of the Far East Command. Afterward MacArthur and Pace talked in private for over two hours; though the topics of their conversation were never revealed, Tokyo correspondents speculated in their dispatches that evening that the Secretary had briefed the general on the mounting storm in Washington. Pace's group went on to Korea the next day.[57] Almond had been in Tokyo since April 2 on a week's leave, visiting his family and conferring with MacArthur. He said that when he visited the UNC chief to bid farewell before returning to the X Corps, MacArthur spoke of a premonition of what was about to happen:

> On the 9th of April, as my leave in Tokyo was about to expire, I went to tell General MacArthur goodbye. He looked rather disconsolate and said to me, "I may not see you anymore, so goodbye, Ned." I said, "I don't understand what you mean, because you have been coming to see me frequently during the past six or eight months." He said, "That isn't the question. I have become politically involved and may be relieved by the President." I said, "Well, General MacArthur, I consider that absurd and I don't believe the President has the intention of taking such a drastic action. We will expect to see you in X Corps headquarters very soon." He said, "Well, perhaps so." And thus we parted.[58]

Perhaps MacArthur's feeling was prompted by Lowe's receipt of a message from Truman to terminate his Far East mission and return to Washington. In what would be one of his last official actions, MacArthur awarded the Distinguished Service Cross to Lowe on April 10. The President's representative was cited for having "distinguished himself by extraordinary heroism in action" in Korea, which was no exaggeration. He had also proven to be a sincere friend and admirer of MacArthur, believing to the end that Truman and the Far East commander could have worked out their differences had it not been for the anti-MacArthur bias of some of the President's key advisers.[59]

The MacArthurs were hosting Senator Warren G. Magnuson (Democrat, Washington) and William Stern, executive vice president of Northwest Airlines, at an embassy luncheon on Wednesday, the 11th, when Huff heard the dismissal news on a commercial radio broadcast and immediately informed Jean. She interrupted the table talk between the three men to whisper the shocking message to MacArthur. After a moment of silence, he remarked aloud but in a gentle tone, "Jeannie, we're going home at last." The rest of the meal was not hurried, but when the guests left, MacArthur telephoned Whitney to meet him at the Dai Ichi. The official notification of his relief was brought to MacArthur before he left the embassy, having reached the GHQ message center over a half-hour after Japanese radio stations had begun interrupting programs with the startling news. When they met in MacArthur's office, Whitney was amazed that "MacArthur wanted only to discuss the problems that would confront *me* after his departure."[60]

Meanwhile, in Korea on the afternoon of April 11, Ridgway, who was with Pace near the front, got his first inkling of the command upheaval when a reporter offered congratulations on his promotion. Not long afterward Pace received a message from Marshall instructing him to inform Ridgway of his succession to MacArthur's commands. A fierce storm was moving through that sector of the front, however, and prevented Ridgway from departing for Tokyo until noon the next day. Late on the afternoon of the 12th, he and MacArthur met for about an hour in the embassy library.[61] Ridgway was impressed by MacArthur's attitude:

He [MacArthur] received me at once, with the greatest courtesy. I had a natural human curiosity to see how he had been affected by his peremptory removal from his high post. He was entirely himself — composed, quiet, temperate, friendly, and helpful to the man who was to succeed him. He made some allusions to the fact that he had been summarily relieved, but there was no trace of bitterness or anger in his tone. I thought it was a fine tribute to the resilience of this great man that he could accept so calmly, with no outward sign of shock, what must have been a devastating blow to a professional soldier standing at the peak of his career.[62]

Ridgway later said he "wholeheartedly" concurred in MacArthur's comment in a letter to Republican Senator Harry P. Cain of Washington in May: "I do not know how there could have been any more complete cooperation, devotion, and loyalty both ways than between General Ridgway and myself."

MacArthur liked "fighting commanders," so he was undoubtedly satisfied with the selection of Van Fleet as the new Eighth Army commander. He had earned citations for heroism in World War I, and during the campaign from Normandy into Germany, from 1944 to 1945, he had been outstanding as a leader at the regimental, then divisional, and finally corps command levels. From 1948 to 1950 he had headed the American Army advisory group in Greece, where Communist forces were set back in the long civil war in that country. When appointed to the Korean command, Van Fleet was commanding the Second Army in the States. Like Ridgway, his principal prior roles of distinction had been in the European theater, but he was surely the type MacArthur sought from 1942 onward to command his armies — bright, aggressive, and combat-proven. Van Fleet arrived in Korea about noon on April 14 and took over the Eighth Army from Ridgway, who returned to Tokyo that day to assume MacArthur's former positions, Hickey having served as acting commander in Tokyo during the interim.[63]

On the whole, MacArthur's reaction that week did reflect an "indomitable spirit" and a "lack of rancor and resentment," as Ridgway described it. In a personal memorandum for the record, however, Ridgway noted that during their talk on the 12th MacArthur claimed that "an eminent medical man" had informed him that Truman "was suffering from malignant hypertension," which "was characterized by bewilderment and confusion of thought" and was so serious that "he wouldn't live six months."

Sebald recalled that when he conferred with MacArthur on the afternoon of the 11th the general "expressed irony and bitterness over the *method* that had been used to send him home" and remarked that "he would have retired without protest, if the President had given the slightest intimation that he wished him to do so." Sebald commented, "Watching and listening to him was the most painful interview I have had." In his memoirs MacArthur quoted at length a *New York Times* article of December 9, 1950, about Truman's threat to assault a music critic who had not liked his daughter's singing. The general used the incident in the context of his dismissal, maintaining, "I realized that I was standing at the apex of a situation which could make me the next victim of such an uncontrollable passion." MacArthur also expressed in his autobiography the kind of response expected from an aristocrat mistreated by a commoner: "The actual order I received was so drastic as to prevent the usual amenities incident to a transfer of command, and practically placed me under duress. No office boy, no charwoman, no servant of any sort would have been dismissed with such callous disregard for the ordinary decencies."[64] Few would argue that the communication of the relief news to him could have been handled better.

On the evening of April 11, Truman delivered a radio address to the nation that, concludes one historian, "was a complete flop" to the many listeners who wanted to hear his explanation for relieving the general. Instead, following Acheson's counsel, the President focused on the larger theme of his administration's policy in the war. Truman tried to talk plainly to the people, he said, about "what we are doing in Korea and about our policy in the Far East." But 55 percent of the 84,000 letters to the White House in the wake of his speech were pro-MacArthur, and the mail to congressmen in the immediate aftermath of the dismissal and the speech ran as high as ten to one against Truman. For a while at least, the President would not be able to convince a large segment of the nation that policy and strategy in Korea were more important than MacArthur's ouster.[65]

MacArthur had appointed Hickey as acting commander at GHQ promptly after getting the official word of his relief. For the next five days he spent most of the time at the embassy with his family and closest staff friends, returning to the Dai Ichi Building only twice and then just to oversee the movement of his personal effects to the embassy. With Whitney, Bunker, and Huff, he prepared the departure plans and delegated the details of the arrangements for the long trip to New York, where the MacArthurs would stay at the Waldorf-Astoria Hotel, at least temporarily. From city officials in San Francisco and New York he received word that welcome celebrations were being planned; from Congress he got an invitation to address a joint meeting of the House and the Senate on April 19, which he readily accepted. The ROK National Assembly and the Japanese Diet both passed resolutions praising him; Syngman Rhee, Shigeru Yoshida, and other top officials of those nations wrote him to express regret and gratitude; Japan's two largest newspapers, *Asahi Shimbun* and *Mainichi Shimbun,* as well as a number of other periodicals in that country, paid tribute to his leadership and expressed disappointment that he could not have been retained as SCAP until the Japanese peace treaty was signed; and Emperor Hirohito paid a farewell visit to him — a signal honor, explains an authority, because "this was the first time in history that a Japanese monarch had called upon a foreigner who held no official capacity." On Sunday, the 15th, many members of his GHQ staff and their wives called at the embassy to say good-by; Mrs. MacArthur received them and, observed Sebald, "as usual, was gracious and friendly, without the slightest hint of bitterness or resentment."[66]

Before sunrise on Monday, April 16, throngs of Japanese began lining the route from the embassy through the southern part of Tokyo to Haneda Airport; estimates of the total number of persons ranged from 400,000 to over a million. Many of the Japanese wept as they waved farewell to the general when his car passed. At the airport a big crowd waited behind the fence, and beside MacArthur's plane two lines of American, Japanese, and allied military and civilian dignitaries and their spouses were formed according to the dictates of protocol. On MacArthur's order of the previous day, his aircraft's name had been changed back immediately from *SCAP* to *Bataan,* and the freshly painted letters gleamed on the nose. At 7:00 A.M. sharp, the MacArthurs' automobile arrived. Ridgway and Hickey escorted MacArthur on a review of the honor guard, a platoon of select American soldiers. Then he and Jean proceeded slowly down each of the lines of of-

ficials, shaking hands and saying a few words to each person.
MacArthur's deportment was poised, sincere, and positive as he
said his farewells. He remarked to Ridgway, his successor in commanding the occupation of Japan and the UNC forces in Korea:
"I hope when you leave Tokyo you will be Chief of Staff. If I had
been permitted to choose my successor, I'd have selected you."
Many of the ladies were weeping, and some of the men were close
to tears. A nineteen-gun salute was rendered, and eighteen F-80
and F-86 jet fighters and four B-29 bombers flew low over the field
in precise formations. In the meantime, Colonel Anthony Story,
MacArthur's pilot and close friend, Major William E. Gregg, the
copilot, and the rest of the plane crew had boarded the Constellation to make their preflight checks. At about 7:20, Huff, Canada, and their wives, together with Whitney, Bunker, and Ah Cheu,
began to climb aboard. As MacArthur, Jean, and Arthur moved
toward the plane's ramp, the Army band began "Auld Lang Syne."
The general waved and quickly guided his little family into the
plane, the door swung shut, and the *Bataan* was soon taking off
for its first destination, Oahu, on the flight to New York. Sebald
observed, "The chilling moment was over. Officers and wives slowly
trooped away, the flags were furled, the troops were dismissed —
and the working day began." As Ridgway's personal belongings
were moved into the embassy, some American and Japanese admirers of his predecessor sadly began to realize that, after all, even
MacArthur was expendable.[67] But as his last scene in Japan, the
Haneda departure, demonstrated, MacArthur was at his best in
the role of the aristocrat in uniform: he had been stripped of his
commands, but he left with grace and dignity.

PART IV

Fading Away

CHAPTER XIX

The Excitement of the Season

1. Return of the Hero

THE PRESIDENT'S RELIEF OF MACARTHUR set off a nation-wide cacophony of howls of indignation, shrieks of hysteria, and screams of anger that at first created such a racket that the quieter sounds of sorrow and reason were barely heard. Truman was hanged in effigy in San Gabriel, California; at the University of Washington in Seattle a dummy dressed in an Army uniform and with a corncob pipe in its teeth was found dangling from a campus tree. The state legislatures of Texas and Wisconsin adopted resolutions extolling MacArthur and inviting him to address them; while the Oklahoma Senate killed a resolution commending the general. At least eleven state legislatures debated resolutions supporting MacArthur and criticizing Truman, or vice versa. Although the National Maritime Union backed Truman, the International Longshoremen's Association declared a two-hour work halt on the New York docks in protest against the President's action. Pro-MacArthur congressmen inserted in the *Congressional Record* numerous telegrams and letters from irate constituents who demanded the impeachment of Truman and referred to him in such terms as "the imbecile," "the Judas," "the red herring," and "the little ward politician." As expected, the Hearst, McCormick, and Scripps-Howard newspapers portrayed MacArthur as a martyr and Truman and Acheson as arch villains. On the other hand, some of the nation's principal papers defended the President's decision;

they included the *New York Times,* New York *Herald Tribune,* Washington *Post, Christian Science Monitor,* Boston *Globe,* Minneapolis *Tribune,* Denver *Post,* and Atlanta *Journal.* A Gallup poll of April 14 found that 66 percent of those surveyed disapproved of Truman's removal of the general and only 25 percent approved of it. Truman and MacArthur, both keen students of history, undoubtedly were aware that national paroxysms in America had long demonstrated a pattern of declining rapidly. Eben Ayers, on the White House staff, recorded in his diary on April 16: "The President did not seem too upset by the uproar that has resulted throughout the country from his recall of General MacArthur from Tokyo. He has suggested that within the Administration nothing be said to keep the fire going." MacArthur was pleased by the huge protest over his relief but also was surprised by its size.[1]

The *Saturday Review of Literature* polled 332 American correspondents assigned to Washington, Korea, Japan, and the United Nations on their reactions to Truman's recall of the general. They were almost solidly behind the President's action: 85 percent thought Truman was right, and 13 percent said he was wrong in the matter. According to an analysis of the survey by Elmo Roper Associates, "The main reason Truman was right, the reporters said, was that MacArthur obviously didn't agree with American policies, and we must preserve the constitutional right of the Commander-in-Chief to remove an insubordinate general." Interestingly, 76 percent of the correspondents in Korea and Japan supported Truman's decision, and 21 percent opposed it. The Roper study found that among this group "another major justification for MacArthur's removal was given," namely, his incompetence as military commander of the Korean War. In summing up, the Roper analysts noted that the "working press" in the areas surveyed "overwhelmingly supported Harry Truman, and many thought he should have done it sooner."[2]

Among the enlisted men of the Eighth Army in Korea, the news of the Far East chief's ouster was a surprise, but few were greatly disturbed, particularly since the highly respected Ridgway was to be his successor. "I don't recall feeling anything about it [MacArthur's relief]," remarked one soldier who was at the front at the time, "and I don't think anybody else [in the Eighth Army] did either really. We weren't that close to MacArthur." Most senior officers of the American forces in Korea, if those interviewed were typical, said they were "astonished" or "shocked," because they were too busy at the front to keep up with news developments elsewhere and, besides, they were not privy to the high-level messages between Tokyo and Washington that might have indicated an imminent change. A number of Tokyo GHQ officers who had been close to MacArthur shortly requested retirement or transfers. For instance, Willoughby chose to retire; he left Tokyo in late May. Stratemeyer soon suffered a heart attack and had to return to the States. Almond became commandant of the U.S. Army War College that summer.[3]

An event that perhaps unleashed the new round of partisan ugliness that took place on Capitol Hill was the death of Senator Arthur H. Vandenberg of Michigan on April 18. He had backed MacArthur for the Republican presidential nomination in 1944, but later he had proved outstanding as a champion of bipartisan foreign policy, and his leadership had been greatly valued by the Democratic administration in building strong congressional support for the Marshall Plan and NATO. Not surprisingly, the Republican right wing was vociferous in condemning Truman's "firing" of the general. McCarthy figured the "son of a bitch" was drunk on "bourbon and benedictine" when he decided to get rid of MacArthur. Martin called it "a colossal executive blunder." On the Senate floor William E. Jenner (Republican of Indiana) demanded the impeachment of Truman and exclaimed that "this country today is in the hands of a secret inner coterie which is directed by agents of the Soviet Union." Senator Nixon futilely introduced a resolution calling on the President to restore MacArthur to his commands. He remarked, "The happiest group in the country . . . will be the Communists and their stooges. . . . The President has given them what they always wanted — MacArthur's scalp." Nixon wrote a friend that during the first three days after the dismissal he "received more than five thousand telegrams and ten thousand letters, running almost one hundred to one in support of General MacArthur and in opposition to the President." Taft acknowledged that Truman "had every right" to relieve the general, but he charged that the action "has led the world to believe we are looking in the direction of appeasement." Senator Everett M. Dirksen (Republican of Illinois) labeled

MacArthur's ouster "a great victory" for Britain and observed that "our State Department is becoming a branch of Downing Street."

Robert S. Kerr, a freshman Democratic senator from Oklahoma, was the first person in the upper house to defend Truman and attack the body's Old Guard Republicans, who were talking of impeaching the President. Kerr challenged the right-wingers to submit a resolution favoring a declaration of war against Communist China or calling for "open warfare" against her. "If they do not," he asserted, "their support of MacArthur is a mockery." Though some Democrats in Congress felt, as one grumbled, that "they're taking the rap for another of Truman's bunglings," slowly pro-administration voices began to be heard in both houses on the MacArthur issue, and Truman could take some assurance from the fact that his party had control of the Senate and the House. House Speaker Sam Rayburn, perhaps the most influential of all congressmen of that day, took his stand firmly with Truman, stating, "We must never give up [the principle] that the military is subject to and under control of the civilian administration."[4]

In Peking and most other Communist capitals the radio and press statements about MacArthur's fate were expectedly gleeful. Ambassador Alan G. Kirk in Moscow, however, wrote Acheson on April 13 that "the Soviet press has been singularly quiet" on the subject. Later Soviet statements maintained that there was little hope the command shake-up would bring a change in the "imperialist aggression" of the United States. Press dispatches from Western correspondents in Japan, South Korea, and Formosa indicated widespread grief over the loss of MacArthur's leadership in the Far East and some uneasiness over whether it portended a lessening of the American presence in their region. In the United Kingdom, Canada, and the Continental Western European nations, reactions by officials and journalists, not surprisingly, were largely ones of relief, for MacArthur had been regarded in those countries as trying to influence the United States government to decrease its assistance to NATO in favor of broadening the war in East Asia. When the news of the general's dismissal was announced by Foreign Secretary Herbert Morrison in the British House of Commons, spontaneous cheering broke out from members of both sides of the chamber. *The Economist* of London said, "General MacArthur frightened Europeans and had become the focus of anti-American feeling" in Great Britain. The initial reaction in France and the Low Countries was generally one of "profound relief." Truman's action received "wide support" among Italians, many of whom saw his move as reaffirming "Washington's conviction that the defense of Europe has priority over the defense of Asia." In West Germany, however, there was reportedly serious concern that unless the MacArthur controversy subsided soon, the Truman administration might be forced by public pressure to reduce its aid to that nation.[5]

While MacArthur was en route from Japan to Hawaii, he exchanged radio messages of best wishes with John Foster Dulles, who was flying to Tokyo to reassure leaders there and to continue work on the Japanese peace treaty. When the *Bataan* touched down at Hickam Air Force Base in Oahu on the evening of April 16, Admiral Radford and other brass of the CINCPAC and Hawaiian headquarters were on hand to greet MacArthur and his party. Radford said the general tried to work on his speech to Congress during every spare moment, but they proved to be few. The next day MacArthur rode in a twenty-mile parade through the Honolulu–Pearl Harbor area that attracted about 100,000 viewers, received an honorary doctorate of civil laws from the University of Hawaii (actually awarded in absentia in 1946), and led a wreath-laying ceremony at the large World War II cemetery at the Punchbowl. That afternoon he and his traveling group of family and friends departed aboard the *Bataan*, with MacArthur again scribbling notes for his congressional address. They arrived at San Francisco International Airport about 8:30 P.M. on the 17th. For MacArthur and his wife, it was their first return to the United States in fourteen years; Arthur, now thirteen years old, had never before been to America. As the general was greeted at the bottom of the plane ramp by General Albert Wedemeyer and other officers of his Sixth Army command, the large, ecstatic crowd broke through the police lines to try to get close to him. On the way to the St. Francis Hotel downtown, where the MacArthur party spent the night, mobs and traffic jams made the fourteen-mile trip a two-hour extemporaneous parade, with approximately 500,000 people coming out to welcome him from the airport into the city. Another massive turnout occurred for the city's ticker-tape parade in his honor through the main business district the following morning. Flanked by municipal and state officials, he made a short speech outside City Hall to an assemblage of over 100,000 citizens. At one point in his talk he referred to a reporter's query that morning about his political plans and remarked, "I do not intend to run for any political office. . . . The only politics I have is contained in a simple phrase known to all of you — 'God bless America!' " While he was in San Francisco, an officer in the Pentagon telephoned MacArthur and informed him that he was to submit his speech to Congress for advance scrutiny, according to the President's December directive. MacArthur flatly refused to do so, challenging the directive's applicability to him in his current status. Truman later admitted that he had instructed Pace to obtain an advance copy for him.

That afternoon the MacArthur party flew on to Washington and landed at National Airport about 12:15 A.M. on the 19th. An official welcoming party was waiting, made up of Marshall, all the Joint Chiefs, and Major General Harry H. Vaughan, Truman's military aide. General Jonathan Wainwright was spotted in the crowd and asked to join them. They barely had time to say a few words to MacArthur when the mob of over 12,000 surged past the police and restraining ropes and rushed toward the *Bataan*. It took the police nearly a half-hour to escort the MacArthur group to waiting cars nearby, during which time MacArthur became separated briefly from his wife and son, and Whitney was shoved to the ground by the throng. More crowds and traffic snarls slowed their trip to the Statler Hotel, where they spent the few remaining hours of the night.[6]

The media buildup for the General's address to the joint meeting of Congress on April 19 had been tremendous, and about 20 million Americans witnessed the dramatic occasion on television as many other millions listened by radio. At noon in the House chamber of the Capitol the representatives and senators began to take their seats. Soon Mrs. MacArthur, amid much applause, was seated in the gallery. Arthur came in several minutes later with Whitney, Huff, Bunker, and other officers who had served under and been close to MacArthur; they were seated in chairs on the chamber floor usually taken by members of the Cabinet, all of whom were conspicuously absent. At 12:31 P.M., MacArthur was announced by the House doorkeeper and strode to the podium, escorted by several congressmen. He was given a thunderous ovation, especially by the Republican members of Congress and the visitors in the now-packed public galleries. Speaker Rayburn introduced him, and the five-star officer, wearing a trim Eisenhower jacket bare of ribbons or medals, stepped forward, looking somber and dignified. After standing silently before the battery of microphones for nearly three minutes while the audience stood and applauded again, he began the thirty-seven-minute address that would be ranked later as one of the most impressive and divisive oratorial performances of recent American times.

He spoke in an unhurried, yet incredibly forceful manner, his voice sounding deeply resonant and his phrases and sentences blending eloquence and sincerity, emotionalism and sweeping generalizations, in a way that moved even many listeners who found his logic and his proposals faulty or downright dangerous. As one account says, "From his first words, it was clear that he was in complete command of the situation." Before he finished speaking, he was interrupted by applause or cheers at least fifty times. Like the printed texts of some of the greatest sermons, the following excerpts from the speech indicate the substance of his main points but in no way convey the drama and emotion that swept his audience, for the charisma was in the speaker himself, an already legendary figure expressing convictions, deeply held, that had cost him his military career.[7]

MacArthur began by identifying his cause with the essence of the American heritage, with the clear, if indirect, implication that it was the President's course, not his, that was an aberration:

Mr. President [of the Senate], Mr. Speaker, distinguished members of Congress, I stand on this rostrum with a sense of deep humility and great pride; humility in the wake of those great American architects of our history who have stood here before me; pride in the reflection that this forum of legislative debate represents human liberty in the purest form yet devised.

Here are centered the hopes, and aspirations, and faith of the entire human race.

I do not stand here as an advocate of any partisan cause, for the issues are fundamental and reach beyond the realm of partisan consideration. They must be resolved on the highest plane of national interest if our course is to prove sound and our future protected. I

trust therefore that you will do me the justice of receiving that which
I have to say as solely expressing the considered viewpoint of a fellow
American. I address you with neither rancor nor bitterness in the
fading twilight of life with but one purpose in mind, to serve my
country.[8]

Boldly venturing into the realm of global strategy in countering
Communist expansionism, he maintained that it was "defeatism" to
"claim our strength is inadequate to protect on both fronts," Asia
and Europe. The strategic issues were "so interlocked that to consider the problems of one sector oblivious to those of another is
but to court disaster for the whole." Obviously having in mind the
American forces going to NATO that he had wanted for his theater, he argued, "You cannot appease or otherwise surrender to
communism in Asia without simultaneously undermining our efforts to halt its advance in Europe." He went on, however, to focus on the anti-Communist struggles solely in East Asia, praising
the efforts of the leaders and peoples of South Korea, Japan, the
Philippines, and Nationalist China and stressing the strategic significance of Formosa, which "under no circumstances" must be allowed to fall to the Communists.

As for the Korean conflict, he praised Truman's decision to intervene in June 1950 as a "sound" one "from a military standpoint." But he lamented Washington's failure to produce "new
decisions in the diplomatic sphere" after the CCF intervention
created "an entirely new situation." He expounded on the restrictions imposed on his forces, the alleged absence of clear and consistent directives for the conduct of the war, and his unsuccessful
pleas for reinforcements. He set forth a toned-down version of his
plan for driving the Communist forces out of Korea, now calling
for an accelerated economic blockade of Communist China, imposition of a naval blockade against it, aerial reconnaissance of
Manchuria and the Chinese coastline, and the use of Chiang's forces
in mainland operations with American logistical support. He emphasized that "no man in his right mind would advocate sending
our ground forces into continental China," and, in what proved
to be perhaps his most controversial point, he claimed that his
proposals for achieving victory in Korea were "fully shared in the
past by practically every military leader concerned with the Korean campaign, including our own Joint Chiefs of Staff."[9]

MacArthur's emotion-packed climax was based on his old false-dilemma technique of posing his strategic ideas, which would produce victory and end the slaughter, in contrast to the administration's supposed lack of policy, which would mean a long, indecisive war and the needless sacrifice of many American boys:

. . . Efforts have been made to distort my position. It has been said in effect that I was a warmonger. Nothing could be further from the truth. I know war as few other men now living know it, and nothing to me is more revolting. I have long advocated its complete abolition as its very destructiveness on both friend and foe has rendered it useless as a means of settling international disputes. . . .

But once war is forced upon us, there is no other alternative than to apply every available means to bring it to a swift end. War's very object is victory — not prolonged indecision. [Applause.] In war, indeed, there can be no substitute for victory. [Applause.]

There are some who for varying reasons would appease Red China. They are blind to history's clear lesson. For history teaches with unmistakable emphasis that appeasement but begets new and bloodier war. It points to no single instance where the end has justified that means — where appeasement has led to more than a sham peace. Like blackmail, it lays the basis for new and successively greater demands, until, as in blackmail, violence becomes the only other alternative. Why, my soldiers asked of me, surrender military advantages to an enemy in the field? I could not answer. [Applause.] Some say to avoid spread of the conflict into an all-out war with China; others, to avoid Soviet intervention. Neither explanation seems valid. For China is already engaging with the maximum power it can commit and the Soviet will not necessarily mesh its actions with our moves. Like a cobra, any new enemy will more likely strike whenever it feels that the relativity in military and other potential is in its favor on a world-wide basis.

. . . Of the nations of the world, Korea alone, up to now, is the sole one which has risked its all against communism. The magnificence of the courage and fortitude of the Korean people defies description. [Applause.] They have chosen to risk death rather than slavery. Their last words to me were "Don't scuttle the Pacific." [Applause.]

I have just left your fighting sons in Korea. They have met all tests there and I can report to you without reservation they are splendid in every way. [Applause.] It was my constant effort to preserve them and end this savage conflict honorably and with the least loss of time and a minimum sacrifice of life. Its growing bloodshed has caused me the deepest anguish and anxiety. Those gallant men will remain often in my thoughts and in my prayers always. [Applause.]

I am closing my 52 years of military service. [Applause.] When I joined the Army even before the turn of the century, it was the fulfillment of all my boyish hopes and dreams. The world has turned over many times since I took the oath on the plain at West Point, and the hopes and dreams have long since vanished. But I still remember the refrain of one of the most popular barracks ballads of that day which proclaimed most proudly that —

"Old soldiers never die; they just fade away." And like the old soldier of that ballad, I now close my military career and just fade away — an old soldier who tried to do his duty as God gave him the light to see that duty.

Good-by.[10]

A considerable number of congressmen and people in the galleries were weeping as the general ended his address. Representative Dewey Short, a Missouri Republican who had studied at Harvard, Oxford, and Heidelberg, made the remark most often quoted of the many adulatory responses: "We saw a great hunk of God in the flesh, and we heard the voice of God." Herbert Hoover's reaction was a close second among the paeans; the former President exclaimed that MacArthur was "the reincarnation of Saint Paul into a great General of the Army who came out of the East." Truman made a point to let people know that he and Acheson had been in conference at the time and did not have a television or a radio on during the broadcast. In the immediate aftermath of the speech the President wisely refrained from public comments about it, but later he said that when he read a copy of the text he had concluded that it was "nothing but a bunch of bull shit" and that "once all the hullabaloo died down, people would see what he was." Acheson dismissed it as "a demagogic speech" and "more than somewhat bathetic." MacArthur's reference to the JCS produced the only official reaction: the Pentagon promptly released a statement that "the action taken by the President in relieving Gen. MacArthur was based upon the unanimous recommendations of the President's principal civilian and military advisers including the Joint Chiefs of Staff." One reporter predicted the speech would cause great divisiveness among Washington politicians, and on April 22 the weekly radio show "Meet Your Congress" proved his point. It featured a debate on MacArthur's proposed Far East strategy, with Republican Senators Taft and Homer E. Capehart (Indiana) on the affirmative side and Democratic Senators Hubert H. Humphrey (Minnesota) and Herbert H. Lehman (New York) on the negative. Tempers flared throughout the program, and afterward Taft had to help separate the other three, who engaged in a "cream-puff brawl" replete with "more hot words . . . to the accompaniment of pushing, shoving, grappling, and arm-flailing."[11]

After his address to Congress, MacArthur had lunch that day with Martin and forty congressmen and friends in the Senate dining room. Later that afternoon he spoke briefly to an assembly of the Daughters of the American Revolution in Constitution Hall, and in a ceremony on the Mall, witnessed by a vast crowd, he was presented a silver tea set and the official key to the city by Washington officials. As his motorcade moved slowly down Pennsylvania Avenue, an estimated 250,000 persons were on hand, many cheering or waving American flags, and a formation of Air Force jets flew over in a salute to him. Then he, his family, and his accompanying officers and their wives from Tokyo flew on to New York City that evening. The mail awaiting him at the Waldorf-Astoria Hotel amounted to 150,000 letters and 20,000 telegrams, and messages continued to arrive by the sackload daily for weeks. The next day, April 20, he was accorded a wildly enthusiastic reception in New York City during a nineteen-mile parade through Manhattan. Stops were made at City Hall, where the mayor awarded him the city's gold medal of honor and a scroll for distinguished service, and at St. Patrick's Cathedral, where he was greeted by Francis Cardinal Spellman, an old friend and the highest ranking Roman Catholic prelate in America. The crowds along the parade route were estimated by the New York Police Department at 7.5 million, a record for the city known for some huge welcoming parades for heroes and visiting heads of state. The city's Sanitation Department figured that 2852 tons of confetti, ticker tape, and other pieces of paper were picked up by its workers along the parade route afterward, which surpassed the tonnage for the parades in honor of Howard Hughes in 1938 and Charles Lindbergh in 1927, the former record-holders. At 3:00 P.M., after four hours of the Manhattan motorcade, MacArthur was taken to the

Starlight Roof of the Waldorf-Astoria, where he was the guest of honor at a luncheon for 800 people. After a brief talk to the guests and some afterdinner conversations with friends, the weary MacArthur was finally allowed to retire to his suite on the thirty-seventh floor in the Waldorf Towers.

The hotel management, which normally charged $133 per day for his spacious suite, No. 37-A, provided it to him for $450 a month as a permanent home. He resided there until his death, thirteen years later, and Mrs. MacArthur continued to live at the hotel afterward. Although a Manhattan hotel suite was not viewed by some of his friends as the place where they thought he would likely settle, actually MacArthur had been residing in the heart of large cities for over two decades — Washington, Manila, Melbourne, Brisbane, and Tokyo. And, besides, his well-to-do Waldorf neighbors included a man he greatly admired and formerly had worked for, Herbert Hoover.[12]

Entrepreneurs and hucksters alike were quick to exploit the public excitement over MacArthur in New York, as elsewhere across the nation. Vendors hawked corncob pipes, pictures of the general, "Welcome Back, Mac" buttons and pennants, Toby jugs and dolls shaped in his likeness, and scores of other knickknacks bearing his name or image. Of course, printed texts and phonograph recordings of his address to Congress were fast-selling items, and Gene Autry, the cowboy actor-singer, sang the ballad "Old Soldiers Never Die" on a popular Columbia recording. Several books about MacArthur were rushed into print. One released in late April sold 14,000 copies in its first two weeks on the market; most of the "quickies" were made up largely of pictures. One of the works published before the year's end, however, was, in view of the short span of its preparation, a well-written, thought-provoking study — *The General and the President and the Future of American Foreign Policy,* by two talented liberal writers, Richard H. Rovere of the *New Yorker* and Arthur M. Schlesinger, Jr., of the Harvard history department. After being given "the first copy" of the anti-MacArthur book, Truman wrote Schlesinger on November 5, "I think you analyzed the situation just as it is." Whitney, Willoughby, and other defenders of MacArthur were soon at work on adulatory works about the general.[13]

On April 21, Arthur got some publicity when he accompanied

Story and the Huffs to a baseball game between the Brooklyn Dodgers and the New York Giants at the Polo Grounds, where he was allowed to throw out the first ball amid the crowd's cheers. Leo Durocher, the Giants' manager, presented him with a Giant jacket, cap, glove, and team-autographed ball. At Griffith Stadium in Washington that day, where the New York Yankees played the Washington Senators in the season opener, Truman threw out the first ball amid a mixture of applause and catcalls, but he was roundly booed as he departed in the eighth inning. Old-time baseball buffs said it was the first time a President had been booed at a game since it happened to Hoover in 1931. For General MacArthur, too, the day was not too pleasant: the *New York Times* published correspondent Anthony Leviero's story on the Wake Island conference of October, in which he used a copy of Bradley's compilation of the Washington participants' notes that a White House staff member had given him. For the first time from an authoritative source the public learned that MacArthur had been quite wrong about Communist China's plans in October, though from the Bradley record the readers, of course, got no glimpse of the version of the Wake meeting from the viewpoint of MacArthur and those of his staff who were there. On behalf of MacArthur, Whitney issued a press statement charging the White House staff with leaking classified documents and with trying to smear the general prior to the inquiry into his relief which the Senate was discussing and would authorize four days later.

At first MacArthur let Whitney handle reporters for him at his office in the Armed Services Building at 90 Church Street. Even MacArthur must have been taken aback when, in response to persisting press skepticism about his chief's absence of political aspirations, Whitney told a group of reporters to read John 20:20–29. It was the story of the doubting disciple, Thomas, who did not believe Jesus had been resurrected until he appeared and let Thomas touch him. H. L. Hunt, the Dallas oil tycoon and ultraconservative Republican, wrote MacArthur on April 27: "If press releases were curtailed, there would be some less discussion concerning you. . . . If you yourself attend to the interviews it would be safer and better" than Whitney "speaking for you." Thereafter MacArthur kept a closer control over his new situation in press relations, and less was heard from Whitney, who meant to serve his boss well but was not patient or tactful with correspondents.[14]

After resting a few days and enjoying informal reunions with old comrades who visited his suite, MacArthur flew to Chicago on April 26. There he was honored with a twenty-three-mile parade that attracted about 2 million people and that night addressed a crowd of 55,000 at Soldiers Field, defending his proposed Far Eastern strategy and criticizing the administration's policy "vacuum." The next day he spoke and paraded before large turnouts in Milwaukee, where he had once lived and had sometimes considered retiring. At both Chicago and Milwaukee, which had been important centers in the MacArthur-for-President booms of 1944 and 1948, he denied any interest in running for political office. On the 30th the MacArthurs flew to Stewart Air Force Base in central Tennessee and journeyed by car to nearby Murfreesboro, the town of about 13,000 residents where Mrs. MacArthur's home was located. Up to 50,000 people attended the parade and other festivities the town staged in honor of the MacArthurs. The general did his best to stay in the background for a change, making no major speech and letting Jean be the center of attention. After returning to New York, MacArthur kept his activities to a minimum for the next two days, for by then he had been scheduled as the opening witness at the Senate hearings, which would convene on May 3. According to Whitney, "He prepared for this inquiry just as he had prepared for the conference at Wake Island, which is to say that he prepared not at all. He went to Washington, as he had to Wake Island, with only the information that he carried in his head." And, he might have added, in Whitney's head, for the ever-faithful staff officer went with him to the Senate interrogation.[15]

The national eruption that followed MacArthur's dismissal was complex and by no means reflected only public anger over the President's action. Many people reacted negatively at first because the news hit them like a shock wave; they had not been prepared at all for the sudden ouster of a long-revered figure. Some were upset, too, when they learned the details of the graceless, bungling manner in which MacArthur had been notified. The unprecedented welcome given to him in city after city was probably, for most participants, not necessarily a signal of their agreement with his views but rather a sincere outpouring of gratitude to an old warrior who had become the first major American hero of World War II and one of the most successful commanders, not only in that conflict but in the occupation of Japan. The underlying reasons for the great excitement following his relief stemmed from the pent-up exasperation and frustration of many people over the nation's course in foreign affairs in the uncertain and frightening era of the atomic bomb and the Cold War. The administration's containment strategy seemed to run counter to the American way of dealing with foreign problems. No longer did traditional principles of foreign and military policy seem so absolutist in the new, unprecedented crises of the post–World War II period. Both Cold War diplomacy and the limited war in Korea involved compromises and limitations in order to maintain fragile relations with allies and to avert nuclear holocaust. The "loss" of mainland China, the end of the American atomic monopoly, the discovery of spies in high places and McCarthy's raucous warnings of many more, and the stage of costly, protracted stalemate that the Korean War seemed to have reached — all these recent developments had left many Americans disillusioned and ready to cheer a respected commander who promised victory and to disparage an unpopular President who appeared to have led a once powerful and purposeful nation into a state of impotence and drift.

2. Inquiry into Cabbages, Kings, and Other Things

The life span of the public excitement over MacArthur seemed to depend on the course of the Senate hearings that conservative Republicans began agitating for soon after his dismissal. On April 25 the Senate unanimously approved a resolution providing for its Armed Services and Foreign Relations committees "to conduct an inquiry into the military situation in the Far East and the facts surrounding the relief" of MacArthur. The chairman of the Armed Services Committee and a highly respected eighteen-year member of the Senate, Richard B. Russell (Democrat of Georgia) was selected as the chairman of the joint investigation, after being nominated by Tom Connally (Democrat of Texas), head of the Foreign Relations Committee. Each committee consisted of eight

Democrats and seven Republicans. Four of the Republicans on each committee were aligned with the party's Old Guard, which had been severely critical of the Democratic administrations' handling of foreign affairs since the Yalta Conference of early 1945 and had opposed American military help to NATO during the recent Great Debate. In a sense, the so-called MacArthur Hearings constituted the later phase of the Great Debate, since the Far East inquiry proved to be an extension of the arguments over the global priorities and containment strategy of the Truman administration. Neither Taft nor McCarthy was a member of the committees, but some of their views were voiced by various Old Guard senators during the hearings. McCarthy managed to insert himself into the picture by delivering a long, vicious speech in the Senate on June 14 against Marshall as a key leader in "the great conspiracy" of the past decade to yield America and the free world to the Communists. Not really a response to the Secretary of Defense's testimony at the hearings on May 7–14, McCarthy's "audacious derogation" of Marshall, suggests one historian, was, instead, "a means of sustaining his place in the limelight."[16]

Hoping to exploit MacArthur's rhetorical skills and the huge wave of popularity he was riding, the Republican committee members wanted the hearings conducted in open sessions and with radio and television coverage. But the Democratic majority, arguing that sensitive security issues and documents would be involved, voted for closed hearings and censorship of the transcripts of the sessions before their release to the press. Interestingly, in view of his future position when in the White House, Richard Nixon opposed the Democrats' insistence on closed sessions and censorship, and he remarked on April 22, in reference to the documentation that the executive branch indicated it would make available, "The new test for classifying documents now seems to be not whether the publication of a document would affect the security of the nation but whether it would affect the political security of the Administration." The inquiry was officially terminated in August, and in the fall the bulk of the record of the hearings and its many supplementary documents, which was unclassified and amounted to over 2 million words in print, was published by the Senate, though the transcript deletions and some appendices were not declassified and opened to researchers until 1973.[17]

The hearings began on May 3 in the caucus room of the Senate Office Building, with MacArthur as the first witness. At his request the senators continued his interrogation through lunch and into the early evening hours each day. He completed his testimony on the 5th, having commuted daily from New York City with Whitney, who sat beside him at the inquiry as his counsel and adviser. During the period of May 7 to June 9, the administration's seven witnesses were called: Marshall, Bradley, Collins, Vandenberg, Sherman, Acheson, and Adrian S. Fisher, the last being the State Department's legal adviser, who was questioned briefly about a matter of document declassification. The final group of six witnesses, who testified from June 11 to June 25, were Wedemeyer, Sixth Army commander and Republican party adviser on military and foreign affairs who had headed U.S. forces in China and had been Chiang's chief of staff from 1944 to 1946 and had returned to China on a special mission in 1947; Johnson, Secretary of Defense from 1949 to 1950 and, earlier, Assistant Secretary of War; Vice Admiral Oscar C. Badger, the Navy's Eastern Sea Frontier commander, who had handled negotiations and delivery of surplus war matériel to Chiang following World War II; General David Barr, 7th Division commander in Korea until February and chief of the American military advisory mission with the Nationalist Chinese from 1948 to 1949; Patrick J. Hurley, a Republican who had been ambassador to China from 1944 to 1945, and earlier Hoover's Secretary of War; and General Emmett O'Donnell, Fifteenth Air Force commander, who had until recently headed the FEAF Bomber Command in the Korean War.

Compared with MacArthur's three days of testimony, which took up 318 pages in the Senate's published edition of the hearings, the administration's witnesses gave twenty-eight days of testimony, amounting to 1779 pages in print, and the last six witnesses provided nine days and 772 pages of testimony. Acheson was questioned for eight days, Marshall for seven, and Bradley for six; their interrogation makes up 46 percent of the total printed pages of the inquiry. (The appendices and index are 15 percent, leaving 39 percent for the other eleven witnesses.) As measured by days and pages of testimony, MacArthur ranked next, followed by Wedemeyer (three days and 264 pages) and Collins (two days and 189 pages). The selection of Wedemeyer and the five witnesses who followed him seemed to be based, in part, on expectations by the Old Guard that most of them would buttress MacArthur's (and their) views and, apparently more important to those senators, that they would criticize the administration's China policy since World War II. Most of the last six witnesses had been in China before the withdrawal of Chiang to Formosa in late 1949, and much of the questioning concerned United States relations with China from 1944 to 1949. In fact, about half of all the testimony at the MacArthur Hearings was related to the administration's China policy, with MacArthur's position on various issues often fading into the background as Old Guard senators bored into the alleged blunders of both the Roosevelt and Truman administrations in dealing with the China situation.[18]

In their blatant pursuit of the factors underlying the alleged "loss" of mainland China and inadequate support of Chiang's regime on Formosa, the senators called no witnesses who could have provided solid support for MacArthur's testimony; no senior officers of his Tokyo GHQ were asked to testify. More important, the two men who had key roles in the liaison between MacArthur and Washington were not asked to appear, namely, Lowe, the President's special emissary at MacArthur's headquarters, and Sebald, the State Department's senior official in Tokyo. If they, together with Harriman, the other member of Truman's Big Four, had testified, the general trend of the hearings may not have been altered, but surely there would have been more perceptive insights into MacArthur's motivation and judgments, and less time would have been consumed on matters irrelevant to his dismissal or the current situation in the Far East.

The MacArthur inquiry was reminiscent of the general session at Wake in the absence of agendas, the rapid movement from one subject to another, and the frequent straying from the topics that should have been considered basic. Although Russell was an exemplary chairman — polite, fair, and nonpartisan — he was bound by the joint decision of the participating committees to recognize a senator from the Armed Services Committee and then one from the Foreign Relations Committee, alternating by seniority during the interrogation. This method, of course, produced a disconnected array of questions, which could have been averted by following topical approaches. Moreover, because some senators were prone to leave the caucus room frequently to take care of other work, witnesses were often subjected to repetitious questioning; Acheson, for instance, faced virtually the same question six times. As the hearings moved into the interrogation of the last six witnesses in June, the senators' absenteeism became more flagrant and so did the repetition of questions. After the completion of Acheson's testimony on June 9, most newspapers, responding to declining reader interest, relegated the hearings farther and farther from the front page, which they had commanded at first. In fact, the inquiry was moved after the appearances of MacArthur, Marshall, and Bradley from room 318, the caucus room, to room 212, a less spacious and impressive location. By the time of the fourteenth and final witness, General O'Donnell on June 25, most of the participating senators, as well as the public, had grown tired of the inquiry.

During his three-day appearance before the senators, MacArthur, according to an authority on the hearings, "never seemed to tire or show any strain; he never appeared irritated." Senator Alexander Wiley (Republican of Wisconsin) remarked, "At the end of 3 days he was just as fresh as when he started." Senator John C. Stennis (Democrat of Mississippi) remembered the general as being "very dignified and impressive" during his testimony. The senators, for the most part, were "utterly dazzled" by his "Olympian manner and finely turned phrases," says one account. Although all were courteous to him, Democratic Senators J. William Fulbright (Arkansas) and Brien McMahon (Connecticut) were not reluctant to ask him "barbed or embarrassing questions." Unexpectedly deferential toward the general was tough Senator Wayne Morse, the maverick Republican from Oregon, who sometimes was almost apologetic when posing frank queries to him. Marshall, the Joint Chiefs, and Acheson were interrogated more sharply than MacArthur; the Old Guard senators occasionally displayed animosity or contempt toward them, particularly in their exchanges with the Secretary of State.

Leaders in Moscow, Peking, and Pyongyang must have been delighted by the unprecedented wartime investigation that, despite the reviewers' deletions, revealed much about United States military and foreign policy planning. But any reader of the record of the inquiry, whether American or foreign, then or afterward, was bound to be baffled by the confusing lines of questioning and the meandering from topic to topic. Contemporary and later attempts to summarize or analyze the hearings, confronted the difficulty, if not impossibility, of presenting in a clear, coherent manner that which was wholly lacking in order from start to finish. The framework used in this book was devised on the assumption that there were three principal dimensions to the confrontation between MacArthur and his superiors: Korean War strategy, civil-military relations, and the chain of command. It must be emphasized, however, that the potpourri of issues touched on during the MacArthur Hearings includes many that do not fall into any of these three dimensions, such as United States–China relations prior to 1949.[19]

As for his past strategic planning and leadership in the Korean War, MacArthur simply admitted to no mistakes on his part. Questioned about his splitting of the X Corps from the Eighth Army in the advance toward the Yalu, he reiterated his argument, stated previously in messages to the JCS, that terrain difficulties in central Korea and lack of adequate troops made it infeasible to maintain a continuous line across the peninsula. Besides, in both their late October and late November attacks the CCF divisions had not advanced through the gap between his forces, but had struck and routed the ROK units on the flank of Walker's army. He defended, too, the subsequent withdrawal as orderly and made with minimum losses, charging that "the concept that our forces withdrew in disorder or were badly defeated is one of the most violent prevarications of the truth that ever was made." As in past statements, he asserted that with adequate warning through political intelligence agencies in Washington about Communist China's plans to enter the conflict and with the removal of restrictions on his air forces in attacking the Yalu bridges and the CCF's air and supply bases in southern Manchuria, his troops would not have had to retreat from North Korea. He remained convinced that his four-point proposal to the JCS in late December would have led to the CCF's ouster from Korea and to the avoidance of a long, costly stalemate. Those courses of "decisive" action were, it will be recalled, naval blockade of Communist China, air and naval bombardment of military and industrial targets on the Chinese mainland, use of Chiang's troops in Korea, and support of Nationalist

Chinese "infiltrative" operations across the Formosa Strait. As in his address to Congress, he now played down the deployment of Nationalist units in Korea, favored an expanded economic blockade of Red China, and wanted aerial reconnaissance of portions of Manchuria and Communist China. From his exchanges earlier with the Joint Chiefs, he was aware that they had a low regard for the effectiveness of Chiang's soldiers, which would be borne out again in the later testimony by Marshall and the JCS, and felt that air and naval attacks directly on Communist China might well bring the USSR into the war.[20]

MacArthur insisted that his proposed courses of action, which would involve no American ground forces outside Korea, would produce "a decisive end without the calamity of a third world war." Senator Lyndon B. Johnson of Texas asked what he would advocate if the CCF were pushed out of Korea but Peking still refused to terminate hostilities. MacArthur dismissed his query as "very hypothetical," maintaining, "I can't quite see the possibility of the enemy being driven back across the Yalu and still being in a posture of offensive action." When Senator Wiley raised "the most serious question" of whether his plan would trigger the Soviet Union's entry and bring on World War III, the general confidently asserted that Moscow's decision to go to war against the West would be decided by its own "timetable" and not by such actions as he contemplated, which he stressed would still leave the conflict with China at a limited-war level. He claimed his strategy would "tend to not precipitate a world war, but to prevent it," because the risk of global conflict would increase if the war were allowed to "go on indefinitely in Korea" or "if we practice appeasement" of Red China. Besides, he observed, Moscow's leaders would probably be uneasy "if China became too powerful" and might be pleased to see "this new Frankenstein" dealt a setback in Korea.

MacArthur's speculation about relations between Moscow and Peking would be borne out, in part, by the heightening of Sino-Soviet tensions later in the 1950s. His contention that Moscow was not "sufficiently associated" with Peking and Pyongyang in the Korean struggle to see its interests so menaced as to compel its entry into the war ran counter to the thinking of both the administration leaders and the Old Guard Republicans, as well as of most Americans in the spring of 1951, that global Communism was a monolithic creation inspired and controlled by the decision-makers in the Kremlin. A distinguished liberal historian observed that "the most powerful point" MacArthur made in the hearings was his assertion "that there was no world Communist plan and that China and Russia had separate policies and objectives."[21] Although twisted to his own purposes and presented simplistically, the viewpoint espoused by MacArthur, darling of anti-Communists in America, was actually an early revisionist one of the Soviet Union's links with other Communist states.

MacArthur testified that victory in the Korean War meant destroying the Communist armies in Korea or driving them above the Yalu, not conquering Manchuria, much less Communist China. Such a triumph would make possible the creation of a united, independent, and democratic Korea, as called for by the UN General Assembly in its October resolution, which had been quietly shelved but not rescinded. The defeat of the CCF in Korea would also curb or dampen Peking's expanionist urges toward Indochina and Formosa and, on the other hand, would encourage non-Communist nations of Asia. According to Whitney, when Mac-Arthur heard the news of the Korean armistice in July 1953, he remarked, "This is the death warrant for Indochina." MacArthur also saw the crippling of Communist China's war-making potential as essential to the security of Formosa, which he steadfastly argued was of vital strategic significance to America's Pacific defense line. "I believe that from our standpoint," he told the senators, "we practically lose the Pacific Ocean if we give up or lose Formosa."[22]

By no means an isolationist, he believed that unless victory were attained in Korea, we would see "the beginning of the downfall of Europe," for the fight to contain Communist expansionism "will roll around to Europe as sure as the sun rolls around." He asserted, "You can't let one half of the world slide into slavery and just confine yourself to defending the other. You have got to hold every place." He would, in other words, have the United States assist in the security of West Europe but not at the sacrifice of East Asia, which was really "the first line of defense" for the Europeans. When Senator Theodore F. Green (Democrat of Rhode Island) asked what should be the United States government's recourse if its allies rejected an acceleration of the Korean War to attain his version of victory, he replied emphatically that America, "alone, if necessary," should undertake the mission of driving the CCF out of Korea. Although he possessed a fairly accurate general knowledge of the strength of the American military establishment, he did not elaborate on how such limited ground, sea, and air units could help to hold the line globally and at the same time, with possibly only South Korean assistance, defeat the Chinese and North Korean forces.[23]

As often mentioned in this biography, MacArthur was a master at role-taking, and in discussing strategy at the hearings he played to the hilt the role of America's foremost authority on East and Southeast Asia, which most of the senators seemed to accept as beyond dispute. After all, over half of his fifty-three years of military service had been spent in the Far East. But in reality, a huge portion of that time had been restricted to the confines of two cities, Manila and Tokyo. "Later suggestions by General Marshall and Secretary Acheson," observes a careful student of the hearings, "that the general might not have been well-informed about China, the country at the center of the controversy, seemed to make no impression."[24] Also, few senators took MacArthur to task when he roamed freely and judged sweepingly about the Soviet Union, West Europe, and the global aspects of containment strategy. One challenger, Senator McMahon, reminded him that he had been wrong in his prediction in October about Communist China's intentions, which led to an unusually candid exchange and a weakening of the general's role as premier authority on things global as well as Asian:

> Senator McMahon: . . . If you happen to be wrong this time and we go into all-out war, I want to find out how you propose in your own mind to defend the American Nation against that war.
> General MacArthur: That doesn't happen to be my responsibility, Senator. My responsibilities were in the Pacific, and the Joint Chiefs of Staff and the various agencies of this Government are working day and night for an over-all solution to the global problem.
> Now I am not familiar with their studies. I haven't gone into it. I have been desperately occupied over on the other side of the world, and to discuss in detail things that I haven't even superficially touched doesn't contribute in any way, shape, or manner to the information of this committee or anybody else.

Senator McMahon: General, I think you make the point very well that I want to make; that the Joint Chiefs of Staff and the President of the United States, the Commander in Chief, has [sic] to look at this thing on a global basis and a global defense.

You as a theater commander by your own statement have not made that kind of a study, and yet you advise us to push forward with a course of action that may involve us in that global conflict.[25]

Whereas Truman, his principal four advisers, and the service chiefs had considered MacArthur's repeated violations of the President's muzzling directive of early December as threatening civilian supremacy over the military, MacArthur professed to be a firm believer and faithful practitioner of that hallowed principle of American military policy. He told the senators, "Any idea that a military commander in any position would possess authority over the civil functions of this Government is a treasonable concept in my mind." Senator Bridges asked him whether he questioned the President's right to relieve him. The general responded, "Not in the slightest. The authority of the President to assign officers or to reassign them is complete and absolute. He does not have to give any reasons therefor or anything else." Later he remarked in an exchange with Senator Morse, "I do not know why I was recalled. . . . So far as I know, I have completely implemented, to the best of my ability, every directive, every policy that was given to me." At another point he had proclaimed, "I have . . . to the best of my ability, carried out every order that was ever given me. No more subordinate soldier has ever worn the American uniform."[26] If Truman and Acheson read the testimony, they undoubtedly chose the last sentence as the most outlandish utterance made during the inquiry.

Regarding his public pronouncements, including his surrender ultimatum to the Chinese and his letter to Martin, MacArthur professed utter puzzlement as to why his superiors became so excited over such remarks. But, while claiming they had overreacted to his public statements, he used the hearings to lash out again at the administration's alleged lack of policy: "I was operating in what I call a vacuum. I could hardly have been said to be in opposition to policies which I was not aware of even. I don't know what the policy is now." Because of the restrictions that kept his forces from defeating the enemy in Korea, he said he "could not go on ordering men to their deaths by the thousands, in such a complete vacuum of policy decision." He charged that the administration endorsed "the concept of a continued and indefinite campaign in Korea . . . that introduces into the military sphere a political control such as I have never known in my life or have ever studied." On several occasions he maintained that the military conduct of the war had been handicapped by "politicians" who were "interfering" with the commanders. "When politics fails, and the military takes over, you must trust the military," he insisted. Later in his testimony he commented, "There should be no non-professional interference in the handling of troops in a campaign. You have professionals to do that job and they should be permitted to do it."[27]

MacArthur pictured the situation as if he and the Joint Chiefs, as well as most of America's senior military brass, were in agreement on policy and strategy, but Truman and his civilian advisers, especially Acheson, were responsible for the stalemate and indecision in Korea. "I had made certain recommendations, most of which — in fact, practically all, as far as I know — were in complete accord with the military recommendations of the Joint Chiefs of Staff, and all other commanders," he claimed. Referring to the JCS memorandum of January 12 on possible courses of action if the situation worsened, MacArthur said, "The position of the Joint Chiefs of Staff and my own, so far as I know, were practically identical." He went on to portray the dealings between himself and the Joint Chiefs as wholly harmonious: "The relationships between the Joint Chiefs of Staff and myself have been admirable. All members are personal friends of mine. I hold them individually and collectively in the greatest esteem. If there has been any friction between us, I am not aware of it."[28] If Truman, Acheson, and Harriman had realized the value of getting the support of Marshall and the JCS before the dismissal action, now MacArthur exposed the chasm in communications between him and his military superiors by proposing that the fundamental quarrel was between the civilian and the military leadership, not between him and the Washington officials both in and out of uniform. Perhaps he was sincerely under the impression that his directives, which he often branded as unclear or outmoded, and his relief had been dictated by Truman and his civilian advisers, or, again, he may have been trying the desperate tactic of dividing the forthcoming witnesses for the administration. Friction between the Pentagon and the State Department was probably more the norm than the exception, and Acheson in particular was not a favorite among many senior military men. If division was his aim, MacArthur was on good historical grounds in figuring that it might work.

But in all three of the principal areas — strategy in Korea, civil-military relations, and chain of command — the administration's witnesses, who followed MacArthur, presented a united front in rebutting his points and in defending staunchly the President's decisions. Marshall, who led off the testimony in behalf of the administration, frankly charged that MacArthur's proposals for taking the war directly to Communist China would "risk involvement not only in an extension of the war with Red China, but in an all-out war with the Soviet Union. He would have us do this even at the expense of losing our allies . . . [and] even though the effect of such action might expose Western Europe to attack." Marshall belittled the assistance Chiang's forces might give, and he added, "The record of the Chinese Nationalist troops for losing equipment furnished them increases the reluctance of the Joint Chiefs to equip them and employ them in battle." The Secretary of Defense effectively rebutted MacArthur's frequent past complaints about the restrictions against air attacks on the enemy's "privileged sanctuary" in Manchuria by pointing out that such action would likely provoke the Chinese into sending their Soviet-made bombers against such highly vulnerable targets as Pusan, the main port and supply base for the UNC forces in Korea. He believed "the loss of advantage with our troops on the ground [if the scattered targets in Manchuria were not hit] was actually more than equalled by the advantages which we were deriving from not exposing our vulnerability to air attacks," especially since UNC targets in Korea were much more concentrated.[29]

Sherman observed, in turn, that the enemy was operating under self-imposed limitations in the naval side of the war, too. He pointed out that if the war were expanded as MacArthur wished, some of the eighty-five or so Soviet Navy submarines in Far Eastern waters would probably be transferred to the Chinese. Sherman also was convinced that a naval blockade, though desirable, would be ineffective if imposed unilaterally by the United States because of the Soviet-controlled ports of Port Arthur and Dairen and British-owned Hong Kong. Hoyt Vandenberg's testimony was particularly devastating to MacArthur's call for air strikes on Manchuria and China. He revealed (in censored remarks) that all the United States possessed was "really a shoestring air force," that the air groups Stratemeyer already had were "about a fourth of our total effort that we could muster today," and that "four times that amount of groups . . . over that vast expanse of China would be a drop in the bucket." By the time Marshall and the Joint Chiefs were finished, MacArthur's strategic thinking, for the first time in his career, had been torn to shreds not by liberal correspondents or politicians but by the top four officers of the American military establishment. As Bradley summed up the JCS position in his now-famous statement, MacArthur's strategy "would involve us in the wrong war, at the wrong place, at the wrong time, and with the wrong enemy."[30]

As for MacArthur's contention that he had not challenged the principle of civilian authority over the military, Marshall severely castigated MacArthur for the half-dozen occasions when his public criticisms of administration policies were obvious violations of the President's December directive. Marshall viewed the statements as unprecedented effrontery by an American military officer toward his superiors, especially toward the commander in chief of the armed services:

> It is completely understandable and, in fact, at times commendable that a theater commander should become so wholly wrapped up in his own aims and responsibilities that some of the directives received by him from higher authority are not those that he would have written for himself. There is nothing new about this sort of thing in our military history. What is new, and what has brought about the necessity for General MacArthur's removal, is the wholly unprecedented situation of a local theater commander publicly expressing his displeasure at and his disagreement with the foreign and military policies of the United States.
>
> It became apparent that General MacArthur had grown so far out of sympathy with the established policies of the United States that there was grave doubt as to whether he could any longer be permitted to exercise the authority in making decisions that normal command functions would assign to a theater commander. In this situation, there was no other recourse but to relieve him.[31]

In his turn, Bradley stated categorically that the dismissal was essential because "General MacArthur's actions were continuing to jeopardize the civilian control over military authorities." Although, just as in the five days of deliberations preceding MacArthur's relief, the Joint Chiefs did not directly accuse MacArthur of insubordination, they all testified during the Senate inquiry that, in effect, he had flagrantly and repeatedly violated the President's directive regarding clearance of public statements and that his widely quoted criticisms had challenged the authority of Truman. Acheson also testified strongly to the damage MacArthur's public remarks had done to the United States' image in the eyes of its allies, who were uneasy about the extent to which MacArthur's views represented new courses in American policy and how much control the United States government actually had over the volatile Far East commander.[32]

MacArthur's assertion that he and the Joint Chiefs were on the same side in their thinking about strategic directions in the Korean War was contradicted by each of the four members of the JCS. The memo of January 12, on which MacArthur's case heavily rested in this instance, was explained by the Joint Chiefs, as well as by Marshall, as a contingency recommendation for the NSC's consideration if the combat situation became desperate and it was dropped once Ridgway's army showed it could not only stop but also drive back the CCF armies. Collins, when asked whether MacArthur had ever disobeyed an order from the JCS, surprised many in the room by answering bluntly that he had, citing his dispatch of American ground units into the northern provinces of North Korea in violation of a JCS directive that only ROK troops were to be used in those areas. Collins added that this was only "one indication among others" that led the JCS "to fear that just as he violated a policy in this case," he might do so again and under "more serious" circumstances.[33] In addition, Bradley said that MacArthur had been out of line with the JCS in commenting on matters that were in their realm, not his:

> While a field commander very properly estimates his needs from the viewpoint of operations in his own theater or sphere of action, those responsible for higher direction must necessarily base their actions on broader aspects, and on the needs, actual or prospective, of several theaters. The Joint Chiefs of Staff, in view of their global re-

sponsibilities and their perspective with respect to the world-wide strategic situation, are in a better position than is any single theater commander to assess the risk of general war. Moreover, the Joint Chiefs of Staff are best able to judge our own military resources with which to meet that risk.[34]

Much of the interrogation of Acheson strayed far afield of the issues surrounding MacArthur's relief; the Old Guardsmen pounced on the State Department's "writing off" of Nationalist China, especially during the two years preceding the outbreak of the war in Korea. The Secretary of State had long been the scapegoat of the China lobby over the fate of China in particular and of many other critics over the containment strategy in general. Having apparently given up hope of defending MacArthur, the Old Guard senators led the way in what turned into the longest and most grueling interrogation of any witness at what by then could only sardonically be called the MacArthur Hearings. As the principal historian of the hearings states, "Their object was transparent: establishment of their thesis that since about 1944 the Democratic Administrations . . . had taken a 'soft' stance on Communist expansions in East Asia . . . delivered China to the Communists and invited Communist aggression in Korea, and that if not checked . . . the Democratic leadership was apt to continue the discredited policies of the past with equally disastrous consequences." The Old Guard faction and the other members of the two Senate committees became weary even of this exercise in frustration and recrimination, however, and absenteeism of senators was extremely high by the end of Acheson's eight days of testimony. The Washington *Post* reported a survey that showed "widespread lack of interest" in the hearings by June 9, Acheson's final day, and noted that "some people followed the hearings when MacArthur appeared as a witness but apparently stopped when his testimony was concluded." The survey found that 30 percent of those polled no longer read anything about the inquiry.[35]

The final six witnesses, who probably were expected to testify mainly against the administration's China policy, contributed little that was new or substantial on that subject or on the MacArthur matter. Although some of them were sympathetic toward the general's views on certain points, none contributed strong support to his main positions. General Wedemeyer unexpectedly testified, contrary to MacArthur, that neither Formosa nor mainland China was of great strategic value to American interests, and he even favored withdrawal from Korea rather than a protracted, indecisive war. Louis Johnson, long a good friend of MacArthur's, said the President was right to relieve any commander who opposed his policies, and the former Defense Secretary was critical of MacArthur's proposals to use Chiang's troops or to bomb Manchuria. Admiral Badger did not support MacArthur's plan to expand the war and affirmed that the JCS, not the general, had the best grasp of the global strategic problems of the United States. Patrick Hurley, who had been Secretary of War when MacArthur became the Army Chief of Staff in 1930, said little about MacArthur's case, spending much of his time, instead, vociferously defending his record as ambassador at Chungking and assailing the State Department's subsequent position on the situation in China. General Barr opposed the idea of taking the air and naval war directly to Communist China and denounced as hopeless the sending of Chiang's forces back to the mainland. General O'Donnell, who, like Barr, had been a commander in the Korean War, thought the FEAF bombers should have been unleashed against Manchurian targets in the fall of 1950, but he now opposed sacrificing American strategic bombers and crews in raids on China proper as too costly for the meager results that were obtainable.[36]

On August 17 the Armed Services and Foreign Relations committees met for the last time on their joint inquiry into the Far East situation and MacArthur's dismissal. By a vote of 20 to 3, they decided to transmit to the full Senate the record of the hearings, along with the supplementary documents, but to issue no formal majority and minority reports. According to the motion, however, members of the two committees would "be permitted before September 1 to file their views and conclusions with the chairman, and that said views would be printed in the appendix." Negative votes on the motion were cast by Old Guardsmen William Knowland, Styles Bridges, and Harry Cain. Senators Wayne Morse, Henry Cabot Lodge, Jr. (Republican of Massachusetts), and Leverett Saltonstall (Republican of Massachusetts) submitted individual views in support of the administration's position against MacArthur for inclusion in the appendix of the published record of the inquiry.[37]

Despite the above motion, eight Old Guard senators filed a lengthy joint statement on August 19 for the appendix that, in essence, constituted a minority report. These Republican senators were Bridges, Knowland, Cain, Wiley, Smith, Ralph E. Flanders (Vermont), Bourke B. Hickenlooper (Iowa), and Owen Brewster (Maine). They concluded that "the removal of General Mac-Arthur was within the constitutional power of the President, but the circumstances were a shock to the national pride." They charged that "the reasons assigned for the removal of General MacArthur were utterly inadequate to justify the act," that "the 'justification' for removal seems to have been built up after the removal rather than before," and that "there was no serious disagreement between General MacArthur and the Joint Chiefs of Staff as to military strategy in Korea." Of the eight conclusions in their joint statement, however, only two dealt directly with MacArthur; the rest, like the hearings, concerned "glaring mistakes" of the administration in its China policy and its foreign affairs in general.[38]

In fairness to MacArthur, Russell had invited him on June 16 "to again appear before the committees to present any rebuttal testimony that you may think desirable," since the general "had no knowledge of the testimony of the succeeding witnesses" when he was questioned. MacArthur answered on the 19th while Badger was testifying and Barr, Hurley, and O'Donnell were still to appear. The general thanked Russell for the opportunity, but said, "I do not believe it [is] in the public interest for me to do so."[39] He went on to let the inquiry chairman know what he thought of the testimony thus far, which had included the administration's witnesses, as well as Wedemeyer and Johnson:

Certain of the testimony which was given by some of the subsequent witnesses did not coincide with my own recollection and record of the events, and with many of their opinions and judgments I am in direct disagreement. I especially take sharp exception to interpretations of events of campaigns given with little local knowledge thereof by those thousands of miles away from the scene of action. In some cases such witnesses had never even visited the area and none had direct knowledge of the events discussed. I suggest that the bimonthly official reports to the United Nations be incorporated into the committees' proceedings as they represent factually the views of the Commanders on the spot at the time of the actual occurrence of events, entirely uninfluenced by any extraneous issues or pressures. [These reports were included in the appendix.]

Much opinion testimony was given of a nature which was never either by word or deed communicated to me and of which I had no slightest inkling. There has been, too, a lack of accuracy in the paraphrased documentation presented and some lifting from context — which could not fail to have been misleading.

Insofar as the investigation dealt with my relief from the Far East Command, I feel that the full facts have not been elucidated due to the orders of the President silencing the pertinent witnesses as to his own part in the action.[40]

The general's last sentence, of course, buttressed the position of those who considered him implacably hostile toward the President, and it served as the opening barrage in an exchange of insults between him and Truman that would continue until MacArthur's death. The general might well have included the observation that "insofar as the investigation dealt with my relief," that subject had constituted a disappointingly insubstantial portion of the hearings in quantity and quality. Senator Flanders had observed the meandering trend of the inquiry as early as May 13 (near the end of the interrogation of Marshall), when he commented to a reporter on the similarity between the Korean War and the MacArthur Hearings: "There seems to be no way to terminate it [the inquiry]. Our questions are leading us into fields that are vague, indefinite, and purposeless."[41] Since that wayward course continued to the end, in retrospect it seems appropriate that the committees decided not to produce majority and minority reports.

The national uproar over the President's recall of the widely respected commander, regarded by many as the last great hero, faded more quickly than MacArthur's supporters wished. The decline of the issue of his relief in public interest, and the drop in popular support of MacArthur are clearly evident in the letters and telegrams received by the White House, from April 11 to May 8, regarding the dismissal. During the first five days following MacArthur's relief, Truman received 12,999 letters and telegrams on the matter — an average of 2600 per day — with 66.8 percent of them against the President's action and 33.2 percent supporting it, according to figures compiled by the White House staff. For the week of April 16–22, which included the general's address to Congress, the volume rose to 33,374, or 4768 daily, of which 56.6 percent were anti-Truman and 43.4 percent were pro-Truman. In the next week Truman got 21,065 letters and telegrams about the recall of MacArthur, now averaging 3009 a day; 50.4 percent were for the President and 49.5 percent against him. For the week of April 30–May 6, during which the Senate hearings began with MacArthur's testimony, the White House mail about MacArthur totaled 15,436 pieces, or 2205 daily, with 51.3 percent anti-Truman and 48.7 percent pro-Truman. But, for May 7–8, which included two of the final three days of Acheson's testimony as the last of the administration's witnesses, the President received only 1223 letters and telegrams about MacArthur's relief, with the pendulum swinging sharply in favor of the President — 74.7 percent to 25.3 percent. After May 8 the White House mail on the issue fell to insignificant numbers, and the staff no longer recorded the tallies for and against Truman's decision to relieve the general.[42]

A noted scholar on the period has observed that "neither expedition nor enlightenment appeared to be Chairman Russell's principal purpose. His object seemed to be to use the inquiry as a vehicle for calming the passions which the MacArthur controversy had stirred across the republic."[43] If the White House mail was indicative, he succeeded, though, of course, the Senate inquiry was not the only factor in the complex phenomenon of the waning MacArthur excitement. A number of writings have said that the precipitous decline was due to the inquiry's exposure of the flaws in MacArthur's arguments on strategy, civil-military relations, and his role as a theater commander, especially in the rebuttals by the administration's witnesses. That surely may have been true of thinking citizens who followed the testimony as published in censored form the day following each session; by the time Acheson left the hearings, the administration's representatives had presented a solid case against MacArthur's positions, though perhaps it was somewhat exaggerated about the general's plan setting off World War III. But the great majority of the people had lost interest in the inquiry after about a week or two, so the role of the hearings in the decline of interest does not seem to have been paramount. The key is probably in the very nature of the American public's periodical outbursts of emotional and irrational fervor: historically, they have risen and fallen quickly. If there is no convincing explanation for the decline of the MacArthur excitement of the spring of 1951, at least some reasons for its rise can be delineated in the insecure, disillusioned sentiments of the time that were discussed earlier. As for the inquiry, the senators' obfuscation in interrogating the witnesses produced a thick fog over the hearings that left probably the bulk of the American populace wondering where the strange ship was headed and where the shoreline was located. To have striven so long for the spotlight, MacArthur must have been saddened to realize that on the occasion when his cause was to reach its zenith it became only one of many subjects of the inquiry, and especially when compared to the China issue, not the most important problem discussed.

CHAPTER XX

The Periphery of Power

1. Final Months in the Spotlight

DESPITE HIS MOVING FAREWELL before Congress in April 1951, the next fifteen months would show that MacArthur had no intention of fading away. If the President and the Pentagon had been unable to stop his public criticisms of policy while he was in Tokyo, it became impossible, because of political and popular pressures, to silence him after his relief. At the Senate inquiry his testimony against the administration's position on the war and other issues would seem mild in comparison with the scorching attacks he launched during the next year or so.

In fact, neither Truman nor the Defense Department could retire him, because under the laws of 1944 and 1946 establishing five-star ranks, a general of the Army was to be retained on the active list, subject to new duties and missions, the rest of his life. Although he returned his Constellation aircraft to the government, MacArthur continued to draw his salary of $18,761 as a five-star general, and the amount increased over the years as military pay tables were raised. Until February 1952, he had an eight-man military staff; then Pace, on Truman's orders, forced him to cut it to three — Colonel Bunker, Warrant Officer George C. Yount, and Sergeant Francisco M. Valbuena (with Whitney, now retired, a volunteer staff member until he went on the Remington Rand payroll in August 1952 as Board Chairman MacArthur's assistant). He was also given a three-room office, with equipment and supplies, in the First Army's area in the Armed Services Building at 90 Church Street. On July 31, 1951, he was assigned to the Office of the Chief of Staff of the U.S. Army, 8525th Administrative Area Unit, with station in New York City. Most irksome to the Pentagon leaders and to Truman, he continued to wear his uniform while touring the country and denouncing the administration's conduct of the Korean War and of domestic and foreign affairs generally.[1]

A week before General O'Donnell's testimony as the final witness at the Senate hearings, MacArthur embarked on a round of nationwide appearances that lasted until shortly before the Republican National Convention in July 1952. Many of his critics were convinced that he was trying to build up support for another MacArthur-for-President boom, particularly since most of his public remarks were typical right-wing Republican blasts at the Democratic administration's record. According to Whitney, however, MacArthur decided to launch "a blunt, hard-hitting crusade" aimed at "revitalizing the nation." He was deeply concerned because "the same moral dry rot that infected U.S. Korean policy was also eating away at our conduct of affairs at home." Most of his travel expenses, including the use of planes, were covered by ultraconservative, well-to-do Republicans like Texas oilmen H. L. Hunt and Clint Murchison.[2]

Given the home base of his principal financial backers, it is not surprising that he began his crusade in Texas. At Austin on June 13, he addressed the Texas legislature, decrying "appeasement on the battlefield" and declaring, "Our first line of defense for Western Europe is not the Elbe, it is not the Rhine — it is the Yalu." But he hit hard, too, on the subjects of corruption in Washington and spiraling federal budgets and taxes. At Houston the following day he addressed a crowd of about 25,000 in Rice Stadium and participated in a parade in his honor. In his Houston speech he pleased conservatives by warning of the dangers to the free enterprise system posed by an overgrown central government that exercises "despotic power," tramples people's rights, spreads "false propaganda to destroy moral precepts," and exacts excessive taxes. The horror of high, unjust income taxes became a favorite theme of his tour; it was a topic that had not previously excited him during his seventy-one years. Satisfying any devotees of McCarthy in his Houston audience, he added that "these insidious forces working from within," which were more to be feared than "the threat of external attack," included "those who seek to convert us to a form of socialistic endeavor, leading directly to the path of Communist slavery." On the 15th he spoke similarly at San Antonio, where he also enjoyed a brief reunion with Generals Wainwright, Walter Krueger, and Courtney Hodges, and later that day he addressed a crowd of approximately 20,000 in the huge Cotton Bowl in Dallas. The next day he was honored with a parade through Fort Worth and spoke at a local high school stadium to an audience estimated variously between 7500 and 15,000 people. Friends of Truman jubilantly wrote the President that MacArthur's audiences in Texas were often in places where there were far more empty seats than filled ones and that the numbers had declined each day of his itinerary in the Lone Star state. Senator Robert Kerr of Oklahoma said of the general's Texas tour, "If MacArthur's not a candidate for President, there's not a steer in Texas. The Mac-kado rides again!"[3]

On July 25–26 he toured Massachusetts on a special train financed by his supporters. He visited Boston, Chicopee Falls (his father's birthplace), Springfield, and several other cities, where he was welcomed with parades and other festivities and, in turn, gave short speeches. His major address in the state, which Taft later praised as "the most effective of the many powerful speeches you have made," was delivered before the state legislature in Boston on the 25th; again he assaulted the Truman government and also claimed he had been warned that his "outspoken course" would bring "ruthless retaliation." Without giving names, a tactic used by McCarthy, he asserted, "I am told in effect I must follow blindly the leader — keep silent — or take the bitter consequences." But he exclaimed, "I shall raise my voice as loud and as often as I believe it to be in the interest of the American people."[4] No evidence has been discovered, however, that the administration had made any effort to silence his criticisms. Later in his speech he left no doubt how deep was his hostility toward Truman and how distorted was his own interpretation of an American military officer's oath:

Men of significant stature in national affairs appear to cower before the threat of reprisal if the truth be expressed in criticism of those in higher public authority.

For example, I find in existence a new and heretofore unknown and dangerous concept that the members of our Armed Forces owe primary allegiance and loyalty to those who temporarily exercise the authority of the executive branch of Government, rather than to the country and its Constitution which they are sworn to defend.

No proposition could be more dangerous. None could cast greater doubt upon the integrity of the armed services.[5]

In truth, his last two sentences aptly described his own proposition. Welcomed in communities as a great military hero, MacArthur had already tarnished his image by savagely denouncing the President and endorsing extreme rightist political views, even while wearing his uniform. If some had already become disenchanted with him, more shook their heads sadly and left his ranks on hearing or reading his Boston remarks about an officer's duty to his commander in chief. Boston marked a new low in his sagging career. With Taft's encouragement, he was learning mean politics fast.

His affront to the officer's code did not deter the Veterans of Foreign Wars, who honored him with the position of chief reviewing officer at the organization's huge parade in New York on August 28. At a program sponsored by several civic groups in Cleveland on September 6, he addressed an audience of about 10,000 people. He briefly praised Taft — after all, he was in his home state — but it was enough to prompt a letter of thanks from the senator. MacArthur continued his offensive against Truman but expanded his operation, now attacking America's "political and military leaders" since World War II for contributing to the spread of world Communism. *Time* labeled his speech "a slambang, frankly political assault on the Democratic Administration and its works." He received a warm welcome from a huge crowd at a fair in Allentown, Pennsylvania, on September 21, and on October 17 flew to Miami to ride in a large parade and address the annual convention of the American Legion. The audience of 20,000 veterans and their spouses gave him a rousing welcome, and he proceeded once again to defend his management of the Korean War and to slash at "Washington." He charged that his March ultimatum to the CCF had foiled a dastardly conspiracy to turn over Formosa to the Red Chinese and to seat Communist China in the UN. He also attacked "the bombast of violent propaganda and vulgar language which inevitably meets every honest criticism directed at the Government." His forty-five-minute speech was interrupted by the Legionnaires' applause forty-nine times. At a press conference the next day Truman commented, in response to a question about MacArthur's charge of an anti-Chiang conspiracy, that it was "not based on fact" and that "the General knew it." At NATO headquarters Eisenhower remarked privately that MacArthur "now, as always, was an opportunist seeking to ride the crest of the wave." Back in New York, MacArthur spoke before the National Institute of Social Sciences on November 8, repeating what he had said in Tokyo: that he hoped he would be remembered in history more for his leadership in the occupation of Japan than for his many military campaigns.[6] It was sad that the nobler side of the general was not demonstrated more often in his year of crusading.

On a journey to the Pacific Northwest on November 13–16, MacArthur spoke at a Seattle centennial celebration on the campus of the University of Washington. He used the occasion, not intended to be a political one, to launch what *Time* called "his sharpest attack to date" against the Truman administration. Some civic leaders left in disgust during his speech, and afterward a number of Democratic and labor leaders of the region spoke out in rage over his misuse of the invitation. Later at a dinner for 400 in Seattle he refrained from making a speech because, he announced, his wife had told him he had "talked enough in Seattle." At Portland he rode in a parade and visited a veterans' hospital, but he gave no address. *The Nation*'s correspondent covering his Northwest activities reported, "The net effect of the MacArthur pilgrimage to this region has been to reduce not only his own stature but that of those associated with him," especially Senator Harry Cain, whose admiration of the general was likely to hurt his approaching bid for re-election. Representative John W. Mc-Cormack of Massachusetts, the House Democratic leader, remarked after the Seattle fiasco, "It is about time General MacArthur took off his Army uniform when he is making Republican political speeches." Senator Herbert Lehman and Representative Emanuel Celler, New York Democrats, were irritated because he was drawing his general's salary while campaigning to oust the President.[7]

His other appearances that fall and winter were in places more friendly to the general: dedication of a park on the site of his mother's family home at Norfolk on November 18; acceptance of an award from the New York Touchdown Club, December 6; a speech warning of America's "moral decay and political irresponsibility" before the Salvation Army Association in New York, which gave him a citation for distinguished service to humanity, December 12; acceptance of the Poor Richard Club's gold medal of achievement in Philadelphia on January 15, 1952; and a brief nonpolitical talk at the Founders' Day dinner in New York of West Point alumni on March 14. Some among his admirers who had lamented his earlier vituperative remarks against the leadership in Washington hoped that his future appearances would be more like his winter ones.[8]

But, unhappily, his violent anti-Truman feelings seemed to emerge from hibernation with the coming of the spring of 1952. After a flight to Jackson, Mississippi, on March 22 aboard a Hunt-chartered Douglas DC-4 that went through severe turbulence and left him weak from nausea, he rebounded quickly after touching down and delivered a fiery address on the steps of the new state capitol. His audience included both houses of the state legislature and a crowd of about 25,000, who already considered Truman a threat to segregation and states' rights and repeatedly interrupted his speech with enthusiastic applause and "rebel yells." MacArthur gave them his most devastating indictment yet of Truman's policies, especially his domestic ones. He abhorred the high federal taxes, the waste and corruption in Washington, and — playing on the strong "Dixiecrat" sentiments of white Mississippians — the "rapid centralization of power" under Truman, which had left "the state in the position of a supplicant" to the federal government. The *New York Times* declared that "the bitterness of his attack" on Truman in his Jackson address was "a disservice to the public duty" of citizens to challenge governmental policies they considered wrong. Late that afternoon he, Jean, Arthur, and Whitney flew to Natchez, a beautiful town on the Mississippi known for its antebellum homes. There he was honored with a night parade, attended the tourist-packed Old South tableaux and Confederate ball for which the town was famous, and spent the night at Stanton Hall, a stately antebellum mansion. Early the next day the Mac-Arthurs and Whitney flew on to Little Rock, his birthplace, where they attended church and the dedication of MacArthur Park.[9]

On May 15–16, MacArthur addressed the Michigan state legislature at Lansing and spoke in East Lansing and Detroit. In his remarks before the Michigan legislature, he vowed, "There is no politics in me. . . . I plead nothing but Americanism. We have strayed far indeed from the course of constitutional liberty if it be seriously contended that patriotism has become a partisan issue in contemporary American life." Yet he went on to take a slap at Eisenhower's presidential candidacy and once more flailed the Truman administration as a "tragic failure" in domestic and foreign affairs.[10]

Observers were not altogether sure even at that late date in the campaigning for the Republican presidential nomination what MacArthur had actually been trying to accomplish in his appearances across the country (of which only the main ones have been mentioned). He had told the Michigan legislature at the end of what must have been an exhausting and, as the crowds dwindled, somewhat disappointing year of speechmaking: "I have been impelled as a patriotic duty of simple citizenship — and a disagreeable duty it has been — to expose for public consideration the failures and weaknesses, as I view them, which have brought our once righteous and invincible Nation to fiscal instability, political insecurity, and moral jeopardy at home and to universal doubt abroad." Those four topics had surely been his principal themes, repeated with only slight variation from city to city, almost regardless of the occasion. Courtney Whitney and other friends argued that he was sincerely dedicated to crusading for a "revitalized nation." Nevertheless, his frequent attacks against Truman convinced many that he was merely an embittered old man carrying on a personal vendetta. Others believed he had been testing the waters for another try for the Republican presidential nomination. Whether of the liberal or conservative wings of the party, most Republican politicians were happy to exploit his visibility, for not only his slashing speeches but also the very presence of the dismissed commander were reminders of what an awful President the man in the White House was and of the need for ending the two-decade Democratic hold on the presidency. How much the general's vitriolic campaign against Truman contributed to the President's low rating in various polls is moot, but MacArthur must have gotten satisfaction from Truman's announcement on March 29, one week after the general's most severe assault on him in his Jackson address, that he would not seek re-election.[11]

During his first days back in the United States in April 1951, the general had stated repeatedly that he had no political aspirations. Of course, his public reception turned out to be far larger at first than anticipated, his recall and the Senate inquiry had precipitated heated partisan excitement, and his year-long speaking tour was weighted with possible political overtones, at least in the eyes of his die-hard political advisers. Only once did he give the MacArthur-for-President enthusiasts some encouragement: on March 20, two days after Robert Taft had fared poorly in the Minnesota primary, the general told reporters, "I would be recreant to all my concepts of good citizenry were I to shrink because of the hazards and responsibilities involved from accepting any public duty to which I might be called by the American people." As in 1944 and 1948, however, he considered the nomination only in terms of a convention draft; he never announced his candidacy and, indeed, supported Taft for the nomination in several public comments. Numerous old friends interested in getting him into the White House remained undeterred and often wrote him detailed political analyses during the spring of 1952. Although not an active candidate, he was a definite factor in preconvention Republican politics, particularly in the Taft camp, where some of the senator's tacticians thought some form of Taft-MacArthur coalition might become necessary to prevent the nomination of Eisenhower. Though Taft was the favorite of the party's neo-isolationists and domestic conservatives, Eisenhower, who from his NATO headquarters outside Paris let it be known he would accept a convention draft, was the choice of the Republican internationalists and domestic moderates. When he visited the general at his Waldorf suite in December 1951, Taft received MacArthur's pledge that, though he did "not intend actively to campaign," he would give the Ohio senator his "fullest support for the Republican nomination." Subsequently, according to Whitney, the general "did everything in his power to discourage the rising pressures put upon him to declare himself a candidate."[12]

Some of the groups that had been active in the MacArthur presidential boom four years earlier began to stir anew in the winter and spring of 1952, but, as in 1948, the movement lacked leadership, local organizational contacts, and funding, and never posed a threat to the forces of Eisenhower and Taft in any state where a spring primary was to be held. Lar Daly's Chicago organization wanted MacArthur for President and McCarthy for Vice President; Gerald L. K. Smith's ultrarightist Christian Nationalist Party nominated MacArthur as its presidential candidate. Other groups, mostly made up of rabid anti-Communists and Republican malcontents of the extreme right who could not support either Eisenhower or Taft, included the Americans for MacArthur in California; the Demand MacArthur Clubs in Texas; the National Collegiate MacArthur Clubs, led by Communist-hater Bob Munger of Indianapolis; the Fighters for MacArthur, headed by John Chapple, an Ashland, Wisconsin, editor; and a supposedly national organization, which it actually never was, the MacArthur for President Clubs, led by Ervin Hohensee, a certified public accountant in College Park, Maryland. One authority states that the various MacArthur groups "fought each other almost as fiercely as they did the Eisenhower movement" and never achieved any effective unity at the state, much less the national, level. H. L. Hunt allegedly contributed $150,000 to the 1952 MacArthur presidential efforts, but otherwise contributions were meager. Representative Joe Martin was one of the few major politicians to express support publicly for MacArthur's nomination. General Robert Eichelberger, who had been one of MacArthur's key commanders from 1942 to 1948, embarrassed the political supporters of MacArthur by publicly endorsing Eisenhower. Robert Wood and others who had been active in MacArthur's behalf in 1944 or 1948 exhibited some interest for a while, but as Eisenhower's support grew, nourished by Senator Lodge's excellent organizational efforts, most of them threw their support to Taft.

Hunt, the multimillionaire, however, remained convinced that the only hope of blocking Ike's nomination at Chicago in early July was a ballot deadlock between him and Taft, with the latter then withdrawing in favor of MacArthur. Hunt not only bombarded MacArthur with his ideas but also bluntly wrote Taft that he could not beat Eisenhower and should follow the Texan's proposed tactics. Various stories, none provable, circulated during the late stages of preconvention campaigning about deals that were discussed between Taft and MacArthur. One claimed that Taft, desperately in quest of a way to thwart Ike, offered MacArthur the vice presidential slot with him; Whitney reported Taft as offering the general also the position of "deputy commander-in-chief of the Armed Forces" and "a voice" in making foreign policy; and still another story said that Taft made a firm promise to throw his delegates to MacArthur if in the early convention balloting Eisenhower had the lead. The one well-confirmed story is that when MacArthur declined an invitation in early June from the chairman of the Republican National Committee to deliver the keynote address at Chicago, Taft persuaded him to undertake it.[13]

By the time of the convention, Taft and Eisenhower had most of the delegates pledged through primary victories that spring, with Ike, who resigned his NATO command in April but did not start campaigning until June 4, controlling all the large eastern state delegations and favored to win the nomination. Repeatedly that spring MacArthur had told his supporters to vote for Taft and in several cases had asked that slates in his name be withdrawn. Nevertheless, he still got some votes as a write-in candidate in several early Republican primaries. He received 3 percent of the votes in the New Hampshire primary on March 11, finishing fourth behind Eisenhower, Taft, and Harold Stassen; in the Minnesota primary a week later he again was fourth, getting 7 percent of the votes; and on April 22 in the Pennsylvania primary, won easily by Ike, MacArthur again was fourth, getting only about 6000 of the more than 1.2 million votes cast. To objective analysts it was obvious that MacArthur had no chance of winning the nomination, but Hunt and other faithful supporters believed there was still some hope if he produced a keynote speech that excited the convention, if Ike and Taft were deadlocked in the early balloting, and if Taft withdrew hence in favor of MacArthur.[14]

After receiving a thunderous ovation and a planned demonstration when he entered the Chicago convention hall on the evening of July 7, MacArthur mounted the dais to begin his keynote address at 8:00 sharp. The delegates and the millions of television viewers noticed first that he was attired in a civilian suit, his first public appearance out of uniform, and as he began to speak, they soon became aware that he had developed several annoying mannerisms since his address to Congress fifteen months ago, including movement up and down on his toes and gesticulations with his right hand pointed upward. He looked ill at ease, as if he were not comfortable trying to make a speech that would bring together the right and left wings of the party for a unified and victorious campaign. The speech, which seemed to be a synthesis of clichés and generalities from his tour talks, again indicted the Truman administration for its errors and failures. He called for the Republicans to provide the leadership for "a purification of the nation's conscience and a refortification of its will and faith." The text itself was no worse than that of many of his addresses during the previous year's tour or some of the other speeches to be heard at the Chicago convention. But his delivery was so poor and ineffective, in such striking contrast to his performance before Congress, that many delegates lost interest midway through his speech and began moving about and talking loudly to each other. The address did not help his cause nor that of Taft. C. L. Sulzberger of the *New York Times* remarked, "He said nothing but sheer baloney." The correspondent Bob Considine, an ardent admirer of the general, called his performance "rasping and not well-informed." Afterward MacArthur left the hall quickly and was soon on a plane back to New York. Undoubtedly aware that his effort had been unsatisfactory, he refused to answer telephone calls the next day, according to one account. But Whitney claims Taft called him just before the first ballot to say that if he did not get the nomination on the first ballot he would call back to discuss the next step in trying to stop Ike, possibly a withdrawal in favor of MacArthur. The general assured him, "Win or lose, I am with you." Another story says Taft pleaded futilely with MacArthur to return to Chicago and to speak out actively for him. Wood sent MacArthur a telegram urging him to return to the convention to assist the Taft forces, but the general refused to come. Back in Chicago the ballot battle ended quickly: on the first vote, Eisenhower re-

ceived 845, Taft 280, Earl Warren 77, and MacArthur 4, whereupon the convention passed a motion making the nomination of
Ike unanimous.[15]

For five months after the Chicago convention, MacArthur made
no speeches and few public appearances. On August 1, he began
working for Remington Rand as its board chairman. A small group
of dissident Republicans was interested in Colonel Robert Mc-
Cormick's idea of establishing an "American Party" ticket with
MacArthur for President and Senator Harry F. Byrd (Democrat
of Virginia) for Vice President, but neither of the principals was
interested in running. Later a New York *World-Telegram* editorialist observed, "It is a roaring pity that General MacArthur was ever
sucked into even the fringe of politics through the back door, the
side door, or any door by his admirers, for this was no place for
him."[16] Surely after his experiences in the presidential campaigns
of 1944, 1948, and 1952, MacArthur finally realized that the great
majority of Americans who had cheered him were honoring him
as a hero and a commander, not as an authority or a potential
leader in national politics.

In the November contest Eisenhower and Nixon, his running
mate, decisively defeated the Democratic presidential and vice
presidential candidates, Adlai E. Stevenson and Estes Kefauver.
Republican gains in Congress were modest, and in most cases the
party's congressional candidates lagged well behind Eisenhower in
vote-getting. In late October, Ike had promised publicly that if
elected he would "concentrate on the job of ending the Korean
War" and would make "a personal trip to Korea." He kept his
pledge to go to Korea, but his whirlwind three-day visit during
the first week of December — reviewing troops, chatting informally with commanders, and devoting only an hour to serious discussion with Syngman Rhee — did not seem to contribute an iota
toward terminating hostilities.[17]

On the day Eisenhower departed from Seoul, December 5,
MacArthur delivered his first major address as Remington Rand's
board chairman, telling the Waldorf meeting of the National Association of Manufacturers' 57th Congress of American Industry
that it was important to support the incoming Eisenhower administration if free enterprise was to be saved. The highlight of the
speech was his surprising claim that he knew how to end the Ko-

rean conflict. He said his "solution involves basic decisions which I recognize as improper for public disclosure or discussion, but which in my opinion can be executed without either an unduly heavy price in friendly casualties or any increased danger of provoking universal conflict." The President-elect, who already had many friends among the top industrialists who heard MacArthur's speech, was quickly informed of MacArthur's exciting news. On December 7, Eisenhower, who was aboard the cruiser *Helena* in the Pacific, sent a message to MacArthur, saying that he wanted to meet with him about his plan and to "obtain the full benefits of your thinking and experience." MacArthur promptly replied that he would be happy to confer with him and noted that "this is the first time that the slightest official interest in my counsel has been evidenced since my return." At a press conference on the 11th, Truman angrily belittled both Ike's Korean trip and MacArthur's plan as playing politics with the war issue. Bradley wrote MacArthur on December 16 that the JCS was interested in meeting with him if he had found "a clear and definite solution which might end the Korean conflict." MacArthur answered that he would be conferring with the President-elect about his plan on the 17th and "I am confident that he will bring to the attention of the Joint Chiefs of Staff anything suggested by me which he believes appropriately requires their consideration."[18]

MacArthur and Eisenhower met on December 17, with Dulles as host at his town house in Manhattan. Although MacArthur had vigorously opposed Ike's nomination and had not campaigned for him after Chicago, the former Far East chief apparently felt he would get at least a friendly hearing before two men with whom he had worked closely and enjoyed warm friendships for a spell — the President-elect as his assistant in Washington and Manila in the 1930s and the Secretary of State–designate as the principal author of the Japanese peace treaty. MacArthur presented them with copies of his "Memorandum on Ending the Korean War," dated the 14th, which included the following eight proposals:

(a) Call a two-party conference between the President of the United States and Premier Stalin. . . .

(b) That such a conference explore the world situation as a corollary to ending the Korean War;

(c) That we insist that Germany and Korea be permitted to unite under forms of government to be popularly determined upon;

(d) That thereafter we propose that the neutrality of Germany, Austria, Japan and Korea be guaranteed by the United States and the Soviet with all other nations invited to join as co-guarantors;

(e) That we agree to the principle that in Europe all foreign troops should be removed from Germany and Austria, and in Asia from Japan and Korea;

(f) That we urge that the United States and the Soviet undertake to endeavor to have incorporated in their respective constitutions a provision outlawing war as an instrument of national policy, with all other nations invited to adopt similar moral limitations;

(g) That at such conference, the Soviet be informed that should an agreement not be reached, it would be our intention to clear North Korea of enemy forces. (This could be accomplished through the atomic bombing of enemy military concentrations and installations in North Korea and the sowing of fields of suitable radio-active materials, the by-product of atomic manufacture, to close major lines of enemy supply and communication leading south from the Yalu, with simultaneous amphibious landings on both coasts of North Korea);

(h) That the Soviet be further informed that, in such eventuality, it would probably become necessary to neutralize Red China's capability to wage modern war. (This could be accomplished by the destruction of Red China's limited airfields and industrial and supply bases, the cutting of her tenuous supply lines from the Soviet and the landing of China's Nationalist forces in Manchuria near the mouth of the Yalu, with limited continuing logistical support until such time as the communist government of China has fallen. This concept would become the great bargaining lever to induce the Soviet to agree upon honorable conditions toward international accord.[19]

MacArthur said his memo presented "in broadest terms a general concept and outline" that he "would be glad" to expatiate later "as minutely as may be desired." Dulles remarked that Ike "should first consolidate his position as President before attempting so ambitious and comprehensive a program." Eisenhower commented, "I'll have to look at the understanding between ourselves and our allies in the prosecution of this war. . . . We have to make sure that we're not offending the whole free world, or breaking faith." According to Ike, MacArthur "agreed that I was right. . . . There was no argument." Before a group of waiting reporters outside the town house later, MacArthur and Eisenhower exchanged amiable remarks about their continuing friendship and regard for each other.

But MacArthur wrote in his memoirs eleven years later, "From that day to this I have never been further approached on the matter from any source." Eisenhower undoubtedly realized that it would be politically inexpedient for him to endorse MacArthur's plan, which incorporated, besides some quite idealistic notions, the strategic proposals that had been repudiated by the Pentagon and by the Republican wing that was most responsible for his presidential nomination and victory. By then on the periphery of power, MacArthur must have found some vindication the following spring and summer when President Eisenhower was forced to issue several warnings to Peking, implying an expansion of the war beyond the borders of Korea and even possible use of atomic weapons in order finally to bring the two-year negotiations on a Korean armistice to a conclusion. From his lofty, isolated view in the Waldorf Towers, MacArthur could claim, with some justification, that he had contributed to the achievement of two goals very dear to him: getting Truman out of the White House and ending the fighting in Korea.[20]

2. *Still Busy and Controversial*

The MacArthurs' home life in the Waldorf Towers was reminiscent of the tightly controlled environment of their years in the Tokyo embassy. The Towers has its own entrance and elevators, apart from the main Waldorf-Astoria Hotel. Guards screened visitors to the MacArthur suite, and telephone calls to the general were screened first by the hotel operator and then by Mrs. MacArthur. The MacArthurs' apartment, which included quarters for Ah Cheu, consisted of ten spacious rooms. The drawing room was forty-seven feet long and twenty-eight wide; from its windows a beautiful view of the busy city unfolded, with Park Avenue below. Despite the suite's size, there seemed barely enough room for the forty-nine tons of personal belongings that arrived from Japan at the end of May 1951. Guests invariably were impressed by the quantity and quality of the Oriental art, much of it gifts and souvenirs from Japan, the Philippines, and Korea. When the Japanese consul-general presented MacArthur with a high Japanese decoration in a ceremony in the drawing room, a reporter said "members of the consulate staff looked around in wonder" at all the general's "reminders of a lifetime in the Far East: rare objects in ebony, jade, silver, and ivory; delicate Japanese panels." Mrs. Vining remarked that it looked like "a big, expensive curio shop" of Asian objects (most of which would go to the Norfolk museum in his honor later). On his first visit to the general's apartment, Vice President Nixon, having just left Hoover's residence on the floor below, was struck by the contrast: "Hoover's suite was impressive in its simple, uncluttered dignity. MacArthur's, while the same size, was spectacular. The memorabilia . . . gave me the feeling that he rather than Hoover had served in the highest position America could offer."[21]

In outward appearance during his seventies MacArthur was jaunty, debonair, and distinguished, still looking somewhat younger than he was. His mind stayed sharp; indeed, his intellectual faculties were more than a match for the athletic organizations' leaders whose differences President John F. Kennedy assigned him to arbitrate in his early eighties. When a group of cadets brought him greetings from West Point on his eighty-third birthday in 1963, they reported the general to be "looking thin but alert, straight, and healthy." He wore his uniform for speechmaking up to the Republican convention in 1952, but he began purchasing civilian clothes at Saks Fifth Avenue and other fashionable stores soon after he moved into the Waldorf. Although he never picked up his pre-1941 reputation as a dandy, MacArthur dressed well in the fashion of corporate executives of the "gray flannel suit" era.

Television, particularly sports events, now took the place of the nightly movies MacArthur had watched at the Tokyo embassy. He and Jean also played some table games, including pinochle and Parcheesi, his favorites. He attended some baseball games of the Yankees, Giants, and Dodgers, but his "special passion" continued to be football, especially the West Point team. Coach Red Blaik often visited him, keeping him posted on his game plans and his players and at times earnestly seeking his counsel, for instance, during the cheating scandal at the Military Academy in 1951. Blaik and Felix (Doc) Blanchard, his assistant and once All-American back under him, sometimes brought films of Army games to the suite for the general to view. On several occasions MacArthur visited football practices at the academy and made brief, inspiring talks to the players, but most of his sports-watching was now confined to television. During their first few years in Manhattan, he and his wife frequently attended shows and programs at Radio City Music Hall, Carnegie Hall, and the main Broadway theaters, but the general's nonbusiness activities became more and more restricted to the Waldorf by the later 1950s.

At first, the MacArthurs visited the residences of friends in and near the city, but as the years passed, such get-togethers were held at the Waldorf. Whitney and Bunker became, even more than in Tokyo, the general's principal confidants. Other old friends who came to visit often included George Kenney, his Southwest Pacific air chief and later the head of SAC; Charles Kades, a key Government Section official in Japan who later served as the MacArthurs' attorney; Sidney Huff, who returned to the general's staff for a time; Herbert Hoover, with whom the MacArthurs chatted often and dined sometimes; and, among occasional callers, a host of officers who had served under MacArthur, such as Matthew Ridgway, who visited in May 1952 en route to assume the supreme command of NATO forces. Sometimes congressmen, usually conservative Republicans, came to call, and friends from Japan and the Philippines occasionally visited him, including President Epidio Quirino of the Philippines in 1951, Shigeru Yoshida in 1954, Mamoru Shigemitsu the following year, and the Japanese Crown Prince Akihito in 1960. Some callers were distinguished admirers from the Atlantic side, including Field Marshal the Viscount (Bernard L.) Montgomery, who, like Churchill and Field Marshal Sir Alan Brooke, later concluded that MacArthur had been the ablest American commander of World War II. Like other old men, MacArthur was fond of reminiscing, but unlike most, he had a long, rich, and adventure-packed past to recall. He seemed to enjoy most talking about the years in Japan. Mrs. Vining visited him in 1959 and later commented, "Some of the things he told me were those I had heard before in the Dai-Ichi, but now enlarged and emphasized, as if he had sat and thought about them until, like a drawing traced over and over with a soft pencil, the color deepened and the outlines blurred."[22]

During World War II and later in Japan, MacArthur's birthdays had been big ceremonial occasions; his staff gave him a stag party, other top military and political leaders sent greetings, and news articles publicized everything about his day. With advancing age, the birthday high points for the general became the annual visits of cadet groups from West Point and the reunion dinners with his old comrades-in-arms, the latter held usually on the evening of his birthday, January 26. He was still deluged by birthday greetings, too; on his eighty-second birthday he received about 15,000 letters, telegrams, and cards. Major General Leif J. (Jack) Sverdrup, who had succeeded Major General Hugh J. Casey as chief engineer officer at the Southwest Pacific headquarters and later headed a large engineering firm in St. Louis, had been staging reunion dinners on MacArthur's birthday at the Carlton Hotel in Washington since 1948, with sixty or so officers of the Southwest Pacific command attending. The first one at which MacArthur was present was that of 1952, held in a dining room of the Waldorf-Astoria Hotel. He was present at all of them thereafter, and the event was always staged at the Waldorf for his convenience. (The group continued to meet on his birthday until the late 1970s, though the post-1964 dinners were usually in Washington.)

The stag affairs, whose attendance varied between 25 and 140, became somewhat ceremonial but without losing the spirit of informal camaraderie. When MacArthur entered, the group, dressed in tuxedos or their old formal uniforms (in the few cases where they still fitted), snapped to attention, saluted him, and sang "Happy Birthday." MacArthur then moved among them, greeting each man warmly. After a few rounds of drinks they were served an elaborate dinner, with MacArthur flanked by his senior ground, sea, and air chiefs of the war with Japan — General Walter Krueger, Admiral Thomas C. Kinkaid, and General George Kenney — who delivered brief speeches of greetings from their respective services. Telegrams from President Eisenhower and others who had served with the Old Man were read. At MacArthur's last dinner with the group, in January 1964, President Johnson, once a naval officer in the Southwest Pacific who had been decorated with a Silver Star by MacArthur, sent his greetings, adding, "On behalf of the American people, please accept the appreciation of a grateful nation for what you have given and all you have done." The high point came when MacArthur delivered a short address, usually extemporaneous, on their wartime experiences, the traits of military leadership, or the state of current affairs, as his mood dictated. His remarks always got an enthusiastic response. After the swapping of undoubtedly much-embellished war stories in informal talk later, the group ended the evening by rising and singing "Old Soldiers Never Die."[23]

Even more than her husband, Jean MacArthur seemed to age with remarkable grace. In fact, Robert Sherrod, a journalist who talked with her in 1967, was surprised by how little she had changed since he met her in Australia in 1942. Like the excellent Army wife she had been since 1937, during the postdismissal period she was usually beside her husband, or observing quietly nearby, at his many public appearances. The small, attractive lady greeted the legions of people with a sincere smile, talked to many of them, and applauded enthusiastically at the dedicatory ceremonies and other public festivities involving the general. She was able to remain amazingly poised and gracious amid the often hectic situations that developed with huge crowds. Reporters, including those who did not care for her husband, never had an unkind word about her; she treated them courteously, though she never granted personal interviews. Of all her trips across America with the general, the one she probably cherished most was the homecoming to Murfreesboro, Tennessee, at the end of April 1951. Jean epitomized the old Southern ideal of womanhood, pleasantly and devotedly striving to help her husband in every way he needed her and appearing utterly happy in her role. For whatever it meant, the Parents' League of America voted the MacArthurs "the happiest married couple" in the nation in 1951. (The Earl Warrens finished second.) In 1953, Mrs. MacArthur received the prestigious Theodore Roosevelt Memorial Medal "for her great courage in facing untold hardships, for her magnificent bravery under fire and in extreme danger [in the Philippines from 1941 to 1942], and for her abiding faithfulness to her family and her country." Her devotion to the general was matched by her loving concern for Arthur, who had just entered his teens when the family moved to New York. Ah Cheu, who had been with them since Arthur's babyhood in Manila, continued to be an important member of the household and received special attention from Jean. In 1956, Whitney made a comment that really was a tribute to Jean: "The MacArthur family is an idealistic one. Simple, of quiet elegance and of complete unity and devotion."[24]

General and Mrs. MacArthur wanted their son to enjoy a normal life, but his circumstances in New York, as in Tokyo, were far from ordinary. For one thing, the Waldorf Towers was the abode of extremely well-to-do adults in or near their retirement years, the Hoovers and the Duke and Duchess of Windsor being among the more notable residents of that time, and there were few if any other young people among his neighbors. Arthur also had to go through the trauma of attending school with other adolescents for the first time at the age of thirteen, when he entered the private Buckley School on East 74th Street in September 1951. (Mrs. Gibbons, his tutor since 1945, arrived in late May 1951 aboard the ship transporting the MacArthurs' belongings, and she soon accepted a position in upstate New York.) Thrust into the role of a celebrity, Arthur was photographed, beseeched for autographs, given all sorts of gifts, and honored with his parents at public festivities. Newspaper and magazine articles often referred to the family heritage of the MacArthurs; the *New York Times* declared him the "heir to generations of military tradition." Fans of his father even wrote Arthur about what the nation expected of him. One said, "It will be your great privilege to live up to the honor, glory and nobility of that heritage" of the family. Representative James E. Van Zandt, a Pennsylvania Republican, promised the general at the time the boy was fourteen that he would appoint Arthur to the class entering the Military Academy in 1955. An official of the St. Louis Browns baseball club, assuming too much from the boy's attendance at some major league games, wrote Arthur in 1951 that the Browns "would be happy to give you a thorough tryout when you reach your eighteenth birthday." Being the son of a father who was not only a famous general but also a highly controversial one must have been a burden for Arthur; it is unlikely that many of his schoolmates had fathers who had been summarily dismissed by the President.

Nevertheless, Arthur seemed to adjust to his unique pressures, particularly in 1953–1956, when he attended and graduated from the Browning School, a private secondary school on East 62d Street, where he played on the soccer team and performed well academically, winning prizes in history and English. In the fall of 1956 he entered Columbia College, the undergraduate liberal arts school of Columbia University. On a registration card he listed his hobby as "music — piano." One faculty member remarked that he was "an average student, very quiet, soft-spoken, extremely well-mannered." Another professor remembered him as "a sensitive, bright, delicate boy and a fair student . . . very much interested in the theater." He received a bachelor's degree from Columbia in June 1961, having majored in general liberal arts with a concentration in English literature. By then Arthur had developed a life style and a value system quite different from his father's. During the next several years he took other courses at Columbia, mostly in literature, opera, and theater, and he began work on some compositions in music and drama.[25] In one of the few recorded comments by the general about his son during their years in New York, MacArthur remarked to Blaik in the spring of 1953:

> Arthur is not competitive like me, but rather artistically oriented, as his mother is. He has strong convictions and is completely capable of determining his own future. As a youngster, he saw more of war and death than many soldiers, and I have wondered whether it has left a scar on him. Although Arthur is not a robust athlete, he is an excellent swimmer, is president of his class, and an accomplished musician. I am glad that he is not number one in his class standing, as I believe that brings little reward, though he does rank in the first 10 percent and is especially good in the arts.[26]

Although he was then seventy-three and his son fifteen, MacArthur showed an understanding and acceptance of the fact that his son was developing into an individualist who would pursue a life course of his own choosing.

When MacArthur was away from his family, it was usually because of his duties in the realm of big business, to which he adjusted with little difficulty, since he had been in managerial positions in the military for many years. James H. Rand, the founder of Remington Rand, Inc., first approached MacArthur in late 1949 about working for him when he returned to the States. One of the several Remington Rand executives who stayed in close touch with MacArthur until he accepted the firm's board chairmanship after the Chicago convention in July 1952 was Lieutenant General Leslie R. Groves, an old friend who had headed the Manhattan Project, which developed the atomic bomb. On his retirement from the Army in 1948, Groves had become a Remington Rand executive and rose to vice president and member of the board of directors. Whitney, who was given an executive position with the company as MacArthur's assistant, dedicated his book on the general (1956) to Rand, lauding him as an "industrial pioneer, who had the vision to guide MacArthur's brilliant mind toward new horizons after a willful President foreclosed the old."[27]

When Rand, who had been both president and chairman of the board, relinquished the latter position to MacArthur on August 1, 1952, Remington Rand was a vigorous multinational enterprise employing 36,000 people in twenty-two American plants and twenty-three factories in fifteen foreign nations. It was engaged primarily in electronic manufactures for both military and civilian markets and was best known to most consumers for its lines of typewriters, calculators, and office equipment. In mid-1955 it was merged with the Sperry Corporation; MacArthur was elected board chairman of the new Sperry Rand Corporation, and Harry F. Vickers became the president and chief executive officer. The corporate giant had net annual sales of over $1.1 billion in 1960; its contracts with defense and space agencies were responsible for half of all its revenues.[28]

MacArthur received a beginning salary at Remington Rand in 1952 of $45,000 a year, a handsome income for that time. It was supplemented by $19,548 in pay and allowances as a five-star general. Eight years later he was making $89,343 — $68,800 from Sperry Rand and $20,543 from the Army. At first he owned no Remington Rand stock, but after a heckler pointed this out while he was presiding over the annual stockholders' meeting in August 1953, he purchased 800 shares in December at a cost of $12,000, which by the next summer's stockholders' meeting was worth $21,000, owing to the sharp rise in the stock's value. MacArthur had not been in a state of financial want when he joined Remington Rand, thanks to a "bonus" of $500,000 from the Philippine Commonwealth government in early 1942 for his service as military adviser since 1935. His estate in 1964, which included a large number of municipal bonds, was valued at $2,131,942.[29]

When MacArthur and Whitney joined Remington Rand, a chauffeured limousine transported them usually four times a week for lengthy luncheon-business sessions with Rand and his executives at the company offices at Stamford, Connecticut. Often MacArthur went to meetings at Rand's Rockledge mansion at Rowayton, seven miles north of Stamford, and sometimes he and other company leaders accompanied Rand on sailing trips on Long Island Sound aboard the president's plush 130-foot yacht. After the Sperry merger the general often presided over sessions at the Sperry Rand headquarters, 30 Rockefeller Plaza, and sometimes he invited the board of directors to meet in the large drawing room of his Waldorf suite.[30]

In a conversation with Coach Blaik in 1953, MacArthur expounded on his new role as a corporate leader: "My career in the Army began in the Corps of Engineers, and I have returned to that type of work, except, of course, that now I am occupied with electronics, a very interesting and limitless subject." He thought his "importance is far overemphasized" at Remington Rand, but said his contribution to the firm was "more in the nature of advice and at times keeping them from making foolish moves." Leslie Groves recalled that, unlike many retired generals and admirals who were given titular positions in companies and actually were little involved in the decision-making, MacArthur "took an active part in the discussions" of the board and other company executives and that his advice was of "tremendous value." Groves praised him as "a steadying influence" at high-level meetings and as "a senior adviser on such matters as our international relations."[31] Citing a specific instance where MacArthur's advice was crucial to the company, Groves said:

> On this occasion, we were discussing our problems in connection with operations in the Far East, that is, in Australia, India . . . Japan and . . . Hong Kong. . . . He [MacArthur] advised very strongly that we retire as soon as we could from India, and that we not open any new company-owned operations anywhere outside of Japan, Taiwan, the Philippines and Australia. I imagine this advice, which was followed (because we all felt that he knew so much more about the Far East than we did), must have saved the company at least several million dollars in actual cash as well as much more in the dissipation of managerial services because if we had gone in there, we would have had

constant troubles; we would have had many matters being brought to the senior executives constantly. All in all, it was a most advantageous decision. . . . Some of the other executives were anxious to go there since it seemed to be a means of considerable profit. As it turned out, it would have been a considerable loss.[32]

MacArthur found respect and friendship among the corporate officers, most of whom shared his dedication to conservatism and to aristocratic ways. As the years passed and his mind remained keen, he performed admirably in presiding over board meetings and even over the annual stockholders' meetings, though occasionally a stockholder with no great respect for his prestige protested a company policy or one of the general's sometimes lengthy speeches. His corporate colleagues were well pleased, too, with his representation of the firm in speaking engagements, as in December 1954, when he addressed the annual meeting of the National Association of Manufacturers in New York. In a strongly worded speech he attacked the federal government's "incessant encroachment upon the capitalistic system" through labor laws and regulations that "provoke distrust and strife" between management and workers and through the "increasingly oppressive" corporate and personal income taxes that amount to "a series of graduated penalties upon the efficiency and the thrift which produces profit and accumulates capital." Not unexpectedly, he also became a strong believer in the military-industrial complex: "It is an unassailable truth that the science of industry has become a major element in the science of war. . . . The armed forces of a nation and its industrial power have become one and inseparable. The integration of the leadership of one into the leadership of the other is not only logical but inescapable." He undoubtedly did not think much of another five-star general's warning against "the acquisition of unwarranted influence" and "the disastrous rise of misplaced power" in the fast growth of the post-1945 military-industrial complex, as President Eisenhower expressed it in his farewell address in January 1961.

The Society for the Advancement of Management cited MacArthur for his distinguished leadership of Sperry Rand and gave him a plaque at a "gathering of the nation's industrial great" in New York in September 1963. In one of his last major speeches, MacArthur thanked the group and went on to emphasize that "the successful conduct of a military campaign now depends upon industrial supremacy." Moreover, he contended, industry "is the very fabric of our society — the reason why our standards of living, of humanity, of culture are the highest in the world. We must guard it." And he asserted that the huge multinational corporations like his own could "become the leavening influence in a world where war and the threat and fear of war would otherwise completely distort the minds of men and violently react upon the peaceful progress of the human race." MacArthur, like his old boss Hoover, had become sold on the wonders of industry and the new world it promised, whose "limits are as broad as the spirit and imagination of man."[33]

Besides extolling the virtues of big business, MacArthur continued to speak out on the injuries being done against industry, individual liberties, and states' rights by the interventions of a too-powerful federal government, especially through its crippling taxes. Other favorite themes of his were enunciated during his memorable day of three major addresses in Los Angeles on January 26, 1955, his seventy-fifth birthday. Arriving with his wife by plane the previous evening, he spoke on the morning of the 26th at the dedication of a war memorial in MacArthur Park that included a statue of him, a monument with some of his sayings, and a reflecting pool containing tiny replicas of the islands of his World War II campaigns. He told the crowd of 15,000 that the proponents of "internationalism and collective security" were trying to undermine Americanism and that citizens should repudiate the "seductive murmurs . . . that patriotism is outmoded." At a luncheon for 1100 members of the Los Angeles diocese of the Protestant Episcopal Church, held at the Biltmore Bowl, he received an award for distinguished leadership as "a Christian statesman and soldier." In response, he spoke fondly of his efforts to further Christianity in occupied Japan, remarking, "Although I am of Caesar, I did try to render unto God that which was His."[34]

That evening he addressed a large American Legion banquet at the Ambassador Hotel in Los Angeles. The speech, one of his best in delivery and effectiveness, was remembered by many for his quotation of a little-known brief essay that some thought he penned but that was actually composed by a long-deceased Southern business and civic leader, Samuel Ullman. MacArthur asserted that at the age of seventy-five he was still young because he believed (quoting Ullman) that "youth is not entirely a time of life — it is a state of mind. . . . People grow old only by deserting their ideals. . . . In the central place of the heart, there is a recording chamber; so long as it receives messages of beauty, hope, cheer and courage, so long are you young." The general's principal theme before the Legionnaires, however, was the idealistic one he had first proclaimed at the Japanese surrender ceremony in September 1945 — the need to abolish war. In words not unlike those of the advocates of the Kellogg-Briand Pact of 1928, he declared that the United States government should "proclaim our readiness to abolish war in concert with the great powers of the world." The advent of atomic weapons "has destroyed the possibility of war being a medium of practical settlement of international differences. The enormous destruction to both sides of closely matched opponents makes it impossible for the winner to translate it into anything but his own disaster." The problem, he maintained, was in "the world's leaders," who have not shown "the imagination and courage to translate this universal wish for peace — which is rapidly becoming a necessity — into action." He went on to assail the conventional view of the Cold War: "The present tensions, with their threat of national annihilation, are kept alive by two great illusions. The one, a complete belief on the part of the Soviet world that the capitalist countries are preparing to attack them. . . . And the other, a complete belief on the part of the capitalistic countries that the Soviets are preparing to attack us. . . . Both are wrong." For the first time since he had pushed the early liberal reforms in occupied Japan, MacArthur received strongly favorable reviews in liberal newspapers and periodicals. But a writer in the conservative *Christian Century* pointed out that MacArthur, like the drafters of the 1928 pact outlawing war, "failed to tell" his audience "how war can be ended."[35]

The general was called on to address all sorts of political, civic, and fraternal organizations, often in response to an award given to him by the group. For example, he extolled the "stern virtues" of Daniel Webster at the Whooper Dinner of 2000 people at Manchester, New Hampshire, in April 1954, following the governor's presentation to him of a scroll certifying him as an honorary citizen of the state. At its annual Football Hall of Fame dinner, held in New York in December 1959, the National Football Foundation, on whose advisory board MacArthur served, gave him its Gold Medal Award for his contributions to the sport, whereupon he spoke on the value of football, describing it as "a symbol of our country's best qualities — courage, stamina, coordinated efficiency . . . virility and enterprise."[36]

At the commencement exercises of Michigan State University in June 1961 he was awarded an honorary doctorate of laws, and he gave the commencement address, calling once again for the major powers on both sides in the Cold War to work more earnestly toward the abolition of war. In the search for this solution, he stressed, "we must go on or we will go under." At a Waldorf luncheon in April 1963 marking the start of a drive to endow a chair of history in MacArthur's name at Columbia, he spoke on the significance of the discipline of history. Over 125 distinguished leaders of business and academia attended the kick-off luncheon, and the original committee on the chair project was impressive: it was headed by Arnold A. Saltzman, president of the Seagrave Corporation, and included, besides Columbia administrators and faculty, such luminaries as Eisenhower (president of Columbia University from 1948 to 1953), Hoover, Hearst, Bernard M. Baruch, Governor Nelson A. Rockefeller of New York, Roger Blough of United States Steel, and David Sarnoff of the Radio Corporation of America. In spite of its auspicious beginning, however, the drive to obtain funds for the chair's endowment was not overly successful, and the professorship was never filled.[37]

For the first five years or so after his dismissal, MacArthur was repeatedly embroiled in controversies about the recent history he had helped to shape. Of course, as long as he lived controversy surrounded him and much of the writing about him after his death has been highly polemical, but after the mid-1950s he himself seemed to mellow somewhat in his reactions, though a Truman barb could still excite him quickly. In December 1951, *Cosmopolitan* published Charles Willoughby's fiery article denouncing much of the press coverage of the Korean War for allegedly revealing sensitive military data, unjustly criticizing the UNC forces, and even promoting friction between Truman and MacArthur. The article contained a foreword by MacArthur, who proclaimed Willoughby's essay "of the greatest importance," because it exposed "one of

the most scandalous propaganda efforts to pervert the truth in recent times." Two separate interviews with General Lowe, Truman's emissary with the Far East Command in 1950–1951, appeared in newspapers in January 1952, revealing that Lowe was
sympathetic with MacArthur's position and that he blamed the
President's top civilian and military advisers for misleading him
about the Far East chief. Neither MacArthur nor the President
commented publicly about the Lowe interviews, but they created
a stir in Congress, where they were brought up by the general's
defenders on the floor of both the Senate and House as further
evidence of the injustice of his recall. When Senator Harry Byrd
headed a Senate investigation into ammunition shortages in Korea and asked for MacArthur's opinion, the general responded
strongly in a letter in April 1953, criticizing the Pentagon's supply
program for the forces in Korea and flatly contradicting much of
Pace's testimony before Byrd's subcommittee. MacArthur's letter
was made public and provoked heated press reactions; for instance, *Time* called his letter a "valid analysis" of the logistical mess,
but the St. Louis *Post-Dispatch* claimed that his remarks were damaging to the current armistice negotiations. As related in the second volume of this work, MacArthur joined in the renewed Yalta
controversy in 1955, sharply criticizing those who had wanted the
Soviet Union's assistance against Japan in World War II. When
the Pentagon released a study that autumn showing that Mac-
Arthur also had urged Washington several times to try to get Stalin's forces into the war with Japan, some of the general's anti-
Communist followers were stunned, and he sputtered that at least
he was never consulted in advance about the Yalta deals.[38]

A dispute developed between the Department of the Army and
MacArthur in the wake of his return regarding the disposition of
the manuscripts and documents of several large historical projects
that were known to have been under way at his Tokyo GHQ from
1946 to 1951. Willoughby had been editor in chief (with Dr. Gordon W. Prange as one of his senior editors) of the so-called
MacArthur Histories, a four-volume account of Southwest Pacific
operations from 1941 to 1945, and of the occupation of Japan to
1948. According to Willoughby, the volumes were at "finalized page-
proof status" in his G-2 section when MacArthur was relieved in
April 1951. Willoughby had most sets of the galleys and page proofs

destroyed before he left Japan. But thirty-two cabinets of materials, relating to this project, to an extensive series of Japanese war monographs, and to an eighteen-volume history of intelligence in MacArthur's commands from 1941 to 1948, that Willoughby and his G-2 staff had prepared or edited, turned up at MacArthur's Church Street office in Manhattan. Under pressure from the Pentagon, MacArthur yielded the materials in 1953, and most were taken to the Army's Office of the Chief of Military History in Washington. (The intelligence project information went temporarily to Army intelligence's custody.) Willoughby argued in vain that all these items were the property of MacArthur, though the G-2 chief and his subordinates had expended a large amount of duty time in Tokyo and considerable government funds in their preparation, including the employment of Japanese artists, former Imperial Army and Navy officers, translators, and Tokyo printers. When the chief of military history endeavored to secure MacArthur's permission to publish the main four-volume set, he objected that they needed more checking and rewriting by him personally, but Willoughby later admitted that both he and MacArthur feared that the Army historians would drastically alter them. Apparently the matter of custody was not altogether clear, for the Army dropped the matter until after MacArthur's death; the MacArthur Histories were finally published by the government in 1966 under the title *Reports of General MacArthur*. The four volumes bore the same text and format as the original Willoughby version, except for the helpful additions of indices and a foreword by General Harold K. Johnson, the current Chief of Staff, who stated that the Department of the Army, having decreed no textual revisions, had to "disclaim any responsibility for their accuracy."[39]

As the historians of the armed services completed drafts of the first official volumes on the Korean conflict, portions or entire copies of the manuscripts, along with questions about certain unclear points, were sent for comment to key commanders in the particular operations and their planning, ranging from small-unit leaders to the theater commander. In his commentary on the draft of the Army's first volume on the Korean conflict, which covered operations of June to November 1950, MacArthur was brutal in his criticisms at many points, sweepingly contending that "it contains many errors of basic fact and numerous misjudgments of concepts and events" and "constitutes a damning indictment of the courage and reliability of our national security forces." Some of his suggestions were incorporated in the final work, but, for the most part, the Army's chief of military history allowed the author's composition to stand as it was after passing his office's reviewers.

Except for his correspondence with the Army's historical office, MacArthur had little connection with official Army activities, aside from his logistical dependence on the First Army headquarters at his Church Street office. Although, as a five-star general, he was still considered on active duty, the Department of the Army never called on him to perform any function whatsoever. And though he was officially assigned to the Office of the Chief of Staff, there was astonishingly little correspondence or contact between him and the generals who held the position of Chief of Staff from 1951 to 1964, including even Ridgway, who was Chief of Staff from 1953 to 1955.[40]

MacArthur's place in the history of the decade 1941 to 1951 was evaluated in a torrent of books and articles that appeared between his dismissal and his death, with old controversies renewed as many of the books were reviewed in newspapers and large-circulation magazines. Unofficial writings about the occupation of Japan and the Korean War varied greatly in assessing MacArthur's role. Between 1954 and 1962, eight official volumes on Korean operations by U.S. Army, Air Force, Navy, and Marine historians were published. The first scholarly monographs on the Truman-MacArthur controversy were published by Harvard and Oxford University presses in 1959 and 1960. Journalistic biographies of MacArthur, of which there were already a number before 1952, continued to appear. The overall trend of the better writings of the period 1952 to 1963, especially the official volumes and the initial academic studies, was to portray MacArthur's leadership qualities as declining by 1950–1951 and his recall by Truman as regrettable but necessary.[41]

This pattern and the failure of books by two of his key lieutenants to revise the developing interpretation of MacArthur's leadership that appeared likely to be labeled as standard was probably a factor in the general's decision late in life to write his memoirs.

In 1954, Willoughby and John Chamberlain, a journalist-friend, wrote *MacArthur, 1941–1951*, which was published by the Mc-Graw-Hill Book Company. MacArthur read and revised portions of the text as it was being prepared, and in his preface Willoughby quoted MacArthur as urging "full public acceptance" of the authoritativeness of the book. The *Saturday Evening Post* reportedly paid the authors $100,000 for serialization rights, but the magazine editors finally decided against publication. Generally, reviewers in popular periodicals and newspapers gave the book a mixed reception, but its reviews in the major scholarly historical journals were savage, especially about the portrayal of MacArthur as always being right. Two years later Alfred A. Knopf published Whitney's *MacArthur: His Rendezvous with History*, which was even more defensive about MacArthur. Whitney was said to have received a handsome sum from *Life* for the serialization of excerpts that it ran. Whitney used a lot of the same sources that Willoughby had, again provided by MacArthur; in fact, Willoughby later charged that Whitney had leaned too heavily on his work and materials. On the dust jacket of Whitney's book MacArthur was quoted as saying that the author had "full use of my personal records" and that the reader could be assured of "the historical accuracy" of the book. A former SCAP official who knew both Whitney and MacArthur well remarked that the work was valuable as "MacArthur's estimate of himself." Likewise, Hanson Baldwin, military editor of the *New York Times*, commented that, like Willoughby and Chamberlain's book, Whitney's also might have been more accurately entitled *MacArthur on MacArthur*. Reviews by academic historians were consistently negative.[42]

The publication of Truman's *Memoirs* in 1955–1956, in a *Life* serialization and in book form by Doubleday, was upsetting to MacArthur and his friends both because it overshadowed Whitney's publication of the same period in both sales and reviews and because the former President was exceedingly blunt in his comments about MacArthur, openly charging that he had been guilty of insubordination. MacArthur responded angrily in a long essay in the *Life* issue of February 13, 1956, which featured on the cover a picture of him and Truman at the Wake Island meeting and included Truman's account of their controversy as well as the general's. In private, MacArthur called Truman "a vulgar little clown";

Truman told a friend he expected MacArthur's "blowup" over his autobiography, because "when an egotist is punctured, a lot of noise and whistling always accompanies the escaping air." Before and after this episode the two men periodically made cutting remarks about each other. In December 1960, Truman commented on a national television program that MacArthur had wanted to use the atomic bomb against Communist China, whereupon the general replied heatedly in a press release that he had never advocated using atomic weapons and that he could have won in Korea with conventional arms if Truman had not restricted his forces.

Even after MacArthur's death the controversy between the two would continue in strange echoes. While the general's body was lying in state, Hearst and Scripps-Howard newspapers published the interviews he had given separately to correspondents Bob Considine and Jim Lucas in early 1954, containing his harsh remarks about Truman and the general's "betrayal" by "those fools in Washington." At the time MacArthur had stipulated that the interviews be withheld until after his death; the publishers took the condition literally and released them before his body was interred. In the autumn of 1964, Truman harshly criticized Mac-Arthur in a highly publicized television special, whose filming reportedly had been started earlier that year while the general lay desperately ill.[43] The Truman-MacArthur feud must be ranked as one of the most bitter in modern American annals. The person most disheartened about their sorry relationship was surely General Frank Lowe, who liked and admired both men, and sincerely, if naïvely, believed that they could have worked out their differences if not for the prejudices of some advisers to the President.

3. A Full Life to the End

Although not hostile, relations between MacArthur and President Eisenhower from 1953 to 1961 were not close. In June 1953, MacArthur attended a thirteen-guest dinner at the White House, and in March 1954 he was there for a presidential luncheon with nine Pentagon and congressional leaders. The luncheon was preceded by a three-hour private discussion between Ike and Mac-

Arthur, reportedly about Asian problems. MacArthur issued a press statement supporting Eisenhower's order in early 1953 withdrawing the Seventh Fleet from its former mission in the Formosa Strait, and later he backed the President's position in refraining from military intervention in the clashes between the Chinese Communists and Nationalists over the Quemoy and Matsu islands. Nevertheless, when a business executive inquired in 1959 whether Ike consulted him in decision-making on Asian policy, MacArthur replied tersely, "I have never been asked to participate." Before his journey to the Far East in June 1960, Eisenhower conferred with him by telephone about certain Asian leaders, and on landing in Manila the President's first public statement included greetings from MacArthur to the Filipinos. (He had intended to convey MacArthur's greetings to the Japanese, too, before that leg of his trip was cancelled.) Secretary of State Dulles' contacts with MacArthur were minimal from their meeting in December 1952 to May 1959, when Dulles died. Ironically, one of Dulles' closest advisers by 1954 was said to have been Douglas MacArthur II, a rising diplomat and future ambassador who was the son of the general's brother, Arthur, a Navy captain who died in 1923.[44]

On the other hand, Nixon visited MacArthur at the Waldorf Towers on a number of occasions, but later said, "I did not report them to the President, and in fact I cannot recall ever discussing MacArthur with Eisenhower. I always had the distinct impression that any mention of MacArthur would be unwelcome." In June 1960, Nixon notified the general that the Japanese government was awarding him the highest honor it could give to a foreigner who was not a head of state — the Grand Cordon of the Order of the Rising Sun with Paulownia Flowers — for his leadership in Japan's postwar reconstruction and for his promotion of friendly relations between America and Japan. MacArthur replied on June 21: "You have sent me a magnificent message. I have given it to the press to show my complete support of your candidacy for the Presidency. Your chances were never better."[45]

The number and variety of honors conferred on MacArthur during his last thirteen years were enormous. The following represents only a selection from many awards, some significant and others perhaps interesting but unimportant. During the period from 1951 to 1964 he received six honorary doctorates (giving him

a total of twenty-two) and honorary memberships in dozens of civic
and social organizations, as well as plaques, medals, and citations
from all sorts of societies in America and abroad. Among the things
that were named for him were twelve schools, a town on Leyte, a
bridge in St. Louis, six buildings, nine chapters or posts of various
organizations, four parks, an airport on Long Island, and eight
streets, besides five statues of him. The impressive array of American and foreign military decorations awarded to him before 1951
was increased by others bestowed later by many of the United Nations members whose forces had served under him.

Based on a poll of the forty-eight state governors, the Columbia
Broadcasting System awarded him a plaque as "the Man of 1951."
William H. (Alfalfa Bill) Murray, former Oklahoma governor, gave
him a plaque the next year, on behalf of his anti-Communist organization, for his "courageous and continuous fight against communism." Cardinal Spellman announced he was using $50,000 at
his disposal to set up a MacArthur Scholarship for Filipino college
students. The Boy Scouts of America gave him a Silver Buffalo,
its highest adult honor. In the Philippines in 1956 a stamp was
issued and a Leyte monument erected in honor of the general,
and the South Koreans put up a statue of MacArthur at Inchon
the following year. The Morgenstern Foundation's Soldier of
Freedom Award was presented to him in 1961, and the Military
Order of Foreign Wars of the United States established the
MacArthur Medal in 1962, to be given annually to the citizen
making the most "significant contributions to the community in a
non-military field." In 1963 the MacArthur Academy of Freedom,
a museum and historical studies center, was founded at Howard
Payne College in Brownwood, Texas, and in the meantime work
was under way on the MacArthur Memorial in Norfolk, Virginia.
The Department of the Army even got into the act in November
1958, when it produced "The MacArthur Story" for its popular
series "The Big Picture," which went to over 330 television stations and was shown in many motion picture theaters.[46]

Two of the most significant tributes were actions taken by Congress during the last half of 1962. On August 16, following an
hour's chat with President Kennedy, MacArthur was driven to the
Capitol steps, where Vice President Lyndon B. Johnson and House
Speaker John W. McCormack spoke in high praise of his military

record. McCormack then presented him with an engrossed copy of a resolution passed unanimously by both houses of Congress that expressed "the thanks and appreciation of the Congress and the American people" to him for "his outstanding devotion to the American people, his brilliant leadership during and following World War II," and his efforts "to strengthen the ties of friendship" between the Philippines and the United States. (Oddly, the citation omitted his contribution to American-Japanese relations.) In his first appearance on Capitol Hill since April 1951, MacArthur spoke briefly, thanking the congressmen and observing that their tribute to his services "does me too much honor. . . . A general is just as good or just as bad as the troops under his command make him. Mine were great." On October 9, Congress approved a joint resolution authorizing the issuance of a special gold medal to MacArthur in recognition of his "gallant service" to the nation. The resolution stipulated that gold-plated and bronze replicas of the medal also were to be produced by the federal mint and sold through the MacArthur Memorial Foundation, which was chartered that month in Virginia.

During the years 1955 to 1964, partly because of Pentagon opposition on the grounds that such action would be demeaning to other five-star officers, attempts were unsuccessful by various senators and representatives to secure passage of legislation in Congress authorizing the President to appoint MacArthur to the six-star rank of General of the Armies, a grade held only by John J. Pershing. In 1955 Joe Martin was the sponsor of one such bill, and by 1963–1964 a leader in the continuing effort was Senator Stuart Symington, a Missouri Democrat whose action was not exactly pleasing to the former President residing at Independence. In January 1964, Truman allegedly remarked that "if he had anything to do with it, he would demote General MacArthur from five to four stars."[47]

Actions honoring MacArthur were easier to carry off in Norfolk than in Congress, because that city's mayor, W. Fred Duckworth, a hard-driving conservative with strong political power in Tidewater Virginia, was bent on developing a shrine to the general. As early as 1951, Duckworth and some other prominent Norfolk citizens began talking and planning for a MacArthur Square in the heart of the business district. When the general came to the city that November to dedicate a memorial park on the site of Riveredge, his mother's antebellum family home, the Norfolk City Council made him the first honorary citizen in the city's history. In December 1960, MacArthur agreed to give his personal memorabilia and papers to the MacArthur Memorial, a future complex of buildings in downtown Norfolk that at first consisted of the city-renovated courthouse, built in 1850 as a city hall. Mayor Duckworth and Councilman Roy B. Martin, Jr., were instrumental in the negotiations and the establishment of the MacArthur Memorial, which was to be operated under the auspices of the municipal government and the MacArthur Memorial Foundation. It was agreed that MacArthur and his wife would be buried in marble crypts in the rotunda of the old courthouse, which was to be the museum.

The MacArthur Memorial museum was opened to the public in January 1964. The general's papers were stored in the municipal library across the street until an archival building was ready in 1967. The memorial proved to be unique, ironic, and significant: unique as the nation's only municipal museum-archives-mausoleum combination; ironic as the principal MacArthur shrine in a city best known as a Navy town, the Atlantic Fleet headquarters and a number of naval and naval air facilities and shipyards being located there and in the immediate area; and significant to the city as a major tourist attraction (400,000 people visited the museum the first year) and to scholars as the repository of the bulk of MacArthur's considerable records (about 400 linear feet at the beginning, with many accessions later), which are valuable on the history of East and Southeast Asia and on the evolution of the modern American Army. The memorial's main drawbacks were the excessive glorification of the general in the museum exhibits and the absence in the archival records of many items reflecting negatively on him, an omission resulting from the strong influence of Duckworth and Whitney. Later memorial and foundation leaders became more interested in gaining the respect of scholars who viewed the general with less adulation than those two men.[48]

Interestingly, at the time the preparations for the memorial were under way, MacArthur's papers were still growing, because he was amazingly active for a man in his early eighties. The general demonstrated that he could attract record crowds when he visited the

Philippines, on July 3–12, 1961. President Carlos P. García invited him to participate in his republic's celebration of the fifteenth anniversary of Philippine independence. President Kennedy, displaying an interest in MacArthur not seen in the White House for some time, provided the general with a Boeing 707 jet of the Military Air Transport Service for the trip and told him that he would eagerly await his personal report on the Philippines when he returned. En route to and from Manila, the jet stopped briefly at the U.S. Air Force base at Misawa, in northern Honshu, but probably because of the short time it was on the ground, MacArthur did not meet with any Japanese leaders.

MacArthur, Jean, Ambassador Carlos P. Romulo, his wife, and Whitney landed at the Manila International Airport at 4:30 P.M., July 3, where they were greeted by President García, other high-ranking Philippine officials, and a huge crowd. Because of the throngs of Filipinos along the way, it took two hours for the motorcade to travel the five miles from the airport to Malacañan Palace, now the presidential residence, where the MacArthurs and Whitney were guests for the next few days. The following morning MacArthur delivered the main address of the national independence program at Luneta Park in Manila, which was attended by over 1 million people — the largest gathering in Philippine history.

On July 5, the general addressed a joint session of the Philippine Senate and House in the Congress Building. The next day he went with President García and other dignitaries on the presidential train to Lingayen, north of Manila, to dedicate the new MacArthur Highway; he also visited some battle sites of 1941 and 1945 in the Central Luzon Plain and attracted large crowds at every town and village.

On July 7 the MacArthurs and Whitney journeyed by ship to Leyte, where the following day MacArthur dedicated the Leyte Veterans Memorial Building and toured Red Beach, the site of his return to the islands in 1944. They visited Cebu and Panay on July 9–10, where MacArthur participated in ceremonies at military cemeteries, spoke at public rallies, visited old battle sites, and dined with local officials. On July 11, they returned by sea to Manila, passing slowly by Corregidor at the bay entrance — the MacArthurs' "home" during the intense bombardments of early 1942.

The next morning the tired old general, who, according to one report, had "faltered occasionally" during the busy ten-day tour of the islands, boarded the Boeing 707 with his wife, Whitney, and the Romulos to return to the United States.[49]

Another journey laden with memories and deep sentiments was MacArthur's final trip to the U.S. Military Academy, which he and his wife made on May 12, 1962, for the presentation to him of the school's coveted Sylvanus Thayer Award. Wearing a dark business suit and a black homburg, he was driven in a jeep on an inspection of the 2200-cadet corps; then he watched the cadets sharply parade by in a review in his honor on the Plain at West Point. Among others with him were Major General William C. Westmoreland, the academy superintendent and a fervent admirer of MacArthur's, and General Groves, who had retired from Sperry Rand the previous year and was now president of the school's Association of Graduates. Following the inspection and review, which took about forty minutes, they had lunch with the cadets in Washington Hall, after which Westmoreland made some introductory remarks and Groves presented the Thayer Award to MacArthur. It was given annually by the academy alumni society to a distinguished American leader whose service to the nation was characterized by outstanding devotion to the ideals expressed in the academy's motto, "Duty, Honor, Country." Speaking in a low, deliberate, and sincere voice, MacArthur then proceeded to outdo his performance before Congress eleven years earlier in inspiring and moving his audience. By the end of his address, says one account, "there were tears in the eyes of big strapping Cadets who wouldn't have shed one before a firing squad."[50] The following excerpts, like those from his speech to Congress, provide some of the substance of his remarks but, unfortunately, suggest little of the highly emotional atmosphere of the occasion, which none of the listeners was likely to forget:

> No human being could fail to be deeply moved by such a tribute as this. . . . But this award is not intended primarily to honor a personality, but to symbolize a great moral code — the code of conduct and chivalry of those who guard this beloved land. . . .
>
> Duty, honor, country: Those three hallowed words reverently dictate what you ought to be, what you can be, what you will be. They

are your rallying point to build courage when courage seems to fail, to regain faith when there seems to be little cause for faith, to create hope when hope seems forlorn. . . .

. . . They build your basic character. They mold you for your future roles as the custodians of the Nation's defense. They make you strong enough to know when you are weak, and brave enough to face yourself when you are afraid. . . .

They give you a temper of will, a quality of the imagination, a vigor of the emotions, a freshness of the deep springs of life, a temperamental predominance of courage over timidity, of an appetite for adventure over love of ease.

They create in your heart the sense of wonder, the unfailing hope of what next, and the joy and inspiration of life. They teach you in this way to be an officer and a gentleman.

And what sort of soldiers are those you are to lead? . . . Their story is known to all of you. It is the story of the American man-at-arms. . . .

In twenty campaigns, on a hundred battlefields, around a thousand campfires, I have witnessed that enduring fortitude, that patriotic self-abnegation, and that invincible determination which have carved his statue in the hearts of his people. . . .

You now face a new world, a world of change. The thrust into outer space of the satellite spheres and missiles marks a beginning of another epoch in the long story of mankind. . . .

. . . We are reaching out for a new and boundless frontier. We speak in strange terms of harnessing the cosmic energy, of making winds and tides work for us . . . [and] of such dreams and fantasies as to make life [now] the most exciting of all times.

And through all this welter of change and development your mission remains fixed, determined, inviolable. It is to win our wars. Everything else in your professional career is but corollary to this vital decision. . . .

Yours is the profession of arms, the will to win, the sure knowledge that in war there is no substitute for victory; that if you lose, the Nation will be destroyed; that the very obsession of your public service must be duty, honor, country.

Others will debate the controversial issues, national and international, which divide men's minds. But serene, calm, aloof, you stand as the Nation's war guardian, as its lifeguard from the raging tides of international conflict, as its gladiator in the arena of battle. . . .

Let civilian voices argue the merits or demerits of our processes of government: Whether our strength is being sapped by deficit financ-

ing . . . by Federal paternalism . . . by power groups . . . by politics . . . by morals grown too low, by taxes grown too high, by extre-
mists grown too violent. . . .

These great national problems are not for your professional participation or military solution. Your guidepost stands out like a ten-
fold beacon in the night: Duty, honor, country.

. . . From your ranks come the great captains who hold the Nation's destiny in their hands the moment the war tocsin sounds.

The long gray line has never failed us. Were you to do so, a million ghosts in olive drab, in brown khaki, in blue and gray, would rise
from their white crosses, thundering those magic words: Duty, honor,
country.

This does not mean you are warmongers. On the contrary, the soldier above all other people prays for peace, for he must suffer and
bear the deepest wounds and scars of war. But always in our ears
ring the ominous words of Plato, that wisest of all philosophers: "Only
the dead have seen the end of war."

The shadows are lengthening for me. The twilight is here. My days
of old have vanished — tone and tint. They have gone glimmering
through the dreams of things that were. Their memory is one of
wondrous beauty, watered by tears and coaxed and caressed by the
smiles of yesterday. I listen vainly, but with thirsty ear, for the witch-
ing melody of faint bugles blowing reveille, of far drums beating the
long roll.

In my dreams I hear again the crash of guns, the rattle of musketry, the strange, mournful mutter of the battlefield. But in the evening of my memory I come back to West Point. Always there echoes
and re-echoes: Duty, honor, country.

Today marks my final rollcall with you. But I want you to know
that when I cross the river, my last conscious thoughts will be of the
corps, and the corps, and the corps.

I bid you farewell.[51]

Admirers regarded this speech as one of the general's finest; his
detractors dismissed it as unadulterated bathos. Its entry into the
Congressional Record came about in an ironic manner. During his
Senate remarks in July 1963 relating to a floor discussion about
the participation of military personnel in civil rights demonstrations, Mississippi's Senator Stennis, who was on the Armed Services Committee, requested that "this great speech be printed in
the record," because "it will surely go down in history as one of
the best, clearest and truest expositions of the proper role of the

military man in non-military matters."[52] If Truman heard about this, he must have chuckled a long time. Like a cut-glass chandelier prism that refracts sunlight into fascinating multicolored patterns on walls, MacArthur's nature was so complex that people of quite different styles and beliefs could be attracted to or repelled by him. For instance, though Vice President Nixon respected and liked him and later nominated him as one of the great leaders of the century, President Kennedy deeply admired him, too, and solicited his counsel. Kenneth P. O'Donnell, among the most powerful members of Kennedy's White House staff, described the President's impressions of MacArthur in 1961 after their first two meetings:

> President Kennedy first began to have doubts about our military effort in Vietnam in 1961 when both General Douglas MacArthur and General Charles de Gaulle warned him that the Asian mainland was no place to be fighting a non-nuclear land war. There was no end to Asiatic manpower, MacArthur told the President, and even if we poured a million American infantry soldiers into that continent, we would still find ourselves outnumbered on every side.
>
> The President's first meeting with MacArthur [on April 27], a courtesy call on the general in New York after the Bay of Pigs disaster [of April 17–19], turned out to be an agreeable surprise to Kennedy. Like a lot of Navy veterans of the Pacific war, Kennedy had assumed that MacArthur was a stuffy and pompous egocentric. Instead, the President told us later, MacArthur was one of the most fascinating conversationalists he had ever met, politically shrewd and intellectually sharp. Later the President invited the general to the White House for lunch. They talked for almost three hours, ruining the whole appointments schedule for that day [July 20]. I could not drag them apart. The President later gave us a complete rerun of MacArthur's remarks, expressing a warm admiration for this supposedly reactionary old soldier that astonished all of us. MacArthur was extremely critical of the military advice that the President had been getting from the Pentagon, blaming the military leaders of the previous 10 years, who, he said, had advanced the wrong young officers. "You were lucky to have that mistake happen in Cuba where the strategic cost was not too great," he said about the Bay of Pigs. MacArthur implored the President to avoid a U.S. military build-up in Vietnam, or any other part of the Asian mainland, because he felt that the domino theory was ridiculous in a nuclear age. MacArthur went on to point out that there were domestic problems — the urban

crisis, the ghettos, the economy — that should have far more priority than Vietnam. Kennedy came out of the meeting somewhat stunned. That a man like MacArthur should give him such unmilitary advice impressed him enormously.[53]

The only official assignment from Washington that MacArthur received after April 1951 came from President Kennedy, when he appointed the general to arbitrate a bitter "power struggle" between the American Athletic Union (AAU) and the National Collegiate Athletic Association (NCAA) that was threatening the eligibility and training of hundreds of American athletes for the Olympic Games of 1964. Attorney General Robert F. Kennedy asked Red Blaik in December 1962 to recommend someone who could settle the feud, which mainly involved jurisdiction over athletes and meets in track and field. Coach Blaik suggested MacArthur, which both the Attorney General and the President thought was "a splendid suggestion." The President then telephoned MacArthur, who happily agreed to undertake the mission and persuaded Blaik to serve as his key adviser and Whitney as his assistant. Neither the AAU nor the U.S. Track and Field Federation, the latter being the NCAA-sponsored agency in that sport, was enthusiastic about arbitration by a White House appointee, but their leaders finally agreed under pressure from the President.

MacArthur conducted the negotiations in the drawing room of his Waldorf suite, with the officials and attorneys of the two sides battling through several long sessions without making much progress. Finally the general, after letting them try to settle their differences without much interference from him, presented them with a judicious four-point proposal that he and Blaik had developed. Showing his leadership traits of old, MacArthur brought the two sides together in an agreement on January 19, 1963, accepting the settlement, nicknamed the "MacArthur Plan," for at least the period through the Olympics of 1964. The main representatives of both the NCAA and the AAU said afterward that "the agreement was fair to all concerned." One official commented, "It came out like a tie game . . . and the meeting ended with everybody in complete harmony." The next day the two organizations began lifting all suspensions and blacklistings of each other's athletes and meets. The plan provided for future differences before the Olympics to be settled by a "MacArthur Board" of three representatives from each side, the general acting as the final arbiter in case of deadlocks. The Washington *Post,* which had often been critical of MacArthur in the past, praised him "for a good job, done with customary thoroughness and decisiveness." On several occasions that spring and summer he had to arbitrate minor disputes that arose between the two bodies, but generally the MacArthur Plan worked well. Most sports authorities credited MacArthur with having made possible American track and field participation in the Olympics, held in Tokyo in the summer of 1964. President Kennedy proudly remarked that MacArthur's "mediating the dispute so effectively and successfully" was vital in assuring "the highest caliber of American amateur athletic participation both at home and abroad."

The mutual admiration of the old warrior and the young President was deepening into a warm friendship when Kennedy's assassination occurred, in November 1963. MacArthur, on hearing the news, sent the following telegram to his widow: "I realize the utter futility of words at such a time, but the world of civilization shares the poignancy of this monumental tragedy. As a former comrade in arms, his death kills something within me."[54]

As Lyndon Johnson, who also esteemed MacArthur, moved into the Oval Office, the general was busy revising the manuscript of his autobiography. From late 1945 onward, there was repeated speculation in the press as to whether MacArthur would write his memoirs. When asked about it, he or his public relations officers gave the stock response that he was too busy with official duties to undertake such a project. Over the years several publishers had approached him with lucrative offers for his memoirs, but he replied, as he had done to Simon and Schuster in August 1952, that he hoped to "start some writing of my own" someday, but for the present "there is nothing to discuss." As related earlier, however, he was willing to give time to Willoughby and Whitney while they prepared their books, and he claimed to have plans to revise personally the MacArthur Histories that Willoughby and his G-2 staff had written.

Suddenly in the late spring of 1963, Whitney presented Henry R. Luce, editor in chief of Time, Inc., with a 220,000-word manuscript entitled tentatively *MacArthur Reminiscences,* which the general had asked him to deliver. It was unmistakably handwritten by MacArthur, filling hundreds of pages of yellow legal pads and remarkably clean, that is, with very few deletions or changes. At the end of the manuscript was this statement, again in longhand: "This manuscript was commenced about the middle of October, 1962, and completed early in April, 1963. Douglas MacArthur." Both Whitney and Blaik said they were unaware for a long while that he had been working on it, though it is difficult to believe this of Whitney, not only because of his extreme closeness to the general but also because textual analysis indicates strongly that Whitney had more than a negligible part. Of course, his role could have been played during the revision. Acting without a literary agent, MacArthur negotiated the terms of publication directly with Luce, and in mid-August 1963 they signed the contract. Luce, representing Time, Inc., agreed to give him "a sum of $900,000, payable upon the publication of the Work in book form, provided that no payment shall be due and payable before January 20, 1965." Time, Inc., according to the contract, agreed to publish "extracts of the Work" in *Life* within twelve months and "to publish or authorize others to publish the Work in book form" within six months after the completion of the *Life* serialization.

The magazine series appeared in seven installments, the first three in January 1964 and the rest in July. One source indicates that MacArthur was working on revisions for *Life* when he suffered his final illness, which could explain the six-month gap in the *Life* serialization. *Reminiscences* was published by McGraw-Hill in September 1964, with the copyright held by Time, Inc., and with the preface by MacArthur dated March 1964. Pages 408 to 418 of the book were added between the time the galleys appeared, in July, and the publication date, two months later. There are a number of textual differences between the magazine and book versions, mainly matters of syntax but some factual alterations. The *Life* editor who worked on the manuscript was not impressed by McGraw-Hill's concern for historicity in its edition, but he found MacArthur "always amenable to changes in the interest of accuracy." The book was a best seller for a time and, like the *Life* series, revived old controversies in the press and raised new ones among scholars, many of whom still question whether all or parts of the manuscript were actually composed by Whitney and then transcribed in longhand by MacArthur. Such basic errors as "Guadalcanal on Bougainville," they believed, MacArthur would have caught, though not necessarily Whitney, an attorney by profession who did not join the Southwest Pacific headquarters until 1943.

Many of the early journalistic reviews of the book were more descriptive than analytical, and those written by professional historians were generally very critical, emphasizing the many historical inaccuracies, the self-glorification, and the similarities to the works of Willoughby and Whitney. John Chamberlain quipped, "MacArthur is probably the only ghost who ever ghosted for some unadmitted ghosts." A noted historian wrote, "This is a sad book. . . . Hard as he may try, even General MacArthur cannot destroy his own place in history." Even Blaik admitted that the general's memoirs do "not give the true measure of the man, as it might have done had he written [the book] sooner, perhaps in the 50's, when he was closer to events."[55] Louis Morton, long regarded as the dean of historians of the Pacific war, wrote perhaps the best evaluation in a *Harper's* review entitled "Egotist in Uniform." He closed with these observations:

> All his life MacArthur was the center of controversy. . . . The *Reminiscences*, far from stilling the controversies, will only add fresh fuel to the fire. Those who admired and revered him during his lifetime will find in it evidence to support the charges he made and the policies he advocated. Others will find in it confirmation of their worst fears. He was always his worst enemy, and his autobiography will add nothing to his reputation. He should be remembered by his deeds, not his words.[56]

Certainly part of the explanation for the disappointing quality of his autobiography was MacArthur's declining health. In January 1960, for the first time in his life, he became seriously ill. His extreme self-confidence and his deep-set aversion to physicians (except as friends) compelled his wife and Whitney finally to request Lieutenant General Leonard D. Heaton, the surgeon general of the Army, to try to persuade him to get medical treatment. Heaton made a flying trip from Washington and succeeded in talking him into entering Lenox Hill Hospital in New York City for urological tests. He was admitted on January 29, three days after his eightieth birthday, but it took a long while to cure his kidney infection and to get his generally poor condition improved enough for the prostate surgery that was deemed necessary. On March 19, Dr. George W. Slaughter removed a large nonmalignant tumor from his prostate; his recuperation was slow but probably normal for a person of his age. During his hospital stay he received an enormous number of get-well messages, though visitors had to be restricted mainly to close friends like Whitney, Bunker, Blaik, and Hoover. Lieutenant General Blackshear M. Bryan, the First Army commander who had led a division under MacArthur in the Korean action, brought him what was undoubtedly his favorite gift — a West Point bathrobe with a varsity "A" on it. As long as anyone could remember, he had prized such robes and would order or be given a new one as the old wore out. Allowed to return to his Waldorf apartment on April 3, MacArthur said the illness "left me gaunt and haggard" and feeling like "a modern Lazarus," so serious had been his condition for a time.[57]

During the last year of his life the general continued to serve as board chairman of Sperry Rand, successfully completed his mission as the President's special arbiter in the AAU–NCAA dispute, and finished his memoirs — an extraordinary record for an octogenarian, particularly one who was desperately ill by then. Surgeon General Heaton, who had not examined MacArthur since early 1960, was suddenly asked by Whitney in late February 1964 to come to New York and again persuade the general to get medical attention. When Heaton checked him at the Waldorf suite on the 28th, he was shocked by MacArthur's "horrible" physical condition. MacArthur was "extremely jaundiced" and "really was suffering." Later Heaton determined that his serious decline had probably begun some time in 1962, but MacArthur, while residing in the midst of some of the nation's finest medical facilities, had steadfastly refused to permit a physician to be summoned, much less visit one. The surgeon general remarked sadly, "General MacArthur was a victim of medical [self] neglect. . . . It's just unfortunate that a man of his greatness, his knowledge and capacities . . . could be so utterly obsessed and convinced that he should not seek any medical care whatsoever." MacArthur had postponed Heaton's visit until he finished the last revisions of his memoirs; the final dated entry was a moving letter from Yoshida, written on February 20, inviting him to return to Japan and "see with your own eyes how firmly your epochal reforms have taken root."

Heaton wanted him to be flown immediately to Washington for treatment at the Walter Reed Army Medical Center, but he said MacArthur protested that "he was not going to come to Washington, D.C., at the outset because of the way he had been treated by President Truman." The surgeon general finally convinced him that "Truman has got nothing to do with this" and "we are going to see that you get the best." Accompanied by his wife and Whitney, MacArthur traveled to Washington on March 2 aboard an Air Force plane, as arranged on orders from President Johnson. At Walter Reed, he was given a five-room executive suite, and both Jean and Whitney stayed with him during the next four weeks of crises. Arthur joined them the last two weeks.

On March 6, Heaton, assisted by Major General Thomas Whalen, another top Army surgeon, removed his gall bladder. After the surgery MacArthur rallied valiantly and for a while was able to receive some visitors. One of them was President Johnson, who wore the Silver Star ribbon for the award the general had bestowed on him in World War II. MacArthur was sufficiently alert to counsel LBJ, as he had advised Kennedy, that American ground forces should not be committed in Vietnam nor elsewhere on the Asian mainland. Subsequently, after suffering from severe gastrointestinal hemorrhaging, MacArthur underwent emergency surgery on March 23 for the removal of his spleen. But as his recuperation began, he developed other complications, including a serious lung inflammation. Heaton, who attended Dulles in 1959 and Eisenhower in 1969 during their final illnesses, observed that dying persons often "are completely unmasked and they show their true personality and their true characteristics." MacArthur, he said, "showed even more greatness to me during that period of time than . . . either in an official or unofficial capacity" earlier. He was "very warm, understanding, compassionate, and just profoundly grateful for any and all, however little, things that you did for him."

MacArthur was subjected to his third major operation in three weeks on March 29, this time for the removal of a portion of his intestines. On April 3, the general sank into a coma, and at 2:39 P.M., April 5, 1964, he died at Walter Reed. An hour later President Johnson, who had kept closely informed of his condition throughout his hospitalization, ordered the United States flag at the White House lowered to half-mast and issued a statement announcing that "one of the most distinguished soldiers in the history of the United States" had died and would be accorded a state funeral — "buried with all the honors a grateful nation can bestow upon a departed hero."[58]

Defense Department officials, while preparing a new plan for state funerals, had consulted MacArthur in late 1963 about his wishes. For the most part, the general was agreeable to the Pentagon plan, though he made some changes for his funeral: the Defense plan provided for four days of lying in state at the Capitol rotunda and for burial in Arlington National Cemetery, but MacArthur stipulated seven days, with additional lying-in-state periods in New York and Norfolk, and interment in the rotunda of the MacArthur Memorial museum in Norfolk. Also at his request, his body was dressed in one of his old tropical worsted uniforms bearing only the U.S. and five-star insignias. Usually at military funerals the coffin was closed, but it was Whitney's decision, according to an official source, that it be kept open during the lying in state.

As the cortège prepared to leave Walter Reed Hospital late on the afternoon of April 5 for the drive to New York, Mrs. MacArthur and Arthur had just entered the limousine behind the hearse when Mrs. MacArthur suddenly asked Heaton to have someone in the crowd of hospital staff members come to her. It was Lieutenant Bonnie Ritter, the young nurse who had spent long hours in the recovery room during the final efforts to save the general's life and who had become a special friend to Mrs. MacArthur during the preceding weeks. The widow and the nurse exchanged a few words and kissed each other. Then the motorcade departed for New York, where, shortly before midnight, the hearse took the flag-draped casket to the Universal Funeral Parlor. On April 7, MacArthur's body was moved to the 7th Regiment Armory, where, after a private interfaith memorial service, the public was admitted. It was estimated that they came by the coffin at a rate of 3000 an hour until the building was closed, at 11:00 P.M. The next day an elaborate procession marked the movement of the body from the armory to Pennsylvania Station in Manhattan; it involved a horse-drawn caisson, a caparisoned horse, the West Point band, flag-bearing regular troops and veterans' groups, and sidewalk crowds that were huge despite steady rain.

En route to Washington, the funeral train stopped in New Jersey, where the governors of that state and Delaware, together with some other dignitaries, paid their respects briefly; on the outskirts of the national capital President Johnson and Attorney General Kennedy boarded the train for the trip to Union Station. About 100,000 people turned out for the funeral procession to the Capitol rotunda, though the rain was heavy at times. By midnight that day, April 8, about 20,000 people had passed the body laying in state at the Capitol. The rain continued to fall but seemed to deter no one who wanted to pay his respects. The following day President Johnson accompanied the procession to National Airport, whence the body was flown by military transport to Norfolk. Another impressive cortège, replete with caisson, riderless horse, and other state-funeral features, made its way slowly from the Norfolk airport to the MacArthur Memorial downtown; approximately 150,000 people stood along the route. The body lay in state in the memorial rotunda from 6:00 P.M., April 9, until 7:00 A.M. on the 11th, and over 60,000 came to pay their respects. The funeral service was held at three-centuries-old St. Paul's Episcopal Church on the morning of April 11, followed by a brief burial ceremony in the MacArthur Memorial rotunda. To the day, it was the thirteenth anniversary of the general's dismissal by Truman. Those attending the funeral included not only a host of the general's old service friends but also a large number of high-ranking civilian and military officials of the current American government, as well as of many foreign governments. Truman and Eisenhower were not among the mourners at the funeral.

The person whom MacArthur probably would have been most pleased to know was there, aside, of course, from his family and close Army friends, was one who had traveled halfway around the world for the occasion: Yoshida, who had boarded a plane for the United States shortly after receiving the news of the general's passing. There had been many indications in the general's remarks as he grew older that he remembered as his finest hours those spent helping to build a new Japan. In an address of late 1951, when referring to that occupation which was unique and significant for both Japan and America, MacArthur had rendered his own best epitaph: "Could I have but a line a century hence crediting a contribution to the advance of peace, I would gladly yield every honor which has been accorded by war."[59]

APPENDIX

ABBREVIATIONS

BIBLIOGRAPHICAL NOTE

NOTES

INDEX

Appendix

Men Who Had the Most Contact
With MacArthur, 1945–1951

The following people mentioned in General of the Army Douglas MacArthur's Office Diary (in the MacArthur Memorial Bureau of Archives) met with him individually or in a group sixteen or more times, September 3, 1945–April 9, 1951. This list was compiled by Mrs. Judy R. Hotard.

Person	*Service*	*Meetings with DM*
Mr. William J. Sebald	U.S. Govt.	138
Sir Alvary D. Gascoigne	U.K. Govt.	128
Prime Min. Shigeru Yoshida	Jap. Govt.	75
Maj. Gen. William F. Marquat	U.S. Army	72
Lt. Gen. H. C. Horace Robertson	Aus. Army	67
Lt. Gen. Ennis P. Whitehead	U.S. Air Force	64
Lt. Gen. Charles Gairdner	U.K. Army	55
Maj. Gen. Charles A. Willoughby	U.S. Army	51
Adm. C. Turner Joy	U.S. Navy	44
Mr. George Atcheson, Jr.	U.S. Govt.	42
Maj. Gen. Edward M. Almond	U.S. Army	40
Gen. George E. Stratemeyer	U.S. Air Force	38
Lt. Gen. Chu Shih-ming	Chin. Army	36
Maj. O. L. Gentry	U.S. Army	35
Maj. Gen. Paul J. Mueller	U.S. Army	32
Mr. Joseph B. Keenan	U.S. Govt.	31
Rear Adm. Russell S. Berkey	U.S. Navy	29
Lt. Col. Charles J. Blake	U.S. Army	29

Vice Adm. Robert M. Griffin	U.S. Navy	29
Mr. E. Herbert Norman	Can. Govt.	29
Lt. Gen. Zinovi Pechkoff	French Army	29
Col. Sidney L. Huff	U.S. Army	28
Lt. Gen. Robert L. Eichelberger	U.S. Army	27
Lt. Gen. Walton H. Walker	U.S. Army	27
Maj. Gen. Alonzo P. Fox	U.S. Army	25
Maj. Gen. Courtney Whitney	U.S. Army	25
Lt. Gen. Wybrandus Schilling	Neth. Army	24
Maj. Gen. Doyle O. Hickey	U.S. Army	21
Brig. Gen. Frayne Baker	U.S. Army	20
Maj. Gen. William A. Beiderlinden	U.S. Army	18
Mr. Lon H. Moss	U.S. Govt.	18
Mr. Miles Vaughn	U.S. (United Press)	18
Mr. Russell Brines	U.S. (Associated Press)	17
Mr. Patrick Shaw	Aus. Govt.	16
Brig. Gen. Edward H. White	U.S. Air Force	16

Abbreviations

DFC Distinguished Flying Cross
DM General of the Army Douglas MacArthur
DMBP Douglas MacArthur Biographical Papers, Mississippi State University, Mississippi State, MS
DM Misc. 201 Miscellaneous 201 file of Douglas MacArthur, Center of Military History or MacArthur Memorial, as indicated
DS Department of State
ECA Economic Cooperation Administration
EROA Economic Rehabilitation of Occupied Areas
ESS Economic and Scientific Section
FDR President Franklin D. Roosevelt
FEAC Far Eastern Advisory Commission
FEAF Far East Air Forces
FEC Far Eastern Commission
FECOM Far East Command
FRUS *Foreign Relations of the United States*
GARIOA Government and Relief in Occupied Areas
G-1 Personnel and administration section (or chief)
G-2 Intelligence section (or chief)
G-3 Operations and training section (or chief)
G-4 Supply section (or chief)
G-5 Military government and civil affairs section (or chief)
GHQ General headquarters
HCLC Holding Company Liquidation Commission
HNAOJ *History of the Non-Military Activities of the Occupation of Japan*
HSTL Harry S. Truman Library, Independence, MO
IMTFE International Military Tribunal for the Far East
Int(s). Interview(s)
JAG Judge Advocate General
JAS Joint Administrative Services
JCS Joint Chiefs of Staff
JFK President John F. Kennedy
JFL Japan General Federation of Trade Unions
JIC Joint Intelligence Committee
JSPOG Joint Strategic Plans and Operations Group
JUSMAGPHIL Joint United States Military Advisory Group to the Republic of the Philippines
KATUSA Koreans Attached to the United States Army
KMAG United States Military Advisory Group to the Republic of Korea
LARA Licensed Agencies for Relief in Asia
LBJ President Lyndon B. Johnson
LC Library of Congress, Manuscript Division, Washington, DC

LST	Landing ship, tank
Mrs. DM	Mrs. Douglas MacArthur
MARBO	Marianas-Bonins Command
MDAP	Mutual Defense Assistance Program
MMBA	MacArthur Memorial Bureau of Archives, Norfolk, VA
MSFE	*Military Situation in the Far East* (published "MacArthur Hearings")
"MSFE-TD"	"Military Situation in the Far East: Transcript Deletions" (unpublished "MacArthur Hearings")
MSU	Special Collections Department, Mitchell Memorial Library, Mississippi State University
NA	National Archives, Washington, DC
NATO	North Atlantic Treaty Organization
NAVFE	United States Naval Forces in the Far East
NAVJAP	United States Naval Forces in Japan
NAVMARIANAS	United States Naval Forces in the Marianas
NAVPHIL	United States Naval Forces in the Philippines
NCAA	National Collegiate Athletic Association
NSC	National Security Council
OSDIRR	*Office of Strategic Services–State Department Intelligence and Research Reports*
PACUSA	Pacific Air Command, United States Army
PHILRYCOM	Philippines-Ryukyus Command
POL	Petroleum, oil, and lubricants
PPS	Policy Planning Staff
PSF	President's secretary's file
RCT	Regimental combat team
RG	Record group
ROK	Republic of Korea
RYCOM	Ryukyus Command
SAC	Strategic Air Command
SANACC	State-Army-Navy-Air Force Coordinating Committee
SCAJAP	United States Naval Shipping Control Authority for the Japanese Merchant Marine
SCAP	Supreme Commander for the Allied Powers, Japan
SCAPIN	Instructions of the Supreme Commander for the Allied Powers to the Japanese Government
SNAJK	*Summation of Non-Military Activities in Japan and Korea*
SWNCC	State-War-Navy Coordinating Committee
T/O	Table of organization
TAG	The Adjutant General of the United States Army
UNC	United Nations Command
UNCURK	United Nations Commission for the Unification and Rehabilitation of Korea

USACGSC United States Army Command and General Staff College, Fort Leavenworth, KS
USAF United States Air Force
USAFFE United States Army Forces in the Far East
USAFPAC (AFPAC) United States Army Forces in the Pacific
USAFIK United States Army Forces in Korea
USAMGIK United States Army Military Government in Korea
USAMHI United States Army Military History Institute, Carlisle Barracks, PA
USMA United States Military Academy, West Point, NY
USMC United States Marine Corps
USTFF United States Track and Field Federation
VFW Veterans of Foreign Wars
WNRC Washington National Records Center, Suitland, MD
ZI Zone of the Interior

Bibliographical Note

Manuscripts

The starting place for research on Douglas MacArthur is the archives of the MacArthur Memorial, Norfolk, Virginia. The record groups that were mined in preparing this volume were: RG 4, records of GHQ, USAFPAC, 1942–47; RG 5, records of GHQ, SCAP, 1945–51; RG 6, records of GHQ, FECOM, 1947–51; RG 7, records of GHQ, UNC, 1950–51; RG 9, collection of messages (radiograms), 1945–51; RG 10, Douglas MacArthur's private correspondence, 1932–64; RG 14, MacArthur Memorial records; RG 15, documents donated by the general public; RG 21, records of Douglas MacArthur, 1951–64; and RG 23, Charles A. Willoughby papers. Its oral history and photograph collections were also essential.

In federal repositories in Washington, DC, the most frequently used documentary collections were RG 218, records of the Joint Chiefs of Staff, in the National Archives and RG 331, records of SCAP, in the Washington National Records Center, Suitland, Maryland. In the former repository, important MacArthur-related materials were also found in the SWNCC-SANACC documents in RG 59, records of the Department of State; RG 107, records of the Office of the Secretary of War; and RG 165, records of War Department general and special staffs; and in the latter repository, RG 407, post-1917 records of the Office of the Adjutant General. In the Manuscript Division of the Library of Congress, some data were located in the papers of Douglas MacArthur, George V. H. Moseley, Harry S. Truman, and Omar N. Bradley. The files on MacArthur, Robert L. Eichelberger, and several other officers in Japan and Korea, 1945–51, as well as some official historians' interviews and correspondence, in the records of the Center of Military History, Department of the Army, were informative. At the Naval Historical Center, Washington Navy Yard, the Daniel E. Barbey papers, MacArthur Memorial documents file, and miscellaneous Seventh Fleet records were of assistance. A number of oral history transcripts were used at the Marine Corps Historical Center, then at Arlington, Virginia; these and other interviews will be cited in the following section.

Several student papers on MacArthur and the Army in Japan and Korea, 1945–51, at the library of the U.S. Command and General Staff College, Fort Leavenworth, Kansas, were illuminating. A limited amount of data was obtained from the Douglas MacArthur collection in the archives of the U.S. Military Academy, West Point, New York; at that time the bulk of the Omar N. Bradley papers had not been deposited there. Much significant material was found at the U.S. Army Military History Institute, Carlisle Barracks, Pennsylvania, in the papers of Edward N. Almond, Omar N. Bradley, Matthew B. Ridgway, and Charles A. Willoughby, as well as in the oral history collection.

The records of the Harry S. Truman Library, Independence, Missouri, yielded rich data in the Truman presidential papers, especially the David D. Lloyd, Philleo Nash, President's secretary's, and official files; and in the papers of Dean Acheson, Eben Ayers, George M. Elsey, and Theodore Tannenwald, as well as in several interview transcripts. At the Dwight D. Eisenhower Library, Abilene, Kansas, significant information was found in the C. D. Jackson papers and particularly in the Eisenhower papers, including his diaries and the 1916–52 principal files, Ann Whitman files, and President's secretary's files.

As they had been for the Southwest Pacific war previously, the Robert L. Eichelberger papers proved important on occupied Japan; they are in the Manuscripts Department, Perkins Library, Duke University, Durham, North Carolina. A number of interviews in the collections of the Oral History Research Office, Butler Library, Columbia University, New York City, were of value. In the Seeley G. Mudd Manuscript Library, Princeton University, Princeton, New Jersey, considerable information was located in the papers of John Foster Dulles and Arthur Krock, along with some transcripts in the Dulles Oral History Collection. Papers that included MacArthur data at the Hoover Institution on War, Revolution, and Peace, Stanford University, Stanford, California, were those of Clovis E. Byers, Charles M. Cooke, Jr., Robert C. Richardson, Jr., Hubert G. Schenck, and Joseph C. Trainor. (The Bonner F. Fellers papers were acquired later.) Small amounts of photocopied material were obtained by mail from the Herbert C. Hoover Library, West Branch, Iowa; University of Chicago Library, Chicago, Illinois; East Asia Collection, McKeldin Library, University of Maryland, College Park, Maryland; S. L. A. Marshall Collection, Library, University of Texas, El Paso, Texas; and Regional Oral History Office, Bancroft Library, University of California, Berkeley, California.

The Special Collections Department, Mitchell Memorial Library, Mississippi State University, has accumulated a variety of original and photocopied materials related to this project, mostly grouped in the Douglas

MacArthur Biographical Papers. Some of these data were given by people with whom the author was in contact during his research; instrumental to this volume were such files as those donated by Robert Sherrod, Samuel Milner, George Dingledy, and Duane N. Diedrich. Also, this research endeavor has been supported by MSU purchases of a number of sizable microfilm collections, including records of the Homma, Yamashita, and IMTFE trials and of the JCS, SCAP, and State Department documentary series. The Special Collections Department also has the papers of John C. Stennis, Turner Catledge, and Wilson F. Minor, which contain some MacArthur-related items.

Interviews and Correspondence

The research experience was made more helpful and pleasurable by the splendid cooperation of the following people, who kindly granted interviews to the author. A "T" indicates that the interview was tape-recorded. The tapes and transcripts are in the Special Collections Department, Mitchell Memorial Library, Mississippi State University. An "X" denotes additional data provided by the person interviewed, usually copies of documents or personal papers. The author is deeply grateful to these interviewees: Capt. Robert H. Alexander, Norfolk, VA, May 28, 1971 (X); Lt. Gen. Edward M. Almond, Anniston, AL, Aug. 4, 1971 (TX); Prof. Akira Amakawa, Tokyo, Japan, Aug. 18, 1977 (TX); Col. A. D. Amoroso, Atlanta, GA, Dec. 17, 1966; Earl L. Ballenger, Norfolk, VA, May 27, 1971; Dorris Bankston, Starkville, MS, Nov. 23, 1983; Lt. Gen. Earl W. Barnes, Washington, DC, July 1, 1971; Maj. Gen. William A. Beiderlinden, McLean, VA, June 25, 1971 (X); Gen. Frank S. Besson, Jr., Alexandria, VA, June 18, 1977 (T); Adm. Russell S. Berkey, Old Lyme, CT, July 9, 1971 (TX); Brig. Gen. Clifford Bluemel, Yardley, PA, July 8, 1971 (T); Niles W. Bond, Washington, DC, June 16, 1977 (T); Maj. Faubion Bowers, New York, NY, July 18, 1971 (TX); Lt. Gen. Alpha L. Bowser, San Diego, CA, Sept. 3, 1971 (TX); Russell Brines, Arlington, VA, June 18, 1977 (T); Mrs. William E. Brougher, Atlanta, GA, Dec. 16–18, 1966 (X); Philip P. Brower, Norfolk, VA, June 17, 1968 (X); Rear Adm. John D. Bulkeley, Arlington, VA, July 12, 1971 (X); Col. Laurence E. Bunker, Wellesley Hills, MA, July 12, 1971 (T); Lt. Gen. Joseph C. Burger, Virginia Beach, VA, June 5, 1971; Adm. Arleigh A. Burke, Washington, DC, July 2, 1971 (TX); Lt. Gen. Clovis E. Byers, Washington, DC, June 24, 1971 (T); Col. Frank C. Caldwell, Arlington, VA, June 18, 1971; Dr. Verna A. Carley, Walnut Creek, CA, Aug. 23, 1971 (T); Col. James D. Carter, Kentfield, CA, Aug. 23, 1971 (T); Turner Catledge, Starkville, MS, Mar. 25, 1971 (T); Col. Joseph L. Chabot, Washington, DC, Dec. 18, 1966, and July 2, 1971; Vice Adm. Alvin D. Chandler, Virginia Beach, VA, June 5, 1971; Maj. Gen. John H. Chiles, Independence, MO, July 28, 1977 (T); Bernard P. Chitty, Norfolk, VA, May 26–27, 1971; Maj. Gen. James G. Christiansen, Co-

lumbus, GA, Aug. 4, 1971 (T); Brig. Gen. Bradford G. Chynoweth,
Berkeley, CA, Aug. 22, 1971 (TX); Col. James V. Collier, Santa Barbara,
CA, Aug. 20, 1971 (T); Gen. J. Lawton Collins, Washington, DC, Aug.
30, 1967, and June 15, 1971; David W. Condé, Tokyo, Japan, Aug. 17,
1977 (TX); Brig. Gen. John F. Conklin, Chevy Chase, MD, June 22, 1971;
Lt. Gen. Edward A. Craig, El Cajon, CA, Sept. 3, 1971 (TX); Maj. Gen.
Chester A. Dahlen, San Antonio, TX, Sept. 8, 1971 (TX); Vice Adm. Ralph
E. Davison, Pensacola, FL, Aug. 2, 1971 (T); Brig. Gen. Miles M. Dawson,
Columbus, OH, July 21, 1977 (TX); Masaru Debuchi, Tokyo, Japan, Aug.
15, 1977 (T); Gen. Jacob L. Devers, Washington, DC, June 30, 1971; Brig.
Gen. Le Grande A. Diller, Bradenton, FL, May 31, 1977 (T); Joseph H.
Downs, Jr., Starkville, MS, Nov. 17, 1970; W. Fred Duckworth, Norfolk,
VA, Aug. 24, 1967; Gen. Clyde D. Eddleman, Washington, DC, June 29,
1971; Brig. Gen. Hallett D. Edson, Arlington, VA, June 20, 1977 (T); Dr.
Roger O. Egeberg, Washington, DC, June 29–30, 1971 (TX); Gen. of the
Army Dwight D. Eisenhower, Gettysburg, PA, Aug. 29, 1967 (X); Brig.
Gen. John A. Elmore, McLean, VA, June 25, 1971 (T); Maj. Gaetano
Faillace, North Hollywood, CA, Aug. 31, 1971 (TX); Brig. Gen. Bonner
F. Fellers, Washington, DC, June 26, 1971 (TX); Brig. Gen. Louis J. For-
tier, Washington, DC, June 23, 1971 (T); Lt. Gen. Alonzo P. Fox, Wash-
ington, DC, June 26, 1971 (TX); Col. René E. Frailé, Santa Barbara, CA,
Aug. 30, 1971 (TX); Benis M. Frank, Arlington, VA, June 18, 1971 (X);
Toshitaro Fukushima, Tokyo, Japan, Aug. 17, 1977; Tetsuro Furukaki,
Tokyo, Japan, Aug. 17, 1977 (T); Col. A. Dean Gough, Kentfield, CA,
Aug. 23, 1971 (T); Prof. Henry F. Graff, New York, NY, July 13, 1977
(T); Benson Guyton, Decatur, AL, Aug. 5, 1971 (TX); Lt. Col. J. Addison
Hagan, Norfolk, VA, June 3, 1971; Gen. Thomas T. Handy, San Anto-
nio, TX, Sept. 8, 1971 (TX); Amb. W. Averell Harriman, Washington,
DC, June 20, 1977 (TX); Brig. Gen. and Mrs. Benjamin T. Harris, Cocoa
Beach, FL, June 3, 1977 (T); Maj. Gen. and Mrs. George W. Hickman,
Jr., Solana Beach, CA, Sept. 4, 1971 (TX); Brig. Gen. Milton A. Hill, Santa
Barbara, CA, Aug. 30, 1971 (TX); Gen. John E. Hull, Washington, DC,
June 23, 1971; Lt. Gen. Joseph C. Hutchison, Sanford, FL, July 27, 1971;
Amb. and Mrs. Philip C. Jessup, Sr., Norfolk, CT, July 14, 1977 (TX);
Brig. Gen. Dwight F. Johns, Piedmont, CA, Aug. 22, 1971 (TX); Vice Adm.
Felix Johnson, Leonardtown, MD, July 7, 1971 (TX); Gen. Harold K.
Johnson, Washington, DC, Dec. 18, 1966, and Valley Forge, PA, July 7,
1971 (TX); Under Sec. of State U. Alexis Johnson, Washington, DC, June
24, 1971 (X); Col. Charles L. Kades, New York, NY, July 13, 1977 (T);
Shingo Kaite, Tokyo, Japan, Aug. 19, 1977 (T); Amb. Masayoshi Kakit-
subo, Tokyo, Japan, Aug. 15, 1977 (T); Sukejiro Katamoto, Tokyo, Ja-
pan, Aug. 16, 1977 (T); Kinji Kawamura, Tokyo, Japan, Aug. 15–16, 1977
(TX); Col. John M. Kemper, Andover, MA, July 13, 1971 (T); Gen. George
C. Kenney, New York, NY, July 16, 1971 (TX); Shigeo Kimura, Tokyo,
Japan, Aug. 18, 1977 (T); Amb. Shiroshichi Kimura, Tokyo, Japan, Aug.
19, 1977 (T); Masaki Kodama, Washington, DC, June 13, 1977; Kenichi
Kuwashima, Tokyo, Japan, Aug. 17, 1977; Maj. Gen. Thomas A. Lane,

McLean, VA, June 25, 1971 (T); Col. Richard M. Levy, Washington, DC, June 14, 1977 (T); Brig. Gen. James H. Lynch, Augusta, GA, May 24, 1977 (T); Amb. Mike Mansfield, Tokyo, Japan, Aug. 16, 1977 (T); Frederic S. Marquardt, Phoenix, AZ, Sept. 5, 1971 (TX); Maj. Gen. Richard J. Marshall, Leesburg, FL, July 27, 1971 (TX); Col. and Mrs. Sidney F. Mashbir, Laguna Beach, CA, Sept. 1–2, 1971 (TX); Mrs. Hisako Matsudaira, Tokyo, Japan, Aug. 16, 1977; Mrs. Tane Matsumura, Tokyo, Japan, Aug. 18, 1977 (T); H. Freeman Matthews, Washington, DC, June 15, 1977 (T); Col. Aurelio Mendoza, Starkville, MS, Aug. 21, 1972 (X); Gen. John H. Michaelis, St. Petersburg, FL, June 1, 1977 (T); Gen. Frank T. Mildren, Beaufort, SC, May 25, 1977 (T); Chaplain Luther D. Miller, Washington, DC, June 28, 1971; Maj. Gen. Ned D. Moore, Falls Church, VA, June 21, 1977 (T); Brig. Gen. Frederick P. Munson, Washington, DC, July 2, 1971 (T); Col. Virgil Ney, Silver Spring, MD, July 6, 1971 (TX); Col. William Niederpruem, Los Gatos, CA, Aug. 25, 1971 (TX); Adm. Albert G. Noble, Washington, DC, June 24, 1971 (T); Kiichiro Ohba, Tokyo, Japan, Aug. 23, 1977; Sadao Ohtake, Tokyo, Japan, Aug. 17, 1977 (T); Hon. Frank Pace, Jr., New York, NY, July 12, 1977 (T); Gen. Charles D. Palmer, Washington, DC, June 14, 1977 (T); Maj. Gen. Gines Perez, Columbia, SC, May 25, 1977 (TX); Hans E. Pringsheim, Tokyo, Japan, Aug. 15, 1977 (TX); Col. L. Robert Rice, Virginia Beach, VA, June 3, 1971; Brig. Gen. William L. Ritchie, Washington, DC, June 24, 1971 (T); Frank Rizzo, Tokyo, Japan, Aug. 16, 1977 (T); Brig. Gen. Paul I. Robinson, Montgomery, AL, Aug. 3, 1971 (T); Brig. Gen. Crawford F. Sams, Atherton, CA, Aug. 25, 1971 (TX); Shizuo Saito, Tokyo, Japan, Aug. 15, 1977 (T); Gen. Frank C. Schilt, Norfolk, VA, June 5, 1971; Amb. William J. Sebald, Naples, FL, July 30, 1971 (TX); Hajime Seki, Tokyo, Japan, Aug. 20, 1977 (T); Col. Clyde A. Selleck, Chevy Chase, MD, June 22, 1971; Robert Sherrod, Washington, DC, June 17, 1977; Kimpei Shiba, Tokyo, Japan, Aug. 19, 1977 (TX); Adm. H. Page Smith, Virginia Beach, VA, June 5, 1971; Gen. Oliver P. Smith, Los Altos, CA, Aug. 25, 1971 (T); Mrs. William A. Smith, Hilton Head Island, SC, July 25, 1971 (T); Prof. Rinjiro Sodei, Tokyo, Japan, Aug. 18, 1977 (TX); Mrs. Yukika Soma, Tokyo, Japan, Aug. 22, 1977 (TX); Gen. Carl Spaatz, Chevy Chase, MD, June 22, 1971; Sen. John C. Stennis, Washington, DC, June 21, 1977 (T); Col. Anthony F. Story, New York, NY, July 16, 1971; Mrs. George E. Stratemeyer, Winter Park, FL, July 27, 1971 (X); Dr. W. Dupont Strong, Leesburg, FL, July 27, 1971 (T); Adm. Arthur D. Struble, Chevy Chase, MD, June 22, 1971 (T); Tokio Sugase, Tokyo, Japan, Aug. 13, 1977 (TX); Isamu Suzukawa, Tokyo, Japan, Aug. 12, 1977 (T); Amb. Tadakatsu Suzuki, Tokyo, Japan, Aug. 22, 1977 (T); Lt. Gen. Joseph M. Swing, San Francisco, CA, Aug. 26, 1971 (TX); Prof. Hideo Tanaka, Tokyo, Japan, Aug. 22, 1977 (TX); Rear Adm. Raymond D. Tarbuck, Coronado, CA, Sept. 4, 1971 (TX); Vice Adm. Edmund B. Taylor, Virginia Beach, VA, June 5, 1971; Gen. Gerald C. Thomas, Washington, DC, June 15, 1977 (T); Brig. Gen. Elliott R. Thorpe, Sarasota, FL, May 29, 1977 (TX); Brig. Gen. Edward W. Timberlake, Naples, FL, July 29, 1971; Col. John B. B.

Trussell, Carlisle Barracks, PA, May 22, 1980; Yosaku Tsuchiya, Tokyo, Japan, Aug. 12, 1977; Gen. Merrill B. Twining, Fallbrook, CA, Sept. 2, 1971; Gen. James A. Van Fleet, Polk City, FL, May 30, 1977; Brig. Gen. Robert H. Van Volkenburgh, San Francisco, CA, Aug. 26, 1971 (T); Brig. Gen. Harry Van Wyk, Pebble Beach, CA, Aug. 28, 1971 (T); Mrs. Elizabeth G. Vining, Kennett Square, PA, July 8, 1977 (TX); Col. John H. Weber, Ft. Leavenworth, KS, Dec. 10, 1980; Gen. Albert C. Wedemeyer, Boyds, MD, July 6, 1971 (TX); Brig. Gen. Charles J. West, Wilton, CT, July 14, 1977 (TX); Capt. Rexford V. Wheeler, Norfolk, VA, June 3, 1971; Cdr. Justus P. White, Virginia Beach, VA, June 5, 1971; Maj. Gen. Courtney Whitney, Washington, DC, Aug. 28–29, 1967 (X); Dr. Harry E. Wildes, Philadelphia, PA, July 8, 1977 (T); Dr. and Mrs. Justin Williams, Sr., Washington, DC, June 15, 1977 (T); Maj. Gen. Charles A. Willoughby, Washington, DC, Aug. 28, 1967, and Naples, FL, July 30, 1971 (TX); Brig. Gen. Walter F. Winton, Jr., Clearwater, FL, May 31, 1977 (T); Maj. Gen. Roscoe B. Woodruff, San Antonio, TX, Sept. 8, 1971 (TX); Maj. Gen. Edwin K. Wright, Monterey, CA, Aug. 28, 1971 (TX); Lt. Gen. John M. Wright, Jr., Arlington, VA, June 28, 1971 (X); Amb. Thomas K. Wright, Naples, FL, July 30, 1971 (T); Rep. Hisanari Yamada, Tokyo, Japan, Aug. 20, 1977 (T); Brig. Gen. Edwin A. Zundel, Sarasota, FL, May 29, 1977 (T).

A number of interviews conducted by Samuel Milner and Robert Sherrod are in the transcripts of the Douglas MacArthur Biographical Papers, MSU. Used in this book were Milner's interviews with Maj. Gen. David G. Barr, Maj. Gen. William A. Beiderlinden, Col. Hubert Binkley, Col. John D. Davenport, Col. Chauncey E. Dovell, Maj. Gen. George L. Eberle, Lt. Gen. Charles B. Ferenbaugh, Col. Wayne S. Hume, Gen. Paul L. Neal, and Lt. Gen. William W. Quinn. Also helpful were Sherrod's interviews with Col. Laurence E. Bunker, Gener Farmer, Giichi Imae, Col. Charles L. Kades, Nobura Kajima, Shigehara Matsumoto, Col. Anthony F. Story, and Kenzo Suzuki. Substantial data were obtained from the following interviews at the Oral History Research Office of Butler Library, Columbia University: Dr. Lauren V. Ackerman, Roger N. Baldwin, Adm. John J. Ballantine, Joseph Ballantine, Hugh Borton, Maj. Faubion Bowers, Burton Crane, Esther Crane, Eugene H. Dooman, Alvin Grauer, John R. Harold, Harold G. Henderson, Cyrus H. Peake, and Sen. H. Alexander Smith. In the oral history collection of the U.S. Army Military History Institute, considerable information was found in the interviews with Lt. Gen. Edward M. Almond, Gen. Mark W. Clark, Gen. Barksdale Hamlett, Gen. Thomas T. Handy, Lt. Gen. Leonard D. Heaton, Gen. John E. Hull, and Maj. Gen. Hugh M. Milton. Relevant data were in these interviews of the John Foster Dulles Oral History Collection of Princeton University: Pres. Dwight D. Eisenhower, Gov. W. Averell Harriman, Rep. Joseph W. Martin, Jr., Foreign Min. Carlos P. Romulo, Amb. William J. Sebald, and Prime Min. Shigeru Yoshida. Helpful interviews at the U.S. Marine Corps Historical Center were those of Lt. Gen. Alpha L. Bowser, Lt. Gen. Edward A. Craig, Gen. Lemuel C. Shepherd, Jr., and Gen. Oliver

P. Smith. The MacArthur Memorial interviews that were used were those of Lt. Gen. Edward M. Almond, Lt. Gen. Leslie R. Groves, and Gen. Lemuel C. Shepherd, Jr. Interviews of value in the Harry S. Truman Library were those of Amb. John J. Muccio, Gen. Bruce C. Clarke, and Hon. Thomas K. Finletter. Also used was an interview with Lulu Holmes at the Regional Oral History Office, Bancroft Library, University of California, Berkeley; and Louis Morton's interview with Gen. MacArthur at the Army's Center of Military History.

The following people provided assistance in various ways, some through personal counsel but most through correspondence in sending sundry materials: Clay Blair, Brig. Gen. Charles C. Drake, Mrs. Dale M. Hellegers, Mariko Hiramitsu, Col. William Menoher, Dr. Forrest C. Pogue, Prof. E. Daniel Potts, Prof. Paul P. Rogers, Col. Donald P. Shaw, Lt. Col. James C. Shepard, Dr. E. B. Sledge, Robert Smith, Col. William A. Stofft, Col. Harry G. Summers, Jr., and Col. Frederick B. Wiener. The author is also indebted to a large number of American and foreign Army, Navy, Marine, and Air Force officers who were students or faculty members at the U.S. Army War College and U.S. Army Command and General Staff College, 1979–81, and discussed with the author, a visiting professor at those two schools, their knowledge of or prior experiences with Gen. MacArthur or various commanders who served under him. Much was learned, too, from discussions with visiting scholars at the U.S. Army Military History Institute, to which the author was attached in 1979–80.

Published Sources

SCAP publications are voluminous and vary greatly in accuracy on the situation in Japan. Most useful were three sets of SCAP, GHQ, data: *Summation of Non-Military Activities in Japan and Korea* (10 vols., Tokyo, 1948), also printed in monthly summaries, Sept. 1945–Aug. 1948; *History of the Non-Military Activities of the Occupation of Japan* (55 vols., Tokyo, 1951–52), with many of the separate monograph titles cited in the notes herein; and *SCAP Directives to the Imperial Japanese Government, 1945–1952* (2 vols., Tokyo, 1952), containing the 2204 SCAPINS issued during the period. Much relied on also was SCAP, Government Section, *Political Reorientation of Japan, September 1945 to September 1948: Report of Government Section* (2 vols., Washington, 1949). Other helpful SCAP works were *A Brief Progress Report on the Political Reorientation of Japan* (Tokyo, 1949); *Mission and Accomplishments of the Occupation in the Civil Information and Education Fields* (Tokyo, 1950); *Mission and Accomplishments in the Natural Resources Field* (Tokyo, 1950); *Mission and Accomplishments of the Occupation in the Public Health and Welfare Fields* (Tokyo, 1949); *Mission and Accomplishments of the Supreme Commander for the Allied Powers in the Economic and Scientific Fields* (Tokyo, 1950); and *Public Health in Japan* (2 vols., Tokyo, 1948). Other SCAP titles are in the notes.

A wealth of data on MacArthur is in the following volumes of U.S. Department of State, *Foreign Relations of the United States: 1945,* II, IV–VI; *1946,* VII, VIII, X; *1947,* VI, VII; *1948,* VI, VIII; *1949,* I, VII–IX; *1950,* I, VI, VII; *1951,* I, VI, VII. State Department publications on occupied Japan include *The Axis in Defeat: A Collection of Documents on American Policy Toward Germany and Japan* (Washington, 1945); *Report of the United States Education Mission to Japan* (Washington, 1946); *Occupation of Japan: Policy and Progress* (Washington, 1946); *Trial of Japanese War Criminals* (Washington, 1946); *The Constitution of Japan, Effective May 3, 1947* (Washington, 1947); Edwin W. Pauley, *Report on Japanese Reparations to the President of the United States, November 1945 to April 1946* (Washington, 1948); *Report of the Second United States Education Mission to Japan* (Washington, 1950); *Treaty of Peace with Japan, Signed at San Francisco, September 8, 1951, with Related Documents* (Washington, 1952); *The Far Eastern Commission: Report by the Secretary General* (3 vols., Washington, 1947–50); and George H. Blakeslee, *The Far Eastern Commission: A Study in International Cooperation, 1945 to 1952* (Washington, 1953). Also of value were these State Department works on Korea: *Korea's Independence* (Washington, 1947); *United States Policy in the Korean Crisis* (Washington, 1950); *The Conflict in Korea: Events Prior to the Attack on June 25, 1950* (Washington, 1951); *The Record on Korean Unification, 1943–1960: Narrative Summary with Principal Documents* (Washington, 1960); and *A Historical Summary of United States–Korean Relations, with a Chronology of Important Developments, 1834–1962* (Washington, 1962). Other State Department volumes of value were *United States Relations with China, with Special Reference to the Period 1944–1949* (Washington, 1949); and *American Foreign Policy, 1950–1955: Basic Documents* (2 vols., Washington, 1957).

Useful microfilm compilations by University Publications of America were *Office of Strategic Services-State Department Intelligence and Research Reports,* pt. 2, *Postwar Japan, Korea, and Southeast Asia* (6 reels, Frederick, MD., n.d.); and *Records of the Joint Chiefs of Staff,* pt. 2, *1946–1953* (70 reels, Frederick, MD., n.d.).

Many relevant documents are available in the National Archives series *Public Papers of the Presidents of the United States: Harry S. Truman, 1945–53* (8 vols., Washington, 1961–66); *Dwight D. Eisenhower, 1953–61* (8 vols., Washington, 1958–61); *John F. Kennedy, 1961–63* (3 vols., Washington, 1962–64); and *Lyndon B. Johnson, 1963–64,* vol. I (Washington, 1965).

Three U.S. Senate publications were of fundamental importance: *Military Situation in the Far East: Hearings Before the Committee on Armed Services and the Committee on Foreign Relations, United States Senate, Eighty-second Congress, First Session, to Conduct an Inquiry into the Military Situation in the Far East and the Facts Surrounding the Relief of General of the Army Douglas MacArthur from His Assignments in That Area* (5 pts. in 2 vols., Washington, 1951); *Substance of Statements Made at Wake Island Conference on October 15, 1950; Compiled by General of the Army Omar N. Bradley, Chairman of the Joint Chiefs of Staff, from Notes Kept by the Conferees from Washington* (Washington, 1951); and *Representative Speeches of General of the Army Douglas MacArthur,* comp. by Legislative Reference Service, Library of Congress (Washington, 1964). Other Senate publications that were used included Committee on Foreign Relations and Committee on Armed Services, *Assignment of Ground Forces of the United States to Duty in the European Area: Hearings* . . . 82d Cong., 1st Sess. (1951); Committee on the Judiciary, *Institute of Pacific Relations: Hearings* . . . 82d Cong., 1st and 2d Sess. (1951–52); Committee on Foreign Relations, *The United States and the Korean Problem: Documents, 1943–1953,* 83d Cong., 1st Sess., Senate Doc. 74 (Washington, 1954); Committee on Armed Services, Preparedness Subcommittee, *Ammunition Shortages in the Armed Services: Hearings* . . . 83d Cong., 1st Sess. (1953); Committee on the Judiciary, *Interlocking Subversion in Government Departments: Hearings* . . . 83d Cong., 2d Sess. (1953–54). Relevant data also were found in two publications of the U.S. House of Representatives: Committee on Appropriations, *Aid to Korea: Hearings* . . . 81st Cong., 1st Sess. (1949); and Committee on Foreign Affairs, *Background Information on Korea,* 81st Cong., 2d Sess., House Report 2495 (1950). Another U.S. government source that proved valuable was Department of Defense, *Semiannual Reports of the Secretary of Defense, Secretary of the Army, Secretary of the Navy, and Secretary of the Air Force, January 1, 1950–December 31, 1951* (Washington, 1952).

English-language publications of the Japanese government that were of assistance included Ministry of Labor, *The Japanese Labor Legislations, 1949* (Tokyo, 1949); and Ministry of Foreign Affairs, *Documents Concerning the Allied Occupation and Control of Japan* (7 vols., Tokyo, 1949–51).

Varying degrees of information about MacArthur are in a considerable number of published personal papers, memoirs, and firsthand accounts, of which the following are notable: Dean G. Acheson, *Among Friends: Personal Letters of Dean Acheson,* eds. David S. McLellan and David C. Acheson (New York, 1980); idem, *The Korean War* (New York, 1971); idem, *Present at the Creation: My Years in the State Department* (New York, 1969); Sherman Adams, *Firsthand Report* (New York, 1961); John M. Allison, *Ambassador from the Prairie; or Allison Wonderland* (Boston, 1973); Clement R. Attlee, *As It Happened* (London, 1954); idem and Francis Williams, *Twilight of Empire: Memoirs of Prime Minister Clement Attlee* (New York, 1962); Hugh Baillie, *High Tension: The Recollections of Hugh Baillie* (New York, 1959); W. Macmahon Ball, *Japan: Enemy or Ally?* (Melbourne, Australia, 1948); Norman Bartlett, ed., *With the Australians in Korea* (Canberra, Australia, 1960); Keyes Beech, *Tokyo and Points East* (Garden City, NY, 1954); Earl H. Blaik, *The Red Blaik Story* (New Rochelle, NY, 1974); Charles E. Bohlen, *Witness to History, 1929–1969* (New York, 1973); Omar N. Bradley and Clay Blair, *A General's Life: An Autobiography* (New York, 1983); McGeorge Bundy, ed., *The Pattern of Responsibility* (Boston, 1952); James F. Byrnes, *All in One Lifetime* (New York, 1958); idem, *Speaking Frankly* (New York, 1947); Mark W. Clark, *From the Danube to the Yalu* (New York, 1954); Frank Clune, *Ashes of Hiroshima: A Post-War Trip to Japan and China* (Sydney, Australia, 1950); J. Lawton Collins, *Lightning Joe: An Autobiography* (Baton Rouge, LA, 1979); idem, *War in Peacetime: The History and Lessons of Korea* (Boston, 1969); Robert Considine, *It's All News to Me: A*

Reporter's Deposition (New York, 1967); William F. Dean, with William Worden, *General Dean's Story* (New York, 1954); Robert L. Eichelberger, with Milton Mackaye, *Our Jungle Road to Tokyo* (New York, 1950); Dwight D. Eisenhower, *Crusade in Europe* (Garden City, NY, 1948); idem, *Mandate for Change, 1953–1956* (Garden City, NY, 1963); idem, *The Papers of Dwight D. Eisenhower*, vols. VI-IX [1945–48], eds. Alfred D. Chandler, Jr., Louis Galambos, et al. (Baltimore, 1978); John K. Emmerson, *The Japanese Thread: A Life in the U.S. Foreign Service* (New York, 1979); James V. Forrestal, *The Forrestal Diaries*, eds. Walter Millis and E. S. Duffield (New York, 1951); Mark J. Gayn, *Japan Diary* (New York, 1948); Joseph C. Grew, *Ten Years in Japan: A Contemporary Record . . .* (New York, 1944); Leslie R. Groves, *Now It Can Be Told: The Story of the Manhattan Project* (New York, 1962); W. Averell Harriman and Elie Abel, *Special Envoy to Churchill and Stalin, 1941–1946* (New York, 1975); Marguerite Higgins, *War in Korea: The Report of a Woman Combat Correspondent* (Garden City, NY, 1951); Sidney L. Huff, with Joe A. Morris, *My Fifteen Years with General MacArthur* (New York, 1964 [1st ed., 1951]); Emmet J. Hughes, *The Ordeal of Power: A Political Memoir of the Eisenhower Administration* (New York, 1963); E. J. Kahn, Jr., *The Peculiar War: Impressions of a Reporter in Korea* (New York, 1952); Toshikazu Kase, *Journey to the "Missouri,"* ed. David N. Rowe (New Haven, CT, 1950); George F. Kennan, *Memoirs* (2 vols., Boston, 1967–72); Nikita Khrushchev, *Khrushchev Remembers*, trans. and ed. Strobe Talbott (Boston, 1970); Trygve Lie, *In the Cause of Peace: Seven Years with the United Nations* (New York, 1954); Douglas MacArthur, *Reminiscences* (New York, 1964); idem, *A Soldier Speaks: Public Papers and Speeches of General of the Army Douglas MacArthur*, ed. Vorin E. Whan, Jr. (New York, 1965); Harold Macmillan, *Tides of Fortune, 1945–1955* (New York, 1969); S. L. A. Marshall, *Bringing Up the Rear: A Memoir*, ed. Cate Marshall (San Rafael, CA, 1979); Joseph W. Martin, with Robert J. Donovan, *My First Fifty Years in Politics* (New York, 1960); John Morris, *The Phoenix Cup: Some Notes on Japan in 1946* (London, 1947); Robert D. Murphy, *Diplomat Among Warriors* (Garden City, NY, 1964); Richard M. Nixon, *Leaders* (New York, 1982); Harold J. Noble, *Embassy at War*, ed. Frank Baldwin (Seattle, 1975); Alfred C. Oppler, *Legal Reform in Occupied Japan: A Participant Looks Back* (Princeton, 1976); K. M. Panikkar, *In Two Chinas: Memoirs of a Diplomat* (London, 1955); Lester B. Pearson, *Mike: The Memoirs of the Right Honorable Lester B. Pearson*, vol. II, *1948–1957*, eds. John A. Munro and Alex I. Inglis (New York, 1973); Monte M. Poen, *Strictly Personal and Confidential: The Letters Harry Truman Never Mailed* (Boston, 1982); Willard Price, *Journey by Junk: Japan After MacArthur* (New York, 1953); Arthur W. Radford, *From Pearl Harbor to Vietnam: The Memoirs of Admiral Arthur W. Radford*, ed. Stephen Jurika, Jr. (Stanford, 1980); Karl L. Rankin, *China Assignment* (Seattle, 1964); George E. Reedy, *The Twilight of the Presidency* (New York, 1970); Syngman Rhee, *Korea Flaming High* (Seoul, Korea, 1954); Matthew B. Ridgway, *The Korean War: How We Met the Challenge . . .* (Garden City, NY, 1967); idem, with Harold H. Martin, *Soldier: The Memoirs of Matthew B. Ridgway* (New York, 1956); William J. Sebald, with Russell Brines, *With MacArthur in Ja-*

pan: A Personal History of the Occupation (New York, 1965); Kimpei Shiba, *I Cover Japan* (Tokyo, 1952); Mamoru Shigemitsu, *Japan and Her Destiny: My Struggle for Peace*, ed. F. S. G. Piggott and trans. Oswald White (New York, 1958); Cyrus L. Sulzberger, *A Long Row of Candles: Memoirs and Diaries (1934–1954)* (New York, 1969); Maxwell D. Taylor, *Swords and Ploughshares* (New York, 1972); Elliott R. Thorpe, *East Wind Rain: The Intimate Account of an Intelligence Officer in the Pacific, 1939–49* (Boston, 1969); Harry S. Truman, *Memoirs* (2 vols., Garden City, NY, 1955–56); idem, *Off the Record: The Private Papers of Harry S. Truman*, ed. Robert H. Ferrell (New York, 1980); Arthur H. Vandenberg, *The Private Papers of Senator Vandenberg*, ed. Arthur H. Vandenberg, Jr. (Boston, 1952); Elizabeth G. Vining, *Quiet Pilgrimage* (Philadelphia, 1970); idem, *Windows for the Crown Prince* (Philadelphia, 1952); Vernon A. Walters, *Silent Missions* (Garden City, NY, 1978); Grover A. Whalen, *Mr. New York: The Autobiography of Grover A. Whalen* (New York, 1955); Justin Williams, Sr., *Japan's Political Revolution Under MacArthur: A Participant's Account* (Athens, GA, 1979); Shigeru Yoshida, *The Yoshida Memoirs: The Story of Japan in Crisis*, trans. Kenichi Yoshida (Boston, 1962).

Essential United Nations data were located in Andrew W. Cordier and Wilder Foote, eds., *Public Papers of the Secretaries-General of the United Nations*, vol. I, *Trygve Lie* (New York, 1969); United Nations General Assembly, *Official Records*, 1945–51 (55 vols., New York, 1947–52); United Nations Security Council, *Official Records*, 1945–51 (23 vols., New York, 1946–52); idem, *Resolutions and Decisions of the Security Council, 1946–57* (New York, 1965).

Other published sources of consequence to this project were Barton J. Bernstein and Allen J. Matusow, eds., *The Truman Administration: A Documentary History* (New York, 1966); Margaret Carlyle and Denise Folliot, eds., *Documents on International Affairs*, 1947–51 (3 vols., New York, 1952–54); Raymond Dennett, et al., eds., *Documents on American Foreign Relations*, 1945–51 (6 vols., Princeton, 1948–53); Theodore H. McNelly, ed., *Sources in Modern East Asian History and Politics* (New York, 1967); Republican National Committee, *Official Report of the Proceedings of the Twenty-fifth Republican National Convention; Held in Chicago, Illinois, July 7–11, 1952* (Washington, 1952); Arthur M. Schlesinger, Jr., and Roger Bruns, eds., *Congress Investigates, 1927–1974: A Documented History*, vol. V (New York, 1975); Francis O. Wilcox and Thorsten V. Kalijarvi, eds., *Recent American Foreign Policy: Basic Documents, 1941–1951* New York, 1952); and George F. Zook, *Japan and Germany: Problems in Reeducation: Official Summaries of Reports of the United States Educational Missions* (New York, 1947).

Among the preceding published sources, indispensable were the SCAP and *FRUS* volumes; the MacArthur Hearings; the Wake notes; the collections of MacArthur's speeches by the Library of Congress and by Whan; the Japanese Foreign Office's compilation of occupation documents; and the memoirs by Acheson, Blaik, Bradley, Collins, Huff, Kennan, MacArthur, Oppler, Ridgway, Sebald, Thorpe, Truman, Vining, Williams, and Yoshida.

Newspapers and Popular Periodicals

Searches for MacArthur-related articles were undertaken on an almost daily-issue basis in the following newspapers for the periods indicated: Chicago *Tribune*, 1945–64; *New York Times*, 1945–64; Washington *Post*, 1945–64; London *Times*, 1945–51; *Nippon Times* of Japan, 1945–51; and *Stars and Stripes* (Pacific ed.), 1945–51. Short-run searches of paper files or clippings obtained from individuals and repositories provided articles of interest from these newspapers: Baltimore *Sun*, Boston *Globe*, Boston *Herald*, Charleston (SC) *News-Courier*, *Christian Science Monitor*, Fort Wayne (IN) *Journal-Gazette*, Fort Wayne (IN) *News-Sentinel*, Indianapolis *Star*, London *Observer*, Los Angeles *Evening Herald and Express*, *Mainichi Daily News* of Japan, *Manila Times*, Memphis *Commercial Appeal*, Natchez (MS) *Democrat*, New Orleans *Times-Picayune*, New York *Daily Worker*, New York *Herald Tribune*, New York *Journal-American*, New York *Journal Tribune*, New York *World-Telegram*, Norfolk (VA) *Virginian-Pilot*, St. Louis *Globe-Democrat*, St. Louis *Post-Dispatch*, San Francisco *Examiner*, Starkville (MS) *Daily News*, Wasbash (IN) *Plain Dealer*, Washington *Daily News*, Washington *Evening Star*, and Washington *Times-Herald*.

There was no want of attention to MacArthur in popular and general periodicals. Helpful articles were located in *Amateur Athlete*, *American Mercury*, *Business Week*, *Christian Century*, *Collier's*, *Commonweal*, *Cosmopolitan*, *Current History*, *The Economist*, *Editor and Publisher*, *Esquire*, *Fortune*, *Forum*, *Harper's*, *Life*, *Nashville Tennessean Magazine*, *The Nation*, *National Parent-Teacher*, *National Review*, *New Republic*, *Newsweek*, *New Yorker*, *New York Times Book Review*, *New York Times Magazine*, *Parade*, *The Reporter*, *Saturday Evening Post*, *Saturday Review of Literature*, *Sports Illustrated*, *Time*, *U.S. News & World Report*, and *Vital Speeches*. Useful, too, were such government organs as the *Congressional Record*, *Department of State Bulletin*, and *United States Supreme Court Reports*.

Among the principal articles of substance in the above newspapers and periodicals are the following: Robert Considine, " '54 Interview Reveals Bitter MacArthur," Washington *Post*, Apr. 9, 1964; Jerome Forrest and Clarke H. Kawakami, "General MacArthur and His Vanishing War History," *The Reporter*, 8 (Oct. 14, 1952), 20–25; Leland M. Goodrich, "Collective Action in Korea: Evaluating the Results of the UN Collective Action," *Current History*, 38 (June 1960), 332–36; Harry F. Kern, "What's Wrong in Japan? Plenty, Blasts Survey Expert," *Newsweek*, 33 (Apr. 18, 1949), 45; "A Lawyer's Report on Japan Attacks Plan of Occupation . . . Far to the Left of Anything Now Tolerated in America," ibid., 30 (Dec. 1, 1947), 36–38; Jim G. Lucas, "An Interview with MacArthur — The Storm It Provoked," *U.S. News & World Report*, 56 (Apr. 20, 1964), 40–41; Douglas MacArthur, "Formosa Must Be Defended: A Declaration by General Douglas MacArthur, Supreme Commander in Japan for the Allied Powers," ibid., 29 (Sept. 1, 1950), 32–34; idem, "Gen. MacArthur Makes His Reply," *Life*, 40 (Feb. 13, 1956), 94–96, 101–02, 104, 107–08;

ibid., "Japan: An Economy of Survival," *Fortune*, 39 (June 1949), 74–75, 188, 190, 192, 194, 196, 198, 200, 202, 204; ibid., "Reply with Editorial Comment," *Saturday Evening Post*, 222 (July 30, 1949), 4; Helen Mears, "We're Giving Japan Democracy, But She Can't Earn Her Living," ibid., 221 (June 18, 1949), 12; Louis Morton, "Egotist in Uniform," *Harper's*, 229 (Nov. 1964), 138, 142, 144–45; John Osborne, "My Dear General," *Life*, 29 (Nov. 27, 1950), 27–39; "SCAPitalism Marches On: Japan's Economy Will Be Better Off When It Comes Marching Home," *Fortune*, 40 (Oct. 1949), 76–77; Arthur M. Schlesinger, Jr., "The Supreme Cavalier," *Washington Post*, Sept. 27, 1964; Robert Shaplen, "A Reporter at Large: From MacArthur to Miki," *New Yorker*, 51, pt. 1 (Aug. 4, 1975), 60–74; pt. 2 (Aug. 11, 1975), 48–68; pt. 3 (Aug. 18, 1975), 38–65; Beverly Smith, "The White House Story: Why We Went to War in Korea," *Saturday Evening Post*, 224 (Nov. 10, 1951), 22–23, 76, 78, 80, 82, 86, 88; Harry S. Truman, "The Recall of Gen. MacArthur," *Life*, 40 (Feb. 13, 1956), 66–93; "Two-Billion-Dollar Failure in Japan," *Fortune*, 39 (Apr. 1949), 67–73, 204, 206, 208; Alfred L. Warner, "How the Korea Decision Was Made," *Harper's*, 203 (June 1951), 99–106; T. Harry Williams, "The Macs and the Ikes: America's Two Military Traditions," *American Mercury*, 75 (Oct. 1952), 32–39; and Charles A. Willoughby, "The Truth About Korea," *Cosmopolitan*, Dec. 1951, 34–37, 133–39.

Official Histories

In the *United States Army in the Korean War* series of the Department of the Army's Office of the Chief of Military History (later Center of Military History), two volumes were relied upon heavily: James F. Schnabel, *Policy and Direction: The First Year* (Washington, 1972); and Roy E. Appleman, *South to the Naktong, North to the Yalu* (Washington, 1961). Much use was made also of the series by the Historical Division of the Joint Chiefs of Staff, *The History of the Joint Chiefs of Staff: The Joint Chiefs of Staff and National Policy, 1945–1953* (4 vols. in 5, Wilmington, DE, 1979), of which the individual volumes are: vol. I, *1945–1947*, by James F. Schnabel; vol. II, *1947–1949*, by Kenneth W. Condit; vol. III (in 2 pts.), *The Korean War*, by Schnabel and Robert J. Watson; and vol. IV, *1950–1952*, by Walter S. Poole. The Army volume by Schnabel and the JCS one by him and Watson (pt. 1, 1950–51) were indispensable. Other Army publications of value were Russell A. Gugeler, *Combat Actions in Korea* (2d ed., Washington, 1970); James E. Hewes, Jr., *From Root to McNamara: Army Organization and Administration, 1900–1963* (Washington, 1975); James A. Huston, *The Sinews of War: Army Logistics, 1775–1953* (Washington, 1966); John Miller, et al., *Korea, 1950–53* (2 vols., Washington, 1952–56); B. C. Mossman and M. W. Stark, *The Last Salute: Civil and Military Funerals, 1921–1969* (Washington, 1971); and Robert K. Sawyer, *Military Advisors in Korea: KMAG in Peace and War* (Washington, 1962). Helpful, too, were U.S. Eighth Army,

A Short History of the Eighth United States Army, 1944–1954 (Tokyo, 1955); U.S. Military Academy, Department of Military Art and Engineering, *Operations in Korea* (West Point, NY, 1956); and Charles A. Willoughby, ed., *Reports of General MacArthur*, vol. I suppl., *MacArthur in Japan: The Occupation: Military Phase* (Washington, 1966), prepared at Tokyo GHQ, 1946–51.

Other American service histories that were helpful included James A. Field, Jr., *History of United States Naval Operations: Korea* (Washington, 1962); Robert F. Futrell, *United States Air Force Operations in the Korean Conflict, 25 June 1950–30 June 1952* (2 vols., Washington, 1952–53); Benis M. Frank and Henry I. Shaw, Jr., *Victory and Occupation. History of U.S. Marine Corps Operations in World War II*, vol. IV (Washington, 1968); Lynn Montross, et al., *U.S. Marine Operations in Korea, 1950–1953* (5 vols., Washington, 1954–72), especially vols. I-III; and Henry I. Shaw, Jr., *The United States Marines in the Occupation of Japan* (rev. ed., Washington, 1962).

Some illuminating data were found in these official allied histories: Canadian Army Headquarters, Historical Section, *Canada's Army in Korea: The United Nations Operations, 1950–53, and Their Aftermath* (Ottawa, 1956); S. Woodburn Kirby, *The Surrender of Japan. History of the Second World War: United Kingdom Military Series* (London, 1969); Eric Linklater, *Our Men in Korea: The Commonwealth Part of the Campaign* (London, 1952), on BC units; Rajendra Singh, *Post-War Occupation Forces: Japan and South-East Asia. Official History of the Indian Armed Forces in the Second World War* (New Delhi, 1958), includes BCOF in occupied Japan; Thor Thorgrimsson and E. C. Russell, *Canadian Naval Operations in Korean Waters, 1950–1955* (Ottawa, 1965); and Herbert F. Wood, *Strange Battleground: The Operations in Korea and Their Effects on the Defence Policy of Canada. Official History of the Canadian Army in Korea* (Ottawa, 1966).

Other Secondary Works

On MacArthur biographies, see *The Years of MacArthur*, I, 634–35; II, 824, 972. Of the works cited therein, those by Hunt, Long, Kenney, Lee and Henschel, Whitney, and Willoughby and Chamberlain appear in the notes of this final volume, with the latter two books referred to rather often, in spite of their previously mentioned flaws. A perceptive, scholarly recent study is Carol M. Petillo, *Douglas MacArthur: The Philippine Years* (Bloomington, IN, 1981). Two best sellers on MacArthur appeared nearly three decades apart: John Gunther, *The Riddle of MacArthur: Japan, Korea, and the Far East* (New York, 1950), a contemporary view of his proconsulship in Tokyo; and William Manchester, *American Caesar: Douglas MacArthur, 1880–1964* (Boston, 1978), which undoubtedly will long remain the most popular biography of the general. Recent works also include Clay Blair, Jr., *MacArthur* (New York, 1977), a movie tie-in but well done; Sydney L.

Mayer, *MacArthur in Japan* (New York, 1973), a sequel to his earlier brief study in the popular Ballantine series; William S. Phillips, Jr., *Douglas MacArthur: A Modern Knight-Errant* (Philadelphia, 1978), a revised M.A. thesis on chivalry in MacArthur's rhetoric; and Robert Smith, *MacArthur in Korea: The Naked Emperor* (New York, 1982), a vitriolic attack on his wartime leadership, 1950–51. Older writings on MacArthur not cited previously include Edgar J. Fredricks, *MacArthur: His Mission and Meaning* (Philadelphia, 1968), a brief rightist interpretation; Frank Kelley and Cornelius Ryan, *Star-Spangled Mikado* (New York, 1947), a journalistic account of the early phase of the occupation; Norfolk *Virginia-Pilot* and *Ledger-Star* staffs, *Gen. Douglas MacArthur: Last Journey for an Old Soldier* (Norfolk, 1964), a pictorial record of his cortege and burial in Norfolk; and John M. Pratt, ed., *Revitalizing a Nation* (Chicago, 1952), a conservative record of MacArthur's speeches and public appearances during his 1951 nationwide tour.

Studies of other leaders that yielded consequential information were Stephen E. Ambrose, *Eisenhower*, vol. I, *Soldier, General of the Army, President-Elect, 1890–1952* (New York, 1983); John K. Beal, *John Foster Dulles: A Biography* (New York, 1957); Bert Cochran, *Harry Truman and the Crisis Presidency* (New York, 1973); Blanche W. Cook, *The Declassified Eisenhower: A Divided Legacy* (Garden City, NY, 1981); Burke Davis, *Marine! The Life of Lt. Gen. Lewis B. (Chesty) Puller, USMC (Ret.)* (Boston, 1962); Robert J. Donovan, *Conflict and Crisis: The Presidency of Harry S. Truman, 1945–1948* (New York, 1977); idem, *Tumultuous Years: The Presidency of Harry S. Truman, 1949–1953* (New York, 1982); John W. Dower, *Empire and Aftermath: Yoshida Shigeru and the Japanese Experience, 1878–1954* (Cambridge, MA, 1979); Ronald T. Farrar, *Reluctant Servant: The Story of Charles G. Ross* (Columbia, MO, 1969); Louis L. Gerson, *John Foster Dulles* (New York, 1967); Eric F. Goldman, *The Tragedy of Lyndon Johnson* (New York, 1969 [1st ed., 1968]); Richard F. Haynes, *The Awesome Power: Harry S. Truman as Commander in Chief* (Baton Rouge, LA, 1973); Osanga Kanroji, *Hirohito: An Intimate Portrait of the Japanese Emperor* (Los Angeles, 1975); Aubrey S. Kenworthy, *The Tiger of Malaya: The Story of General Tomoyuki Yamashita and "Death March" General Masaharu Homma* (New York, 1953); Peter Lyon, *Eisenhower: Portrait of the Hero* (Boston, 1974); David S. McLellan, *Dean Acheson: The State Department Years* (New York, 1976); Merle Miller, *Plain Speaking: An Oral Biography of Harry S. Truman* (New York, 1973); Leonard Mosley, *Hirohito, Emperor of Japan* (Englewood Cliffs, NJ, 1966); idem, *Marshall: Hero for Our Times* (New York, 1982); Kenneth P. O'Donnell and David F. Powers, with Joe McCarthy, *"Johnny, We Hardly Knew Ye": Memories of John Fitzgerald Kennedy* (New York, 1973 [1st ed., 1972]); Robert T. Oliver, *Syngman Rhee: The Man Behind the Myth* (New York, 1955); Herbert S. Parmet, *Eisenhower and the American Crusades* (New York, 1972); James T. Patterson, *Mr. Republican: A Biography of Robert A. Taft* (Boston, 1972); Cabell Phillips, *The Truman Presidency: The History of a Triumphant Succession* (New York, 1966); Forrest C. Pogue, *George C. Marshall*, vols. II–III (New York, 1965–73); Arthur M. Schlesinger, Jr.,

A Thousand Days: John F. Kennedy in the White House (Boston, 1965); Duane Schultz, *Hero of Bataan: The Story of General Wainwright* (New York, 1981); Gaddis Smith, *Dean Acheson* (New York, 1972); Alfred Steinberg, *The Man from Missouri: The Life and Times of Harry S. Truman* (New York, 1962); W. A. Swanberg, *Luce and His Empire* (New York, 1972); Margaret Truman, *Harry S. Truman* (New York, 1973); Frank C. Waldrop, *McCormick of Chicago* (Englewood Cliffs, NJ, 1966); and William S. White, *The Taft Story* (New York, 1954).

Although the following list of secondary works on the occupation and postwar Japan may seem lengthy, there are many more books in English on the period that were worth checking but had to be passed over because of time pressures: Edward A. Ackerman, *Japan's Natural Resources and Their Relation to Japan's Economic Future* (Chicago, 1953); Thomas F. M. Adams and Hoshii Iwao, *A Financial History of Modern Japan* (Tokyo, 1964); E. J. Lewe van Aduard, *Japan: From Surrender to Peace* (New York, 1954); George C. Allen, *Japan's Economic Expansion* (London, 1965); Joseph L. Anderson and Donald Richie, *The Japanese Film: Art and Industry* (Tokyo, 1959); Asahi Shimbun staff, *The Pacific Rivals: A Japanese View of Japanese-American Relations*, trans. Peter Grilli and Murakami Yoshio (New York, 1972); James E. Auer, *The Postwar Rearmament of Japanese Maritime Forces, 1945–1971* (New York, 1973); Iwao F. Ayusawa, *A History of Labor in Modern Japan* (Honolulu, 1966); Hans H. Baerwald, *Japan's Parliament: An Introduction* (New York, 1974); idem, *The Purge of Japanese Leaders Under the Occupation* (Berkeley, CA, 1959); E. Wight Bakke, *Revolutionary Democracy: Challenge and Testing in Japan* (Hamden, CT, 1968); Mariko Bando, *The Women of Japan — Past and Present* (Tokyo, 1977); Thomas A. Bisson, *Prospects for Democracy in Japan* (New York, 1949); idem, *Zaibatsu Dissolution in Japan* (Berkeley, CA, 1954); Hugh Borton, *Japan's Modern Century: From Perry to 1970* (2d ed., New York, 1970); idem, ed., *Japan* (Ithaca, NY, 1951); idem, et al., *Japan Between East and West* (New York, 1957); Faubion Bowers, *Japanese Theatre* (New York, 1952); Everett F. Briggs, *New Dawn in Japan* (New York, 1948); Russell Brines, *MacArthur's Japan* (Philadelphia, 1948); Martin Bronfenbrenner, *Prospects of Japanese Democracy* (Toronto, 1955); Thomas W. Burkman, ed., *The Occupation of Japan: Educational and Social Reform . . .* (Norfolk, 1982); Noel F. Busch, *Fallen Sun: A Report on Japan* (New York, 1948); Robert J. C. Butow, *Japan's Decision to Surrender* (Stanford, 1954); Bernard C. Cohen, *The Political Process and Foreign Policy: The Making of the Japanese Peace Settlement* (Princeton, 1957); Jerome B. Cohen, *Economic Problems of Free Japan* (Princeton, 1952); idem, *Japan's Economy in War and Reconstruction* (Minneapolis, 1949); idem, *Japan's Post-War Economy* (Bloomington, IN, 1958); Evelyn S. Colbert, *The Left Wing in Japanese Politics* (New York, 1952); Allan B. Cole, *Japanese Society and Politics: The Impact of Social Stratification and Mobility on Politics* (Boston, 1956); idem, et al., *Socialist Parties in Post-War Japan* (New Haven, 1966); idem and Nakanishi Naomichi, comps. and eds., *Japanese Opinion Polls, with Socio-Political Significance, 1947–1957* (Medford, MA, 1958); Alvin D. Coox, *Japan: The Final Agony* (New York, 1970); William Costello, *De-*

mocracy vs. Feudalism in Post-War Japan (Tokyo, 1948); William J. Coughlin, *Conquered Press: The MacArthur Era in Japanese Journalism* (Palo Alto, CA, 1952); William Craig, *The Fall of Japan* (New York, 1967); Wilhelmus H. M. Creemers, *Shrine Shinto After World War II* (Leiden, Netherlands, 1968); Richard L. G. Deverall, *Red Star Over Japan* (Calcutta, 1952); Ronald P. Dore, *Land Reform in Japan* (New York, 1959); Benjamin C. Duke, *Japan's Militant Teachers: A History of the Left-Wing Teachers' Movement* (Honolulu, 1973); Frederick S. Dunn, et al., *Peacemaking and the Settlement with Japan* (Princeton, 1963); Jun Eto, *A Nation Reborn: A Short History of Postwar Japan* (Tokyo, 1974); Miriam S. Farley, *Aspects of Japan's Labor Problems* (New York, 1950); Robert A. Fearey, *The Occupation of Japan: Second Phase, 1948–1950* (New York, 1950); Herbert Feis, *Contest Over Japan* (New York, 1967); Sherwood M. Fine, *Japan's Post-War Industrial Recovery* (Tokyo, 1952); Foreign Affairs Association of Japan, ed., *The Japan Year Book, 1946–1948* (Tokyo, 1949); John W. Gaddis, *Public Information in Japan Under American Occupation: A Study of Democratization Efforts Through Agencies of Public Expression* (Geneva, Switzerland, 1950); Frank Gibney, *Five Gentlemen of Japan: The Portrait of a Nation's Character* (New York, 1953); Grant K. Goodman, comp., *The American Occupation of Japan: A Retrospective View* (Lawrence, KS, 1968); Andrew J. Grad, *Land and Peasant in Japan: An Introductory Survey* (New York, 1952); Eleanor M. Hadley, *Antitrust in Japan* (Princeton, 1970); John W. Hall and Richard K. Beardsley, eds., *Twelve Doors to Japan* (New York, 1965); Robert K. Hall, *Education for a New Japan* (New Haven, 1949); idem, *Shushin: The Ethics of a Defeated Nation* (New York, 1949); Ehud Harari, *The Politics of Labor Legislation in Japan: National-International Interaction* (Berkeley, CA, 1973); Elizabeth A. Hemphill, *The Road to KEEP: The Story of Paul Rusch in Japan* (New York, 1970 [1st ed., 1969]); Dan F. Henderson, ed., *The Constitution of Japan: Its First Twenty Years, 1947–67* (Seattle, 1969); Laurence I. Hewes, Jr., *Japan — Land and Men: An Account of the Japanese Land Reform Program, 1945–51* (Ames, IA, 1955); idem, *Japanese Land Reform Program* (Tokyo, 1950); Hajo Holborn, *American Military Government: Its Organization and Policies* (Washington, 1947); Daniel C. Holtom, *Modern Japan and Shinto Nationalism: A Study of Present-Day Trends in Japanese Religions* (rev. ed., Chicago, 1947); David Horowitz, *The Free World Colossus* (New York, 1965); Charles W. Inglehart, *A Century of Protestant Christianity in Japan* (Tokyo, 1959); Nobutaka Ito, *New Japan: Six Years of Democratization* (Tokyo, 1952); Chalmers Johnson, *MITI and the Japanese Miracle: The Growth of Industrial Policy, 1925–1975* (Stanford, 1982); Kazuo Kawai, *Japan's American Interlude* (Chicago, 1960); William Kerr, *Japan Begins Again* (New York, 1949); Joseph M. Kitagawa, *Religion in Japanese History* (New York, 1966); Akira Kubota, *Higher Civil Servants in Postwar Japan: Their Social Origins, Educational Backgrounds, and Career Patterns* (Princeton, 1969); Dan Kurzman, *Kishi and Japan: The Search for the Sun* (New York, 1960); Richard L. Lael, *The Yamashita Precedent: War Crimes and Command Responsibility* (Wilmington, DE, 1982); John La Cerda, *The Conqueror Comes to Tea: Japan Under MacArthur* (New Brunswick, NJ, 1946); Frank Langdon, *Politics in Japan*

(Boston, 1967); Theodore H. McNelly, *Contemporary Government of Japan* (Boston, 1963); *Mainichi Daily News* staff, *Fifty Years of Light and Dark: The Hirohito Era* (2d ed., Tokyo, 1976); John M. Maki, *Government and Politics in Japan: The Road to Democracy* (New York, 1962); Edwin M. Martin, *The Allied Occupation of Japan* [1945–48] (Stanford, 1948); Richard H. Minear, *Victor's Justice: The Tokyo War Crimes Trial* (Princeton, 1971); John D. Montgomery, *Forced to Be Free: The Artificial Revolution in Germany and Japan* (Chicago, 1957); idem, *The Purge in Occupied Japan: A Study in the Use of Civilian Agencies Under Military Government* (Chevy Chase, MD, 1954); Ivan I. Morris, *Nationalism and the Right Wing in Japan: A Study of Post-War Trends* (New York, 1960); Takafusa Nakamura, *The Postwar Japanese Economy: Its Development and Structure* (Tokyo, 1981); Osamu Nariai, *The Modernization of the Japanese Economy* (Tokyo, 1977); Charles E. Neu, *The Troubled Encounter: The United States and Japan* (New York, 1975); Toshio Nishi, *Unconditional Democracy: Education and Politics in Occupied Japan, 1945–1952* (Stanford, 1982); Masatake Okumiya and Jiro Horikoshi, with Martin Caidin, *Zero!* (New York, 1971 [1st ed., 1957]); Herbert Passin, *The Legacy of the Occupation: Japan* (New York, 1968); John C. Perry, *Beneath the Eagle's Wings: Americans in Occupied Japan* (New York, 1980); Philip R. Piccagallo, *The Japanese on Trial: Allied War Crimes Operations in the East, 1945–1951* (Austin, 1979); Willard Price, *The Japanese Miracle and Peril* (New York, 1971); Harold S. Quigley and John E. Turner, *The New Japan: Government and Politics* (Minneapolis, 1956); Lawrence H. Redford, ed., *The Occupation of Japan . . . and Its Legacy to the Postwar World . . .* (Norfolk, 1976); idem, ed., *The Occupation of Japan: Economic Policy and Reform . . .* (Norfolk, 1980); idem, ed., *The Occupation of Japan: Impact of Legal Reform . . .* (Norfolk, 1978); A. Frank Reel, *The Case of General Yamashita* (Chicago, 1949); Edwin O. Reischauer, *Japan, Past and Present* (3d ed., New York, 1964); idem, *Japan: The Story of a Nation* (New York, 1970); idem, *The Japanese* (Cambridge, MA, 1977); idem, *The United States and Japan* (3d ed., Cambridge, MA, 1965); Richard N. Rosecrance, *Australian Diplomacy and Japan, 1945–1951* (Parkville, Australia, 1962); Walter J. Sheldon, *The Honorable Conqueror: The Occupation of Japan, 1945–1952* (New York, 1965); Saburo Shiomi, *Japan's Finance and Taxation, 1940–1956*, trans. Hasegawa Shotaro (New York, 1957); Archibald T. Steele, *Present-Day Japan* (New York, 1947); Kurt Steiner, *Local Government in Japan* (Stanford, 1965); Peter B. Stone, *Japan Surges Ahead: The Story of an Economic Miracle* (New York, 1969); Richard Storry, *A History of Modern Japan* (Harmondsworth, England, 1960); Arthur R. Swearingen, *Communist Strategy in Japan, 1945–1960* (Santa Monica, 1965); idem, *The Soviet Union and Postwar Japan: Escalating Challenge and Response* (Stanford, 1979); idem and Paul Langer, *Red Flag in Japan: International Communism in Action, 1919–1951* (Cambridge, MA, 1952); Irene B. Tauber, *The Population of Japan* (Princeton, 1958); Otomo Taka and Hideo Tanaka, eds., *The Making of the Constitution of Japan* (2 vols., Tokyo, 1972); Yasuo Tatsuki, *General Trend of Japanese Opinion Following the End of the War; Based Especially on Public Opinion Surveys* (Tokyo, 1948); Lawrence Taylor, *A Trial of Gener-*

als: Homma, Yamashita, MacArthur (South Bend, IN, 1981); Robert B. Textor, *Failure in Japan; with Keystones for a Positive Policy* (Westport, CT, 1972); George O. Totten, ed., *Democracy in Prewar Japan: Groundwork or Facade?* (Boston, 1965); Edward Uhlan and Dana L. Thomas, *Shoriki, Miracle Man of Japan: A Biography* (New York, 1957); Harold Wakefield, *New Paths for Japan* (London, 1948); Robert E. Ward and Frank J. Shulman, comps. and eds., *The Allied Occupation of Japan, 1945–1952: An Annotated Bibliography of Western-Language Materials* (Chicago, 1974); Robert E. Ward, ed., *Five Studies in Japanese Politics* (Ann Arbor, MI, 1957); idem, ed., *Political Development in Modern Japan* (Princeton, 1968); Martin E. Weinstein, *Japan's Postwar Defense Policy, 1947–1968* (New York, 1971); Harry E. Wildes, *Typhoon in Tokyo: The Occupation and Its Aftermath* (New York, 1954); Robert Wolfe, ed., *Americans as Proconsuls: United States Military Government in Germany and Japan, 1944–1952* (Carbondale, IL, 1984); William P. Woodard, *The Allied Occupation of Japan, 1945–1952, and Japanese Religions* (Leiden, Netherlands, 1972); Kozo Yamamura, *Economic Policy in Postwar Japan: Growth Versus Economic Democracy* (Berkeley, CA, 1967); Chitoshi Yanaga, *Big Business in Japanese Politics* (New Haven, 1968); idem, *Japan Since Perry* (New York, 1949); idem, *Japanese People and Politics* (New York, 1956); Shigeru Yoshida, *Japan's Decisive Century, 1867–1967* (New York, 1967); Michael M. Yoshitsu, *Japan and the San Francisco Peace Settlement* (New York, 1982).

The following secondary works on postwar Korea and the Korean War were used: Frank Baldwin, ed., *Without Parallel: The American-Korean Relationship Since 1945* (New York, 1974); C. N. Barclay, *The First Commonwealth Division: The Story of British Commonwealth Land Forces in Korea, 1950–1953* (Aldershot, England, 1954); Carl Berger, *The Korea Knot: A Military-Political History* (Philadelphia, 1957); Malcolm W. Cagle and Frank A. Manson, *The Sea War in Korea* (Annapolis, MD, 1957); Ronald J. Caridi, *The Korean War and American Politics: The Republican Party as a Case Study* (Philadelphia, 1968); Soon Sung Cho, *Korea in World Politics, 1940–1950: An Evaluation of American Responsibility* (Berkeley, CA, 1967); Henry Chung, *The Russians Came to Korea* (Seoul, Korea, 1947); Bruce G. Cumings, *The Origins of the Korean War: Liberation and the Emergence of Separate Regimes, 1945–1947* (Princeton, 1981); idem, ed., *Child of Conflict: The Korean-American Relationship, 1943–1953* (Seattle, 1983); Charles M. Dobbs, *The Unwanted Symbol: American Foreign Policy, the Cold War, and Korea, 1945–1950* (Kent, OH, 1981); David D. Duncan, *This Is War: A Photo Narrative in Three Parts* (New York, 1951); T. R. Fehrenbach, *This Kind of War: A Study in Unpreparedness* (New York, 1963); Robert F. Futrell, *The United States Air Force in Korea, 1950–1953* (New York, 1961); Lloyd C. Gardner, ed., *The Korean War* (New York, 1972); Andrew C. Geer, *The New Breed: The Story of the U.S. Marines in Korea* (New York, 1952); Alexander L. George, *The Chinese Communist Army in Action: The Korean War and Its Aftermath* (New York, 1967); Leland M. Goodrich, *Korea: A Study of U.S. Policy in the United Nations* (New York, 1956); Leon Gordenker, *The United Nations and the Peaceful Unification of Korea: The Politics of Field Operations,*

1947–1950 (The Hague, 1959); Joseph C. Goulden, *Korea: The Untold Story of the War* (New York, 1982); A. Wigfall Green, *The Epic of Korea* (Washington, 1950); Samuel B. Griffith, *The Chinese People's Liberation Army* (New York, 1967); Allen Guttmann, ed., *Korea: Cold War and Limited War* (2d ed., Lexington, MA, 1972); Eric M. Hammel, *Chosin: Heroic Ordeal of the Korean War* (New York, 1981); Robert D. Heinl, Jr., *Victory at High Tide: The Inchon-Seoul Campaign* (Philadelphia, 1968); Francis H. Heller, ed., *The Korean War: A 25-Year Perspective* (Lawrence, KS, 1977); Gregory Henderson, *Korea: The Politics of the Vortex* (Cambridge, MA, 1968); Trumbull Higgins, *Korea and the Fall of MacArthur: A Précis in Limited War* (New York, 1960); Walter Karig, et al., *Battle Report: The War in Korea* (New York, 1952); William W. Kaufman, *Policy Objectives and Military Action in the Korean War* (Santa Monica, CA, 1956); Richard S. Kirkendall, *Harry S Truman, Korea and the Imperial Presidency* (St. Charles, MO, 1975); idem, *Harry S Truman: The Decision to Intervene* (St. Louis, MO, 1979); Michael Langley, *Inchon Landing: MacArthur's Last Triumph* (New York, 1979); Robert Leckie, *Conflict: The History of the Korean War, 1950–53* (New York, 1962); idem, *The March to Glory* [Chosin] (Cleveland, 1960); Richard Lowitt, ed., *The Truman-MacArthur Controversy* (Chicago, 1967); Gene M. Lyons, *Military Policy and Economic Aid: The Korean Case, 1950–1953* (Columbus, OH, 1961); George M. McCune, *Korea Today* (Cambridge, MA, 1950); James McGovern, *To the Yalu: From the Chinese Invasion of Korea to MacArthur's Dismissal* (New York, 1972); S. L. A. Marshall, *The Military History of the Korean War* (New York, 1963); idem, *Operation Punch and the Capture of Hill 440, Suwon, Korea, February 1951* (Baltimore, 1952); idem, *The River and the Gauntlet: Defeat of the Eighth Army by the Chinese Communist Forces, November 1950, in the Battle of the Chongchon River, Korea* (New York, 1953); E. Grant Meade, *American Military Government in Korea* (New York, 1951); Harry J. Middleton, *The Compact History of the Korean War* (New York, 1965); C. Clyde Mitchell, Jr., *Korea: Second Failure in Asia* (Washington, 1951); Lynn Montross, *Cavalry of the Sky: The Story of the U.S. Marine Combat Helicopters* (New York, 1954); Edgar O'Ballance, *Korea, 1950–1953* (Hamden, CT, 1969); George Odgers, *Across the Parallel: The Australian 77th Squadron with the United States Air Force in the Korean War* (Melbourne, Australia, 1953); Robert T. Oliver, *Why War Came to Korea* (New York, 1950); Glenn D. Paige, *The Korean Decision: June 24–30, 1950* (New York, 1968); idem, ed., *1950: Truman's Decision: The United States Enters the Korean War* (New York, 1970); Rutherford M. Poats, *Decision in Korea* (New York, 1954); David Rees, *Korea: The Limited War* (Baltimore, 1970 [1st ed., 1964]); W. D. Reeve, *The Republic of Korea* (New York, 1963); Richard H. Rovere and Arthur M. Schlesinger, Jr., *The MacArthur Controversy and American Foreign Policy* (New York, 1965 [1st ed., 1951, entitled *The General and the President and the Future of American Foreign Policy*]); Walt Sheldon, *Hell or High Water: MacArthur's Landing at Inchon* (New York, 1968); Richard C. Snyder and Glenn D. Paige, *The United States Decision to Resist Aggression in Korea: The Application of an Analytical Scheme* (Evanston, IL, 1956); John W. Spanier, *The Truman-MacArthur Controversy and the Korean*

War (Cambridge, MA, 1959); Denis Stairs, *The Diplomacy of Constraint: Canada, the Korean War, and the United States* (Toronto, 1974); James F. Stewart, *Airpower: The Decisive Force in Korea* (Princeton, 1957); I. F. Stone, *The Hidden History of the Korean War* (New York, 1952); Reginald W. Thompson, *Cry Korea* (London, 1951); Edmund Traverso, ed., *Korea and the Limits of Limited War* (Menlo Park, CA, 1970); Allen S. Whiting, *China Crosses the Yalu: The Decision to Enter the Korean War* (New York, 1960); Charles A. Willoughby, *Aid and Comfort to the Enemy: Trends of Korean Press Reports* (Tokyo, 1951); Guy Wint, *What Happened in Korea? A Study of Collective Security* (London, 1954); Tae-ho Yoo, *The Korean War and the United Nations: A Legal and Diplomatic Historical Study* (Louvain, Belgium, 1965).

Other secondary books of value to this study were Charles C. Alexander, *Holding the Line: The Eisenhower Era, 1952–1961* (Bloomington, IN, 1975); Stephen E. Ambrose, *Ike's Spies: Eisenhower and the Espionage Establishment* (Garden City, NY, 1981); idem, *The Supreme Commander: The War Years of General Dwight D. Eisenhower* (Garden City, NY, 1970); Max Beloff, *Soviet Policy in the Far East, 1944–1951* (London, 1953); C. Joseph Bernardo and Eugene H. Bacon, *American Military Policy: Its Development Since 1775* (Harrisburg, PA, 1955); Harry R. Borowski, *A Hollow Threat: Strategic Air Power and Containment Before Korea* (Westport, CT, 1981); Andrew Boyle, *The Climate of Treason: Five Who Spied for Russia* (London, 1979); idem, *The Fourth Man* (New York, 1980); Bernard Brodie, *War and Politics* (New York, 1973); Seyom Brown, *The Faces of Power: Constancy and Change in United States Foreign Policy from Truman to Johnson* (New York, 1968); Peter Calvocoressi, ed., *Survey of International Affairs, 1947–51* (3 vols., New York, 1952–54); John C. Campbell, Richard C. Stebbins, et al., eds., *The United States in World Affairs, 1945–51* (4 vols., New York, 1947–52); Hadley Cantril, ed., *Public Opinion, 1935–1946* (Princeton, 1951); Congressional Quarterly Service, *Global Defense: U.S. Military Commitments Abroad* (Washington, 1969); Cecil V. Crabb, Jr., *Bipartisan Foreign Policy: Myth or Reality?* (Evanston, IL, 1958); James B. Crowley, ed., *Modern East Asia: Essays in Interpretation* (New York, 1970); Richard M. Dalfiume, *Desegregation of the U.S. Armed Forces: Fighting on Two Fronts, 1939–1953* (Columbia, MO, 1969); Paul T. David, et al., *Presidential Nominating Politics in 1952* (5 vols., Baltimore, 1954); Robert A. Divine, *Foreign Policy and U.S. Presidential Elections, 1940–1960* (2 vols., New York, 1974); Joe C. Dixon, ed., *The American Military and the Far East: Proceedings of the Ninth Military Symposium, United States Air Force Academy, 1–3 October 1980* (Washington, 1982); Herbert Druks, *Harry S. Truman and the Russians, 1945–1953* (New York, 1966); Clyde Eagleton and Richard N. Swift, eds., *Annual Review of United Nations Affairs, 1950–51* (2 vols., New York, 1951–52); Herbert Eaton, *Presidential Timber: A History of Nominating Conventions, 1868–1960* (New York, 1964); John K. Fairbank, et al., *Next Step in Asia* (Cambridge, MA, 1949); Thomas K. Finletter, *Power and Policy: U.S. Foreign Policy and Military Power in the Hydrogen Age* (New York, 1954); Denna F. Fleming, *The Cold War and Its Origins, 1917–1960* (2 vols., Garden City, NY, 1961); Jack D. Foner, *Blacks and the Military in American History* (New York, 1974); John

L. Gaddis, *Strategies of Containment: A Critical Appraisal of Postwar American National Security Policy* (New York, 1982); idem, *The United States and the Origins of the Cold War, 1941–47* (New York, 1972); Robert J. Gilmore and Denis A. Warner, eds., *Near North: Australia and a Thousand Million Neighbors* (Sydney, Australia, 1948); Norman A. Graebner, *The New Isolationism: A Study in Politics and Foreign Policy Since 1950* (New York, 1956); Louis J. Halle, *The Cold War as History* (New York, 1967); Morton H. Halperin, *Limited War in the Nuclear Age* (New York, 1963); Alonzo Hamby, *Beyond the New Deal: Harry S. Truman and American Liberalism* (New York, 1973); Paul Y. Hammond, *Organizing for Defense: The American Military Establishment in the Twentieth Century* (Princeton, 1961); Alan D. Harper, *The Politics of Loyalty: The White House and the Communist Issue, 1946–1952* (Westport, CT, 1969); Louis Harris, *Is There a Republican Majority? Political Trends, 1952–1956* (New York, 1954); Gregg Herken, *The Winning Weapon: The Atomic Bomb in the Cold War, 1945–1950* (New York, 1982 [1st ed., 1980]); Richard G. Hewlett and Francis Duncan, *Atomic Shield, 1947–1952. A History of the United States Atomic Energy Commission*, vol. II (University Park, PA, 1969); Jim D. Hill, *The Minute Man in Peace and War: A History of the National Guard* (Harrisburg, PA, 1963); Roger Hilsman, *Strategic Intelligence and National Decisions* (Glencoe, IL, 1956); R. Gordon Hoxie, *Command Decision and the Presidency: A Study in National Security Policy and Organization* (New York, 1977); Samuel P. Huntington, *The Common Defense: Strategic Programs in National Politics* (New York, 1966 [1st ed., 1961]); idem, *The Soldier and the State: The Theory and Politics of Civil-Military Relations* (Cambridge, MA, 1957); Akira Iriye, *Across the Pacific: An Inner History of American-East Asian Relations* (New York, 1967); Irving L. Janis, *Victims of Groupthink: A Psychological Study of Foreign-Policy Decisions and Fiascoes* (Boston, 1972); Philip C. Jessup, *The Birth of Nations* (New York, 1974); Walter Johnson, *1600 Pennsylvania Avenue: Presidents and the People Since 1929* (Boston, 1963 [1st ed., 1960]); Francis C. Jones, et al., *The Far East, 1942–1946. Survey of International Affairs, 1939–1946*, vol. VII (London, 1955); E. J. Kahn, *The China Hands: America's Foreign Service Officers and What Befell Them* (New York, 1975); Joseph B. Keenan and Brendon F. Brown, *Crimes Against International Law* (Washington, 1950); Young-hum Kim, ed., *Twenty Years of Crises: The Cold War Era* (Englewood Cliffs, NJ, 1968); Russell Kirk and James McClellan, *The Political Principles of Robert A. Taft* (New York, 1967); Joyce Kolko and Gabriel Kolko, *The Limits of Power: The World and United States Foreign Policy, 1945–1954* (New York, 1972); Lawrence J. Korb, *The Joint Chiefs of Staff: The First Twenty-five Years* (Bloomington, IN, 1976); Martin Kyre and Joan Kyre, *Military Occupation and National Security* (Washington, 1968); Walter LaFeber, *America, Russia, and the Cold War, 1945–1966* (New York, 1967); Richard E. Lauterbach, *Danger from the East* (New York, 1947); Robert McClintock, *The Meaning of Limited War* (Boston, 1967); William H. McNeill, *America, Britain, and Russia: Their Cooperation and Conflict, 1941–1946. Survey of International Affairs, 1939–1946*, vol. III (New York, 1953); Harvey Matusow, *False Witness* (New York, 1955); Ernest R. May, *"Lessons" of the Past: The Use and*

Misuse of History in American Foreign Policy (New York, 1975 [1st ed., 1973]); idem, ed., *The Ultimate Decision: The President as Commander in Chief* (New York, 1960); Robert L. Messner, *The End of an Alliance: James F. Byrnes, Roosevelt, Truman, and the Origins of the Cold War* (Chapel Hill, NC, 1982); Lynn H. Miller and Ronald W. Pruessen, eds., *Reflections on the Cold War: A Quarter Century of American Foreign Policy* (Philadelphia, 1974); Walter Millis, et al., *Arms and the State: Civil-Military Elements in National Policy* (New York, 1958); Raymond Moley, Jr., *The American Legion Story* (New York, 1966); Booth Mooney, *The Politicians, 1945–1960* (Philadelphia, 1970); J. Robert Moskin, *The U.S. Marine Corps Story* (rev. ed., New York, 1982); John E. Mueller, *War, Presidents, and Public Opinion* (New York, 1973); Robert W. Mullen, *Blacks in America's Wars: The Shift in Attitudes from the Revolutionary War to Vietnam* (New York, 1973); Maureen Mylander, *The Generals* (New York, 1974); Yonosuke Nagai and Akira Iriye, eds., *The Origins of the Cold War in Asia* (New York, 1977); Richard E. Neustadt, *Presidential Power: The Politics of Leadership* (New York, 1960); Virgil Ney, *Evolution of a Theater of Operations Headquarters, 1941–1967* (Washington, 1967); Lee Nichols, *Breakthrough on the Color Front* (New York, 1954); Robert E. Osgood, *Limited War: The Challenge to American Strategy* (Chicago, 1957); Overseas Press Club of America, *Men Who Make Your World* (New York, 1949); Bruce Page, et al., *The Philby Conspiracy* (Garden City, NY, 1968); Edgar F. Puryear, Jr., *Nineteen Stars* (Washington, 1971); Thomas C. Reeves, ed., *McCarthyism* (Hinsdale, IL, 1973); Elmo B. Roper, *You and Your Leaders: Their Actions and Your Reactions, 1936–1956* (New York, 1957); Eugene H. Roseboom, *A History of Presidential Elections: From George Washington to Richard M. Nixon* (3d ed., New York, 1970); Richard H. Rovere, *Senator Joe McCarthy* (New York, 1959); Ralph L. Roy, *Apostles of Discord: A Study of Organized Bigotry and Disruption on the Fringes of Protestantism* (Boston, 1953); Joseph P. Savage, *A Man Named Savage* (New York, 1975); Arthur M. Schlesinger, Jr., *The Imperial Presidency* (Boston, 1973); idem, ed., *History of American Presidential Elections, 1789–1968*, vol. IV (New York, 1971); Mark Seldon, ed., *Remaking Asia: Essays on the American Uses of Power* (New York, 1971); Robert R. Simmons, *The Strained Alliance: Peking, Pyongyang, Moscow, and the Politics of the Korean Civil War* (New York, 1975); Harold E. Snyder and George E. Beauchamp, eds., *An Experiment in International Cultural Relations: A Report of the Staff of the Commission on Occupied Areas* (Washington, 1951); John C. Sparrow, *History of Personnel Demobilization in the United States Army* (Washington, 1952); Harold Stein, ed., *American Civil-Military Decisions: A Book of Case Studies* (University, AL, 1963); Gay Talese, *The Kingdom and the Power* (New York, 1969); James C. Thomson, Jr., et al., *Sentimental Imperialists: The American Experience in East Asia* (New York, 1981); K. G. Tregonning, *A History of Modern Sabah: North Borneo, 1881–1963* (Singapore, 1965); Tang Tsou, *America's Failure in China, 1941–50* (Chicago, 1963); Andrew Tully, *CIA: The Inside Story* (New York, 1962); Gordon B. Turner, ed., *A History of Military Affairs in Western Society Since the Eighteenth Century* (New York, 1953); idem and Richard D. Challener, eds., *National Security in the Nuclear Age* (New York, 1960); Patricia D. Ward, *The Threat of Peace: James F. Byrnes and the Council of Foreign Ministers, 1945–1946* (Kent, OH, 1979); Alan Watt, *The Evolution of Australian Foreign Policy, 1938–1965* (New York, 1967); Russell F. Weigley, *The American Way of War: A History of United States Military Strategy and Policy* (New York, 1973); idem, *History of the United States Army* (New York, 1967); H. Bradford Westerfield, *Foreign Policy and Party Politics: Pearl Harbor to Korea* (New Haven, 1955); John Wheeler-Bennett and Anthony Nicholls, *The Semblance of Peace: The Political Settlement After the Second World War* (New York, 1974 [1st ed., 1972]); William S. White, *Citadel: The Story of the U.S. Senate* (New York, 1956); William A. Williams, ed., *From Colony to Empire: Essays in the History of American Foreign Relations* (New York, 1972); Elaine Windrich, *British Labour's Foreign Policy* (Stanford, 1952); George Woodbridge, comp., *UNRRA: The History of the United Nations Relief and Rehabilitation Administration* (3 vols., New York, 1950); Gordon R. Young, ed., *The Army Almanac: A Book of Facts Concerning the United States Army* (2d ed., Harrisburg, PA, 1959).

Whereas most secondary books that were used are listed above, the following articles from scholarly, military, and other professional journals are only those that were most essential to this project: Martin Blumenson, "MacArthur's Divided Command," *Army*, 7 (Nov. 1956), 38–44, 65; Ralph J. D. Braibanti, "The Role of Administration in the Occupation of Japan," *Annals of the American Academy of Political and Social Science*, 267 (Jan. 1950), 154–63; Malcolm W. Cagle, "Errors of the Korean War," *U.S. Naval Institute Proceedings*, 84 (Mar. 1958), 31–35; Ronald J. Caridi, "The G.O.P. and the Korean War," *Pacific Historical Review*, 37 (Nov. 1968), 423–43; John W. Dower, "Occupied Japan as History and Occupation History as Politics," *Journal of Asian Studies*, 34 (Feb. 1975), 485–504; Roger O. Egeberg, "General Douglas MacArthur," *Transactions of the American Clinical and Climatological Association*, 78 (1966), 161–71; Wesley R. Fishel, "Japan Under MacArthur: Retrospect and Prospect," *Western Political Quarterly*, 4 (June 1951), 210–25; Alexander L. George, "American Policy-Making and the North Korean Aggression," *World Politics*, 7 (Jan. 1955), 209–32; Morton H. Halperin, "The Limiting Process in the Korean War," *Political Science Quarterly*, 78 (Mar. 1963), 13–39; Leon Hollerman, "International Economic Controls in Occupied Japan," *Journal of Asian Studies*, 38 (Aug. 1979), 707–19; Philip C. Jessup, "Research Note: The Record of Wake Island — A Correction," *Journal of American History*, 67 (Mar. 1981), 866–70; Theodore H. McNelly, "The Renunciation of War in the Japanese Constitution," *Political Science Quarterly*, 77 (Sept. 1962), 350–78; Ray A. Moore, "Reflections on the Occupation of Japan," *Journal of Asian Studies*, 38 (Aug. 1979), 721–34; idem, "The Occupation of Japan as History: Some Recent Research," *Monumenta Nipponica*, 36 (Autumn 1981), 317–28; John Norman, "MacArthur's Blockade Proposals Against Red China," *Pacific Historical Review*, 26 (May 1957), 616–74; Forrest C. Pogue, "The Military in a Democracy," *International Security*, 3 (Spring 1979), 58–80; Harold S. Quigley, "Democracy Occupies Japan," *Virginia Quarterly Review*, 23 (Autumn 1947), 521–31; Clark G. Reynolds, "MacArthur as Maritime Strategist," *Naval War College Review*, 33 (Mar.–Apr. 1980), 79–91; Richard T. Ruetten, "General Douglas MacArthur's 'Reconnaissance in Force': The Rationalization of a Defeat in Korea," *Pacific Historical Review*, 36 (Feb. 1967), 79–93; Michael Schaller, "Securing the Great Crescent: Occupied Japan and the Origins of Containment in Southeast Asia," *Journal of American History*, 69 (Sept. 1982), 392–414; Howard B. Schonberger, "The General and the Presidency: Douglas MacArthur and the Election of 1948," *Wisconsin Magazine of History*, 57 (Spring 1974), 201–19; idem, "The Japan Lobby in American Diplomacy, 1947–1952," *Pacific Historical Review*, 6 (Aug. 1977), 327–59; idem, "Zaibatsu Dissolution and the American Restoration of Japan," *Bulletin of Concerned Asian Scholars*, 5 (Sept. 1973), 16–31; William Stueck, "Cold War Revisionism and the Origins of the Korean Conflict: The Kolko Thesis," *Pacific Historical Review*, 42 (Nov. 1973), 537–60, with rejoinders by Joyce and Gabriel Kolko and by Stueck, 560–75; Philip H. Taylor, "The Administration of Occupied Japan," *Annals of the American Academy of Political and Social Science*, 267 (Jan. 1950), 140–53; H. Pat Tomlinson, "Inchon: The General's Decision," *Military Review*, 47 (Apr. 1967), 28–34; Justin Williams, "Making the Japanese Constitution: A Further Look," *American Political Science Review*, 59 (Sept. 1965), 665–79; John E. Wiltz, "The MacArthur Hearings of 1951: The Secret Testimony," *Military Affairs*, 39 (Dec. 1975), 167–73; idem, "Truman and MacArthur: The Wake Island Meeting," ibid., 42 (Dec. 1978), 169–76; Lawrence S. Wittner, "MacArthur and the Missionaries: God and Man in Occupied Japan," *Pacific Historical Review*, 40 (Feb. 1971), 77–98; Philip Wylie, "Medievalism and the MacArthurian Legend," *Quarterly Journal of Speech*, 37 (Dec. 1951), 473–78.

Besides the above journals, others with useful articles were *Administrative Science Quarterly, Aerospace Historian, American Historical Review, American Journal of International Law, American Journal of Sociology, American Political Science Review, Army and Navy Journal, Association of American Colleges Bulletin, Combat Forces Journal, The Crisis, Far Eastern Quarterly, Far Eastern Survey, Foreign Affairs, Foreign Intelligence Digest, Foreign Policy Bulletin, Forensic Quarterly, Hanover Forum, Harvard Business Review, International Conciliation, International Organization, International Social Science Journal, Journal of Politics, Marine Corps Gazette, Military Collector, Military Government Journal, Orbis, Pacific Affairs, Phi Delta Kappan, Political Quarterly, Proceedings of the Academy of Political Science, Quarterly of the Historical Society of Southern California, Quarterly Journal of the Library of Congress, School and Society, UN Bulletin, UN World, World Affairs,* and *Yale Review.*

Dissertations that provided much data were Roy K. Flint, "The Tragic Flaw: MacArthur, the Joint Chiefs, and the Korean War" (Duke University, 1976); Carolyn J. Mattern, "The Man on the Dark Horse: The Presidential Campaigns for General Douglas MacArthur, 1944 & 1948" (University of Wisconsin, Madison, 1976); John R. Scott, "The Effect of the Cold War Upon the Occupation of Japan" (University of Illinois, 1952); and Eric H. F. Svensson, "The Military Occupation of Japan: The First Years: Planning, Policy Formulation, and Reforms" (University of Den-

ver, 1966). Other graduate works of consequence were John Bowden, "The
SCAP Files of Commander Alfred R. Hussey" (unpublished M.A. thesis,
University of Michigan, 1968); Armel Dyer, "The Oratory of Douglas
MacArthur" (unpublished Ph.D. dissertation, University of Oregon, 1968);
Shirley S. Foster, "Lieutenant General Alpha L. Bowser, USMC, and the
Korean War" (unpublished M.A. thesis, San Diego State University, 1975);
Donald M. Goldstein, "Ennis C. Whitehead, Aerospace Commander and
Pioneer" (unpublished Ph.D. dissertation, University of Denver, 1970); John
F. Hanson, "The Trial of Lieutenant General Masaharu Homma" (un-
published Ph.D. dissertation, Mississippi State University, 1977); Merne
A. Harris, "The MacArthur Dismissal: A Study in Political Mail" (unpub-
lished Ph.D. dissertation, University of Iowa, 1966); Thomas J. Hehman,
"U.S. Security Policy in Postwar Japan: The Making of a Cold War Ally"
(unpublished M.A. thesis, Old Dominion University, 1977); Thomas G.
Henderson, "Editorial Reaction of Selected Major Indiana Daily News-
papers to a National Controversy — the Truman-MacArthur Conflict"
(unpublished Ed.D. dissertation, Ball State University, 1977); Han Mu
Kang, "The United States Military Government in Korea, 1945–1948: An
Analysis and Evaluation of Its Policy" (unpublished Ph.D. dissertation,
University of Cincinnati, 1970); Charles A. Lofgren, "Congress and the
Korean Conflict" (unpublished Ph.D. dissertation, Stanford University,
1966); Matthew E. Mantell, "Opposition to the Korean War: A Study in
American Dissent" (unpublished Ph.D. dissertation, New York Univer-
sity, 1973); Thomas L. Marshall, "The Strategy of Conflict in the Korean
War" (unpublished Ph.D. dissertation, University of Virginia, 1969);
Lawrence H. Redford, "The Trial of General Tomoyuki Yamashita: A
Case Study in Command Responsibility" (unpublished M.A. thesis, Old
Dominion University, 1975); James R. Riggs, "Congress and the Conduct
of the Korean War" (unpublished Ph.D. dissertation, Purdue University,
1972); Stephen Robb, "Fifty Years of Farewell: Douglas MacArthur's
Commemorative and Deliberative Speaking" (unpublished Ph.D. disser-
tation, Indiana University, 1967); Albert L. Sage III, "Policy Formulation
for the Occupation of Japan and Its Immediate Execution" (unpublished
M.A. thesis, Mississippi State University, 1971); Michael S. Twedt, "The
War Rhetoric of Harry S. Truman During the Korean Conflict" (unpublished Ph.D. dissertation, University of Kansas, 1969); Ann C. Wyman,
"The Contribution of General Crawford F. Sams to the Occupation of
Japan, 1945–1951" (unpublished M.A. thesis, Mississippi State University, 1975). In addition, a number of unpublished scholarly papers are
cited in the chapter notes.

Notes

CHAPTER I. *Constraints on the New Shogun*

pages 3–34

1. Maj. Gen. Clovis E. Byers to his wife, Sept. 8, 1945; Lt. Gen. Robert L. Eichelberger to DM, Sept. 7, 1945, Clovis E. Byers Papers, Hoover Institution on War, Revolution, and Peace, Stanford University, Stanford; Robert L. Eichelberger, Diary, Sept. 8, 1945, Robert L. Eichelberger Papers, Duke University, Durham, NC; SCAP, *Political Reorientation of Japan, September 1945 to September 1948: Report of Government Section* (2 vols., Washington, 1949), II, 738; Robert L. Eichelberger, with Milton Mackaye, *Our Jungle Road to Tokyo* (New York, 1950), 264–65. That noon MacArthur had lunch at the Imperial Hotel with nine of the officers who had attended the flag-raising ceremony: Eichelberger, Byers, Adm. William F. Halsey, Lt. Gen. Barney M. Giles, Lt. Gen. Richard K. Sutherland, Brig. Gen. Courtney Whitney, Brig. Gen. Bonner F. Fellers, Col. Sidney F. Mashbir, and Col. Roger O. Egeberg.

2. Ints., Amb. Masayoshi Kakitsubo, Aug. 15, 1977; Sukejiro Katamoto, Aug. 16, 1977; Amb. Tadakatsu Suzuki, Aug. 22, 1977; Bishop John F. O'Hara to DM, Aug. 19, 1946, RG 5, MMBA; *Stars and Stripes* (Pacific ed.), Nov. 29, 1945; Apr. 6, Sept. 24, 1946; *Nippon Times*, Sept. 28, 1946; *New York Times*, Oct. 24, 1945; May 16, Oct. 12, 1946; "Reports from a Neglected Area," *Commonweal*, 45 (Dec. 13, 1946), 219–20; Richard E. Lauterbach, "Letters to MacArthur: Japs Ask Him Favors and Tell Their Troubles," *Life*, 20 (Jan. 14, 1946), 4, 7.

3. Ints., Tokio Sugase, Aug. 13, 1977; Hajime Seki, Aug. 20, 1977; U.S. Strategic Bombing Survey, *Summary Report (Pacific War)* (Washington, 1946), 14–25; Alvin D. Coox, *Japan: The Final Agony* (New York, 1970), 22–41; Robert J. C. Butow, *Japan's Decision to Surrender* (Stanford,

1954), 94–95; William Craig, *The Fall of Japan* (New York, 1967), 22–26.

4. *Mainichi Daily News* staff, *Fifty Years of Light and Dark: The Hirohito Era* (2d ed., Tokyo, 1976), 198–99; Robert Shaplen, "From MacArthur to Miki," pt. 1, *New Yorker*, 51 (Aug. 4, 1975), 62–63; Hugh T. Patrick, "The Phoenix Risen from the Ashes: Postwar Japan," in James B. Crowley, ed., *Modern East Asia: Essays in Interpretation* (New York, 1970), 298–299; Jerome B. Cohen, *Japan's Economy in War and Reconstruction* (Minneapolis, 1949), 417–19.

5. Ints., Suzuki, Sugase; Jun Eto, *A Nation Reborn: A Short History of Postwar Japan* (Tokyo, 1974), 12–13; Edwin O. Reischauer, *The United States and Japan* (3d ed., Cambridge, MA, 1965), 205–18; Masatake Okumiya and Jiro Horikoshi, with Martin Caidin, *Zero!* (New York, 1971 [1st ed., 1957]), 276–77, 300–01.

6. Int., Kakitsubo; Kazuo Kawai, *Japan's American Interlude* (Chicago, 1960), 4–15; Robert E. Ward and Frank J. Shulman, comps. and eds., *The Allied Occupation of Japan, 1945–1952: An Annotated Bibliography of Western-Language Materials* (Chicago, 1974), 716; Douglas MacArthur, *Reminiscences* (New York, 1964), 281, 282; Ray A. Moore, "Reflections on the Occupation of Japan," *Journal of Asian Studies*, 38 (Aug. 1979), 722–23; Reischauer, *United States and Japan*, 220–21; John W. Gaddis, *Public Information in Japan Under American Occupation: A Study of Democratization Efforts Through Agencies of Public Expression* (Geneva, 1950), 88–89.

7. Ints., Harry Emerson Wildes, July 8, 1977; Shingo Kaite, Aug. 19, 1977; Hideo Tanaka, Aug. 22, 1977; DM, *Reminiscences*, 282; George O. Totten, ed., *Democracy in Prewar Japan: Groundwork or Façade?* (Boston, 1965), passim; Yasusaburo Hara, et al., "Japan Looks Back on the Occupation," *Far Eastern Survey*, Feb. 25, 1953, 30, 32; George Atcheson, Jr., to HST, Nov. 5, 1945, in *FRUS, 1945*, VI, 826; John W. Dower, "Occupied Japan as History and Occupation History as Politics," *Journal of Asian Studies*, 34 (Feb. 1975), 486–87; Robert B. Textor, *Failure in Japan; With Keystones for a Positive Policy* (Westport, CT, 1972 [1st ed., 1951]), 16–23.

8. Courtney Whitney, *MacArthur: His Rendezvous with History* (New York, 1956), 213; DM, *Reminiscences*, 282–83.

9. Potsdam Declaration, July 26, 1945, in DS, *The Axis in Defeat: A Collection of Documents on American Policy Toward Germany and Japan* (Washington, 1945), 27–33.

10. Directive to SCAP, Aug. 15, 1945, RG 5, MMBA; Instrument of Surrender, Sept. 2, 1945, in Francis C. Jones, et al., *The Far East, 1942–1946. Survey of International Affairs, 1939–1946*, vol. VII (London, 1955), 498.

11. D. Clayton James, *The Years of MacArthur*, II, *1941–1945* (Boston, 1975), 782–84; Hugh Borton, "Occupation Policies in Japan and Korea," *Annals of the American Academy of Political and Social Science*, 255 (Jan. 1948), 146–47; Policy Decision on Basic Post-Surrender Policy

for Japan, Adopted by the Far Eastern Commission, June 19, 1947, in *DAFR*, IX, 95–103.

12. DS, *The Axis in Defeat*, 107–09.
13. Ibid., 109.
14. Ibid., 110–11.
15. Ibid., 111–14.
16. Ints., Gen. of the Army Dwight D. Eisenhower, Aug. 29, 1967; Col. Sidney F. Mashbir, Sept. 1, 1971; H. Freeman Matthews, June 15, 1977; Niles W. Bond, June 16, 1977; Hajo Holborn, *American Military Government: Its Organization and Policies* (Washington, 1947), 7–15, 91–92; U.S. National Archives, *Federal Records of World War II*, I, *Civilian Agencies* (Washington, 1950), 709; William H. Cunliffe, "Military Planning for the Occupation of Japan" and Milton O. Gustafson, "The State Department and the Occupation of Japan: Pre-Surrender Planning and Post-Defeat" (papers read at Assn. of Asian Studies meeting, San Francisco, Mar. 25, 1975); "Our Occupation Policy for Japan," *Department of State Bulletin*, 13 (Oct. 7, 1945), 538–45; Joseph C. Grew to DM, Aug. 22, 1945, RG 10, MMBA; U.S. Senate, Committee on the Judiciary, *Institute of Pacific Relations: Hearings* . . . 82d Cong., 1st and 2d Sess. (1951–52), 716–47, 2152–55; E. J. Kahn, Jr., *The China Hands: America's Foreign Service Officers and What Befell Them* (New York, 1975), 11–12, 253–56; Dwight D. Eisenhower, *Crusade in Europe* (Garden City, NY, 1948), 435–46, 441; idem, *The Papers of Dwight D. Eisenhower*, vols. VI–IX (1945–48), eds. Alfred D. Chandler, Jr., Louis Galambos, et al. (9 vols., Baltimore, 1978), VI, 220–21.
17. *New York Times*, Nov. 9, 1951.
18. Robert E. Wood to DM, Sept. 4, 1945, RG 10, MMBA.
19. Eisenhower, *Papers*, VI, 50, 414, 285; John C. Sparrow, *History of Personnel Demobilization in the United States Army* (Washington, 1952), 35–37, 306–10; Robert J. Donovan, *Conflict and Crisis: The Presidency of Harry S. Truman, 1945–48* (New York, 1977), 127.
20. DM, Statement, Sept. 17, 1945, in *FRUS, 1945*, VI, 715–16.
21. Dean G. Acheson, Memorandum of Telephone Conversation, Sept. 17, 1945, in ibid., 716–17; Dean G. Acheson, *Present at the Creation: My Years in the State Department* (New York, 1969), 126; *New York Times*, Sept. 18, 19, 23, 1945; "Watch on Tokyo," *Time*, 46 (Oct. 1, 1945), 27–28; London *Times*, Sept. 20, 1945; *Department of State Bulletin*, 13 (Sept. 23, 1945), 423; Donovan, *Conflict and Crisis*, 127–28; Pres. Harry S. Truman, News Conference, Sept. 18, 1945, in U.S. National Archives, *Public Papers of the Presidents of the United States* . . . *Containing the Public Messages, Speeches, and Statements of the President, 1945–64* (20 vols., Washington, 1958–66), *Truman, 1945*, 326.
22. Charles Patton to Sec. of State James F. Byrnes, Sept. 20, 1945; John S. Winant to Byrnes, Sept. 22, 1945, in *FRUS, 1945*, VI, 719–21; Gen. of the Army George C. Marshall to DM, Sept. 17, 1945; DM to Marshall, Sept. 18, 1945, in ibid., 717–18.

23. Washington *Post,* Sept. 19, 1945; Chicago *Tribune,* Sept. 19, 1945; New York *Daily Worker,* Sept. 18, 1945; misc. newspaper editorials reprinted in "Civil vs. Military Control," *Forum,* 194 (Nov. 1945), 262–67.

24. "Good Faith with Japan," *Christian Century,* 62 (Oct. 3, 1945), 1119–20.

25. Gordon R. Young, ed., *The Army Almanac: A Book of Facts Concerning the Army of the United States* (2d ed., Harrisburg, PA, 1959), 625; "Concerning Policy Toward Japan," *Department of State Bulletin,* 13 (Sept. 30, 1945), 479–80; Acheson, *Present,* 126–27; *New York Times,* Sept. 23, 25, 26, 1945; H. Bradford Westerfield, *Foreign Policy and Party Politics: Pearl Harbor to Korea* (New Haven, 1955), 60; David S. McLellan, *Dean Acheson: The State Department Years* (New York, 1976), 57–58; U.S. Senate, *Congressional Record,* 79th Cong., 1st Sess., Sept. 19–24, 1945, passim; James Van Zandt to Fellers, Oct. 10, 1945, RG 5, MMBA.

26. Harry S. Truman, *Memoirs* (2 vols., Garden City, NY, 1955–56), I, 520–21.

27. Gen. Robert L. Eichelberger, Diary, Oct. 20, 1945, Eichelberger Papers. For documents cited in this quotation, see Marshall to DM, Oct. 12, 1945, RG 5, MMBA; U.S. Senate Concurrent Resolution 35, passed Oct. 9, 1945, and U.S. House Concurrent Resolution 92, passed Oct. 10, 1945, RG 4, MMBA.

28. Truman, *Memoirs,* I, 455; *FRUS, 1945,* II, 59–61, 313–15, 336–39, 357–58, 360, 365–70; James F. Byrnes, *Speaking Frankly* (New York, 1947), 91–109, 213–15; Herbert Feis, *Contest Over Japan* (New York, 1967), 35–37, 44–47; John L. Gaddis, *The United States and the Origins of the Cold War, 1941–1947* (New York, 1972), 265–66; Max Beloff, *Soviet Policy in the Far East, 1944–1951* (London, 1953), 109–10.

29. Ints., Maj. Gen. Richard J. Marshall, July 27, 1971; Brig. Gen. Charles J. West, July 14, 1977; int., Faubion Bowers, pt. 2, no. 21, p. 32, CUOHRO; John Gunther, *The Riddle of MacArthur: Japan, Korea and the Far East* (New York, 1950), 22; Frank R. Kelley and Cornelius Ryan, *MacArthur: Man of Action* (Garden City, NY, 1951), 160–61; DM, *Reminiscences,* 285; William J. Sebald, with Russell Brines, *With MacArthur in Japan: A Personal History of the Occupation* (New York, 1965), 128; W. Averell Harriman and Elie Abel, *Special Envoy to Churchill and Stalin, 1941–1946* (New York, 1975), 214; E. J. Lewe van Aduard, *Japan: From Surrender to Peace* (The Hague, 1953), 20.

30. George H. Blakeslee, *The Far Eastern Commission: A Study in International Cooperation, 1945 to 1952* (Washington, 1953), 2–11; Maj. Gen. Frank R. McCoy to DM, Nov. 1, 1945, RG 10, MMBA; "Far Eastern Advisory Commission: Terms of Reference," *Department of State Bulletin,* 13 (Oct. 14, 1945), 561, 580; Samuel S. Stratton, "The Far Eastern Commission," *International Organization,* 2 (Feb. 1948), 3.

31. Byrnes to McCoy, Nov. 27, 1945, in *FRUS, 1945,* VI, 870; McCoy to Sec. of War Robert P. Patterson, Mar. 1, 1946, RG 5, MMBA; *Nippon*

Times, Feb. 13, 1946; "Far Eastern Commission: Summary Report on Trip to Japan," *Department of State Bulletin,* 14 (Mar. 10, 1946), 370–74; Blakeslee, *Far Eastern Commission,* 18–29; Nelson T. Johnson, Memorandum on Interview with Gen. of the Army Douglas MacArthur, Jan. 30, 1946, in *FRUS, 1946,* VIII, 123–27; Dr. George H. Blakeslee, Report on the Far Eastern Commission's Trip to Japan, Dec. 26, 1945–Feb. 13, 1946, in ibid., 163–65.

32. McCoy to Byrnes, Mar. 4, 1946, in *FRUS, 1946,* VIII, 159.

33. Int., Amb. W. Averell Harriman, June 20, 1977; Col. Lloyd A. Lehrbas to DM, Nov. 29, 1945, RG 5, MMBA; Byrnes to Amb. W. Averell Harriman, Oct. 27, 1945, in *FRUS, 1945,* VI, 797–98; Memorandum of Meeting of State, War, and Navy Secretaries, Nov. 6, 1945, in ibid., 832–34; Feis, *Contest Over Japan,* 51–84; James V. Forrestal, *The Forrestal Diaries,* ed. Walter Millis (New York, 1951), 103–08; Byrnes, *Speaking Frankly,* 215–17; Richard N. Rosecrance, *Australian Diplomacy and Japan, 1945–1951* (Parkville, Australia, 1962), 3–45; "Far Eastern Rivalries," London *Economist,* 140 (Nov. 10, 1945), 667–68; Gaddis, *Cold War,* 273–76.

34. Ints., Marshall, Mashbir; Washington *Times-Herald,* Oct. 11, 18, 1945; Chicago *Tribune,* Oct. 11, 1945; Washington *Daily News,* Oct. 11, 1945; Baltimore *Sun,* Oct. 18, 1945.

35. James F. Byrnes, *Moscow Meeting of Foreign Ministers, December 16–26, 1945* (Washington, 1946), passim; William H. McNeill, *America, Britain, and Russia: Their Cooperation and Conflict, 1941–1946. Survey of International Affairs, 1939–1946,* III (London, 1953), 703–06; Byrnes, *Speaking Frankly,* 109–22; Feis, *Contest Over Japan,* 85–110.

36. Agreement of Foreign Ministers on Establishing the Far Eastern Commission and the Allied Council for Japan, Moscow, Dec. 27, 1945, in *DAFR,* VIII, 275–77.

37. Ibid., 277–78.

38. *New York Times,* Dec. 31, 1945; Truman, *Memoirs,* I, 600–06; Byrnes, *Speaking Frankly,* 237–39; James F. Byrnes, *All in One Lifetime* (New York, 1958), 344–45.

39. Truman, News Conference, Dec. 20, 1945, in Truman, *Public Papers, 1945,* 565; *New York Times,* Dec. 22, 1945; *Nippon Times,* Dec. 25, 1945.

40. DM, *Reminiscences,* 292; *New York Times,* Dec. 31, 1945, and Jan. 1, 1946; DM, Statement on Control Plan, Dec. 30, 1945, RG 5, MMBA; London *Times,* Dec. 31, 1945; *Nippon Times,* Jan. 1, 1946; John R. Scott, "The Effect of the Cold War Upon the Occupation of Japan" (unpublished Ph.D. dissertation, University of Illinois, 1952), 97–98.

CHAPTER II. *The World of GHQ*

pages 35–66
1. SCAP, GHQ, Statistics and Reports Section, *Introduction* (HNAOJ; Tokyo, 1952), 6–7; Charles A. Willoughby, ed., *Reports of General MacArthur,* vol. I suppl., *MacArthur in Japan: The Occupation: Military*

Phase (Washington, 1966), 75; Philip H. Taylor, "The Administration of Occupied Japan," *Annals of the American Academy of Political and Social Science*, 267 (Jan. 1950), 140–41.

2. Ints., Suzuki, Marshall; Kinji Kawamura, Aug. 15, 1977; DM, Office Diary, Sept. 3, 1945, RG 5, MMBA; *Mainichi Daily News*, Aug. 18, 1976; Washington *Post*, July 27, 1976; Mamoru Shigemitsu, *Japan and Her Destiny: My Struggle for Peace*, ed. F. S. G. Piggott and trans. Oswald White (London, 1958), 375–77. Citations herein to issues of the *Mainichi Daily News*, May 31–Oct. 4, 1976, refer to its staff-prepared series of 52 installments entitled "The Occupation of Japan."

3. Ints., Suzuki, Marshall; Justin Williams, Sr., *Japan's Political Revolution under MacArthur: A Participant's Account* (Athens, GA, 1979), 5; *SNAJK*, Jan. 1946, 25.

4. JCS Directive to DM, Sept. 6, 1945, in SCAP, *Political Reorientation*, II, 427.

5. *Mainichi Daily News*, Aug. 18, 1976; DM, Press Statement, Sept. 14, 1945, in SCAP, *Political Reorientation*, II, 739.

6. Int., West; Sebald, *With MacArthur*, 127–31; Whitney, *MacArthur*, 242–43.

7. Ints., Maj. Gen. Charles A. Willoughby, July 30, 1971; Brig. Gen. Crawford F. Sams, Aug. 25, 1971; Taylor, "Administration of Occupied Japan," 141, 143; SCAP, GHQ, Gen. Orders nos. 1 and 2, Oct. 2, 1945, RG 5, MMBA; *SNAJK*, Jan. 1946, 16–17, 25; Willoughby, ed., *Reports*, 73, 75–76.

8. Int., Marshall; *Nippon Times*, Oct. 13, 1945; SCAP/FEC, GHQ, *Selected Data on the Occupation of Japan* (Tokyo, 1950), 5–9; Willoughby, ed., *Reports*, 75–76; Ward and Shulman, comps. and eds., *Allied Occupation*, 296; Taylor, "Administration of Occupied Japan," 145. For the first 18 months the Statistics and Reports Section was named the Statistical and Reports Section.

9. Ints., Willoughby; Maj. Gen. Courtney Whitney, Aug. 28, 1967; Brig. Gen. Elliott R. Thorpe, May 29, 1971; Dr. Justin Williams, Sr., June 15, 1977; Charles L. Kades, July 13, 1977; Frank Rizzo, Aug. 16, 1977; SCAP/FEC, *Selected Data*, 174; Williams, *Japan's Political Revolution*, 74, 269.

10. Ints., Willoughby, Thorpe; Willoughby, ed., *Reports*, 76, 79–80; SCAP/FEC, *Selected Data*, 155.

11. Ints., West, Rizzo; Maj. Gen. Frank H. Britton, July 28, 1971; Lt. Gen. Alonzo P. Fox, June 26, 1971; Brig. Gen. Milton A. Hill, Aug. 30, 1971; SCAP/FEC, *Selected Data*, 166–69; Richard E. Lauterbach, *Danger from the East* (New York, 1947), 61–62.

12. Ints., Willoughby, Wildes, Rizzo; Lauterbach, *Danger*, 62; SCAP/FEC, *Selected Data*, 153–54; Willoughby, ed., *Reports*, 80–81.

13. Ints., Sams, West; SCAP, GHQ, Public Health and Welfare Section, *Public Health in Japan* (2 vols., Tokyo, 1948), I, 3–5; Crawford F. Sams, "Medic" (MS memoirs), 338–402, DMBP; Ann C. Wyman, "The Contribution of General Crawford F. Sams to the Occupation of Ja-

pan, 1945–51" (unpublished M.A. thesis, Mississippi State Univ., 1975), 24–40; SCAP/FEC, *Selected Data*, 193–94.

14. Ints., Willoughby; Maj. Gen. William A. Beiderlinden, June 25, 1971; Maj. Gen. William E. Burgin to Lt. Col. Hubert G. Schenck, Nov. 5, 1951, Hubert G. Schenck Papers, Hoover Inst.; SCAP, GHQ, Natural Resources Section, *Mission and Accomplishments in the Natural Resources Field* (Tokyo, 1950), 1–4; SCAP/FEC, *Selected Data*, 186–88; Edward A. Ackerman, *Japan's Natural Resources and Their Relation to Japan's Economic Future* (Chicago, 1953), 569–71.

15. Ints., Bond; Under Sec. of State U. Alexis Johnson, June 24, 1971; Amb. William J. Sebald, July 30, 1971; int., Hugh Borton, pt. 2, no. 19, pp. 33–34, CUOHRO; Max W. Bishop, Memorandum of Conversation [with DM], Apr. 4, 1946, in *FRUS, 1946*, VIII, 188–90; Fleet Adm. William D. Leahy to DM, Oct. 2, 1945, RG 10, MMBA; SCAP/FEC, *Selected Data*, 164; Sebald, *With MacArthur*, 42–43, 49–50, 59–60, 65; Kahn, *China Hands*, 172–74.

16. W. Macmahon Ball, *Japan: Enemy or Ally?* (Melbourne, Australia, 1948), 19; George F. Kennan, *Memoirs* (2 vols., Boston, 1967–72), I, 375.

17. Ints., Willoughby, Wildes; Col. Laurence E. Bunker, July 12, 1971; Claude A. Buss, "Japan — Under the Occupation" (MS, c. Dec. 1945), RG 5, MMBA.

18. Ralph J. D. Braibanti, "The Role of Administration in the Occupation of Japan," *Annals of the American Academy of Political and Social Science*, 267 (Jan. 1950), 158–59; Taylor, "Administration of Occupied Japan," 143–44; John Bowden, "The SCAP Files of Commander Alfred R. Hussey" (unpublished M.A. thesis, University of Michigan, 1968), 4–5; Philip H. Taylor, "Policy Snags in Japan: Efficiency of Administration and Controls Put under Spotlight," *Christian Science Monitor* (magazine sec.), 39 (Jan. 25, 1947), 3, 14.

19. Int., Wildes; Walter J. Sheldon, *The Honorable Conquerors: The Occupation of Japan, 1945–1952* (New York, 1965), 63–64; Robert K. Hall, *Education for a New Japan* (New Haven, 1949), 57; Williams, *Japan's Political Revolution*, 33, 52–53, 77.

20. Harold S. Quigley and John E. Turner, *The New Japan: Government and Politics* (Minneapolis, 1956), 91–92.

21. Ints., Thorpe, Wildes; Hans H. Baerwald, *Japan's Parliament: An Introduction* (New York, 1974), 7; Elliott R. Thorpe, *East Wind Rain: The Intimate Account of an Intelligence Officer in the Pacific, 1939–49* (Boston, 1969), 96; int., Roger N. Baldwin, pt. 2, no. 10, pp. 29–32, CUOHRO; George B. Sansom, "The Political Reorientation of Japan," *Pacific Affairs*, 24 (Sept. 1951), 312; Shigeru Yoshida, *Japan's Decisive Century, 1867–1967* (New York, 1967), 54–55.

22. Kennan, *Memoirs*, I, 390; Harry E. Wildes, *Typhoon in Tokyo: The Occupation and Its Aftermath* (New York, 1954), 24; Shaplen, "From MacArthur to Miki," pt. 1, 64–65.

23. Ints., Marshall, Fox; Amb. Thomas K. Wright, July 30, 1971; Dr. Paul I. Robinson, Aug. 3, 1971; Brig. Gen. Burdette M. Fitch, Aug. 26,

1971; Wildes, *Typhoon,* 20; Braibanti, "Role of Administration," 159–60.

24. Ints., Marshall, Whitney, Fox; Col. Richard M. Levy, June 14, 1977; Hugh Borton, ed., *Japan* (Ithaca, NY, 1951), 304–07; Edwin M. Martin, *The Allied Occupation of Japan* [1945–48] (Stanford, 1948), 9–13; Ward and Shulman, comps. and eds., *Allied Occupation,* 145; Russell Brines, *MacArthur's Japan* (Philadelphia, 1948), 73–81.

25. *SNAJK,* Sept.–Oct. 1945, 5.

26. DM, *Reminiscences,* 294.

27. Ints., Lt. Gen. Clovis E. Byers, June 24, 1971; Lt. Gen. Joseph M. Swing, Aug. 26, 1971; Ralph J. D. Braibanti, "Administration of Military Government in Japan at the Prefectural Level," *American Political Science Review,* 43 (Apr. 1949), 250–74; Jones, et al., *Far East,* 322–23; Willoughby, ed., *Reports,* 194–98; Textor, *Failure,* 233–34; Bowden, "Hussey," 106.

28. Ints., Marshall, West, Beiderlinden, Bunker; *Nippon Times,* Sept. 19, 1945; Noel F. Busch, *Fallen Sun: A Report on Japan* (New York, 1948), 57.

29. Kimpei Shiba, "MacArthur's Carpet" (MS, c. 1976), copy enclosed with Shiba to DCJ, Aug. 27, 1977. According to Shiba, a version of this MS was published in the *Asahi Evening News* sometime in 1976.

30. Sheldon, *Honorable Conquerors,* 56.

31. Gunther, *Riddle,* 55–56.

32. Ints., Willoughby, Whitney, Seki; Isamu Suzukawa, Aug. 12, 1977; Shigeo Kimura, Aug. 18, 1977; *Nippon Times,* Nov. 26, 1945; "Candidate," *New Republic,* 118 (May 17, 1948), 8.

33. Ints., Marshall, Bunker, West; Gunther, *Riddle,* 53; George C. Kenney, *The MacArthur I Know* (New York, 1951), 252; Sheldon, *Honorable Conquerors,* 57.

34. Ints., Marshall, Willoughby, Levy; Lt. Gen. Edward M. Almond, Aug. 4, 1971; Brig. Gen. Benjamin T. Harris, June 3, 1977; int., Maj. Gen. George L. Eberle, Samuel Milner File, DMBP, MSU; int., John R. Harold, pt. 2, no. 88, pp. 34–35, CUOHRO; int., Lt. Gen. Edward M. Almond, pt. 3, pp. 60–62, USAMHI.

35. Int., Gen. Barksdale Hamlett, no. 4, p. 25, USAMHI.

36. Ints., various GHQ, SCAP/AFPAC, officers; int., Burton Crane, pt. 2, no. 48, p. 30, CUOHRO. The Bataan Gang members still with MacArthur were Sutherland, Marshall, Casey, Willoughby, Marquat, Akin, Diller, and Huff.

37. DM Diary, 1945–51, passim; Carl Mydans, "Memento of 25 Years," *Life,* 56 (Apr. 17, 1964), 25; int., Roger N. Baldwin, 1954, pt. 2, no. 10, pp. 11–12, CUOHRO; Lauterbach, *Danger,* 52–53; Frank Clune, *Ashes of Hiroshima: A Post-War Trip to Japan and China* (Sydney, Australia, 1950), 207–12.

38. Hugh Baillie, *High Tension: The Recollections of Hugh Baillie* (New York, 1959), 220–21.

CHAPTER III. *Military Matters*
pages 67–108

1. Ints., West, Beiderlinden; DM Diary, May 5, 1946.

2. SCAP/AFPAC, GHQ, "Summary of Data Presented to Members of the Military Affairs Committee, House of Representatives, Congress of the United States, August 1946," RG 4, MMBA; Eisenhower, *Papers*, VII, 599–606; Willoughby, ed., *Reports*, 62–65, 67–68; DM to Marshall, Jan. 16, 1946, RG 4, MMBA.

3. SCAP/AFPAC, "Summary of Data"; Charles A. Willoughby and John Chamberlain, *MacArthur, 1941–1951* (New York, 1954), 79–80; James E. Hewes, Jr., *From Root to McNamara: Army Organization and Administration, 1900–1963* (Washington, 1975), 129–74.

4. Int., Eisenhower; Eisenhower, *Papers*, VII, 858–62, 1059–66.

5. Eisenhower, *Papers*, VIII, 1260.

6. Ibid., 1296–1300, 1409–12; JCS Directive 1259/27, Dec. 14, 1946, CCS 381 (1-24-42) Sec. 4, RG 218, NA; James F. Schnabel, *Policy and Direction: The First Year*. *United States Army in the Korean War* (Washington, 1972), 46–47; ints., Eisenhower; Maj. Gen. John E. Hull, June 23, 1971; Gen. Thomas T. Handy, Sept. 8, 1971. Hereinafter, to avoid confusion, FECOM will refer to the Far East Command and FEC to the Far Eastern Commission. Official documents of 1947–51 use both FECOM and FEC as abbreviations for the Far East Command.

7. Ints., Almond; Maj. Gen. Edwin K. Wright, Aug. 28, 1971; FECOM Hq., "The Far East Command, 1 January 1947–30 June 1957," 6–14, RG 6, MMBA; JCS Directive 1259/27, Dec. 14, 1946; "Unified Command Roles," *United States News*, 21 (Dec. 27, 1946), 51; Willoughby, ed., *Reports*, 84.

8. Int., Edwin Wright; Schnabel, *Policy and Direction*, 47–48; Robert F. Futrell, *United States Air Force Operations in the Korean Conflict, 25 June–1 November 1950* (Washington, 1952), 9–11.

9. Robert F. Futrell, *United States Air Force Operations in the Korean Conflict, 1 November 1950–30 June 1952* (Washington, 1953), 71–72.

10. C. Joseph Bernardo and Eugene H. Bacon, *American Military Policy: Its Development Since 1775* (Harrisburg, PA, 1955), 442–45, 476–77; Schnabel, *Policy and Direction*, 52–59; Russell F. Weigley, *History of the United States Army* (New York, 1967), 486–87, 561, 569; DM, *Reminiscences*, 327–28.

11. Ints., Adm. Arthur D. Struble, June 22, 1971; Adm. Albert G. Noble, June 24, 1971; Adm. Russell S. Berkey, July 9, 1971; Adm. Charles M. Cooke, Jr., "Narrative History of Seventh Fleet and Naval Forces Western Pacific, 8 January 1946–24 February 1948," 1–46, Charles M. Cooke, Jr., Papers, Hoover Inst.; Samuel E. Morison, *History of United States Naval Operations in World War II*, XV, *Supplement and General Index* (Boston, 1962), 12–21; Willoughby, ed., *Reports*, 277–90.

12. Ints., Gen. George C. Kenney, July 16, 1971; Mrs. George E. Stratemeyer, July 27, 1971; Gen. Carl Spaatz, June 22, 1971; DM to Gen. Hoyt S. Vandenberg, Mar. 21, 1949, RG 5, MMBA; Futrell, *USAF June–Nov. 1950*, 1–4; Willoughby, ed., *Reports*, 268–77. See also Donald M. Goldstein, "Ennis C. Whitehead, Aerospace Commander and Pioneer" (unpublished Ph.D. dissertation, Univ. of Denver, 1970).

13. John Freeman to DM, Dec. 21, 1946, RG 5, MMBA; DM to Eichelberger, June 2, 1948, RG 9, MMBA; Maj. Gen. Paul J. Mueller to Eichelberger, June 1, 1948, Eichelberger Papers; *FRUS, 1945*, VI, 897; "BCOF in Japan," *Department of State Bulletin*, 13 (Feb. 10, 1946), 221–22; Clune, *Ashes*, vii–viii, 56, 68, 76–79, 153–57, 300; Robert J. Gilmore and Denis A. Warner, eds., *Near North: Australia and a Thousand Million Neighbors* (Sydney, Australia, 1948), 342–45; John Morris, *The Phoenix Cup: Some Notes on Japan in 1946* (London, 1947), 52–55; Rajendra Singh, *Post-War Occupation Forces: Japan and South-East Asia* (New Delhi, India, 1958), 101–06; London *Times*, Feb. 1, 1946; May 27, 1950.

14. See numerous negative comments about MacArthur in Eichelberger's diary and correspondence, especially to his wife, 1945–48, Eichelberger Papers.

15. Eichelberger Diary, July 30, 1948. Apparently unknown to Eichelberger, MacArthur recommended him on August 6, 1948, for the Distinguished Service Medal (Oak Leaf Cluster), which was subsequently awarded. DM to Gen. Omar N. Bradley, Aug. 6, 1948, RG 5, MMBA.

16. Eichelberger, *Jungle Road*, 270; Roy E. Appleman, *South to the Naktong, North to the Yalu (June–November 1950). United States Army in the Korean War* (Washington, 1961), 49–50; Eichelberger Diary, Mar. 7, 1948.

17. FECOM Inspector Gen., "Report of Annual General Inspection of Headquarters, Eighth United States Army . . . Fiscal Year 1948," Eichelberger Papers.

18. Henry L. Hill, Jr., "Eighth Army's Role in the Military Government of Japan," *Military Review*, 27 (Feb. 1948), 9–18; DM, *Reminiscences*, 283; Braibanti, "Administration of Military Government in Japan at the Prefectural Level," 250–58, 268; C. K. Huston to Acheson, June 24, 1949, in *FRUS, 1949*, VII, 786; Willoughby, ed., *Reports*, 194–230; Richard Park, "Transition in Japan," *Far Eastern Survey*, 18 (Sept. 21, 1949), 225–26.

19. Ints., Willoughby, Thorpe; SCAP/FEC, *Selected Data*, 88; Willoughby, ed., *Reports*, 231–67; Willoughby and Chamberlain, *MacArthur*, 318–27; SCAP, GHQ, Civil Intelligence Section, "Leftist Infiltration into SCAP," June 1947, RG 23, MMBA.

20. Willoughby, ed., *Reports*, 134–47; *FRUS, 1946*, VIII, 474–76, 513–14; *DAFR*, X, 1956–59; *New York Times*, Dec. 22, 1945; July 15, 1947.

21. JCS to DM, Oct. 31, Dec. 15, 1945; DM to JCS, Nov. 24, 1945, RG 9, MMBA; Leslie R. Groves, *Now It Can Be Told: The Story of the Man-*

hattan Project (New York, 1962), 367–72; *Mainichi Daily News,* June 21, 1976; DM, *Reminiscences,* 286–87.

22. Int., Johnson; Chiang Kai-shek to DM, Mar. 4, 1956, RG 5, MMBA; SCAP/FEC, GHQ, "Two Years of Occupation," G-3 Summary, Aug. 1947, SCAP, GHQ, Administrative Div. Subject File, RG 331, WNRC; *FRUS, 1945,* II, 1210–11; Willoughby, ed., *Reports,* 149–93, 265–67; *Mainichi Daily News,* June 28, July 12, Sept. 8, 1976; Martin, *Allied Occupation,* 18–20; Robert T. Fearey, *The Occupation of Japan: Second Phase, 1948–1950* (New York, 1950), 14–17, 193–94.

23. Misc. messages between DM and DS or JCS in re Soviet repatriation, 1945–51, in "Blue Binder Series" of radiograms, RG 9, MMBA; *DAFR,* XI, 175–76; *FRUS, 1946,* X, 908; *1947,* VII, 990–93; *1948,* VI, 757–60, 924–25; *1949,* VII, 783–84, 908–09; *New York Times,* Oct. 31, 1948; Frank Gibney, *Five Gentlemen of Japan: The Portrait of a Nation's Character* (New York, 1953), 241–45; Sebald, *With MacArthur,* 136–48.

24. DM, Press Release, Dec. 22, 1949, RG 9, MMBA.

25. Int., Mrs. Yukika Soma, Aug. 22, 1977; *Washington Post,* Aug. 20, 1970; *Mainichi Daily News,* July 12, 1976; United Nations, *Yearbook of the United Nations, 1950* (New York, 1951), 566; Shigeru Yoshida, *The Yoshida Memoirs: The Story of Japan in Crisis,* trans. Kenichi Yoshida (Boston, 1962), 231–35; A. Rodger Swearingen and Paul F. Langer, *Red Flag in Japan: International Communism in Action, 1919–1951* (Cambridge, MA, 1952), 232–34.

26. SCAP, GHQ, G-2, "Final Report: Progress of Demobilization of the Japanese Armed Forces," Dec. 31, 1946, SCAP, GHQ, Admin. Div. Subject File, RG 331, WNRC; *DAOCJ,* II, 129–31; Willoughby, ed., *Reports,* 117–34; Martin, *Allied Occupation,* 14–18; Brines, *MacArthur's Japan,* 102–13.

27. Willoughby, ed., *Reports,* 131, 134.

28. Misc. messages between DM and Allied commanders in China and Southeast Asia relating to war crimes trials, 1945–48, "Blue Binder Series," RG 9, MMBA; Harold Wakefield, *New Paths for Japan* (London, 1948), 173–77; S. W. Kirby, *The Surrender of Japan. History of the Second World War: United Kingdom Military Series* (London, 1969), 224–31; George M. Beckmann, *The Modernization of China and Japan* (New York, 1962), 624–25; K. G. Tregonning, *A History of Modern Sabah: North Borneo, 1881–1963* (Singapore, 1965), 217–21. Also see Philip R. Piccagallo, *The Japanese on Trial: Allied War Crimes Operations in the East, 1945–1951* (Austin, 1979).

29. AFPAC Hq., "U.S.A. vs. Tomoyuki Yamashita: Proceedings of the Trial," Oct. 29–Dec. 7, 1945, SCAP, GHQ, JAG File, RG 331, WNRC (microfilm, MSU); DM Diary, Nov. 28, 1945; Green to DM, Feb. 5, 1946, RG 5, MMBA; Whitney to editor, San Francisco *Examiner,* May 1, 1963, RG 21, MMBA; Lawrence H. Redford, "The Trial of General Tomoyuki Yamashita: A Case Study in Command Responsibility" (unpublished M.A. thesis, Old Dominion University, 1975), passim; DM, *Reminiscences,* 295–96; A. Frank Reel, *The Case of General*

Yamashita (Chicago, 1949), 6–8, 15–16, 32–33, 40–42, 76, 84–86, 173–75, 191–99, 202–05, 223–26, 232–39; Courtney Whitney, *The Case of General Yamashita: A Memorandum* (Tokyo, 1949), 1–22. The U.S. Supreme Court opinions are reprinted in full in Reel, *Yamashita*, 251–324, and the AFWESPAC, JAG, review and the UN War Crimes Commission's report on the case appear in Whitney, *Memorandum*, 23–82.

30. DM, Press Release, Feb. 5, 1946, RG 10, MMBA.
31. Ints., Marshall, Willoughby, Mashbir, West; Mrs. Elizabeth Gray Vining, July 8, 1977; Edward J. Smith to DCJ, Sept. 2, 1971; *Mainichi Daily News*, Sept. 22, 1976; Murphy and Rutledge opinions in Reel, *Yamashita*, 286–87, 294–95; Aubrey S. Kenworthy, *The Tiger of Malaya: The Story of General Tomoyuki Yamashita and "Death March" General Masaharu Homma* (New York, 1953), 84–88. Some of the articles on the Yamashita case are listed in Ward and Shulman, comps. and eds., *Allied Occupation*, 343–72, passim.
32. Ints., Col. James V. Collier, Aug. 30, 1971; Col. James P. Carter, Aug. 23, 1971; AFPAC Hq., "U.S.A. vs. Masaharu Homma: Proceedings of the Trial," Jan. 3–Feb. 11, 1946, SCAP, GHQ, JAG File, RG 331, WNRC (microfilm, MSU); John F. Hanson, "The Trial of Lieutenant General Masaharu Homma" (unpublished Ph.D. dissertation, Mississippi State Univ., 1977), passim; "Two Japanese War Criminals," *New Republic*, 114 (Feb. 25, 1946), 269; Morris, *Phoenix Cup*, 8–11; Reel, *Yamashita*, 236–37; *Stars and Stripes* (Pacific ed.), Mar. 22, 1946; *Nippon Times*, Mar. 12, 23, 1946; DM, *Reminiscences*, 296–98.
33. Associate Justice Frank Murphy, "Dissenting Opinion: In re Homma," in *United States Supreme Court Reports . . .* , 110 (New York, 1946), 993.
34. Hanson, "Homma," 197–99; *New York Times*, Mar. 11, 21, 1946; DM, *A Soldier Speaks: Public Papers and Speeches of General of the Army Douglas MacArthur*, ed. Vorin E. Whan, Jr. (New York, 1965), 160.
35. Col. Frederick B. Wiener to DCJ, June 24, July 9, 1974; Aug. 20, Oct. 4, 1977; Frederick B. Wiener, "General MacArthur and the Lesser War Criminals in 1946," 1, 4; Waldemar A. Solf to Wiener, Sept. 19, 1977 (copy), DMBP. See also two recent studies: Richard L. Lael, *The Yamashita Precedent: War Crimes and Command Responsibility* (Wilmington, DE, 1982), containing a critical but fair appraisal of MacArthur's role; and Lawrence Taylor, *A Trial of Generals: Homma, Yamashita, MacArthur* (South Bend, IN, 1981), which is unduly harsh toward MacArthur.
36. Ints., Thorpe, Suzuki; Fellers to DM, Oct. 2, 27, 1945, RG 5, MMBA; JCS to DM, Apr. 25, 1946; Marshall to Atcheson, May 13, 1947; DM to Bradley, Nov. 12, 1948; Marshall to William J. Sebald, Dec. 1, 1948, RG 9, MMBA; Sir William Webb to DM, Mar. 5, 6, 8, 1946; DM to Webb, Mar. 8, 1946; Joseph B. Keenan to DM, Dec. 30, 1948; Apr. 21, 1950, RG 10, MMBA; IMTFE, "Proceedings of the International Military Tribunal for the Far East," pt. 1, 184, 321–23, LC (micro-

film, MSU); Richard H. Minear, *Victors' Justice: The Tokyo War Crimes Trial* (Princeton, 1971), 134, 160–69, 180, 183–84; Joseph B. Keenan and Brendon F. Brown, *Crimes Against International Law* (Washington, 1950), v–vii, 1–13, 26–46, 176–83; Sebald, *With MacArthur*, 151–72; DM, *Reminiscences*, 279–80, 298, 318–19; Brines, *MacArthur's Japan*, 114–26; Sung Yoon Cho, "The Tokyo War Crimes Trial," *Quarterly Journal of the Library of Congress*, 24 (Oct. 1967), 309–10; "Now Told: Secret History of World War II," *U.S. News & World Report*, 70 (Jan. 25, 1971), 40–41; *DAFR*, VIII, 352–58. See also numerous items in *FRUS, 1945,* V, VI; *1946,* VI, VIII; *1947,* VI; *1948,* VI; *1949,* VII.

37. Ints., Suzuki, Whitney; Maj. Faubion Bowers, July 18, 1971; DM Diary, Nov. 9–21, 1946; *Nippon Times*, Dec. 1, 1948; DS, *Trial of Japanese War Criminals* (Washington, 1946), 44.
38. DM, Press Release, Nov. 24, 1948, in *DAOCJ*, II, 260–61.
39. Sebald, *With MacArthur*, 172–76; DS, Div. of Far East Research, "Japanese Reactions to Verdict in Class A War Crimes Trial, December 3, 1948," 4, in *USDIRR*, pt. 2; Hugh S. Borton, *Japan's Modern Century* (2d ed., New York, 1970), 476; Edwin O. Reischauer, *Japan: The Story of a Nation* (New York, 1970), 225; *FRUS, 1948,* VI, 935–36. On additional IMTFE bibliography, see Ward and Shulman, comps. and eds., *Allied Occupation*, 340–74.
40. Ints., Soma, West; Mrs. Tane Matsumura, Aug. 18, 1977; int., Bowers, pt. 2, p. 34, CUOHRO; Senate Joint Res. 94, Sept. 18, 1945, in Theodore H. McNelly, ed., *Sources in Modern East Asian History and Politics* (New York, 1967), 174; *Washington Post*, Sept. 26, 1945; *New York Times*, Sept. 27, 1945; DM, *Reminiscences*, 287–88; Brines, *MacArthur's Japan*, 97; Osanga Kanroji, *Hirohito: An Intimate Portrait of the Japanese Emperor* (Los Angeles, 1975), 134–35; Leonard Mosley, *Hirohito, Emperor of Japan* (Englewood Cliffs, NJ, 1966), 338–42.
41. DM to Gen. of the Army Dwight D. Eisenhower, Jan. 25, 1946, in *FRUS, 1946,* VIII, 395–97.
42. Ints., Suzuki, Soma; *FRUS, 1946,* VIII, 395; telephone call, Eisenhower to DM, June 11, 1960, Ann Whitman Files, Dwight D. Eisenhower Papers, DDEL.

CHAPTER IV. *An Avalanche of Political Reforms*

pages 109–52

1. Int., Mashbir; Sidney F. Mashbir, *I Was an American Spy* (New York, 1953), 315.
2. Ints., Whitney, Marshall, Mashbir; Tetsuro Furukaki, Aug. 17, 1977; DM Diary, Sept. 3–Dec. 31, 1945.
3. DM, *Reminiscences*, 288–89, 293; Shigemitsu, *Japan*, 381; Yoshida, *Memoirs*, 63–64; "Directive from General MacArthur to the Imperial Japanese Government [Oct. 4, 1945]," in *Department of State Bulletin*, 13 (Nov. 4, 1945), 730–32.

4. Atcheson to DM, Oct. 8, 1945, in *FRUS, 1945*, IV, 1941–42; *Nippon Times*, Dec. 17, 1945.

5. Shigemitsu, *Japan*, 377.

6. Yoshida, *Memoirs*, 65; Borton, *Japan's Modern Century*, 344, 352–53, 368, 372, 378; Quigley and Turner, *New Japan*, 83.

7. "Directive from General MacArthur [Oct. 4, 1945]," 371; Atcheson to DM, Oct. 10, 1945, in *FRUS, 1945*, VI, 742–43.

8. DS, Office of Research and Development, "The Problem of Civil Liberties in Japan," Apr. 1, 1946, 26, in *OSDIRR*, pt. 2.

9. SCAP, GHQ, *Administration of the Occupation,'September 1945–July 1951 (IINAOJ;* Tokyo, 1952), 117–18.

10. DM, *Reminiscences*, 294.

11. Martin, *Allied Occupation*, 51–59; *DAOCJ*, II, 219, 224; Ivan I. Morris, *Nationalism and the Right Wing in Japan: A Study of Post-War Trends* (London, 1960), 1–2.

12. SCAPIN 148, Dec. 15, 1945.

13. *Nippon Times*, Jan. 2, 1946; Daniel C. Holtom, *Modern Japan and Shinto Nationalism: A Study of Present-Day Trends in Japanese Religions* (rev. ed., Chicago, 1947), 176–77.

14. SCAPIN 550, Jan. 4, 1946; SCAP, *Political Reorientation*, II, 482–89; Wildes, *Typhoon*, 51–65; Chitoshi Yanaga, *Japan Since Perry* (New York, 1949), 630.

15. John D. Montgomery, *Forced to Be Free: The Artificial Revolution in Germany and Japan* (Chicago, 1957), 26; DM, *Reminiscences*, 289; Williams, *Japan's Political Revolution*, 210–13. For the official account, see SCAP, GHQ, *The Purge, 1945–December 1951 (HNAOJ;* Tokyo, 1952).

16. Morris, *Nationalism and the Right Wing in Japan*, 10–13; Hans H. Baerwald, *The Purge of Japanese Leaders Under the Occupation* (Berkeley, 1959), 106. See also John D. Montgomery, *The Purge in Occupied Japan: A Study in the Use of Civilian Agencies Under Military Government* (Chevy Chase, MD, 1954).

17. Williams, *Japan's Political Revolution*, 101–02, 122–23, 129–31; SCAP, *Political Reorientation*, II, 745; John K. Emmerson, *The Japanese Thread: A Life in the U.S. Foreign Service* (New York, 1979), 274, 277.

18. SCAP, *Political Reorientation*, I, 88–91; Quigley and Turner, *New Japan*, 111.

19. Shiba to DCJ, Aug. 27, 1977; Dale M. Hellegers, "The Konoye Affair," in Lawrence H. Redford, ed., *The Occupation of Japan: Impact of Legal Reform . . .* (Norfolk, 1978), 167–68; Emmerson, *Japanese Thread*, 265. Some accounts claim the misinterpretation occurred during the first meeting between MacArthur and Konoye, Sept. 13, 1945. See *Mainichi Daily News*, Sept. 27, 1976; Wildes, *Typhoon*, 34.

20. Int., Tanaka; Theodore McNelly, "The Japanese Constitution: Child of the Cold War," *Political Science Quarterly*, 74 (June 1959), 179–82; Robert E. Ward, "The Origins of the Present Japanese Constitution," *American Political Science Review*, 50 (Dec. 1956), 984; Bowden, "Hussey," 31, 108–09; Emmerson, *Japanese Thread*, 265–67; Hellegers,

"Konoye Affair," 168–75; *New York Times*, Oct. 26, 1945; New York *Herald Tribune*, Oct. 31, 1945.

21. Williams, *Japan's Political Revolution*, 128; Emmerson, *Japanese Thread*, 265–66; Kelley and Ryan, *MacArthur*, 58–59; Byrnes to DM, Nov. 3, 1945, RG 9, MMBA; Atcheson to Acheson, Nov. 7, 1945, in *FRUS*, *1945*, VI, 837–41.

22. Quigley and Turner, *New Japan*, 114–16; Ward, "Origins of the Present Japanese Constitution," 984–85; SCAP, *Political Reorientation*, I, 91; *Mainichi Daily News*, Sept. 27 and 29, 1976.

23. Atcheson to DM, Dec. 13, 1945, in *FRUS*, *1945*, VI, 882–84.

24. McNelly, "Japanese Constitution," 183; Justin Williams, "Making the Japanese Constitution: A Further Look," *American Political Science Review*, 59 (Sept. 1965), 667; int., Williams; DM to JCS, May 3, 1946, RG 5, MMBA.

25. SWNCC 228: "Reform of the Japanese Governmental System," Jan. 7, 1946, in *FRUS*, *1946*, VIII, 99–101. On Dec. 28, 1945, MacArthur received SWNCC 228/1, a two-page annex by the JCS on immediate and long-range military concerns related to constitutional reforms. The short-term concern was the possibility of civil unrest and violence fomented by SCAP's implementation of the proposed changes. The long-term concern was the need to make certain that ultranationalistic or militaristic elements did not get control of Japan and produce another era of aggression. Williams, *Japan's Political Revolution*, 101.

26. DM, *Reminiscences*, 300, 302; Williams, "Making the Japanese Constitution," 671–73; Williams, *Japan's Political Revolution*, 101–04; Blakeslee, *Far Eastern Commission*, 44–45.

27. SCAP, *Political Reorientation*, I, 98–102; II, 611–23; DM, *Reminiscences*, 300. In Jan. 1946, the Matsumoto Committee completed two conservative, if slightly different, drafts, but neither was available to SCAP in early Feb. They are reprinted in SCAP, *Political Reorientation*, II, 607–10.

28. SCAP, *Political Reorientation*, I, 102.

29. Williams, *Japan's Political Revolution*, 105; Whitney, *MacArthur*, 247; Dr. Kenzo Takayanagi to DM, Dec. 1, 1958, RG 21, MMBA.

30. DM to Takayanagi, Dec. 5, 1958, RG 21, MMBA.

31. SCAP, *Political Reorientation*, I, 103; II, 671–73; Dale M. Hellegers, "Comment," in L. H. Redford, ed., *The Occupation of Japan . . . and Its Legacy to the Postwar World . . .* (Norfolk, 1976), 24.

32. Ints., Whitney, Kades, Tanaka, Furukaki; *Japan Times*, May 3, 1977; Kenzo Takayanagi, "Some Reminiscences of Japan's Commission on the Constitution," in Dan F. Henderson, ed., *The Constitution of Japan: Its First Twenty Years, 1947–67* (Seattle, 1969), 82–88; Thomas J. Hehman, "U.S. Security Policy in Postwar Japan: The Making of a Cold War Ally" (unpublished M.A. thesis, Old Dominion University, 1977), 70–74; Theodore H. McNelly, "American Influence and Japan's No-War Constitution," *Political Science Quarterly*, 67 (Dec. 1952), 593n.

33. Int., Tanaka; DM to Takayanagi, Dec. 5, 1958, RG 21, MMBA; Kenzo Takayanagi, "The Constitution," *International Social Science Journal*, 13 (1961), 7–10; Whitney, *MacArthur*, 257–62; DM, *Reminiscences*, 303–04; Theodore H. McNelly, "The Renunciation of War in the Japanese Constitution," *Political Science Quarterly*, 77 (Sept. 1962), 375–78; Yoshida, *Japan's Decisive Century*, 61.

34. Williams, *Japan's Political Revolution*, 108–13; SCAP, *Political Reorientation*, I, 102–05.

35. Ints., Kades, Tanaka; Whitney, *MacArthur*, 250–55; John W. Dower, *Empire and Aftermath: Yoshida Shigeru and the Japanese Experience, 1878–1954* (Cambridge, MA, 1979), 318–19; *Mainichi Daily News*, Sept. 29, Oct. 1, 1976; McNelly, "Japanese Constitution," 189.

36. Ints., Tanaka; Prof. Akira Amakawa, Aug. 18, 1977; *SNAJK*, Mar. 1946, 18; Ward, "Origins of the Present Japanese Constitution," 1002.

37. DM, "Statement Concerning the Proposed New Constitution, March 6, 1946," in *DAOCJ*, II, 87–88.

38. Int., Amakawa; DM to JCS, Oct. 7, 1946, RG 5, MMBA; Borton, *Japan's Modern Century*, 466–67.

39. *SNAJK*, Nov. 1946, 21–23; *Nippon Times*, May 4, 1946; Yoshida, *Memoirs*, 143–46; SCAP, *Political Reorientation*, II, 669.

40. DS, *The Constitution of Japan, Effective May 3, 1947* (Washington, 1947), 1–13.

41. Int., Wildes; DM, *Reminiscences*, 302, 305; John C. Perry, *Beneath the Eagle's Wings: Americans in Occupied Japan* (New York, 1980), 144; Susan J. Pharr, "A Radical U.S. Experiment: Women's Rights Laws and the Occupation of Japan," in Redford, ed., *Occupation of Japan: Impact of Legal Reform*, 133–34.

42. DM, *Reminiscences*, 302; DM to Asst. Sec. of War Howard C. Petersen, May 18, 1946; Atcheson to Asst. Sec. of State John H. Hilldring, May 21, 1946, RG 5, MMBA; Quigley and Turner, *New Japan*, 121–25; Blakeslee, *Far Eastern Commission*, 48–52.

43. JCS to DM, Apr. 30, 1946, RG 5, MMBA.

44. DM to JCS, May 3, 1946, RG 5, MMBA.

45. Ints., Wildes, Kades; JCS to DM, May 24, 1946, RG 5, MMBA; John C. Vincent to Byrnes, Apr. 20, 1946, in *FRUS, 1946*, VIII, 213–14; SWNCC Secretaries' Note, June 11, 1946, in ibid., 247–53; DM to Japanese Diet, June 21, 1946, in ibid., 256–58.

46. Int., Whitney; Petersen to DM, July 28, Oct. 11, 1946; DM to Petersen, July 30, Nov. 1, 1946; JCS to DM, July 7, Oct. 29, 1946, RG 5, MMBA; Hilldring to SWNCC, July 26, 1946, in *FRUS, 1946*, VIII, 276–78; Hilldring to McCoy, Aug. 12, 1946, in ibid., 289–91; Hilldring to SWNCC, Aug. 13, 1946, in ibid., 292–94; Hilldring to SWNCC, Oct. 7, 1946, in ibid., 334–35; DM to Eisenhower, Oct. 7, 1946, in ibid., 335–36; Hilldring to SWNCC, Dec. 16, 1946, in ibid., 375; Byrnes to Atcheson, Jan. 3, 1947, in *FRUS, 1947*, VI, 156–57.

47. Nobutaka Ito, *New Japan: Six Years of Democratization* (Tokyo, 1952), 33.

48. SCAP, GHQ, Government Section, *A Brief Progress Report on the Political Reorientation of Japan* (Tokyo, 1949), 8–9; Byrnes to Atcheson, Jan. 3, 1947, in *FRUS, 1947,* VI, 156–57; Rosecrance, *Australian Diplomacy,* 36–37; Blakeslee, *Far Eastern Commission,* 61–62.

49. Yanaga, *Japan,* 646–47; Frank Langdon, *Politics in Japan* (Boston, 1967), 61–62, 168–70; *Nippon Times,* Jan. 7, 1947; Martin Bronfenbrenner, *Prospects of Japanese Democracy* (Toronto, 1955), 15–16.

50. SCAP/FEC, *Selected Data,* 21; SCAP, *Brief Progress Report,* 14–15; Kurt Steiner, *Local Government in Japan* (Stanford, 1965), 68; Robert E. Ward, "Some Observations on Local Autonomy at the Village Level in Present-day Japan," *Far Eastern Quarterly,* 12 (Feb. 1953), 183–84; *Asahi Shimbun* staff, *The Pacific Rivals: A Japanese View of Japanese-American Relations,* trans. Peter Grilli and Murakami Yoshio (New York, 1972), 170–73; Terry E. MacDougall, "Perspectives on the Local Government Reforms of the Allied Occupation," in Redford, ed., *Occupation of Japan: Impact of Legal Reform,* 1–26; Wildes, *Typhoon,* 150–59.

51. Int., Amakawa; *Nippon Times,* Feb. 5, Mar. 16, 1946; *Mainichi Daily News,* Sept. 10, 1976; *SNAJK,* June 1946, 49–55; *Asahi Shimbun* staff, *Pacific Rivals,* 148–51; Prime Min. Tetsu Katayama to DM, Sept. 3, 1946; DM to Katayama, Sept. 16, 1946, RG 10, MMBA.

52. DS, Div. of Far East Research, "Progress in Local Government Reform in Japan," Oct. 24, 1947, 1–12; idem, "Situation Report — Japan: Problems of the Japanese Police System," Oct. 8, 1948, 6–17, in *OSDIRR,* pt. 2; SCAP, GHQ, *Police and Public Safety, 1945–October 1951* (*HNAOJ;* Tokyo, 1952) passim; Shuichi Sugai, "The Japanese Police System," in Robert E. Ward, ed., *Five Studies in Japanese Politics* (Ann Arbor, MI, 1957), 4–14; DM, *Reminiscences,* 314; Perry, *Beneath the Eagle's Wings,* 149.

53. DM to Bradley, July 8, 1948, RG 9, MMBA; Alfred C. Oppler, *Legal Reform in Occupied Japan: A Participant Looks Back* (Princeton, 1976), especially chaps. 6–10, 22, 26; idem, "The Judicial and Legal System," in SCAP, *Political Reorientation,* I, 186–245; SCAP, GHQ, *Legal and Judicial Reform, 1945–1951* (*HNAOJ;* Tokyo, 1952) passim; Takeyoshi Kawashima, "Post-war Democratization in Japan: Law," *International Social Science Journal,* 13 (1961), 21–34; Chitoshi Yanaga, *Japanese People and Politics* (New York, 1956), 347–55; B. James George, Jr., "Law in Modern Japan," in John W. Hall and Richard K. Beardsley, eds., *Twelve Doors to Japan* (New York, 1965), 484–536; Richard K. Beardsley, "Japan's Political System," in ibid., 476–77.

54. Oppler, *Legal Reform,* ix–xiii, 35–38; David J. Danelski, "The Constitutional and Legal Phases of the Creation of the Japanese Supreme Court," in Redford, ed., *Occupation of Japan: Impact of Legal Reform,* 49–56.

55. DM, Statement on Lèse Majesté Case, Oct. 9, 1946, in SCAP, *Political Reorientation,* II, 759; Prime Min. Shigeru Yoshida to DM, Dec. 27, 1946, in ibid., 679; DM to Yoshida, Feb. 25, 1947, in ibid., 680; Chief

Justice Tadahiko Mibuchi to DM, Mar. 29, 1948; DM to Mibuchi, Apr. 1, 1948; DM to Yoshida, Apr. 23, 1947, RG 10, MMBA.
56. Ints., Tanaka, Suzukawa; Shaplen, "From MacArthur to Miki," pt. 1, 64; pt. 2, 52–54; Beardsley, "Japan's Political System," 472–75; Bowden, "Hussey," 105; *Asahi Shimbun* staff, *Pacific Rivals*, 139–42, 183–86; *Nippon Times*, Aug. 2, 1952; Yanaga, *Japanese People*, 307–11; Wildes, *Typhoon*, 90–101; John K. Fairbank, et al., *Next Step in Asia* (Cambridge, MA, 1949), 64–65.
57. SCAP, *Political Reorientation*, I, 246–59; II, 578–80; SCAP, GHQ, *Working Conditions, 1945–September 1950* (*HNAOJ*; Tokyo, 1952), 99.
58. Foreign Affairs Association of Japan, ed., *The Japan Year Book, 1946–1948* (Tokyo, 1949), 170–76; SCAP, *Political Reorientation*, I, 314–37.
59. SCAP, *Political Reorientation*, I, 323, 337; II, 767.
60. Alfred B. Clubok, "Japanese Conservative Politics, 1947–1955," in Ward, ed., *Five Studies*, 26–27.
61. Ints., Kakitsubo, Tanaka, Kaite, Wildes, West; Yanaga, *Japanese People*, 239; Textor, *Failure in Japan*, 16–20, 112–17; Tsuyoshi Matsumoto, "Japan's Election," *New Republic*, 114 (Jan. 14, 1946), 46–47; Langdon, *Politics in Japan*, 61–66; DS, Div. of Far East Research, "An Analysis of the 1947 Japanese House of Representatives Election," Sept. 1, 1947, in *OSDIRR*, pt. 2; Dower, "Occupied Japan," 486–87; Harold S. Quigley, "Democracy Occupies Japan," *Virginia Quarterly Review*, 23 (Autumn 1947), 521–31; Thomas A. Bisson, *Prospects for Democracy in Japan* (New York, 1949), 72–74; Allan B. Cole, et al., *Socialist Parties in Post-War Japan* (New Haven, 1966), 15–16; Morris, *Nationalism and the Right Wing in Japan*, 59–60.
62. SCAP, *Political Reorientation*, I, 329.
63. DM to Charles M. Englisby, Feb. 14, 1948, in ibid., II, 785.
64. Perry, *Beneath the Eagle's Wings*, xii.

CHAPTER V. *Efforts Toward Economic Relief, Recovery, and Reform*

pages 153–92
1. Kimpei Shiba to DCJ, Aug. 27, 1977; Kimpei Shiba, "Japan Yesterday and Today," *Asahi Evening News* clipping, n.d. [c. 1966]; Wildes, *Typhoon*, 260–61.
2. Ints., Wildes, Thorpe; Shizuo Saito, Aug. 15, 1977; SCAP/FEC, *Selected Data*, 45–46; Kawai, *Japan's American Interlude*, 133–35; Thomas F. M. Adams and Hoshii Iwao, *A Financial History of Modern Japan* (Tokyo, 1964), 161–63.
3. Ints., Kakitsubo, Saito; Takafusa Nakamura, *The Postwar Japanese Economy: Development and Structure* (Tokyo, 1981), 21–22; David F. Anthony, "Adjustments in the Economic Structure of Japan," in Redford, ed., *Occupation of Japan . . . and Its Legacy*, 70.
4. Int., Kakitsubo; Buss, "Japan — Under the Occupation," 25–27; Adams and Iwao, *Financial History*, 173–74; *Mainichi Daily News* staff, *Fifty*

Years, 211–17; Cohen, *Japan's Economy*, 447–48; DS, Div. of Far Eastern Research, "Current Inflationary Developments in Japan," Apr. 30, 1947, in *OSDIRR*, pt. 2.

5. Int., Kawamura; SCAP, GHQ, *Mission and Accomplishments of the Supreme Commander for the Allied Powers in the Economic and Scientific Fields* (Tokyo, 1950), 25–26; Nakamura, *Postwar Japanese Economy*, 22; Archibald T. Steele, *Present-Day Japan* (New York, 1947), 11–13. Large numbers of Allied prisoners also had been forced to work in the Japanese mincs.

6. Ints., Kimpei Shiba, Aug. 19, 1977; Saito; *Asahi Shimbun* staff, *Pacific Rivals*, 122–25; Kozo Yamamura, *Economic Policy in Postwar Japan: Growth versus Economic Democracy* (Berkeley, 1967), 1–2; *Mainichi Daily News*, July 2, 1976; *Nippon Times*, Mar. 12 and 16, May 19, 1946.

7. DM, *Reminiscences*, 307.

8. Int., Saito; DM to Yoshida, Mar. 22, 1947; DM to Eisenhower, Mar. 30, 1947, RG 9, MMBA; DS, *Occupation of Japan: Policy and Progress* (Washington, 1946), 37–40; Wildes, *Typhoon*, 234–42; Morris, *Phoenix Cup*, 34–35; Toshio Nishi, *Unconditional Democracy: Education and Politics in Occupied Japan, 1945–1952* (Stanford, 1982), 68–70; *Nippon Times*, May 13, 1946; *New York Times*, Feb. 24, 1947; John C. Campbell, et al., *The United States in World Affairs, 1945–1947* (New York, 1947), 26–28.

9. Cohen, *Japan's Economy*, 492–500; *Mainichi Daily News*, Aug. 2, 1976; DS, *Occupation of Japan*, 45–46.

10. Ints., Kakitsubo, Bunker; Col. Laurence E. Bunker, "Remarks," in Redford, ed., *Occupation of Japan . . . and Its Legacy*, 86; Ernest A. Gross to J. E. Johnson, Aug. 20, 1946, in *FRUS, 1946*, VIII, 298–99.

11. JCS to DM, Aug. 14, 1947, Leahy File 42, RG 218, NA; SCAP/FEC, *Selected Data*, 93; *DAFR*, IX, 111–14; *FRUS, 1947*, VI, 276–79; VII, 257–60.

12. *Nippon Times*, June 10, 1947.

13. Blakeslee, *Far Eastern Commission*, 105.

14. Int., Dr. Roger O. Egeberg, June 30, 1971; DM to Eisenhower, May 1, 1947; JCS to DM, Nov. 13, 1945, RG 9, MMBA; SCAP, GHQ, *Mission and Accomplishments in the Natural Resources Field* (Tokyo, 1950), 15–21; SCAP/FEC, *Selected Data*, 39; Blakeslee, *Far Eastern Commission*, 114–22; *FRUS, 1945*, V, 884–85; *FRUS, 1946*, VII, 524; *FRUS, 1948*, VI, 930–32.

15. Ints., Saito, Harris; SCAP, GHQ, *Fisheries, 1945–1950 (HNAOJ;* Tokyo, 1950), 117–19; Atcheson to U.S. Legation, Wellington, New Zealand, Aug. 19, 1946, RG 9, MMBA; *Nippon Times*, Jan. 27, 1947; Blakeslee, *Far Eastern Commission*, 106–14; *FRUS, 1947*, VI, 164–65, 195–97, 212–16, 235–36; *FRUS, 1948*, VI, 737–38, 747–50, 769–70, 810–11.

16. Ints., Wright, Rizzo, Kakitsubo; Blakeslee, *Far Eastern Commission*, 123–24, 142–51; Cohen, *Japan's Economy*, 419–20; DS, *Occupation of Japan*, 30–31.

17. Edwin W. Pauley to DM, Feb. 24, 1947, RG 10, MMBA; Maj. Gen. William F. Marquat to DM, Mar. 13, 1947, RG 5, MMBA; JCS to DM, Jan. 26, 1946, Leahy File 43, RG 218, NA; *Nippon Times*, Jan. 19, 1946; *FRUS, 1945*, VI, 1004–07, 1010–11; *FRUS, 1946*, VIII, 502–04, 601–04; Edwin W. Pauley, *Report on Japanese Reparations to the President of the United States, November 1945 to April 1946* (Washington, 1948), 1–10; Scott, "Effect of the Cold War," 131–36.

18. DM to Eisenhower, Dec. 21, 1946, Feb. 3, 1947, RG 9, MMBA; Atcheson to Byrnes, Jan. 23, 1946, in *FRUS, 1946*, VIII, 474–76; Blakeslee, *Far Eastern Commission*, 123; Hugh T. Patrick, "The Phoenix Rises from the Ashes: Postwar Japan," in James B. Crowley, ed., *Modern East Asia: Essays in Interpretation* (New York, 1970), 300.

19. Ints., Kawamura, Kakitsubo; Yoshida to DM, Oct. 23, 1946; DM to Yoshida, Nov. 10, 1946, Justin Williams Papers, McKeldin Library, University of Maryland, College Park, MD; Clifford Strike, et al., to Petersen, Feb. 24, 1947 [report of Special Committee on Japanese Reparations], Eichelberger Papers.

20. Strike, et al., to Petersen, Feb. 24, 1947, Eichelberger Papers.

21. JCS to DM, Jan. 14, 1947, Leahy File 42, RG 218, NA; DS, Div. of Far East Research, "A Résumé of Progress in the Japanese Reparations Program," May 23, 1947, in *OSDIRR*, pt. 2; *FRUS, 1947*, VI, 358–60, 370–71, 376–80, 385–87, 389–90; *DAFR*, IX, 109–11; Cohen, *Japan's Economy*, 421–22.

22. Howard B. Schonberger, "Zaibatsu Dissolution and the American Restoration of Japan," *Bulletin of Concerned Asian Scholars*, 5 (Sept. 1973), 16; Thomas A. Bisson, *Zaibatsu Dissolution in Japan* (Berkeley, 1954), 6–32.

23. Pauley, *Report*, 10; Bisson, *Zaibatsu Dissolution*, 239.

24. JCS to DM, Nov. 1, 1947, Leahy File 42, RG 218, NA; Eleanor M. Hadley, *Antitrust in Japan* (Princeton, 1970), 6–10, 120–21; DS, Interim Research and Intelligence Service, "Factors Affecting the Status of the Zaibatsu in Japan," Nov. 5, 1945, in *OSDIRR*, pt. 2; Bisson, *Zaibatsu Dissolution*, 61–79; Martin, *Allied Occupation*, 139–40.

25. Yamamura, *Economic Policy*, 9–10; Bisson, *Zaibatsu Dissolution*, 80–81; Cohen, *Japan's Economy*, 428–29.

26. SCAP, GHQ, *Elimination of Zaibatsu Control, 1945–June 1950* (*HNAOJ*; Tokyo, 1951), 6–28, 31–32; Lauterbach, *Danger*, 118–20; Hadley, *Antitrust*, 125–27.

27. SCAP, GHQ, "Comments on Recommendations of Report on the Mission on Japanese Combines," May 26, 1946, SCAP, GHQ, File, RG 331, WNRC; SCAP, GHQ, *Promotion of Fair Trade Practices, 1945–October 1951* (*HNAOJ;* Tokyo, 1952), 4–5.

28. Mark J. Gayn, *Japan Diary* (New York, 1948), 259.

29. Eleanor M. Hadley, "Trust Busting in Japan," *Harvard Business Review*, 26 (July 1948), 425–26; Schonberger, "Zaibatsu Dissolution," 17–18; Hadley, *Antitrust*, 129–30; Eric H. F. Svensson, "The Military Occupation of Japan: The First Years of Planning, Policy Formulation,

and Reforms" (unpublished Ph.D. dissertation, University of Denver, 1966), 230–32, 235; *Department of State Bulletin*, Nov. 3, 1946, 823–24.

30. DS, Div. of Far East Research, "Progress in the Dissolution of the Zaibatsu," Dec. 20, 1946, in *OSDIRR*, pt. 2; Adams and Iwao, *Financial History*, 169–70; Sheldon, *Honorable Conquerors*, 193–94; Hadley, "Trust Busting," 437; Bisson, *Zaibatsu Dissolution*, 97–104, 110–14, 120–21, 193–95; Hadley, *Antitrust*, 69–73.

31. Yoshida to DM, Nov. 8, 1946; DM to Yoshida, Dec. 26, 1946, Williams Papers; DM to Eisenhower, Sept. 22, 1947, Leahy File 42, RG 218, NA; *SNAJK*, Jan. 1947, 35–36; int., Roger N. Baldwin, 1954, vol. I, pt. 3, p. 494, CUOHRO; Sherwood M. Fine, *Japan's Post-War Industrial Recovery* (Tokyo, 1952), 30–31; *Asahi Shimbun* staff, *Pacific Rivals*, 164–67; Dower, *Empire and Aftermath*, 332; Baerwald, *Purge*, 30–36, 91–94; Hadley, *Antitrust*, 86–88, 96–99; Bisson, *Zaibatsu Dissolution*, 158–62, 175–79; Yoshida, *Memoirs*, 160–63.

32. [Compton Pakenham], "Behind the Japanese Purge — American Military Rivalries," *Newsweek*, 29 (Jan. 27, 1947), 40.

33. DM, Comment on *Newsweek* Article, Jan. 27, 1947, in SCAP, *Political Reorientation*, II, 549.

34. Ints., Wright, Willoughby; Katayama to DM, Sept. 4, 1947; DM to Katayama, Sept. 10, 16, 18, 1947, Williams Papers; SCAP, GHQ, *Deconcentration of Economic Power, 1945–December 1950 (HNAOJ;* Tokyo, 1951), 11–13; Yamamura, *Economic Policy*, 9–14; Hadley, *Antitrust*, 147–48, 370–71; Bisson, *Zaibatsu Dissolution*, 132–33, 197–200; William Costello, *Democracy versus Feudalism in Post-War Japan* (Tokyo, 1948), 15–16, 105–21.

35. Under Sec. of the Army William H. Draper to DM, Mar. 25, 1947, PSF, Harry S. Truman Papers, HSTL.

36. Swearingen and Langer, *Red Flag*, 143; Miriam S. Farley, *Aspects of Japan's Labor Problems* (New York, 1950), 26–27.

37. Cohen, *Japan's Economy*, 436–37.

38. Int., Kaite; SCAP, *Missions and Accomplishments . . . in the Economic and Scientific Fields*, 44–45; Japan Ministry of Labor, *The Japanese Labor Legislations, 1949* (Tokyo, 1949), 94–107, 166–219, 436–55; Yamamura, *Economic Policy*, 15–16; Farley, *Japan's Labor Problems*, 33–43, 57–60; Ehud Harari, *The Politics of Labor Legislation in Japan: National-International Interaction* (Berkeley, 1973), 51–59; Iwao F. Ayusawa, *A History of Labor in Modern Japan* (Honolulu, 1966), 249–54.

39. Yamamura, *Economic Policy*, 16.

40. Compiled from data in SCAP, *Missions and Accomplishments . . . in the Economic and Scientific Fields*, 42; Cohen, *Japan's Economy*, 205, 437; Swearingen and Langer, *Red Flag*, 128, 143.

41. Int., Kaite; Swearingen and Langer, *Red Flag*, 144, 147; Harari, *Labor Legislation*, 61; Farley, *Japan's Labor Problems*, 64–65; Cohen, *Japan's Economy*, 437–38; SCAP, *Mission and Accomplishments . . . in the Economic and Scientific Fields*, 42–43.

42. Ints., Willoughby, Wildes; *Nippon Times*, May 21, 1946; Farley, *Japan's Labor Problems*, 44–47; SCAP, *Police and Public Safety*, 81–82; Arthur R. Swearingen, *Communist Strategy in Japan, 1945–1960* (Santa Monica, CA, 1965), 68–77, 118–21.

43. DM, Warning Against Mob Disorder or Violence, May 20, 1946, in SCAP, *Political Reorientation*, II, 750 (also in *DAOCJ*, II, 239).

44. Gayn, *Japan Diary*, 231–32.

45. *Asahi Shimbun* staff, *Pacific Rivals*, 174–75; Farley, *Japan's Labor Problems*, 50–52, 126–31, 132–34, 146–49; Lauterbach, *Danger*, 142.

46. Int., Sadao Ohtake, Aug. 17, 1977; Col. E. J. Barnette to Eichelberger, Jan. 23, 1947, Eichelberger Papers; DS, Div. of Far East Research, "The Threatened February First Government Workers' Strike in Japan," Feb. 28, 1947, in *OSDIRR*, pt. 2; SCAP, GHQ, *Development of the Trade Union Movement, 1945–June 1951 (HNAOJ;* Tokyo, 1952), 63, 90–91; Lauterbach, *Danger*, 142–43; Farley, *Japan's Labor Problems*, 149–52; Ayusawa, *Labor*, 269–70; Brines, *MacArthur's Japan*, 164–65; Richard L. G. Deverall, *Red Star Over Japan* (Calcutta, 1952), 183–84; Ball, *Japan*, 158–59; Martin E. Weinstein, *Japan's Postwar Defense Policy, 1947–1968* (New York, 1971), 33–42.

47. DM, Statement Prohibiting General Strike, Jan. 31, 1947, in *SNAJK*, Jan. 1947, 174–75.

48. Ints., Bunker, Shigeo Kimura; Eichelberger Diary, Jan. 30, 1947; DM to Eisenhower, Feb. 1, 1947, RG 9, MMBA; Atcheson to Marshall, Mar. 14, 1947, in *FRUS, 1947*, VI, 188; *Nippon Times*, June 30, 1947; *Asahi Shimbun* staff, *Pacific Rivals*, 175–76; Blakeslee, *Far Eastern Commission*, 170–71.

49. Ints., Kaite, Katamoto, Shigeo Kimura; Rinjiro Sodei, Aug. 18, 1977; Kichisaburo Nomura to DM, Feb. 1, 1947, RG 5, MMBA; Dower, *Empire and Aftermath*, 313; Yasuo Tatsuki, *General Trend of Japanese Opinion Following the End of the War; Based Especially on Public Opinion Surveys* (Tokyo, 1948), 35–41; Ayusawa, *Labor*, 271–72.

50. Int., Kaite; Costello, *Democracy*, 7–13; Farley, *Japan's Labor Problems*, 52, 153–54, 616–62; Lauterbach, *Danger*, 145; Brines, *MacArthur's Japan*, 166.

51. Int., Kades.

52. Laurence I. Hewes, Jr., *Japanese Land Reform Program* (Tokyo, 1950), 7, 9–13; DM, *Reminiscences*, 313.

53. Hewes, *Land Reform*, 13–15, 48–51; Ball, *Japan*, 132; Ronald P. Dore, *Land Reform in Japan* (New York, 1959), 130–31; DM, *Reminiscences*, 313.

54. Yoshida, *Japan's Decisive Century*, 61–63; Yoshida, *Memoirs*, 196–200; DS, Div. of Far East Research, "Status of the Japanese Agrarian Reform Program," Mar. 19, 1946, in *OSDIRR*, pt. 2; SCAPIN 411, Dec. 9, 1946; *Mainichi Daily News*, June 28, 1976; SCAP, GHQ, *The Rural Land Reform, 1945–June 1951 (HNAOJ;* Tokyo, 1952), 24–26, 30; Dore, *Land Reform*, 131–32; Laurence I. Hewes, Jr., *Japan — Land and Men:*

An Account of the Japanese Land Reform Program, 1945–51 (Ames, IA, 1955), 51–54.
55. Int., Fox; Hewes, *Japan*, 67–73.
56. Int., Kawamura; *SNAJK*, Oct. 1946, 67, 70; Hewes, *Japan*, 57–64, 75, 82–84, 91–95, 97–111, 112–15, 141–46; SCAPIN 1855, Feb. 4, 1948; SCAP, *Rural Land Reform*, 34–35, 96–97; Dore, *Land Reform*, 137, 169, 171–73; Martin, *Allied Occupation*, 87–92; Fearey, *Occupation*, 87–98; Cohen, *Japan's Economy*, 442–47.
57. Ints., Katamoto; Hans E. Pringsheim, Aug. 15, 1977; DM to Yoshida, Oct. 21, 1949, RG 10, MMBA; Yoshida, *Japan's Decisive Century*, 62; Whitney, *MacArthur*, 278; Herbert Passin, *The Legacy of the Occupation — Japan* (New York, 1968), 29–32; Aduard, *Japan*, 43–47.
58. Ints., Ohtake, Kakitsubo, Wildes, Shigeo Kimura; Wesley R. Fishel, "Japan Under MacArthur: Retrospect and Prospect," *Western Political Quarterly*, 4 (June 1951), 218–19; Willard Price, *The Japanese Miracle and Peril* (New York, 1971), 177–88; Kawai, *Japan's American Interlude*, 170–75; Wildes, *Typhoon*, 221–33; *Asahi Shimbun* staff, *Pacific Rivals*, 145–48; Andrew J. Grad, *Land and Peasant in Japan: An Introductory Survey* (New York, 1952), 201–05; Kennan, *Memoirs*, I, 387–88; Hewes, *Japan*, 129–40.
59. Sidney Klein, "The Educational and Social Aspects of Land Reform in Japan," in Thomas W. Burkman, ed., *The Occupation of Japan: Educational and Social Reform . . .* (Norfolk, 1982), 449.
60. DM, *Reminiscences*, 314; Martin Bronfenbrenner, "The American Occupation of Japan: Economic Retrospect," in Grant K. Goodman, comp., *The American Occupation of Japan: A Retrospective View* (Lawrence, KS, 1968), 16.
61. SCAP press release, June 28, 1947; State Dept. aide-mémoire to Australian Embassy, July 24, 1947, in *FRUS, 1947*, VI, 264–65.
62. SCAP, GHQ, *Agricultural Co-operatives, 1945–December 1950 (HNAOJ;* Tokyo, 1951), 4; SCAP/FEC, *Selected Data*, 42; DM, Statement on Organization of Agricultural Co-operatives, Dec. 15, 1949, in *DAOCJ*, IV, 120–21.
63. Int., Whitney; DM, *Reminiscences*, 313.

CHAPTER VI. *His Second Political Misadventure*

pages 193–217
1. Howard B. Schonberger, "The General and the Presidency: Douglas MacArthur and the Election of 1948," *Wisconsin Magazine of History*, 57 (Spring 1974), 202; DM, *Reminiscences*, 365; Whitney, *MacArthur*, 516; Truman, *Memoirs*, II, 502–03.
2. Carolyn J. Mattern, "The Man on the Dark Horse: The Presidential Campaigns for General Douglas MacArthur, 1944 & 1948" (unpublished Ph.D. dissertation, University of Wisconsin, 1976), 28–143; Arthur H. Vandenberg, *The Private Papers of Senator Vandenberg*, ed.

Arthur H. Vandenberg, Jr. (Boston, 1952), 77–89; James, *Mac-Arthur*, II, 403–40. On his Tokyo office visitors, see DM Diary, sundry entries, 1945–47, RG 5, MMBA.

3. Eichelberger Diary, Feb. 5, 1946.
4. Int., Eisenhower; DM Diary, May 10, 1946; Forrestal, *Forrestal Diaries*, 325.
5. Kenney, *MacArthur*, 248–49.
6. Ints., Whitney, Willoughby; Carl M. Degler, *Affluence and Anxiety, 1945–Present* (Glenview, IL, 1968), 18–19.
7. Ints., Beiderlinden, Willoughby, Bunker, Bowers; Brig. Gen. Bonner F. Fellers, June 26, 1971.
8. Ints., Whitney, Willoughby, Mashbir; Maj. Gen. George V. H. Moseley to DM, June 23, 1946, RG 10, MMBA; *Army and Navy Journal*, June 22, 1946; Hadley Cantril, ed., *Public Opinion, 1935–1946* (Princeton, 1951), 559, 565–66, 585, 643–47; Schonberger, "The General and the Presidency," 203.
9. Fellers to DM, Jan. 19, 1946; Maj. Gen. Charles A. Willoughby to DM, c. Mar. 1946; Eichelberger to DM, Nov. 27, 1946, RG 10, MMBA; Col. Laurence E. Bunker to DM, Nov. 18, 1946, RG 5, MMBA. Also see Eichelberger to DM, Aug. 18, Sept. 29, Oct. 12, Nov. 14, 1947, and Eichelberger Diary, various entries of 1946–47, Eichelberger Papers.
10. Lehrbas to DM, Jan. 4, 1946, RG 5, MMBA; Moseley to DM, Oct. 15, 1945; Philip F. La Follette to DM, Oct. 15, 1945; Herbert C. Hoover to DM, Oct. 17, 1945; Julius Klein to DM, Dec. 7, 1946, RG 10, MMBA.
11. Wood to DM, June 16, 1947, RG 10, MMBA; "Japan: Signals of Economic Storm," *Newsweek*, 29 (Apr. 14, 1947), 37; Mattern, "Man on the Dark Horse," 154–55.
12. Robert R. McCormick to DM, June 18, Aug. 29, 1947; DM to McCormick, Sept. 6, 1947; Eichelberger to DM, Sept. 29, 1947, RG 10, MMBA; "Generals in 1948 Campaign," *United States News*, 23 (Aug. 1, 1947), 22.
13. Int., Gen. Albert C. Wedemeyer, July 6, 1971; Sen. Robert A. Taft to DM, May 4, 1946; Lt. Gen. Albert C. Wedemeyer to DM, Oct. 20, 1947, RG 10, MMBA.
14. Wood to DM, Oct. 17, 1947, RG 10, MMBA; Hanford MacNider to DM, Sept. 18, 1947, quoted in Mattern, "Man on the Dark Horse," 158.
15. DM to Wood, Oct. 15, 1947, RG 10, MMBA; DM to MacNider, Oct. 14, 1947, quoted in Mattern, "Man on the Dark Horse," 158.
16. Wood to DM, Nov. 6, 1947, RG 10, MMBA.
17. DM to Wood, Nov. 16, 1947, RG 10, MMBA.
18. *Nippon Times*, Nov. 19, 1947; *New York Times*, Nov. 16, 1947; "Maybe MacArthur," *Newsweek*, 30 (Nov. 24, 1947), 23; Mattern, "Man on the Dark Horse," 170–71.
19. Byers to Eichelberger, Nov. 4, 1947, Byers Papers; DM Diary, Nov.

2, 9, 12, 1947; *Stars and Stripes* (Pacific ed.), Nov. 3, 1947; Eichelberger to Roy W. Howard, Feb. 14, 1948, Eichelberger Papers; Clark G. Lee and Richard Henschel, *Douglas MacArthur* (New York, 1952), 106; Sidney L. Huff, with Joe A. Morris, *My Fifteen Years with General MacArthur* (New York, 1964 [1st ed., 1951]), 125–26.

20. Eisenhower to Leonard V. Finder, Jan. 22, 1948, in Eisenhower, *Papers*, IX, 2191–94; Roy E. Larsen to Eichelberger, Feb. 5, 1948, Eichelberger Papers; *New York Times*, Jan. 24, Feb. 6, 1948; *Nippon Times*, Feb. 9, 1948.

21. *New York Journal-American*, Mar. 1, 1948; San Francisco *Examiner*, Mar. 1, 1948; Washington *Post*, Mar. 1, 1948; "Booby-Trapped?" *Time*, 51 (Mar. 15, 1948), 72, 75; "MacArthur Is Willing," *Newsweek*, 31 (Mar. 15, 1948), 21.

22. Washington *Post*, Mar. 9, 1948.

23. Whitney, *MacArthur*, 518–19; Washington *Post*, Mar. 10, 1948; *Nippon Times*, Mar. 10, 1948; Schonberger, "The General and the Presidency," 212–13.

24. *New York Times*, Mar. 14, 1948; Russell Splane, "Our Far-Flung Correspondents," *New Yorker*, 24 (Apr. 10, 1948), 90; "Gen. MacArthur," *The Nation*, 166 (Mar. 20, 1948), 318.

25. Ints., Kawamura, Shiba, West; David W. Condé, Aug. 17, 1977; Russell Brines, June 18, 1977; Splane, "Our Far-Flung Correspondents," 90, 92.

26. *Mainichi Daily News*, Oct. 4, 1976.

27. Int., Beiderlinden; int., Maj. Gen. William A. Beiderlinden, Jan. 27, 1967, Milner File, DMBP.

28. Int., Gaetano Faillace, Aug. 31, 1971; sundry correspondence on the MacArthur-for-President movement in RG 10, MMBA, and Eichelberger Papers; Schonberger, "The General and the Presidency," 203–04; Sidney Olson, "The MacArthur Gamble," *Life*, 24 (Apr. 5, 1948), 55; Robert Considine, *It's All News to Me: A Reporter's Deposition* (New York, 1967), 139.

29. Frank C. Waldrop, *McCormick of Chicago* (Englewood Cliffs, NJ, 1966), 6; Schonberger, "The General and the Presidency," 206, 211–12; Mattern, "Man on the Dark Horse," 219–20. The indispensable secondary works on the 1948 MacArthur campaign, as this chapter's notes attest, are Schonberger's article and particularly Mattern's dissertation.

30. Richard H. Rovere, *Senator Joe McCarthy* (New York, 1959), 181n; Mattern, "Man on the Dark Horse," 195–215; Schonberger, "The General and the Presidency," 213–14.

31. Mattern, "Man on the Dark Horse," 207–08.

32. *New York Times*, Mar. 12, 29, Apr. 1, 4, 1948; *Nippon Times*, Mar. 31, 1948; Schonberger, "The General and the Presidency," 215–17; Mattern, "Man on the Dark Horse," 218–26; Robert A. Divine, *Foreign Policy and U.S. Presidential Elections*, vol. I, *1940–1948* (New York, 1974), 191.

33. Washington *Post*, Apr. 7, 8, 1948; Olson, "The MacArthur Gamble," 54–55; Sebald, *With MacArthur*, 106.
34. Washington *Post*, Apr. 15, 1948; Mattern, "Man on the Dark Horse," 248–52.
35. DM to Sen. Styles Bridges, May 28, 1948, PSF, Truman Papers.
36. Lee and Henschel, *MacArthur*, 106–07; Richard S. Kirkendall, "Election of 1948," in Arthur M. Schlesinger, Jr., ed., *History of American Presidential Elections, 1789–1968*, vol. IV (New York, 1971), 3115–16; Mattern, "Man on the Dark Horse," 258–65; Duane Schultz, *Hero of Bataan: The Story of General Wainwright* (New York, 1981), 438; Eugene H. Roseboom, *A History of Presidential Elections: From George Washington to Richard M. Nixon* (3d ed., New York, 1970), 495–98; Herbert Eaton, *Presidential Timber: A History of Nominating Conventions, 1868–1960* (New York, 1964), 410–25.
37. Brig. Gen. Harold E. Eastwood to MacNider, June 20, 23, 1948, and DM to MacNider, June 28, 1948, quoted in Mattern, "Man on the Dark Horse," 264.
38. DM to William Randolph Hearst, June 26, 1948, RG 10, MMBA.
39. Gen. Jonathan M. Wainwright to DM, July 14, Aug. 24, 1948, RG 10, MMBA; *New York Times*, May 5, 1948; *Nippon Times*, May 7, 1948.
40. La Follette to Mrs. DM, Sept. 3, 1948, RG 10, MMBA; Mattern, "Man on the Dark Horse," 265–67.

CHAPTER VII. *Entrenchment of Conservatism*
pages 221–47
1. "Mr. X" [George F. Kennan], "The Sources of Soviet Conduct," *Foreign Affairs*, 25 (July 1947), 566–82; *Department of State Bulletin*, 16 (May 18, 1947), 991–94; JCS to DM, Aug. 14, 1947, Leahy File 42, RG 218, NA; Michael Schaller, "Securing the Great Crescent: Occupied Japan and the Origins of Containment in Southeast Asia," *Journal of American History*, 69 (Sept. 1982), 393–95; Borton, *Japan's Modern Century*, 490; Kennan, *Memoirs, I*, 375–77; Frederick S. Dunn, et al., *Peacemaking and the Settlement with Japan* (Princeton, 1963), 56–65. On a trip to Tokyo in March 1947, Borton showed his draft treaty to MacArthur; shortly afterward, the general issued his call for an early treaty.
2. Schonberger, "Zaitbatsu Dissolution," 22–24; Howard B. Schonberger, "The Japan Lobby in American Diplomacy, 1947–1952," *Pacific Historical Review*, 6 (Aug. 1977), 331–33; Joyce and Gabriel Kolko, *The Limits of Power: The World and United States Foreign Policy, 1945–1954* (New York, 1972), 514–15.
3. DM to Sec. of the Army Kenneth B. Royall, Oct. 24, 1947, RG 10, MMBA; Under Sec. of the Army Tracy S. Voorhees to Sec. of Defense Louis Johnson, Apr. 22, 1950; DM to Johnson, June 20, 1950, SCAP Government Sec., Admin. Div. File, RG 331, WNRC; Col.

Charles L. Kades, Memorandum, n.d., quoted in Schonberger, "Japan Lobby," 334.

4. Schonberger, "Zaibatsu Dissolution," 25–26; "A Lawyer's Report on Japan Attacks Plan to Run Occupation . . . Far to the Left of Anything Now Tolerated in America," *Newsweek*, 30 (Dec. 1, 1947), 36–38; Sen. William F. Knowland, speeches of Dec. 17, 1947, and Jan. 19, 1948, U.S. Senate, *Congressional Record*, 80th Cong., 2d Sess. (1947–48), XCIV, pt. 1, 116–19, 299–301.

5. DM to Sen. Brien McMahon, Feb. 1, 1948, in U.S. Senate, *Congressional Record*, 80th Cong., 2d Sess. (1948), XCIV, pt. 1, 1362.

6. Royall, San Francisco Address, Jan. 6, 1948, in ibid., 1363–64, and *DAOCJ*, II, 4–10; Howard B. Schonberger, "U.S. Policy in Post-War Japan: The Retreat from Liberalism" (unpublished paper read at Organization of American Historians meeting, Detroit, Apr. 1981), 10; Hadley, *Antitrust*, 166–67; Blakeslee, *Far Eastern Commission*, 200–01.

7. DM Diary, Mar. 1, 5, 21, 1948; Kennan, *Memoirs*, I, 382–85.

8. Kennan, *Memoirs*, I, 385–86.

9. Ibid., 376, 389.

10. DM Diary, Mar. 20, 21, 25, Apr. 1, 2, 1948; Kolko and Kolko, *Limits*, 518–19; Schonberger, "Japan Lobby," 337. For Kennan's memo of his talks with DM, Mar. 1, 5, and 21, 1948, see *FRUS, 1948*, VI, 697–712.

11. Schaller, "Securing the Great Crescent," 396–97.

12. George F. Kennan, PPS 28, "Recommendations with Respect to U.S. Policy Toward Japan," Mar. 25, 1948, in *FRUS, 1948*, VI, 691–96, 712–19; Kennan, *Memoirs*, I, 391–93. On PPS 28, see also *FRUS, 1948*, VI, 727–36, 775–81.

13. NSC 13/2, "Report by the National Security Council on Recommendations with Respect to United States Policy Toward Japan," Oct. 7, 1948, in *FRUS, 1948*, VI, 858–62. On NSC 13/2, also see ibid., 878, 890–91, 932–34.

14. Ints., Kawamura, Suzuki, Amakawa, Pringsheim, Willoughby; Gen. Frank S. Besson, Jr., June 18, 1977; Yoshida, *Japan's Decisive Century*; Fearey, *Occupation*, 9–12.

15. Ints., Willoughby, Whitney, Thomas Wright, Matthews; Kennan, *Memoirs*, I, 369–70; Blakeslee, *Far Eastern Commission*, 228–31; Fearey, *Occupation*, 5–6.

16. Rosecrance, *Australian Diplomacy*, 101–06; Feis, *Contest Over Japan*, 143–44; D. C. Watt, "Britain and the Cold War in the Far East, 1945–1958," in Yonosuke Nagai and Akira Iriye, eds., *The Origins of the Cold War in Asia* (New York, 1977), 89–122; Fearey, *Occupation*, 7–9. See also Roger Buckley, *Occupation Diplomacy: Britain, the United States, and Japan, 1945–1952* (Cambridge, England, 1982), which appeared too recently for use in this book.

17. Schonberger, "Japan Lobby," 327–59.

18. Kolko and Kolko, *Limits*, 510, 533; Scott, "Effect of the Cold War," 212–26, 321–25; Dower, *Empire and Aftermath*, 305–68; Schaller, "Securing the Great Crescent," 392–414.

19. Ints., Willoughby, Bunker.

20. Ints., Tanaka, Ohtake, Suzukawa; Fearey, *Occupation*, 17–24, 194–95; Blakeslee, *Far Eastern Commission*, 182–93.

21. Int., Sebald; *DAFR*, XII, 479–80; Sebald, *With MacArthur*, 140–49; Fearey, *Occupation*, 14–17, 193–94.

22. *Nippon Times*, June 7, 1950; Sebald to Acheson, Mar. 7, 1949, in *FRUS, 1949*, VII, 684–85; Baerwald, *Purge*, 99; Scott, "Effect of the Cold War," 176–79; Fearey, *Occupation*, 26–33; Swearingen and Langer, *Red Flag*, 209–12, 242–45, 249–56; SCAP, *Purge*, 121–24; Deverall, *Red Star*, 244–49; *New York Times*, May 2, 1951.

23. DM to Yoshida, June 6, 1950, Williams Papers.

24. Int., Willoughby; DM to Yoshida, June 7, 26, July 18, 1950, Williams Papers.

25. Ints., Suzukawa, Tanaka; DM to Prime Min. Hitoshi Ashida, July 22, 1948; Ashida to DM, July 24, 1948, Williams Papers; *FRUS, 1948*, VI, 837–42, 847–48, 850–52, 866–70, 916–21; Yoshida, *Memoirs*, 214–18; Farley, *Japan's Labor Problems*, 205–06, 250–56; Wildes, *Typhoon*, 90–101; Yanaga, *Japanese People and Politics*, 307–11; Evelyn S. Colbert, *The Left Wing in Japanese Politics* (New York, 1952), 104–05; Aduard, *Japan*, 87–88; Williams, *Japan's Political Revolution*, 67–68.

26. Int., Amakawa; DM to Katayama, Sept. 16, 1947; Yoshida to DM, Aug. 6, 1949; DM to Yoshida, July 8, 1950, RG 10, MMBA; DM to Bradley, July 7, 1949, RG 9, MMBA; *Mainichi Daily News*, Sept. 10, 17, 1976; SCAP, *Police and Public Safety*, 111–13, 129–30; Williams, *Japan's Political Revolution*, 210; Sugai, "Japanese Police System," 6–7; *FRUS, 1949*, VII, pt. 2, 694–96, 771–73; *FRUS, 1950*, VI, 1251–54; *FRUS, 1951*, VI, 808–09, 884–95, 906.

27. DM, Message on Second Anniversary of the Constitution, May 2, 1949, in *FRUS, 1949*, VII, pt. 2, 743–44.

28. Huston to Acheson, May 10, 1949, in ibid., 740–43.

29. *DAFR*, XI, 174–75; Fearey, *Occupation*, 192–93.

30. Ints., Kaite, Kakitsubo; int., Baldwin, 1961, pt. 2, no. 10, p. 103, CUOHRO; Textor, *Failure*, 112–17; Kenneth E. Colson, "The Conservative Political Movement," *Annals of the American Academy of Political and Social Science*, 308 (Nov. 1956), 40–42; Allan B. Cole, et al., *Socialist Parties*, 16–32.

31. Int., Wildes; *Mainichi Daily News*, Sept. 15, 1976; Deverall, *Red Star*, 101–02; Borton, *Japan's Modern Century*, 471–73; Clubok, "Japanese Conservative Politics," 30–33; *New York Times*, Jan. 25, 1949.

32. DM, Statement on Elections, Apr. 27, 1947, in SCAP, *Political Reorientation*, II, 767; *Nippon Times*, Jan. 25, 1949.

CHAPTER VIII. *Stabilizing Japan's Economy*

pages 248–74

1. *DAFR*, X, 160–62, 167; *FRUS, 1948*, VI, 705–06, 710–11, 973–77, 996–1011, 1019–21; Ball, *Japan*, 167–69, 237; Blakeslee, *Far Eastern Commission*, 151–68; Cohen, *Japan's Economy*, 422–27.

2. DM to DA, Dec. 14, 1948, quoted in Bishop to W. W. Butterworth, Dec. 17, 1948, in *FRUS, 1948*, VI, 1064.

3. Ibid., 1065; *FRUS, 1949*, VII, pt. 2, 611–12, 625–26, 633–42, 744, 983–89.

4. McCoy, Statement on Japanese Reparations and Level of Industry, May 12, 1949, in *DAFR*, XI, 180–81. See also *FRUS, 1949*, VII, pt. 2, 766–67.

5. DM to Bradley, July 8, 1948, RG 9, MMBA; Roy S. Campbell to DM, May 16, 1949, RG 5, MMBA; *New York Times*, Sept. 16, 1948; *Nippon Times*, Aug. 4, 1949; SCAP, *Deconcentration of Economic Power*, 21–32, 37–41, 46, 81–83; Kawai, *Japan's American Interlude*, 147; Willard Price, *Journey by Junk: Japan After MacArthur* (New York, 1953), 158–61; Bisson, *Zaibatsu Dissolution*, 144–48; Hadley, *Antitrust*, 142–44.

6. Fearey, *Occupation*, 62–63; Eleanor M. Hadley, "Japan: Competition or Private Collectivism?" *Far Eastern Survey*, 18 (Dec. 14, 1949), 293.

7. Yoshida to DM, Feb. 2, 1949, Mar. 28, 1950; DM to Yoshida, Feb. 4, 1949, Williams Papers; *FRUS, 1948*, VI, 649–53; *FRUS, 1949*, VII, pt. 2, 622–23; Baerwald, *Purge*, 91–93; Yoshida, *Memoirs*, 161–63; Bisson, *Zaibatsu Dissolution*, 176–79.

8. Hadley, *Antitrust*, 201; Bisson, *Zaibatsu Dissolution*, 201–02, 216–17; E. Wight Bakke, *Revolutionary Democracy: Challenge and Testing in Japan* (Hamden, CT, 1968), 207–09.

9. DM, Statement to the Japanese People, Sept. 2, 1949, in Willoughby, ed., *Reports*, 294.

10. Ints., Kakitsubo; Masaru Debuchi, Aug. 15, 1977; George C. Allen, *Japan's Economic Expansion* (London, 1965), 247–48; Fearey, *Occupation*, 123–24, 215–17; Aduard, *Japan*, 88–92.

11. DM to Bradley, July 8, 1948, RG 9, MMBA; DM to Bradley, Sept. 21, 1948, Leahy File 42, RG 218, NA; Aduard, *Japan*, 92–95; Colbert, *Left Wing*, 270–79; Eto, *Nation Reborn*, 23–25; *Asahi Shimbun* staff, *Pacific Rivals*, 189–92.

12. Royall to DM, Dec. 10, 1948, Leahy File 42, RG 218, NA. See also *DAFR*, X, 165–66; *DAOCJ*, III, 26–29.

13. DM to Royall, Dec. 13, 1948, Leahy File 43, RG 218, NA; DM to Yoshida, Dec. 19, 1948, RG 10, MMBA.

14. Royall to DM, Dec. 11, 1948; DM to Royall, Dec. 12, 1948, PSF, Truman Papers.

15. Butterworth to Acheson, Jan. 25, 1949, quoted in Nishi, *Unconditional Democracy*, 75–76; DM Diary, Feb. 1, 19, Mar. 19, May 2, 1949.

16. Int., Crane, pt. 2, no. 48, pp. 31–32, CUOHRO; Osamu Nariai, *The*

Modernization of the Japanese Economy (Tokyo, 1977), 23–24; Fearey, *Occupation*, 128–35; Yamamura, *Economic Policy*, 29–31; Nakamura, *Postwar Japanese Economy*, 37–40; Asahi Shimbun staff, *Pacific Rivals*, 179.

17. Ints., Kawamura, Debuchi; DM to Gen. J. Lawton Collins, Nov. 17, 1949, RG 9, MMBA; *Mainichi Daily News* staff, *Fifty Years*, 244; Ikuhiko Hata, "The Occupation of Japan, 1945–1952," in Joe C. Dixon, ed., *The American Military and the Far East* . . . (Washington, 1981), 104; Yoshida, *Japan's Decisive Century*, 73–75; Farley, *Japan's Labor Problems*, 216–19.

18. Joseph M. Dodge, Statement on Japanese Economic Stabilization, Mar. 7, 1949, in *DAOCJ*, III, 29–33; Fearey, *Occupation*, 135–201; Leon Hollerman, "International Economic Controls in Occupied Japan," *Journal of Asian Studies*, 38 (Aug. 1979), 711–19.

19. DM to Voorhees, Oct. 2, 1949, RG 9, MMBA; DM to DA, May 2, 1949, quoted in Nishi, *Unconditional Democracy*, 77; Asahi Shimbun staff, *Pacific Rivals*, 179.

20. DM to Yoshida, Mar. 21, Apr. 11, 1950, RG 10, MMBA; Yoshida to DM, Sept. 16, 1949, Mar. 18, May 22, 1950; DM to Yoshida, Sept. 15, 1949, Apr. 11, May 25, 1950, Williams Papers; Saburo Shiomi, *Japan's Finance and Taxation, 1940–1956*, trans. Hasegawa Shotaro (New York, 1957), 77–92; Cole, *Socialist Parties*, 156; SCAP, GHQ, *National Government Finance, 1945–March 1951 (HNAOJ;* Tokyo, 1952), 150–51; SCAP, GHQ, *Local Government Finance, 1945–March 1951 (HNAOJ;* Tokyo, 1952), 65–66; Williams, *Japan's Political Revolution*, 223–25, 266; Fearey, *Occupation*, 150–54, 197–98; Yamamura, *Economic Policy*, 31–32.

21. DM to Howard, Jan. 14, 1949, RG 5, MMBA; [Harry F. Kern], "What's Wrong in Japan? Plenty, Blasts Survey Expert," *Newsweek*, 33 (Apr. 18, 1949), 45; Schonberger, "Japan Lobby," 346–47.

22. "Two Billion Dollar Failure in Japan," *Fortune*, 39 (Apr. 1949), 72; DM, "Japan: An Economy of Survival," ibid. (June 1949), 74; Schonberger, "Japan Lobby," 346.

23. DM, "Japan," 188, 190, 192.

24. "Two Billion Dollar Failure," 72, 204; DM, "Japan," 192, 194, 196, 198; "Editors' Comment," *Fortune*, 39 (June 1949), 204.

25. "SCAPitalism Marches On: Japan's Economy Will Be Better Off When It Comes Marching Home," ibid., 40 (Oct. 1949), 76–77; DM to Voorhees, Oct. 2, 1949, RG 9, MMBA.

26. Helen Mears, "We're Giving Japan Democracy, But She Can't Earn Her Living," *Saturday Evening Post*, 221 (June 18, 1949), 12; DM, "Gen. MacArthur Protests *Post* Editorial," ibid., 222 (July 30, 1949), 4.

27. Voorhees to DM, Feb. 23, 1950, RG 10, MMBA; DM, "Japan," 196. The figures on congressional appropriations on this page and the next refer to U.S. fiscal years and are as stated in Fearey, *Occupation*, 218.

28. Voorhees to DM, May 25, 27, 1949, RG 9, MMBA.

29. DM to Voorhees, Dec. 16, 1949; Voorhees to DM, Dec. 17, 1949, RG

9, MMBA; Voorhees to DM, Feb. 14, 1950, RG 10, MMBA; Nishii, *Unconditional Democracy*, 78–79.

30. Voorhees to DM, Apr. 15, Oct. 26, 1950, RG 10, MMBA.
31. DM to Draper, June 12, 1948, in *FRUS, 1948*, VI, 822–23; NSC 13/2, Oct. 7, 1948, in ibid., 859–60.
32. NSC 13/3, "Report by the National Security Council on Recommendations With Respect to United States Policy Toward Japan," May 6, 1949, in *FRUS, 1949*, VII, pt. 2, 730–36.
33. Maxwell M. Hamilton, Draft Memorandum: "State Department Assumption of Control of Non-Garrison Aspects of Military Occupation of Japan: Full Implementation of NSC 13/2," Mar. 2, 1949, in ibid., 674–78.
34. Ints., Willoughby, Whitney.
35. Omar N. Bradley and Clay Blair, *A General's Life: An Autobiography* (New York, 1983), 526.
36. DM to Bradley, June 16, 1949, RG 5, MMBA. See also DM to Acheson, June 16, 1949; DM to Voorhees, June 16, 1949; DM to Under Sec. of Defense Stephen T. Early, June 16, 1949, RG 5, MMBA. MacArthur allegedly sent a similar letter to Johnson, but it was not found in the records.
37. Sebald to Butterworth, July 26, 1949, in *FRUS, 1949*, VII, pt. 2, 808–12.
38. William R. Mathews to John Foster Dulles, June 5, 1950, John Foster Dulles Papers, Mudd Library, Princeton University, Princeton, NJ.
39. Bradley to DM, Aug. 16, 1949; DM to Bradley, Sept. 3, 1949, RG 5, MMBA.
40. Acheson to DM, Sept. 9, 1949, in *FRUS, 1949*, VII, pt. 2, 850–51.
41. Ibid., 852.

CHAPTER IX. *Social and Cultural Encounters*

pages 275–308
1. Int., Sams; Byers to his wife, Sept. 8, 1945, Byers Papers; Rear Adm. A. E. Smith to Cooke, Cooke Papers; int., Col. Chauncey E. Dovell, Milner File, DMBP; Sams, "Medic," 348–50, 403–16, 439; SCAP, GHQ, *Public Health, September 1945–December 1950 (HNAOJ;* Tokyo, 1952), 3–4.
2. Int., Dr. Lauren V. Ackerman, pt. 2, no. 2, pp. 3–15, 27–28, CUOHRO; *Mainichi Daily News*, June 9, 1976; Sams, "Medic," 445–52; SCAP, *Public Health in Japan*, I, 18–23.
3. Wyman, "Sams," 68–72; SCAP, GHQ, *Mission and Accomplishments of the Occupation in the Public Health and Welfare Fields* (Tokyo, 1949), 2–9; Sams, "Medic," 440–45, 452–72, 486–87; Wildes, *Typhoon*, 207–20; DM, *Reminiscences*, 313.
4. Eichelberger Diary, Sept. 11, 1945; Sams, "Medic," 472–85; *Mainichi Daily News*, June 9, 1976; SCAP, *Public Health and Welfare Fields*, 9–

11; Frank Kelley and Cornelius Ryan, *Star-Spangled Mikado* (New York, 1947), 150, 152–54; Ray A. Moore, "The Occupation of Japan as History: Some Recent Research," *Monumenta Nipponica*, 36 (Autumn 1981), 325; Price, *Journey*, 132–33; Sheldon, *Honorable Conquerors*, 118–20.

5. Sams, "Medic," 417–38, 493–603, 625–26; Wyman, "Sams," 41–101 passim; Crawford F. Sams, "Japan's New Public Health Program" [3 pts.], *Military Government Journal*, 1 (Sept.–Oct. 1948), 9–10, 14; 2 (Jan.–Feb. 1949), 7–9; 2 (Summer 1949), 11–12.

6. Irene B. Taeuber, *The Population of Japan* (Princeton, 1958), 369–70; Price, *Journey*, 212.

7. *Nippon Times*, July 2, 1949; Taeuber, *Population*, 370–71; Price, *Journey*, 212–15; "Birth Rate Going Down," *Newsweek*, 35 (May 8, 1950), 42.

8. Ints., Soma, Sugase, Seki; Setsu Tanino, "Post-war Democratization in Japan: Family Life," *International Social Science Journal*, 13 (1961), 57–64; Kazuya Matsumiya, "Family Organization in Present-Day Japan," *American Journal of Sociology*, 53 (1947), 105–10; Shio Sakanashi, "Women's Position and the Family System [in Japan]," *Annals of the American Academy of Political and Social Science*, 308 (Nov. 1956), 130–39; Passin, *Legacy*, 32–35; Kawai, *Japan's American Interlude*, 225–39; *Asahi Shimbun* staff, *Pacific Rivals*, 161–64.

9. Dr. Mary R. Beard to 1st Lt. Ethel B. Weed, Oct. 31, 1946, RG 5, MMBA. See also Beard to Weed, July 19, 1946; Weed to Lt. Col. Donald R. Nugent, Aug. 29, 1946; Col. Herbert B. Wheeler to Nugent, Sept. 17, 1946; Nugent to Wheeler, Nov. 13, 1946, RG 5, MMBA.

10. Ints., Vining, Soma; int., Baldwin, 1961, pt. 2, no. 10, p. 46, CUOHRO; Eto, *Nation Reborn*, 14; Mariko Bando, *The Women of Japan — Past and Present* (Tokyo, 1977), 9–10, 24–25, 31–32; DM, *Reminiscences*, 304–06; *Asahi Shimbun* staff, *Pacific Rivals*, 125–26, 167–70; Edwin O. Reischauer, "Japan and Korea as American Policy Problems," in John K. Fairbank, et al., *Next Step in Asia* (Cambridge, MA, 1949), 65.

11. Int., Soma; Pharr, "Radical U.S. Experiment," 131–32; Lauterbach, *Danger*, 102; *Asahi Shimbun* staff, *Pacific Rivals*, 126–27.

12. *SNAJK*, June 1946, 26–27; *Nippon Times*, May 10, 1946; SCAP, *Political Reorientation*, II, 752, 777, 832.

13. Ints., Wildes, Soma; *Asahi Shimbun* staff, *Pacific Rivals*, 125; Pharr, "Radical U.S. Experiment" [and commentary], 129, 139; Kelley and Ryan, *Mikado*, 162; Sheldon, *Honorable Conquerors*, 46.

14. Roger O. Egeberg, "General Douglas MacArthur," *Transactions of the American Clinical and Climatological Association*, 78 (1966), 170–71.

15. Ints., Egeberg, Bowers, Shiba; int., Baldwin, 1954, vol. I, pt. 3, pp. 452, 454, 495; int., Bowers, pt. 2, no. 21, p. 36, CUOHRO; *Mainichi Daily News*, June 7, 1976; *New York Times*, Apr. 3, 1946; Perry, *Beneath the Eagle's Wings*, 174–76, 184–87; Sheldon, *Honorable Conquerors*, 120–21.

16. Joseph M. Kitagawa, *Religion in Japanese History* (New York, 1966),

271–74; Wilhelmus H. M. Creemers, *Shrine Shinto After World War II* (Leiden, Netherlands, 1968), 43–61; William P. Woodard, *The Allied Occupation of Japan, 1945–1952, and Japanese Religions* (Leiden, Netherlands, 1972), 14–18; Lawrence S. Wittner, "MacArthur and the Missionaries: God and Man in Occupied Japan," *Pacific Historical Review*, 40 (Feb. 1971), 78–79. As the following notes indicate, the works by Woodard and Wittner are indispensable on MacArthur's Christian crusade.

17. Int., Beiderlinden; Gunther, *Riddle*, 76; DM, *Reminiscences*, 276; Woodard, *Japanese Religions*, 243–46, 356–57; Wittner, "MacArthur and the Missionaries," 81–82.

18. *Nippon Times*, Jan. 18, Dec. 3, 1947; Dec. 11, 18, 1948; Nishi, *Unconditional Democracy*, 42–45, 175–76; DM, *Reminiscences*, 310; Wittner, "MacArthur and the Missionaries," 84–91; Woodard, *Japanese Religions*, 243.

19. DM to Eisenhower, Feb. 20, 1947, RG 9, MMBA; *Nippon Times*, Apr. 8, 1947; Woodard, *Japanese Religions*, 245–46, 272–75, 357; Wittner, "MacArthur and the Missionaries," 90, 92–93; Gunther, *Riddle*, 75.

20. DM, Draft Statement on International Christian University, 1949, RG 10, MMBA; Woodard, *Japanese Religions*, 242, 247–48.

21. Dr. William K. Bunce to Nugent, Nov. 18, 1949, quoted in Woodard, *Japanese Religions*, 350–51.

22. Shaplen, "From MacArthur to Miki," pt. 3, 57–58; Wittner, "MacArthur and the Missionaries," 97–98. The figures on religious memberships in occupied Japan vary, but as the following works indicate, the differences on the percentage of Christians range only between 0.4 and 0.6: Kitagawa, *Religion*, 278, 297–306; Nishi, *Unconditional Democracy*, 43; Wittner, "MacArthur and the Missionaries," 30, 97; Kelley and Ryan, *Mikado*, 110–11; Charles W. Iglehart, *A Century of Protestant Christianity in Japan* (Tokyo, 1959), 337; Everett F. Briggs, *New Dawn in Japan* (New York, 1948), 221–26; William Kerr, *Japan Begins Again* (New York, 1949), 161.

23. DM, *Reminiscences*, 311–12; Kawai, *Japan's American Interlude*, 183.

24. Robert K. Hall, "Education in the Development of Postwar Japan," in Redford, ed., *Occupation of Japan . . . and Its Legacy*, 118. See also Hall, *Education*, 69–82.

25. Ints., Wildes, Vining; Wilson Compton to DM, Apr. 29, 1946, RG 5, MMBA; DM to Eisenhower, Mar. 30, 1947, RG 9, MMBA; Willard E. Givens, "Tokyo and Return" [MS on 1946 education mission], T. V. Smith Papers, University of Chicago Library; DM Diary, Mar. 20, 1946; *Nippon Times*, Mar. 23, Apr. 8, 1946; George D. Stoddard, et al., "Report of the United States Educational Mission to Japan," Mar. 30, 1946, SCAP, GHQ, Admin. File, RG 331, WNRC; DM, Statement Concerning the Report of the U.S. Education Mission, Apr. 6, 1946, in *DAOCJ*, II, 212–13; George D. Stoddard, "MacArthur and the U.S. Education Mission to Japan," *National Parent-Teacher*, 41 (Sept. 1946), 22–24; Martin, *Allied Occupation*, 59–61; Benjamin C. Duke, *Japan's*

Militant Teachers: A History of the Left-Wing Teachers' Movement (Honolulu, 1973), 46–49, 70, 218–19; Hall, "Education," 120, 130–31, 135–37; Yoshida, *Japan's Decisive Century*, 64–65; Nishi, *Unconditional Democracy*, 187–93.

26. SCAP, GHQ, *Education, 1945–September 1949 (HNAOJ;* Tokyo, 1952), 93; Isaac L. Kandel, "Revision of Japanese Education," *School and Society*, 64 (Aug. 24, 1946), 134; Hall, "Education," 131–35; Hall, *Education*, 293–401; Reischauer, *United States and Japan*, 268–69.

27. Tatsumi Makino, "Japanese Education," *International Social Science Journal*, 13 (1961), 44–55; Kawai, *Japan's American Interlude*, 183–200; Hall, *Education*, 202–92, 402–82; Robert K. Hall, *Shushin: The Ethics of a Defeated Nation* (New York, 1949), 237–44; SCAP, GHQ, *Mission and Accomplishments of the Occupation in the Civil Information and Education Fields* (Tokyo, 1950), 11–20; Duke, *Teachers*, 207–10, 219–20; Nishi, *Unconditional Democracy*, 288–95; Fearey, *Occupation*, 33–39; Walter C. Eells, comp., *The Literature of Japanese Education, 1945–1954* (Hamden, CT, 1955), iii–iv; Reischauer, *United States and Japan*, 262–68.

28. Ints., Soma, Wildes; Dr. Verna A. Carley, Aug. 23, 1971; Duke, *Teachers*, 75–99, 209–14, 217; Hall, "Education," 127.

29. Int., Lulu Holmes, 1–3, Regional Oral History Office, Bancroft Library, University of California, Berkeley; Makino, "Japanese Education," 47–48; Hall, "Education," 136; Kawai, *Japan's American Interlude*, 201–11; Fearey, *Occupation*, 36–37.

30. Yoshida to DM, Aug. 9, 1949, Williams Papers; DM to Commission on Occupied Areas, Dec. 7, 1949, in Harold E. Snyder and George E. Beauchamp, eds., *An Experiment in International Cultural Relations: A Report of the Staff of the Commission on Occupied Areas* (Washington, 1951), 53–54; Willard E. Givens, et al., "Report of the Second United States Education Mission to Japan," Sept. 22, 1950, 1, Joseph C. Trainor Papers, Hoover Inst.

31. Ints., Carley, Wildes, Suzukawa, Kawamura, Soma; int., Shigeharu Matsumoto, Robert Sherrod File, DMBP; Dower, *Empire and Aftermath*, 348–50; Hall, *Education*, 478–82; Yoshida, *Japan's Decisive Century*, 63–67; Edward Norbeck, "The Social Retrospect," in Goodman, comp., *American Occupation*, 27–28; Marius B. Jansen, "Japan from MacArthur to MacArthur," *Hanover Forum*, Spring 1957, 22–24; Nishi, *Unconditional Democracy*, 261–62; George F. Zook, "The Educational Missions to Japan and Germany," *International Conciliation*, Jan. 1947, 3–19.

32. Daishiro Hidaka, "The Aftermath of Educational Reform [in Japan]," *Annals of the American Academy of Political and Social Science*, 308 (Nov. 1956), 143–55; Makino, "Japanese Education," 55; Hall, "Education," 142–43.

33. Ints., Willoughby, Thorpe; Willoughby, ed., *Reports*, 232–33, 236–41; William J. Coughlin, *Conquered Press: The MacArthur Era in Japanese Journalism* (Palo Alto, CA, 1952), 29–30, 106–07.

34. DM to Imperial Japanese Government, Sept. 10, 1945, SCAP, GHQ, Admin. File, RG 331, WNRC.

35. Ints., Debuchi, Thorpe; *New York Times*, Sept. 22, 29, 1945; *Mainichi Daily News*, June 4, 1976; Coughlin, *Conquered Press*, 15–28, 59–60.

36. Int., Giichi Imae, Sherrod File, DMBP; Draper to DM, Oct. 30, 1947, RG 10, MMBA; DS, Div. of Far East Research, "The *Yomiuri Shimbun* Case," Mar. 6, 1947, in *OSDIRR*, pt. 2; Gayn, *Japan Diary*, 253–54, 334–38; Coughlin, *Conquered Press*, 30–58; Sheldon, *Honorable Conquerors*, 86–89; Kawai, *Japan's American Interlude*, 214–19; Edward Uhlan and Dana L. Thomas, *Shoriki, Miracle Man of Japan: A Biography* (New York, 1957), 156–82.

37. Ints., Willoughby, Shiba, Suzukawa, Pringsheim; Kimpei Shiba to DCJ, Aug. 27, 1977; *Nippon Times*, Sept. 28, 1946; *Stars and Stripes*, Sept. 24, 1946; *New York Times*, Oct. 12, 13, 1946; Gayn, *Japan Diary*, 475–78; Textor, *Failure*, 109–10; Coughlin, *Conquered Press*, 51–56.

38. Ints., Shiba, Ohtake, Kawamura, Suzukawa; int., Kenzo Suzuki, Sherrod File, DMBP; DM, Statement on National Newspaper Week in Japan, Sept. 30, 1949, RG 9, MMBA; Kawai, *Japan's American Interlude*, 215–16, 219; Brines, *MacArthur's Japan*, 246–49; Coughlin, *Conquered Press*, 141–42, 144–46; Yukio Matsuyama, "Communications in the Development of Postwar Japan," in Redford, ed., *Occupation of Japan . . . and Its Legacy*, 31–39. On general views of Japanese newspapers and periodicals, see Ward and Shulman, comps. and eds., *Allied Occupation*, 11–19.

39. Ints., Condé, Pringsheim, Brines, Wildes; Frederic S. Marquardt, Sept. 5, 1971; DM to Hearst, Mar. 24, 1947, RG 5, MMBA; Textor, *Failure*, 33–45; Price, *Japanese Miracle*, 162–69; Williams, *Japan's Political Revolution*, 89, 267–69; Price, *Journey*, 284–91; Coughlin, *Conquered Press*, 111–18, 142–44; Martin Kyre and Joan Kyre, *Military Occupation and National Security* (Washington, 1968), 76–77.

40. DM to Eisenhower, Nov. 2, 1946, RG 21, MMBA.

41. Ints., Brines, Condé, Pringsheim, Williams, Wildes; Brig. Gen. Le Grande A. Diller, May 31, 1977; Robert Sherrod to DCJ, Aug. 8, 1972; London *Times*, June 20, 1950; *New York Times*, Oct. 17, 1945; "MacArthur and the Press," *Newsweek*, 31 (Feb. 9, 1948), 50, 52; Nishi, *Unconditional Democracy*, 105–10; Sheldon, *Honorable Conquerors*, 89–92; Coughlin, *Conquered Press*, 118–40; Keyes Beech, *Tokyo and Points East* (Garden City, NY, 1954), 45–62; Reginald W. Thompson, *Cry Korea* (London, 1951), 100, 191–92.

42. Ints., Shiba, Furukaki, Bowers, Pringsheim, Condé; DM to Collins, June 16, Nov. 14, 1949, RG 9, MMBA; Eichelberger to Roger Baldwin, Aug. 1, 1947, Eichelberger Papers; int., Bowers, pt. 2, no. 21, pp. 43–44; int., Baldwin, 1954, vol. I, pt. 3, 493–94, CUOHRO; *Mainichi Daily News*, June 11, 1976; *New York Times*, May 17, 1946; DS, Div. of Far East Research, "Japan's Press Purge," Dec. 19, 1947, and "The Development of Media Information in Japan Since the Surrender," Oct. 1, 1947, in *OSDIRR*, pt. 2; Kawai, *Japan's American*

Interlude, 219–23; SCAP, *Civil Information and Education Fields*, 7–10; Faubion Bowers, *Japanese Theatre* (New York, 1952), 107–08, 224–30; Brines, *MacArthur's Japan*, 243–46; Rodger Swearingen, *The Soviet Union and Postwar Japan: Escalating Challenge and Response* (Stanford, CA, 1979), 90–95; Gayn, *Japan Diary*, 98–99; Textor, *Failure*, 149, 185; Asahi Shimbun staff, *Pacific Rivals*, 134–36; Hugh Borton, et al., *Japan Between East and West* (New York, 1957), 165–82; Joseph L. Anderson and Donald Richie, *The Japanese Film: Art and Industry* (Tokyo, 1959), 160–64, 424.

43. Gaddis, *Public Information*, 88–109; Kawai, *Japan's American Interlude*, 223–24; SCAP, *Civil Information and Education Fields*, 27–28; Borton, et al., *Japan Between East and West*, 299–314; Ward and Shulman, comps. and eds., *Allied Occupation*, 716–26; Tatsuki, *Japanese Opinion*, 1–4.

44. Allan B. Cole and Nakanishi Naomichi, comps. and eds., *Japanese Opinion Polls with Socio-Political Significance, 1947–1957*, vol. I, *Political Support and Preference* (Medford, MA, 1958), 484, 486–87.

45. Ints., Saito, Katamoto, Sugase; Fishel, "Japan Under MacArthur," 221–25; Moore, "Occupation," 327–28; *Mainichi Daily News*, Oct. 4, 1976; Frederick S. Hulse, "Some Effects of the War upon Japanese Society," *Far Eastern Quarterly*, 7 (Nov. 1947), 35; Kazuo Kawai, "American Influence on Japanese Thinking," *Annals of the American Academy of Political and Social Science*, 278 (Nov. 1951), 23–31; Perry, *Beneath the Eagle's Wings*, 215.

CHAPTER X. *Affairs of State*

pages 309–25

1. DM Diary, 1945–51, passim.

2. Ints., Marshall, Willoughby; DM Diary, Sept. 15, 29, 1945; The Rev. P. J. Byrne, "The Anti-MacArthur Complex" (MS, c. 1947), RG 5, MMBA; Atcheson to Byrnes, Oct. 8, 1945; Atcheson to DM, Oct. 8, 1945, in *FRUS, 1945*, VI, 941–42; Shigemitsu, *Japan*, 381; "The Prince and the Press," *Newsweek*, 26 (Oct. 1, 1945), 48.

3. Ints., Furukaki, Marshall; 1st Lt. Philip H. Snyder to 1st Lt. William P. Hogan, Dec. 31, 1945, RG 5, MMBA; *New York Times*, Mar. 11, 1951; DS, Div. of Far East Intelligence, "The Reorganization of the Shidehara Cabinet," Jan. 23, 1946, in *OSDIRR*, pt. 2; Yoshida, *Memoirs*, 64; Quigley and Turner, *New Japan*, 83; Yanaga, *Japan*, 419, 460, 553, 564, 647, 652–53.

4. Ints., Furukaki, Sodei, Wildes, Willoughby; DM to Eisenhower, Apr. 28, 1947, RG 9, MMBA; Katayama, Statement of the Prime Minister, June 1, 1947; Katayama to DM, Sept. 4, 1947; DM to Katayama, Sept. 10, 16, 18, 1947, RG 10, MMBA; *SNAJK*, May 1947, 27–28; Warren S. Hunsberger, Memorandum of Conversation, Mar. 2, 1948, in *FRUS, 1948*, VI, 954; Ball, *Japan*, 73–79; Colbert, *Left Wing*, 219–20; DM, Statement on Selection of Tetsu Katayama as Prime Minister, May

24, 1947, in SCAP, *Political Reorientation*, II, 770; DM, Statement on Resignation of Katayama Cabinet, Feb. 9, 1948, in ibid., 784.
5. Ints., Wildes, Furukaki, Ohtake, Sugase; DM to Bradley, July 8, 1948, RG 9, MMBA; DM to Bradley, Sept. 21, 1948, Leahy File 42, RG 218, NA; Ashida to DM, Mar. 1948, Williams Papers; DM to Ashida, July 22, 1948, RG 10, 1948; Sebald to Marshall, Feb. 24, 1948, in *FRUS, 1948*, VI, 665–66; Colbert, *Left Wing*, 270–79.
6. Yoshida to DM, July 11, Aug. 9, 1949, Williams Papers; Morris, *Phoenix Cup*, 76–79; Dower, "Occupied Japan," 489; Harley F. MacNair and Donald F. Lach, *Modern Far Eastern International Relations* (2d ed., New York, 1955), 613.
7. Ints., Suzukawa, Shiba, Soma, Furukaki, Matsumura, Shigeo Kimura, Wildes, Pringsheim; Shiroshichi Kimura, Aug. 19, 1977; Kimpei Shiba, *I Cover Japan* (Tokyo, 1952), 109–11; Eto, *Nation Reborn*, 21; Wildes, *Typhoon*, 135–36; Dan Kurzman, *Kishi and Japan: The Search for the Sun* (New York, 1960), 263.
8. Gibney, *Five Gentlemen*, 315–17.
9. Ints., Wildes, Diller, Sodei; Yoshida to DM, Sept. 27, 1946; DM to Yoshida, Sept. 27, 1946, RG 10, MMBA; Yoshida, *Japan's Decisive Century*, 48–55; idem, *Memoirs*, 61–89; Wildes, *Typhoon*, 137; Eto, *Nation Reborn*, 21–22; Ball, *Japan*, 56–70; Dower, *Empire and Aftermath*, 294, 310–11, 328; John Osborne, "My Dear General," *Life*, 29 (Nov. 27, 1950), 127–30, 133–34, 136, 139.
10. Yoshida, *Japan's Decisive Century*, 49.
11. Ints., Sodei, Furukaki; Sheldon, *Honorable Conquerors*, 281–92; Dower, *Empire and Aftermath*, 292–400; Moore, "Occupation," 320; Shaplen, "From MacArthur to Miki," pt. 1, 70–71; Eto, *Nation Reborn*, 21; Robert D. Murphy, *Diplomat Among Warriors* (Garden City, NY, 1964), 344–45.
12. Eisenhower–DM Telephone Conversation Notes, June 11, 1960, Whitman Files, Eisenhower Papers; DM, *Reminiscences*, 315.
13. Sen. H. Alexander Smith to DM, Jan. 7, 1952, RG 21, MMBA. See also Memorandum in re Conference Between Smith and Yoshida, Sept. 1951, in *FRUS, 1951*, VI, 1326–27.
14. Dower, *Empire and Aftermath*, 321, 552.
15. Richard M. Nixon, *Leaders* (New York, 1982), 85–86.
16. Int., Thorpe; Wheeler to DM, Jan. 5, 1946, RG 5, MMBA; Yoshida to DM, Dec. 27, 31, 1946; DM to Yoshida, Feb. 25, 1947, RG 10, MMBA; Kawai, *Japan's American Interlude*, 71–90; *Mainichi Daily News*, Aug. 20, 1976; *Nippon Times*, Jan. 1, 26, 1946; Lauterbach, *Danger*, 37–39; Oppler, *Legal Reform*, 49–55, 166–72; Yanaga, *Japanese People*, 137–43; Tatsuki, *Japanese Opinion*, 19–21; "Japan Loves Mikado, On or Off a Pedestal," *U.S. News & World Report*, 24 (Apr. 16, 1948), 67; Mosley, *Hirohito*, 331–38, 342–50.
17. Ints., Vining, Faillace; Amb. Michael J. Mansfield, Aug. 16, 1977; Fellers to DM, Oct. 2, 1945, Bonner F. Fellers Papers, Hoover Inst.; int., Joseph Ballantine, pt. 1, no. 13, p. 74, CUOHRO; Kenneth Ishii,

"An Emperor's Visit," Fort Wayne (IN) *Journal-Gazette,* Sept. 27, 1964; *New York Times,* Dec. 26, 1971; Dower, *Empire and Aftermath,* 309; Mosley, *Hirohito,* 338–42; DM, *Reminiscences,* 287–88; Murphy, *Diplomat,* 342–43. Some sources give the date of the first MacArthur-Hirohito meeting as Sept. 26, 1945, and the Emperor's car as a Daimler.

18. *Nippon Times,* Sept. 28, 1945; *New York Times,* Oct. 2, 15, 1945; *Stars and Stripes,* Oct. 16, 1945; Kanroji, *Hirohito,* 134–35; Toshikazu Kase, *Journey to the "Missouri,"* ed. David N. Rowe (New Haven, 1950), 265.

19. Ints., Seki, Sodei; *Mainichi Daily News,* Aug. 23, 1976; *New York Times,* Sept. 27, 28, 1945; "Transformation of Hirohito," *Christian Century,* 62 (Oct. 10, 1945), 1147; "Japan: 'Shikata Ga Nai,' " *Time,* 46 (Oct. 8, 1945), 38; Sheldon, *Honorable Conquerors,* 102, 137–38; Richard Storry, *A History of Modern Japan* (Harmondsworth, England, 1960), 247–49; Peter B. Stone, *Japan Surges Ahead: The Story of an Economic Miracle* (New York, 1969), 180.

20. Int., Lt. Gen. Edward M. Almond, MMBA; int., Noboru Kajima, Sherrod File, DMBP; DM to Eisenhower, May 7, 1947, RG 9, MMBA; Miichiji Tajima to DM, Nov. 12, 1948, RG 10, MMBA; *Nippon Times,* Nov. 14, 1947; Jan. 11, Nov. 27, 1949; London *Times,* June 1, 1946; *New York Times,* Apr. 19, 1950; *Stars and Stripes,* Aug. 1, Oct. 17, 1946; Atcheson to DM, Oct. 13, 1945; Atcheson to Byrnes, Oct. 13, 1945, in *FRUS, 1945,* VI, 752–53; *SNAJK,* Oct. 1946, 39; Whitney, *MacArthur,* 286.

21. Ints., Vining, Matsumura, Furukaki, Seki; Yoshida to DM, Dec. 22, 1945; Mrs. DM to Mrs. Caldwell, June 21, 1965, RG 10, MMBA; int., Baldwin, 1961, pt. 2, no. 10, pp. 65–66, 69–70, CUOHRO; Elizabeth G. Vining, *Quiet Pilgrimage* (Philadelphia, 1970), 245.

22. Ints., Soma, Suzuki, West; Rep. Hisanari Yamada, Aug. 20, 1977; Eisenhower–DM telephone conversation notes, June 11, 1960, Whitman Files, Eisenhower Papers; int., Bowers, pt. 2, no. 21, p. 34, CUOHRO; Mrs. Elizabeth G. Vining to DCJ, Dec. 8, 1978; *Nippon Times,* June 29, 1949; Brines, *MacArthur's Japan,* 97; Vining, *Quiet Pilgrimage,* 246–59; Ray A. Moore, "Saving the Imperial Institution" (paper read at Assn. for Asian Studies meeting, Los Angeles, Mar. 1979), 8–23; Elizabeth G. Vining, *Windows for the Crown Prince* (Philadelphia, 1952), 218–23; Yoshida, *Memoirs,* 179.

CHAPTER XI. *War, Diplomacy, and New Hope for Japan*
pages 326–54

1. *Nippon Times,* July 22, Aug. 28, 1950; Sebald, *With MacArthur,* 199; Herbert P. Bix, "Regional Integration: Japan and South Korea in America's Asian Policy," in Frank Baldwin, ed., *Without Parallel: The American-Korean Relationship Since 1945* (New York, 1974), 194–95.

2. Ints., Maj. Gen. Ned D. Moore, June 21, 1977; Gen. Charles D. Palmer, June 14, 1977; Appleman, *South to the Naktong,* 382; David Rees,

Korea: The Limited War (Baltimore, 1970 [1st ed., 1964]), 33; Bix, "Regional Integration," 223; James A. Huston, *The Sinews of War: Army Logistics, 1775–1953* (Washington, 1966), 616–17, 641; Congressional Quarterly Service, *Global Defense: U.S. Military Commitments Abroad* (Washington, 1969), 34.

3. Int., Brig. Gen. Miles M. Dawson, July 21, 1977; int., Gen. Barksdale Hamlett, no. 4, pp. 25–49, USAMHI; DM to JCS, Mar. 31, 1951, RG 9, MMBA; DM to Yoshida, July 8, 1950, RG 10, MMBA; FECOM Hq., "Far East Command," 32; *Nippon Times*, July 7, 1950; Bix, "Regional Integration," 194–95; Huston, *Sinews*, 641, 646, 674–75; Schnabel, *Policy and Direction*, 58–59, 136–37, 207–10, 341; Murphy, *Diplomat*, 347–48; Sebald, *With MacArthur*, 197–99; Walter S. Poole, *The Joint Chiefs of Staff and National Policy*, vol. IV, *1950–1952* (Wilmington, DE, 1979), 470–76.

4. *Nippon Times*, Jan. 9, 1951; Kolko and Kolko, *Limits*, 642–44; Dower, *Empire and Aftermath*, 359–68; Ayusawa, *Labor*, 302–04; Gibney, *Five Gentlemen*, 258–60; Paul F. Langer, "Communism in Independent Japan," in Borton, et al., *Japan Between East and West*, 46–51.

5. Huston, *Sinews*, 639; Schnabel, *Policy and Direction*, 136–37; Fine, *Recovery*, 51–52, 57; Adams and Iwao, *Financial History*, 215; Yamamura, *Economic Policy*, 39n; Shaplen, "From MacArthur to Miki," pt. 1, 70.

6. Sundry letters to commanding general, Japan Logistical Command, Sept.–Dec. 1950, FECOM Correspondence Files, RG 6, MMBA.

7. Acheson to Amb. Philip C. Jessup, Sr., Aug. 22, 1950, in *FRUS, 1950*, VI, 1281; Bix, "Regional Integration," 197; *Mainichi Daily News* staff, *Fifty Years*, 262; *Asahi Shimbun* staff, *Pacific Rivals*, 193–96; Shaplen, "From MacArthur to Miki," pt. 1, 70; Sheldon, *Honorable Conquerors*, 215–19.

8. SCAP, GHQ (Magruder) to DA Office of Occupied Areas (Hamblen), Feb. 10, 1951, RG 5, MMBA.

9. Bix, "Regional Integration," 195–96; Sheldon, *Honorable Conquerors*, 217.

10. Yamamura, *Economic Policy*, 39; Nakamura, *Postwar Japanese Economy*, 41–43; Adams and Iwao, *Financial History*, 218–21; Fine, *Recovery*, 50–51; Nariai, *Modernization*, 24; Huston, *Sinews*, 617.

11. Ints., Katamoto, Suzukawa, Debuchi, Furukaki; DM to Yoshida, Oct. 26, 1950, RG 10, MMBA; Jerome B. Cohen, *Economic Problems of Free Japan* (Princeton, 1952), 1–5; *Mainichi Daily News* staff, *Fifty Years*, 263; Fine, *Recovery*, 52–58; Adams and Iwao, *Financial History*, 216–18; Nakamura, *Postwar Japanese Economy*, 43–46; Yamamura, *Economic Policy*, 39–53. See also Chalmers Johnson's excellent study, *MITI and the Japanese Miracle: The Growth of Industrial Policy, 1925–1975* (Stanford, CA, 1982).

12. Nakamura, *Postwar Japanese Economy*, 48.

13. Int., Vining. A slightly different version of MacArthur's remarks is in Vining, *Quiet Pilgrimage*, 254.

14. DM to Eisenhower, May 16, 1947, Principal Files, Eisenhower Papers; DM to Petersen, Feb. 20, 1947; DM to Draper, Jan. 17, 1948, RG 9, MMBA; DM to JCS, Sept. 1, 1947, Leahy File 42, RG 218, NA; Kennan, *Memoirs*, I, 375–77; Acheson, *Present*, 426–35; Sebald, *With MacArthur*, 242–47; Bernard C. Cohen, *The Political Process and Foreign Policy: The Making of the Japanese Peace Settlement* (Princeton, 1957), 11; Kenneth W. Condit, *The Joint Chiefs of Staff and National Policy*, vol. II, *1947–1949* (Wilmington, DE, 1979), 493–509; Emmerson, *Japanese Thread*, 285; Dunn, *Peacemaking*, 42–94; int., Borton, pt. 2, no. 19, pp. 34–36, CUOHRO; *FRUS, 1947*, VI, 326, 448, 450–56, 461–66, 489–91, 498–503, 512–15, 594; *FRUS, 1948*, VI, 656–60; *FRUS, 1949*, VII, pt. 2, 803–07, 830–40, 862–64, 890–94, 898–99.

15. JCS to Lt. Gen. Alfred M. Gruenther, Dec. 9, 1949, RG 5, MMBA; DM Diary, Dec. 5–8, 12, 1949; *FRUS, 1950*, VI, 1119–22, 1133–35, 1167–71, 1182–84, 1205–07; Kennan, *Memoirs*, I, 394–96; Cohen, *Japanese Peace Settlement*, 235–36; Charles E. Neu, *The Troubled Encounter: The United States and Japan* (New York, 1975), 213–14; Sebald, *With MacArthur*, 247–49.

16. Jessup to Acheson, Jan. 10, 1950, in *FRUS, 1950*, VI, 1114–16. See also Jessup to Acheson, Jan. 9, 1950, in ibid., 1109–14; int., Amb. Philip C. Jessup, Sr., July 14, 1977; DM Diary, Jan. 5, 8, 10, 1950.

17. Cohen, *Japanese Peace Settlement*, 12–13, 125–43, 231–32; Neu, *Troubled Encounter*, 212–13; Sebald, *With MacArthur*, 251; Aduard, *Japan*, 157–58; Dunn, *Peacemaking*, 95–99.

18. DM Diary, June 17–27, 1950; *FRUS, 1950*, VI, 1210–11, 1222–23, 1264–65; Aduard, *Japan*, 158–60; Sebald, *With MacArthur*, 250–53; Cohen, *Japanese Peace Settlement*, 13; DM, *Reminiscences*, 324; John M. Allison, *Ambassador from the Prairie; or Allison Wonderland* (Boston, 1973), 126–39.

19. Dulles to DM, July 4, 1950, and Jan. 27, 1951, RG 10, MMBA; DM, Memorandum on the Peace Treaty Problem, June 14, 1950, in *FRUS, 1950*, VI, 1213–21; DM, Memorandum on Concept Concerning Security in Post-war Japan, June 23, 1950, in ibid., 1227–28.

20. DM, Memo on Peace Treaty Problem, in *FRUS, 1950*, VI, 1213–17, 1219–21.

21. Sebald, *With MacArthur*, 256, 258; Cohen, *Japanese Peace Settlement*, 13; Scott, "Effect of the Cold War," 227–65; Hehman, "U.S. Security Policy," 108–44.

22. DM, Memo on Security in Post-war Japan, in *FRUS, 1950*, VI, 1228.

23. JCS to DM, Dec. 18, 1950; DM to JCS, Dec. 28, 1950, RG 5, MMBA. At their conference on Wake Island, Oct. 15, 1950, Truman and MacArthur made some brief, general remarks about the Japanese treaty issues. Omar N. Bradley, comp., "Substance of Statements Made at Wake Island Conference on October 15, 1950 . . . From Notes Kept by the Conferees from Washington," 16–18, 60, Bradley File, RG 218, NA.

24. Allison, *Ambassador*, 140–54; Cohen, *Japanese Peace Settlement*, 13–14;

Sebald, *With MacArthur*, 259–60, 263; Aduard, *Japan*, 162–82; Acheson, *Present*, 539–42; Dunn, *Peacemaking*, 123–71; Burton Sapin, "The Role of the Military in Formulating the Japanese Peace Treaty," in Gordon B. Turner, ed., *A History of Military Affairs in Western Society Since the Eighteenth Century* (New York, 1953), 751–56; Louis L. Gerson, *John Foster Dulles* (New York, 1967), 54–67; Poole, *JCS 1950–1952*, 437–58; John Wheeler-Bennett and Anthony Nicholls, *The Semblance of Peace: The Political Settlement After the Second World War* (New York, 1974 [1st ed., 1972]), 501–15; *FRUS, 1950*, VI, 1311–13, 1331, 1344–46, 1383–85.

25. Dulles to DM, Nov. 15, 1950; Jan. 30, Mar. 7, 1951, Dulles Papers; Dulles to DM, July 4, 1950; Jan. 3, Jan. 26, 27, Feb. 9, 10, Mar. 18, Apr. 5, 1951; Jan. 4, 1952, RG 10, MMBA; Dulles to DM, Mar. 2, 1951, RG 5, MMBA; DM to Dulles, Sept. 23, 27, 1950; Feb. 10, Mar. 2, 22, 1951, Dulles Papers; Cohen, *Japanese Peace Settlement*, 240–44, 248–49. See also Dulles–DM correspondence in Peace Treaty Messages File, RG 331, WNRC, and *FRUS, 1950*, VI, 1349–52; *FRUS, 1951*, VI, 176–78, 900–03, 909, 931.

26. Int., Shigeru Yoshida, 3–5, 15, 31; int., William J. Sebald, 2–7, 15–18, John Foster Dulles Oral History Collection, Mudd Library, Princeton; Neu, *Troubled Encounter*, 214; Shaplen, "From MacArthur to Miki," pt. 1, 71; Sebald, *With MacArthur*, 260–63; Dower, *Empire and Aftermath*, 373–400; Rosecrance, *Australian Diplomacy*, 195–98; Weinstein, *Defense Policy*, 24–26, 43–63, 137; Yoshida, *Japan's Decisive Century*, 79; Allison, *Ambassador*, 154–57; *FRUS, 1951*, VI, 778–81, 786–87, 800, 805–07, 811–12, 818–25, 863–65, 866, 872, 908–09.

27. Yoshida to DM, July 13, 1951; DM to Yoshida, Aug. 20, 1951, RG 10, MMBA; Dulles, Memorandum on General MacArthur's Relief, Apr. 12, 1951, Dulles Papers; Dulles to Acheson, May 3, 1951, in *FRUS, 1951*, VI, 1038; Sapin, "Role of the Military," 756–57; Cohen, *Japanese Peace Settlement*, 14–15; Sebald, *With MacArthur*, 265–75; Aduard, *Japan*, 182–200.

28. Dunn, *Peacemaking*, 172–86; Cohen, *Japanese Peace Settlement*, 16–17; Scott, "Effect of the Cold War," 266–88; Wheeler-Bennett and Nicholls, *Semblance*, 516–24; Poole, *JCS, 1950–52*, 459–66; Aduard, *Japan*, 201–28; Allison, *Ambassador*, 170–72; Acheson, *Present*, 542–50; Truman, *Public Papers, 1951*, 504–08; Dean G. Acheson, *Among Friends: Personal Letters of Dean Acheson*, eds. David S. McLellan and David C. Acheson (New York, 1980), 265–70, 323–26. On the San Francisco Conference and the peace treaty, see also the many entries in *FRUS, 1951*, VI.

29. Yoshida, *Memoirs*, 243; idem, *Japan's Decisive Century*, 80–81; Cohen, *Japanese Peace Settlement*, 17–25, 198–99; Neu, *Troubled Encounter*, 215–16; Sebald, *With MacArthur*, 282; Poole, *JCS, 1950–52*, 466–69; Scott, "Effect of the Cold War," 289–320, 327–40; Aduard, *Japan*, 229–51; Sapin, "Role of the Military," 757–62. For the texts of the peace and

security treaties of Sept. 1951 and of the agreement and note exchange on security of Feb. 1952, see DS, *American Foreign Policy, 1950–1955: Basic Documents* (2 vols., Washington, 1957), I, 425–40, 885–86; II, 2406–25; DS, *Treaty of Peace with Japan, Signed at San Francisco, September 8, 1951, with Related Documents* (Washington, 1952), 1–25.

30. Yoshida to DM, Sept. 10, 1951, RG 10, MMBA; Dulles to DM, Sept. 8, 1951, RG 21, MMBA.

31. Ints., Bunker, Whitney, Willoughby; Bunker, Press Release, Aug. 21, 1951, Dulles Papers; *New York Times*, Apr. 22, 1951; DM, *Reminiscences*, 389.

32. Dulles, Memorandum of Telephone Conversations Regarding the Invitation to General MacArthur to Attend the San Francisco Conference — Colonel Bunker, General Whitney, Aug. 19, 1951, Dulles Papers. See also *FRUS, 1951*, VI, 1275–77.

33. President's News Conference, Aug. 16, 1951, in Truman, *Public Papers, 1951*, 465; Dulles, Press Release, Aug. 22, 1951, Dulles Papers; Acheson, *Present*, 544; Sebald, *With MacArthur*, 275.

34. Sen. William F. Knowland to Edward R. Browne, Mar. 11, 1952; Sen. Alexander Wiley to DM, Sept. 21, 1951; Wood to DM, Oct. 30, 1951, RG 10, MMBA; DM to Dulles, Mar. 21, 1952, Dulles Papers. On additional writings about the peace treaty, see Ward and Shulman, comps. and eds., *Allied Occupation*, 738–97; For post-1972 works, see bibliographies in *Journal of Asian Studies*.

CHAPTER XII. *Personal Life in Tokyo*
pages 355–84

1. Int., Mansfield; Kenney, *MacArthur*, 252; Whitney, *MacArthur*, 227; Faubion Bowers, "The Late General MacArthur, Warts and All," *Esquire*, 67 (Jan. 1967), 91; Huff, *Fifteen Years*, 112, 126; Joseph C. Grew, *Ten Years in Japan: A Contemporary Record . . . 1932–1942* (New York, 1944), 7–8.

2. Ints., Beiderlinden, Palmer, Harris, Fox, Fellers, West; Maj. Gen. John H. Chiles, July 28, 1977; Brig. Gen. Edwin A. Zundel, May 29, 1977; Brig. Gen. Louis J. Fortier, June 23, 1971; int., DM, 10–11, Dulles Oral History Coll., Princeton; Frederic S. Marquardt, "The MacArthur Story," pt. 5, *Manila Times*, July 29, 1950; Busch, *Fallen Sun*, 117–21; "Japan: One or Many," *Time*, 51 (May 31, 1948), 25; "MacArthur's Role in the Japan of Tomorrow," *Newsweek*, 29 (June 23, 1947), 38; Gunther, *Riddle*, 6–8; Huff, *Fifteen Years*, 126–27.

3. Whitney, *MacArthur*, 233, 239; Huff, *Fifteen Years*, 114; "Assassination Day," *Newsweek*, 27 (May 13, 1946), 50; Faubion Bowers, "How Japan Won the War," *New York Times Magazine*, Aug. 30, 1970, 44.

4. Ints., Vining, Sams, Bunker, Kenney, Diller, Faillace, Bowers, West; DM Passport, June 8, 1961, DM Misc. 201, MMBA; *Nippon Times*, Oct. 14, 1950; *Washington Post*, Mar. 11, 1948; Bowers, "Late General

MacArthur," 91, 93; "Wonderful Figure," *New Yorker*, 27 (June 16, 1951), 24–25; Martin Sommers, "The Reconversion of Douglas MacArthur," *Saturday Evening Post*, 218 (May 25, 1946), 12–13; Clune, *Ashes*, 201–02, 207–12; Kenney, *MacArthur*, 242–44.

5. Ints., Bowers, Vining; DM Diary, June 9, 1950; George Creel, "General MacArthur," *Collier's*, 121 (May 15, 1948), 58; *New York Times*, Oct. 20, 1945; May 4, 1947; Jan. 21, 1950; Mathews to Dulles, June 5, 1950, Dulles Papers; Bowers, "Late General MacArthur," 93; Vining, *Windows*, 89; Vining, *Quiet Pilgrimage*, 248; Gunther, *Riddle*, 48–50; *Nippon Times*, Oct. 14, 1950; Kenney, *MacArthur*, 253.

6. Ints., Sams, Thorpe.

7. Ints., Egeberg, Sams, Diller, Britton; Col. William Niederpruem, Aug. 25, 1971; *New York Times*, Apr. 16, 1951; Gunther, *Riddle*, 48–50; Bowers, "Late General MacArthur," 164; Huff, *Fifteen Years*, 93, 121–22.

8. Ints., Whitney, Bunker, Almond, Dawson, West, Thorpe; Huff, *Fifteen Years*, 113; Anthony F. Story, with Bill Davidson, "My Air Adventure with Gen. MacArthur," *Collier's*, 127 (June 16, 1951), 13.

9. Ints., Beiderlinden, Willoughby, Whitney, Fox, Besson, West; DM Diary, Sept. 3, 1945–Apr. 9, 1951, passim; int., Almond, pt. 4, pp. 7–9, USAMHI; Huff, *Fifteen Years*, 111–12; Kenney, *MacArthur*, 253.

10. Whitney, *MacArthur*, 234; Kelley and Ryan, *Mikado*, 40.

11. Huff, *Fifteen Years*, 116–17.

12. Ints., Maj. Gen. James G. Christiansen, Aug. 4, 1971; Vice Adm. Felix Johnson, July 7, 1971; int., Borton, pt. 2, no. 19, pp. 40–42, CUOHRO; Gunther, *Riddle*, 46, 51–52.

13. Col. Earl H. Blaik to DM, Apr. 19, 1948; Mrs. DM to Mrs. Caldwell, June 21, 1965, RG 10, MMBA; DM to Blaik, Apr. 26, 1948, in Earl H. Blaik, *The Red Blaik Story* (New Rochelle, NY, 1974), 255; *Nippon Times*, Apr. 8, July 12, 1947; June 26, 1948; *SNAJK*, Sept. 1947, 270.

14. Ints., Bunker, Whitney; Mrs. DM to Mrs. Caldwell, June 21, 1965, RG 10, MMBA; *Washington Post*, Mar. 11, 1948; Huff, *Fifteen Years*, 113, 120–22; Kenney, *MacArthur*, 256.

15. Except as noted otherwise, the rest of this chapter section is based on a synthesis of the views expressed by the almost 180 colleagues and contemporaries of DM who were interviewed by the author. Their names are given in the Bibliographical Note.

16. DM to Maj. Henry A. Grace, June 15, 1956, RG 21, MMBA.

17. Some of the better analyses of DM's personal traits by correspondents who knew him are Cornelius Ryan, "MacArthur: Man of Controversy," *American Mercury*, 71 (Oct. 1950), 425–35; Lindesay Parrott, "MacArthur — Study in Black and White," *New York Times Magazine*, Apr. 22, 1951, 9, 43; Carl Mydans, "Memento of 25 Years," *Life*, 56 (Apr. 17, 1964), 25; Weldon James, "General's General: Douglas MacArthur," in Overseas Press Club of America, *Men Who Make Your World* (New York, 1949), 51–67; Brines, *MacArthur's Japan*, 53–71; Beech, *Tokyo*, 53–62.

18. For analyses of DM's rhetoric and oratory, see Stephen Robb, "Fifty Years of Farewell: Douglas MacArthur's Commemorative and Deliberative Speaking" (unpublished Ph.D. dissertation, Indiana University, 1967); Armel Dyer, "The Oratory of Douglas MacArthur" (unpublished Ph.D. dissertation, University of Oregon, 1968); William S. Phillips, Jr., *Douglas MacArthur: A Modern Knight-Errant* (Philadelphia, 1978); Charles B. Marshall, "An Old Soldier's Rhetoric," *New Republic*, 153 (Nov. 20, 1965), 26, 28.

19. Two of the best concise evaluations of DM's assets as SCAP are Kawai, *Japan's American Interlude*, 11–13, and Reischauer, *United States and Japan*, 224–27.

20. On DM's leadership attributes, besides the many biographical works on him, see Edgar F. Puryear, Jr., *Nineteen Stars* (Washington, 1971), 103–51; Williams, *Japan's Political Revolution*, 263–82; T. Harry Williams, "The Macs and the Ikes: America's Two Military Traditions," *American Mercury*, 75 (Oct. 1952), 32–39; Henry A. Grace, "Leadership: Douglas MacArthur and Robert E. Lee" (course paper, U.S. Army Command and General Staff College, 1956), USACGSC Library, Ft. Leavenworth, KS; James H. Toner, "Douglas MacArthur's Theory and Practice of Leadership" (MS study for MacArthur Memorial Foundation, 1973), MMBA. Some of the most perceptive brief critiques of DM's leadership traits have appeared in reviews by noted military historians of books by or about DM, for example, Louis Morton, "Willoughby on MacArthur: Myth and Reality" [review of Willoughby and Chamberlain, *MacArthur*], *The Reporter*, 11 (Nov. 4, 1954), 42–46; S. L. A. Marshall, "The Commander's Case: Aide's Eye View" [review of Whitney, *MacArthur*], *Saturday Review*, 39 (Feb. 4, 1956), 14–15; Louis Morton, "Egotist in Uniform" [review of DM, *Reminiscences*], *Harper's*, 229 (Nov. 1964), 138–45; Forrest C. Pogue, "The Military in a Democracy" [review of Manchester, *American Caesar*], *International Security*, 3 (Spring 1979), 58–80.

21. Ints., Sams, Bunker, Kades, Egeberg, Kenney, Brines, Beiderlinden, Diller, Whitney, Stratemeyer; Maj. Gen. Roscoe B. Woodruff, Sept. 8, 1971; int., Dovell, Milner File, DMBP; int., Esther Crane, pt. 2, no. 49, pp. 50–53, *CUOHRO;* Vining, *Windows*, 89; Huff, *Fifteen Years*, 117; Gunther, *Riddle*, 46, Kenney, *MacArthur*, 254; "The General's Lady Charmed the Japanese," *Life*, 39 (Aug. 22, 1955), 96; Bowers, "Late General MacArthur," 95; Elizabeth A. Hemphill, *The Road to KEEP: The Story of Paul Rusch in Japan* (New York, 1970 [1st ed., 1969]), 107–08. On Mrs. DM's varied public representations, see *Nippon Times,* Sept. 25, 1945; May 21, Sept. 10, Oct. 4, 5, Dec. 4, 1947; Dec. 6, 1948; Apr. 6, Oct. 16, 1949; May 14, Sept. 9, Oct. 2, Nov. 11, 18, 1950; Jan. 17, 1951.

22. "Setting for a Supreme Commander," *Life*, 39 (Aug. 22, 1955), 94–95.

23. Ints., Vining, Diller, Bunker; Mathews to Dulles, June 5, 1950, Dulles Papers.

24. Nora Waln, "The MacArthurs Carry On," *Saturday Evening Post*, 223 (Sept. 2, 1950), 104.
25. *New York Times*, June 1, 1951.
26. Ints., Bunker, Egeberg, Kenney, Diller, Whitney, West, Marquardt, Willoughby; Col. John H. Weber, Dec. 10, 1980; int., Col. Anthony F. Story, Sherrod File, DMBP; int., Adm. John J. Ballantine, pt. 1, p. 551, CUOHRO; *Stars and Stripes*, Apr. 10, 1946; *New York Times*, May 16, June 1, 1951; Washington *Post*, Mar. 11, 1948; Waln, "MacArthurs Carry On," 106; "Reunion," *Newsweek*, 37 (June 11, 1951), 50; Lee and Henschel, *MacArthur*, 75; Whitney, *MacArthur*, 236; Kenney, *MacArthur*, 254.
27. Mrs. DM to Mrs. Caldwell, June 21, 1965, RG 10, MMBA; *Nippon Times*, May 30, 1947; Jan. 27, 1949; Jan. 27, 1950; Jan. 27, 1951; *New York Times*, Jan. 26, 1951; Whitney, *MacArthur*, 236–37; Gunther, *Riddle*, 47; Huff, *Fifteen Years*, 128–29.
28. Huff, *Fifteen Years*, 135–36.
29. Ints., Whitney, Fitch, Bowers, Egeberg, Kenney, Almond, Niederpruem, Bunker, Willoughby, Mashbir, Swing, Britton, Fox, Beiderlinden, Edwin Wright, Marquardt, Kades, Besson, Chiles, Rizzo, Williams, Thorpe, Wildes, West; Adm. Arleigh A. Burke, July 2, 1971; Courtney Whitney, Jr., to DCJ, Sept. 14, 1975; Williams, *Japan's Political Revolution*, 89–90; Gunther, *Riddle*, 73: *New York Times*, Apr. 26, 1951; "MacArthur Spokesman," *U.S. News & World Report*, 30 (May 4, 1951), 37–39.
30. Ints., Bunker, Sebald, Willoughby, Alexis Johnson, Brines, Matsumura, Williams, West, Rizzo, Beiderlinden, Robinson; Maj. Gen. George W. Hickman, Jr., Sept 4, 1971; ints., Col. Laurence E. Bunker, Col. Charles L. Kades, Sherrod File, DMBP; New York *Herald Tribune*, Dec. 22, 1963; Boston *Globe*, Oct. 12, 1977; *New York Times*, Dec. 18, 1963; Oct. 12, 1977.
31. Ints., Almond, Besson, Chiles, Levy, Woodruff, Christiansen, Palmer, Rizzo, Thorpe, Zundel, West, Fortier, Fox, Hickman, Sebald, Niederpruem, Beiderlinden, Willoughby, Edwin Wright; Gen. John H. Michaelis, June 1, 1977; Brig. Gen. James H. Lynch, May 24, 1977; Brig. Gen. Hallett D. Edson, June 20, 1977; Gen. Frank T. Mildren, May 25, 1977; Gen. Gerald C. Thomas, June 15, 1977; Brig. Gen. Walter F. Winton, Jr., May 31, 1977; Lt. Gen. Alpha L. Bowser, Sept. 3, 1971; int., Almond, USAMHI; int., Almond, MMBA; ints., Beiderlinden, Maj. Gen. David G. Barr, Gen. Paul L. Neal, Milner File, DMBP.
32. Ints., Willoughby, West, Harris, Brines, Bunker, Fellers, Alexis Johnson, Besson, Chiles, Rizzo, Thorpe, Whitney, Fortier, Marshall, Hill, Fitch, Egeberg, Mashbir, Niederpruem, Berkey, Britton, Fox, Almond, Beiderlinden, Edwin Wright; Brig. Gen. Robert H. Van Volkenburgh, Aug. 26, 1971; Brig. Gen. Frederick P. Munson, July 3, 1971; Lt. Gen. Edward A. Craig, Sept. 3, 1971; int., Lt. Gen. Charles B. Ferenbaugh, Milner File, DMBP; Gunther, *Riddle*, 74.

33. Ints., Whitney, Hill, Van Volkenburgh, Munson, Britton, Fox, Shigeo Kimura, Harris, Rizzo, Thorpe, Willoughby, West, Levy, Thomas Wright; Whitney, *MacArthur*, 267; Gunther, *Riddle*, 73; Willoughby and Chamberlain, *MacArthur*, 36.

34. Ints., Willoughby, Whitney, Bunker, Fitch, Hill; Rear Adm. John D. Bulkeley, July 2, 1971.

35. Based on the various interviews previously cited in this chapter section.

CHAPTER XIII. *The Road to War in Korea*
pages 387–418

1. Appleman, *South to the Naktong*, 21–30, 36; Rees, *Korea*, 3; Gunther, *Riddle*, 166; DM, *Reminiscences*, 327–28.

2. E. Grant Meade, *American Military Government in Korea* (New York, 1951), 90–93; Bruce G. Cumings, *The Origins of the Korean War: Liberation and the Emergence of Separate Regimes, 1945–1947* (Princeton, 1981), 290–92; James F. Schnabel and Robert J. Watson, *The Joint Chiefs of Staff and National Policy*, vol. III, *The Korean War*, pt. 1 [1950–51] (Wilmington, DE, 1979), 1–9; Soon Sung Cho, *Korea in World Politics, 1940–1950: An Evaluation of American Responsibility* (Berkeley, 1967), 13–60; Carl Berger, *The Korea Knot: A Military-Political History* (rev. ed., Philadelphia, 1964), 31–48; Schnabel, *Policy and Direction*, 6–10; George M. McCune, *Korea Today* (Cambridge, MA, 1950), 44–45; Arthur L. Grey, Jr., "The Thirty-eighth Parallel," *Foreign Affairs*, 29 (Apr. 1951), 482–87; U.S. Senate, Committee on Foreign Relations, *The United States and the Korean Problem: Documents, 1943–1953* (Washington, 1954), 1–3; U.S. House of Representatives, *Background Information on Korea: Report of the Committee on Foreign Affairs . . .* (Washington, 1950), 1–3; DS, *The Conflict in Korea: Events Prior to the Attack on June 25, 1950* (Washington, 1951), 2–3; DS, *The Record on Korean Unification, 1943–1960* (Washington, 1960), 3–4.

3. Robert K. Sawyer, *Military Advisors in Korea: KMAG in Peace and War*, ed. Walter G. Hermes (Washington, 1962), 7; Kolko and Kolko, *Limits*, 279–81; Berger, *Korea Knot*, 48–49; Schnabel, *Policy and Direction*, 13–16; Cumings, *Origins*, 122–29; Gregory Henderson, *Korea: The Politics of the Vortex* (Cambridge, MA, 1968), 122–23.

4. DM, Proclamation No. 1 to the People of Korea, Sept. 7, 1945, Douglas MacArthur Papers, LC.

5. USAFPAC, G-3, Summary of Operations in Korea, Sept. 1945, RG 4, MMBA; *New York Times*, Sept. 12, 1945; Sawyer, *KMAG*, 7–8; Berger, *Korea Knot*, 50–51; Schnabel, *Policy and Direction*, 16–18; U.S. Senate, *Korean Problem*, 3; *FRUS, 1945*, VI, 1044–45; Cumings, *Origins*, 139; Cho, *Korea*, 63–65; Donovan, *Conflict and Crisis*, 153–54; Charles M. Dobbs, *The Unwanted Symbol: American Foreign Policy, the Cold War, and Korea, 1945–1950* (Kent, OH, 1981), 34; Lauterbach, *Danger*, 198–201; A. Wigfall Green, *The Epic of Korea* (Washington, 1950), 51–52.

6. Ints., Britton, Bowers, Almond, Harris, West, Harriman; Lt. Gen. John R. Hodge to DM, July 14, 1946; Mueller to Hodge, July 16, 1946, RG 10, MMBA; DM Diary, Oct. 25, 1945; Apr. 4, 1947; June 21, Aug. 15, 27, 28, 1948; int., Bowers, pt. 2, no. 21, pp. 27–28, CUOHRO; Hodge to DM, Nov. 2, 25, 1945, in *FRUS, 1945*, VI, 1106, 1133–34; DM to Hodge, Nov. 25, 1945, in ibid., 1134; Henderson, *Korea*, 340; Dobbs, *Unwanted Symbol*, 42; Robert T. Oliver, *Syngman Rhee: The Man Behind the Myth* (New York, 1955), 227.

7. Int., Britton; DM Diary, Oct. 14–15, 1945; Syngman Rhee to DM, Sept. 29, 1945; Jan. 14, 1946, RG 5, MMBA; *Nippon Times*, Mar. 19, 1946; Cho, *Korea*, 61–160; Meade, *Military Government*, 49–82; Berger, *Korea Knot*, 51–73; Sawyer, *KMAG*, 8–32; Henderson, *Korea*, 128–29; Schnabel, *Policy and Direction*, 18–23; Schnabel and Watson, *Korean War*, 9–12; Hugh Borton, "Korea Under American and Soviet Occupation, 1945–7," in Jones, et al., *Far East*, 428–72; U.S. House, *Background*, 4–9; U.S. Senate, *Korean Problem*, 4–10; DS, *Record*, 4–7; Cumings, *Origins*, 188–89, 213, 442; *FRUS, 1945*, VI, 1054–57, 1067–68, 1071–91, 1112, 1136–37, 1140, 1144–48, 1154–56; *FRUS, 1946*, VI, 1156–57; *FRUS, 1946*, VIII, 607–48, 717–18.

8. Berger, *Korea Knot*, 74–92; Cumings, *Origins*, 229; Schnabel, *Policy and Direction*, 25–30; Cho, *Korea*, 161–244; DS, *Conflict*, 4–7; DS, *A Historical Summary of United States–Korean Relations, with a Chronology of Important Developments, 1834–1962* (Washington, 1962), 61–76; U.S. Senate, *Korean Problem*, 10–29; U.S. House, *Background*, 9–20; Philip C. Jessup, *The Birth of Nations* (New York, 1974), 19–42; *FRUS, 1947*, VI, 601–06, 622, 627, 639–40, 661–62, 682–84, 696–97, 714–31, 855–56; *FRUS, 1948*, VI, 1116, 1192–95, 1341–43; FECOM Hq., "Far East Command," 3–4, 11–12.

9. Rhee to DM, Aug. 18, Oct. 22, 1948, RG 10, MMBA; DM to Bradley, Aug. 17, 1948, RG 9, MMBA; DM Diary, Aug. 15, 19, 20, 1948; *Nippon Times*, Aug. 16, 1948; *New York Times*, Aug. 13–15, Oct. 21–22, 1948; DM, Address at Seoul, Aug. 15, 1948, in DM, *Soldier Speaks*, 199–201; Dobbs, *Unwanted Symbol*, 149–50; Oliver, *Rhee*, 263.

10. Int., Bond; DA to DM, July 29, 1949, RG 9, MMBA; Dean G. Acheson, Princeton Seminars, Feb. 13–14, 1954, reel 3, track 1, pp. 1–10, Dean G. Acheson Papers, HSTL; Sawyer, *KMAG*, 32–45; *FRUS, 1949*, VII, pt. 2, 942–46, 976–77; *DAFR*, X, 169–79; XI, 555–63; Leon Gordenker, *The United Nations and the Peaceful Unification of Korea: The Politics of Field Operations, 1947–1950* (The Hague, 1959), 115–20.

11. Henry Chung, *The Russians Came to Korea* (Seoul, 1947), 155–75; Han Mu Kang, "The United States Military Government in Korea, 1945–1948: An Analysis and Evaluation of Its Policy" (unpublished Ph.D. dissertation, University of Cincinnati, 1970), 71–72; DS, *Record*, 11–13; Schnabel, *Policy and Direction*, 23–25, 34; Sawyer, *KMAG*, 46–47.

12. Int., Amb. John J. Muccio, 1971, 13–14, HSTL; int., Muccio, 1973, 29, HSTL; Truman, *Memoirs*, II, 375.

13. Meade, *Military Government,* 103–04, 133–34; C. Clyde Mitchell, *Korea: Second Failure in Asia* (Washington, 1951), 13–34; Denna F. Fleming, *The Cold War and Its Origins, 1917–1960,* vol. II, *1950–1960* (Garden City, NY, 1961), 589–93; Berger, *Korea Knot,* 93–102; U.S. House, *Background,* 40–41; Rees, *Korea,* 15–16; Okonogi Masao, "The Domestic Roots of the Korean War," in Nagai and Iriye, eds., *Origins,* 299–320; Bruce Cumings, "American Policy and Korean Liberation," in Baldwin, ed., *Without Parallel,* 39–108; Robert R. Simmons, "The Korean Civil War," in ibid., 143–78; Kolko and Kolko, *Limits,* 277–99. For some arguments in favor of and against the revisionist view on Korea and the coming of war, 1945–50, see the essays by William Stueck and Joyce and Gabriel Kolko in "An Exchange of Opinion," *Pacific Historical Review,* 42 (Nov. 1973), 537–75.

14. Voorhees to DM, Nov. 5, 1949, RG 10, MMBA; Sawyer, *KMAG,* 47–104; U.S. Senate, *Korean Problem,* 29–34; DS, *Conflict,* 7–11; U.S. House, *Background,* 21–40.

15. Rhee to DM, Oct. 24, Dec. 2, 16, 1949; DM to Rhee, Jan. 24, 1950, RG 5, MMBA; Allen B. Moreland, Memorandum of Gen. MacArthur's Briefing of the Huber Congressional Committee, Sept. 5, 1949, in *FRUS, 1949,* IX, 545–46; Robert F. Futrell, *The United States Air Force in Korea, 1950–1953* (New York, 1961), 5.

16. Int., Bond; Truman, *Memoirs,* II, 371–72; Dobbs, *Unwanted Symbol,* 91–92, 96–98, 169–70; Schnabel, *Policy and Direction,* 28–30, 49–50; Truman, *Public Papers, 1952–53,* 945–50; Schnabel and Watson, *Korean War,* 12–22; John L. Gaddis, "Korea in American Politics, Strategy, and Diplomacy, 1945–50," in Nagai and Iriye, eds., *Origins,* 277–83; Trumbull Higgins, *Korea and the Fall of MacArthur: A Précis in Limited War* (New York, 1960), 6–8; Ernest R. May, *"Lessons" of the Past: The Use and Misuse of History in American Foreign Policy* (New York, 1975 [1st ed., 1973]), 52–66.

17. DM to DA, Jan. 19, 1949, RG 6, MMBA; Royall to Acheson, Jan. 25, 1949, in *FRUS, 1949,* VII, pt. 2, 945–46; *New York Times,* Mar. 2, 1949; Gaddis, "Korea," 283–86; Higgins, *Korea and Fall of MacArthur,* 9–14; Schnabel, *Policy and Direction,* 50–52; Schnabel and Watson, *Korean War,* 23–38; Dobbs, *Unwanted Symbol,* 180–81; Acheson, *Present,* 354–58; Robert R. Simmons, *The Strained Alliance: Peking, Pyongyang, Moscow, and the Politics of the Korean Civil War* (New York, 1975), 110–11; Robert J. Donovan, *Tumultuous Years: The Presidency of Harry S. Truman, 1949–1953* (New York, 1982), 95–96; Gaddis Smith, *Dean Acheson* (New York, 1972), 174–77; McLellan, *Acheson,* 209–17; DM, *Reminiscences,* 321–22.

18. Acheson, *Present,* 302–07; Huston, *Sinews,* 575–614; Roy K. Flint, "The Tragic Flaw: MacArthur, the Joint Chiefs, and the Korean War" (unpublished dissertation, Duke University, 1976), 27–45; Donovan, *Tumultuous Years,* 82–113; James F. Schnabel, *The Joint Chiefs of Staff and National Policy,* vol. I, *1945–1947* (Wilmington, DE, 1979), 238; Condit, *JCS, 1947–48,* 561, Harry R. Borowski, *A Hollow Threat: Strategic*

Air Power and Containment Before Korea (Westport, CT, 1981), 201–04; DS, *United States Relations with China; With Special Reference to the Period 1944–1949* (Washington, 1949) passim; Samuel P. Huntington, *The Common Defense: Strategic Programs in National Politics* (New York, 1966 [1st ed., 1961]), 25–47; Russell F. Weigley, *The American Way of War: A History of United States Military Strategy and Policy* (New York, 1973), 363–83; idem, *United States Army*, 485–504.

19. Voorhees to DM, May 26, 1950, RG 6, MMBA; Schnabel and Watson, *Korean War*, 31–41, 47; Poole, *JCS, 1950–52*, chs. 1–2; Huntington, *Common Defense*, 47–64; Bradley and Blair, *General's Life*, 518–19; Donovan, *Tumultuous Years*, 158–61, 241–47; McLellan, *Acheson*, 270–72; Lawrence S. Kaplan, "The Korean War and U.S. Foreign Relations: The Case of NATO," in Francis H. Heller, ed., *The Korean War: A 25-Year Perspective* (Lawrence, KS, 1977), 36–111; Seyom Brown, *The Faces of Power: Constancy and Change in United States Foreign Policy from Truman to Johnson* (New York, 1968), 53–56; John L. Gaddis, *Strategies of Containment: A Critical Appraisal of Postwar American National Security Policy* (New York, 1982), 89–126; Charles E. Bohlen, *Witness to History, 1929–1969* (New York, 1973), 290–91, 303–04.

20. Rovere, *McCarthy*, 6–7, 12–13, 81–82, 123–34, 145–59; Thomas C. Reeves, ed., *McCarthyism* (Hinsdale, IL, 1973), 1–4, 79–82, 126–31; Donovan, *Tumultuous Years*, 162–75; Alonzo L. Hamby, *Beyond the New Deal: Harry S. Truman and American Liberalism* (New York, 1973), 390–409; Westerfield, *Foreign Policy*, 362–69.

21. Sebald to Acheson, Apr. 17, 1950; Cooke to DM, Apr. 27, 1950, RG 10, MMBA; Poole, *JCS, 1950–52*, 379–86; Schnabel and Watson, *Korean War*, 39; Bradley and Blair, *General's Life*, 527–30.

22. Int., Amb. Philip C. Jessup, Sr., July 14, 1977; DM Diary, Jan. 31, May 19, June 2–3, 9, 1950; misc. items, Formosa File, RG 6, MMBA; Sebald to Acheson, June 22, 1950, in *FRUS, 1950*, VI, 366–67; Schnabel and Watson, *Korean War*, 39–40; *New York Times*, May 11, 1951; Poole, *JCS, 1950–52*, 386–87; Lester B. Pearson, *Mike: The Memoirs of the Right Honourable Lester B. Pearson*, vol. II, *1948–1957*, ed. John A. Munro and Alex I. Inglis (New York, 1973), 145–47; C. L. Sulzberger, *A Long Row of Candles: Memoirs and Diaries (1934–1954)* (New York, 1969), 560–74, 687–88; Arthur W. Radford, *From Pearl Harbor to Vietnam: The Memoirs of Admiral Arthur W. Radford*, ed. Stephen Jurika, Jr. (Stanford, CA, 1980), 154.

23. DM, Memorandum on Formosa, June 14, 1950, in *FRUS, 1950*, VI, 161–65. Besides Johnson and Bradley, Dulles also was given a copy of the memo by DM. See Dulles Papers, Princeton.

24. Schnabel and Watson, *Korean War*, 40–41; Bradley and Blair, *General's Life*, 532–33.

25. Rhee to DM, Jan. 4, Feb. 7, 20, 1950; DM to Rhee, Jan. 24, Feb. 26, 1950, RG 5, MMBA; Acheson, *Present*, 358; Truman, *Memoirs*, II, 375; Schnabel and Watson, *Korean War*, 38; Westerfield, *Foreign Policy*, 353–

54, 366–67; Margaret Carlyle, ed., *Documents on International Affairs, 1949–1950* (London, 1953), 624–29; Futrell, *USAF, June–Nov. 1950,* viii.

26. Sawyer, *KMAG,* 67–113; Appleman, *South to the Naktong,* 7–18; J. Lawton Collins, *War in Peacetime: The History and Lessons of Korea* (Boston, 1969), 41–44; Robert Leckie, *Conflict: The History of the Korean War, 1950–1953* (New York, 1962), 32–33.

27. Ints., Palmer, Almond, Fox; Col. Thomas T. Jones, June 16, 1977; int., Almond, pt. 4, pp. 15–17, USAMHI; Schnabel, *Policy and Direction,* 52–60; Schnabel and Watson, *Korean War,* 43–47; Huston, *Sinews,* 615–19; Futrell, *USAF, 1950–53,* 56–59; Futrell, *USAF, June–Nov. 1950,* 1–3; James T. Stewart, ed., *Airpower: The Decisive Force in Korea* (Princeton, 1957), 5–6; James A. Field, Jr., *History of United States Naval Operations: Korea* (Washington, 1962), 42–50; Malcolm Cagle and Frank A. Manson, *The Sea War in Korea* (Annapolis, MD, 1957), 30–32.

28. Int., Almond; DA to DM, Jan. 4, 1950, RG 9, MMBA; DM Diary, Feb. 1–3, 1950; London *Times,* Feb. 3, 14, 1950; Collins, *War,* 5–6; Bradley and Blair, *General's Life,* 523–29.

29. Bradley to DM, Feb. 13, 1950, RG 10, MMBA.

30. Schnabel, *Policy and Direction,* 60.

31. "MSFE-TD," pt. 4, pp. 6777–78, 6819, 6877, 7504–05, 7579; Kennan, *Memoirs,* I, 484–85; Gaddis, "Korea," 286–88; Schnabel, *Policy and Direction,* 61–65; Schnabel and Watson, *Korean War,* 48–53; Donovan, *Tumultuous Years,* 179–83; Amb. John J. Muccio, et al., "From Where I Stood: A Panel," in Heller, ed., *Korean War,* 10–16; Harvey A. DeWeerd, "Strategic Surprise in the Korean War," *Orbis,* 6 (Fall 1962), 436–41; Truman, *Memoirs,* II, 377.

32. Harold J. Noble, *Embassy at War,* ed. Frank Baldwin (Seattle, 1975), 219–37; Glenn D. Paige, ed., *1950: Truman's Decision: The United States Enters the Korean War* (New York, 1970), 30–45; Bradley and Blair, *General's Life,* 530.

33. Ints., Edwin Wright, Fortier, Munson, Matthews; int., Eberle, Milner File, DMBP; DM, *Reminiscences,* 323–24, 330; I. F. Stone, *The Hidden History of the Korean War* (New York, 1970 [1st ed., 1952]), 1–6; idem, "New Facts on Korea," *Nation,* 173 (Dec. 15, 1951), 514–17; Willoughby and Chamberlain, *MacArthur,* 350–55; *New York Times,* Aug. 25, 1950; Schnabel, *Policy and Direction,* 64; Schnabel and Watson, *Korean War,* 50–51; Matthew B. Ridgway, *The Korean War: How We Met the Challenge . . .* (Garden City, NY, 1967), 11–16; Lee and Henschel, *MacArthur,* 195–96; Richard H. Rovere and Arthur M. Schlesinger, Jr., *The MacArthur Controversy and American Foreign Policy* (New York, 1965 [1st ed., 1951]), 112–15; Charles A. Willoughby, ed., *Aid and Comfort to the Enemy: Trends of Korean Press Reports* (Tokyo, 1951), 14–15, 17; Baillie, *High Tension,* 258; Joseph C. Goulden, *Korea: The Untold Story of the War* (New York, 1982), viii, 37–41; Roger Hilsman, *Strategic Intelligence and National Decisions* (Glencoe, IL, 1956), 88–90.

34. Schnabel, *Policy and Direction*, 64, 65.
35. DA to DM, June 3, 1950, RG 9, MMBA; Rhee to DM, June 20, 1950, RG 5, MMBA; *New York Times*, Sept. 15, 1950; Noble, *Embassy*, 231–37; Berger, *Korea Knot*, 98–101; Kolko and Kolko, *Limits*, 574–78; T. R. Fehrenbach, *This Kind of War: A Study in Unpreparedness* (New York, 1963), 11–14; Fleming, *Cold War*, II, 593–94; Schnabel, *Policy and Direction*, 40, 61n; Appleman, *South to the Naktong*, 19–21; Higgins, *Korea and Fall of MacArthur*, 9; Mitchell, *Korea*, 34–36; Goulden, *Korea*, 36–37; Walter LaFeber, *America, Russia, and the Cold War, 1945–1966* (New York, 1967), 96–97. The North Korean attack orders, with some commentary thereon, are in DS, *Conflict*, 26–36.
36. DM Diary, Feb. 16–17, 1950; United Nations General Assembly, *Official Records*, 5th Sess. (New York, 1950) suppl. XVI, 9–10, 19, 25, 210, Stone, *Hidden History*, 1–66, 349–52; Fleming, *Cold War*, II, 592–608; David Horowitz, *The Free World Colossus* (New York, 1965), 114–40; *U.S. News & World Report*, 29 (July 7, 1950), 29; W. D. Reeve, *The Republic of Korea* (New York, 1963), 42; Allen S. Whiting, *China Crosses the Yalu: The Decision to Enter the Korean War* (New York, 1960), 34–46; Cho, *Korea*, 270–75; Robert Smith, *MacArthur in Korea: The Naked Emperor* (New York, 1982), 128–36; Robert R. Simmons, "The Communist Side: An Exploratory Sketch," in Heller, ed., *Korean War*, 197–98, 207; Robert T. Oliver, "Why War Came to Korea," in Kim Young Hum, ed., *Twenty Years of Crises: The Cold War Era* (Englewood Cliffs, NJ, 1968), 71–75; Nikita Khrushchev, *Khrushchev Remembers*, trans. and ed. Strobe Talbott (Boston, 1970), 367–73; Simmons, *Strained Alliance*, 116–24; Richard S. Kirkendall, ed., *The Truman Period as a Research Field: A Reappraisal, 1972* (Columbia, MO, 1974), 44–45, 58–63, 180–81; Alexander L. George, "American Policy-Making and the North Korean Aggression," *World Politics*, 7 (Jan. 1955), 209–32; Beloff, *Soviet Policy*, 182–83; Lloyd C. Gardner, "From Liberation to Containment, 1949–1953," in William A. Williams, ed., *From Colony to Empire: Essays in the History of American Foreign Relations* (New York, 1972), 371–79. See also essays cited in note 13.

NOTES FOR CHAPTERS XIV–XVIII

Basic works in Chapters XIV–XVIII that will not be cited in the notes except when quoted are Dean G. Acheson, *The Korean War* (New York, 1971); Acheson, *Present*, 404–529; Appleman, *South to the Naktong;* Bradley and Blair, *General's Life*, 522–637; Cagle and Manson, *Sea War*, 25–310; Collins, *War*, 1–293; Fehrenbach, *This Kind*, 54–422; Field, *USN: Korea*, 39–345; Flint, "Tragic Flaw"; *FRUS, 1950*, VII; *FRUS, 1951*, VII; Futrell, *USAF, 1950–53*, 7–335; idem, *USAF, June–Nov. 1950;* idem, *USAF, Nov. 1950–June 1952*, 1–82; Goulden, *Korea*, 42–496; Higgins, *Korea and the Fall of MacArthur;* "MacArthur Chronology, 1950–51," David D. Lloyd Files, HSTL; "MacArthur, 1950–51," Official Files, Truman Papers, HSTL;

MSFE and "MSFE-TD" [published MacArthur Hearings and classified transcript deletions therefrom]; DM, *Reminiscences*, 327–96; Lynn Montross, et al., *U.S. Marine Operations in Korea, 1950–1953*, vols. I–IV (Washington, 1954–62); "Record of the Actions Taken by the Joint Chiefs of Staff Relative to the United Nations Operations in Korea from 25 June 1950 to 11 April 1951," CCS 013.36 (4-20-51), RG 218, NA; Rees, *Korea*, 3–221; Ridgway, *Korean War*, 17–160; Rovere and Schlesinger, *MacArthur Controversy;* Sawyer, *KMAG*, 114–69; Schnabel, *Policy and Direction;* Schnabel and Watson, *Korean War*, pt. 1; Sebald, *With MacArthur*, 177–210; John W. Spanier, *The Truman-MacArthur Controversy and the Korean War* (Cambridge, MA, 1959); Truman, *Memoirs*, II, 360–510; Whiting, *China Crosses;* Whitney, *MacArthur*, 315–468; Willoughby and Chamberlain, *MacArthur*, 350–417.

CHAPTER XIV. *Holding the Naktong Line*
pages 419–51
1. Ints., Matthews, Chiles; Amb. John J. Muccio to Acheson, June 25, 1950, in DS, *United States Policy in the Korean Crisis* (Washington, 1950), 11; DM to Irvin, June 25, 1950, in Schnabel, *Policy and Direction*, 65; UN Security Council, Resolution, June 25, 1950, in Paige, ed., *1950*, 64–65; Donovan, *Tumultuous Years*, 189–97; Allison, *Ambassador*, 132; Kennan, *Memoirs*, I, 485–86; Glenn D. Paige, *The Korean Decision, June 24–30, 1950* (New York, 1968), 79–100; Martin Lichterman, "To the Yalu and Back," in Harold Stein, ed., *American Civil-Military Decisions: A Book of Case Studies* (Tuscaloosa, AL, 1963), 579–80; Walter Karig, et al., *Battle Report: The War in Korea* (New York, 1952), 31–34; Clyde Eagleton and Richard N. Swift, eds., *Annual Review of United Nations Affairs, 1950* (New York, 1951), 131–38; Jon Halliday, "The United Nations and Korea," in Baldwin, ed., *Without Parallel*, 125–29; Muccio, et al., "From Where I Stood," 16–23; Merle Miller, *Plain Speaking: An Oral Biography of Harry S. Truman* (New York, 1974 [1st ed., 1973]), 284–99.
2. Int., Harriman; Paige, *Korean Decision*, 101–44; Beverly Smith, "The White House Story: Why We Went to War in Korea," *Saturday Evening Post*, 224 (Nov. 10, 1951), 76, 78, 80; Jessup, Memorandum of Blair House Meeting, June 25, 1950, in *FRUS, 1950*, VII, 160; McLellan, *Acheson*, 273–80; Richard F. Haynes, *The Awesome Power: Harry S. Truman as Commander in Chief* (Baton Rouge, LA, 1973), 165–68; Leland M. Goodrich, *Korea: A Study of U.S. Policy in the United Nations* (New York, 1956), 7–41; Richard C. Snyder and Glenn D. Paige, "The United States Decision to Resist Aggression in Korea: The Application of an Analytic Scheme," *Administrative Science Quarterly*, 3 (Dec. 1958), 356–57.
3. JCS, "Record of Actions," 6–7.
4. Schnabel, *Policy and Direction*, 70.
5. Int., Bond; int., Muccio, 1971, 30–47, 50–55, HSTL; DM to JCS, June

26, 1950, in Truman, *Memoirs*, II, 383; Noble, *Embassy*, 20–84; Donovan, *Tumultuous Years*, 204–08; Smith, "Why We Went to War," 80;
Allison, *Ambassador*, 135–37; Paige, *Korean Decision*, 145–82; Smith,
MacArthur, 171; Haynes, *Awesome Power*, 168–70; Harry J. Middleton, *The Compact History of the Korean War* (New York, 1965), 34–41;
John C. Caldwell, *The Korea Story* (Chicago, 1952), 172–73.
6. JCS, "Record of Actions," 8.
7. DA to DM, June 27, 1950, RG 6, MMBA; Poole, *JCS, 1950–52*, 387–
89; JCS, "Record of Actions," 8–9; Truman, Press Statement, June
27, 1950, in DS, *Korean Crisis*, 18; UN Security Council, Resolution,
June 27, 1950, in Allen Guttmann, ed., *Korea: Cold War and Limited
War* (2d ed., Lexington, MA, 1972), 5; Donovan, *Tumultuous Years*,
208–10; Smith, "Why We Went to War," 80, 82, 86; Noble, *Embassy*,
266; Haynes, *Awesome Power*, 170–77; Edwin C. Hoyt, "The United
States Reaction to the Korean Attack: A Study of the Principles of
the United Nations Charter as a Factor in American Policy-Making,"
American Journal of International Law, 55 (Jan. 1961), 45–76; Paige,
Korean Decision, 183–208; Ronald J. Caridi, "The G.O.P. and the Korean War," *Pacific Historical Review*, 37 (Nov. 1968), 424–26; Leland
M. Goodrich, "Korea: Collective Measures Against Aggression," *International Conciliation*, no. 494 (Oct. 1953), 143–45; Charles A. Lofgren, "Mr. Truman's War: A Debate and Its Aftermath," *Review of
Politics*, 31 (Apr. 1969), 223–30; Richard S. Kirkendall, *Harry S Truman: The Decision to Intervene* (St. Louis, 1979), 9–10; Donald W. Coble,
"Air Support in the Korean War," *Aerospace Historian*, 16 (Summer
1969), 26; Miller, *Plain Speaking*, 299–302.
8. Ints., Almond, Edwin Wright, Willoughby; Noble, *Embassy*, 36, 54, 60–
62, 78–79; Rutherford M. Poats, *Decision in Korea* (New York, 1954),
19–22.
9. Lt. Gen. Edward M. Almond, Testimony, Nov. 23, 1954, in U.S. Senate, Committee on the Judiciary, *Interlocking Subversion in Government
Departments: Hearings Before the Subcommittee to Investigate the Administration of the Internal Security Act and Other International Security Laws*,
83d Cong., 2d Sess. (Washington, 1954–55), pt. 25, pp. 2060–61.
10. Ints., Brines, Edwin Wright, Almond; int., Almond, pt. 4, pp. 12–15,
USAMHI; Oliver, *Rhee*, 372; David D. Duncan, *This Is War: A Photo
Narrative* (New York, 1951), 10–12; Noble, *Embassy*, 85–91; DM,
Reminiscences, 332–34; Marguerite Higgins, *War in Korea: The Report
of a Woman Combat Correspondent* (Garden City, NY, 1951), 30–34;
Smith, "Why We Went to War," 86, 88; *Nippon Times*, June 30, July
1, 1950; George Odgers, *Across the Parallel: The Australian 77th Squadron with the United States Air Force in the Korean War* (Melbourne, Australia, 1953), 16–23; "Over the Mountains: Mountains," *Time*, 56 (July
10, 1950), 12–15; Harry F. Kern, "MacArthur in Action," *Newsweek*,
36 (July 10, 1950), 20–22; David D. Duncan, "U.S. Gets into Fight
for Korea: The First Five Days," *Life*, 29 (July 10, 1950), 26; Walt
Sheldon, *Hell or High Water: MacArthur's Landing at Inchon* (New York,

1968), 30–33; *Time* editors, *Time Capsule/1950: A History of the Year Condensed from the Pages of Time* (New York, 1967), 61–63; Norman Bartlett, ed., *With the Australians in Korea* (Canberra, Australia, 1960), 170–72.

11. JCS to DM, June 29, 1950, in *FRUS, 1950*, VII, 240–41.
12. Lt. Gen. George E. Stratemeyer to Maj. Gen. Earle E. Partridge, June 29, 1950, in Appleman, *South to the Naktong*, 44; Memorandum of NSC Consultants' Meeting, June 29, 1950, in *FRUS, 1950*, I, 328.
13. DM to JCS, June 30, 1950, in Schnabel and Watson, *Korean War*, 111–13.
14. Ints., Harriman, Chiles; Paige, *Korean Decision*, 209–52; Almond, Testimony, in U.S. Senate, *Interlocking Subversion*, 2062; Collins to DM, Telecon, June 30, 1950, in Collins, *War*, 20–23; Smith, "Why We Went to War," 88; Flint, "Tragic Flaw," 85–86; Haynes, *Awesome Power*, 177–80; J. Lawton Collins, *Lightning Joe: An Autobiography* (Baton Rouge, LA, 1979), 360–63.
15. DA to DM, June 30, 1950, RG 6, MMBA; JCS, "Record of Actions," 12–13; JCS to DM, June 30, 1950, in *FRUS, 1950*, VII, 263; Truman, Press Statement, June 30, 1950, in Truman, *Public Papers, 1950*, 513; Donovan, *Tumultuous Years*, 210–18; Schnabel, *Policy and Direction*, 79; Smith, "Why We Went to War," 88; Paige, *Korean Decision*, 253–71; Goodrich, *Korea*, 115–16; Lawrence J. Korb, *The Joint Chiefs of Staff: The First Twenty-five Years* (Bloomington, IN, 1976), 137–39; Haynes, *Awesome Power*, 180–83; Poole, *JCS, 1950–52*, 389–90; Alfred L. Warner, "How the Korea Decision Was Made," *Harper's*, 203 (June 1951), 101–06; McGeorge Bundy, ed., *The Pattern of Responsibility* (Boston, 1952), 248–53; Lloyd Norman, "Washington's War," *Army*, 10 (June 1960), 48; Cabell Phillips, *The Truman Presidency: The History of a Triumphant Succession* (Baltimore, 1969 [1st ed., 1966]), 303–04; Wilber W. Hoare, Jr., "Truman (1949–1953)," in Ernest R. May, ed., *The Ultimate Decision: The President as Commander in Chief* (New York, 1960), 191–93; Walter Millis, et al., *Arms and the State: Civil-Military Elements in National Policy* (New York, 1958), 263–64; Richard S. Kirkendall, *Harry S Truman, Korea and the Imperial Presidency* (St. Charles, MO, 1975), 27–28; Truman, *Memoirs*, II, 391; Acheson, *Present*, 413.
16. Ints., Jones, Christiansen; Rhee to DM, July 15, 24, 1950; DM to Rhee, July 15, 1950, RG 7, MMBA; int., Muccio, 1971, 55–63, HSTL; USMA, Dept. of Military Art and Engineering, *Operations in Korea* (West Point, NY, 1956), 5–10; Berger, *Korea Knot*, 113–15; Leckie, *Conflict*, 50–84; Republic of Korea Army, Office of Information, *Republic of Korea Army*, vol. I (Seoul, Korea, 1954), 47–48; William F. Dean, with William Worden, *General Dean's Story* (New York, 1954), 5–82; Middleton, *Korean War*, 47–74.
17. UN Security Council, Resolution, July 7, 1950, in *FRUS, 1950*, VII, 329; Beloff, *Soviet Policy*, 187–88; Leland M. Goodrich, "Collective Action in Korea: Evaluating the Results of the UN Collective Action," *Current History*, 38 (June 1960), 334–35; Halliday, "UN and

Korea," 129–30; Tae-ho Yoo, *The Korean War and the United Nations: A Legal and Diplomatic Historical Study* (Louvain, Belgium, 1965), 37–42; Richard C. Stebbins, ed., *The United States in World Affairs, 1950* (New York, 1951), 213–17. A Security Council Resolution of July 31, 1950, called for UN members to offer aid for Korean civilian relief, which was administered under MacArthur through Sams's SCAP section, AMIK, and ECA at first and by the UN Civil Assistance Command later. U.S. Senate, *Korean Problem,* 154–68; Gene M. Lyons, *Military Policy and Economic Aid: The Korean Case, 1950–1953* (Columbus, OH, 1961), 20–23.

18. Ints., Jessup; Frank Pace, Jr., July 12, 1977; Gen. J. Lawton Collins, June 14, 1971; Sec. Gen. Trygve Lie to DM, July 12, 1950, RG 10, MMBA; Stone, *Hidden History,* 75–81; Truman, Statement on MacArthur's Appointment, July 8, 1950, in Truman, *Public Papers, 1950,* 520; Schnabel and Watson, *Korean War,* 135; Goodrich, *Korea,* 120–22.

19. DM to Truman, July 11, 1950, RG 7, MMBA.

20. Truman to DM, July 12, 1950, RG 7, MMBA.

21. Dulles to DM, July 10, 1950, Dulles Papers; Diary of Eben Ayers, July 1, 1950, Eben Ayers Files, Truman Papers; Allison, *Ambassador,* 126–39; Phillips, *Truman,* 300.

22. *New York Times,* July 9, 1950.

23. JCS to DM, July 12, 28, 1950, quoted in Schnabel and Watson, *Korean War,* 137, 140; Lichterman, "To the Yalu," 582–83; Haynes, *Awesome Power,* 185–86; Paul Y. Hammond, *Organizing for Defense: The American Military Establishment in the Twentieth Century* (Princeton, 1961), 247–56.

24. DM to Truman, July 19, 1950, RG 6, MMBA; Truman, Address to the American People, July 19, 1950, PSF, Truman Papers; *MSFE,* 11.

25. *MSFE,* 10.

26. Johnson to DM, July 10, 1950, RG 10, MMBA; DM Diary, July 14, 1950; *Nippon Times,* July 15, 1950; Sebald, *With MacArthur,* 191; "MacArthur Accepts U.N. Flag," *UN Bulletin,* 9 (Aug. 1, 1950), 97–98.

27. Schnabel, *Policy and Direction,* 103; Lichterman, "To the Yalu," 583; Virgil Ney, *Evolution of a Theater of Operations Headquarters, 1941–1967* (Washington, 1967), 55–73, 112.

28. DM to JCS, July 2, 1950; JCS to DM, July 3, 7, 1950, RG 9, MMBA; DM to JCS, July 7, 1950, in Schnabel and Watson, *Korean War,* 180–81; Major. Gen. George L. Eberle, "Logistic Problems in Early Phases of Hostilities [Korea, 1950–51]," (National War College paper, 1953), 1–15, Milner File, DMBP; Karig, et al., *Battle Report,* 88–89.

29. DM to JCS, July 9, 1950, in *FRUS, 1950,* VII, 336.

30. Collins to Gen. Wade H. Haislip, July 14, 1950, RG 6, MMBA; Collins to DM, July 11, 1950, RG 9, MMBA; DM Diary, July 13–14, 1950; Collins, *War,* 81–82, 85; Lt. Gen. George E. Stratemeyer, Testimony, Aug. 25, 1954, in U.S. Senate, *Interlocking Subversion,* 1725.

31. DM to Muccio, Aug. 17, 1950, RG 6, MMBA; JCS to DM, June 30, July 12, 15, 30, Aug. 1, 30, 1950; DM to JCS, July 15, 1950, RG 9, MMBA; Trygve Lie, Message on Aid to South Korea, July 14, 1950, in United Nations Security Council, *Official Records*, 5th Year Suppl. (June–Aug. 1950), 99; Huston, *Sinews*, 618–20; Eighth Army, Military History Sec., *A Short History of the Eighth United States Army, 1944–1954* (n.p., 1955), App., pp. xvi–xvii; Trygve Lie, *In the Cause of Peace: Seven Years with the United Nations* (New York, 1954), 336–38; Goodrich, "Korea," 145–47; Schnabel and Watson, *Korean War*, 155; U.S. Senate, *Korean Problem*, 149–53; FECOM Hq., "Far East Command," 22–24; Andrew W. Cordier and Wilder Foote, eds., *Public Papers of the Secretaries-General of the United Nations*, vol. I, *Trygve Lie* (New York, 1969), 351; Jim D. Hill, *The Minute Man in Peace and War: A History of the National Guard* (Harrisburg, PA, 1963), 506–10; Herbert F. Wood, *Strange Battleground: The Operations in Korea and Their Effects on the Defence Policy of Canada. Official History of the Canadian Army in Korea* (Ottawa, 1966), 41–44; Thor Thorgrimsson and E. C. Russell, *Canadian Naval Operations in Korean Waters, 1950–1955* (Ottawa, 1965), 1–28; Harold Macmillan, *Tides of Fortune, 1945–1955* (New York, 1969), 325–26; Clement R. Attlee and Francis Williams, *Twilight of Empire: Memoirs of Prime Minister Clement Attlee* (New York, 1962), 230–32.

32. Int., Almond; DM to DA, July 27, 1950, RG 9, MMBA; int., Almond, pt. 4, pp. 21–22, USAMHI; *Nippon Times*, July 28, 1950; Appleman, *South to the Naktong*, 206, 207–08; "The Battle Crisis," *Newsweek*, 36 (Aug. 7, 1950), 15; Smith, *MacArthur*, 64–67; Sheldon, *Hell*, 35–36.

33. Ints., Lynch, Palmer, Moore, Thomas, Craig, Bowser; Maj. Gen. Gines Perez, May 25, 1977; Eighth Army, *Short History*, App., p. i–ii; Karig, et al., *Battle Report*, 75–158; Lynn Montross, "The Pusan Perimeter," *Marine Corps Gazette*, June 1951, 32–38; Poats, *Decision*, 21–55; J. Robert Moskin, *The U.S. Marine Corps History* (rev. ed., New York, 1982), 446–61; Russell A. Gugeler, *Combat Actions in Korea* (2d ed., Washington, 1970), 3–30; Andrew C. Geer, *The New Breed: The Story of the U.S. Marines in Korea* (New York, 1952), 12–88.

34. Ints., Struble, Almond, Edwin Wright; Futrell, *USAF, 1950–53*, 43, 47.

35. Appleman, *South to the Naktong*, 352–53; Futrell, *USAF, 1950–53*, 131.

36. JCS to DM, July 31, Aug. 16, 29, 1950, RG 6, MMBA; Futrell, *USAF, 1950–53*, 178, 183; Kennan, *Memoirs*, II, 24–25; UN Security Council, *Official Records*, 495th–497th Meetings, Sept. 5–7, 1950. Schnabel and Watson, *Korean War*, 253n, says that Stratemeyer issued the order prohibiting further raids on Rashin; Futrell, *USAF, 1950–53*, 183, asserts the JCS ordered the prohibition.

37. Ints., Craig, Michaelis, Perez; "MSFE-TD," 3111; Coble, "Air Support," 27; USMA, *Korea*, 10–16; Leckie, *Conflict*, 84–104; Middleton, *Korean War*, 75–91; Gugeler, *Combat Actions*, 31–38; Geer, *New Breed*, 89–102; C. N. Barclay, *The First Commonwealth Division: The Story of*

British Commonwealth Land Forces in Korea, 1950–1953 (Aldershot, England, 1954), 200–01; Eric Linklater, *Our Men in Korea: The Commonwealth Part of the Campaign* (London, 1952), 71–74.

CHAPTER XV. *From Formosa to Inchon*
pages 452–85

1. JCS to DM, July 14, 26, 27, 28, 30, 1950; DM to JCS, July 16, 26, 29, 30, 1950, RG 9, MMBA; "Summation of the Remarks of Gen. MacArthur, 13 July 1950," quoted in Schnabel and Watson, *Korean War*, 507; Poole, *JCS, 1950–52*, 391–93.
2. Ints., Chiles, Willoughby, Edwin Wright; int., Almond, pt. 3, pp. 64–67, USAMHI; DM to Maj. Gen. Alonzo P. Fox, Aug. 8, 9, 1950, RG 6, MMBA; DM to JCS, Aug. 11, 1950, RG 9, MMBA; *Nippon Times*, Aug. 1, 2, 1950; *New York Times*, Aug. 1, 1950; Almond, Testimony, in U.S. Senate, *Interlocking Subversion*, 2055–58; Middleton, *Korean War*, 92–101; Kahn, *China Hands*, 226n; Sebald, *With MacArthur*, 123.
3. Ints., Fox, Almond; Sebald to Acheson, Aug. 3, 1950; Acheson to Sebald, Aug. 11, 1950, RG 6, MMBA; JCS to DM, Aug. 3, 1950; Johnson to DM, Aug. 4, 1950; DM to Johnson, Aug. 5, 1950, RG 9, MMBA.
4. Int., Almond; DM to JCS, Aug. 7, 1950; Almond, "GHQ FEC Command and Staff Visit to Formosa, 31 July–1 August 1950," Aug. 1, 1950, RG 6, MMBA; "MSFE-TD," 1855–56; London *Times*, Aug. 9, 15, 1950; Acheson, *Present*, 422; "MacArthur's Detractors," *Life*, 29 (Aug. 21, 1950), 28; Kolko and Kolko, *Limits*, 589–90.
5. Int., Harriman; int., W. Averell Harriman, 15, Dulles Oral History Coll., Princeton; Almond, "Notes on CINC Conference," Aug. 8, 1950, RG 6, MMBA; London *Times*, Aug. 10, 1950; Truman, News Conference, Aug. 3, 1950, in Truman, *Public Papers, 1950*, 568; Truman, *Memoirs*, II, 400–02; Ridgway, *Korean War*, 38; DM, *Reminiscences*, 341; Phillips, *Truman*, 315–18; Donovan, *Tumultuous Years*, 260–62; Willard Shelton, "Notes from Capitol Hill," *Nation*, 171 (Aug. 19, 1950), 162; "The Last Word," *Time*, 56 (Aug. 14, 1950), 8; Considine, *It's All News*, 343–46; Vernon A. Walters, *Silent Missions* (Garden City, NY, 1978), 190–201. Truman briefly considered flying to Tokyo in Aug. 1950. DM to Truman, Aug. 4, 1950, PSF, Truman Papers.
6. Truman, Press Conference, Aug. 10, 1950, in Truman, *Public Papers, 1950*, 580; DM, Press Release, Aug. 10, 1950, RG 6, MMBA.
7. DM, Press Release, Aug. 10, 1950, RG 6, MMBA.
8. DM Diary, Jan. 9, 1946; Aug. 6, 8, 1950; JCS to DM, Aug. 14, 1950, RG 9, MMBA; Boston *Herald*, Jan. 14, 1952; Washington *Daily News*, Jan. 25, 1952; Donovan, *Tumultuous Years*, 262.
9. DM to Truman, Aug. 12, 1950, PSF, Truman Papers.
10. Truman to DM, Aug. 16, 1950, PSF, Truman Papers.
11. Washington *Times-Herald*, Jan. 14, 1952.
12. DM Diary, Aug. 13, 27, 1950; Mar. 8, Apr. 9, 1951; Washington *Daily News*, Jan. 25, 1952; Boston *Herald*, Jan. 14, 1952.

13. Goulden, *Korea,* ix, 157. On Davis' memo to the JCS, for which no date or archival source is given, see ibid., viii–ix, xxii–xxiii.
14. Clyde A. Lewis to DM, Aug. 17, 1950; DM to Lewis, Aug. 20, 1950, RG 7, MMBA. Cf. DM, "Memorandum on Formosa," June 14, 1950, Dulles Papers.
15. Int., Pace; Johnson to DM, Aug. 26, 1950; DM to Johnson, Aug. 27, 1950, RG 6, MMBA; *New York Times,* Aug. 29, 1950; DM, "Formosa Must Be Defended: A Declaration," *U.S. News & World Report,* 29 (Sept. 1, 1950), 32–34; "An Unsinkable Aircraft Carrier," *Time,* 56 (Sept. 4, 1950), 10; London *Times,* Aug. 30, 1950; Truman, *Memoirs,* II, 404, 405; Margaret Truman, *Harry S. Truman* (New York, 1973), 477–79; Donovan, *Tumultuous Years,* 262–65; Caridi, "G.O.P.," 426–27; Millis, et al., *Arms and State,* 270–72; Smith, *MacArthur,* 137–43.
16. DM to Johnson, Aug. 27, 1950; Johnson to DM, Aug. 27, 1950, RG 6, MMBA; Washington *Daily News,* Jan. 25, 1952; *New York Times,* Aug. 29, 1950; Truman, *Memoirs,* II, 406–08, 436.
17. *MSFE,* 989–90, 1217, 2002–03; Acheson, *Among Friends,* 69; Tang Tsou, *America's Failure in China, 1941–50* (Chicago, 1963), 566–67; Simmons, *Strained Alliance,* 148–49; McLellan, *Acheson,* 277–79, 283–84; Denis Stairs, *The Diplomacy of Constraint: Canada, the Korean War, and the United States* (Toronto, 1974), 96–99.
18. Ints., Fortier, Felix Johnson, Chiles, Edwin Wright, Burke, Harriman; JCS to DM, July 20, 22, 1950; DM to JCS, July 21, 23, 1950, RG 9, MMBA; int., Almond, pp. 2–6, MMBA; Almond, "How Inchon Was Chosen," 1–3, RG 6, MMBA; Almond, Testimony, in U.S. Senate, *Interlocking Subversion,* 2065–66; Karig, et al., *Battle Report,* 122, 161–66; Heller, ed., *Korean War,* 24–26; Sheldon, *Hell,* 92–116; Edgar O'Ballance, *Korea, 1950–1953* (Hamden, CT, 1969), 48–50; Geer, *New Breed,* 2, 108; Robert D. Heinl, Jr., *Victory at High Tide: The Inchon-Seoul Campaign* (Philadelphia, 1968), 3–38; Michael Langley, *Inchon Landing: MacArthur's Last Triumph* (New York, 1979), 39–42; Shirley S. Foster, "Lieutenant General Alpha L. Bowser, USMC, and the Korean War" (unpublished M.A. thesis, San Diego State University, 1975), 55–97.
19. Montross, et al., *USMC in Korea,* II, 39; Schnabel, *Policy and Direction,* 148; Geer, *New Breed,* 110–13.
20. Almond, "Notes on CINC Conference," Aug. 23, 1950, RG 6, MMBA; int., Almond, pt. 4, pp. 38–41, USAMHI; Collins, *War,* 123, 125; Langley, *Inchon,* 42–48; Rees, *Korea,* 81; Schnabel, *Policy and Direction,* 149; Karig, et al., *Battle Report,* 166–69; Smith, *MacArthur,* 70–74; Radford, *Pearl Harbor to Vietnam,* 230–37; H. Pat Tomlinson, "Inchon: The General's Decision," *Military Review,* 47 (Apr. 1967), 30–32.
21. DM, *Reminiscences,* 349–50.
22. Ibid., 350; Heinl, *Victory,* 42.
23. JCS to DM, Aug. 28, 1950, RG 9, MMBA; Lt. Gen. Lemuel C. Shepherd, Jr., to DCJ, June 23, 1971; Collins, *Lightning Joe,* 364–67; Burke

Davis, *Marine! The Life of Lt. Gen. Lewis B. (Chesty) Puller, USMC (Ret.)* (Boston, 1962), 249; Clark G. Reynolds, "MacArthur as Maritime Strategist," *Naval War College Review,* 33 (Mar.–Apr. 1980), 86; Collins, *War,* 126.

24. Ints., Almond, Smith, Struble, Beiderlinden; int., Almond, pt. 4, pp. 23–44, USAMHI; Lt. Gen. Edward N. Almond, Diary, Aug. 31–Sept. 14, 1950, Edward N. Almond Papers, USAMHI; Heinl, *Victory,* 44–63, 291–93; Langley, *Inchon,* 52–53, 55–56, 161; Sheldon, *Hell,* 36–38; int., Almond, 6–8, MMBA; Lynn Montross, *Cavalry of the Sky: The Story of the U.S. Marine Combat Helicopters* (New York, 1954), 122–26.

25. DM to JCS, Sept. 6, 1950; JCS to DM, Sept. 5, 7, 1950, RG 6, MMBA; Rhee to DM, Sept. 8, 1950, RG 10, MMBA; Foster, "Bowser," 105–08; Heinl, *Victory,* 63–64; DM, *Reminiscences,* 351.

26. DM to JCS, Sept. 8, 1950, RG 6, MMBA.

27. JCS to DM, Sept. 8, 1950, RG 6, MMBA; DM to Cdr. Malcolm W. Cagle, Mar. 19, 1956, Documents for MacArthur Memorial, Naval Historical Center, Washington, D.C.; Radford, *Pearl Harbor to Vietnam,* 238; Collins, *War,* 128; DM, *Reminiscences,* 352.

28. Int., Gen. Lemuel C. Shepherd, Jr., 15, MMBA; U.S.S. *Mount McKinley,* War Diary, entries of Sept. 12–16, 1950, Documents for MacArthur Memorial, Naval Historical Center; Eberle, "Logistic Problems," 7–8; Sheldon, *Hell,* 159–61, 168–69; Heinl, *Victory,* 65–77; Lynn D. Smith, "A Nickel After a Dollar," *Army,* 20 (Sept. 1970), 25, 32–34; Odgers, *Parallel,* 89.

29. Heinl, *Victory,* 77–86; Langley, *Inchon,* 57–62.

30. DM to JCS, Sept. 15, 1950, RG 6, MMBA; Lynn Montross, "The Inchon Landing: Victory Over Time and Tide," *Marine Corps Gazette,* July 1951, 33–34; Heinl, *Victory,* 87–97; Karig, et al., *Battle Report,* 223; Smith, *MacArthur,* 53–54; Poats, *Decision,* 61–63.

31. Ints., Chiles, Smith, Almond; int., Col. Hubert Binkley, Milner File, DMBP; Montross, "Inchon Landing," 34–35; Almond Diary, Sept. 15–22, 1950; Langley, *Inchon,* 71–130; Heinl, *Victory,* 97–224; Foster, "Bowser," 117–26; Middleton, *Korean War,* 107–14; Geer, *New Breed,* 122–40, 184–91.

32. Ints., Edwin Wright, Almond, Smith, Chiles; int., Shepherd, pp. 16–22, MMBA; int., Almond, pt. 4, pp. 46–49, USAMHI; int., Almond, 8–10, MMBA; Sheldon, *Hell,* 177–82, 221, 226–29; Davis, *Puller,* 260–64; Karig, et al., *Battle Report,* 452.

33. *Nippon Times,* Sept. 23, 1950; Kenney, *MacArthur,* 210–15; Heinl, *Victory,* 188–89, 199–200, 259–60; Geer, *New Breed,* 146–47.

34. Ints., Almond, Smith; Maj. Gen. Edward N. Almond to DM, Sept. 25, 1950, Almond Papers; int., Almond, pt. 4, pp. 48–57, USAMHI; Almond Diary, Sept. 23–28, 1950; Noble, *Embassy,* 198–99; Foster, "Bowser," 126–29; Poats, *Decision,* 66–69; Heinl, *Victory,* 225–51, 257–58; Geer, *New Breed,* 141–83; Davis, *Puller,* 272.

35. Ints., Edson, Michaelis; Maj. Gen. Leven C. Allen, Journal, entries of Sept. 16–26, 1950, Milner File, DMBP; ROK Army, *ROK Army,* I, 70–

71; Middleton, *Korean War,* 115–18; Heinl, *Victory,* 147–48, 246–48; Langley, *Inchon,* 137–41.
36. JCS to DM, Sept. 22, 27, 1950; DM to JCS, Sept. 23, 1950, RG 9, MMBA; Schnabel, *Policy and Direction,* 184.
37. Int., Muccio, 1971, 78, HSTL; int., Beiderlinden, Milner File, DMBP; *New York Times,* Sept. 29, 1950; *Nippon Times,* Sept. 29, 30, 1950; DM, *Reminiscences,* 355, 356; DM, Address at Seoul, Sept. 29, 1950, in *MSFE,* 3481; Noble, *Embassy,* 194–95, 200–04; Almond Diary, Sept. 29, 1950; Baillie, *High Tension,* 224–25; "Liberation," *Time,* 56 (Oct. 9, 1950), 34; Kenney, *MacArthur,* 215–20; Davis, *Puller,* 281–82; Thompson, *Cry Korea,* 83–89.
38. Truman to DM, Sept. 29, 1950, in *MSFE,* 3482; JCS to DM, Sept. 29, 1950, quoted in Appleman, *South to the Naktong,* 538; DM, *Reminiscences,* 356n; Washington *Post,* Oct. 1, 1950.
39. Int., Whitney; DM, *Reminiscences,* 356n–357n; Heinl, *Victory,* 263–67; Malcolm W. Cagle, "Inchon: The Analysis of a Gamble," *U.S. Naval Institute Proceedings* 80 (Jan. 1954), 47, 50–51; Leonard Mosley, *Marshall: Hero for Our Times* (New York, 1982, 459–60; James F. Schnabel, "The Inchon Landing: Perilous Gamble or Exemplary Boldness?" *Army* 9 (May 1959), 51, 59; Robert D. Heinl, Jr., "Inchon," *Marine Corps Gazette,* Oct. 1967, 50; Adm. C. Turner Joy, Testimony, Dec. 29, 1954, in U.S. Senate, *Interlocking Subversion,* 2134–35; Collins, *War,* 141–42.

CHAPTER XVI. *The Optimism of October*
pages 486–517
1. Acheson, Princeton Seminars, reel 3, track 1, pp. 9–10, track 2, pp. 1–3, Acheson Papers, HSTL; *New York Times,* Aug. 18, Sept. 2, 1950; Truman, Broadcast to the Nation, Sept. 1, 1950, in Truman, *Public Papers, 1950,* 231–32; Tsou, *America's Failure,* 569–70; McLellan, *Acheson,* 285–87.
2. NSC 81, "United States Courses of Action with Respect to Korea," Sept. 1, 1950, in *FRUS, 1950,* VII, 685–93; NSC 81/1, Sept. 9, 1950, quoted in Schnabel and Watson, *Korean War,* 227; *MSFE,* 718; Kennan, *Memoirs,* II, 487–90; Lichterman, "To the Yalu," 584–85, 592–93; Fleming, *Cold War,* II, 655–58; Kolko and Kolko, *Limits,* 593–99.
3. JCS to DM, Sept. 27, 1950, in *FRUS, 1950,* VII, 781–82, 792–93; Radford, *Pearl Harbor to Vietnam,* 239–40; Walter LaFeber, "Crossing the 38th: The Cold War in Microcosm," in Lynn H. Miller and Ronald W. Pruessen, eds., *Reflections on the Cold War: A Quarter Century of American Foreign Policy* (Philadelphia, 1974), 83–84; Haynes, *Awesome Power,* 194–98; Donovan, *Tumultuous Years,* 268–80; Heller, ed., *Korean War,* 26–29; Smith, *MacArthur,* 143–47.
4. DM to Marshall, Sept. 30, 1950, RG 6, MMBA; DM to JCS, Sept. 28, 1950, RG 9, MMBA; Marshall to DM, Sept. 29, 1950, in *FRUS, 1950,*

VII, 826; int., Almond, pt. 4, pp. 58–59, 65–66, USAMHI; Collins, *Lightning Joe*, 367–70; Lichterman, "To the Yalu," 586–88.

5. JCS to DM, Sept. 27, 1950; DM to Almond, Sept. 28, 1950, RG 6, MMBA; DM to JCS, Sept. 28, Oct. 2, 1950, RG 9, MMBA; Washington *Post*, Oct. 1, 2, 1950; CIA Director to Truman, Oct. 12, 1950, quoted in Schnabel and Watson, *Korean War*, 262; Whiting, *China Crosses*, 108; James McGovern, *To the Yalu: From the Chinese Invasion of Korea to MacArthur's Dismissal* (New York, 1972), 38–47; K. M. Panikkar, *In Two Chinas: Memoirs of a Diplomat* (London, 1955), 109–13; Truman, News Conference, Sept. 28, 1950, in Truman, *Public Papers, 1950*, 658–60; ROK Army, *ROK Army*, I, 78–79; Karig, et al., *Battle Report*, 291–92; Leckie, *Conflict*, 132–46; Fleming, *Cold War*, II, 614–15, 655–56; Samuel B. Griffith, *The Chinese People's Liberation Army* (New York, 1967), 117–21; Louis J. Halle, *The Cold War as History* (New York, 1967), 220–23.

6. UN General Assembly, Resolution, Oct. 7, 1950, in *DAFR*, XII, 459–61. See also Austin's speech, Sept. 30, 1950, in ibid., 454–58.

7. Washington *Post*, Oct. 9, 1950; Goodrich, *Korea*, 133–34; Rees, *Korea*, 108; Stone, *Hidden History*, 133–38; Lichterman, "To the Yalu," 588–91, 593–97; Irving L. Janis, *Victims of Groupthink: A Psychological Study of Foreign-Policy Decisions and Fiascoes* (Boston, 1972), 55–65; Yoo, *Korean War*, 42–49; Richard E. Neustadt, *Presidential Power: The Politics of Leadership* (New York, 1960), 123–51.

8. Ints., Mildren, Almond, Palmer, Smith, Bowser, Craig, Lynch; ints., Beiderlinden, Col. Wayne S. Hume, Milner File, DMBP; Col. Maury Holden to DCJ, Aug. 28, 1981; int., Almond, pt. 4, pp. 58–59, USAMHI; DM to Howard, Feb. 1, 1951, RG 5, MMBA; DM to Sen. Harry F. Byrd, Apr. 19, 1953; DM to Maj. Gen. E. W. Snedeker, Feb. 24, 1956, RG 21, MMBA; DM to Cagle, Mar. 19, 1956, Naval Historical Center; Foster, "Bowser," 129–34; Smith, *MacArthur*, 80–83, 183–85; Karig, et al., *Battle Report*, 298–302, 330–31; Thorgrimsson and Russell, *Canadian Naval Operations*, 20; "Foreign History and Leverage," *Time*, 61 (May 4, 1953), 22; Martin Blumenson, "MacArthur's Divided Command," *Army*, 7 (Nov. 1956), 38–44, 65; Lynn Montross, "Wonsan to the Reservoir: Red China Enters the Fight," *Marine Corps Gazette*, Oct. 1951, 31–32; S. L. A. Marshall, *The Military History of the Korean War* (New York, 1963), 29–30; Malcolm W. Cagle and Frank A. Manson, "Wonsan: The Battle of the Mines," *U.S. Naval Institute Proceedings*, 83 (June 1957), 598–611; Malcolm W. Cagle, "Errors of the Korean War," ibid., 84 (Mar. 1958), 31–32.

9. Ints., Mildren, Jones; Gen. Harold K. Johnson, July 7, 1971; int., Hume, Milner File, DMBP; Barclay, *First Commonwealth Division*, 17–29; Collins, *War*, 177; Collins, *Lightning Joe*, 370–72; Middleton, *Korean War*, 119–26; Poats, *Decision*, 71–86; Leckie, *Conflict*, 146–47, 151–53.

10. Ints., Edwin Wright, Mildren; Rhee to DM, Oct. 20, 1950, RG 7,

MMBA; *Nippon Times,* Oct. 21, 1950; Washington *Post,* Oct. 21, 1950; DM's DFC citation, Oct. 29, 1950, in U.S. Senate, *Congressional Record,* 8th Cong., 2d Sess. (1960), 106, pt. 1, 1248; ROK Army, *ROK Army,* I, 83–85; Thompson, *Cry Korea,* 176–77; Oliver, *Rhee,* 307.

11. Acheson to Muccio, Oct. 29, 1950, RG 5, MMBA; Brig. Gen. Kenneth B. Bush to Lt. Gen. Walton H. Walker, et al., Oct. 28, 1950, RG 6, MMBA; Rhee to Acheson, Oct. 31, 1950, RG 7, MMBA; JCS to DM, July 2, 4, Oct. 10, 20, 1950; DM to JCS, Oct. 11, 21, 1950, RG 9, MMBA; int., Muccio, 1973, pp. 25–27, HSTL; FECOM Hq., "Far East Command, 1947–57," 28–29; Lyons, *Economic Aid,* 24–26; Wood, *Strange Battleground,* 261–62; Leckie, *Conflict,* 153–54.
12. JCS to DM, Oct. 21, 1950; DM to JCS, Oct. 22, 1950, RG 6, MMBA; DM to JCS, Oct. 24, 25, 1950; JCS to DM, Oct. 24, 1950, RG 9, MMBA; DM to Walker, et al., Oct. 19, 1950, quoted in Schnabel and Watson, *Korean War,* 274; Lichterman, "To the Yalu," 600–01; Stone, *Hidden History,* 151–55; Haynes, *Awesome Power,* 202–04; Tsou, *America's Failure,* 580–82; David S. McLellan, "Dean Acheson and the Korean War," *Political Science Quarterly,* 83 (Mar. 1968), 24–25.
13. DM to JCS, Oct. 25, 1950, RG 9, MMBA.
14. Schnabel and Watson, *Korean War,* 276; *MSFE,* 1300; Collins, *War,* 180.
15. Lt. Cdr. William M. Rigdon, comp., "Log of President Truman's Trip to Wake Island, October 11–18, 1950," 8–11, CMH; DM, *Reminiscences,* 360–61; Truman, *Public Papers, 1950,* 665–66; John E. Wiltz, "Truman and MacArthur: The Wake Island Meeting," *Military Affairs,* 42 (Dec. 1978), 170–71, 174; Stone, *Hidden History,* 139–44.
16. Rigdon, "Log," 49.
17. Ibid., 77.
18. JCS to DM, Oct. 9, 1950, RG 9, MMBA; Truman, *Memoirs,* II, 413.
19. Rigdon, "Log," 19, 21, 47. The people who made the trip to Wake from the U.S., including the presidential party, the press corps, and the plane crews, are listed in "Trip of the President, October 11–18, 1950," PSF, Truman Papers.
20. Rigdon, "Log," 18–21, 47; Truman to Adm. Arthur W. Radford, Oct. 23, 1950; "President Truman's Trip to the Pacific to Meet General MacArthur, October 11–18, 1950" [White House staff compilation of newspaper items], 1–3, PSF, Truman Papers; Truman, *Public Papers, 1950,* 669–72; Whitney, *MacArthur,* 385; Wiltz, "Truman and MacArthur," 171.
21. Ints., Harriman, Jessup; Wiltz, "Truman and MacArthur," 170; " 'No Truth to Story, Says General's Aide [Bunker]," Starkville (MS) *Daily News,* Jan. 6, 1973; Robert Sherrod, "Truman Story Doesn't Jibe," Memphis *Commercial Appeal,* Dec. 15, 1973; Heller, ed., *Korean War,* 30–32. The popularizations were Miller, *Plain Speaking,* one of the top best sellers of 1973; Samuel Gallu's stage production, *Give 'Em*

Hell, Harry! (1975); and the ABC television historical drama, "Collision Course: Truman vs. MacArthur" (1976).

22. Ints., Pace, Harriman; "Pres. Truman's Trip," 4; Rigdon, "Log," 45, 47; *New York Times*, Oct. 15, 1950; Truman, "Memorandum on Wake Island," Nov. 25, 1950, in Harry S. Truman, *Off the Record: The Private Papers of Harry S. Truman*, ed. Robert H. Ferrell (New York, 1980), 200; Truman *Memoirs*, II, 416; Wiltz, "Truman and MacArthur," 172; DM, *Reminiscences*, 361; [Robert Sherrod], "The General Rose at Dawn," *Time*, 56 (Oct. 23, 1950), 19; "What Happened at Wake," *Newsweek*, 36 (Oct. 23, 1950), 21.

23. Int., Harriman; Dean Rusk, "Memorandum of [Wake] Conversation, Oct. 14 [15], 1950," in *FRUS, 1950*, VI, 533–34; *MSFE*, 41; Truman, *Off the Record*, 200; idem, *Memoirs*, II, 416; Donovan, *Tumultuous Years*, 285–86; Whitney, *MacArthur*, 387.

24. Ints., Jessup, Harriman, Pace, Whitney; int., Story, Sherrod File, DMBP; DM, *Reminiscences*, 361; Philip C. Jessup, "Research Note: The Record of Wake Island — a Correction," *Journal of American History*, 67 (Mar. 1981), 866–70; Whitney, *MacArthur*, 388; Gen. of the Army Omar N. Bradley, "Substance of Statements Made at Wake Island Conference on 15 October 1950, Compiled from Notes Kept by the Conferees from Washington," 1–23, Bradley File, RG 218, NA. The preceding Bradley File also contains several earlier drafts with editorial changes, as well as some individuals' notes used in the compilation. A published edition, with the same title as Bradley's MS compilation but with some textual deletions, was prepared by the JCS for the Senate Armed Services and Foreign Relations committees in conjunction with the MacArthur Hearings. The letter of submittal from Bradley to Chairman Richard B. Russell is dated May 2, 1951. The complete Bradley compilation is in *FRUS, 1950*, VII, 948–60.

25. Bradley, "Substance," 1–10; Walters, *Silent Missions*, 202–10; Radford, *Pearl Harbor to Vietnam*, 240–45.

26. Bradley, "Substance," 10–12.

27. Ints., Whitney, Willoughby; DM to Maj. Gen. R. W. Stephens, Nov. 5, 1957, RG 21, MMBA; Bradley, "Substance," 12–23; Charles A. Willoughby, "The MacArthur Notes on the Wake Island Meeting," *Foreign Intelligence Digest*, Sept. 1971, 3–6.

28. Ints., Harriman, Jessup, Pace; int., Muccio, 1971, 78–91, HSTL; int., Muccio, 1973, 21–22, 26–27, HSTL; Acheson, Princeton Seminars, reel 3, track 2, pp. 3–7; W. Averell Harriman, "Notes Made at Wake Island, Oct. 15, 1950" (photocopy, DMBP); Rusk, "Addendum to Notes of Wake Conference, October 14 [15], 1950," in *FRUS, 1950*, VII, 961–62; Bradley and Blair, *General's Life*, 576–77.

29. DM to Truman, Oct. 18, 1950, RG 5, MMBA; Mrs. DM to Truman, Oct. 16, 1950, PSF, Truman Papers; Rigdon, "Log," 49, 55, 71–93; "Pres. Truman's Trip," 5–9; *Nippon Times*, Oct. 16, 1950; *New York Times*, Oct. 16, 1950; Washington *Post*, Oct. 16, 1950; Truman, *Public*

Papers, 1950, 672–82; int., Vernice Anderson, 1971, HSTL, quoted in Jessup, "Research Note," 870; Wiltz, "Truman and MacArthur," 173–74; Spanier, *Truman-MacArthur Controversy,* 112; "The Mysterious Voyage," *Life,* 29 (Oct. 30, 1950), 34; DM, *Reminiscences,* 363; Ronald T. Farrar, *Reluctant Servant: The Story of Charles G. Ross* (Columbia, MO, 1969), 216.
30. Bradley to DM, Oct. 19, 1950, RG 5, MMBA.
31. Truman to DM, Oct. 23, 1950; DM to Truman, Oct. 30, 1950, RG 5, MMBA.
32. DM to Snedeker, Feb. 24, 1956, RG 21, MMBA; Boston *Herald,* Jan. 14, 1952; Washington *Daily News,* Jan. 25, 1952; DM, *Reminiscences,* 362; Acheson, *Present,* 456; *MSFE,* 439–40; Wiltz, "Truman and MacArthur," 174–75; Stone, *Hidden History,* 145–50; Truman, *Off the Record,* 196, 199.
33. Whitney, *MacArthur,* 395; Wiltz, "Truman and MacArthur," 174–75; Donovan, *Tumultuous Years,* 284; [Sherrod], "The General Rose at Dawn," 20; "Political Hue of the Flight to Wake," *Newsweek,* 36 (Oct. 23, 1950), 27; "Political 'It' and Glory: MacArthur's Lure for Presidents," *U.S. News & World Report,* 29 (Oct. 20, 1950), 36, 38. The accounts of the Wake conference by Wiltz and Donovan are the best, as well as the most recent.

CHAPTER XVII. *"An Entirely New War"*
pages 518–59
1. Ints., Smith, Mildren, Almond, Palmer, Perez; int., Almond, pt. 4, pp. 66–68, USAMHI; Almond Diary, Oct. 25–Nov. 6, 1950; Almond to DM, Oct. 30, 1950, Almond Papers; Allen Journal, Oct. 26–Nov. 9, 1950, Milner File, DMBP; Gen. Walton H. Walker to DM, Nov. 6, 1950, in Schnabel, *Policy and Direction,* 235; Lie, *In the Cause of Peace,* 347–49; Griffith, *Chinese People's Liberation Army,* 123–37; McGovern, *To the Yalu,* 38–66; Leckie, *Conflict,* 149–66; Berger, *Korea Knot,* 122–24; Stone, *Hidden History,* 151–74; Poats, *Decision,* 87–94; Goodrich, *Korea,* 140–42; Geer, *New Breed,* 194–95.
2. JCS to DM, Nov. 3, 1950; DM to JCS, Nov. 4, 1950, RG 9, MMBA; Karig, et al., *Battle Report,* 374–75; UN Security Council, *Official Records,* 518th Meeting, Nov. 6, 1950, pp. 3–5.
3. JCS to DM, Nov. 6, 1950, RG 9, MMBA; *New York Times,* Nov. 6, 1950; Futrell, *USAF, 1950–53,* 209; Truman, *Memoirs,* II, 426–27; DM, *Reminiscences,* 369–70; McGovern, *To the Yalu,* 73–76; Haynes, *Awesome Power,* 205–07; Middleton, *Korean War,* 137–39.
4. DM to JCS, Nov. 6, 1950, RG 9, MMBA (reprinted, among other places, in Truman, *Memoirs,* II, 427–28).
5. JCS to DM, Nov. 6, 1950, RG 9, MMBA; DM to JCS, Nov. 7, 1950, in *FRUS, 1950,* VII, 1076–77; Stratemeyer, Testimony, Aug. 25, 1954, in U.S. Senate, *Interlocking Subversion,* 1720–23, 1728–30; Truman,

Memoirs, II, 428; Bradley and Blair, *General's Life*, 587; Donovan, *Tumultuous Years*, 298–300.

6. Marshall to DM, Nov. 7, 1950; DM to Marshall, Nov. 8, 1950, RG 6, MMBA.

7. DM to JCS, Nov. 7, 1950; JCS to DM, Nov. 7, 1950, RG 9, MMBA; Thompson, *Cry Korea*, 208–13; Goodrich, *Korea*, 149–55; Haynes, *Awesome Power*, 207–09; Stone, *Hidden History*, 175–84; Poats, *Decision*, 96–97; Mosley, *Marshall*, 474–75.

8. JCS to DM, Nov. 8, 1950, in *FRUS, 1950*, VII, 1098; DM to JCS, Nov. 9, 1950, in ibid., 1108.

9. Thomas L. Marshall, "The Strategy of Conflict in the Korean War" (unpublished Ph.D. dissertation, Univ. of Virginia, 1969), 176–80; Acheson, *Korean War*, 68; Schnabel and Watson, *Korean War*, 306; Janis, *Groupthink*, 64–65; McGovern, *To the Yalu*, 78–79; McLellan, "Acheson and the Korean War," 27–29; Neustadt, *Presidential Power*, 140–46.

10. DM to JCS, Nov. 7, 1950, quoted in Schnabel, *Policy and Direction*, 239.

11. Ints., Mildren, Smith, Edson, Michaelis, Perez, Lynch, Zundel, Palmer, Pace; DM to JCS, Nov. 18, 1950, RG 9, MMBA; Allen Journal, Nov. 9–22, 1950; Middleton, *Korean War*, 140–42.

12. Sebald, Memorandum of Conversation [with DM], Nov. 14, 1950, in *FRUS, 1950*, VII, 1148–49.

13. Muccio, Memorandum of Conversation [with DM], Nov. 17, 1950, in ibid., 1175.

14. Schnabel and Watson, *Korean War*, 309.

15. Laurence S. Kaplan, "Korean War and U.S. Foreign Relations," in Heller, ed., *Korean War*, 52, 68–70; Kolko and Kolko, *Limits*, 601–02; Poats, *Decision*, 94–95; Stairs, *Diplomacy*, 132–36; Smith, *Acheson*, 210; Watt, "Britain and the Cold War in the Far East," 104; Elaine Windrich, *British Labour's Foreign Policy* (Stanford, CA, 1952), 223.

16. Ints., Pace, Harriman, Jessup, Matthews; JCS to DM, Nov. 24, 1950, in *FRUS, 1950*, VII, 1222–24; DM to JCS, Nov. 25, 1950, in ibid., 1231–33; Bradley and Blair, *General's Life*, 597; Janis, *Groupthink*, 65–66; Tsou, *America's Failure*, 587–88; McLellan, "Acheson and the Korean War," 31–35.

17. Caridi, "G.O.P.," 429–32; Stebbins, ed., *U.S. in World Affairs, 1950*, 412–13; Huntington, *Common Defense*, 56–64. See also Spanier, *Truman-MacArthur Controversy*, 151–56.

18. Ints., Mildren, Smith, Almond, Lynch, Perez, Palmer, Michaelis; int., Neal, Milner File, DMBP; int., Almond, pt. 4, pp. 6–7, USAMHI; Almond Diary, Nov. 24–25, 1950; Allen Journal, Nov. 24–26, 1950; Lichterman, "To the Yalu," 607–09; Leckie, *Conflict*, 166–72; USMA, *Korea*, 22–24; Poats, *Decision*, 101–04; McGovern, *To the Yalu*, 92–106; Donovan, *Tumultuous Years*, 302–05; Fleming, *Cold War*, II, 621–22.

19. Int., Col. Anthony F. Story, July 16, 1971; Washington *Evening Star*,

Nov. 25, 29, 1950; *New York Times*, Nov. 24, 25, 1950; Ray Henle to
DM, Nov. 29, 1950, RG 7, MMBA; Whitney, *MacArthur*, 416; DM,
Reminiscences, 372; Huff, *My Fifteen Years*, 132–33; Thompson, *Cry
Korea*, 235–36. Stratemeyer awarded the Distinguished Flying Cross
to DM after his Yalu flight, his second DFC in five weeks.

20. DM, Communiqué No. 12, Nov. 24, 1950, RG 9, MMBA (reprinted,
among other places, in *MSFE*, 3491–92, and *New York Times*, Nov.
24, 1950).

21. Ints., Lynch, Mildren, Smith, Michaelis; JCS to DM, Nov. 24, 1950;
DM to JCS, Nov. 25, 1950, RG 9, MMBA; Almond Diary, Nov. 25–
Dec. 11, 1950; Allen Journal, Nov. 26–Dec. 10, 1950; Leckie, *Conflict*, 172–88; Middleton, *Korean War*, 146–54; Gugeler, *Combat Actions*, 45–79; McGovern, *To the Yalu*, 107–16, 123–34; Alexander L.
George, *The Chinese Communist Army in Action: The Korean War and Its
Aftermath* (New York, 1969 [1st ed., 1967]), 2–7; Griffith, *Chinese People's Liberation Army*, 138–44; Eric M. Hammel, *Chosin: Heroic Ordeal
of the Korean War* (New York, 1981), 48–49; Barclay, *First Commonwealth Division*, 30–42. For one of the best small-unit studies of the
Korean War, see S. L. A. Marshall, *The River and the Gauntlet: Defeat
of the Eighth Army by the Chinese Communist Forces, November, 1950, in
the Battle of the Chongchon River, Korea* (New York, 1953).

22. DM to JCS, Nov. 28, 1950; DM, Communiqué No. 14, Nov. 28, 1950,
RG 9, MMBA; int., Almond, pt. 5, pp. 11–12, USAMHI; int., Beiderlinden, Milner File, DMBP; *New York Times*, Nov. 29, 1950; Lichterman, "To the Yalu," 617–19; Donovan, *Tumultuous Years*, 304–06,
313–15.

23. JCS to DM, Nov. 29–30, Dec. 1–4, 6, 1950; DM to JCS, Nov. 30, Dec.
3, 5, 1950, RG 9, MMBA; Ridgway, *Korean War*, 62. As elsewhere
herein, some of the JCS-DM messages are reprinted in full in *FRUS,
1950*, VII, and in excerpts in Schnabel, *Policy and Direction*, and
Schnabel and Watson, *Korean War*.

24. Collins to JCS, Dec. 8, 1950, quoted in Schnabel and Watson, *Korean
War*, 368; DM Diary, Dec. 4, 1950; Collins, *War*, 231–32; Collins,
Lightning Joe, 373–74.

25. Bradley and Blair, *General's Life*, 599; McLellan, *Acheson*, 295–96;
Haynes, *Awesome Power*, 213–14.

26. Truman, *Memoirs*, II, 450; Truman, Press Conference, Nov. 30, 1950,
in Truman, *Public Papers, 1950*, 726–27; Bundy, ed., *Pattern*, 267–
70; London *Times*, Nov. 30, 1950; Truman, *Truman*, 495–98; Goodrich, "Korea," 167–68; John E. Mueller, "Trends in Popular Support
for the Wars in Korea and Vietnam," *American Political Science Review*,
45 (1971), 360–62; "Key to Conflict — and Its Significance," *Newsweek*, 36 (Dec. 4, 1950), 29; Gregg Herken, *The Winning Weapon: The
Atomic Bomb in the Cold War, 1945–1950* (New York, 1982 [1st ed.,
1981]), 332–33; Kolko and Kolko, *Limits*, 603–04; Farrar, *Ross*, 216–
21; Richard G. Hewlett and Francis Duncan, *Atomic Shield, 1947–1952*.

A History of the United States Atomic Energy Commission, vol. II (University Park, PA, 1969), 532–34.

27. London *Times*, Dec. 13, 1950; Panikkar, *In Two Chinas*, 118–19; Marshall, "Strategy," 35–36; McLellan, *Acheson*, 298–99; Higgins, *Korea and Fall of MacArthur*, 88; Clement R. Attlee, *As It Happened* (London, 1954), 280–83; Donovan, *Tumultuous Years*, 308–10, 316–18; Bert Cochran, *Harry Truman and the Crisis Presidency* (New York, 1973), 325.

28. DM to David Lawrence, Dec. 1, 1950; DM to Hugh Baillie, Dec. 1, 1950; DM to Arthur Krock, Dec. 2, 1950; DM to Barry Farris, Dec. 4, 1950, RG 7, MMBA; DM to Snedeker, Oct. 17, 1956; DM to Stephens, Nov. 15, 1957, RG 21, MMBA; DM to Cagle, Mar. 19, 1956, Naval Historical Center; Stratemeyer, Testimony, Aug. 25, 1954, in U.S. Senate, *Interlocking Subversion*, 1724–25; Washington *Post*, Nov. 29, Dec. 3, 1950; New York *Herald Tribune*, Dec. 2, 1950; Washington *Evening Star*, Nov. 29, 1950; London *Times*, Dec. 2, 1950; *Nippon Times*, Dec. 3, 7, 1950; *New York Times*, Dec. 2, 1950; "MacArthur's Own Story," *U.S. News & World Report* 29 (Dec. 8, 1950), 16–22; "The Shape of Things," *Nation*, 171 (Dec. 2, 1950), 497; Higgins, *War*, 176–78; "War at Home Between the Achesons and the MacArthurs," *Commonweal*, 53 (Dec. 15, 1950), 245–46; "On the Griddle," *Time*, 56 (Dec. 11, 1950), 26; Baillie, *High Tension*, 225–26; Thompson, *Cry Korea*, 252–53. On the limitations imposed by both sides during the war, see Morton H. Halperin, "The Limiting Process in the Korean War," *Political Science Quarterly*, 78 (Mar. 1963), 13–39.

29. *New York Times*, Dec. 2, 1950; "MacArthur's Own Story," *U.S. News & World Report*, 29 (Dec. 8, 1950), 16–22; Richard T. Ruetten, "General MacArthur's 'Reconnaissance in Force': The Rationalization of a Defeat in Korea," *Pacific Historical Review*, 36 (Feb. 1967), 79–93.

30. JCS to DM, Dec. 6, 1950, Official Files, Truman Papers; JCS to DM, Dec. 8, 1950, RG 6, MMBA; Lucius D. Battle, Memorandum, Dec. 4, 1950, in *FRUS, 1950*, VII, 1346; Truman, *Memoirs*, II, 435, 437; idem, *Off the Record*, 210; idem, *Truman*, 493; Phillips, *Truman*, 329–30; Haynes, *Awesome Power*, 247–49.

31. DM to JCS, Dec. 12, 1950, RG 6, MMBA; JCS to DM, Dec. 11, 1950, RG 9, MMBA; DS, *American Foreign Policy*, II, 2627–42; UN Security Council, *Official Records*, 527th Meeting, Nov. 28, 1950, pp. 20–23; Lichterman, "To the Yalu," 618–19; Stebbins, ed., *United States in World Affairs, 1950*, 416–19; Poats, *Decision*, 119–21; McGovern, *To the Yalu*, 141–42; McLellan, *Acheson*, 300–01.

32. Ints., Chiles, Harriman, Mildren, Perez, Smith, Michaelis; Truman to DM, Dec. 26, 1950, RG 6, MMBA; DM to Almond, Dec. 18, 1950, RG 7, MMBA; DM to JCS, Dec. 12, 1950; Almond to DM, Dec. 24, 1950, RG 9, MMBA; ints., Barr, Col. John D. Davenport; Allen Journal, Dec. 12–23, 1950, Milner File, DMBP; int., Almond, pt. 5, pp. 19–20, 24, USAMHI; int., Shepherd, 33–43, MMBA; Almond Diary, Dec. 12–24, 1950; *New York Times*, Dec. 12, 1950; Karig, et al.,

Battle Report, 423–25; William McCallam, Jr., "The Evacuation of Hungnam," *Combat Forces Journal,* Aug. 1951, 32–35; Lynn Montross, "The Hungnam Evacuation," *Marine Corps Gazette,* Dec. 1951, 18–27; Poats, *Decision,* 108–15, 123–24; Stone, *Hidden History,* 223–31; Cagle, "Errors," 32–33; Thorgrimsson and Russell, *Canadian Naval Operations,* 37–40; Robert Leckie, *The March to Glory* [Chosin] (Cleveland, 1960), passim.

33. DM to Lt. Gen. Matthew B. Ridgway, Dec. 23, 1950, Matthew B. Ridgway Papers, USAMHI; DM Diary, Dec. 26, 1950; Matthew B. Ridgway, with Harold H. Martin, *Soldier: The Memoirs of Matthew B. Ridgway* (New York, 1956), 195–96, 201; Middleton, *Korean War,* 163–64; Leckie, *Conflict,* 204–05; McGovern, *To the Yalu,* 148–51; Radford, *From Pearl Harbor to Vietnam,* 247–48.

34. Ridgway, Memorandum of Conference with MacArthur, Dec. 26, 1950, Ridgway Papers (reprinted in Ridgway, *Korean War,* 81–83).

35. DM to JCS, Nov. 29, 1950; JCS to DM, Nov. 30, Dec. 19, 22, 1950, RG 9, MMBA; DM to Haislip, Dec. 18, 1950, quoted in Schnabel, *Policy and Direction,* 300; Truman, Press Conference, Dec. 19, 1950, in Truman, *Public Papers, 1950,* 751–54; Poole, *JCS, 1950–52,* 221–24; Phillips, *Truman,* 330–31; Herbert Druks, *Harry S. Truman and the Russians, 1945–1953* (New York, 1966), 235–39; Cecil V. Crabb, Jr., *Bipartisan Foreign Policy: Myth or Reality?* (Evanston, IL, 1958), 87–91; R. Gordon Hoxie, *Command Decision and the Presidency: A Study in National Security Policy and Organization* (New York, 1977), 99–102; Stairs, *Diplomacy,* 205–06; Syngman Rhee, *Korea Flaming High* (Seoul, Korea, 1954), 219; O'Ballance, *Korea,* 156–57.

36. JCS to DM, Jan. 4, 1951; DM to JCS, Jan. 6, 1951, Official Files, Truman Papers, HSTL; DM to Henry Haylitt, editor of *Freeman,* Apr. 5, 1951, Lloyd Files, HSTL; JCS to Marshall, Jan. 17, 1951, in *FRUS, 1951,* VII, pt. 1, 106–07; *New York Times,* Mar. 31, 1951; Haynes, *Awesome Power,* 224.

37. Ints., Winton, Perez; int., Muccio, 1971, 93–95, HSTL; Ridgway, *Soldier,* 202–08; Heller, ed., *Korean War,* 29–30, 34–35; Middleton, *Korean War,* 164–68; Poats, *Decision,* 126–34; Leckie, *Conflict,* 205–11; Stone, *Hidden History,* 232–47; Griffith, *Chinese People's Liberation Army,* 151–53; Mosley, *Marshall,* 481–82; Thompson, *Cry Korea,* 277–79.

38. JCS to DM, Dec. 29, 1950, in *FRUS, 1950,* VII, 1625–26.

39. DM, *Reminiscences,* 378; Smith, *MacArthur,* 126–27.

40. DM to JCS, Dec. 30, 1950, Ridgway Papers, USAMHI (reprinted in *FRUS, 1950,* VII, 1630–33).

41. DM to JCS, Jan. 3, 1951, RG 9, MMBA; Collins, *War,* 247; Millis, et al., *Arms and State,* 303–14; McGovern, *To the Yalu,* 151–53.

42. JCS to DM, Jan. 9, 1950, RG 9, MMBA; Lichterman, "To the Yalu," 619–21; Donovan, *Tumultuous Years,* 344–45. For critiques of DM's proposals of Dec. 30, see John Norman, "MacArthur's Blockade Proposals Against Red China," *Pacific Historical Review,* 26 (May 1957), 161–74; Alvin J. Cottrell and James E. Dougherty, "The Lessons of

Korea: War and the Power of Man," *Orbis*, 2 (Spring 1958), 39–60.
43. DM to JCS, Jan. 8, 10, 1951, RG 6, MMBA; Ridgway to DM, Dec. 8, 1950; DM to JCS, Dec. 8, 1950, RG 9, MMBA. Ridgway's communiqué of Jan. 21 is reprinted in Ridgway, *Korean War*, 264–65.
44. DM to JCS, Jan. 10, 1951, RG 6, MMBA.
45. Truman, *Memoirs*, II, 492; *MSFE*, 329, 1600; Acheson, *Present*, 515; Donovan, *Tumultuous Years*, 346; Lichterman, "To the Yalu," 622–23.
46. JCS to DM, Jan. 12, 1951, RG 9, MMBA.
47. *MSFE*, 1396–97; Haynes, *Awesome Power*, 227–28; Schnabel, *Policy and Direction*, 328.
48. Truman to DM, Jan. 13, 1950, in Truman, *Memoirs*, II, 493, 495; DM, *Reminiscences*, 382; Acheson, *Korean War*, 98; Phillips, *Truman*, 334–35; Hoare, "Truman," 202; Haynes, *Awesome Power*, 226–27.
49. Int., Michaelis; Middleton, *Korean War*, 168–69; Poats, *Decision*, 137; Leckie, *Conflict*, 219–21; Schnabel, *Policy and Direction*, 326.
50. Int., Collins; DM Diary, Jan. 17, 1951; Collins to Bradley, Jan. 17, 1951, quoted in Bradley and Blair, *General's Life*, 623; Collins, *War*, 253–55; Adm. C. Turner Joy, Testimony, Dec. 29, 1954, in U.S. Senate, *Interlocking Subversion*, 2136–37; Odgers, *Parallel*, 140–41; Haynes, *Awesome Power*, 228–29.
51. DM, *Reminiscences*, 383; McGovern, *To the Yalu*, 162; Smith, *MacArthur*, 125–26.
52. *MSFE*, 324; Collins, *War*, 255.
53. Rees, *Korea*, 183.
54. Schnabel and Watson, *Korean War*, 439–40.

CHAPTER XVIII. *The Furies of Self-Destruction*
pages 560–604
1. Lt. Gen. Pedro A. del Valle to Capt. Miles Duval, Apr. 30, 1969, RG 15, MMBA.
2. Del Valle to DM, Dec. 14, 1950; Feb. 10, 1951, RG 10, MMBA; Andrew Tully, *CIA: The Inside Story* (New York, 1962), 30.
3. DM Diary, Jan. 15, 17, 1951. Smith's pre-CIA activities and relations with Marshall, Bradley, and Eisenhower are prominently mentioned in Eisenhower, *Papers*, vols. I–IX; Bradley and Blair, *General's Life*; Forrest C. Pogue, *George C. Marshall*, vols. II–III (New York, 1965–73); Stephen E. Ambrose, *The Supreme Commander: The War Years of General Dwight D. Eisenhower* (Garden City, NY, 1970); and several volumes of the official series, *U.S. Army in World War II*.
4. DM to Howard, Feb. 1, 1951, RG 5, MMBA; *MSFE*, 123, 241; *New York Times*, May 4, 11, 1951; Joseph C. Harsch, "MacArthur Authority Sags . . ." *Christian Science Monitor*, Jan. 22, 1951; Truman, News Conference, May 3, 1951, in Truman, *Public Papers, 1951*, 262; Stephen E. Ambrose, *Ike's Spies: Eisenhower and the Espionage Establishment* (Garden City, NY, 1981), 169–71, 176; Tully, *CIA*, 185–90; Mosley, *Marshall*, 470–72.

5. JCS to DM, Nov. 15, 1950; DM to JCS, Nov. 15, 1950, RG 9, MMBA; *MSFE*, 123.

6. Ints., Willoughby, Jessup, Bond, Pace, Harriman, Fortier; int., Lt. Gen. William W. Quinn, Milner File, DMBP; int., Muccio, 1971, 91–92, HSTL; int., Almond, pt. 4, pp. 66–68, USAMHI; *New York Times*, Mar. 30, 1951; *MSFE*, 18; Appleman, *South to the Naktong*, 757; Tully, *CIA*, 178–83; H. A. DeWeerd, "Lessons of the Korean War," *Yale Review*, 60 (June 1951), 597–601; idem, "Strategic Surprise," 445–52; Truman, *Off the Record*, 303; Griffith, *Chinese People's Liberation Army*, 124–30; Lichterman, "To the Yalu," 612–14; McGovern, *To the Yalu*, 88–90.

7. Willoughby, Brief of "Trends of High-Level Washington Estimates of Chinese Communist Intervention in Korea," Feb. 23, 1951, RG 6, MMBA. In the same file, see also Willoughby to DM, Feb. 22, 23, 1951; and Willoughby's full report covering Aug. 10–Dec. 7, 1950, dated and entitled the same as above ("Trends . . .").

8. Charles A. Willoughby, "The Truth About Korea," *Cosmopolitan*, Dec. 1951, 134.

9. Jim G. Lucas, "An Interview with MacArthur — The Storm It Provoked," *U.S. News & World Report*, 56 (Apr. 20, 1964), 40; Robert Considine, " '54 Interview Reveals Bitter MacArthur," *Washington Post*, Apr. 9, 1964; DM, "General MacArthur Makes His Reply," *Life*, 40 (Feb. 13, 1956), 101; *Chicago Tribune*, Apr. 11, 22, 1964; *London Times*, Apr. 10, 1964; "MacArthur v. Truman," *Time*, 67 (Feb. 20, 1956), 19–20; "Top Secret," *Newsweek*, 47 (Feb. 20, 1956), 31–32; "Heroes," *Time*, 83 (Apr. 17, 1964), 40–41; McGovern, *To the Yalu*, 120–21. Lucas and Considine each interviewed MacArthur in Jan. 1954, but at the general's request publication was withheld until after his death.

10. Andrew Boyle, *The Climate of Treason: Five Who Spied for Russia* (London, 1979), 359; Bruce Page, et al., *The Philby Conspiracy* (Garden City, NY, 1968), 186–89, 192, 216–17, 228; Marshall, "Strategy," 60–61. See also Andrew Boyle, *The Fourth Man* (New York, 1980).

11. Int., Brines; DM to Howard, Feb. 1, 1951, RG 5, MMBA; DM to Milburn P. Akers, July 16, 1950, RG 6, MMBA; DM to DA, RG 9, MMBA; *Nippon Times*, July 17, 1950; Thompson, *Cry Korea*, 100, 191–92; Beech, *Tokyo*, 182–83. Marguerite Higgins of the New York *Herald Tribune* left Japan for Korea shortly after MacArthur lifted his ban on women correspondents in the combat zone on July 19, 1950. *Nippon Times*, July 20, 1950.

12. DM to DA, Sept. 28, 1950, RG 9, MMBA.

13. Ints., Brines, Pringsheim; DM to Collins, Dec. 15, 1950; DM to Howard, Feb. 1, 1951, RG 5, MMBA; Robert U. Brown to DM, Mar. 17, 1951, RG 6, MMBA; DM to DA, Jan. 10, 1951, RG 9, MMBA; *London Times*, Dec. 5, 1950; *New York Times*, Jan. 19, 1951; *Nippon Times*, Jan. 20, 1951; Gay Talese, *The Kingdom and the Power* (New York, 1969), 40.

14. DM to Brown, Jan. 10, 1951, RG 6, MMBA.

15. DM to Stephens, Nov. 16, 1957, RG 21, MMBA.
16. Willoughby, *Aid and Comfort;* idem, "Truth About Korea," 34–37, 133–39; London *Times,* Nov. 29, 1951.
17. Thurgood Marshall, "Summary Justice: The Negro GI in Korea," *The Crisis,* 58 (May 1951), 297–304, 350–54; Jack D. Foner, *Blacks and the Military in American History* (New York, 1974), 190–91; Richard M. Dalfiume, *Desegregation of the U.S. Armed Forces: Fighting on Two Fronts, 1939–1953* (Columbia, MO, 1969), 206–07.
18. Ints., Hickman, Michaelis, Moore, Smith, Almond; int., Milner with Beiderlinden, Milner File, DMBP; Marshall, "Summary Justice," 354–55; Foner, *Blacks,* 188–92; Lee Nichols, *Breakthrough on the Color Front* (New York, 1954), 20–21, 111–17; Dalfiume, *Desegregation,* 201–10; Robert W. Mullen, *Blacks in America's Wars: The Shift in Attitudes from the Revolutionary War to Vietnam* (New York, 1973), 60–61.
19. DM's interview of May 22, 1951, Pittsburgh *Courier,* May 27, June 2, 1951, quoted in *New York Times,* May 28, June 4, 1951; Dalfiume, *Desegregation,* 206; Nichols, *Breakthrough,* 113–14; S. L. A. Marshall, *Bringing up the Rear: A Memoir,* ed. Cate Marshall (San Rafael, CA, 1979), 184–85; Smith, *MacArthur,* 228, 233–34.
20. *New York Times,* Jan. 6, 8, Apr. 5, 1951; U.S. Senate, Foreign Relations and Armed Services committees, *Assignment of Ground Forces of the United States to Duty in the European Area: Hearings . . .* 82d Cong., 1st Sess. (1951) passim; UN General Assembly, Resolution, Feb. 1, 1951, in McNelly, ed., *Sources,* 259–60; Poole, *JCS, 1950–52,* 221–26; *DAFR,* XIII, 13–25; Crabb, *Bipartisan Foreign Policy,* 87–97; Druks, *Truman and the Russians,* 235–39; James T. Patterson, *Mr. Republican: A Biography of Robert A. Taft* (Boston, 1972), 476–81; Ronald J. Caridi, *The Korean War and American Politics: The Republican Party as a Case Study* (Philadelphia, 1968), 135–38; Kaplan, "Korean War and U.S. Foreign Relations," 60–64; Donovan, *Tumultuous Years,* 321–24; Rees, *Korea,* 196; Stairs, *Diplomacy,* 220–29; Fleming, *Cold War,* II, 629–34; Pearson, *Mike,* II, 179–83.
21. Ints., Chiles, Palmer, Michaelis; DM to Ridgway, Feb. 3, 1951; DM to Maj. Gen. Maxwell D. Taylor, Feb. 11, 1951, RG 6, MMBA; Gugeler, *Combat Actions,* 80–136; Leckie, *Conflict,* 222–24; Stone, *Hidden History,* 253–55, 265–66; John Miller, et al., *Korea, 1950–53* (2 vols., Washington, 1952–56), II, 8–16; Griffith, *Chinese People's Liberation Army,* 150–61; S. L. A. Marshall, *Operation Punch and the Capture of Hill 440, Suwon, Korea, February, 1951* (Baltimore, 1952), passim.
22. Ints., Mildren, Michaelis, Almond, Smith, Palmer; Rhee to DM, Mar. 15, 1951; DM to Rhee, Mar. 16, 1951, RG 5, MMBA; Ridgway to DM, Mar. 22, 1951; DM to Ridgway, Mar. 23, 1951, RG 6, MMBA; Stratemeyer to DM, Feb. 16, Mar. 18, 1951, RG 10, MMBA; *MSFE,* 3195; Lichterman, "To the Yalu," 625; Gugeler, *Combat Actions,* 137–43; Middleton, *Korean War,* 171–74; Poats, *Decision,* 145–50, 173–81; Stone, *Hidden History,* 255–59, 264–68; Miller, et al., *Korea,* II, 17–22; Cagle, "Errors," 34–35.

23. Ints., Smith, Mildren, Palmer; Foster, "Bowser," 166–69; Miller, et al., *Korea*, II, 23–26; USMA, *Korea*, 31–35.
24. Ints., Whitney, Smith, Michaelis, Palmer; *Nippon Times*, Jan. 21, 29, Feb. 14, 21, Mar. 8, 25, Apr. 4, 1951; Montross, et al., *USMC in Korea*, IV, 90–92. MacArthur flew to Korea on Feb. 8 but could not land because of a snowstorm, so he returned to Tokyo — a nonstop flight for his Constellation of nearly seven hours. *Nippon Times*, Feb. 10, 1951.
25. Int., Gen. Oliver P. Smith, 235–36, U.S. Marine Corps Historical Center, Washington, D.C.
26. *Nippon Times*, Feb. 21, 1951; Ridgway, *Korean War*, 108, 109.
27. DM to JCS, Feb. 15, 26, 1951; JCS to DM, Feb. 21, Mar. 1, 1951, RG 9, MMBA; *FRUS, 1951*, VII, pt. 1, 221–23; Mark W. Clark, *From the Danube to the Yalu* (New York, 1954), 25–27; Schnabel, *Policy and Direction*, 354. For MacArthur's 16th report to the UN Security Council, dated Mar. 26 and covering operations of Feb. 16–28, 1951, see *MSFE*, 3460–62; UN Security Council, *Official Records*, Suppl. (Jan.– Mar. 1951), Doc. S/2053, Mar. 26, 1951, pp. 53–56.
28. *MSFE*, 920; Schnabel, *Policy and Direction*, 349, 350; Lichterman, "To the Yalu," 625–26.
29. Dr. Frederick Lemere to DM, Dec. 1, 1950, RG 6, MMBA; Lucas, "Interview with MacArthur," 40; Considine, " '54 Interview," Washington *Post*, Apr. 9, 1964; Hanson W. Baldwin, "Atom's Role in Tactics," *New York Times*, June 13, 1950; "Atomic Death Belt Urged in Korea," ibid., Apr. 17, 1951; Akira Iriye, *Across the Pacific: An Inner History of American-East Asian Relations* (New York, 1967), 290; Kolko and Kolko, *Limits*, 603–04, 608; Smith, *MacArthur*, 154–55, 191–92.
30. DM to Brig. Gen. F. R. Zierath, Sept. 7, 1960, RG 21, MMBA; *MSFE*, 77, 260; Chicago *Tribune*, Dec. 24, 1960; Considine, " '54 Interview," Washington *Post*, Apr. 9, 1964; Hewlett and Duncan, *Atomic Shield*, 538–39; Donovan, *Tumultuous Years*, 308–09; Morton H. Halperin, *Limited War in the Nuclear Age* (New York, 1963), 47–50; DM, "Memorandum on Ending the Korean War," Dec. 14, 1952, Whitman Files, Eisenhower Papers.
31. DM, Statement, Feb. 13, 1951, in *MSFE*, 3539; *Nippon Times*, Feb. 15, 21, 1951; *New York Times*, Feb. 14, 1951; Lichterman, "To the Yalu," 626; Smith, *MacArthur*, 125–26.
32. DM, Statement, Mar. 7, 1951, in *MSFE*, 3540–41; *Nippon Times*, Mar. 8, 1951; *New York Times*, Mar. 8, 1951.
33. Gen. Matthew B. Ridgway, Diary, Apr. 3, 1951, Ridgway Papers; *New York Times*, Mar. 6, 1951; London *Times*, Mar. 16, 1951; *Nippon Times*, Apr. 4, 1951; *FRUS, 1951*, VII, pt. 1, 234; Rees, *Korea*, 189; Leckie, *Conflict*, 227–29.
34. London *Times*, Mar. 10, 1951. A work completed too recently to be used in this book is Hakon Osthom, "The First Year of the Korean War: The Road Toward Armistice" (unpublished Ph.D. dissertation, Kent State University, 1982).
35. Hoare, "Truman," 203; Lichterman, "To the Yalu," 626–29; Good-

rich, *Korea*, 169–70, 181; Smith, *Acheson*, 270–72; Haynes, *Awesome Power*, 230–33; McLellan, *Acheson*, 309–10; Richard C. Stebbins, ed., *The United States in World Affairs, 1951* (New York, 1951), 91–93. On the 38th Parallel issue, Feb.–Mar. 1951, see *FRUS, 1951*, VII, pt. 1, 152–251. On the proposed presidential peace overture, see ibid., 246, 251–55, 263–64.

36. JCS to DM, Mar. 20, 1951, RG 6, MMBA (reprinted in *MSFE*, 3541; *FRUS, 1951*, VII, pt. 1, 251).

37. DM to JCS, Mar. 21, 1951, RG 6, MMBA (reprinted in *FRUS, 1951*, VII, pt. 1, 255–56; Schnabel and Watson, *Korean War*, 526).

38. DM, Statement, Mar. 24, 1951, MacArthur Chronology, 1950–51, Lloyd Files, Truman Papers (reprinted in *MSFE*, 3541–42; *New York Times*, Mar. 24, 1951).

39. DM, *Reminiscences*, 387; Whitney, *MacArthur*, 467; Rees, *Korea*, 211; Smith, *MacArthur*, 155–57; Marshall, "Strategy," 206–07; Lee and Henschel, *MacArthur*, 223–26.

40. HST to George M. Elsey, Apr. 16, 1951, George M. Elsey Papers, HSTL; Truman, News Conference, May 17, 1951, in Truman, *Public Papers, 1951*, 287–89; Truman, *Memoirs*, II, 501; Acheson, *Korean War*, 102; Stone, *Hidden History*, 268–71; McGovern, *To The Yalu*, 169–74; Mosley, *Marshall*, 489–92; Kolko and Kolko, *Limits*, 609; Truman, *Off the Record*, 303; "Tricks and Dupes," *Time*, 57 (Apr. 9, 1951), 32; "The Shape of Things," *Nation*, 172 (Mar. 31, 1951), 289; Edward Weintal, "How the General Scooped the President," *Newsweek*, 37 (Apr. 2, 1951), 26, 29; Cochran, *Truman*, 326; Haynes, *Awesome Power*, 250–51; Truman, *Truman*, 511–13.

41. JCS to DM, Mar. 24, 1951, PSF, Truman Papers (reprinted in *MSFE*, 3542).

42. Ints., Willoughby, Whitney; Higgins, *Korea and Fall of MacArthur*, 112; Acheson, *Korean War*, 101.

43. Rep. Joseph W. Martin, Jr., to DM, Mar. 8, 1951, RG 6, MMBA (reprinted in *MSFE*, 3543; *FRUS, 1951*, VII, pt. 1, 298–99); Martin, Speech at Brooklyn, NY, Feb. 12, 1951, in *MSFE*, 3176–79; Joseph W. Martin, with Robert J. Donovan, *My First Fifty Years in Politics* (New York, 1960), 199–212; McGovern, *To the Yalu*, 164, 167–71, 174–75; Kolko and Kolko, *Limits*, 608–09.

44. DM to Martin, Mar. 20, 1951, Official Files, Truman Papers (reprinted in *MSFE*, 3544; *FRUS, 1951*, VII, pt. 1, 299).

45. Bradley, Memorandum for the Record, Apr. 24, 1951, Omar N. Bradley Papers, USAMHI; *New York Times*, Mar. 28, 29, 1951; Truman, *Off the Record*, 207–08, 210–11; DM, *Reminiscences*, 386; Acheson, *Korean War*, 103; Truman, *Memoirs*, II, 506; *MSFE*, 113; Stone, *Hidden History*, 274–76; Poats, *Decision*, 162–64; Middleton, *Korean War*, 178–80; Frazier Hunt, *The Untold Story of Douglas MacArthur* (New York, 1954), 513–14; Cochran, *Truman*, 326; Haynes, *Awesome Power*, 233–34, 251–52; Truman, *Truman*, 513–14; McLellan, *Acheson*, 311; Phillips, *Truman*, 346–47.

46. Hazlitt to DM, Mar. 31, 1951; DM to Hazlitt, Apr. 5, 1951, RG 6, MMBA (reprinted in *MSFE*, 3544); *New York Times*, Apr. 5, 1951; Washington *Evening Star*, Apr. 7, 1951; London *Daily Telegraph*, Apr. 5, 1951, quoted in Acheson, *Korean War*, 103; Truman, *Memoirs*, II, 510. On Mar. 31, 1951, the *New York Times* reported that 120,000 troops were being released from the ROK Army because of insufficient arms.

47. Bradley Memo, Apr. 24, 1951.

48. Int., Harriman; Harry S. Truman, Diary, Apr. 5–6, 1951, PSF, Truman Papers; Bradley Memo, Apr. 24, 1951; Truman, *Memoirs*, II, 507; Bradley and Blair, *General's Life*, 629; Donovan, *Tumultuous Years*, 352–53; Mosley, *Marshall*, 493–94; Phillips, *Truman*, 340–47; Acheson, *Among Friends*, 105.

49. Int., Harriman; Truman Diary, Apr. 7, 1951; Bradley Memo, Apr. 24, 1951; Truman, *Memoirs*, II, 508; Acheson, *Korean War*, 105; Haynes, *Awesome Power*, 253.

50. Int., Collins; Bradley Memo, Apr. 24, 1951; Collins, *War*, 283; Bradley and Blair, *General's Life*, 634.

51. Bradley Memo, Apr. 24, 1951. For Bradley's revision of this memo, dated May 16, 1951, see Bradley and Blair, *General's Life*, 634–35.

52. Int., Collins; Truman Diary, Apr. 8, 1951; Bradley Memo, Apr. 24, 1951; Donovan, *Tumultuous Years*, 353–54; Marshall, *Bringing Up the Rear*, 209–10.

53. Int., Pringsheim; London *Times*, Apr. 7, 1951; London *Observer*, Apr. 8, 1951; Stebbins, ed., *United States in World Affairs, 1951*, 99–100.

54. Ints., Pace, Harriman; int., Almond, pt. 5, pp. 43–44, USAMHI; Acheson, Memorandum of Conversation with Senators McCarran and Bridges, Apr. 10, 1951, Acheson Papers; Bradley Memo, Apr. 24, 1951; Truman Diary, Apr. 9–10, 1951; Truman, *Truman*, 515; Acheson, *Among Friends*, 106; Monte M. Poen, *Strictly Personal and Confidential: The Letters Harry Truman Never Mailed* (Boston, 1982), 55–56; Donovan, *Tumultuous Years*, 355–59; Middleton, *Korean War*, 181–82; Haynes, *Awesome Power*, 254–55; McLellan, *Acheson*, 314.

55. Bradley to DM, Apr. 10, 1951, PSF, Truman Papers (reprinted in *MSFE*, 3546, among many places).

56. Truman, Statement on the Relief of Gen. MacArthur, Apr. 10, 1951, PSF, Truman Papers (reprinted in *MSFE*, 3547, among many places).

57. Ints., Pace, Hull, Beiderlinden; DM Diary, Apr. 9, 1951; *New York Times*, Apr. 10, 1951; *Nippon Times*, Apr. 10, 1951.

58. Int., Almond, pt. 5, p. 43, USAMHI.

59. *New York Times*, Apr. 15, 1951; Washington *Times-Herald*, Jan. 14, 1952. Lowe departed from Tokyo on Apr. 16, 1951, shortly after MacArthur's exit.

60. Int., Whitney; *Nippon Times*, Apr. 12, 1951; DM, *Reminiscences*, 395; Whitney, *MacArthur*, 472; Huff, *My Fifteen Years*, 137.

61. Ints., Hull, Pace; int., Gen. John E. Hull, no. 7, pp. 31–34, USAMHI; Ridgway to DM, Apr. 11, 1951; Ridgway Diary, Apr. 10–13, 1951;

Marshall to Ridgway, Apr. 10, 1951, PSF, Truman Papers; Marshall, *Korean War*, 59, 61.

62. Ridgway, *Soldier*, 223.
63. Ridgway to DM, Apr. 14, 1951, RG 10, MMBA; Lt. Col. William F. Winton, Jr., "Narrative Summary of [Eighth] Army Commander's Activities, 1–14 April 1951," Ridgway Papers; Ridgway Diary, Apr. 14, 1951; Ridgway, *Korean War*, 159; Leckie, *Conflict*, 242–43.
64. Ridgway, Memorandum for Diary, Apr. 12, 1951, Ridgway Papers; DM, *Reminiscences*, 394, 395; Sebald, *With MacArthur*, 229; Ridgway, *Korean War*, 158; Donovan, *Tumultuous Years*, 311–12; Smith, *MacArthur*, 163.
65. *New York Times*, Apr. 12, 13, 1951; Truman, Radio Address to the Nation, Apr. 11, 1951, in Barton J. Bernstein and Allen J. Matusow, eds., *The Truman Administration: A Documentary History* (New York, 1966), 455–61; Bradley and Blair, *General's Life*, 637; Donovan, *Tumultuous Years*, 359–60; Poats, *Decision*, 166–68.
66. Ints., Whitney, Bunker; *New York Times*, Apr. 12, 13, 15, 1951; Huff, *My Fifteen Years*, 137–38; Spanier, *Truman-MacArthur Controversy*, 213; Sebald, *With MacArthur*, 234.
67. Ints., Bond, Williams, Sebald, Bunker; Mrs. Almond to Almond, Apr. 12, 1951, Almond Papers; Sams, "Medic," 722, 724; *Mainichi Daily News*, Oct. 4, 1976; *Nippon Times*, Apr. 17, 1951; *New York Times*, Apr. 16, 1951; Story, "My Air Adventure," 40; Sebald, *With MacArthur*, 235–36; Ridgway, *Korean War*, 159; Huff, *My Fifteen Years*, 138–40; "Homeward Bound," *Time*, 57 (Apr. 23, 1951), 23; "Banzai to MacArthur," *Newsweek*, 37 (Apr. 23, 1951), 28.

CHAPTER XIX. *The Excitement of the Season*

pages 607–40
1. Ayers Diary, Apr. 16, 1951, Ayers Files, Truman Papers; William J. Hopkins to Joseph H. Short, Apr. 26, 1951, Philleo Nash Files, Truman Papers; sundry press items re MacArthur's relief, Apr.–May 1951, MacArthur Folder, PSF, Truman Papers; *New York Times*, Apr. 12, 13, 16, 17, 28, 1951; *Washington Post*, Apr. 12, 13, 16, 17, 1951; *London Times*, Apr. 12, 1951; James F. Reston, "Memorandum to General MacArthur," *New York Times Magazine*, Apr. 12, 1951; "A White House Announcement at 1 A.M.," *Life*, 30 (Apr. 23, 1951), 36–37; "Millions for MacArthur," *Newsweek*, 37 (Apr. 23, 1951), 24; "AFL Longshoremen 'Strike' for MacArthur," *Business Week*, Apr. 21, 1951, 34; Rovere and Schlesinger, *MacArthur Controversy*, 3–9, 12–13; Booth Mooney, *The Politicians, 1945–1960* (Philadelphia, 1970), 118–19; John E. Mueller, *War, Presidents, and Public Opinion* (New York, 1973), 229–30; W. A. Swanberg, *Luce and His Empire* (New York, 1972), 311–16; Hamby, *New Deal*, 424–25. See also Thomas G. Henderson, "Editorial Reaction of Selected Major Indiana Daily Newspapers to a National Controversy — the Truman-MacArthur Conflict" (unpub-

lished Ed.D. dissertation, Ball State Univ., 1977). Cited in the notes
for this chapter is the revised edition of the Rovere and Schlesinger
work, *The MacArthur Controversy and American Foreign Policy,* which
appeared in 1965.

2. Elmo Roper Associates, "A Report and Analysis of the *Saturday Review's* Survey of Correspondents on the Dismissal of Gen. MacArthur" (n.d., c. July 1951), Principal Files, Eisenhower Papers; Elmo Roper and Louis Harris, "The Press and the Great Debate," *Saturday Review of Literature,* 34 (July 15, 1951), 6–9, 29–31.

3. Ints., Lynch, Jones, Dawson, Chiles, Mildren, Palmer, Perez; Gordon W. Prange to Col. S. L. A. Marshall, May 30, 1951, S. L. A. Marshall Papers, University of Texas, El Paso; Willoughby to DM, Apr. 11, 1951; Stratemeyer to DM, Apr. 14, 1951, RG 10, MMBA; Los Angeles *Evening Herald and Express,* Apr. 27, 1951; *New York Times,* Apr. 12, 15, 17, 27, 1951; E. J. Kahn, Jr., "Letter from Korea," *New Yorker,* 27 (Apr. 21, 1951), 122; idem, *The Peculiar War: Impressions of a Reporter in Korea* (New York, 1952), 3–4.

4. Sen. Richard M. Nixon to Dr. John F. Fahey, n.d. (c. May 1951), RG 10, MMBA; *New York Times,* Apr. 12, 13, 21, 23, 27, May 6, 1951; "What They Said," *Time,* 57 (Apr. 23, 1951), 28; "On Trial: Big Men and Big Issues," *Business Week,* May 12, 1951, 26; William Costello, "The Facts About Nixon, Part XI: The MacArthur Affair," *New Republic,* 141 (Dec. 14, 1959), 13; James R. Riggs, "Congress and the Conduct of the Korean War" (unpublished Ph.D. dissertation, Purdue University, 1972), 212–31, 410–11; Patterson, *Mr. Republican,* 486–88; William S. White, *The Taft Story* (New York, 1954), 43; Rovere, *McCarthy,* 12; Russell Kirk and James McClellan, *The Political Principles of Robert A. Taft* (New York, 1967), 174–77.

5. Ints., Willoughby, Fox, Pringsheim, Thomas Wright; Amb. Alan G. Kirk to Acheson, Apr. 13, 1951, Acheson Papers, HSTL; Rhee to DM, Apr. 12, 1951; Yoshida to DM, Apr. 14, 1951, RG 10, MMBA; *Nippon Times,* Apr. 14, 1951; London *Times,* Apr. 12, 13, 1951; *New York Times,* Apr. 12, 13, 20, 21, 24, 29, 1951; Stairs, *Diplomacy,* 230–35; London *Economist,* Apr. 28, 1951; Ernest K. Lindley, "MacArthur and Our Allies," *Newsweek,* 37 (May 21, 1951), 30; "Japan Without MacArthur," *U.S. News & World Report,* 30 (Apr. 20, 1951), 23; miscellaneous articles on world reactions in *Foreign Policy Bulletin,* 30 (Apr. 13–June 22, 1951); Karl L. Rankin, *China Assignment* (Seattle, 1964), 100–01; Odgers, *Parallel,* 189–93; "Foreign Reaction: Cheers, Few Tears," *Newsweek,* 37 (Apr. 23, 1951), 28, 31; "Jubilation — and Foreboding," *Time,* 57 (Apr. 23, 1951), 34; Panikkar, *In Two Chinas,* 133–34; Beloff, *Soviet Policy,* 79.

6. Ints., Wedemeyer, Thomas, Marquardt; int., Shepherd, pp. 43–44, MMBA; Radio Telephone Exchange Between Dulles and MacArthur, Apr. 16, 1951, Dulles Papers; Washington *Post,* Apr. 19, 1951; *New York Times,* Apr. 17, 18, 19, 1951; Story, "My Air Adventure,"

40–41; "The Crowds Cheer," *Newsweek*, 37 (Apr. 30, 1951), 18; DM, *Soldier Speaks*, 241–42; Whitney, *MacArthur*, 482, 483; Huff, *My Fifteen Years*, 140; Donovan, *Tumultuous Years*, 361; McGovern, *To the Yalu*, 182–83; Hunt, *Untold Story*, 520–21; Miller, *Plain Speaking*, 336–37.

7. Ints., Diller, Bunker, Whitney; int., Bunker, Sherrod File, DMBP; *New York Times*, Apr. 20, 1951; Washington *Post*, Apr. 20, 1951; Spanier, *Truman-MacArthur Controversy*, 216.

8. DM, Address to Joint Meeting of Congress, Apr. 19, 1951, in *MSFE*, 3553.

9. Ibid., 3553–57.

10. Ibid., 3557–58. MacArthur's speech to Congress is reprinted in many works, such as DM, *Reminiscences*, 400–05; DM, *Soldier Speaks*, 243–52; *DAFR*, XIII, 26–29; Bernstein and Matusow, eds., *Truman Administration*, 461–69. Copies of the stenographic transcript of the speech can be found in DM Misc. 201 File, CMH; PSF, Truman Papers; and RG 10, MMBA.

11. William Klein to Truman, Apr. 28, 1951, Official Files, Truman Papers; *New York Times*, Apr. 20, 23, 27, 1951; Washington *Post*, Apr. 20, 1951; New York *Herald Tribune*, Apr. 27, 1951; London *Times*, Apr. 21, 1951; "The General Sows Confusion," *Nation*, 172 (Apr. 28, 1951), 388; "The Old Soldier," *Time*, 57 (Apr. 30, 1951), 21, 23; "MacArthur States His Case," *Newsweek*, 37 (Apr. 30, 1951), 19; Donovan, *Tumultuous Years*, 361–62; Rovere and Schlesinger, *MacArthur Controversy*, 15–16; Miller, *Plain Speaking*, 338–39. See also F. W. Haberman, "General MacArthur's Speech: A Symposium of Critical Comment," *Quarterly Journal of Speech*, 37 (Oct. 1951), 321–31; Philip Wylie, "Medievalism and the MacArthurian Legend," ibid. (Dec. 1951), 473–78.

12. Ints., Kades, Bunker, Whitney; *New York Times*, Apr. 20–23, 1951; "The Crowds Cheer," *Newsweek*, 37 (Apr. 30, 1951), 18–19; "The Heartiest Welcome Ever," *Life*, 30 (Apr. 30, 1951), 30–31; Grover A. Whalen, *Mr. New York: The Autobiography of Grover A. Whalen* (New York, 1955), 249–57; Haynes, *Awesome Power*, 257; McGovern, *To the Yalu*, 185–88; Rovere and Schlesinger, *MacArthur Controversy*, 9–10.

13. Truman to Arthur M. Schlesinger, Jr., Nov. 5, 1951; Schlesinger to Truman, Nov. 28, 1951, MacArthur Folder, PSF, Truman Papers; *New York Times*, Apr. 21, 1951; McGovern, *To the Yalu*, 186; "MacArthur Starts a Retail Sales Boom," *Business Week*, May 5, 1951, 22.

14. H. L. Hunt to DM, Apr. 27, 1951, RG 10, MMBA; Baillie, *High Tension*, 226–27; *New York Times*, Apr. 21–22, 24–27, 1951; Truman, News Conference, Apr. 26, 1951, in Truman, *Public Papers, 1951*, 243; Rovere and Schlesinger, *MacArthur Controversy*, 23.

15. Eastwood to Bunker, Apr. 30, 1951, RG 10, MMBA; DM, Address at Soldiers Field, Chicago, Apr. 26, 1951, George Dingledy File, DMBP; *New York Times*, Apr. 27, 28, May 1, 1951; Washington *Post*, May 1, 1951; Larry Daughtrey, "Why They Cut the Umbrella Tree [Mur-

freesboro visit]," *Nashville Tennessean Magazine*, Nov. 21, 1965; "Mac Rolls On," *Life*, 30 (May 7, 1951), 44; Story, "My Air Adventure," 41; Whitney, *MacArthur*, 488.

16. Sen. Richard B. Russell to Marshall, Apr. 13, 14, 1951; Marshall to DM, Apr. 13, 1951; DM to Marshall, Apr. 14, 15, 1951, PSF, Truman Papers; *New York Times*, Apr. 23, 25, 26, 30, 1951; Acheson, *Present*, 524; Rees, *Korea*, 264; John E. Wiltz, "The MacArthur Inquiry, 1951," in Arthur M. Schlesinger, Jr., and Roger Bruns, eds., *Congress Investigates: A Documented History, 1792–1974*, vol. V (New York, 1975), 3593–96, 3630–31; Alan D. Harper, *The Politics of Loyalty: The White House and the Communist Issue, 1946–1952* (Westport, CT, 1969), 215–17; Caridi, *Korean War*, 153–58, 298–99.

17. Marshall to Russell, May 1, 1951, Official Files, Truman Papers; int., H. Alexander Smith, pt. 1, pp. 232–36, *CUOHRO*; *New York Times*, Apr. 26, 1951; McGovern, *To the Yalu*, 194; Arthur M. Schlesinger, Jr., *The Imperial Presidency* (Boston, 1973), 356; William S. White, *Citadel: The Story of the U.S. Senate* (New York, 1956), 246; "Trial by Transcript," *Time*, 57 (May 14, 1951), 52; John E. Wiltz, "The MacArthur Hearings of 1951: The Secret Testimony," *Military Affairs*, 39 (Dec. 1975), 168, 171–72. Vice Adm. Arthur C. Davis of the JCS staff, assisted by Adrian S. Fisher, DS legal adviser, was in charge of the review and censorship of the transcripts of the sessions.

18. Int., Sen. John C. Stennis, June 21, 1977; *New York Times*, May 5, 1951; "Shifts and Middle Ground," *Time*, 57 (May 7, 1951), 23–24. Each of the 14 witnesses except Fisher, Johnson, and Hurley was accompanied by an assistant or staff officer.

19. *MSFE*, 307–08, 324–78, 1368; Wiltz, "MacArthur Inquiry," 3602–03, 3626–27; Sulzberger, *Long Row*, 635, 644; Rees, *Korea*, 265; "What MacArthur Believes In — and Why He Believes It's Best," *Newsweek*, 37 (May 14, 1951), 26; "The General's Case," *Time*, 57 (May 14, 1951), 19–20; Freda Kirchwey, "The General's Sanctuary," *Nation*, 172 (May 12, 1951), 435–36.

20. *MSFE*, 12–21, 39–42, 82, 165–67, 179, 239–42, 246–47; "MSFE–TD," 40–41, 62–64, 74; Wiltz, "MacArthur Inquiry," 3603–04, 3605–09, 3633; Wiltz, "Secret Testimony," 168; Ernest K. Lindley, "Behind the MacArthur Strategy," *Newsweek*, 37 (May 14, 1951), 31; "War to the Death," *New Republic*, 124 (May 14, 1951), 5; Robert E. Osgood, *Limited War: The Challenge to American Strategy* (Chicago, 1957), 177–78; Robert McClintock, *The Meaning of Limited War* (Boston, 1967), 203. Copies of the transcript deletions ("MSFE–TD") are in DMBP and John C. Stennis Collection, MSU, and U.S. Senate Foreign Relations Committee Records, RG 46, NA.

21. *MSFE*, 9, 41–45, 58–60, 69, 81, 135–37, 197–98, 211–12, 218, 251; Wiltz, "MacArthur Inquiry," 3629–30; Arthur M. Schlesinger, Jr., "The Supreme Cavalier," Washington *Post*, Sept. 27, 1964, "Book Week," p. 10.

22. *MSFE*, 32, 52–53, 80–83, 183–86, 211–21, 250; Whitney, *MacArthur*, 509.

23. *MSFE*, 42–43, 81, 263, 297–98; Wiltz, "MacArthur Inquiry," 3605; Osgood, *Limited War*, 174–76.

24. *MSFE*, 31–32, 146, 186, 262–64; "MSFE–TD," 1856, 2506–07; Wiltz, "MacArthur Inquiry," 3627–29.

25. *MSFE*, 76.

26. *MSFE*, 26–28, 53, 69–71, 282–84, 289; Wiltz, "MacArthur Inquiry," 3604; Maxwell D. Taylor, *Swords and Ploughshares* (New York, 1972), 157.

27. *MSFE*, 30, 39–40, 45, 67–68, 82–83, 283. See also William W. Kaufman, "Policy Objectives and Military Action in the Korean War" (Rand Corp. study no. P-286; Santa Monica, CA, 1956).

28. *MSFE*, 12–16, 165–67, 283; Wiltz, "MacArthur Inquiry," 3634.

29. *MSFE*, 324–25, 355, 435; "MSFE–TD," 840, 876, 1272, 1300–02, 1626–30, 1652; Wiltz, "MacArthur Inquiry," 3609–10; "Challenge by Colleagues," *Newsweek*, 37 (June 4, 1951), 18.

30. *MSFE*, 355, 730–32, 745, 751, 892, 898, 1224, 1378–79, 1392, 1401–05, 1441–42, 1503, 1512–15, 1524–25, 1528–31; "MSFE–TD," 2322, 2324–25, 2435–36, 2579–83, 3124, 3469–70, 3524–25, 3952, 4193, 4334–35, 4344–45; Wiltz, "MacArthur Inquiry," 3613–16; Wiltz, "Secret Testimony," 168–71; Harper, *Politics of Loyalty*, 210–12; Fleming, *Cold War*, II, 641–42; Ernest K. Lindley, "The JCS Verdict on MacArthur," *Newsweek*, 37 (June 4, 1951), 19.

31. *MSFE*, 325.

32. *MSFE*, 341, 416–17, 752–53, 878–79, 893, 989–91, 1041–44, 1095, 1138, 1187, 1194–95, 1314–15, 1630, 1791–92, 1862–63, 3192–93, 3665–67; "ABC's of the Big Debate," *U.S. News & World Report*, 30 (May 18, 1951), 20; Wiltz, "MacArthur Inquiry," 3614–15; Haynes, *Awesome Power*, 262–63.

33. *MSFE*, 324, 329–41, 735–38, 1119, 1189, 1216–17, 1239–41, 1300, 1394–97, 1531–33; "JCS Unshaken," *Combat Forces Journal*, I (July 1951), 10–11.

34. *MSFE*, 730.

35. *MSFE*, 1755, 1762–63, 1765–66, 1769–71, 1838–59, 1866–76, 2152, 3217–24; Washington *Post*, June 10, 1951; "Impatient Audience," *Time*, 57 (June 4, 1951), 22; Spanier, *Truman-MacArthur Controversy*, 255–56; Bundy, ed., *Pattern*, 275–89; Coral Bell, "Korea and the Balance of Power," *Political Quarterly*, 25 (Mar. 1954), 22–23; Rovere and Schlesinger, *MacArthur Controversy*, 312–35; Acheson, *Present*, 524–28; McLellan, *Acheson*, 315–18; Wiltz, "MacArthur Inquiry," 3616–20.

36. *MSFE*, 2362–63, 2474, 2514–15, 2604, 2632, 2739, 2744, 2827–45, 2958, 2978–79, 3064–68, 3072–74, 3257; "MSFE–TD," 6865, 7368–69, 7810; Wiltz, "MacArthur Inquiry," 3620–25.

37. *MSFE*, 3162–63, 3558–60, 3659–65; *New York Times*, Aug. 19, 1951.

38. *MSFE*, 3567–3605; London *Times*, Aug. 21, 1951; "MacArthur

Hearings: What Eight Republicans Found," *Time*, 58 (Aug. 27, 1951), 18–19.
39. *MSFE*, 2825–26; *New York Times*, June 21, 1951.
40. *MSFE*, 2826.
41. *New York Times*, May 14, 1951. See also *MSFE*, 946–47.
42. Hopkins to Truman, May 8, 1951, PSF, Truman Papers. For an analysis of Truman's mail about the relief of MacArthur, see Merne A. Harris, "The MacArthur Dismissal: A Study in Political Mail" (unpublished Ph.D. dissertation, University of Iowa, 1966).
43. Wiltz, "MacArthur Inquiry," 3626; George E. Reedy, *The Twilight of the Presidency* (New York, 1970), 51–53. For a good summary of the White House staff's view of the main points of the MacArthur Inquiry, see Theodore Tannenwald, Jr., "Analysis of the MacArthur Hearings" (n.d., c. July 1951), Theodore Tannenwald Papers, HSTL.
As evident from the preceding notes on the hearings, the principal works on the subject are the two essays by Wiltz. Other writings on the inquiry include Rovere and Schlesinger, *MacArthur Controversy*, 177–251; Higgins, *Korea and Fall of MacArthur*, 122–76; Spanier, *Truman-MacArthur Controversy*, 221–56; Goulden, *Korea*, 513–47; Schnabel and Watson, *Korean War*, 546–58, 561–62; Caridi, *Korean War*, 153–75; Acheson, *Present*, 524–28; Rees, *Korea*, 264–83; Collins, *War*, 287–93; Bernard Brodie, *War and Politics* (New York, 1973), 81–91.

CHAPTER XX. *The Periphery of Power*
pages 641–90
1. TAG to DM, July 23, 1948; July 31, 1951, DM Misc. 201 File, MMBA; Sec. of the Army Frank Pace, Jr., to DM, July 8, Oct. 31, 1951; G. A. Sullivan to DM, Nov. 2, 1951; U.S. Senate, Committee on Military Affairs, Report Accompanying S. 1354, Sept. 12, 1945, RG 21, MMBA; *New York Times*, June 11, 13, 1951; Feb. 23, June 3, 12, 18, 1952; "A Question of Subordination," *Time*, 57 (May 14, 1951), 24; "The Political Generals," ibid., 59 (June 23, 1952), 9. In 1967 the *Bataan* was converted into a flying electronic laboratory for NASA. Chicago *Tribune*, July 21, 1967.
2. Whitney, *MacArthur*, 490–91; Huff, *My Fifteen Years*, 141–42. See also DM, *Revitalizing a Nation: A Statement of Beliefs, Opinions and Policies Embodied in the Public Pronouncements of General of the Army Douglas MacArthur*, ed. John M. Pratt (Chicago, 1952).
3. Maury Maverick to Truman, June 15, 1951; George O. Wilson to Truman, June 16, 1951; Harry N. Seay to Truman, June 17, 1951, PSF, Truman Papers; Wood to DM, Apr. 27, 1951; Hunt to DM, May 24, June 6, 1951, RG 10, MMBA; DM, Speech to Texas Legislature, June 13, 1951, in U.S. Senate, *Representative Speeches of General of the Army Douglas MacArthur*, comp. Legislative Reference Service, Library

of Congress (Washington, 1964), 20–26 (also in DM, *Soldier Speaks*, 262–72); Washington *Post*, June 17, 1951; *New York Times*, June 14–17, 26, 1951; Whitney, *MacArthur*, 491–92, 498; "Eyes on Mac-Arthur," *Newsweek*, 37 (June 25, 1951), 17; "A Delightful Trip," *Time*, 57 (June 25, 1951), 21–22; "Texas Unconquered," *New Republic*, 124 (June 25, 1951), 7; John McCully, "Not So Deep in the Heart of Texas," *Nation*, 172 (June 30, 1951), 605–06.

4. Keenan to DM, July 25, 1951; Wood to DM, July 25, 1951; Taft to DM, Aug. 9, 1951, RG 10, MMBA; *New York Times*, June 11, July 26–29, 1951; DM, Speech to Massachusetts Legislature, July 25, 1951, in U.S. Senate, *Speeches*, 27–33 (and Rovere and Schlesinger, *MacArthur Controversy*, 336–44); "MacArthur Blast," *Newsweek*, 38 (Aug. 6, 1951), 15–16; "Logic or Language," *Commonweal*, 54 (Aug. 10, 1951), 421.

5. DM, Speech to Massachusetts Legislature, July 25, 1951, in U.S. Senate, *Speeches*, 30.

6. Taft to DM, Sept. 12, 1951, RG 10, MMBA; DM, Speech at Cleveland, Sept. 6, 1951, in U.S. Senate, *Speeches*, 33–39 (and DM, *Soldier Speaks*, 273–82); DM, Speech at Miami, Oct. 17, 1951, in U.S. Senate, *Speeches*, 39–46; *New York Times*, Aug. 29, Sept. 7, 9, 22, Oct. 18, 19, 1951; Truman, Press Conference, Oct. 18, 1951, in Truman, *Public Papers, 1951*, 584; MacArthur Memorial Foundation, "The MacArthur Memorial" (pamphlet, n.d.), 3, DMBP; Whitney, *MacArthur*, 494; "MacArthur for Taft," *Time*, 58 (Sept. 17, 1951), 25; "A Critic Predicts," ibid. (Oct. 29, 1951), 20; Sulzberger, *Long Row*, 685; Raymond Moley, Jr., *The American Legion Story* (New York, 1966), 298–301.

7. Walter Gates to Truman, Nov. 14, 1951, PSF, Truman Papers; Dr. Horace Greeley, Press Statement, Aug. 4, 1952; Russell B. Corey to Sen. Herbert Lehman, Aug. 6, 1952; Corey to Rep. Emanuel Celler, Aug. 6, 1952, RG 10, MMBA; DM, Speech at Seattle, Nov. 13, 1951, in U.S. Senate, *Speeches*, 47–51; *New York World-Telegram*, Aug. 5, 1952; *New York Times*, Sept. 20, Nov. 14–17, 21, 1951; Richard L. Neuberger, "When MacArthur Remained Silent," *Nation*, 173 (Nov. 24, 1951), 436–37; "The General in Seattle," *Time*, 58 (Nov. 26, 1951), 24–25.

8. DM, Speech at Norfolk, Nov. 18, 1951, in DM, *Soldier Speaks*, 283–84; DM, Speech to Salvation Army Association, New York, Dec. 12, 1951, in ibid., 285–88; DM, Speech at USMA Founders' Day Dinner, New York, Mar. 14, 1952, in U.S. Senate, *Congressional Record*, 83d Cong., 1st Sess. (1953), 99, pt. 2, 2077–78; *New York Times*, Nov. 18, 19, Dec. 7, 13, 29, 1951; Jan. 16, 1952; "Honored," *Newsweek*, 39 (Jan. 28, 1952), 65.

9. Int., Dorris Bankston, Nov. 23, 1983; DM, Speech to Mississippi Legislature, Mar. 22, 1952, in Wilson F. Minor Papers, Special Collections, MSU (reprinted in U.S. Senate, *Speeches*, 51–58); New Orleans *Times-Picayune*, Mar. 24, 1952; *New York Times*, Mar. 23, 24, 1952; "For the Old Folks," *Newsweek*, 39 (Jan. 28, 1952), 44; "MacArthur Speaks

Out," ibid. (Mar. 31, 1952), 21; "Prospect and Retrospect," *Time,* 59 (Mar. 31, 1952), 22; Considine, *It's All News,* 349–50.

10. Taft to DM, May 16, 1952; Dorsey R. Rodney to DM, May 16, 1952, RG 10, MMBA; DM, Speech to Michigan Legislature, May 15, 1952, in U.S. Senate, *Speeches,* 58–65; "The General v. Generals," *Time,* 59 (May 26, 1952), 24; "Citizen MacArthur Speaks Up," *Life,* 32 (May 26, 1952), 41.

11. Int., Whitney; DM, Speech to Michigan Legislature, May 15, 1952, in U.S. Senate, *Speeches,* 59; Donovan, *Tumultuous Years,* 396–97; Goulden, *Korea,* 605–06.

12. Moseley to DM, July 30, 1951, RG 10, MMBA; *New York Times,* Sept. 16, 1951; "MacArthur: Prefers Taft, Likes Ike, Hates Harry," *Newsweek,* 39 (Feb. 25, 1952), 28; Whitney, *MacArthur,* 522–23; Herbert S. Parmet, *Eisenhower and the American Crusades* (New York, 1972), 66; Kirk and McClellan, *Taft,* 174–77; Elmo B. Roper, *You and Your Leaders: Their Actions and Your Reactions, 1936–1956* (New York, 1957), 241–42; Louis Harris, *Is There a Republican Majority? Political Trends, 1952–1956* (New York, 1954), 56–57; Paul T. David, et al., *Presidential Nominating Politics in 1952* (5 vols., Baltimore, 1954), I, 26, 186–87; Martin, *My First Fifty Years,* 168–71.

13. Lar Daly to DM, June 24, 1952; Willoughby to DM, June 23, 1952; Hugh S. Jennings to DM, June 23, 1952; Emer Yeager to DM, Jan. 14, 1952; Whitney, Press Statement, June 23, 1952; Wedemeyer to DM, May 3, 1952; Hunt to Taft, May 31, 1952; Hunt to DM, Feb. 26–July 5, 1952 (16 letters); Stephen Goodyear to DM, June 22, 1952; Bob Munger to Bunker, Aug. 10, 1952, RG 10, MMBA; Indianapolis *Star,* July 23, 1952; *New York Times,* Sept. 25, 1951; Washington *Post,* June 22, 1952; Sept. 9, 1973; "Unfading Old Soldier," *Time,* 59 (Feb. 11, 1952), 19; Whitney, *MacArthur,* 523–25; Ralph L. Roy, *Apostles of Discord: A Study of Organized Bigotry and Disruption on the Fringes of Protestantism* (Boston, 1953), 118–19, 124–26, 294–97, 329–31; David, et al., *Nominating Politics,* II, 33–34; Patterson, *Mr. Republican,* 549; Robert A. Divine, *Foreign Policy and U.S. Presidential Elections,* vol. II, *1952–1960* (New York, 1974), 61–62; William Manchester, *American Caesar: Douglas MacArthur, 1880–1964* (Boston, 1978), 685–86.

14. Fellers to DM, Mar. 13, 1952; Christine Perry to Sen. Owen Brewster, Feb. 24, 1952; Brewster to DM, Feb. 27, 1952; Sen. Harry P. Cain to DM, July 4, 1952; Rep. Carroll D. Kearns to DM, June 24, 1952; Wood to DM, May 2, June 11, 1952; Hoover to DM, May 12, 1952, RG 10, MMBA; *New York Times,* Mar. 2, Apr. 12, 1952; "Who's for Whom," *Time,* 59 (Mar. 10, 1952), 24; Barton J. Bernstein, "Election of 1952," in Schlesinger, ed., *Presidential Elections,* IV, 3227–29; Peter Lyon, *Eisenhower: Portrait of the Hero* (Boston, 1974), 459–60; Parmet, *Eisenhower,* 54–82; David, et al., *Nominating Politics,* I, 32–33, 54; II, 37, 271; IV, 137, 168; Sulzberger, *Long Row,* 733–34; Patterson, *Mr. Republican,* 529–31, 551; Blanche W. Cook, *The Declassified Eisenhower: A Divided Legacy* (Garden City, NY, 1981), 100–10.

15. Ints., Whitney, Wedemeyer, Marquardt; int., Lt. Gen. Leslie R. Groves, 13–14, MMBA; Haskell L. Nichols to DM, June 20, 1952; DM to Nichols, June 20, 1952; J. E. Dooley to DM, July 8, 1952; Kenneth Colegrove to Bunker, Aug. 11, 1952; Cain to DM, July 4, 1952; Wood to DM, July 8, 1952, RG 10, MMBA; Chicago *Tribune*, Apr. 10, 1964; *New York Times*, June 11, 15, July 8, 1952; Truman, Informal Remarks, Oct. 3, 11, 21, 1952, in Truman, *Public Papers, 1952–53*, 654, 694, 905; DM, Speech at Chicago, July 7, 1953, in U.S. Senate, *Speeches*, 65–74; Republican National Committee, *Official Report of the Proceedings of the Twenty-fifth Republican National Convention; Held in Chicago, Illinois, July 7–11, 1952* (Washington, 1952), 66–76; Whitney, *MacArthur*, 526–31; Roseboom, *Presidential Elections*, 508–13; Clay Blair, Jr., *MacArthur* (New York, 1977), 353–54; Patterson, *Mr. Republican*, 547–66, 570–71; Parmet, *Eisenhower*, 83–101; Walter Johnson, *1600 Pennsylvania Avenue: Presidents and the People Since 1929* (Boston, 1963 [1st ed., 1960]), 247–52; Bernstein, "Election of 1952," 3229–34; Manchester, *American Caesar*, 686, 688; Roper, *Leaders*, 116–17; Lyon, *Eisenhower*, 468–72; Sulzberger, *Long Row*, 769–71; Dwight D. Eisenhower, *Mandate for Change, 1953–1956* (Garden City, NY, 1963), 40; Considine, *It's All News*, 350–51; Blaik, *Blaik Story*, 494–95; Milton Friedman, "MacArthur Patriots," *Nation*, 175 (July 19, 1952), inside cover; Eaton, *Presidential Timber*, 432–53; Nixon, *Leaders*, 127–30. Fred L. Coogan of Oklahoma gave the nominating speech for MacArthur for the presidential nomination, with seconding speeches by McGinnis Hatfield of West Virginia and Thomas W. Thompson of Georgia.

16. Patrick J. Hurley to DM, Oct. 16, 1952; Hunt to DM, July 19, 1952; McCormick to DM, July 24, 1952; Taft to DM, July 18, 1952; Wedemeyer to DM, Aug. 11, 22, Sept. 18, Oct. 21, 1952, RG 10, MMBA; New York *World-Telegram*, Aug. 9, 1961; Whitney, *MacArthur*, 532; Emmet J. Hughes, *The Ordeal of Power: A Political Memoir of the Eisenhower Administration* (New York, 1963), 36.

17. Parmet, *Eisenhower*, 144–45, 150–57; Truman, *Memoirs*, II, 575–76, 583–85; Goulden, *Korea*, 624–26; Bernstein, "Election of 1952," 3257–66; Matthew E. Mantell, "Opposition to the Korean War: A Study in American Dissent" (unpublished Ph.D. dissertation, New York University, 1973), 195–234; Eisenhower, Campaign Speech on Korea, Oct. 24, 1952, in Bernstein and Matusow, eds., *Truman Administration*, 483–87; Caridi, *Korean War*, 209–45; Norman A. Graebner, *The New Isolationism: A Study in Politics and Foreign Policy Since 1950* (New York, 1956), 100–01.

18. Wedemeyer to DM, Dec. 8, 1952, RG 10, MMBA; Eisenhower to DM, Dec. 7, 1952; DM to Eisenhower, Dec. 7, 1952 (also in DM, *Reminiscences*, 409); Bradley to DM, Dec. 16, 1952; DM to Bradley, Dec. 16, 1952 (also in DM, *Reminiscences*, 412–13); Eisenhower to DM, Dec. 10, 1952, RG 21, MMBA; DM, "Memorandum on Ending the Korean War," Dec. 14, 1952, Whitman Files, Eisenhower Papers (also in

RG 21, MMBA, and DM, *Reminiscences,* 410–12); DM, Speech to 57th Congress of American Industry, New York, Dec. 5, 1952, in U.S. Senate, *Speeches,* 75–80; *New York Times,* Dec. 6, 11–13, 1952; Truman, Press Conference, Dec. 11, 1952, in Truman, *Public Papers, 1952– 53,* 1073–76; Sherman Adams, *Firsthand Report* (New York, 1961), 47– 48; James E. Pollard, "Truman and the Press: Final Phase, 1951–53," *Journalism Quarterly,* 30 (Summer 1953), 283; Alfred Steinberg, *The Man from Missouri: The Life and Times of Harry S. Truman* (New York, 1962), 417; "Ike Sure of Korean Results As He Settles Down at Home," *Newsweek,* 40 (Dec. 22, 1952), 15–16; "Businessman at Bat," ibid. (Dec. 15, 1952), 74.

19. DM, "Memorandum on Ending the Korean War," Dec. 14, 1952, Whitman Files, Eisenhower Papers.

20. Int., Eisenhower; int., Dwight D. Eisenhower, 8–9, Dulles Oral History Coll., Princeton; Eisenhower to DM, Jan. 19, 1952; DM to Eisenhower, Jan. 29, 1952, Principal Files, Eisenhower Papers; *New York Times,* Dec. 11, 18, 1952; DM, *Reminiscences,* 412, 414; Goulden, *Korea,* 628–29; Parmet, *Eisenhower,* 158, 195, 299, 303; Blaik, *Blaik Story,* 495–98, 505–08; "Electors Are Counted and So Is MacArthur," *Life,* 33 (Dec. 29, 1952), 18–19; "Two Old Soldiers," *Time,* 60 (Dec. 29, 1952), 10; "Meeting with Ike," *Newsweek,* 40 (Dec. 29, 1952), 13; Lyon, *Eisenhower,* 498–500; Eisenhower, *Mandate,* 180; Considine, *It's All News,* 351–55; Charles C. Alexander, *Holding the Line: The Eisenhower Era, 1952–1961* (Bloomington, IN, 1975), 35; John R. Beal, *John Foster Dulles: A Biography* (New York, 1957), 181–84.

21. Ints., Kades, Vining, Whitney; Julius Ochs Adler, Talk with Gen. MacArthur, May 23, 1951, 1–2, Arthur Krock Papers, Princeton; Mrs. DM to Mrs. Caldwell, June 21, 1965, RG 10, MMBA; *Nippon Times,* Aug. 23, 1951; Fort Wayne (IN) *Journal-Gazette,* Jan. 17, 1960; *New York Times,* Apr. 23, June 1, 21, 1951; June 22, 1960; Jan. 27, 1964; Jan. 27, 1967; Blaik, *Blaik Story,* 525; Nixon, *Leaders,* 90; Murphy, *Diplomat,* 340; Rep. W. J. Bryan Dorn, Remarks, Jan. 18, 1960, in U.S. House, *Congressional Record,* 86th Cong., 2d Sess. (1960), 106, pt. 1, A424. McCarthy's "Voice of America" probe in 1953 was directed largely in the Waldorf Towers suite of the parents of G. David Schine, one of the senator's key assistants. Harvey Matusow, *False Witness* (New York, 1955), 208.

22. Ints., Kenney, Whitney, Bunker, Wedemeyer, Harriman, Vining, Almond, Sams, Hickman; int., Almond, pt. 6, pp. 6–7, USAMHI; Adler, Talk with MacArthur, May 23, 1951, 2, Krock Papers; *Chicago Tribune,* Feb. 13, 1961; *New York Times,* May 13, 27, Aug. 20, Sept. 19, 1951; Apr. 23, May 27, 1952; Dec. 4, 1954; "International," *Newsweek,* 44 (Nov. 15, 1954), 50; "Dogwoods and Ball Games," *Time,* 57 (May 21, 1951), 24; "People," ibid., 65 (Jan. 24, 1955), 34; "Reunion at the Waldorf," ibid., 66 (Sept. 12, 1955), 27; "Wonderful Figure," *New Yorker,* 27 (June 10, 1951), 24–25; DM, *Soldier Speaks,* 321–22; Blaik, *Blaik Story,* 297, 299–300, 521–27; Whitney, *Mac-*

Arthur, 546–47; Vining, *Quiet Pilgrimage*, 258; Considine, *It's All News*, 359; Yoshida, *Memoirs*, 120–23; Murphy, *Diplomat*, 340–41.

23. Ints., Bunker, Burke, Dawson, West, Struble, Whitney; Gen. Clyde D. Eddleman, June 29, 1971; int., Maj. Gen. Hugh Milton, no. 8, pp. 43–44, USAMHI; L. J. Sverdrup to DM, Sept. 16, 1949; Nov. 14, 1951; DM to Sverdrup, Oct. 7, 1949; Sverdrup to Bunker, Dec. 27, 1951; Invitation List, MacArthur's Birthday Party, Jan. 1952, RG 5, MMBA; Sverdrup to DM, July 27, 1951; Gen. Lyman L. Lemnitzer to DM, Jan. 25, 1960; DM to Lemnitzer, Jan. 26, 1960, RG 10, MMBA; Membership List and By-Laws of MacArthur Commemorative Dinner Group, Oct. 1966, Barbey Papers, Naval History Div.; Attendees at MacArthur Birthday Dinner, Jan. 26, 1967, Sherrod File, DMBP; Eisenhower to DM, Jan. 18, 1960; DM to Eisenhower, Jan. 26, 1960, PSF, Eisenhower Papers; Ft. Wayne (IN) *Journal-Gazette*, Jan. 17, 1960; *New York Times*, Jan. 26 or 27 issue annually, 1952–64; Chicago *Tribune*, Jan. 27, 1963; Egeberg, "MacArthur," 171; DM, *Soldier Speaks*, 366–67; "Five-Star Feast," *Newsweek*, 47 (Feb. 6, 1956), 29; "Salad Days," ibid., 63 (Feb. 10, 1964), 48; " 'Old Soldier' MacArthur Passes the 80-Year Mark," *U.S. News & World Report*, 48 (Feb. 8, 1960), 22; "Salute to a Soldier at 80," *Life*, 48 (Feb. 8, 1960), 119; Eisenhower, Statement on MacArthur's 80th Birthday, Jan. 26, 1960, in Eisenhower, *Public Papers, 1960–61*, 124. MacArthur's speech at the reunion dinner in Jan. 1959 is on tape and transcribed in DCJ int. with Dawson, MSU. The only civilian to attend a dinner was Hoover in Jan. 1960. Adm. Arleigh A. Burke was the only regular member of the dinner group who had not served under MacArthur. *New York Times*, Jan. 26, 1960; int., Burke.

24. Ints., Bunker, Whitney, Vining, Kenney, Stratemeyer, Egeberg, Kades, Bowser; Sherrod to Mrs. DM, May 9, 1967, Sherrod File, DMBP; Mrs. DM to Dulles, Dec. 23, 1952, Dulles Papers; Washington *Post*, Apr. 20, May 1, 1951; *Nippon Times*, Aug. 23, 1951; *New York Times*, Apr. 20, 21, 30, May 1, June 21, 1951; Jan. 18, Nov. 14, 1953; "Man of the Hour," *Time*, 57 (May 7, 1951), 25; John G. Rodgers, "The General's Widow," *Parade Magazine*, Mar. 12, 1967, 12–13; Whitney, *MacArthur*, 546.

25. Ints., Egeberg, Whitney, Bunker, Vining, Kenney; Prof. Henry F. Graff, July 13, 1977; Frank H. Mills to Arthur MacArthur, Apr. 20, 1951; Alexander C. Young to Arthur MacArthur, Apr. 23, 1951; Jim Russo to Arthur MacArthur, Apr. 28, 1951, RG 10, MMBA; Van Zandt to DM, June 19, 1952; DM to Van Zandt, June 23, 1952, RG 10, MMBA; *Nippon Times*, Aug. 23, 1951; Washington *Post*, Apr. 20, 1951; *New York Times*, Apr. 21–24, May 9, 16, 28, June 1, 1951; Washington *Daily News*, Apr. 8, 1964; "Reunion," *Newsweek*, 37 (June 11, 1951), 50; "Newsmakers," ibid., 44 (Aug. 9, 1954), 44; " 'The Sergeant' Discovers U.S.," *Life*, 30 (Apr. 30, 1951), 28–29; DM, *Reminiscences*, 408.

26. Blaik, *Blaik Story*, 526.

27. Int., Groves, 9–10, MMBA; Willoughby to DM, Aug. 5, 1952; Bunker
to Edward S. Shattuck, Aug. 14, 1952; J. R. Smith to DM, Aug. 2,
1952; Bridges to DM, Aug. 11, 1952, RG 10, MMBA; *Nippon Times*,
Dec. 26, 1949; May 31, 1950; *Mainichi Daily News*, June 1, 1951; *New
York Times*, Apr. 13, 1951; Aug. 1, 1952; "Businessman MacArthur,"
Newsweek, 40 (Aug. 11, 1952), 24; "The Military Businessman," *Fortune*, 46 (Sept. 1952), 128, 130; Whitney, *MacArthur*, v. MacArthur
allegedly vetoed a guest appearance by Truman on the television
program "What's My Line?" when it was sponsored by Sperry Rand.
New York Times, Apr. 4, 1967.
28. E. L. Parker to DM, Apr. 16, 1959; DM to Parker, Apr. 22, 1959;
Col. William C. Lucas to DM, June 15, 1959; Merrill Lynch, Pierce,
Fenner and Smith, Stock Comment No. 128, Apr. 1, 1959, RG 10,
MMBA; Memphis *Commercial Appeal*, Aug. 17, 1967.
29. Int., Kades; Dunn to Sherrod, May 9, 1967, Sherrod File, DMBP;
Chicago *Tribune*, Oct. 11, 1964; Dorn, Remarks, Jan. 18, 1960, in U.S.
House, *Congressional Record*, 86th Cong., 2d Sess. (1960), 106, pt.1,
A424–25; "Loud Minority Voice," *Newsweek*, 42 (Aug. 10, 1953), 66;
"The General and the Heckler," *Time*, 66 (Aug. 10, 1955), 88, 90;
"Old Soldiers Sometimes Buy," ibid., 64 (Aug. 9, 1954), 71; Carol M.
Petillo, "Douglas MacArthur and Manuel Quezon: A Note on an Im-
perial Bond," *Pacific Historical Review*, 48 (Feb. 1979), 107–17; idem,
Douglas MacArthur: The Philippine Years (Bloomington, IN, 1981), 204–
11. MacArthur sold $1,040,000 worth of stock in Consolidated Mines,
Inc. (engaged in Philippine gold mining) on the Manila exchange in
Sept. 1955. According to Norfolk, VA, court records, the inventory
and appraisal of MacArthur's personal estate in 1964 showed his largest
holding in bonds as $176,295 worth of Los Angeles Metro Trust Au-
thority bonds and his largest holding in stocks as $180,259 worth of
General Motors Corp. common stock (2205 shares). *New York Times*,
Sept. 18, 1955; Oct. 11, 1964.
30. Int., Whitney; int., Groves, 8–9, MMBA; *New York Times*, Nov. 12,
1952; "People," *Time*, 65 (Jan. 24, 1955), 34; Fort Wayne (IN) *Journal-Gazette*, Jan. 17, 1960; Considine, *It's All News*, 352–53.
31. Int., Sams; int., Groves, 7–13, MMBA; J. R. McMicking to DM, June
4, 1959; DM to McMicking, June 9, 1959; W. C. Schmidt to DM, June
3, 1959, RG 10, MMBA; *New York Times*, Oct. 8, 1955; "Businessmen
in the News," *Fortune*, 53 (Feb. 1956), 60.
32. Int., Groves, 9–10, MMBA.
33. DM to Fred C. Riley, May 4, 1959, RG 10, MMBA; Eisenhower, Pre-
Press Conference Notes, July 31, 1957, Whitman Files, Eisenhower
Papers; DM, Speech to the Society for the Advancement of Management, New York, Sept. 14, 1963, RG 21, MMBA; DM, Speech to
Sperry Rand Corp. Stockholders' Meeting, New York, July 30, 1957,
in DM, *Soldier Speaks*, 323–37; Whitney, *MacArthur*, 532–35; Eisenhower, Farewell Address to the American People, Jan. 17, 1961, in
Eisenhower, *Public Papers, 1960–61*, 1035–40; Nixon, *Leaders*, 93;

"Plain Talk from the General," *Nation*, 185 (Aug. 17, 1957), 62; Samuel P. Huntington, *The Soldier and the State: The Theory and Politics of Civil-Military Relations* (Cambridge, MA, 1957), 361–64; Maureen Mylander, *The Generals* (New York, 1974), 280.

34. DM, Speech to Episcopal Diocese, Los Angeles, Jan. 26, 1955, in U.S. Senate, *Speeches*, 80–82 (and DM, *Soldier Speaks*, 308–11); DM, Speech at MacArthur Park, Los Angeles, Jan. 26, 1955, in U.S. Senate, *Speeches*, 82–84; *New York Times*, Jan. 26, 27, 1955; Gustave O. Arlt, ed., "Los Angeles Pays Tribute to General Douglas MacArthur," *Quarterly of the Historical Society of Southern California*, 37 (Mar. 1955), 3–22.

35. Louis B. Mayer to Eisenhower, Feb. 8, 1955; Judge Roger A. Pfaff to Eisenhower, Feb. 14, 1955, PSF, Eisenhower Papers; DM, Speech to American Legion, Los Angeles, Jan. 26, 1955, in U.S. Senate, *Speeches*, 80–84 (also in DM, *Soldier Speaks*, 312–20; *Vital Speeches*, 21 [Feb. 15, 1955], 1040–43); "What MacArthur Didn't Tell," *Christian Century*, 72 (Feb. 23, 1955), 227–28; "The General's Moment," *Newsweek*, 45 (Feb. 17, 1955), 22; "Notes and Comment," *New Yorker*, 30 (Feb. 5, 1955), 21–22; John Cogley, "The MacArthur Speech," *Commonweal*, 61 (Feb. 25, 1955), 550; "As Young as Your Faith," *Time*, 65 (Feb. 7, 1955), 14; David Lawrence, "Yes, We Can Abolish War!" *U.S. News & World Report*, 38 (Feb. 11, 1955), 132. MacArthur first quoted Ullman's essay in a speech at a Remington Rand officials' dinner in Nov. 1952. Samuel Ullman (1840–1924) was born in France, came to the U.S. in the 1850s, and became a merchant and educational leader in Natchez, MS, and later Birmingham, AL. *New York Times*, Nov. 12, 1952; Natchez (MS) *Democrat*, Aug. 4, 5, 1982.

36. DM, Speech at Football Hall of Fame Dinner, New York, Dec. 1, 1959, in DM, *Soldier Speaks*, 338–43; *New York Herald Tribune*, May 31, 1963; *New York Times*, Apr. 30, 1954; July 1, 1958; Dec. 2, 1959; May 20, 1961; Nov. 9, 13, 1962; U.S. Senate, *Speeches*, 104; "MacArthur Carries the Ball," *Sports Illustrated*, Dec. 14, 1959, 26, 28; "Two Generals' Views of Humor," *Life*, 45 (Nov. 10, 1958), 45. The Order of Lafayette consists of U.S. officers who served in France in World War I or II.

37. Int., Graff; George W. Hibbitt to DM, June 6, 1962; John G. Palfrey to DM, July 2, 1962; Arnold A. Saltzman to DM, Oct. 31, 1962; Columbia College Luncheon Program Honoring Gen. MacArthur and List of Guests, Apr. 19, 1963, RG 21, MMBA; DM, Commencement Address at Michigan State Univ., June 11, 1961, in U.S. Senate, *Speeches*, 90–95; DM, Speech to Columbia College Luncheon, Apr. 19, 1963, RG 21, MMBA (also in DM, *Soldier Speaks*, 361–65); Michigan State Univ., "Commencement, 1961" (pamphlet; Lansing, MI, 1961), RG 21, MMBA; Chicago *Tribune*, Apr. 20, 1963. Columbia University conferred an LL.D. on MacArthur in 1947 (given to him in 1958).

38. Joseph Fearon to DM, Aug. 8, 1952, RG 10, MMBA; Robert T. Ross to DM, Oct. 18, 1955; Byrd to DM, Apr. 13, 1953; DM to Byrd, Apr.

19, 1953, RG 21, MMBA; Washington *Times-Herald,* Jan. 14, 1952; Oct. 21, 1955; Washington *Daily News,* Jan. 25, 1952; Oct. 20, 1955; Washington *Post,* Mar. 25, Oct. 20, 21, 1955; St. Louis *Post-Dispatch,* Apr. 24, 1953; *New York Times,* Nov. 29, 30, 1951; Apr. 25, 1953; Mar. 24, Oct. 20, 1955; Rep. Lawrence E. Smith, Remarks, Jan. 14, 30, 1952, in U.S. House, *Congressional Record,* 82d Cong., 2d Sess. (1952), 98, pt. 8, A92, A521–22; Cain, Remarks, Jan. 28, 1952, in U.S. Senate, ibid., 527–30; Willoughby, "Truth about Korea," 34–37, 133–39; "For History and Leverage," *Time,* 61 (May 4, 1953), 22; "Real Story of MacArthur and the Russians," *U.S. News & World Report,* 39 (Oct. 28, 1955), 31–36; "The Yalta Story: MacArthur's Role," *Newsweek,* 45 (Apr. 11, 1955), 34; Neal Stanford, "Yalta Lessons for Pentagon," *Foreign Policy Bulletin,* 35 (Dec. 1, 1955), 43; "MacArthur and Yalta," *Commonweal,* 63 (Nov. 4, 1955), 109; DM, *Reminiscences,* 261–62; James, *MacArthur,* II, 763–65. The Yalta controversy was stirred anew by the DS volume of 1955, *The Conferences at Malta and Yalta, 1945.*

39. Ints., Willoughby, Whitney, Marquardt; Col. John M. Kemper, July 13, 1971; Willoughby to DM, Nov. 22, 1951; Aug. 5, 7, Sept. 17, 1952; Maj. Gen. Orlando Ward to Willoughby, July 15, 1952; Willoughby to Almond, Nov. 29, 1971; numerous articles by Willoughby in *Foreign Intelligence Digest,* 1966–71, in re *Reports of General MacArthur,* RG 10, MMBA; Sherrod, Notebook, Apr.–May 1967, Sherrod File, DMBP; Dr. Stanley L. Falk to Acting Chief of Military History, Apr. 22, 1959; Falk to DCJ, Mar. 12, 1979, DMBP; *New York Times,* Nov. 14, 1952; *MSFE,* 285–86, 294–95; Charles A. Willoughby, "The MacArthur Reports" (pamphlet; Washington, 1966); Truman, Press Conference, Nov. 20, 1952, in Truman, *Public Papers, 1952–53,* 1059; Jerome Forrest and Clarke H. Kawakami, "General MacArthur and His Vanishing War History," *Reporter,* 8 (Oct. 14, 1952), 20–25.

40. Cagle to DM, Feb. 28, 1956; DM to Cagle, Mar. 19, 1956, Naval Historical Center; int., DM, DM Misc. 201, CMH; Snedeker to DM, Feb. 7, Mar. 5, 1956; May 31, 1957; DM to Snedeker, Feb. 24, Oct. 17, 1956; June 6, 1957; Stephens to DM, Oct. 8, Nov. 25, 1957; DM to Stephens, Oct. 18, Nov. 15, 1957, RG 21, MMBA.

41. Among these works of 1952–63 were Wildes, *Typhoon in Tokyo;* Kawai, *Japan's American Interlude;* Whiting, *China Crosses the Yalu;* Montross, et al., *U.S. Marine Operations in Korea, 1950–53,* vols. I–IV; Field, *History of U.S. Naval Operations: Korea;* Cagle and Manson, *The Sea War in Korea;* Futrell, *The United States Air Force in Korea, 1950–53;* Appleman, *South to the Naktong, North to the Yalu;* Spanier, *The Truman-MacArthur Controversy and the Korean War;* Higgins, *Korea and the Fall of MacArthur;* Lee and Henschel, *Douglas MacArthur;* Hunt, *The Untold Story of Douglas MacArthur.*

42. Ints., Willoughby, Whitney, Bunker, Williams; Eichelberger to Samuel Milner, Nov. 10, 1954, Gen. Robert L. Eichelberger Misc. 201 File, CMH; C. D. Jackson to Whitney, May 5, 1955; Whitney to Jackson,

May 10, 1955; Jackson to Cal Whipple, Sept. 13, 1955, C. D. Jackson Papers, DDEL; DM to Pres., McGraw-Hill Book Co., Jan. 15, 1954, RG 21, MMBA; Sherrod to DCJ, Nov. 16, 1971; Charleston (SC) *News-Courier*, Mar. 3, 1964; Hanson W. Baldwin, "Gen. MacArthur's Decade of Glory," *New York Times*, Oct. 3, 1954; idem, "With MacArthur in War and Peace," ibid., Jan. 22, 1956; Morton, "Willoughby on MacArthur," 46; S. L. A. Marshall, "Apologia for Doug," *Saturday Review*, 37 (Oct. 9, 1954), 12–13; idem, "The Commander's Case," 14–15; Rovere and Schlesinger, *MacArthur Controversy*, 253–64; Willoughby and Chamberlain, *MacArthur*, vi–vii; James A. Field, Jr., review of *MacArthur, 1941–51*, *American Historical Review*, 60 (Apr. 1955), 630; H. A. DeWeerd, review of *MacArthur: Rendezvous with History*, ibid., 62 (Oct. 1956), 163–65; Robert F. Cocklin, combined review of Willoughby and Chamberlain's book and Whitney's, *Military Affairs*, 20 (Winter 1956), 235–36.

43. DM to Almond, Apr. 28, 1952, Almond Papers; London *Times*, Apr. 9, 10, 1964; Los Angeles *Times*, May 4, 1952; New York *Journal-American*, Apr. 8, Nov. 19, 1964; New York *World-Telegram*, Apr. 8, 1964; Washington *Post*, Apr. 9, 14, 1964; *New York Times*, Jan. 10, 1953; Feb. 9, 1956; Apr. 9, 10, Dec. 1, 1964; Chicago *Tribune*, Jan. 26, Dec. 23–25, 1960; Apr. 11, Nov. 16, 1964; Wabash (IN) *Plain Dealer*, Dec. 23, 1960; Lucas, "Interview with MacArthur," 40–41; R. A. Aurthur, "Harry Truman Chuckles Dryly," *Esquire*, Sept. 1971, 136–39, 256–62; "MacArthur v. Truman," *Time*, 67 (Feb. 20, 1956), 19–20; "The President's Week," ibid., 84 (Nov. 20, 1964), 70–71; "Heroes," ibid., 83 (Apr. 17, 1964), 40–41; Harry S. Truman, "The Recall of Gen. MacArthur," *Life*, 40 (Feb. 13, 1956), 66–93; DM, "Gen. MacArthur Makes His Reply," ibid., 94–108; "Here Is What MacArthur Really Meant," ibid., 56 (Apr. 24, 1964), 4; "Top Secret," *Newsweek*, 47 (Feb. 20, 1956), 31–32; "The Crossing of the Yalu," *National Review*, 16 (May 5, 1964), 342–44; Truman, *Off the Record*, 322–24; Considine, *It's All News*, 355–57.

44. Telephone Conversation Between Eisenhower and MacArthur, June 11, 1960, Whitman Files, Eisenhower Papers; DM, Press Statement, Jan. 31, 1953; Sen. Everett M. Dirksen to John F. McCullough, Aug. 24, 1959; McCullough to DM, Aug. 26, 1959; DM to McCullough, Aug. 26, 1959, RG 21, MMBA; DM to Prof. Duane M. Diedrich, Oct. 17, 1960, Duane M. Diedrich File, DMBP; Chicago *Tribune*, Sept. 6, 1959; London *Times*, Mar. 19, 1954; *New York Times*, June 9, 1953; Mar. 17, 19, 25, 1954; Oct. 24, 1960; Eisenhower, Press Conference, Mar. 24, 1954, in Eisenhower, *Public Papers, 1954*, 348; Eisenhower, Remarks at Manila Airport, June 14, 1960, in ibid., *1960–61*, 477; "Old Soldiers . . . New Problems," *U.S. News & World Report*, 36 (Mar. 26, 1954), 18; Martin, *My First Fifty Years*, 230–31; Sulzberger, *Long Row*, 957–58.

45. Nixon to DM, June 21, 1960; DM to Nixon, June 21, 1960, RG 21, MMBA; Nixon, *Leaders*, 91. The Grand Cordon was presented to

MacArthur by Consul-Gen. Mitsuo Tanaka in a ceremony at the General's Waldorf suite on June 21, 1960. Consul-Gen. Mitsuo Tanaka to DM, June 17, 1960; Tanaka, Press Release, June 17, 1960; Remarks by Tanaka and MacArthur at Grand Cordon Ceremony, June 21, 1960, RG 21, MMBA.

46. Rhee to DM, Sept. 16, 1955; DM to Rhee, Sept. 16, 1955; Guy D. Newman to DM, Apr. 5, 1962; DM to Newman, Apr. 17, 1962, RG 21, MMBA; DA, Press Release on "The MacArthur Story," Nov. 21, 1958, DM Misc. 201, CMH; W. Fred Duckworth, "The MacArthur Memorial Foundation Program" (brochure, n.d. [c. 1964]), DMBP; New York *Herald Tribune,* May 31, 1963; *New York Times,* Jan. 28, May 6, 1952; Oct. 28, 1956; Apr. 28, Sept. 15, Nov. 7, 1957; Jan. 24, 1958; Feb. 21, 1961; Feb. 4, Apr. 11, 1962; May 25, 1963; "Man of 1951," *Newsweek,* 39 (Jan. 7, 1952), 30. On MacArthur's honors and decorations, see misc. data in DM Misc. 201, MMBA.

47. Sen. Thomas J. Dodd to DM, Dec. 19, 1963; DM to Dodd, Dec. 26, 1963, RG 10, MMBA; Rep. John W. McCormack, Tribute to Gen. MacArthur, Aug. 16, 1962; U.S. House Concurrent Resolution 347, July 11, 1962; U.S. House, Armed Services Committee, Report Accompanying House Concurrent Resolution 347, July 17, 1962; U.S. Senate Joint Resolution 228, Oct. 9, 1962, RG 21, MMBA; Sec. of the Army Cyrus R. Vance to Rep. Carl Vinson, Aug. 6, 1963, DM Misc. 201, CMH; St. Louis *Globe-Democrat,* Jan. 18, 1962; Chicago *Tribune,* Aug. 17, 1962; *New York Times,* June 26, July 18, Aug. 17, 1962; Joint Congressional Resolution of Thanks to Gen. MacArthur and His Response, Washington, Aug. 16, 1962, in DM, *Soldier Speaks,* 359–60; "Stars in His Eyes," *Newsweek,* 45 (May 23, 1955), 32; "Old Soldier, Young Man," ibid., 60 (Aug. 27, 1962), 22; "From Congress to General MacArthur — A Vote of Thanks," *U.S. News & World Report,* 53 (Aug. 27, 1962), 6; DM, *Reminiscences,* 406–08. In Aug. 1954, Democratic Reps. Herman Eberharter (PA) and Emanuel Celler (NY) succeeded in blocking a House bill to extend thanks to MacArthur. *New York Times,* Aug. 5, 1954. On speeches and bills regarding MacArthur's promotion to six-star rank, see *Congressional Record,* 1955–56, 1958, 1960, 1963–64.

48. Ints., Whitney, Bunker; Capt. Robert H. Alexander, May 28, 1971; W. Fred Duckworth, Aug. 24, 1967; Philip P. Brower, June 17, 1968; Philip P. Brower to DCJ, Sept. 14, 1971; Norfolk *Virginian-Pilot,* Mar. 17, 1968; Washington *Post,* Dec. 27, 1960; Mar. 26, Apr. 23, 1972; Chicago *Tribune,* July 9, 1961; *New York Times,* Jan. 1, 1961; Jan. 26, Apr. 6, 14, July 22, 1964; Jan. 14, June 2, 1966; Mar. 22, 1969; "Norfolk's MacArthur Memorial," *Lawyers Title News,* Mar. 1968, 15–17; "MacArthur's Memorial," *U.S. News & World Report,* 50 (Jan. 9, 1961), 22; "The Virginian," *Newsweek,* 57 (Jan. 9, 1961), 26. For data on the origin and early history of the MacArthur Memorial and the foundation, see RG 14, MMBA. Fred Duckworth headed the foundation until his death in 1972; his successors were Larry Bunker and

Roy Martin. Gen. Robert E. Wood was the first chairman of the foundation's National Advisory Board, which included Herbert Hoover, Senators Harry Byrd and A. Willis Robertson of VA, Henry Luce, Arnold Saltzman, Harry Vickers, actor Joe E. Brown, and fourteen other business, political, and military leaders. Mrs. MacArthur later became the honorary chairman of the Advisory Board.

49. Official Program of the Visit of Gen. MacArthur to the Philippines, July 3–12, 1961; DM, Press Statement, July 15, 1961, RG 21, MMBA; DM, Speech at Luneta Park, Manila, July 4, 1961, in U.S. Senate, *Speeches*, 95–97 (also in DM, *Soldier Speaks*, 347–51; *Vital Speeches*, 27 (Aug. 1, 1961), 619–20); DM, Speech Before Philippine Congress, Manila, July 5, 1961, in RG 21, MMBA (reprinted in U.S. Senate, *Speeches*, 97–100); New York *Herald Tribune*, July 2, 9, 1961; Fort Wayne (IN) *News-Sentinel*, July 12, 1961; Wabash (IN) *Plain Dealer*, July 15, 1961; Washington *Evening Star*, July 5, 1961; Manila *Times*, July 10, 1961; *New York Times*, May 25, July 2, 4–8, 10, 14, Oct. 20, 1961; Carl Mydans, "General's Shared Memories with a 'Life' Comrade," *Life*, 51 (July 14, 1961), 42–47; "Sentimental Journey," *Time*, 78 (July 14, 1961), 23–24; "An Old Soldier Talks About the Next War," *U.S. News & World Report*, 51 (July 17, 1961), 70–71; Cornelio M. Ferrer, "MacArthur Returns," *Christian Century*, 78 (Aug. 9, 1961), 964; Blair, *MacArthur*, 354; DM, *Reminiscences*, 419–20.

50. *New York Times*, May 13, 1962, Apr. 6, 1964; New York *Journal Tribune*, May 1, 1967; Considine, *It's All News*, 359–61; Taylor, *Swords*, 254–55. The four previous Thayer Award winners were Dr. Ernest O. Lawrence, noted nuclear physicist; John Foster Dulles; Henry Cabot Lodge, Jr., senator and UN representative; and Eisenhower.

51. DM, Thayer Award Speech at U.S. Military Academy, May 12, 1962, in U.S. Senate, *Speeches*, 100–03 (also in DM, *Reminiscences*, 423–26; DM, *Soldier Speaks*, 352–58; *Vital Speeches*, 28 [June 15, 1962], 519–21).

52. Sen. John C. Stennis, Senate Floor Statement, July 18, 1963, Public Series, Stennis Collection, MSU.

53. Kenneth P. O'Donnell, "LBJ and the Kennedys," *Life*, 69 (Aug. 7, 1970), 51. On the JFK-MacArthur relationship, see also Kenneth P. O'Donnell and David F. Powers, with Joe McCarthy, *"Johnny, We Hardly Knew Ye": Memories of John Fitzgerald Kennedy* (New York, 1973 [1st ed., 1972]), 13–14, 320; Arthur M. Schlesinger, Jr., *A Thousand Days: John F. Kennedy in the White House* (Boston, 1965), 339; Blaik, *Blaik Story*, 498–99; Taylor, *Swords*, 217–18; Chicago *Tribune*, May 8, 1961; *New York Times*, July 21, 1961.

54. Blaik to Whitney, Mar. 1, 1963; DM to Blaik, Feb. 25, 1964; DM to Pres. John F. Kennedy, Jan. 21, 1963; DM, Press Statements on AAU–NCAA Arbitration, Jan. 18, June 4, 1963; Donald F. Hull to DM, June 5, 1963; Hull to Whitney, Jan. 6, 1964; DM to Robert F. Ray, Jan. 14, 1963; Ray to DM, Mar. 8, 1963; DM to Louis J. Fisher, Mar. 12, 1963; Fisher to DM, May 13, 1963; A. O. Duer to DM, Apr. 24, 1963;

DM to William W. Russell, Mar. 11, 25, June 7, Oct. 11, 1963; Jan.
8, 1964; Russell to DM, Mar. 12, 18, 20, June 6, Oct. 9, Dec. 16, 1963;
DM to Mrs. John F. Kennedy, Nov. 22, 1963, RG 10, MMBA; Pres.
John F. Kennedy, Press Conference, Dec. 12, 1962, in Kennedy, *Public Papers, 1962*, 866; idem, Press Conference, Mar. 21, 1963, in ibid.,
1963, 276; idem to DM, Jan. 9, 1963, ibid., 7; Washington *Post*, Dec.
26, 1962; Washington *Evening Star*, Dec. 13, 1962; Jan. 21, 1963; *New
York Times*, June 5, 1963; Chicago *Tribune*, Jan. 21, 1963; "AAU, NCAA
Reach Agreement," *Amateur Athlete*, Feb. 1963, 5; Louis J. Fisher, "Gen.
MacArthur's Ruling Saves U.S. Olympic Development Effort," ibid.,
July, 1963, 8–9; "Olympian Challenge," *Newsweek*, 61 (Jan. 7, 1963),
57; Blaik, *Blaik Story*, 470–73. At the time William W. Russell was
president of the USTFF, Robert F. Ray of the NCAA and Louis J.
Fisher of the AAU.

55. Ints., Whitney, Bunker, Willoughby; ints., Bunker, Kades, Gene
Farmer, Sherrod File, DMBP; int., Lt. Gen. Leonard D. Heaton, vol.
II, pp. 10–11, USAMHI; DM to Frederic S. Marquardt, Aug. 21, 1948,
MMBA; Henry R. Luce to DM, Apr. 6, 1951; Arthur H. Sulzberger
to DM, Apr. 17, 1951; Richard L. Simon to DM, Aug. 7, 1952; DM
to Simon, Aug. 12, 1952; DM, Addenda to "Reminiscences," n.d.;
Edward K. Thompson to Whitney, Aug. 14, 16, 1963; MacArthur–
Time, Inc., Contract on "Reminiscences," Aug. 14, 1963, RG 10,
MMBA; Marion C. George to DM, July 23, 26, Aug. 21, 1963, RG
21, MMBA; Jackson to DM, Aug. 20, 1963; DM to Jackson, Aug. 29,
1963; Sandy Clark to Jackson, Oct. 7, 1963, Jackson Papers; Sherrod
to DCJ, Nov. 16, Dec. 17, 1971; May 21, 1973; Washington *Evening
Star*, Aug. 21, 1963; New York *Herald Tribune*, Aug. 21, 1963; *New
York Times*, Nov. 29, 1945; Aug. 21, Sept. 11, 1963; Apr. 17, 1964;
Jan. 11, 1965; *Nippon Times*, Dec. 2, 1945; Chicago *Tribune*, Sept. 27,
1964; Washington *Post*, Sept. 27, 1964; "MacArthur Writes His Life
Story," *Editor and Publisher*, 96 (Aug. 24, 1963), 14; "The Old Soldier's Memoirs," *Time*, 82 (Aug. 30, 1963), 37; Rovere and Schlesin-
ger, *MacArthur Controversy*, 265–73; Blaik, *Blaik Story*, 527–28; Con-
sidine, *It's All News*, 358–59; Smith, *MacArthur*, 62. On reviews of
Reminiscences, see those by Forrest C. Pogue in *American Historical Review*, 70 (July 1965), 1140–41; by Thomas P. Govan in *Journal of
American History*, 52 (June 1965), 163–64; by Mark Watson in *Satur-
day Review*, 47 (Sept. 26, 1964), 42–43; by Hanson W. Baldwin in *New
York Times Book Review*, Sept. 27, 1964; and by John Chamberlain in
National Review, 16 (Dec. 15, 1964), 1112; and also review excerpts in
Book Review Digest, 60 (1964–65), 759–60.

56. Louis Morton, "Egotist in Uniform," *Harper's*, 229 (Nov. 1964), 145.

57. Eisenhower to DM, Feb. 1, Mar. 24, 1960, PSF, Eisenhower Papers;
The Rev. John A. Lavender to DM, Nov. 4, 1960, RG 21, MMBA;
Sherrod, Notes on MacArthur, Jan. 30, 1967, Sherrod File, DMBP;
New York Times, July 6, 1949; Mar. 3, 1957; Jan. 30, 31, Feb. 1, 2, 6,
8, Mar. 20, Apr. 4, 1960; DM, *Reminiscences*, 418–19.

58. Int., Heaton, vol. II, pp. 2–19; Almond to DM, Mar. 16, 1964, Almond Papers; Whitney, "Profile of Gen. MacArthur," n.d., Sherrod File, DMBP; Chicago *Tribune*, Mar. 7, 1964; Washington *Post*, Apr. 1, 4, 5, 1964; *New York Times*, Mar. 3–7, 24–27, 30–31, Apr. 4–6, 1964; Pres. Lyndon B. Johnson, Statement on the Death of Gen. MacArthur, Apr. 5, 1964, in Lyndon B. Johnson, *Public Papers, 1963–64,* I, 444; Egeberg, "MacArthur," 171; Blaik, *Blaik Story,* 534–35; "The Bleeding Gullet," *Time,* 83 (Apr. 3, 1964), 79; "MacArthur," ibid. (Apr. 10, 1964), 24–25; "Hail from the Chief," *Newsweek,* 63 (Mar. 23, 1964), 56; "MacArthur: An Old Soldier Dies," ibid. (Apr. 13, 1964), 34–35; Eric F. Goldman, *The Tragedy of Lyndon Johnson* (New York, 1969 [1st ed., 1968]), 472–73.

59. Ints., Whitney, Bunker; int., Heaton, vol. II, p. 12, USAMHI; DM, Speech to National Institute of Social Sciences, New York, Nov. 8, 1951, RG 10, MMBA; New York *Herald Tribune*, Apr. 9, 1964; Chicago *Tribune*, Apr. 7, 10, 12, 1964; Washington *Post,* Apr. 9, 1964; *New York Times,* Apr. 6–12, 1964; "Home Is the Soldier," *Newsweek,* 63 (Apr. 20, 1964), 43–44; Mydans, "Memento," 25; "Threnody and Thunder," *Time,* 83 (Apr. 17, 1964), 40–41; "Notes and Comments," *New Yorker,* 39 (Apr. 18, 1964), 39–40; B. C. Mossman and M. W. Stark, *The Last Salute: Civil and Military Funerals, 1921–1969* (Washington, 1971), ix–x, 216–62, 404; Considine, *It's All News,* 357–58; Blaik, *Blaik Story,* 483–85; Norfolk *Virginian-Pilot* and *Ledger-Star* staffs, *Gen. Douglas MacArthur: Last Journey for an Old Soldier* (Norfolk, 1964). For contemporary appraisals and eulogies of MacArthur, see the issues of most major newspapers and news periodicals in America and abroad, which are far too voluminous to cite. Of course, the publication of the Lucas and Considine interviews precipitated a new flurry of editorials and articles about the Truman-MacArthur controversy of 1950–51.

Index